THE OXFORD COMPANION TO SPIRITS AND COCKTAILS

THE OXFORD COMPANION TO
SPiRITS
AND
cocktails

EDITOR-IN-CHIEF
DAVID WONDRICH

ASSOCIATE EDITOR
NOAH ROTHBAUM

OXFORD
UNIVERSITY PRESS

OXFORD
UNIVERSITY PRESS

Oxford University Press is a department of the University of Oxford. It furthers
the University's objective of excellence in research, scholarship, and education
by publishing worldwide. Oxford is a registered trade mark of Oxford University
Press in the UK and certain other countries.

Published in the United States of America by Oxford University Press
198 Madison Avenue, New York, NY 10016, United States of America.

Library of Congress Cataloging-in-Publication Data
Names: Wondrich, David, editor. | Rothbaum, Noah, editor.
Title: The Oxford companion to spirits and cocktails /
editor in chief, David Wondrich, associate editor, Noah Rothbaum.
Description: New York, NY, United States of America :
Oxford University Press, [2022] | Includes index. |
Identifiers: LCCN 2021033610 (print) | LCCN 2021033611 (ebook) |
ISBN 9780199311132 | ISBN 9780190670405 (epub) |
ISBN 9780190670399 (pdf)
Subjects: LCSH: Cocktails. | LCGFT: Cookbooks.
Classification: LCC TX951 .O99 2021 (print) | LCC TX951 (ebook) |
DDC 641.87/4—dc23
LC record available at https://lccn.loc.gov/2021033610
LC ebook record available at https://lccn.loc.gov/2021033611

DOI: 10.1093/acref/9780199311132.001.0001

1 3 5 7 9 8 6 4 2

Printed by Sheridan Books, Inc., United States of America

CONTENTS

FOREWORD

Throughout my career as a chef, I've noticed many similarities between mixology and cooking. When building cocktails, you have different ingredients and spirits that you layer to evoke an emotion, a feeling, or a story. There is history and tradition in each of those parts, magic in their alchemy, and creativity coming from behind the bar, all into one glass. Dave Wondrich, Noah Rothbaum, and these amazing contributors have brilliantly succeeded in capturing all that in this informative and engaging guide that people will refer to time and time again.

These experts (and my NYC neighbors) were able to boil down the distillation, fermentation process, history, and consumption of spirits in all of its complexities in one compelling and definitive read. This deep dive into the origin of spirits and cocktails will enable you to enhance your drinking experience by learning about not only the broad cultures they stem from but the specific bartenders behind the world's most popular drinks.

I typically drink cocktails when celebrating with family, friends, and loved ones as we gather around and break bread. What I find most enjoyable when pairing cocktails with food is how it can bring an added dimension to the dining experience by introducing those bitter, sweet, salty, sour, or umami notes. With the help of the *Oxford Companion*, these drinks will transport you to different periods of time and countries around the world without you leaving your bar stool. Crack these pages and delve into everything from the history of Grey Goose, to the lore of moonshine, to what makes the Paloma cocktail so singular, to exploring the role of the Stork Club and the history of the spirits trade, to name a few. Like me, I hope you'll get lost in the pages of this book, which will take you beyond your taste buds on a delicious journey.

Marcus Samuelsson

INTRODUCTION

Distillation is much older, more widespread, and easier than most people, including many historians, realize. Spreading the technology of it, which tends to be regarded as some arcane alchemy that requires years of apprenticeship to master, can be as simple as by telling someone that if they boil their local beer or wine and collect the first part of the steam, they will end up with something stronger, easier to transport, and far less likely to turn into vinegar. As for that steam collecting: you don't need an expensive, elaborately worked copper still, complete with complex condensing coil, to do it. It has been done with two clay bowls and a swatch of tree bark, or a clay pot, the bottom of another, broken one, and a bamboo tube, or—well, there are as many ways as there are human imaginations.

As a result, the world of spirits is vast: they can be, and have been, made from anything that has some kind of sugar in it, or even starch that can be converted to sugar. The raw material doesn't have to taste good; a great deal of perfectly clean spirit is made from beet molasses, the foul muck left over from extracting the sugar from sugar beets. But you don't even have to distill and filter a questionable-tasting spirit to neutrality to make it palatable; sometimes all you have to do is stick it in a wooden barrel and forget about it for a few years, or simply mix it with some citrus juice and sugar, or a healthy splash of ginger ale.

The Oxford Companion to Spirits and Cocktails is our quixotic attempt to squeeze this whole world of spirits between the covers of a book. And by "whole world" we do mean whole world: here you will find detailed coverage of not just cognac and scotch whisky or London dry gin, bourbon, and Caribbean rum—the types of spirits you'll find in any halfway-decently stocked liquor store—but also of Philippine lambanog and Nigerian ogogoro, Maryland peach brandy, Indian feni, and Chinese baijiu. The things that a great many people around the world drink but which don't make it to Duty Free. To the best of our knowledge, nobody has been foolhardy enough to try that since Samuel Morewood back in 1838, at least not in any detail.

But the book's title isn't the *Oxford Companion to Spirits*; it's the *Oxford Companion to Spirits and Cocktails*, which means it also encompasses how spirits are consumed. Unlike beer and wine, spirits are most commonly mixed into various delightful little potions, not poured straight from the bottle. To cover the fermentation (all spirits begin with fermentation), distillation, and maturation that go into making spirits without also covering the mixology that completes the circuit between the maker and the consumer seems wrong. So spirits and cocktails (a term we are using in its loosest sense, to cover any mixed drink based on spirits, plus a few key fellow travelers). That means not only origin stories of the various popular mixtures, each with a recipe, but also biographies of famous bartenders and histories of influential bars. Most influential bartenders make their marks on the world not by writing books or talking to the press but one interaction at a time, one customer at a time. Their drinks and their bars are their resumes, and we are proud to present a great deal of new information on both, along with detailed looks at things such as the various bar tools, the techniques of mixing drinks, and even the theories that underpin the art (it does have them).

That's a lot of ground to cover, even with some 1,150 entries and eight hundred–odd pages in which to do it. Spirits are made (and consumed) on every continent, in all but a handful of countries, from an incredible variety of base materials, and as anybody who has perused a modern cocktail list will know, the drinks known to the world's mixologists are as the sand of the sea, which cannot be numbered nor measured. To cover all this in detail would take a shelf of books the size of this one.

Like a road-map, therefore, the master list of entries for the *Companion* contains both highways and byways. We've tried to include all of the highways—the big topics everyone's going to expect to find. In a perfect world, we'd also include all the byways; all the obscure liqueurs, midwestern tiki bars, micro-distilleries, and whatnot. But this is a mid-scale map, which means we've included only the most scenic byways—that is, the interesting and colorful ones: the ones that follow along the rivers and go through the old villages, not past the modern industrial park. When it comes to spirits, we've kept the focus on explaining what's actually in your glass. That means entries devoted to production and history, not sociology. We know alcohol of any kind can be problematic, and distilled spirits particularly so, but the body of literature on spirits and their effects on society, on Prohibition and licensing and so forth, is already vast; the *Companion* will defer to it.

Likewise, the *Companion* is not a catalog of mixed drinks; we've covered a great many—almost 250 of them—but our selection is limited to the most important historically, plus (again) a few scenic byways. Spirits and cocktails are made by people, but here we've had to be selective as well. The most important aspect of that is that among the distillers, bartenders, brand launchers, writers, and other individuals who receive individual entries here, you won't find any who made their mark after 2004, when the modern cocktail renaissance and the micro-distilling revolution that went with it really got off the ground. After that, there are so many individuals who have made their marks that were we to include them, the book would end up like those top-100-of-all-time lists one sees where fully 60 percent of the entries are from the last twenty years. Such individuals do, however, appear by name in other entries, whether they're devoted to chronicling the modern spirits and cocktail worlds or to

individual drinks, brands, or techniques with which they have been involved.

But let's move on to how we've covered the great many things we have been able to cover. Since this is the first *Oxford Companion to Spirits and Cocktails*, that has given us a chance to try something new. The twenty-first century seen the digitization of vast amounts of material from the past—books, periodicals, corporate records, government documents, and on and on. This has enabled us to incorporate primary sources—that is, ones that were based on reporting, rather than pieced together later from other books—to an unprecedented degree for a work of this type. That means that what you find in here will often contradict the conventional wisdom. But rest assured that when you come across an assertion such as that rum was invented in Asia, not the Caribbean; that American rye whisky owes far more to Pennsylvania's German settlers than to its Scotch-Irish ones; or even that the cocktail is named after a disreputable and unsanitary practice London horse-dealers used to perk up a tired nag before sale, it has been checked and double-checked. (Yes, we've seen that story on Wikipedia. We didn't use it because we looked into it and it was wrong.) We've done our best to make sure everything here is documented, providing references to the most useful sources we know for further reading and also to many of those obscure primary documents, particularly where they offer new information. And, speaking of Wikipedia, since we live in a world in which it and Google and the like exist, we've lightened up on the sorts of lists on which books like this usually gorge. Rather than use the limited space here to repeat things that are easily looked up online, we've focused on the things that are not: origins, early history, context, analysis.

Having touched on the what and the how, let's talk about the who. It took some 150 people to write this book (and nine years, but who's counting?), and that's not including editors, designers, proofreaders, photographers, and such. Our writers include a large proportion of the most familiar names in the field of drinks writing, whether they usually write for academic audiences or general ones. But we've also reached out to distillers, blenders, spirits merchants, bartenders, brand owners, collectors, spirits geeks, cocktail fiends, poets, critics, bar owners, raconteurs, and a couple of people we really can't pigeonhole at all. There has been surprisingly little academic study of the history of distilled spirits and their trade, and even less of the history of mixed drinks, but on the other hand there is a ready corps of extremely knowledgeable people working in the field, and we have recruited widely from among them, including many individuals who have been pivotal in making the cocktail world and the spirits world what they are today. You'll find them all in our list of contributors, and many of them among our entries as well. Sadly, there are three in that list who did not make it to the end of the journey, Tomás Estes, Nicholas Faith, and Gary Regan. We wish we could raise a glass with them rather than to them.

How to Use This Book

You can use this book as a cocktail book, to be sure. The recipes we've provided are basic and, we hope, noncontroversial. (They're also metric, but they've been designed to be easy to convert to ounces, should that be how you measure your ingredients; we've included a conversion table on page xxv.) Or you can pour yourself a glass of something—kirschwasser, shochu, cachaça, plain old whisky—read the appropriate entry, and start following the cross-references. Each entry will send you to one or more—sometimes many more—other relevant entries. Thus RYE WHISKY rapidly leads you to THREE-CHAMBER STILL, which leads you to KORN, which leads you to HERRENGEDECK, which leads

you to BOILERMAKER, and so forth. Or you can pick a region and start exploring its drinks—the spirits it makes and the drinks into which it mixes them. You'll find a list of regions that shows how we've carved up the world on page xxiv. Appendix 1, a list of the world's spirits broken down by their raw materials, gives you another way in, as does Appendix 2, a historical timeline of distillation and the spirits trade. Again, follow the cross-references; the book is designed to help you wander, harvesting morsels of information along the way.

You can also engage with the book by helping us to correct it. This book being the first of its name, it is new to the world and awkward in spots. We've tried to be accurate in all matters large and small, but this book is a human endeavor, and perfect accuracy is not a characteristic of such things. If there is any blame to be assigned, it belongs to the editor-in-chief, whose job it was to trim the loose ends, nail down what needed nailing down, and make sure everything in here is shipshape. If you will let us know about any places where the cargo is loose, so to speak, we shall do our best to correct it in any subsequent editions—unless, that is, your issue is the fact that we've spelled American and Irish whiskies without the "e." That, we're afraid, is policy. See WHISKY.

David Wondrich
EDITOR-IN-CHIEF

ACKNOWLEDGMENTS

It takes a lot of people to complete a project such as this—contributors, editors, advisers, correspondents, authors, researchers, forerunners of all sorts, even friends and family. Space precludes me from thanking all of them by name, but it cannot limit how deeply grateful I am for all of their help, patience, and understanding. That said, here are some names.

There are a few people without whom there would be no book at all. At their head stands Noah Rothbaum, my friend, associate editor, and sounding board for most of the years it took to pull this book together. Without his wisdom, intelligence, and encyclopedic knowledge of the spirits business and those who work in it, this book would have sunk in mid-voyage. My old friend and neighbor Garrett Oliver was the one who suggested the voyage in the first place, and my agent Janis Donnaud made it possible for me to undertake it. Max Sinsheimer, Mary Kate Garmire, and Elise Levy of Oxford University Press USA saw the ship crewed, out of port, and on its way. Jo Payne, Joanna Harris, and Eleanor Brine of Oxford University Press UK took over in rough waters and skillfully guided the ship safely into port.

Without a great many other people the book would not be what it is. Our editorial board figured out the scope of the project and parceled the vast world of spirits and cocktails out into some 1,200-odd entry topics. Additionally, many of its members tackled those entries in numbers far beyond reasonable expectation. In this regard, I would like to extend particular thanks to Dave Mahoney, Doug Frost, and Matt Rowley, all paladins. But each of the book's more than 150 contributors provided something crucial to it, both those who wrote the big entries and those who wrote the smaller ones. You need stones of all sizes to build a dry-stone wall. Eric Medsker provided the stunning cover and spine photographs and those of all the barware. Brady McNamara designed the cover and Farzana Razak the text. Don Lee drew up the clean and lucid still diagrams. I am most grateful to them, and also to all those who contributed pictures. And special thanks to Ursula Reshoft-Hegewisch for the Kiderlen's Pure Holland Geneva bottle that anchors the cover and Marcus Samuelsson for his kind foreword.

Finally, I owe more thanks than I can ever acknowledge to my parents, Virginia Bugliarello-Wondrich and the late Dr. Giorgio Bugliarello-Wondrich, for raising me in a house full of books and so many other things, and to my dear wife, Karen, and my equally dear daughter, Marina, for their support and their patience with a project that has taken far too much of my attention away from those with whom it most properly belongs.

To all of yinz, next round's on me!

—David Wondrich

Seven years ago, when David Wondrich approached me about coming on board to help him edit this book, I thought I knew a lot about the world of spirits and cocktails. I naively envisioned it taking us a couple of years—tops—to pull together. No problem.

Seven years later, I realize just how much there is to learn about the world of drinks and how much we still don't know.

The experience of working on this book was a rare opportunity to give spirits and cocktails their proper due and to set the record straight on many long-held myths, legends and misconceptions. If there was any lingering doubt, this book should conclusively prove that drinks are worthy of serious academic study. I'm truly excited that you have all of this knowledge at your fingertips, and hope you enjoy reading these many entries.

At times, I wasn't sure we'd ever finish this book. But I'm also a bit sad to be done. The countless hours I spent talking and strategizing with Dave were incredibly enjoyable—like a masterclass. I would like to thank him for allowing me to go on this amazing and unique journey with him. I'd also like to thank the Oxford University Press team, our wonderful writers, and our colleagues and our friends who helped in large and small ways. We could never have pulled this off without all of you. Drinks are on us!

I'd also like to thank my wife and family for their unending support and love. None of my work would be possible without them. I hope I've made them proud.

—Noah Rothbaum

TOPICAL OUTLINE OF ENTRIES

Entries in the body of *The Oxford Companion to Spirits and Cocktails* are organized alphabetically. This outline offers an overview of the *Companion*, with entries listed in the following categories:

Bartenders, Mixologists,
and Mixographers
(Contemporary)
Bartenders, Mixologists, and
Mixographers (Historical)
Brands and Spirits Companies
Cocktail Bars

Cocktails
Distillation, Blending, and
Maturation
General and Miscellaneous
Mixers and Garnishes
Mixology Culture, Theory,
Technique, and Tools

Spirits
Spirits Institutions
Spirits Personalities
The World of Spirits and
Cocktails, by Region

Bartenders, Mixologists, and Mixographers (Contemporary)

Abou-Ganim, Tony
Ankrah, Douglas
Barnard, Alfred
Berry, Jeff "Beachbum"
Bradsell, Dick
Brown, Jared
Calabrese, Salvatore
Collins, Wayne
DeGroff, Dale
Dorelli, Giampiero "Peter"
Downey, Jonathan

Field, Colin Peter
Foley, Ray
Grimes, William "Biff"
Haigh, Ted
Hamilton, Edward "Ed"
Harrington, Paul
Hess, Robert
McMillian, Chris
Miller, Anistatia, and
    Brown, Jared
Petraske, Sasha

Rea, Brian
Reed, Ben
Regan, Gary
Reiner, Julie
Saunders, Audrey
Schumann, Charles
Stenson, Murray
Strangeway, Nick
Ueno, Hidetsugu
Uyeda, Kazuo

Bartenders, Mixologists, and Mixographers (Historical)

Abeal y Garcia, Jose "Sloppy Joe"
Alexander, Cato
Amis, Kingsley
Antone, Donato "Duke"
Arthur, Stanley Clisby
Ashley, James
Baker, Charles Henry, Jr.

Beach, Donn
Beebe, Lucius
Bergeron, Victor "Trader Vic"
Boadas, Miguel
Boothby, William
    T. "Cocktail Bill"
Brigham, Peter Bent

Bullock, Tom (Thomas
    Washington)
Chicote, Pedro "Perico"
Clarke, Edwin "Eddie" J.
Coleman, Ada
Craddock, Harry Lawson
Crouch, Jasper

Brands and Spirits Companies

Distillation, Blending, and Maturation

ABV
acetaldehyde
acidity
adulteration
agave
aging
aldehydes
alembic
añejo
angel's share
apples
Armagnac still
aroma
Aspergillus oryzae
azeotrope
bananas
barley
barrel
barrel rotation
barrel storage systems
bathtub gin
Baudoinia compniacensis
beets
blending
boisé
bonificateur
botanical
bottled in bond
bouquet
Brix
bubble test
capel still
caramel
caraway
Carter-head still
cellarmaster
cereals
charcoal filtration
charring, toasting (and
    recharring)
chauffe-vin
chill filtration
Chinese still
Christian Carl
citric acid
closures
Coffey still
column still

compounding
condenser
congeners
conversion
cooking
cooper
copper
cork
corn
craft distilling
creosote
cryoextraction
cut
da qu
diffuser
distillate
distillation
distillation, history
distillation, process
distillers' dried grains
double distillation
doubler, thumper, keg, or
    retort
draff
dunder
eau-de-vie still
egg still
elder
élevage
ellagic acid
ellagic tannins
enzymes
essential oils
esters
ethanol
eugenol
falca
fermentation
filtration
flavor
flavorings
floor malting
Forsyths Ltd.
fractional distillation
freeze distillation
furfural
fusel oil
gallic acid

Gandharan still
Geographical Indication (GI)
    and Protected Designation of
    Origin (PDO)
gibberellins
glycerin
grapes
heads
heart
heat exchangers
Hellenistic still
high wines
hogo
hogshead
holandas
home distilling
hong qu
hops
hors d' age
hue/color
hydrometer
jiu qu
juniper
ketone
kilning
koji
lactobacillus
lactones
legs
light-aroma-style baijiu
lignin
Lincoln County process
log still
low pressure distillation
low wines
maître de chai
malting
mark
mash
mash bill
mashing
master blender
master distiller
maturation
methanol
methylated spirits
micro-oxygenation
millet

General and Miscellaneous

Mixers and Garnishes

Mixology Culture, Theory, Technique, and Tools

Spirits

nalivka
nipa
obstler
oghi
ogogoro
okolehao
Old Tom gin
oro or gold liqueurs
orujo
ouzo
pacharán
parfait amour
pastis
peach brandy
pimento dram
pineau des charentes
pinga
pisco
pitorro
Plymouth gin
poire Williams
pomace brandy
ponche
prunelle
punsch
quetsch
raicilla

raki
rakija
raksi
ratafia
rhum agricole
rock and rye
root-based spirits
rosolio
rum
rum, demerara
rum, Jamaica
rum, Medford
rum, navy
sambuca
samogon
samshoo
Santa Cruz rum
schnapps
schnapps, Schiedam
shochu
singani
slivovitz
sloe gin
soju
sotol
starka
Swedish Punch

tafia
tequila
triple sec
tuber-based spirits
tuica
usquebaugh
vermouth
crème de violette
verschnitt
vodka
wacholder
waragi
whisky
whisky, blended
whisky, bourbon
whisky, Canadian
whisky, corn
whisky, grain
whisky, Irish
whisky, Japanese
whisky, pot still
whisky, rice
whisky, rye
whisky, scotch
whisky, single-malt, global
whisky, Tennessee
Żubrówka

Spirits Institutions

American Distilling Institute
BarSmarts
bartending schools
Beverage Alcohol
    Resource (BAR)
cocktail contests

DrinkBoy Forum
expositions and world's fairs
IBA
International Wine and Spirit
    Competition
Police Gazette Bartender's Medal

regulating bodies
Tales of the Cocktail
United Kingdom
    Bartenders' Guild
United States Bartenders' Guild
Wine and Spirit Education Trust

Spirits Personalities

al-Zahrāwī
Arroyo Valdespino, Rafael
Bayly, Phil
Booker Noe II, Frederick
Bronfman family
Cellier-Blumenthal, Jean-Baptiste
Coffey, Aeneas
Coolhaes, Caspar Janszoon
Cooper, Ron
Cowdery, Charles K.
Crockett, Barry

Crow, James C.
Crowgey, Henry Gundry
Difford, Simon
Faith, Nicholas
Ford, Simon
Frank, Sidney
Hamilton, Edward "Ed"
Hansell, John
Jackson, Michael
Lull, Raimund
MacDonald, Aeneas

Martin, John G.
Munier, Etienne
Murray, Jim
Nichol, Tom
Olson, Steven "Steve"
Pacult, F. Paul
Ray, Cyril
Rosenstiel, Lewis
Roux, Michel
Rupf, Jörg

Saintsbury, George Edward
   Bateman
Sylvius, Franciscus

Taketsuru, Masataka
Taylor, Col. E. H.
Washington, George

Wiley, Harvey W.

The World of Spirits and Cocktails, by Region
(beginning at the International Date Line and following the sun)

Micronesia
Australia and New Zealand
Philippines
Indonesia
Japan
Korea
China
Southeast Asia
India and Central Asia
Middle East

North Africa
Central and East Africa
South Africa
Russia and Eastern Europe
Caucasus
Greece
Scandinavia
Germany, Switzerland, and
   Austria
Italy

France
Scotland and Ireland
England
Iberian Peninsula
United States and Canada
Caribbean
Mexico
Central America
Brazil
Andean South America

A NOTE TO THE READER ON MEASURES

Except where historical discussion requires it, all quantities in this book are in the metric system. For those accustomed to using the old ounces-pints-and-quarts imperial measures, however, know that we have tried to make this as easy as possible, particularly in the recipes for mixing drinks. There, we have used quantities that are easily convertible to ounces and such. Thus, we have used the following equivalents for standard imperial bartender's measures:

　　5 ml = 1 teaspoon = 1 barspoon
　　7 ml = ¼ ounce
　15 ml = ½ ounce
　22 ml = ¾ ounce
　30 ml = 1 ounce
　45 ml = 1½ ounces
　60 ml = 2 ounces

With larger quantities, where absolute precision is not required, we have used the rough equivalent of 1 liter = 1 quart and 4 liters = 1 gallon; where it is required, of course, 1 liter = 1.057 quarts, and 3.8 liters = 1 gallon.

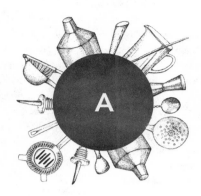

Abeal y Otero, Jose "Sloppy Joe" (1886–1942), was the founder and proprietor of Sloppy Joe's bar in Havana, a famous watering hole frequented by American movie stars and other tourists during (and after) Prohibition. See SLOPPY JOE'S. Of Spanish birth, he worked in Havana and then New Orleans and Miami before opening the bar in 1917. In 1937, he sold the bar and returned to Spain, where he died.

David Mahoney

Abou-Ganim, Tony (1960–), is an American bartender who was an influential figure in the early days of the craft cocktail revivals in San Francisco and Las Vegas. A would-be actor who first tended bar at his cousin's tavern in Port Huron, Michigan, he further honed his trade in San Francisco in the 1980s and '90s at Balboa Café and Harry Denton's, Bay Area bars where the classic cocktail canon was still plied. In 1996, he was tapped for the relaunch of the Jazz Age Starlight Room atop the Francis Drake Hotel. Like with Dale DeGroff at the Rainbow Room in New York, the owners set Abou-Ganim and his fellow bartenders on a pedestal. See DEGROFF, DALE. Abou-Ganim's classical standards and infallibly gracious, expert service filtered down to the staff, which, over the years, would include some of the best bartenders San Francisco produced in the twenty-first century, including Marcovaldo Dionysus and Thomas Waugh. While at the Starlight, Abou-Ganim created his best-known drink, the Cable Car, made of spiced rum, curaçao, and lemon juice, with a sugared rim. He brought the craft cocktail gospel to Las Vegas in 1998, when he was asked to take command of the many bars at the Bellagio hotel and casino. There, he applied a rigorous bartending training system and a commitment to fresh juices and quality spirits theretofore not seen in the city. He, along with Francesco Lafranconi, also helped revive the United States Bartenders' Guild by founding a chapter in Las Vegas. He left the Bellagio in 2004 and has since worked as an itinerant cocktail and bartending authority. See UNITED STATES BARTENDERS' GUILD (USBG).

See also CRAFT COCKTAIL.

Simonson, Robert. *A Proper Drink: How a Band of Bartenders Saved the Civilized World*. Emeryville, CA: Ten Speed Press, 2016.

Robert Simonson

abricotine is today a term applied to the clear, colorless brandy made from apricots in the Valais area of Switzerland, although similar products are made in Austria and Hungary (as *Marillenbrand* and *barack pálinka*). The spirit's origins lie in the wave of fruit distilling that swept through the region in the sixteenth and seventeenth centuries.

From the mid-nineteenth century until 1975, however, "Abricotine" was a proprietary term belonging to the French house of Garnier, which applied it to an apricot-flavored grape brandy liqueur; with the closure of the company, the Swiss had the field to themselves. Since 2003 abricotine has been designated with an AOP (appellation d'origine protégée, or protected designation of origin). Abricotine AOP is made with at least 90 percent Luizet apricots and must be a minimum 40 percent

ABV. Cultivation of the fruit, fermentation, distillation (in hybrid eau-de-vie stills), and bottling all take place exclusively within the canton of Valais.

Abricotine tastes of apricot with a touch of almond and is best appreciated as a digestif neat and chilled, but it incorporates well in cocktails and desserts.

"Abricotine AOP (apricot brandy)." Valais.com. https://www.valais.ch/en/about-valais/local-products/quality-labelled-products/abricotine-apricot-brandy (accessed March 16, 2021).
"Distillerie Garnier." Enghien-les-Bains.com, February 8, 2019. https://www.enghienlesbains.fr/fr/actualites/distillerie-garnier (accessed March 16, 2021).

Jack Robertiello

absinthe is a distilled neutral spirit flavored with *Artemisia absinthium*—a species of wormwood—and aniseed, with other botanicals playing supporting roles. It is intended for dilution and imbibing as a light drink to cleanse the palate and stimulate the appetite. It contains no added sugar and so is not a liqueur, but rather an aperitif spirit.

Due to controversies over public health issues, absinthe was banned in much of the world for most of the twentieth century. These health concerns have since been solidly debunked by modern scientific analysis and historical research. Absinthe has enjoyed a resurgence in interest and manufacture during the first decades of the twenty-first century.

Origins

Absinthe takes its name from the *Artemisia absinthium* plant, a member of the sagebrush genus. Absinthe reached its peak popularity in France, where the name under which absinthe was sold in the 1800s was *extrait d'absinthe*, "wormwood extract," alluding to its concentrated strength. It began, however, as a medicinal tonic in late-medieval Europe. It has been claimed that Switzerland is its birthplace; however, it is more accurate to say that France and Switzerland are absinthe's adopted homes.

Wormwood has been in medicinal use since the times of the ancient Egyptians. The use of *A. absinthium* together with aniseed for gastrointestinal health goes back to at least the mid-1600s, and formulas for "aqua absinthii" appear in pharmacopeias from all over Europe, England, and the United States. In 1653, the English herbalist Nicholas Culpeper gave a formula consisting only of *A. absinthium* and aniseed. This could be regarded as the earliest known absinthe recipe. By the late 1700s the popularity of the combined flavors of wormwood and aniseed evolved into beverage use, and several French and Swiss entrepreneurs began promoting it as a "health drink," bridging the gap between therapeutic tonic and recreational beverage. By the early 1800s absinthe had taken on a new life as a fashionable and healthy drink.

Controversy

The popularity of absinthe grew in France during the early 1800s. By the mid-1840s it had become a favorite among the soldiers of the French campaign to colonize Algeria (1844–1847). Its abuse among many of the soldiers—owing to its great strength—led to criticism from temperance activists. Yet at the same time absinthe became associated with victorious veterans, and it acquired a rakish, patriotic appeal.

To complicate matters, in the mid-to-late 1850s the grape vine parasite phylloxera decimated the vines in France and threatened the wine industry with collapse. Increased wine costs drove up the price of grape spirits, causing most producers of liqueurs to switch to a more economical beet-sugar spirit base, thereby bringing the price of absinthe within the budget of the common person, even impoverished artists.

As demand for absinthe increased, inferior faux absinthes were created using flavor extracts and harmful colorings such as copper arsenate, a popular but poisonous dye known as Scheele's Green. These faux absinthes, consumed habitually in quantity and at higher than recommended strength, likely resulted in a great number of illnesses and deaths.

While these faux absinthes were in the extreme minority, the concerned wine interests and the nascent temperance movement did not hesitate to denounce all absinthe as the cause of the illnesses, and the national problem with alcoholism in general. This was made easier by the unique ingredient, wormwood, which made a convenient scapegoat. Despite the fact that millions of people drank genuine absinthe every day for over a century with no apparent ill effect, a decades-long campaign of politically motivated sensational propaganda accompanied by false science manipulated public opinion and finally resulted in a ban on absinthe in nearly every country where it had become popular. Absinthe was banned in Belgium in 1906, the Netherlands in 1909, Switzerland in 1910, the United States in 1912, and France in 1915.

Manufacture

Botanicals are macerated in a base of neutral spirits, traditionally grape spirits, which is then re-distilled, during which the volatile botanical oils vaporize along with the ethanol vapor and are re-condensed. The resulting clear distillate is infused, or "finished," with other herbs, providing additional flavors and aromas as well as the green color for which absinthe is famous, a result of chlorophyll extracted from the leaves. The canonical pre-ban absinthe ingredients were grand wormwood (*A. absinthium*), aniseed, and fennel seed, for the maceration/distillation stage, and petite wormwood (*A. pontica*), lemon balm, and hyssop for the finishing infusion. See MACERATE; DISTILLATE; and INFUSION. Absinthe is bottled at high proof in order to better preserve the infused constituents, particularly the chlorophyll. Typically bottled at 55–72 percent ABV, absinthe is customarily diluted at a ratio of approximately five parts water to one part absinthe, as shown on absinthe labels from the pre-ban era. This makes a drink at 11–15 percent ABV, about the same range typical of wine. Classic absinthes are formulated with this dilution in mind. Alternatively, absinthe is used in small amounts as a cocktail ingredient, much like bitters. Its concentrated flavors make it a poor choice as a base spirit in cocktails, as it easily overwhelms any other ingredients.

Modern Myths

Aside from the early-era apprehensions about absinthe being poisonous, there is a commonly-held modern misbelief that absinthe is or was a sort of hallucinogenic or psychedelic drug. However, no evidence has been found to suggest that anyone at the time regarded absinthe as a drug as we would define it today, with recreational effects beyond those of alcohol. The ingredients of nineteenth-century absinthe are known and well-documented in historical texts, and none of them are hallucinogens or psychedelics.

Thujone, a compound found in wormwood, is often cited for absinthe's alleged effects. Thujone is a lethal neurotoxin in high concentrations, but such concentrations would not exist in properly made absinthe, owing to thujone's resistance to distillation. Absinthes dating from the early 1900s, as well as modern absinthes made to the same formulas and standards, have been analyzed and found to be well within normal and safe limits for all ingredients used.

See also APERITIF AND DIGESTIVE; HEALTH AND SPIRITS; and WORMWOOD.

Conrad, Barnaby, III. *Absinthe: History in a Bottle*. San Francisco: Chronicle Books, 1988.
Nathan-Maister, David. *The Absinthe Encyclopedia*. Burgess Hill, UK: Oxygenee Press, 2009.
Wormwood Society. http://www.wormwoodsociety.org (accessed January 7, 2021).

Gwydion Stone

Absinthe Drip has been the customary method of preparation since absinthe first came into use as a beverage in the late 1700s. It is made by slowly adding ice-cold water to a portion of absinthe until the desired strength and appearance is achieved. The ratio most commonly used, as suggested by historical absinthe labels, is five parts water to one part absinthe. While this level of dilution may seem unusual, classic-style absinthes—unlike other spirits—are formulated with this level of dilution in mind. See LOUCHE. This preparation method makes a drink at around 11–15 percent ABV, similar to a glass of wine. The Absinthe Drip is customarily drunk leisurely as a light aperitif, much in the same way as wine is drunk.

Although there are specially made absinthe glasses, the most common glass used for serving absinthe is a stemmed water goblet or wine glass. Plain, straight-sided glasses such as the Old-Fashioned glass are less desirable for aesthetic reasons; the shape does not exhibit absinthe's unique refractory properties to best advantage, whereas the curved stemware globe will enhance the drink's beautiful gem-like opalescence particularly in natural daylight. See GLASSWARE.

Absinthe itself—when properly produced—contains no sugar or sweeteners, and the Absinthe

Drip may be sweetened or not, according to the preference of the drinker. In the early 1800s absinthe was sweetened by the addition of simple syrup or gum syrup and the water added from a carafe or pitcher. See SIMPLE SYRUP and GUM SYRUP. Later, after the introduction of the sugar cube, the Absinthe Spoon was created in order to dissolve the sugar at the same time as the water was added. Still later in the 1880s, the absinthe fountain was devised to further simplify the process for busy bartenders.

Recipe: Pour 30 ml of absinthe into a glass with at least 240 ml capacity. If sugar is to be used, place the spoon on the rim of the glass and the sugar cube on the spoon. Slowly add 150 ml of ice-cold water. This may be done by pouring a thin, steady stream from a carafe or pitcher, or with an absinthe fountain. Adding the water slowly allows the botanical oils in the absinthe to come out of solution more fully and form a more flavorful and aromatic drink.

See also ABSINTHE and ABSINTHE FOUNTAIN.

Child, Theodore. "Characteristic Parisian Cafés." *Harper's New Monthly Magazine,* April 1889, 687–703.
Conrad, Barnaby, III. *Absinthe: History in a Bottle.* San Francisco: Chronicle Books, 1988.
Thomas, Jerry. *The Bar-Tenders Guide, 2nd ed.* New York: Dick & Fitzgerald, 1876.

Gwydion Stone

absinthe fountain is an ornamental iced-water dispenser used to slowly add water to a glass of absinthe. It came into vogue in French cafés in the latter 1800s, as the increasing popularity of absinthe demanded a more efficient means of service. Prior to the arrival of the fountain, absinthe was prepared by pouring iced water from a carafe or pitcher by hand. With the fountain, a server could prepare up to six or eight glasses at a time, or take the fountain to the table, allowing the guests to prepare their absinthes together, without waiting for a carafe to be passed.

The fountain's most common form comprises a clear glass globe for holding ice and water with two to six spigots, all supported on a single, turned metal leg. In rural Switzerland, thrown pottery types are also found and often have many more spigots on the larger versions.

See also ABSINTHE and ABSINTHE DRIP.

Conrad, Barnaby. *Absinthe: History in a Bottle.* San Francisco: Chronicle, 1988.

Gwydion Stone

Absinthe Frappé is an absinthe-based drink that enjoyed great popularity in the late 1800s and early 1900s and was among the first mixed drinks that featured absinthe as a base rather than as a modifying ingredient. See BASE and MODIFIER. Following the debut of the Absinthe Cocktail in the 1870s, the Absinthe Frappé developed as a simple variation; an 1895 recipe calls for the drink to be made with 30 ml each of absinthe and water and 2 dashes of anisette, rolled between mixing glasses filled with fine ice and then strained into a serving glass and topped with seltzer. (Other recipes call for shaking the mixture or agitating the mix with shaved ice using a barspoon, and many add sugar syrup to the drink, in place of or in addition to the anisette.) After finding some appeal as a morning restorative, the Absinthe Frappé made the leap to popular culture in 1904, when Victor Herbert and Glen MacDonough dedicated a song to the drink in their musical *It Happened in Nordland*; the song "Absinthe Frappé" subsequently spread via sheet music and recorded versions. The drink's popularity was interrupted by the US ban on absinthe in 1912, though it retained its appeal in places such as New Orleans, where recipes for versions calling for anise liqueurs such as Ojen or absinthe substitutes such as Herbsaint long remained in use. With absinthe's legal return to the US and other markets in the early twenty-first century, the Absinthe Frappé reentered limited circulation, in some cases prepared with the addition of muddled fresh mint leaves to the mix.

Recipe: Roll 30 ml absinthe, 30 ml water, and 2 dashes of anisette between mixing glasses filled with fine ice. Strain into serving glass and top with seltzer.

Arthur, Stanley Clisby. *Famous New Orleans Drinks and How to Mix 'Em.* New Orleans: Harmanson, 1937.
Kappler, George J. *Modern American Drinks.* Akron, OH: Saalfield Publishing, 1895.
Wondrich, David. *Imbibe!* New York: Perigee, 2007.

Paul Clarke

The classic French absinthe spoon, ca. 1890, designed to hold a cube of sugar over the glass so that water can be dripped through it. Wondrich Collection.

absinthe spoon is a piece of flatware used in preparing an Absinthe Drip when a sugar cube is used for sweetening. It is usually flat and trowel-shaped, with perforations to allow the water and melting sugar to pass into the absinthe below, and a small raised area in the handle to hold it in place on the edge of the glass.

The absinthe spoon became widely popular in the latter half of the nineteenth century, after the invention of the sugar cube in 1843. Prior to this, absinthe was typically sweetened with simple syrup or gum syrup. See SIMPLE SYRUP and GUM SYRUP. Hundreds of designs were made, some very simple and some fanciful, but most were inexpensive utilitarian pieces, comparable to today's stainless steel restaurant flatware. Few examples of fine flatware absinthe spoons have been recorded. Nonetheless, vintage examples are highly collectable these days.

An absinthe "grille" was created around the same time as the absinthe spoon. It usually consisted of a very shallow metal dish with decorative perforations, suspended by three prongs on the top of the glass and was used in the same way as the absinthe spoon.

Also common was the *brouilleur*, or "absinthe glass," as it is called in early mixology treatises. The brouilleur is a small glass or metal bowl with a single small hole in the center to deliver a very thin stream of water slowly into the absinthe below. It is made to sit directly on top of the absinthe glass.

See also ABSINTHE and ABSINTHE DRIP.

Conrad, Barnaby, III. *Absinthe: History in a Bottle*. San Francisco: Chronicle Books, 1988.
Nathan-Maister, David. *The Absinthe Encyclopedia*. Burgess Hill, UK: Oxygenee Press: 2009.

Wormwood Society. http://www.wormwoodsociety.org (accessed January 7, 2021).

Gwydion Stone

Absolut is a brand of vodka distilled in Åhus, Sweden, from winter wheat. As of 2015, it is the second-best-selling vodka in the world (behind Smirnoff), with sales of just over 11 million cases annually. Absolut makes dozens of different bottlings, including flavored vodkas like Absolut Citron, which, according to legend, was the base spirit in Cheryl Cook's influential recipe for the Cosmopolitan, as well as the unflavored Absolut Elyx, distilled in a copper still from wheat grown on a single estate. See COSMOPOLITAN.

Absolut traces its history to Lars Olsson Smith, a successful vodka merchant in Sweden who launched his own brand, Absolut Rent Bränvin ("absolutely pure vodka" in Swedish), in 1879. The original Absolut Rent Bränvin disappeared in the early twentieth century, but Swedish spirits producer V&S Group sought to revive the name in the mid-1970s. The modern incarnation of Absolut launched in 1979 as one of the first vodka brands focused on purity and smoothness. It was (and still is) packaged in a distinctive bottle modeled after an eighteenth-century apothecary bottle. Absolut found much early success thanks to an iconic series of advertisements featuring a photo of the bottle with a simple slogan using "Absolut" as a pun (the first read "Absolut Perfection"). The company has since run thousands of variations of the ad, among them designs created by famed artists including Andy Warhol and Keith Haring.

The brand has partnered with several different major spirits companies for distribution, including Seagram from 1994 to 2001 and Fortune Brands from 2001 to 2008. In 2008, V&S Group was purchased by Pernod-Ricard, and Absolut is today the top-selling brand in that company's portfolio. See PERNOD-RICARD.

See also VODKA.

Absolut. "The Story of Absolut." http://www.absolut.com/us/News/Drinks/The-Story-of-Absolut/ (accessed January 8, 2021).

Jason Horn

ABV is an abbreviation for "alcohol by volume," which is a measurement of the relative amount of alcohol (i.e., ethanol) contained in an alcoholic beverage. Most countries require that the ABV of any spirit be stated on the label, typically as a percentage followed by "alc./vol." or "alc. by vol."

See also ETHANOL and PROOF.

Lee, Tiffany K. "Alcohol by Volume." In *The Sage Encyclopedia of Alcohol: Social, Cultural, and Historical Perspectives*, ed. Scott C. Martin, 58–60. Thousand Oaks, CA: SAGE Publications, 2015.

David Mahoney

accent describes an ingredient in a cocktail that enhances the overall drink and is utilized in small amounts. It is not intended to play a major role in the overall flavor profile, but instead is used either as a background note to stand slightly in counterpoint of the other flavors in the drink as a highlight or as a bridge between two flavors within the drink that might otherwise be slightly incompatible. Nor does an accent necessarily have to be an ingredient within a cocktail. It can also come in the form of a garnish that releases aroma from an essential oil (as in the case of a citrus twist), an ingredient such as floral water that can be misted, dashed, or dropped on/in the drink from an atomizer, or even smoke. See ATOMIZER (MISTER) and SMOKE.

Orange flower water provides the accent in a Ramos Fizz, providing a slightly hidden yet alluring flavor that stands out from the rest. See ORANGE FLOWER WATER and RAMOS GIN FIZZ. Bitters would be considered the accent in the Old-Fashioned, providing a bridge between the whisky and the sugar. See BITTERS and OLD-FASHIONED COCKTAIL. Orgeat is the accent in the Mai Tai that provides the drink with a unique personality that distinguishes it from simply a sour-based drink. See ORGEAT and MAI TAI.

In *The Fine Art of Mixing Drinks* (1948), David Embury proposes a classification of three different types of ingredients that go into a cocktail: base, modifier, and special flavoring or coloring agent. This final item could also be referred to as an accent. See EMBURY, DAVID A.

One of the defining features of the new mixology since 2010 is the use of multiple contrasting or parallel accents in a drink. While the results can taste muddy and unfocused, when done well, as, it is, for example, at London's 69 Colebrooke Row, this can yield drinks of an uncommon richness.

See also BASE and MODIFIER.

Conigliaro, Tony, *69 Colebrooke Row*, London: Ebury Press, 2014.

Audrey Saunders

acetaldehyde is an organic compound that is closely related chemically to ethanol, so called "drinking alcohol." This relationship is reflected in the systemic name for acetaldehyde, which is ethanal. Although the compositional difference is slight, merely two hydrogen molecules, the impact on the way the compound smells, tastes, and feels is dramatic. Acetaldehyde smells and tastes solvent-like, with a distinct "green apple" note. In concentration, it is generally considered to be an off flavor in beer, wine, and spirits. In small amounts, however (roughly, less than 250 milligrams per liter), it is considered an important part of the flavor of some spirits, whiskies in particular, and is also thought to contribute positively to mouthfeel. It is one of the compounds whose concentration increases as a spirit ages in wood. See TEXTURE.

Acetaldehyde is an intermediate product of all alcoholic fermentations, formed in the yeast cells and then converted to ethanol by a facilitating enzyme called nicotinamide adenine dinucleotide (NAD+ or NADH). It will therefore be present in some amount in every alcoholic fermentation.

The concentration of acetaldehyde can be minimized during fermentation by providing yeast with the best possible environment to fully complete the fermentation process, which includes controlling the available nutrients, managing temperature, and selecting the appropriate duration for fermentation. Acetaldehyde is more volatile than ethanol and can therefore also be effectively removed by either a batch distillation process (with most of the acetaldehyde being removed in the "heads") or by a continuous distillation process with a side stream that selectively removes acetaldehyde and other high-volatility compounds.

See also DISTILLATION.

Nykänen, Lalli, and Heikki Suomalainen. *Aroma of Beer, Wine, and Distilled Alcoholic Beverages*. Berlin: Akademie Verlag, 1983, 52–53.

Piggott, J. R. *The Science and Technology of Whiskies.* Harlow, UK: Longman Scientific & Technical, 1989.

White, Chris, and Jamil Zainasheff. *Yeast: The Practical Guide to Beer Fermentation.* Boulder, CO: Brewers Publications, 2010.

Nicole Austin

acidity describes the concentration of acid (a compound with the ability to donate a hydrogen ion, or proton, to another) present in a liquid, expressed as a pH value or as a percentage of the total solution. A liquid with a pH lower than 7 is usually referred to as "acidic," with acidity increasing as the pH drops.

Beyond such chemical considerations, acidity holds an exalted position in alcohol beverages; it provides flavor, texture, and even structure. Acidity brings sourness to the collection of flavors and balances the sweetness inherent in most cocktails. Many tasters report that acidity tends to give a sense of "sharpness" to textures as well. In cocktails, acidity may come from fruits (most notably from citrus, including lemon and lime) that may provide citric, malic, and other acids; other modifiers such as vinegar, which gives a boost of acetic acid; or dairy products with lush, sour lactic acid. See SHRUB. Even spirits themselves may provide acidity, which plays a strong role, possibly providing stability and even longevity to fruit flavors and aromas.

See also ACIDS; CITRUS; and pH.

American Chemical Society. https://www.acs.org (accessed January 8, 2021).

Doug Frost

acid phosphate was a compound created in 1868 by Professor Eben Norton Horsford (1818–1893) of Cambridge, Massachusetts, as a tonic for dyspepsia, nervousness, and seasickness and an ingredient for various culinary uses. Made originally by treating bone ash with sulfuric acid, which yielded a mixture of phosphoric acid and subsidiary phosphate salts of calcium, magnesium, potassium, and sodium, it first found a use in food as a substitute for vinegar but was quickly adopted by soda fountains as a shelf-stable substitute for lemons and limes, to which it had a similar level of acidity (around pH 2.0).

Acid phosphate solution became popular because it was shelf-stable in a time when refrigeration or rapid shipping of citrus fruit was not practical. Its popularity continued with pharmacists in the nineteenth century because citric acid powders were often made by evaporating lemon and lime juice in tin pans, which contained lead, and it was safe from the possibility of such contamination. See CITRIC ACID.

Acid phosphate has pure sour flavor with a unique flavor-enhancing effect from the dissolved mineral salts. It was often described as adding a "sparkle" to soda drinks because it can produce a subtle tingling sensation on the tongue.

Though acid phosphate was immensely popular at soda fountains, it found sparse use in cocktail bars, with rare exceptions such as the Angostura Phosphate, a hangover remedy offered at some bars, and the Montauk Riding Club Cocktail published in the Waldorf Astoria Bar Book in 1934, with brandy, Calisaya, and gum syrup. See WALDORF ASTORIA. Modern bartenders have taken a more accepting approach to incorporating acid phosphate in cocktails as a replacement for citrus juice, although its use is still rather uncommon.

Recipe (Angostura Phosphate): Place in short highball glass: 3 ml acid phosphate, 5 ml Angostura bitters, and 30 ml lemon syrup. Fill with chilled sparkling water. Some modern drinkers prefer this with ice added to the glass.

Crockett, Albert Stevens. *Waldorf Astoria Bar Book.* New York: Aventine, 1934.

Hiss, Emil. *Standard Manual of Soda and Other Beverages.* Chicago: G. P. Engelhardt, 1897.

O'Neil, Darcy. *Fix the Pumps.* N.p.: Art of Drink, 2009.

Darcy O'Neil

acids are highly reactive molecules that produce a sour taste in the food we eat and the beverages we drink. Besides supplying the obvious sour taste— one of the basic tastes recognized by the palate, along with sweet, salty, bitter, and savory or umami—acids do three fairly basic things physiologically: they increase salivation, stimulate the appetite, and refresh the taste buds, allowing them to experience flavors better. This is what makes many high-acid cocktails good choices to enjoy before a meal.

The opposite of acidity is alkalinity. Measuring the acid/alkaline ratio is typically accomplished with the fourteen-point pH scale, with pure acid at 0 and pure alkaline at 14. A reading of 7 means that acid and alkaline are in balance, or neutralized. Very few edible ingredients score above 7, in the alkaline range. Lemon juice has an approximate pH of 2, tomato juice 4, coffee 5; water, sugar, and even ethanol are 7 (neutral). Milk can sometimes measure at 8, baking soda at 9; ammonia has a pH of 11, and bleach comes in with a pH of 13.

While a pH meter measurement might be a good scientific means for specifically identifying how acidic something is, it doesn't directly translate into just how sour it might actually taste. Sourness appears to be more associated with what is known as "titratable acidity," a chemical term that refers to the overall concentration of the acid and not just its pH level. Exactly how sourness is registered by the taste buds isn't quite fully understood, however, and currently there is no real consensus as how to define how sour something might be perceived on the palate based on chemical measurements alone.

There are several different types of acid that are typically found in beverages: citric (commonly found in lemon juice), malic (apples), tartaric (grapes), ascorbic (vitamin C), acetic (vinegar), and lactic (pickles).

Both lemons and limes are commonly used in mixed drinks, and they are fairly concentrated with approximately 6 percent acid. In addition to the citric acid also found in lemons, limes also contain malic and succinic acids. It is the succinic acid in limes that contributes their distinctly bitter-salty flavor. Oranges and grapefruits (both with an approximate pH of 3.5) have less acidity and more sugars than lemon and lime, which allows them to be enjoyed directly for their actual flavor profiles, whereas the acids from lemon and lime function more as a boost to the flavors of other substances with which they are combined.

In the mid-1800s, phosphoric acid was diluted and blended with salts of calcium, magnesium, and potassium into a solution referred to as "acid phosphate." With a pH of approximately 2, it has an acidity comparable to that of lime juice and serves as the foundation of what once were some of the most popular soda fountain drinks, which went by the name "phosphates." One could easily find a cherry phosphate at the soda fountain shop and an Angostura phosphate at a bar. See ACID PHOSPHATE.

Aperitif wines, aromatized wines, and fortified wines are frequently utilized in aromatic cocktails and, depending on their respective categories, will range from a pH of somewhere between 3 and 4. The acidity factor will also vary from one brand to another as well. While they blend seamlessly into aromatic cocktails, their lower acidity allows them to be enjoyed on their own as well (and as they were originally intended). See APERITIF AND DIGESTIVE.

Other sources of acids used in the bar include acidic fruits such as passion fruit, mango, and tamarind, or their juices; sour beers; and champagne or other high-acid sparkling wines. Acids can also be commingled for differing effects, as in the case of the French 75, which combines the acids from both lemon juice and champagne. See FRENCH 75.

Acidity is also present in many spirits, to varying degrees. Levels tend to be higher in pot-stilled and barrel-aged ones, the former due to some acids coming in with the tails and the latter due to extraction from the oak. In general, the resulting acidity is considered a positive, giving the spirit structure, although occasionally the levels can cross into overt sourness. Whiskies, for example, have a pH range from around 3.5, where one might find an old American straight rye, to around 4.5, where one of the lighter Irish blends might be. (Some column-distilled spirits, and in particular vodkas, have a little bit of added citric acid, to brighten their flavor.)

See also CITRUS and PH

Arnold, Dave. *Liquid Intelligence*. New York: W. W. Norton, 2014.

Da Conceicao Neta, Edith Ramos, Suzanne D. Johanningsmeier, and Roger F. McFeeters. "The Chemistry and Physiology of Sour Taste: A Review." *Journal of Food Science* 72, no. 2 (2007): R33–R38.

O'Neil, Darcy. *Fix the Pumps*. N.p.: Art of Drink, 2009.

Sowalsky, Richard A., and Ann C. Noble. "Comparisons of the Effects of Concentration, pH and Anion Species on Astringency and Sourness of Organic Acids." *Chemical Senses* 23, no. 3 (1998): 343–349.http://chemse.oxfordjournals.org/content/23/3/343.full.pdf (accessed April 20, 2021).

Stuckey, Barb. *Taste: Surprising Stories and Science About Why Food Tastes Good*. New York: Atria, 2012.

Audrey Saunders

adulteration, as it applies to distilled spirits, refers to the process of amending any liquor with artificial coloring, flavoring, or other additives, typically to stretch cheap spirits and confuse the consumer. Adulterated spirits may have merely been diluted with water, but in many instances began with a young, high-proof neutral spirit mixed with cheap ingredients to add color, flavor, and sometimes additional pharmacological effect, often to mimic traditional types of spirits, especially aged whiskies and brandies.

Now quite rare in most developed countries, adulterated imitation spirits were common in the second half of the nineteenth century around the world, prompting legislation that articulated legal classifications for many spirits, especially spirits that are typically aged. As with milk, butter, sugar, and other common commodities, advances in chemistry and industrial production in the era of rapidly increasing mechanization and urbanization created financial incentives for manufacturers to use chemistry to improve yields and costs of traditional spirits. One of the most important of those advances was the introduction of truly neutral spirit, made possible by the column still. The product from these stills, while inexpensive to produce, was often flavorless, or nearly so—comparable to today's vodka. Distillers would sell this almost-pure alcohol, sometimes called Cologne spirits or Berlin spirits (Germany was a prime producer), for a variety of beverages, but also for industrial purposes such as perfumes, solvents, and medicines.

For beverage purposes, distillers rarely sold products to consumers directly before 1900, but rather to rectifiers, whose job, among other things, was to produce spirits at a variety of price points, chiefly by stretching out the relatively expensive pure spirits produced by traditional means with this high-proof spirit and water, making up the difference between this compound spirit and the pure one with colorings, sugar, and flavoring agents. See WHISKY, BLENDED. Less scrupulous rectifiers would go further than blenders by dispensing with the pure spirits altogether and using artificial colors and flavors to imitate the traditional whiskies and brandies. These imitation spirits would then be sold as wholesale products, typically by the barrel, for distribution to taverns, saloons, and public houses, whose proprietors might further dilute or adulterate the spirits.

In England, the 1860 Act for Preventing the Adulteration of Articles of Food or Drink began to address what had widely been perceived as a problem. After the act proved to be mostly unenforceable, an amendment in 1872 began to address the situation more seriously. Publicized testing of consumer spirits found high concentrations of methanol (toxic but inexpensive), sulfuric acid, lead, copper, and zinc. Arthur Hill Hassall's 1855 and 1876 books on adulterations in food and beverages also brought attention to the issue and forced some political attention to the problem, which affected gin, rum, brandy, and whiskies. In 1872, the *North British Daily Mail* tested thirty samples of whisky, and only five came back described as pure whisky, but only two of those samples were not "excessively diluted" with water.

The problem was just as severe on the other side of the Atlantic. For example, a recipe for imitation bourbon, published in 1860, calls for 40 gallons of proof spirits, tincture of hickory nut, 1 gallon domestic brandy, 1 pint wine vinegar, and 1 pound white glycerin with 12 drops oil of cognac. Caramel coloring was added according to preference. This example is one of the more reputable recipes. Other rectifiers added prune juice, burnt sugar, wood shavings, acetic acid, creosote, and other chemicals. Heavily diluted whisky can become cloudy as alcohol-soluble fusel oils and esters drop out of suspension and emulsify at lower proof. So alum, carbonate of potash, and lead acetate might be added to help clarify the liquid.

In the United States, growing sentiment against adulterated foods found common cause with an aggressive political temperance movement, as well as a progressive movement that wanted to see social reforms, curbs on unscrupulous business practices, and more government oversight of food, beverages, and drugs. Leading the movement was H. W. Wiley, a charismatic chemist whose advocacy dovetailed with the Kentucky distillers, led by Col. E. H. Taylor Jr., whose traditional, unadulterated whisky was being undermined in the marketplace by imitation spirits. See WILEY, HARVEY W., and TAYLOR, COL. E. H. Above all, both sides wanted the government to define, once and for all, what could be labeled as whisky. Although the resulting 1897 Bottled-in-Bond Act didn't quite do that, it nonetheless set a government-backed standard for pure whisky, while still allowing other kinds to be sold.

See BOTTLED IN BOND. Along with the subsequent 1905 Pure Food and Drug Act, it set a policy of defining but not prohibiting: you could sell adulterate (but not poisonous) whisky, but you would have to tell people what was in it and couldn't call it anything it wasn't—only pure bourbon could be called bourbon.

In the United Kingdom, the 1908 Royal Commission on Whiskey and Other Potable Spirits served a similar purpose, setting definitions and labeling requirements without outlawing blending or preventing column-still spirit from being labeled as whisky.

While the makers of traditional whiskies often aligned themselves with the pure food movement, suggesting that American straight whiskies or scotch single malt were more authentic and traditional and therefore "healthier," rectifiers pointed to the fact that pot-distilled whisky often has more congeners—the chemicals that create flavor but are difficult for the body to metabolize and contribute to hangovers. See CONGENERS. But in the intervening years, and through decades of marketing, the authenticity argument has prevailed. Simulated or imitation whiskies are far less popular than sugar substitutes, margarine, and other categories of synthesized food alternatives.

Today, outright adulteration is rare, at least in legal spirits. When adulteration does occur, it is generally connected either to counterfeiting of spirits to avoid high taxes or to unscrupulous or lax production of moonshine. All too often, bootleggers have added chemicals like methanol in an effort to cheaply stretch a spirit. Deaths have been reported in India, Haiti, and eastern Europe from this kind of adulterated, bootleg alcohol. See MOONSHINE.

Mainstream spirits are not, however, entirely free from manipulation: for many categories, additives are permitted up to a certain threshold that varies by country. In the United States, products labeled vodka can contain trace amounts of sugar or citric acid without disclosing those ingredients on the label. Rye whisky (but not straight rye whisky) made in the United States may have up to 2.5 percent of its volume as "harmless coloring/flavoring/blending materials" without disclosing those ingredients on the label. Even single malt scotch, perhaps the most constrained category of whisky anywhere, can still have coloring added.

See also DILUTION and RECTIFICATION.

Burns, Edward. *Bad Whiskey: The Scandal that Created the World's Most Successful Spirit*, 3rd edition. Castle Douglas, UK: Neil Wilson Publishing, 2012.

Department of the Treasury, Alcohol and Tobacco Tax and Trade Bureau. *The Beverage Alcohol Manual (BAM): A Practical Guide*, vol. 2. Washington, DC: Department of the Treasury, Alcohol and Tobacco Tax and Trade Bureau, 2007.

Dick, William B. *Encyclopedia of Practical Receipts and Processes.* New York: Dick & Fitzgerald, 1900.

Veach, Michael. *Kentucky Bourbon Whiskey: An American Heritage.* Lexington: University Press of Kentucky, 2013

Young, James Harvey. *Pure Food: Securing the Federal Food and Drugs Act of 1906.* Princeton, NJ: Princeton University Press, 1989.

Colin Spoelman

agar (or **agar-agar**) is a thickening or clarifying agent derived from red algae. As a vegan substitute for gelatin, it is typically used for gels and foams and can be sold as powder, strips, or flake. Unlike animal-based gelatin, agar remains solid at relatively high temperatures. With no color and little discernable flavor, agar is popular in molecular gastronomy and can be used to clarify fruit juices for cocktails. Agar has roots in Japan where, in 1658, it is said that a Japanese innkeeper discovered its use after retrieving excess seaweed jelly he had thrown out, which had frozen. After he thawed and boiled it, the result was clearer than its first form.

Arnold, Dave, and Travis Huggett. *Liquid Intelligence: The Art and Science of the Perfect Cocktail.* New York: W. W. Norton, 2014.

Myhrvold, Nathan. *Modernist Cuisine: The Art and Science of Cooking.* Bellevue, WA: Cooking Lab, 2011.

Tan, Ria. "Wild Fact Sheets: Agar-Agar Red Seaweeds." *Wild Singapore.* http://www.wildsingapore.com/wildfacts/plants/seaweed/rhodophyta/gracilaria.htm (accessed March 16, 2021).

Alexi Friedman

agave is a genus of succulents indigenous to the Mesoamerican highlands, an area located in what is now central and western Mexico. Currently there are approximately two hundred species of agave recognized with approximately 75 percent of those found in the region stretching from southwestern United States, through Mexico, and into South America. The majority of the species are endemic to specific regions and habitats, having adapted to the arid environments in which they are most prevalent.

Naming

The names for agave in Mesoamerica are as numerous and diverse as the peoples who populate this region, but many are known only on a local or regional level. Although Spanish is the official language of Mexico, the Mexican government recognizes sixty-eight indigenous languages, which all have a word for agave. The Nahuatl word for agave, however, has stood the test of time perhaps due to its role in the provenance of the word *mezcal*, derived from the Nahuatl words for agave (*metl*) and oven-cooked (*ixcalli*). See MEZCAL.

Prior to their arrival in Mesoamerica, the Spanish first encountered agave in the Caribbean. There the indigenous Taíno of Greater Antilles (Cuba, Jamaica, and Hispaniola) called agave *maguey*. See CARIBBEAN. The Spanish introduced the word maguey in what is now central Mexico, and it remains the most commonly used word for the plant.

The name agave was bestowed on this genus by taxonomist Carl Linnaeus in 1753. Agave derives from the Greek *agauē*, meaning noble or illustrious, a name truly suitable for this prolific plant.

Taxonomy and Characteristics

For many years agaves were a moving target in the taxonomy world, having been previously classified in the lily (Liliaceae) and amaryllis (Amaryllidaceae) families prior to temporarily receiving their own home as Agavaceae. In 2009 the third version of the modern plant-based taxonomy system, APG III, was published. In APG III the Agavaceae were incorporated into the larger family Asparagaceae, where *Agave* is one of eighteen genera in the subfamily Agavoideae. The confusion in regard to where and how the plant should be classified can quickly be understood when looking at the diversity of the genus. From the petite, variegated leaves of the *cupreata* to the upright palm tree characteristics of the *karwinskii* to the dark, curvy *pencas* of the *marmorata*, the differences between agave can seem greater than their similarities. There are, however, commonalities that hold this genus together.

Agaves are characterized by basal rosettes of thick *pencas*, or leaves, that are arranged in an overlapping pattern emitting from the central axis at the golden angle of 137.5°. Individual pencas are most commonly edged in spines before terminating at a sharp point. The alignment of the spines and the shape of the pencas, spines, and terminating points are used by farmers and botanists to distinguish varieties within a species.

Agaves are monocots, flowering plants whose seeds contain a single embryonic leaf. Each rosette will mature slowly, with some varieties taking upwards of thirty years to reach full maturity. Agaves are monocarpic, meaning that upon maturity each rosette will flower once and then die. A spectacular *quiote*, or flowering stalk, will flourish from the center of the rosette. The development of the quiote begins internally before there is external growth. Prior to the shooting of the inflorescence, the internal cluster of leaves at the center of the rosette will become thinner and narrower. The quiote will grow rapidly, up to 20 cm a day for some varieties, and can reach heights of 2–10 meters. The flowers of the agave vary in color from light green to yellow to red. Pollen and nectar are produced at night, with the flowers sometimes smelling like rotting fruit. For these reasons agaves are predominately pollinated by nocturnal animals, the most common being bats. Additional pollinators include hawkmoths, hummingbirds, songbirds, bees, and opossums. Depending on the variety of agave, the flowers will result in seedpods or bulbils, small bulbs that can result in a new plant.

Many types of agave can also reproduce asexually through cloning. The mother plant will send out rhizomes, or underground stems, from which offshoots will grow. Typically the mother plant will begin producing clones at the age of two or three and on average will produce three to four offshoots per year. The offshoots will be carefully removed when they reach 50–120 centimeters in height, stored for a period of time, then replanted in the fields.

Agave and Humankind

Agave and humans have had a symbiotic relationship for thousands of years in Mesoamerica. The Tehuacán-Cuicatlan Valley of Puebla hosts the area of the greatest diversity of agave species as well as a human history of 12,000–14,000 years. Archaeological remains of masticated agave fibers have been discovered on cave floors and in coprolites (fossilized human excrement) in the layers of earth associated with human habitation of this area some 10,000 years ago. For many reasons the use of agave as a food source is not surprising. The plant was prevalent, and one needed only heat and water to convert the starches to sugars for consumption. Once prepared, one could use what was needed and dry what remained into cakes to be consumed at a later time or to be traded with neighboring communities. Agave can still be used as a food source in times of poor harvests of standard seed crops or during turbulent years when access to other food sources is interrupted. However, its role as a food source is now an ancillary one. Standard seed crops are inter-planted with agave, utilizing the relatively shallow root systems of the agave to minimize erosion and water runoff. In return, the seed crops replenish nutrients in the soil that have been consumed by the agave.

Beyond being a food source, every part of the agave plant offers something useful to humankind. By 7000 BCE agave fibers were being used in multiple ways, and many of those uses continue to this day. The fibers are woven into baskets, bags, blankets, clothing, and other textiles. Dried fibers can be made into hair- and paintbrushes. By taking the point of a penca and pulling it down the leaf, one could have a needle and thread. Agave fibers have been used as the strings on a musical instrument constructed from a hollowed quiote. The quiote, when dried, can be used as a type of log to build fences and shelter, while agave pencas can thatch the roof. The *aguamiel*, or honey water, is medicinally beneficial as an anti-inflammatory and to treat digestive conditions.

The dispersion of the varieties of agave within Mesoamerica and beyond accelerated after the arrival of the Spanish. As the Spanish spread throughout Mesoamerica, they would take indigenous laborers, interpreters, and farmers who would migrate with their favored type of agave. The Spanish and Portuguese, in turn, took agave overseas for ornamental and fiber purposes. Succulents became popular in public and private gardens throughout Europe in the nineteenth century, while colonial interests established agave fiber industries in the Philippines and Indonesia around the same time and in East Africa by the twentieth century. See INDONESIA and CENTRAL AND EAST AFRICA.

Today modern technologies have allowed for even more diverse uses of the plant. Agave is rich in sapogenins, a compound used in soap production but which also contains base molecules from which cortisone and sex hormones such as estrogen can be synthesized. Additionally, agave is rich with the prebiotic inulin. The pencas of the agave are high in fermentable sugars and therefore can be used in the production of industrial ethanol.

Agave Beverages

Beverages made from the agave plant come in many varieties. Fermented or distilled, they each have a long mythology and history as well as great social and economic impacts.

Pulque is an ancient fermented beverage made from the *aguamiel* of any of six varieties of agave, the most common being *Agave salmiana*. Prior to the Spanish arrival, Aztec nobles and priests consumed the beverage as part of religious ceremonies; its intoxicating effects were meant to bring drinkers closer to the gods. Upon their arrival the Spanish took a liking to this fermented beverage and introduced pulque agaves as they subsequently moved through Mesoamerica.

Distilled agave beverages have a long but somewhat clouded history. In the past the prevailing belief was that distillation technology was a gift from the Spanish. Currently, dissenting scholars debate about the origins of distillation in Mesoamerica. What is certain is that agave distillation has been a cottage industry in Mexico providing economic opportunity for hundreds of years. See DISTILLATION, HISTORY.

The Future of Agave

The abundance and utilitarian nature of agave resulted in its central role in the lives of Mesoamerican peoples. As a primary resource with myriad uses, the plant has been respected and protected for thousands of years. The years since 2010 have seen significant growth in the international interest in agave distillates, resulting in a significant increase in the production and sale of the agave spirits of Mexico. Financially, this has offered economic opportunities for individuals involved in all aspects of their production. Unfortunately it has also resulted in significant pressures on Mexico's ecosystems.

As global demand and profits have risen, traditional harvesting practices and communal land management are facing pressure to adapt or lose these resources that have always been a part of local surroundings. With two hundred species within the genus of *Agave*, genetic diversity is one of its most distinguishing features. In 1975 the Denomination of Origin of Tequila was created, mandating the use solely of *Agave tequilana*. As the category of Tequila grew, so did the need for more plants. In the course of expansion, differing species of agave were eradicated, thus reducing the biodiversity within the states of the DO. Additionally, producers ceased using reproduction through the inflorescence, which led to two adverse effects: in doing so they removed a primary food source for *Leptonycteris* bats, resulting in a dramatic shift in their migratory paths and thereby altering the ecosystem of central Mexico; and without sexual reproduction and cross-pollination, the genetic diversity of crops waned, weakening the plant and making it susceptible to disease.

The Denomination of Origin of Mezcal was established in 1995. Although the DO is only a few decades old, the pressure to increase production, paired with a lack of respect for the lengthy lifecycle of the agave, has resulted in diminishing populations of multiple species.

The future of agave is dependent on all of us who consume it in its many forms. Respecting tradition and educating oneself about the products we purchase are the keys to ensuring the future of this noble plant and the livelihood of those who depend on it for survival.

Colunga-Garcia, Marín, Alfonso Larqué Saavedra, Luis E. Eguiarte, and Daniel Zizumbo-Villarreal, eds. *En lo Ancestral Hay Futuro: Del Tequila, Los Mezcales y Otro Agaves*. Mérida, Mexico: Centro de Investigación Científica de Yucatán, 2007.

García-Mendoza, Abisaí. "Distribution of the genus *Agave* (Agavaceae) and its endemic species in Mexico." *Cactus and Succulent Journal* 74 (2002): 177–187.

Gentry, Howard Scott. *Agaves of Continental North America*. Tucson: University of Arizona Press, 1982.

Valenzuela Zapata, Ana, and Gary Paul Nabhan. *Tequila!: A Natural and Cultural History*. Tucson: University of Arizona Press, 2004.

Misty Kalkofen

agave nectar or syrup is a sweetener made from the sap of the agave plant. Known in Mexico as *aguamiel* (honey water), it is intensely sweet and amber in color and slightly less viscous than honey. While raw aguamiel has been used for millennia, commercially manufactured agave nectar undergoes varying degrees of refining and filtering. Commonly made from blue agave, the variety used to make tequila, agave nectar is marketed as a healthy sugar alternative thanks to a low glycemic ranking, but its health benefits are hotly debated, as the nectar's high fructose content has been linked to heart disease and obesity. Agave nectar may be used as a cocktail ingredient, such as in a Tommy's Margarita, where it replaces orange liqueur, adding extra agave punch to the drink's flavor. See MARGARITA.

See also AGAVE.

Diana, Richard. *Healthy Joints for Life: An Orthopedic Surgeon's Proven Plan to Reduce Pain and Inflammation, Avoid Surgery and Get Moving Again*. Toronto: Harlequin, 2014.

Chantal Martineau

aging, typically in barrels, is an essential step in the production of brown spirits such as whisky. See also BARREL; MATURATION; and WHISKY.

aguardiente and **aguardente** (roughly "firewater"; see AQUA VITAE) are generic terms in use for spirits wherever Spanish or Portuguese are spoken, though on brand labels there are often regulations controlling the terms' usage. Brazil's cachaça, for example, may be colloquially known as *aguardente de caña*, but there are different legal definitions for each: cachaça is made from sugar cane juice, while aguardente de caña càn be made from sugar cane juice, syrup, or molasses. Additionally, cachaça is bottled at 38–48 percent ABV, while aguardente de caña can be bottled at 38–54 percent ABV. See BRAZIL and CACHAÇA.

Mexico also utilizes the term *aguardiente de caña* to describe sugar cane–derived spirit, among other terms. See CHARANDA, HABANERO, and CHINGUIRITO. Colombia's aguardiente is a popular sugar cane–based spirit of between 24 percent and 29 percent ABV flavored with anise. Ecuador has its own popular aguardiente brands without anise flavoring; and one of El Salvador's top spirits, Tic Tack, is an aguardiente de caña at 30 percent ABV. El Salvador uses the term *guaro* (a slang term for aguardiente shared with other Latin American countries) for their sugar cane spirit. Puerto Ricans refer to their high-proof *ron* (rum) as *pitorro*. See PITORRO.

In Spain and Portugal, the terms have legal definitions, referring to spirits distilled from wine (alcohol fermented from fruit), though lees and other solids are allowed in the distillation in other countries. EU regulations stipulate that wine rather than pomace is used in order to be labeled as aguardente. In Portugal, if pomace is used, the country's regulations require that the product is labeled aguardente bagaçeira, or merely bagaçeira. See BAGAÇEIRA.

In Portugal, the EU has demarcated six aguardente-producing regions, each with its own delimited boundaries: Aguardente de Vinho Douro, Aguardente de Vinho Ribatejo, Aguardente de Vinho Alentejo, Aguardente de Vinho da Região dos Vinhos Verdes and Aguardente de Vinho da Região dos Vinhos Verdes de Alvarinho (made solely from the Alvarinho grape variety), and Aguardente de Vinho Lourinhã.

Aguardiente is the Spanish equivalent, and the rules are roughly the same. The only two regional Spanish demarcated examples are aguardiente de sidra de Asturias (or apple-based spirit from Asturias) and a liqueur: aguardiente de hierbas de Galicia (a sweet herb liqueur).

See also ORUJO and POMACE BRANDY.

Mistesterio da Agricultura, do Desenvolvimento Rural e das Pescas. "Vinhos e Aguardentes de Portugal: Anuário 2010|11." http://www. winesofportugal.info/anuario_2011.pdf (accessed June 1, 2016).
Regulation (EC) No 110/2008 of the European Parliament and of the Council. http:// eur-lex.europa.eu/legal-content/en/TXT/ ?uri=CELEX%3A52001PC0760.

Doug Frost

Air Mail is a tropical take on the Champagne Cocktail that first saw print in a 1930 recipe pamphlet published in Cuba by the Bacardi company. See BACARDI; CHAMPAGNE COCKTAILS. Since Cuba also began air mail service in 1930, it is tempting to assume that this was the year the drink's anonymous creator gave it wings. But the pamphlet offers no provenance. The original recipe remains largely unchanged today and has become a popular serve in craft cocktail bars.

Recipe: Shake 15 ml lime juice, 5 ml liquid honey (or 5 ml honey dissolved in 5 ml warm water), and 45 ml gold, Cuban-style rum with ice. Strain into a tall glass, and top with champagne.

Bacardi and Its Many Uses. Santiago de Cuba: Compañía Ron Bacardi, 1930.
Wondrich, David. *Esquire Drinks: An Opinionated and Irreverent Guide to Drinking.* New York: Hearst, 2002.

Jeff Berry

akpeteshie (Ga: "something hidden") is a home-distilled liquor that has become common throughout West and Central Africa's coastal zone since the 1930s. See HOME DISTILLING. The Ga term *akpeteshie* is specific to southern Ghana; other names include: "local gin," *kelewele, sodabi, ogogoro, kai kai,* and *mongorokom*. See OGOGORO. Most names refer either to the drink's history as an illegal product or to its strength. Akpeteshie is single-distilled from fermented palm juice or sugar cane using improvised stills made from metal barrels and copper pipes. The finished drink is a strong liquor of varying strength (between 30 percent and 50 percent ABV), which is poured into unlabeled and recycled bottles for storage and sale. Akpeteshie tastes rough and has a local reputation for being potentially harmful. It is usually distilled by farmers for whom it offers extra income and consumed by the poor, wage laborers, farmers, and fishermen. Distillation first occurred during the 1910s in small quantities. The colonial governments of the time relied heavily on import taxes from foreign alcohol and thus declared akpeteshie illegal. There is little evidence of its production during the 1920s when African crops fetched good prices on the world market and farmers could afford imported liquor. Illegal akpeteshie distillation spread rapidly during the 1930s global recession. It was a symbol of resistance against colonialism during decolonization. It has remained a symbol of popular culture and of protest to governments in West Africa.

See also CENTRAL AND EAST AFRICA and WEST AFRICA.

Akyeampong, Emmanuel. "What's in a Drink? Class Struggle, Popular Culture and the Politics of Akpeteshie (Local Gin) in Ghana, 1930–67." *Journal of African History* 37 (1996): 215–236.
Korieh, Chima J. "Alcohol and Empire: 'Illicit' Gin Prohibition and Control in Colonial Eastern Nigeria." *African Economic History* 31 (2003): 111–134.
Leis, Philip E. "Palm Oil, Illicit Gin, and the Moral Order of the Ijaw." *American Anthropologist*, n.s., 66, no. 4, pt. 1 (1964): 828–838.

Dmitri van den Bersselaar

akvavit is a variant spelling of aquavit, the caraway-flavored Scandinavian spirit. See AQUAVIT.

The **Alaska Cocktail**, with gin and yellow Chartreuse, never achieved significant fame but did manage to putter along for several decades. Though the drink was not unknown on the menus of fashionable West Coast hotel bars, it existed less in the glass than on the page. It is one of those drinks that, once included in a bartender's guide, gets copied into other compendia, which leads to further copying into mixology manuals to come. A fairly sweet version of the drink, made with Old Tom gin, Chartreuse, and orange bitters, can be found in the 1913 *Straub's Manual of Mixed Drinks*. By the time it was copied into the famous *Savoy Cocktail Book* in 1930, it had become a drier drink made with 3 parts dry gin to 1 part Chartreuse. "So far as can be ascertained this delectable potion is NOT the staple diet of the Esquimaux," the book joked. "It was probably first thought of in South Carolina—hence its name." Lame joshing aside, the Alaska is a worthy Martini variation, especially if one reduces the sweetness dramatically by dialing back the Chartreuse, and indeed it is something of a cult drink among modern cocktail aficionados. It is best at 6 or 8 parts gin to 1 part yellow Chartreuse, especially if one restores the dash of orange bitters (a nicety that got lost sometime during Prohibition).

Recipe: Stir 75 ml dry gin and 22 ml yellow Chartreuse with ice and strain into a chilled Martini glass.

Craddock, Harry. *The Savoy Cocktail Book*. London: Constable & Co, 1930.
"Fashions in Mixed Drinks." *Guthrie Daily Leader*, October 18, 1905, 2.

Eric Felten

alcopop is a blanket term, common in the United Kingdom, for mass-produced canned and bottled drinks often with low alcohol content. The sweetened beverages are named for their resemblance to soda pop. These include flavored malt beverages, wine coolers, and spirit-based, ready-to-drink cocktails (known in the trade as RTDs). The category has existed since at least 1981, when E & J Gallo launched Bartles & Jaymes wine coolers, but it experienced explosive growth in the mid-1990s, led in the United States by Zima, released in 1993, and in the UK by Hooper's Hooch, launched in 1995. Other major brands include Smirnoff Ice, Bacardi Breezers, and Mike's. See SMIRNOFF and BACARDI.

Alcopops tend to appeal to younger (and often underage) drinkers; one British study found that alcohol consumption among eleven- to fifteen-year-olds increased by 63 percent between 1992 and 2001, led largely by alcopop consumption. This led many countries to increases taxes on, and institute strict regulations about, alcohol content, advertising, and labeling of alcopops, which drove many brands out of business. Brands such as Jim Beam, Jack Daniels, Wild Turkey, and Johnnie Walker continue to make such drinks, while newer brands such as Ballast Point, Life of Reilley, Punching Mule, and Hochstadter's are revitalizing the category. See JIM BEAM; JACK DANIEL'S; and JOHNNIE WALKER.

Duffy, Jonathan. "What Happened to Alcopops?" *BBC News Magazine*, November 9, 2005. http://news.bbc.co.uk/2/hi/uk_news/magazine/4419578.stm (accessed January 27, 2021).
Koerner, Brendan. "The Long, Slow, Torturous Death of Zima." *Slate*, November 26, 2008. http://www.slate.com/articles/life/drink/2008/11/the_long_slow_torturous_death_of_zima.html (accessed January 27, 2021).

Jason Horn

aldehydes, like ketones, represent a group of organic compounds usually created by the oxidation of alcohols. The term is credited to the nineteenth-century chemist Justus von Liebig, from "dehydrogenated alcohols." As with ketones, aldehydes can have remarkably powerful aromatics, from fruits to nuts, cheese, vegetables, and flowers. Acetaldehyde is the most common of these; its aromas seem fruity at low levels but at higher levels take on the aromas of nuts and even bruised and rotten apples. See ACETALDEHYDE. Wines and spirits marked by oxidation, such as oloroso sherry, madeira, cognac, and Armagnac, have high levels of acetaldehyde as well as other aldehydes.

See also KETONE and OXIDATION.

American Chemical Society. https://www.acs.org (accessed January 27, 2021).

Buxton, Ian, and Paul S. Hughes. *The Science and Commerce of Whisky*. Cambridge: RSC, 2015.

Jeffrey, David W., Gavin Sacks, and Andrew Waterhouse. *Understanding Wine Chemistry*. Oxford: Wiley, 2016.

Doug Frost

alembic is an old name for the classic pot still. See STILL, POT. The name remains in general use in some countries and is used by some producers in others. It is derived from the Arabic *al-anbîq*, which is in turn derived from the Greek *ambix*, or cup.

Alexander, Cato (1780–1858), was a key member of the founding cohort of the American school of mixing drinks, running establishments that pleased New Yorkers and travelers foreign and domestic with his exceptional drinks and cuisine for over forty years. Born enslaved, probably in New York, Alexander was raised in the world of inns and taverns (as a youth he frequently waited on George Washington when the president lived in New York). See WASHINGTON, GEORGE. He gained his freedom in 1799 and, sometime before 1811, leased a substantial, two-story house and an acre or two of land on the Boston Post Road four miles north of New York City (today it corresponds roughly to Second Avenue and Fifty-Fourth Street in Manhattan). He would run a tavern there for the next three and a half decades.

In its long heyday, Cato's Tavern was an integral part of the city's social life. It was a popular destination for weekend family excursions and a venue for balls, auctions, and funerals. It was also, however, a key part of the infrastructure of the city's sporting life, as a goal for impromptu carriage races, a meeting point for foxhunts in the wilds of northern Manhattan, and a gathering point for the raffish, the high-spirited, and the dissolute.

Alexander himself enjoyed a general respect infrequently accorded to African Americans at the time. As was common with African American caterers, he supervised both the kitchen and the bar. His reputation as a chef was high, but as a mixologist it was even higher. While Alexander was often praised for his traditional punches, his chief acclaim was for his way with the new, peculiarly American drinks that were transforming the country's drinking culture. The Irish actor Tyrone Power, who frequented his establishment in the early 1830s, summed up the general opinion when he called Alexander "foremost amongst cullers of mint, whether for julep or hail-storm; second to no man as a compounder of cock-tail, and such a hand at a gin-sling!" See COCK-TAIL and GIN SLING. His only rival as a popularizer of these drinks was Orsamus Willard, of New York's famous City Hotel. See WILLARD, ORSAMUS.

In the mid-1840s, Alexander was forced to sell his business after losses incurred, rumor had it, from lending incautiously to his patrons. After a stint as a farmer on Long Island, east of the city, he returned to New York in 1852 and opened a modest oyster house on Broadway. It lasted barely a year, and after that he disappeared from the public eye. Alexander's original tavern and its popular proprietor, however, remained large in the memory of New Yorkers well into the twentieth century.

"Death of Cato of 'the Road.' " *New York Herald*, February 17, 1858.

Mott, Hopper Striker. "Cato's Tavern." *Americana*, April 1916, 123.

Power, Tyrone. *Impressions of America during the Years 1833, 1834, and 1835*. London: R. Bentley, 1836.

David Wondrich

The **Alexander Cocktail**, with gin or brandy, crème de cacao and heavy cream, is notable for pioneering the use of cream as a cocktail ingredient. First appearing in print in the United States in 1914 (there was an earlier, more conventional drink of the same name with rye and Bénédictine), the Alexander was not the first cocktail to use cream, with which "the Only William" had already experimented in the 1890s. See SCHMIDT, WILLIAM. It was, however, certainly the first to gain a broad popularity both in the United States and in Europe (it is found there by the early 1920s), and it would prove both influential and controversial in equal parts. The drink's origins are much disputed, but the best-supported claim traces it to Rector's, one of New York City's "lobster palaces," where bar manager Troy Alexander created it for some officials of the Lackawanna Railroad, then famous for its advertising campaign featuring "Phoebe Snow," a (fictional) young lady who could ride the railroad's trains in a spotless white gown due to its use of smokeless coal. Alexander therefore created a drink that was perfectly white. The year is uncertain, but he was at Rector's on and off from at least 1904 until it closed in 1913. The formula seems to have gotten into the wild only loosely attached to the name, as it is found in Hugo Ensslin's invaluable 1916 compendium of what they were drinking in New York under three different names, including also the "Panama" (making it one of several drinks circulating under that name) and the "Stonewall Jackson."

The Alexander was not universally beloved. Some objected to the gin: Harry MacElhone, for one, who in his 1922 *ABC of mixing cocktails* replaced it with brandy. See MACELHONE, HARRY. This version, too, would become quite popular. Most, however, objected to the crème de cacao and the cream, which together earned the Alexander the reputation as a drink for, as one 1930 American drink guide put it, "tender young things, who have just been taken off stick candy." In 1934, *Esquire* magazine listed it as number two in its list of the "ten worst cocktails" of the year. Nonetheless the Alexander did not go away, at least not the brandy version, which survived long enough as a popular drink for Jack Lemmon to get Lee Remick hooked on alcohol with them in the 1962 film *Days of Wine and Roses* and to be one of the mainstays of the fern bar. Only with the cocktail revival of the twenty-first century did its popularity finally fade, despite its impeccable pre-Prohibition pedigree.

Recipe: Shake 30 ml ea. London dry gin or brandy, white crème de cacao, and heavy cream. Strain and serve up. For a Brandy Alexander, grate nutmeg on top.

Elliott, Virginia, and Phil D. Strong. *Shake 'Em Up: A Manual of Polite Drinking*. N.p.: Brewer & Warren, 1930.

Ensslin, Hugo R. *Recipes for Mixed Drinks*. New York: Mud Puddle Books, 1916.

Montague, Harry. *The Up-to-Date Bartenders' Guide*. In *New Bartender's Guide . . . 2 Books in One*. Baltimore: I & M Ottenheimer, 1914.

Winchell, Walter. "Your Broadway and Mine" (syndicated column), March 22, 1929.

David Wondrich

almond liqueurs, better known by the Italian name amaretto, are indigenous to Saronno, in Lombardy, and purportedly date back to the Renaissance. There are a number of brands that make up this nut-flavored cordial category, but the most famous one is Disaronno, which employs a recipe of herbs and fruits steeped in crushed apricot kernel oil—although amaretto is commonly thought of as almond-flavored, it is generally made from apricot kernels macerated in brandy and then sweetened; the error is understandable given that apricots and almonds are closely related members of the drupe family of stone fruits. Another brand, Lazzaroni, uses an infusion of Amaretti di Saronno cookies. The liqueur is most famously used in 1980s cocktails such as the Amaretto Sour, made with lemon juice and sweet and sour mix, as well as the Alabama Slammer, made with Southern Comfort, sloe gin, and orange juice, and the Godfather, where it is paired with scotch whisky. See AMARETTO SOUR. Beyond boozy libations, almond liqueurs spice up desserts like tiramisu and everyday cups of coffee.

See also CORDIALS.

Food Network Canada Editors. "A Brief History of Amaretto." foodnetwork.ca (accessed March 28, 2011).

Alia Akkam

al-Zahrāwī, Abū al-Qāsim Khalaf ibn al-ʿAbbās (also known as **Abu al-Qasim** or **Abulcasis**, 936–1013), was a physician from Moorish Andalusia (modern-day Spain), author of one of the most important medical texts of the Middle Ages. His medical encyclopedia *Kitab al-Tasrif* became extremely influential in medieval Europe, and some of the techniques he described are still in use today. He also described distillation methods, including a mention of wine distillation, and is among the Arab pioneers cited in traditional Western histories of distillation.

The pharmacological volume of *al-Tasrif*, often published separately in translation as *Liber Servitoris*, does briefly mention the distillation of wine. After describing the distillation of vinegar to produce acetic acid, al-Zahrāwī adds, "In this way wine can be distilled by anyone who wants it distilled."

This cursory reference to wine distillation and others in Arab alchemical literature that are similarly brief have led to debate over whether the Arabs produced distilled alcohol before Europeans did. Some scholars have suggested that if Arab chemists found the product of wine distillation so unremarkable, perhaps they were allowing the ethanol to escape and only collecting the "tails" of the vapors, due to insufficient cooling. However, experimental results indicate that it would not have been difficult to isolate ethanol with the alembic stills used in the Arab world. Furthermore, by the eleventh century references to the "araq" of wine (distilled alcohol) had begun to appear in the Arabic, so it is quite possible that al-Zahrāwī was aware of distilled alcohol and simply didn't think it needed description. See DISTILLATION, HISTORY OF.

Little is known about the life of al-Zahrāwī. He spent most of his days in Cordoba, where he was court physician to Caliph Al-Hakam II. He is credited with either inventing or first documenting more than a hundred surgical instruments. *Al-Tasrif* contains the first known descriptions of ectopic pregnancy, the hereditary nature of hemophilia, the use of "catgut" (animal intestine) for internal stitching, "Kocher's method" of treating a dislocated shoulder, and the "Walcher hanging position" for giving birth. In these things, it may be argued, lies the true value of his works.

Cosman, Madeleine Pelner, and Linda Gale Jones. *Handbook to Life in the Medieval World*, vol. 2. New York: Infobase, 2009.

Forbes, R. J. *Short History of the Art of Distillation*. Leiden: E. J. Brill, 1948.

Sam Eilertsen

The **Amaretto Sour**, originally a simple mix of two parts amaretto liqueur to one part lemon juice, was introduced by the importer of Amaretto di Saronno (later Disaronno Originale) in 1974 and would go on to become one of the standards of the 1980s. See ALMOND LIQUEURS. By then, of course, most bartenders ditched the lemon juice for commercial sour mix. Like other popular liqueur highballs of the time, such as the Midori Sour, it was a one-dimensional easy-drinker that tasted mostly of the liqueur from which it was made. The Amaretto Sour can be greatly improved by going back to fresh lemon juice (use 30 ml lemon juice along with 15 ml simple syrup) and adding a little (15 ml) lightly-whipped egg white and 22 ml good cask-strength bourbon.

See also SOUR MIX; CRÈME DE NOYAUX.

Recipe (standard): Mix 45 ml amaretto and 90 ml sour mix, serve over ice, and garnish with a cherry and an orange or lemon wedge.

Sardi, Vincent, with George Shea. *Sardi's Bar Guide*. New York: Ballantine, 1988.

Jeffrey Morgenthaler

amaro, the Italian word for "bitter," also denotes an Italian form of—no surprise here—potable bitters. See BITTERS. Traditionally served as a digestive, amari have been enthusiastically embraced as cocktail ingredients by contemporary mixologists. See also HERBAL LIQUEURS.

ambergris is produced in the digestive tract of sperm whales, where it is thought to accrete around sharp objects, such as the beaks of giant squid, in order to protect the internal organs of the whale, much like pearls are formed around irritating grains of sand inside the shells of oysters. When fresh—despite the descriptions in *Moby Dick*—it is fatty and smells like feces. Whales expel ambergris, which floats and develops a pleasant sweetness as it ages that seems, by the sheer number of adjectives used to capture its aroma, to defy description. It is commonly said to be both earthy and marine, like rich, smooth rubbing alcohol, but without the astringency. Ambergris is staggeringly expensive, was used for centuries as a fixative in perfume, and was thought to ward off the plague. It appears, very occasionally, in early recipes for punch.

See also PUNCH.

Melville, Herman. *Moby Dick*. Oxford: Oxford University Press, 2008.

Wondrich, David. *Punch: The Delights (and Dangers) of the Flowing Bowl*. New York, Penguin, 2004.

Max Watman

The **American Distilling Institute** is a trade organization founded by Bill Owens (1938–), an influential American photographer and journalist, in 2003 to promote the interests of American distillers, particularly those on the smaller, "craft" end of the spectrum. Through its membership forums, online resources, newsletter, *Distiller* magazine, annual conference, distilling workshops, and other events, ADI provides distillers with technical and regulatory guidance, as well as information on potentially relevant legislation. The organization also organizes an annual judging of craft spirits by panels of industry experts. Awards are given for both spirits and packaging.

The definition of craft distilling is nebulous, but the ADI has addressed the issue with a craft spirit certification program. To receive certification, distillers and blenders must be independently owned, operate at a small scale in both sales and total production, and employ hands-on production techniques. Certified producers are permitted to advertise their status on their product labels.

See also CRAFT DISTILLING.

American Distilling Institute. https://www.distilling.com (accessed December 30, 2016).

Jacob Grier

Americano is an Italian drink combining vermouth with an aperitive or digestive bitter, seltzer, and ice. See APERITIF AND DIGESTIVE. The name, Italian for "American-style" or "in the American way," is an acknowledgment of the drink's origin, which is as an Italian riff on the 1860s American practice of adding bitters to vermouth to turn it into a Vermouth Cocktail. This led to Italian producers making a pre-bittered "vermouth Americano," mostly for their domestic markets. Yet many Italian

drinkers agreed with the oenologist Arnaldo Strucchi's opinion that it was better for "whoever enjoys drinking a vermouth with some modification or special flavor" such as bitters to have the drink made to order by adding "a little of the preferred liqueur to it." By the end of the 1880s (at least according to Parisian bartender Émile Lefeuvre, writing in 1889), many Italians were doing just that and stretching out the resulting drinks with soda and ice. This marks the first fusion between the Italian *aperitivo* and American mixology.

Originally, a variety of bitters were used in the drink—Fernet Branca was one popular option—but by the 1930s Campari had largely driven out the others. That was perhaps due to the influence of the drink known in Turin as the "Torino Milano" and in Milan as the "Milano Torino," which combined Turin's vermouth and Milan's Campari, but without the sparkling water.

The Americano was quite popular, both in Italy and abroad, through the 1960s, when it began to fade as drinkers switched to one of its variants, the Negroni. See NEGRONI. Nowadays, its role as a light, refreshing, and flavorful aperitif is usually played by the Aperol Spritz. See APEROL SPRITZ.

Recipe: Combine 45 ml Italian vermouth, 45 ml Campari bitters, and a splash of soda in an ice filled Highball glass. Garnish with a twist of lemon peel or an orange wheel.

Grassi, Elvezio. *1000 misture*. Bologna: Cappelli, 1936.

Lefeuvre, Émile. *Méthode pour composer soi-même les boissons Américaines*. Paris: 1889.

Mazzon, Ferruccio. *Il barista*. Trieste: Nazionale, 1920.

Strucchi, Arnaldo. *Il vermouth di Torino*. Casale Monferato: Cassoni, 1907.

Leo Leuci and David Wondrich

Amis, Kingsley (1922–1995), probably the greatest English comic novelist of the late twentieth century, was also a poet, a restaurant critic, and a passionate proselytizer for drink. Among Amis's prodigious output—twenty-five published novels, seven books of poetry, and eleven nonfiction books, not to mention many thousands of letters and articles—were several books on liquid refreshment: *On Drink* (1972), *How's Your Glass* (1984), and *Everyday Drinking* (1983). One handy posthumous volume,

Everyday Drinking: The Distilled Kingsley Amis (2008), combines the three.

As Amis's friend Christopher Hitchens, himself no slouch when it came to liquid consumption, remarked in his introduction to the compilation, "Booze was his muse." The hangover scene in Amis's first novel, *Lucky Jim* (1954), remains one of the most outstanding depictions of this unfortunate condition ever written. Amis's personal tastes in cocktails were both radically simplistic and defiantly ritualistic—no road trip was complete without a cocktail hamper from which drinks had to be served at a precise hour. While most would differ with his preference for stirring all drinks with ice in a large jug and object as vigorously to the idea of tomato ketchup in a Bloody Mary as to a premade Martini, Amis's columns in *Penthouse* and the *Telegraph* did much to demystify both cocktails and spirits in beery 1970s Britain.

Amis's heavy, ultimately addictive drinking contributed not only to his marriage breakup and death but also to his daughter Sally's alcoholism and early death. It casts his recommendation of a Milk Punch for breakfast in a rather darker light. See MILK PUNCH.

See also SPIRITS WRITING.

Leader, Zachary. *The Life of Kingsley Amis*. London: Jonathan Cape, 2006.

Theodora Sutcliffe

Anchor Distilling Company is the spirits division of Anchor Brewers & Distillers, based in San Francisco, California. The company's roots reach back to 1965, when Fritz Maytag purchased the faltering Anchor Brewery and turned it into a craft-beer vanguard. In 1993, Maytag established the Anchor Distilling Company, based in part on his long interest in rye whisky and early American spirits. Following a series of experiments with pot-distilling whisky, the distillery began production of a 100 percent malted rye whisky in 1994; determined to follow Colonial-era practice, Anchor bottled the whisky after only one year of aging, and in subsequent years two additional expressions were added, all sold under the Old Potrero label; this, the first modern microdistilled whisky to reach market, was an early—perhaps too early—shot across the bows of the American whisky industry, signaling the coming of a new generation of small-scale, creative whisky makers.

In 1996, Anchor released Junípero, one of the first craft-distilled gins in the United States, followed shortly by Genevieve, a genever-style spirit based on unaged whisky. In 2010, Maytag retired and sold Anchor Distilling to the Griffin Group, headed by Keith Greggor and Tony Foglio. The new owners entered a co-distribution arrangement with London merchants Berry Bros. & Rudd, expanding global distribution of Anchor's spirits while also adding a range of more than four hundred other spirits to Anchor Distilling's portfolio, including whiskies from Scotland, Japan, and Taiwan, along with a number of absinthes, liqueurs, rums, and other spirits. See BERRY BROS. & RUDD. Under head distiller Bruce Joseph (first hired by Anchor in 1980), the company also expanded its own range of products, adding Hophead Vodka (a hopped vodka produced in collaboration with Anchor Brewing) in 2012, and Anchor Old Tom Gin in 2014.

Abate, Tom. "Anchor Brewing Co. Sold to Greggor, Foglio." *San Francisco Chronicle*, April 27, 2010. http://www.sfgate.com/news/article/Anchor-Brewing-Co-sold-to-Greggor-Foglio-3266099.php (accessed January 28, 2021).

Anchor Brewers and Distillers website. http://www.anchorbrewersanddistillers.com/ (accessed April 14, 2021).

Ross, Andrew S. "Anchor Brewing Acquisition Is Official." *San Francisco Chronicle*, August 11, 2010. http://www.sfgate.com/business/bottomline/article/Anchor-Brewing-acquisition-is-official-3178996.php (accessed January 28, 2021).

Paul Clarke

Andean South America stretches from the very northern end of the continent to the very southern one, with the mountains beginning in Venezuela and running through Colombia, Ecuador, Peru, and Bolivia before ending at the southern tips of Chile and Argentina. The region is primarily known for pisco, the grape brandy produced in Peru and Chile, but significant amounts of sugar-cane spirits are produced throughout the region along with some agave spirits in Venezuela and Colombia and a range of European-style aperitifs and digestives in Argentina and, to a lesser extent, Chile. See APERITIF AND DIGESTIVE.

Unlike in Central America, there is broad agreement that distillation only came into South America after 1532, when the Spanish began their invasion and destruction of the Inca Empire. Along with the Spanish settlers came the "frutos de Castilla," as they labeled the package of Iberian crops with which they intended to replace, or at least supplant, the "frutos de tierra"—the local crops. Along with such staples as wheat and the olive, these included the mission or listán prieto grape, which was planted widely in what is now Peru and Bolivia in the late 1530s and 1540s (with the creation of the Viceroyalty of Peru in 1542, Spain folded all of Andean America, or at least all the parts that it controlled, under one administration, centered in Lima). As Spanish rule extended to the coastal region south of the large and arid Atacama desert (1540) and the eastern slopes of the Andes (1573), so did the vine.

We do not know exactly when or where distillation began in the viceroyalty (records are scarce), but the two earliest known mentions of stills in the region—one in Santiago and the other in Ica, now the heart of Peru's pisco industry—are connected to wineries, and they show that making brandy, or pomace brandy, was a standard part of viticulture in parts of the viceroyalty by the last quarter of the 1500s, despite a government policy of suppressing distilling. This was designed to protect the monopoly on selling spirits in the Americas it granted, for a hefty price, to Spanish producers. At any rate, by the mid-1600s, grape-based "aguardiente" was in wide production both for local use and for illicit export to other parts of Spanish America. As the different parts of the viceroyalty developed their own cultural identities, this aguardiente evolved as well, into pisco in Peru and Chile, singani in Bolivia, and aguardiente de Catamarca in the Catamarca province of northwestern Argentina, each with its own preferences in grape varietals, distillation, and maturation, but all sharing a great many common characteristics: they are aromatic, floral, and generally undisguised by oak. Each has its idiosyncrasies—the Chileans, for instance, tend to use hybrid stills and do in fact sometimes age their pisco in oak barrels; the Bolivians insist that the moscato de Alejandría grapes for singani must be grown and the spirit distilled at 1,600 meters above sea level

or higher; and the Peruvians distill to bottling proof and sometimes use the primitive style of still known as a falca. See PISCO.

Along with the frutos de Castilla, the Spanish also included a ringer: sugar cane, an Asian crop that had grown poorly in Spain itself but exceedingly well in Spain's Atlantic and Caribbean islands. As early as 1549, there were four trapiches—cane mills—operating in Peru. By the end of the century, Peru had a great many large sugar estates, including twenty-three run by the Jesuits alone. At some point after that—here there are even fewer records than for grape distillation—sugar-cane spirits started to be distilled. This seems to have been the province of the enslaved and indentured African and Native American workers and their lower-class European managers, who turned the unwanted skimmings from the pots where cane juice was crystallized (the cachaza) or the juice of canes grown for the purpose into aguardiente de caña. (Molasses was not used at this point, since it belonged to the sugar-mill owners and there was a thriving market for it in Europe.) See RUM.

These spirits did not make it into the historical record until the beginning of the 1600s, at which point their use was widespread. By the 1630s, sugar-mill owners had taken notice of them and begun to co-opt and commercialize their manufacture, initiating two centuries of conflict with the colonial authorities. One of the drivers of this trade was the insatiable demand for spirits created by the massive silver mines at Potosí in Bolivia, founded in 1545. By the early 1600s, there were over 50,000 workers there, struggling with the altitude—the mines were 4,000 meters (2.5 miles) up—and the perpetual cold and desperate for the fleeting comfort a swig of raw spirit can give.

By the nineteenth century, cane spirits had become deeply ingrained in the cultures of many South American countries, and they remain that way today. Their variety is dizzying. Some, such as Peru's cañazo, and guaro, shared by Colombia and Ecuador with various Central American nations, are cane-juice based. See CENTRAL AMERICA. Some are molasses based and barrel aged (these usually go by ron, or rum). Paraguay's caña is made from cane syrup, which must be reduced over an open flame; it, too, can be barrel aged. Some of these spirits are flavored with anise, frequently with added sugar. See ANISE SPIRITS.

Of course, South America is a big place and a very diverse one, with many remote corners with traditions of distilling whatever the land produces, be it grains, manioc, indigenous or introduced fruits, or agave. With the possible exception of Venezuela's agave-based *cocuy*, these spirits are purely regional affairs, made for their local markets. See SPIRITS TRADE, HISTORY OF.

Andean South America also has a vibrant tradition of turning spirits into mixed drinks. Punch gained an early foothold there, with *ponches* of aguardiente (grape- or grain-based) in wide popular use by the eighteenth century, as did egg drinks and heavily spiced variations on the Hot Toddy. See PUNCH and TODDY. The region also proved fertile territory for North American–style iced drinks, with "American bars" appearing in its major cities in the last half of the nineteenth century. And not just the major ones: in 1898, a correspondent for the *Brooklyn Eagle* found Manhattan Cocktails being served at Punta Arenas, at the tip of Patagonia.

Andean South America's most popular and enduring cocktail creation is, of course, the Pisco Sour, from Lima. See PISCO SOUR. Most of the others involve North American–style carbonated soft drinks: Peru's Chilcano, which dates back to the 1930s, and Bolivia's Chuflay both use ginger ale. Others use cola, including the Rum and Coca-Cola that was already popular in Venezuela by 1911, Argentina's Fernet and Cola, Chile's self-explanatory Piscola. But many of the cities in the region have thriving modern cocktail cultures, some with a long tradition (Buenos Aires and Lima's involvement with cocktail culture are particularly significant), and it is easy to find state of the art mixology being practiced there.

"City of the Magellans." *Brooklyn Eagle*, October 30, 1898, 15.

Giovannoni, Tato. *Cocteleria argentino*. Buenos Aires: Sudamericana, 2014.

Mix, Ivy. *Spirits of Latin America*. Berkeley, CA: Ten Speed, 2020.

Pierce, Gretchen, and Áurea Toxqui, eds. *Alcohol in Latin America*. Tucson: University of Arizona Press, 2014.

David Wondrich

añejo, the Spanish word for "aged" or "mature," is used as a descriptor for several different types of aged spirits. By law, tequila and mezcal must be aged in wooden containers for a minimum of one year to be called añejo. There are also añejo rums; these spirits are generally aged for a significant amount of time, but there is no legal regulation of the use of the term with rum.

See also MEZCAL; RUM; and TEQUILA.

Jason Horn

angel's share is an evocative expression (from the French, *la part des anges*) for the volume of alcohol that evaporates from spirits aging in barrels. It is usually expressed in percent per year. Generally, spirits stored in wooden barrels (usually oak), through indirect contact with the air, decrease in alcoholic strength and volume.

The angel's share varies in quantity and quality depending on the temperature and humidity. In a more humid cellar, the angel's share will contain more alcohol, thus favoring the progressive drop in proof of the spirit in the barrel. A drier cellar will cause relatively more water to evaporate through the wood, resulting in a slightly "spicier," and of course stronger, spirit.

The angel's share varies in quantity depending on the climate. For instance, each year in Cognac, the "angels" consume about 2.5 percent of the total stock, the equivalent of thirty million bottles. In the Caribbean, the angel's share is 7 percent per year on average and can sometimes be as high as 10 percent per year.

To compensate for evaporation, the casks are sometimes topped up regularly with fresh spirit. This technique is sometimes referred as the solera system.

A fungus, *Torula compniacensis*, feeds on alcohol vapors. On the roofs and walls of the cellars, a light black veil signals its presence.

See also AGING and BARREL.

Ray, Cyril. *Cognac*. New York: Stein & Day, 1974.

Alexandre Gabriel

Angostura Bitters has been the dominant aromatic or cocktail bitters worldwide for well over a century and a half, having replaced the earlier Stoughton's and Boker's Bitters. See STOUGHTON'S

BITTERS. Its iconic bottles, with their oversized white paper labels, are omnipresent in bars around the globe. In its native Trinidad, a bottle of the intensely bitter, reddish-brown tincture graces every table, for cooking and as a condiment. Although most recipes call for a few dashes, Angostura also sells its namesake in five-gallon pails and 55-gallon drums.

The Angostura bitters story begins in 1820 in Angostura, Venezuela, when the German surgeon Dr. Johann Siegert (1796–1870) joined Simon Bolivar's forces in the war for Venezuelan independence from Spain. Stomach ailments were a frequent malady, for which Siegert developed a rum-based medicinal tincture of gentian and other spices, preparing his first commercial batch in 1824. As early as 1830, the bitters were exported to England as a remedy for "anemia, colic, colds, fever, malaria, and sea sickness."

In its initial decades only a few hundred cases sold annually. But after Johann's first son, Carlos Dámaso Siegert (1830–1905), took over marketing, it won an Honourable Mention in the Great London Exhibition of 1862, which gained it British distribution in 1863, with American distribution following right after. Numerous international exhibition awards followed.

While the bitters continued to be marketed as a stomachic, it quickly found off-label use as a drink enhancer in things such as Pink Gin and cocktails. See COCKTAIL. Angostura's success forced Siegert and his heirs to vigorously defend their trademark for many decades against infringers such as Abbott's Angostura bitters, founded in Baltimore in 1872. To this day, the bitters' recipe is a tightly held secret, known only to a handful of Angostura executives.

Soon after bringing Carlos into the business in 1867, the elder Siegert died. Facing political upheaval in Venezuela, Carlos and his younger brother Alfredo escaped to Trinidad in 1875, moving Angostura's operations with them. By 1878, Siegert's Bouquet, a bottling of the same Trinidad rum used in the bitters, was part of the company's portfolio.

The bitters' trademark oversize label originated as a mistake—the brothers had independently designed both a new bottle and a label without consulting each other on the dimensions. They lost a subsequent competition, but a judge noted that the oversized label was good for brand identity—it has remained that way since. Mark Twain was an early admirer, requesting of his wife that she have them present in his bathroom, along with scotch whisky, lemon, and sugar, upon his 1874 return to the United States.

Circa 1878, Angostura's Venezuelan agent, George Diogracia Wuppermann (1838–1915), and his American wife moved to New Jersey (and later Manhattan) to manufacture and distribute the bitters in North America; under his stewardship, the brand went from being *a* cocktail bitters to being *the* cocktail bitters. Wuppermann's son Frank became a vice president in the highly successful family firm in 1934, and five years later, under his stage name, Frank Morgan, played the title role in the MGM film, *The Wizard of Oz*. The Angostura-Wuppermann company left family hands in the 1970s, while in Trinidad the last Siegert retired in 1990. Today the brand is owned by a Trinidad-based holding company, CL Financial.

Angostura's early portfolio included Carypton, a bottled Green Swizzle base of rum, lime juice, sugar, and "indigenous herbs of the West Indies." That was trademarked in 1907. See GREEN SWIZZLE. In 1947, the company's ever-growing need for rum, for both bitters and their rum brands, led them to build their own distillery; today the company markets a wide range of rums, some of them highly regarded.

Despite its 44.7 percent ABV strength, Angostura bitters is not classified as a potable alcoholic beverage in the United States. Seeing opportunity as Prohibition encroached in 1920, a Washington, Wisconsin, bar owner obtained a pharmacist's license to dispense Angostura shots to his "patients," a tradition still continued at Nelsen's Hall Bitters Pub.

A few dashes of Angostura bitters are de rigueur in numerous classic cocktails, including the Manhattan and the Old-Fashioned. A float of Angostura bitters crowns the iconic Queen's Park Swizzle, concocted at the Trinidad hotel of the same name. Angostura bitters is a staple in many of the tiki drink recipes that emerged in post–World War II America, including the Zombie and Three Dots and a Dash, both created by Donn Beach. See ZOMBIE; BEACH, DONN.

The early twenty-first-century craft cocktail movement found Angostura bitters pushed to the forefront of cocktail ingredients. Italian bartender Valentino Bolognese won Angostura's 2008 European competition with his Trinidad Especial, containing a full 30 ml of Angostura bitters (most cocktails use less than a tenth of that), along with pisco, orgeat, and lime juice, with the bitters' high alcohol content acting as a base spirit.

Bologuese's recipe inspired Giuseppe Gonzalez of New York City's Clover Club to create the Trinidad Sour in 2009, utilizing 45 ml of Angostura bitters, orgeat, rye, and lemon juice. Although not an immediate sensation, it eventually penetrated craft cocktail menus and spawned many variations.

Thirty ml or more of Angostura can overwhelm a recipe unless it is balanced with copious amounts of sweet ingredients such as orgeat or cream of coconut. Modern tiki recipes like Zac Overman's Angostura Colada further popularized the bitters' upfront flavors. Toward that end, in 2015 Angostura introduced Amaro di Angostura, a less-concentrated, liqueur-based variation designed for cocktail use.

See also BITTERS.

De Verteuil, Anthony. *The Germans in Trinidad*. Port of Spain, Trinidad: Litho, 1994.

"Dr. Siegert's Angostura Bitters" (advertisement). *San Francisco Bulletin*, December 16, 1863, 2.

"Made a Fortune from a Formula—and She Never Knew What It Was." *St. Louis Post-Dispatch*, October 11, 1936, 87.

Siegert, R. W. "The Company and You" (presentation). Angostura archives, June 1966.

"Venezuelan Bitters" (advertisement). *London Sporting Gazette*, July 11, 1863, 16.

Willis, Resa. "Mark and Livy: The Love Story of Mark Twain and the Woman Who Almost Tamed Him." New York; Routledge, 2003.

Matt Pietrek

Angostura Holdings Limited

Angostura Holdings Limited is a Trinidadian company. It is known primarily for its production of the world-famous Angostura bitters, which became popular as one of the many elixirs of life to emerge in the nineteenth century. Started in Venezuela by Dr. J. G. B. Siegert, the company moved to Trinidad in 1875. Bitters remained the primary focus of J. G. B. Siegert and Sons until the 1930s, when Robert Siegert purchased a multi-column still in Leventille, Trinidad, and began to explore the art of rum making. In 1949, they established Trinidad Distillers Limited (TDL) and began producing their White Oak brand. An offshoot variety of White Oak was their Old Oak rum, which came in a multicolored, hand-painted bottle in the form of a limbo drummer complete with a bright yellow hat reminiscent of the bright yellow cap found on bottles of Angostura bitters. In 1973, Trinidad Distillers Limited acquired Fernandes Distillers Limited, a family-owned Trinidadian distillery from Forres Park Estate. The merger added several new rums to TDL, including Fernandes Black Label and Vat 19. In recent years, they have penetrated international rum markets with such fine award-winning aged rums as Angostura 1919 and Angostura 1824. All of Angostura's rums are column-distilled and aged in bourbon barrels. At their best, they have a medium-rich texture and a unique, and appealing, tarry fruitiness.

See also ANGOSTURA BITTERS and RUM.

Parsons, Brad Thomas. *Bitters: A Spirited History of a Classic Cure-All, with Cocktails, Recipes, and Formulas.* Berkeley: Ten Speed Press, 2011.

Smith, Frederick H. *Caribbean Rum: A Social and Economic History*. Gainesville: University Press of Florida, 2005.

Frederick H. Smith

anise spirits

anise spirits form one of the oldest and most widespread categories of spirit, emerging from the medieval Mediterranean to root itself throughout the world. As a result, they come in a wide variety: sweetened, unsweetened, high-proof, low-proof, based on grapes, grape pomace, grain, beets, dates, figs, sugar-cane juice, molasses. What's more, the anise they're flavored with isn't always anise. The seeds (or actually the seedlike fruits) of *Pimpinella anisum* are rich in anethole, the compound that gives them their characteristic fresh, licorice-like flavor. But so are the seeds of fennel (*Foeniculum vulgare*), a relative; star anise (*Illicium verum*), not a relative at all; and licorice roots themselves (*Glycyrrhiza glabra*).

Anethole is soluble in alcohol and will pass through a still alongside it. It is not, however, soluble in water, and when water—particularly cold water—is added to a distillate containing it, it will spontaneously form a microemulsion, with tiny droplets of it coming out of solution. This makes the liquid turn cloudy—the "louche" effect, as it is known (it can be prevented by chill-filtering the spirit).

One of Palermo's *acquaioli*, or water sellers, ca. 1915. The jug holds water, the tall bottle with the quill top *zammu*, or anise spirit. Wondrich Collection.

The origin of anise spirits is as cloudy as they are. There are some who trace their origin to India in antiquity, although evidence for that is scarce and dating uncertain. At the least, aniseed arrack seems to have predated European colonization of India. See INDIA AND CENTRAL ASIA. In China, star anise has long been one of the common ingredients in medicinal *paojius*. See PAOJIU AND YAOJIU. Similarly, in Europe green anise was a common component in the multi-ingredient, medicinal *aquae compositae*, or "compound waters," that characterized the early years of the European spirits industry. Its "simple" version, *aqua anisi*, or anise water, is common in fifteenth- and sixteenth-century European medical texts, many of them from Arab sources. Yet this is not always alcoholic, and it can be difficult to tell which version is being called for.

In any case, anise doesn't appear to have become a dominant flavoring in spirits until the seventeenth century. Then it flourished. Having the advantage of being cheap and, to many at least, tasty, anise became the flavoring of choice for spirits all around the Mediterranean, in both its Ottoman eastern and southern parts and its Italian, French, and Iberian northern and western ones. It conquered the Iberian possessions of the New World as well, and "aniseed water" was even among the earliest spirits to come into recreational use in England. When English colonists in Barbados began distilling rum, in the 1640s, some of it may have been anise flavored—as was a portion of the arrack the Dutch were shipping to Europe from Batavia (modern Jakarta), their base in the East Indies. See ARRACK, BATAVIA. It was even one of the key flavorings of Irish *usquebaugh*, the flavored forerunner of whisky. See WHISKY.

By the late eighteenth century, some of this tide of anise-flavored spirits had receded. Spirits such as Batavia arrack, Caribbean rum, and Celtic whisky no longer needed a "cover" to mask the uneven quality of their distillation. But the particularly refreshing nature of anise spirit when mixed with cold water ensured its popularity around the Mediterranean. Turkish *rakı*, Lebanese *'araq*, Greek *ouzo*, Italian *anice* and *sambucca*, French *pastis* and *anisette*, Moroccan *mahia*, and Spanish *chinchón* and *anis* amply demonstrate its prevalence. By the nineteenth century, a common sight in any town in the region was the water seller, circling the streets with a sweating earthenware jug of water and a tray of little bottles with which to flavor it, always including one of anise spirit. See ARRACK; MAHIA; OUZO; PASTIS; and SAMBUCA. Colombia's cane-based *aguardiente* and the *anisado* made in the Philippines by rectifying nipa-palm spirit with anise demonstrate the enduring influence of the Spanish version. See ANDEAN SOUTH AMERICA and PHILIPPINES.

The modern age has been less kind to anise spirits than to many others. The availability of clean water and ice have made their sanitizing and cooling virtues less unique, and they tend to seem a little archaic. Yet that cooling virtue is undiminished, and there are few things more pleasant than to be sitting in one of Palermo's baroque piazzas and sipping a glass of *acqua cu zammu*—ice water with a healthy splash of the unsweetened, 60 percent ABV Anice Unico Tutone, made in the same small factory in the heart of town for over two hundred years.

See also ABSINTHE.

Mitra, Rājendralāla. *Indo-Aryans: Contributions towards the Elucidation of their Ancient and Mediæval History.* London: E. Stanford, 1881.

Stewart, Amy. *The Drunken Botanist.* Chapel Hill, NC: Algonquin, 2013.

Zat, Erdir. *Rakı, the Spirit of Turkey.* Translated by Bob Beer. Istanbul: Overteam, 2012.

David Wondrich

Ankrah, Douglas

Ankrah, Douglas (1970–), is a British bartender and founder of London Academy of Bartenders (LAB) and Townhouse, two London bars that became famous in the late 1990s as breeding grounds for new bartending talent thanks to their extensive cocktail lists and high standards of service. Ankrah is also the creator of the Porn Star Martini, a 1990s classic made with vanilla-infused vodka, champagne, and passion fruit liqueur, which can still be found on cocktail menus the world over. A former manager and tender at influential 1990s bars including Planet Hollywood, the Hard Rock Café, and Dick's Bar at the Atlantic Bar & Grill, Ankrah now works as a bar consultant and in brand innovation. He is also the author of *Shaken and Stirred: Douglas Ankrah's Cocktails.* See ATLANTIC BAR & GRILL.

See also MARTINI.

Ankrah, Douglas. *Shaken and Stirred: Douglas Ankrah's Cocktails.* London: Kyle Cathie, 2004.

Alice Lascelles

Antone, Donato "Duke"

Antone, Donato "Duke" (Dominic Donald Paolantonio; 1917–1992), was a postwar American bartender and mixologist-for-hire who for many years ran the Bartending School of Mixology in his home town of Hartford, Connecticut. His true claim to fame, however, is as the most likely candidate for creating the basis of the Harvey Wallbanger, one of the most popular drinks of the twentieth century. Antone may have first concocted the simple highball (vodka, orange juice, and a float of Galliano) in the late 1940s or early 1950s at the Black Watch cocktail lounge on Sunset Boulevard in Hollywood, California, which he either owned or worked at. He originally called it the Duke Screwdriver, since it is, of course, just a twist on the classic Screwdriver. Antone later did work for both Galliano and Smirnoff in support of the drink. See SMIRNOFF.

Antone's claims about his early career—that he won national mixology championships in the late 1940s; that he founded his school in 1949; that he created several famous drinks (among them the Rusty Nail, the Golden Cadillac, the Freddy Fudpucker, and the Kamikaze)—are cast in doubt by the fact that in 1955 he was sentenced to six years in federal prison for running a heroin ring while tending bar in Hartford. It further must be conceded that he was far from a mixological wizard. His provable liquid inventions bordered on the ham-fisted, typically involving sweet liqueurs and cream. (His Italian Fascination, for example, contained only Galliano, Kahlua, triple sec, and sweet cream.) But in the 1960s he did promote bartending and mixology as worthy pursuits at a time when few in the United States did. He is also significant as an early exemplar of the kind of hand-in-hand partnership between bartenders and brands that, for better or worse, has become commonplace in the twenty-first century.

See also GALLIANO; HARVEY WALLBANGER; and SCREWDRIVER.

"4 Dope Peddlers Get Terms of 5, 6 Years." *Bridgeport (CT) Post*, January 11, 1955, 18.

Simonson, Robert. "Banging My Head against a Wall." *Lucky Peach* 12 (August 2014), 96–99.

Tucker, Jean. "School of Pourmanship." *Hartford Courant*, December 11, 1966, B1.

Robert Simonson

aperitif and digestive

aperitif and digestive are the English equivalents for the French *apéritif* and *digestif* and the Italian *aperitivo* and *digestivo*, terms designating a spirit or other drink taken before a meal to stimulate the appetite or after one to aid digestion. On the one hand, these can be just about anything—a cold glass of crisp lager beer, a balloon glass of rich old Armagnac, a Dry Martini, a Stinger. The terms are also, however, applied to two dedicated, if overlapping and closely related, categories of spirit- or wine-based alcoholic tonics that are infused with bitter botanicals (in many cultures, bitter substances are believed to facilitate digestion, not without some scientific basis). In general, aperitifs are less sweet than digestives and lower in proof (they range from about 10 percent to 25 percent ABV, while digestives range from 25 percent to 45 percent, and sometimes as high as 70 percent), although some are quite sweet and some digestives are quite low in proof. The use and production of these drinks, it must be noted, are by no means confined to France and Italy: although those countries might be their most ardent advocates, such drinks also have, or have had, a place in the drinking cultures of many other countries, notably including Germany, the Netherlands, Spain, the Czech Republic, China, Argentina, and even England. In the European tradition, these tonics stem from the *aquae compositae*, or "compound waters," of the Middle Ages, spirits distilled with or infused with multiple medicinal botanicals (Chinese *paojiu* and *yaojiu*, of similar or even greater antiquity, often also include animal elements). See BOTANICAL and PAOJIU AND YAOJIU.

Aquae compositae were highly complex medicines, and expensive. The six detailed by Michele Savonarola (ca. 1385–ca. 1466) in the fascinating study he made in the 1440s of distilling in northern Italy are a good example. These used an average of 21.5 botanicals, as well as precious stones, silver, and gold. Nonetheless, the formulae for such remedies were circulated widely, particularly after the introduction of printing. By the seventeenth century, they were being collected in "pharmacopoeias": apothecary's manuals pulling together all of the various medicinal formulae circulating in a town or country. At the same time, the sheer number of botanicals used began to diminish somewhat as formulae became more focused. Nonetheless, in 1690, when the young London apothecary Richard Stoughton (1665–1716) wished to make a bitter stomachic elixir—combining aperitif and digestive properties—he apparently used twenty-two ingredients (alas, he kept his precise formula a secret). His spirit-based "bitters," as people came to call them, were (or so he claimed) "of a delicate pleasant bitterish taste" and sold well, not just in London but throughout Britain, in Britain's North American and Caribbean colonies, and in several other European countries. In 1712, he obtained a royal patent to protect his formula and its packaging from the many imitators who had arisen, thus making his elixir the first branded spirit. See STOUGHTON'S BITTERS.

By the 1730s, however, formulae for Stoughton's Elixir were appearing in pharmacopoeias and recipe collections. These had radically reduced ingredient counts—the first one to circulate widely used but four ingredients: brandy, bitter orange peel, gentian root, and cochineal for color. Such formulae, which relied more on ingredients of proven efficacy and less on ones chosen according to medieval medico-alchemical theory, were much easier and cheaper to prepare than the older ones, and generally tasted better as well. Even if their medical value was small, as was still too common, at least taking a dram of one just in case, as it were, could be a pleasant thing to do. Stoughton-style bitters, with gentian and/or one or two other bittering agents (wormwood, quinine-rich cinchona bark, Virginia snakeroot, etc.), plus a flavoring agent or two, such as rhubarb or hyssop, and some citrus peel to freshen up the taste, became extremely common. These "aromatic bitters" were still very concentrated, as they were meant to be taken mixed with water, wine, tea, spirits, or some other diluting, softening medium. See BITTERS. Some apothecaries, however, took to adding water (or more spirit) and a big splash of sugar syrup to balance out the bitterness and bottling them as potable bitters, particularly once books such as the influential *Il confetturiere Piemontese* (The Piedmontese confectioner) published in Turin in 1790, spread the idea of compound spirits as epicurean drinks rather than strictly medicinal ones. (Of course, some makers kept to the older tradition and used many more botanicals, but they were increasingly in the minority.)

It is at the end of the 1700s that we see the rise of absinthe, essentially a strong wormwood bitter, and vermouth, a light wine-bitter. Vermouth was essentially a pre-bottled version of Wine and Bitters, a preparation already recommended by Richard Stoughton in 1690 and a standard pre-dinner aperitif in Britain and its American colonies, at least. In 1783, when the British were negotiating the surrender of New York City to George Washington and his army, at the end of the first day of talks (as William Smith, a member of the British delegation recorded in his diary) "Washington pulled out his watch, and observing that it was near Dinner Time, offered Wine and Bitters." But the British already appeared to have a preference for mixing their drinks to order, while the French and the Italians and the Spanish preferred to have them premixed and bottled (indeed, *Martini Cocktails*, the first cocktail booklet published by the Martini & Rossi company, contains recipes only for bottled cocktails). See ABSINTHE; COCK-TAIL; and VERMOUTH.

Until the middle of the nineteenth century, aperitif and digestive drinks were, with few exceptions, the products of enterprises like the typical Italian *distillatore-liquorista*, who compounded liquors for sale both by the drink over the bar and in bulk for the local market. But with the opportunities for increased distribution and the move toward branding and trademarking that came in the 1860s and 1870s, one after another of these enterprises took their versions of the traditional formulae and essentially privatized them, enclosing the commons as it were. In France, this trend resulted in aperitifs such as the quinine-spiked Dubonnet (created in 1846), Lillet (1872), Byrrh (1866), and Suze (registered in 1898) and digestifs such as Amer Picon (created in 1840; trademarked in 1872). See PICON and SUZE. In Italy, seemingly every town in the peninsula ended up with its own aperitivo and bitter digestive *amaro*. The path followed by Gaspare Campari can be taken as typical: taking a standard formula for a "Stoughton di Holanda," or "Dutch Stoughton bitters," he adapted it in stages, making it lighter and more palatable—and selling more of it—each time. Eventually, it just became "Bitter Campari," the iconic aperitif. Averna and Fernet Branca underwent similar evolutions. See AVERNA; CAMPARI; and FERNET.

The late nineteenth and early twentieth centuries saw branded aperitifs and digestives thrive and proliferate beyond France and Italy. Some notable examples include Germany's Jägermeister, now the most popular spirit in that country; Hesperidina Bagley, Argentina's bitter-orange-flavored aperitif, invented in Buenos Aires in 1864 (Melvin Sewell Bagley, the American who invented it, talked the Argentine government into passing a trademark law to protect it); and Chile's Amargo Araucano (invented in 1920 by Fritz Hausser, a German, based on local botanicals).

Today the medicinal value of these drinks pales compared to the products of the modern pharmaceutical industry, and they are enjoyed mostly for their gustatory value—although with a few of the digestives there is some dispute whether they have that at all (Fernet, for example, is notoriously polarizing). Campari and some of the other aperitifs were adopted as cocktail ingredients in the early twentieth century. See APEROL SPRITZ; DUBONNET COCKTAIL; NEGRONI; and VESPER. The attempt made then to treat digestives the same way didn't take root until the early twenty-first century: now, they are a mainstay of modern mixology.

The Complete Family-Piece and Country Gentleman and Farmer's Best Guide, 2nd ed. London: 1737.

Jones, Andrew. *The Aperitif Companion*. London: Quintet, 1998.

Martini Cocktails. Torino: Martini & Rossi, ca. 1900.

Parsons, Brad Thomas. *Amaro*. Berkeley, CA: Ten Speed, 2016.

Piccinino, Fulvio. *Amari e bitter*. Torino: Graphot, 2019.

Savonarola, Michele. *Excellentisimi medici Michaelis Savonarolae libellus singularis de arte conficiendi aquam vitae*. Grossenhain: 1532.

David Wondrich

Aperol is an Italian bitter *aperitivo*, or aperitif, introduced in 1919 by brothers Luigi and Silvio Barbieri, who had inherited their father's liqueur company in Padua seven years earlier. See APERITIF AND DIGESTIVE. They derived its name from the French *apéro* (short for *apéritif*). Vibrantly orange in color, Aperol is supposedly still infused with the original recipe of oranges and bitter barks and roots (chiefly chinchona, rhubarb, and gentian). Compared to Campari, another long-popular aperitivo, Aperol is less bitter and considerably lower in alcohol (ranging from 11 percent to 15 percent ABV, depending on where it's sold); indeed, in Italy it has always been promoted as an "aperitivo poco alcolico"—a "lightly alcoholic aperitif." See CAMPARI.

In the 1950s, Aperol began to appear as a component in the Aperol Spritz, the drink with which it eventually became indelibly linked. See APEROL SPRITZ. It was only after the brand's acquisition by Gruppo Campari in 2003 and Campari's canny promotion of the spritz that Aperol achieved its remarkable global success, catapulting to the leading position in the company's spirits portfolio.

Parsons, Brad Thomas. *Amaro: The Spirited World of Bittersweet, Herbal Liqueurs*. Berkeley: Ten Speed, 2016.

David Mahoney

Aperol Spritz traces its roots back to the 1840s with the original "Spritzer," composed of white wine and seltzer water. The German term *Spritz* means "splash" or "squirt," and the drink came about when Austro-Hungarian soldiers, based in Italy's northeast and accustomed to beer, began adding sparkling water to the stronger wines of the area to reduce their alcohol content and make them more refreshing.

After the unification of the Italian Kingdom in 1861, the drink remained popular with Italians, especially for the farmers around the regions of Friuli–Venezia Giulia, Trentino–Alto Adige, and the Veneto, who wanted to soften the strength of the wine drunk while working in the fields.

At the beginning of the twentieth century Italians started to add locally produced vermouths, bitters, and liqueurs to the original concoction. One of the most popular of these versions is the Spritz Veneziano, a Spritz with some kind of bitter added (the Select brand, from the region, was often used, as was Campari). Gradually the Spritz Veneziano spread to the bordering regions and, by the 1970s, everywhere in northern Italy.

Meanwhile, in 1919 in the city of Padua, in the Veneto, a light bitter called Aperol was developed by the Barbieri family. For decades, it was generally drunk with soda and a slice of orange, often from a glass rimmed with sugar. At some point near the end of the twentieth century—it is difficult to establish exactly when—beach bars on the Venetian Riviera began using Aperol in their Venetian Spritzes and serving the drink with ice in a large wine glass. The resulting drink spread rapidly throughout the region, and then the country.

After the 2003 acquisition of Aperol by the Campari company, the drink started to be marketed not only as the perfect way to serve Aperol but as the quintessential Italian summer drink. By the second decade of the century this campaign had largely succeeded, in no small part because the Aperol Spritz really does combine most of the most popular elements of Italian drinking: it is refreshing, low in alcohol, lightly bitter, and based largely on wine. It is now ubiquitous in Italy. Since the exports of Aperol started in the 2000s, it is also now wildly popular around the world.

See also AMERICANO and CAMPARI.

Recipe: Pour 120 ml prosecco, 30 ml Aperol, and 60 ml soda into an ice-filled wine goblet or Collins glass and garnish with an orange slice.

Baiocchi, Talia, and Leslie Pariseau. *Spritz*. San Francisco: Ten Speed Press, 2016.

Cremonesi, Marco. "Quel drink diventato un simbolo italiano." *Corriere della sera*, June 29, 2019, 38.

Leo Leuci

applejack, a spirit distilled from apples, is, historically speaking, as American as apple pie. Variously known as cyder spirit, cider brandy, apple brandy, or apple whisky, the apple-based spirit was a fixture of American life from colonial days all the way up to Prohibition. It fueled the enthusiasm of voters at campaign rallies and conventions, and was even reputed to have its best vintages in presidential election years.

Applejack is said to have derived its name from a crude method of concentrating the alcohol in hard cider, called "jacking," that involves freezing it and removing the frozen water. Commercial applejack producers, however, typically employed copper pot stills or wooden three-chamber stills to distill their fermented cider, and they mellowed the resulting spirit in oak barrels. See STILL, POT, and STILL, THREE-CHAMBER. (General consensus has long held that applejack reaches its peak of potability after roughly four years in the barrel.)

Although applejack has traditionally been produced in several states along the Eastern Seaboard, including New York and Connecticut, its deepest roots are in the Garden State, New Jersey—hence its nickname, "Jersey lightning," a moniker that may been inspired by the potency of the unaged spirit. "As the liquor runs from the tail of the still it is as limpid as the purest water, and fully as innocent-looking, but it is the most deceptive stuff imaginable," a *Jersey City News* reporter opined in 1892, when there were more than seventy applejack distilleries in New Jersey alone. "It will make a strong man wince to take a mouthful of it if he is not a confirmed liquor drinker."

Throughout much of the nineteenth century, applejack distilleries were a common sight at many family farms in New Jersey and nearby states. Apple farmers who didn't operate their own distilleries could sell their surplus crop to neighbors who did, and they frequently took their payment in applejack. But with the advent of a federal excise tax on alcohol imposed during the Civil War and competition from cheap imitations artificially "aged" by rectifiers with burnt sugar or peach pits, the number of applejack distilleries dwindled, leaving only a few still in operation when Prohibition took effect and shut those down as well.

Until the relatively recent resurgence of interest in applejack by craft distillers, the venerable Laird & Company was the only post-Prohibition producer of applejack in the country. See also APPLES and LAIRD'S. At the dawn of the twenty-first-century cocktail renaissance, the acquisition of a bottle of Laird's Bonded Apple Brandy was a rite of passage for a young mixologist and the gateway to mixing up a number of forgotten classics, including the Jack Rose, the Widow's Kiss, the Star (an applejack Manhattan), and the lethal Diamondback (with applejack, rye, and yellow Chartreuse). See JACK ROSE and WIDOW'S KISS.

"Jersey Lightning." *Jersey City News*, November 23, 1892, 3.

Weiss, Harry Bischoff. *The History of Applejack or Apple Brandy in New Jersey from Colonial Times to the Present.* Trenton: New Jersey Agricultural Society, 1954.

David Mahoney

apples are the fruit of *Malus domestica*, a deciduous tree whose origins can be traced to the mountains of central Asia. Most apple production is for table use, cooking, or juice, which is sometimes used as a mixer for spirits (particularly in Europe). Some of the fruit, however, is destined for a higher purpose and used to make fermented and distilled beverages.

When fermented, apple juice makes cider (or, in the United States, "hard cider"—apple juice being generally drunk there unfermented). Cider's first recorded consumption was by the ancient Greeks, and it was popularized by the Romans; its current strongholds include the west of England, the north of Spain, and the northeastern United States. Just about any of the more than 7,500 apple cultivars grown throughout the temperate world can be used in the production of cider, but the traditional and arguably best varieties for the purpose have a good amount of tannin and are high in sugar and acid.

Cider is also distilled to make spirits, although some of the most prized apple brandies are made from varietals too acidic to yield a drinkable cider. Like grape brandy, the beverages distilled from fermented apples have many names depending on geographic origin. The main types are cider brandy (England), apple brandy or applejack (the United States), batzi (Switzerland), obstler (in which apples are combined with other orchard fruits; Germany), and eau-de-vie de pomme and calvados (France). Of these, the last is unquestionably the best regarded, although American apple brandy also has its dedicated adherents. See APPLEJACK, CAL-VADOS, and OBSTLER. Apples are also occasionally used to flavor liqueurs, as in the German apfelkorn, which is naturally flavored, and the American green-apple schnapps, which is most assuredly not.

Roasted apples were incorporated into one of the foundational drinks of American mixology, the Apple Toddy, where they were muddled with sugar and mixed with hot water and rum or apple brandy. Today, they usually appear thinly sliced as a garnish, as in the Apple Martini, a 1990s Los Angeles favorite that is made by combining vodka and apple schnapps or another, less artificial, substitute.

Fournier, Adam. "Is Apple Brandy the Next Big Thing." *Daily Beast*, October 9, 2018. https://www. thedailybeast.com/is-apple-brandy-the-next-big-thing (accessed March 16, 2021).

Neal, Charles. *Calvados: The Spirit of Normandy*. San Francisco: Wine Appreciation Guild, 2011.

Jason Grizzanti

Appleton Estate rum is the oldest and one of the most widely recognized rums of Jamaica. Appleton Estate is located in the fertile Nassau Valley region of Jamaica on the edge of the rugged Cockpit Country. As with fine French brandies linked to particular vineyards in France, Appleton Estate rum embraces the idea of *terroir* because, unlike many other rum brands, Appleton uses sugar cane grown only in its own region. In 1655, the British captured Jamaica from the Spanish and immediately began establishing sugar estates. At that time, rum distilling was already considered an integral part of sugar plantation operations in other parts of the British Caribbean, especially in Barbados. A large number of Barbadians took part in the invasion and capture of Jamaica and migrated there to establish new sugar estates. They brought with them capital, enslaved laborers, and knowledge of how to make sugar and distill rum. Among them was Francis Dickenson, who received the lands that would become Appleton Estate as payment for his services. The property remained in the Dickenson family for more than a century. The earliest evidence for rum making at Appleton Estate is from 1749, though rum distilling there probably began much earlier. In the early twentieth century, Appleton Estate became part of J. Wray and Nephew Ltd., a family-owned Jamaican company with a history of rum making and tavern keeping dating back to the early nineteenth century. Through the early twenty-first century, Appleton's master blender has been Joy Spence, perhaps the first woman to hold such an illustrious position in the spirits industry. Appleton's Wray & Nephew White Overproof is by far the most popular rum in Jamaica and is something of a cultural institution on the island.

In 2012, Gruppo Campari, the fast-growing Italian spirits conglomerate, acquired a controlling share of Appleton Estate and its Appleton, Wray & Nephew and Coruba brands. See CAMPARI.

See also RUM, JAMAICA; and TERROIR.

Smith, Frederick H. *Caribbean Rum: A Social and Economic History*. Gainesville: University Press of Florida, 2005.

Frederick H. Smith

apricot brandy is a distilled spirit made from apricots and apricot pomace. The high sugar content of apricots led to the production of fermented apricot wines in ancient Europe. Because of its curved shape and sweet flesh, the apricot was widely considered an aphrodisiac and, as with grape wine, believed to increase amorous affections. Apricot brandy is considered a true eau-de-vie or fruit brandy, and it contains little residual sugar. Regional variations of this clear spirit can be found throughout Europe, especially northern Europe, where, for example, it is found under the names *barack pálinka* in Hungary and *Marillenschnaps* or *Marillenbrand* in Austria. See ABRICOTINE. Apricot brandy can also be made of a neutral spirit, fruit brandy, or a blend of the two, which is then flavored with apricot juice, sweeteners, and natural flavors. As a result, this spirit might more reasonably be called apricot liqueur than apricot brandy. It is sweet, peach or apricot in color, and commonly and appropriately labeled as "apricot-flavored brandy."

Apricot-flavored brandy is a staple at bars and restaurants because it is an essential ingredient in many classic cocktails, including the Baltimore Bang, Hotel Nacional, and Fairbanks. It is a key ingredient in the Georgia Mint Julep, which is made with apricot brandy, cognac, syrup, lime juice, bitters, and mint. In most cases, the liqueur can be replaced with the eau-de-vie for a less sweet and more delicate cocktail.

Popular brands of apricot-flavored brandy include DeKuyper Apricot Brandy and Apricot Brandy XO, Bols Apricot Brandy, Marie Brizard Apry, Rothman & Winter Orchard Apricot, G. E. Massenez Liqueur d' Abricot, and Giffard Abricot du Roussilon.

Dominé, André. *The Ultimate Guide to Spirits and Cocktails*. Königswinter, Germany: Ullmann, 2008.

Derek Brown

aquavit is a distilled spirit flavored with caraway seeds or dill seeds, usually complemented by additional botanicals, and bottled in both unaged and barrel-aged expressions. See CARAWAY. It has its roots in Scandinavia, where it developed as an allegedly medicinal infusion of spices into alcohol. Like whisky and eau-de-vie, its name derives from the Latin for "water of life." See AQUA VITAE. An early written reference to the spirit is found in a 1531 letter to the archbishop of Trondheim in Norway from a Danish officer of the crown, Eske Bille, who sent a sample of aquavit with a promise of its remarkable healing qualities.

Early production was widespread and informal, with thousands of stills operating in homes and farms throughout Scandinavia. Over the course of the nineteenth century production shifted to commercial distilleries, due to taxes, bans on home distilling, and shifts toward more capital-intensive production methods. See HOME DISTILLING.

Regulations in the European Union require only that aquavit be flavored with caraway or dill (American regulations are more restrictive, specifying only the use of caraway). Beyond that, distillers enjoy a great deal of freedom in how their aquavits are produced. Other botanicals that are often found in aquavit include cumin, fennel, anise, coriander, juniper, and citrus peel. The botanicals are usually macerated in neutral spirit, which is then redistilled, although sometimes there is additional infusion after distillation.

Sweden and Norway have passed additional geographic protections for spirits bearing the designations "Swedish aquavit" or "Norwegian aquavit," respectively. Qualifying Swedish aquavits must include fennel among their botanicals. Qualifying Norwegian aquavits must be made from Norwegian potatoes and spend a minimum of six months aging in barrels. Some Norwegian aquavits also undergo the unique "linie" process of aging at sea, in which casks of aquavit cross the line of the Equator twice as deck cargo. According to lore, the process was discovered by the Lysholm family in the early 1800s during a failed attempt to export Norwegian potato spirits to the East Indies; finding no buyers, the spirit was returned to Norway and discovered to have improved in taste over the course of the journey.

Denmark is also a significant producer of aquavit, and the spirit has roots in Germany and Iceland as well. Broadly speaking, Swedish aquavit tends to be somewhat mild and sweet; Norwegian aquavit is typically barrel aged; and Danish, German, and Icelandic aquavit tends to be assertive and crisp.

The most traditional way to drink aquavit is neat, often taken as a small, chilled shot all at once with a toast of "Skål!" (The pronunciation rhymes roughly with "bowl" in English.) It appears frequently at social occasions such as Christmas, midsummer (the longest day of the year), communal crawfish boils, and Þorrablót (an Icelandic midwinter feast). Swedes are famous for their festive drinking songs that break out with they drink aquavit together. In Nordic countries, bottlings of aquavit are often marketed to pair with specific foods, such as grilled meats, seafood, fermented fish, lamb, or pork.

Distillation of aquavit has arisen among craft distilleries in the United States, especially in areas that have significant Scandinavian populations, such as Chicago, Minnesota, Wisconsin, Washington, and Oregon.

While there are few firm definitions of aquavit styles, some to be aware of are: taffel aquavits, which are clear and typically unaged with prominent notes of caraway; dill aquavits, which use dill as the primary flavor component; and jule aquavits, created especially for Christmas, which use holiday spice blends. Beyond those three is a very diverse range of spirits, using a variety of botanicals and aging processes.

Though aquavit appears rarely in the canon of classic cocktails, the spirit is versatile for mixing. Its spice notes lend it to use in savory drinks such as the Bloody Mary, while its distillation with various botanicals makes it a promising substitute for gin. Barrel aged aquavits may also be used to good effect in place of aged spirits such as whisky, brandy, or rum.

See also LINIE AQUAVIT and SCANDINAVIA.

Brandt, Tova, ed. *Skål! Scandinavian Spirits*. Elk Horn, IA: Museum of Danish America, 2015.

Grier, Jacob. "Aquavit in the US." *Aquavit Week*. http://aquavitweek.com/aquavits-in-the-us (accessed January 28, 2021).

Jacob Grier

aqua vitae, Latin for "water of life," is (along with *aqua ardens*, "burning water") one of the oldest European terms for distilled spirits, its first documented use coming in the 1270s in a series of similar treatises on distillation variously, and loosely, attributed to Taddeo Alderotti (1223–1303) and Teodorico Borgognoni (1205–1298), both physicians practicing in Bologna. It was originally an alchemico-medical term, referring to the magical stimulant, solvent, and preservative properties perceived in spirits. While aqua ardens was the favored term in the Iberian Peninsula and southern Europe, aqua vitae was almost universal in the north, and indeed gives us the Scandinavian word *aquavit*, the French *eau de vie*, and the English "whisky" (via the Gaelic *uisce beatha*). See AQUAVIT; EAU-DE-VIE; and WHISKY.

Although aqua vitae was originally applied chiefly to spirits distilled from wine, giving rise to many a play on words with *aqua vitis*, "water of the vine," the development of grain spirits in the fourteenth and fifteenth centuries saw the term extended to them as well. Indeed, it was used indiscriminately for spirit whatever its source. Only with the increased sophistication and diversification of the spirits market in the seventeenth century did it begin to be replaced by individual, base material–specific terms such as "brandy," "rum," and "arrack." In England, where it is first recorded in 1471, aqua vitae remained the legal term for spirits through the eighteenth century.

Forbes, R. J. *Short History of the Art of Distillation*. Leiden: E. J. Brill, 1948.

Wilson, C. Anne. *Water of Life*. Totnes, UK: Prospect Books, 2006.

David Wondrich

Armagnac is a grape brandy produced in the heart of the Gascony region in southwestern France. It is France's oldest commercial spirit, predating its more famous rival cognac by at least 150 years. See CO-GNAC. Armagnac was born out of the convergence of three cultures: the Romans, who introduced the vine to the region; the Arabs who are believed to have introduced, or reintroduced, the alembic still; and the Celts, who brought barrels for storage and aging.

Records indicate that wine was being distilled in the Armagnac region as far back as the fourteenth century for its healing benefits. In 1310, Prior Vital Du Four (1260–1327), a doctor and ordained cardinal in the town of Eauze, in the heart of the region, wrote *De conservanda sanitate* ("On preserving health"), a treatise on medicine, which includes the forty virtues of "aqua ardens" and instructions for making it from wine, using multiple distillations. See AQUA VITAE and DISTILLATION, HISTORY. Commercialization of Armagnac can be traced to the fifteenth century, when it was commonly sold in local markets. The seventeenth and eighteenth centuries saw growth in both domestic and export markets, with increased transport through the ports of Bordeaux, primarily by Dutch traders. By the mid-nineteenth century, the Gers was France's largest wine-growing region, but the arrival of phylloxera in 1870 resulted in a dramatic reduction of vineyards, with only a quarter of the original 247,105 acres being replanted.

In 1909, the Fallières Decree delimited the zones of Armagnac production, with appellation d'origine contrôlée status being granted in 1936. With these decrees, production rules were laid down, and the three regions of Armagnac were designated: Bas-Armagnac, Armagnac-Ténarèze, and Haut-Armagnac.

Production in the Region

Today the vineyards designated for Armagnac production cover 5,200 hectares (12,849 acres). There are 800 producers (500 are independent, with the remaining 300 associated with six cooperatives and 40 trading houses). The annual average production is 19,000 hl of pure alcohol, equivalent to approximately 6.8 million bottles.

The Armagnac Appellation

The region experiences an ideal climate for viticulture: long, warm springs; hot, humid summers; and long, sunny autumns followed by short and relatively mild winters. The appellation is comprised of three *terroirs*; previously each *terroir* held its own appellation. However, since December 2014, there is now only one unique designation, Appellation d'Origine Contrôlée (or AOC) Armagnac, while the three regions, Bas-Armagnac, Armagnac-Ténarèze, and Haut-Armagnac, are now protected geographical indications. Additionally, blanche Armagnac, an un-aged Armagnac, has been recognized since 2005 as a category. Finally, the simple Armagnac appellation is used for spirits that come from more than one of the three regions.

The Three Terroirs

The Bas-Armagnac is the region farthest west and has a relatively flat terrain. The soil is a mix of sand with iron-rich pockets, known as "tawny sands," with some areas of *boulbènes*, a rock-like mix of sand, silt, and clay. This region is said to produce a lighter, more elegant style of Armagnac and represents 67 percent of the overall planting in the Armagnac appellation.

Armagnac-Tenarèze lies to the east of Bas-Armagnac, and its rolling hills account for approximately 32 percent of the vineyards producing Armagnac. The soils typically consist of *boulbènes* along with clay-limestone, and the spirit produced here is fuller bodied and requires longer aging to reach maturity.

Haut-Armagnac is the region farthest to the east and south. Armagnac vineyards are sparse and spread out across limestone-covered hills. This region accounts for only 1 percent of production, though it produces a sizable amount of table wine.

The Grapes of Armagnac

The AOC rules state that ten grape varieties are permitted in the production of Armagnac. In practice, most Armagnac is produced from four main grape varieties: ugni blanc, baco blanc, folle blanche, and Colombard. This diversity offers Armagnac producers a range of options in their blending decision.

Ugni blanc produces wines with high acidity and low alcohol, making it ideal for distillation. It produces an elegant and high quality eau-de-vie, which contributes body, weight, and age-ability to the blend. Ugni blanc represents 55 percent of the distillation in the region.

Baco blanc (previously called baco 22A) is the only hybrid grape (the product of the folle blanche and Noah varieties) allowed in the French AOC system. It produces wines that are very high in acidity and low in alcohol and is especially well adapted to the sandy soils of Bas-Armagnac. The spirit from baco tends to be round and rich with subtle aromatics and a long finish, typically showing their best after ten to twelve years of aging. Baco accounts for 35 percent of the wine destined for distillation.

Folle blanche, also known as picquepoult, or "lip-stinger," which suggests its highly acidic nature, was the traditional grape variety before the arrival of phylloxera, but due to its fragility and difficulty in grafting post-phylloxera, it now accounts for only 5 percent of the region's production. Folle blanche creates spirits with floral and fruity notes that show best in their youth.

Colombard is better known for producing still wines in the area due to its ability to achieve higher sugar levels. Colombard is responsible for just under 5 percent of the wine destined for distillation. In a blend it contributes fruit, spice, and vegetal nuances. Six other varieties are also permitted: plant de graisse, meslier St-François, clairette de Gascogne, Jurançon blanc, mauzac blanc, and mauzac rosé, accounting between them for less than 1 percent of plantings.

Distillation of Armagnac

After a traditional vinification (addition of sulfur is prohibited by AOC law), the naturally low-alcohol base wines (usually between 9–10 percent ABV) remain in contact with their lees until distillation. Ninety-five percent of production in Armagnac is carried out using a type of continuous still known as the alambic Armagnacais. See ARMAGNAC STILL.

The remaining 5 percent use a double distillation pot still, the same type of distillation used in cognac. The spirit generally comes off the still at 52–60 percent ABV, although regulations allow it to go up to 72 percent. All distillation must be complete prior to March 31 of the year following the harvest. These lower distillation strengths yield a spirit rich in flavor compounds. With aging in oak barrels, historically sourced from the local Monlezun oak forests in Gascony, and today increasingly from the Limousin region, the spirit will mature to develop a wide range of aromas and flavors and will gain in color and complexity.

Maturation of Armagnac

The freshly distilled eau-de-vie goes into new 400-liter oak barrels, for a minimum of six months and up to two years (less for the more aromatic varieties). The spirit is then moved into older, more neutral barrels, to continue aging. See ÉLEVAGE.

During its maturation in barrels, Armagnac extracts tannins, aromatic compounds, and color. Extended maturation softens the spirit, while an average 2 percent evaporation (known as the "angel's share") enriches the aromas and concentrates the spirit. With time, rancio notes begin to develop while the color deepens. See ANGEL'S SHARE and RANCIO.

Styles of Armagnac

Armagnacs come in a range of styles, from blended ones to single-vintage ones that can date back many decades.

A VS or 3 *** must be aged for a minimum of one year in oak barrels; a VSOP must be aged for a minimum of four years in oak barrels. Napoleon and XO must both spend a minimum of six years in oak barrels, while the minimum legal age of the youngest eau-de-vie in an hors d'age Armagnac is ten years old. Single vintages, produced entirely from grapes grown in the vintage year indicated on the label, may not be sold if under ten years old.

The younger styles of Armagnac are used for cooking, baking, mixing in cocktails, while the more mature styles of Armagnac are usually drunk on their own or at the end of a meal paired with dessert or cheese courses. While more than 95 percent of the cognac made in an average year is exported, almost half the Armagnac stays home in France.

See also EAU-DE-VIE; FRANCE; HEALTH AND SPIRITS; and TERROIR.

Andrew, Joseph, Natalino Maga, and Jean-Louis Puech. *Armagnac: The Gers Region of Southwest France, the People, the Brandy.* Monpellier, France: AVL Diffusion, 2007.

Bureau National Interprofessionnel de l'Armagnac. *Armagnac: Come to Your Senses.* http://www.armagnac.fr/en (accessed April 20, 2021).

Lebel, Frédéric. *L'esprit de l'Armagnac.* Paris: Cherche Midi, 2011.

Neal, Charles. *Armagnac: The Definitive Guide to France's Premier Brandy.* San Francisco: Flame Grape, 1998.

May Matta-Aliah

Armagnac still, also known as an alambic armagnacais, is a small hybrid still, a pot with a continuous feed topped off with a short rectifying column, unique to the Armagnac region of France. It is sometimes set on a wheeled conveyance, allowing it to travel from one vineyard to another. The alambic armagnacais is inefficient for a continuous still, producing eau-de-vie only at alcohol levels between 52–60 percent ABV. See also ARMAGNAC and STILL, CONTINUOUS.

The **aroma** of a spirit or mixed drink is the perceived sum of the diverse volatile compounds contained within it to which the human nose is sensitive (sometimes it is called the drink's "nose"). Because people differ widely in their abilities to smell and identify many compounds, in this context aroma can only ever be an imprecise term: one person's "burnt rubber and road tar" is another person's "pineapple and hogo." See HOGO.

The word "aroma" also has a specific and limited application in the wine industry, where it is used to describe the primary odorants of a young wine; as the wine ages, aroma evolves into "bouquet" as a secondary set of odorants slowly replaces the primary ones.

The spirits industry lacks a similar technical vocabulary, which is to a degree understandable due to the great diversity of base materials and flavor compounds. Nonetheless, there are commonalities between spirits stemming from factors such as length of fermentation, type of distillation, and length of aging that could serve as a basis for such a vocabulary. It would be welcome.

See also AGING; BOUQUET; SENSORY EVALUATION; SMELL, THE SENSE OF; and TASTING SPIRITS.

Finger, Thomas, and Wayne Silver. *Neurobiology of Taste and Smell.* Malabar, FL: Krieger, 1991.

Wolfe, Jeremy, Keith Kluender, and Dennis Lem. *Sense and Perception*, 3rd ed. Sunderland, MA: Sinauer, 2011.

Doug Frost

arrack, a word of Arabic origin meaning "distilled spirit," is the first widely accepted umbrella term used to differentiate spirits from fermented beverages. From Morocco to Mongolia, India to Indonesia, during the centuries when Arabic was the lingua franca of trade in the Mediterranean, Red Sea, Indian Ocean, and beyond, the word 'araq (translated variously as "sweat," "sap," "essence," or "spirit") was used as a general term but also beaten into many local shapes to fit many different tongues and many different distillates.

In Delhi in the 1280s, the 'araq that wine sellers from Meerut and Aligarh were bringing into town was made from raw sugar; strong and sweet-smelling, it was said to be two or three years old. In 1326, it was two loads of arakı that the Ottoman sultan Orhan Bey sent Geyikli Baba, the great dervish who had just taken part of the Byzantine fortress of Bursa; that was almost certainly a grape spirit. In Mongolia, it became arkhi, and it was made from milk; that was in the 1330s. At some point that century, an anonymous Bulgarian scratched the words "at the feast I drank . . . rakinya" on his drinking cup; that rakia (as it's now called) could have been from grapes or from any one of a number of other fruits. In Baghdad in the 1510s, the Azeri poet Fuzuli wrote it as arak. That same decade, in Goa it was being made from palm wine, and it was orraca, or at least that's how the Portuguese heard it. The strong, clear rice-based spirit Antonio Pigafetta, Ferdinand Magellan's Venetian assistant, came across in the Philippines in 1522 was arach. Whatever it was that the version they were making in Algiers in the 1580s was based on, the Spanish heard its name as arraquin.

In the 1600s, the word entered English as "rack" or "arrack," and there it has stayed. At the same time, four of these local arracks entered the system of global trade in spirits that was then being established. The first was the palm arrack from Goa and other ports in southern and western India. As noted already, Portuguese traders had included this spirit, which had been in local and international commerce in India and Southeast Asia for over half a millennium, in their cargos since the very beginning of that country's trade with India; the English and the Dutch would join them by the early 1600s. At first, the trade was simply a matter of selling off excess ships' stores (the Portuguese, Dutch, and English all stocked their ships with the spirit for the long return journeys to Europe), but by the 1700s markets had been formed in Europe for "Goa arrack," and it was in regular commerce. Some considered it to be the original spirit for making punch (which it almost certainly was), and the best (here there was room for debate). This trade lasted into the nineteenth century but faded out by 1900. Today the version made in Sri Lanka is the most common outside the region. See ARRACK, COCONUT; and FENI.

The second type was the cane arrack from northeast India. As "Bengal arrack," this spirit—stronger than Goa arrack, but also rougher—saw some trade with Europe, but was mostly shipped around Asia, where it was used to ration soldiers and sailors and the like. When Great Britain colonized Australia at the end of the eighteenth century, Bengal arrack, or "Bengal rum," as it was commonly known, provided a large part of the colony's early alcohol trade. See RUM.

The third was the protean spirit known to the Ottoman Turks as *rakı*, to their Balkan subjects as *rakia* (spelled variously), and to their Levantine Arab ones as *'araq*. This spirit, usually distilled from grapes or raisins but also from dates and, in the Balkans, from plums, cherries, or just about any fruit that grew in the region, was made and traded widely around the eastern Mediterranean, in spite of Islamic prohibitions on alcohol. Although the early versions were flavored with all kinds of different herbs, singly or in combination, or left unflavored, by the eighteenth century anise had become the dominant flavor, as it was around the Mediterranean, and the spirit had often gained a fairly stiff dose of sugar. See MARASCHINO; RAKI; RAKIJA; and SLIVOVITZ.

Finally, there was Batavia arrack. A Dutch modification of a Chinese spirit made in Indonesia and consumed mostly in Europe, Batavia arrack was the world's first international luxury spirit. See ARRACK, BATAVIA. The spirit itself was a complex one, involving palm sap whose fermentation was started with rice-based qu in the Chinese manner and encouraged by the addition of molasses and other sugar byproducts. See QU. In its journey from Batavia—modern Jakarta—to Amsterdam, it spent many months aging in the large teak-wood *leggers* in which it was shipped. In London in 1730, a bowl of punch made with a quart of French brandy or Jamaican rum generally cost six shillings, while one with Batavia arrack cost eight. This price superiority lasted well into the nineteenth century, by which point the spirit's palm component had fallen out of use. The market for Batavia arrack collapsed after the Second World War, but in recent years the spirit has received new attention from punch makers and tikiphiles. See PUNCH and TIKI.

All of these spirits preceded the rise of brandy, genever, rum, and whisky, the European (or European-controlled) spirits that would become mainstays of the global spirits trade. Although Batavia arrack provided a bridge between the old, predominately Asian spirits trade, or trades, that flourished from approximately the ninth century CE through the sixteenth and the new, European-dominated trade that has developed since the seventeenth century, in general the newer trade networks supplanted the older ones, and the various arracks fell back on their local markets (with the exception of Batavia arrack, which had given those up in the 1600s).

See also SPIRITS TRADE, HISTORY OF.

Habib, Irfan. *The Economic History of Medieval India, 1200–1500.* History of Science, Philosophy and Culture in Indian Civilization 8, part 1. New Delhi: Pearson-Longman, 2011.

Konstantinova, Daniela. "Bulgarians Knew the Rakiya as Early as 14 c." *Radio Bulgaria*, October 18, 2011. https://bnr.bg/en/post/100128465/bulgarians-knew-the-rakiya-as-early-as-14-c (accessed February 9, 2021).

Wondrich, David. *Punch.* New York: Perigee, 2010.

Wondrich, David. "Rediscovering the World's First Luxury Spirit: Batavia Arrack," *Daily Beast*, October 2, 2017. https://www.thedailybeast.com/rediscovering-the-worlds-first-luxury-spirit-batavia-arrack (accessed February 9, 2021).

Zat, Erdir. *Rakı, the Spirit of Turkey*. Translated by Bob Beer. Istanbul: Overteam, 2012.

David Wondrich

arrack, Batavia, a pungent, intensely flavorful sugar cane–rice spirit from Indonesia, has been traded internationally and even intercontinentally since the 1600s, making it one of the oldest spirits in global commerce. It is also the first and, so far, only Asian spirit to gain broad acceptance in the West (although that acceptance peaked in the eighteenth century). Perhaps that is because of its cosmopolitan origin: created by overseas Chinese distillers applying their native techniques to Indonesian ingredients and financed by Dutch capital, Batavia arrack (it takes its name from Batavia, the Dutch colony that evolved into the modern Jakarta) is as much a product of the colonial age as its relative rum.

We do not know the precise circumstances of the spirit's creation. It is not mentioned by Ibn Battuta, who visited Java in the 1300s, or by Fernão Mendes Pinto or any of the other Portuguese who recorded their experiences on the island in the 1500s. It was only during that century, however, that significant numbers of Chinese settled in Java, working as artisans, merchants, and farmers. Among the trades the Chinese brought was distilling. They used a compound base for their spirit, adding palm wine to the rice used for distilling in southern China. In the early 1600s, when the Dutch financed a Chinese-managed sugar industry on the island, the distillers began adding the molasses and other byproducts thrown off by the sugar-making, possibly at Dutch instigation. See also LAMBANOG.

A handful of detailed accounts of the spirit's production from the early nineteenth century give some insight into the hybrid nature of the resulting process, although it is unknown how closely they tally with the original sixteenth-century manufacture. First, glutinous rice is piled in a heap and moistened with water that has been mixed with molasses, and yeast is added (presumably in the form of *jiuqu*) for a dry fermentation in the Chinese style. Separately, more molasses is combined with palm sap and water, for a liquid Western-style fermentation (it should be noted that the Chinese in Java had been making sugar from mixed sugar cane juice and palm sap since at least the 1500s). Proportions varied, but four parts molasses to two parts rice and at the very most one part palm sap is common.

The liquid thrown off by the rice is combined with the molasses-palm mix for further fermentation and then distillation in Chinese-style egg-shaped stills modified by European condensing coils. The low wines are then usually redistilled

This very rare, murky picture shows the still room at the OGL or KWT arrack distillery in Jakarta. The bollard-shaped heads of the Dutch-style pot stills can just be made out at *center right* and *center left*, with sticks used to tension the wires holding them onto the still. Wondrich Collection.

twice or thrice (like most Chinese spirits and un-like most South Asian arracks, Indonesian arrack is quite strong, at over 50 percent ABV) and the distillate placed in teak-wood vats for aging or wooden casks for shipping.

The resulting spirit found favor with some native Javanese, but was even more prized by the Dutch and English merchants and sailors who began colonizing the island in the early 1600s, at least once they got used to it (Edmund Scott, who encountered it in Batavia in 1604 at the distillery-tavern kept by his Chinese neighbor, described it unenthusiastically as "a kind of hott drink that is used in most of those partes of the world, in stead of wine"). At first, Dutch and English ships stocked up on it for shipboard use out of necessity. Once the simple formula for making punch was in universal circulation, however, sailors actively sought the spirit out, so that by the middle of the seventeenth century Batavia, with its numerous punch houses and arrack selling for eight pence a gallon, was a hotly anticipated port of call.

Batavia was the capital of the arrack trade, but considerable production was also centered on Cirebon in West Java and Surabaya in East Java. In both of those regions, however, the molasses used came from large, Dutch-run sugar plantations, while the distillers in Batavia bought theirs from smaller, family-run plantations. The latter, due to less efficient processing, had more residual sugar and produced a higher-quality spirit.

By the end of the seventeenth century, Batavia arrack was being shipped to Europe in considerable quantities, mostly by the Dutch, who had control of the island of Java, but also by the English. From the Netherlands, it went on to Scandinavia and Germany, while the English re-exported it to their American colonies. The spirit enjoyed an enviable reputation for quality. Indeed, in London, the world's greatest spirits marketplace, Batavia arrack sold in punch houses for eight shillings a quart, while the finest French brandy cost only six. The spirit's primacy endured in Britain through the eighteenth century and well into the nineteenth. Although its dry tang was not appreciated by all, arrack was nonetheless the punch connoisseur's choice (see REGENT'S PUNCH). Meanwhile, in northern Europe, arrack was commonly drunk in tea or coffee, and Arrack Punch was so well established as to become a pillar of local drinking customs (indeed it is still sold in bottled form, as Swedish Punch). In America, arrack's deep pungency made it challenging to incorporate in the standard spectrum of American cocktails, Juleps, and the like. Indeed, "it is but little used . . . except to flavor punch," wrote Jerry Thomas in 1862, although it "is very agreeable in this mixture."

Over the course of the nineteenth century the arrack trade, by then entirely in Dutch hands, saw a good deal of streamlining and consolidation. At some point, palm sap fell out of the formula. In 1899, the main distilleries, KWT and OGL (the names represent the initials of their Chinese founders), were consolidated under the umbrella of the Batavia-Arak Maatschappij, or BAM, the leading purveyor of the spirit until World War II. After that war, which entailed years of German occupation of the Netherlands and Japanese occupation of Indonesia, the industry emerged much smaller than before, although Batavia arrack still had and has significant uses in the confectionery and tobacco industries. Some arrack is still also drunk, mostly in Scandinavia and Germany, either straight, premixed into punch, or "verschnitt"—cut with neutral spirits. All of these markets are supplied by a handful of now Indonesian-run distilleries in Java, all of which export through E. & A. Scheer, the heir to BAM and indeed the entirety of the arrack trade.

Batavia arrack is also one of the "lost" ingredients to benefit from the cocktail renaissance, with it returning to the American market in 2008 after a hiatus of at least fifty years. It is seen as a rewarding challenge among bartenders to feature its burly funkiness in cocktails and tiki drinks, usually as an accent rather than a main ingredient. The spirit also features in some rum blends, where a touch of it adds desirable complexity and aromatics.

Campbell, Donald M. *Java: Past and Present*. London: Heinemann, 1915.

Raffles, Thomas Stamford. *The History of Java*, vol. 1. London: Black, Parbury & Allen, 1817.

Scott, Edmund. *An Exact Discourse of the Subtilties, Fashions, Pollicies, Religion, and Ceremonies of the East Indians*. London: 1606.

Verhoog, Jeroen. *Walking on Gold: The History of Trading Company E & A Scheer*. Amsterdam: E & A Scheer, 2013.

Wondrich, David. *Punch*. New York: Perigee, 2010.

David Wondrich and Jacob Grier

Distilling *tadi* (palm wine) into coconut arrack at the Dadar Central Distillery, Mumbai, 1908. Note the modified Gandharan-style still, with the pot at the *right* and the receiver sitting in its bowl of cooling water at *center*, with more being ladled on top from the reservoir beneath. Wondrich Collection.

arrack, coconut is the most widespread and historically significant representative of one of the earliest categories of spirits, those distilled from palm sap. (Besides the coconut palm—*Cocos nucifera*—the nipa, date, and African raffia or oil palms are also of commercial and historical importance as sources for distillation. See AKPETESHIE, NIPA, and OGOGORO.) Spirits distilled from the coconut palm are or have been made throughout the tropics, from South and Southeast Asia to the Indonesian and Philippine archipelagos, Central America, the Caribbean, and equatorial Africa. Their earliest appearance, however, is in Asia.

In the absence of a detailed history of distillation in Asia, we cannot say precisely (or even imprecisely) when the first palm spirits were made, or where. While evidence of a spirits trade in the India of antiquity is fragmentary, what there is does not suggest palm spirits were known, nor is there any evidence that they were known in China. The earliest, rather ambiguous, notices of the spirit appear in the 900s CE, when Abu Zeyd Hassan, a Basra-based chronicler, records an Arab sailor's notice of a Sri Lankan drink made from "palm-honey, boiled," and Chinese merchants may have been importing it from Siam via ports on the Andaman Sea. Less tenuously, in the 1410s the Chinese navigator Ma Huan (1380–1460) recorded that Siam was producing coconut-palm spirit, and Bengal coconut- and nipa-palm spirit. In any case, by 1510, when the Portuguese established their colony in Goa, they found coconut-palm "arrack" (the Arab word for "distilled spirit" was used) being made, drunk, and traded throughout eastern and southern India.

The traditional way of making palm arrack is by climbing mature coconut palms, cutting the "spathes"—the stalks from which the tree's flowers grow—and collecting the sap that runs out. This ferments quickly with environmental yeasts, yielding a palm wine or "toddy," as it is known, of about 8 percent ABV, which must be distilled within twenty-four hours, before it goes sour. Traditionally, a clay external-condensation pot still is used identical to the Gandharan one of antiquity. See STILL, POT. In Goa, there were three grades of arrack, depending on if it was single-, double-, or triple-distilled (ranging from under 30 percent to over 60 percent ABV). See FENI.

The Europeans took to the spirit right away. In 1518, the Portuguese trader Francisco Corbinel, who had been in Goa from 1510 through 1515, returned to Lisbon and was released from his debts in return for an impressive list of Indian goods he had shipped home, including 2,426 jars of "orraca." With these initial intercontinental shipments began the global spirits trade.

The Portuguese, however, never developed their commerce in arrack, as it was in conflict with the royally protected wine trade. It fell to the English to make Indian coconut arrack a standard item of commerce a century later. With the establishment of "factories"—trading posts—at Mumbai and elsewhere on the Indian coast, the East India Company (founded 1600) began provisioning its ships with coconut arrack. Eventually, this created a market in England for what was not consumed, spurred by the English embrace of punch—originally, arrack with sugar, citrus, water, and (usually) spices. See PUNCH. By the late 1600s, "Goa arrack" or "Colombo arrack," as Indian or Sri Lankan coconut arrack was known (as opposed to "Batavia arrack," the Dutch-imported palm-and-molasses product from Java), was bringing a premium price on the London market. See ARRACK, BATAVIA. In 1712, for instance, one London merchant was selling Colombo arrack for a princely 14 shillings a gallon, with Batavia arrack bringing 12; the only other spirit that brought comparable prices was the oldest French brandy. As that peerless observer of the world around him, the explorer William Dampier (1651–1715), noted in 1697, no other arrack was "so esteemed for making Punch" as the Goa kind, although the "most delicate" punch made with it "must have a dash of brandy to hearten it," as it was not strong enough to make good punch on its own (clearly the triple-distilled version was not getting around). Eventually, Batavia arrack, all of which was fairly high proof, largely drove the Indian version out of the market, and by the beginning of the nineteenth century it was a rarity.

In the meanwhile, the production of coconut-palm spirit had spread to the Philippines, where it was common by the 1570s, and from there to Mexico with the fleets that tied Spain's vast maritime empire together. Today, a great deal of coconut *lambanog*, as it is known, is still made in the Philippines, but Mexico has moved on to other spirits. See LAMBANOG and MEXICO. Some coconut arrack is still made in Goa, although it is rarely exported.

The leader of the modern industry is undoubtedly Sri Lanka, which has turned coconut arrack into a modern spirit (some spirit is also made from palmyra and kitul palms). Both pot and column stills are used, the latter having been introduced in the 1920s. Their products are (generally) blended and then aged in large teak or *halmilla*-wood (*Berrya*

ammonilla) vats for anywhere from six months to seven years; after two years it can be called "old arrack." The resulting products are generally mild and subtle, with a slight lactic tang and a hint of funk. The contemporary bump in interest in spirits with local traditions and historical resonance has cracked the door of the global spirits market for Sri Lankan arracks, and they can now be found in the United Kingdom and some markets in the United States.

See also WEST AFRICA.

Dampier, William. *A New Voyage round the world.* London: 1697.
"Datas da primeira occupação de Goa." In *O Oriente Portuguez*, vol. 2, nos. 1–2: 337–40. Nova Goa: Imprensa Nacional, 1905.
Needham, Joseph, et al. *Science and Civilization in China*, vol. 5, part 4, *Chemistry and Chemical Technology.* Cambridge: Cambridge University Press, 1980.
Renaudot, Eusebius, ed. *Ancient Accounts of India and China.* London: 1733.
Samarajeewa, U. *Industries Based on Alcoholic Fermentation in Sri Lanka.* Colombo: Natural Resources and Science Authority, 1986.

David Wondrich

Arrack Punch, most likely the earliest kind of punch, was popular from the beginning of the seventeenth century to the middle of the nineteenth, when it was still able to earn an entry in Jerry Thomas's pioneering bartender's guide in 1862. Its principal ingredient is either palm arrack or the more popular Batavia arrack. See also ARRACK, BATAVIA; and ARRACK, COCONUT.

Arroyo Valdespino, Rafael (1892–1949), has arguably had a greater influence on modern rum production than any other figure. As head of the Agricultural Experiment Station of Puerto Rico in the 1940s, Arroyo made significant advances that are still the backbone of the industry today. Cuban born but educated in Louisiana, Arroyo was best known for his seminal 1945 text, *Studies on Rum*, as well as for patents held for heavy rum production.

Arroyo's *Studies* sought to reveal the mysteries of distillation of both commodity rums and fine rums at every stage of production. Commodity rums benefited from his examination of molasses pretreatment techniques to prevent detrimental scaling of continuous column equipment, which at the time created maintenance problems that frequently shut down operations. Fine rums benefited from his explorations of (and possible experimentations with) the yeast *Schizosaccharomyces pombe*, as well as symbiotic fermentation of aroma-beneficial bacteria and molds. Arroyo was able to unlock the secrets of the much admired Jamaican rums and achieve comparable results in Puerto Rico under controlled conditions that could scale dramatically upward.

The progressive process of slow, meticulous advancement was expounded by Arroyo, and he illustrated methods for homing in on optimal production parameters. Much success was attributed to the use of novel micro-distillation analysis techniques in the laboratory, and Arroyo was among the first to put significant emphasis on rum oil as a congener class while others were focused primarily on esters. Rum oil, to which Arroyo attributed the "suavity" of great rum, was only maximized by careful attention to every stage of production and integrated into decisions regarding every other congener class.

Arroyo's efforts to improve the art of rum distilling were cut short by his untimely death in 1949 at the age of fifty-seven while still completing his ambitious work.

See also RUM and CONGENERS.

Arroyo, Rafael. *Studies on Rum*. Rio Piedras: University of Puerto Rico, Agricultural Experiment Station, 1945.
"Necrology." *Chemical and Engineering News* 27 (1949): 3643.

Stephen Shellenberger

Arthur, Stanley Clisby (1881–1963), was the first person to pay serious attention to the origin and the history of the cocktail and of American mixed drinks in general. He is a particularly apt figure to stand at the head of the field of cocktail history in that his writing on the topic, contained in his 1937 book, *Famous New Orleans Drinks and How to Mix 'Em*, encompasses both the genre's (rare) strengths and its (common) faults. Arthur, a newspaper reporter and photographer by training from Merced, California, parlayed his wildlife photographs and interest in John Audubon into an appointment first as Louisiana's state ornithologist, in 1915, then as director of the state Department of Wildlife, and then, in 1934, as the regional director of the Federal Survey of Archives under the Works Progress Administration.

The last position, which led to *Famous New Orleans Drinks*, grew out of his archival research on Audubon and also spawned two other books, *Old Families of Louisiana* (1931) and *Old New Orleans: A History of the Vieux Carré* (1936). Like them, his drinks book was lively, anecdotal, and detailed, offering historical commentary on just about every drink. No book had done that before, and much of what he wrote contains invaluable nuggets of history. But Arthur was never a particularly meticulous researcher, and the book is riddled with easily avoidable errors. Worse, he was prone not only to jumping to conclusions and printing supposition as fact but also to altering the evidence to support his conclusion, as when he omitted the identifier "Stoughton's" from a description of the bitters used in an early New Orleans cocktail so that he could imply that Peychaud's bitters were used in the drink. Unfortunately, these faults have been perpetuated in the genre he did so much to found, but so, on occasion, have his breezy style, his wit, and his deft hand with an anecdote.

See also SAZERAC COCKTAIL.

Arthur, Stanley Clisby. *Famous New Orleans Drinks and How to Mix 'Em*. New Orleans: Harmanson, 1937.
Wondrich, David. "Is the Sazerac a New Orleans Cocktail?" *Daily Beast*, April 24, 2017, https://www.thedailybeast.com/is-the-sazerac-a-new-orleans-cocktail (accessed October 31, 2017).

David Wondrich

arzente is an Italian term for brandy, derived from the medieval *acqua arzente*, "burning water," which was in turn derived from the Latin *aqua ardens*. See AGUARDIENTE. The term, which had been dormant, was resurrected in 1921, when the Italian Distillers' Association asked the poet Gabriele D'Annunzio (1863–1938) to come up with a replacement for *cognac*, then used in Italy to designate domestic aged grape brandy. See COÑAC. D'Annunzio chose *arzente* not only for its historical resonance but also because it was a cognate to *arzillo*, "sprightly" or "tipsy," and "also 'the idea of ardor,'" as was reported at the time.

While Italian brandy is no longer called "cognac," neither is it frequently called "arzente." Under

Mussolini's Fascists, such linguistic purification later became a government policy, forcing such substitutions as *mistura*, "mixture," and *arlecchino*, "harlequin," for "cocktail"; *bottiglieria*, "bottle shop," for "bar"; and another of D'Annunzio's, *sangue morlacco*, "Morlach blood," for "cherry brandy" (Morlacchia being the region in Dalmatia where the spirit originated). This ended up rather tainting the whole idea.

See also BRANDY.

"D'Annunzio Turns His Guns on the Dictionary." *New York Herald*, October 16, 1921, 22.
"Minor Notes." *The Living Age*, October 15, 1921, 129.

David Wondrich

Ashley, James (1698–1776), kept the London Punch House on Ludgate Hill in the center of that city, the most famous establishment of its kind, for forty-five years. There, he pioneered and popularized the practice of mixing spirits with other ingredients to order in individual portions, making him responsible, perhaps more than any other person, for the creation of the modern bar. A native of Northamptonshire, in the English Midlands,

James Ashley as portrayed by Thomas Worlidge, ca. 1740.
© The Trustees of the British Museum.

Ashley was working in London by 1720. At some point he got into the wholesale cheese business, but that apparently did not satisfy his ambitions, and in 1731 he took out the lease on a large old tavern on Ludgate Hill and renamed it "The London Coffee House, Punch House, Dorchester Beer and Welch Ale Warehouse." Before long, the coffee, beer, and ale ceased to be central to the enterprise. and it was known simply as the London Punch House.

Before Ashley, punch was retailed only in relatively large quantities, at de facto fixed prices, so that a quart of Batavia arrack made into punch cost eight shillings and one of rum or brandy six; furthermore, the smallest quantity generally made was based on a half pint of spirits, for one and a half or two shillings. See ARRACK, BATAVIA. Even skilled workers frequently made less than two shillings a day at the time, so these prices were prohibitive. When he opened his punch house, Ashley charged only six shillings for a quart of arrack made into punch and four for brandy or rum. What's more, as his advertisements claimed, he was willing to sell smaller amounts, with prices "in Proportion, to the smallest Quantity, which is a half Quartern," or an eighth of a pint. That half-quartern, like all his punch whatever the quantity, was mixed in front of the customer, allowing him to verify the proportion and quality of the spirits used. The result, following Ashley's standard proportions of one part spirit to two parts other ingredients, was a nice cup—roughly 180 ml—of punch that cost as little as three pence—half the price of one of his bottles of Dorchester beer. This put punch within the reach of a great many more people and, as Ashley later boasted, "raised its reputation" with the general public. (Ashley could afford to charge so little because he had extensive cellars and could buy his spirits in large lots and age them himself.)

Ashley's precise punch recipe has not been preserved, although from circumstantial evidence mined from advertisements and descriptions of the bar we know that it was always made with a premixed, bottled, and cellared "Sherbett" or shrub based on the peels and juice of sour Seville oranges. See SHRUB. This enabled his bartenders, the chief of whom was one Mrs. Gaywood, to have the punch, whatever the quantity, "as soon made as a Gill of Wine can be drawn." That speed was necessary: the London Punch House was large and well-situated and had a reputation for high quality at a low price, all of which meant that it was perpetually thronged with customers. Its clientele ranged from dissolute youths like the young James Boswell (who recorded drinking "three threepenny bowls" of punch there in his journal) all the way to celebrities such as Benjamin Franklin and Oliver Goldsmith. Indeed, the London Punch House was one of the fixtures of the city, celebrated in prose and verse (alas, most of it doggerel). Its popularity and fame helped to spread the practice and techniques of punch making and the cult of punch drinking throughout England and the English-speaking world.

James Ashley was said to be an "intelligent and cheerful man," although too much given to litigation and obsessed with his reputation—indeed, he had a large inscription painted on the front of the punch house recounting his achievement in lowering the price of punch and popularizing it, "Pro Bono Publico," as it stated. For a time in the 1750s, he passed the management of the bar to his son and concentrated on dealing in spirits from his cellars, but at his death in 1776 he was back running the bar, along with his son. The London Punch House continued to operate until the mid-nineteenth century.

See also PUNCH.

Advertisement. *Grub St Journal*, March 9, 1731.
"Biographical Anecdotes of Thomas Worlidge." *Monthly Magazine*, April, 1796, 217.

David Wondrich

Aspergillus oryzae is filamentous fungus that excretes enzymes to produce food, including alcohol. The major enzyme *A. oryzae* produces is an alpha amylase, which hydrolyzes (breaks down) starch into smaller chains of sugar units and which is critical for yeast fermentation. But there are other interesting enzymes that *A. oryzae* produces such as proteases, glucanases, or hemicellulases that encourage yeast growth and reduce viscosity in whole-grain mash. The fungus is grown either in a solid state or in a liquid culture and usually requires further processing to purify the enzyme for the purpose of alcohol production.

The use of *A. oryzae* to hydrolyze starch and promote fermentation of grains was discovered and perfected in China during the early Zhou dynasty, at the beginning of the first millennium BCE, and has been a bedrock of Chinese alcohol production

ever since. See BAIJIU and QU. In the mid-twentieth century, it was experimented with in some North America distilleries, particularly those of the Seagram company. See SEAGRAM COMPANY LTD.

Today, purified sources of enzyme are sometimes used in place of malt or in conjunction with it in spirits that use grain in the fermentation process. For example, in producing vodka or some whisky categories, it is allowed to use enzymes that are produced by a fungus. This gives latitude to distillers to change ratios of malted and unmalted cereals and ultimately the flavors in the final product.

Huang, H. T. *Science and Civilization in China*, vol. 6, part 5, *Fermentations and Food Science*. Cambridge: Cambridge University Press, 2000.
Machida, M., O. Yamada, and K. Gomi. 2008. "Genomics of *Aspergillus oryzae*: Learning from the History of Koji Mold and Exploration of Its Future." *DNA Research* 15, no. 4 (2008): 173–183.
Monterio de Souza, P., and P. de Oliveira Magalhaes. 2010. "Application of Microbial α-Amylase in Industry: A Review." *Brazilian Journal of Microbiology* 41, no. 4 (2010): 850–856.
Willkie, Herman F., and Joseph A. Prochaska. *Fundamentals of Distillery Practice*. Louisville, KY: Joseph E. Seagram & Sons, 1943.

Don Livermore

The **Astor House** hotel—the latest word in modern hotels—opened on Broadway in 1836 in New York; one of its proprietors was Charles Stetson, former head bartender at Boston's Tremont House. Nonetheless, the hotel went against common practice and displaced the bar from the lobby to a small, secluded room of its own. This was considered a sop to the nascent temperance movement, whose supporters disliked checking into the hotel at the bar as was customary. Liquor sales nonetheless remained high, and in 1845 the bar was moved to larger quarters in the basement. Presiding over the bar was Sherwood "Shed" Sterling (1801–1856), the "Napoleon II" of barkeepers, as one old habitué dubbed him (the original Napoleon being Orsamus Willard), and "an expert maker of fancy drinks and cocktails" who "knew everybody and could name them." See WILLARD, ORSAMUS.

In 1852, the hotel moved the bar again, to the center of a showy new iron and glass rotunda

The Astor House, New York, as portrayed in *Gleason's Pictorial*, 1854. Wondrich Collection.

occupying the former central courtyard. After a slow start, the statue-studded and elaborately gilded 50-foot (15-meter) black walnut bar, reputedly the largest in the city, became a mainstay of the downtown cocktail route for the next sixty years. See COCKTAIL ROUTE. In the 1880s, the bar took in from $700 to as much as $7,000 a day, depending on the season (and which estimate one believes). At the time, 25 cents was a high price to pay for a drink, and a bar that made $50 a day was considered a smashing success.

The Astor House bar was not an engine for drink innovation—in 1889, for instance, when two Englishmen ordered scotch whisky cocktails, then coming into vogue, the head bartender had never heard of such a thing—but it was a great popularizer of drinks such as the Collins and the Manhattan, adopting them early and selling them in large numbers. See COLLINS and MANHATTAN. A great many young bartenders, including Jim Gray, began their careers there, learning their trade from head bartenders such as George Alexander in the 1850s, Billy Flynn in the 1880s, and Edward Buchanan (a grand nephew of President James Buchanan) in the late 1900s and early 1910s. See GRAY, "COLONEL" JIM. In 1913, after almost eighty years of operation, the bar closed when the badly outdated Astor House was sold for development. The bar, however, was still as busy as it ever was.

"Bar of Old Astor House Recalls Drinkers of Ante-Bellum Days." *New York Press*, May 11, 1913, 7.
"Caught at Last." *New-York Herald*, August 27, 1836, 2.
"Liquor Drinking in New York." *Decatur (IL) Daily Republican*, February 1, 1882.
"New York City: Its Ancient Taverns and Modern Hotels." *The Caterer and Household Magazine*, 1885, 311.

David Wondrich

Atholl brose is a Scottish liqueur. Brose (also brewis, browse, or brewst) is a traditional Scottish dish made by pouring water or milk over grains, such as oats or oatcakes, that may be served plain or with simple embellishments. Atholl brose liqueur, however, combines the same oatmeal and water with honey and scotch whisky. See WHISKY, SCOTCH. Variations are legion. Some contain no oats, while others include cream, milk, or eggs. Some are spiced; most are not. Modern executions sometimes deploy oat or nut milks and veer into the realm of desserts with whipped cream. All, however, boast whisky and honey. Beverages such as Atholl brose may have existed previously, but John Stewart, the first earl of Atholl, is credited for its invention. In 1475 Atholl captured the renegade earl of Ross, Iain MacDonald. Custom holds that Atholl's spies discovered a well where MacDonald drank at night, then spiked the well with a mix of honey, oatmeal, and whisky. Rendered unconscious by the resulting nectar, the rebel earl was readily seized. That boozy brose has been dubbed Atholl ever since. During her

1842 visit to Scotland, England's Queen Victoria sampled the famous liqueur. History does not record whether the monarch also succumbed to the brose.

Recipe: Soak ½ cup steel-cut oats in 360 ml water overnight. Strain the oats from this concoction, then stir 30 ml heather honey and 240 ml single-malt Scotch whisky into the "brose," or oat water—with a silver spoon, some insist—until the blend is homogenous. A day's rest allows the mix to achieve a more harmonious balance.

See also LIQUEUR; SCOTLAND; and WHISKY.

Atholl, J. *Chronicles of the Atholl and Tullibardine families*, vol 1. Edinburgh: Ballantyne, 1908.
Baker, Charles H. *The Gentleman's Companion*, vol. 2. New York: Crown, 1946.
Davidson, Alan. *The Oxford Companion to Food*. Oxford: Oxford University Press, 2014.
"The Queen's Progress." *Yorkshire Herald*, September 17, 1842, 2.
Wilson, C. Anne. *Food and Drink in Britain*. Constable, London, 1973.

Matthew Rowley

The **Atlantic Bar & Grill**, one of the incubators of the twenty-first century cocktail revolution, was opened in 1994 by Irish nightclub and restaurant impresario Oliver Peyton (1961–) at 20 Sherwood Street off Piccadilly Circus in London. It occupied a magnificent art deco ballroom that had lain dormant under the Regent Palace Hotel until Peyton painstakingly restored it to its former lavish, gilt-edged glory.

Catering to cabinet ministers and artists, transvestites and rock stars, the Atlantic had no late-night cover charge, unusual for London at the time, nor was it a private members' club. But it did have a strict door policy, making it the ultimate celebrity hideaway.

Determined to create the ultimate hedonistic temple to food and drink, Peyton convinced Chris Edwardes to leave the Groucho Club, a members' only bastion of music, TV, and film celebrities to head up the Atlantic's bar team, which at varying points included bartenders Douglas Ankrah, Dré Masso, and Jamie Terrell, all of whom would go on to bar-world stardom. He also lured the "godfather of London cocktails," Dick Bradsell, to preside over the eponymous lounge, Dick's Bar. Bradsell was not alone. His roster of protégés included current luminaries Nick Strangeway, Tony Conigliaro, and Angus Winchester, as well as his assistant bar manager Spike Marchant.

The Atlantic's doors closed in 2005 when its landlord, the Regent Palace Hotel, decided to refurbish the property. The space was converted and reopened in 2012 as Brasserie Zédel. Retaining its original art deco décor, Dick's Bar was also reopened and renamed Bar Américain.

See also BRADSELL, DICK; and STRANGEWAY, NICK.

Barber, Lynn. "Interview: Peyton's Place." Guardian, June 16, 2002. http://www.theguardian.com/lifeandstyle/2002/jun/16/foodanddrink.features6 (accessed January 29, 2021).
Personal interviews with Dick Bradsell and Oliver Peyton dated 15 January 2011 and 9 February 2011.

Anistatia R. Miller and Jared M. Brown

An **atomizer (mister)**, an item found in many modern bartenders' toolkits, disburses a mist by pumping air into a liquid-filled dispenser. The resulting pressure forces the liquid through a mesh screen, dispersing it into a mist. As a method of coating a glass with an aromatic liquid, this both provides better control and creates less waste than the traditional "rinse," where a larger volume of liquid is swirled into an empty glass to "season" or aromatize it. This use of atomizers in cocktail preparation became popular in the 1990s when it was mistakenly believed that the best Martinis should contain only a whisper of vermouth. An atomizer could dispense the slightest amount of vermouth via a mist into a glass before the addition of chilled vodka or gin. See MARTINI.

In twenty-first century drink preparation, many bartenders utilize an atomizer to add a flavor component that can play a role similar to a garnish. The mist can either be sprayed into the glass before the drink is poured into it (a "coat") or sprayed over the top of the drink once it has been poured as an aromatic (a "lid" or "cover"), diffusing the aromatics in the liquid.

Audrey Saunders

Australia and New Zealand, both former British colonies, have spirits industries whose histories are coextensive with British colonization. While small quantities of palm arrack were brought to Indigenous communities in northern Australia by Makassan traders prior to British colonization, those traders did not bring distilling technology with them, and the first European explorers of New Zealand noted a complete absence of alcoholic beverages in Māori life as they encountered it.

In Australia, rum played a significant role in the colony's foundation and early years (1788–1808). In the absence of quantities of British currency, "rum"—in the New South Wales colony, a catch-all term for distilled spirits—functioned as a trading and bartering medium, which, in the words of New South Wales governor William Bligh, "added to its pernicious effects . . . beyond all conception." The military body charged with maintaining order in the colony, the New South Wales Corps, held a de facto monopoly on the importation and illicit production of spirits; the "Rum Corps," as they became known, resisted Bligh's attempts to curb this corrupt trade. This internecine conflict culminated in an 1808 rebellion that would later come to be known as the "Rum Rebellion"—the only successful armed insurrection in Australia's history.

Bligh's successor, Lachlan Macquarie, legalized the distilling of spirits in Australia, and by the late 1820s and early 1830s distilleries operated throughout the colonies: whisky distilleries in Van Diemen's Land (now Tasmania), rum distilleries in Queensland, and gin and grape brandy distilleries in New South Wales. See WHISKY; RUM; GIN; and BRANDY, GRAPE. Each of these nascent industries experienced vicissitudes of fortune: in 1839, Van Diemen's Land governor John Franklin outlawed distilling on the island; rum production boomed with the expansion of Queensland's sugar cane industry (which in turn owed much of its success to enslaved Kanaka laborers brought to Australia by so-called blackbirders); brandy production grew alongside the growth of the nascent Australian wine industry in New South Wales, Victoria, and South Australia in the 1840s and 1850s, particularly for use in fortified wines; and in 1830 colonial newspaper *The Australian* lamented that gin distiller Robert Cooper had ceased production "in consequence of the very little encouragement given to his laudable exertions by the publicans and the public."

The federation of Australia's colonial states into the Commonwealth of Australia in 1901 saw the establishment of uniform federal laws regarding distilling; these laws demanded that a licensed distiller be capable of exhausting at least 150 imperial gallons (680 liters) of wash in an hour. This legal restriction ensured that throughout most of the twentieth century Australian distilling was the sole province of large industrial operations such as Bundaberg Rum, Château Tanunda Brandy, and Corio Whisky. Hefty tariffs on imported spirits protected this local industry until the trade liberalization reforms of the 1970s. These reforms created a crisis in the industry; cheaper imports saw Australian consumers disdaining local brands, which started to compete on price rather than quality. According to a report by the Australian Government's Industries Assistance Commission, whisky production in Australia had effectively ceased by 1977, and the commission temporarily imposed stiff tariffs on imported brandies in an unsuccessful attempt to stimulate demand for local brandy.

In the early 1990s Tasmanian distiller Bill Lark successfully lobbied the Australian government to ease the still size requirements of the 1901 Distillation Act; several craft distillers soon followed in Lark's footsteps, producing highly regarded spirits such as Tasmanian whiskies (including Sullivans Cove French Oak single cask whisky, which was awarded World's Best Single Malt Whisky at the 2014 World Whisky Awards), boutique rums, a wide variety of gins (including several that feature native Australian botanicals), vodkas, and other oddities such as Italian-style aperitivo bitters flavored with native Australian plants. See VODKA and BITTERS. Economies of scale and Australia's taxation regime ensure that these spirits are often significantly more expensive than their mass-produced or imported competitors; the Australian craft spirit industry's strategy is, for the most part, to ensure that their products' quality justifies their prices.

New Zealand's spirits industry is, by comparison to Australia's, underdeveloped; craft distilling remains something of a cottage industry, albeit one with pleasing prospects. Scots immigrants in the South Island's Southland area, particularly in the Hokonui Hills around Gore, brought with them a tradition of moonshining that prevailed throughout the late nineteenth and early twentieth centuries. New Zealand's twentieth century spirits industry mirrored Australia's in many ways: a small number of industrial distillers dominated, although these fared less well than their Australian counterparts. New Zealand's last large-scale whisky distillery, Willowbank, shut down in 1997, not long after legislative changes made the possession of stills for home use legal and kickstarted a small craft distilling industry. Aside from the commercial vodka behemoth 42 Below, New Zealand's current craft distilling scene favors inventiveness and novelty; products from the country include a gunpowder-infused rum, a gin flavored with native horopito flowers, and a liqueur flavored with native tītoki berries.

Brady, Maggie. *First Taste: How Indigenous Australians Learned about Grog*, vol. 3, *Strong Spirits from Southeast Asia*. Deakin, Australia: Alcohol Education and Rehabilitation Foundation, 2008.

Gately, Iain. *Drink: A Cultural History of Alcohol*. New York: Gotham, 2008.

Hutt, Marten. *Maori and Alcohol: A History*. Wellington: Health Services Research Centre for Kaunihera Whakatupato Waipiro o Aotearoa / Alcohol Advisory Council of New Zealand, 1999.

McCarthy, Luke. *The Australian Spirits Guide*. Richmond: Hardie Grant Books Australia, 2016.

Chad Parkhill

Averna, or **Amaro Averna**, has been the best-selling or second best-selling brand of Italian digestive bitter since the 1970s. See APERITIF AND DIGESTIVE. It was founded in Sicily in 1868 when Salvatore Averna, a textile merchant from Caltanissetta, began producing a cordial at his country house at nearby Xiboli. According to company lore, it was based on a recipe given him by the head of the Capuchin abbey just up the road (the Abbazia di Santo Spirito), but since the last monk there died in 1904, this cannot be independently confirmed. In any case, it is not the only herbal liqueur founded at the time to claim monastic roots. See BÉNÉDICTINE.

Averna added the famous Sicilian oranges and lemons to the bitter herbs and roots characteristic of Italian amari, making for a product that was still pleasant and sweet to the palate. Under the management of Salvatore's son, Francesco, Averna first gained the favor of Sicilians and then, in 1895, a medal of recognition from the Italian king, Umberto I. In 1912, King Vittorio Emanuele III granted the company the coveted Royal Trademark.

By 1958, when the Averna family incorporated their business, it had become one of the leading amari in Italy and one of Sicily's most successful businesses, although it would not begin exporting its product until the 1980s. At that point, Averna owned 25 percent of the Italian amaro market. All production remained at Xiboli (where a new facility was built in 1970) until 2010, when the brand moved all stages of production but the compounding of botanicals and alcohol to a new bottling facility in northern Italy. Then, in 2014, the Averna family sold the brand to Gruppo Campari. For now, at least, the compounding still occurs at Xiboli.

Amaro Averna. https://www.amaroaverna.com (accessed January 29, 2021).

De Luca, Saverio. "Il Gruppo Campari acquisisce la Fratelli Averna." *Gambero rosso*, April 15, 2014. https://www.gamberorosso.it/notizie/il-gruppo-campari-acquisisce-la-fratelli-averna-firmato-l-accordo-per-103-7-milioni-di-euro/ (accessed January 29, 2021).

"Una forma secolare per un amaro genuine." *Corriere della sera*, December 30, 1970, 22.

Leo Leuci

The **Aviation Cocktail**, made with gin, lemon juice, maraschino liqueur, and, originally, crème de violette, is one of a handful of obscure old formulae revived by the early proponents of the twenty-first-century cocktail revolution and used as a sort of secret handshake of the movement. See FORGOTTEN CLASSIC. The original formula for the classic Aviation first appears in New York bartender Hugo Ensslin's 1916 *Recipes for Mixed Drinks*, one of at least four different formulae with the same name circulating at the time (the earliest of them appears in print in 1911, when aviation was in its first infancy as a sport). See ENSSLIN, HUGO RICHARD.

As far as can be determined, Ensslin's drink did not enjoy broad popularity before Prohibition. Its fortunes improved somewhat in the 1930s, chiefly due to its being one of the many drinks from Ensslin incorporated by both Harry Craddock and Patrick Gavin Duffy into their popular drink books at the time. See DUFFY, PATRICK GAVIN, and CRADDOCK, HARRY LAWSON. By the 1950s, however, it had sunk into obscurity. Craddock's version, which omitted the crème de violette, was the one that was revived by Paul Harrington in his influential online column for *Wired* magazine, and it helped to propagate the cocktail revolution, calling as it did for gin and maraschino liqueur, the one untrendy and the other obscure. See HARRINGTON, PAUL.

The 2003 rediscovery of Ensslin's book and the subsequent reintroduction of crème de violette to the American market have worked to make the Aviation something of a shibboleth for the generational divide between the first wave of modern cocktail aficionados, who tend to follow Craddock's formula, and the subsequent ones, who follow Ensslin's.

Recipe: Shake 50 ml London dry gin, 15 ml lemon juice, 8 ml maraschino liqueur, and 5 ml crème de violette (opt.) with ice. Strain and serve.

Craddock, Harry. *Savoy Cocktail Book.* London: Constable, 1930.

Duffy, Patrick Gavin. *Official Mixer's Manual.* New York: Ray Long & Richard R. Smith, 1933.

Ensslin, Hugo R. *Recipes for Mixed Drinks.* New York: Mud Puddle, 1916.

Harrington, Paul, and Laura Moorhead. *Cocktail: The Drinks Bible for the 21st Century.* New York: Viking, 1998.

David Wondrich

awamori, Japan's first spirit, is a distillate made from long-grained indica rice and black koji (*Aspergillus awamori*) on the tropical islands of Okinawa. See KOJI. Formerly the Ryukyu Kingdom, the islands are thought to have received distillation technology through their role as a South China Sea trade hub. However, the exact year awamori production began is still disputed, theorized domestically as sometime between 1477 and 1534. Importantly, awamori is thought to be the direct ancestor of Japan's most popular spirit, shochu. See SHOCHU.

Several accounts from the sixteenth to nineteenth centuries attest to the importance of awamori in the culture, serving as an aristocratic tipple poured liberally when foreign emissaries were greeted. Ryukyu awamori is now protected under the World Trade Organization's Appellation of Origin Control strictures. Requirements are a single-mash fermentation using Thai rice and black koji, followed by a single distillation in a pot still, almost always at atmospheric pressure rather than with the vacuum-assisted lower-temperature distillation used so often for shochu. Most awamori is bottled at 30 percent ABV. Awamori is known for its sweet aroma and earthy notes and is generally enjoyed on the rocks or mixed with cool water. A versatile liquor that can accompany meals, awamori can hold its own against bitter or heavily seasoned dishes.

Okinawa also boasts a centuries-old fractional blending tradition employing multiple earthenware aging pots. This creates a savory product, labeled *kūsu* when aged for at least three years. The devastation of World War II claimed the longest aged awamori, some of it more than 150 years old, but the practice was restarted along with the postwar reinvigoration of the industry.

See also JAPAN; MASH; and STILL, POT.

"Characteristics and Production Methods of the Main Varieties of Honkaku Shochu and Awamori." http://www.honkakushochu-awamori.jp/english/pdf/no_4.pdf (accessed January 29, 2021).

Pellegrini, Christopher. *The Shochu Handbook: An Introduction to Japan's Indigenous Distilled Drink.* N.p.: Telemachus, 2014.

Christopher Pellegrini

An **azeotrope** is a liquid compound whose boiling point is either above or below those of its component parts, meaning that its proportions cannot be altered by simple distillation. Ethanol and water form a so-called positive azeotrope, one whose boiling point is lower than that of either compound, at 95.63 percent of the former and 4.37 percent of the former. Pure 100 percent alcohol, then, is impossible to create through normal distillation: the ethanol that volatilizes and comes through the still is in fact actually the ethanol-water azeotrope. All normal distillation can do is separate the azeotrope from any water above that 4.37 percent. That final portion of water can only be removed by breaking the azeotrope with vacuum distillation or other heroic measures, such as adding benzene or cyclohexane to the liquid to be distilled.

See also ETHANOL.

American Chemical Society. https://www.acs.org (accessed January 29, 2021).

Rowley, Matthew B. *Moonshine!* New York: Sterling, 2007.

Doug Frost

bacanora is a Mexican agave spirit regulated since 2005 by Norma Obligatoria Mexicana (NOM-168-SCFI-2004). Legal to produce only since 1992, bacanora gained Denomination of Origin (DOB) protection in 1994. The ancient Hohokam people of the arid region now divided between the Mexican state of Sonora and the American state of Arizona had already domesticated several agave species for food and fermented beverages circa 1000 CE. See AGAVE. Bacanora is named after a small village in east-central Sonora, whose name means "reed-covered slope" in the language of the indigenous Opata people of the region. The Opata and other peoples of northern Mexico have a long and cherished tradition of production of mezcal-type alcohols traditionally called *vitzo* or *cuviso*. The term bacanora was first applied to a bootleg mezcal made in Sonora and adjacent Chihuahua from *Agave angustifolia* var. *Pacifica*, sometimes mixed with *A. palmeri*. The DOB restricts production by geography and plant species; bacanora as such may only be produced in a few dozen Sonoran locales and must be prepared exclusively from *Agave angustifolia*. In addition to the restrictions of the NOM and DOB, bacanora production is limited but growing slowly.

In the latter part of the seventeenth century, Spanish missionaries and indigenous people in the region drank mezcal. Missionaries distributed mezcal and aguardiente to indigenous people to increase their dependency on the Spaniards. The beginning of the twentieth century saw the first important boom in tequila export to the United States. See TEQUILA. At the same time Sonoran mezcal was also exported. Traditional markets are the major cities of Sonora and Arizona. Bacanora production was almost one million liters in first decade of the twentieth century. In the 1930s and 1940s, the proud tradition of Sonoran mezcal was prohibited; producers were persecuted, punished, and even put to death. Illegal production continued for almost fifty years until the creation of the DOB. During bacanora's clandestine period, bootleggers sold poor quality liquors, and the product's reputation suffered. These spirits were called pejoratively *tumba Yaquis*, or "fallen Yaquis," after the strongest and most resistant tribal people of Sonora. Bacanora production remained illegal until 1990, and, as such, the industry is still young. In the Sonoran-Arizona desert, wild plant populations from within the local pastoral system have been used for millennia; however, conversion from wild to cultivated agave is a big challenge for the cowboys and *ganaderos*, or "ranchers," of the production area. Research institutions and producers have introduced in vitro propagation and created pilot plantations.

As a kind of mezcal, bacanora is produced from the fleshy stems and leaves of agave plants and not, as has been reported, from the sap of the plants as is the case for the *pulques* or *aguamiels* of the central Mexican plateau. In traditional bacanora production, the material is cooked in deep ovens to convert the starches into fermentable sugars. After roasting, the fiber is removed from the plant material through manual or mechanical means and the starchy component set to ferment with water either in underground receptacles called *barrancos* or in plastic containers. Bacanora exists in four types, all of which may be diluted with water to between 38 percent and 55 percent alcohol after distillation. Closest to the original northern Mexican tradition is the *blanco* (silver). More modern grades have adopted characteristics from the tequila tradition and include *oro* (gold), which is sweetened; *reposado* (aged), matured for two months in wood containers; and *añejo* (extra aged), matured at least one year in 200-liter wooden barrels. Local consumption is typically at festivals. See ORO OR GOLD LIQUEURS; REPOSADO; and AÑEJO.

Bacanora's flavors are directly related to the wild agave plants from which it is produced: dry, but sweet and smoky from the mesquite wood used for roasting. Water quality and still technologies are also especially important. In many cases, wild harvest and few added products make bacanora one of the most organic mezcal products of Mexico.

In 2005 300,000 liters were reported by three thousand producers.

See also AGAVE; AGUARDIENTE; MEZCAL; and TEQUILA.

Nuñez, Luis, Vidal Salazar, and Evelia Acedo. *El Bacanora: Cultivo, Regulación y Mercados.* Hermosillo: Ed. CIAD Mexico, 2008.

Nuñez, Luis, and Vidal Salazar Solano. "La producción y comercialización de bacanora como estrategia de desarrollo regional en la sierra sonorense." *Estudios Sociales* 1 (2010: 206–219).

Ana G. Valenzuela-Zapata

Bacardi is a multinational spirits company with roots in mid-nineteenth-century Cuba. The brand is noted for elevating the perception of rum from a rough-edged, generally unwholesome drink of sailors to a lighter, more refined drink of sophisticated urban sippers. While the company remains closely associated with its Bacardi brand rum, in recent decades it has expanded and now also owns other prominent global spirit brands.

The company was founded by patriarch Facundo Bacardi y Maso, who emigrated with his family from Catalonia in Spain to Santiago de Cuba on the island's southeast coast in 1836. In his twenties, he became a wine importer and merchant. By 1862 he had partnered with a brother to acquire a small distillery then owned by John Nunes, an Englishman.

Bacardi's distillery flourished. Among his innovations was a visual logo in the form of a bat. Family lore ascribes this to the presence of bats in the Santiago distillery. The move proved sage in establishing the brand in an era when much rum was sold solely as a bulk commodity and in a region where many consumers were illiterate but could easily recognize and request the "rum with the bat."

Bacardi also was acknowledged to produce a rum superior in taste to other Cuban rums then commonly available. He did this through careful attention to distilling, using traditional pot stills (Bacardi apparently did not introduce column stills until the late 1910s) and by filtering the distillate after maturation (presumably through charcoal and sand) to strip out some of the heavier congeners that then characterized rum, yielding a more refined product. "Beginning as a thick, dark-brown drink to make pirates drunk, and passing through its phase as a universal medicine, rum, by the grace of a family named Bacardi and of American Prohibition, had become, in fact, a gentleman's drink," wrote cocktail scribe Basil Woon in 1928. See PROHIBITION AND TEMPERANCE IN AMERICA.

Bacardi's rum won recognition at the 1876 World's Fair in Philadelphia and continued to gain adherents through the late nineteenth century. But it was American Prohibition that boosted the brand's fame far beyond earlier achievement. When the taps closed and liquor shelves emptied in the United States in 1919, the nearest place for many Americans to order a drink was in Cuba, ninety miles south of Florida. Seaplanes, steamers, and ferries fed a booming tourist trade, and many visitors were surprised to find upon arrival a refined rum. They brought back stories (and smuggled bottles).

Following the repeal of Prohibition, the emphasis on spirits branding became more prominent, and with its head start Bacardi grew to dominate the rum market. (This was aided by a distribution agreement with Schenley Distillers Corp., one of the most influential United States liquor companies.)

In the 1930s the Bacardi corporation sought to escape the heavy tariff on liquor imported into the United States by establishing a distillery in American territory. After considering Pennsylvania, Louisiana, and Florida, the family opted to set up operations in the US territory of Puerto Rico in 1936. The shift proved prescient; when political turmoil roiled Cuba in the late 1950s—first with consolidation of power around corrupt political strongman Fulgencio Batista, followed by the revolution led by Fidel Castro—the Bacardi family was well prepared to abandon Cuba, with both intellectual property and production facilities safely situated abroad.

In the post-Castro years, Bacardi has been managed under a complex corporate arrangement involving a holding company and various units (mostly for tax purposes). Not until 1997 was a non–family member brought in to head the corporation.

More recently, the corporation has been engulfed in a legal battle with the government of Cuba over ownership of the Havana Club brand, to which Bacardi laid claim following its abandonment by the Arechabala family in 1973. Rulings by various national and international bodies have gone both for and against Bacardi. In the meantime it has expanded sales of its Havana Club rum. In recent years Bacardi has also sought to expand by moving aggressively into non-rum brands, including Bombay gin, Dewar's whisky, and Grey Goose vodka. See DEWAR'S and GREY GOOSE.

See also HAVANA CLUB and RUM.

Foster, Peter. *Family Spirits: The Bacardi Saga, Rum, Riches, and Revolution.* Toronto: McFarlane, Walter & Ross, 1990.

Gjelten, Tom. *Bacardi and the Long Fight for Cuba: The Biography of a Cause.* New York: Viking, 2008.

Noel, John Vavasour. "Who Discovered 'Bacardi?'" *The South American,* November 1916, 24.

Woon, Basil. *When It's Cocktail Time in Cuba.* New York: Liveright, 1928.

Wayne Curtis

Bacardi Cocktail may originally have been nothing more than a Daiquiri made with Bacardi rum, though somewhere along the line grenadine found its way into the mix. See DAIQUIRI; BACARDI; and GRENADINE.

bagaçeira, or aguardente bagaçeira, is a grape-based marc made in Portugal that is distilled to no higher than 86 percent and bottled at no less than 37.5 percent ABV (and rarely exceeding 54 percent). No flavoring or additional alcohol can be added. Bagaçeira can be found as both an artisanal spirit and a large-scale industrial distillate, with varying methods of distillation employed, from small pot stills to large column stills. Raw materials may vary among both red and white grapes, as well

as the amount of distillate retained (rather than that which is set aside for disposal or redistillation); indeed, distillers sometimes use fully fermented wine (generally called aguardente vinica), leftover grape pomace after fermentation, and a limited amount of spent lees, though bagaçeira is intended to be made from pomace, or *bagaço*. See MARC and POMACE BRANDY.

The EU provides for demarcated regional bagaçeira under its 2008 regulations. These include Aguardente Bagaçeira Bairrada, Aguardente Bagaçeira Alentejo, Aguardente Bagaçeira da Região dos Vinhos Verdes, and Aguardente Bagaçeira da Região dos Vinhos Verdes de Alvarinho (made solely from the alvarinho grape variety).

In Portugal, bagaçeira is viewed as a common and even rustic product (indeed, the word can be used to connote something poor or substandard), but that does not preclude some producers from making very skillful and lovely bagaçeira spirits. Increasingly, as with grappa in Italy, high-quality wine producers are participating, and some, such as Herdade de Mouchão, make single variety bagaçeira. Some producers will age the spirit in used oak and sell the resulting brandy as a more rarefied product called bagaçeira velha (or even velhissima).

Additionally, licor de bagaçeira is a grape beverage that is made sweet (often through the addition of grape-based spirit to interrupt the fermentation process) and bottled at 18–54 percent ABV.

See also AGUARDIENTE, and GRAPPA.

Regulation (EC) no 110/2008 of the European Parliament and of the Council of 15 January 2008. https://eur-lex.europa.eu/legal-content/EN/ALL/?uri=celex%3A32008R0110 (accessed January 29, 2021).

Doug Frost

Bagpiper, a leading Indian "whisky" brand, was launched in 1976 by Vittal Mallya's United Spirits Limited (USL). It is a blend of Indian and scotch malt whisky and neutral spirit made from molasses. This places it outside the internationally recognized definition for whisky.

Mallya bought United Breweries in 1947 and began to move into distilling in the early 1950s, initially with the purchase of McDowell's. ISL was taken over by Diageo in 2014; Mallya has since been removed from control of the business.

Bagpiper sells in the region of nine million cases a year. Any consideration for moving into export was thwarted in 2016 when Diageo stopped selling it outside of its home market. This was as a result of concerns raised by the scotch Whisky Association regarding the use of "Scottish names" on non-scotch whiskies.

Woodard, Richard. "Indian Whisky: Why It Matters to Scotch." *Scotchwhisky.com*, April 12, 2016. https://scotchwhisky.com/magazine/in-depth/8924/indian-whisky-why-it-matters-to-scotch/ (accessed January 29, 2021).

Dave Broom

The **Bahama Mama**, which, naturally, originated in the Bahamas, is an example of a drink that, though it gained popularity in the United States in the 1970s after the heyday of the tiki bar was over, nicely fits the definition of an exotic cocktail. Exotic cocktails, as defined by tiki godfather Donn Beach, are, at their heart, riffs on the traditional Planter's Punch: one of sour, two of sweet, three of strong, four of week, and often "a bit of spice to make it nice." The British Colonial Hotel in Nassau was serving a Bahama Mama in 1960, as was the Beverly Hills Trader Vic's in 1961 (served in its own wooden mug), but neither formula was recorded, and their relation to each other and to subsequent iterations of the drink is not known. See TRADER VIC'S. Recipes for the Bahama Mama begin to appear in print in the United States in the early 1970s, and in the middle of the decade ads from the Bahamas Tourist Board began calling for you to "Drink a Goombay Smash or a Bahama Mama" (the name probably comes from Wolfe Gilbert and Charles Lofthouse's long-lived 1932 novelty hit song of the same name, with which tourists landing in Nassau were routinely greeted). There appears to be no definitive recipe for the Bahama Mama, but most recipes include lemon or lime, giving the drink the requisite sour, and feature a blend of rums as the strong component (also following in the tradition of Donn Beach and his fellow legendary tiki barman Trader Vic), and many use sugar, grenadine, or a coffee, coconut, or orange liqueur for the sweet, pineapple and/or orange juice as the weak, and bitters for the spice.

However, when made poorly, the Bahama Mama can and should be lumped in with the sweet and slushy "boat drinks" of the 1970s like the Mudslide or Lava Flow, which don't have enough of a sour component to balance out their sweet core. And, like many of its exotic cocktail brethren, by the mid-late 1980s you see variants of the Bahama Mama that have completely devolved from their Planters Punch–style origins, introducing nontraditional ingredients like pink lemonade, tequila, and Southern Comfort.

See also BEACH, DONN, and BERGERON, VICTOR "TRADER VIC".

Recipe: Shake well with ice: 15 ml dark rum, 15 ml coconut liqueur, 7 ml coffee liqueur, 15 ml fresh lemon juice, and 120 ml pineapple juice; strain into ice-filled Collins glass, float 7 ml 151-proof rum on top, and garnish with maraschino cherry.

Berry, Jeff. *Beachbum Berry's Potions of the Caribbean: 500 Years of Tropical Drinks and the People behind Them.* New York: Cocktail Kingdom, 2014.
"Holiday Spirits." *Tampa Times*, December 23, 1960, 8.
Katz, Betty. "Press Previews Resort Wear to Calypso Beat," *Van Nuys (CA) Valley News*, April 20, 1961, C26–27.
Pogash, Jeffrey, and Rick Rogers, eds. *Mr. Boston Official Bartender's Guide: 75th Anniversary Ed.* Hoboken, NJ: John Wiley, 2012.

Martin Cate

baijiu is a category of Chinese grain spirit notable for its use of solid-state fermentation. Baijiu (literally, "white spirits") is most commonly distilled from sorghum but is also often made from rice, wheat, corn, and millet. See SORGHUM. The production techniques differ significantly by region and style, but all baijiu is fermented with *qu*, cakes of wheat or rice inoculated with naturally harvested cultures of airborne yeast and microorganisms, including the *Aspergillus oryzae* fungus. See ASPERGILLUS ORYZAE; QU. Most baijiu is also distilled in a solid state using traditional Chinese pot stills, which pass steam directly through the fermented grains (rather than a wash, as used elsewhere for grain distilling) to create alcoholic vapor. See CHINESE STILL. The distilled liquor is produced in batches, which are aged separately and blended together to create a finished

North Vietnamese President Ho Chi Minh (*left*) and Zhou Enlai, prime minister of the People's Republic of China, drinking baijiu in Hanoi, 1960. Getty Images.

product. It is traditionally served neat at room temperature, consumed alongside meals through a series of communal toasts.

Owing principally to the immense population of the nation that created it, baijiu is the world's most popular liquor by volume, with annual outputs that exceed that of vodka and whisky—numbers 2 and 3, respectively—combined. Yet outside of Asia baijiu remains largely unknown and misunderstood. This is due in part to a categorical confusion: baijiu and Western spirits, broadly defined, are fundamentally different alcohols. In terms of production, ingredients, flavor, and aroma they bear little in common. Thus for one born in a land that enjoys gin and brandy, baijiu is usually an acquired taste, and vice versa.

Origins

Prehistoric Chinese began producing alcoholic beverages about nine thousand years ago. When the nation was first unified in 221 BCE, there already existed a complex and varied winemaking tradition within its borders. It was around this time that qu-fermented grain alcohol called *huangjiu* ("yellow wine") became China's preferred tipple. Qu allowed

Chinese brewers to perform dual action on grains, converting starches to sugars and sugars to alcohol simultaneously, processes that have always been performed separately when making huangjiu's Western counterpart: beer. China's elaborate bureaucracy allowed for rapid dissemination of production techniques, and regional winemakers across China developed countless variations.

According to the earliest known reference to baijiu, written during the sixteenth century, the Chinese began distilling the spirit during the Mongolian Yuan dynasty (1271–1368), but there is archaeological evidence, including two bronze stills from the Eastern Han dynasty (25–220 CE) that it is very considerably older than that, and other evidence to suggest it may have already begun to spread throughout the region during the Tang dynasty (618–907 CE). See DISTILLATION, HISTORY. There is even the faint possibility that Marco Polo, who traveled through Mongolian China, tasted proto-baijiu when he wrote of a rice alcohol that was "clear, bright, and pleasant to the taste, and being (made) very hot, has the quality of inebriating sooner than any other."

Whatever liquor first warmed Chinese bellies, it likely bore only faint resemblance to today's baijiu.

The earliest *shaojiu* ("burnt wine"), as liquor was then known, was likely just distilled huangjiu. Details of what happened next are sketchier. According to the nineteenth-century French missionary Évariste Huc, a Chinese peasant in Shandong Province invented solid-state fermentation by accident while trying to make brandy from grains that had grown moldy and undrinkable during a botched fermentation cycle. He goes on to claim that wheat-based "big qu," which is used to ferment the majority of modern baijius, appeared shortly thereafter just south of Shandong, in Jiangsu or Henan. Sichuan Province, some two thousand miles upstream of Jiangsu on the Yangtze River, makes a competing claim on big qu's invention.

These developments facilitated solid-state fermentation and distillation, and by the beginning of the Ming dynasty (1368–1644) China possessed a drink resembling modern baijiu. The ruling scholar-bureaucrat caste still favored the more delicate huangjiu and would continue to do so until the twentieth century, but baijiu found an eager reception among the nation's peasantry. Farmers and laborers appreciated that spirits required less grain to produce more potent drinks. Baijiu spread to all corners of the empire and absorbed local ingredients and winemaking techniques along the way. Thus emerged a number of distinct spirits in China, divided mainly along regional lines.

Modern Baijiu

After centuries of gradual evolution, baijiu changed radically following the fall of the Manchu Qing dynasty in 1912. China's fledgling republic saw a resurgence of nationalism, and reformers attempted to create modern industrial enterprises to compete with those of foreigners in China's colonized ports. Earlier baijiu had come almost exclusively from small family-run workshops, but during this period private investors created some of the nation's first modern distilleries, such as what would later become Xinghuacun Fenjiu Distillery in Shanxi Province.

Political instability, Japanese invasion, and later civil war temporarily disrupted efforts at full-scale industrialization, which began in earnest with the birth of the People's Republic of China in 1949. In the first decade of Chairman Mao's tenure the state created most of today's major distilleries—Luzhou Laojiao, Jiannanchun, Xifengjiu, and others—by consolidating private baijiu workshops into massive state-run distilleries across the country. Stainless steel replaced wood, cranes replaced wheelbarrows, but the fundamentals of production remained intact. Most work was still performed by hand, only on a grander scale.

Baijiu, which had always been a proletarian tipple, firmly established itself as the national drink. Distilleries with patriotic bona fides, like Kweichow Moutai and Redstar Erguotou, received official promotion and became household names. Production techniques were recorded, improved upon, and codified, and the government created the first classification systems. Yet during the lean years of Mao's China, grain was scarce, and the government rationed baijiu consumption, forestalling the possibility of connoisseurship.

It was only with the advent of President Deng Xiaoping's "Reform and Opening Policy," which reintroduced market economics to China in the late 1970s and 1980s, that baijiu entered full maturity. The number of private distilleries exploded during this period; early 1990s estimates place the number as high as 36,000. For the first time average Chinese had access to baijius produced in distant provinces, spurring innovation that created entire new varieties of spirits.

The industry has since moved toward consolidation and expansion, particularly in the premium segment. Baijius that once retailed for no more than a single US dollar began selling for hundreds. This was due mainly to rising demand from businessmen and government officials, who made a point of having top-shelf baijiu on hand for any important meeting. Starting in 2013, Beijing enacted measures to limit extravagant state expenditures on alcohol, which disrupted this trend and led to a general reshuffling of the market.

The next chapter of baijiu's story will doubtless be written overseas. In the first decade of the twenty-first century three international spirits corporations—Diageo, LVMH, and Pernod Ricard—entered the baijiu market, with varying degrees of success. See Diageo and Pernod-Ricard. Early in the second decade, a handful of independent investors launched baijiu brands with the aim of expanding the category's reach overseas. More are sure to follow, as bartenders discover the category and begin incorporating it into their menus.

Production

A distiller begins the process of making baijiu by washing and steaming the grains. After steaming, grains are spread out to cool on a stone platform. Once they have reached a temperature that will not inhibit yeast activity, qu is added to the grains and the fermentation begins.

Fermentation technique is one of the key distinctions between different styles of baijiu. In the southwestern provinces of Sichuan and Guizhou, as well as along much of the east coast, distillers bury and seal fermenting grains in large subterranean pits for at least a month. Elsewhere in China grains are fermented in large stone jars for days or weeks.

Once the mash has been collected, it is loaded into a pot still, usually the same device in which the initial steaming was performed. The base of the pot is a perforated surface, often covered with a layer of wheat chaff to prevent mash from slipping through. The pot is placed over boiling water, and as the steam elevates the mash's temperature, alcoholic vapor rises from the top of the mash. At this point a lid is affixed to the pot that will collect the vapor and pipe it into a condenser, generally a coiled tube running through a tank of cold water. The workers collect the spirit from a spigot running from the condenser, discarding the head and the tail.

The spirit distilled from each pot of mash is stored and aged separately, traditionally in terracotta clay jars left in dark, humid cellars or caves. Clay is a highly porous material that allows for significant interaction between the spirit and its surrounding environment, which can help break down aldehydes and develop sweeter flavors by improving ester concentration. Lower-end baijiu is often aged in stainless steel containers. Although there are no official aging requirements for baijiu, most Chinese spirits are aged at least six months, and premium brands are typically aged at least three to five years.

All baijiu is blended before bottling. As baijiu is distilled in batches, the quality and taste of the distillate can vary greatly. With many styles of baijiu a mash will be fermented and distilled multiple times (sometimes with the addition of fresh grain), generating flavors ranging from sour to smoky. Thus in achieving the proper balance of flavors, the role of a distillery's master blender is essential. Most distilleries create a range of blends, using more of their best batches in top-shelf products and often using neutral spirit as filler for lower-end products. Water is also added before bottling to reduce baijiu's strength, with common ABVs ranging from 38 to 65 percent; premium products are almost always over 50 percent.

Classification of Baijiu

Today there are four principal styles of baijiu, grouped by fragrance: strong aroma, light aroma, sauce aroma, and rice aroma. There are also at least a dozen minor categories and subcategories, some so specific as to refer to the liquor of a single distillery. The government introduced this classification system in the late 1970s to replace a 1952 system that defined a category by its representative distillery (Moutai fragrance, Luzhou fragrance, etc.). Awkward though the names may be in literal English translation, the contemporary categories are defined by concrete differences in production. Strong-aroma-style baijiu uses sorghum and other grains fermented in subterranean mud pits, whereas sauce-aroma-style baijiu is made from a sorghum mash mixed with wheat-based qu, fermented in pits lined with stone bricks. See STRONG-AROMA-STYLE BAIJIU and SAUCE-AROMA-STYLE BAIJIU. Rice-aroma and light-aroma styles are both traditionally fermented in earthenware jars, but the former is distilled from rice fermented with small qu and the latter sorghum fermented with big qu. See RICE-AROMA-STYLE BAIJIU and LIGHT-AROMA-STYLE BAIJIU. Also many light-aroma distilleries have adopted pit fermentation to increase yields. By mixing regional methods, distillers have produced new styles like small-qu light-aroma style, sesame-aroma style, and mixed-aroma style, to name but a few.

See also CHINA.

Dudgeon, John. *The Beverages of the Chinese*. Tianjin: The Tientsin Press, 1895.

Huang Faxin, David Tiande Cai, and Wai-Kit Nip. "Chinese Wines: Jiu." In *Handbook of Food Science, Technology, and Engineering*, vol. 4, ed. Yiu H. Hui: 173-1–52. Boca Raton, FL: CRC, 2005.

Huang, H. T. *Science and Civilization in China*, vol. 6, part 5, *Fermentations and Food Science*. Cambridge: Cambridge University Press, 2000.

Huc, Évariste Régis. *The Chinese Empire*. London: Longman, Brown, Green, Longmans, & Roberts, 1859.

Polo, Marco. *The Travels of Marco Polo*. Translated by William Marsden. New York: Barnes & Noble, 2005.

"Pouring a Big One." *China Economic Review*. May 1, 2008.

Ruan, Victoria. "China to Ban Public Purchases of 'High-End' Alcohol." *Bloomberg Businessweek*, March 27, 2012.

Xu Ganrong and Bao Tongfa. *Grandiose Survey of Chinese Alcoholic Drinks and Beverages* (中国酒大观目录, Chinese and English versions). Jiangnan University, 1998.

Zhang Wenxue 张文学 and Xie Ming 谢明, eds. *Zhong Guo Jiu Ji Jiu Wen Hua Gai Lu* 中国酒及酒文化概论. Chengdu: Sichuan Daxue Chuban She 四川大学出版社, 2010.

Derek Sandhaus

Baker, Charles Henry, Jr. (1895–1987), was an American writer who traveled around the world collecting recipes and experiences that became the foundation of his best-known works, *The Gentleman's Companion* (1939) and *The South American Gentleman's Companion* (1951). Part travelogues, part cookbooks, and part manuals for budding bon vivants, Baker's *Companions* have inspired generations of bartenders and spirits professionals with tales of mixological adventure in exotic locales, written with the unbridled enthusiasm of the passionate amateur.

Born in Zellwood, Florida, to a family of wealthy Northeastern industrialists, Baker was educated at Trinity College in Connecticut and worked as a mechanical engineer for Norton Abrasives before moving to New York to pursue a life in letters. He was a tall, athletic, and handsome man, an avid sailor and fisherman, who often sported a pencil-thin mustache and bore a striking resemblance to the actor John Barrymore. In the 1920s, he worked as a freelance writer, a magazine editor, and an interior decorator before an unexpected inheritance allowed him to take an around-the-world cruise aboard the steamship *Resolute* in 1925.

On this journey, he made a discovery that would inform his life's work, told here in his characteristic, charming prose: "All really interesting people—sportsmen, explorers, musicians, scientists, vagabonds, and writers—were vitally interested in good things to eat and drink," and "this keen interest was not solely through gluttony, the spur of hunger or merely to sustain life, but in a spirit of high adventure . . . That was all we needed to start us on this pleasant madness of recipe collection."

In this spirit, he went to work for the Hamburg American Line steamship company, and on the numerous cruises that followed he recorded recipes for food and cocktails that he encountered in exotic ports of call.

In 1932, he met a young heiress named Pauline Paulsen aboard the SS *Resolute*, and the couple were married when they arrived back in the States. They settled in Coconut Grove, Florida, at the house they christened Java Head, a manorial estate built to Baker's own exotic design.

After the publication of *The Gentleman's Companion*, Baker continued to chronicle his frequent travels, penning columns for *Gourmet*, *Town & Country*, and *Esquire* in the 1940s.

At the invitation of Pan-American Airlines, Baker took a multi-month junket to South America in 1946; the recipes he gathered there would become the basis of *The South American Gentleman's Companion*.

Baker's notable contributions to the cocktail canon include the Remember the Maine ("a Hazy Memory of a Night in Havana during the Unpleasantness of 1933, when Each Swallow Was Punctuated with Bombs Going off on the Prado"), the Colonial Cooler (an improvised Pimm's Cup created by the officers of the Sandakan Club in British North Borneo, 1925), and the Death in the Gulf Stream (contributed by Baker's friend Ernest Hemingway during a 1937 fishing trip in Key West).

Far more significant, however, is the contribution of his inimitable wit, romantic sensibility, and unfettered spirit to cocktail culture in general. In *The South American Gentleman's Companion*, Baker describes the transformative effects of his Maracaibo Champagne Punch thus: "Feuding females actually beam on one another; tycoons unbend and remember when they made their first million; husbands forget the fretful pass of years; the petty-peckings, bills, taxes . . . even the waning hurly-burly of the marriage-bed, and lead their astonished brides of yesteryear out into the patio to sniff the frangipani blossoms or to inhale the intoxicating swoon of night-blooming jasmine." Baker reminds his readers that a passion for cocktails can inspire adventure and that well-made drinks, in good company, have the potential to change lives.

See also PIMM'S CUP.

Baker, Charles H., Jr. *The Gentleman's Companion*, 2nd ed. New York: Crown, 1946.

Baker, Charles H., Jr. *The South American Gentleman's Companion*, 2nd ed. New York: Cocktail Kingdom, 2014.

Fichtner, Margaria. "Gentleman's Gentleman." *Miami Herald*, March 18, 2002.

St. John Frizell

balance is one of the most important goals to achieve when preparing a cocktail. Balance, the art of proportioning the sweet, bitter, alcoholic, sour, spicy, fruity, creamy, effervescent, and other ingredients so that they are in harmony, with none of them dominating or masking any other, takes a mixed drink that might otherwise taste ordinary and elevates it into a crisp, lively, memorable culinary expression. The overall combination of individual flavor components selected should certainly provide a deliciously pleasurable experience, but the negotiation of balance between those very same flavors should be so pleasing and so thirst-quenching that you would happily order another of the same.

The original recipe for a cocktail was a fairly straightforward one, made simply from a spirit, sugar, and bitters. See COCKTAIL. Water came in the form of dilution from melting ice and tied the entire drink altogether. Yet even in such a simple framework, the balance achieved through the understanding of its components allowed the cocktail to become the figurehead of all mixed drinks today. The sweetening had to be perceptible enough to counter the alcohol in the spirit without being cloying; the bitters had to be used deftly enough so as to add just the right degree of complexity; and the ice had to not only chill everything down but also soften the heat of the spirit and provide just enough dilution to round out the edges of the overall drink without allowing it to become flabby.

The major flavor components the bartender works with are sweet, sour, strong, and bitter. On occasion umami is included as well, which is the work of glutamic acid. Glutamic acid, found in things such as cheese, eggs, and tomato juice, provides an enticing "meaty" flavor. It is the reason why a drink as simple as the Bloody Mary (when properly made) can be so satisfying. See TOMATO JUICE and BLOODY MARY.

It is paramount to consider flavors and their counterpoints. Sweetness acts as a counterpoint to both sour and bitter. Yet too much sweetness can turn a perfectly good drink into a cloying one, as its overuse will dull the taste buds, suppress the appetite, and flatten the drink's overall flavor. Consider the sugar levels of any given sweetener (or for that matter, any ingredient), and adjust the other components accordingly. Sourness will aid in cleaning the palate and engage the taste buds as well as allowing other flavors to be better received, yet too much sour will overwhelm the palate and make it difficult to taste anything else. Bitterness has the ability to cut through other flavors, reduce perceived sweetness, and overall "point a drink up." But bitters can also quickly overpower a drink and, like salt, cannot be negated once added into the recipe.

Alcohol's bite can be desirable in certain situations, but is not meant to be overpowering within a balanced drink, so proof should be considered as well. Higher-proof spirits will cut through other flavors, enhancing "dryness" on the palate and amplifying the bitter and sour components and at the same time suppressing the sweeter ones. Water (or other soft ingredients) can tone down the sharp edges of alcohol, but too much and the drink becomes flabby and lacking in character.

Balance can also be dependent upon the type of spirit being used, or even varying brands within the same spirit category. A Manhattan cocktail made with the softness of bourbon has balancing characteristics different from one made with the spicier rye, and adjustments are necessary as a result. See MANHATTAN; WHISKY, BOURBON; and RYE. Viscosity in any form can amplify the perception of sweetness, so when working with eggs or cream, one might consider reducing the sweetening agent in the recipe. Understanding the relationship between all of these factors and bringing them together in complete harmony is where culinary artistry enters the picture and balance takes its rightful place.

Embury, David A. *The Fine Art of Mixing Drinks.* New York: Mud Puddle Books, 1948.

Regan, Gary. *The Joy of Mixology*. New York: Clarkson Potter, 2018.

Audrey Saunders

The **Bamboo Cocktail** is a simple mixture of sherry, vermouth, and bitters. So is the Adonis, the Rosa, the New York Athletic Club, the Armour, the Arkwood, and the Harvard. Doubtless there are others. This profusion of sherry-vermouth drinks is due to the popularity of the Manhattan and the fact that the substitution of sherry for whisky in a cocktail as a way of keeping its intensity but significantly lowering its proof was one of the most useful, and used, items in the late-nineteenth-century bartender's bag of tricks. The first of these drinks on record is the Adonis, created by Joseph F. McKone (1860–1914) of New York's famous Hoffman House in 1884 or 1885 to celebrate the Broadway show of the same name. See HOFFMAN HOUSE. (As a point of trivia, it should be noted that *Adonis*, the first modern musical, opened in the Bijou Theater, which was formerly the Thomas Brothers' saloon.) See THOMAS, JEREMIAH P. "JERRY". The Bamboo is the second, recorded in 1886. According to San Francisco bartender and mixographer "Cocktail Bill" Boothby, writing in 1907, it was invented by Louis Eppinger (1830–1908), a German immigrant who kept a famous bar on Halleck Street in that city in the 1870s before decamping to Portland, Oregon, and then Yokohama, where he managed the Grand Hotel from 1890 until his death. See BOOTHBY, WILLIAM T. "COCKTAIL BILL" and GRAND HOTEL. On the other hand, in the 1890s the drink was sometimes known as the Boston Bamboo, which casts some doubt upon a San Francisco origin.

Historically, there was a great deal of variation in the styles of vermouth, sherry, and bitters used in these drinks and in their proportions, even when the name was the same. The earliest recorded version of the Bamboo, for instance, called for 3 parts sherry to 1 part vermouth, presumably sweet (as in most of the pre-Prohibition recipes), but most later versions used equal parts. In modern times, while proportions still vary, most mixologists make their Bamboos with dry vermouth, reserving the name "Adonis" for the sweet-vermouth version. Whatever the precise details, the combination of vermouth, sherry, and bitters, after virtually disappearing with American Prohibition, has come back strongly with the second wave of the modern cocktail revolution and its keen interest in the drink's three component parts. See COCKTAIL RENAISSANCE.

Recipe: Stir 45 ml ea. sherry and vermouth and 2 dashes orange bitters with ice and strain into a chilled cocktail glass. Twist lemon or orange peel over the top.

See also BITTERS; SHERRY; and VERMOUTH.

Boothby, William T. *The World's Drinks and How to Mix Them*. San Francisco: Pacific Buffet, 1908.
"Disturbing Sunday Drinks." *New Haven Register*, July 27, 1885, 2.
"Poems in Cocktails." *St Paul Globe*, September 16, 1886, 16.
Sanders, Dinah. *The Art of the Shim*. San Francisco: Sanders & Gratz, 2013.
"What Will It Be?" *St Louis Post-Dispatch*, October 22, 1893, 29.

David Wondrich

bananas have been used for centuries as a fermentable raw material in making beer and wine, particularly in regions of East Africa. See CENTRAL AND EAST AFRICA. In the mid-nineteenth century, there are references to banana syrup being added to spirits (such as banana brandy) published in liquor manufacturing guides (such as Dr. Lewis Feuchtwanger's 1858 *Fermented Liquors*). Early in the twentieth century, recipes for crème de banana appear, in which banana is infused in neutral spirit and sugar and vanilla added. Soon after, cocktail recipes that include crème de banana or banana liqueur are published in European cocktail guides such as the 1913 *Lexikon der Getränke*.

There are reports of distillation of bananas in the early twentieth century, such as a 1912 pharmacy journal, *Merck's Report*, which notes that banana "is a possible source of alcohol. It is reported that a very good spirit has been obtained from bananas unfit for any other purpose in Guatemala." Perhaps the best-known example of the distillation of bananas is in the form of a banana gin known as *enguli* or *waragi* made by the indigenous people of Uganda.

Although many artificially flavored banana liqueurs are on the market today, some of the older European brands, such as Giffard, continue using traditional production methods that incorporate real bananas.

Narayana, Cherukatu Kalathil, and Michael Pillay. "Postharvest Processed Products from Banana." In *Banana Breeding: Progress and Challenges*, ed. Michael

Pillay and Abdou Tenkouano, 269–284. Boca Raton, FL: CRC, 2011.

Willis, Justin. "Banana Wine." In *Alcohol and Temperance in Modern History: An International Encyclopedia*, ed. Jack S. Blocker, David M. Fahey, and Ian R. Tyrell, 1:84–86. Santa Barbara, CA: ABC-CLIO, 2003.

Martin Cate

The **bang** (properly written "bang!") is a class of mixed drink created, or at least identified and named, by American drinks writer John J. Poister (1924–2011), wherein the ingredients include more than one iteration of the same basic flavor. His Cherry Bang, for example, contains gin, cherry Marnier, kirschwasser, and maraschino liqueur. See KIRSCHWASSER and MARASCHINO. A characteristic innovation of the disco drink era, the bang is occasionally still seen.

Poister, John J. *New American Bartender's Guide*. New York: Signet, 1989.

David Wondrich

Bank Exchange was, during the 1850s and 1860s, the first stop on San Francisco's cocktail route and, along with Barry and Patten's nearby saloon, one of the premiere bars on the West Coast of the United States. See COCKTAIL ROUTE. It enjoyed a second period of prominence as a beloved local institution and the home of Pisco Punch from the 1890s until Prohibition forced its closure in 1919.

The first Bank Exchange, a saloon and pool hall, was opened by Burlin Brown on Montgomery Street in the heart of the city's commercial district in 1850; it closed a few months after his death in 1852. The second Bank Exchange opened at the end of 1853 in the new, fireproof Montgomery Block at the corner of Montgomery and Washington streets. It is unknown what, if any, connection Patrick Kilduff, its proprietor, had with Brown or Smith, but like the first one it featured large oil paintings on classical themes, or at least the ones that allowed for lightly draped female figures, and billiard tables, along with a marble floor and $1,500 mahogany bar that were carried to San Francisco around Cape Horn. John Torrence and Thomas Parker took over the bar in 1854 and ran it until Parker's death in 1860. During those years it served as one of the main foci of the sporty, often brawling social life of the new city.

Another Parker, George, ran the saloon from 1860 until he went bankrupt in 1872; by then, the commercial center of the city had moved farther down Market Street and the area was no longer fashionable. After two years as an auction house, the bar reopened under the management of George Brown and George Perkins. In 1886 Brown brought Duncan Nicol into the business, Perkins having died two years before. Nicol (1852–1926) was a close-mouthed Glaswegian who had worked for a number of years behind the bar at the venerable Parker House Hotel, a San Francisco institution. By 1896, he was the Bank Exchange's sole proprietor.

Under Nicol's meticulous, conservative supervision, the Bank Exchange became famous again, this time as a precious remnant of the city's fast-disappearing Gold Rush past. To cement that reputation, Nicol specialized in serving Pisco Punch, a drink known in the city and its surrounds since 1849 but no longer in vogue. It is unknown if Nicol inherited the drink along with the saloon or brought it with him, but Torrence and Parker had stocked and sold pisco, and the bar was known as "Pisco John's" (whether from Torrence or from the bar's first telephone number, "John 3246," is also unknown).

By the 1910s, the bar had become a quiet, gentlemanly place—so gentlemanly, in fact, that ladies, too, were allowed to drink there. Despite its various bankruptcies and sales, the bar retained a great deal of memorabilia, among which Nicol held court, mixing his Pisco Punches one at a time, always with a fresh-squeezed lemon. When he closed the bar in 1919, the city was heartbroken. He died in 1926, taking his formula for the Pisco Punch with him to the grave. The Montgomery Block fell to development in the 1960s, and now the Transamerica Pyramid occupies the site.

See also NICOL, DUNCAN and PISCO PUNCH.

"His Ambition Not Dulled by Years." *San Francisco Chronicle*, February 4, 1921, 9.

"In San Francisco: Splendid Paintings." *Sacramento Transcript*, April 25, 1851, 3.

Jacobson, Pauline. "A Fire-Defying Landmark." *San Francisco Bulletin*, May 4, 1912.

David Wondrich

barack palinka is a popular type of apricot brandy from Hungary, distilled from—rather than flavored with—apricots. See APRICOT BRANDY.

Barbayanni is one of the leading brands of ouzo, founded in 1860 by Efstathios Barbayannis (1805–1873) in Plomari, on the Greek island of Lesbos. Barbayannis had worked as a distiller in the Russian city of Odessa and, following time served as a sailor during the Greek-Turkish War, began crafting and selling distilled products. Later a politician and philanthropist, Barbayannis built a company that remains dominant in the Greek spirit industry to this day. Five generations later, the family continues to keep secret the recipes for the firm's classic Barbayanni Blue Label and its four other expressions of ouzo, other than stating that they are based on raisin spirit, rectified with anise in pot stills.

See also ANISE SPIRITS and OUZO.

Ouzo Barbayanni. https://www.barbayanni-ouzo.com (accessed February 1, 2021).

Doug Frost

barley (*Hordeum vulgare*) is the base for a variety of whiskies because of the same qualities that make it the best grain for brewing beer. It is relatively easy and reliable to malt, so much so that malted barley is simply known as "malt," while other malted grains are called by name, such as "malted rye." Malted barley has high levels of the enzymes needed for converting starches to sugars in the mashing process. It has fairly low gluten content and is not as doughy as other grains when mashed (this also means it is not particularly good for bread production, meaning less competition for alcohol production uses). It is hardy and grows in a wide variety of climates. It also has a husk that serves as a natural filter after the mashing stage of brewing. All of these have led to barley being the grain of choice for brewing, and thus for spirits production.

Russia is the top producer, with Germany, France, Canada, and Spain in a dead heat for second place. Barley grows in both temperate and tropical climates but is not as well adapted to truly cold climates as rye is. There are two major types of domesticated barley: two-row and six-row, named for the numbers of rows of kernels on the ears. The six-row has higher protein content and is the preferred type for animal feed. Barley is the primary feed grain in Europe, Canada, and the northern United States. Agronomists are constantly creating new barley cultivars with improved traits for both feed and beverage use.

The origins of barley are deeply embedded in the historical and archaeological records of the Fertile Crescent, the area comprising what is considered the cradle of human civilization in modern-day Iraq, Syria, southeastern Turkey, Lebanon, Israel/Palestine, and Egypt. Wild barley (*Hordeum spontaneum*) is still found in these areas. Barley has been domesticated for about ten thousand years, one of the original crops from the dawn of agriculture. Humans have been turning it into beer for almost as long; indeed, some scholars have speculated that the demand for beer may have driven the start of agriculture.

It is not known precisely when or where distilling from grain—from beer, in effect—began in Europe, but the practice was widespread by the mid-1400s, documented in Germany, the Netherlands, Ireland, and Scotland. In Germany, some varieties of korn are still made from barley malt, while Dutch jenever was traditionally distilled from a mash of barley malt supplemented with malted or unmalted rye (for that matter, until the mid-nineteenth century English gin was made from rectified barley malt spirit). See KORN and GENEVER. Scotch whisky is still centered on malt, especially in the single malt and blended malt varieties, which are, by law, made from 100 percent malt. (The same can be said for Japanese whisky, which took the scotch whisky model as a starting point.) See WHISKY, SCOTCH, and WHISKY, JAPANESE. The malt may be simply pale malt, or it may be peated, with smoke from smoldering peat introduced during the kilning process, imbuing the distillate with a distinct smoky, iodine-like aroma.

Irish whisky also uses a large percentage of malt, but there is a type of Irish whisky called "single pot still" (formerly known as "pure pot still") that uses a mixture of malted barley and unmodified barley in the mash, which gives a fresh and fruity character to the whisky, along with a certain oiliness. See WHISKY, IRISH and SINGLE POT STILL. The practice became widespread in Ireland after the imposition of a tax on malt in 1785, but it appears to have been used before, presumably for reasons of flavor rather than costs.

American whiskies such as bourbon and rye usually have between 5 and 15 percent malt, but it is used largely for the enzymes malt delivers in the mash rather than for flavor. There is a small but growing trend among small American distillers to make all-malt whiskies. See WHISKY, BOURBON and WHISKY, RYE.

See also WHISKY.

Badr, A., et al. "On the Origin and Domestication History of Barley (*Hordeum vulgare*)." *Molecular Biology and Evolution* 17, no. 4 (2000): 499–510.

Bamforth, Charles. *Beer: Tap into the Art and Science of Brewing*. New York: Insight, 1998.

Buxton, Ian, and Paul S. Hughes. *The Science and Commerce of Whisky*. Cambridge: Royal Society of Chemistry, 2013.

Hayden, B., N. Canuel, and J. Shanse. "What Was Brewing in the Natufian?" *Journal of Archaeological Method Theory* 20 (2013): 102.

O'Connor, Fionnán. *A Glass Apart: Irish Single Pot Still Whiskey*. Mulgrave, Australia: Images, 2015.

Lew Bryson

The **bar meeting**, regular and well run, is an important component for discussing the business matters of the bar as well as creating a cohesive bar program. These allow bartenders (and perhaps the rest of the staff) to agree upon drink recipes and standards of service. Such meetings also allow bar management to explain changes in the menu and offerings. A bar meeting is an opportunity to provide tune-up training as well as hands-on experience with any new products or recipes coming on board.

A "bar meeting" is also bartender's slang for any given moment behind the bar, usually in the middle of fast-paced service, when the bartenders all agree that it is time take a quick drink together, whether it is a shot of spirits or a short mixed drink. It can be a planned moment or called impromptu by one of the bartenders, and it can also include the rest of the staff.

Audrey Saunders

Barnard, Alfred (1837–1918), was an English journalist who is regarded as the first "whisky writer"; his work forms the template for numerous books.

In 1885, he was commissioned by *Harper's Weekly Gazette*, a London journal "devoted to the interests of the wine, spirit, and brewing trade," to conduct an epic tour of all of the whisky distilleries in Britain. His reports, gathered in *The Whisky Distilleries of the United Kingdom*, were published two years later. They form the earliest and most accurate account of the industry at what was a major turning point in the fortunes of scotch and Irish whiskies.

His writing is notable for its precision in detailing the minutiae of much of the equipment within each of the distilleries. The virtual absence of any mention of casks gives an indication of how unimportant they were considered at that time in the creation of a whisky's character.

In addition to the technical information, Barnard peppers his accounts with evocative descriptions of his journey. For all his persnickety love of detail, these descriptive passages reveal him to be a gregarious man of not inconsiderable humor. The book can also therefore be read as a fascinating travelogue through the industrial and rural parts of Britain. His descriptions of Ireland, for example, speak at length about the rising nationalist movement.

Between 1889 and 1891, Barnard embarked upon a similarly grandiose endeavor, completing a tour resulting in *The Noted Breweries of Britain and Ireland*.

Barnard was ultimately a jobbing freelance journalist, and he also wrote numerous smaller publications for individual distilleries including Highland Distillers, Craigellachie, Glenfarclas, and Dalmore. He also wrote a short account of blending scotch with a focus on Lagavulin and profiles of blending houses such as John Walker & Son, Pattison, and George Morton of Dundee. These shorter works, which also offer invaluable insights into the industry at a pivotal moment in its evolution, are now being reprinted.

Barnard, Alfred, *The Whisky Distilleries of the United Kingdom*. 1889; repr., Edinburgh: Mainstream, 1987.

Dave Broom

barrel is the popular term for a cylindrical container assembled from wooden slats—"staves"—hooped together with steel or wooden bands that can be used to transport and mature spirits. Properly, barrels are a subset of casks (the generic term for all such built—"coopered"—wooden containers) and contain between 119 and 300 liters, depending on what they are designed to hold. The standard bourbon barrel, used for aging spirits throughout the world, holds 53 US gallons, or 200 liters; the standard cognac *barrique* now holds 300 liters.

The barrel's roots stretch back to Mesopotamian and Egyptian Antiquity, but barrels, usually made of oak, came into widespread use for storing and shipping spirits in the sixteenth century as the European spirits trade with Asia and the Americas grew. Their advantages were manifest. The barrel is one of the most sophisticated and successful pieces of design ever conceived. A modern whisky barrel weighs 50 kg empty and holds 186 kg of water, a ratio of 1 to 3.72. With a typical clay wine amphora, the barrel's main competitor until modern times, the ratio is more like 1 to 1.375. That's a lot of energy spent hauling around clay. What's more, if laid on its side, the barrel, pivoting as it does on a single point, can be moved and maneuvered easily by one person; if stood upright, one person can still rock it across a warehouse floor on its rim. Empty or full, it will float, which means it can easily be landed on a beach or floated out to a boat where no port facility is available. If it springs a leak, it can usually be patched without having to empty it. Barrels can be stacked five or six high, even when full. See BARREL STORAGE SYSTEMS.

Three things that a barrel is not, however, are cheap, sterile, and non-reactive. To make a watertight container out of separate pieces of wood is a tour de force of woodworking that requires great skill and years of apprenticeship, which means money. As master cooper Kenneth Kilby put it, "There are no amateur barrel makers." (The chief cooper was typically one of the highest-paid men at a distillery.) No matter the elegance of their structure, barrels did nothing to stop water, beer, or wine stored in them from spoiling on long ocean voyages (this led, at the end of the eighteenth century, to experiments with charring the inside of the barrel, which largely worked, at least for water). Spirits did not spoil, but barrels proved to be a dynamic container for them in a way that earthenware jars like the ones used for shipping spirits in Asia and parts of South America were not. See PISCO. Barrels are slightly porous, like the jars were, but in addition to the oxidation that came from that, the spirits leached a good deal of color and tannins, lignins, and other compounds from the oak. That took some

getting used to: spirits that came off the still as clear as water came out of the barrel tan and woody. But they were also smoother and richer in texture. See MATURATION.

At the height of the coopered cask's use as a container for shipping spirits, it came in an impossible thicket of sizes and names, as this sentence from the 1790 *Ship-Owner's Manual* demonstrates: "The aume is reckoned at Amsterdam for 8 steckans, or 20 verges or veerteels; or for one-sixth of a tun of 2 pipes, or 4 barrels of France or Bordeaux; which one-sixth is called at the latter tierçon, because three of them make a pipe or 2 barrels, and 6 make the tun." Easy. Spirits casks varied according to nation and spirit, and a merchant's warehouse could easily contain elongated, 300-liter *pieces* of cognac, large puncheons of Jamaica rum (400 liters), even larger teakwood "leaguers" of Batavia arrack (this was the Dutch *legger*, which held about 575 liters), smuggled Highland whisky in cigar-shaped 40-liter ankers, perfect for hanging off a pony's back, and more. See ARRACK, BATAVIA.

Today, barrels are rarely used for shipping spirits, having been replaced mostly by the 1,000-liter (275-gallon), steel-framed plastic "tote" (with a ratio of 1:16.25, clearly very efficient indeed, although it requires a forklift to move). Millions of barrels are of course still in use for maturing spirits. It's safe to say that most of these began their working lives as bourbon barrels: the United States requirement that straight whiskies be aged in new, charred oak containers means that barrels cannot be reused. Most of the ones that are emptied are broken down back into staves and hoops and shipped to Scotland, Ireland, Canada, Japan, the Caribbean, and a great many other places where spirits are matured. In Scotland, it is common to raise four larger barrels out of the staves from five standard ones; these 250-liter barrels are known as "hogsheads," an older measure that used to equate to a barrel and a half, or 300 liters. Supplanting this "American oak" cooperage, as it's known, is "French oak," used for cognac, Armagnac, and calvados (some of the oak used is in fact from eastern Europe, but European oak nonetheless).

In some parts of the world, such as Brazil, oak is supplemented by other, more local woods. See OAK ALTERNATIVES. Smaller barrels are also found in use, mostly by newer distilleries wishing to give their product the appearance of maturity as quickly as possible (the smaller the barrel, the greater the ratio of oak area to spirit, which creates more extraction of barrel compounds). Spirits left too long in such barrels can become very woody.

Kilby, Kenneth. *The Cooper and His Trade.* London: J. Baker, 1971.

Ship-Owner's Manual. Newcastle-Upon Tyne, 1790.

Stevens, Robert White. *On the Stowage of Ships and Their Cargoes,* 7th ed. London: Longmans, Green, 1878.

Work, Henry H. *Wood, Whiskey and Wine.* London: Reaktion, 2014.

David Wondrich

barrel-aged cocktails, a fixture of high-end cocktail bars in the early 2010s, are precisely what they appear to be: cocktails (and occasionally other styles of mixed drink) that have been premixed and then put in a small oak barrel (these range from four liters [one gallon] to as much as twenty liters [five gallons]) and left to mature for a time. At the turn of the twentieth century, when branded bottled cocktails were introduced and rose to instant popularity, some of the top-selling brands, including Heublein's Club Cocktails, the market leader, used the fact that they were aged in wood before bottling in their advertisement. Thus the Cook & Bernheimer company claimed the success of its Gold Lion Cocktails was the result of "long expert experience in blending the choicest materials," and, of course, "sufficient ageing in wood." See BOTTLED COCKTAILS.

While this might be simply making marketing out of necessity (stainless steel was still in the future, and the cocktails had to be kept in something before they were bottled), there was also some scientific basis to it. Even if stored in well-used barrels, the cocktails would take on some sweet oak notes, and the oxidation that occurred as they rested in the barrels would eliminate some of the spikier, more volatile compounds in the mixture.

The second coming of barrel-aged cocktails was unconnected to the first. It began in 2009, when the influential Portland, Oregon, bartender Jeffrey Morgenthaler (1971–) visited a new bar in London. Tony Conigliaro (1971–), the owner of 69 Colebrooke Row and one of the pillars of London's craft cocktail movement, had been experimenting with aging cocktails in

bottles for long periods. Says Conigliaro, "Bottle aged cocktails were born of the idea that oxidization could be used in a positive way for premixed cocktails, if the process was controlled in the same way that it is with wine when it ages." He even subjected his bottled cocktails to gas chromatography, which showed that the sharp peaks that marked the chemical reactions between the ingredients greatly subsided over time. This signals "a final product that has an incredible smoothness and encourages a new direction for flavors that are already present in the cocktail."

Having tried Conigliaro's five-year-old Manhattan, Morgenthaler, back at Clyde Common, his bar in Portland, thought he would try aging a cocktail, but in a one-gallon barrel in which he had been aging Madeira. After some experimentation, he and his bartenders hit on six weeks as the ideal period (longer and the wood begins to dominate).

The barrel-aged Manhattan was an immediate success, and before long bars all around the United States were experimenting with barrel-aging cocktails, and then all around the world. Perhaps the most popular drink to receive the treatment is the Negroni. See NEGRONI.

See also COCKTAIL RENAISSANCE; MANHATTAN COCKTAIL; and MATURATION.

"Club Cocktails" (advertisement). *New York Clipper,* September 14, 1912, 14.

Conigliaro, Tony. Personal communication with author, May 2016.

"Gold Lion Cocktails" (advertisement). *New York Press,* December 4, 1901, 5.

Simonson, Robert. "The Aged Cocktail's Barrel Zero." *Punch,* June 19, 2019. https://punchdrink.com/articles/aged-cocktails-barrel-zero-clyde-common-portland/ (accessed April 20, 2021).

David Wondrich

barrel rotation is the practice, largely confined to the whisky industry, of moving barrels around in the warehouse during maturation. The placement of a newly filled barrel in the warehouse can have a great effect on the mature whisky, especially in large distilleries with multiple warehouses or warehouses of great size, like the nine-floor behemoths in

Kentucky. Temperature and humidity differences among warehouses in sometimes far-flung areas or in the different floors of a large warehouse can make the whisky in a barrel evaporate faster, extract more or less from the wood (and at varying rates), or even allow the whisky to mature to an age beyond normal.

Barrel rotation is one way to balance these effects, albeit a labor-intensive one. The warehouse manager will devise a scheme to shift the barrels in lots from one area to another. The rotation evens out the effects of being in a cool bottom floor with some time in a hot, dry top floor, or balances a few years in the south side of the warehouse with a few in the north. The desire is to have the whiskies coming out of the barrel be as similar as possible.

Barrel rotation is not widely used, especially in non-palletized warehouses, because of the labor and risks involved in manhandling the heavy barrels. Other methods for achieving aging similarity include tightly spaced single-story warehouses, where smaller groups of barrels experience a relatively similar environment, and heated warehouses, which artificially create a uniform temperature and humidity throughout.

See also BARREL; ÉLEVAGE; MATURATION; and WHISKY.

Broom, Dave. *The World Atlas of Whisky: The New Edition*. London: Mitchell Beazley, 2014.

Lew Bryson

barrel storage systems. The standard 200-liter oak barrel might be remarkably easy to move, given its weight, but when it is not moving it has, to be kept somewhere, and once there are more than two or three lying around, that requires a storage system. See BARREL.

The oldest and simplest system in use dates back to the origins of barrel aging, when the barrels used were primarily shipping containers. To maximize the amount of space in a ship's hold, they would be laid on their sides in rows, bungs up, with more barrels placed on top of them, cradled in the hollows between each pair and locked in place with wooden wedges. (For storing spirits, wood is always preferable to metal due to the danger posed by sparks in an environment saturated with the alcohol vapor that transpires through the pores of the barrels.) This "pyramid stacking" is still used in France and several European countries, where warehouses are characterized by long rows of barrels stacked between two and five high (they are seldom stacked higher). With this system, individual barrels are difficult to move without dismantling the whole pyramid, but as the bungs of the barrels are all accessible, spirit can easily be pumped out of them for blending—it is the system used in Spain for solera aging—or to go into a different kind of barrel or cellar environment (e.g., from a "wet" cellar to a "dry" cellar). See BRANDY DE JEREZ and ÉLEVAGE.

In Scotland, the traditional "dunnage" system is a variation of the pyramid system, with the barrels stacked on top of each other three high. Each layer is separated by long wooden runners fitted out with wedges. Since the casks are stacked belly over bung, it is not a system for moving the spirit around often; it is one for sticking it in the warehouse and leaving it there until it is ready.

Because of the difficulty of moving the barrels, the pyramid and dunnage systems are best in low warehouses where barrel position is not much of a factor in aging. In Kentucky, a different system is used, the "rickhouse" system, where the barrels are held in multistory warehouses. There they rest in vertical wooden racks, which can be as much as seven stories high, with each story being three barrels high. The simplest rickhouses feature a unitary construction, where the racks are all connected so as to form the inner core of the building with the floors themselves attached to that framework and the whole thing covered with a skin of brick, wood, or corrugated tin.

Where in pyramid stacking the heads of the barrels are turned to the aisles between them, in rickhouses it is the bellies of the barrels. This allows them to easily be rolled out of the racks and moved to a different position in the warehouse—from the intensely hot top floor, for instance, to the relatively cool bottom. This allows for balanced aging, as does the great amount of air circulation that rickhouses allow. See WHISKY, BOURBON.

There are other systems in use, but they are generally variations on these. One modern exception that is finding more and more use (e.g., by Irish distillers and several Canadian distillers) is palletized storage, where anywhere from four to nine barrels are placed upright on a wooden pallet, strapped down, and then stacked vertically on top of each other. These pallets can of course only be moved mechanically, but they can be packed very tightly, saving warehouse space, at the expense of air circulation.

Sachs, Tony, "Whisky Barrel 101: All About Warehouses." *Whisky Magazine*, June 11, 2020. https://www.whiskyadvocate.com/all-about-whisky-warehouses/ (accessed March 28, 2021).
Veach, Michael R. *Kentucky Bourbon Whiskey: An American Heritage.* Lexington: University Press of Kentucky, 2013.

David Wondrich

BarSmarts is an online bartender education program created by the partners of Beverage Alcohol Resource (BAR) for Pernod-Ricard. See BEVERAGE ALCOHOL RESOURCE (BAR); BARTENDING SCHOOLS; and PERNOD-RICARD.

BarSol is a pisco brand from the Bodega San Isidro distillery in the town of Pueblo Nuevo in Ica Province, Peru. The bodega is firmly documented in the town archives as a pisco producer from 1919, when the property last changed hands, but some evidence exists for pisco production at the bodega in the nineteenth century.

Bodega San Isidro produces several varietal (or puro) piscos as well as an acholado (blend) and mosto verde, all under two brands: BarSol and Mendiola. Only BarSol is presently exported to the United States.

In the 1940 the distillery was operated by the Mendiola family. Master distiller Doña Mendiola created several celebrated and award-winning piscos. There remains a tradition of female distillers in Peru today with the sisters Melanie and Lizzie Asher producing pisco at Macchu Pisco.

Peru's military coup in 1968 brought the growth of the pisco trade to a grinding halt. The land that supported the vineyards was nationalized and turned into cooperative farms. Eventually many of these large farms failed; small subsistence farms followed, tended by individual families.

The vineyards remaining provided only enough grapes for personal use. The political situation only worsened in the decades following the military coup with the emergence of the Shining Path and Tupac Amaru groups. The ongoing struggle between these groups and the central government made business all but impossible, and exports virtually ceased. Only by the end of the twentieth century had the political situation improved.

Taking advantage of the improving climate for business in 2002, partners Diego Loret De Mola and Carlos Ferreyros purchased small tracts of land from different families to revive Bodega San Isidro and resume the production of premium pisco for export to the United States. BarSol Pisco was the spark that ignited the entrepreneurial spirit in Peru and inspired other like-minded Peruvians now reviving the once moribund pisco industry.

"Authentic Peruvian Pisco Brought to Life through a Diverse Range of Traditional Expressions." Anchor Distilling Company website. http://www.anchordistilling.com/brand/barsol/ (accessed April 23, 2021).
BarSol Pisco website. https://www.barsolpisco.com/ (accessed February 1, 2021).
Museo del Pisco website. https://museodelpisco.org/ (accessed May 5, 2021).

Dale DeGroff

A **bar spoon** is a long spoon with a small bowl and (usually) a twisted handle used to stir cocktails and direct the flow of poured ingredients for drinks like pousse-cafes. See POUSSE CAFÉ.

The implement has been in common use behind the bar since the mid-nineteenth century and is thought to have evolved from a particular design of apothecary spoon.

In traditional stirring technique, the back of the bowl of the bar spoon tracks, but does not press, the inside of the mixing glass. This technique moves the ice without agitating it and guides the liquid along with the ice, thus introducing less air into the cocktail. See STIRRING.

Bar spoons come in many shapes and sizes. The ends of some are covered in little red rubber knobs, others with intricate shapes significant to the brand that ordered them. Many ends, like the teardrop, trident, and coin-shaped flat disk have specific bartending applications as sugar-breaker, muddler, olive fork, and the like, but others are purely ornamental.

The spiraled handle used on most bar spoons prevents splashing when liquor or syrup is poured down it. It also allows the spoon to move within the mixer's hand, maintaining form while allowing the spoon to rotate within the liquid.

Within the cocktail world, a bar spoon has a secondary use as a unit of measurement of approximately 4–7 mL, or ⅛–¼ ounce. However, results will vary: the volume of most bar spoons, like most jiggers, is not quality controlled and can vary widely even within single bars.

See also MIXOLOGY (HOW TO MIX DRINKS).

Arnold, Dave. *Liquid Intelligence.* New York: W. W. Norton, 2014.
Klopfer, Brady. "The History of Bar Spoons." https://drinkedin.net/blog/41264-the-history-of-bar-spoons.html (accessed April 15, 2021).
Uyeda, Kazuo. *Cocktail Techniques.* Translated by Marc Adler. New York: Mud Puddle, 2010.

Clair McLafferty

bartender culture (twenty-first century) is experiencing a zenith; current wisdom says that the twenty-first century is the second golden age of bartending (the first being roughly 1862–1929). Having finally gained much of the same respect and professional stature accorded to chefs and sommeliers, bartenders are once again admired for their skills, not just for their position as dispensers of social lubricants.

No longer the stop-gap job of the young, the uncertain, or the socially flawed, bartending is now a fully fledged career and profession that is attracting motivated and passionate individuals. It could be argued that this is be the first real golden age, as the bartenders of the twenty-first century would, on many levels, surpass their nineteenth- and twentieth-century forebears.

Certainly, if one looks at the knowledge of the bartenders of today, there is no competition at all. The internet has effectively allowed human knowledge to be freely shared and accessible to all, no matter how arcane the topic. Between websites, discussion forums, social media, and databases of books and periodicals, information on almost any brand, drink, liquid, or trend, much of it accurate, is available to anyone with wi-fi, fingers, and curiosity. Now bartenders can discuss mash bills, the different species of agave plants, the terroir of botanicals in gin, and the specifics of distillation with an ease and confidence that would often set even a master

distiller on the back foot. Whereas early bartenders relied upon the railroad for the dissemination of ideas, now the information superhighway is the font of all knowledge.

It is not just new media that has gotten on board. Whereas in the late twentieth century there were very few bartending books (normally hiding quietly at the end of the wine section), a quick visit to any decent bookshop (or a search on Amazon) will show a huge array of books from coffee-table-style cocktail porn to hardcore in-depth tomes on previously recondite categories.

As drinks companies have grown in size and sophistication, the bartender has come to be recognized as the ultimate salesperson, someone who can make a guest love or hate a certain brand. As such, vast resources have been expended educating and inspiring them—from sending brand ambassadors or roving master distillers to talk to them, to creating schools and classes for them, to global bartending competitions that share recipes and techniques from around the world.

Technique has also always been an important component of a bartender's skills, and in this modern era mixologists are streets ahead of their nineteenth-century counterparts. Bartenders now know the "why" behind the "how" and the science of shaking and stirring, layering and muddling are now understood and incorporated into drink making. But also the skills, tools, and creativity of the kitchen have been incorporated into the bartender's repertoire. Creatively as well, the twenty-first-century bartender has an almost unfair advantage over his or her historical predecessors. The vast array of products, both alcoholic and non-, from around the world, available often year round due to global shipping and modern farming advances, gives the mixologist a vastly expanded palette from which to choose. And, as with the foodie in culinary circles, the drinking public has shown an increasing thirst for the bold and the new and the creative. No longer is a bartender judged only by their classics and staple drinks but also by their signature creations and envelope-shredding new concoctions.

But if one sees the function of the bartender as a key provider of hospitality rather than primarily a creator of consumable concoctions, then perhaps we are not as advanced as the giants of the past upon whose shoulders we stand. There has developed an increasing focus by the bartending community on the product and not the person. Drinks snobbery is becoming alarmingly commonplace, and focus on the guest is becoming increasingly rare. But this is a trend that food and wine have already encountered and have overcome, and no doubt the bartender, always known for his or her adaptability, will overcome this to provide the perfect cocktail of product, service, and ambience.

Morgenthaler, Jeffrey. *The Bar Book: Elements of Cocktail Technique.* San Francisco: Chronicle, 2014.

Petraske, Sasha. *Regarding Cocktails.* London: Phaidon, 2016.

Soloarik, Frankie. *Bar Chef.* New York: Harper, 2015.

Angus Winchester

bartending schools are trade schools for aspiring bartenders and ongoing professional enrichment for existing bartenders. In some cases the school may be part of a self-organized bartender association or trade union, part of a larger government-supported catering or hospitality/tourism school, or (the most common) a privately owned stand-alone institution run as a for-profit business. A new development has been ongoing on- and offline bartending teaching programs originated by, or financially supported by, liquor brands. These courses are often offered free or drastically discounted, the costs being underwritten by the brands, which feature to a larger or smaller degree in the teaching materials.

The first paid-for bartending instruction was almost certainly as part of a butler/valet's larger apprenticeship in their trade. In fact, one of the earliest mentions of bartender training was in an 1885 New York newspaper, recounting how a wealthy Brazilian man about town hired the legendary bartender Harry Johnson to teach his valet mixology skills. See JOHNSON, HARRY. New York newspaper articles and advertisements from the late 1890s confirmed the existence of dedicated bartending schools offering courses of around a month's duration. Bartending associations (which invariably offered training as well as trade-union benefits) began forming around this time as well, coalescing into national organizations such as the Internationale Barkeeper-Union (forerunner of the Deutsche Barkeeper Union) founded in Cologne, Germany, in 1909. The International Bartender's Association

(IBA), an association of national bartending associations, came into being in 1951.

America's Prohibition put a halt to the bartending-school business but stimulated bartending outside the United States, as experienced US bartenders emigrated. Cuba's Club de Cantineros association, founded in 1924 in Havana, had a strong element of training, insisting students learn English in addition to their trade skills. After the end of Prohibition in December 1933, there was an understandable boom in bartending schools all over the United States. See PROHIBITION AND TEMPERANCE IN AMERICA.

Given the undeniable importance of a lengthy on-the-job apprenticeship in learning all aspects of the bartender's profession—mixology, hospitality, hygiene, speed, efficiency, financial control, and responsible service, to name but a few—a good bartender school will simply equip its graduates with the basic skills and correct mindset to acquire and "survive" their first job as a junior bartender. Then, employed, those selfsame students can learn on the job and progress. The claims of some schools to train "master mixologists" from scratch are to be treated with the skepticism they deserve.

The curricula of schools vary wildly, as do the teaching methods; only a tiny minority of bartending schools are validated by educational authorities. Some teach only the most rudimentary of drink-making techniques; others concentrate on mixology, and still others put more of a focus on beer, wine, and coffee than on spirits and cocktails. Since at least the 1960s and "Duke" Antone's Bartender School of Mixology, it has been traditional for most bar schools to use colored water instead of liquor when teaching, which puts students at a disadvantage, as many of them have little knowledge of how spirits taste or why various combinations are successful. See ANTONE, DONATO "DUKE."

As with all types of schools, a common criticism of bartending schools is that they are teaching skills and knowledge that were last relevant ten or even twenty years ago. In their defense, there is often a variance between the most currently fashionable type of bartending (at the time of writing, craft-cocktail mixology is very much in vogue) and the type of bartending that offers the highest earnings for the smallest investment of time and effort (such as nightclub bartending). Many schools see it as their duty to help students get the most lucrative jobs as quickly as possible, and such (usually) for-profit schools often advertise bartending as a good part-time job, not as a full-time profession.

See also AMERICAN DISTILLING INSTITUTE and BEVERAGE ALCOHOL RESOURCE (BAR).

"Bartending School" (advertisement). *New York World*, October 25, 1894.
"Before the Bar." *National Police Gazette*, October 3, 1885, 14.
Brown, Jared, Anistatia Miller, and Dave Broom. *Cuba: The Legend of Rum*. London: Mixellany, 2009.
"Historie." https://www.dbuev.de/dbu-ev/historie/ (accessed February 1, 2021).
"A History of the IBA." https://www.iba-world.com (accessed February 1, 2021).
"Odd Ways of Odd People." *Brooklyn Daily Eagle*, June 4, 1894, 4.

Philip Duff

The **base** of a mixed drink is the spirit present in it in the largest quantity or the most dominant ones in equal quantity. In the case of a Manhattan this is whisky; for a Martini, it is gin or vodka, and for a Margarita it is tequila. See MANHATTAN; MARTINI; and MARGARITA. In common usage, there are six primary base spirits: brandy, gin, rum, tequila, vodka, and whisky, but there are of course regional variations to this list.

The vast majority of classic cocktails rely on just one base spirit, with only a few examples (such as the Vieux Carré's whisky mixed with brandy) of using two or more spirits as a base. In most punches and a great many tall drinks, such as Collinses, coolers, fizzes, highballs, and the like, the base spirit will comprise considerably less than 50 percent of drink's the total volume. In cocktails proper, that is much less common, although there are a few prominent examples there where the spirituous component takes a back seat to another ingredient.

Some of the early versions of the Martini, for example, called for more sweet vermouth than gin. In such a situation the sweet vermouth would be considered the base and the gin simply the modifier. Consider the Martinez from the 1887 third edition of Jerry Thomas's *Bartender's Guide*, which utilized a "pony" (30ml) of Old Tom gin and a "wineglass" (60ml) of vermouth. See MARTINEZ; OLD TOM GIN; and VERMOUTH.

"Base" can also refer to the type of alcohol that is used as the foundation for a liqueur or similar products. For example, the base spirit of Grand Marnier is cognac, while the base spirit for Cointreau (and most triple secs) is a neutral spirit. See GRAND MARNIER; COGNAC; and COINTREAU.

See also BRANDY; GIN; RUM; TEQUILA; VODKA; and WHISKY.

Embury, David. *The Fine Art of Mixing Drinks*. Garden City, NY: Doubleday, 1948.

Audrey Saunders

The **Batanga** is a 1950s Mexican take on the Cuba Libre, replacing the rum with tequila and employing an unorthodox method of stirring. A variation on the Changuirongo—a 1940s-vintage Mexican name for tequila mixed with ginger ale, cola, or any other sweet soda—it is the creation of Don Javier Delgado Corona, proprietor of La Capilla, a bar in the town of Tequila from the 1950s until his death in 2020. Don Javier, as he was universally known, mixed his version with a large iron utility knife, used to cut limes, chiles, avocados, and anything else in the bar that needed cutting. Habitués of La Capilla claim that this gives the drink a certain irreproducible *je ne sais quoi*.

The Batanga was discovered by journalists in the early 1990s and is often encountered in Australia and Europe but only rarely in the United States. Aficionados insist, however, that the only place one may secure a perfectly executed version is, of course, at La Capilla.

Recipe: Combine 60 ml 100 percent–agave, blanco tequila and 15 ml lime juice in a tall, salt-rimmed, ice-filled glass. Add 90 ml chilled Coca-Cola (Mexican preferred) and stir with a large, (non-stainless) steel utility knife.

See also CUBA LIBRE.

Porter, Gabi. "Twist of the Knife: Tequila's Authentic Batanga." *Saveur*, May 9, 2013. http://www.saveur.com/article/Wine-and-Drink/The-Authentic-Batanga (accessed February 1, 2021).

David Wondrich

batching is the art of preparing multiple servings of a mixed drinks in advance of when it is to be served. Whether the batch is prepared to increase speed of service or because the drink is to be served in a situation that makes building drinks from scratch difficult—or, as when large crowds must be accommodated, both—it requires taking the same precision and care used in measuring out the ingredients for one perfectly crafted cocktail for one guest and multiplying that service by the hundreds and sometimes the thousands. Done properly, it is a technique that bartenders can use to ensure efficient and consistent drink service to their guests.

Batching has a rich history that goes back to the beginning of modern mixed drinks. Punch, which dates at least to the 1600s, is a batched drink, and most modern drinks are descended from it. See PUNCH. In the nineteenth century, bars used to sell bottled cocktails, which are of course batched drinks. See BOTTLED COCKTAILS. Batching really came into its own during the tiki era, when entrepreneurs such as Don the Beachcomber and Trader Vic and their largely Filipino bar staffs made extensive use of full and partial batches (where some of the ingredients of a drink are batched and the rest are added à la minute). Their drinks were highly complex and their bars large and popular, and without batching they would have lost business. See BEACH, DONN; TIKI; and BERGERON, VICTOR "TRADER VIC."

The basic techniques of batching have not changed that much over its history, but bartenders have become more creative in some of the tools they use and, often, in their choice of ingredients. Over the last five decades the beverage industry has seen countless new liqueurs and spirits introduced, from every base imaginable. Furthermore, some of the ingredients have themselves changed: canned juices, prepared syrups, frozen fruits, and fruit purees are all available to speed up batch preparation, although sometimes to the detriment of the quality of the drink.

Now in the craft cocktail era, batching has been used as a way of getting good, cocktail-bar-quality drinks into the hands of the crowd, whether it's at a backyard party, a booth at a culinary festival, or even a concert venue—from a lobby bar at a single performance to a dozen bars scattered around an all-weekend music festival, with potential customers that number in the tens of thousands.

With batching, how to proceed depends on the drink and the situation. With some drinks—those that are basically all spirits, such as the Old-Fashioned and the Sazerac, or those that are made up of spirits and fortified wines, such as the Martini, the Manhattan, and the Bamboo—there is no reason not to batch them completely and bottle them. They are shelf-stable and will keep for months at room temperature (leave the garnishes out, of course, and for the Sazerac save the absinthe for rinsing the glass or plastic cup it will be served in). Others should never be completely batched. The only way to batch a Ramos Gin Fizz is in parts: the gin, citrus, sugar, and orange flower water can go in one container, but the egg whites and cream must go in another or they will curdle, and the sparkling water must go in on its own, as always with carbonated ingredients. With regular sours, where cream and egg whites play no part, to batch them in parts or completely depends on the situation.

For standard bar service or a situation such as the all-weekend festival, a set of partial batches may be the best solution. Generally, one mix is used for the syrups and sweet ingredients, another mix for all the juices, and a third for all the spirits. (It is important to take note of hygiene and to use food-safe containers, including buckets.) It is best practice to keep citrus and other fresh juices separate from the sweet ingredients or the spirits, because batching them together gives those ingredients a limited shelf life. Thus, a Mai Tai that normally takes five steps to build (lime juice, orgeat, curaçao, two separate rums) can be built in three (lime juice, orgeat, rum-curaçao mix). Determining the shelf life of citrus juices is complicated, but it is not long (some eight to eighteen hours, depending on storage conditions). Partially batched drinks have the advantage of longevity, since everything but the citrus is stable for the duration of service.

Punch is a bit of a special case: here, one can keep the "shrub" on which it is based, an equal-parts sugar and citrus juice mix, refrigerated for several days. To assemble a batch, one merely has to add spirits, water and any carbonated ingredients, and ice and grate a little nutmeg over the top. In this case, the spirits can also be batched with the shrub if desired, but the water should be reserved until needed, as once it is added the punch goes stale fairly quickly.

For an event with a predetermined number of cocktails and a fairly brief, set period of service, it might be a better idea to pre-batch full recipes even for the sours. This is useful for parties, weddings, shows, and other large events. Besides being extremely fast to serve, full-cocktail batches have another advantage over making drinks from scratch. With any cocktail, there is a window of acceptability and error in terms of its measurements. Jiggers can only be accurate to about within an eighth of an ounce (4 ml). With most ingredients, that is an acceptable tolerance, and a good bartender will adjust afterward if necessary. Obviously, the busier the bar, the more likely those tolerances are to be exceeded and the less likely that adjustment will be made. But with a large-scale recipe, mixers have the option of using measurements they could never use in an individual recipe. Rather than calculating down to the eighth of an ounce, they can use decimal fractions of ounces or metric measurements (even in countries that use the metric system, many bartenders prefer imperial measures for their speed). That means, for example, you can have a recipe calling for 0.62 of an ounce of pineapple juice per drink, a quantity that cannot be measured for a single drink.

For example, let's say you want to make a classic Pegu Club Cocktail, as found in *The Savoy Cocktail Book*, for 75 people. Here is the recipe precisely as it appears in the book:

> 1 dash Angostura Bitters.
> 1 dash Orange Bitters.
> 1 Teaspoonful Lime Juice.
> 1/3 Curaçao.
> 2/3 Dry Gin.

Assuming that the thirds here are of a 1 ½-ounce jigger, this gives you a metric recipe that looks like this:

> 1.2 ml Angostura bitters
> 1.2 ml orange bitters
> 5 ml lime juice
> 15 ml curaçao
> 30 ml dry gin

Let's say you taste this and find it unbalanced (most will) and after tinkering come up with the following formula:

> 1.2 ml Angostura bitters
> 1.5 ml orange bitters
> 15 ml lime juice
> 18 ml curaçao
> 52 ml dry gin

This would be extremely hard and slow to mix from scratch in a bar, involving eyedroppers and graduated cylinders. Yet it's easy to make seventy-five of them (rounding to the nearest 5 ml):

> 90 ml Angostura bitters
> 115 ml orange bitters
> 1,125 ml lime juice
> 1,350 ml curaçao
> 3,900 ml dry gin

Once there is a universal measurement, batches can be sized according to the vessels being used for storage or serving. This Pegu Club can also easily be adapted to 125 guests if ticket sales surge or 45 if rain is in the forecast. See Pegu Club Cocktail.

It is important to note that sugar, citrus, and bitter ingredients have to be treated carefully. These ingredients, on a very large scale, can multiply their potency over time in the batch. Regular tasting is key in ensuring that the batch is not too rich or satisfying. A drink that is too rich will keep the drinker from ordering another. Guests will either feel full in the stomach from the sugar or, if too much citrus is consumed, their palate and throat will be overpowered, pushing them to drink something lighter like soda, champagne, or wine.

It is also important to pay attention to one of the largest ingredients in any cocktail, if not the largest: water. There are many ways to add it. Shaking a drink adds 25–60 percent dilution. Stirred drinks add 20–40 percent dilution. A lot of that variation depends on the ice used. Large, cold cubes will melt fairly slowly but can chill the drink more than "hotel ice" can (soft chips, cylinders, and such). If you have the good cubes, it will speed service if you pre-dilute the drink to a degree. When using "hotel ice" or faster-melting cubes then refrigerating the batch to pour over said ice will be helpful. Ice can vary in different establishments, so the only real way to ensure proper execution is to check by taste before the guests. See Ice, science of its use.

When making syrups for batch recipes, it is easier to stick to 1:1 syrups (where water and sugar are in equal parts) rather than the common 2:1 syrups used in bars (two parts sugar to one of water), so water addition, or dilution, can be easier and more consistent. Events and venues tend to have larger-sized glassware, making it necessary for syrup recipes to have the full amount of water. Often, purees and prepackaged syrups require adjusting depending on their thickness, sugar levels, and potency of flavor. Batching purees with juices and syrups to control their sweet and sour elements is necessary. Batching fresh fruit elements with spirits or liqueurs flavored with the same spirit is a great way to control costs and add fresh fruit elements to a product designed for shelf stability and cost over flavor. Often fortification with alcohol is necessary in some of the batches to extend their shelf lives and help hold consistency.

Batching ensures efficiency and fast delivery of perfectly balanced cocktails. A list of ingredients and a common unit of measuring, plus the general knowledge of the drink's history, are all that is needed to create delicious product to be enjoyed by multitudes of guests.

See also MIXOLOGY (HOW TO MIX DRINKS).

Reiner, Julie. *The Craft Cocktail Party*. New York: Grand Central, 2015.

Wondrich, David *Punch!* New York: Perigee, 2010.

Leo DeGroff

bathtub gin represents the lowest point in our collective drinking shame more clearly than almost any drink. During Prohibition, when Americans were forbidden from purchasing intoxicating beverages, they could concoct rough gin in secret with little more than neutral spirits, water, and essence or essential oil of juniper berries. Though such compounded gins could be more nuanced, especially when made with additional essential oil or botanicals, they both predated and survived Prohibition. Unlike other ersatz spirits of Prohibition, homemade gin remained popular after repeal. "Bathtub" may refer to actual tubs in which gin was sometimes blended or to the only faucet in a home that could accommodate carboys too tall to fit under a kitchen tap.

See also GIN; PROHIBITION AND TEMPERANCE IN AMERICA and RECTIFIER (DEVICE).

"Repeal of Prohibition in Practical Effect in N.Y." *San Bernardino County Sun*, October 14, 1933, 3.

Rowley, Matthew. *Lost Recipes of Prohibition: Notes from a Bootlegger's Manual*. New York: Countryman, 2015.

Matthew Rowley

Batida is a Brazilian drink made from cachaça (or any other spirit) shaken up, or more commonly blended, with lime or other fresh tropical fruits and sugar (its name comes from the Portuguese word for "beaten" or "shaken"). The drink's origin goes back to the late nineteenth or early twentieth century; today, its variations are almost without number; the ones that seem most popular feature the addition of coconut milk or condensed milk. Like the Piña Colada, which it resembles, the Batida is a fresh, frothy, sweet treat.

Recipe (Batida de Coco): Combine in blender 60 ml cachaça, 15 ml lime juice, 30 ml coconut cream, 30 ml coconut milk, 7 ml passion fruit puree, and 250 ml cracked ice. Blend until smooth and pour into tall glass.

See also CAIPIRINHA.

Costa, Roberto. *Traçado geral das batidas*. Rio de Janeiro: Civilização Brasileira, 1974.

Ivy Mix

Baudoinia compniacensis is a black fungus that frequently grows on warehouses where barrels (or permeable clay jars, in the case of baijiu) of spirits are aging, feeding on the ethanol vapors known as the angels' share. See ANGEL'S SHARE. Antonin Baudoin was the first to identify the mold, originally called *Torula compniacensis*, in the 1870s. It was renamed in the 1990s after it was discovered that it is not in fact a *Torula* fungus at all (it is related only to a fungus that grows in Antarctica).

It is believed that the fungus can use nutrients other than ethanol and that ethanol alone is not sufficient to provide adequate support for it. (The fungus being millions of years old and large-scale ethanol production being a relatively recent phenomenon, this must be the case.) The angel's share will vary widely depending upon the alcohol strength of a barreled spirit and the materials, temperature, humidity, airflow, and other influences of a warehouse environment, and there seems no simple formula by which to predict *Baudoinia* growth, due perhaps to the sheer complexity of all these variables.

The mold is essentially harmless, and indeed some distillers believe it adds to the character and aromas of their aging spirits; many point to its vigorous growth as an endorsement of the quality of their spirits. Not everyone is a fan, though: in 2013, some Louisville, Kentucky, residents sued the Brown-Forman company, saying the mold was unsightly and that removing it from their cars and homes involved frequent cleaning, shortening the life of those objects. See BROWN-FORMAN.

See also ETHANOL.

Rogers, Adam. *Proof*. New York: Houghton Mifflin Harcourt, 2014.

Doug Frost

Bayly, Phil (1954–), is an influential Australian bar owner whose key contribution to contemporary cocktail culture was the promotion of tequila in Europe and Australia. Born in Adelaide, Bayly moved to Amsterdam in 1979 to pursue an interest in painting, which led to a chance encounter with Tomas Estes, who had just opened Cafe Pacifico. Developing a passion for tequila, Bayly toured Mexico in 1982, seeking out traditional cantinas and immersing himself in Mexican bar culture. He and Estes went on to open fifteen more tequila bars across Europe, North America, and Australia in the 1980s and 1990s, educating their customers along the way.

See also ESTES, TOMAS; and TEQUILA.

"Café Pacifico to Close after 15 Years." *Australian Bartender*, April 12, 2013. https://australianbartender. com.au/2013/04/12/cafe-pacifico-to-close-after-15- years/ (accessed February 1, 2021).

Pat Nourse

Beach, Donn, né Ernest Raymond Beaumont-Gantt (1907–1989), was a mixologist and restaurateur who almost single-handedly created the post-Prohibition "tiki drink" category, launching a faux-Polynesian cocktail craze that influenced American culinary culture for over four decades. See TIKI.

The son of a New Orleans hotelier turned Texas oilman, Donn was born in Mexia, Texas, on February 22, 1907. At age eighteen he squandered his college fund on a trip around the world. His travels ended in Los Angeles, where in 1934 he opened Don the Beachcomber's, a South Seas–themed bar

Donn Beach as he liked to be portrayed. From a Don the Beachcomber's menu, ca. 1948. Wondrich Collection.

whose "Rhum Rhapsodies"—wildly original exotic cocktails with Polynesian names but Caribbean roots—enchanted the Hollywood movie colony. By 1937 the Beachcomber's was nationally famous and nationally imitated.

While Donn actually had combed beaches in Polynesia, it was in Jamaica that he found his "tiki" drink template: the Planter's Punch. Donn built on this simple mix of lime juice, sugar, and rum by blending multiple juices, multiple sweeteners, and multiple rums in the same glass. He created over thirty complex, layered Planter's variations, most famously the Zombie; other popular inventions included the Navy Grog, Rum Barrel, Pearl Diver, and Missionary's Downfall. These were appropriated by hundreds of copycat tiki bars and restaurants that sprang up across America from the late 1930s well into the 1970s.

By 1980 a chain of Don the Beachcomber's restaurants stretched from Chicago to Waikiki, but Donn was living in the shadow of his most successful imitator, Trader Vic, whose Mai Tai had replaced the Zombie as the most famous tiki drink. On June 7, 1989, Donn succumbed to liver cancer in Honolulu. See Mai Tai and Bergeron, Victor "Trader Vic".

See also Planter's Punch and Zombie.

Berry, Jeff. *Beachbum Berry's Sippin' Safari*. San Jose, CA: Club Tiki Press, 2007.

Bitner, Arnold. *Scrounging the Islands with the Legendary Don the Beachcomber*. Lincoln, NE: iUniverse, 2007.

Bitner, Arnold, and Phoebe Beach. *Hawaii Tropical Rum Drinks and Cuisine by Don the Beachcomber*. Honolulu, HI: Mutual Publishing, 2001.

Jeff Berry

Beebe, Lucius (1902–1966), was a premier historian of America's railways, a columnist, an editor, and an ostentatious gourmand and bon vivant. Born into a wealthy New England family, Beebe was dismissed from Harvard and Yale, where he kept a roulette wheel and well-stocked bar in his room. He went on to write from 1929 to 1950 for the *New York Herald Tribune*, where he coined the term "cafe society." "Luscious Lucius" also contributed tales of gossip, food, and drink to the *San Francisco Examiner*, the *New Yorker*, *Gourmet*, and other publications. His 1946 *Stork Club Bar Book* remains one of the classic cocktail books.

"Lucius Beebe." http://www.wakefieldlibrary.org/wikipedia/index.php/Lucius_Beebe (accessed June 2, 2017).

"Lucius Beebe Demanded 'the Best' as He Saw It." *Kansas City Times*, February 25, 1966.

Matthew Rowley

beef broth plays a prominent role in two mid-twentieth-century cocktails, the Bloody Bull and the Bull Shot, as well as in the meaty creations of some contemporary mixologists. See Bullshot. Traditionally, canned broth, or even canned consomme, is used.

Beefeater is an iconic London dry gin that is consistently among the world's top ten best-selling gins. According to the company's current owners, the brand's history began in 1863, when London pharmacist James Burrough (1835–1897) bought the Cale Street distillery from John Taylor, who had founded it in 1820 (the year noted on the current bottle). Burrough had previously at least experimented with making gin, as his recipe books include an 1849 formula for black-currant gin. At Cale Street he made a variety of spirits, including, by 1876, Beefeater and a few other marks of gin, with Beefeater soon becoming the company's leading brand, winning prizes and cracking the American market in 1917.

The James Burrough company's advertising, however, suggests that the Beefeater brand, whenever it was created, was not the company's priority until the mid-1920s, when one first comes across advertisements for it. Before that, the company primarily dealt in bulk alcohol and scotch and Irish whisky, although it did have a damson gin that it promoted. A 1933 American trademark filing claims that the brand was first in commerce in 1909.

The brand entered, or re-entered, the American market in 1933, but its greatest growth came after World War II. By the early 1960s, three of every four bottles of gin imported to the United States were Beefeater. The Burrough family sold the brand to Whitbread in 1987, who in turn sold it to Pernod Ricard in 2005. It is unique among major old-line gin brands in offering tours of its modern distillery in Kennington, London. The Beefeater name evokes a sense of patriotism among the British people with its iconic beefeater red jacket, an item that even in the nineteenth century invoked strong feelings and memories of "Old London."

Beefeater is an unapologetically traditional London gin. A widely cited 1895 gin recipe from Burrough's formula book includes the nine botanicals still used to make Beefeater today: juniper, angelica root and seeds, coriander, licorice, almond, orris root, and the rinds of lemons and bitter Seville oranges, which together lace Beefeater's distinctive and classic juniper with a touch of soft citrus. Now as then, Beefeater begins as a purchased neutral grain spirit in which, famously, all nine botanicals steep in pot stills for twenty-four hours before distillation.

Formerly, these were Carterhead stills, but now those are only used for some special bottlings.

The product line under the Beefeater name has expanded greatly since the 1990s with products such as Crown Jewel, Wet, Summer and Winter editions, London Market, and an oak-rested variant known as Burrough's Reserve, which is distilled in James Burrough's original copper still with the same botanical blend as Beefeater Dry before resting in barrels that formerly held Lillet. In 2008 Beefeater 24 debuted, so called because of the aforementioned twenty-four-hour steeping period, adding grapefruit peels, Japanese sencha, and Chinese green teas to the nine botanicals featured in Beefeater Dry.

See also LONDON DRY GIN and PERNOD-RICARD.

Harper's Directory and Manual. London: Harper, 1920.
"James Burrough Limited." *Official Gazette of the United States Patent Office*, September 12, 1933, 278.

Aaron Knoll

beer is a moderately alcoholic beverage derived from grain. By volume and expenditure, it is the world's most popular alcoholic beverage. It is a cousin to whisky, which can be described as "distilled beer," and to Japanese sake. Most beers are flavored with hops, giving the drink its bitterness and a wide range of flavors and aromas. Many mass-marketed beers, similar in origin, color, and flavor, are bowdlerized versions of Czech-German pilsner. Over the mid-twentieth century, this class of beer assumed a bland sameness, especially in the United States, the country now leading recovery of traditional beer flavor through the insurgent "craft beer movement." Now the flavor spectrum of beer is the broadest of any class of alcoholic drinks except, perhaps, for cocktails.

Most beers are based upon barley (or, less frequently, wheat). Mass-market beers may incorporate large portions of corn or rice, which lighten flavor and body. Before it is ready to use for brewing, most barley is malted. It may also be roasted or caramelized to make malts of varying flavors, colors, and uses. Once the grist of barley and other grains is established and blended, it is then milled to crack the grains and expose starches within. The crushed grist is then mixed with water into a porridge called mash in which natural enzymes convert starches to sugars. Rinsed from the grain husk, these sugars yield a liquid called "wort." The wort is then boiled, flavored with hops in the kettle, and cooled. Added yeast ferments the wort into beer over three to twelve days. After brief aging, most beer is then filtered, carbonated, and packed in bottles or kegs. Despite inevitable outliers, most beers are between 2.5 and 15 percent ABV.

If the brewing process is interrupted at the mashing stage and the mash cooled and fermented, the resulting mash is suitable for distillation into whisky. In bourbon production, the fermented mash, now containing about 9 percent ABV, is typically referred to as "the beer," while in scotch whisky making it is referred to as "the wash."

Beer is a natural partner to whisky at the bar. When served together, beer may simply be deployed as a chaser, but they are sometimes further entwined into an alliance known as the Boilermaker—generally a glass of beer accompanied by a shot of whisky. A more committed version involves dropping the entire shot glass into the beer and then downing the mix in one draught. See BOILERMAKER.

Around the world, beer is used to "chase" many drinks. In the American Midwest a beer chaser may follow the Bloody Mary, while in the Netherlands it follows genever in a revered combination called a *kopstootje* ("little head-butt"). See BLOODY MARY; HERRENGEDECK; and KOPSTOOT. In Mexico the chaser follows tequila, though it also sometimes takes the lead position in the Michelada. See MICHELADA.

Though their history is long and storied, beer cocktails are controversial. There are many old recipes for ale-based punches, and the modern cocktail movement has minted a few new classics, such as the Black Flip (stout, egg, and rum). Still, many beer cocktails can have a forced gimmicky quality about them, as if the beer were included as a stunt or show of cleverness. Better beer cocktails use the beer's specific qualities—roasted flavors, citric hop flavor, bitterness, or even acidity—to drive the cocktail's flavors.

In a good cocktail bar, a short, focused beer list can be a fine feature. The beers can step into longer evenings as a brief pause in the march of cocktails, allowing the evening to progress more pleasantly. A good choice of beers can reflect the personality of the bar—old-school, funky, geeky, steampunk-ish, and so on. Just as a cocktail menu often expresses a point of view, so can the cocktail bar beer list, thus becoming an essential part of the bar's offering of fine drinks and best evenings.

See also ABV; BARLEY; CORN; FLIP; GENEVER; HOPS; MALTING; RICE; WHISKY, SCOTCH; WHEAT; and WHISKY.

Byson, Lew. *Tasting Whiskey: An Insider's Guide to the Unique Pleasures of the World's Finest Spirits*. North Adams, MA: Storey, 2014.

Grier, Jacob. *Cocktails on Tap: The Art of Mixing Spirits and Beer*. New York: Abrams, 2015.

Meehan, Jim, and Chris Gall. *The PDT Cocktail Book: The Complete Bartender's Guide from the Celebrated Speakeasy*. New York: Sterling Epicure, 2011.

Oliver, Garrett. *The Oxford Companion to Beer*. New York: Oxford University Press, 2011.

Garrett Oliver

beer cocktail. Beer and spirits have always been happy bar mates, not infrequently in front of the same imbiber. That said, each tends to be looked upon with wariness, especially by its own respective adherents, when someone suggests their combination into a single drink. The image of a frat party looms, perhaps unfairly. Simple beer and spirit combinations are not entirely without pedigree, from the Pop-In of 1600s England (the spirits apparently "popped into" a mug of ale) to various combinations of porter and gin. A favorite of mid-twentieth century-America, the Depth Charge featured an actual full shot glass of whisky sent plummeting to the bottom of a beer mug. See BOILERMAKER.

If these concoctions are found wanting, a more favorable history may be found within the realm of classical punch, where beer was used in a few classic recipes. One Ale Punch recipe from 1862 naturally shows ale as the lead ingredient, followed into the bowl by white wine, brandy, capillaire (maidenhair fern syrup), lemon juice, grated nutmeg, and a bit of toasted bread. The tasty Billy Dawson's Punch (1863) combined stout, rums of different characters, decidedly funky arrack, cognac, lemons, and demerara sugar. See PUNCH.

The past two centuries have spawned less complex combinations of varying popularity. The Black Velvet (stout and champagne) sounds worrying on its face but can be very pleasant when made with excellent beer and wine. See BLACK VELVET. The Michelada, a popular "folk drink" from Mexico, blends beer over ice with lime juice, Worcestershire sauce, hot sauce, and soy sauce or various "oriental seasonings," with many variations coming to vaguely resemble the Bloody Mary. See MICHELADA and BLOODY MARY. The Calgary Red Eye or Red Beer, now largely faded from the scene, is a simple blend of beer and tomato juice. The German Radler (cyclist) is a blend of pilsner and lemonade and, as the name suggests, is considered a sort of sports drink.

Whether these latter examples, which omit spirits, are really cocktails per se, they are certainly mixed drinks, and it makes sense to speak of them here. The modern professional mixologist may not reject these older drinks, but newer inventions are more likely to use beer more thoughtfully. When beer cocktails truly work, it is almost always where beer is used as a unique ingredient rather than as an ersatz replacement for seltzer water or sparkling wine. For example, stouts, which feature roasted malts that impart strong chocolate and coffee flavors to the beer, can be used to bring those flavors to a cocktail. India pale ales (IPAs), which are built around bitterness and bold citrus-like aromatics, can row in well with bitters and lend a boost to citrus zest. Newly popular "sour" beer styles such as the mildly acidic Berliner weisse, the slightly salty gose, or the zingy, fruity new Florida weisse style are able to play very well with all manner of spirits, sometimes replacing citrus juices.

Beer, which has very different foaming properties than sparkling water or wine, can be difficult to use to finish cocktails, even when the flavor combinations are pleasant. Beer-based foams, if not stabilized by ingredients such as egg whites, tend to start well, but many break down quickly in an unsightly fashion. As a result, in some cocktails the beer is degassed before mixing. Jim Meehan, of the influential New York cocktail bar PDT, has created an excellent modern classic in the Black Flip. It combines imperial stout, dark rum, an egg (the defining ingredient of a flip), and demerara syrup, shaken with ice into an egg nog–like creamy drink and topped with freshly grated nutmeg. Balanced, rich, and undeniably tasty, it is the quintessential modern beer cocktail, where the omission of the beer would ruin the very point of the drink. As the craft beer culture and modern mixology barrel forward on parallel tracks, it is to be expected that we'll see other new classics rise from behind the best bars of the day.

Recipe (The Black Flip): Combine in shaker 60 ml Brooklyn Black Chocolate Stout, 45 ml blackstrap rum, 15 ml demerara sugar syrup, and 1 egg. Swirl to release carbonation, dry shake without ice, shake again with ice, strain into a fizz glass, and grate nutmeg over the top.

Bevill, A. V. *Barkeeper's Ready Reference*. St. Louis: A. V. Bevill, 1871.

Oliver, Garrett. *The Oxford Companion to Beer*. New York: Oxford University Press, 2012.

Thomas, Jerry. *How to Mix Drinks*. New York: Dick & Fitzgerald, 1862.

Garrett Oliver

Bee's Knees—equal parts gin, lemon juice, and honey—is a cocktail that the great mid-century cocktail authority David A. Embury denounced as a "pernicious recipe." It was, he explained, one of those Prohibition drinks, like the Alexander and the Orange Blossom, designed to cover up "unutterably vile" bootleg liquor (in fact, it does first appear in print during Prohibition, ascribed to socialite Margaret "The Unsinkable Molly" Brown). This explains the use of "sweetened, highly flavored, and otherwise emollient and anti-emetic ingredients" such as honey. If you must have one, Embury recommends a dry version: eight parts gin and two parts lemon juice to one part honey; "Cocktail Bill" Boothby's version, with three parts gin to one part each honey, lemon juice, and orange juice, is also an improvement. Make it with rum instead of gin and add champagne and you get an Air Mail Cocktail; or, use maraschino liqueur instead of honey to make an Aviation. See AIR MAIL and AVIATION COCKTAIL.

Recipe: Shake 45 ml gin, 22 ½ ml lemon juice, and 7 ½ ml honey over ice and strain into a chilled cocktail glass.

"Bars in Paris for 'Madame' Close Doors to Mere Male," Brooklyn NY *Standard Union*, April 23, 1929, p. 23.

Embury, David A., *The Fine Art of Mixing Drinks*, 2nd ed., Garden City, NY: Garden City Books, 1952.

Eric Felten

beets, the bulbous roots of the *Beta vulgaris*, supply sugar that is used to make spirits and an earthy, intensely red juice that is sometimes used as an accent in cocktails of the more artistic variety.

The root of the (white) sugar beet—*B. vulgaris altissima*—can contain over 20 percent sucrose, chemically identical to the sugar derived from the sugar cane. Developed in the eighteenth century in a process of selective breeding initiated by the German scientist Andreas Marggraf (1709–1782), the sugar beet could be grown in the landlocked areas of Europe, requiring neither tropical colonies nor access to an extensive shipping industry. Nonetheless, production was low until the Napoleonic Wars, when a British naval blockade prompted the French to start a beet-sugar industry to replace the cane sugar no longer coming in from the Caribbean.

By the middle of the nineteenth century, spirit was being distilled in Europe, North America, and Australia from the pressed juice of shredded sugar beets or from the notoriously nasty molasses left over from making beet sugar. This spirit was generally distilled in column stills to high proof and then rectified to neutrality. It was held in low repute until the 1870s, when the phylloxera aphid put an end to the supply of cheap grape neutral spirit and Continental distillers had to switch to beet spirit as a base for their liqueurs, bitters, and absinthes and as a blending medium for other, more flavorful spirits. Many market-leading brands, such as Cointreau, never switched back. See ABSINTHE, COINTREAU, and VERSCHNITT.

In the twenty-first century, a number of American craft distilleries, such as Brooklyn, New York's Industry City, and Montana Distillery in Missoula began experimenting with sugar beets to craft their small-batch vodkas. Many of these are not entirely neutral in flavor, a new direction for beet spirits.

Byrn, M. La Fayette. *The Complete Practical Distiller*. Philadelphia: Henry Carey Baird, 1868.

Dietsch, Michael. "The *Serious Eats* Guide to Rum." *Serious Eats*, January 19, 2012. https://drinks. seriouseats.com/2012/01/guide-to-rum-basics-types-history-regions-terms-rum-cocktails.html (accessed February 2, 2021).

Alia Akkam

The **Bellini** was created around 1945 by Giuseppe Cipriani (1900–1980), founder of the legendary Harry's Bar in Venice. By mixing a puree of fresh white peaches with prosecco, he created a cocktail that was refreshing and glamorous in equal measures. The Bellini was named for the fifteenth-century Venetian painter Giovanni Bellini, as the drink's dream-like peach hue resembled one characteristic of the painter's work.

To achieve the Bellini's signature rich foam and for good integration of flavor, the ingredients are best stirred slowly in a mixing glass and gently poured into a champagne flute or tumbler. The flavor profile of sparkling wine allows for many delicious variations on the Bellini, with purees of pear, almond, and raspberry drawing out different aspects of the prosecco.

Recipe: Combine 50 ml fresh white peach puree and 100 ml chilled prosecco in a mixing glass and gently stir. Strain into a champagne flute.

Cipriani, Arrigo. *The Harry's Bar Cookbook*.
London: John Blake, 2000.

Tony Conigliaro

Bell's is one of the pioneering brands of blended scotch whisky. In 1825, Thomas Sandeman (a cousin of the founder of the port house) set up as a wine and spirit merchant in Perth, Scotland. In 1845, Arthur Bell (1825–1900) joined the firm as a traveler. By 1851 he was a partner and had started to blend whiskies.

It was his son, A. K. (Arthur Kinmond; 1868–1942), who expanded the business, with the help of his brother Robert. Although Arthur Sr. had created brands such as Curler, he could not be persuaded to put his own name on a bottle. It wasn't until after his death that Arthur Bell & Sons launched Bell's Extra Special.

The firm branched into distilling in the 1930s with the purchase of Blair Athol, Dufftown, and later Inchgower distilleries. It would also build the now-silent Pittyvaich. By 1954, Bell's was in 130 markets—it had a strong following in South Africa—but its main focus was the United Kingdom. By the 1970s, under the dynamic leadership of managing director Raymond Miquel (1931–), it became the United Kingdom's top-selling blend, and the company began diversifying into the hotel industry.

As it was gearing up for an export push in 1985, Bell's was bought by Guinness and then became absorbed within Diageo and remained a UK-focused brand. It carried an eight-year-old age statement between 1994 and 2008.

"A Guide to Bell's." Diageo website. https://www.diageobaracademy.com/en_zz/know-your-liquid/our-brands/bells/ (accessed April 15, 2021).

Dave Broom

Bénédictine is a liqueur whose original formula, according to company claims, dates back to a recipe developed in 1510 by the Benedictine monk

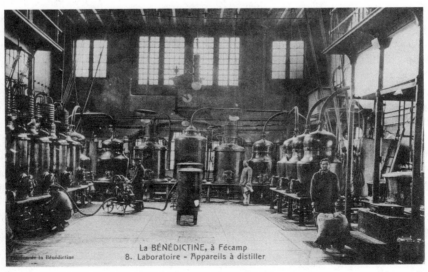

The Bénédictine distillery at Fécamp, Normandy, ca. 1900; note the rank of state-of-the-art steam-heated pot stills to the *right*. Wondrich Collection.

Dom Bernardo Vincelli at the Abbey of Fécamp in Normandy, France. This recipe, which combined local herbs and spices with exotic ingredients, supposedly became famous throughout the region and was prepared by the abbey long after his death until production was halted during the French Revolution in 1789.

In 1863, a French merchant and collector of religious artifacts named Alexandre Legrand claimed to have discovered the recipe for Vincelli's elixir amid hundreds of pages of gothic script written by the monk on subjects ranging from alchemy to hermeticism and to have recreated it after numerous experiments. Against these claims, maintained by the company to this day, we must balance the fact that it has never produced the original document, either in whole or in part, and no independent trace of Vincelli or his liqueur has been found.

Whatever the truth of the formula's origin, Legrand named it Bénédictine, in tribute to the order (and to appropriate some of the cachet of Chartreuse, which was in fact made by monks) and built a mock-Medieval palace in Fécamp to produce it. See CHARTREUSE. This burned to the ground four years later in 1892. Undeterred, he hired architect Camille Albert to design a larger palace and production facility that opened in 1898, the year he died. Here, in gothic splendor, the liqueur is still produced from the original recipe, with twenty-seven different plants and spices, including angelica, hyssop, saffron, cinnamon, nutmeg, and clove.

The manufacturing process encompasses maceration, multiple distillations in century-old copper pot stills, barrel aging, and blending, ending with the addition of honey, saffron, and other spices. See MACERATION and AGING. The mixture rests for four months before it is filtered and bottled at 40 percent ABV. Bénédictine is one of the first liqueurs to find its way into the cocktail and is one of the handful that Rochester, New York, bartender Patsy McDonough suggested dashing into a cocktail to "improve [it] in flavor." That was in 1883; it soon became common practice. Bénédictine is essential in classic cocktails such as the Chrysanthemum, Vieux Carré, Singapore Sling, and Bobby Burns. In the 1930s, Bénédictine released B&B, a drier combination of Bénédictine and French Cognac, which is still available today.

See HERBAL LIQUEURS.

Bénédictine website. https://www.benedictinedom.com (accessed February 2, 2021).
McDonough, Patsy. *McDonough's Bar-Keeper's Guide*. Rochester, NY: Post-Express, 1883.
Ridgewell, Mark. *Spirits Distilled*. Oxford: Infinite Ideas, 2014.

Jim Meehan

Bergeron, Victor "Trader Vic" (1902–1984), was arguably the most famous—and inarguably the most financially successful—celebrity mixologist of the mid-twentieth century. From the 1940s through the 1970s Bergeron made millions as a restaurateur, recipe book author, and seller of bottled tropical drink mixes. After Donn Beach, Bergeron was the second great pioneer of post-Prohibition "tiki" drinks—and the creator of that category's best-known drink, the Mai Tai (Beach's widow Phoebe disputes this claim). See TIKI and MAI TAI.

Bergeron was born on December 10, 1902, in San Francisco, to a French mother and a French Canadian father. A sickly child, he lost a leg and a kidney to tuberculosis before dropping out of high school. After a series of short-lived jobs selling everything from paint to tires, in 1934 he finally found success as proprietor, bartender, and chef of an Oakland barbecue shack called Hinky Dink's. A 1937 visit to Don the Beachcomber's, Donn Beach's popular South Seas–themed Hollywood nightspot, inspired Bergeron to jump on the tiki bandwagon, and in 1938 he turned Hinky Dink's into Trader Vic's. Unlike Beach's other imitators, who stole his secret bespoke recipes by poaching his bartenders, Bergeron drew on his own culinary skills to create original tiki drinks, most famously the Fog Cutter, Scorpion, and Mai Tai. See FOG CUTTER.

By the time Bergeron died in 1984, he'd opened more than twenty Trader Vic's restaurants across North America, Europe, and Japan. The chain has survived into the twenty-first century, but unfortunately none of his eight lively, insightful books are still in print (his *Bartender's Guide* remains a classic of its kind).

See also BEACH, DONN.

Bergeron, Victor J. *Frankly Speaking: Trader Vic's Own Story*. New York: Doubleday, 1973.

Berry, Jeff. *Beachbum Berry's Potions of the Caribbean.*
New York: Cocktail Kingdom, 2014.

Jeff Berry

Berry, Jeff "Beachbum" (1958–), is a drink historian specializing in exotic cocktails of the mid-century, commonly called "tiki" drinks. He's the author of seven books covering their history and featuring definitive recipes; these include *Beachbum Berry's Grog Log* (1998), *Beachbum Berry Remixed* (2009), *Beachbum Berry's Sippin' Safari* (2007), and *Beachbum Berry's Potions of the Caribbean* (2014).

Berry was born in Albany, New York, but grew up in Southern California, watching "adults ordering these amazing-looking exotic cocktails served with ice cones molded around straws, fancifully garnished with flaming lime shells," he recalls. By the time he was old enough to order these himself, the tiki drink culture had begun to fade, with tiki bars shuttering and drinks in most remaining restaurants evolving into debased versions of the originals.

In his twenties and thirties, Berry began researching how the original drinks were crafted. He visited existing tiki bars that still made tiki drinks with integrity and interviewed retired bartenders who worked at the hallowed locales in their glory days. Where the original bartender was not available, Berry often interviewed their children and others who knew their recipes and how to decipher them (many were written in code). In the 1990s, while working his day job as a screenwriter, he started meeting and exchanging notes with fellow cocktail historian Ted Haigh, along with tiki design expert Sven Kirsten and designer-writer-producer Otto Von Stroheim. See HAIGH, TED.

Berry's first books were published in spiral-bound format, which he and his wife, Annene Kaye, designed using photocopied type and graphics in a mix-and-match collage style. His first, *Grog Log*, contained recipes for classics such as Trader Vic Grog, La Florida, Boo Loo, and the Mai Tai (which had been badly corrupted by later bartenders, thanks to Victor "Trader Vic" Bergeron's penchant for secrecy about the ingredients in his creation and his refusal to publish a recipe for many years). See BERGERON, VICTOR "TRADER VIC," and MAI TAI.

Berry has made a convincing case that tiki drinks were among the original "craft cocktails" and deserving of placement alongside others in the classic canon. See CRAFT COCKTAIL. He has insisted on the use of quality ingredients in every drink, reflecting the care with which they were originally made (often using rums considered old and rare today). "Always squeeze your own lime juice," Berry wrote during a time when concentrates were common. "The difference is crucial to the fresh, crisp, 'alive' taste you're after."

Berry said that it took ten years and three books to nail down the origins of the Zombie, a drink first created by Don the Beachcomber. Berry searched for the original Zombie recipe ("Nobody really seems to know what went into . . . the Zombie" he wrote in 1998). See ZOMBIE. In a chapter devoted to the Zombie published in *Sippin' Safari*, he revealed an early recipe he found in a self-published three-ring-binder cookbook from 1950, which gave a recipe in which the author thanked Don the Beachcomber for his "generous assistance." Berry subsequently turned up additional Zombie recipes, including a 1934 Zombie Punch and a 1956 recipe he unearthed in *Cabaret Magazine*.

Berry is credited for decoding many other classic tiki drinks, especially those popularized by Don the Beachcomber, including the Nui Nui.

Berry left both screenwriting and Los Angeles in 2007. In something of a reverse migration of Don the Beachcomber (a New Orleans native who ended up in Los Angeles), Berry and his wife eventually moved to New Orleans. In 2015 they opened Latitude 29, a restaurant and bar in the city's French Quarter where guests sample both original creations and potions laboriously recreated from past recipes of tiki's golden era.

See also TIKI and BEACH, DONN.

Berry, Jeff. *Potions of the Caribbean.* New York: Cocktail Kingdom, 2014.
Berry, Jeff. *Sippin' Safari.* San Jose, CA: Club Tiki, 2007.

Wayne Curtis

Berry Bros. & Rudd (BBR) is Britain's oldest wine and spirit merchant. Founded by the Widow Bourne in 1698 at no. 3 St. James's Street, London—the address that still serves as its headquarters today—it is the holder of two royal warrants and has been supplier of wine and spirits to the royal family since the reign of King George III. The firm's famous customers have included Lord Byron, William Pitt the Younger, and the Aga Khan.

The company began life as a grocer supplying the neighboring coffee houses of St. James's (a fact attested to by the "Sign of the Coffee Mill," which still hangs outside the shop), before second cousins Francis Berry and Charles Walter Berry made the decision to specialize in wines and spirits in the late 1800s. In 1920 they were joined in business by the wine merchant Hugh Rudd.

While Berry Bros. & Rudd is best known as a wine merchant today, it has made a number of significant contributions to the world of spirits in the last hundred years, including the creation of the Cutty Sark Scotch whisky blend in 1923 and the reinvention of Speyside's Glenrothes as a "vintage" single malt in the 1990s. BBR is also responsible for the King's Ginger, a fiery liqueur created for King George VII in 1903 at the behest of his physician, who wished for something to keep His Highness warm during long drives in his new motor car. Other spirits in the BBR stable include the single-estate Mauritian rum Penny Blue XO, No. 3 Gin, Pink Pigeon Rum, and a large range of own-label malts, brandies, and rums.

More than three hundred years after it was founded, the company is still family-owned and run, with outposts in Hong Kong, Singapore, and Japan as well as a sizeable online business.

Berry Bros. & Rudd. http://www.bbr.com/about/history (accessed February 2, 2021).

Alice Lascelles

The **Between the Sheets** cocktail, with white rum, another spirit (either gin or brandy), Cointreau, and, usually, lemon juice, was—with its potent formula and its suggestive name—one of the signature cocktails of the Jazz Age, both in America and in Europe. Like many cocktails introduced at the time, there is an unusual degree of variation among the oldest recipes, whether because different bartenders took the name and added their own mixology or because of the adaptations imposed by American Prohibition. See ALEXANDER COCKTAIL and WHITE LADY.

The cocktail's origin is unclear. In the 1950s, American bartender Johnny Brooks claimed he invented it while working at a speakeasy in New Rochelle, New York, but also admitted that others

had claimed it. The New York newspaperman O. O. McIntyre mentioned in a 1931 column that it was a specialty of a particular New York speakeasy but declined to name it. It first appears in print in America in 1929, in *Drawn from the Wood* by Frank Shay; there, the recipe called for gin, Bacardi rum, and Cointreau. But when the recipe traveled to Europe, it was modified to become very similar to the Sidecar, with the gin being replaced by cognac and the addition of lemon juice. Harry Craddock was the first to publish this new version, in his *Savoy Cocktail Book*.

In 1934, Patrick Gavin Duffy mentioned the later recipe, but he marked it with an asterisk, indicating that he didn't recommend it. His reasoning was that it combined two spirits in the same drink, and "drinking different strong liquors at one session often brings on sudden intoxication and sick headaches afterwards." See DUFFY, PATRICK GAVIN. Such drinks were relatively uncommon at the time, at least outside the world of punch (where cognac and rum had been happily mixed together since the 1700s). Today, Duffy's taboo is no longer respected, but this has still not brought the Between the Sheets back into common use.

Recipe: Shake 45 ml white rum, 45 ml cognac, 45 ml Cointreau and 45ml fresh lemon juice. Strain. Garnish with twist of orange peel.

See also SIDECAR.

Brooks, Johnny. *My 35 Years Behind Bars.* New York: Exposition, 1954.

Duffy, Patrick Gavin. *The Official Mixer's Manual.* New York: Long & Smith, 1934.

McIntyre, O. O. "New York Day by Day." *Akron Beacon-Journal*, October 3, 1930, 4.

Shay, Frank. *Drawn from the Wood.* New York: Macaulay, 1929.

Fernando Castellon

Beverage Alcohol Resource (BAR) is an education and certification program in distilled spirits and mixology founded in 2005 by a quintet of notable experts in the field: drinks historian David Wondrich, pioneering bartender Dale DeGroff, author and wine expert Doug Frost, restaurant and bar consultant Steven Olson, and author/editor F. Paul

Pacult; they were quickly joined by bartender and educator Andy Seymour. See DeGroff, Dale; Olson, Steve; and Pacult, F. Paul. Its intensive 5-Day Certification Program in New York may be the cocktails and spirits equivalent of the Master Sommelier and Master of Wine certifications.

BAR has run the 5-Day program twenty-one times as of 2021, with almost 650 students receiving certifications in total, including a great many of the bar industry's most influential figures. In 2008, the organization added BarSmarts, an intermediate-level certification that has also been used as a prerequisite for the 5-Day Certification and can be done online or in one-day "BarSmarts Advanced" classes held throughout the United States. And in 2015, the organization created BarStarts, a customized training program for bar and restaurant groups. As of the beginning of 2021, the two programs have certified over sixty-five thousand graduates between them.

See also BARTENDING SCHOOLS.

"Beverage Alcohol Resource." https://
    beveragealcoholresource.com/ (accessed
    February 3, 2021).

Jason Horn

bierschnaps is a spirit distilled from finished beer, whose hop content makes the schnaps easily distinguishable from whisky even though the other ingredients—malted barley, yeast, water—might be the same. It is traditionally a specialty of small Bavarian breweries (which often have their own stills), and many versions are only available at each brewery's own taproom or gift shop. These spirits are typically 40–50 percent ABV, and classical versions are unflavored, though they are sometimes oak aged. By the late 1990s, American craft brewers had begun to offer their own variations. American bierschnaps, now fairly common, are sometimes flavored with beer wort, caramel, or other flavors. Iterations can be found worldwide from Japan to Brazil. While bierschnaps are occasionally used in cocktails, they are largely considered novelty spirits outside Bavaria.

See also ABV; BEER; and GERMANY, SWITZERLAND, AND AUSTRIA.

Garrett Oliver

The **Bijou Cocktail**, with gin, green Chartreuse, and Italian vermouth, is the one of the many drinks associated with master bartender Harry Johnson most often encountered in the modern age. The drink appears to have been Johnson's adaptation of a cocktail that was first recorded in St. Louis and Cincinnati in the spring of 1895. The original version was nothing more than a mixture of the then-new Grand Marnier with cognac (the St. Louis version) or in equal portion with Plymouth gin and Italian vermouth (the Cincinnati one). Johnson's take on the drink, which appeared in the 1900 edition of his *Bartender's Manual*, replaces the Grand Marnier in the Cincinnati version with green Chartreuse, thus turning a rich and pleasant drink into a spicy and invigorating one.

For the next three or four decades, Johnson's Bijou would battle it out in the pages of American and European drink books with variations on the Cincinnati version until the fashion for drier, less complex-tasting cocktails doomed them both to obscurity. In the 2000s, Johnson's version, at least, was woken from hibernation by history-minded bartenders and pressed back into service, its bold intensity and use of trendy ingredients—gin, Chartreuse—making it a good companion for other once-forgotten drinks such as the Aviation and the Last Word. See AVIATION COCKTAIL and LAST WORD.

Recipe: Stir 30 ml ea. Plymouth gin, Italian vermouth, and green Chartreuse and 2 dashes orange bitters with ice. Strain into chilled cocktail glass and twist lemon peel over the top.

See also GRAND MARNIER and JOHNSON, HARRY.

"Drinks That Keep You Cool." *Cincinnati Enquirer*, May
    12, 1895, 28.
Johnson, Harry. *Harry Johnson's New and Improved
    Bartenders' Manual*. New York: Harry Johnson, 1900.
Lawlor, Chris. *The Mixicologist*. Rev. ed.
    Cincinnati: Lawlor, 1895.
"Summer Drinks That Promise to Be the Rage." *St. Louis
    Republic*, May 5, 1895, part 2, 16.

David Wondrich

Bilgray's Tropico, formally known as Bilgray's Tropic Bar, was one of the twin pillars of the

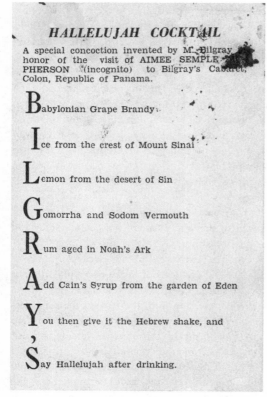

HALLELUJAH COCKTAIL

A special concoction invented by M. Bilgray in honor of the visit of AIMEE SEMPLE McPHERSON (incognito) to Bilgray's Cabaret, Colon, Republic of Panama.

Babylonian Grape Brandy

Ice from the crest of Mount Sinai

Lemon from the desert of Sin

Gomorrha and Sodom Vermouth

Rum aged in Noah's Ark

Add Cain's Syrup from the garden of Eden

You then give it the Hebrew shake, and

'

Say Hallelujah after drinking.

Bilgray's Hallelujah Cocktail, as memorialized on a postcard, 1930. Wondrich Collection.

freewheeling bar culture that gave Panama the reputation it carried in the 1930s and 1940s for raunchy, boozy fun. Located on the notorious Balboa Street, alias "Bottle Alley," in Colon, Bilgray's served the Caribbean end of the (dry) Canal Zone, while Mamie Kelley's Ritz, in Panama City, took care of the Pacific end. Max Bilgray (1885–1958), an Austrian who in the years before Prohibition kept saloons first in the Chicago suburbs and then in Wyoming, set up in Panama in 1921 after seeing a fellow speakeasy proprietor get five years in jail for doing just what he was doing. There, as *Time* magazine recounted in 1956, Bilgray "earned his fame by making the Tropic into a serious drinkingman's bar—an honest saloon that scorned chromium, jukeboxes and B-girls. Its sights and sounds were shiny brass, dark wood panels, man-to-man talk and softly whirling fans." If that was too staid for some customers, in 1938 he opened Bilgray's Garden, an open-air cabaret with dancing and the same sort of risqué floor shows featured at Kelley's Ritz.

Bilgray's enjoyed a large and enthusiastic military clientele, which included such future eminences as General Dwight David Eisenhower and Admiral William F. Halsey, both junior officers at the time. Actors and other celebrities were also frequently found there, such as William Powell, Errol Flynn, and Groucho Marx. In 1930 American radio evangelist Aimee Semple McPherson visited the bar, hiding behind a false name. She was nonetheless recognized, whereupon Bilgray dedicated a drink to her, the Hallelujah Cocktail, and had the recipe printed on postcards. A threatened legal action never materialized.

Bilgray, an unassuming, soft-spoken man (though, as reporter Ernie Pyle noted, "immensely profane"), sold the bar in 1955 after suffering a stroke. It limped along until 1974 but never regained the reputation it enjoyed under its charismatic founder.

Karrer, Bob. "Have a Drink with Max," *Isthmian Collectors' Club Journal*, 2008, 41–47.

Pyle, Ernie. "Touring with Pyle." *El Paso Herald-Post*, January 20, 1940, 6.

Jeff Berry and David Wondrich

biscuits (punch), or toasted biscuits, were a baked good historically served floating in communal drinks, such as punch, or presented on the side as an individual-serving alcohol-infused cake. An account of Admiral Edward Russell's famous fountain punch of 1694 documents that three hundred toasted biscuits were among the ingredients. These may have been traditional double-baked flour-and-water sea biscuits, but a more likely candidate is what the *Dictionaire Oeconomique* (1718) refers to as a "Common Bisket," a combination of eggs, sugar, and flour beaten into a white paste and baked in molds. Variations on this recipe date from the late sixteenth century to the twentieth century, including Auguste Escoffier's punch biscuit paste. While recipes differ on the incorporation of beaten egg whites, most agree on the inclusion of some sort of flavoring, such as citrus zest, aniseed, or rose water, and on double-baking the biscuits, as with biscotti or the aforementioned sea biscuits. In use, punch biscuits both exchange flavors with the punch in which they are placed and absorb the punch, ultimately producing a dessert akin to a rum cake.

See also PUNCH.

Chomel, Noel. *Dictionaire Oeconomique or, The Family Dictionary*. Edited and translated by R. Bradley. London: D. Midwinter, 1725.

Escoffier, Auguste. *A Guide to Modern Cookery*. London: William Heinemann, 1907.

May, Robert. *The Accomplisht Cook*, 5th ed. London: Obadiah Blagrave, 1685.

David Solmonson

bitter lemon soda, a carbonated mixer of nineteenth-century British origin and flavored with lemons and quinine, is often paired with gin (in place of the more common tonic water) or used in making a Pimm's Cup. See GIN; TONIC WATER; and PIMM'S CUP.

bitters, also known as "cocktail" or "aromatic" bitters, are liquid essences generally produced by macerating various herbs, spices, and other botanicals in a base spirit. The result is a liquid with a fairly concentrated flavor that is most commonly measured into drinks by dashes. They are referred to as "bitters" because they almost always include as a core ingredient something that lends a bitter flavor, traditionally ingredients such as gentian, cinchona bark, or wormwood. The cocktail (as a category of mixed drinks) was the first recreational beverage to specifically require the use of bitters. This requirement held, until the onset of American Prohibition. See COCKTAIL.

The original cocktail bitters were an offshoot of digestive bitters, often with little other than their intended use distinguishing one from another. (Cocktail bitters predate the cocktail itself and thus were often simply referred to as "bitters.") Stoughton's Stomachic Bitters were the foundational example of digestive bitters and of their crossover capacity; the brand was established on apothecary shelves around 1690 and was almost immediately used mixed with spirits. See COCK-TAIL.

Digestive bitters (which include the amari category) are a potable spirituous beverage that includes a variety of botanical ingredients and were believed to have medicinal or tonic value; non-potable bitters, the type now used in cocktails, were often touted specifically for an advertised medicinal purpose and promoted as a medicine instead of as a beverage. See AMARO. Bitters were also known as "patent medicines," since they would often receive (or claim to have received) "letters patent" from a royal personage that assumedly gave them authorization for producing their products as well as making claims regarding their medicinal merits.

Patent Medicines

During the 1600s and 1700s, bitters, or patent medicines, were compounded utilizing the best medical knowledge of the day in an attempt to treat or prevent various physical ailments. The compulsion to push the medicinal value of a product to include additional ailments was great, and gradually the list of cures a particular bitters promised would grow until some patent medicines would even claim to cure all diseases. In addition to various herbs and botanicals, many of these formulas would include opium, cocaine, and cannabis. Patent medicines also often used high-proof grain alcohol as a base, providing the illusion of further benefit via a high-octane kick.

Stoughton's are widely considered the product that defined the category and indeed became so popular, and their ownership so loosely managed, that by the mid-1700s many knock-off elixirs were being sold in competition; by the end of the century, they were a standard apothecary's formula, compounded at every pharmacy in Britain and North America. Stoughton's Bitters lasted in common use through most of the 1800s until they were buried by the competition from proprietary brands.

The medicinal use of non-potable bitters greatly benefited from the efforts of the temperance movement, which, starting around 1820, aimed to curb or abolish the recreational use of alcohol. Bitters conveniently skirted this issue, since they were considered medicinal, not recreational.

It is perhaps due to the purported medicinal properties of non-potable bitters that they were first added to a drink and christened as a "cocktail." Cocktails were originally considered a morning beverage, and so downing a medicinal drought upon rising in the morning could be seen as a good way to start the day. Because these types of bitters weren't intended to be palatable straight and instead required mixing with other ingredients, diluting the medicine with a little whisky, water, and sugar made perfect sense for many. See HEALTH AND SPIRITS.

Behind the Bar

During the 1800s, many of the bitters which had previously been utilized as patent medicines found new life behind the mahogany. Over the years, additional bitters came to market, and eventually found their way into cocktails as well. Some of these later entries would include Angostura (1824, 1853 in the United States), Boker's (1828), Peychaud's (1838), Hostetter's (1853), and Abbott's (1872). See ANGOSTURA BITTERS and PEYCHAUD'S BITTERS.

Boker's Bitters were introduced in 1828 by John G. Boker and quickly became a favorite of bartenders. In the 1862 *How to Mix Drinks*, Jerry Thomas referenced Boker's Bitters for use in a number of his cocktail recipes (although a publishing or transcription error converted it to "Bogart's"). See THOMAS, JERRY. Boker's Bitters would continue to be produced up until American Prohibition, and the company finally closed in 1920.

In 1853, Dr. Jacob Hostetter from Lancaster, Pennsylvania, developed Hostetter's Bitters together with his son David and began large-scale production. By this time, the cocktail had already caught on, but these bitters were still being specifically marketed as a health tonic. By the time of the Civil War they'd become a bestseller, marketed as "a positive protective against the fatal maladies of the Southern swamps, and the poisonous tendency of the impure rivers and bayous." Hostetter's Bitters appear to have survived until the 1950s, at which point they were sold simply as a tonic.

Abbott's Bitters were introduced by the C. W. Abbott's company in, or slightly before, 1872. Coming to the party a little late, they had some catching up to do. Angostura by this time had already become fairly popular, and Abbott's attempted to capture some of that market by referring to themselves as "Abbott's—the original Angostura Bitters." Their rationale was that they actually included angostura bark in their recipe, while Angostura bitters took their name from their town of origin, without utilizing any angostura bark whatsoever in their formula. Though some claim that Abbott's were the original bitters used for the Manhattan, no actual evidence appears to

back that up, aside from some early recipes which simply indicate its use.

Prior to Prohibition

In 1935, Albert Crocket Stevens wrote *The Old Waldorf-Astoria Bar Book*, which provides insights into the drinking culture and the cocktails in use at the bar of New York's Waldorf-Astoria hotel until it closed with the onset of Prohibition. See WALDORF-ASTORIA. Of note is a passage regarding gin-based cocktails and their use of bitters:

> Bitters of one kind or another was considered a necessary ingredient of most Gin cocktails. The favorite was Orange Bitters, which appears in something like one hundred different recipes. A distant second was Angostura. Then there were Calisaya, Boonekamp, Boker's, Amer Picon, Hostetter's, Pepsin, Peychaud, Fernet Branca, and so on.

This provides some insight into the lengthy list of cocktail bitters still in common use through the early 1900s.

Prior to Prohibition, there were two major categories of bitters: aromatic and orange. While orange bitters—originally a Dutch creation and introduced to America in the 1860s—were often produced by a variety of companies (for example, Holland House Orange Bitters), aromatic bitters were usually branded and identified by name, as seen in Angostura, Peychaud's, and Abbott's. Other styles of bitters occasionally crop up, such as peach and celery, as well as various branded bitters such as Khoosh, Boker's, and Stoughton. At Prohibition's end, however, the bitters industry as a whole was much smaller, with only a handful surviving.

Twentieth Century

Passage of the Pure Food and Drug Act of 1906 posed the first challenge to cocktail bitters (or patent medicines, as most were still considered to be). The law required products containing an array of potentially dangerous ingredients (including morphine, opium, cannabis, and alcohol) to clearly list these ingredients on the label and curbed some of overtly misleading or fraudulent claims on labels and for marketing.

The next setback would be American Prohibition, which began in 1920. While non-potable bitters skirted the law because of their purported medicinal use, demand for the bitters was understandably reduced. See PROHIBITION AND TEMPERANCE IN AMERICA. Probably the final straw was the revision of the Food and Drug Act in 1936, which banned ingredients known to be dangerous, including some botanicals used in bitters. Some products reworked their recipes to avoid these ingredients; the once-popular Abbott's Bitters altered their recipe to be in full compliance, but their popularity declined, leading to the brand's demise in the 1950s.

By the latter half of the 1900s, only Angostura bitters could commonly be found behind most bars, and even then it was rarely used. Peychaud's Bitters could be found in bars in and around New Orleans in order to make the Sazerac cocktail, but few bars outside the region had much call for Sazeracs or Peychaud's. By the 1980s, the non-potable bitters that had once been a defining ingredient of the cocktail had all but disappeared.

The Cocktail Resurgence

During the cocktail resurgence that started in the late 1990s, bartenders and cocktail enthusiasts rediscovered classic pre-Prohibition cocktails. They learned that many of those recipes called for styles and brands of bitters aside from Angostura and Peychaud's. Among these cocktails was the Dry Martini, which in its earliest incarnations called for the use of orange bitters as a necessary ingredient. Many thought that orange bitters were out of production, only to discover that Fee Brothers in Rochester, New York, had been producing orange bitters since Prohibition. With orange bitters now available for their Martinis, cocktail enthusiasts began looking for other classic bitters, as well as ways to best use them in classic and modern cocktails.

This led to uncovering recipes from the 1800s for making bitters, and after figuring out some of the odd ingredients these recipes called for, many bartenders and cocktail enthusiasts tried making their own. Gradually, this home-brew batch of bitters led to some of the more adventurous to coming out with their own commercial line of bitters. Some such brands include Regans' Orange Bitters no. 6, Scrappy's, the Bitter Truth (aka Berg & Hauk's in the United States), Dr. Adam Elmegirab's, and many others. Where once cocktail enthusiasts bemoaned the difficulties in finding any bitters at all, there now exists a cottage industry with dozens of different bitters available, and the difficulty is trying to decide which bitters would work best in a particular cocktail.

Crockett, Albert Stevens. *The Old Waldorf-Astoria Bar Book*. New York: New York Lithographic Corporation, 1935.

Dr. Adam Elmegirab's. https://www.doctoradams.co.uk/ (accessed February 3, 2021).

Thomas, Jerry. *How to Mix Drinks*. New York: Dick & Fitzgerald, 1862.

Wondrich, David. *Imbibe!*, rev. ed. New York: Penguin, 2015.

Robert Hess

Bix is a San Francisco bar and restaurant founded in 1988 by local restaurateur Douglas "Bix" Biederbeck (1952–) and known for the elegant, formal bar service and classic drinks that helped lay the foundation for the coming West Coast cocktail revival. In a city known for its casual style, Bix instead draws inspiration from the swanky, tuxedoed nightlife of the 1930s, 1940s, and 1950s. Its location, on a quiet alley in the former Barbary Coast neighborhood, just steps away from the site of the old Bank Exchange, proffers a modest speakeasy vibe, with an unassuming front door belying Bix's interior grandiosity—a dark, voluminous, mahogany-paneled interior is anchored by towering columns and a baby grand piano (live jazz is a staple). See BANK EXCHANGE and SPEAKEASY (NEW). In the open dining area, waiters bustle between white-tablecloth-covered tables. Yet Bix's physical and spiritual heart is its long, arcing mahogany bar. On it ready-and-waiting cocktail glasses nestle, stems up, in massive bowls of crushed ice. Bartenders, many of whom have held court there for decades, sport white jackets and black bowties. Excelling in the preparation of classic cocktails, they stir and shake Martinis and Manhattans in endless profusion, while the drink menu perpetually lists standards such as the Pisco Punch, La Floridita Daiquiri, and Blood and Sand. Neither a center of cocktail creativity or spirit-world exploration, Bix is San Francisco's bastion of the urbane, sexy cocktail culture of another era.

See also COCKTAIL RENAISSANCE.

O'Neill, Eve, and Doug "Bix" Biederbeck. *Bixology*, San Francisco: Chronicle, 2009.

Jordan Mackay

Black Strap, also known as Black Stripe, is a primitive mixture of rum, hot or cold water, and molasses that went on to become one of the cornerstone drinks of rural New England. ("Strap" was a seventeenth-century English slang term for wine.) When it first appears, in Charles Johnson's pseudonymous 1724 *General History of the Pyrates*, it is described as "a strong Liquor" consumed by sailors in Newfoundland waters, "made from Rum, Molossus, and Chowder [i.e., spruce] Beer." The spruce beer, a popular antiscorbutic, places it in the same family as Flip, another sailor's drink, but once Black Strap made it to shore and found its way inland, it rapidly split into two drinks: Calibogus with the spruce beer, Black Strap without. See FLIP.

So widespread was Black Strap's popularity in rural New England that in the late eighteenth and early and mid-nineteenth centuries, it became almost as much a part of the popular image of the canny Yankee countryman as the Mint Julep was of the southern cavalier. Although Jerry Thomas (a Yankee himself) printed a recipe for it (as Black Stripe) in his 1862 book, from which it was repeatedly plagiarized, it is doubtful if anyone in America but nostalgic old Vermonters drank it then or any time after, although it would continue to appear in American bar guides well into the twentieth century. See THOMAS, JEREMIAH P. "JERRY".

As a sailor's drink, however, Black Strap got around; indeed, Charles H. Baker Jr. recorded a version of it, sophisticated with ice and bitters, still being served in Jamaica in the 1930s, and it appeared in European bar guides with enough variation in the formulae to suggest that it was still occasionally served. After the Second World War it is heard from no more. See BAKER, CHARLES HENRY, JR.

Recipe: In tumbler, stir 15 ml molasses with 15 ml warm water until molasses has dissolved. Add 60 ml dark aromatic rum and fill with shaved ice. Garnish with nutmeg. For hot Black Strap, substitute 90 ml boiling water for warm water and ice.

Baker, Charles H., Jr. *Gentleman's Companion*, vol. 2. New York: Derrydale, 1939.
Farmer, John S. *Slang and Its Analogues*, vol. 1. N.p., 1890.
Johnson, Charles. *General History of the Pyrates*. London: 1724.
"Mr. Hill." *Concord (NH) Patriot*, February 27, 1810, 3.
Thomas, Jerry. *How to Mix Drinks*. New York: Dick & Fitzgerald, 1862.

David Wondrich

The **Blackthorn Cocktail** was once popular enough to spawn a slew of drinks all confusingly going by the same name. The 1947 Trader Vic *Bartender's Guide* has no fewer than five wildly different recipes for the Blackthorn. There's a Blackthorn made of gin, Dubonnet, and kirschwasser; there's a Blackthorn of gin, sloe gin, dry vermouth, and orange bitters; there's one with sweet vermouth instead of dry; there's one with both sweet and dry vermouth; and then there's an entirely different Blackthorn— Irish whisky and dry vermouth with a dash each of Angostura and Pernod. The great Blackthorn debate goes back the better part of a century. In his 1922 *Cocktails: How to Mix Them*, Robert Vermeire, the barman at the Embassy Club in London, allows that "the Blackthorn is a very old cocktail, which is made in two different ways." See VERMEIRE, ROBERT. One is attributed to the legendary barman Harry Johnson and calls for equal parts Irish whisky and dry vermouth with 3 dashes each absinthe and Angostura bitters. See JOHNSON, HARRY. The other version, credited to "Cocktail Bill" Boothby of San Francisco, is made with equal parts sloe gin, dry and sweet vermouth, and a dash each orange and Angostura bitters. See BOOTHBY, BILL. Boothby himself—in the 1908 edition of his manual, *The World's Drinks and How to Mix Them*—gave the honors for the sloe-gin version to William Smith, bartender at the Royal Hawaiian Hotel in Honolulu.

Recipe (Smith's Blackthorn Cocktail): Stir 30 ml ea. sloe gin, red Cinzano vermouth and try vermouth and 2 dashes orange bitters and one dash Angostura bitters with ice. Strain into a chilled cocktail glass and twist lemon peel over the top.

"New Things in Tipples." *New York Herald*, November 21, 1897, section 5, 8.
"Shun Blackthorn Cocktail." *Los Angeles Herald*, December 13, 1905, 4.

Eric Felten

Black Velvet, a simple mixture of champagne and stout or porter, first surfaces in the 1830s as a German student's drink, under the name *Menschenfreund*, or "Philanthropist." A favorite with the future chancellor Otto von Bismarck, it had a reputation for fueling irresponsible behavior. The combination did not, as far as can be determined, catch on outside Germany until Bismarck stepped out on the world stage in the 1870s, when it was invariably pointed to as one of the symptoms of his "wild" youth in the many biographies of him that appeared in the popular press in Britain and America. While some called it a "strange and almost incredible beverage," others, such as arch-colonialist Cecil Rhodes, latched onto it as the proper drink for a man of destiny. In the United Kingdom and its possessions, it was known by various names, including Bismarck, the mixologically precise Imperial Shandy, and Velvet, which accurately described its texture. American drinkers, most of them from the so-called sporting fraternity (boxers, gamblers, and their ilk), preferred the last of these.

The drink remained a minority taste, almost a curiosity, until the 1920s, when as Black Velvet (first attested to in 1922) it came into fashion in London, although there were still dissenters such as George Saintsbury, who considered the drink "at once vicious and vulgar" and a waste of good champagne. Presumably, Americans who encountered it at the Savoy and the Café Royal and the like brought it back across the Atlantic, and once Repeal ensured the easy availability of its ingredients, it rapidly gained popularity in America as well, in particular as a morning drink. While the Black Velvet's popularity has fallen off since its peak in the 1930s, it is still found wherever fancy brunches are served.

Recipe: Half-fill a tall glass with chilled stout or porter; slowly top off with chilled champagne.

See also SAINTSBURY, GEORGE EDWARD BATEMAN.

"Eine Excursion in das Gebiet der Spitznamen." *Nurnberger Presse*, September 7, 1872, 2–3.
"Facing the Music." *Leeds Mercury*, March 3, 1902.
Johnson, Harry. *New and Improved Illustrated Bartender's Manual.* New York: Harry Johnson, 1888.
Klaczko, M. Julian. *The Two Chancellors: Prince Gortchakof and Prince Bismarck.* London: Chapman & Hall, 1876.
Saintsbury, George. *Notes on a Cellar-Book.* London: Macmillan, 1920.

David Wondrich

Blanton's became the first "single barrel" bourbon brand when it was introduced in 1984. The brand's genesis came in 1983 after two liquor executives, Ferdie Falk and Robert Baranaskas, purchased the Albert B. Blanton Distillery in Frankfort, Kentucky, and decided to start their own business. This distillery has had many names over the years, but was changed to Buffalo Trace in 1999. Elmer T. Lee, a longtime distillery employee who had worked under Albert Blanton, the outfit's former namesake, guided the creation of the brand. Blanton had worked in the industry for over fifty years, starting in 1897, and was remembered for the practice—not uncommon among distillery executives of his era—of bottling whisky from a single, particularly appealing barrel for personal use or as gifts to industry insiders. Whisky to be sold under the Blanton's name was chosen accordingly, from single barrels that had all aged in the same metal-clad warehouse and fell within a specific flavor profile. Blanton's arrived on store shelves after a long slump in American whisky sales, when some market watchers began noticing an uptick in the popularity of niche offerings. This new higher-end market was particularly big in Japan, where drinkers gravitated toward whiskies perceived as more exclusive. Later that decade, the brand was sold to Japanese investor Takara Shuzo but continued to be made at the same facility.

See also WHISKY, BOURBON; BUFFALO TRACE DISTILLERY; and SINGLE BARREL.

Apple, R. W., Jr. "Bourbons in the Cognac League." *New York Times,* September 17, 1997.
"Buffalo Trace Master Distiller Emeritus Elmer T. Lee, Creator of Blanton's, Passes at 93," *Business Lexington,* July 16, 2003.
Fabricant, Florence. "Boutique Bourbons Win Prestige at Home and Sales Abroad." *New York Times*, December 16, 1992.
Van Gelder, Lawrence. "Long Islanders; Catering to Shifts in Drinking Tastes." *New York Times,* January 15, 1984.
Veach, Michael. *Kentucky Bourbon Whiskey: An American Heritage.* Lexington: University Press of Kentucky, 2013.

Vitello, Paul. "Elmer T. Lee, Whose Premium Bourbon Revived an Industry, Dies at 93." *New York Times*, July 21, 2013.

Reid Mitenbuler

blending is a long-practiced art form by spirits producers whereby different lots of spirits, either from the same distillery but with different maturation or from different distilleries and, commonly, with different styles or lengths of maturation are combined to form a harmonious whole. Blending dates back at least to the eighteenth century, when British rectifiers made a practice of stretching out expensive imported brandy and arrack with cheap domestic molasses spirit and Dutch brandy wholesalers "adjusted, that is, mixed, coloured, sweetened and made up" their spirits before resale, according to W. A. Smyth's *Publican's Guide.* See RECTIFICATION. The next century saw the British apply the art to rum and whisky and the French adopt it in brandy making, where it is now one of the building blocks of the trade. See ÉLEVAGE.

Blending gained a new prominence in the middle of the nineteenth century with the widespread adoption of the column still in Britain and the cheap, light, relatively clean whisky it produced. In 1860, by act of Parliament (23 and 24 Victoria, cap 114), British rectifiers were allowed to blend pot- and column-produced spirits in bond; this was the beginning of the modern blender's art (and the end of the old one: the same act forbade the blending of British and foreign spirits). See EXCISE, TAXES, AND DISTILLATION. While Ireland and Jamaica both resisted the column still until the 1950s, blended pot- and column-still spirits rapidly became the norm in Scotland, Canada, and parts of the British Caribbean.

Nowadays many spirits are pot-column blends, where the pot-still product provides the intense flavor and the column-still one lightens it, brings out accents in it, and—just as importantly—makes it available at a manageable price. Many scotch and Irish whiskies, a number of popular rums, and most American applejacks and Dutch and Belgian jenevers are blends of this sort. Nowhere has the blender's art been more important than in Canada, where it has been at the heart of Canadian whiskey making since at least the 1890s. In fact, we can use Canadian practice as a model for blending in general.

Modern blending is not simply pouring barrels of whisky into a vat and stirring. It requires consideration of all the variables in production from the largest to the smallest. A master blender has to have a keen understanding of all the distillery's processes and how the flavors from source grain, brewing and fermentation, and distillation interact with the aging process.

By this standard, blending starts with the selection of raw materials. In general, for whisky production corn gives a sweet-creamy expression, barley a nutty-cereal note, rye a spicy character, and wheat a bready nuance. The quality of the raw material is also important, as negative characteristics can impact the flavor of final blends. For example, when fungus grows on poor-quality grain, it produces geosmin or 2-methylisoborneol (MIB), which survive distillation and give whisky a musty character. If these compounds are at detectable levels in the finished product, a blender can either mix the whisky with better batches or, in a worst-case scenario, send it to be redistilled.

Fermentation is also important to the blender. Along with ethanol and carbon dioxide, yeast also produces compounds with fruity, floral, grassy, soapy, or sulfurous character. Brewers in a whisky operation can influence these flavors by manipulating a number of fermentation parameters such as temperature and pH or oxygen levels, so it is important for the brewer to work with the master blender to establish a consistent baseline of flavors that are generated by the fermentation process. See FERMENTATION.

The master distiller will also influence the final flavor of the whisky by selecting the method of distillation. See MASTER DISTILLER. Two passes through a column still creates a lighter spirit that removes the majority of the yeast congeners and grain characteristics; this is often termed a "base whisky"; it will usually be made from corn. "Flavoring whiskies," on the other hand, can get one pass through a column still, which produces a full flavored spirit that has retained a good deal of the grain and yeast characteristics, or they can go through a pot still, to concentrate the desired characteristics and remove the unwanted heads and tails (these whiskies perform the role in a Canadian blend that malt whiskies do in a scotch one). No matter the type of distillation method, the master blender must be able to understand how to work with the spirits that are produced by the distiller to maintain existing recipes or to create unique whisky styles.

Prior to the aging process a blender has to decide the strength of alcohol that spirit should be diluted to, as it effects the interaction with the barrel over time. The last consideration a blender has is barrel type. Even if just employing bourbon barrels, as is standard in Canada, a blender has choices to make. An unused barrel will provide four or five times as many vanilla, caramel, and toffee notes as a once-used one. However, a once-used barrel will infuse the spirit with some characteristics of the mature spirit it previously contained, which can make for a complex, interesting whisky, especially if the barrel was filled with a spirit of a different category. Although it has fewer extractive compounds, a barrel that has already been used several times tones down the acidic tannins and can allow flavors from the raw material, fermentation, or distillation to shine through. See BARREL.

Finally, after aging the master blender will construct a recipe by mixing percentages of whisky from specific grain types, brewing parameters, distillation methods, and barrel types. Blenders are like a conductor with an orchestra where all the parts, whether great or small, are considered in the final development of the whisky recipe.

See also WHISKY.

Cooper, Ambrose. *The Complete Distiller*. London: 1757.

Kunze, W. *Technology Brewing and Malting*. 2nd ed. Berlin: VLB Berlin, Verlagsabteilung, 1999.

Livermore, D. *Quantification of Oak Wood Extractives Via Gas Chromatography: Mass Spectrometry and Subsequent Calibration of Near Infrared Reflectance to Predict the Canadian Whisky Ageing Process*. Edinburgh: Heriot-Watt University Life Sciences, 2012.

MacKinnon, T. L. *The Historical Geography of the Distilling Industry in Ontario: 1850–1900*. Waterloo, ON: Wilfrid Laurier University, 2000.

Piggott, J. R, K. Y. Lee, and A. Paterson. "Origins of Flavour in Whiskies and a Revised Flavour Wheel: A Review." *Journal of the Institute of Brewing* 107 (2001): 287–313.

Smyth, William Augustus. *Publican's Guide*. London: 1781.

Don Livermore

The **Blood and Sand** cocktail, with equal parts of blended scotch whisky, cherry brandy, Italian vermouth, and orange juice, is a drink of unknown parentage that first appears in the *Savoy Cocktail Book* in 1930. All that is known about its creation is that it was apparently named after the successful silent film of the same name starring Rudolf Valentino. The film, first screened in 1922, was based in turn on the widely popular 1909 novel *Sangre y arena* by the Spanish author Vicente Blasco Ibáñez. The possibility that the drink was named after the book and not the film cannot be dismissed.

Although it has its passionate defenders, the Blood and Sand—one of the few classic scotch whisky cocktails—has an unusual number of detractors. Even many of its defenders admit that the drink could use some tweaking, in either its ingredients, its proportions, or both. The most common fixes are to use more whisky and better whisky, substituting single malt for blended. Even with these tweaks, the drink's critics find it unfocused and muddy-tasting.

Recipe: Shake well with ice 45 ml blended scotch whisky, 45 ml cherry brandy, 45 ml Italian vermouth, and 45 ml fresh-squeezed orange juice. Strain and garnish with a cherry.

Craddock, Harry. *Savoy Cocktail Book*. London: Constable, 1930.

Fernando Castellon and David Wondrich

Bloody Bull is a cross between the Bloody Mary and the Bull Shot combining beef broth and tomato juice. See BLOODY MARY; BULLSHOT; BEEF BROTH; and TOMATO JUICE. Its origin is claimed, not entirely without evidence, by Brennan's Restaurant in New Orleans.

The **Bloody Caesar**, a variation on the Bloody Mary with a blend of clam and tomato juices in place of the straight tomato juice, is widely considered to be the national drink of Canada. The drink's immediate story is well known and largely unchallenged: it was invented in 1969 by Walter Silin Chell (1925–1997), the Montenegro-born, European hotel school–educated manager of the Owl's Nest restaurant in the Calgary Inn, at the time the finest restaurant in Calgary, for the opening of Marco's, an Italian restaurant in the same hotel. Within five years, it was popular throughout western Canada, with the *Calgary Herald* declaring it "Calgary's favorite mixed drink" in 1974. In 1976, the Mott's corporation, with whose Clamato (a premixed, canned blend of clam and tomato juices) the drink was usually made, promoted it in advertisements in major publications in the United States and Canada. That same year, the Campbell's Soup Company introduced their "Caesar's Choice" to compete with Clamato. While this marketing push had little effect in the United States, it succeeded in establishing the drink throughout Canada, where it has remained popular ever since. In 2009, its fortieth anniversary, there was a concerted, if ultimately fruitless, effort to have Canadian parliament declare it the country's official cocktail.

The question is: What exactly did Chell invent? If he recorded his original recipe, it has not been circulated. There are claims that his drink used juiced whole clams, not Clamato, and that it was spiced with oregano, not Tabasco sauce. These are small hooks on which to hang a claim of invention. The idea of a spiced clam juice–tomato juice–vodka cocktail was not new. Setting aside a long tradition of nonalcoholic drinks involving clam juice and bottled condiments, including Tabasco and Worcestershire sauces and ketchup, and clam juice and tomato juice, and even the Fire Island Clam Juice, a Bloody Mary with clam juice instead of the tomato (attested to in the early 1950s), there is the Smirnoff Smiler, touted by American gossip columnist Walter Winchell in 1953: tomato juice, clam juice, a dash of "Wooooshhhtasheer sauce," and, of course, vodka. "The best pickmeup since Eve winked at Adam," he pronounced it. That one did not quite catch on. More successful was the Clam Digger, heavily promoted by the Mott corporation in 1968 and 1969 as a use for their newly introduced "Clamato." Its ingredients? Vodka and Clamato. While these creations might invalidate any claim to true originality and introduce a good deal of skepticism regarding the story that Chell labored for months on the drink's formula, they cannot undermine his credit for naming, or renaming, the drink and launching it on its journey to becoming a symbol of Canadian identity.

In the twenty-first century, the "Caesar," as it is generally known, has served as a focal point for the creativity of Canada's bartenders and amateur mixologists and in particular for their spicing and garnishing skills. The traditional spices are often supplemented or replaced by everything from horseradish and wasabi to pickle brine to various bottled condiments, while garnishes range from the traditional celery stick and lime wedge to pickled vegetables to boiled shrimp to a gamut of eye-popping stunt garnishes similar to the ones that the Bloody Mary has been subjected to, although often with a nautical cast (think whole lobster tails).

Recipe: Roll or gently shake 45 ml vodka, 120 ml Clamato, 2 dashes Worcestershire sauce, and 2 dashes Tabasco sauce with ice. Strain into a salt-rimmed highball glass full of ice. Add a celery stalk, a lime wedge, and a straw.

See also Bloody Mary.

Haesecker, Fred. "Alberta Drinkers Take Whisky First, Vodka Second." *Calgary Herald*, December 31, 1974.

O'Brian, Jack. "Voice of Broadway" (syndicated column). September 7, 1968.

O'Neil, Darcy S. "Caesar Cocktail." Art of Drink, February 17, 2016, https://www.artofdrink.com/cocktail/caesar-cocktail (accessed February 3, 2021).

Winchell, Walter. "On Broadway" (syndicated column). December 11, 1953.

David Wondrich

The **Bloody Mary**, a spiced mix of vodka and tomato juice, is one of the drinks that, in the mid-twentieth century, turned vodka from an eastern European spirit into a global one. Indeed, it is undoubtedly one of the world's most popular mixed drinks. Even after voluminous research and debate, though, its history remains as murky as the drink itself. As with the Margarita, there are many claimants to its invention, and its origin is a long-vexed question. See Margarita. The evidence, spread between the usual cultural detritus from which cocktail history is constructed—a heterogeneous mass of bartender's guides, nightlife columns, marketing brochures, diaries, pulp novels, liquor-store advertisements, and the like—is both copious and contradictory.

In such cases, it is often best to begin at the end of the process that led to the drink's rise to popularity and work backwards. The first time we find the Bloody Mary's three essential components—vodka, tomato juice, and its distinctive name—united is in Dorothy Kilgallen's Voice of Broadway column, November 1939, where she writes that the "newest hangover cure to entrance the headholders" at New York's 21 Club "is called a 'Bloody Mary'—tomato juice and vodka." Within days of this mention, columnists Lucius Beebe and Walter Winchell would chime in to say the same thing. See BEEBE, LUCIUS. Also in 1939, in a little compendium of drinks he assembled for New York's famous Cotton Club, veteran bartender Charlie Connolly (1879–1969) included a drink he called George Jessel's Pick-Me-Up—vodka, tomato juice, Tabasco sauce, and lemon juice. The mixture of vodka and spiced tomato juice had arrived—but from where?

George Jessel and Fernand Petiot

The most serious claimants to being that point of origin are George Jessel (1898–1981), an American entertainer, and Fernand "The Frog" Petiot (1900–1975), a French bartender who worked at Harry's New York Bar in Paris and then the St. Regis Hotel in New York from 1934 until his retirement in 1966. See HARRY'S NEW YORK BAR. Jessel claimed to have first mixed vodka and tomato juice in Palm Beach, Florida, in 1927, while Petiot claimed that he was the one who invented the "real" Bloody Mary by taking that vodka and tomato juice mixture and adding the spices (others later claimed that he came up with the base combination as well when he was at Harry's). Unfortunately, there is no contemporary evidence for either claim, although Jessel was strongly associated with the vodka–tomato juice combination by 1939, and possibly as early as 1934, while the St. Regis had a vodka bar under Petiot's tutelage in 1936, and the drink, spices and all, was a documented specialty of the hotel since at least 1941. In the absence of further evidence, the evaluation of their claims must rest there.

A Hangover Cure

If, however, we set aside the personalities, the general outline of the drink's early history is much clearer. It begins in the early 1920s, with hungover American drinkers prying open cans of stewed tomatoes, straining out the liquid in them and drinking it for its vitamins (canned tomato juice was then a rare novelty). By the end of the decade, the canned juice had taken off and was widely available. It had made it into the speakeasies, as evidenced by the sign columnist Odd McIntyre saw in one in 1927: "Try tomato juice for that hangover." The next step was inevitable. McIntyre again, from 1929: "A popular cocktail diversion of the moment is composed of equal parts tomato juice and gin. . . . Broadway seizes on any panacea for the day-after throb." It is possible, of course, that the idea of thus fortifying the tomato juice came from Jessel, a denizen of those same Broadway speakeasies, but the sporty crowd that patronized such places could certainly be counted on to discover the idea without outside prompting. Indeed, as the head of the Department of Agriculture's Food and Drug Control Division noted in 1928, while "non alcoholic cordials" such as tomato juice were very popular, "in many cases people add alcohol" to them.

The Tomato Juice Cocktail

But alcohol wasn't the only thing that Americans were adding to their tomato juice. Once it became a popular drink, it fell victim to the American propensity for tinkering, and beginning in 1927 the press made frequent references to a non-alcoholic "Tomato Juice Cocktail" (this may have been the creation of Chicago hotelier and restaurateur Ernest Byfield). Served as an appetizer, it was intended to provide the stimulating kick of a real cocktail without running afoul of the dry law. Recipes varied in detail, but the *Trenton Evening Times* summed up the general consensus in 1928 when it noted that "many like to chill the [tomato] juice and season." The seasonings? "Salt, lemon juice, Tabasco and Worcestershire sauce."

This, too, would soon get alcoholized: *Cocktail Parade*, a 1933 booklet, contains a gin-spiked "Tomato Juice Pick Me Up" with lemon and Worcestershire. From there, it was a short step to using vodka (the mix first appears in print in the 1936 account New York financial advisor Dwight Farnham published of country-house life in Connecticut) and spicing the whole thing à la Tomato Juice Cocktail. In a 1964 interview, Petiot claimed that the spices were his particular contribution to the Bloody Mary and that the tomato juice–vodka combination and the name belonged to Jessel (at the St. Regis, the drink was known as the Red Snapper).

A Popular Drink

By the end of World War II, the Bloody Mary was widely known, if not always accepted: he-man columnist Robert Ruark summed up the opposition in 1949 when he dubbed it a "nauseous blend," perhaps attributable to "dastardly foreign forces." In 1951, Jack Townsend, president of the Bartenders Union of New York, was still lumping it in among the so-called freak drinks. By that time, the members of his union must have served hundreds of thousands of them, since less conservative drinkers had made the drink a sensation. Indeed, along with the Moscow Mule, the Bloody Mary would largely facilitate the stunning growth vodka enjoyed in the American market (and in cocktail bars everywhere) in the 1950s. See MOSCOW MULE.

When, in the late 1960s and early 1970s, the canon of popular drinks was largely renegotiated, sending the old Manhattan and Old-Fashioned and their ilk out to pasture, the Bloody Mary, freak no more, stood at the head of the new order (even if, as *New York Magazine* discovered when it tested the versions local bars were turning out, its actual vodka content was often minimal). At the same time, the usual variations that accrue to such a widely popular formula began to appear. Some have their own names: replace the vodka with tequila and you have the Bloody Maria; replace the tomato juice with Clamato juice and you have the Bloody Caesar; with beef broth, the Bull Shot (invented at Detroit's Caucus Club in the mid-1950s) and the Bloody Bull (with a 50-50 mix of broth and tomato). See BLOODY CAESAR; BULLSHOT; and BLOODY BULL. There are many more. Among the most common additions to the basic formula is horseradish (attested to in the Tomato Juice Cocktail since at least 1934), but the spices attempted are legion. Garnishes originally began with a simple lemon wedge, moved on through the now-iconic celery stalk (used in Tomato Juice Cocktails from 1929 and also attributed to Ernest Byfield) and various pickled vegetables, and now have evolved, if that's the right word, into cantilevered arrangements of skewered food items such as shrimp, bacon, chicken wings, fried chicken, cheeseburgers, and pizza. This is perhaps not a sign of health.

Nonetheless, although the cocktail revolution of the twenty-first century has somewhat dimmed the Bloody Mary's luster, it is still almost universally available and remains one of the few drinks almost every ordinary drinker knows how to make.

Recipe: Roll or gently shake 45 ml vodka, 120 ml tomato juice, 15 ml lemon juice, 3 dashes Tabasco sauce, and 3 dashes Worcestershire sauce with ice. Pour into a highball glass. Garnish at will.

See also TOMATO JUICE and VODKA.

Cocktail Parade. Scarborough, NY: Canapé Parade, 1933.
Farnham, Dwight. *A Place in the Country*.
    New York: Funk & Wagnalls, 1936.
Jessel, George. *The World I Lived In*.
    Chicago: Regnery, 1975.
Kilgallen, Dorothy. "The Voice of Broadway" (syndicated column). November 22, 1939.
McIntyre, O. O. "New York Day-by-Day" (syndicated column). June 22, 1927, and January 19, 1929.
"The Talk of the Town." *New Yorker*, July 18, 1964.
"Tomato Juice Is Very Popular." *Trenton Evening Times*, October 18, 1928.

David Wondrich

Blow My Skull, or **Blow My Skull Off**, is a drink from the early colonial period of Australia's history—or, rather, it is a pair of drinks connected by nothing more than a common name, one that undoubtedly must be parsed, in consideration of their formulae, as a wish.

Blow My Skull I, if we may call it that, was the brainchild of Lieutenant Colonel Thomas Davey (1758–1823), lieutenant governor of Van Diemen's Land (as Tasmania was then known) from 1813 to 1817. According to Edward Abbott (1801–1869), an eccentric Tasmanian landowner, legislator, and *bon viveur* who published the first Australian cookbook in 1864, Davey had a peculiar procedure when he held session. He would have a wattle hut erected out in the bush and sit therein behind a table bearing a barbecued pig. At his right hand would be a cask of his Blow My Skull, a punch containing rum, brandy (or, by another account, whisky), porter, citrus juice, sugar, and water. When a petitioner approached, he would receive a large tumbler of Blow My Skull, and he and Davey would drink, not stopping until their tumblers were empty. "The governor having an impenetrable cranium, and an iron frame," as Abbott recalled, he "could take several goblets of the alcoholic fluid, and walk away as lithe and happy as possible." His petitioners were seldom so fortunate. See PUNCH.

Davey's drink might have been strong, but it was not vicious. The same cannot be said for Blow My Skull II, or Blow My Skull Off. A drink of the first Australian gold rush in the early 1850s, it contained (as one observer claimed) "Cocculus indicus, spirits of wine, Turkey opium, Cayenne pepper, and rum." *Cocculus indicus* and opium being stupefacients, even served diluted with five parts of water, as was the practice, this formula would have earned its name. By the end of the nineteenth century, Australia was fortunately beyond such intoxicants, and Blow My Skull would remain dormant until around 2000, when the influential mixographers Gary Regan and Mardee Haidin Regan came up with their (Almost) Blow My Skull Off, a tribute to the gold miners' drink combining cognac, peach schnapps, and Jägermeister. There, for now, the story rests. See REGAN, GARY.

Recipe (Davey's Blow My Skull): Dissolve 180 g demerara sugar in 500 ml boiling water. Let cool; add 180 ml lime or lemon juice, 500 ml ale or porter, 500 ml dark, aromatic rum, and 250 ml brandy or lightly-aged scotch malt whisky.

See also AUSTRALIA AND NEW ZEALAND.

An Australian Aristologist [Edward Abbott]. *English and Australian Cookery*. London: Sampson, Low, Son & Marston, 1864.

Bannerman, Colin. *Australian Dictionary of Biography*, s.v. "Abbott, Edward." http://adb.anu.edu.au/biography/abbott-edward-12762 (accessed February 3, 2021).

"The Green Ponds Municipality: Original Correspondence" *Cornwall Chronicle* (Launceston, Tasmania), April 1, 1865.

"My Holiday Trip to Victoria and Tasmania." *Australian Town and Country Journal*, April 9, 1870.

Reed, C. Rudston. *What I Heard, Saw and Did at the Australian Gold Fields*. London: T. & W. Boone, 1853.

David Wondrich

The **Blue Blazer**, one of the more spectacular drinks in the bartender's repertoire, is ultimately nothing more than a hot, scotch-whisky Toddy, set ablaze and poured back and forth between mugs in as broad an arc as the maker can manage. See WHISKY, SCOTCH; and TODDY. The drink, strongly associated with Jerry Thomas, enjoyed broad popularity from the 1860s until the beginning of the twentieth century. It was not revived again until the cocktail revolution, when it once again became a popular and highly visual way for bartenders to demonstrate their skill.

The Blue Blazer first appeared in print in 1862, in Thomas's *How to Mix Drinks*, accompanied by an engraving of the author mixing one, evidently based on a photograph Thomas displayed behind his bar. While he apparently claimed, in his lost 1863 second book, that "this drink is solely my own," that might not be strictly true. The American naval officer William Augustus Weaver recalled his fellow sailors during the War of 1812 drinking a "blue blazes." Admittedly, he gives no description of the drink, but it does raise the possibility that Thomas adapted his drink from something he picked up during his years before the mast. (Another possibility is that he learned it in the late 1850s from the bartenders at New York's famous St. Nicholas Hotel, just down the street from his job at the Occidental Hotel, who were famous for lighting their Toddies on fire—unless it was he who taught it to them.)

In 1862, Thomas wrote that "a beholder gazing for the first time upon an experienced artist compounding this beverage would naturally come to the conclusion that it was a nectar for Pluto rather than Bacchus." That devilish display was always the drink's strong suit, but it was not the only rationale advanced during its heyday for setting the whisky ablaze. As one Chicago barman claimed in 1885, the fire "burns out the sting—the fusel oil, you know." See FUSEL OIL. Considering that almost all the scotch whisky sent to the United States at the time was undiluted and unaged, there may be something to that idea. Nonetheless, it is clear that the drink's greatest appeal was the fact that preparing it made the bartender appear, in the words of the *New York Sun* from 1882, like "a necromancer working up something fine to please the heated tastes of his Satanic boss."

By the 1880s, however, the flamboyant style of American bartending was becoming increasingly unfashionable, and the Blue Blazer with it. "This drink is seldom called for over a first-class bar," one Chicago bartender sniffed in 1883. "It is a great country drink, as the 'jays' think more of watching the blaze than they do of the drink." Upon receiving an order for one, Matt Higgins, a cocky young New York mixologist of the new school, would even go so far as to mix it out of the customer's sight. As a standard bar drink, the Blue Blazer did not make it out of the nineteenth century.

Nor did the Blue Blazer benefit much from the revival of interest in classic formulas that came with the repeal of Prohibition. There may be a practical reason for that: the Blue Blazer had a secret, and that secret was lost. In order for the whisky to ignite, it must be either specially preheated (a trick unknown at the time) or quite high in proof—over 54 percent ABV. By the 1930s, the fiery, strong, unaged malts that had burned so well were a thing of the past as far as scotch whisky exports were concerned, with the business moving almost exclusively to blended whiskys that were rarely bottled at more than 43.4 percent ABV. The Blue Blazer did not emerge from hibernation until the twenty-first-century, when Dale DeGroff discovered the pre-heating technique and with it made the drink one of his many showpieces. See DEGROFF, DALE. By 2007, detailed investigation of Thomas and his drinks had uncovered the original (and much easier) high-proof method, and the drink once again entered bartenders' repertoires, where it resides primarily as a late-night spectacle. While cask-strength scotch whisky is often used as the base spirit, one also encounters everything from rye whisky to Jamaican rum to green Chartreuse to baijiu. See CHARTREUSE and BAIJIU.

Recipe: Take a pair of metal pint mugs with handles and flaring rims. Pour 120 ml of boiling water into one of a matched pair of metal pint mugs with handles and flaring rims. Quickly add 150 ml cask-strength scotch whisky to the same mug and ignite with a long match or grill lighter. Pick up both mugs and carefully pour three-quarters of the contents of the flaming one into the other. Now pour three-quarters of that back into the first mug, from a greater distance. Repeat four or five times, increasing the distance each time. Snuff each mug with the bottom of the other and pour into four small glasses, each prepared with 5 ml sugar and a twist of lemon peel. Stir and serve.

See also THOMAS, JEREMIAH P. "JERRY".

"The Barkeeper." *Chicago Tribune*, November 25, 1883.

"Barmaids." *Salt Lake Tribune*, April 30, 1885 (reprinted from *Chicago Tribune*).

Campbell, Charles B. *The American Barkeeper*. San Francisco: Mullin, Mahon, 1867.

"The Kinnickabine Bake." *New York Sun*, November 19, 1882.

Thomas, Jerry. *How to Mix Drinks*. New York: Dick & Fitzgerald, 1862.

Weaver, William Augustus. *Journals of the Ocean and Other Miscellaneous Poems*. New York: George C. Morgan, 1826.

David Wondrich

The **Blue Moon** cocktail, a combination of gin and—well, nobody is quite sure—was one of the fashionable drinks of the 1910s and enjoyed a wide popularity. It entered the public eye as the house drink at Joel's, the legendary theatrical and bohemian restaurant on West Forty-First Street in Manhattan. The drink's startling blue color did nothing to hinder its notoriety. Going back as far as 1911, recipes for the drink abound, with very little agreement between them. The lack of consensus can be attributed to the fact that the original formula, as far as can be determined, was simply equal parts of gin and Crème Yvette, a deep blue American liqueur flavored with berries and violets. This yielded a drink that was fairly potent but sweet and unharmonious. There most common amendments were to add egg white to the drink or, much better, to cut the gin and liqueur with an equal part of dry vermouth. After a brief revival in the 1930s the drink quickly faded away. The revival of Crème Yvette in 2010 (it had suspended production in 1969) has not materially improved the Blue Moon's fortunes.

Recipe: Shake 45 ml ea. London dry gin and Crème Yvette or crème de violette with ice and strain into a chilled cocktail glass.

McIntyre, Odd. "Big Town Stuff." *El Paso Herald*, June 23, 1925, 9.

David Wondrich

Boadas, Miguel (1895–1967), was a Spanish bartender born in Cuba and the safekeeper of the throwing technique, which involves tossing a cocktail from one ice-filled tin to an empty one until the drink is perfectly cold and diluted. He learned bartending in 1908 when his father put him to work at El Floridita in

Ladies may come alone—but you can also bring your wife or sister—understand?

THE MUSIC ROOM OF "JOEL'S" SEATING 1000

The Bohemian life at Joel's, the home of the Blue Moon, as portrayed on one of its postcards, 1911. Wondrich Collection.

Havana, then owned by his cousins. See Floridita. In 1922, he left for Spain and settled in Barcelona, where he opened his own bar, Boadas, in 1933. At this Barcelona institution—still open today—he and his successors, including daughter Maria Dolores and her husband, Pep Maruenda, kept the Cuban throwing technique alive when it had fallen into disuse, paving the way for its recent revival. Boadas was also the founder of the Catalonian Bartender's Club.

"Miguel Boadas." ABE: Órgano oficial de la Asociación de Barmen españoles: 21 (1966). Torns, Miquel. El besavo va anar a Cuba. Girona, Spain: Hermes Comunicacions, 1999.

François Monti

Boadas Cocktails, or simply Boadas, as most people shorten its name, is an institution among Barcelona bars. It is hard to believe that Boadas was even smaller than its current (tiny) incarnation when it first opened its doors in 1933, but what this bar lacks in space it more than makes up in atmosphere and history. Boadas takes its name from Miquel Boadas (1895–1967), its first owner, who had learned his chops as a teenager in Cuba at the Floridita bar, a hub of Catalan immigrants from Lloret de Mar such as Narcís Sala Parera, the bar's founder, and Constantí Ribalaigua. See Boadas, Miguel; Floridita; and Ribalaigua y Vert, Constante.

Unlike them, Miquel Boadas moved back to Spain, where he brought a flair for the Cuban technique of throwing or tossing a drink, which still can be seen in use today at many of the city's other bars, and a knack for attracting visiting artists, writers, and musicians, such as Josephine Baker and Joan Miró. See tossing.

After a short stint behind the stick at the trendy spots of the era, such as Maison Dorée, Canaletes, and Nuria in Las Ramblas, Miquel opened Boadas in 1933. The press at the time describes the place as "quaint and elegant," and indeed it wouldn't be much more than a long corridor with a bar attached to it until after the end of Spain's civil war, when it would gain a few precious meters and become the triangle it is now.

Miquel Boadas was also an organizer, and he was the first president of el Club del barman, a Spanish bartending association that is now affiliated to IBA. At his death, his daughter Maria Dolors (1935–2017), a fine, skilled bartender in her own right, took over the bar. Maria Dolors held firmly the helm of Boadas until shortly before her death, always keeping her father's eye for detail and warm hospitality. Her legacy continues in the work of today's owner and manager Jerónimo Vaquero (who started as an apprentice in 1970) and that of his team. Like Miquel Boadas, they throw their drinks, shun jiggers, and will make one feel in a different universe from Barcelona's most crowded street, just steps away: Boadas is the complete opposite of a tourist trap.

[Catalan spelling has been used throughout this entry.]

"Boadas cocktail." Boadas Cocktails website. http://boadascocktails.com/en/history/ (accessed March, 10, 2017).

Boadas, María Dolors. *Los cóctels del Boadas Cocktail Bar.* Barcelona: Muchnik, 1990.

"Gacetillas." *La vanguardia*, August 23, 1933.

Mar Calpena

Bobby Burns, a cocktail made with scotch whisky and sweet vermouth, is a close cousin to the Rob Roy, with Bénédictine taking the place of the bitters. See VERMOUTH; ROB ROY; and BÉNÉDICTINE. It first appears in Hugo Ensslin's 1916 *Recipes for Mixed Drinks*. See ENSSLIN, HUGO RICHARD; and WHISKY, SCOTCH.

Boilermaker is the North American name for a glass of beer accompanied by, or sometimes invaded by, a shot of whisky. The Boilermaker seems too simple and straightforward—too elemental—to have a history, to have been introduced and tested and approved and propagated in the manner of normal cocktails. And yet, for all its old-as-the-hills airs, it is a relative latecomer to American drinking. While the Scots and the Irish had no qualms about washing their "ball" of whisky down with a mug of beer or ale, American drinkers traditionally used iced water for that function, and indeed thought beer to be an outlandish substitute. When, for example, one New Englander was visiting Scotland in 1846 and had, at one gentleman's house, "both whisky and beer set before [him]," he found it remarkable—and not just because the gentleman was a clergyman. Even fifty years later the *New York Herald* could publish a story about a man who went into a saloon and ordered "beer n' whisky," side by side, and the consternation such an order caused in the bartender and the regulars. "I've heard of queer drinks in my time," one of the latter observes.

But American drinking habits were changing, and as the German and central European immigrants who came to America in such numbers assimilated the idea of drinking (German) beer and (Irish/American) whisky together became less outlandish.

Sometimes the two were even mixed, a concoction at first known by various names—Bohemian Cocktail (1896), Rough Rider Cocktail (1904), and Puddler's Cocktail (1915; although sometimes the last one, a Pittsburgh favorite, was unmixed). By the 1950s, it had become a Depth Bomb or Depth Charge, with the shot glass dropped into the beer. (This would later give rise to a whole "bomb" class of college-student drinks, such as the Irish Car Bomb, with a mixed shot of Irish whisky and Irish cream liqueur dropped in a pint of Guinness Stout, and the "Jägerbomb," with Jägermeister and Red Bull energy drink.)

It wasn't until the 1930s that the unmixed combination got a name that stuck. "Boilermaker and His Helper" was the original version, a boilermaker being a skilled sort of industrial metalworker who was often accompanied by extra muscle. This was colorful enough to catch on and long enough to require abbreviation. By the 1940s it was simply "Boilermaker," although the fact that in 1948 showman-turned-columnist Billy Rose still had to explain to his readers that the name referred to "straight rye with a beer chaser" indicates that it was not yet in universal use.

As the American art of the cocktail went into eclipse in the 1950s and 1960s, the Boilermaker grew in popularity, if not in elegance. It was still primarily a working-class drink, although it also colonized bohemia (Bob Dylan, for instance, recalled drinking "shooters of Wild Turkey and iced Schlitz" between sets back in his early Greenwich Village days).

As the modern cocktail revolution has evolved, its excesses have driven some drinkers back to the old Boilermaker, only now it comes as a menu item, with spirits and beers paired in various and creative ways. See COCKTAIL RENAISSANCE. Fortunately, some of those still involve a shot of rye and a glass of lager beer.

See also HERRENGEDECK and KOPSTOOT.

"A False Alarm." *New York Herald*, April 5, 1896, 4.

Dylan, Bob. *Chronicles: Volume 1.* New York: Simon & Schuster, 2004.

"Glasgow: From Mr. Schouler's Letters." *Portland (ME) Advertiser*, October 20, 1846.

"Locals Pray for Old Soupbone." *Brooklyn Eagle*, April 17, 1938.

"Pitching Horseshoes with Billy Rose." *Utica (NY) Observer*, January 26, 1948.

Spring, William A. "This and That," *Yonkers (NY) Herald-Statesman*, December 12, 1933.

David Wondrich

boisé is a legal additive utilized in aged spirit production which can intensify or mimic the character of barrel aging; it is made by boiling down oak chips in water into a thick, woody brown liquid that can be then mixed with eau-de-vie and liquid sugar. As a traditional and common component of many brandies, it is legally controlled and defined by French law for use in all French brandies. Though a "liquid oak extract" called boisé is reported as having been "invented" (undoubtedly patented) by Antoine Descoffre in 1902 in the Poitou-Charentes (Cognac) region, oak maturation is such an integral part of brandy manufacture that it is difficult to fix starting lines for boisé and similar treatments.

Brandy is by French law a grape-based spirit that has been aged and matured in oak barrels. See ÉLEVAGE and MATURATION. In the case of cognac, Armagnac, and calvados the shape, size, origin, and manufacture of those barrels is at least partly defined by law, as is the maturation of each. See BARREL. But time is money. Boisé exists to enhance brandy aroma and flavor and to accelerate the aging process. Unsurprisingly, discussion around boisé is charged, as some consider it useful and even essential and others believe it is somehow dishonest.

One cognac house has been accused of "tampering" with their cognac by soaking oak chips in brandy in a stainless steel vat instead of extracting oak chips with a water solution. This is by no means uncommon, but the rules since 1921 (and re-established in 1990) are such that a gentle water extraction is legal while a more robust alcohol or brandy extraction is not. Most use hot or nearly boiling water; some use an ambient temperature. The defendants have maintained that an alcohol or brandy extraction of oak chips is historical; it is also allowed by EU rules. The matter is not settled. See OAK CHIPS.

But the use of boisé remains widespread, while candor is not. Consider that Cognac and other brandies require amelioration with water: these "petits eaux" are sometimes themselves aged in barrel, extracting oak character, albeit gently. It is no great leap to allowing oak pieces to be in the barrel too; records suggest such practices go back more than a century and a half. Like other such activities, secrecy has given the air of deceit to the use of "oak additives." But the aromas are hardly foul; the characteristics of vanilla, caramel, butterscotch, clove, allspice, and all the other myriad smells of traditional oak aging can be mirrored by boisé.

The counterargument is that boisé can only duplicate raw oak aromas and is unable to offer the oxidative process that exemplifies oak aging. So far, data suggest only partial support for this view: true *rancio* is not wholly duplicated by boisé, but many of its constituent elements are. See RANCIO.

Wood chips, inner staves (new staves inside older barrels), and wood powder are commonly used in wine production in the New and Old Worlds. Likewise, such tools have been in the brandy maker's kit bag for as long as records have been kept and likely before. According to some, wood chips are more recent innovations (though the 1921 regulations speak directly to their use or misuse), while inner staves date back to the mid-nineteenth century and "are quite mastered." These are toasted to the same specifications as the barrel staves themselves, and serve to "refresh" any used and depleted barrel.

Today, many micro-distillers use wood infusions created by pressure-cooking wood chips in spirit; this is fairly described by traditional producers as heavy-handed and creates a new kind of boisé of excess bitterness and imbalance.

See also BRANDY and COGNAC.

Faith, Nicholas. *Cognac: The Story of the World's Greatest Brandy*. Oxford: Infinite Ideas, 2013.
"The State-of-the-Art Estate Winery." *Vinovation*, http://www.vinovation.com/equipment.htm (accessed April 18, 2016).

Doug Frost

Bols, the leading Dutch spirits company, is known for its genevers and for its wide range of liqueurs. Based in Amsterdam, it can trace its documented history there at least back to 1640, when Pieter Jacobz Bulsius was registered as arriving in the city. He was the son of a family named Bulsius, Bultius, or Bulsies who had fled political unrest in their home in what was then the Netherlands region of northern Flanders (modern-day Belgium) to resettle near Cologne, Germany. (The Bols firm publicize the date "1575" and "Lucas Bols," but the only known evidence from 1575 is a request to the Cologne Protestant synod by a local congregation of Belgian refugees, which probably included a widow named Bulsius/Bultius/Bulsies, to clarify if brewing and distilling from grain was allowed by religious law.)

Pieter simplified his name to "Bols" and, after apprenticing with a renowned distiller, built a prosperous company. The first known Lucas Bols was born in Amsterdam in 1652. The company fell into a decline after the family lost control in the early 1800s. The firm was sold to financier Gabriel van 't Wout in 1813, who rejuvenated it by focusing on exports and concentrating on the production of quality liqueurs instead of just the jenever and simpler "alcoholic waters" it had begun with. Production moved out of Amsterdam in 1964 and has since been almost entirely outsourced. Although the Bols name is on a wide range of spirits such as vodka, gin, and brandy, the majority of its income derives from Bols-range liqueurs. Most Bols-brand liqueurs are produced either in the Netherlands or (in a similar bottle and label but with a significantly different liquid, aroma, and flavor) under license by Brown-Forman in the United States. In 2008, the company, Dutch-owned once more after years of foreign ownership, reinvigorated the jenever category with its launch of Bols Genever, a rich genever in the classic style aimed at craft cocktail bars.

See also GENEVER.

Bols heritage research findings by the Fluitschip historical research bureau, www.fluitschip.nl (accessed April 16, 2021).
Bols Prospectus for IPO, February 2015. http://www.lucasbols.com/investors/ipo (accessed April 16, 2021).

Philip Duff

bonificateur is a cognac term used liberally for material used as an addition in blending, typically small in volume and powerful in character, to improve overall quality. In the most traditional sense bonificateur may consist of reserved, extended age, exemplar spirits that are added in small amounts to add depth and dimension to the final spirit. In more liberal applications of the word this can include additives such as dosage, house-made or purchased

boisé and rancio, coloring, or flavoring agents. Traditional methods include creating concentrated teas or extracts (for example from dried fruit or vanilla beans) to blend into spirits to improve smoothness and flavor or soften character.

See also BOISÉ and RANCIO.

Dialogue with Hubert Germain-Robin, n.d.
Heath, B. Henry. *Source Book of Flavors*. New York: Van Nostrand Reinhold, 1981.

Maggie Campbell

Booker Noe II, Frederick (1929–2004), known universally as "Booker," was among an extraordinary post–World War II generation of visionary distillers including Jimmy Russell of Wild Turkey, Elmer T. Lee of George T. Stagg (now Buffalo Trace), Parker Beam of Heaven Hill, and Jim Rutledge of Four Roses. Of this whisky-maker pantheon, none was larger, in every way, than Jim Beam's grandson, Booker Noe, with his six feet four (193 cm) frame and personality to match.

Born in Springfield, Kentucky, just outside of Bardstown, during the height of Prohibition, Booker went on to football stardom at the University of Kentucky and then became assistant distiller to T. Jeremiah Beam in 1950. After mastering every aspect of distilling, he was named Jim Beam's master distiller in 1965, becoming the sixth generation of Beam family members to guide the legendary Kentucky distillery. Known for his fiercely candid wit as well as his unbridled love of fishing, playing "jug bluegrass" with his musician friends, and smoking hams in his backyard smokehouse in Bardstown, Noe turned legendary by the 1980s. He often described his illustrious grandfather as a "stuffed shirt" due to Jim Beam's peculiar habit of going fishing in a white shirt and tie.

Noe's most significant contribution to the American whisky historical record was certainly the creation of Booker's Bourbon. First released in 1988, Booker's Bourbon was the initial American whisky left uncut (not diluted with water) and unfiltered. "Straight from the barrel," Noe would say, "the way bourbon used to be." It was doused with a splash of branch water, and Noe described his personal bourbon as "Kentucky tea." Booker's Bourbon helped to unleash the small-batch bourbon revolution.

See also JIM BEAM.

Prial, Frank J. "F. Booker Noe II, 74, Master Bourbon Distiller." *New York Times*, February 27, 2004.

F. Paul Pacult

boomerang is a drink sent by the bartender at one bar to the bartender at another via customer courier. The drink is typically served in a glass covered in cling wrap, and often placed in a to-go food container for the sake of stealth. This clandestine and largely illegal practice has probably existed for some time but gained notoriety in the late 2000s thanks to the cocktail community in New York City's East Village. The term most likely derived from the idea that a drink sent to a friend working at the same time would most certainly be returned in some fashion.

Jeffrey Morgenthaler

Boothby, William T. "Cocktail Bill" (1862–1930), was a man of many talents: minstrel, tailor, realtor, streetcar conductor, San Francisco assemblyman. But he was best remembered as San Francisco's premier bar man. Boothby's Bay Area bartending career began across the bay at Byron Hot Springs Hotel, thirty miles southeast of Oakland, where he catered to the rich and famous in1889. After a short stay in 1890 at the Silver Palace on Geary Street in San Francisco, he became the head barkeeper at the prestigious Hotel Rafael Club House in Marin County.

During employment at these three locations, Boothby began keeping notes of cocktail recipes, valuable secrets for liquor dealers, and tips to members of the trade with the thought of publishing a bartending guide. His first publication, *Cocktail Boothby's American Bar-Tender*, came out in 1891, priced at 50 cents. (Only two known copies still exist, both in the California Historical Society.)

After serving a one-year term as a California State assemblyman in 1894–1895, Boothby opened the Parker House on Union Square. Soon thereafter, he was elected president of the Unity Club, a protection group for the "white apron club." He reprinted his book twice in 1900 with two separate editions. After the 1906 San Francisco earthquake and fire destroyed most of his books, and the printing plates were destroyed in the Call Building on Market Street. He published a 1908 edition, followed a few years later by a second "1908" edition; both were titled *The World's Drinks and How to Mix Them* and are now known as The "Honorable" William "Cocktail Bill" Boothby. His employment as a bartender continued at the Fairmont Hotel, Pacific Buffet, and Palace Hotel before he closed out his career serving soft drinks during Prohibition at the Olympic Club and Far Western Travelers Club—a tragic end for San Francisco's premier bartender. Boothby died in August 1930 and was buried at Greenlawn Memorial Park in Colma. His funeral was attended by bartenders from throughout the country.

Boothby, William T. *"Cocktail Bill" Boothby's World Drinks and How to Prepare Them*. San Francisco: Boothby's World Drinks, 1930.

Boothby, William T. *Cocktail Boothby's American Bar-Tender*. ed. David Burkhart. 1891; repr., San Francisco: Anchor Distilling, 2009.

Boothby, William T. *Cocktail Boothby's American Bar-Tender*. San Francisco: Pacific News, 1900.

Boothby, William T. *The World's Drinks and How to Mix Them*, 2nd ed. San Francisco: Pacific Buffet, 1908.

Boothby Collection, California Historical Society San Francisco.

John C. Burton

Booth's lays claim to the oldest origin story of all major gin brands. F. J. Kelly, testifying on behalf of the Booth's distillery before the Royal Commission on Whiskey and Other Potable Spirits in 1908 said, "We take our date from 1740." Even though a Booth family member wouldn't be listed as a distiller in London until Philip Booth and John Mootham established the Cow Cross Distillery in Clerkenwell in 1772, the Booth family included established brewers, victuallers, and coopers in London in the decades prior, all professions that had close ties to the eighteenth-century gin scene. By 1792, in an early example of vertical integration, the Booths had taken a rare step among gin rectifiers and added a malt distillery to their portfolio and were the ninth-largest producers of raw grain spirit in the country.

By the early nineteenth century Booth & Co. was the largest gin distillery in London. As head of the immensely successful company, Sir Felix Booth, Philip's youngest son, would finance Captain John Ross's 1829 arctic expedition, becoming the only gin magnate to have several places named after him, including the Gulf of Boothia and Cape Felix in Nunavut, Canada. Popularized fictions of Ross's voyage imagined the captain pouring "himself a double portion of Booth's best cordial gin."

Over the years the product line changed along with changing tastes. It was known as Booth's English Gin by 1801; while Booth's Old Tom was popular in the mid-nineteenth century, and Booth's Finest Old Dry Gin was widely sold in the early twentieth century. Booth's Finest was marketed as "the only matured gin" and described as "bonded for many years." Changing fashions in the 1940s and 1950s led Booth's to release their "crystal clear" High and Dry Gin, "the driest gin of all."

Once one of the world's best known gins, the Booth brand fell in esteem in the twentieth century. The Booth family was no longer associated with the gin bearing its name, and in 1937 Booth's Distilleries was acquired by the Distillers Company Ltd. See DISTILLERS COMPANY LTD (DCL). The distillery on Cow Cross was badly damaged in World War II, and although it was rebuilt shortly thereafter and christened the Red Lion Distillery in honor of the Booth family crest, operations subsequently moved, and it was demolished in the 1990s.

Currently owned by Diageo, the brand is now distilled only at their Plainfield, Illinois, plant.

See also GIN and OLD TOM GIN.

"Clerkenwell Road." In Survey of London, vol. 46, South and East Clerkenwell, ed. Philip Temple, 385–406. London: London County Council, 2008.
The House of Commons. Accounts Relating to Distillation in England, Scotland and Ireland: No 1– to No. 11. 1822.
Huish, Robert. The Last Voyage of Capt. Sir John Ross, R.N. Knt. to the Arctic Regions. London: John Saunders. 1835.
"Revenue Statement." London Evening Mail, September 12, 1792, 1.

Aaron Knoll

Bortolo Nardini (Ditta Bortolo Nardini Spa, to give it its full corporate name) is Italy's first grappa house, founded in 1779 on the banks of the Brenta River in Bassano in the northern Veneto region. Bortolo Nardini (1739–1812) was previously a distiller in his home town of Segonzano, in Trentino. Passing through Bassano on business, he was taken with the town and decided to settle there, purchasing the Osteria del Ponte beneath the town's central bridge. There he created and sold an *acquavite di vinaccia*, or pomace spirit—what is today known as grappa. See GRAPPA. While grappa had been made in Italy previously, Nardini was the first to regularize its production and market it as a quality spirit, rather than as a poor farmer's attempt to squeeze every drop of alcohol from his harvest. The primacy of his effort is reflected in the town's name: it is now called Bassano del Grappa.

The Nardini family continued to help grappa to innovate, adopting steam (indirect) distillation in 1860, introducing double distillation in 1915, and by the 1960s implementing vacuum distillation in order to improve the character of this once rustic spirit. In the postwar years, the firm was also a pioneer in barrel-aging grappas. It built a new distillery just outside of town in 1964 (now adorned with a pair of futuristic giant blue glass bubble pods that hold a laboratory and a meeting room), and in 1991 it acquired and modernized the Monastier distillery in Treviso, with six times the capacity of the Bassano one. Today the seventh generation of the family continues to own and run the company, which makes a number of amari, liqueurs, and other spirits, although 95 percent of its production continues to be grappa, most of it unaged.

See also ITALY and POMACE BRANDY.

Beyrendt, Axel, and Bibiana Beyrendt. Grappa: A Guide to the Best. New York: Abbeville, 2000.
"Ditta Bolo. Nardini SPA." Camera di Commercio, Industria, Agricoltura e Artigianato. https://www.unioncamere.gov.it/impresa/P48A0C0S738I2016/ditta-bortolo-nardini-spa.htm (accessed March 25, 2021).

Doug Frost

Boston shaker is the two-part cocktail mixing tool, consisting of a mixing glass and mixing tin, favored by most bartenders. See also COCKTAIL SHAKER; MIXING GLASS; and MIXING TIN.

botanical is the generic term used to describe the plants or their parts (including fruits, leaves, flowers, roots, seeds, and barks) or other organic substances that are used to flavor spirits. Historically, botanicals were used for their curative properties, as well as to act as adjunct flavorings to improve the taste of medicinal distillates. Medieval monasteries cultivated extensive gardens of medicinal plants, and monks drew heavily on them in making early European spirits. See APERITIF AND DIGESTIVE.

Botanicals contain complex, volatile organic chemical compounds in the form of concentrated hydrophobic liquids, or "essential oils," as they are known. Essential oils are stored in the oil cells, glands, or vessels of the plant, where they act as powerful attractors of insects, to ensure pollination, or as chemical defenses to stop the plant being eaten by a predator, or as warning signals to other plants that there is a predator about. These essential oils also contain the plant's aromas and flavors.

Growing regions and the climate and soil conditions that come with them play a large part in the sensory profile of an essential oil. Since photosynthesis is responsible for the formation of the hydrocarbons that make up the oils, a change in hours or intensity of sunlight can create a change in the balance of their component compounds. The soil the plant grows in yields the other elements that go into the oils, such as sulfur and nitrogen. A change in terroir can make the same botanical—juniper berries, for example—much more or much less aromatic.

Essential oils are commonly extracted via steam distillation, cold pressing, and solvent extraction or maceration, where they are steeped in high-proof alcohol. Essential oils are not normally miscible in water; the ethanol acts as the solvent and hence carrier of flavor. Generally, spirit producers use steam distillation, cold or hot steeping (macerating), or a combination thereof, to extract the essential oils and chemically attach them to ethanol to form a flavored spirit. However, any spirit that comes into contact with a natural substance uses organic chemical compounds to some degree, whether that be the pinene flavors from juniper berries or vanillin flavors produced by oak casks.

See also GIN; PHENOLS; and TERPENES.

Williams, David G. *Chemistry of essential oils,* 2nd ed. Weymouth, UK: Micelle, 2008.

Sean Harrison

bottled cocktails are ready-to-drink alcoholic beverages that have been packaged for later consumption, originally in bottles, and later also in cans. Since at least the late eighteenth century, punches have been bottled for later enjoyment. See PUNCH. The 1827 book *Oxford Night Caps* collects several recipes that were well known at the university, including clarified milk punches to be bottled for later use; indeed, the status of bottles Milk Punch was such in Britain that in the 1840s one Mr. Hudson of Chichester and London was appointed manufacturer of Milk Punch to the queen. See MILK PUNCH and MIXOGRAPHY. The Cock-Tail itself, having nothing perishable in its makeup, proved particularly amenable to bottling, and bottled Cock-Tail was sold by most high-end bars in the United States; Jerry Thomas's 1862 cocktail manual lists several large-gauge recipes for bottling, most notably "Recipe no. 106, Bottle Cocktail." See COCK-TAIL and THOMAS, JEREMIAH P. "JERRY".

It is not until the 1890s, however, that the modern era of commercially available, premixed and pre-diluted cocktails gets going. In 1892 the Heublein Hotel of Hartford, Connecticut, took advantage of advances in packaging technology to launch its Club Cocktail line of bottled cocktails; as the G. F. Heublein Co., they enjoyed large sales nationwide that lasted through the 1980s (and went on to spearhead the vodka revolution in America after their purchase of the Smirnoff brand). See SMIRNOFF. Liquor companies have sought to capitalize on their well-known brands by marketing bottled versions of popular drinks, most notably the Sazerac Cocktail in the United States and Campari Soda in Italy, launched in its signature conical bottle in 1932. See CAMPARI and SAZERAC COCKTAIL.

The use of soda cans starting in the 1930s increased the availability and variety of ready-to-drink highballs, most especially canned Bourbon and Cola and canned Gin and Tonic. See GIN AND TONIC and HIGHBALL. Later non-spirits trends, such as the wine cooler fad of the 1980s or the flavored-malt-liquor blip of the 1990s are debatable as proper bottled cocktails, but they certainly helped to keep ready-to-drink concoctions in front of consumers. A remaining technical hurdle is the inclusion of citrus juice in these beverages, as the fruit solids will separate and oxidize. Refined citric acid is used as a more stable substitute, but without achieving the citrus flavor of a freshly made drink. The twenty-first-century cocktail renaissance has brought an even wider variety of premixed cocktails to the market, particularly once the Covid-19 pandemic of 2020–2021 drove bars to a takeout-only model. See COCKTAIL RENAISSANCE. Some are new flavors of highballs, such as the Moscow Mule, while others return to premixed, pre-diluted versions of spirit-forward cocktails such as the Manhattan or the Negroni, constituting a growing panoply of store-bought cocktails furnished by liquor companies, bars, bartenders, and celebrities alike. See MANHATTAN, MOSCOW MULE, and NEGRONI.

"Milk Punch Royal" (advertisement). *Liverpool Standard*, October 9, 1840, 1.

Oxford Night Caps. Oxford: 1827.

House of Heublein: An American Institution. Hartford, CT: G. F. Heublein & Bro., n.d. [ca. 1960].

Thomas, Jerry. *How to Mix Drinks*. New York: Dick & Fitzgerald, 1862.

David Moo

bottled in bond is a term that indicates a spirit (typically whisky) meets certain US legal requirements, originally established by the Bottled-in-Bond Act of 1897, which protected consumers against inferior and adulterated products made by rectifiers and other purveyors. Although the legislation has since undergone some revisions, it still guarantees that any spirit labeled as "bottled in bond" is made up of a single type of liquor, produced in a single distilling season by a single distiller, aged in wood for at least four years, and unadulterated except for the addition of pure water to lower the alcohol volume to the required bottling strength of 100 proof.

See also BOTTLES, LABELING, AND PACKAGING.

US National Archives and Records Administration. *Code of Federal Regulations*, Title 27. Alcohol, Tobacco Products and Firearms. 2015.

David Mahoney

bottles, labeling, and packaging are so much a part of the spirits industry today, forming an integral part of many a product's identity, that it is difficult to imagine a time when they were an afterthought; something almost entirely unconnected to the distiller's business. Yet until the second half of the nineteenth century, distillers in most countries sold their products wholesale, by the barrel or large earthenware jar (such as the 10–12 liter *pisquitos* in which pisco was shipped from Peru to San Francisco). See BARREL and PISCO. If they sold smaller quantities—in Britain, this was essentially forbidden—it was to the local market, to neighbors who usually supplied their own bottles or jugs or used returnable ones from the distillery. The distillery's bulk-package customers, who included everything from rectifiers (who would blend and flavor and otherwise monkey with the product), to wine and spirits merchants, saloons and restaurants, and pharmacies, groceries, and department stores, would fill and label their own bottles, either for use behind the bar or for sale over the counter. See RECTIFIER.

There were of course exceptions to this general process. Many Dutch genever distillers and blenders exported their product in square-shouldered "case bottles," so named because they could be packed together tightly in a case with no wasted space. These often had the distiller's monogram or logo molded into them. Japanese shochu distillers sold their product in returnable earthenware *tokkuri* jars, emblazoned with the distillery's name in large characters. Beginning in the 1690s, London apothecary Richard Stoughton sold and shipped his Magnum Elixir Stomachicum, the progenitor of all modern bitters, in uniform, sealed bottles. See GENEVER; SHOCHU; and STOUGHTON'S BITTERS. For the rest, though, bottles—the spirit's last-mile container—were the customer's concern.

From the thirteenth-century revival of the ancient art of glassblowing to the mid-nineteenth century, European spirits bottles came in a few traditional shapes, sized approximately (as any free-blown bottle must be) to one of the measures used in the place they were made or destined for. Such shapes include "shaft and cylinder," with a long neck on a cylindrical body (some have a long shaft on a short body, others the reverse); "shaft and globe" (a long neck on a globular body with a flattened bottom), and "onion" (the same but with the globe's bottom further flattened). Other than the case bottles, always associated with gin, the broad-shouldered "flowerpot" bottle preferred for calvados, and the "chestnut" for Armagnac (essentially an onion with flattened sides), most European and American bottle shapes were not closely associated with particular spirits. In Asia, earthenware or porcelain containers were preferred, and these too had traditional shapes. In China, for example, baijiu usually came in small, un-necked cylinders with paper seals over the closures.

Since it was retailers who generally bottled spirits, it was also retailers who labeled or otherwise marked the bottles, unless they left that to their customers. Merchants and wealthy customers with large cellars could have glass seals with their monograms or marks molded into them attached to the bottles as they were being made. See MARK. Paint and handwritten or printed paper labels were also used. By the early nineteenth century, preprinted labels were increasingly common. Often these had the merchant's name or mark, but otherwise the information they conveyed was generic, identifying only the type of spirit in the bottle (e.g., "French Brandy," or "Old Monongahela Whisky"). Since bottle capacity and proof were variable, that information was not included. As the century unfolded, however, the name of the distiller became an increasingly common addition, at least for top-shelf goods. Some distillers even supplied labels with their barrels.

The mid-nineteenth century brought advances in bottle-molding, label-printing, and branding, all of which worked together to completely transform the way spirits presented themselves. Bottles could be made in proprietary shapes and, with the introduction of chromolithography, bright, multicolor labels printed cheaply. Rectifiers, merchants, and even distillers were quick to take advantage. Why not emboss a big American eagle on the bottle that contained American peach brandy, or even shape the whole thing like George Washington's head? And why bottle your blend of various scotch whiskies as, say, "Thomas's Old Scotch Whisky" with a picture of your shop on the label when you could slap a bright, three-color picture of a Highland glen on the bottle and call it "Thomas's Dew of Glen Dochart"? By the 1870s, such a name could be trademarked, as could a unique bottle design.

The last decades of the nineteenth century saw a proliferation of distillery brands, as improved transportation, cheaper bottles, and trademarking made such things worthwhile. Just as some distillers took traditional formulae and made them proprietary, some laid claim to traditional bottle shapes: thus, for example, Bénédictine staked a claim in the flowerpot bottle and Cointreau in the square one. See BÉNÉDICTINE and COINTREAU. Others, such as the French aperitif Suze, created entirely new and distinctive bottles (its bottle was trademarked in 1913). See SUZE. Eventually, the taste for novelty subsided somewhat, and considerations of economic efficiency reasserted themselves. The introduction of fully automated bottle making helped that process, with machines such as the one patented in 1903 by Michael Owens of Toledo, Ohio (1859–1923), which could churn out 102,000 bottles a day, revolutionizing the trade. Bottles were now, for the first time, cheap, particularly if one avoided doing anything fancy with them. At the same time, consumer protection laws such as the American Pure Food and Drug Act (1906) placed an effective restraint on what one could claim on a label. In some countries, Prohibitionist sentiment came to tightly constrain trade dress, mandating plain labels and a rigid adherence to the truth (see, for example, Iceland's Brennvin, an aquavit that is labeled in the severest black by government mandate). See AQUAVIT.

Fanciful packaging had a comeback in the 1960s, with the brightly painted figural holiday gift decanter, which could take on any shape imaginable—a game fish, a distillery, Elvis Presley—and, arguably, saved the American bourbon industry at its time of greatest crisis. See WHISKY, BOURBON.

Today, most spirits are packaged in either standard, off-the-rack bottles (so to speak) or proprietary bottles that are slight variations of them (the smooth, cylindrical, high-shouldered Absolut vodka bottle, for example, or the Tanqueray gin bottle, which is plain enough save for the flange running around its shoulder, designed to make it resemble a cocktail shaker). Bottles that are too unusual can be difficult to ship and challenging for bartenders to fit in their bars. Prestige brands will often encase the basic bottle in a lavishly printed cardboard shipping canister, or even a wooden box. This protects the bottle but also takes up more shelf space in a store, making the brand more visible, and gives the marketing department a greater canvas upon which to practice its art. The more expensive the brand, the more expensive the bottle it goes into and the more lavish the surrounding packaging (although there are exceptions).

Most countries today adopt a set of standard metric bottle sizes: 50 ml, 200 ml, 350 ml (or 375 ml, in countries where the 750-ml bottle is in use), 500 ml, 700 ml (or 750 ml), 1 liter, 1.75 liters, 3 liters. Labels are also to a degree internationalized, with, at minimum, information such as the volume of the container, the proof of its contents, and the address of its producer being almost universally required by law, and bar codes by commerce. Some countries require a good deal more than that, including distillery numbers, notes on ingredients, health warnings, and the like.

The twenty-first century has seen a rise in interest in sustainable packaging. Glass is recyclable, but it is very heavy to ship. The largest bottles have been replaced in some countries by bag-in-box packages, while in parts of Asia and Africa the smaller sizes are often replaced by plastic sachets. In many places, plastic bottles are common, but not for premium spirits, whose marketing tends to rely on appealing to perceptions of status. There is, however, a good deal of experimentation, including things such as the ecoSPIRITS system being tested in parts of Asia, where spirits are delivered to bars in returnable and reusable 4.5-liter mini-totes, from which bottles are refilled for service. As history has taught us, such a system can be very effective.

See also CLOSURES and SPIRITS TRADE, HISTORY OF.

Albert Pick & Co. *General Catalog Enlightening the Hotel, Restaurant and Saloon World*. Chicago: Albert Pick, 1913.

Hamilton, Carl. *Absolut: Biography of a Bottle*. New York: Texere, 2000.

Liang, Alice. "Eco-Friendly Distribution Technology ecoSPIRITS Introduced in Asia." *The Drinks Business*, June 29, 2020. https://www.thedrinksbusiness.com/2020/06/eco-friendly-distribution-technology-ecospirits-introduced-in-asia/ (accessed April 24, 2021).

Moss, Robert F. "The Origins of the Package Store." Robert F. Moss website, June 4, 2016. https://www.robertfmoss.com/features/The-Origins-of-the-Package-Store (accessed April 24, 2021).

van den Bossche, Willy. *Antique Glass Bottles*. Woodbridge, UK: Antique Collectors' Club, 2001.

David Wondrich

boukha is a fig brandy made in Tunisia, where it is typically associated with the Jewish community. See also BRANDY, FIG AND DATE, and NORTH AFRICA.

bouquet describes aromas that develop as wine ages in the bottle, although identical aromas can develop as wine ages in any container, including a barrel. The thousands of such possible aromas are not "primary;"; that is, they are not derived from the grape character, condition, and identity. Rather, they result from interactions between the wine's constituent elements and other compounds and molecules, including oxygen. Spirits connoisseurs use the term to describe the creation of complex aromas during and after a spirit's aging, particularly with reference to cognacs and other fine brandies.

See also AROMA.

Peycaud, Emile. *The Taste of Wine: The Art and Science of Wine Appreciation*. San Francisco: Wine Appreciation Guild, 1997.

Robinson, Jancis. *How to Taste: A Guide to Enjoying Wine*. New York: Simon & Schuster, 2008.

Doug Frost

Bourbon Street drinks are a loose, louche, and deceptively strong family of mixtures typically sold on Bourbon Street in New Orleans. Aptly named (though for the French royal lineage, not the whisky), Bourbon Street is one of the world's legendary drinking thoroughfares. The ten-block stem that stretches from Canal Street to St. Philip Street (the location of Lafitte's Blacksmith Shop Bar, said to be the oldest structure housing a tavern in America) has been the site of countless first drinks, no doubt a few last ones, and an incalculable number of tipples in between. The street is almost as awash in alcoholic folklore as it is actual in booze—a reputation that had its start in the 1917 destruction of New Orleans's notorious Storyville red-light district, which pushed the business of vice into the French Quarter. For better and worse, the indulgences of Bourbon Street defined and sold the identity and allure of the Crescent City to the world for generations.

Individual cocktails have long played their part in Bourbon Street's legend. It may not be true, despite the insistence of local tour guides, that Andrew Jackson and the privateer Jean Lafitte planned the Battle of New Orleans over absinthe frappes at the Old Absinthe House, but countless other schemes, realistic and otherwise, have certainly since been hatched in the same manner in that establishment's two-hundred-year history, at two Bourbon Street locations. See Old Absinthe House. Likewise, over Sazeracs and flaming Café Brûlot at Galatoire's Restaurant, opened in 1905, or highballs at the burlesques and nightclubs that lined Bourbon Street through the 1950s and 1960s, or the inventions of bartender Chris Hannah, who oversaw the city's twenty-first-century cocktail revival from Arnaud's French 75 Bar, a hundred yards off Bourbon, on Bienville Street. See Sazerac Cocktail.

None of these, however, can strictly be said to be "Bourbon Street Drinks." That designation is reserved for an altogether more lurid, potent genre of cocktail that gained popularity as the public life of Bourbon Street shifted from the inward-facing cloisters of restaurants and nightclubs to the public pageant of a twenty-four-hour street promenade. The first and most famous of these was the Hurricane, perhaps invented but certainly popularized by Pat O'Brien's. An accommodation to the whisky shortages (and rum surpluses) of World War II, the Hurricane was a bright red, proto-tiki combination of rum, citrus, and passionfruit. It set the Bourbon Street standard for high proof, high sugar and high theatricality, with its instantly recognizable hurricane-lamp glass which became a self-sustaining sidewalk advertisement. See Hurricane.

The Hurricane was inspiration for Earl Bernhardt and Pam Fortner, who opened Tropical Isle on the corner of Toulouse Street in 1984. The pair introduced the technicolor Hand Grenade, served in a bright green plastic version of that weapon, which soon became the most visible accessory on Bourbon Street—helped by Bernhardt and Fortner's irrepressibly amateur TV commercials and their very professional commitment to bringing litigation against imitators. (A sign at Tropical Isle offered rewards to customers willing to act the snitch.) Lesser known, but with a local cult following, was Tropical Isle's Shark Attack, a simple concoction of sour mix and vodka transformed into an operatic high-seas drama with the addition of literal bells and whistles rung and blown whenever one was ordered, plus a plastic alligator and shark and copious amounts of "blood" in the form of grenadine syrup.

By the late 2010s, the pantheon of gimmicky drinks included the Fish Bowl, the Jester, the Mango Mango Lady, the Yard Dog, the Willie's Cocktail, the self-explanatory Huge Ass Beer, and more—each in a distinctive container hoping to achieve the lucrative iconicity of the Hurricane or Hand Grenade. Vulgar, trashy, and mass produced, these drinks are the very antithesis of the craft cocktail. Yet in a city that insists on participation—the ethos that every consumer is also a part of the show—they may be the most authentic New Orleans drinks of all.

Curtis, Wayne. "Remembering Earl Bernhardt, the Cocktail King of Bourbon Street." *Daily Beast*, January 28, 2020. https://www.thedailybeast.com/remembering-earl-bernhardt-the-cocktail-king-of-bourbon-street (accessed March 17, 2021).

Brett Martin

Bowmore is a whisky distillery on the Scottish isle of Islay, in the Inner Hebrides. The distillery is located in the town of Bowmore, on the shore of Loch Indaal, and its 1779 founding makes it one of the oldest distilleries in Scotland, and the oldest on Islay. The distillery was first established by David Simson and was later taken over by James Mutter; the Mutter family retained the distillery until 1887, when it was sold to John Sherriff of Campbeltown, and in 1963 the Bowmore Distillery Company was acquired by Stanley P. Morrison. Today, Bowmore is owned by Morrison Bowmore Distillers, a holding company that also owns the Auchentoshan and Glen Garioch distilleries, which was purchased by Suntory (now Beam Suntory) in 1994. See Suntory. The distillery produces a highly regarded malt whisky using its own floor-malted barley grown on the island, supplemented by malted barley from the Scottish mainland; per Islay tradition, Bowmore uses a peated malt, giving its whisky a distinctive smoky edge. See FLOOR MALTING. The distillery's water source is the River Laggan, and the whisky is distilled using two wash stills and two spirit stills; annual capacity is around two million liters. Bowmore's maturation warehouses are adjacent to the Atlantic Ocean; during the Second World War, the distillery was closed and the buildings were utilized by the RAF Coastal Command.

See also SCOTLAND AND IRELAND.

"Bowmore Distillery." Whisky.com. https://www.whisky.com/whisky-database/distilleries/details/bowmore.html (accessed April 16, 2021).

Bowmore website. https://www.bowmore.com/ (accessed February 4, 2021).

Jackson, Michael. *Whiskey: The Definitive World Guide.* New York: DK, 2005.

Paul Clarke

Bradsell, Dick (1959–2016), is widely regarded as the godfather of London's cocktail renaissance. Born in Bishop's Stortford, northeast of London, and raised on the Isle of Wight, Dick was a delinquent adolescent. His mother sent the eighteen-year-old Bradsell off to London in 1977 to live under the watchful eye of his ex-RAF uncle, who managed London's Naval & Military Club (aka the "In and Out Club") at Cambridge House. But working as a chef trainee did not suit hm.

Three years later, his flatmate Sophie Parkin offered to train Bradsell as a barman at the new members' club the Zanzibar. He discovered David Embury's *The Fine Art of Mixing Drinks* and felt that he found his true calling. See EMBURY, DAVID A. Bradsell became a fixture in London's emerging bar scene, with stints at the Groucho Club, Fred's Club, Café de Paris, Detroit, the Moscow Club, the Flamingo, the Pharmacy, the Player, Match Bar, and, of course, Dick's Bar at the Atlantic Bar & Grill. Every place he presided over felt his passion for drink. See ATLANTIC BAR & GRILL. His creations such as the Detroit Martini, the Bramble, the Wibble, Vodka Espresso (also known as Pharmaceutical Stimulant and Espresso Martini), and Raspberry Martini have circumnavigated the world's bar menus. See BRAMBLE and ESPRESSO MARTINI.

In the 2000s, Bradsell held court at the legendary avant-garde members' club the Colony Rooms, a miniature Soho hideaway filled with artwork contributed by its members in exchange for drinks, including Lucian Freud, Damien Hirst, and Tracy Emin. Bradsell eventually found himself at the helm of another members' club—the Pink Chihuahua—secreted in the cellar of El Camion, a Mexican eatery in his beloved Soho. Bradsell died of brain cancer at his London home in April 2016.

See also COCKTAIL RENAISSANCE.

Bradsell, Dick. Personal interview, January 15, 2011, and June 6, 2015.

Parkin Vink, Sophie, Personal interview, January 25, 2016.

Anistatia R. Miller and Jared M. Brown

The **Bramble** was created by British bartender Dick Bradsell in 1989 while working at Fred's Club in London's Soho, which had opened the year before. Bradsell based the drink on a version of the Singapore Sling he made previously at the Zanzibar, a private members' club. It was at this Great Queen Street landmark that he met Fred Taylor, who wanted to open a members' club for a younger clientele. Dick was hired as the opening bartender at Fred's Club. There, he moved the Zanzibar's Singapore Sling to a shorter Old-Fashioned glass, dropped the soda and Bénédictine, and gave it a more British name. Garnished with a lemon slice and fresh blackberries, this streamlined version more clearly resembled a classic Gin Fix or Sour. The drink was intended to be a salute to British flavors: despite lemons that hailed from Spain, the crème de mûre evoked memories for Bradsell of the blackberries that grow on the Isle of Wight.

Recipe: Pour 60 ml dry gin, 30 ml lemon juice, and 15 ml rich simple syrup over crushed ice in a double Old Fashioned glass; drizzle 15 ml crème de mûre (blackberry liqueur) on top and garnish with a blackberry and a lemon slice.

See also BRADSELL, DICK; FIX; SINGAPORE SLING; and SOUR.

Bradsell, Dick. Personal interview, January 15, 2011.

"Dick Bradsell and His Bramble." https://www.youtube.com/watch?v=zuP3YWHnBk8 (accessed February 4, 2021).

Anistatia R. Miller and Jared M. Brown

A century-old French brandy distillery as illustrated in 1894. Note the twin Dutch-style "Moor's head" still tops protruding from the stone firebox and the lack of a wine-warmer to feed the stills. Wondrich Collection.

brandy is the general term for spirits distilled from the fermented juice, mash, pulp, or wine of fruit (or from its residue); taken together, these spirits represent one of the major historical categories of distilled spirits, along with rum, whisky, and the like. See SPIRITS. The word *brandy* is derived from the Dutch *brandewijn* or *gebrande wijn*, meaning burned (that is, distilled) wine. From the most elegant *hors d'age* cognac to rowdy young California brandies destined for Wisconsin's celebrated Old-Fashioned cocktail, brandy is most famously made from grapes. See OLD-FASHIONED. The argument that brandy must be made from grapes, however, is a regional prejudice that does not reflect global practice; any fruit with sufficient natural sugars may be fermented and distilled into brandy. Brandy may be wrested from dried fruits such as dates, raisins, or figs when mixed with water and fermented, but because brandies are more typically made from delicate fresh fruit that may suffer damage from rough handling during long transport, its production is overwhelmingly local and seasonal.

The distillation of brandy in Europe is often thought to have emerged in the Middle Ages as an efflorescence of Arab rose-water-distilling techniques, but Herman Diels and C. Anne Wilson separately argue that a text written in Greek around 200 CE, attributed to the Christian theologian Hippolytus, describes wine distillation. Such grape distillates, however, were not brandy as we understand it today. Rather, Wilson writes, they were part of secret Gnostic fire rituals with even deeper roots reaching back to the philosopher-chemists of Hellenistic and Roman Egypt. Or so the argument goes. Meanwhile, in the 600s, brandy making seems to have become a specialty of the Uighur silk-road oasis of Turpan, where grapes were mixed with qu, the traditional Chinese fermentation starter, and then "steamed." Large-scale production of brandies closer to the beverage we know began in earnest in the 1500s when Flemish, English, and other traders came to favor strong, young eaux-de-vie from Charente in western France. By that time, the Dutch had gained an international reputation as skilled distillers who could transform sour or lackluster wines into spirits consumed as eau-de-vie or reconstituted with water to make ersatz wine. See DISTILLATION, HISTORY, and EAU-DE-VIE.

Brandy Defined

It is difficult to concisely define such a broad category. Cognac, for example, must be distilled twice in open-flame copper pot stills, but no final proof is specified (in practice, it ends up at between 68 percent and 75 percent ABV). According to American regulations, brandy (made from grapes, unless otherwise specified) must be distilled at less than 95 percent ABV and bottled at no less than 40 percent ABV and must have "the taste, aroma and characteristics generally attributed to brandy," but no still type is required. As with most countries, when it comes to dealing with imported brandies, US regulations generally defer to the laws and regulations of the countries from which they originate. Brandy de Jerez, for example, must be in compliance with Spanish laws concerning its production and labeling.

In broad strokes, distillers make brandies intended either to mature over the course of years as aromatic brown spirits or to be consumed relatively young as "white" spirits. The latter are colorless brandies either wholly unaged or rested in containers made of inert materials such as stainless steel, glass, or clay. Such resting allows these spirits to stabilize and mellow without acquiring aroma and flavor compounds typical of barrel aged spirits. The French term eau-de-vie (meaning "water of life" and often abbreviated EDV) may describe the hearts cut of a brandy distillation run, but is more popularly ascribed to colorless fruit spirits made from spirits such as cherry, apricot, and plum. Well-made eaux-de-vie capture the essence of fruits at the height of their aroma and flavor. See AQUA VITAE; HEART; OBSTLER; and SCHNAPPS.

When barrel aged for decades, brandies may acquire rich, lush aromas, tastes, and textures during their physical and chemical interactions with the barrels and surrounding environments. During this long maturation, they take on autumnal hues, while the distinct fresh fruit aromas of young fruit brandies diminish as more complex aromas emerge. Others yet may be bottled relatively young, after perhaps a year or two in wooden barrels. Such young spirits lack the structure and nuance of aged brandies but may shine in mixed drinks. See BARREL; ÉLEVAGE; and MATURATION.

Brandy Fruits

Grape brandies, often aged in French or American oak, dominate the market. They may be made from pressed juice, a mix of juice and pulp, or pomace (the skins, stems, seeds, and pulp left from pressing grapes for white wine or recovered from red wines fermented on the skin). Examples include cognac, Armagnac, and marc from France; Italian grappa; Peruvian and Chilean pisco; and Spanish brandy de Jerez. See ARMAGNAC; BRANDY DE JEREZ; COGNAC; GRAPPA; MARC; and PISCO. Some, especially some cognacs, are distilled on lees, a residue of dead yeast cells produced during fermentation and critical for creating rancio, a prized attribute of aged brandies. Americans prefer the Italian term *grappa* for pomace brandies rather than the French *marc*, though both are used. Grape brandies may be aged, unaged, flavored, or not. They are often made at wineries as a value-added product or to use in-house for fortified wines such as port. Such fortifying brandies, distilled between 85 percent and 95 percent ABV, are known in the liquor trade as "neutral brandy" and may be used as the base spirit for cordials, liqueurs, and flavored brandies. See BRANDY, POMACE; WINES, FORTIFIED; and RANCIO.

Non-grape brandies are collectively known as fruit brandies. They include the following:

Pome fruit brandies are made from fleshy fruits with a core containing seeds. Apple and pear are the most important for commercial distilling, but quince, crabapples, and others are also used. Of the pome fruit brandies, cider-based calvados from northwestern France is arguably the best known globally, but apple brandies are also made in England, Australia, Japan, and other places where apples are grown. See CALVADOS. Applejack may refer to American apple brandy, but the federally designated class of "blended applejack" is merely neutral spirits flavored with apple brandy. See APPLEJACK. Distillers sometimes make "imprisoned" apples and pears by covering a single bud with an empty bottle until the growing fruit ripens. They then cut the fruit's stem and fill the bottle with brandy of the same type. See POIRE WILLIAMS.

Stone fruit brandies include peach, apricot, plum, cherry, and other fruits with a single large kernel. From the seventeenth century until the twentieth, aged peach brandy was America's native luxury spirit. See PEACH BRANDY. In German, the designation -*wasser* (as in kirschwasser) may be used to describe eaux-de-vie of stone fruits. See APRICOT BRANDY; CHERRY BRANDY; KIRSCH; and SLIVOVITZ. Brandies made of softer fruits without such stones and with too little sugar to ferment profitably alone may be macerated in alcohol and re-distilled. In German, these spirits are designated -*geist* (as in *Himbeergeist*, a clear raspberry brandy).

Flavored brandies (made by macerating fruits or other ingredients such as blackberry, Douglas-fir tips, coffee, or apricot in grape spirits) have long enjoyed popularity around the world. Some are excellent. Experimental brandies infused with arresting ingredients such as foie gras or Dungeness crab get some play among distillers but are unlikely to see commercial production. See COFFEE LIQUEURS.

Drinking Brandy

Brandy is often consumed neat, that is, without ice or mixers. However, aged brandies in particular make excellent base spirits and have had a starring role in mixed drinks for centuries. Brandy makes, for instance, the foundation of a particularly suave punch and was the spirit most commonly associated with the Mint Julep when it was at the peak of its popularity. Other drinks that use or may use brandies include the Alexander, Crusta, Highball, Jack Rose, Japanese Cocktail, Milk Punch, Sidecar, and Stinger. See ALEXANDER COCKTAIL; CRUSTA; JACK ROSE; HIGHBALL; JAPANESE COCKTAIL; MILK PUNCH; JULEP; PUNCH; ROSE COCKTAIL; SIDECAR; and STINGER.

Beverage Alcohol Manual. https://www.ttb.gov/images/pdfs/spirits_bam/chapter4.pdf (accessed March 18, 2021).

Dominé, A., A. Faber, and M. Schlagenhaufer. *The Ultimate Guide to Spirits and Cocktails*. [Königswinter, Germany]: H. F. Ullmann, 2008.

Germain-Robin, Hubert. *Traditional Distillation: Art and Passion*. N.p.: White Mule, 2012.

Germain-Robin, Hubert. *The Maturation of Distilled Spirits: Vision and Patience*. N.p.: White Mule, 2016.

Huang, H. T. *Science and Civilization in China*, vol. 6, part 5, *Fermentations and Food Science*. Cambridge: Cambridge University Pres, 2000.

Jarrard, K. *Cognac: The Seductive Saga of the World's Most Coveted Spirit*. Hoboken, NJ: Wiley, 2005.

Neal, Charles. *Calvados: The Spirit of Normandy*. Flame Grape, 2011.

Wilson, C. A. *Water of Life: A History of Wine-Distilling and Spirits, 500 BC–AD 2000*. Totnes, UK: Prospect, 2006.

Matthew Rowley

brandy, grape, is the most familiar form of fruit-based spirit—so much so, in fact, that it typically is referred to simply as brandy. See BRANDY.

Brandy Alexander is a popular variation of the Alexander cocktail, combining brandy, crème de cacao, and cream. See also ALEXANDER COCKTAIL; BRANDY; and CRÈME DE CACAO.

The **Brandy Crusta** is an elaboration on the original Cock-Tail that is accented with liqueur and lemon juice and served in a glass whose rim has been fitted with a broad collar of lemon peel and dipped in sugar. See COCK-TAIL. It is one of three drinks in Jerry Thomas's 1862 *Bartenders Guide* attributed to New Orleans bartender and saloon-keeper Joseph Santini (ca. 1818–1874); Thomas had worked in New Orleans in the 1850s and may well have encountered the drink then. See THOMAS, JERRY. Although the Crusta never enjoyed wide popularity in the United States, it held on as an epicure's or connoisseur's drink until Prohibition (there were also gin and whisky versions, the first appearing more often than the second). It did, however, enjoy a surprising afterlife in Australia, where it was a standard drink from the 1930s until the 1980s, although the antipodean version substituted orange juice for the original lemon juice and Australian brandy for the canonical French.

Some mixographers have pointed to the Crusta, the first recorded Cock-Tail variant to include citrus, as the ancestor of the Sidecar and the Margarita and other such citrus cocktails. See SIDECAR and MARGARITA. In the original Crusta, however, the amount of citrus juice is so small as to render it merely an accent, not a full-blown modifier; the ancestry of the Sidecar et al. is better traced through the Daisy. See ACCENT; MODIFIER; and DAISY.

Recipe: Prepare a narrow-mouthed, stemmed cocktail or sour glass by fitting a wide ribbon of lemon peel in its mouth as in illustration. Rub the rim of the glass and the protruding peel with lemon juice and roll in sugar. Chill glass. Stir with ice: 60 ml brandy, 5 ml maraschino, 5 ml lemon juice, 2.5 ml rich simple syrup, 2 dashes bitters. Strain into prepared glass.

"Perfumed Cocktails." *Sydney Evening News*, February 25, 1931, 8.

David Wondrich

brandy de Jerez is a traditional Spanish spirit distilled from wines grown anywhere in Spain but aged in the Jerez region in the south of the country. Distilling in Spain may date back to the period of Muslim rule, from the eighth to the fifteenth centuries, but the first recorded sale of spirit dates from 1580. The origin story that is widely accepted in the spirit's home region traces it to an unsold brandy from Pedro Domecq Loustau (destined for an export client in Holland, naturally), subsequently stored in sherry barrels for a decade or more. In 1874 it was bottled and sold as "Coñac Fundador" (Spain only stopped labeling its brandies thus in the 1970s). See COÑAC. The success of the brandy was enough to spark the growth of a category that eventually received its DO (*denominación de origen*) status in 1987. Brandy de Jerez has enjoyed great domestic popularity but is less well known in international markets.

The specific character of brandy de Jerez is not dependent upon its base material, usually the innocuous airen grape, and only occasionally sherry's primary grape, palomino. Those grapes are reliable for providing acidity, at least, but otherwise work more or less as a blank canvas for aging. That is done in old sherry barrels that have long held intensely aromatic and oxidative amontillados or olorosos. Some brands will add a proportion of barrels that held the sweet and treacly Pedro Ximénez (PX). Unsurprisingly, brandy de Jerez ranges from somewhat sweet to distinctly so, though total residual sugar can be no more than 3.5 percent by volume.

Barrels used for aging are made from American oak, are less than 1000 l in volume, and must have previously held some type of sherry. All but a few are traditional 500 l or 600 l *botas*. Jerez laws allow some latitude, and so though these *botas* might have contained sherry for only a month or two, in practice, they have generally held sherry for at least one year, and most barrel stocks are an average of at least three years old.

The spirit is distilled in either continuous or (less frequently) traditional pot stills (called *alquitaras*) and is labeled and classified based upon the percentage of each. Each base spirit is distilled once in order to retain flavor and aroma compounds (with minimums required). The classifications are as follows:

Holandas: distilled in either alquitaras or continuous stills to no more than 70 percent ABV with significant volatile substances (2–6 g/l)

destilados: distilled in continuous stills (usually) to between 70 percent and 86 percent ABV, with measurable volatile substances

aguardientes : distilled in continuous stills to more than 90 percent ABV with few volatile substances

Those spirits are blended to create labeled categories of:

brandy de Jerez solera: at least 50 percent Holandas by alcoholic strength, aged more than six months in barrel

brandy de Jerez solera reserva: at least 75 percent Holandas, aged more than one year in barrel

brandy de Jerez solera gran reserve: 100 percent Holandas, aged more than three years in barrel

Here, too, the authorities require minimums of volatile substances (responsible for aromas and flavors) in increasing amounts for each type. Bodegas will most often purchase these spirits for aging in their cellars, though a few do at least some of their own distilling or are affiliated with distillers.

Most brandy de Jerez goes into the barrel at around 53 percent alcohol by volume. The humid conditions in the bodegas that nurture the *flor* that typifies fino and manzanilla sherries also provide for significant evaporation of alcohol when brandy is aged there (up to 4.5 percent per year).

Brandy de Jerez is also greatly influenced by the solera system, in which aged brandies are commingled through the *rocios* or *sacas* process—a portion (usually one-third or less) is drained from the oldest barrel once or twice a year and replaced with brandy from the next oldest barrel, which is then topped up with the next oldest barrel and so on. This practice can obviate specific age statements but also adds to the complexity of the spirit and reflects a practice long utilized to nurture sherry types. See MATURATION.

Current annual sales of brandy de Jerez are less than 10 million liters. Solera accounts for just under half of that; solera reserva is over one-third of that volume, and solera gran reserva provides the remainder.

As sales of brandy de Jerez (like those of its kin, sherry) have slowed over the last half century, the average age of this distinctive spirit has increased. Experimentation has also followed with brands specifying barrel type (amontillado, PX, oloroso barrels), but so too have some houses moved to lower-alcohol offerings (lower than 36 percent), preventing brands such as Osborne's Veterano or Gonzalez Byass's Soberano from being labeled as brandy de Jerez, or even brandy at all.

See also BRANDY.

Epstein, Becky Sue. *Brandy: A Global History*. London: Reaktion, 2014.
Saldaña Sánchez, César, ed. *The Big Book of Sherry Wines*. N.p.: Ministry of Agriculture and Fisheries (Spain), 2006.
Saldaña Sánchez, César. Private correspondence with author, May–October 2020.

Doug Frost

brandy, fig and date, though much less common than brandy from other fruits like grapes or apples, can be found throughout North Africa, eastern Europe, and the Middle East. While brandy made from dried fruits has been produced in significant volumes in the past, today such brandies are more often made in small quantities by small-scale or even illegal distillers. See MOONSHINE. There are few that are commercially available outside of their areas of production.

Especially in Muslim North Africa, fig brandy was often made by Jewish communities, as Islam forbids alcohol consumption. This is true of both boukha, a fig brandy from Tunisia, and mahia, a fig brandy from Morocco.

See also BRANDY.

Kramer, Sarah Kate. "Distilling the Taste of Morocco." *Tablet*, October 3, 2012. http://www.tabletmag.com/jewish-life-and-religion/112829/distilling-the-taste-of-morocco (accessed February 4, 2021).

Jason Horn

Brandy Smash, a mixture of brandy, sugar, and mint shaken up with ice, is first recorded in 1844 and went on to become the American drink sensation of the 1840s and early 1850s. See SMASH.

Brazil, with an area of 8,515,767 km², has a diverse geography, a complex sociocultural demography, and a long and complex history of producing alcoholic beverages. For thousands of years before the arrival of the Portuguese, the indigenous peoples of Brazil made drinks, such as *cauim* and *caxiri*, from fruits and roots that were chewed by women and left to ferment. These drinks were used for social and spiritual purposes, as well as to facilitate epic parties that led to exhaustion in a sonorous joy of tribal companionship.

The first Portuguese settlers arrived in 1500. In the sixteenth century, the Portuguese had a strong and longstanding tradition of wine drinking, and distilled brandy and fortified wines from the Atlantic islands, especially Madeira, were increasing in popularity. Once in contact with the Portuguese, the indigenous peoples of Brazil began to enjoy wine and distilled spirits that came from Europe and incorporate these imported drinks into their traditional

alcohol-based ceremonies and cultural practices. These drinks were also commonly used as a bargaining chip in trade negotiations. The ancient "ethylic regime" of indigenous Brazilians—moderate, ritualized, and serving as a central element of their cultures—was virtually destroyed by imported alcoholic beverages and, later, by alcoholic drinks produced in Brazil from sugar cane juice and molasses. The sixteenth century also saw the arrival of enslaved Africans brought mainly from the Congo region and other parts of Central Africa. As with the Portuguese, enslaved peoples in Brazil came from societies with long traditions of alcohol use, especially fermented palm wine and grain-based beers. With the arrival of sugar cane agriculture and distillation technology, sugar cane–based alcoholic drinks, especially cachaça and aguardiente, were used to facilitate new social and spiritual alcohol-based practices that blended Portuguese, African, and indigenous traditions. See CACHAÇA and AGUARDIENTE.

The first sugar plantation in Brazil was established in the Captaincy of São Vicente (near the present port of Santos), where Martim Afonso de Souza built the first sugar mills. The distillation of cachaça—today the most iconic Brazilian spirit—seems to have begun alongside the first sugar mills in the 1530s, in southern Brazil, between Paraty and São Paulo, with the help of Dutch and Portuguese investors. The word *cachaça*, however, is distinctly Brazilian and probably derives from the turbid, abundant foam formed by boiling sugar cane juice (known as *cagassa*). It is also possible that the name *cachaça* came from the designation of a lower-quality wine distillate of that time in Spain known as *cachaza*. Brazilian-made cachaça and the lower-grade aguardiente would eventually become central items of commerce in the colony's extensive slave trade with Africa.

Today, cachaça is produced in nearly every Brazilian territory, commercially and privately and at both artisanal and industrial scales. Estimates for the number of distilleries in the country vary, but five thousand is an often-cited figure. While production has fallen somewhat in recent years, it is still in the region of a billion liters a year, making Brazil one of the world's most important spirits producers.

In addition to cachaça, the production of fruit liquors has become common in Brazil. Distillers use native and exotic fruits, which they mix with cachaça or grain alcohol to extract various compounds from the pulps. As a legacy of Amerindian culture, the production of *tiquira*, the distilled beverage made from fermented cassava, is still performed, especially in the state of Maranhão. Wine distillates are produced in the southern region of Brazil, which reflects the influence of the large number of Italian migrants who came to Brazil in the late nineteenth and twentieth centuries. The Italian influence in southern Brazil is also evident in the widespread production of grappa or *graspa* (brandy made from fermented wine dregs). Today, other rectified spirits (especially gin) have introduced new varieties of spirits, including some that incorporate cachaça and Brazilian botanicals in their recipes.

Cascudo, L. C. *História da alimentação no Brasil*. São Paulo: Global Ed., 2004.
Venturini Filho, W. G. *Bebidas alcoólicas: Ciência e Tecnologia*. São Paulo: Blucher, 2010.
Vaissman, M. "Licit and Illicit Beverages in Brazil." In *Moonshine Markets: Issues in Unrecorded Alcohol Beverage Production and Consumption*, ed. A. Haworth and R. Simpson, 84–99. New York: Brunner-Routledge, 2004.

Cauré Portugal

The **Breakfast Martini** is a cocktail combining gin, Cointreau, lemon juice, and orange marmalade. Though the gin is the only ingredient the cocktail shares with the classic Martini, it is so named because it is served in a Martini glass. The Breakfast Martini was created in 1996 at the Lanesborough hotel in London by noted bartender Salvatore Calabrese and rapidly joined the pantheon of modern classics, spreading to bars and bartenders all over the world. Because of its light flavor and the inclusion of orange marmalade, the Breakfast Martini is a popular brunch and lunchtime drink.

The Breakfast Martini's recipe is also fairly similar to the Marmalade Cocktail, which appeared in Harry Craddock's *The Savoy Cocktail Book*, published in 1930. See CRADDOCK, HARRY LAWSON.

Recipe: Add 50 ml gin, 15 ml Cointreau, 15 ml fresh lemon juice, and 1 barspoon of thin-cut orange marmalade to a shaker and stir to dissolve the marmalade. Fill with ice, shake, and strain into a chilled cocktail glass. Garnish with shredded orange peel.

See also CALABRESE, SALVATORE; and MARTINI.

Calabrese, Salvatore. *Classic Cocktails*. London: Prion, 1997.
Craddock, Harry. *The Savoy Cocktail Book*. London: Constable, 1930.

Jason Horn

Brigham, Peter Bent (1807–1877), set the canon of American drinks for a generation in 1842 when the extensive list of "Fancy Drinks" (a term he popularized) offered at his Oyster Saloon in Boston caught the attention of the national press. It would serve as a source of both moral indignation and commercial imitation for the next twenty years, and as a de facto checklist of what Americans were drinking. Saloons copying the list could be found from coast to coast, and as far away as Paris. It would not be superseded until 1862, with the publication of Jerry Thomas's *Bar-Tenders Guide*. See THOMAS, JERRY.

Brigham, a native of Vermont, opened his first oyster counter in Boston in 1828. By 1836 he was the lessee of the large, old Concert Hall in the center of the city, and it is there where he opened the Oyster Saloon in 1842, "fitted up in a style of splendour unequalled in the Union," as his advertisements claimed. Here there were not only oysters of all origins and preparations but also "other Refreshments," served both in the large "gentlemen's gorgeous and neat saloon," as one patron called it, and the smaller "Ladies' Saloon" around the corner. Those included the fancy drinks.

On offer were least eighteen mixed drinks, including six different kinds of punch, plus such oddities as Tippe na Pecco, Tip and Ty, Fiscal Agent, and Wormwood Floater. When Charles Jewett, a prominent Prohibitionist, criticized the list in print, Brigham responded by adding a Jewett's Fancy. By the end of 1843, the list had stretched to encompass eleven kinds of julep (including such elaborations as Capped Julep and Race Horse Julep), five cobblers, and seventeen other drinks. See JULEP and COBBLER. It had also been printed in newspapers all around the United States. Unfortunately, none of his recipes are known to survive.

Brigham never married, devoting his life to his business. As a saloonkeeper he was known for his hands-on management and his constant battles with Boston's many and vocal Prohibitionists. See PROHIBITION AND TEMPERANCE IN AMERICA.

In 1869, Brigham retired from the saloon business and devoted himself to investing in local real estate. This made him a fortune, which upon his death went to the endowment of a hospital. Today, the Brigham and Women's Hospital is one of the most famous and respected in America.

"Progress of Temperance." *New Orleans Daily Picayune*, October 31, 1843.
"Peter Bent Brigham." *Boston Journal*, May 25, 1877.

David Wondrich

Brix is a unit of measurement for the concentration of sugar in a liquid, which is important in the production of wines and other distillers' washes, liqueurs, bar syrups, and a great many other things besides. (Beer producers most often use a closely related and functionally identical unit called Plato.) The unit is named for Adolf Ferdinand Wenceslaus Brix (1798–1870), a Prussian engineer and mathematician who made detailed measurements of sugar solutions' specific gravity in the mid-1800s.

Sugar concentration is expressed in degrees: 1° Brix (abbreviated as 1° Bx) is the concentration of a solution of pure water and 1 percent sucrose by mass; thus in theory a simple syrup made up of equal parts by weight of sugar and water is at 50° Brix, while a rich simple syrup, with two parts sugar to one of water, is at 66° (in practice they are a little lower—48° Bx and 64° Bx—due to the chemical interaction of sugar and water). Brix is most often measured using a hydrometer or refractometer, which analyzes the specific gravity of a liquid to determine its sugar concentration; both instruments are commonly calibrated to the Brix scale. Such instruments actually measure the total amount of dissolved solids in a solution, not just sugar, and so measurements of Brix are generally somewhat inexact.

See also RICH SIMPLE SYRUP; SIMPLE SYRUP; and SUGAR.

Karmarsch, Karl. "Brix, Adolf Ferdinand Wenceslaus." *General Deutsche Biographie 3* (1876), 335. Available online at https://www.deutsche-biographie. de/gnd11763199X.html#adbcontent (accessed February 4, 2021).

Reid, Matt. "Brix." In *The Oxford Companion to Sugar and Sweets*, ed. Darra Goldstein, 77–78. New York: Oxford University Press, 2015.

Jason Horn

The **Bronfman Family** was one of the driving forces in the twentieth-century globalization of the spirits industry. In 1889 Yechiel Bronfman, a Bessarabian tobacco farmer, brought his family to Canada to escape anti-Semitic pogroms. Though they struggled to survive, his children would later achieve enormous financial success building the world's largest spirits business.

During the early 1920s, "boozoriums" that his sons Samuel (1889–1971) and Harry (1885–1983) established along the US border generated monthly revenues approaching $400,000, selling compounded spirits to American bootleggers. By 1928, "Mr. Sam"—now clearly in charge—had acquired several distilleries, including Joseph E. Seagram & Sons. He called the newly merged firm Distillers Corporation–Seagram's Limited. At the height of their success the Bronfmans operated a global empire from their thirty-eight-38-story Park Avenue headquarters in New York. With wineries and thirty-nine distilleries around the world, including several it built in the United States and Scotland, the company earned billions annually from such brands as Seagram's VO, Four Roses, Chivas Regal, and Mumm champagne.

By the time of his death, Mr. Sam had methodically eliminated his brothers and their families from leadership roles in the firm and had appointed his son Edgar (1929–2013) as CEO. However, overlooked family members created rival fortunes in real estate. In 1989 Edgar appointed his own son, another Edgar (1955–), as president of Seagram's, then in 1994 as CEO. In a series of disastrous moves Edgar Jr. sold Seagram's largest profit center (shares in DuPont Corporation) for $12 billion, to finance Seagram's 1995 entry into the entertainment business. Then in 2000 Bronfman sold Seagram's to Vivendi Corporation for $42 billion, mostly in shares. In the financial implosion that followed, the family watched billions disappear as the spirits business passed briefly to Pernod-Ricard, and eventually to Diageo, minus several key brands. Many of Seagram's brands, such as Chivas Regal whisky and Captain Morgan rum, remain vital in other hands, although Seagram's itself is a rapidly fading memory of a once celebrated spirits enterprise, and the Bronfmans stand as examples of how to build and destroy a business empire.

See also CHIVAS REGAL; PERNOD-RICARD; and SEAGRAM COMPANY LTD.

Faith, Nicholas. *The Bronfmans: The Rise and Fall of the House of Seagram*. New York: St. Martin's, 2006.

Marrus, Michael R. *Samuel Bronfman: The Life and Times of Seagram's Mr. Sam*. Lebanon, NH: University Press of New England, 1991.

Newman, Peter C. *King of the Castle: The Making of a Dynasty; Seagram's and the Bronfman Empire*. New York: Atheneum, 1979.

Davin de Kergommeaux

The **Bronx Cocktail**, essentially a Perfect Martini with added orange juice (or other orange flavor), was the cocktail sensation of the 1900s and 1910s and was the drink that, in the United States, took the cocktail from the barroom to the sideboard, helping to sell untold numbers of cocktail shakers in the process. See COCKTAIL SHAKER. Indeed, such was the Bronx's popularity that, as one journalist noted in 1914, one could "order one with confidence and get it with prompt familiarity in any part of the civilized world."

As is so often the case with such a highly popular drinks, the question of the Bronx's invention is a vexed one, with many claimants—at least eleven of them, each with a scrap or two of documentation. The earliest of them, however, is John E. "Curly" O'Connor (1870–1941), head bartender at New York's Waldorf-Astoria, who in 1901—a full five years before the cocktail achieved national popularity—participated in a sort of summit of the city's top mixologists, brought together to come up with a "Carrie Nation Cocktail." O'Connor's ticket to entry was his fame as "inventor of the Bronx Cocktail." Since two other Waldorf-Astoria bartenders, John J. Solan (1875–1951) and Philip M. Kennedy (1875–1922), also turn up among the drink's putative fathers, it is at least very likely that the Bronx came out of that famous bar.

The Bronx's popularity remained high during Prohibition but declined precipitously after Repeal—indeed, *Esquire* magazine placed it first on its list of the ten worst cocktails of 1934. Nor has it prospered

during the twenty-first-century cocktail renaissance, whether because it is a difficult drink to balance properly (too much orange juice and it is insipid, too little and it is merely a neither-flesh-nor-fowl Perfect Martini) or because even if properly balanced it is a light and pleasant drink, not a spectacular one. See COCKTAIL RENAISSANCE and COSMOPOLITAN.

Recipe: Cut an orange wheel in 8 pieces and muddle in cocktail shaker. Add 60 ml London dry gin, 15 ml each sweet and dry vermouth and 2 dashes Angostura bitters. Shake with ice and strain into a chilled cocktail glass.

See also MARTINI; PERFECT; and WALDORF-ASTORIA

"A 'Carrie Nation Cocktail.'" *Kansas City Star*, February 7, 1901, p7.

Shay, Frank. "Ten Best Cocktails of 1934." *Esquire*, December, 1934, 40.

David Wondrich

Brooklyn Cocktail is a name that has been applied to a great many drinks saluting New York City's most populous borough. The only thing that most of them have in common is their inventors' desire to create a drink to rival the Manhattan and the Bronx Cocktail. The earliest on record, a rum Manhattan, dates to 1883 but apparently never left the hushed precincts of the Brooklyn Club, where it was created. In 1908, Manhattan bartender Jack Grohusko got in on the act with a harmonious combination of rye whisky and sweet vermouth accented with maraschino and Amer Picon. See PICON. His was not the last word—over the next few years, various compounds would be invented, christened as Brooklyns, and floated in the pages of American newspapers, only to be ridiculed, dismissed, and forgotten. See GROHUSKO, JACOB ABRAHAM "JACK".

After Repeal, the *Brooklyn Eagle*, the borough's leading newspaper, wondered why there wasn't a Brooklyn Cocktail and invited submissions. In the process, Grohusko's old recipe was excavated from the pages of Harry Craddock's *Savoy Cocktail Book*. Unfortunately, Craddock had pinched the drink not from Grohusko directly but from Jacques Straub's 1914 *Drinks*, where it was altered to use dry vermouth instead of sweet, yielding a rather awkward drink. Neither it nor any of the other Brooklyns caught on, not then and not in 1945, when the

Bronx borough president reopened the question by taunting Brooklyn in print over its lack of a signature drink. See CRADDOCK, HARRY LAWSON.

The modern cocktail renaissance happening to coincide with a renaissance of Brooklyn the borough, there has also been a renewed interest in Brooklyn the cocktail. See COCKTAIL RENAISSANCE. Grohusko's old warhorse has been dusted off, its resurrection hampered only by the need to work around the Amer Picon (altered from its original state and, in any case, unavailable in America), but modern mixologists have also taken to inventing their own riffs on his formula, naming them after the neighborhoods of Brooklyn, such as Red Hook and Greenpoint. In fact, these variations are probably more popular than the Brooklyn itself, bringing the matter of the Brooklyn Cocktail back to square one.

Recipe (Grohusko's): Stir with ice 45 ml each straight rye whisky and sweet vermouth and 5 ml each Amer Picon or substitute (such as Amaro CioCiaro) and maraschino. Strain into chilled cocktail glass and twist lemon peel over the top.

See also BRONX COCKTAIL and MANHATTAN.

Currie, George. "George Currie's Brooklyn." *Brooklyn Eagle*, December 13, 1945.
Grohusko, Jacob A. *Jack's Manual*. New York: J. A. Grohusko, 1908.

David Wondrich

Brown, Jared, has written more than thirty books about cocktails and spirits with his wife, Anistatia Miller. He is also the master distiller for London's Sipsmith distillery. See also MILLER, ANISTATIA AND BROWN, JARED.

Brown Derby refers to two different cocktails: a rum-based drink created on the East Coast during the 1930s and a bourbon concoction often linked to "the golden age of Hollywood."

This later version reputedly was invented in Hollywood during the 1930s and named for the Brown Derby restaurant, whose original location was shaped like an actual derby hat. The Tinseltown connection seems to have come from a single source, George Buzza Jr.'s *Hollywood Cocktails* (1933),

which claimed to be a collection of recipes for cocktails served at famous Hollywood nightclubs and restaurants. In reality, Buzza copied dozens of recipes from *The Savoy Cocktail Book*, including the De Rigueur, which he renamed "the Brown Derby," although there is no evidence that it was ever served at the Brown Derby or anywhere else in Hollywood.

The Brown Derby was rediscovered in the early 2000s. Dale DeGroff published it in his pioneering volume *The Craft of the Cocktail* (2002), and it soon made its way into other bartenders' guides, including Jim Meehan's influential *PDT Cocktail Book* (2011), thereby "reviving" a classic cocktail that never actually existed.

In 1930s New York City, however, there was an actual cocktail called the Brown Derby, though it was made from dark rum, maple sugar, and lime juice. The drink was mentioned in *Esquire*'s "Painting the Town" column in 1935, in which the author mentioned drinking one at the "Amen Corner of the Fifth Avenue Hotel." Four years later, the magazine published a recipe for the drink in Murdock Pemberton's "Potables" column. That recipe would appear periodically in bartender's guides and magazine articles until the 1990s, but it never achieved lasting popularity.

Recipe (faux-Hollywood version): Combine 60 ml bourbon whisky, 30 ml fresh grapefruit juice, and 15ml honey syrup in a shaker with cracked ice. Shake well, strain into a cocktail glass, and serve.

Recipe (East Coast Rum version): Combine 60 ml dark rum, 30 ml fresh lime juice, and 5 ml maple syrup in a shaker with cracked ice. Shake well, strain into a cocktail glass, and serve.

See also CRADDOCK, HARRY LAWSON; DEGROFF, DALE.

Craddock, Harry. *The Savoy Cocktail Book*. London: Constable, 1930.
DeGroff, Dale. *The Craft of the Cocktail*. New York: Clarkson Potter, 2002.
Pemberton, Murdock. "Potables." *Esquire*, June 1939.
Wondrich, David. "Brown Derby." *Esquire*, November 5, 2007, http://www.esquire.com/food-drink/drinks/recipes/a3656/brown-derby-drink-recipe/(accessed February 4, 2021).

Robert F. Moss

Brown-Forman, one of the world's biggest liquor companies, began its ascent during the 1870s, when pharmaceutical salesman George Garvin Brown joined his half-brother J. T. S. (John Thompson Street) Brown selling liquor in Louisville. The company's early success was built on sales of Old Forester bourbon (originally called Old Forrester), which it first sourced from outside producers but began making on its own shortly after the turn of the century. After weathering Prohibition, Brown-Forman was helmed by members of the Brown family for most of the remaining century, diversifying into all manner of alcoholic beverages, buying into and selling out of numerous brands and operations along the way, including Woodford Reserve, Early Times, Herradura tequila, Finlandia vodka, and many others. In 1956, Brown-Forman paid $20 million for the Jack Daniel Distillery (which then produced only fifty-four barrels per day), an acquisition that helped fuel the company's growth as Jack Daniel's grew to sell twelve million cases per year by 2015.

See also JACK DANIEL'S and OLD FORESTER.

Zoeller, Chester. *Bourbon in Kentucky: A History of Distilleries in Kentucky.* Louisville, KY: Butler, 2010.

Cecil, Sam K. *Bourbon: The Evolution of Kentucky Whiskey.* New York, NY. Turner Publishing Company, 2010

"Owsley Brown, Noted in Distillery Field," *Associated Press,* reprinted in the *New York Times,* November 2, 1945.

"Brown-Forman Corp.: Company Acquires the Jack Daniel Distillery," *New York Times,* August 29, 1956.

"Distiller is 110 and Still Growing," *New York Times,* August 1, 1980.

Ward's Business Directory of U.S. Private and Public Companies, 55th edition, 2012.

Reid Mitenbuler

bruising is one of the zombie ideas of mixing drinks, namely, that shaking a Martini might "bruise" the gin. The term, first documented in a 1931 novel, recalls another popular idea, that it is undesirable to muddle or "bruise" the mint when constructing a Mint Julep. One school of Julep purists believed that mint should appear only on top of the drink as a nosegay, allowing the essential oils to seep into the cup only though its stems. To them, the act of crushing (muddling) the mint was almost blasphemous, and (as in Tom Bullock's 1917 bartender's guide) it was referred to as "bruising the mint." However the term found itself extended to gin and the Martini, it has caused many a bartender and cocktail aficionado to scratch their heads and wonder exactly how gin can get bruised. See JULEP, MUDDLER, and SHAKE.

Ironically, whether the command "and don't bruise the gin" was meant as a joke or not, it might have some validity to it. There are two schools of thought as to how. One holds that the term describes over-dilution. When fine ice shards are transferred from the shaker into a cocktail glass after shaking, they melt into the drink, leaving behind excess water in its wake. See DILUTION. The other focuses on the aeration in a shaken drink, whereby the combination of oxygen and carbon dioxide create air pockets in suspension. When a cocktail is instead stirred, it provides a smooth, silky texture. Shaking negates this pleasurable silkiness, offering bubbles instead.

Perhaps the best explanation is that the combination of over-dilution and aeration delivers a blow to any aromatic drink. But one person's poison is another person's pleasure, and in today's bars, there are fans of each.

Arnold, Dave. *Liquid Intelligence.* New York: Norton, 2014.

Wilson, Harry Leon. *Two Black Sheep.* New York: Cosmopolitan, 1931.

Audrey Saunders

bubble test is a visual method for calculating the percentage of alcohol in a distilled spirit by shaking the solution and evaluating the size of the resulting bubbles. A distilled spirit is a combination primarily of ethanol and water. Due to their molecular structure and polarity, water molecules tend to congregate, thereby creating strong surface tension. Ethanol has similar tendencies but to a lesser degree and thus has a lesser surface tension. This allows the two substances to mix but with variable surface tension depending upon the concentration of alcohol in the solution. As the alcohol concentration rises in an ethanol/water solution, the surface tension drops. When this is agitated, larger bubbles form. Although many factors such as temperatures and additives can alter the results, an experienced analyst can determine alcohol percentage by volume through the size of the bubbles.

The practice has a long history. A 1738 English manual instructs distillers to evaluate the "blebs" to determine if they are using proofgoods in their stills. In the United States, the bubble test was, and to a small degree still is, associated with moonshine production. See MOONSHINE. American folk distillers may refer to the bubbles as frog's eyes or goose eggs. Today, mezcal producers throughout Mexico still use the bubble test as the method for determining proof. Using a *venencia*, an approximately 50-centimeter-long piece of the native plant *carrizo* that has been dried and fashioned into a pipette, the mezcalero will pull the mezcal into the pipette using his breath. The mezcal will then stream through the narrow opening of the *venencia* into a dried, hollowed out gourd to create *las perlas*, or the pearls, on the fluid's surface for evaluation. See MEZCAL.

See also ETHANOL and PROOF.

Smith, George. *A Compleat Body of Distilling, Explaining the Mysteries of That Science, in a Most Easy and Familiar Manner; Containing an Exact and Accurate Method . . .* 2 vols. London: 1738.

Misty Kalkofen

buchu brandy and buchu gin are two separate substances. Buchu brandy, or *boegoebrandewyn*, has been made in what is now South Africa since at least the eighteenth century, although now it is scarce. It is prepared either by infusing brandy with the leaves of the buchu bush (*Agathosma betulina*) or by distilling them with grape pomace and wine lees, and it is a traditional remedy for urinary problems when taken internally and wounds when taken externally. Its flavor partakes of black currants and peppermint. Buchu gin, a rather more cynical affair, was an American drink of the late nineteenth century that traded on the medicinal reputation of the South African herb to sell a drink that was essentially a bottled cocktail. It was first marketed in 1896 with the Buchu, Gin and Juniper of the Murray Drug Co. of Columbia, South Carolina (like buchu, juniper was widely held to benefit the kidneys and bladder). By far the most successful brand, however, was Dr. C. Bouvier's Buchu Gin, introduced by the Rosenbaum Bros. of Louisville, Kentucky, in 1900

or thereabouts (as far as can be determined, there was no Dr. Bouvier). This was advertised as a preparation of the "best leaves of buchu" and "the purest old Holland gin," and as delicious in a Fizz or Rickey, even for those who were not drinking for medical reasons. See FIZZ and RICKEY. ("Drink all you want," the ads advised.) A 1916 analysis, however, found that it was almost 40 percent alcohol, with sugar, "coloring matter," and "a very small amount of buchu." By then, it was no longer sold in bars and was exclusively a patent medicine. It did not survive Prohibition.

See also HEALTH AND SPIRITS and SOUTH AFRICA.

Louisiana State Board of Health. "Quarterly Bulletin." September 1916, 77.
Stephenson, John, and James Moss Churchill. *Medical Botany*. London: John Churchill, 1831.
Sullivan, Jack. "The Elusive Dr. C. Bouvier and the Rosenbaum Brothers." *Those Pre-Pro Whiskey Men!* (blog), October 14, 2013, http://preprowhiskeymen.blogspot.com/2013/10/the-elusive-dr-c-bouvier-and-rosenbaum.html (accessed February 4, 2021).

David Wondrich

The **Buck** is a variant of the Rickey combining spirits with lime juice and ginger ale. Its original and most popular version by far, the Gin Buck, is first documented in July 1903 when it is identified in a Kansas City, Missouri, newspaper as "the only new drink called for at the leading hotels in Kansas City." Already in 1901 the *New York Sun* had identified gin and ginger ale as one of the new hot-weather "combinations that are called for constantly," and *Life* magazine's nostalgic 1925 recollection of pre-Prohibition "ginger-ale highballs at the bar" of the Hotel Buckingham in that city perhaps sheds some light on the drink's name and origins, although there is no proof. (Broadway columnist O. O. McIntyre's claim that it was invented at New York's Hotel Van Cortlandt when it was under the management of playwright and lowlife saint Wilson Mizner is impossible, as the hotel didn't open until September, 1903.) In any case, the Gin Buck didn't start to gain broad popularity until the 1910s, when this "Gin Rickey with a college education," as the *New Orleans Item* dubbed it, regularly appears in drink books and newspaper stories. It wasn't until Prohibition was enacted in 1919 that it really took off, though. See PROHIBITION AND TEMPERANCE IN AMERICA.

If there was one thing that American drinkers agreed on during the great drought, it was that ginger ale was the perfect mixer for bootleg liquor. From 1919 to 1933, gin and buck went together like ham and eggs. In Washington, DC, the Gin Buck was the house specialty of the Mayflower Club, the most elegant speakeasy in town, which sold them for thirty-five cents apiece, ten cents above the going rate. (For that extra dime, you got a proper splash of fresh lime juice, rather than the "few drops of lemon juice" most places used.) The drink was ubiquitous, though. Indeed, in 1926, Americans drank 1.25 billion pints of dry ginger ale; in 1918, right before prohibition, the figure was only ninety-nine million. Of course, much of that ginger ale was mixed with whisky or rum, but the Gin Buck must have accounted for a sizeable proportion of the total. After Prohibition, the drink's popularity faded quickly, as if people wanted to forget it. The Gin Buck has not benefitted from the cocktail renaissance, but San Diego bartender Erick Castro's bourbon-based Kentucky Buck has become something of a modern classic. See COCKTAIL RENAISSANCE.

Recipe: Combine 60 ml London dry gin and 15 ml lime juice in a tall glass with ice. Fill with ginger ale.

See also GINGER BEER AND GINGER ALE; GIN BUCK; and RICKEY.

"Drinks for Hot Weather." *New York Sun*, July 7, 1901, 9.
"A Few Recollections of the Distant Past." *Life*, May 14, 1925, 6.
" 'Gin Buck' A New Drink." *Kansas City Star*, July 25, 1903, 2.
"How 'Dry' America Made 'Dry' Ginger Ale a Billion Dollar Industry." *Helena (MT) Independent*, July 29, 1928 ,18.

David Wondrich

Buffalo Trace Distillery sits along the bank of the Kentucky River on the outskirts of Frankfort, Kentucky. It is best known for its eponymous bourbon, Blanton's small batch bourbon, and the annual release of the Antique Collection of five distinct whiskies. It also produces the famed

Van Winkle whiskies in partnership with the Van Winkle family.

The oldest building on the distillery grounds dates to 1792. Distilling may have taken place on site in the early 1800s; the first documented distillery was built on the grounds in 1858. Colonel E. H. Taylor bought this distillery in 1870 and renamed it OFC (for "Old Fashioned Copper" or "Old Fire Copper," both of which the company used) Distillery. Taylor sold to George T. Stagg in 1878; in 1904 the distillery was renamed for Stagg. It was sold to Schenley Distillers in 1929, then in 1992 to the Sazerac Company, which renamed it Buffalo Trace seven years later. See SAZERAC CO. After much research, the distillery was confirmed as a National Historic Landmark in 2013.

Buffalo Trace has a well-funded experimental program encompassing all aspects of whisky production, including wood, grain, temperature, yeast, and distillation. The program includes small releases of test whiskies (the Experimental Collection) and full-bottle releases of the Single Oak Project: whiskies aged in carefully tracked barrels made from single oak trees. The distillery also encompasses the E. H. Taylor micro-distillery and Warehouse X, a small, five-bay warehouse testing the effects of light, air, and temperature on aging whisky.

A large expansion is underway on newly acquired land across the river, ensuring future capacity for a long time to come.

See also BLANTON'S; WHISKY, BOURBON; and TAYLOR, COL. E. H.

Buffalo Trace website. http://www.buffalotrace.com/ (accessed February 4, 2021).
Personal interviews with Mark Brown and Harlen Wheatley.

Lew Bryson

Bullock, Tom (Thomas Washington) (1872–1964), was an African American bartender who penned a celebrated cocktail book just before the Volstead Act banned the profession that he'd thoroughly documented. He was born in Louisville, Kentucky, and it is believed that Bullock worked at both the Pendennis and Kenton clubs there beginning in the mid-1890s before moving to Missouri in around 1904 and working at the St. Louis Country

Club. It was here that Bullock would write *The Ideal Bartender*, which is the first known tome written by a Black man dedicated to the art of mixing beverages. Although just writing the book would be an accomplishment for any bartender, Bullock's talents were further validated by having the prominent banker and businessman George Herbert Walker (grandfather of United States president George H. W. Bush) write its forward, which praised Bullock's mixology skills. This gesture showed that Bullock was respected by the elite members within the community even at a time when racial segregation and Jim Crow laws were in full force. Indeed, when Sir Frederick Smith, the British attorney general, toured America in 1918, he was brought to the country club and was introduced to Bullock, who was, his hosts claimed, "the greatest artist in the United States in the manufacture of cocktails." Smith thought that "he certainly seemed very resourceful."

Written in 1917, *The Ideal Bartender* is one of the last cocktail books written before Prohibition, and it serves as a snapshot of drinking styles before the thirteen-year drought. In fact, Bullock's publication may be credited with helping to preserve the tradition of American mixology and the types of concoctions that would have otherwise been lost during Prohibition. There are many stories yet to be discovered about the contributions of Black bartenders to US cocktail history. Tom Bullock is a fine example of a prominent bartender whose profession suffered the mayhem of Prohibition (he seems to have found work, as the law took force, as a waiter on the Pennsylvania Railroad). Fortunately, he recorded his skills and knowledge in *The Ideal Bartender*, which serves to guide future generations of mixologists.

Smith, Frederick. "British Attorney General Discovers New United States in a Fighting Mood." *New York Sun*, April 20, 1918, 8.

Duane Sylvestre

The **Bullshot** or **Bull Shot**, an eccentric mix of vodka, beef broth, and, usually, Bloody Mary spices, was invented at the Caucus Club in Detroit, Michigan, when John Hurley, an advertising executive charged with selling more Campbell's canned consommé, was discussing his problem with the club's owner, the legendary restaurateur Lester Gruber (1907–1983). That was in 1954 or 1955. The drink made it into print in 1956 and soon became a favorite among ad men, movie stars, and all kinds of other people who wanted something flashy and different to drink.

Recalls Dale DeGroff:

I first encountered the Bullshot in the late 1960s at Charlie O's Restaurant in Rockefeller Center in New York, which was run by another legendary restaurateur, Joe Baum (1920–1998), and his company Restaurant Associates. Baum, who opened the place in 1966, wanted a classy Irish bar and if the Bullshot was classy enough for the Caucus Club then it belonged in Charlie O's, although we ended up favoring a variant of the drink, the Bloody Bull, which swapped out half the Campbell's beef broth for tomato juice.

I was leery of that at first because tomato juice loses its integrity if it is shaken hard. But I was wrong; the drink tasted wonderful shaken and it looked great. It actually "set up" like a pint of Guinness in the glass. The Caucus Club claimed to have their own spice mix, but like most people we spiced ours—both Bullshot and Bloody Bull—similarly to a Bloody Mary. We left out the salt, since the broth was so salty.

Charlie O's kept both drinks popular until they closed in 1989. They can still be found in older New York steakhouses such as Ben Benson's, Keens, and Mortons.

In 1984, as head bartender for Baum's fine dining restaurant, Aurora, DeGroff wanted to recreate the Bullshot he had loved so much at Charlie O's. "Baum was skeptical," he explains. "He didn't like the idea of canned beef broth being served in his upscale joint, what with its Michelin-star chef, Gérard Pangaud. Gérard liked the idea but wanted it made with pheasant consommé and so it was for a while. We dubbed it the 'Foul Shot' (and that is the cleaned up version)." At least one special customer, celebrated art director Milton Glazer, enjoyed it, and that was good enough for Baum. When DeGroff finally got back to beef broth, "Joe still wasn't satisfied: he claimed the lime or lemon didn't work as garnish. I stumbled on the solution in a Chinese restaurant; I scanned the menu and my gaze landed on beef with orange. I started garnishing my Bullshot with orange peel and left out the Worcestershire sauce, and Joe was satisfied." As with the Bloody Mary, there is a lot of "creativity" when it comes to recipes for the Bull Shot. Here is DeGroff's:

Recipe: Shake well with ice: 45 ml vodka, 100 ml beef broth (canned or house-made) or, for a Bloody Bull, 60 ml broth and 40 ml tomato juice, 5 ml fresh-squeezed orange juice, 5 ml medium dry sherry, 2 dashes Tabasco sauce, and a pinch of black pepper. Strain into ice-filled highball glass and twist orange peel over the top.

See also: BLOODY MARY.

Wondrich, David. "Why the Bullshot Cocktail Is No Joke." *Daily Beast*, April 10, 2017, https://www.thedailybeast.com/why-the-bullshot-cocktail-is-no-joke (accessed February 4, 2021).

Dale DeGroff and David Wondrich

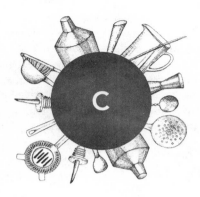

cachaça, otherwise known as *pinga* (among many other names), is a sugar-cane-based spirit made in Brazil and is among the world's leading spirits in production volume, with between 1 billion and 1.4 billion liters a year being made, almost entirely for the domestic market. In 2001, the Brazilian government formally specified that it must be made from pure sugar-cane juice, as is modern practice, and has been petitioning the World Trade Organization to recognize it as an exclusively Brazilian product due to its historical and cultural roots in that country. While those roots are undeniably deep, cachaça was historically also made from molasses and the skimmings from sugar refining. Indeed, in Brazil *cachaça* (a Portuguese word for grape pomace) was originally a term for those skimmings, which were fermented and drunk (as *garapa*). See SKIMMINGS. The name, therefore, demonstrates how early Portuguese colonists in Brazil applied Old World mental models to describe New World products.

It has been posited that Brazilian cachaça was the earliest form of sugar-cane-based spirit made in the New World. Is it, in fact, the first rum? Historians have speculated about the origins of New World rum making and often assume that it emerged immediately alongside sugar production. Staking claim to the origins of rum making carries a strong sense of nationalistic pride, and Brazilian claims are steeped in this nationalism. Much of the confusion surrounding the origin of New World rum making stems from the gradual evolution of rum prototypes, fermented sugar-cane-based alcoholic beverages, such as garapa, that were produced on a small scale in the early years of colonization, and from the almost parallel ascent of

rum distilling in the different parts of the Americas in the seventeenth century.

Brazil developed a highly productive sugar industry in the sixteenth century, beginning in the 1530s with large *engenhos*, or sugar works, in the south; by the 1570s, the center of the industry had moved to Pernambuco in the north. It has been claimed that distillation began with the founding of the engenhos, as a byproduct of sugar making. But while the Portuguese had certainly already encountered sugar-cane spirits in northern India (where they are attested to in the Delhi Sultanate in the late 1200s) and had plenty of general experience with distillation both at home and on the Portuguese island of Madeira, what textual evidence exists for them in sixteenth-century Brazil is weak and confused, while the known archaeological evidence is nonexistent. In 1587, Gabriel Soares de Sousa recorded the presence of numerous large sugar factories and eight smaller syrup factories in the Rencôncavo region of Bahia, but his detailed account of the industry made no specific references to alcohol production in them. Nor is there any mention of alembics or tools necessary for distillation in the extensive sixteenth-century records of the large Sergipe plantation, one of the most productive sugar factories in the Rencôncavo. Distillers are not listed among the artisans at *engenho* Sergipe, and the earliest reference to an "alambique" there appears in 1651, although by 1622–1623 there is a record of the enslaved workers being given "aguardente" (it is not impossible that that was a Portuguese wine-based product, although a local cane one is far more likely). Without further archaeological research, we must conclude that if cachaça was produced in

Brazil in the sixteenth century, the industry was small and limited to meeting the demands of the local population.

The earliest firm evidence of distillation in Brazil comes from a 1611 São Paulo will. By the late 1630s, however, Brazilian sugar planters were clearly distilling cachaça in volume and, in 1646, Portuguese officials already considered it such a threat to the social and economic stability of Brazil that they attempted to ban its production. (The ban was apparently never implemented, probably because cachaça was integral to Brazilian social life and because it had already found a strong market in west central Africa.) It is possible that the Brazilian industry got a boost from the Dutch, who controlled the northern sugar-growing province of Pernambuco from 1630 to 1634 and had long experience with distillation in general with cane spirits from their colony in Java. See ARRACK, BATAVIA.

For much of its history cachaça's reputation was as a cheap firewater suitable only for peasants and the enslaved. By the early nineteenth century, however, Brazilian distillers had considerable experience with the spirit, and the Rev. Robert Walsh, encountering it in 1828, albeit pronouncing it "an inferior kind of rum," also conceded that it was "cheap and accessible" and "not . . . an unwholesome or unpalatable liquor." In 1869, the explorer Richard Burton went further and provided a taxonomy of Brazilian cane spirits, reserving "cachaça" for the lowest grade, made from molasses. Above it, he ranked "caninha" (still a popular nickname for the spirit), which was made from cane juice, and finally there were "restilo" and "lavado," which were redistilled to higher strengths.

The rise of the Brazilian coffee industry in the late nineteenth century drew energy and investment from the sugar industry, which shrank to the point that it cut off the supply of molasses for distillation. From the end of the century, cachaça became exclusively a sugar-cane-juice spirit. By this point, it had become an essential, if complicated, icon of Brazilian identity, both loved for its deep traditions and scorned for its perceived rusticity and backwardness.

At present, there are thousands of distilleries in Brazil that produce cachaça. No accurate count can be supplied, as the vast majority of them are semi-legal at best: small-volume backwoods operations that refill customers' bottles straight from the still.

Commercial cachaça comes in two unofficial grades, industrial and artisanal. The former, whose manufacture is centered in the northeast, is made on a huge scale in modern column stills. Many of these distilleries also further refine their spirit into ethanol for motor fuel. Industrial cachaça is extremely cheap and ranges in quality from raw and fiery, with a strong hogo, to reasonably smooth and pleasant. See HOGO.

Artisanal cachaça, a small but growing part of the market, is made in pot stills (often traditional Portuguese-style ones, with water-cooled heads that allow a single distillation to proof). Fermentation with ambient yeasts is common, as is (in some regions) the addition of a little maize to help with fermentation. At its best, it is a subtle, soft, and even lovely expression of the cane it is made from.

Most cachaça, artisanal or industrial, is rested in either stainless steel or neutral wood containers before bottling. Many artisanal cachaças, and a few industrial ones, are also aged in reactive wood for anywhere from a year to twelve years. The barrels used are often (imported) oak ones, but a wide variety of Brazilian hardwoods are also commonly used, including *amburana*, *jequitiba*, *ipê*, and a number of others. Some of these are fairly neutral, but others impart strong flavors and even unusual colors to the spirit. Amburana, for instance, gives a strong black-cherry note to cachaça aged in it.

By Brazilian law cachaça must be between 38 and 48 percent alcohol by volume. Other legal definitions include: *adoçada* (sweetened) (6–30 g/L sugar concentration); *envelhecida* (minimum 50 percent wooden-aged cachaça); *premium* (100 percent wood-aged cachaça); *extra premium* (at least three-year 100 percent wooden-aged cachaça). There are currently three officially recognized indications of origin for cachaça, including Paraty (Rio de Janeiro), Salinas (Minas Gerais), and Abaíra (Bahia).

Cachaça is the base spirit in a number of uniquely Brazilian drinks. Most of these are of fairly recent origin: as Burton noted, the Brazilians had a long-standing "prejudice against mixing" cachaça into punches and the other common mixed drinks of the Americas. Only in the twentieth century did that prejudice ease, helped by the rise of the *batida*, wherein cachaça is shaken or beaten together with sugar, fruit juices, and other ingredients. The most popular of these, the Batida Paulista, is better known by its alternate name, the Caipirinha, a drink that made it onto the global stage in the 1970s, by which point cachaça was suffering from one of its periodic bouts of unfashionableness in Brazil. See CAIPIRINHA. That unfashionableness is passing now, and with the global mixology craze, Brazilian bartenders are turning to it to create a local take on the art.

See also BRAZIL; RUM; and SUGAR CANE.

Burton, Richard F. *The Highlands of Brazil.* London: Tinsley Bros, 1869.
Curto, José Carlos. "Alcohol and Slaves: The Luso-Brazilian Alcohol Commerce at Mpinda, Luanda, and Benguela during the Atlantic slave trade c. 1480-1830 and its impact." PhD diss., UCLA, 1996.
Du Tertre, Jean-Baptiste. *Histoire generale des Antilles: 1667–1671.* Fort de France: Societe D'histoire de la Martinique, 1958.
Maranhão, Piaul. *Documentos para a história do açúcar.* Vol. 2: *Engeho Sergipe do conde livro de contas (1622–1653).* Rio de Janeiro: Instituto do açúcar e do álcool, 1956.
Schwartz, Stuart B. *Sugar Plantations in the Formation of Brazilian Society: Bahia, 1550–1835.* Cambridge: Cambridge University Press, 1985.
Soares de Sousa, Gabriel. *Notícia do Brasil.* Edited by Piraja da Silva. São Paulo: Empresa Gráfica da Revista dos Tribunais, 1974.
Smith, Frederick H. *Caribbean Rum: A Social and Economic History.* Gainesville: University Press of Florida, 2005.
Walsh, Robert. *Notices of Brazil in 1828 and 1829.* London: Westley & Davis, 1830.

Frederick H. Smith

Café Brûlot, sometimes also known as Café Brûlot Diabolique or Café Brulé, is a spectacular coffee service presented tableside that involves warming brandy-laced coffee in a special pan over an alcohol fire, setting it alight, and ladling the flaming liquid down a spiral-cut lemon peel held over the pan. Its invention has been ascribed to Jules Alciatore, the son of the founder of Antoine's Restaurant in New Orleans, Louisiana, opened in 1840 and fortunately still thriving on St Louis Street in the heart of the city's famed French Quarter. Its roots lie in the nineteenth-century French café drink, *brûlot de café*, a simple mix of coffee and *eau-de-vie* that was served flaming, but with influence from the elaborate flaming Punches popular in mid-century France.

There are a number of other classic New Orleans restaurants, such as Galatoire's and Commander's Palace, that also prepare this classic recipe. To many, a Café Brûlot is an essential part of experiencing New Orleans's unique culinary culture.

The drink is not easy to reproduce because of the special apparatus the "show" requires, a copper bowl with a Sheffield silver lining and a special decorative cradle supported by brass figures. The drink is quite labor-intensive to fix, since it requires most the ingredients to marinate for several hours beforehand and has several intricate steps, but it is worth all the work and preparation.

Recipe: Marinate 3 cinnamon sticks (broken into pieces), 1 whole lemon peel and 1 whole orange peel for several hours in 240 ml VS-grade cognac and 120 ml kirschwasser. Prepare a second orange peel, cut in a spiral, by studding it with 12 cloves and threading one end of it on the tines of a serving fork. Have 1.5 liters of French roast coffee flavored with chicory hot and ready in warmers. Place the brandy, kirsch, lemon peel, and un-studded orange peel in the upper bowl of a Brûlot set and heat it by pouring 60 ml 151-proof rum in the lower bowl and igniting it. When the brandy is warmed enough it will ignite. Hold the studded orange peel over the bowl and using the ladle pour the flaming brandy mixture over it. Repeat this several times. The bursting oil cells on the skin of the orange will sparkle, and the cloves will begin to glow, providing a wonderful light show for your guests. Pour the coffee into the bowl to put the flame out, sweeten to taste with demerara-sugar syrup, and serve in demitasse cups.

"Plusiers limonadiers du quartier," *Le droit* (Paris), December 30, 1840, p. 3.
"Light My Fire: The Spectacle and Tradition of Café Brûlot." French Quarter.com. http://www.frenchquarter.com/tradition-cafe-brulot/ (accessed February 22, 2021).

Dale DeGroff

The **Caipirinha**, a mix of cachaça, sugar, ice, and muddled pieces of lime (and often other fruits), is considered by non-Brazilians to be the national drink of that country. See CACHAÇA. In Brazil, however, the Caipirinha is merely the most famous member of a large, native class of mixed drinks, the batidas, which Roberto Costa defined in his pioneering 1974 *Traçado geral das Batidas* as a "cold aperitive that is essentially made with cachaça, sugar, fruits, juices or essences and ice, shaken in a cocktail shaker or mixed in a blender." See APERITIF AND DIGESTIVE. Indeed, one of the Caipirinha's original names appears to have been "Batida Paulista"—roughly, "São Paulo Shake." That was in the 1950s. Before that, it appears to have been identified simply by its most distinctive ingredients, as *pinga com limão*, "pinga (one of cachaça's many other names) with lime."

It is a quirk of Brazilian drinking that this simple, basic way of drinking sugar-cane spirit appears to be of no great antiquity. Where almost all the other Latin American countries where cane was grown had their own, naturalized versions of punch by the eighteenth century, Brazil seems to have by and large ignored the drink. See PUNCH. It is only in the mid-nineteenth century that one begins to find *pinga com limão*, as in the folksong "O meu boi morreu" ("My ox died"), where it is lauded as a cure for the evil eye, or when, in 1856, the town of Paraty was forced to issue it during a cholera epidemic so that people wouldn't drink the water, or when, thirty years later, the English traveler James William Wells came across a "a *refresco* [cooling drink] of cachaça, lemon, sugar, and water" in Paraíba, in the easternmost part of Brazil.

As that "Batida Paulista" implies, however, it was much further south, in São Paulo, that the drink became cemented as an institution, in the first half of the twentieth century. The Batida Paulista, however, showed the influence of American mixology, and not only in its incorporation of ice. Some versions had the sugar added in the form of simple syrup, while others had the "sophisticated" (as the great Brazilian poet Mario de Andrade characterized them in 1944) additions of egg white and a "splash" of gin; this would require mixing in a cocktail shaker. Some drinkers, however, rejected such innovations.

That created a dynamic very much like the one that gave rise to the Old-Fashioned in the United States, with the old *pinga com limão* playing the ancestral role of Cock-Tail and the Batida Paulista as the evolved Manhattan and its ilk. See OLD-FASHIONED COCKTAIL; COCK-TAIL; and MANHATTAN COCKTAIL. And, as in the United States, there was a third way, one that incorporated the ice from the new drink into a

nostalgic, rustic preparation built simply in the glass. In the United States, that was an Old-Fashioned; in Brazil, a "caipirinha," or (roughly) a "Little Hillbilly" ("Caipira" is a southern Brazilian epithet for a person from the rural hinterlands). The name was in occasional use by the 1950s and widespread by the end of the 1960s. By then, the drink was known throughout Brazil.

It would take another twenty years for the Caipirinha to catch on abroad, at least outside of Brazilian expatriate communities. In the 1980s, it enjoyed a strong vogue in Europe, where it remains popular, and in places that look to Europe for drinking trends. In Kenya, a variation, the Dawa, went so far as to become the national drink. In the United States, however, despite frequent efforts from cachaça importers, it remains a drink more mentioned than served. See DAWA.

Meanwhile, in Brazil the drink was evolving. Fashionable city dwellers found cachaça too rustic and backward-looking for their tastes and preferred vodka, thus making the drink a "Caipiroska," which first appears in the early 1980s. Others went for imported white rum (for a "Caipirissima") or replaced the lime with other fruits, such as passionfruit, pineapple, strawberries, grapes, and so forth, at which point it merges back into the general category of batida.

Andrade, Mario de. "Os eufemismos de cachaca." *Hoje* (São Paulo), April, 1944.

Costa, Roberto. *Traçado geral das batidas*. Rio de Janeiro: Civilização Brasileira, 1974.

Jannuzzi, Felipe. "A história da caipirinha—versão Paratiense." *Mapa da cachaca*, January 17, 2014, https://www.mapadacachaca.com.br/artigos/qual-a-origem-da-caipirinha-versao-paratiense/ (accessed February 22, 2021).

Wells, James William. *Exploring and Travelling Three Thousand Miles through Brazil*. London: Sampson Low, Marston, Searle, & Rivington, 1887.

David Wondrich

Calabrese, Salvatore, born on Italy's Amalfi Coast in 1955, is one of the world's most celebrated bar professionals. He is past president of the United Kingdom's Bartenders Guild, a keeper of the quaich, chevalier du cognac, and chevalier du champagne and has been awarded numerous distinctions, notable among them Lifetime Achievement Award from Tales of the Cocktail. He is known as much for the exuberance of his personality as for the classic elegance of his technique. See UNITED KINGDOM BARTENDERS GUILD (UKBG) and TALES OF THE COCKTAIL.

Calabrese's first bar job in the United Kingdom was at the legendary Duke's Hotel; he helped the hotel bar to establish its reputation as the source of some of London's top Martinis. James Bond author Ian Fleming was a regular at Duke's; lore is that Bond's shaken-not-stirred martini was the invention of a Dukes bartender. See DUKES BAR.

In the early 2000s, while director of the famous Library Bar at the Lanesborough Hotel in London, Calabrese began acquiring antique spirits, particularly old cognacs dating back to the dawn of that spirit's production in the late eighteenth century. That collection came in handy in 2012 when Calabrese was operating Salvatore at Playboy in London's Playboy Club and used it to create a cocktail named Salvatore's Legacy. Sold to a guest for £5,500, the drink earned Calabrese a spot in the *Guinness Book of World Records* as creator of world's most expensive cocktail.

Calabrese went on to open signature bars in Las Vegas, London, and Hong Kong. He has also written drink-related articles for several British publications, including the *Sunday Times*, and twelve drink-related books. His 1997 *Classic Cocktails* is one of the most widely read bartender's guides of the modern era, and was recently reprinted in a new edition.

Calabrese's celebrity is not unnoticed by film and television producers. He was also approached by the producer of the remake of the James Bond thriller *Casino Royal* to shake the famous shaken-not-stirred Bond Martini but refused to participate because he would never shake a Martini.

Salvatore Calabrese's website. https://salvatore-calabrese. co.uk (accessed February 22, 2021).

Dale DeGroff

The **Calimotxo** or **Kalimotxo** is a mixture of red wine and cola in equal parts, usually served over ice. It is believed to have originated in Spain's Basque Country, where it is immensely popular. Although it is likely that Spaniards had already been mixing cola and wine for decades (since the 1920s

at least), according to Jonathan Miles, writing in the *New York Times* in 2007, "The drink was supposedly created—or at least named—at a festival in Algorta, Spain, in 1972, when some young entrepreneurs discovered that the wine they had planned to sell tasted not just bad but toxic, and added Coca-Cola and ice to mask the flavor."

Franck Celhay elaborates on the story, citing *La verdadera historia del kalimotxo* (The true story of the Kalimotxo), edited by the not very authoritative-sounding Bilbao artists' collective Funky Project. But since *bilbotarras* are serious about the Calimotxo, let us take Funky Project at their word when they explain that the inventors of the Calimotxo that fateful day at the festival were members of a group called Antzarrak, and that the drink was initially called "Rioja Libre" or "Cuba Libre del Pobre" (poor man's Cuba libre), but was christened "Kalimotxo" by combining the nicknames of two members of the gang: "Kalimero" and "Motxo" (others say that it was Kalimero alone responsible, and that the name came about from another of his nicknames, "Motz," Basque for "short" or "stumpy"). In any case, the name stuck. Variations on this origin story are in circulation, but Funky Project's version is considered the most reliable.

The drink's taste has been likened to sangria, and it's the favored cheap buzz of young people in the Basque Country, who sometimes mix it in great quantity in plastic shopping bags. But the appeal of this plonk-and-coke combo is widespread, if not universal: in many former Yugoslav republics it's "bambus." Chileans call it "jota," Hungarians "vadász." And Romanians know it as motorină—"diesel fuel."

Recipe: Pour equal parts red wine and Coca-Cola into a tall, ice-filled glass. Stir.

Miles, Jonathan. "If Bacchus Drank Cola." *New York Times*, December 2, 2007.
Celhay, Franck. "Le kalimotxo: cocktail hérétique ou nouvelle opportunité pour la filière vin?" *Décisions marketing*, October–December 2008, 67–71.

Rosie Schaap

call drink is a mixed drink made with a specified brand of liquor "called" for by the guest, instead of allowing the bartender to use the house's standard "well" or "rail" brand. These drinks tend to be more expensive than well drinks because they generally use premium or super-premium liquor. Example: instead of ordering a Gin and Tonic, a guest will call for a "Beefeater and Tonic." Some establishments feature "you call it" specials, where the guest "calls" for what they want.

Regan, Gary. *The Joy of Mixology*, 2nd ed. New York: Clarkson Potter, 2018.

Chad Solomon

calvados is a cider-based brandy that comes from Normandy in northern France. The region is largely surrounded by the English Channel, which creates a cool and humid environment that is not hospitable for grape growing. Such a climate, however, along with soils that contain silt, clay, granite, flint, and limestone, provides an ideal atmosphere for the cultivation of both apple and pear trees.

Although distilled cider (or *eau de vie de bouche*) was made in Normandy as early as 1553, the word *calvados* first appeared in early 1800s. Although it was once overflowing with calvados distillers, migration to urban areas, temperance laws, and increasing grain and beet cultivation led to a decline in apple orchards and other fruit trees in Normandy.

Increasing interest in calvados led to greater regulation in the nineteenth century. A number of specific regions were identified around Normandy, and most distilled calvados once in column stills. Differences in apple varieties and soil types created different regional characteristics in calvados that were formally recognized by the French government as regulated regions. The first official appellation was established in 1942 and called Calvados Pays d'Auge. To bear its name, the fruit must have been grown in a circumscribed area and the cider must have been double distilled. In 1984, the regulated regions were combined into a second appellation simply known as AOC Calvados that generally required that calvados go through a single distillation. A southern region known for its unusually high plantings of pear trees was granted the appellation Calvados Domfrontais in 1998. Regulations required that its cider contain at least 30 percent pears and be distilled once in a column still.

Traditional apple trees have tall trunks (*hautes-tiges*) and long branches under which cows can graze. The milk from these cows is used not only for cream and butter but also for the region's well-known cheeses Camembert, Pont l'Eveque, Livarot, and Neufchâtel. Since the 1980s, farmers have increasingly planted their orchards with dwarf trees (*basses-tiges*) that produce fruit at a more rapid rate and take up less space.

About thirty varieties of apples and ten varieties of pears are commonly grown in the Calvados region. The apples and/or pears are harvested and crushed, and their juice is extracted from the pulp. Fermentation takes place in stainless-steel tanks or neutral oak barrels. When the cider is completely dry, it is distilled in either pot stills or column stills, depending upon the region. The clear exiting spirit is placed into oak barrels where, over time, it begins to pick up its darker color. After two years in barrel, the spirit can be released as calvados (marked as three stars, "Trois pommes," or "Fine"), although the majority is aged in these oak barrels for much longer periods of time; after four years, it may be labeled as "VO," "Vieille reserve," or VSOP; after six, as "XO," "Napoléon," "Hors d'age," or "Age inconnu."

Until the mid-twentieth century, calvados had a poor reputation in France: it was often distilled clandestinely and drunk without any aging at all. Referred to as *calva*, it was akin to American moonshine and often served alongside, or often in, coffee (in Normandy, there was even a "Café de la Mort," where calvados replaced the water used to make the coffee). See MOONSHINE. Stricter appellation laws, tighter controls, and diminished orchard acreage have largely reduced the amount of mediocre calvados on the market.

While calvados is often used in cooking and is found in several classic cocktails, it is typically consumed on its own at the end of a meal similar to fine brandies. The balloon snifter is widely used for consuming calvados, but a sherry copita also works well. As with other fine brandies, aromas and flavors develop as the spirit ages: green apple and fresh pear are often coupled with vanilla and honey blossom in calvados up to ten years old. Adolescence sees emerging aromas of baked orchard fruit, often paired with some nuttiness, a whiff of smoke, and spice. Calvados more than twenty years old is rare and quite difficult to find.

Examples of well-aged calvados tend to have deep aromas of red apple, concentrated pear, mirabelle plum, licorice, vanilla, walnuts, and well-integrated touches of smoke.

See also APPLEJACK; ÉLEVAGE; and FRANCE.

Mattson, Henrik. *Calvados: The World's Premier Apple Brandy*. Malmö, Sweden: Flavourrider.com, 2004.
Neal, Charles. *Calvados, The Spirit of Normandy*. N.p.: Flame Grape, 2011.
Nouraisson, Didier. *Le buveur du XIXe siècle*. Paris: Albin Michel, 1990.
Stamp, Matt. "Booze a la Normande: Calvados, Cidre, Poire and Pommeau." Guildsomm, May 31, 2011. https://www.guildsomm.com/stay_current/features/b/stamp/posts/booze-224-la-normande-calvados-cidre-poir-233-and-pommeau (accessed February 22, 2021).

Charles Neal

Campari, the iconic bright-scarlet, bitter aperitif, is the flagship brand of the Italian drinks conglomerate Gruppo Campari. See APERITIF AND DIGESTIVE. Campari has been a fixture in Italian life, both as a drink and, through its ubiquitous advertisements, as a part of the country's visual environment, since the end of the nineteenth century. It is a key component in the Negroni, Italy's main contribution to the global cocktail canon.

The Campari company was founded by Gaspare Campari (1828–1882), a farmer's son from Novara, between Milan and Turin. When he was fourteen, he became the apprentice distiller at the elegant and popular Caffè Liquoreria Bass in Turin; according to some sources, one of his fellow apprentices there was Alessandro Martini (1824–1905), cofounder of the vermouth brand. Returning to Novara in 1856, he established his own business, following the same traditional Italian model as Bass, wherein cafes made their own liquors in all the popular types, plus a few of their own.

In 1862, Campari moved his business to Milan, finally settling in a space in an old arcade on the city's cramped main square, across from the cathedral. When the arcade was demolished, three years later, he moved the shop to temporary quarters until

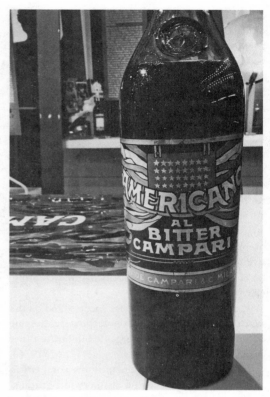
Bottled Americano (Campari and Vermouth) in the Campari Museum, Sesto San Giovanni, Milan, ca. 1910. Wondrich Collection.

1867, when the new and modern Galleria Vittorio Emanuele opened on the site of his former shop. As someone displaced by its construction, Campari had first crack at one of the new commercial spaces in the Galleria. He took a prime space next to the main entrance facing the cathedral. This, along with the new formula he had developed while away from the square, was the foundation of his, and his company's, fortune.

That formula was for a "Bitter all'Uso d'Olanda" ("Holland-Style Bitter"), as it was initially known, which was rapidly simplified to "Bitter Campari" and then just "Campari." Normally, such a formula would have used bitter orange peel as its main bittering agent, as in the "Bitter de Hollande" published by Pierre Duplais in his benchmark 1855 *Traité des liqueurs*. However, Gaspare's notebooks, which have been preserved in the Campari museum, show a somewhat different initial title: "Stoughton d'Holanda." Stoughton's Bitters were not Dutch, but rather English, with a formula dating to the 1690s; by the late 1700s, unauthorized recipes for them had proliferated to the point that they had become a standard apothecary's and distiller's formula. See STOUGHTON'S BITTERS. In fact, Campari's initial recipe is virtually identical to the "Elisire amaro Stoughton" ("Stoughton bitter elixir") found in Pietro Valsecchi's distiller's and liqueur maker's manual, published in Milano in 1857, which supplemented the orange peel with gentian, germander, and wormwood (Valsecchi in turn seems to have taken his recipe from James Rennie). Yet penciled-in annotations show that Campari adjusted the botanicals, used less sugar, and added more dilution, turning a thick, intensely bitter digestive into a lighter, brighter aperitif. At some point, he also added the drink's distinctive red coloring, using cochineal.

Campari's bitter was a great success, and by the time of his death he was not only selling it at the cafe but also wholesaling it in large demijohns to other cafes in the city. His son Davide (1867–1936), who took over the management of the company in 1888 after apprenticing at a distillery in Bordeaux, transformed Campari from a local success into an international one. In part, he did that by emphasizing only two of the company's many products: the bitter and a new, French-style "Cordial Campari," flavored with raspberries and saffron (in 1920, all the others were discontinued). He also displayed an early and sophisticated dedication to advertisement.

In 1904, Davide moved the company's manufacturing out of the cafe basement and another auxiliary site to a large new factory in the Milan suburbs. By then, Bitter Campari was being shipped as far away as San Francisco and Buenos Aires, and the firm's splashy posters were ubiquitous in Italy and in Paris, where the bitter was aggressively marketed. He sold the Milan cafe in 1919, in order to concentrate on the producing side of the business, and discontinued all products except the bitter and the cordial the next year. In 1923, the company built a satellite factory outside Paris, and in the 1920s and early 1930s Bitter Campari was widely used in Parisian cocktail bars, to the point that the American humorist Nina Putnam Wilcox could write about her visit to France in 1933 that "all Gaul was divided into three parts: one part gin, one part vermouth, and one part Italian bitters."

Meanwhile, in 1932 the company launched a premixed Campari soda, in an instantly iconic single-serving conical bottle, which brought its fortunes to new heights. World War II, however, almost destroyed them: in 1945, sales were half what they were in the 1920s, the French branch was gone, and exports were at a halt. Yet Campari was one of the success stories of the postwar Italian economic miracle, and with the help of the Negroni cocktail, the quintessential *dolce vita* drink, the company went on to new heights, becoming an essential bar staple in every part of the world. See NEGRONI.

In 1976, the company began a process that saw its control passing from the Campari family to the Garavoglia family, with whom it rests today. In 1992 it ceased producing the cordial, which had been languishing for decades, and soon after embarked on an aggressive series of acquisitions, buying brands in Europe and the Americas. As a result, Gruppo Campari, as it is now known, is one of the leading multinational spirits companies, with brands as diverse as Wild Turkey American whiskies, Grand Marnier, Appleton Jamaican rum, Skyy vodka, and Aperol, the Italian low-alcohol aperitif, which it built into an Italian and then international institution through its canny promotion of the Aperol Spritz. See APEROL SPRITZ and GRAND MARNIER.

Duplais, Pierre. *Traité des liqueurs*. Paris: 1855.

Jones, Andrew. *Aperitivi: guida agli aperitivi di tutto il mondo*. Milan: Idealibri, 1998.

Putnam, Nina Wilcox. "Bouncing Checks." *Minneapolis Star-Tribune*, December 17, 1933, 20.

Rennie, James. *A New Supplement to the Complete Pharmacopoeias*. London: 1829.

Valsecchi, Pietro. *Nuovo ed unico manuale completo del distillatore liquorista*. Milan: 1857.

Vergani, Guido. *Thirty Years and a Century of the Campari Company*, 3 vols. Milan: Campari Advertising, 1990.

Wondrich, David. "The History of how the Negroni Conquered America." *Daily Beast*, June 10, 2019. https://www.thedailybeast.com/the-history-of-how-the-negroni-conquered-america (accessed February 22, 2021).

Leo Leuci and David Wondrich

Canadian Club is one of the leading brands of Canadian whisky, launched in 1882 by Hiram Walker (1816–1899), a Massachusetts-born whisky merchant. As Canada's oldest surviving whisky brand, it is wreathed in mythology. Walker introduced Club whisky as a seven-year-old blend of corn and rye spirits, intending to make a whisky so flavorful it would recover market share lost when US tariffs raised the price of imported whisky. Initial sales were small compared to less expensive American and Canadian whiskies. Walker added the word "Canadian" to the Club label in 1888, and within a year sales had quadrupled over the 1886 volume (though still only a meager 3,156 cases). Walker promoted Canadian Club aggressively, resulting in sales to 155 countries, most of which still sell it today. In the United States, it became a Prohibition staple given the distillery's size and proximity to the border. See PROHIBITION AND TEMPERANCE IN AMERICA. Now called "Premium" in Canada, it appeared frequently on American television, reminding audiences of its popularity during the Roaring Twenties and the 1960s. In 2014 a robust but value-priced version of Canadian Club appeared to supplant the standard blend and the other, longer-aged bottlings; it was named 100% Rye, to reflect how it was made. Canadian Club whisky distilled in the 1950s and bottled in 2014 for exclusive release in Australia is the oldest known Canadian whisky ever bottled for commercial sale. In 2005 ownership of the Windsor, Ontario, distillery, one of the largest in North America, passed to the French drinks giant Pernod-Ricard, while Beam Suntory took ownership of the Canadian Club brand. The distillery continues to produce Canadian Club whiskies under contract to Beam Suntory.

See also HIRAM WALKER AND SONS; PERNOD-RICARD; SUNTORY; and WHISKY, CANADIAN.

De Kergommeaux, Davin. *Canadian Whisky, Second Edition: The New Portable Expert.* Vancouver: Appetite by Random House, 2017.

Davin de Kergommeaux

cane-based spirits comprise a far-flung family of distillates made from any of the several species of *Saccharum*, the perennial grasses more commonly known as sugar cane, which thrive in tropical and subtropical climates. See SUGAR CANE. These spirits may be distilled from various fermented sugar-cane derivatives, such as molasses, cane syrup, or freshly pressed cane juice. See MOLASSES and cane syrup. See CANE SYRUP. Their names are legion, too many to collect here.

The standard-bearer for the category is rum, the Caribbean's contribution to the global pantheon of great spirits. See RUM. Now produced in all corners of the world, from Austria to Australia, rum is most often distilled from the same raw material used in the seventeenth century to make the first documented rums on Barbados and neighboring islands: molasses, a byproduct of sugar production. In some places, such as Guatemala and Paraguay, rum is distilled from the boiled-down version of cane juice known as cane syrup (in Paraguay it must be reduced over an open flame).

In the latter part of the nineteenth century, a decline in the value of sugar from French possessions in the Caribbean led to the production of rum distilled from fresh sugar-cane juice, which became known as rhum agricole. See RHUM AGRICOLE. Brazil's national spirit, cachaça, which traces its history back at least as far as Caribbean rum, is also made from fresh cane juice, though it is usually distilled to a lower proof than rhum agricole and may be aged in barrels made of indigenous woods. See CACHAÇA.

While most Caribbean and Latin American nations produce rums aged for varying lengths of time, much of which is exported, many of these countries also make more rustic versions of cane-based spirits for domestic consumption. In Colombia, for example, anise-flavored aguardiente (which translates loosely as "firewater") is the cane-based spirit of choice, typically knocked back in shots. Aguardiente is also popular in neighboring Ecuador, where it tends to be unflavored and mixed into hot drinks. See AGUARDIENTE. A similar spirit in Costa Rica goes by the name of *guaro*, made almost exclusively by a government-owned distillery. See GUARO. Elsewhere in South America, locally distilled cane juice spirit is known simply as *caña*, or "cane."

In Haiti, which exports rums of cognac-like refinement, the people's choice is clairin, a cane-based moonshine often sold in reused bottles. See CLAIRIN. Panama, too, sends its rums around the world, though Panamanians are just as likely to drink *seco*, a relatively neutral cane spirit traditionally mixed with milk.

Unlike most of its Latin American brethren, Mexico is best known for its agave-based spirits. However, the country formerly made vast amounts of *chinguirito* from cane juice or skimmings, and the state of Michoacán makes a cane spirit called charanda, though the number of distilleries making charanda has been declining for many years. See CHARANDA; CHINGUIRITO; and SKIMMINGS.

While Asia might not spring to mind as a hotbed of cane-based spirits, there is evidence to suggest that the progenitors of the category may have first been made in India. And Indonesia's Batavia arrack once rivaled or even surpassed the reputation of Caribbean rum. Although made, like most rum, from molasses, Batavia arrack employed fermented rice cakes to trigger the fermentation process. See ARRACK, BATAVIA. A staple of eighteenth- and nineteenth-century punch recipes, it later faded into obscurity. Only in recent years, in response to demand from historically minded mixologists, has Batavia arrack reemerged.

Africa, too, has its share of cane spirits, including the homemade cane juice of Liberia. South Africa produces a vodka-like spirit from sugar cane called simply cane spirit; made with continuous column stills, it is essentially neutral in flavor. Across the Mozambique Channel, Madagascar makes a great deal of *toaka gasy*, a much more rustic spirit. See CENTRAL AND EAST AFRICA.

In many countries around the world, including the United States, the ready availability of table sugar makes it a popular raw material for making illicit moonshine. Several national variations of sugar-based hooch can be found throughout eastern and northern Europe, such as Finnish *pontikka* and Russian *samogon*. See MOONSHINE and SAMOGON.

Buglass, Alan J. *Handbook of Alcoholic Beverages: Technical, Analytical and Nutritional Aspects*. Hoboken, NJ: John Wiley & Sons, 2011.

Minnick, Fred. *Rum Curious: The Indispensable Tasting Guide to the World's Spirit*. Minneapolis: Voyageur, 2017.

Smith, Frederick H. *Caribbean Rum: A Social and Economic History*. Gainesville: University Press of Florida, 2005.

David Mahoney

cane syrup is partially evaporated sugar cane juice. It ranges in color from light amber, resembling grade A maple syrup, to a deep brown-black, not unlike thick molasses.

Making cane syrup was traditionally a way to preserve and store the sweetness of sugar-cane juice, especially when making crystalized sugar was impractical. In the American South cane syrup has often been used for cooking or to sweeten dishes such as grits and cornbread; in the West Indies cane syrup allows rum distillers to store cane juice in bulk far after the sugar harvest concludes. (This may be called "sugar-cane honey.") In parts of South America, this *miel de caña* is used to make aguardiente, a (mostly) unaged cane spirit. It is particularly prevalent in Paraguay, where (as *caña*) it is the national spirit and is sometimes aged to mellow maturity.

The boiling down of cane juice adds burned sugar notes to the syrup. Lighter cane syrup is called for in some tropical drinks, notably ti' punch, a popular drink in the French West Indies. See TI' PUNCH.

See also SUGAR CANE.

Ferris, E. B. *Sugar Cane for Syrup Making*. Jackson: Mississippi Agriculture Experiment Station, Bulletin no. 129, 1909.

Wayne Curtis

Caol Ila, the largest-volume malt whisky distillery on the Scottish island of Islay, was built in 1846 by Hector Henderson on the Sound of Islay, from which the distillery took its Gaelic name (pronounced cull-EE-lah). "Caol Ila Distillery stands in the wildest and most picturesque locality we have seen," Alfred Barnard rhapsodized in his exhaustive 1887 survey of the United Kingdom's distilleries. "It is situated . . . on the very verge of the sea, in a deep recess of the mountain, mostly cut out of the solid rock. The coast hereabouts is wild and broken, and detached pieces of rock lie here and there of such size that they form small islands."

Six years after Caol Ila's founding, it was sold to the owner of the Jura distillery on the neighboring island, and then again in 1863 to the Glasgow firm of Bulloch, Lade, & Co., which operated the distillery for the next fifty-seven years. In the 1920s, it was acquired by Distillers Company Limited (DCL), the predecessor to Diageo, the giant spirits conglomerate that owns Caol Ila today. See DISTILLERS COMPANY LTD (DCL). The old distillery was demolished and then rebuilt and expanded in the early 1970s. The expansion tripled the number of stills from two to six, which are housed in a glass-fronted structure that offers visitors spectacular views across the sound to the rounded hills known as the Paps of Jura.

Throughout the DCL/Diageo era, the lion's share of Caol Ila's production has gone toward Johnnie Walker and other Scotch whisky blends. It wasn't until 2002 that an official single malt bottling was released. See SINGLE MALT. Although the malt used by Caol Ila for its standard twelve- and eighteen-year-old offerings tends to be heavily peated, the smoky flavor component of these whiskies is relatively tame by Islay standards.

See also PEAT.

Barnard, Alfred. *The Whisky Distilleries of the United Kingdom.* London: Harper's Weekly Gazette, 1887.

David Mahoney

The **Cape Codder** is a mixed drink made with vodka, cranberry juice, and sometimes a lime wedge or lime juice and occasionally a splash of soda water. The name, which dates back to at least 1964, derives from its use of cranberry juice, as Cape Cod is home to cranberry bogs and grower associations. The drink itself has many predecessors, including the Red Devil, which is made with the same ingredients as the Cape Codder and is mentioned in *Ocean Spray's Cranberry Cooperative News* in 1945. Later mention of a similar drink includes famed bartender Trader Vic's "Rangoon Ruby" in 1956. See BERGERON, VICTOR "TRADER VIC." As the Cape Codder, the drink enjoyed its greatest popularity during the "preppie" craze of the early 1980s. Other, related cocktails include the Madras (a Cape Codder with a splash of orange juice), Sex on the Beach, and Cosmopolitan. See SEX ON THE BEACH and COSMOPOLITAN. In the twenty-first century, as New England has faded as a leader of American popular culture, the drink is most often ordered as a plain "Vodka Cranberry."

Recipe: Combine in an ice-filled highball glass 45 ml vodka, 15 ml lime juice, and 75 ml cranberry juice. Stir. Garnish with lime. (Optional: top off with chilled sparkling water.)

Popik, Barry. "Cape Codder (cocktail)." *The Big Apple*, August 10, 2014. http://www.barrypopik.com/index.php/new_york_city/entry/cape_codder_cocktail (accessed February 22, 2021).

White, Donald. "Ocean Spray." *Boston Globe*, November 19, 1964, 26.

Wondrich, David. *Esquire Drinks.* New York: Hearst, 2002.

Derek Brown

Capel still is a form of hybrid pot/column still used in Chile to make pisco. See PISCO. It combines a cylindrical pot, topped with a globular still head, with a rectifying column through which distillate may be (but does not have to be) routed. It takes its name from Capel, the giant Chilean pisco-producing cooperative. See also STILL, HYBRID.

caperberry, the fruit of the caper bush, generally sold pickled in brine, is sometimes used in place of the more conventional olive as a garnish in cocktails such as the Martini. See MARTINI.

capillaire, known as sirop de capillaire or maidenhair syrup, is a flavoring and sweetener, originally made using the tincture of a delicate fern. True capillaire has distinctive aromas of black tea, pine tar, and dried flowers. It evolved from a medicinal Renaissance-era respiratory tonic into a fashionable European drink flavoring of the eighteenth and nineteenth centuries. Capillaire was so often used (and its recipe modified) by cafes and street vendors for tea and *eau sucré*, as well as by public houses and distilleries for sweetening grogs, punches, and liqueurs that written references to capillaire became almost synonymous with simple or clarified sugar syrup.

The medicinal plant *Adiantum capillus-veneris* was used in ancient Greece, Persia, and southern Europe and documented by Pliny under the name adiantum. Capillaire de Montpellier, its French name, paid tribute to the city of medical schools where the syrup gained its fame with European royalty.

To treat pulmonary ailments, early sixteenth-century pharmacists prepared *serapium adiantinum* or *syrupus capillorum veneris* by soaking the dried capillaire leaves in boiling water, mixing this "tea" with a tincture of licorice root, and then combining the liquid with sugar or honey. See HEALTH AND SPIRITS. Licorice was later replaced by orange-flower water, its floral aroma so dominant in the syrup that even the use of the eponymous fern was considered unnecessary by many makers toward the late 1700s.

The legend of a Bavarian prince who visited the elegant Parisian Café Procope in the early 1700s and asked for his tea to be sweetened with the syrup instead of sugar sparked capillaire's transition from medicinal use to recreational use in France. The resulting Bavarois à l'Eau and its hot cream and chocolate-flavored drink variations became highly esteemed and their recipes included in nineteenth-century bar manuals. Capillaire was also used in the once celebrated digestive liqueur Elixir de Garus.

The syrup was often imported to England from France and served alone with water or used to sweeten punch and liqueurs. In 1649, English physician Nicolas Culpeper recommended syrup of maidenhair to "open stoppings of the stomach" and declared that it "strengthens the Lungues." But in 1747, Dr. Robert James wrote, "As it is a very trifling Medicine, I have only given it a Place here for the Satisfaction of some who have an Opinion of it." Canadian maidenhair, a more aromatic species, was highly prized by French syrup makers and once so common in the upper regions of North America that it was used for packing material. "The Syrup of Capillaire, sold in the Coffee houses," Dr. James declared, "ought to be made of the Canada Maidenhair—and Orange flower Water." Even so, capillaire does not appear to have ever enjoyed the popularity in the Americas as it had in Europe.

During the eighteenth-century Scottish Enlightenment, the Capillaire Club of Edinburgh mocked local intellectual societies, cheekily promoting the syrup's recreational consumption while listening to the *Capillaire Minuet*, played at its elegant, often bawdy, parties. In nineteenth-century France, *sirop de capillaire* remained a tonic often prepared by pharmacists, and adherence to the official pharmacological recipe, consisting only of dried fern, water, and sugar, was enforced by the courts, though it did little to stop the commercial alterations. The deviations were more extensive in England; in 1854 the *Pharmaceutical Journal* reproached, "It is doubtful if Capillaire be ever rightly made this side of the Channel."

In 1862, Jerry Thomas offered recipes for capillaire, calling for orange flower water or substituting other ingredients for the fern as diverse as bitter almond and curaçao. See CURAÇAO. Indicating sweetening the Oxford Punch recipe he shared, the entry shows clearly that capillaire had lost its unique association with the fern and that syrup variations would change the taste of the punch. See THOMAS, JEREMIAH P. "JERRY".

By the early twentieth century, capillaire was recognized as having limited, if any, medical benefits, and the fern was difficult to source. Due to recipe modifications and an unclear understanding of a single, "true" flavor profile, the majority of historic drink recipes calling for *sirop de capillaire* would expect the floral aroma of orange flower or a utilitarian unflavored simple syrup.

The syrup is virtually unknown today outside of Lisbon and former Portuguese colonies, where, under the name *xarope de capilé*, a version is served from street kiosks mixed with water as a nostalgic soft drink once favored by the noted nineteenth century Portuguese writer Eça de Queiroz.

See also SIMPLE SYRUP.

Culpeper, Nicolas. *A Physical Directory*. London: Peter Cole, 1651.
Barton, Benjamin H., and Thomas Castle. *The British Flora Medica*, vol. 2. London: E. Cox, 1838.
Demachy, M. *Art du Distillateur Liquoriste* [Art of the distiller liquor maker]. Paris: J. Moronval, 1819.
James, Robert. *Pharmacopoeia Universalis, or A New Universal English Dispensatory*. London: J. Hodges, 1747.
Legré, Ludovic. *La Botanique en Provence aux XVIe Siècle* [Botany in Provence during the sixteenth century]. Marseille: H. Aubertin & G. Rolle, 1899.
Read, George. *The Guide to the Trade: The Confectioner*. London: Charles Knight, 1842.
Thomas, Jerry. *How to Mix Drinks*. New York: Dick & Fitzgerald, 1862.

Peter Schaf

Captain Morgan is a spiced rum brand somewhat incongruously named after Henry Morgan (1635–1688), the rapacious English privateer who burned cities and tortured civilians throughout the Spanish Main. It was introduced by Seagram's in 1944 as a brand for the dark, rich rums made at the company's Long Pond distillery in Jamaica. See SEAGRAM COMPANY LTD. It has traveled far from those origins. Today, the brand's ever-expanding product portfolio ranges from Black Spiced and 100 Proof Spiced to Private Stock and Cannon Blast. These are all variations on Captain Morgan Original Spiced: Virgin Islands rum bottled at 35 percent ABV and flavored with a proprietary spice blend, dominated by cinnamon and vanilla. Original Spiced, which Seagram's created in 1984 (reviving the dormant Captain Morgan brand to do it), was the first and remains the most mixable Captain Morgan expression, especially in cola—the way most consumers drink it—but also in cocktails like the Cable Car (a Sidecar with spiced rum instead of cognac). In 2000 Diageo purchased the brand from Seagram and launched an aggressive marketing campaign that perhaps played some small part in making Captain Morgan the second-biggest-selling rum in the world by 2014, with a 34 percent market share (after Bacardi's 67 percent). In 2015 Captain Morgan introduced a line of fruit-flavored rums.

See also DIAGEO; RUM; and SIDECAR.

Diageo. "Our History." https://www.diageo.com/en/our-business/our-history/ (accessed April 20, 2021).
Kapner, Susan. "Diageo and Pernod Buy and Divide Up Seagram Beverage Assets." *New York Times*, December 20, 2000.

Jeff Berry

caramel coloring is a colloid commonly used to color spirits including brandy, rum, and some whiskies, especially scotch whisky (as well as beer, soft drinks, and a wide range of foods). Caramel is an amber to dark-brown liquid or solid prepared by carefully heating food-grade carbohydrates (sugars such as sucrose, glucose, malt syrup, and molasses are all permitted), sometimes in the presence of alkalis or salts to assist the caramelization process. Under regulations defined by the United Nations Joint Food and Agriculture Organization / World Health Organization Expert Committee on Food Additives (JECFA), caramel used in spirits manufacture can be plain caramel or spirit caramel (category E150a), made without the use of ammonium or sulfite compounds, or caustic sulfite process caramel (category E150b), made in the presence of sulfite compounds but without the use of ammonium. (E150a is used in whisky and other high-proof spirits, and E150b is more typically used in cognac, as well as in sherry and other wines.) On its own, caramel is an intensely colored substance with an acrid aroma and a bitter flavor, and only a very small amount is needed to color a bottle of spirits. Caramel is usually deployed for one of two reasons: to achieve a consistent appearance in an aged spirit that otherwise would show some variability in color and to give a spirit a darker hue, sometimes implying the spirit shows greater age or quality.

See also HUE/COLOR.

CFR—Code of Federal Regulations Title 21, last modified April 1, 2016, http://www.accessdata.fda.gov/scripts/cdrh/cfdocs/cfcfr/CFRSearch.cfm?fr=73.85.
"Physical & Chemical Properties of Caramel Color." Sethness Roquette. http://www.sethness.com/caramel_color_facts/properties.php (accessed September 30, 2016).

Paul Clarke

caraway seed (actually a fruit) is a traditional flavoring agent for northern European spirits, particularly aquavit and kümmel. See AQUAVIT and KÜMMEL.

carbonation, in the context of spirits and cocktails, refers to a process in which carbon dioxide gas is dissolved into a liquid under pressure. When a carbonated liquid is subsequently exposed to normal atmospheric pressure, the carbon dioxide comes out of solution, and small bubbles form.

Several factors influence the rate and size at which the bubbles of carbonation form, the two most important being the temperature of the liquid and the prevalence of nucleation sites. At temperatures above freezing, the solubility of carbon dioxide in water increases as temperature decreases, leading to slower release of carbon dioxide at lower temperatures. Nucleation points consist of microscopic imperfections or dust on the interior surface of glassware, particles present in the liquid, and features on the surface of ice cubes, garnishes, and other items that may be introduced into the liquid. These sites contain small pockets of trapped gas that increase in size with the addition of carbon dioxide until they grow large enough for a portion to break away and rise to the surface as a bubble, after which the process repeats with the portion of gas that remains trapped. Carbon dioxide therefore comes out of solution at a slower rate for colder liquids and liquids with fewer nucleation sites compared to warmer liquids and liquids with more nucleation sites, and as a result such liquids retain carbonation for a longer period of time.

Carbonation has several characteristic effects on flavor. Small bubbles bursting on the tongue produce a "fizzy" or "prickly" sensation that involves both the tactile and pain senses. The release of carbon dioxide can influence retronasal olfaction, the process in which odor molecules pass upward from the oral cavity to olfactory receptors in the back of the nasal cavity. Carbonation also produces a mildly sour flavor as a result of carbon dioxide and water reacting to form low concentrations of carbonic acid, in addition to which there is some evidence that carbonation itself may have a direct effect on the sour-sensing taste receptors in the mouth.

Carbonation may be achieved by a variety of means including introduction of carbon dioxide from an external supply of pressurized gas, by sealing the ingredient together with a limited amount of dry ice or as a byproduct of natural fermentation. Because most edible ingredients contain a substantial proportion of water, these techniques can also be used to carbonate non-liquid foods such as fruits and vegetables that may then be used as a garnish or other component of a drink preparation.

The most common way carbonation is incorporated into a mixed drink is through the inclusion of a pre-carbonated liquid such as seltzer water, soda, or sparkling wine, which practice has given rise to several canonical families of drink such as the highball, fizz, daisy, and rickey, to name a few. See COLLINS; DAISY; FIZZ; HIGHBALL; and RICKEY. Bartenders have also begun to experiment with carbonating entire cocktails using specialized equipment, in which case care must be taken that the ingredients have been treated to contain minimal particulate matter, which would otherwise cause the rapid dissolution of carbon dioxide due to an overabundance of nucleation sites.

See also MOLECULAR MIXOLOGY and WINES, SPARKLING AND STILL.

Arnold, Dave. *Liquid Intelligence.* New York: Norton, 2014.

Myhrvold, Nathan, Chris Young, and Maxime Bilet. *Modernist Cuisine: The Art and Science of Cooking.* Bellevue, WA: Cooking Lab, 2011.

Samuel Lloyd Kinsey

The **Caribbean** is a region of some thirty million people living in the islands stretching from the Bahamas to Trinidad, as well as the continental enclaves of French Guiana, Surinam, and Guyana. The continental coastal areas from Venezuela to Belize are also often thought of as Caribbean. Despite its great cultural, racial, and linguistic diversity, the Caribbean exhibits broad social and economic similarities born of its history of colonialism and slavery. The region is known for its tropical climate, beautiful beaches, and bright blue waters, but the Caribbean is also the birthplace of rum and a variety of popular cocktails. See BACARDI; DAIQUIRI; PUNCH; RIBALAIGUA Y VERT, CONSTANTE; and SLOPPY JOE'S.

At the time of European contact, Carib Indians occupied the Caribbean from the Orinoco Delta region of mainland South America through the island chain of the Lesser Antilles, perhaps as far north as the eastern tip of Puerto Rico. The Caribs, as far as can be determined, knew fermentation but not distillation. Before the large-scale transition to sugar production, British, French, and Spanish colonists in the Caribbean experimented with the alcoholic potential of a variety of local plants, including plums, plantains, pineapples, and sweet potatoes. Christopher Columbus carried sugar cane to the Caribbean on his second voyage in 1493. Sugar production was a small cottage industry in some parts of the Spanish Caribbean in the sixteenth century, but there is no evidence that it was accompanied by distillation of the cane juice or the byproducts of sugar making. Instead, Spanish colonists and enslaved Africans used molasses and skimmings to produce a fermented drink called *guarapo.* It was in the British Caribbean colony of Barbados that cane spirits were first turned into an article of global commerce, when in the 1650s Barbadian sugar-planters began exporting the spirit they were distilling from sugar-waste (by then a common practice in the Caribbean and in Latin America) to the British colonies in North America and then to Europe. Today rum is made throughout the region in a great variety of styles.

See also RHUM AGRICOLE; RUM; and SUGAR CANE.

Smith, Frederick H. *The Archaeology of Alcohol and Drinking.* Gainesville: University Press of Florida, 2008.

Smith, Frederick H. *Caribbean Rum: A Social and Economic History.* Gainesville: University Press of Florida, 2005.

Smith, Frederick H. "European Impressions of the Island Carib's Use of Alcohol in the Early Colonial Period." *Ethnohistory* 53, no. 3 (2006): 543–566.

Frederick H. Smith

Carter-head still is a type of still developed in the nineteenth century specifically to make gin. It employs a separate botanical basket to infuse the heated vapor leaving the top of the still. See also BO-TANICAL and STILL, POT.

Caucasus is a catchall term for countries lying along the Caucasus Mountain range, stretching from the Black Sea to the Caspian. Georgia, Azerbaijan, and Armenia sit on the mountainous south side, while the northern side includes some of Russia's fertile steppe. Many of the region's spirits are based on grapes, an outgrowth of millennia of winemaking traditions. In Georgia, "chacha" means both pomace from winemaking (the grape skins, seeds, and stalks) as well as distillates made from it. See POMACE BRANDY. Once strictly a family activity, chacha is growing in economic significance since the introduction of an official geographical indication in December 2011, applicable to chacha made from grape pomace within ten officially recognized Georgian wine-growing regions. The rise of chacha has also sparked an artisan spirits movement, with chic bars in Tbilisi pouring Georgian-made absinthe, gin, and herbal liqueurs. To the south, Armenia shares Georgia's deep ties to wine, but brandy is the drink of choice: Ararat, made by the Yerevan Brandy Company since 1887, is the primary producer. The distillery, run by Pernod-Ricard since 1998, offers ten bottlings made from grapes double-distilled and aged in barrels made from local oak in the distillery's own cooperage. See PERNOD-RICARD. Many Armenian families distill *oghi* (brandy) from grapes or fruits such as mulberries and cornelian cherries. The bounty in both countries is a stark contrast to Azerbaijan and the northern Caucasus, both of which have long winegrowing histories but have never recovered from Soviet prohibition practices, thanks to both their unstable political scenes and large Muslim populations. When people do drink, vodka is the common choice, although samogon (Russian moonshine) may be more popular. See SAMOGON.

See also CHACHA; GRAPPA; HOME DISTILLING; MARC; and RUSSIA AND EASTERN EUROPE.

McGovern, Patrick E. *Ancient Wine: The Search for the Origins of Viniculture*. Princeton, NJ: Princeton University Press, 2007.
World Health Organization. *Global Status Report on Alcohol and Health*. http://www.who.int/substance_abuse/publications/global_alcohol_report/en/ (accessed February 23, 2021).

Tara Q. Thomas

The **cellarmaster** has an essential place in the production of aged spirits as the person most knowledgeable regarding the varied inventories in any aging cellar. He or she is thus both temple keeper and time keeper, a specialist in barrel aging and tasting, and a creator of new blends. Cellarmasters are also central in that they guarantee the style and quality of the brand by managing the stock of aging spirits to insure full flavor development. They will inevitably be in charge of blending the different barrels to elaborate the finished cognac, rum, or whisky, ensuring that it is expressive and true to the signature taste of the house. In cognac it is customary to require at least fifteen years of training in order to become a fully fledged cellarmaster. In many markets, they have taken on additional duties as privileged ambassadors for the producer.

See also AGING and BLENDING.

Alexandre Gabriel

Cellier-Blumenthal, Jean-Baptiste (1768–1840), is generally credited with inventing (in 1808) and patenting (in 1813, with improvements in 1818) the first practical continuous column still. During the first decade of the nineteenth century there was keen interest in France in developing more efficient stills that could operate continuously for the production of industrial alcohol and potable spirits. The drive to develop the continuous still led to what has been described as "an avalanche of patents." The base material was almost invariably wine: in 1818 the French distilled more than half a million liters of it.

Cellier was drawn to the subject as a way of refining beet sugar alcohol, and his first stills were built in partnership with a Dutch sugar trader, Armand Savalle, who would later become a global still manufacturer. Twice Cellier and Savalle were nearly killed by explosions while testing their new distilling equipment.

Cellier's apparatus had a common pot still surmounted by a column containing nine perforated rectifying plates with bubble caps. Wine was fed from the top of the column, while alcohol vapor rose from the pot through the descending liquid, stripping it of alcohol and preheating it. The patent was improved in 1818 with fractionating plates and draff/residue outlets. Cellier then sold his patent to a Parisian apothecary, Louis-Charles Derosne, who commercialized the product.

Eau-de-vie, Armagnac, and cognac distillers soon adopted Cellier's still, which was found to be "most suitable for the production of wine spirit." See EAU-DE-VIE; ARMAGNAC; and COGNAC. However, Cellier's column still was not limited to distilled wine. Rum distillers in Guyana, for example, were quick to embrace this new distilling technology, as were bourbon distillers in the United States. Cellier's transformational invention remains the basis for the modern column still.

See also COFFEY, AENEAS; COLUMN STILL; and RUM.

Forbes, R. J. *Short History of the Art of Distillation from the Beginnings up to the Death of Cellier Blumenthal.* Leiden: Brill, 1948.

Smith, Frederick H. *Caribbean Rum: A Social and Economic History.* Gainesville: University Press of Florida, 2005.

Strengell, Teemu. "Sugars in Whisky." *Whisky Science,* December 10, 2016. http://whiskyscience.blogspot.com/2016/12/sugars-in-whisky.html (accessed February 23, 2021).

Charles MacLean

Central America is made up of a series of Spanish-speaking countries including Guatemala, Honduras, El Salvador, Nicaragua, Costa Rica, and Panama, as well as the English-speaking enclave of Belize. The development of sugar industries in Central America in the late nineteenth and early twentieth centuries produced a great deal of molasses and thus spurred the rise of rum distilling. Flor de Caña began its operations at the San Antonio sugar factory in Chichigalpa, Nicaragua, in

1890, and in Guatemala Ron Zacapa began its operation in 1876. The building of the Panama Canal, at a time when sugar production was expanding, probably increased the regional demand for rum. Many of the workers came from the rum-producing islands of Jamaica and Barbados, and those laborers no doubt sought rum to help them cope with the grueling work of canal building. Illicitly produced sugar-cane-based spirits, such as guaro, may have also emerged in peripheral areas of Central America to meet the needs of indigenous laborers. Although sugar making and rum distilling began late in Central America, many of the award-winning rums in the world today come from this region.

See also GUARO and RUM.

Smith, Frederick H. *Caribbean Rum: A Social and Economic History.* Gainesville: University Press of Florida, 2005.

Frederick H. Smith

Central and East Africa, a vast and vastly diverse swath of territory stretching from Chad, Sudan, and Ethiopia in the north down to Angola, Zambia, and Madagascar in the south, is often considered one of the great blank spots on the world map of distilled spirits. In fact, the region is home to a number of distinct distilling traditions. If they are obscure, it is because very little of what they produce makes it abroad, the only notable exception being the significant amounts of rum exported by Mauritius and some of the other African islands in the Indian Ocean.

As with West Africa, the region has a long tradition of making beers and wines from a wide variety of starches and fruits but does not have an indigenous one of distilling them into spirits. But while West Africa participated in the Atlantic spirits trade from a very early date, it appears to have taken until the nineteenth century for distilling and spirits drinking to make any significant penetration into East Africa or any but the Atlantic Coast parts of Central Africa. In the north, the end of that century saw Ethiopia begin to make *katikala* and its more refined derivative, *areqe*, from various combinations of wheat, sorghum, and maize, flavored with the pounded leaves of the ghesho shrub (*Rhamnus prinoides*, or shiny buckthorn) and distilled once or twice in clay pot stills to as much as 70 percent ABV. Even before that, low-level distilling from dates or grain had trickled up the Nile from Egypt—a date and sugar-cane distillery was operating in South Sudan by 1840 and a grain one by 1868—and anise-flavored date *arequi* is still made in relatively small quantities in Sudan and Chad. See ARRACK.

Distillation was slower to move upriver into Central Africa. In 1864 when the English explorer Samuel Baker set up an improvised distillery in the camp of Kumarasi, the king of Bunyoro-Kitara in western Uganda, to make sweet potato spirit for his daily medicinal Hot Toddies, it was treated as a great novelty. By the 1890s, however, European and local spirits were moving south through the region from Sudan. In the meanwhile—after Baker, but probably not because of him—the practice of distillation began spreading through the Bantu villages of the East African Highlands and the Congo Basin. Distillation may follow industrialization, as the drink historian's rule of thumb holds, but it also follows certain other forces that break apart traditional societies, including colonization and war, two forces to which the region is unfortunately no stranger. There is still a great deal of unbranded, village-level distilling in the region, mainly the one known in various parts of the Congo as kwete, lotoko, or rutuku, made from maize and cassava chips, but also banana "gin" and a wide variety of other spirits. None are industrialized. See KACHASU and KWETE.

The former Portuguese colonies of Angola and Mozambique are also responsible for a good deal of small-scale, unbranded distilling, only there the raw materials are sugar cane and—as in Goa, another former Portuguese colony—cashew fruit. See FENI. Most of the cane distilling in Africa, however, is done on islands, both the Atlantic ones and the ones in the Indian Ocean. Madagascar, the largest of them, had a working distillery as early as 1821 and imported a good deal of spirit for the consumption of the royal household (Amer Picon was a favorite), but its characteristic *toaka gasy*—cane juice rum, often flavored with tamarind or other fruits or herbs—appears to have arisen only after the French took over the island in 1895. See AMER PICON. The French had already turned the island of Réunion, which had begun making sugar cane "raque" in the early 1700s, into a high-volume sugar and rum

producer to replace the supply lost with the Haitian Revolution. Today, its production, from three distilleries, has been eclipsed by that of Mauritius, which became a sugar island under Dutch rule in the early 1600s, albeit a struggling one. In the 1700s, under the French, Mauritius exported more rum than sugar; that proportion was reversed in the next century, with the British in charge. Today, the country's six modern distilleries produce a good deal of rum (column still, from molasses) for export, but the industry is eclipsed in the local economy by tourism and financial services.

Mauritius is not the only country in the region with modern distilleries. East Africa has a belt of industrializing and urbanizing economies running south from Ethiopia through Kenya, Tanzania, Zambia, and Zimbabwe, and each has at least one modern, high-volume distillery, making spirits in various international categories, including gin, vodka, and blended whisky (where imported scotch whisky is mixed with local grain spirit in the Indian style). Some are entirely locally owned, but a number are partnerships with multinational spirits companies or brewers. In most cases, this sector of the industry serves as a sort of bridge between imported spirits and unbranded, local ones. Very little of what it produces is exported, except to other countries in the region. If history is any guide, however, it is only a matter of time before one of these companies succeeds in marketing a modernized version of one of the region's myriad village spirits internationally; indeed, with products such as Kenya's new, local-botanical Procera gin and Nigeria's Pedro's ogogoro, the process is already beginning. See OGOGORO and SPIRITS TRADE.

Baker, Samuel. *The Albert N'Yanza*, London: 1867.

Haworth, Alan, and Ronald Simpson, eds. *Moonshine Markets: Issues in Unrecorded Alcohol Beverage Production and Consumption.* New York: Brunner-Routledge, 2004.

Huetz de Lemps, Alain. *Boissons et civilizations en Afrique.* Bordeaux: Presses Universitaires de Bordeaux, 2001.

Patrick, James. "The Bootleggers of Madagascar." *Roads and Kingdoms*, March 5, 2018. https://roadsandkingdoms.com/2018/the-bootleggers-of-madagascar/ (accessed March 18, 2021).

David Wondrich

cereals are the domesticated grasses that are cultivated for human or animal food. Their starchy seeds or grains, the parts most commonly used, are generally high in carbohydrates and relatively low in proteins, with a varying amount of oils. Cereal grains are widely used in the production of spirits such as whisky, vodka, gin, aquavit, baiju, shochu, and others. See AQUAVIT; BAIJIU; GENEVER; GIN; SHOCHU; VODKA; and WHISKY.

Major cereals used for making spirits include corn/maize, rice, barley, wheat, sorghum, and rye. The process for using their grains involves breaking up the starches in the grain by cooking and enzymatic conversion, fermentation, and distillation. The resulting spirit may be aged in wood, or not. That is not, however, the only way they are used: the sweet sap that fills their stalks before they produce their seed-laden ears can also be squeezed out and fermented. This is still done with sorghum, and in the early United States it was done with maize, making "cornstalk rum" or "cornstalk whisky"—it is not obvious under which of those categories it falls.

There are also a few so-called pseudo-cereals—quinoa, buckwheat, amaranth—that have been used by US distillers to make spirits. These spirits have often been labeled as "whisky," but their definition is a bit of a gray area, given that the spirit regulations define "whisky" as made from a fermented mash of "grain" without defining that word as a "cereal."

"Cereal." *Britannica*. https://www.britannica.com/topic/cereal (accessed March 18, 2021).
27 CFR 5.22: The Standards of Identity.

Lew Bryson

chacha is an eau-de-vie from Georgia, in the Caucasus, and can be made from sea buckthorn or mulberry, but most frequently, like grappa or marc, is made from the leftover detritus of winemaking. See GRAPPA and MARC. Since Georgia was the wine basket for the former Soviet Union, the chacha tradition remained strong.

Taste chacha alongside its European equivalents, and the difference is apparent. The secret is the way the Georgians traditionally make their wine. Instead of pressing the grapes, wringing them dry, they pump the juice off the skins. This translates into a plump spirit, especially if you're a wine maker with a generous nature.

The traditional production method is to place the leftover wine-making material in a sealed bin to re-ferment over a month, though some people let it go much longer. Then, the concoction is moistened with wine or vinegar and poured into a wood-fired rustic pot still. The best chacha is aged for two years, in either *qvevri* (the buried clay vessel in which locals make wine) or in old barrels, since they won't give the spirit any pronounced woody flavors. At 45–65 percent ABV, it's potent stuff, but as the locals say, "Chacha is the direct path to heaven." And sometimes it's also a path to healing, as it is the first course of treatment for ailments from indigestion to random fevers. See HEALTH AND SPIRITS.

See also EAU-DE-VIE.

Feiring, Alice. *For the Love of Wine: My Odyssey through The World's Most Ancient Wine Culture*. Lincoln, NE: Potomac, 2016.

Alice Feiring

champagne cocktails must be divided into two traditions: the Champagne Cocktail proper, where the wine is the main ingredient, and cocktails (and other mixed drinks) where champagne is a modifier or other component. See MODIFIER.

The Champagne Cocktail

The first description of a Champagne Cocktail we have, with ice and bitters-saturated sugar, is from an American bar in Panama in 1855, around the time champagne was becoming the dry, fizzy drink we know today. (The recipe was published in 1862 by Jerry Thomas.) Its origins are obscure but may have something to do with the nature of champagne at the time: historically, frequent bad vintages had meant the wine was often hard and green. To make the champagne more attractive, winemakers added sugar, and until the 1840s, champagne was preferred sweet. If too sweet, it was best served almost frozen. The idea of a cocktail—spirits with sugar, bitters, and ice—with champagne in place of the spirits fit right in with those practices.

There is another factor. Bubbles are the primary characteristic of any Champagne Cocktail, but the distinctive fizz is a relatively recent development. Champagne was originally "brisk," "delicate," with a "prickling on the palate"; these bubbles gave champagne a unique selling feature to royalty and the rich. A gentle fizz was preferable to a frothy wine, an indication of too much sugar during vinification. However, as creating fine bubbles was mastered, they became important to the cocktail's mouthfeel. Thomas's instruction (1862) to shake the cocktail would re-energize the fizz, as would the use of granulated sugar in the drink, as he recommends (the sugar provides nucleation points for bubbles to form).

Improved viticulture and vinification meant that by the mid-nineteenth century a drier style began to emerge, and drinkers who were used to a sweet, icy drink would have had to add their own sugar. This would have helped the spread of the Champagne Cocktail. As "brut" champagne, initially disliked, became fashionable, it made additional ice less important. In the posthumous 1887 edition of Jerry Thomas's book, the amount of ice used was reduced, and heroic measures were not needed to stimulate bubbles. Only gentle stirring was advised, while Boothby (1908) stipulated NO stirring. See BOOTHBY, BILL.

The Champagne Cocktail remained a sporting-life favorite (one of its nicknames was "chorus girl's milk") well into the twentieth century, and it is still encountered, particularly in Europe.

Cocktails with Champagne

In the parlance of the bar, a cocktail or other drink topped off with champagne is known as a "Royal x" or an "x Royale" (sometimes "Imperial" is used instead). The roots of this usage stretch back to seventeenth-century England, where a drink normally made with beer or ale, when made with wine, was dubbed "royal"; thus punch made with wine instead of water was "Punch Royal." By the end of the eighteenth century, champagne was frequently used for Punch Royal, particularly in France and Germany; it helped that champagne's acidity gave essential balance to the punch, reducing the need for (often scarce) lemons. See REGENT'S PUNCH and CHATHAM ARTILLERY PUNCH.

It's unclear precisely when the addition of champagne jumped from the punch bowl to the individual cocktail or fizz or cooler, but the practice seems to have been greatly facilitated by the introduction of the "champagne tap," a French invention of the mid-nineteenth century that made it to the United Kingdom in the 1860s and United States in the 1870s. A spigot that was screwed through the cork, the tap allowed bartenders to pour small quantities of champagne without killing the wine's carbonation. By 1882, Harry Johnson was instructing bartenders to "squirt a little champagne" into a Fancy Brandy Cocktail, while Bill Boothby's Boothby Cocktail from the 1910s was simply a "Manhattan with a champagne float." See BOOTHBY, WILLIAM.

Among the classic drinks enhanced with champagne are the intoxicating French 75, the soothing Black Velvet, and any number of "pick me ups" (champagne was a popular hangover remedy). Among modern classics, the Seelbach cocktail and Audrey Saunders's 2004 Old Cuban are perhaps the best known. See SAUNDERS, AUDREY.

Although purists frequently claim that true champagne is wasted in cocktails and that they deserve only prosecco or other sparkling wines, the acidity of a good champagne, which serves to balance sweet ingredients, and its tight fizz, which adds texture, usually make champagne the expert's choice.

Recipe (Champagne Cocktail): Place a sugar cube in the bottom of a large champagne flute, add 3 dashes of Angostura bitters, and fill with cold champagne. Twist lemon peel over the top.

Baker, Charles H. *The Gentleman's Companion*, vol. 2: *Jigger, Beaker and Glass.* 1946; repr., Lanham, MD: Derrydale, 1992.

Boothby, William T. *The World's Drinks and How to Mix Them.* San Francisco: Pacific Buffet, 1908.

Thomas, Jerry. *How to Mix Drinks.* New York: Dick & Fitzgerald, 1862.

Tomes, Robert. *Panama in 1855.* New York: Harper & Brothers, 1855.

Elizabeth Gabay

chang'aa is a traditional distilled spirit from Kenya made from a base of fermented millet, maize, or sorghum that is generally pot-distilled in improvised equipment made out of oil drums. Potent and clear in color, chang'aa is similar to American moonshine and has a similarly illicit and often sordid past: indeed, *chang'aa* is Swahili for "kill me quickly." It is also known as "poison brew," a name earned by the frequency with which it is contaminated with methanol and, at least according to rumor, everything from jet fuel to embalming fluid. Until 2010, when the 1980 Chang'aa Prohibition Act was repealed, the moonshine was banned and sold illegally on the black market. Since legalization, it's been subject to a spate of safety and production regulations, although plenty of illegal chang'aa continues to be produced. See CENTRAL AND EAST AFRICA; KWETE; and MOONSHINE.

Aarhus, Paige. "Really Strange Brew." *Vice*, October 30, 2011. https://www.vice.com/en_us/article/bnyzwz/ really-strange-brew-0000009-v18n10 (accessed February 23, 2021).

Hibbert, Celeste. "In Pictures: Kenya's Deadly Drink." *Al Jazeera*, February 27, 2013. https://www. aljazeera.com/indepth/inpictures/2013/02/ 201322783655966424.html (accessed February 23, 2021).

Anna Archibald

The **channel knife and zester** are used to create different types of cocktail garnishes. The knife has, instead of a traditional blade, a small, raised scoop with a sharp edge that will—when it is pulled over the face of a lemon, lime, or other citrus fruit—dig into the rind and create a beautifully long strand of peel, only 3–5 millimeters wide. The zester is also a small hand tool with a line of small, sharp-edged cutting holes. It can be used like the channel knife but creates more delicate strands of the colored zest and without any of the pith.

See also GARNISH.

DearMartiniKitchen. "How to Use a Channel Knife." https://www.youtube.com/watch?v=eYtUR4zZMdk (accessed February 23, 2021).

Dietsch, Michael. "Knives You Need to Make Drinks." Serious Eats, June 16, 2011. http://drinks.seriouseats. com/2011/06/cocktail-101-knives-for-cocktails.html (accessed February 23, 2021).

Morgenthaler, Jeffrey. "The Channel Knife." Jeffrey Morgenthaler website, April 7, 2006. http://www. jeffreymorgenthaler.com/2006/the-channel-knife/ (accessed February 23, 2021).

Dale DeGroff

Chapin and Gore were iconic Chicago liquor dealers and saloonkeepers from the middle of the nineteenth century to the middle of the twentieth. James J. Gore (1830–1891), a teamster, met the more established Gardner Spring Chapin (1833–1895), a broker in mining stocks, in the early 1850s in the gold fields of California. In 1866, the two met again in Chicago, and Chapin took in Gore, then dealing faro, as a partner in his grocery store at the corner of State and Monroe, in the heart of what is now the Loop. Gore convinced Chapin to add a retail and wholesale liquor department, which was an immediate success. They soon launched their own 1867 Sour Mash brand of whisky. The reputation of Chapin and Gore's liquor brought a national audience to its brands that would include Old Reserve, launched in the early 1890s, and Old Jim Gore, trademarked in 1904; the latter survived until the late 1950s, and the former into the 1990s. The partners would eventually acquire their own distillery in Breckinridge County, Kentucky.

Legend has it that Jim Gore saved a good deal of the firm's stock from the Great Chicago Fire of October 1871 by hiring a group of men to roll hundreds of barrels full of their bourbon and rye into Lake Michigan to keep them safe from both flames and looters. Whether that is true or not—the contemporary newspapers are silent, although they do report that John McDevitt, "at one time the champion billiard-player of America," died at Chapin and Gore's when his friends couldn't rouse him to escape the flames—the firm did reopen its retail operation within a month, on Twenty-Second Street outside the burned zone.

The partners rebuilt at their original location as soon as possible. The new Chapin & Gore Café became the leading saloon in Chicago, and one of the most famous in America. According to Chicago historian Stephen Longstreet, this establishment had a reputation for being "high toned." It was host to such illustrious patrons as William McKinley (later to be the doomed president), Mark Twain, and Wild West showman William "Buffalo Bill" Cody, and it was famous for its extensive collection of caricatures of all the celebrities of the day. At the same time, the partners turned their temporary post-fire store on Twenty-Second Street into a saloon as well. This was so successful that, before long, they had branches not only throughout Chicago but in several other midwestern cities.

A bit of lore surrounding Chapin and Gore's cafe is that it was the birthplace of the Old-Fashioned cocktail, due in part to the fact that the first known published Old-Fashioned recipe can be credited to Theodore Proulx (1861–1918), the cafe's head bartender. This, however, only goes to show that Proulx was the first to write down the recipe, not that he or anyone at the bar actually invented the cocktail.

After the deaths of its founders, the company continued to be successful and in 1905 built the Prairie School–style Nepeenauk Building, at 65 East Adams Street, in the bustling heart of the Loop, to house its offices and warehousing (it still stands, a National Historic and Chicago Landmark). On the street level was the large and ornate Nepeenauk Bar, which featured a long wooden bar and fine cut-glass spirit glasses stacked on the backbar, that continued to offer Chapin and Gore whiskys as well as the popular cocktails of the day, with a special focus on the Old-Fashioned cocktail.

The company was forced to shut down by Prohibition, but its whisky brands at least were resurrected in 1934 by the McKesson-Robbins corporation, using whisky produced by Schenley Distilleries. What was left of the brand was sold when McKesson went out of the spirits business in the late 1980s.

"The Dead of Chicago." *New York Times*, November 17, 1871.

Hernandez, Joseph. "Historic Chicago Cocktails." *Chicago Tribune*, May 15, 2017. http://www.chicagotribune.com/dining/drink/ct-food-0517-historic-chicago-cocktails-20170512-story.html (accessed February 23, 2021).

Minnick, Fred. *Bourbon Curious*. Minneapolis: Zenith Press, 2015.

Proulx, Theodore. *The Bartender's Manual*, rev. ed. Chicago: 1888.

Sullivan, Jack. "Chapin and Gore: Kings of the Chicago Saloon." *Those Pre-Pro Whiskey Men*, July 9, 2013. http://pre-prowhiskeymen.blogspot.com/2013/07/chapin-and-gore-kings-of-chicago-saloon.html (accessed February 23, 2021).

Martin Duffy

charanda is a Mexican rum distilled chiefly from cold-extracted, fermented sugar-cane juice, although sugar-cane byproducts, including molasses and piloncillo, can also be used. To be considered charanda, the sugar cane must be grown within its appellation of Michoacán, Mexico, and undergo double distillation (some producers use pot stills, others column; some charandas blend the two distillates). Made since the mid-nineteenth century, charanda was first called that in 1907, when Cleofas Murguíra Riera opened a distillery in Uruapan and used the name for his cane distillate. It received a protected designation of origin in 2013. See PDO. In the native Purépecha language its name denotes the red-hued soil of the region. Popular brands include Tarasco and Uruapan, which are still primarily found in Mexico. Until recently, charanda's market was purely domestic, but the rise in interest in artisanal rum seen in the 2010s has brought it into foreign markets, where it has won accolades among the cognoscenti.

See also CHINGUIRITO; MEXICO; and RUM.

"Charanda." In *Denominaciones de Origen: Orgullo de Mexico*, 95–107. Mexico City: Tirant lo Blanch, 2016.

Anna Archibald

charcoal filtration is a method of removing substances from a liquid by exposing it to charcoal, a porous black material comprised of carbon and ash that is obtained by the controlled slow burning of wood or other organic matter in a low-oxygen environment. As liquid flows into the charcoal, certain molecules bond with and are trapped by the carbon at the surface through a process known as adsorption. Because it works primarily through chemical attraction, charcoal filtration is effective at removing some substances but not others, depending on their molecular properties. Once all the available surface binding sites have been used up, the charcoal medium is no longer effective at filtration and must be replaced.

In the production of spirits, charcoal filtration may be used prior to distillation to purify water. It may also be used after distillation of unaged spirits such as vodka, prior to barrel aging as in the Lincoln County process used to make some Tennessee whiskies, or after aging in order to produce a lighter flavor and remove color from spirits such as white rum. The effect of charcoal filtration can be different depending upon the source material and the form and purity of the charcoal (e.g., the birch charcoal traditionally favored by Russian vodka distillers, or the maple charcoal used by Jack Daniel's Tennessee whisky), as well as the chemical properties of the liquid undergoing treatment and the filtration procedure itself. Even aging in charred-wood barrels may be understood as including an element of charcoal filtration, as the spirit interacts with the carbonized material created by the charring process.

See also BACARDI; JACK DANIEL'S; and LINCOLN COUNTY PROCESS.

Pokhlebkin, William. *A History of Vodka*. Translated by Renfrey Clarke. London: Verso, 1991.

Samuel Lloyd Kinsey

charring, toasting (and recharring) refers to heating the inside of a wooden barrel prior to the addition of spirits or wine. Toasting is an original part of barrel making, the staves being hooped together at one end and then inverted over a low fire to relax the wood enough so that they can be bent together at the other end (now many barrels are steamed instead, although French wine barrels are still toasted). Deliberate charring dates to the end of the eighteenth century, when it was introduced as a way to keep casked water pure; by the 1820s, charred barrels were being used in America to age rye whisky. See WHISKY, RYE.

The most efficient way to heat a barrel is to use a flame at various intensities. Heating barrels with an electric coil imparts less aroma from the heat source. Depending on its maturity, white oak, the standard material for whisky barrels, is made up of cellulose (40–53 percent), hemicellulose (15–30 percent), lignin (7–30 percent), and minor chemicals such as fats, oils, resins, proteins, and ash (5–11 percent). Cellulose and hemicellulose are rather large molecules that can be up to ten thousand sugar units in length. Lignin cements together wood's cellulose and hemicellulose, much like mortar in a brick wall. It is the most abundant non-carbohydrate in the world and is made up of five thousand units of connected phenols. The primary purpose of heating a barrel is to break down the cellulose, hemicellulose, and lignin into their

building blocks, termed "wood extracts." A good analogy is the game Jenga, which involves a series of stacked blocks. Imagine each block piece represents either the sugar from cellulose, hemicellulose, or phenol from lignin. Each piece that is pulled out of the tower would represent a wood extract dissolving into the ethanol. Eventually the tower will crumble, and, as in real life, so does a barrel when used long enough.

Controlling the level of wood extracts from a cask can be difficult, especially when casks have been reused multiple times. How the barrel is heated is very important for creating flavors for the spirit or wine. There are two fundamental methods. The first method is charring: when a barrel is burnt with such intensity that it blackens the surface and transforms the hemicellulose, cellulose, and lignin to pure carbon. The second method is toasting: burning a barrel with a less intense heat, which turns the surface of the wood brown or red rather than the blackened surface of a char.

Wood flavor is controlled by temperature of the burn. When wood temperature reaches 100° C, its physical strength starts to change and its lipids, oils, lactones, and resins degrade. At 140–260° C hemicellulose breaks down into simple sugars and starts to brown (toasting), which creates caramel and toffee notes. Lignin degrades in the range of 150–300° C and creates vanilla and phenolic (smoky) notes. At 275° C wood catches fire, and the degradation of cellulose to wood sugars occurs. Cellulose breaks down from 275 to 350° C. Above 475° C all the components will degrade into pure black carbon, which absorbs any sulfur from the sprit or wine. There is a temperature gradient across the width of a burned barrel stave. It may be above 475° C at the surface and creating char, but several millimeters underneath there is a layer with a red hue that contains the wood extracts. When classifying barrels for purchase, specifications are based on millimeter of burn depth.

Barrels may also be heated to remove unwanted flavors from a previous barrel fill. Barrels act like a sponge, so that what was in the first fill of the barrel will diffuse into the second. The simplest way to remove unwanted flavor is to burn a barrel again—this is recharring. Sometimes blenders want to finish their product in a used barrel to create unique flavor combinations.

In the United States, where straight whiskies must be aged in new, charred oak barrels, there are four levels of char, of increasing thickness, culminating in the no. 4, or "alligator," char. An important part of the American cellarmaster's art is choosing the proper level of char for his or her whisky.

Arcticus [pseud.]. "Literary Intelligence from Russia: Purifying Water." *The Bee*, January 16, 1793, 108.

Di Blasi, C. "Combustion and Gasification Rates of Lignocellulosic Chars." *Progress in Energy and Combustion Science* 35 (2009): 121–140.

Gerhards, C. C. "Effect of Moisture Content and Temperature on the Mechanical Properties of Wood: An Analysis of Immediate Effects." *Wood Fiber* 14 (1982): 4–36.

Holtzapple, M. T. "Lignin." In *Encyclopedia of Food Science and Nutrition*, 2nd ed., ed. Benjamin Caballero, 3535–3542. London: Academic Press.

Parker, M. *The Arcana of Arts and Sciences, or Farmers' & Mechanics' Manual*, Washington, PA: 1824.

Raven, P. H., R. F. Evert, and S. E. Eichhorn. *Biology of Plants*, 5th ed. New York: Worth, 1992.

Schniewind, A. P. *Concise Encyclopedia of Wood and Wood-Based Materials*. Elmsford, NY: Pergamon.

Shebani, A. N., A. J. Van Reenen, and M. Meincken. "The Effect of Wood Extractives on the Thermal Stability of Different Wood Species." *Thermochimica Acta* 471 (2008): 43–50.

Don Livermore

Chartreuse is a French monastic herbal liqueur produced in Aiguenoire, in the Chartreuse Mountains, under the supervision of Carthusian monks—although most employees of the distillery are laypeople. There are two main styles, green Chartreuse and yellow Chartreuse. Both are based on a mix of 130 botanicals. The liqueurs are distilled, sweetened, and naturally colored according to a secret formula known only to a handful of monks. They are also aged for an undetermined amount of time.

According to brand lore, a French nobleman, François-Annibal d'Estrées, bequeathed the formula for a "long life" elixir to the Carthusian order in 1605. Known today as the Elixir Végétal de la Grande Chartreuse, it has been sold by the order at least since 1764. This elixir, intense and medicinal, inspired the monks to create a more pleasant liqueur, first sold in 1840. It became known as the green Chartreuse. The yellow version, sweeter and lower in alcohol (43°, compared to 55° for green Chartreuse), quickly followed. A white Chartreuse was also available until the end of the nineteenth century. Since the 1960s Chartreuse has produced extra-aged expressions of both liqueurs, called VEP (for "vieillissement exceptionnellement prolongé," or "exceptionally long aging"). This main range coexists with numerous limited or special editions.

Although Chartreuse has been produced in the foothills of the French Alps for most of its history, a conflict between the French state and the Catholic Church saw the Carthusian order expelled from France in 1903. They relaunched production in Tarragona, Spain, where they kept a distillery until 1989. They were first allowed back in France to open a distillery in Marseille in 1921, but only in 1932 were they able to resettle their operation in the Chartreuse Mountains. Since 2018, Chartreuse has been produced at a new distillery in Aiguenoire.

Both styles of Chartreuse are mostly drunk straight, as a digestive. Locally, yellow and green Chartreuse are sometimes mixed in a drink called an Episcopale. The liqueurs don't appear in cocktail books until the 1880s, when authors such as Harry Johnson or George Kappeler called for them in recipes such as the Bijou or the Widow's Kiss (although a "Punch Chartreuse," with the liqueur mixed with cold tea and sugar, appears in a French punch book in 1866, as a drink popular in Lyon). See Bijou and Widow's Kiss. Their striking colors also made them popular choices for layered Pousse Cafés. See Pousse Café. But Chartreuse's cocktail golden age has undeniably been the cocktail renaissance. Spurred by Murray Stenson's rediscovery of the Last Word, bartenders have increasingly turned to these monastic liqueurs for inspiration. See Last Word and Stenson, Murray. Marcovaldo Dionysos's green Chartreuse–based Chartreuse Swizzle and Joaquin Simo's Naked and Famous, featuring the yellow version, have become modern classics. Chartreuse was born as a "long life" elixir. It's quite fitting that it probably has never been more popular than it is now, in its fifth century.

Galiano, Martine, et al. *Chartreuse: La Liqueur*. Voiron, France: Chartreuse, 2019.

Turenne [pseud.]. *La véritable manière de faire le Punch*. Paris: 1866.

François Monti

Chatham Artillery Punch, a nineteenth-century specialty of Savannah, Georgia, bears one of the most famous and, to those who have consumed it, formidable names in the annals of mixology. While there is a great deal of variation among the older recipes for it, they all agree in deploying copious amounts of mixed spirits, minimally cut with lemon juice and sugar, and lengthened with champagne.

The two early accounts of the drink's origins (from 1883 and 1900) differ slightly in detail, but triangulating between them yields the following account. The punch was created when the Chatham Artillery, a volunteer militia manned by socially prominent young men, was welcomed back to Savannah after an 1859 trip to Nashville. Alonzo B. Luce (1816–1879), an honorary member of the company who owned and tended bar at the Marshall House, the city's finest hotel, brewed the punch from spirits provided by wholesaler William Murray Davidson, the son of one of Admiral Nelson's officers at Trafalgar and a lieutenant in the company. At its inception the punch's formula was simple: according to the 1883 account in the *Augusta Chronicle*, "One of the horse buckets of ordinary size [12–16 liters] was filled with finely crushed ice; a quart of good brandy, whisky and rum each was poured into the ice, and sugar and lemon added. The bucket was filled to the brim with champagne, and the whole stirred into delirious deliciousness." The 1900 account, from the *Savannah Morning News*, gives the same ingredients, plus "a gallon of some light wine." In any case, as the *Chronicle* noted, in Savannah, "from that day artillery punch has been a regular convivial institution . . . and as a vanquisher of men its equal has never been found."

Savannah was exporting bottled versions of Artillery Punch to the rest of Georgia by the late 1860s. Five years later, it was known throughout the South. By the 1880s, its fame was nationwide. It helped that it had become a custom in Savannah to test visiting dignitaries against "Old Artillery Punch." Many, including ex-president Chester A. Arthur; Admiral Dewey, fresh from his victory at Manila Bay; and a selection of senators, governors, and justices, went up against it and were found wanting.

By the 1890s, Luce's simple formula seems to have been modified, judging from published recipes in which catawba wine has replaced the brandy and things such as green tea, pineapples, oranges, strawberries, and maraschino cherries have been added. The results were somewhat less immediately intoxicating, and deliberately so, "experience," as one recipe writer explained in 1907, "having taught the rising generation to modify the receipt of their forefathers to conform to the weaker constitutions of their progeny."

With temperance on the rise in Georgia in the 1900s and 1910s, Chatham Artillery Punch began to fade as a civic institution in Savannah. By 1912, it was served no more at official banquets. It made something of a comeback after Repeal, but by then it bore little relation to its former self. Recipes from

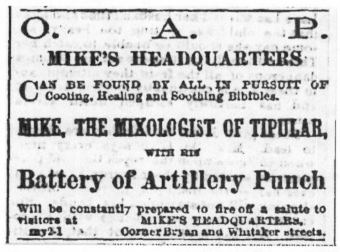

Advertisement for Mike "The Mixologist of Tipular" Quinan's "O.A.P." (Old Artillery Punch), Savannah, Georgia, 1870. Wondrich Collection.

the time offer a catchall mixture of gin, rye whisky, light rum, Bénédictine, and the now-canonical tea, lemons, and oranges. There is little left of Luce's simple, elegant formula but the champagne—and, once again, the potency. This version has survived as an occasional social drink in parts of the South. Modern attempts to revive Luce's formula have proven that its reputation was in no way exaggerated.

See also PUNCH.

Recipe: Seal the peels of 4 lemons and 180 ml sugar in a jar overnight. Add 180 ml lemon juice and shake to dissolve. Pour into a 4-liter bowl half full of roughly cracked ice. Add 250 ml each aged, pot-distilled rum, bourbon whisky, and VSOP cognac. Stir and top with 750 ml chilled champagne.

"Artillery Punch and Other Things." *Atlanta Constitution*, March 22, 1900, 6.
Hammond, Percy, and George C. Wharton. *Poker, Smoke and Other Things*. Chicago: Reilly & Britton, 1907.
"Punch Has Lost Potency." *Savannah Morning News*, April 1, 1900, 9.
"Savannah Salad." *Augusta Chronicle*, February 18, 1883, 2.

David Wondrich

chauffe-vin ("wine-heater" in French) is a large, turnip-shaped enameled copper chamber, through which the lyne arm of a cognac still passes on its way to the condenser, preheating the wine held within prior to the inaugural distillation. Introduced in the late nineteenth century, the chauffe-vin lowers fuel costs and increases the efficiency of the condenser. Some cognac distillers, however, believe that it puts wines at risk of oxidizing and do not use it.

See also ALEMBIC and COGNAC.

Baudoin, A. *Les eaux-de-vie et la fabrication du cognac*. Paris: J. B. Baillière et fils, 1893.
"What Is Cognac Made Of?" Cognac Expert website. https://www.cognac-expert.com/what-is-cognac-made-of/ (accessed April 20, 2021).

Alia Akkam

cherry brandy is a term applied both to a distilled spirit made from cherry fruit or pomace and to what is essentially a cherry-flavored liqueur.

True Cherry Brandy

True cherry brandy is distilled from cherries, which are pressed (the pits are often cracked in the process), fermented, and, generally, pot-distilled. Sour morello cherries (*Prunus cerasus*) are the preferred varietal, but others can be used as well. The resulting spirit is customarily bottled without barrel aging or added sugar and is strong and nutty, the pits contributing almond-like notes, and of a peculiar deep pungency. The acknowledged world capital of cherry-brandy making is a belt that stretches from Alsace in France, through the Black Forest in Germany, and into the northern cantons of Switzerland, with outposts in Austria and all the way down into Croatia and Serbia. It is also made in the United States. See KIRSCHWASSER.

Cherry-Flavored Brandy

The second, more generally popular form of cherry brandy is made by macerating cherries in a grape brandy or other spirit or infusing it with cherry juice and sweetening the result to make a dark-red, often somewhat cloudy cordial. In England, this first appears in the late seventeenth century as "cherry bounce," with "cherry brandy" following shortly after. Although French brandy was preferred as the base spirit, it was also often made with English "brandy," a rectified and doctored malt-based spirit. In England's American colonies, of course, rum was the preferred spirit, although raw whisky or whatever else was available seems to have been considered an acceptable substitute if no rum was to be had. Indeed, a 1777 list of tavern prices from western Maryland includes a line for "all liquors intermixed with cherries" (as well as one for "apple & cherry [brandies]," which suggests that true cherry brandy was also being served).

This cherry brandy was and is not confined to England: as "guignolet," it is also a specialty of central France. Originally, this had a brandy base, but today beet neutral spirit appears to be more common. Poland and eastern Europe in general also specialize in the spirit, which is there based on vodka and known as wishniak. Much of Europe, however, adopted the English name for the spirit.

The leading historic brand of cherry brandy, Cherry Heering, was founded in 1818 by Peter Heering (1792–1875) in Copenhagen, who at first made it primarily for export. Cherry Heering, as it came to be called, has been produced in Denmark ever since, although today it is based on neutral spirit and is owned by the Dutch DeKuyper company. The Dutch Bols company was also famous for its Dry Cherry Brandy, where the cordial was blended back with plain brandy. Both of these were widely exported and, by the end of the nineteenth century, found extensive use in the "American bars" of Europe and around the world, although rather less in the United States.

Finally, it should be noted that there is a third type of cherry brandy: maraschino, originally a specialty of Dalmatia, on the Adriatic coast, this is distilled from cherries like a true cherry brandy and is likewise clear in color but is heavily sweetened and used as a liqueur. See MARASCHINO.

In Cocktails

Most drink recipes that call for cherry brandy employ the cherry-flavored version, including the legendary Singapore Sling, the Blood and Sand, and the Remember the Maine. See BLOOD AND SAND and SINGAPORE SLING. In recent times, however, bartenders have become more accustomed to using the clear, dry cherry brandies in their cocktails. The Cuzco cocktail, for example, created by bartender Julie Reiner uses kirschwasser as a rinse for the glass. See REINER, JULIE.

Dominé, André. *The Ultimate Guide to Spirits and Cocktails*. Cambridge: H. F. Ullman, 2008.

Everts, Louis H. *A History of Western Maryland*, vol. 1. Philadelphia: Louis H. Everts, 1882.

Smith, George. *A Compleat Body of Distilling*. London: 1738.

Derek Brown and David Wondrich

Chicote, Pedro "Perico" (1899–1977) was the most important Spanish bartender of the twentieth century. Over a career spanning more than six decades, he wrote five books, traveled the world, and amassed over twenty thousand bottles that he housed in his Madrid bar until his death.

Born on May 13, 1899, in Madrid, Chicote lost his father at an early age and had to take a variety of small jobs to provide for his family. Through a friend, he became a waiter and, in 1916, started work at the bar of the Ritz, where he received the first bottle of his collection. See RITZ.

From 1923, he worked as a full-fledged bartender in various establishments patronized by Madrid's higher classes, which had taken to cocktails during World War I. During summers, he followed his clientele to the resort town of San Sebastian. It was at Pidoux, the first serious American bar in Madrid, that Chicote really made a name for himself. During his stint there, he wrote the first of his eight books, *El Bar Americano en España*, and became quite the celebrity—he even had his own perfume.

In 1931, with the money he earned at Pidoux, he opened Chicote on Gran Via, then Madrid's most modern avenue. (Later renamed Museo Chicote, the art deco bar exists to this day.) Cocktails were then in fashion, and those were Chicote's golden years, although he is better known for the visits he received from figures such as Dwight D. Eisenhower or Ava Gardner in the 1950s, when he became a poster boy for the Franco regime. (His politics, though, remain vague: the preface of his second book was written by the left-wing Nobel Prize laureate Jacinto Benavente, and it was under the republic that he was handed the parliament's catering—which he kept under the dictatorship.)

Although Spanish bartenders still follow some of his precepts (such as twisting citruses with ice tongs instead of hands), none of Chicote's recipes, most of them variations on the Perfect Martini, are classics. See PERFECT. It was his uncanny ability to connect with clients of all walks of life that ensured his popularity. His funeral on Christmas Day 1977 was a very public affair, and he is probably the only bartender to have a commemorative plaque placed on the house where he lived.

Gomez-Santos, Marino. *Perico Chicote*. Barcelona: Ediciones Cliper, 1958.

J.M.O. [pseud.]. "Con Chicote murió una parte de la historia de Madrid." *Blanco y Negro*, January 4, 1978, 44.

"Pedro Chicote." *ABE : Órgano oficial de la Asociación de Barmen españoles* 1 (1965).

François Monti

chill filtration is a process in which barrel-matured spirits are chilled to between −10° C to 4° C and then filtered through a membrane to remove molecular compounds such as fatty esters and other sediments suspended in the liquid. These compounds can cause whisky to haze when exposed to low temperatures, as in the addition of cold water or water. Distilleries that skillfully chill-filter can tweak the filter material, its porosity, its thickness, and the pressure and temperature of filtration—all conditions that will reduce the haze-inducing elements but also subtly alter the taste and texture of the final product. This increased clarity, improved liquid stability, and, its proponents claim, enhanced flavor are the main goals of chill filtration. Opponents of the process—and there are many—believe that eliminating the fatty esters and other molecular compounds diminishes mouth feel and taste. However, in a 2014 comparative blind tasting of over a thousand whiskies by 111 whisky connoisseurs, the chill-filtered whiskies received essentially the same ratings as non-chill-filtered whiskies.

Lüning, Horst. "Study on the Chill Filtration of Scotch Single Malt Whiskies: Comparative Assessment of a Blind Tasting." Whisky.com, 2014. https://www.whisky.com/information/knowledge/science/study-on-the-chill-filtration-of-scotch-single-malt-whiskies.html (accessed February 24, 2021).

Heather Greene

China is the world's largest producer and consumer of spirits by volume, particularly those of the homegrown category known as baijiu. China has frequently conquered and been conquered by its neighbors and later fell victim to imperialist incursions, but it has retained a contiguous cultural identity throughout its long history. The nation's stability has facilitated rapid innovation in the field of alcohol fermentation and distillation, and its cultural influence aided in the proliferation of these techniques across East Asia.

History

The origins of Chinese alcohol are murky. We have only a rough sketch of the first several millennia, stitched together from later histories, legends, and archaeological inference. As early as 7000 BCE civilizations along the Yellow River began brewing the world's oldest documented alcohol, and by the time Emperor Qin Shihuang unified China in 221 BCE, the nation's winemakers had already developed the technique of fermenting grains using naturally harvested yeast cultures, or *qu*. See QU. This technique produced alcoholic beverages far more potent—as high as 15 percent ABV—and more flavorful than the primitive brews that preceded it. This new drink, known as *huangjiu*, or "yellow wine," remained the preferred tipple of the Chinese elite until the twentieth century, though it was never widely consumed by the peasantry. China has always had a large population and limited arable land, so the cereals used to brew huangjiu (principally rice, wheat, millet, and sorghum) were more prized as food sources. See CEREAL.

Historians disagree as to how and when the Chinese began distilling alcohol, but they believe that spirits were introduced to China as early as the second century CE and no later than the eleventh. See DISTILLATION, HISTORY OF. Early Chinese spirits were probably similar to the arrack of their day but soon evolved into something more distinctive: *shaojiu* ("burnt wine"), or what we now call *baijiu* ("white spirits"). See ARRACK. With baijiu the Chinese peasant finally had a drink of his own, a rough-around-the-edges economic alternative to aristocratic huangjiu. Baijiu's production required a similar expenditure of grain as huangjiu, but it was stupefyingly strong—sometimes exceeding 70 percent ABV.

Modern Chinese Alcohol

In the early twentieth century, a few baijiu distillers began applying a modern approach to their craft, but full-scale industrialization of Chinese alcohol did not begin until after the Chinese Revolution under Chairman Mao Zedong in 1949. Baijiu was formerly the drink of the proletariat, which perfectly suited the needs of the ruling Communist Party. The government consolidated numerous small family-run distilleries, some of which had operated independently for centuries, into massive state-run distilleries. By the 1950s, the Chinese state had created most of today's leading baijiu producers. China had finally developed the capability to produce spirits on a massive scale, but most consumption was rationed and limited to provincial or regional spirits.

The Chinese alcohol industry began resembling a modern commercial enterprise following the death of Mao Zedong, with China's so-called

Reform and Opening Up policies of the late 1970s and early 1980s. With the reintroduction of private ownership and market economics, the state-run distilleries began to compete for hundreds of millions of new consumers by diversifying their products, improving old recipes, and inventing entire new spirit categories. National brands gained currency, and new distilleries opened. During the first three decades of this experiment, the Chinese spirits industry experienced rapid profit growth, largely on the strength of large government orders, and by 2012 some estimates suggested that Chinese distillers were producing more than 11 billion liters each year, a greater volume than the global production of vodka and whisky combined.

But the "opening up" of the post-Mao era was not confined to baijiu. Foreign liquors and wines entered the Chinese market with great success, with French cognac and scotch whisky far in the lead. Western-style bars have opened in major cities, and beer has become the most popular alcoholic beverage in China. On the strength of their sales in China, three international spirits giants—Diageo, Pernod-Ricard, and LVHM—entered joint-venture agreements with Chinese distilleries to create new baijiu brands in the mid-2000s. See DIAGEO and PERNOD-RICARD.

At the outset of the twenty-first century, alcohol's place in Chinese society reflects a number of larger social trends, namely, a generational divide between tradition and modernity, nationalism and globalization. Chinese drinks like baijiu and huangjiu are as popular as ever, but their consumption is almost exclusively limited to traditional Chinese meals and banquets. Foreign drinks are served at international venues, like bars, nightclubs, and the ever-popular karaoke parlor, or KTV. Moreover, younger generations are eschewing baijiu for its less aggressively flavored and lower-proof foreign counterparts. Various attempts are underway to reverse this trend, such as a move toward incorporating baijiu into cocktail menus and improving its visibility overseas, but only time will determine the viability of this approach.

See also BAIJIU.

China: The IWSR's Annual Report on Consumption of Alcoholic Drinks. London: International Wine & Spirit Research, May 2012.

Gately, Iain. *Drink: A Cultural History of Alcohol.* New York: Gotham, 2008.

Fu Jianwei. *Intoxicated in the Land of Wine.* Translated by Orientaltrans. Beijing: China Publishing Group, 2009.

McGovern, Patrick E., Juzhong Zhang, Jigen Tang, Zhiqing Zhang, Gretchen R. Hall, Robert A. Moreau, Alberto Nunez, et al. "Fermented Beverages of Pre- and Proto-Historic China." *Proceedings of the National Academy of Sciences USA* 101, no. 51 (2004): 17593–17598.

"More Chinese Drinkers Turning to Imported Spirits, but Baijiu Still King." *Jing Daily*, May 4, 2012.

Xu Ganrong and Bao Tongfa. *Grandiose Survey of Chinese Alcoholic Drinks and Beverages* (中国酒大观目录, Chinese and English versions). Jiangnan University, 1998.

Derek Sandhaus

Chinese still is an early form of still in which the distillate drips into a catch bowl placed inside the heating chamber and then runs out through a tube to a receiving vessel. See STILL, POT.

chinguirito is the old Mexican vernacular name for *aguardiente de caña*, or rum. Although the name first appears in the early eighteenth century, the spirit is considerably older, dating to sometime between 1524, when cane was introduced to Mexico, and 1600, when it is first mentioned. It was traditionally distilled from the *mieles*—syrups—that were byproducts of sugar production: molasses and skimmings, but sometimes also from reduced sugar-cane juice. As late as 1800, some distillers were still using Chinese-style wooden pot stills. See MOLASSES; SKIMMINGS; and STILL, POT.

In the seventeenth and eighteenth centuries, production was both very large and very widespread, although it was centered in a broad belt running from Veracruz in the east, through Cuernavaca, south of Mexico City, to Michoacán in the west. It is impossible, however, to provide statistics for this production, as almost all of it was illicit: between 1631 and 1796, the Spanish crown issued an increasingly drastic series of decrees explicitly prohibiting the manufacture, distribution, and possession of cane spirits, occasionally even accompanying them with funds for enforcement, which was draconian. Chinguirito was so easy to make, cheap, and abundant that it drastically reduced the colonial market for Spanish wines and brandies, the licensing of which provided a significant portion of the royal revenue.

While production continued in the nineteenth century, gradually agave spirits took over much of chinguirito's role in Mexican drinking, although there are still areas where considerable quantities of cane are distilled, either on its own or as part of the wash from which *mixto* tequila is made. Some of this production is artisanal and of very high quality.

Traditionally, chinguirito was most popular in Mexico's cities, where it was consumed both on its own and in *mistelas*, some of the mixed drinks in which Mexico abounds, many of them incorporating pulque and others variations on punch.

See also CHARANDA; HABANERO; MEXICO; PUNCH; and RUM.

Armendares, Teresa Lozano. *El chinguirito vindicado*. Mexico City: Universidad Nacional Autónoma de México, 2005.
Palomo, Jose Jesus Hernandez. *El aguardiente de caña en México*. Seville: Escuela de Estudios Hispano-Americanos, 1974.

David Wondrich

Chivas Regal is one of the most established and respected brands of blended scotch whisky, with a history going back to the early nineteenth century. See WHISKY, SCOTCH. The whisky started life as a house brand for a grocery store in Aberdeen, Scotland, that was established in 1801 and specialized in luxury goods, from coffee to Caribbean rums. James Chivas worked there and ultimately acquired the business in the mid-nineteenth century, and he eventually ran it with his brother John under the name Chivas Brothers. The business started producing its own blended whisky, using casks that James Chivas had laid down in the cellar. While the brothers passed away—John in 1862, James in 1886—the business continued on as Chivas Brothers.

In 1909, Chivas Brothers introduced Chivas Regal 25 Year Old, a whisky "designed to woo the high societies of the United States," according to Scotchwhisky.com. The business was severely impacted by Prohibition (although the brand was one of the highest-priced spirits on the American black market), but in the post-Prohibition era, Chivas relaunched in the United States with Chivas Regal 12 Year Old, which went on to become a global icon. Chivas Brothers was later acquired by Seagram in 1949 and then by Pernod Ricard in 2001. See SEAGRAM'S and PERNOD RICARD. Throughout the years, the brand has expanded its portfolio with a series of ongoing and limited releases, including Chivas Regal 18 Year Old Gold Signature, Chivas Regal 25 Year Old Original Legend, Chivas Regal Extra, and Chivas Regal The Icon. As of 2015, Chivas Regal ranked as the third-best-selling scotch whisky brand.

"Chivas Regal." Scotchwhisky.com, https://scotchwhisky.com/whiskypedia/2340/chivas-regal/ (accessed February 24, 2021).
Chivas Regal website, http://www.chivas.com/en/int/ (accessed February 24, 2021).
Hopkins, Amy. "Top 10 Best-Selling Scotch Whisky Brands". *The Spirits Business*, June 22, 2015. http://www.thespiritsbusiness.com/2015/06/top-10-best-selling-scotch-whisky-brands/9/ (accessed February 24, 2021).

Charles Passy

The **Chocolate Martini**, with vodka, chocolate liqueur, or syrup, and sometimes another liqueur, was created by Rock Hudson and Elizabeth Taylor in Texas in 1955 on the set of the film *Giant*. That at least is the claim Taylor advanced in her 1987 diet book *Elizabeth Takes Off*, although there is no known corroborating document published during the three decades between. Taylor described their original combination of vodka, Kahlúa, and Hershey's chocolate syrup as "the best drink I ever tasted." See KAHLUA. Hudson later explained, "We were really just kids, we could eat and drink anything and we never needed sleep."

In the 1960s, some San Franciscans took to jocularly applying the name to the Black Russian, but the term never reached the wider culture. Nonetheless, this usage might have got the name around. It is difficult to otherwise explain the 1972 *Eek & Meek* comic strip in which a bar patron's order of a Chocolate Martini gets him booted out the door. (This does accurately reflect the general disdain for this drink held by cocktail traditionalists.)

The drink did not gain momentum until around 1995, at the height of the sweet Martini craze of the 1980s and 1990s. While some of these later

Chocolate Martinis strove for a clear or at least translucent form, combining vodka with chocolate liqueur and/or crème de cacao, others included dairy or cream liqueurs such as Bailey's in the mix, approaching the concept behind the Alexander of the 1910s. See ALEXANDER. The presentation was often gussied up with a cocoa or chocolate-syrup rim, chocolate-syrup-drizzled interior, and/or a solid, grated, or powdered chocolate garnish. Moreover, Taylor's coffee liqueur element was seldom utilized. Gary Regan offered up his adaptation of a 1993 recipe from Max's South Beach, Miami, as follows (although many recipes drop the liqueur amount down to as low as a half ounce or split it with a chocolate cream liqueur such as Godiva). See REGAN, GARY.

Recipe: Stir 60 ml vodka and 45 ml white crème de cacao with ice, strain into a cocoa-rimmed cocktail glass, and garnish with a Hershey's Hug candy.

Caen, Herb. "These Things I Like." *San Francisco Chronicle*, July 4, 1966, sec. 2, 25.
Regan, Gary. *The Joy of Mixology*. New York: Clarkson Potter, 2003.
Ross, Fiona. *Dining with the Famous and Infamous*. Lanham, MD: Rowman & Littlefield, 2016.
Schneider, Howie. *Eek & Meek*, April 29, 1972.
Taylor, Elizabeth. *Elizabeth Takes Off*. New York: Putnam, 1987.

Frederic Yarm

Christian Carl (CARL GmbH) is a manufacturer of stills and distillation equipment. First established in Göppingen, Germany, in 1869, the company split into two competing companies in 1916, one headed by the founder's son Christian Carl and the second by Christian's brother, Jacob, with both companies working with the brewing and distilling industries. In 2002, Jacob Carl GmbH declared bankruptcy and was acquired by its longtime competitor, and in 2008, Christian Carl Ing GmbH relocated to the neighboring industrial park of Eislingen and rebranded as CARL GmbH. The company provides equipment and services to industrial distilleries as well as smaller distilleries, and Carl stills and equipment are used by many research and craft distilleries worldwide. Indeed, the firm's Capel-style hybrid stills, where the vapor from a pot still can be fed into a separate rectification column if needed, are a modern craft distillery staple. See CAPEL STILL and STILL, HYBRID.

CARL website. https://carl.info/de/ (accessed September 13, 2016).

Paul Clarke

Ciro's was a chain of restaurants that from the 1890s through the 1950s was as famous for the quality of its bars as it was for the excellence of its cuisine and the exclusivity of its clientele, and it was instrumental in naturalizing the American cocktail in Europe. With outposts in Monte Carlo, Paris, London, the French resorts of Deauville and Bagnères de Luchon, and eventually Berlin, Hollywood, and New York, Ciro's was well placed to cater to the one-percenters of its day: royalty, aristocrats of all stripes, industrialists, celebrities of stage and, eventually, film, and ladies and gentlemen of elegant leisure. By the 1930s, the name "Ciro's" had become so synonymous with luxury that it was widely appropriated by businesses unconnected with the original chain. At one point in the late 1930s there were wildcat Ciro's operating in Philadelphia, Chicago, Miami Beach, Honolulu, Acapulco, Mexico City, and a host of other places.

Ciro's began with one man: Ciro Capozzi (1855–1938), a sea captain's son from Vico Equense on the Bay of Naples. In 1885 or thereabouts, the management of the Café de Paris, facing the Casino in Monte Carlo, opened a small American Bar with Capozzi as the head bartender. Unlike many who staffed so-called American bars in Europe, Capozzi had actually worked in America as a bartender, and always prided himself on that experience. See AMERICAN BAR. In fact, as he told a reporter for the Paris edition of the *New York Herald* in 1898, he "learnt [his] business with Jerry Thomas." See THOMAS, JERRY. His boast drew letters from Parisian bartenders disputing the claim (one of them implied that the closest he had come to Thomas was his book, "which is to be found in a drawer behind his bar").

Yet New York immigration records do show one "C. Capozzi" arriving in the city in May of 1883, from Napoli, and Thomas died in 1885, so the claim is not impossible. It is also worth noting that Capozzi, a skilled mixologist, served drinks that were far simpler and closer to what Thomas served than the fantasies encountered at most European bars. When other bars were offering "Heaps of Comfort" and "Flip Flaps," he was introducing Europe to the Manhattan and the Martini. (Other sources have him working in San Francisco, and others at the famous Delmonico's, also in New York, which can be seen as a model for Capozzi's future establishment.)

In 1888, Capozzi opened his own bar in the Galerie Charles III, just off the square dominated by the Casino (the Café de Paris bar would eventually be run by Leo Engel, another bartender who claimed to have worked with Jerry Thomas in New York). See ENGEL, LEO. Capozzi added the space next door the next year, where he began serving elegant breakfasts and lunches, made from the finest ingredients, many of them imported specially from London's top purveyors: Capozzi's clientele was very strongly English and included the prince of Wales, who would show him cocktails he had learned. With the prince and American press baron James Gordon Bennett as regulars, he rapidly attracted the cream of Monte Carlo's seasonal society. After a further expansion in 1897, Ciro's became a true moneymaker. With his wife Clotilde as the cashier and his brother Salvatore as bar manager, things ran smoothly and profitably for Capozzi until 1911, when he sold the operation to a syndicate of investors from London and retired to his villa nearby, where he lived quietly for another twenty-seven years.

In 1912, the London syndicate opened a branch of Ciro's in Rue Daunou in Paris, with the same formula: a top-class bar, a stellar kitchen, the best of everything. As the *Tatler* put it at the time, "The opening of a new Ciro's was more than an event, it was the date of a new epoch for Paris *de luxe*." It instantly became one of the city's top attractions (of its two large rooms, the one with the bar was where the elite sat; if that was full, they would go elsewhere rather than sit in the other one). In 1913, a seasonal branch at the Normandy seaside resort of Deauville followed, open only during the three weeks in summer when the races were held there. The next year saw another such establishment opened at Luchon, a then-fashionable spa town in the French Pyrenees; it would prove to be short-lived.

In 1915, the syndicate opened the lavish Ciro's London. Organized as a private club to get around strict wartime closing hours, this establishment too was an immediate success. A good part of that was due to its head bartender, a young Scot with experience in France and New York. Harry McElhone was an expert at cocktails and knew how to treat the club's clientele. Ciro's was closed for a time in 1917 for violating licensing laws, by which time McElhone had already left to fight in France; he would return after the war, working there and at the Deauville branch until 1923, when he took over the famous New York Bar in Paris. See MCELHONE, HARRY.

The Ciro's empire continued successfully through the 1920s. In the early 1930s, it added loosely affiliated outposts in Hollywood and Berlin, but the first fell afoul of the Depression (it reopened as a private club for celebrities on the London model in 1940, but its degree of affiliation cannot be established), and the second did not survive the next war. In mid-1939, as war in Europe loomed, the Ciro's consortium opened one last branch, on Central Park South in Manhattan. It was intended as a refuge for the high-flying social set that had frequented the European branches, out of range of the Luftwaffe but, as the *New York Sun* noted in early 1940, it "succeeded in being so exclusive that it failed for lack of trade."

The Monte Carlo, Paris, and London Ciro's all closed in the immediate postwar years. The Hollywood one made it into the 1960s, when it became one of the city's premiere rock and roll clubs. Only the Deauville one still survives.

Before Capozzi's, there were numerous American bars in Europe, but their clientele was largely composed of American expatriates and their drinks were viewed as novelties. With his charm, skill, and hospitality, Ciro Capozzi had the leverage to move the culture when the time was right to move it. It might be an exaggeration to say that he made the cocktail fashionable in Europe, but it would not be much of one. Before him, it was the rare aristocrat who would be seen drinking one; after him, sitting kings were lending their names to mixed drinks.

"A Bit of History—and the Moral." *Tatler*, May 8, 1912, ix.
"Ciro at His Post on the Riviera." *New York Herald*, Paris edition, November 30, 1890, Sunday supplement, 1.
"Current Architecture." *Architectural Review*, May 1915, 93–96.
Davenay, G. "Ciro's à Paris." *Le Figaro*, April 12, 1912, 1.
"How to Prepare Real Cocktails." *New York Herald*, Paris edition, April 27, 1898, 3.
Johnson, Malcolm. "Café Life in New York." *New York Sun*, March 11, 1940, 21.
Wakefield, George. Letter, *New York Herald*, Paris edition, April 30, 1898, 5.

David Wondrich

citric acid ($C_6H_8O_7$) was first isolated from lemon juice by the Swedish chemist Carl Wilhelm Scheele in 1784. Modern industry uses the *Aspergillus niger* mold to produce mass quantities of citric acid. It is used as an acidity regulator in beverages, notably in vodkas. For example, American TTB regulations allow up to 1,000 ppm of citric acid in vodka as a "smoothing agent." See VODKA.

Citric acid is also sometimes used in cocktail preparation. In precisely measured amounts, it can be used to increase the acidity of sweeter juices (like apple or pineapple), as a shelf-stable source of tartness, or as an additive to fresh juice to extend freshness.

ATF Ruling 97-1. "The Bureau of Alcohol, Tobacco and Firearms (ATF) Has Been Asked to Interpret the Phrase 'A Trace Amount of Citric Acid.'" www.ttb.gov/images/pdfs/rulings/97-1.htm (accessed March 18, 2021).

Janzen, Emma. "How to Use Citric Acid in Cocktails." *Imbibe*, August 5, 2019 https://imbibemagazine.com/how-to-use-citric-acid-in-cocktails/ (accessed March 18, 2021).

Lew Bryson

citrus refers to a fruit group known as hesperidia, characterized by segments containing juice-filled vesicles held together by a spongy pith (albedo) and surrounded by a leathery peel, generally containing a high concentration of aromatic oils in the outermost layer (flavedo); the juices and the oils are among the most important non-alcoholic ingredients in mixed drinks. Current taxonomy is debated here, but commonly used citrus fruits are descended from either three or four parent species: citron, mandarin, and pomelo, with papeda as a probable ancestor as well. The citrus varieties used most often in cocktails—lemons, limes, oranges, and grapefruit, roughly in that order—are typically a cross between two of these parent species.

Citrus is used in cocktails primarily as an acidifier, although each variety adds its own flavor. See ACIDITY. For citrus-driven drinks, the more sweet ingredients such as syrups and liqueurs are used, the more citrus needs to be added to create balance. See BALANCE. Lemon and lime are the most acidic and the lightest in flavor; grapefruits can range widely in their acidity; and oranges are the sweetest and often benefit from the addition of lemon or lime to bolster their acid. Citrus fruits contain both citric acid and ascorbic acid (vitamin C). Refined citric acid can be used in cocktails to replace fresh juice and is the typical acidifier in bottled tonic water. Citric acid on its own provides sourness without a distinct flavor. Other, less common acidifiers include lactart (lactic acid, found in dairy and lambic beer), malic acid (found in apples, grapes, and rhubarb), and acid phosphate (partially neutralized phosphoric acid with mineral salts added, used in cola and some soda fountain drinks). See LACTART and PHOSPHATE.

Citrus oil, dispersed across the surface of a drink by twisting a strip of zest a few inches above the surface and rubbing the rim of the glass with it, is a common garnish for Martinis, Old-Fashioneds, and other aromatic stirred drinks. The oil can also be extracted mechanically or by macerating citrus zest in sugar. See SUGAR. Sugar is hygroscopic and will draw out the moisture in the zest when left in contact for several hours. The resultant liquid is called an oleo-saccharum, an oil and sugar mixture. See OLEO-SACCHARUM. Traditional punch is started by making an oleo-saccharum, usually with the zest of the citrus juice that will be included in the drink. See PUNCH.

Varieties of Citrus

Citron, one of the parent species of both lemons and limes, is a large, thick-skinned citrus variety used primarily for its pith. The flavedo, or zest, is highly aromatic and used in perfumery. See ZEST. The flesh is proportionately small and dry with many seeds. Its most common use is candying or glacéing the pith, then serving in wedges or dicing for use in fruitcakes or other desserts. Buddha's hand, also called fingered citron, is an unusual and beautiful variety prized for its aroma and brought to prominence in the spirits world when St. George Spirits released its Hangar One vodkas. See ST. GEORGE SPIRITS. In Jewish culture, citron plays a vital part in the holiday of Sukkot.

The mandarin, parent of the orange and grandparent of the grapefruit, is the sweetest of the four original citrus varieties. This characteristic is the reason it has been used in so many common hybrids, including the satsuma, Meyer lemon, rangpur lime, and clementine. Mandarins are most often eaten fresh and are characterized by a thin, weak pith, making them easy to peel. The peel can be dried and used as a spice. Mandarin juice is rarely called for in cocktails.

Pomelo, also known as shaddock, is parent to both the orange and the grapefruit. It most closely resembles a large, mild grapefruit with very thick pith. The peel and pith can be candied, and the flesh is eaten as-is. While "forbidden fruit" was a nickname for grapefruit, it was pomelo that was used in the defunct liqueur of the same name.

Papeda is native to Asia and responsible for many of the exotic citrus hybrids coming out of that part of the world, like yuzu, kaffir lime, and sudachi. Papeda itself is bitter and generally not used for eating but lends important characteristics for rootstock and breeding.

The lime used by today's bartenders is the Persian lime, also known as the Bearss lime, developed by John T. Bearss in California in 1895. He bred them to be larger and hardier than the key lime, without seeds and with a greater juice yield. Ironically, key limes were the variety cultivated in Persia, but when Columbus brought them to America via the Florida Keys, they were renamed. The key lime was the only widely available lime variety for centuries, until hurricanes decimated Florida's groves in 1926 and 1928. The Persian lime filled the void and has been the common lime used in cocktails in the United States ever since. In the rare instances of pre-1930s American cocktails that call for limes, key limes are the variety that would have been used. Cocktails from tropical climates almost always use key limes.

Key lime juice is both sweeter and more acidic than Persian lime juice and is higher in aromatic compounds that are associated with sweet things, like vanilla and strawberries. When substituting one for the other, less key lime juice, and therefore less sweetener, is necessary to create a balanced cocktail.

Lemon, a cross between a sour orange and a citron, is historically the most common source of citrus juice called for in cocktails, as limes were not widely available until the 1930s. Lemons, cultivated in the Middle East and the Mediterranean for a thousand years, were part of Columbus's freight and were then disseminated throughout the Caribbean. Along with sour, or "Seville," oranges, lemons were the original souring agent for punch and had the additional advantage of being a potent antiscorbutic, something known to British sailors as early as 1601 and only acknowledged by the British Admiralty in 1794, after which punch was issued to all sailors.

In cocktails, certain spirits lend themselves better to lemon rather than lime juice, especially whisky. See WHISKY. One category of drinks, the ginger highball, which includes Bucks and Mules, is frequently distinguished only by the use of lemon juice for Bucks and lime for Mules, although these titles are not firm; modern bartenders tend to use the terms interchangeably. See BUCK.

Grapefruit, crossed from pomelo and mandarin, has a stronger flavor than lemon or lime, slightly less acidity, and a higher sugar content. Darker, redder fruits are sweeter than pale varieties.

"Ruby" varieties of grapefruit originated by treating grapefruit bud stems with radiation, then selecting and breeding the varieties that mutated with the richest color. Unlike genetically modified organisms, radiated crops show no evidence of manipulation. Mutant ruby grapefruit now accounts for 75 percent of all grapefruit grown in Texas, the second largest producer of grapefruit in the United States. See WHISKY, IRISH, and WHISKY, SCOTCH.

When using grapefruit as the sole acidifier in a drink, more juice is necessary to add enough acid to balance a cocktail's typical sugar content. Because grapefruit itself is sweeter than lemon or lime, less added sweetener is required. Thus, grapefruit cocktails tend to be more focused on the flavor of the fruit than drinks using lemon or lime as the acidifier.

Oranges, crossed from pomelo and mandarin, are grouped into two categories: sweet and bitter/sour. Sweet oranges, like Valencia and navel, are used for juice and eaten fresh. Bitter/sour oranges are typically used for their aromatic zest.

Sweet Oranges

Navel oranges are a sweet orange seedless clone, grown through grafting, and are firmer and easy to peel and therefore are best eaten fresh. Due to higher concentrations of limonin and other bitter phytochemicals, plus the firmer texture of the flesh, juice yields from navel oranges are low, and it degrades more quickly.

Valencia oranges were hybridized in the mid-1800s in Santa Ana, California, and named for Valencia, Spain, which is known for its sweet oranges. The juice quality and yield are very high. Valencias are the most popular juicing orange in the United States, and it is the most common juice used in cocktails.

The Sicilian blood orange, originally a natural mutation but now generally a hybrid, has a characteristic deep red color and flavorful, slightly acidic juice, often with berry-like notes. Blood orange juice can generally be substituted for Valencia orange juice in cocktails, when available (the oranges are generally available only in winter and early spring). The moro is the most common variety found in the United States.

Bitter Oranges

Bitter/sour oranges include the Seville, chinotto, and bergamot varieties. The zest of bitter oranges is high in essential oils, bitter, and very aromatic, and it is also used in perfumery and cleaning products. Seville oranges, generally only available in winter, are high in pectin and are prized for making marmalade. Sour orange juice is rarely used in the United States but is sometimes used in cooking in Central and South America. In the eighteenth century, however, it was considered the best citrus juice for making punch. See ASHLEY, JAMES. The rangpur lime is often mistaken for a sour orange due to its orange flesh, but it is in fact a variety of lime.

The bergamot orange is a hybrid; its oil is an analgesic and antiseptic, and it is used to flavor Earl Grey tea. See TEA. Chinotto oranges are used to flavor an Italian soda brand of the same name, owned by San Pellegrino.

The peel from bitter orange varieties is used to make orange bitters, and it is often included in aromatic bitters as well. Orange bitters often use sweet orange peel as well as bitter.

Orange flower water (also called orange blossom water) is made by water-distilling orange blossoms. See ORANGE FLOWER WATER and ESSENTIAL OILS. Orange flower water is used in a Ramos Fizz and is a common ingredient in Orgeat, the almond syrup used in the Mai Tai and the Japanese Cocktail. See

JAPANESE COCKTAIL; MAI TAI; ORGEAT; and RAMOS FIZZ. Orange flower water was also used to flavor capillaire, a defunct cocktail syrup made from maidenhair fern. See CAPILLAIRE.

See also CITRIC ACID.

Broad, William J. "Useful Mutants, Bred with Radiation." *New York Times*, August 28, 2007. http://www.nytimes.com/2007/08/28/science/28crop.html (accessed February 24, 2021).

Brown, Jared, and Anistatia Miller. "Lost Ingredients: Forbidden Fruit." *The Historians*, June 20, 2014. http://thehistorians-jaredbrown.blogspot.com/2014/06/lost-ingredients-forbidden-fruit.html (accessed February 24, 2021).

Bailey, David G., George Dresser, and J. Malcolm O. Arnold. Grapefruit-Medication Interactions: Forbidden Fruit or Avoidable Consequences? *Canadian Medical Association Journal* 185 (2013): 309–316. http://www.cmaj.ca/content/185/4/309 (accessed February 24, 2021).

Colliau, Jennifer. "Why Your Daiquiri Isn't the Same as Hemingway's." *Punch*, January 10, 2014. http://punchdrink.com/articles/why-your-daiquiri-isnt-the-same-as-hemingways/ (accessed February 24, 2021).

Integrated Taxonomic Information System. *Rutaceae of North America Update, database (version 2011)*.

Purdue University Center for New Crops and Plant Products. "*Citrus aurantifolia* Swingle." https://hort.purdue.edu/newcrop/morton/mexican_lime.html (accessed February 24, 2021).

Jennifer Colliau

City Hotel, on lower Broadway in New York City, almost from its opening in 1794 until it was demolished in 1849, was the home of one of the most influential bars in the world, presided over by the famous "Willard of the City Hotel." See WILLARD, ORSAMUS.

clairin is a Haitian spirit distilled from fermented sugar-cane juice that is similar to, though less refined than, rhum agricole. To make clairin, sugar-cane juice is fermented for four to eight days before it is distilled in a pot still and filtered. Clairin is produced in small, largely unregulated distilleries all across Haiti for local consumption and is typically not aged. Once the distillation process is complete, it is shipped to markets and street vendors in plastic jugs, where it is then often sold in recycled vessels such as liquor and soda bottles. It is also purported to be used in certain voodoo rituals. The renewed interest in rum seen in the late 2010s meant that for the first time significant amounts of clairin began to be exported to Europe and North America and sold—and appreciated—as an artisanal product.

See also RHUM AGRICOLE.

Chery, Dieu Nalio. "AP PHOTOS: Moving Haiti's Rustic, Rum-Like Clairin to Market." *AP News* , July 12, 2017 (accessed February 24, 2021).
Hall, Michael R. "CLAIRIN." In *Historical Dictionary of Haiti*, 64. Lanham, MD: Scarecrow, 2012.

Anna Archibald

clarification is a technique used to improve the cosmetic appearance of a liquid. Clarification is often done in combination with filtration. Clarifying methods can be less aggressive in removing flavor compounds than filtration and often work better on visible materials that are suspended in the liquid.

Traditional methods used natural flocculants like gelatin, egg whites, agar, or isinglass as fining agents. Some chemicals, like aluminum sulfate or iron chloride, can also be used as clarifying agents. When added to a hazy liquid, these compounds will agglomerate the suspended materials, making it easier to remove them using a coarse filter such as cloth or paper. Some fining agents cause the visible matter to settle to the bottom of the vessel, allowing the clear liquid to be decanted. These methods are beneficial for finishing macerated spirits and liqueurs, giving them a more refined appearance.

Mechanical methods can also be used to clarify liquids. A centrifuge is commonly employed to remove suspended solids by spinning the liquid at high speed, thus using centrifugal force to pull them out of the liquid and concentrate them at the bottom of their container. This method is not common in the production of spirits but has found some use at bars to produce unique ingredients for cocktails, such as clarified lime juice. With the introduction of the Spinzall, Dave Arnold's cheap, bar-optimized centrifuge, one can expect to see more clarified ingredients in drinks.

See also FILTRATION.

Arnold, Dave. *Liquid intelligence*. New York: Norton, 2014.

Darcy O'Neil

Clarke, Edwin "Eddie" J. (ca. 1908–ca. 1972), head bartender of the American Bar at London's Savoy Hotel in 1939 and 1940, wrote three cocktail books and a valuable book on bar management and owned and operated the Albemarle Club, alias Eddie's Club, in London's Piccadilly. See SAVOY. By his own account, Clarke started his career as a ship's bartender in 1926, was a president of the United Kingdom Bartenders Guild, opened the first cocktail bar in Dublin, and was head bartender in London at the Berkeley Hotel, the London Casino, and the American Bar before serving as a captain in the Royal Artillery in World War II. In 1946 Eddie became head bartender at London's fashionable Albany Club, leaving to open the Albemarle Club in 1954, which he ran until his retirement in 1970 or thereabout. Though he was well regarded by his peers and won at least one major cocktail competition, few of Clarke's drinks have endured: perhaps his best-known is the Comet, a blend of brandy, Van der Hum, grapefruit juice, and Angostura.

See also UNITED KINGDOM BARTENDERS GUILD (UKBG).

Clarke, Eddie. *Shaking in the 60s*. London: Cocktail Books, 1963.

Theodora Sutcliffe

classic cocktail is subjective in its definition and has been hotly debated, but the establishment of a canon of classics was an important part of the success of the twenty-first-century cocktail renaissance. Despite the debate, there is broad agreement that, to be considered a classic, a cocktail should satisfy several different requirements. It should be familiar enough among average customers that they order it even when it is not listed on the cocktail menu. Bartenders from high-end craft bars to neighborhood pubs should know its recipe, and the ingredients should be commonly found in most bars. Most importantly, however, it should be well respected and widely accepted as being delicious.

There is no official list of classic cocktails, but pre-Prohibition drinks such as the Old-Fashioned, Manhattan, Martini, Sidecar, Daquiri, and Mojito and more recent ones such as the Bloody Mary, Margarita, and even Cosmopolitan have indisputably achieved this status. (Equally, popular drinks such as the pre-Prohibition Angel's Tit and Coffee Cocktail and the more modern Godfather and Long Island Iced Tea have been excluded. See COFFEE COCKTAIL.) Some drinks, such as the Sazerac, Negroni, Rob Roy, Pisco Sour, and Caipirinha may be long-standing recipes and considered as worthy of this distinction in some circles but are unknown in others. Other old drinks that have appealed to modern tastes are often ranked as "forgotten classics." See FORGOTTEN CLASSIC. With the modern cocktail resurgence, there are a number of new drinks that have been widely discussed as candidates for eventually becoming classics themselves, including the Bramble, Jasmine, Old Cuban, Penicillin, Trident, Chartreuse Swizzle, Little Italy, Red Hook, and Seelbach (which began as a forgotten classic until its rediscoverer admitted that he had in fact invented it). A cocktail becomes a classic not by somebody declaring it so but through the knowledge of its recipe spreading organically through bartenders and customers across the country.

DeGroff, Dale. *The Craft of the Cocktail*. New York: Clarkson Potter, 2002.
Embury, David. *The Fine Art of Mixing Drinks*. New York: Doubleday, 1948.
Regan, Gary. *The Joy of Mixology*. New York: Clarkson Potter, 2003.

Robert Hess

Clear Creek Distillery, based in Portland, Oregon, specializes in fruit brandies (both barrel aged and unaged eaux-de-vie), grappas, and fruit liqueurs. Founded in 1985 by Steve McCarthy, Clear Creek was among the earliest pioneers in what was to become a boom in craft distilling in the United States. See CRAFT DISTILLING. After studying brandy distillation in Europe, McCarthy founded Clear Creek with the plan of making brandy using produce from his family's fruit orchards. The distillery's first product was an unaged pear brandy akin to Poire Williams, made from Oregon-grown Bartlett pears; Clear Creek's Pear Brandy remains the most popular of the company's products. In subsequent years, Clear Creek began producing apple brandy from Golden Delicious apples, a mirabelle eau-de-vie and a slivovitz-like brandy from blue plums, a kirsch made from Washington- and Oregon-grown cherries, an Islay-style heavily peated single-malt whisky, and a Douglas fir eau-de-vie made by clipping young buds from Douglas fir trees and then macerating and distilling them in grape distillate. In 2006, the distillery relocated to a larger facility and doubled its capacity, adding a line of liqueurs flavored with cassis, pear, cherry, cranberry, raspberry, marionberry, and loganberry. In 2014, Clear Creek was purchased by Hood River Distillers, based in Hood River, Oregon, and McCarthy retired from the company.

See also BRANDY and EAU-DE-VIE.

Asimov, Eric. "An Orchard in a Bottle, at 80 Proof." *New York Times*, August 15, 2017.
Clear Creek Distillery website. http://clearcreekdistillery.com (accessed February 24, 2021).
Young, Molly. "Hood River Distillers Acquires Portland-Based Clear Creek Distillery." *Oregonian*, January 24, 2014.

Paul Clarke

A **Clinebell ice machine** is used to create large blocks of crystal-clear ice. It was invented in 1983 by Virgil Clinebell after he observed how ice freezing atop rivers and streams is usually clear.

Clear ice from a non-moving body of water, like a lake or a pond, is usually an indicator of a slow freezing process. As ice crystals form, the lattice grows tighter, leaving little room for air or minerals to make their way inside. Oxygen bubbles and impurities are pushed away, and they eventually become trapped in the last sections of the ice to freeze. If the water is moving, as in the case of a river or stream, clear ice results because the water movement is similarly causing the ice to form slowly, as well as preventing impurities from being trapped inside.

Unlike clear ice found in nature, most home-frozen ice cubes develop a cloudy center because the water is freezing from the outside in. This relegates the air bubbles and impurities to the middle portion of the cube. When the last bit of water on the inside of the cube turns to ice, small fissures and striations develop and branch outward. Impurities and oxygen bubbles then attempt to forcibly defect from the core as this water expands during the freezing process, lending the eye of the cube an overall cloudy appearance.

In 1955, Virgil Clinebell (1931–2014) was running a small refrigeration business in Illinois and would occasionally provide emergency ice service to customers in need. In 1964 he developed a machine that could freeze a fifteen-pound block of ice that was then sealed in a plastic bag for convenient transport and easy storage. In 1970 Clinebell formed the Arctic Belle ice company in Loveland, Colorado, which grew to become a major regional ice distributor.

Throughout his years in the ice business, Clinebell had been interested in the clear ice that came from fast-flowing rivers and streams. This inspired him to imagine a machine that could somehow replicate this behavior and yield similar results via an inversion of the natural top-down freezing process. His now-famous CB300X2D carving block ice maker (aka "Clinebell machine") was initially conceptualized in 1983 and was brought forth to the general public in 1984. His company also underwent a name change to become Clinebell Equipment, Inc., and it is still in business today.

The Clinebell machine freezes water in the opposite manner from a lake or river—from the bottom up, via a cooling plate at the base of the machine. The machine is constructed of galvanized steel, and it features an insulated cover that is lifted to reveal two large cabinets, each lined with a disposable neoprene bag that is filled with forty gallons of water at the beginning of each cycle and replaced after each harvest. Circulating pumps are positioned at the ends or corners of the cabinets in order to constantly circulate and agitate the water. Proper placement of the circulating pumps is critical to achieving optimal clarity in the final product, and the position of the pumps should be adjusted every day of the cycle, as they serve to prevent oxygen bubbles and impurities from forming within the block. These unwanted elements are subsequently relegated to the final and top layer of water to reach a solid state, which is later sliced off and discarded prior to harvesting the blocks within. At the end of its two- to four-day cycle, the Clinebell machine produces two crystal-clear blocks, each weighing 136 kg (300 lbs.). The blocks are removed from the machine via a steel hoist that liberates the finished blocks from their chamber.

The manifest purpose of the Clinebell machine was to create a product that would benefit the ice sculptor. In recent times, a number of modern bartenders have become rather fond of its merits and adopted this machine into their cocktail programs as a means to produce a superior caliber of clear ice that may be cut to all needed sizes and shapes.

Boccato, Richard. "The Cold War (or How I Learned to Stop Worrying and Love the Ice)." In *Gaz Regan's Annual Manual for Bartenders 2013*, ed. Gaz Regan et al. N.p.: Mixellany, 2013.

Clinebell Equipment Company website. http://clinebellequipment.com/ (accessed February 24, 2021).

Gosnell, Mariana. *Ice: The Nature, the History, and the Uses of an Astonishing Substance* Chicago: University of Chicago Press, 2007.

Marling, Karal Ann. *Ice: Great Moments in the History of Hard, Cold Water*. St. Paul, Minnesota: Borealis, 2008.

Richard Boccato

closures are the devices that keep liquid in bottles and oxygen out of them. The great historical virtue of alcoholic beverages is their relative stability, enabling distant and even global commerce, although that stability is reliant on strictly controlling the amount of oxygen to which they are exposed. Long distance transportation relies upon containers matched with particular closures. Whether the answer is amphorae sealed with wooden plugs coated with pine tar, hardwood barrels with softwood bungs, hand-blown glass bottles and corks, or machine-extruded bottles with uniform aluminum screw caps and beyond, the closure still represents the point of greatest vulnerability in the system for transporting spirits.

The ancient Mediterranean use of wood plugs covered in pitch or resin, sometimes supplemented by oil-soaked cloths, is reflected in the continued consumption of retsina, a Greek wine that contains a tiny amount of pine tree resin, and in mastika, a Mediterranean spirit that utilizes the resin of the eponymous tree for its aromas and flavors. In the pioneering South Asian spirits trade, as the circumnavigator William Dampier observed in 1697, the earthenware jars used were similarly fitted with wooden stoppers that were sealed with treated paper and then covered with clay. See SPIRITS TRADE, HISTORY OF. A variant of this method is still used for sealing the large, lightly glazed jars in which Chinese baijiu ages. See BAIJIU. The oaken barrels used to mature and occasionally still transport spirits are sometimes bunged with softwood "shives" in the traditional manner, although synthetic substitutes are often preferred. See BARREL.

The handblown glass bottles that came into increasing use in the seventeenth century (for transporting small amounts of spirits and storing them for ready use) were made with slightly flared necks that could be sealed with plugs made from the spongy bark of the cork oak (*Quercus suber*). This was not a new method; corks date back to antiquity, and indeed many of those amphora-sealing wooden plugs were cork bark, but it had fallen out of use, as had the glass bottle itself. With the increasing trade ushered in by the early modern period, the advantages of both were rediscovered. Cork was, as Walter Riley noted in 1906, "light and impermeable to gases and liquids, elastic, and without taste and smell."

That elasticity was essential, since there was as yet no way to make bottles of precisely uniform dimensions, and the cork had to be able to adjust to the bottle's neck. This often left a little play in the fit, and corks needed to be tied down or dipped in wax to ensure that they stayed put. Only in the late nineteenth century did it become possible to achieve true uniformity of both bottle and cork.

The ability to make perfectly cylindrical bottlenecks and uniform, machine-cut corks meant that a slightly tapered cork with an end a bit wider than the bottle's neck could be squeezed in a press until it could be inserted into the bottle wide-side first, whereupon it would expand to grip the sides of the neck tightly but still be extractable with a corkscrew. This system, now associated with wine, was adopted for spirits as well, and it continues to be found with a few old-school European bottlings.

But unlike wine or beer bottles, spirits bottles had to be resealable, at least in most countries (there are those where it is considered bad form to not discard the closure and empty the bottle once it is opened, but they are the minority). Corks can be difficult to reinsert and are often damaged by the act of extracting them. A traditional solution was the ground glass stopper, where the end that fit into the bottle had to be machined to fit each individual one. This was of course expensive. By the middle of the

nineteenth century, it was largely supplanted by the "shell cork and stopper" closure, where a cork was drilled out and fitted permanently into the bottle and a tapered glass stopper pressed into the opening.

At the same time, advances in bottle molding made it possible to use screw caps. These too were not entirely new—as early as the sixteenth century, some bottles were fitted with threaded pewter neck bands and screw caps, but these had to be custom-fitted to each bottle. Samuel A. Whitney's 1861 US patent for an internally threaded bottleneck and a glass stopper with rubber gasket ushered in a new era of cheap, effective closures. Indeed, the transition from merchant bottling to distillery bottling that came in the late nineteenth century would not have been possible without such things. See SPIRITS TRADE, HISTORY OF.

New closures introduced at the time included nonresealable but very cheap crown caps, still used for spirits in some countries, resealable swing-top "lightning" stoppers (patented by Charles de Quillfeldt in 1874), and externally threaded bottlenecks with caps that screwed down over them. These last would become the industry standard, in metal or, later, in plastic, for all but luxury brands, which would continue to use cork stoppers, perhaps with the hope that such stoppers suggest higher-quality brands, as they have traditionally done for wine (the type most favored is the so-called T-top, where a short cork is glued to a wooden, plastic, or metal knob that enables the cork to be pulled from the bottle).

For some premium brands, however, the risk of counterfeiting trumps the risk of seeming low-class. For them, there is the nonrefillable closure, patented as far back as 1898 and in use since at least 1912, when Johnnie Walker used it. See JOHNNIE WALKER. This type of closure was perfected by Earl Unger for Seagram's in 1971, who used a clever arrangement of barriers and a ball valve to ensure that the bottle can be poured from, but not into (Unger's patent drawing featured a Chivas Regal bottle). See CHIVAS REGAL and SEAGRAM COMPANY LTD. A simpler version also in use features a tamper-evident plastic insert that the cap screws onto that cannot be replaced without breaking the bottle.

The T-top itself has seen changes in recent years as well. With an increased awareness of TCA contamination, natural cork is seen as inconsistent, and while incidents of corked spirits are less common than of corked wine, contrary to popular supposition they do occur. In recent years, the cork in T-tops has been at least partially supplanted by plastic and synthetics or the closures replaced by glass stoppers with silicon gaskets or even the humble screwcap (most often aluminum Stelvin closures, where the top is part of a capsule that fits over the neck). As screwcaps become the norm for everyday wines, and as agglomerated corks and sterilized (TCA-free) corks are becoming the norm in more expensive wines, the adoption of alternative closures in spirits can be expected to continue.

See also BOTTLES, LABELING, AND PACKAGING; and TCA (2, 4, 6-TRICHLOROANISOLE).

Dampier, William. *A New Voyage round the World*. London: 1697.
Jeffrey, David W., Gavin Sacks, and Andrew Waterhouse. *Understanding Wine Chemistry*. Chichester, UK: Wiley, 2016.
Jackson, Ronald. *Wine Science: Principles and Applications*, 4th ed. San Diego: Academic Press Elsevier, 2014.
Lindsey, Bill. "Types of Bottle Closures." Bureau of Land Management/Society of Historical Archeology Historic Glass Bottle Identification and Information Website. https://sha.org/bottle/closures.htm (accessed March 15, 2021).
Riley, Walter A. "The History and Use of Corks and Other Stoppers." *Journal of the Institute of Brewing* 12 (1906): 172–207.

Doug Frost and David Wondrich

The **Clover Club**, a frothy pink concoction of gin, lemon juice, raspberry syrup, and egg white, was created as the signature drink for the club of that name sometime around the turn of the last century. The Clover Club was a Philadelphia-based association of prominent journalists dedicated to good eating, deep drinking, and giving politicians a hard time. The first notice we have of its eponymous cocktail is from 1901, from Michael Killackey, head bartender at the Waldorf-Astoria in New York. That hotel was managed by George Boldt, who had previously managed the Philadelphia's Bellevue-Stratford Hotel, where the club met, so Killackey's recipe can be considered authentic. In any case, the Waldorf-Astoria popularized the drink, and by 1910 it was ubiquitous.

The Clover Club cocktail did not survive Prohibition. It didn't help that *Esquire* named it one of the "ten worst cocktails" in 1934, just as American

drinking was getting back on track again. The drink was more or less dead until 2007 or 2008, when Julie Reiner gave its name to her new Brooklyn, New York, bar and adopted it as the house drink. See REINER, JULIE. The establishment has gone on to become an institution, winning many awards and granting the drink a new lease on life.

Recipe: 60 ml Plymouth gin, 15 ml lemon juice, 10 ml raspberry syrup, 10 ml egg white. Shake, strain, up. In 1909 Paul Lowe suggested substituting 15 ml dry vermouth for half the gin; this is the version Reiner uses.

"How to Mix Your Own Drinks." *New York Press*, June 21, 1901.
Lowe, Paul E. *Drinks: How to Mix and Serve*. Philadelphia: Mackay, 1909.
Shay, Frank. "Ten Best Cocktails of 1934." *Esquire*, December, 1934, 40.

David Wondrich

The **cobbler** is a nineteenth-century American drink consisting of wine (or sometimes a spirit) shaken or tossed with sugar, ice, and citrus peel or slices and elaborately garnished with berries and slices of fruit. Along with the cocktail and the julep, it was one of the cornerstones of American drinking and did more than any other to spread the gospel of iced drinks mixed to order around the world. See COCKTAIL and JULEP. It was also the drink that did more than any other to popularize the use of the straw, through which it was invariably drunk.

The first record we have of the drink is from 1837, when a New York newspaper mentions a "Madeira Cobler [*sic*]," with the implication that it is something new. The Sherry Cobbler turns up the next year, but by 1839 is so popular in New York and beyond that one suspects that it had already been circulating for a while. See SHERRY COBBLER. It would go on to be the cobbler's most popular manifestation by far, consumed anywhere the weather was warm and there was ice to be had (the Madeira Cobbler, on the other hand, sank without a trace).

The origin of the cobbler is obscure and its creator unknown. It has been posited that it was an American adaptation of Cobbler's Punch, a British drink of the early nineteenth century, but there is no evidence that the latter drink was known in America, and there is little commonality between

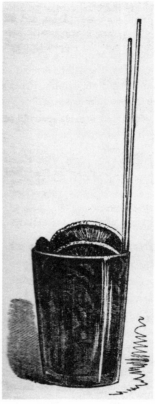

Jerry Thomas's Sherry Cobbler (probably drawn by himself), 1862. Wondrich Collection.

against the drink's strong point, which was as a lighter, less intoxicating alternative to its hot-weather companion, the mighty julep. There were also those who wanted the drink lighter still, and Claret, Hock, Catawba, and even Champagne Cobblers had their vogue in the years after the American Civil War. The occasional specialized version appears, including the Pineapple Cobbler (1851) and the Cranston Cobbler (with champagne and "a cordial"; 1861), but by and large cobblers were simple drinks, with little elaboration (although Harry Johnson did like to make his with flavored syrups instead of plain sugar, and a float of port wine was sometimes also deployed). See JOHNSON, HARRY, and FLOAT. In the last decade of the nineteenth century, the Cobbler saw itself largely supplanted by other, newer iced drinks, such as the rickey, the highball, and various coolers. See RICKEY; HIGHBALL; and COOLER (INC. BREEZES). By Prohibition, in 1919, it was a musty antique: something one would find in the pages of a bartender's guide but not in an actual bar. The cocktail renaissance has reawakened interest in it, to a degree, with bartenders spinning variations on the basic formula, although none has displayed any signs of becoming part of the canon. See COCKTAIL RENAISSANCE. Bellocq, the elegant New Orleans bar devoted to the cobbler that opened in 2012 was forced to broaden its focus in short order.

"Burton—the late William H.—invented Sherry Cobblers." *Washington Evening Star*, March 24, 1860, 1.

"The Weather." *New York Morning Herald*, August, 9, 1837, 1.

Thomas, Jerry. *How to Mix Drinks*. New York: Dick & Fitzgerald, 1862.

David Wondrich

the beverages. See COBBLER'S PUNCH. It is more likely that it takes its name from the "cobbles," or pebbles of ice in it (the form of the name is analogous to "smasher," an alternate name for the SMASH). In any case, judging from the concentration of early mentions there, New York City appears to have been its home, although its spread was rapid and wide. (A detailed and not implausible story circulating in the mid-nineteenth century that the drink was invented by actor William H. Burton at "Dicky" Harbourd's saloon in Philadelphia is undermined by the fact that Harbourd did not arrive in America until 1839.)

In the early 1840s, the popularity of the Sherry Cobbler inspired a raft of other variations, most based on wine or fortified wine. In 1843, however, Peter Brigham added arrack and brandy versions to the famous 1843 list of drinks served at his Boston saloon. See BRIGHAM, PETER. The latter of those took on a certain popularity, particularly in Europe, while in America the Whisky Cobbler had its adherents. These spirituous versions, however, rather militated

cobbler shaker

cobbler shaker is a nineteenth-century term synonymous with cocktail shaker. See COCKTAIL SHAKER. Although it first appears in America (in 1873), its use was chiefly British. In his widely influential 2002 *Craft of the Cocktail*, however, Dale DeGroff tethered the term to what was previously known as a "patent" or "3-piece" shaker: the type with a strainer and pour spout built into the top and a cap to seal it, patented by Charles J. Hauck of Brooklyn, New York, in 1884. See DEGROFF, DALE. That usage was quickly adopted by others and is now general.

"A New Drink." *Leavenworth (KS) Times*, July 16, 1873, 4.

David Wondrich

Cobbler's Punch is a British term originally applied to an impromptu punch made from cheap gin sweetened with treacle and soured with vinegar (although occasionally the canonical sugar and lemon juice are found). First recorded in 1788, the drink may be of naval origin, while its name is derived from its cobbled-together nature. By the mid-nineteenth century, its specificity had greatly dissipated. As Mr. Venus says in Charles Dickens's *Our Mutual Friend* (1864), "It's difficult to impart the receipt for it . . . but the groundwork is gin." Indeed, the name was often applied in Victorian years to what was elsewhere called Dog's Nose—gin or whisky and ale or porter—or Stone Fence—gin or whisky and cider. See STONE FENCE.

Baker, Anne E. *A Glossary of Northamptonshire Words and Phrases*. London: 1854.

Grose, Francis. *A Classical Dictionary of the Vulgar Tongue*, 2nd ed. London: 1788.

David Wondrich

cocktail in modern parlance is a very loose term, often meaning nothing more specific than "a mixed drink containing alcohol," or even one that doesn't have alcohol but imitates the presentation of those that do. More narrowly, it is applied to a little pool of iced spirits, mixed with bits of this and that and poured into an elegant stemmed glass or over crystal crags of ice, that when first sipped gives one the feeling of bursting into full bloom (as the American humorist George Ade wrote in his 1902 play *The Sultan of Sulu*) "like a timid little flower kissed by the morning sunlight." Of all the myriad classes of mixed drink, the cocktail maintains the most perfect balance between delight and efficacy, and that has made it an icon; a symbol for mixed drinks and what they can do to provide a measure of momentary solace for at least some of the difficulties of adult life.

The cocktail began as one specific drink: spirits (for the most part, Dutch-style gin) mixed with sugar, bitters, and water or ice. See COCK-TAIL. The idea of combining spirits, sugar, and bitters was English, but the idea that such a beverage could be a pillar of drinking culture is pure American. Between its debut in the years after the American Revolution and the 1830s, when it became popular enough to become a symbol of the strange things Americans

PUTTING IN THE BITTERS.
This illustrates the making of a cocktail.

Charles Mahoney of New York's Hoffman House bar building a cocktail, beginning with the bitters, 1905. Wondrich Collection.

did with drinks, it changed very little. But that decade saw American drinking transformed with, for example, African American bartenders such as William Walker of Washington, DC, introducing the fancy "Hailstorm Julep" and New York City bartenders producing the Sherry Cobbler, both of which used unprecedented amounts of ice. See JULEP and COBBLER.

Up to this point, the Cocktail (we'll capitalize it, as it was not yet generic) was not iced. Ice was reserved for slow-sipping hot-weather coolers, not short drinks such as the Cocktail, which was meant to be slammed down first thing in the morning, with repeat doses applied if and as needed later in the day. By the 1840s, however, ice began to appear even there. The iced Cocktail is first mentioned in print in New York in 1840, and by 1843, when the *New York Sunday Mercury* defined a Cocktail as "compounded of brandy, sugar, absynthe, bitters, and ice," it was a matter of course. Indeed, they even iced their Cocktails at the bar on the tugboat that pulled steamships into New York Harbor, as one British traveler found in 1844.

By then, the other ingredients of the drink were changing, as the *Sunday Mercury*'s Cocktail demonstrates with its dash of "absynthe." See SAZERAC COCKTAIL. Dashes of curaçao or maraschino were being incorporated into the drink, and perhaps other things as well. In the fanciest saloons, the flashy, cocky young men behind the bar were mixing the drink by pouring it rapidly back and forth between glasses so that it looked like they were throwing it in an arc. See TOSSING. When they had finished, they strained it into a small wine or champagne glass and dropped a thin paring of lemon peel into the glass after rubbing it around the rim. If they weren't doing that, they were replacing the gin or brandy that was customary with chilled French champagne. In other words, the Cocktail had arrived.

Up to this point, the julep had been the reigning monarch of American drinks—the one that leapt first to people's lips, both physically and metaphorically. For the rest of the world, it still was. In the United States, however, the Cocktail was now king. In his groundbreaking *Bar-Tender's Guide*, Jerry Thomas offered thirteen variations on the drink: plain ones, fancy ones, a champagne version, a "Japanese Cocktail," and three versions of the Crusta, "an improvement on the Cocktail," which Thomas attributed to Joseph Santini of New Orleans. See CRUSTA.

Unlike many other classes of American drink of the time—the Rover, the Blush, the Champarelle—the Cocktail in its new, sleek, and icy form worked its way into the permanent fabric of American life. Reasons for such things are never crystal clear, but perhaps it was because the Cocktail was, at root, an extremely simple drink that used no perishable ingredients. Perhaps it was also that whatever it is that a mixed drink can do, the Cocktail did it the most quickly and with the least amount of fuss.

It should be emphasized, however, that Cocktails and saloon drinking in general were confined to a subset of the male population. For many men, and most women, the Cocktail was a vulgar drink that was consumed by louche and outlandish men in disreputable circumstances. But the years after the American Civil War brought a great deal of change to the country, including a growing respectability for the saloon and drinkers of the Cocktail who were more settled and middle class than the raffish,

sporty set that propped up the bar before the war. By the 1870s, in many of the major cities, the habit had even spread to "respectable" women, who could get served a Cocktail (or a julep, a glass of punch, whatever) in tea rooms, cafes, restaurants, the table-service back rooms of some saloons, and even at dress shops and hat makers, such as the milliner's where, according to the *Cincinnati Post*, an order for "French lace, pointed" resulted in a Brandy Sling and "straw goods" in a Sherry Cobbler.

But now its new devotees and the increasing pace of technological change in urban life conspired to expose the Cocktail's greatest weakness—which from another perspective also happened to be its greatest strength. The Cocktail was just too potent. One Cocktail—a full wineglass (60 ml) of spirits—was already a pretty stiff belt, but due to the custom of drinking in rounds, where acquaintances at the bar would take turns to pay for drinks (or roll dice for it), drinkers rarely stopped at one. One solution was the Vermouth Cocktail, first documented in 1868 at a New York luncheon for the Sorosis, the pioneering professional women's club. But this was perhaps going too far in the other direction. By the beginning of the 1880s, the solution had been found, in the form of the Manhattan and the Martini and the Metropole, Cocktails that were divided equally between vermouth and whisky, gin, or brandy, respectively. See MANHATTAN COCKTAIL and MARTINI. These were, needless to say, very successful, and by the end of the century they had essentially killed off the plain Cocktail, except for the deliberately retro version served as the Old-Fashioned, and New Orleans's stubborn Sazerac. See OLD-FASHIONED and SAZERAC.

Ironically, it was only at this point that the true Cocktail took off outside the United States. American-style bars had been popular in Paris since the 1840s, but they mostly served American expatriates. In London, for the most part they struggled, although the American bar at the Criterion in Piccadilly had a certain longevity. See CRITERION. With the exception of the Prince of Wales, the people who had the greatest influence over British mores had treated American drinks, and the Cocktail in particular, as curiosities. See PRINCE OF WALES. The tipping point seems to have come when the upper crust of British society took to drinking at the little bar maintained in the fashionable resort of Monte Carlo by Ciro Capozzi (1855–1938), an Italian who might have worked for Jerry Thomas in New York and made a specialty of the simple Cocktail. See CIRO's and THOMAS, JERRY. Those Cocktails led to the emergence of Manhattans and Martinis, and soon the establishment of an "American bar" at the Savoy Hotel in 1903. See SAVOY HOTEL'S AMERICAN BAR. (As the New York World wrote in 1885, "Thus it is that the American bar-room gradually subjugates and civilizes the semi-barbarians of the Old World.")

By then, however, the very definition of the Cocktail was changing. It was two new drinks that made it happen: the Bronx and the Daiquiri, both of which contained citrus, something heretofore confined to sours, punches, and the like. See BRONX and DAIQUIRI. Once these became accepted as Cocktails, the drink came to assume its narrower modern definition, with its broader one following not long after: once "cocktail lounge" becomes an acceptable synonym for "bar," as it did in the 1920s, "Cocktail" must be spelled "cocktail." This allowed the cocktail category to encompass an even wider selection of drinks over the coming decades. See COSMOPOLITAN; DAWA; LAST WORD; LONG ISLAND ICED TEA; MARGARITA; NEGRONI; and ZOMBIE.

The modern cocktail renaissance, in another irony, brought back every variety of old-school Cocktail except the original, spirits-sugar-bitters-up version. The Old-Fashioned reached dizzying heights of popularity, and the Sazerac got declared the state cocktail of Louisiana, but the just plain Cocktail is rarely ordered.

Recipe (Ciro Capozzi's Cocktail, 1898): Combine in mixing glass full of cracked ice, 2 dashes aromatic bitters, ½ barspoon (4 ml) orange curaçao, scant ½ barspoon rich simple syrup (3 ml), and 60 ml genever, cognac, or straight American whisky (rye or bourbon). Stir well, strain into chilled cocktail glass, and twist lemon peel over the top.

Ade, George. *The Sultan of Sulu.* New York: R. H. Russell, 1903.
Cooke, Henry. "Notes of a Loiterer in New York." *Bentley's Miscellany* 16 (1844): 597.
"How to Prepare Real Cocktails." *New York Herald*, April 27, 1898, 3.
" 'Straws' and 'Laces.' " *Cincinnati Post*, August 16, 1883, 2.
Wondrich, David. *Imbibe!*, 2nd ed. New York: Perigee, 2015.

"Yankee Nectar, from the New York *World*." *St Louis Post-Dispatch*, May 16, 1885, 10.

David Wondrich

Cock-Tail, a simple mixture of spirits, sugar, bitters, and water, is the primitive ancestor of the vast class of mixed drinks that travels today under a streamlined version of its name. While the drink first appears under its name in the United States at the beginning of the nineteenth century, its formula can be traced back to seventeenth-century London, and to Richard Stoughton, creator of the first patent bitters. See STOUGHTON'S BITTERS. One of the ways Stoughton suggested in his prolific advertisements that his bitters be used was added to beer, wine, or even brandy as a way to settle the stomach in the morning, particularly after a night of excessive drinking. With brandy (which was generally sweetened before being sold) or (sweet, fortified) Canary wine, it must be noted, this produces something practically indistinguishable from the early-nineteenth century American Cock-Tail, itself primarily an eye-opener or morning drink. All it really lacks is the name.

By the middle of the 1700s, the combination of Stoughton's Bitters and sweet wine, brandy, or even gin (which was sold even more heavily sweetened than brandy) was well established in Britain and its American colonies, as either eye-opener or preprandial tonic. Indeed, in 1783, when negotiating the surrender of New York City with the city's British governor, General George Washington "pulled out his watch, and observing that it was near Dinner Time, offered Wine and Bitters"—the first cocktail hour on record. See WASHINGTON, GEORGE.

Over the following twenty years, drinkers in a rough triangle between New York City; Albany, New York (150 miles / 240 km to the north); and Boston, Massachusetts, attached a name to this formula: "Cock-Tail." This was a bit of sporting-life British slang denoting a stimulant or pick-me-up, derived from the horse-trader's practice of covertly inserting a "feague" of ginger or cayenne pepper in an old or tired horse's anus to make it cock its tail up and act lively (its earliest figurative use dates to 1790). The first unambiguous appearance in print of the formula and name together is in the river town of Hudson, New York, in 1806, when a local newspaper defines Cock-Tail as "a stimulating liquor, composed of spirits of any kind, sugar, water, and bitters." (There exists a 1798 mention of a drink called "Cock-Tail" in a London newspaper, but its price indicates that it could not be based on spirits or wine and was probably a nonalcoholic ginger decoction; indeed, as late as 1828 the name was still being used in Britain for ginger extract added to a drink.)

At first, the conception of the drink seems to have been rather fluid—early descriptions exist that omit the bitters (yielding a drink indistinguishable from the Sling) or substitute cayenne pepper for them, but by 1820 the formula had stabilized. See SLING. By 1830, it had spread throughout the United States. Indeed, the Cock-Tail was, along with the Mint Julep and the Apple Toddy, one of the canonic drinks that would bring the American art of the bar into global repute. See MINT JULEP and TODDY.

Recipe: In a small Old-Fashioned glass, muddle 1 cube of raw sugar with 10 ml water and 3 dashes bitters; add 60 ml brandy, genever, or young whisky and cold water to taste. Stir.

See also COCKTAIL.

"Journal of a Tour through the Eastern States, by an English Woman." *St Tammany's Magazine*, December 17, 1821.

Croswell, Harry. "Communication." *Balance & Columbian Repository*, May 13, 1806.

Grose, Francis. *A Classical Dictionary of the Vulgar Tongue*. London: 1785, s.v. "feague."

Smith, William. *William Smith's Historical Memoirs, 1778–1783*. Edited by William H. Sabine. New York: New York Times & Arno Press, 1971.

Veritas [pseud]. "In the Clerical Line." *Ipswich Journal*, June 29, 1790.

David Wondrich

The **cocktail app** is downloadable digital software, generally used on mobile devices such as phones or tablets, that disseminates information from drink recipes and cocktail histories to mixological tips and special deals at local bars. The cocktail app is the twenty-first-century equivalent of the bar book: a helpful, convenient source of information for bartenders and cocktailians, both amateur and professional.

At the turn of the twenty-first century, the easiest place to find a cocktail recipe was still a physical book, as had been the case since Jerry Thomas published his *Bar-Tenders Guide* in 1862. See THOMAS, JERRY. Bars were discovered through word of mouth, local newspapers, and magazines or a look through the phone book. That all began to change with the advent of the World Wide Web in the 1990s. Cocktail sites such as CocktailDB and chatrooms like Robert Hess's DrinkBoy became places for the global cocktail community to form, meet, and exchange information. See HESS, ROBERT, and DRINKBOY FORUM. In the early 2000s, however, wireless internet access was rare, and computers were largely laptop or desktop affairs.

The introduction of Apple's App Store for iPhone in July 2008 transformed how software was created and consumed. Apple provided a software development kit for users to create their own apps, which they could sell or give away through the App Store. The response was overwhelming; from an initial library of five hundred–plus apps, more than a million apps were available by 2013.

Cocktail apps sprang up quickly. Among the earliest were Cocktails (created by CocktailDB), Gary Regan's Flip 'N Drink, and cocktail blogger Jimmy Patrick's 101 Cocktails. Presenting new and classic cocktail recipes on devices that were easy and quick to use, these apps made the world of cocktails newly accessible to novices and professionals alike, whether they were preparing drinks at home or behind the bar during a busy shift.

Over subsequent years, apps were created for virtually every aspect of the cocktail industry. Liquor Cabinet and My Bar, for example, keep track of which spirits users have on hand, recommend cocktails that can be made with them, and can suggest missing ingredients for additional cocktails. See REGAN, GARY. Distiller can recommend bottles users do not own with reviews and descriptions written by top spirits and cocktail writers, while Thirstie, an on-demand alcohol delivery app, allows users to purchase those bottles without leaving their homes.

Cocktail magazine apps are an invaluable source for enthusiasts and professionals to stay on top of the latest developments behind the bar and in the spirits industry, from publications well known in print such as *Imbibe* and *Saveur* to iPhone- and iPad-exclusive publications like *Bohemian Bar Magazine*, which achieved a graphic look impossible to achieve in print.

For all the apps aimed at amateur mixologists, many are designed for professionals and serious drink scholars. Apps like PDT Cocktails and Modern Classics feature recipes presented by established bartenders and cocktail writers for more serious mixologists, and charge accordingly ($9.99 per app, which is in the upper tier of paid apps). Apps are able to satisfy every niche in the cocktail community. By and large, however, inexpensive apps aimed at amateur mixologists are the norm in the app world.

Doudoroff, Martin. Email interview, July 25, 2016.

Friedman, Lex. "The App Store Turns Five: A Look Back and Forward." *Macworld*, July 8, 2013.

Winship, Doug. "iPhone App: Cocktails Made Easy." *The Pegu Blog*, March 30, 2009. https://www.killingtime.com/Pegu/2009/03/30/cocktails-made-easy/ (accessed February 25, 2021).

Tony Sachs

cocktail contests have existed almost as long as modern bartending; as far back as 1869, celebrity bartender Harry Johnson boasted of winning a competition in New Orleans and subsequently

The winners of an amateur cocktail competition held at the Hotel Adlon in Berlin, 1930. The actress Lilian Harvey, *second from left*, came in first with her Hocus Pocus Cocktail (equal parts gin, Cointreau, and lemon juice; see White Lady). Wondrich Collection.

being crowned the best bartender in America. See Johnson, Harry. Almost as long ago, bartenders and judges began complaining that the recipes entered in cocktail competitions are needlessly complicated; an 1889 New York newspaper reports disapprovingly of a cocktail contest entry requiring "eggs of a certain age, laid at the change of the moon, and by chickens of a certain breed."

Cocktail contests generally require competitors to create a new cocktail or cocktails, sometimes with surprise ingredients, and (because most contests are sponsored) usually featuring a sponsor's brand. Moving with the times, modern-day competitions may also reward, in whole or in part, a bartender's ability to pair cocktails with food, get branded cocktails listed on their establishment's menu, or publicize such cocktails; even a bartender's potential appeal as an ambassador of the contest itself, the sponsoring brand, or its parent company comes into play. Vagaries of national laws allow some contests to offer multiple large cash prizes, while others may not offer any financial incentive beyond bragging rights.

Perhaps the longest continually running international cocktail contests have been those conducted under the auspices of the International Bartenders Association (IBA), which was founded in 1951 and to which national bartender guilds associate themselves. The IBA World Cocktail Championships (WCC) are open to member bartenders only and are held annually; national guilds hold contests to select that country's delegate(s) to the world finals. The gap between the spirit-forward, classically inspired cocktails that became popular in modern bars starting in about 1990 and the kinds of recipes that typically win the WCC continues to widen. WCC-winning cocktails typically feature layers of flavor dependent on sugar from syrups, juices, or liqueurs and generally relegate the base spirit from a leading to a supporting role in the cocktail. See IBA. The longest almost continually running international branded cocktail contest is the Martini & Rossi vermouth company's annual Martini Grand Prix, which began as the Paissa Prize in 1966 and is open to all bartenders. See Martini & Rossi.

With a global shift to drinking in bars rather than at home, branded competitions have proliferated to saturation point. These heavily sponsored contests have led to a backlash, with many bartenders declining to enter for fear of appearing to have "sold out." There have even been some self-organized, aggressively unsponsored contests where each entrant pays an entry fee and the winner takes all. Winning—or even just placing—in a large, well-respected, contest, however, has huge value to a bartender. In addition to any prize money or trips, he or she gets to meet senior marketing staff from the brand, gets profiled in the media (often worldwide), and may get the chance to be hired to teach about the contest in countries that host it in subsequent years. Competing may also give entrants exclusive access to unique tastings, trainings, and distillery visits. Brands' return on investment is an enhanced reputation among, and relationships with, bartenders; inspiration for new products or signature cocktails; and publicity, which can spill over into consumer awareness.

Cocktail contest judges can evaluate every aspect of a cocktail accurately except the experience of enjoying drinking it in a bar, which is almost impossible to simulate in a contest setting. In a contest, the cocktail is often judged in isolation, frequently by a "blind" jury, whose members do not know the name or bar of the cocktail's creator, do not see it made, and do not know the recipe, or, for contests in which competitors submit a written recipe online, the recipes may be made (by a stand-in bartender) and judged behind closed doors all at once. However, environmental and experiential factors are perhaps the most important in enjoying a cocktail in real life: better an average cocktail with friends in a cozy bar with a good jukebox than an amazing concoction drunk alone in a sterile over-designed hellhole piping lounge "jazz" played by studio musicians working for scale through the speakers. It is telling that in over 145 years of cocktail competitions, fewer than a handful of winning recipes have become well known even to professionals, let alone popular in bars. Perhaps the most successful one, the Commodore, won the Police Gazette Bartender's Medal in 1903 and was popular until Prohibition. It has not been revived since.

Archives of Martini. "From Paissa Prize to the Martini Grand Prix." PDF, 2015.

Johnson, Harry. *The New and Improved Bartenders Guide.* New York, 1882.

The International Bartenders' Association website. https://iba-world.com (accessed February 25, 2021).

"Recognising a New Art." *Brooklyn Eagle*, 1889.

Philip Duff

cocktail creation—the process of creating a new drink—follows many different inspirations. Some of the most common include responding to limits on the available ingredients; accommodating a new ingredient; playing with variations on an existing cocktail; pairing with a certain dish; paying tribute to a person, place, or event; aiming for a certain flavor profile; or even just plain whimsy. Yet the majority of cocktails that have survived the test of time have done so because they follow a simple, balanced formula of sweet, sour (or bitter), and spirit. Such formulae are flexible enough to accommodate the growing global availability of ingredients and technological advances and can help to create happy permutations, which expand and encourage an evolving world of flavor.

Just as great chefs first learn to perfect core recipes before creating their own variations, the foundational structure of various classic recipes should first be grasped before setting out to create something new. This requires an understanding of all of the facets of what makes a cocktail great. Perhaps most important is a solid understanding of each class of ingredient: not just what it goes well with, what it clashes with, and how it affects the flavor, aroma, and texture of a drink but also the various meanings it carries. Sometimes the response to a drink can be influenced more by the provenance or perceived social class of an ingredient than by its flavor. By understanding the totality of the characteristics each product brings to the drink, one will better understand how to incorporate them into the overall creation.

Then there is the drink's family or pattern. Consider some of the foundational families of classic cocktails: the aromatic (Manhattan, Martini), the sour (Whisky Sour, Daiquiri), and the bitter (Negroni). The lineage of almost any cocktail can be traced back to or through one of these. With few exceptions, all new cocktails reflect in one way or another a foundation resting on an already-established classic recipe. By far the most popular way of creating a new cocktail recipe is to bend or mutate a classic formula or already-established recipe. This mutation may occur through a deliberate choice, where the mixer changes the recipe slightly by using the same ingredients but shifting their quantities or makes a slight variation in style of the original ingredients. A good example of this is switching the crème de cassis in a Kir Royale to crème de mure. The flavor of the Kir Royale shifts with the switch in accent from blackcurrant to blackberry, but the substituted ingredient works in essentially the same way.

The mutation can also occur by accident, through a historical misreading of the recipe, miswriting of an original recipe, or mistaken substitution of an ingredient. This can be as simple as accidentally switching the proportions of a cocktail's ingredients, for example, transferring it from a dry drink into a sweeter version.

Mutations can also happen in a more fundamental way, where a key ingredient, such as the base spirit, is changed completely. This may be the case because an ingredient isn't available at the time, such as the legend of the Daiquiri, which is said to have been first drunk in Cuba when Jennings Stockton Cox, an American engineer, ran out of gin while entertaining American guests and substituted the Bacardi white rum made nearby, transforming the usual cocktail from something like a Gimlet to a Daiquiri. See DAIQUIRI and GIMLET. This, too, may be subject to accident: according to Henry Madden, the Tijuana bartender who is credited with inventing the Tequila Daisy and hence possibly the Margarita, the Daisy came about when he reached for the wrong bottle under the bar, grabbing tequila when he was presumably aiming for gin. See TEQUILA DAISY.

In some cases, these variations coalesce, turning a single drink into a family of them, each keeping the structure of the original but differing in its base ingredient or some other element. A classic example is the Collins family, where a simple Old Tom gin punch made tall with soda water metastasized into a whole shelf-full of drinks based on everything from bourbon to Batavia arrack. See COLLINS.

Imitation is another fruitful technique. The most common form of cocktail imitation involves a referencing rather than a mirroring. An example is the Rossini, which references the structure of its friend the Bellini but with strawberry puree instead of the Bellini's peach. See BELLINI. The muted peach hues favored by the Venetian painter Giovanni Bellini, which inspired the naming of the Bellini, are held in mind in the naming of the Rossini—whose pure red color is also part of its name, *rosso* being the Italian for red, and also of the Italian painter John Rossini.

Addition and subtraction of ingredients used in a classic cocktail recipe is also a very common way to create new drinks, and an easy and logical one, as are changing its service style so that, for instance, a cocktail becomes a fizz or an aromatic a punch with the addition of citrus juice. Yet some of the most popular drinks follow neither logic nor pattern and seem unhinged when you read their recipes on the page, with balance and flavor-harmonizing thrown overboard. However, when they are made, they often taste wonderful, even if it's a mystery why they work so well. These cocktails are crazy stews. The Trinidad Sour exemplified this perfectly, where the Angostura bitters that should be an accent are used as the base ingredient. Its huge proportion of bitters seems absurd on the page but somehow works successfully in real life.

In general, though, to play it safe it is important to keep in mind the functionality of the base, modifier, and accents that are being used. The base spirit should always be a distinctive component of the final drink and not be hidden behind the other ingredients. The modifiers should be used to enhance the base and allow it to express the overall inspiration for the drink. The choice for accent ingredients should be such that they provide interesting flavor highlights without specifically drawing any attention. Bitters, orange-flower water, and orgeat are examples of accents that aren't in themselves specifically noticeable but if omitted would make it clearly obvious that the drink was missing something.

For the final drink to be seen as a success, it should be one that achieves a clear balance of all of the ingredients it contains, with each one serving a specific purpose. It should also be a drink that leaves the customer wishing there was a little more left as they take their last sip.

See also COCKTAIL; MIXOLOGY, HISTORY OF; and MIXOLOGY (HOW TO MIX DRINKS).

Craddock, Harry. *The Savoy Cocktail Book*. N.p.: Girard & Stewart, 2015

Day, Alex, Nick Fauchald, and David Kaplan. *Cocktail Codex*. Berkeley, CA: Ten Speed, 2018.

Embury, David. *The Fine Art of Mixing Drinks*. New York: Faber & Faber, 1958.

Wondrich, David. *Imibe!*, 2nd ed. New York: Perigee, 2015.

Woon, Basil. *When It's Cocktail Time in Cuba*. New York: Horace Liveright, 1928.

Tony Conigliaro and Audrey Saunders

cocktail music is a term that encompasses a variety of styles of "mood music" originally produced from the late 1940s through the late 1970s. Technology helped to birth the genre via the 33 1/3-rpm long playing vinyl record album, introduced by Columbia Records in 1948, then a new medium for sound reproduction. The LP, as it was known, could hold over forty minutes' worth of material over two sides, as opposed to the six to eight minutes offered by the two-sided shellac 78-rpm record it replaced. This format was envisioned for releases of orchestral/classical works, which previously had to be reconstructed over multiple 78s. But in short order a new breed of "concept albums" appeared, many marketed as "music for relaxation"—especially since you no longer had to get up off of the couch every five minutes to change the record. These records could also set the mood at social gatherings, such as dinner parties—and particularly for cocktail parties.

Popular songs about spirits existed long before the dawn of high fidelity. During the first seventy years of audio reproduction, songs about drinks and drinking were often humorous and bawdy, especially in the "rhythm & booze" worlds of what were then known as "race" and "hillbilly" platters. In these styles one could hear tunes such as Amos Milburn's "One Scotch, One Bourbon, One Beer," George Jones's "White Lightning," or the Four Deuces paean "WPLJ," a blend of white port and lemon juice that was enjoyed for being both high octane and economical. The first major hit song about a cocktail, albeit not an actual one, appeared early in 1942 when the Glenn Miller Orchestra released "Moonlight Cocktail" (adapted into an actual cocktail, a riff on the Aviation, by bartender/author Gary "Gaz" Regan some sixty-five years later). See AVIATION COCKTAIL and REGAN, GARY. Lyrically, the song related the mixing of a cocktail to a budding romantic relationship; curiously, it was banned by the BBC as being "sentimental slush." In 1945, the swinging Andrews Sisters recorded "Rum and Coca-Cola," a ribald Trinidadian calypso hit. Many radio networks initially refused to play a song about an alcoholic beverage, but the public thrilled to its lilting tropical rhythm and drove the song to the top of the pops.

In contrast, most cocktail music of the 1950s was instrumental, comprised of relaxed, slightly swinging jazz, sometimes with Latin (and later Brazilian bossa) accents: artists such as George Shearing, Buddy Cole, the Three Suns, Sid Bass, and accordionist Art Van Damme's quintet (whose mid-'50s LPs *Martini Time*, *Manhattan Time*, and *Cocktail Capers* exemplify the sound and attitude) provided cool grooves on popular hits that could be complemented by the sound of a cocktail shaker joggling in the background. Bandleader Cedric Dumont took this concept a step further, when his "Musical Cocktail Party" (1956) featured the sound of the shaker recorded and mixed as a percussion instrument. The flamboyantly influential Spanish/Cuban musician Xavier Cugat doubled down on this and produced an album entitled *Cugi's Cocktails* (1963), on which every song was named after a cocktail—not only classics such as "One Mint Julep" and "Rum and Coca-Cola" but new pieces including "Daiquiri," "Grasshopper," "Singapore Sling," and "Zombie." See MINT JULEP; DAIQUIRI; GRASSHOPPER; SINGAPORE SLING; and ZOMBIE. Legendary New Orleans saxophonist Plas Johnson, renowned for his performance of "The Pink Panther Theme," concocted an album titled *Blue Martini* with composer John Neel, with the cocktail photographed on the album cover in all its aquamarine splendor.

Stereophonic LPs were introduced in late 1957, showcasing a new type of gimmick—sounds and instruments traveling from speaker to speaker, hurtling across the room like Sputniks in space. These recordings delighted hi-fi enthusiasts, especially those who might have a few highballs under their belts (by the psychedelic '60s, the same technique applied on rock recordings would thrill listeners experiencing mind-altering drugs). Arranger Bob Thompson released an LP titled *On the Rocks*, adorned with an iconic "woman in a cocktail glass" on the cover. Mexican composer/arranger Esquivel! (yes, only one name and always with an exclamation point) added electronic instruments and effects, wordless vocals, and bodacious production techniques to his "sonorama" space-age arrangements. The space age was on everyone's mind during that time, and records such as *Music from Outer Space* (Frank Comstock), *Moon Gas* (Dick Hyman and Mary Mayo), *Fantastica* (Russ Garcia), and *Music for Heavenly Bodies* (Paul Tanner) sonically explored the cosmos; Les Baxter's *Space Escapade* even featured astronauts drinking fluorescent, dry-ice garnished libations on another planet, surrounded by pink- and green-skinned moon maidens.

Many of these records were made with seduction in mind, designed to be played as a romantic aperitif for listeners before heading to the boudoir. Comedian Jackie Gleason, an amateur musician with a hit TV show, conducted a series of records with just that concept in mind. Armed with luxurious arrangements, dripping with saccharin, and bathed in reverb, Gleason's music was there to help listeners get the job done over dozens of LPs; choice titles included *Music, Martinis & Memories*, *Music to Change Her Mind*, *Music for the Love Hours*, *Aphrodesia, Music for That Moment*, *Opiate D'amour*, and the whisperingly titled *Oooo!* Improbably, Gleason somehow managed to continue recording into the days of incense and peppermints, producing an album of soft rock laced with sitars, tablas, and other groovy sonics entitled *The Now Sound . . . for Today's Lovers*.

Another new style of music, which later came to be called exotica, was first heard on the album *Ritual of the Savage*, by Hollywood composer Les Baxter, in 1952. Fusing imitation orchestral film music with "exotic" rhythms/percussion loosely (very loosely) based on the music of the South Pacific, South America, Africa, Asia, and the Caribbean, Baxter crafted a colorful and relaxing if inauthentic hybrid. In the mid-1950s, pianist Martin Denny, working in Honolulu cocktail lounges, took Baxter's themes and rearranged them in a light jazz motif, replete with the band members imitating bird calls and monkey squeals, replicating a tropical jungle. Hawaii reacted to Denny's group with SRO crowds packing their performances at the Kaiser Aluminum Dome at Waikiki nightly. Their recording debut, the LP *Exotica*, along with its 45-rpm single "Quiet Village," topped the pop music charts in 1958, quickly followed by *Hypnotique*, *Afro-desia, Forbidden Island, Primitiva*, and more. The record industry jumped on the trend, and soon the record bins were overflowing: *Jun'gala* (Marty Wilson), *Surfer's Paradise* (Alex Keack), *Taboo* (Arthur Lyman), *Tropicale* (Tommy Morgan), and *Voodoo* (Robert Drasnin) were among the best. The music became synonymous with tiki, as it provided the soundtrack at Polynesian restaurants around the world. To this day, it's considered the perfect aural accompaniment to a Mai Tai, Zombie, and the like. See MAI TAI and TIKI.

By the late 1960s/early 1970s, cocktail culture had declined, eclipsed by the rise of recreational drug use. The popularization of the Moog synthesizer in 1967 produced a wellspring of electronic mood records, including Martin Denny's *Exotic Moog* and Les Baxter's *Moog Rock* among them. The era's sexual revolution was amalgamated into heavy breathing "orgasm" records, the mod sound of seduction. Acts like the Mystic Moods Orchestra, who often recorded in four-channel quadraphonic sound, and the 101 Strings, whose *The Sounds of Love* LP is perhaps the ultimate absurd artifact of this kind, filled the gap between Serge Gainsbourg/Jane Birkin's 1969 hit international bedroom heavy-breather "Je t'aime . . . moi non plus" and the disco porn of Donna Summer's 1975 big O-fest "Love to Love You Baby." Poet Rod McKuen celebrated gay sexuality in the same way on his *(Crisco) Disco* LP. But if the music was changing, so were the cocktails: tiki drinks were out, and Harvey Wallbangers were in—and soon Sex on the Beaches and, inevitably, Screaming Orgasms. See HARVEY WALLBANGER.

The musical landscape changed as the 1970s chugged along, with disco and punk on the outside looking in at the AOR mainstream, while cocktail music lost much of its appeal. During the 1980s, hipsters immersing themselves in thrift stores and flea markets began picking up the "moldy oldie" LP's, lured by the kitschy cover art and cheap prices. When combined with other mid-century detritus found in these shops—1950s/1960s clothing, mod furniture, cheesy bric-a-brac, cool kitchen/barware, grimy paperback books, and so on—one could decorate a pretty groovy living space curated from the discarded past. Ultimately, that would make a cool place to throw a retro cocktail party for your friends.

As it turns out, that's exactly what happened. The revival of the cocktail in the late 1980s coincided with the (some would say ironic) hip appreciation of cocktail music, alongside other remnants of the era (bowling shirts, grindhouse/drive-in movies, Googie coffee shops, neon signage, etc.) that had been relegated to history's scrap heap. As the 1990s progressed, record companies dug into their vaults to reissue compilations of this "space age bachelor pad music" (a term coined by Los Angeles artist Byron Werner as the title of a mixtape he recorded of his cocktail music favorites, copies of which traveled throughout the tape traders collective in the early 1980s). Many of the CD packages enclosed cocktail recipes, some vintage, some not. Young musicians updated old sounds—the band Combustible Edison referred to their fans as "the Cocktail Nation." They even had their own eponymous signature cocktail, consisting of brandy,

Campari, and lemon juice and printed the recipe on the back cover of their 1994 debut album. "Lounge Music" sections grew in record shops as more and more albums were distributed. Capitol Records, for example, released twenty-five volumes in their Ultra Lounge series. An electronic version called "lounge-core" became a dance club style and boutique hotel accessory, especially in Japan and Europe, with producers/DJs (Ursula 1000, Thievery Corporation, the Karminsky Experience, Tipsy, Fantastic Plastic Machine, the Gentle People, and Nicola Conte among them) sampling the vintage LPs for sounds and beats. The new sound of cocktail music was paired with the revitalized cocktail scene at parties around the globe.

Countryman, Dana, ed. *Cool and Strange Music* magazine. 28 issues, 1996–2003.

Jones, Dylan. *Ultra Lounge: The Lexicon of Easy Listening.* New York: Universe, 1997.

McKnight-Trontz, Jennifer. *Exotiquarium: Album Art from the Space Age.* New York: St. Martin's Griffin, 1999.

Vale, V., and Andrea Juno. *Incredibly Strange Music.* 2 vols. San Francisco: RE/SEARCH, 1993–1994.

Wick, Sam, David Wick, and Bradley Temkin, eds. *Lounge Magazine.* 13 issues, 1994–1997.

Wooley, John, Thomas Conner, and Mark Brown. *Forever Lounge: A Laid Back Price Guide to the Languid Sounds of Lounge Music.* Norfolk, VA: Antique Trader, 1999.

Brother Cleve

cocktails on tap merge the realms of draft beer and cocktails—with the latter compiled in bulk and served at the pull of a handle or the push of a button. Also called kegged or draft cocktails, such mixtures enable bartenders to prepare large quantities of (sometimes complicated) cocktails, store them chilled in pressurized metal kegs, and serve them with great speed and in large numbers without loss of consistency. And as with beer or wine on tap, the preparation gives bartenders a way to let customers sample a cocktail before committing to a full serving. Spirit-forward drinks, such as Manhattans and Negronis, are best suited to the approach, eliminating the shelf-life and storage concerns that come with using citrus juice or other perishable ingredients, and highball-style drinks that benefit from carbonation also lend themselves to the tap approach (one of the most common cocktails

served on tap is the Moscow Mule). Tap cocktails also present their own unique sets of challenges: unbalanced ratios, inaccurate levels of dilution, and a lack of cleanliness in the storage and serving system all pose peril to the practice. Tap cocktails began to spread into bars around 2010, led by bartenders such as Tad Carducci and Paul Tanguay via their Tippling Bros consultancy, with venues such as Marriott Hotels and larger restaurants and clubs utilizing the system. In addition, Road Soda—a New York–based company that serves drinks at large events such as parties, concerts, and festivals—utilizes a tap system to dispense cocktails en masse.

See also BATCHING; MOSCOW MULE.

Smith, Erin Geiger. "Mixed Drinks on Tap." *Wall Street Journal*, September 10, 2014. http://www.wsj.com/articles/mixed-drinks-on-tap-faster-manhattans-negronis-and-more-1410391659 (accessed February 25, 2021).

Van Buren, Alex. "Everything You Need to Know about Draft Cocktails." *Travel and Leisure*, February 2, 2016. http://www.travelandleisure.com/articles/draft-cocktails (accessed February 25, 2021).

Paul Clarke

cocktails on the internet. The rebirth of interest in cocktails that began in the 1990s, and the subsequent and evolving worldwide cocktail subculture, are inextricably entwined with the popularization of the internet. As Ted "Dr. Cocktail" Haigh says, "the cocktail revival . . . could not have happened as it did but for the Internet and World Wide Web." See HAIGH, TED.

Craig Goldwyn's Food & Drink Network on AOL appeared in the early 1990s. In 1995, *Wired* magazine launched the first ambitious suite of early web publications, among which was CocktailTime, a website built from the work of the San Francisco–area bartender Paul Harrington. See HARRINGTON, PAUL. Inspired by the work of Dale DeGroff and Charles Schumann, Harrington published a new mixed-drink recipe each week, each including a short history and illustration. See DEGROFF, DALE, and SCHUMANN, CHARLES. CocktailTime only ran for about a year, but it reached tens of thousands of people, some of whom went on to be deeply involved in the cocktail movement. Also in 1995, P. C. Loberg launched the Webtender, the first web-based cocktail recipe database.

Robert Hess started the Drinkboy Forum in 1999 which, as AOL waned, largely took over as the main message board for cocktail enthusiasts. See HESS, ROBERT; and DRINKBOY FORUM. Beginning in 2001, Drinkboy was complemented by eGullet, a culinary forum founded by Steven Shaw and Jason Perlow that has hosted a lively and often sophisticated cocktail discussion. In the early years of the twenty-first century, committed independent online publishers and bloggers such as Chuck Taggart, Hanford Lemoore, Jamie Boudreau, Jeffrey Morgenthaler, Jimmy Patrick, Paul Clarke, Erik Ellestad, Darcy O'Neil, Marleigh Riggins, Michael Dietsch, Rick Stutz, Natalie Bovis-Nelson, Lauren Clark, Camper English, Craig Mrusek, Jeff Berry, Gabriel Szaszko, Blair Reynolds, Gary Regan, and Sonja Kassebaum emerged, each building followings and spreading inspiration and knowledge.

Online archives of old newspapers and enthusiast-prepared libraries of PDF-based scans of old cocktail books, bar manuals, and distiller's handbooks have been a boon for researchers. On the flip side, the ad hoc, casual semipermanence of internet content has also facilitated the spreading of misinformation, plagiarism, and mythology, as has the voracious need for content to drive traffic to the many culinary web magazines of the 2010s, although those at least are edited.

As commercial interest in mixed drinks and cocktail culture has risen, so has the proliferation of "shovelware" and other low-grade content online. HTML, the lingua franca of the Web, offers no special value to the representation of recipes, the organization of spirits and cocktail information, or even representations of authorship, and as yet no technological standards have emerged to further deepen discourse.

Haigh, Ted. *Vintage Spirits and Forgotten Cocktails: Deluxe Revised and Expanded Edition.* Beverly, MA: Quarry, 2009.

Martin Doudoroff

The **cocktail party**, derisively defined by the *New York Times* in 1922 as "a gathering of persons who can have a 'good time' only when highly stimulated by strong waters," did not have its start in a great metropolis. The credit goes neither to New York nor London (where, apocryphally, Alec Waugh was supposed to have invented the cocktail party in the 1920s). No, the first cocktail party so conceived and so called was held in the American Midwest—in St. Louis, Missouri, on a Sunday afternoon sometime in the first few months of 1917. (We may set aside the after-theater hotel-room "cocktail party" documented in St. Joseph, Missouri, in 1903 and the "cocktail party" a Brooklyn, New York, schoolteacher held for her pupils in 1906 as atypical of the genre, and not just because both ended in deaths.) Mrs. Julius S. Walsh Jr., a socialite, was "responsible for the innovation," according to a local newspaper. Clara Bell Walsh had tried out other party themes before hitting on the cocktail idea (her notion of having guests dress up as babies and drink from bottles wasn't quite the enduring success that her "cocktail party" would be).

Some fifty guests attended the to-do at the Walsh mansion, where cocktails were served from noon to 1:00 p.m. (when "dinner" was then served). The drinks on offer were mostly of the moment—Bronx cocktails and Clover Leaf cocktails (Clover Clubs with mint leaves floating on top). See BRONX COCKTAIL and CLOVER CLUB. Mrs. Walsh, we might note, was up to date in her knowledge of cocktail fashion, living as she did half the year in New York's Plaza Hotel. Also served at the party were highballs ("some with Scotch and some with rye or Bourbon whisky"), Gin Fizzes, Martinis, Manhattans, and even, for the hide-bound oldsters at the event, a few Sazeracs and Mint Juleps. See HIGHBALL; GIN FIZZ; MARTINI; MANHATTAN COCKTAIL; SAZERAC COCKTAIL; and JULEP.

"A Cocktail Party: Mrs. Walsh of St. Louis Has Hit on a New Feature in Way of Entertainment." *Wichita Beacon*, April 3, 1917, 12.

Dietler, Michael, and Brian Hayden, eds. *Feasts: Archaeological and Ethnographic Perspectives on Food, Politics, and Power.* Tuscaloosa: University of Alabama Press, 2001.

"An Innocent Word Is Maltreated," *New York Times*, June 27, 1922.

"Killing Results from Cocktail Party." *Decatur (IL) Daily Review*, November 16, 1903.

Eric Felten

cocktail proportions are the ratios of ingredients that are needed for a drink. They are typically written using ounces (in the United States) and either milliliters or centiliters throughout the rest of the world. There are also recipes that are listed in "shots" or even simply in fractions, as seen in the recipe for the Sidecar from the *Savoy Cocktail Book* (1930): "¼ Lemon Juice. ¼ Cointreau. ½ Brandy. Shake well and strain into a cocktail glass." In this example, the unit of measure is up to the mixologist. Since ¼ + ¼ + ½ = 1, the recipe simply takes the "whole" drink and splits it up into the proportions of ingredients needed for it. If you want to make a 120-ml drink, then you would use 30 ml lemon juice, 30 ml Cointreau, and 60 ml of brandy.

Another variation of this is to reference the recipe in "parts," with a "part" being the unit of measure. For example, in *The Fine Art of Mixing Drinks* by David Embury, the Sidecar recipe is 1 part Cointreau, 2 parts lemon juice, and 8 parts Cognac. To make a reasonably sized drink here utilizing Embury's ratios, your "part" might be 10 ml, which would result in 10 ml Cointreau, 20 ml lemon juice, and 80 ml cognac—making this particular Sidecar recipe a fairly dry and sour one.

By understanding and following the proper proportions of a cocktail recipe, it is easier to scale that recipe up (or down) in order to make more than one drink at a time. By keeping the proportions properly in sync, it will ensure that the resultant drink will always be properly balanced, provided that the original recipe is a good one.

When writing cocktail recipes, always use measurements that are of a similar type; otherwise it can be difficult to understand what is intended or how to scale the drink if necessary. For example, a recipe that lists 1 part of X, 2 parts of Y, and 1 *teaspoon* of Z is technically impossible to recreate properly, since the relationship between a "part" and a "teaspoon" is unexplained. Similarly, recipes that use measures of indeterminate size are impossible to recreate properly. The term "splash" can mean different things to different people, particularly with different ingredients.

Sometimes recipes will state "juice of half a lemon" (or lime). This reference should only be viewed in very loose terms in a recipe. The size of fruit can vary considerably, with one piece of fruit yielding only 1/2 ounce of juice and another providing more than 2 ounces. Trying to follow such a recipe verbatim can quickly disrupt the cocktail's balance.

While there are basic parameters for the proportions of a sweet + sour + strong (or any recipe for that matter), they are also mutable. Over the last couple of decades, most drinks seem to have become stronger and drier. A good example is the formula for a classic sour: The standard recipe fifteen years ago for a fresh-juice sour was: 22 ml sour (lemon or lime juice) + 30 ml sweet (simple syrup or liqueur) + 45 ml strong (spirits). Today an oft-utilized standard recipe is: 22 ml sour + 22 ml sweet + 60 ml strong. On the other hand, drinks from the Manhattan family have generally gotten softer and sweeter: fifteen years ago, it was common to find a formula like 5 ml maraschino cherry syrup + 10 ml vermouth + 75 ml whisky, with no bitters, where now the older style generally prevails: 2 ounces (60 ml) whisky + 1 ounce (30 ml) vermouth + 2 dashes bitters (these proportions are sometimes known as the "212" formula, which happens to be the area code for Manhattan).

Yet even those ratios are subjective. Having basic parameters for drink proportions is very useful, but the most important outcome is that it pleases the individual imbiber. While Embury's Sidecar may perhaps be a bit on the tart side for most people, he said it best here:

> The truth of the matter is, of course, that the proportion of sweet and sour is best which best pleases the taste of the individual drinker, provided always, that for the aperitif cocktail the final blend with the liquor base will produce a drink that is dry, not sweet. Just how dry, again, is a question of personal preference, but let it never be sweet. This is a matter not of ruining the drink but of ruining the appetite and the digestion.

We agree.

See also COCKTAIL RECIPES; EMBURY, DAVID; MANHATTAN; and SOUR.

Embury, David. *The Fine Art of Mixing Drinks*. New York: Doubleday, 1948.

Audrey Saunders

cocktail recipes were created—first in the form of spoken jingles or rhymes, later written down and published—to make mixed drinks reproducible. The earliest were approximate, as seen in the oldest punch recipes, such as "Two of sour, and one of sweet, / One of strong, and two of weak" from 1756.

By the time the first bartending manual, Jerry Thomas's 1862 *How to Mix Drinks*, had appeared, certain conventions were beginning to evolve regarding consistency, documenting ingredients, measures, methods, and recipe formats. See THOMAS, JERRY. Thomas, for example, preferred to list the ingredients with their quantities and then explain how they were to be assembled; others, such as Harry Johnson, preferred to diagram the process as it unfolded, working ingredients and instructions together. These approaches are both still in use. While early bar manuals attempted to be precise in their details, not every recipe included what are now considered essentials—details about ingredients such as "aromatic bitters" or "Jamaican rum," preparation method, glassware, and garnish.

As the art of mixing drinks evolved, obsolescent measures such as the wineglass (2 ounces, or 60 ml) began to be replaced and vague ones to take on definition. Over time, American recipe writers moved to listing quantities in ounces, while British ones tended to prefer "parts." (France and Spain, the other major producers of drink books, eventually followed British practice.) See COCKTAIL PROPORTIONS. Currently in the United States, recipes generally call for ingredients in quarter-ounce (7 ml) increments, and additionally, ingredients used in small amounts—the so-called drops and dashes—are now often given in fractions of a teaspoon (5 ml) as well. Throughout the rest of the world, metric measures allow more precise increments of 5 ml, with 30 ml—equivalent to about 1 ounce—being very common.

Two additional practices have emerged in modern cocktail books worldwide: listing the dominant alcoholic ingredient first and supplying headnotes that convey more detailed information about the drink. This information can include the drink's inventor and other details of creation, the original cocktail from which it was adapted, and substitution recommendations. Today cocktail recipes don't just narrate the making of the drink; they help the reader understand what makes it distinctive.

See also WINEGLASS; COCKTAIL PROPORTIONS; and MIXOLOGY (HOW TO MIX DRINKS).

Kaplan, David, Nick Fauchald, and Alex Day. *Death & Co.: Modern Classic Cocktails*. Berkeley: Ten Speed, 2014.

Masson, P. *Le Parfait Limonadier: Ou le maniere de preparer le thé, le caffé, le chocolat, & autres liqueurs chaudes & froides*. Paris: C. Moette, 1705.

Morgenthaler, Jeffrey. *The Bar Book: Elements of Cocktail Technique*. San Francisco: Chronicle, 2014.

Terrington, William. *Cooling Cups and Dainty Drinks: A Collection of Recipes for "Cups" and Other Compounded Drinks, and of General Information on Beverages of All Kinds*. London: G. Routledge, 1869.

"The Unforgettables." International Bar Association website. http://iba-world.com/iba-cocktails/ (accessed February 25, 2021).

Wondrich, David. *Imbibe!*, rev. ed. New York: Perigee, 2015.

Dinah Sanders

cocktail renaissance is a term for the period at the beginning of the twenty-first century, from roughly 2004 through 2019, when the classic American art of mixing drinks was reconnected with its traditions and re-prioritized in bars around the world. In the process, old recipes were revived, forgotten spirits remembered and reintroduced, and the culture of sophisticated cocktail-sipping revisited, so that Manhattans, Old-Fashioneds, and hand-shaken Daiquiris displaced in turn the Mudslides, Long Island Iced Teas, and slushie-machine Daiquiris that had displaced them a generation or two before. Most immediately, the renaissance inspired a boom in brick-and-mortar bars and fostered cocktail-industry job creation, security, and advancement. Peripherally, it helped to send a ripple of investment through the global bar and restaurant industry and heightened tourism in cities around the United States, and around the world, as well as revitalizing the spirits industry. More generally, the cocktail renaissance changed the way people drink, perhaps for good.

Inspired in part by the last golden age of cocktails, around the turn of the twentieth century, and in part by the culinary revolution of the 1970s and 1980s, the cocktail renaissance came together as a generally (but not always) harmonious movement dedicated to bringing bars back to what they were when they were at the apex of nightlife—and to making the drinks as elegant as they were then, but with perhaps an extra shot of creativity (that part is where friction sometimes occurs between the two wings of the movement). It is that culinary element that helps the movement transcend nostalgia and ensures that the cocktail renaissance as an era is much more nuanced than a predictable reminiscence for simpler times,

Cocktail renaissance pioneer, Sasha Petraske (kneeling, in white), pictured in 2015 with a posse of veterans of Milk & Honey and some of his other bars. Among the group are *Oxford Companion to Spirits and Cocktails* contributors Eric Alperin (kneeling behind Mr. Petraske) and Chad Solomon (with prospector's hat). Photograph by Gabi Porter.

while the dedication to tradition and heritage keep it grounded and give it a cultural foundation.

The result is not just the revitalization of classic old bars but also the opening of thousands of new ones around the world dedicated to serving hand-made drinks mixed from quality ingredients and served with pride and style. While the bulk of them might be concentrated in major cities, the movement has spread to the small-town and even the rural level, aided by the fact that it is self-evangelizing: once a person has had a truly well-made cocktail, it's hard to go back.

Catalysts

While it may not be possible to pinpoint a single catalyst for the cocktail renaissance, three of the most important ones are the culinary revolution of the 1970s, the rise of the craft beer industry, and the introduction of the internet and social media. Together, these separate historic circumstances created a perfect storm for cultural change.

Beginning as a reaction to the processed foods that dominated postwar, mid-twentieth-century America, the culinary revolution led to a new appreciation of fresh ingredients—and, in turn, a curiosity about where those ingredients came from that was sometimes pushed to the point of dogmatism. But along with that came a new passion for careful execution in cooking and a new attention to presentation. In many ways, the culinary world's late-twentieth-century moment of reevaluation paved the way for similar moments in the worlds of wine and beer, and finally cocktails. It is telling that in the 1980s and 1990s, when bartender Dale DeGroff was popularizing classic cocktails as well as inventing new ones and doing it with premium ingredients and (something long out of fashion in drinks) fresh juices, he was doing it under the aegis of pioneering restaurateur Joe Baum (1920–1998), who in the late 1950s and 1960s had blazed the trail for the culinary revolution with the Four Seasons and the Fonda del Sol. See Degroff, Dale.

Meanwhile, following President Jimmy Carter's 1978 legislation permitting home brewing, America saw the birth and boom of the craft beer movement, in turn inspiring healthy competition in the corporate beer world. This was dedicated to the idea that consumers have the right to ask more of their drink brands—that they don't have to accept lowest-common-denominator products and that tradition and history can be drawn from to make better tasting, more substantial, and far more interesting products. What's more, the successful revival of India pale ales, porters, hefeweizens, and the like proved that such historically oriented products could actually sell enough to support themselves.

Finally, as the World Wide Web opened previously closed portals to information and ideas, the bartender's thirst for knowledge increased exponentially. Before the web, if you were behind the bar and somebody asked you for a White Lady, you could look it up in the tattered Mr. Boston book kept under the cash register, and that was about it. Now, after your shift you could find not only a stack of recipes for the drink but also what the story was behind it, who drank it, and the like. A London bartender could post her methodology for making a respectable Manhattan on Robert Hess's Drinkboy.com site, and it would be instantly accessible to a bartender in, say, San Francisco, and the Californian's take on the drink could then be seen back in London—or in Miami, Rome, Mumbai, Singapore, or Melbourne, for that matter; the internet made cocktail chatter a global conversation. And with sites devoted to drink history such as Ted Haigh's at AOL.com, Paul Harrington's at Wired.com, and David Wondrich's at Esquire.com, the archival distance between a classic cocktail's past and present was minimized, allowing modern-day bartenders to openly interpret their forerunners' greatest hits. See HAIGH, TED; HARRINGTON, PAUL; and HESS, ROBERT. This quickly boosted the popularity of not only Prohibition-era classics (Bee's Knees, Negroni, etc.) but drinks introduced much earlier (Old Fashioned, Sazerac, Clover Club) and much later (Moscow Mule). Many of these drinks made appearances on menus alongside craft cocktails of the bar staff's own design, which were often credited accordingly.

Success

After bartenders and bar owners gave patrons a literal taste for what they had been missing, interest grew in an all but invisible industry: distilling. So many of the old drinks called for ingredients that were poorly distributed at best, such as maraschino liqueur or rye whisky, or entirely unavailable in most markets, if not all of them. Crème de violette might have been available in France, if you knew where to look, but it wasn't in the United States. American straight rye was almost as hard to find in Europe, and Old Tom gin hadn't been made since World War II. See GIN, OLD TOM; JACK DANIEL'S; CRÈME DE VIOLETTE; and WHISKY, RYE. In America, twentieth-century consolidation had drastically shrunk the number of distilleries and the range of products that they made, and the same forces were at work in Europe, the Caribbean, and elsewhere. This created an opening, and people rushed in. In the late 1980s, the number of new distillery applicants in America was typically one or two a year, and in 2000 there were but twenty-four operational distilleries in the whole country; by 2010, however, there were more than two hundred, and in 2020 there were more than two thousand. The distillery boom is not isolated to the United States. Ireland, for example, went from just four distilleries in 2010 to thirty-two operational distilleries in 2020. Beyond bars and booze, the cocktail renaissance changed the perception of the occupation of bartending itself. The blue-collar job once relegated to those who couldn't succeed in traditional nine-to-fives was suddenly an enviable position, particularly since those office jobs had lost their stability in the new tech economy. Spirits manufacturers began to promote careers in the industry via so-called brand ambassadors: individuals willing to peddle a product from bar to bar, sometimes across the globe, wining and dining prospective buyers to feature their brands in original craft cocktails. Senior bartenders found careers as beverage managers, overseeing multiple, complex "cocktail programs" and creating elaborate training programs to meet the higher standards of a clientele that, thanks to the internet, was often as educated about the drinks as the bartenders.

One can see the growth in the high end of the bar industry in the story of Tales of the Cocktail, an informal cocktail convention organized in 2002 in New Orleans to introduce writers of drink books to their readers. In the first year, it was presented essentially by a handful of friends and drew a couple hundred people. At its peak a dozen years later, Tales of the Cocktail hosted upward of fifteen thousand attendees from all over the world, representing hundreds of distilleries, brands, and bars. See TALES OF THE COCKTAIL.

Bars and Bartenders

The most romantic legacy of the cocktail renaissance is the reimagining of the speakeasy: an homage to the hidden, dimly lit barrooms that existed by necessity during Prohibition. The most important of these was Milk & Honey, a dark, narrow shoebox of a bar hidden in plain sight in New York City's Lower East Side. Milk & Honey, which opened at the end of 1999, was modeled after Angel's Share, another New York City "speakeasy" opened in 1993—ahead of its time, as far as the movement was concerned. See MILK & HONEY and SPEAKEASY (NEW).

Far more successful were less retiring interpretations of the trend, such as Julie Reiner's Flatiron Lounge (2003) and Audrey Saunders's Pegu Club (2005), which appropriated the retro glamour of the speakeasies but without the secret doors. See PEGU CLUB; REINER, JULIE; and SAUNDERS, AUDREY. Those doors came back with Bourbon & Branch in San Francisco (2006), with Jon Santer and Dominic Venegas as opening bartenders, and PDT ("please don't tell") in New York, which Jim Meehan, a Pegu Club veteran, opened in 2007 behind the phone booth in a downtown hot dog joint. That same year, Chicago saw the opening of the (speakeasy-ish) Violet Hour with bartender Toby Maloney, a veteran of both Milk & Honey and Pegu Club. In fact, those bars served as seminaries, training bartender-missionaries who spread across America opening bars and imbuing more bartenders with the gospel of the craft cocktail, as did Bourbon & Branch, PDT, and the Violet Hour in turn. This process would be repeated around the world. See MATCH.

Of course, not all of these new bars were the same. By the early 2010s, there were clear subcultures on display. To catalog them all is beyond the scope of this entry, but let's take a quick glance at Chicago, as an example, with the understanding that the same subdivisions could be found in London, New York, San Francisco, or Sydney. A cocktail renaissance bar crawl around Chicago at the time would have included straight cocktail bars, of course, such as the Drawing Room, with Charles Joly and Lynn House behind the bar, both of them trained in part by brand ambassador and educator Bridget Albert (a Tony Abou Ganim protégée; see ABOU GANIM, TONY). There would be a whisky bar, such as the rock-and-roll-friendly Delilah's. Shelby Allison and Paul McGhee's Lost Lake would answer any tiki needs. The fine-dining–chemistry-lab fusion that characterized so many of the more culinary-influenced bars at the time was on full display at the Aviary, opened in 2011 by the Michelin-starred chef Grant Achatz. Drawing a direct line from the culinary world to that of cocktails, Achatz opened the Aviary, a molecular mixology bar that featured expensive cocktails created using scientific methods and technology: smoke infusers, sieve traps, Clinebell block-ice makers, and the like. See CLINEBELL ICE MACHINE.

By that point, the cocktail renaissance had created a whole self-perpetuating infrastructure, with new products (and newly rejuvenated old ones), educational institutions, consultants, books, and magazines all cooperating to spread the gospel. See AMERICAN DISTILLING INSTITUTE; BEVERAGE ALCOHOL RESOURCE (BAR); and MIXOGRAPHY.

Legacy

The cocktail renaissance changed the way people drank, and not just in bars. (The last time both microbreweries and micro-distilleries existed en masse was before Prohibition, when alcohol manufacturing had few limitations and laws.) By the late 2010s, the battles had been won. Craft cocktails were officially mainstream. Corporate restaurant chains such as Chili's, Denny's, and Ruby Tuesday featured craft cocktail menus, and rare was the neighborhood restaurant that didn't have at least a few original cocktails on the menu, not to mention a cursory interpretation of a Moscow Mule. But there were signs that another transformation was brewing, as issues of equity and inclusion, of sobriety and work-life balance began to be raised in the bartending world. Then came the Covid-19 pandemic, which pretty much shut the whole industry down; in 2020 alone, upward of a hundred thousand restaurants and bars closed permanently. As bars reopen, there is little doubt that it will be as avatars of a new era.

Clarke, Paul. *The Cocktail Chronicles*. Nashville, TN: Spring House, 2015.

Clarke, Paul. "Remembering Pegu Club. 2005–2010." *Imbibe*, April 30, 2020. https://imbibemagazine.com/pegu-club-2005-2020/ (accessed June 2, 2021).

Harry, John. "Jimmy Carter: American Homebrew Hero?" National Museum of American History website, September 30, 2019. https://americanhistory.si.edu/blog/papazian (accessed June 2, 2021).

Kinstlick, Michael. "The U.S. Craft Distilling Market: 2011 and Beyond." Coppersea Distilling website. https://coppersea.com/wp-content/uploads/2012/04/Craft_Distilling_2011_White_Paper_Final.pdf (accessed June 2, 2021).

Simonson, Robert. "New York's Pioneering Angel's Share, 24 Years Later." *Punch*. https://punchdrink.com/articles/review-angels-share-nyc-cocktail-bar-24-years-later/ (accessed June 2, 2021).

Simonson, Robert. *A Proper Drink*. Berkeley, CA: Ten Speed, 2016.

Viera, Lauren. "Achatz's Aviary Mixes Drinks with a Sense of Whimsy." *Chicago Tribune*, April 24, 2011. https://www.chicagotribune.com/dining/ct-xpm-2011-04-24-ct-live-0425-aviary-opens-20110424-story.html (accessed June 2, 2021).

Lauren Viera

cocktail route is an American term from the 1880s. At first, it referred to any drinker's habitual peregrination from saloon to saloon, but by the turn of the twentieth century it had come to refer to the loose group of 25-cent saloons (when that was a lot to pay for a drink), hotel bars, and other drinking establishments favored by a town's most dedicated social drinkers. The largest and sportiest cities would have more than one such route; to have none would mark a town as sleepy. Cocktail routes, their stops and their travelers were ever changing, but their pillars—bars such as New York's Hoffman House, San Francisco's Bank Exchange, and Harry's New York Bar in Paris—tended to remain constant year in and year out. See Hoffman House; Bank Exchange; and Harry's New York Bar.

David Wondrich

The **cocktail shaker**, a dedicated container for shaking spirits and other ingredients with ice in order to homogenize them, chill them, and dilute them to a more palatable proof, is generally considered the heart of the mixologist's toolkit. It comes in a great number of styles, which we shall attempt to navigate below. All, however, share the same basic operating principle: the rapid melting that occurs when an ice-liquid mix is agitated violently not only chills the liquid with maximum efficiency but also shrinks the volume of the mix (ice taking up more space than water) and creates a vacuum. This is sufficient to hold the parts of the shaker without leaking, yet not so strong that, in a well-designed shaker, the parts cannot be easily separated.

In its first iteration, which we shall call type 1, the cocktail shaker was remarkably basic: a flared, flat-bottomed glass, large or small (i.e., roughly 180 or 360 ml) and a gently flared tin cup sized so that its mouth fit easily over that of the glass. Build the drink in the glass, add ice, cover with the tin, and press it down until it grips the glass. Shake. A little sideways pressure on the glass will flex the tin and break the seal. Remove the tin and slide the glass to the customer or strain the drink into another glass.

We do not know when this simple bartender's trick was first conceived. Its use is first recorded, however, in New York City, in 1850, when low-life journalist George Foster described a city bartender "pulling long ribbons of julep out of a tin cup" (the normal method of mixing drinks at the time involved pouring them back and forth between glasses; here, it seems that the bartender was shaking his drinks before pouring them from the tin into the glass). By the next year this bit of improvisation had become formalized, and one finds the tin cups being referred to as "cobbler mixers"—it took a while for everyone to agree on the name "cocktail shaker," particularly since cocktails were more often stirred than shaken until the twentieth century. Other names included just plain "mixer" or "shaker," "punch" or "Milk Punch shaker," "lemonade shaker," and "eggnog shaker."

These shakers, generally soldered together from thin pieces of sheet tin or brass and then silver-plated, were flimsy and very easy to distort out of round, making them leak (some superior, but expensive, versions were hammered out of sterling silver). By the late nineteenth century manufacturing technology had improved, and they were stamped—or even better spun—from thicker metal. Generally this was nickel silver (an alloy of copper, tin, and zinc, electroplated in silver), or "EPNS," as it was known. Yet this still deformed fairly easily, unless it was made so thick that it lacked the flexibility necessary to allow the vacuum to be broken. Only in 1919 with the introduction of the first stainless steel mixing tins was a material found that was light, flexible, and durable, although it lacked the older alloy's beauty, weight, and thermal conductivity.

In the meanwhile, other styles of shaker had come into use. Type 2 was first described by the London journalist George Augustus Sala, who came across it on a transatlantic crossing in 1865: a pair of "tall silver mugs in which the ingredients of . . . a 'cocktail' . . . are mixed, shaken together, and then scientifically discharged." These, made either of silver or EPNS, were designed so that the rim of one cup fit snugly into the other, resting just inside it (the rims were sometimes flanged, to make them more difficult to bend out of round). European silversmiths had been making similar pairs of cups, often detailed to look like a barrel when assembled, for centuries. Whatever they had been used for, however, it was not mixing iced drinks, making this another example of the improvisatory nature of the bartender's kit. When used for that, they have the advantage of having greater thermal efficiency than the metal and glass version and make drinks very cold, very fast.

Type 2 was quite popular in Europe, and particularly in the United Kingdom, where it only faded from use in the 1960s, but it never really caught on in America. Nonetheless, its most popular variation—type 3—seems to have been invented in the United States: it first appears, at least, in an 1878 American silver catalogue. Instead of a second metal cup like the first, it has a top shaped like a bulbous, pinch-headed cowbell. An elegant shaker, it was particularly favored in France, Germany, Italy, and Argentina, and vintage examples, heavy and thickly-plated, remain in favor among top mixologists such as Salvatore Calabrese. See CALABRESE, SALVATORE.

In 1884, Edward J. Hauck, a Brooklyn, New York, metalworker, patented what would become the final style of shaker to be accepted into widespread professional use when he came up with a version of the type 3 that had a strainer built into the top, with a small, separate cap to fit over that; this obviated the need for a separate strainer—we shall call it type

4. See COCKTAIL STRAINER. Hauck's patent was only one of at least twenty the United States granted between 1870 and 1920 for attempts to improve the basic cocktail shaker, most of them employing moving parts or other features that do not stand up to hard use. But Hauck's was simple and fairly rugged, and it was widely adopted for both home and bar use (although bartenders had a habit of misplacing the top cap). It was also widely imitated in America and around the world, patent or no patent. Hauck's original version was quite utilitarian, being made in thin-gauge, plain or nickel-plated brass, and it was relatively small; the substantial, well-plated EPNS versions the great European drinkware manufacturers, such as Loftus of London, Christofle of Paris, and WMF of Germany, began turning out in the years before the First World War added elegance to the utility.

Many variations on the shaker have been introduced since Hauck's, but almost all of them are variations on his idea or on the Type 2/3 shaker. Most of those are aimed at home use and to appeal to the consumer, and they add shortcuts (embossed drink recipes, built-in juicers, etc.) or decorative frills, such as cut or colored glass (for the bottom of the shaker), chrome plating, and odd shapes—zeppelins, airplanes, rockets, lighthouses, firehose-nozzles, artillery shells, naval cannon, and a whole host of other things. Also intended for home use was one final type of shaker that was enormously popular in America during Prohibition: pitcher-shaped, it had a cork plug top and a pour spout projecting from the side (usually with screw cap). This type 5 shaker worked poorly—the spout poured slowly and was prone to blockage with ice—but it did not obviously look like a cocktail shaker, and at the time that was desirable.

Type 5 excepted, over the course of the twentieth century, bartenders' jargon found names for the various types of shakers. Unfortunately, in the absence of a central, controlling authority, these names kept getting tangled up. Type 1 (with a pint glass and a large, stainless steel tin) was used by the vast majority of American bars, from the most humble to the most august, and was known there simply as a "cocktail shaker." Elsewhere, it was the "American" shaker, at least through mid-century; after that, it was the "American-type Boston shaker" and then simply the "Boston shaker." Originally, however, the name "Boston shaker" belonged strictly to type 2, although nobody is sure why. It can be traced back to advertisements labeling the shaker as such that the W. R. Loftus company placed in two influential 1920s British cocktail books, those by Harry McElhone and Robert Vermiere, but we do not know why Loftus called it that. See McELHONE, HENRY "HARRY"; and VERMIERE, ROBERT.

When the type 2 shaker faded away, in the 1960s and 1970s, the type 1 inherited its name. This British usage then crossed the Atlantic with the cocktail renaissance and was popularized by Dale DeGroff in the late 1990s. See COCKTAIL RENAISSANCE and DEGROFF, DALE. Ironically, the cocktail renaissance also saw the pint glass largely replaced by a smaller "cheater" tin, also stainless steel, thus turning the American Boston shaker into an improvised facsimile of the British one (this usage seems to have been pioneered by the New York bar Milk & Honey). See MILK & HONEY.

Type 3, which acquired the name "Parisian" shaker due to its prevalence behind that city's more elegant bars, faded away in the 1970s and 1980s. With classic mixology in eclipse, there were few new buyers, while the fact that Parisian shakers are practically indestructible meant that the elegant old bars that still used them had no need for replacements. Indeed, the old EPNS Christofle and WMF versions still remain unchallenged as the pinnacles of practical shaker design.

Finally, the type 4 shaker. This did not have a distinctive name until the turn of the twenty-first century. Before that, it was simply a "cocktail shaker" or a "three-piece shaker." While rarely used in American bars, it was found frequently elsewhere, and almost universally in Japan. In the late 1990s, Dale DeGroff began calling it a "cobbler shaker," one of the names formerly used for it in England (the name was generic, and not exclusive: it was also applied to type 1 and type 2 shakers). This usage caught on and is now general.

At present, most modern cocktail bars use the large tin–small tin Boston shaker, except in Japan, where the Cobbler shaker, rarely used elsewhere, is standard. The type 2 Boston shaker and the Parisian shaker, however, are showing signs of revival, albeit in stainless steel. There have, however, been experiments with EPNS, a material not used in fifty years, and it is possible that that, too, will be revived.

Foster, George G. *New York by Gaslight*. Edited by Stuart M. Blumin. Berkeley: University of California Press, 1990.

Rogers, Smith & Co's Illustrated Catalogue. Meriden, CT: 1878.

Sala, George Augustus. "New Application and Change of Terms, Words, Etc." *Notes and Queries*, October 24, 1868, 400–401.

Visakay, Stephen. *Vintage Bar Ware*. Paducah, KY: Collector Books, 1997.

David Wondrich

The **cocktail strainer**, used to hold back the ice while pouring drinks from a cocktail shaker or mixing glass, comes in two main kinds, the "julep strainer" and the "Hawthorne strainer," each with enough variations to give some insects a run for their money.

The julep strainer is the oldest style, appearing by name as early as 1860 and, as a "cocktail strainer," four years before that; it is so named not because one ever strained a julep, but rather because it would be placed in the julep glass before it was served, so as to keep the ice back from the customer's teeth (this usage did not last long, straws being just as effective and much cheaper to replace). All it is is a short-handled, perforated, broad oval or round spoon (indeed, another early name for it was "ice spoon"). It came in two main sizes, each with its own style. The smaller one, sized to fit the small (roughly 180-ml) bar glass, had a scalloped bowl and a decided kink in its handle to enable it to sit well inside the glass. It was probably derived from the sugar sifter, a standard part of a silverware kit. The bigger one, sized to fit the large (roughly 480-ml) bar glass, had a smooth, concave bowl and no kink in the handle. It is difficult to say which of these came first, but originally both were handmade from coin silver, leading to a good deal of variation in detail. By the 1870s, though, both were standardized, silver-plated brass or alloy stampings. What little variation there was is of interest only to collectors. The small bar glass began to fall out of favor as a mixing vessel in the 1880s, and this eventually killed the scalloped strainer. The larger one returned after Prohibition, only now it was stamped out of thin stainless steel, and the silver plating was gone. Used exclusively for drinks stirred in the mixing glass, it fell by the wayside as stirring did. By the end of the twentieth century, it was a rarity, found almost exclusively in bars on the East Coast of the United States, and not too many of those.

With the cocktail renaissance, however, stirring returned to fashion, and with it the julep strainer; now there are many styles available, most of them well manufactured and some even silver plated. See COCKTAIL RENAISSANCE. There has even been an attempt to revive the smaller, scalloped version, for mixing Sazeracs. See SAZERAC COCKTAIL.

Perhaps just as old as the julep strainer is the cup strainer, which is nothing more than a handled silver-plated cup with a perforated bottom, and sometimes a flange around its middle so it can rest on top of the serving glass. This was used with some frequency in the nineteenth century, briefly revived after Prohibition, and then was seen no more.

In the late nineteenth century, as the bartender's craft became more complicated, there was clearly a perceived need for a more flexible strainer, one that could be adapted to the various sizes of mixing vessels in use. Numerous patents were granted, most of them dead ends. In 1889, Charles Lindley of Connecticut came up with a solution: simply thread a coil spring around the edges of the Julep strainer, and, as his patent application claimed, it will adjust itself "to various styles and shapes of glasses, and . . . fit closely around the entire inner edge of [the] . . . glass, no matter at what angle the strainer may be placed." In 1892, William Wright of Boston improved Lindley's design by making the spring easily removable for cleaning. He assigned his patent to another Bostonian, Dennis P. Sullivan. Sullivan was the manager of the popular Hawthorne Café on Avery Street in that city. Instead of having the holes in the strainer arranged in a star pattern, as in Wright's patent, he had them arranged to spell "Hawthorne." The name stuck. The final refinement was to give the strainer a pair of prongs so that it would rest on top of the glass, rather than inside it; a pair of 1907 patents took care of that.

The Hawthorne strainer quickly crossed the Atlantic, where it went through the same process of improvement in materials and aesthetics that the cocktail shaker did (Europeans preferred theirs without prongs). See COCKTAIL SHAKER. But cocktail bars were specialty bars there; in America every bar was expected to be able to mix a drink, and the quest was therefore to make bar equipment as cheap

and simple as possible. The introduction of stainless steel in 1919 saw the end of silver plating and fancy materials. From the end of Prohibition through the 2000s, the industry standard was a steel stamping (with ears, of course) that got thinner and thinner with every passing decade, just as the spaces between the coils of its spring got wider and wider. As with the julep strainer, the cocktail renaissance has reversed that. Materials are better, coils are tighter, and there is another wave of design innovation.

"Rodgers', Wostenholm's and Needham Bros.' cutlery" (advertisement). *San Francisco Daily Evening Bulletin*, September 6, 1856.
"Hawthorne Julep Strainer." *Iron Age*, April 26, 1894, 823.
Lindley, C. P. Julep strainer. US Patent no. 404,204, May 29, 1889.

David Wondrich

cocktail variation, one of the main ways new mixed drinks get introduced, can refer to anything from adaptation of accepted proportions in a known recipe, to the use of alternate brands or subcategories of a spirit, to wholesale substitution or omission of an ingredient on a categorical level. Variation can be premeditated, based on a mixological understanding of how the ingredients can be altered without changing the fundamental identity of the recipe, or it can result from necessity (the lemons didn't come that day) or error, resulting in a variety of outcomes ranging from an unhappy patron to a new recipe or accepted variation upon the original. Before addressing variation, it's important to note that it's common for a cocktail to be "created" simultaneously by bartenders unaware of the existence of a similar recipe elsewhere and for these parallel recipes to circulate under different names. Usually one variation is eventually accepted as canonical, based on factors ranging from the superiority of its recipe to a catchier name. The inclusion of a recipe in an important book or exposure from a marketing campaign are common tipping points for this process, which can take years. See MARGARITA.

Many bars and bartenders pride themselves on deliberate and idiosyncratic variations on a particular classic, which often involve adding an additional ingredient to an accepted recipe, such as the curaçao in the Manhattan made at the New York bar Employees Only (which was actually included in the original 1884 recipe), or the bourbon added to an Amaretto Sour at Pepe Le Moko in Portland, Oregon. See AMARETTO SOUR and EMPLOYEES ONLY. In such instances, admiration for the bartenders who popularized the variations can lead others to offer it at their bars, or even to substitute it for the house version without mentioning it's a twist on a more widely accepted recipe. Over time, a new standard can thus be established. See DAISY.

Another common point of differentiation between bars and bartenders is achieved through manipulating the proportions of a classic recipe: either incrementally in quarter- to half-ounce measures, creating a stronger, sweeter, more sour or bitter version of a cocktail, or by more drastic measures involving inverting proportions or serving them in equal parts. Two-ingredient cocktails such as the Rusty Nail and Stinger are excellent examples of recipes that can be served sweet, in place of dessert at equal parts, or strong, as potent digestives when the liqueur is deployed sparingly, while still retaining the recipe's original identity.

Sometimes a bar will consciously replace one of the components in a known cocktail with an ingredient of a different type and ignore the mixological rule of thumb that holds that if you change a major ingredient, you must also change the name of the drink. One example of this is Julio Bermejo's Tommy's Margarita, which uses agave nectar in place of the traditional Cointreau or triple sec and yet is still called a Margarita. While that variation violates custom, the bartending community has accepted Bermejo's logic that an agave-based sweetener belongs in an agave-based cocktail, and his version of the Margarita, with or without the Tommy's moniker, is served in place of the classic recipe in bars all over the world.

This kind of ingredient switching is known among bartenders as the "Mr. Potato Head" method of creating new recipes, after the popular toy, which gives one a selection of facial features that may be substituted for one another. Take the brandy out of a Sidecar and add pineapple rum and it is a new drink. Then you can change it further by replacing the Cointreau with mandarin orange liqueur and the lemon juice with calamansi juice, and so on ad infinitum.

Lastly, there are multiple mixing methods including shaking, stirring, blending, throwing, rolling, or building a cocktail, any alteration in which can greatly change the quality and character of a cocktail. The difference between a blended and a hand-shaken Daiquiri is dramatic to the point of making them two different drinks.

See also COCKTAIL RECIPES and COCKTAIL PROPORTIONS.

Kaplan, David, et al. *Death & Co*. New York: Ten Speed, 2014.

Jim Meehan

coconut water is the naturally occurring liquid found inside coconuts, especially when they are young and green. Sometimes called *coconut juice*, it is not the same as coconut milk, coconut cream, or cream of coconut, though it is often confused with all three. The people of coastal tropic communities around the globe drink the water straight from the coconut, which has often been chilled and opened with a machete by street vendors. In recent decades, coconut water has been packaged in aluminum cans, bottles, and Tetra Paks, making it available to consumers all over the world. Packaged varieties may sometimes contain bits of coconut pulp or added sugar.

Coconut water is subtle on the palate, with hints of grass, nuts, and salinity that are lost if it is paired with strong flavors. Nonetheless, in the Caribbean and the countries that border on it one will find it mixed with everything from the local rum to gin to tequila to scotch whisky. In the drink often called a Rum Coco, a simple highball found in various forms all around the Caribbean and Latin America, it is mixed with rum, lime, and sometimes sugar. Although coconut water is less commonly used as a mixer in Asia, in Sri Lanka there is a tradition of mixing it with Ceylon arrack, and one sometimes finds it mixed with various rice- or cane-based spirits in Southeast Asia.

As coconuts are abundant in many parts of the world with strong tourism industries, coconut water has often been employed in concoctions aimed at the tastes of tourists. Coconut water's flavor is usually overpowered by the other ingredients in these drinks, such as in the variety of examples named Coco Loco, which might contain any or all of the following in addition to coconut water: rum, tequila, vodka, coconut milk, cream of coconut, lime juice, pineapple juice, orange juice, and grenadine syrup.

The twenty-first-century cocktail renaissance has brought some more focused uses of coconut water, as some enterprising bartenders have achieved the trick of mixing it with various ingredients without entirely masking its natural flavor. See COCKTAIL RENAISSANCE.

See also TIKI.

Ceylon Arrack. https://www.ceylonarrack.com (accessed February 25, 2021).

David Moo

cocuy or **cocoy** is an agave-based spirit made in Venezuela from *Agave cocui*, which grows in the northwest corner of the country. See AGAVE. It is produced in various strengths, sometimes from 100 percent agave and sometimes from a mix of agave and sugar cane, and is sometimes aged in oak barrels. There are at least eight registered brands in production, along with a good deal of unregistered production. See ANDEAN SOUTH AMERICA.

The **Coffee Cocktail**, a late nineteenth-century favorite, has—as newspapers at the time seemed to never tire of pointing out—not a drop of coffee in it, but is rather composed of brandy, port, sugar, and an egg (and sometimes crème de cacao, a later addition), which when shaken together and strained into a glass bears a strong resemblance to café au lait. It is first mentioned in print in a Boston newspaper in 1885, but its invention was also attributed to New Yorker "Major" Flynn, bartender at the sporty Shakespeare Inn, at Broadway and Twelfth Street. The Coffee Cocktail was the first popular drink identified as a cocktail to omit bitters. Its popularity, which rested largely on its novelty, was erased by Prohibition. See PROHIBITION AND TEMPERANCE IN AMERICA.

Recipe: Shake 1 raw egg, 60 ml ruby port, 30 ml brandy, and 15 ml simple syrup with ice. Strain into large cocktail glass and grate nutmeg on top.

"Finest in the City." *Denver Daily News*, August 21, 1901 [attribution to Flynn].
Thomas, Jerry. *The Bar-Tender's Guide.* New York: Dick & Fitzgerald, 1887.

David Wondrich

coffee drinks have played a role in bars since the earliest years of mixology. Christian Schultz's *Manual for the Manufacture of Cordials*, appended to the early editions of Jerry Thomas's 1862 *How to Mix Drinks*, includes recipes for coffee creams, syrups, and spirits, though evidence is lacking that these things—well known in Europe—were actually used in American bars. See THOMAS, JERRY. Harry Johnson's 1882 *Bartender's Manual* has a recipe for a "Soldier's Camping Punch," with coffee, brandy, and rum, and he adds a Coffee Cobbler in the 1900 edition of the book. See JOHNSON, HARRY. The Coffee Cocktail, a late nineteenth-century American bar staple, contained no coffee, it must be noted, but merely looked like it did. See COFFEE COCKTAIL.

There is, however, a long tradition of mixing coffee and spirits in Europe. A Coffee Punch (with brandy) was among the handful of drinks the London bartender Leo Engel added to the many he plagiarized from Jerry Thomas in his 1878 *American and Other Drinks*, while in France it was common to add brandy, calvados, or eau-de-vie to hot coffee (as a *café arrosé*, or "irrigated coffee") or to a Mazagran (coffee in a tall glass with cold water). The most prominent European coffee drink, however, is undoubtedly the Irish Coffee, which was introduced to the United States in the 1950s and remains the signature drink at the Buena Vista in San Francisco. Relatives of the Irish Coffee include the flaming Spanish Coffee, now a specialty of Huber's in Portland, Oregon, and New Orleans's much older Café Brulot, a brandy, coffee, and spice mix that is also set alight in a highly ornate ritual. See CAFÉ BRULOT; IRISH COFFEE; and SPANISH COFFEE.

In the mid-1980s, London barman Dick Bradsell pioneered the modern coffee cocktail when he created the Vodka Espresso (commonly known as an Espresso Martini), which calls for vodka, Kahlua, and a fresh shot of espresso; this drink is particularly widespread in Australia. See BRADSELL, DICK. As mixologists of the early twenty-first century became more experimental, coffee showed up more commonly as a cocktail ingredient.

See also ESPRESSO MARTINI.

Johnson, Harry. *Bartender's Manual.* New York: 1882.
Nourraison, Didier. *Le buveur du XIXe siècle.* Paris: Albin Michel, 1990.

Robert Simonson and David Wondrich

coffee liqueurs are low-alcohol, coffee-flavored cordials. See CORDIALS. Many brands exist and are popular modifiers in a range of cocktails, especially after-dinner drinks. See MODIFIER. Base spirits range from neutral grain spirits to aged rum, tequila, and brandy. Some examples are more strongly sweetened than others. Their coffee flavors may be derived from coffee beans, brewed coffee, or extracts and concentrates.

The best-known coffee liqueur globally is perhaps Kahlúa, a rum-based spirit created in Mexico in 1936. The Black Russian cocktail calls for Kahlúa mixed with vodka (add cream to make a White Russian). Other notable brands include Tia Maria, a Jamaican liqueur made with local rum; Patrón XO Cafe, made with silver tequila; and Galliano Ristretto, an "espresso liqueur" made from two types of coffee beans. A coffee liqueur called Allen's Coffee Brandy is the best-selling spirit in the US state of Maine, where it's commonly mixed with milk. Dozens of American craft distilleries, including St. George Spirits, Old Harbor, and Koval, make coffee liqueurs, cordials, and coffee-flavored spirits. See ST. GEORGE SPIRITS. Recipes for homemade Kahlúa knockoffs have circulated for decades in the United States; bottles of the resulting DIY "Kahlúa" remain popular gifts around Christmastime. See KAHLÚA.

Popular cocktails calling for coffee liqueurs include the Espresso Martini, which mixes it with vodka and espresso; the Mind Eraser, which tops coffee liqueur and vodka with club soda; the Mudslide, a blended mix of coffee liqueur, vodka, Bailey's Irish Cream, and milk; and San Francisco bartender Jon Santer's Revolver, which combines coffee liqueur, bourbon, and orange bitters.

See also ESPRESSO MARTINI; MODIFIER; and WHITE RUSSIAN.

"A Maine Tradition." http://www.allenscoffeebrandy.com/a-maine-tradition/ (accessed February 25, 2021).

George, Anita. "A Brief History of Coffee and Booze." *Paste*, October 17, 2013. https://www.pastemagazine.com/articles/2013/10/a-brief-history-of-coffee-and-booze-1.html (accessed February 25, 2021).

Regan, Gary. "Behind the Drink: The Black Russian." Liquor.com. http://www.liquor.com/articles/behind-the-drink-the-black-russian/#gs.hHmCHTo (accessed February 25, 2021).

Jason Horn

Coffey, Aeneas (1780–1852), invented the first commercially viable continuous still adapted to distilling grain and patented it in 1830. The first steps in this direction had been taken two years earlier by Robert Stein of Kilbagie Distillery at Alloa in Scotland (1770–1854), building on the general principles pioneered by Jean-Baptiste Cellier-Blumenthal; Coffey greatly improved this design and made it more robust. See CELLIER-BLUMENTHAL, JEAN-BAPTISTE. Born in Dublin (one source describes him as a "French-born Irishman"), Coffey entered the lowest level of the excise service in 1800 as a "land-waiter, guager and searcher," receiving several bayonet wounds during the "*poitín* wars" with smugglers. In 1809 he was appointed surveyor for Dublin City and in 1819 inspector-general of excise in Ireland. Five years later (at the age of forty-four) he left the excise service and bought the Dodder Bank Distillery in Dublin.

His prototype stills were made of wood and iron and consisted of a single column, like Stein's heated by steam injection (Cellier-Blumenthal relied on the traditional direct-heated boiling pot). This was soon replaced by double columns—the analyzer and the rectifier—made from copper, with perforated copper plates replacing Stein's earlier horsehair ones and rectifying pipes to remove the residual oils during distillation. Coffey stills were simpler, more robust, and easier to manufacture; they produced a stronger and purer spirit, were more economical to heat, and had better rectifying qualities.

The leading Irish distillers initially scorned Coffey's stills. In its polemic treatise *Truths about Whiskey* (1878), the "Big Four" Dublin firms stated, "These things no more yield whiskey than they yield wine or beer." However, within ten years of registering his patent, thirteen Irish distilleries had adopted the new still. The first Scottish distillery to install a Coffey still was Grange in 1834, and by 1850 eleven others had followed suit. Aeneas Coffey moved his business to London and died in Bromley, Middlesex, in 1852. His company went to his son Philip and then, in 1872, to John Dore, his last foreman, who built it into one of the leading British makers of stills. As John Dore & Co., Ltd., it is still in business.

See also COFFEY STILL and STILL, CONTINUOUS.

Craig, Charles. *The Scotch Whisky Industry Record.* Dumbarton: Index, 1994.

John Jameson & Co., William Jameson & Co., John Power & Co., and George Roe & Co. *Truths about Whiskey*. London: Sutton, Sharpe, 1878.

Rothery, E. J. "Aeneas Coffey, 1780–1852." *Annals of Science* 24 (1968): 53–72.

Charles MacLean

Coffey still, an elaboration of Cellier-Blumenthal's column still patented by Irishman Aeneas Coffey in 1831, revolutionized the British spirits industry by making continuous distillation commercially viable. See also CELLIER-BLUMENTHAL, JEAN BAPTISTE; COFFEY, AENEAS; and STILL, CONTINUOUS.

cognac has been recognized as the finest, most complex and interesting brandy in the world for over three hundred years, even though brandy can be—and is—made not only from grapes grown in many places and climates but from a wide range of other fruits, and almost any spirit made from fruit has the potential to achieve great complexity through proper maturation, something that grain spirits achieve only with exceptional care. All of those other fruit spirits, however, follow a trail blazed by cognac, whose producers are inheritors of the longest-standing traditions of any fine spirit makers in the world.

Cognac itself is a relatively small town in western France on the banks of the Charente River. Its fame is due not to its beauty or history but to the grapes grown on slopes on both sides of the river. For the quality of cognac, like that of any other grape-based beverage, depends on its "terroir"—that untranslatable blend of soil, subsoil, and microclimate. In the case of cognac the "terroir" is based on chalky soils, which store water deep and provide vines with few nutrients, making for a lean, acidic, and subtle wine that only blossoms with distillation. As a result, the heart of the cognac vineyard is a small semicircle of vines in the Grande Champagne region, where the slopes are of a particularly deep sort of chalk called Campanian, named after a region north of Rome famous for the depth of its chalky soils full of fossils. The Santonian chalk in the Petite Champagne region that surrounds the Grande Champagne on three sides is less deep and intense (brandies labeled Fine Champagne must include at least half brandies from the Grande Champagne and the rest from the Petite Champagne).

The Fins Bois, the next ring of the circle of land which alone is allowed to produce cognac, is by far the biggest subregion and very varied in quality—historically the brandies produced north of the river Charente at Jarnac east of Cognac and in the east-southeast of the region, known locally as the "Petits Champagnes de Blanzac," have been highly valued. The terroir of the Bons Bois, the next ring, is much less chalky, while the outer ring, Bois Ordinaires, which reaches west to the coast of the Bay of Biscay, is too sandy to produce worthwhile cognac. Today, apart from vineyards on the offshore islands of l'Ile de Ré and Ile d'Oleron it is, effectively, free of vines. There is one notable exception to the rule that chalk is essential, the Borderies, a little quadrangle of chalky clay to the northwest of Cognac, capable of producing long-lived brandies with overtones of nuts and violets that can be almost too rich on their own.

Cognac's history and its geography made it an ideal center for a world-famous product. It was situated on a navigable river with direct access to the Bay of Biscay and thus to countries in northern Europe. In the Middle Ages the region had been famous for producing the finest salt, a vital product for preserving meat and fish. Then from the twelfth century, as part of an empire that included Aquitaine as well as England, the Charente region had produced vast quantities of wine for the thirsty British. Moreover during the Middle Ages successive monarchs favored Cognac as a royal town—in contrast with its major competitor, Jarnac, a few miles upriver, which remained a feudal appendage until 1789.

In the sixteenth century the Dutch, then masters of the seas, were looking for brandy as a less bulky alternative to the wine they carried to quench their sailors' thirst. They soon found that the acidic white wines grown on the slopes above Cognac were ideal for distilling into "brandwijn," so they brought in their own stills and taught the locals how to use them. In the late seventeenth century London's thirsty aristocrats hailed the superiority of "Coniack brandy" as part of a general trend to other novel—and superior—drinks like Bordeaux aged in oak and port wine, tastes that survive to this day.

The region flourished in the eighteenth century, a time when many of today's most famous firms like Martell and Hennessy were founded, often by outsiders. See MARTELL and HENNESSY. Their families survived the revolution and by 1815 had established a duopoly that dominated the cognac business until after 1945. During the nineteenth century, and above all after 1860 when Britain reduced its duties on brandy, sales soared and new legislation allowed firms to establish their own brands. By the 1870s the vineyard growing grapes to make cognac sprawled over an amazing 280,000 hectares (700,000 acres), then the biggest single vineyard region in the world.

But the phylloxera louse proved a disaster, and it took over a decade to find a rootstock—in Texas of all places—that would suit the deep chalk soils of the region. The region's previous grape variety, the floral Folle Blanche, proved unsuitable for grafting, as the bunches of grapes were so tight that they were susceptible to rot. As a result, it was replaced by the much less aromatic Ugni Blanc. By 1893 the vineyard was down to 40,000 hectares. Recovery was slow and fitful, hampered by the way that other inferior brandies had usurped the name of cognac when supplies of the real stuff ran out, and it took a series of legal measures by the French government to provide cognac with proper legal protection against imitations.

By the 1930s the brandy's qualities had been defined as part of the Appellation d'Origine Contrôlée regulations depending on their ages rather than where the grapes had been grown. The AOC rules ensured that to be sold as XXX—now called VS—brandies had to have been lodged in wood for a minimum of two years, VSOP for four, and superior qualities like XO at a minimum of six years (an age that rose to ten in 2018). At first, these designations were widely exceeded, with the reputable houses selling their VSOPs, for example, with very high proportions of ten- to twenty-year-old brandies in their blends, but those norms faded rapidly in the 1960s. See VS; VSOP; and XO.

After 1945 Cognac, like so much of France, enjoyed three decades of increasing prosperity. Demand everywhere, in Europe, in the United States, and among the Chinese diaspora in the Far East, notably in Hong Kong, soared, and the size of the vineyard doubled, reaching 110,000 hectares (270,000 acres) by 1976.

At the same time Martell and Hennessy were successfully challenged by two competitors. The long-established firm of Courvoisier enjoyed a boom, largely by exploiting its supposed connection with Napoleon Bonaparte. For its part Rémy Martin

revolutionized the market. It relied on the previously neglected VSOP level and sold exclusively brands classed as Fine Champagne. See RÉMY MARTIN. The story since 1973 has been a roller coaster. Sensibly, the Cognacais steadily reduced the size of the vineyard by nearly a third to 76,000 hectares (190,000 acres) of the most suitable, mostly chalky, soils—though it is still by far the biggest vineyard in France devoted to a single product, above all one from a single grape variety.

As a result the quality of eaux-de-vie going into virtually all the cognacs on the market has greatly improved. At the same time, reduced demand from the "Big Four" firms—who still account for five-sixths of cognac's sales—encouraged small distillers, especially in the Grande Champagne, to sell their brandies directly to the public for the first time.

The region survived the 1980s thanks largely to increased demand for the better brandies from Japan, but when the Japanese economy crashed in 1990, it created a crisis that lasted fifteen years. Fortunately, sales above all of the better brandies have soared, thanks largely to the phenomenal rise in the Chinese market—and by the encouragement given to VS as part of hip-hop culture in the United States, whose taste for cognac was born in the country's ghettos, always the unpublicized center of cognac consumption. Today cognac is drunk throughout the world, although the French prefer scotch whisky and the country now accounts for a mere 2 percent of sales.

Even today the production process would be familiar to the pioneers. The grapes may now be harvested by machine—but they should still not be too ripe, and the wine pressed from them should not be too strong in alcohol, ideally between 9 and 10 degrees, or the resulting brandies will not have the right balance of fruit and acidity. The wines are made without any sulfur and so cannot be kept too long before they are distilled—the legal limit is March 31 the year after the harvest, but the best distillers try to complete the process by the end of February. The wines are distilled twice in small pot stills, the first distillation producing the "brouillis" of about 30 percent alcohol; the second "la bonne chauffe" results in warm grapey, fiery brandies, which legally have to be between 68 and 72 percent alcohol. See DOUBLE DISTILLATION and STILL, POT.

Two types of oak are used: the Limousin, a wide-grained wood from the local forests, and the tighter-grained wood from the forests of Tronçais oak in central and northern France, which provides a more neutral spirit. The warehouses, the "chais," generally must be humid and not too draughty or the maturing spirit loses its flavors rather than its strength (although dry warehouses have their uses as well). Luckily for the Cognacais, their original warehouses were built by the Charente to enable the casks to be shipped downriver. New casks provide a strong dose of tannin and vanillin, but even the oldest wood ensures a steady, if minimal, flow of oxygen, which "oxidizes" the brandy and adds mellowness over the years. It then has to be diluted to 40 percent, the level at which most cognacs are sold. See ÉLEVAGE; OXIDATION; TANNIN; and VANILLIN. This process has to be done delicately and slowly, because the brandy tends to repel the water. The cognac is now ready for blending to match the different styles favored by each firm.

At the basic level, VS cognac is not designed to be sniffed, sipped, and savored but is an ideal spirit as a base for long drinks. Until well after 1945 "Fine à l' Eau," brandy with water, was a French favorite. The Anglo-Saxon equivalent, "B&S," brandy and soda—or any other sparkling water—remains a very refreshing drink, above all in summer, while cognac combines well with ginger ale to provide a "winter warmer"—a Horse's Neck. The authorities in cognac have also had some success in promoting drinking brandy with tonic water. See FINE À L' EAU; GINGER ALE AND GINGER BEER; and TONIC WATER.

VSOP cognacs have greater depth and concentration than VS and so are ideal for acting as the base for cocktails, as cognac blends happily with a wide variety of other tastes, such as orange or lemon, apple, cream, coffee, and chocolate—which in solid form is a delightful accompaniment to cognac. Cognacs of VSOP level are more complex; their aromas should be absorbed before they are sipped to appreciate their depth and complexity. After a few decades those from the Grande Champagne and the best brandies from the Borderies develop what the locals call "rancio," with qualities reminiscent of rich fruit cake—nuts, almonds, and dried/candied fruit among its other ingredients—to provide an incomparably long and complex experience. See RANCIO.

See also BRANDY; FRANCE; and TERROIR.

Bernard, Gilles. Le Cognac, Une Eau de Vie Prestigieuse. Pessac: Presses Universitaire de Bordeaux, 2008.
Coussie, Jean Vincent. Le Cognac et les Aleas de l'Histoire. Cognac: BNIC, 1996.
Cullen, Louis. The Brandy Trade under the Ancien Regime. Cambridge: Cambridge University Press, 1998.
Cullen, Louis. The Irish Brandy Houses of Eighteenth-Century France. Stoneybatter, Ireland: Lilliput, 2000.
Delamain, Robert. Histoire du Cognac. Paris: Librairie Stock, 1935.
Faith, Nicholas. Cognac. Oxford: Infinite Ideas, 2014.
Jarrard, Kyle. Cognac: The Seductive Saga of the World's Most Coveted Spirit. Oxford: John Wiley & Sons, 2005.
Sepulchre, Bruno. Le Livre du Cognac. Paris: Hubschmid & Bouret, 1983.

Nicholas Faith

Cohasset Punch, a mixture of rum, sweet vermouth, and lemon juice served with a piece of preserved peach in the glass, was a Chicago fixture from the 1890s until 1986, when the last saloon to serve it was demolished. The drink's origins are unusually clear: it was invented in the 1890s when Louis Williams, who kept a saloon in the heart of that city's theater district, was one of a group of bibulous sports the noted comic actor William H. Crane was entertaining at his summer house at Cohasset, on Massachusetts Bay. The party got to discussing punch and reached the conclusion that New England made the best ones. Williams was not satisfied with the verdict, and he wired his partner, Tom Newman, to ask him to come up with a counterargument in the form of a new punch and to ship a keg of it express. Newman's Medford Rum–based concoction arrived and rapidly won over the crowd. See MEDFORD RUM. Before long, it won over Chicago as well, both at the Williams & Newman saloon and through a bottled version, introduced by them in 1899 (by 1905 that version would be in national distribution, if modestly).

A recipe for the Cohasset Punch saw print in 1901, but habitués of Williams & Newman's saloon agreed that neither it nor the bottled version did the drink true justice. For one thing, the "preserved peach" the recipe calls for was usually interpreted as half a canned peach, jammed into the bottom of a cocktail glass. At the bar, however, one got "an eighth section of a peach that had been soaked in brandy and some liqueur until it had become soft and thoroughly saturated" (brandied peaches, it should be noted, were an early American specialty then fading into the past). Where most bartenders would shake the drink, containing citrus as it did, Williams & Newman's bartenders always stirred it, and at length. Finally, according to one frequenter of the bar, the "bartender always put in a dash of something from a brown bottle that did not appear in the list of ingredients."

In 1916, Williams and Newman retired, selling the formula and rights to their drink to the Ladner brothers, operators of another downtown Chicago saloon. The Ladner Bros. Tavern revived the drink after Repeal, placing a huge neon sign on the front of the saloon with a picture of a lighthouse and the legend "Home of Cohasset Punch." The sign, and the punch, was a Chicago fixture until 1986, when the bar was torn down for development.

Recipe: Muddle ½ lemon cut in pieces in mixing glass. Add 60 ml amber rum, 60 ml sweet vermouth, 5 ml rich simple syrup, 1 dash orange bitters. Stir and strain into large champagne coupe with slice of brandied or canned peach.

Fougner, G. Selmer. "Along the Wine Trail." *New York Sun*, November 11, 1938.
"The Origin of Cohasset Punch." *Bonfort's Wine and Spirit Circular*, August 10, 1902, 305.
Parnell, Sean, "Ladner Bros.: In Memoriam." Chicago Bar Project. http://www.chibarproject.com/Memoriam/ LadnerBros/LadnerBros.html (accessed February 26, 2021).
Sheridan, J. E. *Complete Buffet Manual*. Chicago: Henneberry, 1901.

David Wondrich

Cointreau, the proprietary curaçao that is one of the world's iconic liqueur brands, traces its origins back to 1849, when Edouard-Jean and Adolphe Cointreau expanded their three-century-old family business from cakes and confectionary to liqueurs, beginning with a wild-cherry-based "Guignolet" that became their first commercial success. The Cointreaus went on to produce over fifty different liqueurs in the years ahead, many from fruit grown near their production facilities in Angers, France.

In 1875, Edouard, the son of Edouard-Jean, created his version of the then-fashionable orange "triple sec," a less-sugary version of the "triple" orange liqueurs (where the flavoring is obtained in three separate extractions, rather than the single extraction used in the common brandy-based orange curaçaos) that had been made by French distillers since the 1830s. With both critical acclaim and brand visibility from the family's pioneering marketing efforts, "Cointreau" grew to so dominate the category that its name became synonymous with "triple sec," although the company could not trademark the term. It eventually dropped "triple sec" from its labels in the 1960s.

Edouard's award-winning formula, which is still followed today by master distiller Bernadette Langlais, is produced by macerating fresh sweet orange peel for several months before combining it with dried sweet and bitter orange peels in neutral beet spirit and water, which infuse overnight before distillation. The distillate is blended with sugar, water, and more neutral spirit to yield an aromatic, clear liqueur bottled at 40 percent ABV.

Today, sixth-generation owner Alfred Cointreau carries on his family legacy with new liqueurs such as Cointreau Noir, which includes brandy in its blend, and historic offerings including Chamomile and Guignolet marketed as the Collection D'Edouard. Their triple sec is called for in hundreds of cocktails, such as the White Lady, Sidecar, Margarita, and Cosmopolitan and remains the most premium offering on the market. See COSMOPOLITAN; MARGARITA; SIDECAR; and WHITE LADY.

See also CURAÇAO and TRIPLE SEC.

"Curaçao Saintoin Triple Sec" (advertisement). *Le Constitutionnel* (Paris), February 12, 1867, 4.
Rondeau, Matthieu. *Cointreau, l'unique*. Paris: Éditions Ipanema, 2013.

Jim Meehan

cola gets its name from the kola nut, which gives cola beverages their distinct flavor. Historically, the interest in this nut, native to Africa, was due to its caffeine content. The nuts were consumed whole or ground into a powder, to provide an energy boost. In the 1800s, American pharmacies began using the kola nut to produce stimulating tonics that became common at the soda fountain.

In 1885, John Stith Pemberton of Atlanta, Georgia (1831–1888), created a soda syrup that contained kola nut and coca leaf extract that he named Coca-Cola. Within a few decades, Coca-Cola became one of the most popular beverages in the world, and other companies, like Pepsi, followed that success with similar products.

The Cuba Libre (rum, cola, lime) is the best example of cola in a mixed drink, though colas work well with most distilled spirits such as whisky (cola and bourbon or Tennessee whisky is enormously popular), tequila (yielding the Batanga), and (of course) vodka. See BATANGA and CUBA LIBRE. Part of the appeal is that cola is sweet and can be used to cover up harsh spirit flavors or mask the flavor of alcohol for people who do not appreciate it. It is also a versatile mixer due to its complex flavor and has been used to create unique combinations such as Calimotxo (equal parts red wine and cola). In the Long Island Ice Tea, cola's main purpose is to add a splash of color and a touch of sweetness.

See also CALIMOTXO and LONG ISLAND ICED TEA.

King, Monroe M. "John Stith Pemberton (1831–1888)." *New Georgia Encyclopedia*, June 13 2017. http://www.georgiaencyclopedia.org/articles/business-economy/john-stith-pemberton-1831-1888 (accessed February 26, 2021).

Darcy O'Neil

Coleman, Ada (1874–1966), was the most famous female bartender in Britain and, arguably, the world during her 1920s heyday: in 1925, Britain's *Daily Express* described her as "the last of the famous barmaids." Her father died in 1899, leaving his spinster daughter in need of an income. Rupert D'Oyly-Carte, a family friend, found her employment in one of his father's hotels, Claridge's, where she began by making gentlemen's boutonnières in the flower shop before she was moved to the hotel's bar. There, Fisher, the hotel's wine butler, taught her how to make a Manhattan. In 1903, "Coley," as she was widely known, moved to the American Bar at the Savoy, where she rose to the position of head bartender before being displaced by Harry Craddock in January 1926 (she went on to run for a time the American Bar at Gatti's popular restaurant in the Strand). Coley was a bubbly, vibrant woman whose home was full of parties; her best-known cocktail is the aromatic, cheekily named Hanky Panky.

See also CRADDOCK, HARRY LAWSON; and HANKY PANKY.

"Most Famous Barmaid to Retire." *Daily Express*, December 17, 1925.
Lounger [pseud.]. "Club talk." *Sporting Times*, June 5, 1926, 2.

Theodora Sutcliffe

The **Collins** family of drinks—spirits, lemon juice, sugar, ice, and sparkling water, in a large tall glass—has its origin in the notoriously rowdy and aristocratic Prince of Wales Coffee House and Limmer's Hotel, at the corner of Conduit and George streets in London. Founded in 1784 or thereabouts by Stephen Limmer (1748–1818), the hotel lasted in one form or another until 1904. From 1807, if not before, through the 1830s, the head waiter and bar manager was John Collin (1769–1843), "than whom a more respectable, kind-hearted creature never existed," as one patron recalled. One of Collin's—or Collins's, as history remembered his name—specialties was his Gin Punch, attested to as early as 1834. But Gin Punch was fashionable—Byron had favored it, and that was more than enough recommendation for London's beau monde—and any popular watering hole had to serve it.

What set the Limmer's version apart wasn't the recipe so much as the surroundings: its "coffee room," as the bar was known, was small, low-ceilinged, and dark, with sand on the bare floor (a patron had shoveled hot coals on the carpet, causing it to burn) and a clock that was stopped (the same patron, Lord Waterford, had shot it). But it was packed: anyone who could get past the one-legged doorman, who only let in aristocrats and sportsmen, would end up perched on a table or even the mantelpiece, a tankard of punch in hand and surrounded by gamblers hard at work. It was heady and memorable, and John Collin was the man who issued the tankards. Indeed, he was celebrated in verse as such, by the sons of Richard Brinsley Sheridan—Limmer's regulars both.

At some point the still water that had been standard in the punch was replaced by soda water. Judging from what scraps of information are available, that was in the 1830s, after the Garrick Club Punch showed the way. See GARRICK CLUB PUNCH. It's also possible that, at least at one point, the punch was sweetened with capillaire (French maidenhair-fern syrup). But the drink went underground for twenty years after Collin's death, first reappearing in 1864 at the famous Dolly's Tavern in Montreal, popular among young officers, and at the North Australian Club in Ipswich, outside of Brisbane (both sightings were written up in 1865). In that period, it reached its classical form, described above, with Old Tom gin as its driving spirit and plain sugar as its only sweetener.

Collin's drink next appeared in the "wine room" of the famous Delmonico's, in New York, in the hot summer of 1872, and soon after all over that city. While its new fans at the establishment made it with the original Old Tom gin, many others used genever or a domestic imitation, Old Tom not yet being universally available in America. See GENEVER. Before long, that led to a split: the genever version took the name John Collins, while the Old Tom version became, logically, the Tom Collins. See OLD TOM GIN. There were also brandy and whisky and rum Collinses, the last of which was heavily promoted in the 1930s by the Jamaican rum industry.

With the decline in genever as a part of American drinking culture, by the end of the 1940s the American whisky Collins took over the "John Collins" name, while the decline in Old Tom meant that the Tom Collins was now made with dry gin. By the 1970s, the Collins family was as described by Stan Jones: "There are a number of other names attached to the Collins depending on which liquor is used: Colonel Collins (Bourbon), Mike Collins (Irish whiskey), Sandy Collins (Scotch whisky), Pedro Collins (rum), Pierre Collins (brandy) and Jack Collins (applejack), etc." Few of these names, or the drinks they describe, are still in wide use, although the gin Collins still flourishes.

Recipe (original John Collins; for other versions, substitute the appropriate spirit): In a large, tall glass, stir 5 ml sugar in 22 ml lemon juice. Add 60 ml Old Tom gin, fill with ice, and add 90–120 ml chilled soda water. Stir lightly; add straw and lemon wheel.

See also JOHN COLLINS and TOM COLLINS.

"A Victorian's Opinion of Ipswich." *Brisbane Courier*, March 11, 1865, 6.

"Echoes of the Week." *Illustrated London News*, August 12, 1865, 135.

Jones, Stan. *Jones' Complete Barguide*. Los Angeles: Barguide Ent., 1977.

"The Melting Metropolis." *New York Sun*, July 4, 1872, 2.

Saron. "Diamond Cut Diamond." *Ulster Gazette*, December 30, 1844, 4.

"Wine!" *Tait's Edinburgh Magazine*, January, 1834, 25.

David Wondrich

Collins, Wayne (1970–), is a British bartender, brand ambassador, and educator. He is best known for playing a key role in the UK bar renaissance of the 1990s, driving up service standards and improving product knowledge in the industry with the Mixxit training and education program he developed for Maxxium UK. Born and bred in the Camden district of North London, Collins has tended bar all over the world. He was behind the opening of a number of influential bars in the 1990s, including London's Navajo Joe's, which at the time reputedly boasted the largest tequila selection outside of Mexico. Blessed with a strong work ethic and a gift for gab, Collins has also made many TV appearances and hosted his own cocktail slot on the BBC's *Something for the Weekend* television program for five years.

See also COCKTAIL RENAISSANCE.

"Wayne Collins." Mixxit. http://www.mixxit.co.uk/our-experts/wayne-collins (accessed February 4, 2016).

"Wayne's World: An Interview with Wayne Collins." *Imbibe*. http://imbibe.com/news-articles/drinks/features-waynes-world-interview-wayne6399/ (accessed February 4, 2010).

Alice Lascelles

column still is a type of still developed in the nineteenth century that allows for continuous (as opposed to batch) distillation. See also STILL, CONTINUOUS.

Compass Box is an independent whisky producer that sources, blends, bottles, and markets scotch whisky. Under the helm of American John Glaser (1964–), a former Johnnie Walker marketing executive, Compass Box does not actually distill its own spirit; rather, it sources a variety of malt whisky from malt distilleries such as Ardmore, Caol Ila,

Clynelish, Dailuaine, Glen Elgin, Laphroaig, and Teaninich, as well as various grain whiskies. Glazer blends these at his London headquarters in different combinations to produce an idiosyncratic and dynamic range of whiskies.

Glaser's fans consider him a hero and a maverick for his championing of scotch transparency, energizing the category, and releasing modern, whimsically named blended malts and malt-grain whisky blends such as "Peat Monster," "Flaming Heart," and "This Is Not A Luxury Whiskey," as well as "Hedonism," a pioneering, and idiosyncratic, blend of grain whiskies. Glazer drew the ire of the Scotch Whiskey Association in 2005 when he took a page from the winemakers' book by inserting toasted French oak staves into aging barrels. In 2015, after Glazer disclosed all the constituent components that go into two of his whiskies on his website, the Scotch Whiskey Association once again informed him that he was breaking the law, which allows disclosure of only the youngest whisky in a blend—a regulation that Glazer says keeps whisky consumers in the dark.

See also WHISKY, GRAIN; and WHISKY, SCOTCH.

Adams, Paul. "Scotch Maverick Reinvents a Once-Conservative Drink." *Wired*, October 12, 2007. https://www.wired.com/2007/10/scotch-maverick-reinvents-a-once-conservative-drink/ (accessed February 26, 2021).

Heather Greene

compounding is the process of adding flavorings and aromatics to a spirit or otherwise modifying the spirit (not including dilution) without the use of distillation. Gin, for example, may be produced through distillation (by utilizing juniper berries and other ingredients in the distillation process) or through compounding, by adding the ingredients (either whole or in the form of extracts, essences, or oils) to a neutral spirit prior to bottling and sale. Compound spirits are typically defined by regulatory bodies and are taxed similarly to distilled spirits. Since distillation equipment, expertise, and licenses aren't needed to produce a compound spirit (but other licenses are typically required), these spirits are usually cheaper to produce than distilled spirits, often with a corresponding compromise in quality. The simplicity

of manufacture has made compounding attractive to some startup producers, as well as to makers of illicit spirits. Compounding was widely used in making adulterate spirits in the nineteenth century, when manuals listing a vast variety of compound imitations of distilled spirits were widely available for those without a still or the knowledge necessary to operate one. After such things were curtailed by pure food and drug laws in the early twentieth century, they reappeared in America during Prohibition, when compound "bathtub gin," made by adding (legal) juniper extract to an (illegal) alcohol base was widely popular.

See also ADULTERATION and RECTIFICATION.

"Guidance: Spirits Duty." GOV.UK, November 9, 2009. https://www.gov.uk/guidance/spirits-duty(accessed February 26, 2021).

Paul Clarke

Coñac (also **cogñac**, or **konyak**, or even **cognac**) is used by a number of countries to denote a locally made, pot-distilled, aged grape brandy. The tradition goes back to the late eighteenth century, when the fame and reputation of French cognac led to widespread imitation of the techniques used to make it and even more widespread appropriation of its name, over strenuous French objection. Germany abandoned the term in 1919 and Italy soon after. See ARZENTE. Spain, on the other hand, persisted in marketing its brandies as coñac through the 1970s, but with its integration into the European Union it was forced to abandon the practice, although the word is still in popular usage to describe domestic brandy. It still survives in commercial use in South America, where examples of aged, pot-stilled grape brandy are still marketed as coñac. Some examples: In Chile the Mitjans company, in operation since 1897, has the Tres Palos brand, bottled at 38 percent ABV. Argentina offers the Reserva San Juan, at 39.5 percent ABV, from Mendoza, made since 1933 (the brand was originally launched with investment and technology from the French Otard Dupuy Cognac company). Both of these remain relatively popular. In Peru, the last survivor seems to be the vestigial Cogñac del Nonno brand from the Cuneo distillery in Tacna, known mostly for its pisco. See PISCO. None of these spirits are destined for the export market, which one may be certain is the only reason they can still bear the word "coñac" on their labels.

The same situation prevails to a degree in Georgia and Armenia, where aged brandies are still labeled *konyak* (in the Cyrillic alphabet) for sale in the former Soviet Union.

See also COGNAC.

David Wondrich

A **condenser** in some form is an essential component of every apparatus for distilling alcohol: from the most rudimentary two-gallon jungle still to the modern multi-column system capable of producing millions of liters of spirits, all need condensers to convert the hot, ethanol-rich vapors that emerge from the still into the liquids that become whisky, brandy, mezcal, vodka, rum, or other familiar spirits.

There are two broad types of condenser: the internal one, where it is a part of the architecture of the still, and the external one. The most basic internal condenser, whereby the alcohol-rich vapors are condensed within the still itself, is the curved bottom of a pot full of cold water used to seal off the top of the boiling pot. The most basic external one, whereby the vapors are drawn off from the still before they are condensed, is a long, straight pipe that leads from the top of the boiler to a collection vessel. This is generally cooled by air and may be made from materials as diverse as wood, stone, ceramic, glass, or metal.

The same boiler may be outfitted with a longer length of tubing (usually metal) that is bent skillfully into a coil. Such coils—sometimes called worms or various cognates such as serpentines for their twists—provide greater surface area to cool the vapors arising from the still more efficiently. While most professional distillers prefer copper worms, glass and stainless steel examples have their proponents. Immersed in a tub of cool water, a coil condenser becomes far more efficient. A distiller may instead choose to replace the water used to cool the coil with wine, mash, or wash intended to be run through the still on the next immediate run. As hot vapors in the coil convert to liquid, the surrounding liquid heats, thereby reducing the time needed to bring it to temperature for the next distilling run.

The most efficient external condensers are modern "heat exchangers," which take advantage of the steady availability of cold running water to the modern distiller to create an ultra-efficient version of the coil condenser. The "shell and tube" style, where cold water is circulated under pressure around a series of parallel tubes that vapor passes through, is the most common for spirits use.

See also CHAUFFE-VIN; REFLUX; and STILL, POT.

Dabney, Joseph Earl. *Mountain Spirits: A Chronicle of Corn Whiskey from King James' Ulster Plantation to America's Appalachians and the Moonshine Life.* New York: Charles Scribner's Sons, 1974.
Germain-Robin, H. *Traditional Distillation: Art and Passion.* N.p.: White Mule, 2015.
Klar, M. *The Technology of Wood Distillation.* Translated by A. Rule. London: Chapman & Hall, 1925.

Matthew Rowley

congeners are produced (excreted) by yeast along with ethanol during fermentation and contribute flavor to alcoholic beverages. The formation of congeners depends on the genetic makeup of the yeast culture and on fermentation conditions such as temperature, type of raw material, carbohydrate concentration, fermenter design, pH, oxygen, and growth nutrients. There are five main categories of yeast excretion byproducts that influence flavor: higher alcohols, esters, carbonyls, organic and fatty acids, and sulfur-containing molecules. All of these compounds affect the quality and uniqueness of alcoholic beverages.

Higher alcohols are also called fusel oil, an older term derived from the old German word *Fusel*, "rotgut" or "hooch." High concentrations of fusel oil can contaminate beverage alcohol with harsh flavors, but smaller amounts can make a beverage distinctive. The main fusel oils include propyl alcohol, isobutyl alcohol, amyl alcohols, and phenyl ethyl alcohol; however, forty different types of alcohols made by yeast have been identified. These contribute subtle winey, fruity, banana, or floral notes to alcoholic beverages when in the parts per billion (ppb) to parts per million (ppm) range. When fermentation conditions are favorable for yeast growth, such as higher temperatures or increased oxygen or nitrogen levels, those yeast tend to excrete higher concentrations of fusel oils. Likewise, conditions that do not favor yeast growth prevent higher alcohol production.

In general esters impart fruity or flowery characters such as strawberry, apple, banana, pineapple, lilac, or pear notes to alcoholic beverages. The main esters are ethyl acetate, isoamyl acetate, isobutyl acetate, ethyl caproate, and phenylethyl acetate, but as many as 90 different esters have been identified. Even small changes in ester concentrations can influence the quality of the alcoholic beverage, as they are very potent in terms of flavor profile—thus fermentation consistency is critical.

Carbonyls include various aldehydes, diacetyl, and vicinal diketones. Over two hundred have been identified. Even in small quantities, these compounds can have a negative effect on alcoholic beverages. Acetaldehyde is the most important aldehyde and is an intermediate in the production of ethanol, but at its threshold level it imparts an undesirable green-grass note to alcoholic beverages. Diacetyl, considered a defect in most beverages that gives a buttery impression, is the second notable carbonyl compound. See ACETALDEHYDE.

Over 110 organic and fatty acids have been identified in yeast. Yeasts produce short chain acids such as pyruvic, succinic, citric, or acetic acids when they consume carbohydrates. These can give a spirit structure. They also form longer-chain acids that, as they break down with exposure to oxygen, influence the flavor of spirits maturing in barrels.

Occasionally yeast also produces sulfur-containing molecules, which contribute a significant flavor to alcoholic beverages. Even levels as low as one part per trillion (ppt) can give rise to unpleasant off odors. Some major sulfur defects are sulfur dioxide (burnt match), hydrogen sulfide (rotten egg), dimethyl sulfide (cabbage), or mercaptans (rubber). Sulfur aromas are not necessarily byproducts of yeast metabolism; they may also arise from feedstock or exposure to ultraviolet light.

Hazelwood, L. A., J. M. Daran, A. J. A. van Maris, J. T. Pronk, and J. R. Dickinson. "The Ehrlich Pathway for Fusel Alcohol Production: A Century of Research on *Saccharomyces cerevisiae* Metabolism." *Applied and Environmental Microbiology* 74, no. 8 (2008): 2259–2266.

Mauricio, J. C., J. Moreno, L. Zea, J. Ortega, and M. Medina. "The Effects of Grape Must Fermentation Conditions on Volatile Alcohols and Esters Formed by *Saccharomyces cerevisiae*." *Journal of Science and Food Agriculture* 75 (1997): 155–160.

Saerens, S. M., F. R. Delvaux, K. J. Verstrepen, and J. M. Thevelein. "Production and Biological Function of Volatile Esters in *Saccharomyces cerevisiae*." *Microbial Biotechnology* 2 (2010): 165–177.

Stewart, G. G., and I. Russell. *An Introduction to Brewing Science and Technology. Series III: Brewer's Yeast.* London: Institute of Brewing, 1998.

Van Meer, G., D. R. Voelker, and G. W. Feigenson. "Membrane Lipids: Where They Are and How They Behave." *National Review Molecular Cell Biology* 9 (2008): 112–124.

Don Livermore

conversion is the process by which starches in grain are changed into fermentable carbohydrates. In order for this to happen, the cereal needs to be physically broken down in a mill and the starch gelatinized, making it available to enzymes. The enzymes convert the starch into sugars and dextrin, while proteins are broken down into amino acids and nitrogen-rich elements, which will be required during fermentation.

Only endogenous enzymes (contained within the grain) are permitted in scotch whisky, which is generally based on enzyme-rich barley malt. Exogenous enzymes (i.e., not contained in the grain) are permitted to be added in Canadian, American, and Irish whiskies, all of which are primarily based on raw (i.e., unmalted) grains (as is scotch grain whisky).

In malt whisky distilling, the conversion takes place in a mash tun. The malted barley is ground into grist, then hot water at 63.5° C is added. This gelatinizes the starch while the enzymes within the malt hydrolyze it. The liquid is then drained off as wort.

In scotch grain whisky production (much as with other whiskies that are not made primarily from malt), conversion takes place immediately after the main cereal component has been cooked. Should this grain slurry be allowed to cool, the starch can revert, making it impossible for the enzymes to work. It is then mixed with the malt slurry (making up 10 percent of the total mash) either in a stream flowing through a continuous tube convertor or in a conversion tank where it is held for up to 30 minutes at 62–65° C for the conversion to take place. This temperature is critical. Too low and full conversion will not take place. Excessive temperature will break down some enzymes and adversely affect the early stages of fermentation where they still continue their activity.

See also ENZYMES and MASH.

Buxton, Ian, and Paul S. Hughes. *The Science and Commerce of Whisky*. London: Royal Society of Chemistry, 2014.

Russel, Inge, and Graham Stewart. *Whisky: Technology, Production and Marketing*, 2nd ed. Kidlington, UK: Elsevier, 2014.

Dave Broom

cooking a starch (grain, agave, potatoes, etc.) is the most common method of saccharification, or converting the starch to sugar, so that the yeast can convert that sugar into alcohol. Spirits that use cooking include whiskies, genevers, and other grain spirits; tequilas; and vodkas, among others. Neither fruit- nor sugar-cane-based spirits typically cook, since their sugar content is readily available. However, American moonshiners do cook fruits and molasses.

In whisky, the process begins with milling the grains to increase enzyme activity and surface area, which allows water to more easily hydrate the starch granules. Some American whisky distillers begin the corn cook at around 100° C, add rye and lower the temperature to 77°, and then add the malted barley, at the same time further lowering the temperature to 66°. For malt-only whiskies, the crushed malt is typically cooked between 66° and 77°.

Potatoes are mashed and boiled, liquefying them to make saccharification easier, and are then cooked at a temperature as high as 152°.

Agave plants are cooked at around 93° for 24–36 hours, crushed, and the juice extracted.

How the various spirit bases are cooked varies according to tradition, country, and available equipment, but the cooking process starts the congener development and greatly impacts the final flavor.

See also FERMENTATION; MASHING; and SACCHARIFICATION.

Lea, Andrea, and John Raymond. *Fermented Beverage Production*. New York: Kluwer Academic / Plenum, 2003.

Lee, Byong H. *Fundamentals of Food Biotechnology*, 2nd ed. Oxford: Wiley, 2015.

Potter, Denny. Private interview, 2015.

Fred Minnick

The **cooler** is one of the less well-defined categories of mixed drink, both historically and mixologically, but the drinks that fall into it—light, cold, and (generally) made long with soda water or ginger ale—were both popular and influential. By the 1880s, when the term first starts appearing attached to specific drinks, the julep and the large glass of punch, two of the mainstays of traditional summer drinking, were starting to fade from favor—too heavy, too alcoholic, too complicated to make. See JULEP and PUNCH. Even the cobbler, which was none of those things, had its issues: sherry was expensive and domestic wines inconsistent in quality. See COBBLER.

The first coolers on record come from the 1884 *Modern Bartender*, by the pseudonymous O. H. Byron, which seems to have been compiled in New York. The Brunswick Cooler—perhaps named after the fashionable hotel of that name—is simply lemon, sugar, and ginger ale, with no alcohol (this later cropped up as the Saratoga Cooler and, in Chicago, the Auditorium Cooler), while the Rocky Mountain Cooler repeats the lemon and sugar but adds an egg and hard cider. The category didn't take off until later that decade with the Remsen Cooler, first attested to in 1889. Made by peeling a lemon in a spiral, pressing the peel against the inside of a tall glass to extract some of the oil, and filling the glass with ice, Old Tom gin, and soda water, it was invented by William Remsen, of New York's august Union Club (1815–1895), although some say it was invented by his son, William Jr. It rose to broad popularity in the mid-1890s. It was easy to make, cheap, light, and very refreshing and pointed the way to the highball. See HIGHBALL. The unfamiliarity of its name, however, led to its being frequently mangled and to some mistaking "Remsen" for "Ramsay" and making the drink with Ramsay scotch whisky from Islay.

Between them, the Remsen Cooler and the Brunswick Cooler set some general parameters for the category: it would have soda water or ginger ale, a shot of spirits, ice, and some citrus presence, although usually not the juice. By the 1890s, however, these parameters overlapped with those of the Collins as well as the new highball and rickey. See COLLINS and RICKEY. Those were all well-defined and immensely popular, and the cooler was neither. As a result it drifted into being a catch-all for long, refreshing drinks that didn't quite fit into any of those better-known categories, such as the Panama Cooler printed by Charley Mahoney of New York's Hoffman House, with two kinds of wine, orange juice, lime juice, maraschino liqueur, and no carbonation at all. See HOFFMAN HOUSE. The eighteen coolers printed in Hyman Gale and Gerald Marco's 1937 *The How and When*, for example, are as motley a collection of recipes as ever assembled under one heading, and the same holds true for the hundred-odd coolers printed forty years later in Stan Jones's mammoth *Complete Bar Guide*. Few of these new coolers are memorable or achieved any popularity.

Indeed, the only cooler to achieve true classic status and to be revived in the cocktail renaissance is the Florodora Cooler, and it was invented in 1901 (Susie Drake, one of the stars of the smash hit musical of that name, was in a New York City cafe one night after the show and refused to drink anything unless the bartender invented something just for her; Jimmy O'Brien, the technician in question, obliged).

Recipe (Florodora Cooler): Combine in highball glass 10 ml raspberry syrup, 30 ml lime juice, and 45 ml Plymouth gin; fill with cracked ice, add 60 ml ginger ale, and stir lightly.

Boothby, William T. *Cocktail Boothby's American Bartender*, San Francisco: 1891.

"Latest summer drink." *Cortland (NY) Evening Standard*, July 11, 1901, 3.

New York Press, September 16, 1889, 2.

David Wondrich

Coolhaes, Caspar Janszoon (1536–1615),

author of the influential distilling manual *Van seeckere seer costelijcke wateren* (published in Amsterdam in 1588), became a distiller only when the politics of religion robbed him of his profession as a theologian. Born in 1536 in Cologne, he studied in Düsseldorf and worked as a Reformation minister in various regions of southwestern Germany before accepting a professorship at Leiden university in the Netherlands in 1574. There, he disagreed with purist Calvinists, who felt the church should also be responsible for civic order and punishment,

and subsequently Coolhaes was excommunicated in 1582. Coolhaes, however, was not a man to stand still; in that same year he started a distillery making both medicinal and recreational spirits. Six years later he published his manual, which as well as being influential and frequently reprinted is today principally remembered for bemoaning the fact that *korenbrandewijn* (grain distillate) was by 1588 being bought, paid for, and enjoyed at the same price and in the same way as grape brandy. Initially, when alcoholic distillates were used more medicinally than recreationally, the highest quality distillates were made from grapes. This is probably why, in his book, Coolhaes (who started out as a medicinal distiller himself), clearly disapproved of grain distillates being regarded in the same light as grape distillates, even though this development would allow a distiller like himself higher profits. One of the first known references to distilled recreational spirits in Europe is from the Netherlands in 1495, and that recipe strongly stressed using a wine base. Coolhaes's book is the earliest known to confirm that grain had replaced grape as the base ingredient of choice; hence we now know by what approximate date the Netherlands had switched to grain. Coolhaes went on to found an Amsterdam distillery in 1591 and sold it to his son Adolph in 1608, who in turn sold it to his son, Johannes. Caspar himself died in Leiden (or possibly Amsterdam) in 1615.

See also GENEVER.

Rogge, H. C. *Caspar Jansz. Coolhaes, de voorloper van Arminius en der remonstranten*. Amsterdam: CP Burger, 1856.

van Schoonenberghe, Eric. *Jenever in de Lage Landen*. Oostkamp, Belgium: Stichting Kunstboek, 1996.

Philip Duff

A **cooper** is a skilled worker who makes and repairs oak barrels. Modern coopers have fewer varieties of barrel to turn out and more machines to help them, but they retain the experience, talents, and often tools that connect them with their ancestors. Barrels of oak and other woods have been an integral part of international commerce for more than two thousand years and are described by Herodotus (500 BCE) and Pliny the Elder (23–79 CE), who describes the hooped wooden vessels the Celts developed, which the Romans adopted. See OAK.

The cooper's trade became more complicated in the ensuing millennia, with a maddening variety of tools needed to build and repair a bewildering variety of barrels. Each barrel for wine or spirit had its own precise shapes/sizes and other notable specific requirements of wood origin, aging and seasoning, hoop width, placement and materials, spire and bung location, and so on. See BARREL.

Cooperages purchase and prepare oak for barrel making, or they may purchase prepared staves (the individual, shaped boards that are bound together to make a barrel). Whether staves are air- or kiln-dried (they are often both), the wood's moisture content must be reduced to 10–12 percent. Air-drying staves over several years leaches many phenols from the wood, lightening its bitter, freshly sawn wood character, allowing a distillery to create more complex spirits from the resulting barrels. Wine barrel staves are toasted during and just after barrel assembly. Those for whisky barrels are steamed until the barrel is complete. Then the barrel is fired to the customer's preferred char level.

The modern distillery movement and craft brewers' barrel expressions help drive cooperages' comeback, but fewer skills are required to create the slim diversity of sizes and shapes compared to those of even a century ago.

Kilby, Kenneth. *The Cooper and His Trade*. Fresno, CA: Linden, 1990.

Twede, Diana. "The Cask Age: The Technology and History of Wooden Barrels." *Packaging Technology and Science* 18 (2005): 253–264.

Doug Frost

Cooper, Ron (1943–), founded Del Maguey Single Village Mezcal, one of the first artisanal mezcal brands to launch in America. See DEL MAGUEY. Equal parts outspoken and contemplative, the enigmatic New Mexico–based artist is commonly referred to as the "godfather of mezcal," thanks to his dogged quest to shepherd traditional mezcal from the remote villages of Oaxaca to America. Through his efforts to build the brand, Cooper helped foster an appreciation for Mexico's native spirit amongst US bartenders, which in turn laid the foundation for other agave spirits to flourish in the American market. See MEZCAL.

With jet-black hair wound tightly in a small bun and his signature uniform of loose-fitting jeans and white cotton shirt defining his outward demeanor, Cooper is a character in his own right. Born in New York and raised in California, the artist and car enthusiast helped usher in the California light and space movement, creating works that eventually landed in permanent collections at the Guggenheim and LACMA. As an art student in the 1960s, his thirst for adventure carried him south of the border, where he first discovered mezcal, but it wasn't until 1986 when in Oaxaca for the holidays with friends that he discovered the pure, unadulterated version of the spirit (not the industrial firewater that was pervasive at the time) that would eventually become Del Maguey.

Captivated by the nuances of the vibrant indigenous spirit, Cooper launched the Single Village brand with the import of fifty-four cases from the villages of Chichicapa and San Luis Del Río in 1995. For years the spirit gathered a cult following until Vida, an espadín-based mezcal distilled to a lower proof, launched in 2010. Bartenders clamored for the cocktail-friendly product, and Del Maguey became a permanent fixture at most metropolitan cocktail bars, sparking the beginning of a nationwide thirst for mezcal.

Cooper's work in paving the road for the mezcal boom in America was recognized in 2016 when the James Beard Foundation presented him with the award for Outstanding Wine, Beer, or Spirits Professional. In 2017, he sold a majority stake of the company to Pernod Ricard, and the following year, his memoir *Finding Mezcal: A Journey into the Liquid Soul of Mexico* (written with Chantal Martineau) was published. Del Maguey now ships to over thirty countries around the world, but Cooper's attention remains on the spirit and the people who make it—ask him about facts and figures related to the business, and he'll direct the questions elsewhere. He is content simply being "the keeper of the customs."

Cooper, Ron, with Chantal Martineau. *Finding Mezcal*. New York: Ten Speed, 2018.

Freedman, Brian. "The Story behind Pernod Ricard's Recent Ownership Deal with Del Maguey Mezcal." *Forbes,* June 6, 2017. https://www.forbes.com/sites/brianfreedman/2017/06/12/the-story-behind-pernod-ricards-recent-ownership-deal-with-del-maguey-mezcal (accessed April 21, 2021).

Emma Janzen

The **Cooper Spirits** Co. was founded in 2006 by entrepreneur Robert J. Cooper (1976–2016). Its marquee product, introduced the next year, was St-Germain, an elderflower liqueur that mixed well with sparkling wine and many spirits. It became so commonplace in American craft bars that bar wags jokingly referred to it as "bartender's ketchup." The eye-catching and statuesque bottle was supposedly based on a perfume bottle Cooper bought in Paris. Having built the brand to near ubiquity, he sold it to spirits conglomerate Bacardi in 2013.

Cooper Spirits continued to produce the violet liqueur Crème Yvette but focused on rye whisky and rock and rye. Rye whisky was a personal favorite of Cooper, who was an early supporter of the category even when it seemed on the brink of disappearing. The company's Lock Stock & Barrel, produced in Alberta, Canada, was one of the first premium straight rye whiskies on the market. Cooper liked to say that he tasted through a warehouse full of barrels to find the special ones. See WHISKY, RYE.

Hochstadter's Slow & Low Rock and Rye was inspired by a conversation Cooper had with bartender Chad Solomon about bottling an Old-Fashioned cocktail. Rock and rye, a popular nineteenth-century concoction of rye whisky and rock candy syrup, is arguably an Old-Fashioned without bitters. See OLD-FASHIONED COCKTAIL and ROCK AND RYE.

That Cooper Spirits took the drinks industry by storm was no surprise; Robert Cooper came from a long line of distillers and spirits merchants. The family traces its roots to the early 1900s, when his grandfather, Maurice "Buck" Cooper, started a brewery in Pennsylvania, and the family went on to own the Charles Jacquin company of Philadelphia, the creators of the original Crème Yvette at the turn of the twentieth century. After Cooper's untimely death, the management of the business passed into the hands of his wife, Katie, who continues to introduce new products.

See also BACARDI.

Simonson, Robert. "Robert J. Cooper, 39, Creator of Popular Elderflower Liqueur, Dies." *New York Times*, April 27, 2016.

Noah Rothbaum

copper has been the main material used in the manufacture of stills since the fifteenth century. Initially it rose to prominence because it is a metal that is easily worked and conducts heat well. In recent years, however, it has been shown to have an active involvement in the creating of spirit character.

Not all stills are made of copper. The earliest distillers often used clay or glass, while stainless steel is used in the production of baijiu and shochu, for example. Some artisanal mezcal producers use wooden and ceramic bodies for their distillations, while Bundaberg rum in Australia has pot stills with cast-iron bases. Lead was widely used for repairing stills in the Caribbean in the seventeenth and eighteenth centuries, and even for condensing coils, before it was discovered that lead toxins leaching into the spirit was the cause of the fatal "dry bellyache."

Copper is a reactive material and is believed to help remove potentially unwanted (sulfur-derived) compounds from the spirit. It can also help reduce mercaptan-derived off notes such as those that suggest rotting vegetables. Some phenolic compounds can also be reduced by interaction with copper. See CONGENERS.

It is believed that the longer the spirit vapor spends in contact with copper, the less of these "heavy" compounds will be carried forward to be condensed. This process is therefore closely interrelated with reflux. This interaction between vapor and copper can be manipulated in a number of ways. The size and shape of the still, the angle of its lyne arm, its condensing system, the fill level of the liquid in the still, and the speed of the distillation will all have an impact. See REFLUX.

A distiller wishing to maximize copper interaction would ideally have a tall still with an upward-facing lyne arm, leading to a shell-and-tube condensing system. The still would then only contain a relatively small amount of liquid, which would be distilled slowly. See CONDENSER.

The height of the still prolongs contact, and the upward facing lyne arm helps to increase reflux, while there is a large amount of copper in a shell-and-tube condensing system. The low fill means a greater head space, again opening up more opportunities for copper interaction, while the slow distillation increases the time for that interaction to take place.

Conversely, the ideal still setup for a distiller wishing to make a heavy spirit would comprise a small still with a downward-facing lyne arm, leading into a worm tub. The fill level would be high and distillation quick. All of these elements will reduce the amount of available copper.

There are many variations on these two extremes. A light spirit, for example, can be made in a small still with worm tubs by having a low fill level and keeping the water in the worm tubs warm, thereby prolonging the interaction between vapor and copper. A distiller could also open the manhole on the still after distillation to allow air to refresh the copper and make it active once again. Still designs can incorporate "boil bulbs" in the lower neck of the still, which increase reflux, or pinched waists, making a "lamp glass" shape, again to increase reflux. The shape of the head on an alembic Cognacais will also have impact on the amount of reflux produced.

Although stainless steel is used extensively in column stills, even there the rectifying column will contain copper. This helps to reduce the potential carcinogenic ethyl carbonate (EC). The copper could be in the form of the plates, which separate each reflux chamber, or the use of copper wool, also known as "sacrificial copper." The shape of the bubble caps—which also can be made out of copper—in each of the chambers will also influence the vapor flow and create different forms of reflux and copper interaction.

Buxton, Ian, and Paul S. Hughes. *The Science and Commerce of Whisky*. London: Royal Society of Chemistry, 2014.

Handler, Jerome S., Arthur C. Aufderheide, Robert S. Corruccini, Elizabeth M. Brandon, and Lorentz E. Wittmers. "Lead Contact and Poisoning in Barbados Slaves: Historical, Chemical, and Biological Evidence." *Social Science History* 10, no. 4 (1986): 399–425.

Russel, Inge, and Graham Stewart. *Whisky: Technology, Production and Marketing*, 2nd ed. Kidlington, UK: Elsevier, 2014.

Dave Broom

cordials, in the realm of spirits and cocktails, can mean either of two things. In the United States, cordials are sweet, low-alcohol liqueurs. Flavoring agents include nuts, cream, spices, roots, coffee, chocolate, vanilla, fruits, and herbs. They are generally consumed after a meal, in place of dessert, and they are often named for the flavor used to infuse the alcohol. Base liquors include whiskies, brandies, and neutral grape or grain spirit.

In the United Kingdom and the former possessions of the British Commonwealth, the word cordial has a different meaning—a nonalcoholic sweet drink, usually uncarbonated. Perhaps the most famous example is Rose's Lime Juice Cordial, which is made by preserving lime juice with sugar in place of alcohol. The Gimlet cocktail is traditionally made with Rose's Lime Juice Cordial. (In the United States, the product is known as Rose's Sweetened Lime Juice, owing to the differences in the way US English and UK English use the word *cordial*. The US product additionally uses high-fructose corn syrup in place of the original sugar, which is still used in the United Kingdom and Canada.)

Other nonalcoholic cordial flavors include cucumber, rosehip, cherry, cranberry, rhubarb, ginger, elderflower, nettle, and black currant, to name a few. Alcohol-free UK-style cordials can be sipped with still or sparkling water as a soft drink or mixed into cocktails in a way similar to how you would use a fruit-based syrup.

In the United States, the distinction between cordial and liqueur is small enough to be considered hair splitting. As the bartender and cocktail and spirits writer Gary Regan wrote in his book *The Bartender's Bible*, "In America, a cordial, usually served as an after-dinner drink, is what the rest of the world calls a liqueur—a sweetened liquor." See REGAN, GARY. In the United Kingdom, at least, a cordial is strictly nonalcoholic, and a liqueur is alcoholic. In the United States, both cordials and liqueurs have alcohol; the only difference is that *cordial* tends to refer to an after-dinner drink. But a given spirit can be called either a liqueur or a cordial, depending on the context. A triple sec such as Cointreau, for example, can be a cordial when sipped after dinner but a liqueur when thought of as a cocktail ingredient. And in the United Kingdom, of course, it wouldn't be called a cordial at all. See COINTREAU.

The word *cordial* derives from the Latin *cor*, or heart. Historically, alcohol-based cordials were used as medicines, thought to stimulate the heart, and hence the name. Distilled spirits were flavored with spices and herbs. Some cordials even included gold flakes and pearls, harking back to the alchemical principle that these materials purified the soul and promised eternal life. Gold flakes are still an "ingredient" in some liqueurs, such as goldwasser.

Cordials were produced by apothecaries during the Renaissance, who at that time were medical professionals who both compounded and dispensed medicines. These distilled "cordial waters," as they were known to Renaissance writers, contained a litany of ingredients. A 1600 recipe for Rosa Solis, for example, contained the herb rosa solis (also known as sundew), cinnamon, ginger, cloves, rosehips, and grains of paradise—all steeped along with sugar in a gallon of distilled alcohol. Cordials were also prescribed as aphrodisiacs, which eventually led to them being enjoyed in social settings in addition to for medical purposes. Gradually these medical elixirs became recreational drinks.

Alcohol-based cordials can be sipped alone or mixed into cocktails. Cordial cocktails—usually served after dinner or at brunch—include the Stinger (brandy and crème de menthe), Grasshopper (crème de menthe, crème de cacao, and cream), B52 (coffee liqueur, Irish cream, and triple sec), Black Russian (coffee liqueur and vodka), White Russian (coffee liqueur, vodka, and cream), Brandy Alexander (brandy, crème de cacao, and cream), Harvey Wallbanger (vodka, Galliano herbal liqueur, and orange juice), Kir (crème de cassis and white wine, or crème de cassis and sparkling wine, for the Kir Royale), Mud Slide (vodka, coffee liqueur, and Irish cream), and the Amaretto Sour (amaretto almond liqueur, lemon juice, and sugar). See Amaretto Sour; Brandy Alexander; Grasshopper; Harvey Wallbanger; Kir; Stinger; and White Russian.

Nut-flavored cordials include amaretto (almond), Castries peanut rum creme, Frangelico (hazelnut), Nocello (walnut and hazelnut), and Nocino (green walnuts). Fruit and berry cordials include Amarula (marula fruit), Cherry Heering, Cointreau (orange), Grand Marnier (orange), limoncello (lemon), Midori (melon), sloe gin, Chambord (raspberry), crème de cassis (currant), and Lillehammer (lingonberry). Flower cordials include crème de violette, Rosolio (rose), and St-Germain (elderflower). Cordials also include such flavors as honey (Drambuie), coffee (Kahlúa), and licorice (Sambuca). See Cointreau; crème de cassis; Grand Marnier; limoncello; and sloe gin.

"Drinking Heritage Inspires New Cordials for Gin from Sipsmith." Bar Magazine, January 22, 2015. http:// barmagazine.co.uk/drinking-heritage-inspires-new-cordials-gin-sipsmith/ (accessed March 1, 2021).

Regan, Gary. The Bartender's Bible. New York: HarperTorch, 2003.
Price, Rose. "Savvy Shopper: Additive-Free Cordials." Telegraph, June 24, 2006. http://www.telegraph. co.uk/foodanddrink/healthyeating/3326434/ Savvy-shopper-additive-free-cordials.html (accessed March 1, 2021).

Michael Dietsch

cork has been the dominant choice of closure for beverage containers for centuries. Its flexibility, strength, and durability have made it an ideal closure, particularly in irregular glass bottles in the years before machines provided greater bottle uniformity. It is made from the bark of cork oak, legally protected trees in Portugal since the thirteenth century, and which today account for more than 20 percent of that country's forested landscape. Although natural cork only accounts for about 5 percent of the spirits closures market, it is used in a great many of the most prestigious spirits: single-malt scotch whiskies, small-batch bourbons, old brandies, sipping rums, añejo tequilas, and the like. Spirits corks generally take the form of a short cork glued to a wooden, plastic, or metal flange that enables the user to pull it out without a corkscrew.

Cork oak (*Quercus suber*) is a renewable resource; its bark can be stripped away for a century or two without damaging the tree. The industry norm sees a first stripping at twenty-five years old, a second stripping at thirty-four years old (both of which are used for other industrial purposes), and then subsequent strippings every nine years for the creation of bottle corks. Its cambium structure contains pentagonal and hexagonal cells (Richard Hooke's eighteenth-century study of cork led to his coining of the term "cell" for life's building blocks), almost a billion in each cork, which gives cork its useful properties of lightness, flexibility, resistance, and modest impermeability.

From the early 1980s onward, wine buyers began identifying cork closures that exhibited the wet cardboard-like, off aromas of TCA (or 2,4,6-trichloroanisole), and the market reacted by adopting synthetic corks and screwcap closures. Contrary to popular belief, the high alcohol content of spirits does not prevent TCA from forming or spirits from getting corked. The incidence of this is lower than that with wine, since fewer spirits producers use cork closures, preferring metal or plastic screwcaps, but when it does occur, it is likely to affect higher quality, or at least more expensive, spirits, as those are the ones most likely to use corks.

While wine producers have been inhibited from generally abandoning corks by issues with synthetic corks (often difficult to remove from the bottles) and screwcaps (many wines under screwcap began exhibiting "reductive" aromas), these issues are not generally applicable to spirits; the persistence of high-end spirits producers in using cork is generally image driven.

The large cork producers have responded to the TCA issue by altering their processes to decrease its incidence; estimates of 5–10 percent TCA occurrence (in wine) now seem much closer to 1–2 percent, and at least one producer touts a brand that is guaranteed to be 100 percent free of detectable TCA. Other changes have taken hold in the industry. Chlorine bleaching of corks to create standard coloration, for instance, has been discontinued (chlorine is a TCA precursor compound). Sterile conditions in the cork factories and even in the harvest fields (e.g., cutting no lower than 1.3 meters from the ground) have improved matters as well.

Despite these challenges, cork remains the most common wine bottle closure and is also increasingly used for spirits as the industry trend toward premiumization continues. Tasters have noticed an increase in corked spirits. As the wine industry has learned vigilance, spirits producers will have to do the same.

Amorim Cork. Institutional Presentation, 2014.

Jackson, Belinda. "The New Zealand Screwcap Wine Seal Initiative—Ten Years On." *Wine Business Monthly*, February 2011. https://www.winebusiness.com/news/?go=getArticle&dataid=83546 (accessed March 1, 2021).

Johnson, Hugh. *The World of Trees*. London: Mitchell Beazley, 2016.

Doug Frost

corn (*Zea mays*), known as maize in Europe and elsewhere outside America, is a giant grass that grows taller than most humans, with each plant producing hundreds of grains—kernels—grouped in several ears. It was domesticated and bred over thousands of years from a Central American grass called *teosinte*, which can still be found growing wild in that region. Corn has become the world's most important cereal crop, with a greater total harvest weight than any other grain, and it is grown on every populated continent. The United States harvest accounts for about 40 percent of the total.

Corn is also a major component of both American and Canadian whiskies. It is generally not malted but milled and cooked under pressure to gelatinize the starches in the endosperm. In mashing, these now-soluble starches are converted to sugars by enzymes from an addition of barley malt, or by enzymes added directly to the cooking corn. It has a distinctly sweet flavor that carries through to the distiller's beer and then to the distillate. See ASPERGILLUS ORYZIAE and MASH.

Bourbon whisky, by US regulation, must be at least 51 percent corn (most have substantially more), and corn whisky must be at least 80 percent corn (some are made entirely from corn). Most American rye whiskies have a significant amount of corn in their formulation. Canadian whiskies vary in composition, but the most common grain used overall in the industry is corn. Corn is also used in Scotland and Ireland as a component in grain whisky and in the United States to make vast quantities of grain neutral spirits, or GNS. In Brazil, some producers in the state of Minas Gerais add small amounts to the sugar-cane juice from which they distill cachaça.

See also CACHAÇA; WHISKY; WHISKY, BOURBON; WHISKY, GRAIN; and WHISKY, RYE.

Pollan, Michael. *The Omnivore's Dilemma: A Natural History of Four Meals*. New York: Penguin, 2006.

27 CFR 5.22: The Standards of Identity. *Lew Bryson*.

Corpse Reviver was a nineteenth-century American drink that was unknown in America. It appears to have been an actual drink, served at an American, or American-style, bar in Piccadilly, London, in the late 1850s. Before long, even as the drink itself was forgotten, its name was enrolled by British journalists in their clichéd list of typical American drinks. Yet when British visitors tried to order one over a bar in America, they were invariably greeted with comments like the "What's that?" from a bartender at the Hoffman House in 1895.

Eventually, "corpse reviver" became a generic term on both sides of the Atlantic for a morning drink, akin to "eye-opener" or the older "anti-fogmatic." In 1930, Harry Craddock tethered the term to a couple of actual recipes in his *Savoy Cocktail Book*, one of which—the Corpse Reviver no. 2—has become a modern classic after being revived by Ted Haigh and others in the early 2000s.

Recipe (Corpse Reviver no. 2): Shake with ice: 22 ml each London dry gin, Lillet Blanc, Cointreau, and lemon juice and one dash absinthe; strain into chilled cocktail glass.

See also SAVOY HOTEL'S AMERICAN BAR.

"Could Not Get a Yankee Drink." *New York Herald*, October 6, 1895, section 6, 12.

Craddock, Harry. *The Savoy Cocktail Book*. New York: Richard Smith, 1930.

"European Gossip." *Detroit Free Press*, December 11, 1859, 1.

Haigh, Ted. *Vintage Spirits and Forgotten Cocktails*. Gloucester, MA: Quarry, 2004.

"How I Stopped the Brownes from Asking Me 'to Come in the Evening.'" *Chambers's Edinburgh Journal*, April 5, 1862, 223.

Dinah Sanders

Cosmopolitan is a sour made of lemon-flavored vodka (historically Absolut Citron), fresh lime juice, Cointreau, and cranberry juice, served up, and known colloquially as the "Cosmo." It is the only cocktail of the last years of the twentieth century to have attained the status of a household name. As such, it served as a bridge drink of sorts, linking the dark ages of mixology with the beginnings of the craft cocktail revival. See CRAFT COCKTAIL.

Like most famous cocktails, it has a confused and contested history, with American bartenders from coast to coast laying claim to either the invention or popularization of the drink. However, most of these claims lack any supporting evidence. The recipe that came to be known and served as the Cosmopolitan worldwide was most likely formulated in 1988 by bartender Toby Cecchini at the Odeon in TriBeCa, then one of the most chic and notorious restaurants in Manhattan. (The establishment was even famously pictured on the cover of the paperback edition of Jay McInerney's 1984 novel *Bright Lights, Big City*, which

perfectly captures that era; Cecchini applied for a job there because he recognized it from the book.) Armed with Absolut Citron, which was released in 1988, he re-engineered a cruder vodka drink from San Francisco that he had learned of, also called the Cosmopolitan. As described by Jesse Selvin of the *San Francisco Chronicle*, who encountered it at the popular Julie's Supper Club in 1987, this was simply "a Kamikaze with cranberry juice," served in a cocktail glass. See KAMIKAZE. Besides switching the vodka, Cecchini replaced the bottled Rose's Lime Juice with fresh and the cheap triple sec with Cointreau. Meanwhile, the cocktail began to spread, making a couple of appearances in print the next summer, once as the "Cosmo" and once with rum in place of the vodka; both versions were still using Rose's rather than fresh juice. By 1990, the improved Odeon version of the drink was ubiquitous in New York, its dissemination greatly assisted by its adoption at the famed Rainbow Room by Dale DeGroff (who may have latched on to the original, Rose's version of the drink and performed similar operations to Cecchini's). Variations such as the Metropolitan (using Absolut Kurant) began popping up, and many bars offered their personal spin on the drink.

The improved cocktail attained international fame when it became the drink of choice for the widely popular HBO series *Sex and the City*. Its recurring cameo rendered the concoction a totem of urban sophistication to the show's many impressionable viewers.

The Cosmo's role in introducing a new generation of drinkers (who had grown up in a beer and wine world) to cocktails cannot be underestimated. Nonetheless, because of its vast popularity and use of flavored vodka and processed cranberry juice, the drink was rejected by the brash young mixologists of the 2000s. Early craft cocktail bars such as Milk & Honey went so far as to refuse to carry cranberry juice, so as not to be forced to make the drink. See MILK & HONEY.

Recipe: Combine 60 ml Absolut Citron, 30 ml Cointreau, 30 ml fresh lime juice, and 30 ml cranberry juice in cocktail shaker with ice and shake vigorously. Strain into a chilled coupe.

See also ABSOLUT; COINTREAU; and VODKA.

Cecchini, Toby. *Cosmopolitan*. New York: Broadway Books, 2004.

"Ice Adds Extra Flair to Drinks." *Augusta (GA) Chronicle*, August 9, 1989, B-7.

Selvin, Jesse. "Parties, Aussie Rock at the Clubs." *San Francisco Chronicle*, October 23, 1987, E-16.

Simonson, Robert. *A Proper Drink*. San Francisco: Ten Speed, 2016.

Turek, Sonia. "Drinks on the Rum." *Boston Herald*, July 2, 1989, 15.

Robert Simonson and David Wondrich

Courvoisier is the smallest of the so-called "big four," as the four largest cognac houses are known (the others are Hennessy, Martell, and Remy Martin). See HENNESSY; MARTELL; and RÉMY MARTIN. Its origin dates to 1843, when Felix Courvoisier became managing partner of a new cognac trading company based in a chateau on the bank of the Charente River in the town of Jarnac, where the company still has its headquarters. The company remained in control of Courvoisier and his heirs until 1909, when it was sold to the Simons, an English family.

It was the Simons who solidified the brand's connection with Napoleon Bonaparte, who supposedly was enamored of the cognac sold by Felix's father, Emmanuel. They created a new "Napoleon" grade of cognac and incorporated a silhouette of the erstwhile emperor into the brand's logo. In the early years of this century, after the brand was acquired by Allied Domecq, Courvoisier's successful targeting of young African American consumers culminated in the release of Busta Rhymes's hit rap song "Pass the Courvoisier, Part II." Courvoisier is now owned by Beam Suntory and sells in the vicinity of 12 million liters of cognac a year. Courvoisier's cognacs tend to be rich and fruity, with some heat when young but with an appealing brightness and juiciness in the older expressions.

See also COGNAC.

Bonin, Hubert, and Isabelle Précigoux. "Un symbole de l'économie marchande de la côte atlantique: La société de cognac Courvoisier (des années 1830 aux années 1980)." In *Négoce, ports & océans, XVIe–XXe siècles: Hommages à Paul Butel*, ed. Silvia Marzagalli and H. Bonin, 113–132. Bordeaux: Presses universitaires de Bordeaux, 2000.

David Mahoney

Cowdery, **Charles K.** (1951–), known to all as Chuck, is a writer, filmmaker, and leading American whisky expert. In 1991, he began work on what he thought would be a coffee-table book about bourbon. This project became the documentary *Made and Bottled in Kentucky*, which Cowdery wrote, directed, and produced. The documentary aired on Kentucky Public Television in June of 1992 and is still in rotation. In 1994, he launched the *Bourbon County Reader*, a newsletter focused exclusively on American whisky, which is published to this day. He is the author of *Bourbon, Strange: Surprising Stories of American Whiskey* (2014), *The Best Bourbon You'll Never Taste: The True Story of A. H. Hirsch Reserve Straight Bourbon Whiskey, Distilled in the Spring of 1974* (2012), and *Bourbon, Straight: The Uncut and Unfiltered Story of American Whiskey* (2004).

Cowdery is a frequent contributor to *Whisky Advocate Magazine*, among other publications. His work, in both books and magazines, is notable for the depth of his research and expertise and for his determination to maintain a critical distance even from a topic for which he clearly has a strong affection.

Cowdery's work has earned him the title of Kentucky colonel and an induction to the Bourbon Hall of Fame in 2009. He also works as an attorney in private practice and as a marketing writer.

See also WHISKY, BOURBON.

Cowdery, Chuck. *Bourbon, Straight; The Uncut and Unfiltered Story of American Whiskey*. Chicago: Made and Bottled in Kentucky, 2004.

Cowdery, Chuck. *Bourbon, Strange; Surprising Stories of American Whiskey*. Chicago: Made and Bottled in Kentucky, 2014.

Max Watman

Craddock, Harry Lawson (1876–1964) was largely responsible for igniting interest in cocktails among London's Bright Young People during the 1920s and 1930s. The "dean of cocktail shakers" was born in Stroud in the English Cotswolds. Arriving in New York in March 1897, Craddock worked his way from waiting tables to bartending. By 1906, he had joined the bar team at New York's prestigious Hotel Knickerbocker and then worked briefly at the Hoffman House. By 1918, he was bar manager at the prestigious Holland House, where he remained until Prohibition closed the doors on the bar and his American career. Despite having become a naturalized American citizen in 1916, Craddock returned to England in 1920 and was hired immediately to work the dispensary bar at London's Savoy Hotel. See KNICKERBOCKER and HOFFMAN HOUSE.

With his acquired American accent, naturalization papers, and bar training, Craddock delivered what his expat customers craved. To accommodate Americans who felt women should not work in bars, the Savoy retired its two female bartenders in 1925 and installed Craddock at the helm.

Five years later, management asked him to compile his drinks recipes into a single volume. The result, *The Savoy Cocktail Book*, presented a kaleidoscopic view of the era's mixed drinks (it also drew heavily on Hugo Ensslin's 1916 *Recipes for Mixed Drinks*, the last important New York cocktail book before Prohibition). See ENSSLIN, HUGO. Determined to elevate the quality of British bartending, Craddock joined Café Royal head barman William J. Tarling in 1934 to found the United Kingdom Bartenders Guild, which trained and provided professional support for the country's growing legion of bartenders. See TARLING, WILLIAM JAMES "BILLY" and UNITED KINGDOM BARTENDERS GUILD (UKBG).

In 1939, Craddock took over the bar at the Dorchester, where he served its temporary wartime residents Prime Minister Winston Churchill, members of his cabinet, and US general Dwight D. Eisenhower. In 1951, Craddock opened the refurbished bar at Brown's Hotel, another Mayfair landmark. He spent his final years living on National Assistance, secluded in a South Kensington nursing home, until his death from a cerebral hemorrhage in 1963.

"'King' of Cocktail Mixers." *Pall Mall Gazette*, June 11, 1920, 7.

New York Passport Office. US Passport Application 5108, May 30, 1920.

Percy, H. L. "Britons Slake Thirst in Sea of New Drinks." *Ogden Standard Examiner*, May 31, 1935, 17.

Anistatia R. Miller and Jared M. Brown

craft cocktail is the most common contemporary term for drinks made according to the standards ushered in by the cocktail renaissance of the early twenty-first century. See COCKTAIL RENAISSANCE. A cocktail counts as "craft" when it is mixed from quality, consciously chosen liquors, fresh citrus juice and the like, and dense, cold ice. (Some might add, gratuitously, that it must be mixed by a bartender with tattoos.) It can be as simple and classic as a well-stirred rye Manhattan or as complex and innovative as a coconut milk fat-washed bourbon-yuzu sour topped with amaretto air.

The term entered wide use only in 2008, when the cocktail renaissance had become established enough to need a concise term for what it was doing that was more inclusive than "retro cocktails" or "culinary cocktails," terms that saw some use previously. The term probably stems from the widely used "craft beer," with a very strong boost from Dale DeGroff's seminal 2002 book *The Craft of the Cocktail*. After DeGroff's book one began to hear of bartenders "crafting" their drinks, and it was a short step from describing the process to describing its result.

See also -TINI.

David Wondrich

craft distilling is a movement of small-volume distilleries that emerged in the late twentieth and early twenty-first centuries. By the 1980s, distilling had become a highly industrialized process dominated by large corporations. Much like craft beer, artisan cheese, and the slow food movement, the craft distilling movement reacted against this large-scale industrialization by emphasizing small-scale production, distillation in alembic or pot stills, sourcing of local ingredients, and quaint backstories.

In the United States, some of the earliest craft distilleries were Germain-Robin (founded in 1984) and Anchor (1993) in California and Clear Creek (1985) and Edgefield (1998) in Oregon. See CLEAR CREEK DISTILLERY and GERMAIN-ROBIN. These earliest distilleries tended to focus on brandy and whisky. Craft distilling saw a boom in the 2000s, and by 2016 there were close to one thousand craft distilleries in the United States and Canada, as well as growing numbers throughout the globe. In Europe, there had long been small brandy and schnapps producers who could be considered craft distillers, but the craft distilling movement in America led to a wider variety of spirits being produced on small European stills, including a number of single-malt whiskies.

Craft distilling has had a profound impact on the spirits industry by fueling innovation. These new distillers have unearthed old recipes, used alternative ingredients, and sought to create "grain to glass" spirits in which the distiller manages the production from the growth of the grain (or fruit) through bottling. Among the early innovators, Charbay in California distilled bottle-ready beer with added hops, creating a hop-flavored whisky; Corsair in Kentucky and Tennessee and Balcones in Texas have experimented with smoked whiskies using a variety of smoking agents; and many distilleries have experimented with alternative ingredients, from spelt and sorghum to Douglas fir and citron.

While craft distillers have received plaudits for innovation, there have been questions about quality. Critics, particularly of craft whiskies, have often noted harsh, tannic qualities that can be the result of failing to properly age the spirit or attempting to hasten aging by using small barrels, wood chips, or similar techniques. As time has passed and the movement has matured, more distillers have released spirits aged longer in full-sized barrels. A number of craft distillers are now producing bonded spirits, which are required to be aged for at least four years.

Some small companies have been criticized for implying they are craft distillers when in fact their product is sourced from one of the large industrial distilleries. In 2014, a widely circulated article in the *Daily Beast* highlighted the large number of "craft distillers" that did not disclose that their rye whisky was actually distilled by Midwest Grain Products, a large industrial distillery in Indiana. The article went viral and was followed by a number of lawsuits against spirits companies challenging the representation of particular spirits as craft distilled. Few such lawsuits succeeded.

It didn't take long for the large spirits companies to take note of the craft distilling movement, and a number of larger companies have purchased craft distilleries. In one of the first such purchases, in 2010, New York's Tuthilltown Distillery sold its line of Hudson Whiskies to scotch giant William Grant & Sons. Since then, there have been more buyouts: Campari purchased Canadian craft distiller Forty Creek in 2014, and in 2016 Constellation Brands purchased Utah's High West, Remy Cointreau bought the Westland Distillery in Washington, and Pernod Ricard purchased a majority share of the Smooth Ambler Distillery in West Virginia.

Based on the massive proliferation of craft distillers in the early twenty-first century, the movement is likely to continue to thrive. However, as craft distillers continue to multiply, grow, and—in some cases—be purchased by large corporations, it will likely raise questions of who is and isn't a craft distiller.

American Craft Spirits Association. https:// americancraftspirits.org (accessed March 1, 2021).

American Distilling Institute. https://distilling.com/ (accessed March 1, 2021).

Felten, Eric. "Your 'Craft' Rye Whiskey Is Probably from a Factory Distillery in Indiana." *Daily Beast*, July 28, 2014. https://www.thedailybeast.com/your-craft-whiskey-is-probably-from-a-factory-distillery-in-indiana (accessed March 1, 2021).

Sku [pseud.]. "The Complete List of American Whiskey Distilleries and Brands," *Sku's Recent Eats*, May 6, 2017. http://recenteats.blogspot.com/p/the-complete-list-of-american-whiskey.html (accessed March 1, 2021).

Ury, Steve. "Most Craft Whiskeys Suck!" *Whisky Advocate*, August 30, 2010.

Steve Ury

cream liqueurs (not to be confused with dairy-free crème liqueurs) are quite a recent invention, only dating back to the 1970s. The union of cream and spirits became popular during Prohibition, when the poor quality of the available booze led to the development of drinks like the Alexander, a gin- and cream-based concoction that evolved into the Brandy Alexander, which is still relatively popular today, and the Cowboy cocktail, raw whisky shaken with cream, which is not. See ALEXANDER COCKTAIL.

Bottling dairy-based liqueurs, however, posed a problem: how to create a stable product that wouldn't curdle or separate in the bottle.

It wasn't until 1974 that Gilbey's of Ireland, a division of International Distillers and Vintners

(IDV) figured it out, and Baileys Irish Cream—the first cream liqueur—was born (it was based on a prototype created by David Gluckman and Hugh Reade Seymour-Davies, a pair of London marketing men, who shook together a mixture of Irish whisky, heavy cream and Cadbury's Powdered Drinking Chocolate and thought it had potential). A mix of chocolate, dairy cream, Irish whisky, and other ingredients, Baileys could remain stable for months or even years without refrigeration. It was launched in Britain in 1975 and the United States in 1977; success was not immediate, but by 1983 over a million cases were sold worldwide.

Today, Baileys is still far and away the world's most popular cream liqueur (in fact, it is the most popular liqueur, period), but the category has expanded. Rum creams, made with rum base instead of whisky or neutral spirits, are now almost as ubiquitous as Irish whisky–based creams. Among the most popular is RumChata, a mix of Caribbean rums, Wisconsin dairy cream, and spices, based on the traditional Mexican drink horchata. Fruit-based cream liqueurs, such as the South African Amarula, made from the fermented marula fruit, are also quite popular.

Cream liqueurs are generally intended as an after-dinner drink, whether served chilled, poured into coffee, or even on top of ice cream.

Blue, Anthony Dias. *The Complete Book of Spirits*. New York: Harper Collins, 2004.
Gluckman, David. "In 1973, I Invented a 'Girly Drink' Called Baileys." *Irish Times*, October 2, 2016.
Grimes, William. *Straight Up or on the Rocks*. New York: Simon & Schuster, 1993.
"The Top 10 Best-Selling Liqueur Brands." *The Spirits Business*, July 8, 2015. https://www.thespiritsbusiness.com/2015/07/top-10-best-selling-liqueur-brands/ (accessed April 20 2021).

Tony Sachs

crème de cacao is a chocolate-flavored liqueur with a high sugar content. As its name implies, it was first made in France, at least as early as 1807, when a published recipe called for cacao, vanilla, and cinnamon, in addition to sugar, water, and eau-de-vie. See EAU-DE-VIE. Current-day commercial offerings come in white and dark iterations—the white typically made through re-distillation of the base spirit with cacao, and the dark through percolation (similar to how drip coffee is made).

Although crème de cacao began cropping up in cocktail recipes around the turn of the twentieth century, later sweet-toothed concoctions such as the Brandy Alexander and the Grasshopper really put it on the mixological map. See ALEXANDER COCKTAIL and GRASSHOPPER. It was perhaps used to best advantage by London bartender Charles A. Tuck in his beguiling Twentieth Century cocktail, first memorialized in the *Café Royal Cocktail Book* of 1937. See TARLING, WILLIAM JAMES "BILLY."

See also LIQUEUR.

Bouillon-Lagrange, Edme Jean Baptiste. *L'art de composer facilement, et a peu du frais, les liqueurs de table*. Paris: 1807.

David Mahoney

crème de cassis is a blackcurrant liqueur, originally from Burgundy, France. Blackcurrants (*Ribes nigrum*) are first macerated in neutral alcohol. Solids are then filtered out, and sugar is added. Blackcurrants are particularly tart, and crème de cassis is consequently made with more sugar than other fruit liqueurs—French law states a minimum of 400 grams of sugar per liter. There are currently three protected geographical indications for crème de cassis: cassis de Dijon, cassis de Bourgogne (both in Burgundy), and cassis de Saintonge (in the Cognac region).

Blackcurrants were traditionally grown in vineyards and turned into homemade liqueurs by Burgundian families. In the 1840s, local distiller Denis Lagoute launched the first commercial version, and many others followed. With the phylloxera crisis, which first hit Burgundy in 1878, many Burgundian vine growers saw the blackcurrant as a good opportunity to diversify. This led to a production boom.

Although when drunk on its own, crème de cassis is a digestive, the liqueur is central to French aperitif culture. From the late nineteenth century until World War II, crème de cassis was frequently mixed with aromatized wines and spirits. Today, it's mostly known for its association with the Kir and the Kir Royal, but mixed drinks such as the Vermouth Cassis or the Suze Cassis were once widely popular. See KIR. It was also mixed with spirits such as cognac. Its impact on cocktail culture has been more discreet, with the tequila-based El Diablo the only well-known cocktail calling for it (cassis mixes well with tequila in general, and in fact it was a component in the original Tequila Sunrise). See EL DIABLO and TEQUILA SUNRISE.

"Du cassis de Bourgogne." *La feuille de tout le monde,* August 8, 1861, 4.

Légifrance. *Décret du 28 juillet 1908 pris pour l'application de la loi du 1er août 1905 sur la répression des fraudes dans la vente des marchandises en ce qui concerne les liqueurs et sirops.* https://www.legifrance.gouv.fr/loda/id/LEGITEXT000006071230/1936-02-16/ (accessed March 18, 2021).

François Monti

crème de menthe is a sweet liqueur flavored with mint of French origin, available in a clear version but more commonly seen in its bright green form, the color furnished either by mint leaves or artificially. Its roots go deep: mint is among the earliest botanicals used to flavor spirits and impart their medicinal value to them, and "water of red mint" is among the formulae included in Hieronymus Brunschwig's pioneering 1512 book on distillation. See BOTANICAL. By the 1700s, mint distillates had moved beyond strict medicinal use, as a 1721 reference to the "dram of rum and mint-water" served at a Boston tavern demonstrates. As the century progressed, the spirit was more likely to be sweetened. In 1757, London distiller Ambrose Cooper wrote of his recipe, "You may dulcify it with sugar if required." On the other hand, the liqueur version could not yet have been a standard spirit: when Jacques-Francois Demachy, a French pharmacist, published a recipe for it in 1775, he added, "I believe I am the first person to have imagined this liqueur." Pippermint Get, a mint liqueur created in Revel, France, in 1796 (it assumed its present name many years later), appears to be an early commercial example of the type. Its bottle advertised its ability to rid the body of myriad ailments, including cholera. Another prominent early brand was Menthe-Pastille, created by Emile Giffard, in 1885 in Angers.

Crème de menthe is typically made by infusing peppermint or Corsican mint in water, distilling it, and mixing the result with grain alcohol, which is then sweetened (the mint can also be infused directly in alcohol, which is then rectified in the same way). It comes in two varieties, green and white (the latter was traditionally of higher proof). Crème de menthe, which enjoyed a vogue in American bars in the 1890s, is a critical ingredient in a handful of classic cocktails, typically of the after-dinner variety, including the Stinger, the Grasshopper, and, of course, the Crème de Menthe Frappé (where it is shaken with ice and poured into a glass full of fine ice). The liqueur was also popular as a stand-alone aperitif (Agatha Christie's fictional detective Hercule Poirot favored it). Its reputation suffered in the mid-twentieth century when naturally rendered versions were replaced by artificially flavored and colored brands.

See also GRASSHOPPER and STINGER.

Brunschwig, Hieronymus. *The Vertuose Boke of Distyllacyon.* Translated by Laurence Andrew. London: 1527.

Demachy, Jacques-Francois. *L'Art du distillateur liquoriste.* Paris: 1775.

"To the Readers of the *Courant* in New Hampshire." *New England Courant,* December 18, 1721, 3.

Robert Simonson and David Wondrich

crème de noyaux are among the first "secular" liqueurs, as distinct from the monastic liquors elaborated in the secrecy of the monasteries, made in France in the middle of the seventeenth century. At the time, it was common to use the almond-like hearts of certain fruit kernels such as peaches, apricots, cherries, and prunes to make liqueurs. Their almond taste and aroma come from benzaldehyde, a naturally occurring molecule contained in the kernels. Some of these specialties, such as *crème de noyaux de Poissy, liqueur de noyaux de Vernon,* or *crème de prunelle de Bourgogne,* often enjoyed only very local popularity yet have managed to pass through the centuries. Historically, producers have used either maceration or distillation to create these cordials. In the first case, the hearts are crushed and infused for a few weeks, often commingled with their broken hulls, in a brandy (cognac or Armagnac, for example) before adding sugar syrup to achieve a liqueur with 35 percent ABV with a slight amber color. The other method is to macerate the kernels in alcohol (by adding, if necessary, vanilla, rose buds, etc.) and then to proceed with the distillation. After reduction and addition of sugar syrup, the liqueur is clear and is usually bottled at 40 percent alcohol. American examples are typically colored red (thus lending the Pink Squirrel cocktail its signature color), although quality ranges widely. Crème de noyaux is sipped straight and used in some cocktails such as the Old Etonian, the Mikado, and the Jockey Club.

See also ABV; Armagnac; cognac; France; and liqueurs.

Demachy, Jacques-François. L'art du distillateur-liquoriste. Paris: 1775.

Alexandre Gabriel

crème de violette is a liqueur with the aroma, flavor, and deep purple hue of violets (*Viola odorata*), generally made by adding alcohol to a syrup of the flower. Cordials and syrups of violets date to at least the 1600s, and by the middle of the next century it was an established French specialty. Though isolated shipments of the liqueur had shown up in America since the 1780s, it only found its way into the cocktail bar around the turn of the twentieth century, when imported French crème de violette was used in such American drinks as the Aviation and the widely popular Blue Moon. See Aviation Cocktail and Blue Moon. After enjoying a certain vogue in America and in Europe, the liqueur's cocktail use tapered off by the 1930s, when its heavy floral scent had begun to seem old-fashioned (violets contain ionone, a compound that to some people tastes of soap). In 2007, responding to a small but persistent demand from modern mixologists, the American importer Haus Alpenz reintroduced the liqueur, uncommon even in Europe, to the United States as a cocktail ingredient, with the Austrian Rothman and Winter brand. Although it is still not used often, when crème de violette does appear in a cocktail, its strong scent and flavor and its distinctive color ensure that even in small amounts it will play a crucial role in the drink, and often a defining one.

See also Haus Alpenz; and parfait amour.

Déjean [Antoine Hornot?]. Traité raisonné de la distillation. Paris: 1753.

Doudoroff, Martin. "Crème de Violette." Martin's New and Improved Index of Cocktails and Mixed Drinks from the First Golden Age of the American Bar. App for iPad.

Punch staff. "Bringing It Back Bar: What to Do with Violet Liqueur Crème de Violette." Punch, September 21, 2015. http://punchdrink.com/articles/bringing-it-back-bar-creme-de-violette-cocktail-recipe-history/ (accessed February 5, 2021).

Stewart, Amy. The Drunken Botanist. Chapel Hill, NC: Algonquin, 2013.

Dinah Sanders

creosote, derived from wood tar, was in the nineteenth century one of several noxious additives that might be used by an unscrupulous rectifier to give flavor and color to neutral spirit in an attempt to pass it off as whisky or another spirit; it was particularly used to imitate scotch whisky. See rectification.

The **Criterion** restaurant complex, opened by Australian caterers Felix William Spiers and Christopher Pond in 1873, was a jewel in the heart of London's Piccadilly Circus, and its impressive American bar (aka the Long Bar) was a London fixture for many years. Theater architect Thomas Verity designed both the bar and the five-story restaurant, with its cavernous Marble Hall and "glistering" gold mosaic ceiling, in a neo-Byzantine style to match its adjoining theater. When the American bar opened, a year after the restaurant did, it was the first fully-realized American bar in London. With the German American import Leo Engel as manager, who had worked for Jerry Thomas, the bar was prepared to make any known American drink in the most correct style, along with a few of Leo's own. Creator of the Ladies' Blush, Alabazam, and other classics, Engel would go on to compile more than two hundred recipes, including many that he compounded for Criterion patrons (and many that he pinched from Thomas), in his book *American and Other Drinks*. See Engel, Leo.

In Sir Arthur Conan Doyle's 1887 novel *A Study in Scarlet*, Dr. John Watson stands at the "Criterion Bar" and learns of his prospective roommate Sherlock Holmes. The bar also appears in G. K. Chesterton's 1914 novel *The Flying Inn*. The novel is set in a future England, in which an Islamic sect dominates the government, which bans alcohol sales "except when demanded under a medical certificate from one of the doctors licensed by the State Medical Council, or in the specially excepted case of Claridge's Hotel and the Criterion Bar, where urgency has already been approved."

The Criterion Restaurant saw its last days of lovingly restored glory in the hands of developer Irakli Sopromadze, winning accolades from London food critics in 2011 when it reopened its doors. However, it went into administration a few years later and remains closed despite a planned reopening.

"Piccadilly, South Side." In *Survey of London, vols. 29–30m St James Westminster, Part 1*, ed. F. H. W. Sheppard, 251–270. London: Athlone, 1960. Available online at *British History Online*. http://www.british-history. ac.uk/survey-london/vols29-30/pt1/pp251-270#h3-0005 (accessed March 1, 2021).

Engel, Leo. *American and Other Drinks*. London: 1878.

Chesterton, G. K. *The Flying Inn*. London: Methuen, 1914, 30.

"Miss Fanny Montague, of the Montague Sisters . . ." *London and Provincial Entr'acte*, April 4, 1874, 7.

Neilan, Catherine. "Piccadilly's Criterion Restaurant Enters Administration after 60 Percent Rental Hike by landlord Criterion Capitol." *CityA.M.*, June 24, 2015. http://www.cityam.com/218715/piccadillys-criterion-restaurant-enters-administration-after-60-cent-rental-hike-landlord (accessed March 1, 2021).

Anistatia R. Miller and Jared M. Brown

Crockett, Barry

Crockett, Barry (1948–), the former master distiller of Irish Distillers Limited (IDL), was the third generation of his family to work at the Midleton distillery. His father, Max, was master distiller before him, and Barry was born in the distiller's cottage opposite the original plant. See IRISH DISTILLERS LIMITED (IDL).

He started to work at the distillery in 1965 at age seventeen, dealing with the farmers who supplied the distillery's barley. In 1975, he oversaw the transition of operations from the "old Midleton" site to a purpose-built new distillery. By 1981 Crockett had succeeded his father as master distiller.

Regarded as one of the world's most technologically advanced whisky distilleries, the new Midleton site was set up to produce a wide variety of Irish whisky styles to be used in IDL's many brands—the most notable being Jameson, Power's, and Paddy. This required a highly flexible regime in which various grain whiskies and single pot still whiskies of different characters could be crafted in a single facility. Crockett also oversaw the whiskies made for the first Irish super-premium blend, Midleton Very Rare.

While the blends were the major focus of production, he and his colleagues closely safeguarded the old Irish style of single pot still and implemented a long-term strategy geared at its revival. When, in 2011, IDL brought this strategy to fruition by launching its single pot still range, one particular whisky, typifying the old Midleton style, was named Barry Crockett Legacy after the man who had kept the style alive.

In 2013, Crockett retired after being part of the team that supervised another major expansion of the distillery. The new Midleton stillhouse was named in his honor. He has subsequently taken a degree in archival studies and is now a member of IDL's archive team. Its base is his childhood home.

"The Revival." *Irish Independent*, November 20, 2015.

Dave Broom

Crouch, Jasper

Crouch, Jasper (ca. 1800–ca. 1860), was in his day the leading caterer in Richmond, Virginia, earning particular renown as a mixologist. A "free person of color," Crouch was the drink mixer for the Richmond Quoit Club, which boasted the chief justice of the United States Supreme Court, John Marshall, as a member, among other dignitaries, and for the Richmond Light Infantry Blues, a militia unit recruited from socially prominent families. Crouch was famous for his Mint Juleps, a favorite of Marshall's, and his punch, which he made, according to one old Richmond resident, "of the freshest lemons" and the "best old cognac brandy and Jamaica rum," mixed "in the proportion of four-fifths of brandy to one of rum, and a dash of old Murdock Madeira just to give it a flavor and tone, and to take off the fiery edge." Dilution and cooling for the "strong and sweet" punch were provided "by pouring into the capacious bowl at least one-third of transparent ice." In the 2010s, Crouch's Quoit Club Punch found a new popularity, particularly in the American South.

See also JULEP and PUNCH.

Munford, George Wythe. *The Two Parsons*. Richmond, VA: J. D. K. Sleight, 1884.

Wondrich, David. *Punch*. New York: Perigee, 2010.

David Wondrich

Crow, James C. (1789–1856), was born in Inverness, Scotland. He graduated from Edinburgh University in 1822 with a degree in medicine and emigrated to the United States. Crow had an affinity for chemistry, and for scientific investigation in general, and by 1823 he had gravitated to Kentucky, where he quickly got a job in the growing distilling industry. Crow is often credited with "inventing" the sour mash process, but it is more likely that he refined and standardized the practice through the use of proper scientific instruments, experimentation, and recording results. The Old Crow brand of bourbon is named for him.

See also OLD CROW and SOUR MASH.

Cowdery, Charles K. *Bourbon, Straight: The Uncut and Unfiltered Story of American Whiskey*. Chicago: Made and Bottled in Kentucky, 2004.

Lew Bryson

Crowgey, Henry Gundry (1916–2012), was the author of *Kentucky Bourbon: The Early Years of Whiskeymaking*, published by the University Press of Kentucky in 1971. It is considered one of the outstanding academic works on the early history of bourbon and a model for historical writing on spirits in general.

Crowgey was born in Emory, Virginia. In 1936, he joined the United States Navy and became a pilot. He served through the end of World War II and was discharged with the rank of lieutenant commander. While studying to achieve his PhD in history from the University of Kentucky, he grew apples for twenty years in North Carolina. In 1967, he took a position teaching history at the University of North Carolina in Wilmington.

Kentucky Bourbon, which was based on Crowgey's 1968 dissertation, was not only Crowgey's best-known book but his only one. As a scholarly work, it has survived the years and is still in print. His research relied heavily on contemporary writing of those early years: letters, diaries, wills, newspaper articles, bills of sale. As one reviewer put it, "Crowgey got his hands dirty." It is a deep look at the first fifty years of Kentucky bourbon that explores how whisky distilling advanced, how frontier folk drank their whisky, and how it was used as an early form of currency during the early years of the Republic.

But the real reason the book is still in print (and makes its author worthy of an entry here) is the way Crowgey artfully balanced academic thoroughness with engaging readability. *Kentucky Bourbon* was, and remains, a book for both scholars and aficionados.

See SPIRITS WRITING and WHISKY, BOURBON.

Crockett, Norman L. Review of *Kentucky Bourbon: The Early Years of Whiskeymaking*, by Henry G. Crowgey. *Indiana Magazine of History* 68, no. 2 (1972): 154–155.

"Dr. Henry Gundry 'Harry' 'Gus' Crowgey." *Bristol (VA) Herald Courier*, November 6, 2012.

Lew Bryson

Crown Royal is the world's bestselling Canadian whisky brand. Its flagship blended whisky, packaged in an iconic purple pouch and bottled at 40 percent ABV, was created in 1939 by Seagram president Sam Bronfman to coincide with a visit to Canada by King George VI and Queen Elizabeth of England. For the next twenty-five years, it was sold only in Canada, before beginning to be exported in 1964. A complex blend of lighter and heavier corn whiskies as a base, flavored with Coffey-still rye whisky, modern column-still rye whisky, and a bourbon-like-mash-bill whisky, Crown Royal today surpasses all other imported whiskies in the United States in terms of dollar sales.

Originally produced at Seagram's Waterloo distillery in Ontario, Crown Royal whisky is now made at the Gimli distillery on Lake Winnipeg in Manitoba. Acquired by Diageo in 2001 along with other former Seagram's brands, Crown Royal has expanded to include other blended whiskies, flavored whiskies, and a rye whisky. See SEAGRAM COMPANY LTD.

See also BRONFMAN FAMILY and WHISKY, CANADIAN.

Faith, Nicholas. *The Bronfmans: The Rise and Fall of the House of Seagram*. New York: St. Martin's Griffin, 2007.

David Mahoney

crusta is a family of mixed drinks created in the 1850s by Joseph Santini, an Italian-born New Orleans bartender, when he was working at the St. Louis Hotel or at his own bar, the Jewel of the South. Recipes for Brandy, Whisky, and Gin Crustas first appeared in print in Jerry Thomas's 1862 *Bar-Tender's Guide* (misspelling the name of its creator), although it is the brandy version that endured. See THOMAS, JERRY. If it is to its presentation—a sugar-rimmed small wineglass garnished with the peel of half a lemon arranged as a sort of collar inside the glass—that the drink owes its fame and, indeed, its name ("crusta" means crust in various Italian dialects), its importance in the annals of mixology runs far deeper.

Santini built on the classic, fancy cocktail formula of spirit, syrup, aromatic bitters, and orange curaçao (maraschino can also be substituted, as per later recipes) but took the then-revolutionary step of adding "a dash" (in Thomas's words) of lemon juice, paving the way for the Sidecar and other citrus-forward cocktails.

Although by the 1930s, Harry McElhone was calling for a quarter of a lemon, and today's bartender often go up to 30 ml, a more historically faithful recipe would call for 5 ml, as per David Wondrich's *Imbibe!* See MCELHONE, HENRY "HARRY." In terms of popular success, the crustas never really caught on, but they could be found in Europe as early as 1873 and were important enough to be featured in most cocktail books until World War II. Their popularity has risen with the recent cocktail renaissance. See COCKTAIL RENAISSANCE.

Recipe: Stir well with cracked ice 60 ml brandy, genever, or American whisky, 5 ml rich simple syrup, 3 ml orange curaçao, 2 dashes Aromatic bitters, and 3–5 ml lemon juice. Strain into chilled small wineglass prepared as in text above.

See also SIDECAR.

C. C. F. "American Drinks at Vienna." *Alexandria Gazette*, July 12, 1873.
Wondrich, David, *Imbibe!* New York: Perigee, 2007.

François Monti

cryoextraction is the practice of extracting water from a liquid destined for fermentation to concentrate its sugars or from an alcoholic beverage to concentrate its alcohol. Winemakers in very cold climates such as Germany and Canada extract juice from frozen grapes to achieve higher sugar concentrations. In historical American apple-jack production, fermented cider could be partially frozen during winters; its water (solidified as ice) could be separated from its unfrozen alcohol. The resulting high-proof spirit was rich in (toxic) heads and tails and was known colloquially as skull-pop or Yankee antifreeze. The technique has deep historical roots, being practiced in Russia during the Middle Ages and China during the Eastern Han dynasty (25–220 CE). See HEADS and TAILS.

See also APPLEJACK and DISTILLATION, HISTORY.

Brook, Stephen. *Liquid Gold: Dessert Wines of the World*. Sag Harbor, NY: Beech Tree, 1987.

Doug Frost

Cryovac is a proprietary brand of chamber vacuum sealer, used in some high-end cocktail bars for preparing cocktail ingredients. See VACUUM SEALER.

The **Cuba Libre**—also known as "Rum and Coca-Cola," after its two main ingredients (the others being ice and, sometimes, lime juice)—is one of the most popular mixed drinks in the world. The Bacardi company has long backed the story that it was invented by an American soldier in Havana in 1898 or 1900, but there are discrepancies in the details, and the story is without contemporary documentation. See BACARDI. There is, however, a record of a "Cuba Libre cocktail" being served to a Cuban delegation in Washington, DC, in 1898 (*Cuba libre*, "Free Cuba," was the slogan of the forces opposed to Spanish rule of that country), but the only description of it we have mentions that it was refreshing and was served in frosted glasses with crossed Cuban and American flags with sprigs of mint between them.

In fact, the combination of rum and Coca-Cola does not appear in print as the Cuba Libre until the late 1920s. The combination is considerably older than that: American adventurer Dean Ivan Lamb recalled being introduced to it in Venezuela in 1906, and Coca-Cola's Midwest distributor was pushing the "Coca Cola Highball" in the United States, albeit with whisky or gin, by 1902. See HIGHBALL.

Nonetheless, Coca-Cola was available in Cuba from 1900 on, and the combination is a natural one, so an early Cuban origin cannot be discounted. In any case, the drink reached its apogee in America during World War II, when the availability of Coca-Cola and cheap rum (and the lack of bourbon or rye), along with a catchy song to promote it, rendered its use near-universal. After the war, Americans took to replacing the rum with whisky, while the increased penetration of Coca-Cola into Central and South America and indeed many other parts of the world saw the drink made with local spirits and even wine. See BATANGA and CALIMOTXO. Conversely, after the Cuban Revolution bartenders there had to re-place the Coca-Cola with a local equivalent.

Recipe: Squeeze half a lime into an ice-filled high-ball glass. Add 60 ml white rum and 60–75 ml cold Coca-Cola, stir briefly, and insert the squeezed-out lime shell and a straw.

"Cuba's Commission." *Washington Evening Star*,
    December 1, 1898, 1.
Lamb, Dean Ivan. *The Incurable Filibuster*.
    New York: Farrar & Rinehart, 1934.
"Pure Food Attracted Hundreds." *Detroit Free Press*,
    November 11, 1902, 11.

David Wondrich

curaçao (sometimes spelled **curaçoa**), originally a liqueur flavored with the dried peels of the laraha orange, a particularly bitter offshoot of the Seville orange native to the Caribbean island of Curaçao, has become an umbrella term for orange liqueur in general. As such, it is one of the most important branches of the liqueur family, both historically and commercially.

According to the early nineteenth-century French culinary chronicler Alexandre Grimod de la Reynière, curaçao "originated in Flanders, which is to say Tournai, Brussels, Douai, etc.," where prox-imity to Holland gave distillers easy access to the necessary peels (Curaçao was a Dutch colony at the time). And in fact, some of the earliest known mentions of it by name are found in newspaper advertisements from Ghent, in Flanders, from the mid-1790s. These advertisements present it without explanation, which implies that it must have been known for some time. (Of course, the fact that merchants in Curaçao were exporting dried orange peels strongly suggests that the idea of flavoring spirits with them was already known on that island, at least for local use.)

Spirits flavored with orange peel in general were nothing new: there are German recipes for orange- and lemon-peel-flavored "Pomeranzenwasser" from the late 1500s (although that had other highly aro-matic ingredients as well). Nonetheless, such things were not in universal use: as one English distiller wrote in 1731, "Orange-water" was "not much known, or used in [this] country," despite "the agreeable flavour, or relish thereof."

By the first decade of the nineteenth century, however, curaçao had become fashionable in Paris, and that meant in London as well. It is possible that the French occupation of Curaçao from 1795 to 1800 and the British one from 1800 to 1816 during the Napoleonic Wars greatly assisted its dissemina-tion. In any case, by 1820 curaçao was, along with maraschino di Zara and crème de noyaux, one of the canonical liqueurs, available everywhere and taken on all occasions. See MARASCHINO and CRÈME DE NOYAUX. That popularity led to widespread imita-tion, and by the middle of the century very little of the curaçao sold had any connection with the island beyond sharing a name. As with any popular liqueur in an age before brands, there were as many versions as there were distillers and merchants, using a wide variety of orange and other citrus peels in their composition.

The earliest version, described by Grimod de la Reynière, was made by distilling the peels in unaged brandy and reducing and sweetening the resulting spirit; this would have been colorless. Almost con-temporary, however, was the version treating it as a ratafia, where the peels were infused in brandy without redistillation; this would have been orange or green depending on the ripeness of the oranges peeled. See RATAFIA. By the middle of the century, the state-of-the-art technique involved combining the methods: the bitter-orange peels were distilled, along with some supporting spices (e.g., cinnamon, cloves, mace) in unaged brandy or neutral spirit, and the result was blended with a lesser quantity of an infusion of the peels of sweet, or Valencia, oranges, again in new brandy or spirit. In 1891, the well-regarded Paris *liquoriste* Louis-Alexandre Marnier elaborated on this in the curaçao he created for the exclusive Café Royal in London by replacing the neutral spirit in the infusion with aged cognac from that establishment's cellars. This was widely imitated. See GRAND MARNIER.

By the end of the nineteenth century, curaçao was widely manufactured in Europe and America and marketed in a dizzying variety of styles and grades. It is difficult to categorize them, not least because, in the absence of regulations to hold manufacturers to their claims, there is no guarantee that what was in the bottle corresponded with what was on the label. Thus, for example, "double" curaçao, which ostensibly used twice as much flavoring matter as usual, generally did not, as one distiller noted in 1900, "in reality contain double the aromatics of ordinary curaçao." Different printed recipes for the same designation rarely agree in detail regarding process, quantities, or types of aromatics, quantity of sugar, percentage of alcohol, or anything else.

While most of these styles are of historical interest only, one that remains in use, at least nominally, is the colorless "triple sec," a French innovation of the 1850s, which began, as far as can be determined, as a higher-proof, more concentrated blend of three separate distillations of different kinds of orange peels in neutral spirit (it is *sec*, "dry," not because there is less sugar in it but because there is more bitter-orange flavor and more alcohol). While the highest-quality brands still use some variation of this process, "triple sec" has become an essentially meaningless term, in that the great majority of the versions on the market are cheap, low-proof, thickly sweet compounds of neutral spirit and flavoring essences.

Another common style is blue curaçao, first introduced by the Dutch Lucas Bols firm in 1912 to supplement the existing red and green varieties, which were artificially colored to heighten the natural colors of the peels of the ripe or unripe oranges on which they were ostensibly based. This, too, is usually of poor quality. There are exceptions: the Senior company of Curaçao, the island's only commercial producer since 1945, uses real laraha peels in their product. The two most prominent curaçao producers, however, long ago exempted themselves from the category, Curaçao Marnier becoming Grand Marnier in the 1890s and Curaçao Triple Sec Cointreau becoming simply Cointreau some thirty years later. "Curaçao" had become generic to the point it was detrimental to branding. See GRAND MARNIER and COINTREAU.

Curaçao in its various forms is used in some of the most popular mixed drinks in circulation, including the Margarita, the Mai Tai, the Long Island Iced Tea, and a host of others. See MARGARITA; MAI TAI; and LONG ISLAND ICED TEA. Indeed, this has been one of its most important uses since it was first introduced: one of its main vectors to popularity was its use in punch, and in particular in some of the early versions of the punch that the British prince regent, a connoisseur of that beverage, habitually drank. See REGENT'S PUNCH.

A good orange curaçao adds richness and subtle spice notes to a drink without making it overly orangey, while in a proper triple sec the orange will be more overt. Neither should be too sugary or syrupy on the one hand or hot and harsh on the other.

Annales du propriété industrielle. Paris: A. Rousseau, 1899.

Appers, Jan, advertisement. *Gazette van Ghent,* July 7, 1796, 6.

Arnou, Leon. *Manuel du confiseur liquoriste.* Paris: Baillière & fils, 1905.

Grimod de la Reyniere, Alexandre. *Almanach des gourmands, sixième année.* Paris: 1808.

Sebzius, Melchior. *Siben Bücher von dem Feldbau.* Strasburg: 1579.

Smith, G. *Compleat Body of Distilling.* London: 1731.

Victor, Sébastian. *Guide pratique du fabricant d'alcools.* Montpellier: Camille Coulet, 1900.

David Wondrich

The **cut** is the moment when the distiller decides to separate the different parts of a distillate. Like a tree that is trimmed so that it gives the finest fruits, the art of distillation is based largely on selection: keeping the best while removing the least desirable fractions. This operation of rectification will intervene several times during the distillation cycle. Take the example of the distillation of cognac, which is carried out in two stages. The first distillation produces a low wine (brouillis), a liquid with an ABV between 27 and 35 percent—undrinkable as such, though it contains all the aromatic components of the final product. The second distillation consists of refilling the pot with the first distillate and heating it again to obtain the unaged spirit.

In distilling, "cutting heads" is to collect the first liters of alcohol flowing from the still after the first rising of vapors into the swan neck. On the first distillation (the low wine), the cut consists of the removal of the heads. On the second distillation, cutting heads proves far more difficult to achieve, for if the first liters give off an unpleasant odor, we also know that this part of the second distillation contains compounds—esters of fatty acids—responsible for the aromatic complexity of the distillate. When is the best time to cut? When is the perfect time to remove unwanted elements while preserving the important organoleptic characteristics? This is where a distiller's experience and talent come into play. Depending on the year and the quality of the wines, but also the chosen distillation method, the distiller will take 8–20 liters of heads or more during the second distillation. The cutting of heads is usually done at the still using the nose and palate of the distiller. After a few liters, the distiller checks, liter after liter, the arrival of pleasant odors. Once the cutting of heads has been completed, the heart will flow. But the distillation process does not stop there. It is now necessary to separate the heart from the tails by cutting the tails. In cognac, the tails are accounted in two fractions, the "secondes" and the tails, since at the end of the distillation perfumes change again. Animal scents appear, which are called

secondes. To properly cut the end of the heart, the distiller will first resort to the ABV indicated by the hydrometer as a first indication. From 66/65 percent ABV on, the distiller will lower the fire under the boiler to slow down distillation. The spirit flows more slowly, and the final selection by the master distiller's nose is facilitated. There is no remedy for failed selection of that moment, hence the extreme attention paid by distillers to the cuts of the second distillation. With a pot still, the cut is done at the beginning and end of the distillation; the column still completes this process automatically.

In cognac, there are several distillation methods which will define what is then done with the heads, secondes, and tails.

Generally, the secondes are put back into the brouillis. The heads and tails return to the wine. However, each cognac distiller has a secret way to work with these elements.

See also HEADS and TAILS.

Baudoin, A. *Les eaux-de-vie et la fabrication du cognac.* Paris: J. B. Baillière et fils, 1893.

Alexandre Gabriel

D

The **Daiquiri** is the king of Cuban cocktails and simplicity itself: rum, lime juice, and sugar. From its fluke birth at a Cuban iron mine to its glory days as the favorite drink of Ernest Hemingway and the Kennedy White House—and from its devolution into a creamy disco drink to its rehabilitation at the hands of craft cocktail revivalists—the Daiquiri has endured to take its rightful place alongside the Martini and the Manhattan as the quintessence of satori in a stemmed glass.

People in the Caribbean had been combining rum, lime, and sugar for over two hundred years before Jennings Stockton Cox Jr. (1866–1913) made the first Daiquiri—or at least supervised its making—in 1896, so it's a stretch to call him the drink's father. But he was at least its midwife. Cox ran John D. Rockefeller's Spanish-American Iron Company near Daiquiri, a harbor town on Cuba's east coast. According to Cox's step-granddaughter Carmen Puig, who in 1970 told the story to Time-Life cookbook author Linda Wolfe, Cox improvised the drink for some American visitors after discovering he was out of gin. He did have Bacardi Carta Blanca rum, fresh from the distillery twenty-eight miles away in Santiago, "but he feared that it would not be to the taste of the Americans. To disguise the rum somewhat, he picked limes from a tree in his garden, added some juice and some sugar to his rum," then swizzled it all in a pitcher with shaved ice. He may have had help in the process: as Robert H. Lyman Jr., who was one of the six Yanqui engineers on Cox's staff at the mine, recalled in 1935, the drink was more of a group creation with credit to be shared among the "Siete Solteros," the "Seven Bachelors," as Cox and his crew were known. In any case, "It was an immediate success." See CARIBBEAN.

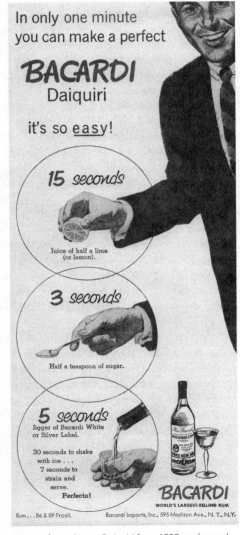

Instructions for making a Daiquiri from 1952, and sound ones. Wondrich Collection.

While their details vary, newspaper accounts from the 1920s through the 1950s quote other sources who confirm Cox's obstetrics—and note that for twelve years after he first made the drink, he'd never thought to name it, just calling it his "rum sour." He had, however, been introducing it to the bars of Santiago. There the bartender at the San Carlos Club streamlined Cox's pitcher full of rum, lime, and sugar into a single-serving drink; according to a chemist named Josh Linthicum, who worked and drank with Cox, in 1908 that same bartender finally gave the drink a name: "Ron à la Daiquiri." A slightly different account, in Basil Woon's 1928 book *When It's Cocktail Time in Cuba*, claims that a barman at Santiago's Venus Hotel streamlined the Daiquiri and that Cox himself named the drink. This Santiago version—shaken with brown sugar and poured over crushed ice in a champagne flute—found its way to Havana, where bartenders there modified it yet again into the Daiquiri as we know it today: shaken with white sugar, strained, and served up. Several Havana barmen were credited with this refinement, but the two most likely were the Plaza Hotel's Emilio "Maragato" González (1869–1940) and Bar La Florida's Constantino "Constante" Ribalaigua Vert. While Maragato had the local reputation as the drink's perfector, it was Ribalaigua's version that enchanted Prohibition revelers in the 1920s, when his bar became known as "the cathedral of the Daiquiri" and the drink became the rage in Havana and US speakeasies. (It had been known to clubmen in Washington and New York since 1909, when Lucius Johnson and John Manchester, a pair of navy doctors, brought it to Washington's Army-Navy Club after Cox introduced them to it at his house in Daiquiri.)

Shortly after Repeal, Ribalaigua employed the latest in cutting-edge culinary technology—the electric blender—to create the first frozen Daiquiris. His Daiquiri no. 3, frappéd with maraschino and grapefruit juice, beguiled Ernest Hemingway, who began drinking them in 1938 and didn't stop until shortly before his death in 1960. (Hemingway's customized version, with no sugar and double the rum, became famous as the "Papa Doble.") See HEMINGWAY DAIQUIRI. The Daiquiri's star rose even higher when President John F. Kennedy cited it as his favorite preprandial drink. But the industrial food complex of the 1970s—coupled with the disco era's penchant for sweet, fruity, lactic cocktails—deformed the Daiquiri beyond recognition with artificial sour mix, frozen strawberries, and whipped cream. The drink languished in this state until the beginning of the twenty-first century, when the burgeoning craft cocktail renaissance brought the classic Cuban shaken-and-strained version back onto American bar menus. See CRAFT COCKTAIL.

Recipe: Stir one teaspoon (5 ml) sugar into the juice of half a lime (ca. 15 ml), add 60 ml white rum, shake with ice and strain into a cocktail glass.

See also MARASCHINO and RIBALAIGUA Y VERT, CONSTANTE.

Berry, Jeff. *Potions of the Caribbean*. New York: Cocktail Kingdom, 2014.

Cuddy, Jack. "Cuba's Cocktail King Tells Cuddy Daiquiri Recipe." *Rome (NY) Sentinel*, May 3, 1937.

Fougner, G. Selmer. "Along the Wine Trail." *New York Sun*, February 11, 1935, 29.

Pegler, Westbrook. "Fair Enough." *Billings Gazette*, October 23, 1956.

"What's in a Name." *All Hands: The Bureau of Naval Personnel Information Bulletin*, April 1951, 54.

Jeff Berry

dairy in the form of milk and cream has been consumed in alcoholic beverages for thousands of years. In kumis, an ancient mare's milk drink from the Central Asian steppe that is still produced, it is the dairy itself that is made alcoholic through fermentation. Milk and cream have been mixed with separately fermented beverages such as wine or ale throughout Europe for many centuries, and they have been among the principal ingredients used to increase the palatability of hard spirits since the beginning of widespread European spirits drinking in the late Middle Ages. The acidity of many fermented beverages, as well as of acidic ingredients, such as lemon juice, that may be added to dairy drinks, will often cause the dairy to curdle. In some traditional recipes, the curds were consumed as part of the beverage, such as in the medieval English drinks posset or syllabub. See POSSET and SYLLABUB.

This curdling of milk solids has been used as a method of preservation, such as in clarified Milk Punch, in which citrus juice, often assisted by heating, causes the formation of curds, which are then strained off and sometimes further removed through the use of an egg white raft (and more recently a centrifuge), leaving behind a clear, brightly flavored, alcoholic punch that is shelf-stable at room temperature for several months. See Milk Punch.

Most dairy beverages, however, are unclarified, not only because of the difficulty of clarification but because the milk fat that is strained out in the curds is responsible for the quality of creaminess that dairy lends to drinks. Scailtin, a warm milk punch from Ireland, is thought by some to be the progenitor of many unclarified milk punches, such as Brandy Milk Punch and Bourbon Milk Punch. Some drinks pair dairy with eggs, as in Eggnog, a Christmas punch that employs both dairy and whole eggs, or the Ramos Gin Fizz, which elevates the classic egg white fizz with the addition of heavy cream. See Eggnog and Ramos Gin Fizz.

Though butter is not a common ingredient in the cocktail world, there are several examples of drinks that employ butter to lend them a rich flavor and unctuous mouthfeel. Most of these drinks seem to be variations on the centuries-old Hot Buttered Rum. See Hot Buttered Rum.

As mixology developed through the twentieth century, dairy became increasingly associated with the dessert or after-dinner drink, beginning in the 1910s with the Alexander and its more popular offspring, the Brandy Alexander, and soon followed by the Grasshopper. Cream has become a popular pairing with coffee liqueur, as in the Sombrero, with Kahlua and cream; the White Russian, with vodka, coffee liqueur, and cream; and the Mudslide, which is essentially a White Russian variation, wherein the cream has been replaced by Irish Cream, a shelf-stable, bottled mixture of Irish whisky and cream. See Alexander Cocktail; cream liqueurs; Grasshopper; and White Russian. The Mudslide can also be made as a frozen drink and has been almost since its inception in the 1950s, with the addition of ice and/or ice cream and the use of an electric blender. See Frozen Drinks, Blender Drinks. A series of alcoholic milkshakes has followed through the years, pairing ice creams of many flavors with almost any spirits or liqueurs imaginable. The 1950s also brought the Irish Coffee, the best-known exemplar of an entire class of hot coffee drinks, all of which are spiked with alcohol and topped with whipped cream. See Irish Coffee. Recent developments have found cocktail bartenders using Calpis, a Japanese brand name for a yogurt-like dairy beverage, as a mixer in cocktails both simple and complex, bringing the history of dairy and alcohol full circle to its Central Asian roots in kumis.

Buttery, Neil. "Possets." *British Food: A History* (blog), April 28, 2012. https://britishfoodhistory.com/2012/04/28/possets/ (accessed March 19, 2021).

Buttery, Neil. "Syllabubs." *British Food: A History* (blog), January 3, 2013. https://britishfoodhistory.com/2013/01/03/syllabubs/ (accessed March 19, 2021).

Ensslin, Hugo R. *Recipes for Mixed Drinks*, 2nd ed. N.p.: 1917. Available online at https://euvs-vintage-cocktail-books.cld.bz/1917-Recipes-for-Mixed-Drinks-by-Hugo-R-Ensslin-second-edition (accessed March 19, 2021).

Kozlik, Erik. " Episode 076: The Milk Punch Episode." Modern Bar Cart (podcast), November 24, 2018. https://www.modernbarcart.com/podcast/episode-076-the-milk-punch-episode (accessed March 19, 2021).

Ringmar, Erik. "How to Make Kumis." History of International Relations website. http://ringmar.net/irhistorynew/index.php/welcome/introduction-4/from-temujin-to-genghis-khan/5-2-a-nomadic-state/how-to-make-kumis/ (accessed March 19, 2021).

David Moo

The **Daisy**—a sour sweetened with a liqueur or flavored syrup, lightened with a splash of sparkling water, and served in a cocktail glass—is a close cousin to the fizz and, like that drink, is an American drink of the 1870s. See sour and fizz. While its origin has not been definitively proven, a credible claim was advanced in 1883 that it was created ten years before at Fred Eberlin's popular bar, around the corner from the New York Stock Exchange, when one Billy Taylor imparted to bartender Frank Haas (1847–1924) the idea he had for a new drink. The Daisy first appeared in print in the 1876 second edition of Jerry Thomas's *Bar-Tender's Guide*, in versions made with brandy, whisky, gin, and rum, all sweetened with orange liqueur. See Thomas, Jerry. Haas's version, upon which he built a long career, was specifically a whisky drink, with lime juice, raspberry syrup, soda water, and at least one other ingredient, but the brandy version also enjoyed some popularity, while other sweeteners found in the drink's early years include yellow Chartreuse and orgeat. See Chartreuse and orgeat.

The Daisy enjoyed a wide popularity in the 1870s and 1880s, fell out of favor in the 1890s, and came back with a vengeance in the first part of the next decade. This time, it was primarily a gin drink, sweetened with grenadine, and now it was served in a tall glass, or even a beer stein, full of crushed ice, and it generally featured lime juice instead of the lemon used in the earlier version. See GRENADINE. This new version was variously attributed to a bar on lower Broadway in Manhattan and to the editor Frederick Upham Adams (1859–1921); it is first attested to in print in 1902.

Neither version survived Prohibition in its original form, but both proved surprisingly influential: the first is one of the progenitors of the Sidecar and the Margarita, while the second spawned the Tequila Sunrise and the Tequila Daisy. See SIDECAR; MARGARITA; TEQUILA SUNRISE; and TEQUILA DAISY. Neither version, however, has been prominent in the twenty-first-century cocktail renaissance. See COCKTAIL RENAISSANCE.

Recipe (Whisky Daisy): Shake with ice: 60 ml rye whisky, 15 ml lime juice, 10 ml orange curaçao, 15 ml raspberry syrup. Strain into large cocktail glass and add 25 ml sparkling water.

Recipe (Gin Daisy): Shake with ice: 45 ml London dry gin, 15 ml lime juice, 15 ml grenadine. Strain into tall glass full of cracked ice and add 45 ml sparkling water. Garnish elaborately.

"Brooklyn at Last Gets Its Cocktail." *New York Herald*, September 9, 1910, 2.

Ensslin, Hugo. *Recipes for Mixed Drinks*. New York: Mud Puddle, 1916.

"Mysterious and Fascinating Drink." *Rochester Democrat*, October 8, 1902, 6.

"What Brokers Drink." *Chicago Daily Tribune*, September 25, 1883, 5.

David Wondrich

da qu ("big qu") is a type of solid-state fermentation starter made from wheat or barley (sometimes supplemented by peas) used in the production of the Chinese spirit baijiu. See also BAIJIU and QU.

Dark and Stormy is a highball made with dark rum (traditionally Gosling's Black Seal) and ginger beer (some recipes add lime juice to the mix). The drink purportedly originated among British sailors on shore leave in Bermuda after World War I (another origin story places the date earlier, in the nineteenth century), and in the intervening century the drink has served not only as a summer refresher but as a means to test the limits of copyright law related to cocktails. In 1991, the Gosling family—which founded Gosling's in Bermuda in 1806—claimed a trademark for the cocktail's recipe, and the family has repeatedly turned to the United States Patent and Trademark Office to protect its claim. In 2015, E. Malcolm Gosling Jr. and his brother filed a complaint in US federal court in Massachusetts, claiming that Pernod Ricard had committed federal trademark infringement for including a recipe for the Dark and Stormy on the company's website, using Malibu Island Spiced Rum.

Recipe: Combine 60 ml dark rum, juice of ½ lime (note that Bermudians take their Dark and Stormies without the lime), and 120–180 ml ginger beer, to taste, in an ice-filled highball glass and stir to combine. Garnish with a lime wheel or lime wedge (or not).

See also HIGHBALL and GINGER ALE AND GINGER BEER.

Fessenden, Marissa. "There's Only One Way to Make a Dark 'n' Stormy Without Breaking the Law." *Smithsonian*, June 8, 2015.

Haglage, Abby. "Will the Real Darn N' Stormy Please Stand Up?" *Daily Beast*, September, 22, 2015. https://www.thedailybeast.com/will-the-real-dark-n-stormy-please-stand-up (accessed March 2, 2021).

Martineau, Chantal. "The Era of Copyrighted Cocktails?" *Atlantic*, August 31, 2010.

Miles, Jonathan. "The Right Stuff (by Law)." *New York Times*, July 2, 2009.

Volz, Michael. "A Courtroom Cocktail: Gosling Brothers and a Dark, Stormy Message." *Lehrman Beverage Law*, November 17, 2015. https://bevlaw.com/bevlog/a-courtroom-cocktail-gosling-brothers-and-a-dark-stormy-message/ (accessed March 2, 2021).

Paul Clarke

The **Dawa** (from the Swahili word for medicine) is a Kenyan take on the Caipirinha, or rather the Caipiroska, introduced at the Carnivore restaurant in Nairobi in 1980 (the owner had just been to Brazil) and now essentially the national drink. It combines vodka or local triple-distilled cane spirit with muddled lime pieces, sugar, and ice and is served with a "Dawa stick," made of plastic or wood, which has been dipped in local honey and stuck in the glass.

Recipe: Cut a lime into quarters and muddle in a heavy-bottomed rocks glass with 5–15 ml sugar, to taste. Fill glass with ice, add 60 ml vodka, and stir. Serve with a "Dawa stick" (a length of dowel approximately 15 mm by 90 mm) that has been dipped in honey.

See also CAIPIRINHA.

Bethune, Meredith. "The Dawa: Kenya's Beloved Boozy Cocktail." *Eater*, March 23, 2016. http://www.eater.com/drinks/2016/3/23/11290110/dawa-cocktail-kenya-vodka (accessed March 2, 2021).

David Wondrich

Death in the Afternoon, an Ernest Hemingway invention, was originally published in the 1935 literary celebrity cocktail book *So Red the Nose, or, Breath in the Afternoon*. Hemingway claimed it "was arrived at by the author and three officers of H.M.S. *Danae* after having spent seven hours overboard trying to get Capt. Bra Saunders' fishing boat off a bank where she had gone with us in a N.W. gale." The *Danae* was a British cruiser that later provided naval gunfire off of Sword Beach, Normandy, during the D-Day landings (coincidentally, Hemingway covered the assault on nearby Omaha Beach as a war correspondent for *Collier's*). The drink is named for Hemingway's 1932 treatise on bullfighting.

Recipe: Pour 45 ml of absinthe into a champagne flute. Slowly add 120 ml of chilled champagne. Garnish with a lemon peel (optional).

See also ABSINTHE and CHAMPAGNE COCKTAILS.

North, Sterling, and Carl Kroch. *So Red the Nose, or, Breath in the Afternoon*. New York: Farrar & Rinehart, 1935.

Philip Greene

DeGroff, Dale (1948–), is an American bartender, author, and drinks educator who is widely credited with being a catalyst, if not the catalyst, for the renaissance in mixology that ushered in the twenty-first century. Born the son of a navy pilot at Quonset Point, Rhode Island, DeGroff grew up in places as far afield as Kwajalein in the Marshall Islands; Pensacola, Florida; and Spain and Morocco. DeGroff began acting while at the University of Rhode Island, which led him to New York City, where he did a little bartending among numerous other jobs, and then Los Angeles, where a stint behind the bar at the Hotel Bel Air turned a day job into a career.

In 1985, DeGroff returned to New York and secured the head bartender spot at Aurora, a fine-dining restaurant being opened by the legendary restaurateur Joe Baum (1920–1998). Baum tasked him to set up a "nineteenth century cocktail bar" using fresh juices and classic recipes, both well out of fashion, and told him to get Jerry Thomas's book for guidance, not mentioning that it was from 1862 and its last edition was from 1928. See THOMAS, JERRY. In 1988, when Baum reopened the Rainbow Room atop the art deco skyscraper at the heart of Rockefeller Center, he made sure that DeGroff ran the bar. In the decade DeGroff worked there he demonstrated not only that it was possible to run a bar without the shortcuts and compromises that had crept into the heart of the craft, but that it was good business—in fact, it was great business.

With the critical and popular success of the Rainbow Room bar, DeGroff found himself in the bully pulpit, so to speak, when it came to the American cocktail. He became the bartender of first resort for the media at a time when the Martini was getting a second look, and with it the craft that produced it. See MARTINI. The craft could not have asked for a better spokesperson. DeGroff proved to be immensely knowledgeable, humble, generous to his younger peers, charming in a way that was both courtly and quotably Runyonesque, and deeply connected to the traditions of the bar. Unlike many traditionalists, however, he was not crotchety when faced with change. When the Cosmopolitan surfaced, rather than reject the rather slapdash mix of vodka, cranberry juice, triple sec, and Rose's bottled lime juice, he improved it, substituting fresh lime for

Dale DeGroff at the Rainbow Room. Courtesy of Dale DeGroff.

the Rose's and Cointreau for the triple sec, and for good measure flamed an orange peel over the top, a trick he learned from Pepe Ruiz, the long-time bartender at Chasen's in Los Angeles. See COSMOPOLITAN and FLAME OF LOVE MARTINI.

Ironically, DeGroff's influence only grew when the Rainbow Room closed in 1998. After a stint at the short-lived Blackbird, a high-end bar and grill in which he was a partner, DeGroff began consulting on bar programs, including that at the London branch of New York's influential Milk & Honey and evangelizing for the bartender's craft. In 2002, he published his first book, the seminal *Craft of the Cocktail* (*The Essential Cocktail* followed in 2008 and a revised edition of *Craft* in 2020). In 2004, he spearheaded the founding of the Museum of the American Cocktail. See MUSEUM OF THE AMERICAN COCKTAIL. In 2005, he became one of the founding partners of Beverage Alcohol Resource, through which he has taught and influenced literally thousands of younger bartenders. See BEVERAGE ALCOHOL RESOURCE (BAR). DeGroff continues to teach and to inspire bartenders worldwide, but he also keeps exploring new ingredients, techniques, and pockets of lore.

See also COCKTAIL RENAISSANCE.

DeGroff, Dale. *The Craft of the Cocktail*, 2nd ed. New York: Clarkson Potter, 2020.
Numerous conversations with the author, 2001–2020.

David Wondrich

De Kuyper, a Dutch liqueur and genever producer run continuously by the same family for eleven generations, can trace its documented origin back to 1695 in Horst, in the south of the Netherlands, when Petrus de Kuyper registered a cooperage business (de Kuyper literally means "the cooper" in Dutch). In 1752, the family got into distilling genever when Petrus's son Jan started or bought a distillery in Schiedam (accounts differ), the satellite town of Rotterdam where local authorities had decreed all the distilleries should site themselves, instead of in

Rotterdam's city center. Schiedam grew to be one of the world's powerhouse distilling cities, with almost four hundred distilleries by the end of the 1800s, and De Kuyper flourished. The company concentrated on genever but, like their Amsterdam-based competitor Bols, would produce market-specific versions of whatever would sell: vodka, gin, and other products. The company began concentrating on liqueur production in 1920 and currently produces the world's most extensive range of liqueurs by some distance. As with Bols, liqueur production has also been largely outsourced to flavor houses and third parties. In 1933, in a partnership with the National Distillers Corporation, De Kuyper began also manufacturing their products in the United States for the North American market. When the James B. Beam Distilling Co. (now Beam-Suntory) bought National Distillers in 1986, they also acquired De Kuyper's American operation. De Kuyper liqueurs produced by Beam-Suntory for the US market in the United States differ significantly in packaging and contents from what is produced in the Netherlands, which more or less supplies the rest of the world.

See also GENEVER and BOLS.

De Kuyper website. https://www.dekuyper.com (accessed March 2, 2021).

Philip Duff

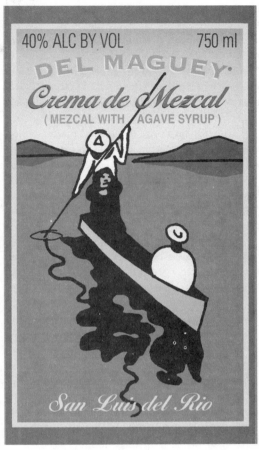

One of the iconic labels artist Ken Price created for Del Maguey Mezcal. Courtesy of Ron Cooper.

Del Maguey Mezcal, which brought the characteristic spirit of the highlands of Oaxaca to the world's notice, is the creation of Ron Cooper, who creates art in almost all he does. See COOPER, RON. It was the artist and adventurer in Cooper that compelled him to Mexico and to the villages where mezcal was still made in the most deeply traditional ways. In 1962 Cooper first discovered agave spirits at Hussong's Cantina on the Baja California coast, sixty miles south of Tijuana. But it wasn't until 1990 that he tasted mezcal in a cafe in Tlacolula, Oaxaca, and was thoroughly hooked.

By 1996 he was importing "single village mezcal," as he called it, into the United States under the Del Maguey label, beginning with four types, each made in a different Zapotec village in the highlands of Oaxaca. Cooper's way was, and is, to find great mezcal and bring it to the market as is, rather than blending it to suit a brand. His model was Armagnac; he wanted each batch to be unique and

different. See ARMAGNAC. And he saw mezcal as capable of transforming the drinker the way art does its viewer. At the same time, he has transformed the communities from which he purchases his wares.

Del Maguey created a business model for premium, artisanal mezcals to find global markets, positioning the category for others to follow (at the time, the only Oaxacan mezcal widely available outside of Mexico was the industrial Monte Alban brand, whose main selling point was the agave worm in the bottom of each bottle). This was not just a replica or variation of tequila; it was a new category and a game changer. Others had to follow the Del Maguey example if they wanted to compete. "Mezcal is intrinsic to Mexican culture but rarely—speaking in general terms—[are] Mexicans . . . aware of this," one member of the indigenous mezcal industry acknowledges, speaking off the record. "It took an American like Ron Cooper to discover what Mexicans had in their culture forever. He made this awareness." The effects have been profound. Emigration patterns have been turned around by giving vitality to "farmer-produced" mezcal. Impoverished communities have seen their young people return, drawn home—often from the United States—by suddenly attractive wages and a rediscovered sense of pride.

Charging a high price for artisanal mezcal has forever altered the category, creating an expectation of super premium returns on expenses, despite the vagaries of farming. The diversity manifested by "single village" and single-varietal mezcals has been a boon to the "slow food" movement, as has the artisanal, craft, small batch, old-school nature of Del Maguey's mezcals.

Cooper's emphasis on "single village" and "single mezcalero"—one who makes mezcal—has defined the mezcal category by distinguishing it from tequila, its more industrialized family member. Del Maguey has made economic, agricultural, and even social sustainability a focus of its mission. Virtually all of modern mixology's brain trust is fixated on mezcal; its reputation is as an artisanal, historical, and culturally pure spirit, as a product with meaning, with real substance.

Del Maguey blew life into a magical spirit that has gone from less than half a million liters in 2005 to double that number in 2015. Mezcal brands increased 48 percent between 2011 and 2014 to 362. Not long ago Mexicans, even Oaxacans, showed little interest in the spirit; today mezcalerias have opened in Mexico City, San Francisco, London, New York, and beyond. The art of Del Maguey transformed the global mezcal category from proletariat industrial to indigenous chic.

In 2017, Del Maguey, a company that sold 6,400 bottles its first year, sold a majority stake in the company to Pernod-Ricard, the French spirits conglomerate, with the provisos that Cooper still call the shots and that Pernod-Ricard protect Del Maguey's indigenous employees and their traditional practices.

See also COOPER, RON; MEXICO; MEZCAL; and PERNOD-RICARD.

López, Antonio. "A Rare Creation." *Santa Fe New Mexican*, February 15, 1998, D2.

"Press." Del Maguey website. https://delmaguey.com/press/ (accessed March 2, 2021).

Tomas Estes

Dewar's is a brand of blended scotch whisky currently owned by Bacardi. Started by wholesaler John Dewar Sr. in 1846 and grown by his sons, John Dewar Jr. and Tommy Dewar, the company has long been one of the largest blended scotch brands. After John Sr.'s death in 1880, John Jr. provided practical business savvy, while Tommy (1864–1930) traveled around the world to promote the brand and hire salespeople along the way. In 1894, Tommy published a book, *A Ramble Round the Globe*, recounting his journey, which furthered his and the brand's notoriety. Restless and curious, the highly quotable Tommy was among the first in England to own an automobile and commissioned the first motion picture advertisements for a spirits brand. Both brothers entered politics, but Tommy—made Baron Dewar in 1919—is most remembered as a conservative member of Parliament for his staunchly anti-immigrant positions.

The Dewar bothers expanded the business by starting or buying distilleries, first with Aberfeldy in 1896, which remains the primary component of Dewar's blends. After setbacks during the First World War and American Prohibition, the company eventually joined with the powerful Distillers Company Limited in 1925. See DISTILLERS COMPANY LIMITED (DCL). That company, which merged with Guinness to become United Distillers in the 1980s, eventually became the spirits behemoth Diageo in 1997. See DIAGEO. Dewar's was sold to Bacardi the next year in a large liquidation of redundant spirits brands and to satisfy antitrust requirements. In addition to Aberfeldy, Bacardi's John Dewar & Sons subsidiary currently owns the Macduff, Aultmore, Craigellachie, and Royal Brackla distilleries.

Dewar's has marketed its primary point of differentiation as aging whiskies further in barrels after marrying, as opposed to merely mixing the blends in tanks before bottling. Current offerings are the flagship white label, 12-, 15-, and 18-year varieties, as well as a "scratched cask" label, designed to have spicier, more robust barrel flavors typically associated with American whiskies.

See also BACARDI and WHISKY, SCOTCH.

Buxton, Ian. *The Enduring Legacy of Dewar's: A Complete History*. Glasgow: Angel's Share, 2010.

Dewar, Thomas R. *A Ramble Round the Globe*. London: Chatto & Windus, 1894.

Dewar's website. https://www.dewars.com/ (accessed March 2, 2021).

Difford's Guide website. https://www.diffordsguide.com (accessed March 2, 2021).

Roskrow, Dominic. *The World's Best Whiskies: 750 Essential Drams from Tennessee to Tokyo.* New York: Stewart, Tabori & Chang, 2010.

Colin Spoelman

Diageo is the world's largest spirits company. Its huge portfolio of brands includes numerous top sellers, including Smirnoff vodka, Tanqueray gin, Captain Morgan rum, Bulleit whisky, Crown Royal Canadian whisky, Don Julio tequila, and numerous other staples, as well as major beer and wine brands, including Guinness stout. Diageo's scotch holdings are particularly impressive: in addition to the Johnnie Walker and J&B brands, it owns twenty-nine distilleries in Scotland. The conglomerate's Italianate name is actually a mashup of the Greek word for "through," *dia*, and *ge*, the root of the Greek name for the earth.

The company, which is based in the United Kingdom, was formed on May 13, 1997, when Grand Metropolitan and Guinness merged. (Guinness dates back to 1759, when founder Arthur Guinness agreed to a now legendary nine-thousand-year lease for his eponymous Dublin brewery.) The deal, according to the *New York Times*, was worth $22.27 billion and the fifth largest merger in history at the time. The paper wrote that this was done out of necessity, since the two firms were facing "a steady decline in liquor consumption in their traditional markets." The *Times* went on to say, "The driving force behind the surprise announcement today is the generational divide that has plagued the liquor business for years. Basically, distilled spirits are popular with people 60 and older, while younger drinkers tend to prefer wine, wine coolers, beer or nonalcoholic drinks—a trend that does not bode well for future growth."

While the paper's forecast couldn't have been worse, the new combined company was certainly perfectly set up as spirits sales started to take off in the new century. Despite opposition from chief rival Seagram, the merger went through. To satisfy regulators, Diageo did have to sell off Dewar's and Bombay gin to Bacardi for $1.9 billion in March of 1998. See DEWAR'S and BACARDI. (That move

helped Bacardi grow from a top rum and vermouth producer to a major company in the wider liquor business.) Diageo also had to satisfy Bernard Arnault, the head of LVMH, who held a sizable piece of both Guinness and Grand Metropolitan. LVMH received $810 million as well as a lucrative distribution deal. At the start, the new company sold much more than just alcohol. Grand Metropolitan brought to the deal a number of major food brands, including, reportedly, nearly ten thousand Burger King locations, frozen-food line Green Giant, Pillsbury, and Häagen-Dazs Ice Cream. Despite initial promises not to sell off these businesses, over the next few years Diageo shed nearly all its non-alcohol investments and used some of the revenue generated to buy more liquor brands when Seagram liquidated its holdings.

It now has production facilities in more than thirty countries around the world. Diageo continues to grow by both creating new alcohol brands, such as Ciroc vodka, as well as acquiring other brands, such as Casamigos tequila. The company has also built large new distilleries for existing brands, including Bulleit's large new facility in Kentucky.

See also CAPTAIN MORGAN; CROWN ROYAL; DON JULIO; GORDON'S; JOHNNIE WALKER; SMIRNOFF; and TANQUERAY GORDON & CO.

Hays, Constance, L. "Diageo May Sell Dewar's to Bacardi for $1.9 Billion." *New York Times*, March 30, 1998.

Steinhauer, Jennifer. "International Business: LVMH Now Backs Merger of Grand Met and Guinness." *New York Times*, October 14, 1997.

Ibrahim, Youssef, M. 1997. Guinness and Grand Met in $22 Billion Deal. *The New York Times*, May 13.

Noah Rothbaum

Difford, Simon (1965–), is a British drinks entrepreneur and publisher of *Difford's Guide*, one of the world's most visited websites about spirits, cocktails, and bars. After an early venture in the frozen-fish business, Difford launched his first drinks wholesale company, Little Tipple, in 1989, before selling it to Coe Vintners in 1995. In 1997, he launched a magazine, *CLASS*, which quickly established itself as the voice of the UK bar trade, before selling it to William Reed Business Media in 2001 (it is now operated by Drinks International). Later the same year, Difford launched the Diffordsguide drinks book series, which includes Diffordsguide Cocktails, a compendium of more than three thousand recipes that remains a key reference book for bartenders worldwide. The digital version followed in 2010. Difford also founded London Cocktail Week, a festival now owned and operated by ABV Global.

See also COCKTAILS ON THE INTERNET.

Difford, Simon. *Diffordsguide Cocktails #11.* London: Diffordsguide, 2013.

Alice Lascelles

A **diffuser** extracts the sugars from shredded, sugar-bearing plant matter by circulating and recirculating hot water through it as it moves along a conveyor belt. This type of hydrolysis technology is traditionally used to extract high-sugar-concentration juice in the cane ethanol industry, but has been increasingly adopted by high-volume tequila makers in place of tahonas or presses. While its use is controversial because aficionados sometimes declare tequilas made with diffusers inferior products, diffusers appeared in the tequila industry in 1999–2003 in response to a real production problem: an agave shortage in the late 1990s. A diffuser allows distillers to extract more fermentable sugars from agave hearts than traditional methods allow. The raw or cooked agave is relieved of up to 99 percent of the agave sugars. When raw agave is used, the resulting fluid is transferred to an autoclave for cooking prior to fermentation. The diffuser can also be redesigned to use acid catalyst hydrolysis for saccharification, thereby eliminating the need of post-diffuser cooking. See COOKING. The further producers go from traditional methods, needless to say, the more controversial the use of a diffuser is.

See also AGAVE; SAUZA; and TEQUILA.

Maxwell, Khrys. "There May Be Too Much Agave in Your Tequila or Mezcal." MuchoAgave.com. http://www.muchoagave.com/the-difusor---there-may-be-too-much-agave-in-your-tequila-or-mezcal.html (accessed March 2, 2021).

Misty Kalkofen

dilution is the process of reducing the concentration or strength of a solution. In the context of cocktails and spirits, dilution most commonly refers to a lowering of alcoholic strength through the addition of water or other ingredients of lower proof.

Dilution has many effects on the organoleptic properties of a beverage and is an important tool of the bartender in preparing an alcoholic drink. Among the most significant effects are changes in viscosity, chemically sensed qualities such as alcoholic "burn," and the volatility of various aromatic molecules, all of which have a significant influence on perceived flavor. For this reason bartenders attempt to control for the effects of dilution in both design and execution of cocktails in order to produce a desired result.

The most common source of dilution in chilled drinks is ice, which achieves almost all of its cooling effect through melting. This is due to a concept of physics known as the heat of fusion, which is that it takes far more thermal energy to induce a phase change from solid to liquid than it does to raise the temperature of a substance to a similar extent without a phase change. Thus, melting ice chills a drink far more effectively than any material that does not melt. When ice is maintained at or near the temperature of freezing, another significant source of dilution is the liquid water already present on the surface of the ice.

In some instances, dilution may even cause certain dissolved substances to come out of solution. A familiar example of this phenomenon is the so-called louche effect produced when water is added to solutions such as absinthe containing a high concentration of dissolved hydrophobic oils, causing the oils to come out of solution and form a milky microemulsion.

See also LOUCHE.

Arnold, Dave. *Liquid Intelligence: The Art and Science of the Perfect Cocktail.* New York: W. W. Norton, 2014.
Liu, Kevin K. *Craft Cocktails at Home: Offbeat Techniques, Contemporary Crowd-Pleasers, and Classics Hacked with Science.* N.p.: Kevin Liu, 2013.
Moore, John T. "Mixing Matter Up: Solutions." In *Chemistry for Dummies.* Hoboken, NJ: Wiley, 2016.

Samuel Lloyd Kinsey

The **dip**, a mixture of whisky, syrup, and ice with orange peel, is one of the more obscure categories of mixed drinks, but in that very obscurity it serves to illustrate the difficulties of writing drink history and the assumptions upon which one must rely in the process. In 1884, a Philadelphia publisher issued a bartender's guide by one Albert Barnes, about whom nothing is known other than the fact that he worked at the Metropolitan Hotel in New York and the strong possibility that he was a Philadelphian. The *Complete Bartender* was, as many such books were, almost entirely plagiarized from Jerry Thomas (who had also worked at the Metropolitan). See THOMAS, JERRY. Tucked in at the end of his drinks section, however, are a few new, individual drinks, including a Whisky Dip and a Cape May Dip (a Whisky Dip with added Jamaica syrup). It would be easy to dismiss these as Barnes's own creations, save for a second book, *Mixology*, by Joseph L. Haywood (1866–1916).

Haywood, who tended bar and ran saloons in Wilmington, Delaware, included a "Whiskey Dip" and a Cape May Dipsey in his book, neither of them identical to Barnes's versions. They do not appear in any other book, or indeed anywhere else. There are two possible conclusions: either the dip was a genre of drink peculiar to the small triangle between Philadelphia, Wilmington, and Cape May, New Jersey, or Haywood simply copied the recipes from Barnes, directly or indirectly, editing them as he saw fit. Based on the evidence we have, there is no way to definitively state which is correct.

This situation is an extreme version of one common with many lesser-known drinks and categories of drinks. Because they keep appearing in drink books, modern mixographers often assume they enjoyed a wide and enduring popularity, when in fact it is just as possible that the drink lived only in those books and had either never caught on or had already seen its heyday come and go. Absent independent confirmation from other contemporary sources, to choose one option or the other is to jump to conclusions. As for the dip, we include it as a caution and as a tribute to either a part of America underexplored by drink historians or a pair of skilled, if obscure, bartenders enterprising enough to get their drinks in print. It is also, it must be noted, the first American iced drink on record to include scotch whisky.

Recipe (Whisky Dip): Combine in rocks glass with cracked ice: 60 ml scotch whisky and 5 ml pineapple syrup. Stir and twist orange peel over the top.

Barnes, Albert. *The Complete Bartender*. Philadelphia: Crawford, 1884.

Haywood, Joseph L. *Mixology*. Wilmington, DE: Press of the Sunday Star, 1898.

David Wondrich

distillate is the liquid product of distillation. Distillates that fall under the category of beverage alcohol are called spirits. See SPIRITS.

distillation is the process by which the ethanol in a fermented substance is extracted and concentrated through successive heating and cooling. See also DISTILLATION, PROCESS; and ETHANOL.

distillation, history. There exists no accurate, comprehensive, and detailed history of distillation as it applies to alcohol, and without considerable primary archaeological and archival research in South and East Asia, Africa, Europe, and Central and South America one cannot be written. It may be impossible even with such work: at its most basic level, distillation is so simple an idea that its gist can be conveyed in a single sentence: "Bring wine or beer to a boil, collect the first part of the steam, and let that cool." There are a great many ways to do this, few of them difficult to conceive and many of them not even requiring special equipment.

Indeed, it is possible to make crude spirits by cleverly arranging three ordinary clay pots, or even a pair of pots, a large roll of tree bark, and an agave leaf (as Carl Lumholtz found the Cora people of northern Mexico doing in the 1890s to make sotol). This makes the geographical origin of distillation and its early range very difficult to determine: as S. Mahdihassan asked in 1972, "When such objects are excavated who could interpret them as having been used in distillation?" It is thus at least technically possible that distillation goes back deep into the Bronze Age, if not earlier. Indeed, recent reevaluation of a style of pot widely distributed in second-millennium BCE archaeological sites from Mesopotamia through to southeastern Europe, in which the mouth is surrounded by an annular gutter that is provided with a spout, suggests that it may have been intended as the bottom half of an internal-condensation still. See STILL, POT. Certainly, modern experimental archaeologists have succeeded in using replicas of these to obtain spirits of a relatively high proof.

One cannot, however, build a history on potential. Until further archaeological research and chemical analysis tell us what these things were actually used for, we must set them aside to focus on historic times—although here, too, there are difficulties. In most languages, the dedicated vocabulary for distillation developed many centuries later than the technology for it, so that, for example, spirits are referred to as "waters" and "wines," and the act of distilling as "boiling," "burning," "steaming," or the like. Factor in distillation's long association with alchemy and the mystification and secrecy long associated with that art, and one has a situation where documentary references tend toward the veiled and the ambiguous.

Nonetheless, between archaeological and textual sources there are enough pieces of evidence, none of them decisive in their own right, that when taken together allow us to sketch out at least a rough and provisional picture of if not the birth of the art, then at least its childhood and adolescence. To do so we shall focus on three main regions, each of which had its own chain of development: South and East Asia, the Middle East and the Mediterranean, and Central and South America.

It is in the Indian subcontinent, China and its southern neighbors, and the East Indies that distillation seems to have been first fully adapted to the production of beverage alcohol. Certainly by the time European travelers first explored the area in numbers, they found it awash with distilled spirits, much of it being produced in stills identical to the ones used more than a thousand years before (what happened in between is largely unknown, due to the lack of a comprehensive history of distillation in Asia, one of the great holes in the scholarship of drink).

The strongest evidence of ancient distillation in India comes from the Gandharan civilization, in the Peshawar Valley at the headwaters of the Indus. At the Shaikhan Dheri archaeological site, the remnants of clay external-condensation "elephant's head" stills, along with numerous condenser/storage jars and drinking cups, provide particularly strong evidence when combined with other sources that, as F. R. Allchin wrote in 1979, "Distillation was known and used for the strengthening of alcohol in North India . . . since the fifth century" BCE. The elephant's

head itself is documented from the second century BCE (a piece of such a still from the first century BCE was also found in Mysore, in southwest India). This same type of still—a pot, a clay head with a spout, and a clay or bamboo tube that joins the head to a sealed clay receiver placed in a water-cooled basin, where the vapors condense into spirit—was used to make palm arrack on the east coast of India well into the twentieth century. See ARRACK and GANDHARAN STILL.

With the present state of archaeological research, it is unclear precisely what the Gandharans were distilling. The drinking cups found at Shaikhan Dheri were "marked with stamped corn-ears," according to Allchin, which would indicate a grain distillate (as does the textual evidence regarding surā, the ancient Vedic name for distilled spirit)—unless those "corn-ears" were actually the tops of sugar canes; the Gandharans were early masters of the art of extracting sugar from cane (it was one of the things Alexander the Great's troops found remarkable about them in the late fourth century BCE). In the seventh century CE, anyway, Xuanzang, the great Chinese Buddhist traveler, found people in the region drinking what was apparently some kind of sugar-cane distillate, and cane spirits were ubiquitous enough during the time of the Moghul sultan 'Ala'uddin Khalji (1296–1316) to earn his specific prohibition.

China, too, has an early history of using distilled spirits, although the approximate starting point is more difficult to fix. By the second century CE, at least, spirits made by freezing wine were common in the northwestern parts of China, while recent archaeological evidence suggests that spirits were also made through conventional distillation in the southeast. After some experimentation with an annular-gutter-type still (see below), China settled on a different, simpler style of internal-condensation still, where the spirit collected on the bottom of a concave basin of cold water that sealed the top of the still and dripped into a cup suspended or placed on a shelf beneath. By the Tang dynasty (618–907 CE), this "Mongol still," as it is known—the Mongols were great consumers of kumiss arrack—was in wide use, although in southern China, at least, it was soon supplanted by an improved version, where the collecting cup is provided with a tube leading out through the side of the still, thus allowing the distillation to be monitored as it proceeds. (By this point, grape spirits had been largely replaced by ones distilled from grain.) It is unsure precisely when the side-tube Chinese still was introduced; Lu and the Needhams posit that it was in use by the tenth century CE. It was certainly early enough to have spread throughout East Asia and the East Indies by the 1500s, where European explorers found it used to produce an array of rice, palm, and cane spirits.

Settled historical opinion holds that the distillation of alcohol was unknown in Greco-Roman antiquity and only reached Europe in the twelfth century CE, through Arab mediation. This hypothesis is predicated on one major assumption, that the well-documented use of stills by Hellenistic-era alchemists in Alexandria and elsewhere did not lead to wine distillation because those stills did not incorporate water-cooled condensation and thus ran too hot for recovering alcohol. This conclusion is backed up by the perceived absence in surviving Greek and Roman writings of references to distillation or its products.

Neither of these objections is conclusive. The type of still most favored by those early Greco-Egyptian alchemists, usually made of glass, has a large, separate head (an *ambix*, whence is derived the Arabic word that is the source of "alembic") with an annular gutter around the bottom that is fitted with an exit spout (in this case, the gutter and spout are part of the head of the still, rather than the pot as in earlier styles), so that the vapor rises through the narrow neck between the body and head, expands to fill the ambix, and, provided that the temperature is carefully controlled, partially condenses on its inside surface, running down the sides to collect in the gutter and drain out the exit tube. This is therefore an internal-condensation still, even though it has a separate head, but it is quite possible that the general idea of a separate still head with outflow pipe was derived from Gandharan stills, as the region was one of Alexander's conquests and later maintained a regular trade with the Roman Empire. Furthermore, a careful examination of the written record discloses numerous anomalies that seem to describe distilled spirit or its manufacture, from Pliny the Elder's claim about the famous Falernian wine that "alone among wines burns when exposed to flame" to a number of references to the use by religious mystery cults of a water that burns, a paradox according to the theory of the four elements prevalent at the time, and hence miraculous. As usual, though, none of these hints approach certainty, while it is incontrovertible that if spirit was being made, it was kept quiet, a trade secret or an alchemist's trick, and did not openly influence the culture of the Mediterranean world at large.

In Central America, the situation is similar in that if spirits were made in antiquity, they do not appear to have been in everyday use, being reserved rather for ritual or ceremonial consumption. The archaeological evidence is highly suggestive of the likelihood that distillation was indeed known, usually based on agave, with stills similar to the three-pot system used in ancient India, where the top pot or bowl is the cold-water condenser. Furthermore, in 1529, only eight years after the Spanish conquest of Mexico, Charles V issued an edict forbidding the natives from making agave distillates; that is far too short a time for a new technology to be adopted, mastered, and diffused to the point that it has become a problem, particularly considering the slow speed of communications at the time.

There's also the question of that technology. If the Mexicans learned distillation from the Spanish, one would expect that they would use Spanish-style external-condensation alembic stills. Yet even to this day, many rustic distillers in western Mexico make their mescal in Chinese-style, internal-condensation, side-tube stills (e.g., the bark-and-agave Cora still mentioned above). In the nineteenth century, some were even found still using the three-pot system. It has been posited that Mexicans learned this technology through the Spanish trade route between Mexico and the Philippines. Yet that was inaugurated only in 1564/5, which would mean that if the Mexican distillers condemned by Charles V learned to distill from the Spanish, they set aside that technology and arbitrarily replaced it with another, less efficient one. That makes little sense. If indeed the technology is pre-Columbian, the open question is whether the Mexicans developed it independently or learned it through pre-Columbian contact with Asia.

But we are getting ahead of ourselves. The Muslim conquest reached the headwaters of the Indus in the seventh and eighth centuries; at the same time, Arab scholars in Baghdad and elsewhere began delving into the technological parts of alchemy, drawing on surviving Hellenistic texts. Eventually, their texts and experiments began filtering into Europe. While the Arabs did not focus on distilling wine, the Europeans seized on that minor part of the art, possibly because it reinforced something already known, albeit darkly: there is good evidence that *aqua ardens*—"burning water"—was used by adherents of the widespread, heavily persecuted, and secretive neo-Gnostic Bogomil and Cathar heresies for ritual fire baptisms. In any case, distillation was one of the many new technologies that characterized Europe's "twelfth-century Renaissance," the revival in European civilization that laid the groundwork for the Renaissance of the fifteenth century.

In the late thirteenth century, finally, the focus of wine distillation moved from ritual to medicinal use. In this, it was sped along by a number of short treatises on the topic written in the Italian university town of Bologna. These (the most important of them was attributed to the Florentine physician Taddeo Alderotti) contained a number of other novelties. For one, *aqua ardens* was replaced by a new term, *aqua vitae*—"water of life." Instead of a single distillation, they advocated two or three redistillations, at least for the most efficacious medicine. Most importantly, they introduced a new modification of the still. Heretofore, Europeans had been using the air-cooled ambix, with its internal gutter. To this, the treatises added a new component: a "canale serpentinum," a serpentine outflow pipe that was cooled in a tub of water. (Michele Savonarola, whose detailed 1440s treatise on distillation deserves to be translated, distinguished between aqua vitae, made in the air-cooled still, and *aqua vitis*, "water of the vine," made in the new still with its coiled, vine-like condenser; he believed both were ancient.) The coil greatly increased the efficiency of the still: the heat no longer had to be so tightly controlled, and now no vapor could escape without condensation. Before long, the annular internal gutter disappeared from most still heads, simplifying their construction. The air-cooled ambix did not disappear entirely until the eighteenth century, but when it was used, it was expanded into a very large cone, the so-called rosenhut, that was big enough for the pointed top to remain cool during even prolonged distillations; alternatively, some turned the air-cooled ambix into a water-cooled one by surrounding its top with a water chamber; this was known as the "Moor's head" (that term was also later applied to a still head in the form of an inverted trapezoid). Ultimately, though, the simplicity and efficiency of external condensation won the day in Europe.

By the early fourteenth century, distillation in northern Italy had moved out of its experimental stage and into the commercial one; indeed, before long Michele Savonarola would be bemoaning that "aqua ardente" was being sold in the piazzas "to poor and miserable people." From Italy, it jumped the Alps and spread through the Rhine valley, in the process adding a new base material, grain, and also spread east and west around the Mediterranean. These early European spirits were not, as far as we know, sold unflavored. Rather, they relied on a "cover" to mask the taste of the raw spirit; a medicinally justified botanical that was pungent and, just as importantly, cheap. See COVER. In the Mediterranean, this was generally aniseed; the Germans and Dutch preferred juniper, while the Scandinavians, when distillation reached there, went with caraway or cumin seeds. Through the seventeenth century, European spirits were not distinguished by base material: grain, grape, or other fruit spirits were all known as aqua vitae or aqua ardens (or the vernacular equivalents, e.g., the Gaelic *usquebaugh* and the Spanish *aguardiente*) or "strong water."

In the seventeenth century, copper decisively displaced glass and ceramics as the main material for the construction of European stills. The century was transitional for European distilling in other ways, too: in some regions, double distillation became the norm for commercial production, yielding purer spirits and higher proofs—indeed, the very concept of proof appears to date to that period. In others, producers began deliberately maturing their spirit in oak barrels. See COGNAC. This may have been prompted by the example of imported spirits, which spent months and even years in the barrel before reaching Europe. By this point, of course, Europeans had colonized or at least established extensive commercial connections with large parts of Asia and the Americas. Everywhere they went in Asia, they found distillation practiced and spirits an ordinary part of commerce. See ARRACK, BATAVIA. Through the medium of punch, spirits became the long-haul sailor's drink: while beer and wine spoiled on long sea voyages, spirits mellowed, and they took up less space to boot.

During the eighteenth century, most European distilleries worked roughly along the same lines: they were family-run; they made a range of products—usually the dominant spirit of the region plus a number of standard cordials—and they were relatively small-scale, with two or three stills, seldom larger than 200 liters. They sold their product locally through tied houses or to rectifiers and brokers who handled all further sales. The great exception to this model was Britain, which, after the so-called gin craze of the early eighteenth century, used excise laws to tightly control the number of distilleries. As a result, the few that existed were massive affairs; in 1792, for instance, the firm of Hatch, Smith & Co. was distilling almost 40,000 liters of grain wash a day. This industrialization and its demand for efficiency led to rapid technological change. With copper, stills could be built in enormous sizes and complex shapes, including extremely wide, shallow ones that boiled very quickly, so that the still could be charged many times a day (this was useful when distillers were taxed on the internal volume of their stills).

Whatever the size of the distillery, most of the spirit made would have been of poor quality by modern standards: many distilleries still used only a single distillation, or if they did redistill their high wines, they combined them first with fresh wash. Tails were often used to reduce stronger spirits to proof, rather than distilled water. Worst of all, an extensive, although not comprehensive, survey of early distillers' manuals fails to disclose any consensus on the need (first mentioned by Alderotti) to discard the heads—the most alcoholic part of the distillation, but also the one with the greatest amount of toxic, foul-tasting, impurities—until the 1820s. After that, it is orthodoxy. See HEADS. Most do not mention it at all. (Of course, the practice might have been a part of the distillers' private lore, a rule-of-thumb deemed not worth mentioning or better reserved for the true adepts, but even the most empirically focused distillers, such as Étienne Munier, ignore it.) See MUNIER, ETIENNE.

The British industrial mentality soon caught on in America as well. There, however, innovation took a different turn: with copper expensive and spirits prices low, distillers began experimenting with wooden stills, coopered chambers into which live steam was injected and the alcohol collected by outflow pipes at the top leading to condensers (the Dutch-German chemist Johann Rudolph Glauber had already provided a diagram for a primitive steam-injection wooden still in 1646, although there is no evidence it was put in widespread use; it was, however, reproduced in John French's influential

1651 *Art of Distillation*). By the 1830s, this had been refined into the simple but effective chamber still, which used stacked distillation chambers to perform multiple distillations in the same still before sending the distillate out for condensation. Normally, the spirit went through a "dephlegmator" (known in America as a "thumper"), a simple device of French invention that fed the alcohol-rich vapor into a precondensing chamber where enough reflux occurred for the hot vapor to bubble through a layer of its own condensate, stripping out alcohol and leaving behind water and other compounds. See DOUBLER, THUMPER, KEG, OR RETORT. What reached the final condenser was thus twice distilled.

Meanwhile, in Britain, France, and the rest of northern Europe the possibilities of steam received a thorough exploration, both for heating traditional pot stills via coils or jackets and for injection directly into the still. This culminated in the development of the continuous-operation column still. See COLUMN STILL. This was invented by Jean-Baptiste Cellier-Blumenthal, a Frenchman, and perfected by, among others, Aeneas Coffey, an Irishman. See CELLIER-BLUMENTHAL, JEAN-BAPTISTE; and COFFEY, AENEAS. In operation, it is complex, yet the concept is simple: use steam to strip the alcohol out of the wash, and use the cold wash, dripping down through pierced horizontal plates, to condense the alcohol-bearing vapor. In practice, these new stills proved revolutionary: not only could they be run continuously, but they could be used to produce a steady stream of nearly pure spirit, stripped of heads, tails, and congeners.

This technology was so powerful as to be disruptive. Over the course of the nineteenth century it became clear that pot or even chamber stills could not compete in terms of price or absolute purity with the new "patent" stills, even with various efficiency-boosting tweaks. Yet they were not entirely replaced by the new technology: indeed, there are records of American rye whisky distilleries ripping out their column stills after a few years and reverting to chamber ones. Although through careful calibration column stills could be made to yield a rich spirit, that meant foregoing some of their advantages, and even then the resulting spirit was not as rich and flavorful as a well-made pot-distilled spirit.

By the beginning of the twentieth century, the spirits industry had developed a rough three-tier system. At its base were the people who more or less kept doing things the way they had always been done: fermenting, distilling in whatever version of the pot still people used in their part of the world, and selling the resulting spirit to their neighbors. Producers tended to be fairly small, although in the aggregate distilling activity was often quite extensive, as in, for example, China or Brazil. See BAIJIU and CACHAÇA. Some of these producers moved on to steam distillation, and some—often the same ones—sold their product in bulk. Their customers represented the second tier, merchants or négociants who purchased spirits made by others, matured, blended, and otherwise rectified it, and either bottled it and sold it under their own brands or sold it on to others who did so. Finally, there were the companies that distilled their own spirits and marketed them on a national or international level. These were highly efficient, technologically sophisticated commercial enterprises, selling for the most part either a pure column-still product or one that had its flavor bolstered by blending with pot-still products, although there were some traditional pot-distilled spirits whose production was successfully scaled up to meet the needs of international commerce (e.g., cognac). Many of these brands are still with us: e.g., Hennessy cognac, Bacardi rum, Dewar's whisky, and Gordon's gin. See SPIRITS TRADE, HISTORY OF.

The same general conditions persist in the twenty-first century, although there is an uptick in the number of small pot distilleries in America and Europe, while most of the local markets have been incorporated into the global spirits trade, and some of those formerly-local spirits have become mainstays of the trade. See TEQUILA. Distilling technology has changed relatively little, although computer control has allowed it to be operated more efficiently. The only true technological advance, vacuum distillation (which allows distilling at room temperatures), is actually not that new in principle, a less-extreme version having been used in Japan for shochu making for at least a century. See LOW-PRESSURE DISTILLATION. For other spirits, its best uses have yet to become apparent. At the very least it allows us to say that technologies from at least three millennia coexist in making the spirits we drink.

Allchin, F. R. "Stamped Tangas and Condensers: Evidence of Distillation at Shaikhan Dheri." In *South Asian Archaeology*, ed. M. Taddei, 755–797. Naples: Istituto Universitario Orientale, 1979.

Butler, Anthony R., and Joseph Needham. "An Experimental Comparison of the East Asian, Hellenistic, and Indian (Gandhāran) Stills." *Ambix*, July 1980, 69–76.

Forbes, R. J. *Short History of the Art of Distillation*. Leiden: E. J. Brill, 1948.

French, John. *Art of Distillation*. London: 1651.

Habib, Irfan. *The Economic History of Medieval India, 1200–1500*. New Delhi: Pearson-Longman, 2011.

Huang, H. T. *Science and Civilization in China*, vol. 6, part 5, *Fermentations and Food Science*. Cambridge: Cambridge University Press, 2000.

Mahdihassan, S. "The Earliest Distillation Units: Pottery in Indo-Pakistan." *Pakistan Archaeology*, 1972, 159–68.

Needham, Joseph, Gwei-Jen Lu, et al. *Science and Civilization in China*, vol. 5, part 4, *Chemistry and Chemical Technology*. Cambridge: Cambridge University Press, 1980.

Samorini, Giorgio. "Distillatori arcaici." Giorgio Samorini Network. http://samorini.it/site/archeologia/varie/distillatori-arcaici (accessed March 2, 2021).

Savonarola, Michele. *I trattati in volgare della peste e dell' acqua ardente*. Edited by Luigi Belloni. Rome: *Società Italiana di Medicina Interna*, 1953.

Wilson, C. Anne. *Water of Life*. Totnes, UK: Prospect, 2006.

Zizumbo-Villarreal, Daniel, Fernando González-Zozaya, Angeles Olay-Barrientos, Laura Almendros-López, Patricia Flores-Pérez, and Patricia Colunga-GarcíaMarín. "Distillation in Western Mesoamerica before European Contact." *Economic Botany* 63 (2009): 413–426.

David Wondrich

distillation, process. Distillation is a method of separating chemical components of a mixture into fractions based on their relative volatility, most commonly achieved by the application and removal of heat. A substance's volatility is related to its boiling point, but not precisely equivalent. In engineering, the pertinent physical property of a chemical is termed vapor pressure, which is defined as the pressure that it exerts at a given temperature when both liquid and vapor phases are present.

To better understand the practical meaning of this technical term, picture a perfectly sealed and insulated container, partially filled with only water and nothing else. At room temperature most of the water molecules will be in liquid form, sloshing around at the bottom of the container, but some will have enough energy to escape the surface of the liquid and bounce around in the empty space above it. The individual molecules will be constantly exchanging places, some careering into the surface of the liquid to be buried deep while knocking others free from their surrounding fellows in the process, but the total number of molecules in the liquid space and molecules in the vapor space will stay relatively constant.

The vapor pressure is a way of expressing, for an individual chemical, how many of the molecules will be in the liquid phase and how many will be in the gas phase. If a substance has a low vapor pressure, most of it will be a liquid. If a substance has a high vapor pressure, most of it will be a gas. Vapor pressure is a physical property (i.e., it can be measured), but it is not a constant one. When the temperature increases, vapor pressure goes up as well. The increased temperature gives molecules more energy, allowing more of them to vaporize—to make the leap from the surface of the liquid and become a gas. A liquid boils when its vapor pressure is equal to the air pressure in the room. Liquids with high vapor pressure, commonly described as volatile, will boil at lower temperatures than liquids with low vapor pressure. When a liquid is boiling, the transition from liquid to gas will occur not just on the surface but throughout the whole bulk of the liquid (picture the gas bubbles of a rolling boil).

The relationship between liquid and gas becomes more interesting and complex when the liquid is made up of more than one component. Consider an equal mixture of two different components, such as ethanol and water, where one has a low vapor pressure and the other has a high vapor pressure. See ETHANOL. Although the total number of molecules is the same, the relative concentrations are different in the vapor space and the liquid space. The higher vapor pressure component (ethanol) dominates the vapor space, while the lower vapor pressure component (water) dominates the liquid.

If the mixture is unequal, that will also impact the relative concentrations in the vapor space. If there is not very much alcohol present in the ethanol/water mixture, then it will not matter how high its vapor pressure is; both the liquid and the vapor space will still be dominated by the component that is present in greatest abundance.

Understanding how vapor pressure, temperature, and concentration allow us to predict the gas and liquid makeup of a mixture is the foundation of distillation competency. The process of distillation generally manipulates temperature (and sometimes pressure) in order to physically separate components of a mixture based on their relative volatility.

Consider a sample that begins as a 50/50 mixture of two substances that have different volatilities (such as ethanol and water). When heat is applied to that mixture, the more volatile substance will vaporize more quickly, and its concentration in the vapor space will be higher than the less volatile substance. A still provides a way for this vapor to escape the pot to where the heat can be removed, so that the vapor cools and condenses back into a liquid and can be collected, or a cool surface within the pot where the vapor can condense and be drawn off.

The liquid that started as a 50/50 mixture has now been separated into two containers, one that contains mostly the less volatile component and one that contains most of the more volatile component. After this single distillation, the substances have been at least partially separated from one another. This is an example of a batch distillation in a pot still, where one single batch of liquid was placed into the pot still, then the distillation was conducted to produce a single batch of distillate. See STILL, POT.

A column still acts like a series of pot stills placed on top of each other, with the liquids vaporizing and condensing over and over again on each tray inside the column. This setup allows column stills to achieve greater distillation efficiency. See STILL, CONTINUOUS.

Distillation is a versatile and simple means of separation, but its applicability is limited. It does not work well for separating components whose vapor pressures are very similar. It is not efficient for separating components whose vapor pressures are so low that it takes an excessive amount of energy to vaporize them (perhaps even so much energy that it damages the component) or whose vapor pressures are so high that it takes a lot of energy to get them to condense into liquid. Some molecules also have a tendency to be attracted to one another, and the more volatile molecule can sometimes "carry" the less volatile one up into the vapor space, making it difficult to separate them by distillation. In these cases, other means of physical separation might be more appropriate, such as fil-tration, absorption, adsorption, membrane separation, or extraction.

See also AZEOTROPE; DISTILLATION, HISTORY; and REFLUX.

Kiss, Anton Alexandru. *Advanced Distillation Technologies: Design, Control and Applications*. New York: John Wiley & Sons, 2013.

McCabe, Warren L., Julian C. Smith, and Peter Harriott. *Unit Operations of Chemical Engineering*. Boston: McGraw-Hill, 2005.

Nicole Austin

Distillers Company Ltd (DCL) was conceived in 1877 as a primarily defensive alliance of six of the largest Scottish grain whisky distillers. It grew to become the largest whisky company in the world by the 1930s, with a stable of world-leading blended scotches, and gins such as Gordon's, Booth's, and Tanqueray, in addition to specialties such as Pimm's Cup. See BOOTH's; GORDON's; PIMM's CUP; and TANQUERAY GORDON & CO. This was a reluctant transformation for a business that had avoided participation in the branded spirits market, seeing itself as a stabilizing force in the production of both blended scotch and gin through its controlling influence in the grain whisky and neutral spirit market. That role was imperiled by the 1898 "Pattison Crash," however, in which the failure of the highly leveraged independent whisky bottler Pattison, Elder & Co. brought down a number of distilling companies. Though DCL was fully aware of Pattison's circumstances several years before its final failure, the company was still involved with Pattison and suffered from its collapse. Between that, the hostile post–World War I fiscal environment and the increasing cost of advertising by the main competing blending houses, DCL found that its path to survival led through branded spirits. This led to the acquisition of Scottish Malt Distillers, the Distillers Finance Corporation (with extensive Irish whisky interests), Tanqueray Gordon & Co, and eventually the "Great Amalgamation" of 1925. This saw John Dewar & Sons, James Buchanan & Co., and John Walker & Sons merge with the DCL, which had already acquired the Haig blending business; White Horse Distillers and MacDonald Greenlees were soon to follow, as were Booth's Distilleries (including William Sanderson) in 1937. See DEWAR's and JOHNNIE WALKER.

Overseen by William H. Ross (1862–1944), in effect the architect of today's scotch whisky industry, the "Great Amalgamation" was in part a visionary piece of business rationalization in the face of increasingly hostile trading conditions. However, the management structure that was put in place ("The respective companies will continue to conduct their business on the same individual lines as formerly"), with a top-heavy DCL main board representing all the once-competing interests, left much to be desired, and eventually became a recipe for ossification.

The 1920s and 1930s saw the company consolidate its leadership position in scotch in the domestic and key export markets, notably the United States, where the importance of Prohibition to its long-term success, euphemistically referred to as "the Special Trade," cannot be understated. At the same time Ross welcomed the advent of "the alcohol age" over the "whisky age" as the company began a widespread program of diversifications into motor fuels, pharmaceuticals, and a range of chemical products, much through the acquisition or licensing of German patents, championed and masterminded by Sir Alexander Walker (1869–1950). As such, the company became increasingly focused on the Anglo Persian Oil Company, ICI, and IG Farben as its competitive set. The sometimes mixed success of these ventures also set the precedent that led to the company signing a deal in 1957 with the German company Chemie *Grünenthal* to distribute the drug thalidomide in the United Kingdom. Prescribed by GPs for morning sickness, the drug had a devastating impact on fetal development, and the subsequent mishandling of the affair by the DCL in the face of a concerted campaign by the *Sunday Times* would cast a long and damaging shadow over the business.

By this time the DCL had become a bastion of the British business establishment, ensconced in St James Square (the birthplace of the Queen Mother, where she was royally entertained to lunch by the DCL main board each year on her birthday) with the offices of its constituent blending house (by now mostly bereft of any family connections) dotted around it in the streets of London's club land. But its reputation was mortally wounded by thalidomide, and the staunchly conservative approach to the scotch business saw its share of the UK market fall from 54 percent to 15 percent in the ten years leading to 1984, as brands like Bells and Famous Grouse stole share, and the first million case selling brand in the United Kingdom, Haig Gold Label, almost disappeared from shelves. They refused to take the rise of single malts seriously and until the mid-1980s staunchly held out against encouraging public visitors at distilleries (one long-serving manager commented that the only sign at his office door said "Fuck off"). Similarly, its position in the United States was under threat from "upstart" lighter Prohibition-era blends such as J&B, Cutty Sark, and Chivas Regal. With an elderly board of questionable talent or energy—largely domiciled among the manicured golf courses of the Home Counties—who rarely, if ever, visited Scotland (or for that matter markets, apart from the occasional mid-winter "fact finding missions" to the Cape), the DCL was completely out of touch, and more often than not out for lunch.

The arrival of John Connell (1924–2014) as chairman in 1983, who, coming from Tanqueray Gordon was the first non-whisky man to hold the position, came too late to stave off the circling predators, despite attempts at innovation in scotch and business acquisitions within the drinks world. The final indignity was that the once-great leviathan of scotch was toppled in 1987 by an illegally financed takeover, which saw the principal players jailed and the chief architect of the affair (Ernest Saunders) experience a miraculous recovery from Alzheimer's disease. What emerged from the ruins under the ownership of Guinness was United Distillers & Vintners, a tougher, marketing-focused business that brought a new spirit of innovation to the scotch category, in both blends and malts. And in turn, following the merger of Grand Metropolitan and Guinness ten years later, Diageo was born. But that is another story altogether.

Today, of the original six distilleries that formed DCL (Cambus, Cameronbridge, Carsebridge, Glenochil, Kirkliston, and Port Dundas), only Cameronbridge is still in operation.

Craig, H. Charles. *The Scotch Whisky Industry Record.* Dumbarton, UK: Index, 1994.

Pugh, Peter. *Is Guinness Good for You?* London: Financial Training, 1987.

Weir, R. B. *The History of the Distillers Company, 1877–1939.* Oxford: Clarendon, 1995.

Nicholas Morgan

distillers' dried grains (DDG) is an industry term for distilling waste that has been dried for use as animal feed. When cooked fermented grain mash passes through a column still, it leaves behind spent grains (also called whole or thick stillage): protein-rich, starch-depleted grain and yeast residues. Fed to livestock, these residues are a source of easily digestible amino acids (protein), fat, and minerals. Early whisky makers often maintained feedlots or sold their residues to local farmers as a side business. Today, these residues are typically dried and then processed into animal feed. After exiting the column still as a slurry depleted of alcohol, the mass passes through a centrifuge that separates solid and liquid components. The resulting liquid (called thin stillage) is concentrated in evaporators, then mixed back with the previously removed solids (called wet cake) and dried, generally using heat. This mixture is known as distillers' dried grains with solubles (DDGS). As in the past, this co-product of distillation is an additional income source. Drying reduces handling costs and spoilage, making distant and export sales lucrative, since volumes by weight roughly equal those of the alcohol produced from the original grain.

Experienced distillers carefully monitor the color and aroma of their distillers' dried grains, which should be sweet and golden caramel in color. Changes in color or aroma alert them to the possibility of overheating during drying, which upsets the nutrient balance, or of incomplete fermentation, which in turn results in lower outputs of alcohol.

Jacques, K. A., T. P. Lyons, and D. R. Kelsall. *The Alcohol Textbook,* 4th ed. Nottingham: Nottingham University Press, 2003.

Davin de Kergommeaux

Don César is a family-owned brand of pisco from Tacna, located in the southernmost district of Peru near the Chilean border. Don César produces single-varietal pisco, called *pisco puro,* from a highly aromatic grape, Italia, as well as *acholado* blends of negra criolla, Italia, and quebranta grapes and a partially fermented distillate, *mosto verde*, from negra criolla and Italia grapes. Renowned bartender Gary "Gaz" Regan has professed his fondness for Don César in pisco cocktails, especially the Pisco Sour.

Don César Alejandro Chiarella Arce and his wife, Violeta Yacub de Chiarella, founded Bodega San Antonio in 1982. Their son and current manager, Cesar Antonio Chiarella Yacub, recounted the story of the bodega's creation in a 2007 interview. In 1981, Yacub recounted, a visiting friend from Yugoslavia named Giovanni Terlevick saw that the Chiarellas had negra criolla grapes on their table at home as well as a small still kept for decoration in their Rancho San Antonio restaurant, where he had eaten lunch. Realizing that they had all the component parts to complete both fermentation and distillation, Giovanni asked the elder César to try a run. The next day he did. Under advisement from a local producer and friend, Don Pedro Liendo Potales, Don César implemented a full distillery, and the brand Don César was born. Don César was one of the first artisanal Peruvian piscos to appear in the American market and helped pave the way for many others.

See REGAN, GARY; PISCO; and PISCO SOUR.

Heimark, Katrina, trans. 'Guest Producer.' *El Piscos del Peru* (blog), April 8, 2007. http://www.elpiscoesdelperu.com/web/index.php?ver_opt=det_noticia&id=621 (accessed March 2, 2021).

Regan, Gary. *The Cocktailian Chronicles: Life with the Professor*. London: Jared Brown, 2010.

Derek Brown

Don Julio is a brand of tequila produced at the La Primavera distillery (registered as NOM 1449) in the municipality of Atotonilco al Alto, Jalisco, Mexico. Founder Don Julio González (1925–2012) started working in his uncle's distillery at the age of seven and purchased his first distillery in 1942 at the age of seventeen by securing a loan from a local businessman. Construction began on the current distillery in 1947 and González registered his first brand of tequila four years later, a mixto named Tres Magueyes. See MIXTO. In 1985, the 100 percent blue agave Tequila Don Julio was introduced

to family and friends in honor of Don Julio's sixtieth birthday. Two years later, Tequila Don Julio launched in its unique short, square, hand-blown glass bottle in Mexico. The US release followed in 1995. González entered into a partnership with the giant Seagram's organization in 1999, staying on as master distiller. See SEAGRAM COMPANY LTD. He retired in 2003, naming Enrique de Colsa his successor as master distiller. At the same time, Diageo, which had acquired the brand with the collapse of Seagram's, sold a 50 percent share to the José Cuervo company, taking it back in 2015 in exchange for the Bushmills Irish whisky brand. See DIAGEO; JOSE CUERVO; and SPIRITS TRADE, HISTORY OF.

Tequila Don Julio is widely respected for its horticultural practices. Currently Tequila Don Julio owns approximately eight million agave plants that are growing on leased land. The use of leased land allows for soil replenishment through crop rotation. Once harvested, the agave is steam-cooked for seventy-two hours in masonry ovens. The sugars are extracted in a mechanical mill before a twenty-four- to thirty-hour fermentation using proprietary yeasts in stainless steel fermenters. Tequila Don Julio is distilled twice in copper pot stills. Don Julio offers four American white-oak-aged expressions: an eight-month reposado; an eighteen-month añejo; Tequila Don Julio 1942, aged for twenty-four to thirty months; and Tequila Don Julio 70 Crystal Añejo, which is aged for eighteen months followed by charcoal filtering.

See also AGAVE; MEXICO; and TEQUILA.

Zandona, Eric. *The Tequila Dictionary*. London: Mitchell Beazley, 2019.

Misty Kalkofen

dop is South African slang for a tot—a short drink—of wine or spirit of any kind. Historically, it was particularly applied to pomace brandy, commonly known as "dop brandy" or "Cape dop." See DRAM; POMACE BRANDY; and SOUTH AFRICA.

Anna Archibald

Dorelli, Giampiero "Peter" (1940–), has worked in the bar industry for over fifty years.

Trained initially in accounting, Dorelli left Rome and a future in the family banking business when he was eighteen to start a new life in the United Kingdom. After spending some time working in hospitality in the English countryside, Dorelli landed a position with the Savoy Hotel Group in Soho, London, where he made a name for himself as a bartender at the Pebble Bar at Stones Chop House. Here he honed his craft making cocktails and charming the clientele for fifteen years (while there, he earned drinks writer John Doxat's "personal trophy" for his "99.9 percent perfect" Dry Martinis). After the bar closed, he was offered a position at the Savoy Hotel's American Bar, where he became infamous as a bartender of extraordinary skill, wit, and charm. Dorelli is a perfectionist and a man who truly loves his craft. Since leaving the Savoy, Dorelli has taken on an educational role in the UKBG, judging competitions and continuing to stir many a perfectly executed cocktail. See UNITED KINGDOM BARTENDERS GUILD (UKBG).

Doxat, John. *Stirred, Not Shaken*. London: Hutchinson, 1976.

Peter Dorelli website. https://www.peterdorelli.com (accessed March 3, 2021).

Tony Conigliaro

double distillation is a common spirits distillation process incorporating two runs through a still (usually a pot still), with the second yielding a distillate that has a significantly higher concentration of ethanol than the first. See also DISTILLATE; DISTILLATION, PROCESS; and ETHANOL.

doubler, thumper, keg, and **retort** are all terms for a reflux chamber inserted between the still and the condenser to perform what is in effect a second distillation (hence the American term, "doubler"). It usually takes the form of a cylindrical chamber with the vapor pipe from the still entering through the top and running almost to the bottom of the chamber. Vapor enters from the still and expands to fill the chamber, allowing reflux to occur and water and other heavier compounds to condense. As these build up, they soon rise above the mouth of the inflow pipe, and the incoming vapor then bubbles through the liquid, leaving behind more condensate and taking any alcohol that has remained behind with it through an exit pipe to the condenser. Usually there is a third pipe leading back to the still so any excess condensate can be redistilled.

In the nineteenth century, "retorts" were commonly used with the pot stills making rum in Jamaica and elsewhere in the British Caribbean. These were usually paired, with the "low wines" retort receiving vapors from the wash still, rectifying them, and passing them on to the "high wines retort" for further purification before going to the condenser. With this setup, a full, high-proof distillation could be accomplished in one pass. Single retorts were also used for making some scotch malt whiskies. Retorts are still sometimes used in the Caribbean, but not in Scotland.

In North American practice, the column stills used for making straight whiskies are generally run "dirty"—that is, tapped in such a manner that the vapor coming off of them is less pure and lower proof than the machine is capable of producing—and doublers or "thumper kegs" (so called from the sound made by the vapor bubbling through the condensate) have traditionally been used to partially rectify that vapor. Many bourbon and rye distilleries still use them. They were also standard with the three-chamber still.

See also DISTILLATION, PROCESS; STILL, POT; and STILL, THREE-CHAMBER.

Wiley, H. W. *Foreign Trade Practices in the Manufacture and Exportation of Alcoholic Beverages and Canned Goods*. Washington, DC: Government Printing Office, 1906.

Willkie, Herman F., and Joseph A. Prochaska. *Fundamentals of Distillery Practice*. Louisville, KY: Jos. E. Seagram & Sons, 1943.

Wray, Leonard. *Practical Sugar Planter*. London: Smith, Elder, 1848.

David Wondrich

double straining, also known as "fine straining," is the technique of passing a shaken or stirred cocktail through either a Hawthorne or julep strainer as well as a fine mesh strainer suspended above the glass to prevent pulp, fruit, herbs, and ice chips from entering a finished cocktail. Not to be confused with passing fresh-pressed citrus through a chinois to remove pulp before service, double straining is recommended for muddled preparations, which produce flecks of herbs and organic residue that are small enough to pass through a traditional strainer yet large enough to affect the clarity of a cocktail. Some bartenders have taken it to an extreme, double straining even clear, stirred drinks. With a good julep strainer, that is not necessary.

Morgenthaler, Jeffrey. *The Bar Book*. San Francisco: Chronicle, 2014.

Arnold, David. *Liquid Intelligence*. New York: Norton, 2014.

Jim Meehan

Downey, Jonathan (1965–), is a bar owner who, beginning in 1997, became an influential figure in the early years of the London cocktail revival. He was unique in the movement in that he was not bartender or restaurateur but a lawyer and businessman. He was an exacting taskmaster, and his bars achieved a reputation for a high level of cocktail quality and service, in part because he enlisted into partnership first Dick Bradsell, the leading London bartender of the time, and later Dale DeGroff, who held equal status in the United States. See BRADSELL, DICK; and DEGROFF, DALE. After visiting the New York cocktail bar Milk & Honey during its early days, he teamed up with owner Sasha Petraske to open, in 2002, a London branch of the bar, thus introducing the haute speakeasy concept to the United Kingdom. In just a few years, he commanded an empire that included the Player; Trailer Happiness, an influential modern tiki bar; Sosha, a club in the east London neighborhood of Shoreditch, which later became a cocktail hotbed; and his cornerstone, Match. With the 2020 Covid-19-related closure of Milk & Honey, the only dedicated cocktail bar remaining in his portfolio, most of Downey's energies are now devoted to Street Feast, a company that creates enclosed, open-air eating-and-drinking night markets in disused industrial spaces throughout London, and to advocating for the restaurant industry.

See also MILK & HONEY and PETRASKE, SASHA.

Simonson, Robert. *A Proper Drink: How a Band of Bartenders Saved the Civilized World*. New York: Ten Speed, 2016.

Robert Simonson

draff is the Scottish term for the spent grain left after the fermented wort has been drawn off for making whisky. It is often used as feed for farm animals. See DISTILLERS' DRIED GRAINS (DDG); WHISKY, SCOTCH; and WORT.

dram, originally a liquid measure equaling one-eighth of an ounce (3.7 ml), saw its meaning extended by the late 1500s to encompass any single dose of liquid taken medicinally. Since such things were often spirituous, by the 1620s or so the term was being applied to any single serving of spirits, whether medicinal or recreational. This soon led to it being stretched again to cover the spirit being served. Thus in 1666 the Virginia Assembly, setting regulations for the colony, divided spirits into locally made "Virginia drams" (e.g., peach brandy), imported grape brandy, and English spirits.

A century later, we find the Pennsylvania German farmer-distiller Friedrich H. Gelwicks recording sales of "ebbeldram" (i.e., apple dram) and "korntram" (*korn* dram), by which he meant rye whisky. By then, in America at least, "dram shop" was a common, somewhat pejorative, synonym for tavern, while a "dram drinker" was a habitual or even degenerate spirits drinker. As a result of these negative connotations, the term eventually fell out of American usage. In the United Kingdom and Ireland, however, "dram" is still used, generally with affection, for a glass of spirit.

Like the modern "shot," which covers roughly the same lexical territory, a dram was elastic in quantity. One can nonetheless posit that most drinks to which the term was applied would fall into a range of 15–75 ml.

See also PEACH BRANDY and WHISKY, RYE.

Henning, William W. *The Statutes at Large . . . of Virginia*, vol. 2. New York: 1823.

Neff, Larry M., and Frederick S. Weiser. *Friedrich Heinrich Gelwicks: Shoemaker and Distiller.* Breinigsville, PA: Pennsylvania German Society, 1979.

David Wondrich

The **DrinkBoy Forum**, active from 1999 to 2008, was an online message board initiated by cocktail enthusiasts under the guidance of Microsoft employee Robert Hess on Microsoft's MSN Groups web service. This forum was where many participants in the nascent "cocktail renaissance" of the late 1990s and early 2000s found their voices, and it was the place where many of those people first met each other. See COCKTAIL RENAISSANCE.

The first wave of forum participants included Robert Hess, Gary Regan, Mardee Regan, Bob "Magoo" McCarthy, Kevin "Tantris" Brown, Bryan Cabrera, Martin Doudoroff, Marko "Kristian" Susimetsä, Robert Semmes, and Steve Visakay. They were soon joined by Audrey Saunders, Cheryl Charming, Rafael Ballesteros, occasionally Dale DeGroff, and also Ted "Dr. Cocktail" Haigh, who had been leading a similar group within the America Online network.

A second wave of active correspondents began appearing around 2002, including Chuck Taggart, David Wondrich, Kevin Verspoor, Fernando Castellon, Philip Duff, Eben Klemm, Angus Winchester, Darcy O'Neil, Chris Carlsson, Adam Elmegirab, Jared Brown and Anistatia Miller, Gonçalo de Sousa Monteiro, and Joerg Meyer, along with many others, some of whom were silent observers.

Popular topics over the years included blue curaçao, maraschino cherries and alternatives, the Margarita, the Singapore Sling, molecular mixology, infusions and tinctures, the Aviation, grenadine, bitters, flavored vodka, Jerry Thomas, Harry Johnson, muddlers, and contemporary bars and bartenders. A couple of bitters brands, the Museum of the American Cocktail, and the annual Tales of the Cocktail event were all inspired or influenced by the milieu. See MUSEUM OF THE AMERICAN COCKTAIL and TALES OF THE COCKTAIL.

In 2008, with the termination of the MSN Groups web service, the DrinkBoy forum was retired and officially replaced by the new Chanticleer Society message board, loosely affiliated with the Museum of the American Cocktail.

See also HESS, ROBERT; and COCKTAILS ON THE INTERNET.

Martin Doudoroff

dry is a sensory descriptor mostly understood intuitively because it has attributes that cut across the multisensory perception of flavor. The term's origins are in winespeak. When a wine is fermented to *dryness,* all sugar is metabolized into alcohol. When two dry wines are compared, the wine with more acidity is typically perceived as *dryer,* though different acids exert different perceived forces. When the acidities are neck and neck, the influence of aroma starts to become more prominent because of a tendency to categorize olfaction in terms of gustation. Other sensory contributors like tannin can exert influence on dryness until the word is abandoned for something more salient like bitter or astringent. Dry vermouths are not *bone dry* but have the minimum of added sugar to enhance their aroma. Dry martinis are defined by an absence of dry vermouth, despite vermouth contributing attributes that may make one wine seem dryer than other.

In spirits, dry is most typically associated with gin and rum categories. Dry gins have no added sugar or appreciable acidity, but the aromas in them that draw the most attention are those that converge with gustatory dryness—piney juniper, lemon peel, black pepper. Rums marketed as dry have an absence of both added sugar and weighty aromas that contribute to body. *Dry* may be chosen over *light* because it connotes sophistication.

Dry when applied to a cocktail generally denotes the use of dry vermouth as a mixer or, in the case of mid-twentieth-century Martinis, the absence of any vermouth at all. See MARTINI. It is also applied to cocktails that downplay sweet elements or suppress them entirely. Drying strategies can be applied to cocktail recipes by replacing a spirit that is perceived as sweet, such as bourbon or cognac, with another perceived as relatively dryer, such as rye whisky or mezcal. Even though the actual sugar content of the drink may remain the same, its perceived sweetness will change. Sour drinks can be made dryer by either decreasing their sugar or increasing their acidity.

See also TASTING SPIRITS and TEXTURE AND MOUTHFEEL.

Auvray, Malika, and Spence. "The Multisensory Perception of Flavor." *Consciousness and Cognition* 17 (2008): 1016–1031.

Stephen Shellenberger

dry shake, also more obscurely known as the "mime shake," is a technique devised to emulsify egg whites by shaking all the ingredients without ice. All the ingredients are first put into a cocktail shaker and shaken vigorously without ice. This is then immediately followed by a second, more traditional shake that utilizes ice. Agitating all of the ingredients together in this manner enables the proteins in the eggs to denature and aerate, creating a foam akin to a meringue. Excluding ice from the process allows for more time to unfurl the protein bonds of the eggs without the limiting factor of dilution. Though not the creator of this technique—the instructions for the Hotel Georgia cocktail in Ted Saucier's 1951 *Bottoms Up* noted that the technique gives the drink "a nice top," and a version of it had been recommended the year before by Henri Babinski to take the funky edge off of "paraty," or cachaça—bartender Chad Solomon, formerly of New York's Milk & Honey and Pegu Club, discovered it independently and helped popularize the dry shake in the early 2000s. See MILK & HONEY and PEGU CLUB. Popular thought maintains that the dry shake produces a loftier foam than the traditional shake with ice, although in recent years the "reverse dry shake" has seen an uptick in usage.

See also EGGS.

Ali Bab [Henri Babinski]. *Gastronomie pratique*, 9th ed. Paris: Flammarion, 1950, s.v. "Cocktail au paraty."
Kamholz, Roger. "Is There a Better Way to Make an Egg White Cocktail?" *Punch*, March 13, 2017. https://punchdrink.com/articles/how-to-make-egg-white-cocktail-reverse-dry-shake-flip/ (accessed March 3, 2021).
Morgenthaler, Jeffrey. *The Bar Book*. San Francisco: Chronicle, 2014.
Saucier, Ted. *Bottoms Up*. New York: Greystone, 1951.

Chloe Frechette

The **Dubonnet Cocktail**, in its most common form a mix of equal parts Dubonnet (the French aperitif wine) and gin, is yet another New York City creation, this one from the first decade of the twentieth century. Drink lore has long maintained that it was a creation of New York's fashionable and sophisticated Café Martin. In this case, at least, that lore may well be correct: Jean-Baptiste Martin (1857–1918), one of the two French-born brothers who ran the cafe, was certainly a heavy promoter of Dubonnet and various drinks made with it, and when he left the business in 1912 when it moved uptown from Madison Square, it was to become Dubonnet's American importer.

In any case, the Dubonnet Cocktail is first recorded in New York, in 1904, along with what has become its twin, the Waldorf-Astoria bar's Zaza Cocktail, christened after the 1899 Broadway musical of the same name, then in revival. See WALDORF-ASTORIA. In fact, it was the Zaza that originally owned the Dubonnet-and-gin formula, while the Dubonnet Cocktail mixed the aperitif with either brandy or sherry, depending on whether you ordered it in New York or San Francisco; it wouldn't be until the next decade that gin came into the formula.

The Dubonnet Cocktail was enormously popular in the 1910s, both in the United States and in Europe. While its European popularity continued unabated until World War II, it was seldom seen in America during Prohibition but vigorously revived there during the 1930s. During the war, it disappeared in Europe but, thanks to the manufacture of Dubonnet in the United States, was quite popular there. After the war, it lived on mostly in the pages of drink books, and one encounters it infrequently anywhere else. It has not played a role in the cocktail revival, in large part because until recently the American market got only the same domestically manufactured substitute it got during World War II, which lacked the cachet of other aperitifs, all imported. This was recently upgraded, albeit still being made domestically; it is too soon to tell if a revival in the Dubonnet Cocktail will ensue.

Recipe: Stir with cracked ice 45 ml Dubonnet, 45 ml London dry gin, and (optional) 2 dashes orange bitters. Strain into a chilled cocktail glass and twist lemon peel over the top.

Boothby, William T. "Cocktail." In *The World's Drinks and How to Mix Them*. San Francisco: San Francisco News Co, 1907.

Crockett, Albert Stevens. *Old Waldorf Bar Days*. New York: Aventine, 1931.

Muckensturm, Louis. *Louis' Mixed Drinks*. Boston: Caldwell, 1906.

"Spring Fashions in Drinks." *New York Times*, May 8, 1904.

David Wondrich

Duffy, Patrick Gavin

Duffy, Patrick Gavin (1868–ca. 1955), born Patrick Joseph Duffy, is best remembered today as the author of the widely influential 1933 *Official Mixer's Manual*, which he wrote under the Patrick Gavin Duffy pseudonym, for whatever reason. Born in Ireland, he started his career at New York's Ashland House, one block from Madison Square, in 1884, at age sixteen, eventually becoming head bartender. His clientele included actors, boxers, circus folk, and horse traders, along with some of the biggest celebrities of his day: Oscar Wilde, John L. Sullivan, J. P. Morgan, Richard Croker, and Maurice Barrymore. An advocate of fastidious service and white-jacket formality, he was described by a contemporary as "a natty little fellow with waxed moustache and vandyke, always wearing a carnation bud in his coat lapel." In 1893, he hopped across Fourth Avenue to open the Lyceum Cafe, adjoining Daniel Frohman's Lyceum Theater. From that establishment, he provided E. H. Sothern's next-door rehearsals with two-gallon bowls of his original Brandy Punch, as described in his *Manual*. Other original recipes include the Blinker, DF, Janet Howard, Montauk Riding Club, and W. Johnson Quinn cocktails; the Hotel Empire Peach Cup; the popular Herald Punch; and, of course, the Patrick Gavin Duffy Punch. He famously claimed to have served the first Scotch Highball ever mixed in America, at the request of British actors frequenting his cafe in 1894 (see, however, HIGHBALL). In 1901, he headed uptown to run the bar at the Hotel Empire, near Columbus Circle and in 1904 opened his second cafe, at the current location of Alice Tully Hall. Then, in 1907, he returned to Ireland, coming back to New York in 1921 to run rooming houses in Brooklyn and work on his magnum opus. The *Official Mixer's Manual* was one of the most important works for re-establishing the American art of the bar after Prohibition, remaining in continuous publication in various formats for forty years—apropos for a work whose author claimed to have been "forty years behind the bar."

Duffy, Patrick Gavin. *The Official Mixer's Manual*. New York: Long & Smith, 1933.

Duffy, Patrick J. "Dear Old New York!" Unpublished hand-typed 110-page monograph.

Duffy, Patrick J. Letter to the editor. *New York Times*, October 25, 1927.

Interview with Patrick Gavin Duffy, *Brooklyn Daily Eagle*, December 1, 1933.

Richardson, Matthew Darrin. "'Round Town . . ." *Elmira Star-Gazette*, Thursday, May 31, 1934.

Doug Stailey

And with all that, there was a strange something about the face that suggested piety or saintliness. The figure was thin--almost frail-and of over medum height. While he spoke to me he looked longingly at the mint and I suggested at once a fine Mint Julep made with twelve year old Hennessy Brandy. He agreed and watched me select the sprigs of mint, crush them with a wooden crusher in a goblet, with a little sugar and water. Then poured a stiff drink of the brandy and after shaking all in cracked ice I poured the whole into a fancy tall glass and dressed the top with sliced fruit and more fresh mint.

Patrick Gavin Duffy meets the great tragedian Edwin Booth (1833–1893): a paragraph from *Dear Old New York*, Patrick Gavin Duffy's unpublished, hand-corrected (and much xeroxed) autobiography, ca. 1935. Public Domain.

The **Dukes Bar** is a classic cocktail bar on the ground floor of Dukes Hotel, a boutique hotel in London that has operated out of Mayfair's exclusive St James's Place since 1908.

The international reputation of the Dukes Bar rests on its Martini ritual, in which the drink is prepared on a tableside trolley by a white-jacketed bartender using a dasher of vermouth, frozen gin, or vodka poured straight from bottle to glass, and a lemon twist, without any shaking or stirring. The result is a Martini of unusual strength and concentration, a fact that necessitated the introduction of the bar's famous house rule of two Martinis, maximum, per guest. The Dukes Martini ritual was developed by former head bartenders Gilberto Preti and Salvatore Calabrese in the 1980s. In 1988, Kingsley Amis pronounced the bar "one of the best spots of its kind in London, if not the best of all."

Dukes Bar originally operated more like a private club than a bar, and even though it has been open to the public for many decades, that air of clubbiness remains. Numerous movie stars, politicians, and royals have sought refuge in its intimate, wood-paneled surroundings, but its most celebrated regular remains James Bond author Ian Fleming, who could often be found drinking Martinis at Dukes in the 1950s.

It's often claimed that the Martini Vesper featured in Fleming's *Casino Royale* (1953) was created here by Gilberto Preti, but this is a myth, since the recipe was published long before Preti was working behind the bar. Dukes' head bartender is currently Alessandro Palazzi, who has been in the role since 2007.

See also CALABRESE, SALVATORE; and MARTINI.

Amis, Kingsley. "Restaurants: Tranquil Haven in St. James's." *Illustrated London News*, March 1, 1988, 56.
Dukes Hotel website. http://www.dukeshotel.com/dukes-bar/ (accessed March 3, 2021).

Alice Lascelles

dunder is a Jamaican rum term for leftover liquid after distilling a batch of rum; its use in sugar cane fermentation creates a "high ester" rum and differentiates such rums from all others. Advocates see it as an integral component to the development of the powerful character and even "hogo" aromas of traditional rum from Jamaica and other Caribbean Islands. Described in the texts as "spent lees" from the stills (stillage), it might historically have encompassed virtually all leftovers from a finished distillation, whether from the still or from one or both retorts, where those are part of a still's architecture.

Dunder was demonstrably utilized since the eighteenth century in Jamaica and the Windward Islands (historically comprising Martinique, St. Lucia, St. Vincent, the Grenadines and Grenada), with the accepted understanding that (as Bryan Edwards wrote in 1794) it was "of the same use in the making of rum, as yeast in the fermentation of flour. . . . [it] causes the sweets [i.e., skimmings and molasses], with which it is combined, to yield far more spirit than can be procured without its assistance." In the mid-nineteenth century Whitehouse and others identified its ability to alter not only yields but also flavors, aromas, and other fundamental characteristics.

Jamaica traditionally used greater portions of dunder and skimmings (or scummings, froth and residue removed from sugar boilers) than any other rum producing island. Whereas Colonel Martin describes Windward Island fermenters being filled with roughly one-third each water, scummings, and dunder; Edwards describes the Jamaican recipe as being 50 percent dunder, 36 percent scummings, 6 percent molasses, and 12 percent water.

Dunder's utilization by Jamaican distillers required storage, giving rise to the mythology surrounding muck pits, holes in the ground where dunder was left to fester and grow bacteria before being used (in fact, only a small amount of the dunder, the heaviest part, goes into the pit; the rest is stored in normal casks or tanks). Eric Seed, who revived the nineteenth-century brand Smith & Cross, believes that "the dunder/skimmings or 'muck,' if you will, are as indispensable as the ambient yeast, and the pot-still process."

The term "muck pit" is also historical; it has referred to any dump of organic waste and reflects farmers' use of natural bacteria to break down organic materials for further use. Today Jamaican muck pits are few or at least elusive, and mythology has sprung up around them, with apocryphal tales of animal carcasses thrown in to add flavor. As the surviving pit at the Hampden distillery demonstrates, such things are not needed: bacterial transformation of spent molasses and distillation lees (*Clostridium butyricum* and *Clostridium pasteurianum* are two that often occur) has been shown to create high esteric content and to provide greater complexity and even hogo to rum when a small amount of muck from the pit is added to the fermenters.

See RUM, JAMAICA.

Edwards, Bryan, and Taylor, Thomas. *An Abridgment of Mr. Edwards's Civil and Commercial History of the British West Indies.* London: J. Parsons and J. Bell, 1794.

Greg, Percival H. *A Contribution to the Study of the Production of the Aroma in Rum.* Bulletin of the Botanical Department, Jamaica, vol. 2, no. 8, 1895.

Innes, R. F. "The Agricultural Utilization of Dunder." *International Sugar Journal* 53 (1951): 99–101.

Sloane, Hans. *A Voyage to the Islands Madera, Barbados, Nieves, S. Christophers and Jamaica.* London: 1707.

Muspratt, Sheridan, and Eben Norton Horsford. *Chemistry, Theoretical, Practical, and Analytical: As Applied and Relating to the Arts and Manufactures.* Glasgow: W. Mackenzie, 1860.

Nielson, Patrick. "On the Manufacture of Rum in Jamaica." *Sugar Cane, a Monthly Magazine* 3 (1871).

Pietrek, Matt. "Days of Dunder." *Cocktailwonk.com,* March 11, 2016. https://cocktailwonk.com/2016/03/days-of-dunder-setting-the-record-straight-on-jamaican-rums-mystery-ingredient.html (accessed March 3, 2021).

Whitehouse, W. F. *Agricola's Letters and Essays on Sugar-Farming in Jamaica.* Jamaica Times, 1845.

Doug Frost

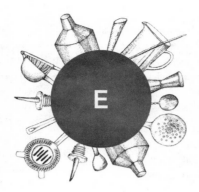

E & A Scheer, a Dutch firm, provides the hidden infrastructure of much of the global rum trade and all of the trade in Batavia arrack. See ARRACK, BATAVIA. For any rum brand that does not have its own distillery, the chances are very good that the product itself, as distinct from its branding or marketing, will have been developed in conjunction with, and supplied by, Scheer. For arrack brands, it is a certainty.

Evert Scheer (ca. 1735–1788), a distiller, and his brother Anthonie (ca. 1740–1783), a wine and spirits merchant, were born in northwest Germany and married into the prosperous distilling and trading Kappelhof family of Amsterdam. The Scheer brothers had their own general shipping and trading company by 1773 (the firm maintains that it was founded in 1712, but it is impossible at this remove to determine what that is based on). The business, a thriving one, remained within the family until 1862, when it passed into the hands of the Huijsser family, who still have a large stake in the privately held company.

In 1818, the company began trading in arrack from Batavia, in the Dutch East Indies (modern-day Jakarta), which enjoyed wide popularity in northern Europe, primarily as a punch ingredient. See PUNCH. This would soon become the heart of its business and remain so until the late twentieth century. In 1895, E & A Scheer was responsible for half

E. & A. Scheer Batavia Arrack label, ca. 1930. Courtesy of Carsten Vlierboom.

of the arrack that the Netherlands imported (and thus a very large part of world production, almost all of which passed through that country), warehousing it and blending it and selling to retailers and wholesalers in Germany and Scandinavia; it also dealt in rum from the West Indies, although it was not a major part of the business. As the twentieth century progressed, however, the arrack trade began to falter due to internal price wars, world events (among them wartime blockades, German occupation, and the upheaval caused by Indonesian independence), and sharply declining demand, and Scheer devoted itself more and more to dealing in rum. It did not abandon the arrack trade entirely, though, and by the early 1980s, having absorbed its competitors, it found itself the last European arrack merchant in operation, the sole heir to a trade more than three centuries old.

By the 1970s, Scheer was Europe's leading blender and broker of sugar-cane spirits. In 2001, with the acquisition of the Main Rum Co. in Liverpool, England, it was able to add long-aged rums from the former British West Indies to its portfolio. Today it sells the equivalent of thirty-three million bottles of rum, arrack, and cachaça a year, not only to spirits brands and marketers but also to the flavor and fragrance, confectionery, and tobacco industries, which use high-ester rums (one of the company's particular specialties) and the lower-ester but pungent arrack in their products. See CACHAÇA and ESTERS. It buys it stocks from over twenty-five distilleries worldwide, importing more than ten million liters of spirits a year.

For customers who know precisely what kind of rum or arrack they want, Scheer acts essentially as a broker. For others, the company determines the desired flavor profile, prepares several blends from the "parcels"—preliminary blends of similar age and flavor—in their warehouses, and works with the customer to refine their preferred one. Its orders range from a single cask to lots exceeding one million liters.

See also RUM.

Pietrek, Matt. "The Most Important Rum Company You've Never Heard Of." *Cocktail Wonk*, February 18, 2016. http://cocktailwonk.com/2016/02/the-most-important-rum-company-youve-never-heard-of-ea-scheer-rum-merchants-to-the-world.html (accessed May 16, 2017).

Verhoog, Jeroen. *Walking on Gold: The History of Trading Company E & A Scheer*. Amsterdam: E & A Scheer, 2013.

David Wondrich

East India Cocktail, with brandy, bitters, curaçao and maraschino liqueurs, and raspberry syrup, was "a great favorite with the English living in the different parts of East India," according to Harry Johnson, who included it in his 1882 *Bartender's Manual* (what authority he had for that statement is unclear; his book marks the drink's first known appearance in print). In the 1888 second edition of his book, he replaced the raspberry syrup with pineapple syrup, a variation that was widely, but not universally, accepted. By 1930, the recipe, as printed in the influential *Savoy Cocktail Book*, had evolved from an extra-"improved" brandy cocktail, with the classic combination of maraschino and curaçao, to a sort of tropical punch, with pineapple juice replacing pineapple syrup and no maraschino liqueur. While easier to procure, pineapple juice pales in comparison to syrup as a cognac modifier and transforms this noble old warrior into a flaccid boat drink. Advantage Johnson.

While not one of the superstars of the cocktail renaissance, the East India is nonetheless well regarded and has appeared on numerous contemporary cocktail lists.

Recipe: Combine 60 ml cognac, 7 ml pineapple gum syrup, 7 ml orange curaçao, 2 dashes of Angostura bitters (or Boker's if available), and 2 dashes of maraschino liqueur; stir with ice and strain into a chilled cocktail glass. Garnish with a brandied cherry and a lemon twist.

See also COCKTAIL; CRADDOCK, HARRY LAWSON; and JOHNSON, HARRY.

Jim Meehan

eau-de-vie ("water of life") is a general term that is the French equivalent of the English *spirit*, the German *Geist*, *Wasser*, or *Schnaps*, and the Latin *aqua vitae*, of which it is a translation. See AQUA VITAE. While it can be applied to spirits that have been barrel aged, it usually denotes one that is unaged. By far the most common use of the term is for the unaged fruit spirits made in Alsace and elsewhere along France's eastern border from cherries (kirsch), plums (quetsch, prune, and mirabelle), apples, pears (poire Williams), quinces (coing), raspberries (framboise), strawberries (fraise), a number of other berries and fruits, and even wine lees (lie) or beer draff (fleur de bière). See FRANCE. These French borderlands, however, are merely the northern tip of a fruit-distilling belt that runs south through Bavaria and Switzerland, then east through Austria and Hungary, and south again into the Balkans. To treat all the individual eaux-de-vie from all the individual countries in detail would require a good deal of space and entail a good deal of repetition; we shall use France as a case study. See DRAFF; KIRSCHWASSER; MIRABELLE; POIRE WILLIAMS; and QUETSCH.

Collectively, the roots of the traditional eaux-de-vie of the French-German borderlands can be traced to the 1400s and 1500s, when distilling in Europe got out of the hands of the alchemists and doctors and into those of the farmer. In works such as Melchior Sebisch's 1579 *Sieben Bücher von dem Feldbau*, we can see the earlier, multi-botanical spirits sharing space with things such as *Erdbeerwasser*, or strawberry spirit, for which the formula is simply "Take ripe strawberries and put them in a glass container; let them putrefy, throw in a little salt or sugar, and distill them." Sebisch, it should be noted, was from Strasbourg, in the heart of eau-de-vie country. By the 1700s, making eaux-de-vie from the abundant fruits of the region was a local specialty.

Then as now, most of the distillers were farmers who distilled as a way of preserving a short-lived crop and making a little extra money. Pot stills remain the norm, most of them relying on indirect heat, although one occasionally still finds the old type of direct-fired still, with the still head peculiar to the region, where the vapor pipe is doubled, like a side-by-side double-barreled shotgun. There are also some larger producers using hybrid stills. See STILL, HYBRID; and STILL, POT.

Most eaux-de-vie are made essentially as they were in Sebisch's day, but there are some that use a two-step process: fruits and berries that lack the necessary sugars for fermentation are macerated for several weeks in neutral spirit (for the larger, more commercial producers) or new cherry or quince spirit (for farm producers, although this is fairly rare) before distillation. The fruits used are chiefly raspberries, but also bilberries, the berries of the whitebeam tree (*Sorbus aria*), which make "one of the finest and most elegant of eaux-de-vie," as Paul

Eschbach wrote in 1992, and a few others. The larger commercial producers produce their spirit using maceration, while some artisanal farmhouse producers still ferment. See MACERATION.

After distillation the spirits are diluted and matured, often for years. Traditionally, this is done in glass demijohns, which are left uncorked for the first few months of aging, allowing some of the more volatile compounds to escape. Large casks of ash wood (which is fairly nonreactive and does not color the spirit) were also used. Today large producers generally use stainless steel tanks. The finished spirits are bottled at between 40 percent and 46 percent ABV.

Eaux-de-vie are generally drunk after meals in small glasses. Their flavors can be quite subtle, but pot distillation means that there is a lot of it: they tend to be paradoxically delicate yet pungent. They also tend to be quite expensive, due to the artisanal nature of their production. Both of these factors limit their use in cocktails, although kirsch does turn up in some punches and in the classic Café Brûlot—and in the Rose cocktail, practically the signature drink of Paris in the 1920s and 1930s.

See also BARACK PALINKA; GERMANY, SWITZERLAND, AND AUSTRIA; JELÍNEK; KOSHER SPIRITS; OBSTLER; RAKIJA; SLIVOVITZ; and TUICA.

Andreae, Illa. *Alle schnäpse dieser welt.* Zurich: Transitbooks, 1973.

Eschbach, Paul. *Les eaux de vie d'Alsace et ailleurs.* Strasbourg: Editions Coprur, 1992.

Sebisch, Melchior. *Siben Bücher von dem Feldbau.* Strasbourg: 1579.

David Wondrich

eau-de-vie still is a hybrid pot/column still. The most prominent manufacturer of them is Arnold Holstein in Germany, whose stills are frequently used to make eau-de-vie, giving rise to the popular term. See also EAU-DE-VIE and STILL, HYBRID.

Edrington (formerly the **Edrington Group**) is an independently owned spirits company best known for its scotch whisky brands, particularly the Macallan. It was established in 1961 by Elspeth, Ethel, and Agnes Robertson as a holding company for their inherited business interests. The sisters donated their shares in the company, named for a family farm in Scotland, to a charitable trust that they created at the same time. (The Robertson Trust, which maintains a controlling interest in Edrington, is the largest such trust in Scotland.)

The company traces its history back to intertwining companies founded in whole or in part by the Robertson sisters' grandfather, W. A. Robertson, starting with the formation of the Glasgow partnership of Robertson & Baxter in 1861. Initially wine and spirits wholesalers, the firm eventually expanded its portfolio to include whisky blending and, ultimately, distillation, leading the effort to build the Bunnahabhain distillery in the early 1880s. In 1887, Robertson became the first chairman of Highland Distilleries Co., adding the Glenrothes distillery to his purview.

Robertson & Baxter and Highland Distilleries Co. continued to be major players in the scotch whisky industry throughout the twentieth century, with varying degrees of connection and separation. They were firmly reunited in 1999 with Edrington's acquisition of Highland Distillers (as it was then known), along with its Highland Park, Macallan, Glenrothes, and Famous Grouse whisky brands. Edrington has since acquired stakes in other spirits brands, including Brugal rum.

See also WHISKY, SCOTCH; and MACALLAN.

MacLean, Charles. *The Robertson Trust*. Edinburgh: Maclean Dubois, 2001.

David Mahoney

egg liqueurs, as well as egg syrups and wines, have been part of European diets for centuries. Egg liqueurs blend distilled spirits and sometimes wine; whole or separated eggs (typically from the domestic chicken); a sweetener such as sugar, honey, or condensed milk; and sometimes flavorings such as nutmeg, orange flower water, and vanilla. They may be served as pourable, drinkable liqueurs about the consistency of cream or venture into dessert territory with almost custard-like thickness. Delicious egg liqueurs may be whipped up à la minute, but most benefit from a rest to allow flavors to marry— and to allow the mixture to be chilled. Some are aged for years before serving.

German *Eierlikör* and Dutch advocaat for the export market are practically identical; both are pourable drinks that may be consumed chilled or mixed. The Snowball, for example, is a British Yuletide concoction of one part advocaat to two parts British lemonade (a clear, carbonated citrus

soft drink, though bitter lemon is the better option). Italian zabaglione is popular, but its lesser known Venetian cousin, *vov*, deserves sampling; it is made with whole eggs, including shells, dissolved in lemon juice before mixing with brandy and sugar.

See also EGGNOG and EGGS.

Fabiani, Gilbert. *Élixirs et Boissons Retrouvés*. Barbentene, France: Équinoxe, 1998.
Vicario, Renato. *Italian Liqueurs: History and Art of a Creation*. Sansepolcro, Italy: Aboca, 2011.

Matthew Rowley

Eggnog is a drink made from beaten eggs, sugar, cream or milk, and spirits. An American invention, Eggnog emerged in the mid-Atlantic region in the late colonial era, a cousin of the egg flip and Tom and Jerry. See TOM AND JERRY. The first printed references to a drink called Eggnog appear in New Jersey and Pennsylvania newspapers in 1788, and it seems to have been popular in New England as well, where it often went by the name "Egg Pop."

By the early nineteenth century, Eggnog had become closely associated with the Christmas holiday, especially in Virginia and other southern states. In many homes it was the tradition to make a large bowl of the drink early on Christmas morning for all the members of the household as well as any guests who dropped by to visit.

The standard recipe was established by 1815. Six or more eggs were separated, and the yolks were beaten with sugar, then blended with spirits (rum being most common but brandy or whisky, or a combination, was used as well, sometimes with the addition of Madeira or sherry) and either milk or cream. Finally, the beaten whites of the eggs were gently folded in, and the finished drink was flavored with nutmeg or lemon zest. Hot Eggnog made with warmed milk was a common variant, as was the single-glass version, where a whole egg was shaken up with sugar, milk, and spirits.

The popularity of Eggnog began to fade in the twentieth century, and the arrival of Prohibition largely put an end to welcoming Christmas guests with a bowl of potent spirits-based nog. Numerous recipes for nonalcoholic versions were published during these dark years, and by the time of Repeal, as far as most of America was concerned, Eggnog had evolved into an egg- and dairy-based beverage, usually bought premixed, that may or may not be "spiked" with alcohol—a far cry from its heritage as a fundamentally alcoholic drink. In parts of the Northeast and Upper Midwest, however, the original drink lies much closer to the surface. Some families in the region even age their Eggnog for a year or more under refrigeration before consuming it.

Recipe: Separate 10 eggs. Whip the yolks with 180 g sugar until sugar has dissolved. Stir in 500 ml brandy and 250 ml Jamaican rum, then 1 l whole milk. In a separate bowl, whip the egg whites until they form stiff peaks. Fold them into the yolk mixture and refrigerate for 1 hour. Grate nutmeg over the top and serve. Whisky or other spirits may be used in place of the brandy and rum.

"The Dram Shop." *New Haven Federal Gazette*, April 9, 1796, 6.

"Elizabeth-Town, March 26." *New-Jersey Journal*, March 26, 1788, 2.

Wondrich, David. *Imbibe!*, 2nd ed. New York: Perigee, 2015.

Robert F. Moss

eggs have been used raw in alcoholic beverages at least as far back as the thirteenth century. They are used not for flavor, of which they have very little, but rather to provide a velvety texture and a measured degree of viscosity in a drink, and to increase its nutritional value (this is much less of a concern today than it was in the past). The whites also provide an attractive white foam on the top of the drink. In general, eggs are most often included as ingredients in sours, fizzes, flips, and Eggnogs. See SOUR; FIZZ; and EGGNOG.

In late nineteenth century England, one could find either a white or a whole egg in a nonalcoholic recipe for "Egg Tea." In this instance the egg was used as a substitute for milk in standard tea service. Aside from providing an ethereal texture, an added benefit is that the polyphenols (tannins) from the tea leaves would bind with the proteins in the egg white before they could affect salivary proteins and thus prevent palate fatigue. Tea is traditionally served with milk for this reason, and this same binding action on particulates has historically been utilized to clarify wine, beer, and mead. This is a useful understanding when constructing tea-based cocktails.

The use of real eggs fell out of favor in the mid-twentieth century, when cocktail "foamers" became popular. These synthetic foamers provided bartenders with a quick and easy replacement of the egg via ready-to-use product yet ultimately proved to be a poor substitute. Some of these foamers tasted soapy or chemical, lessening the overall quality of whatever drink they were inflicted on. Gradually, the very idea of any sort of foam (whether natural or artificial) fell out of favor. See FOAMS. But the twenty-first-century craft cocktail renaissance has rediscovered the merits of egg-based drinks, whisking the egg back into the cocktail shaker and restoring its esteemed position in both drinks as well as history. See COCKTAIL RENAISSANCE.

A recipe for a classic sour doesn't traditionally include an egg white, but it can be added as an option; it is, however, an essential component of the classic Pisco Sour. See PISCO SOUR. A Silver Fizz is another sour-based drink that adds an egg white and is topped with soda water. See SILVER FIZZ. A Golden Fizz follows the same recipe as a Silver Fizz but instead uses an egg yolk in lieu of the white. A Royal Fizz uses both white and yolk. Flips traditionally use an entire egg, along with a spirit, sugar, and optional ale, and the entire drink is poured back and forth between two vessels to provide aeration to the egg, resulting in foam. Eggnogs also utilize an entire egg in addition to milk, cream, or both.

Raw egg whites foam faster and better than pasteurized or instant whites, whose proteins have been altered by heat. When shaking a cocktail that includes an egg white, the same basic principle causes the egg white to produce a foam in the drink yet is not quite as robust as if the white was whipped by itself. Part of this is because the protein unfolding is hampered by the other liquids in the drink, and also because of the coldness that the ice provides. This is why many bartenders initiate their drinks with what is known as the "dry shake." See DRY SHAKE.

While a drink containing an egg is a wonderful experience on the palate, it should be enjoyed in a timely manner. If left sitting too long in a glass, it begins to warm up and releases unpleasant sulfuric compounds reminiscent of the smell of a wet dog. It is thought that the use of aromatic bitters atop a Pisco Sour in the warm South American climate was adopted for this reason.

These days, many bartenders are taking this to another level and decorating the foam with fanciful designs produced by swirling a toothpick or straw through the bitters. Some bartenders are going the extra mile and placing a special stencil over the drink and spraying bitters through it with an atomizer to leave the design on top of the foam, a practice pioneered in the 1890s by William Schmidt. See ATOMIZER (MISTER); and SCHMIDT, WILLIAM. But for the at-home user who might not have bitters at hand, spraying the oil from a citrus twist over the top of the drink is another viable option.

The major concern in using raw eggs is the possible danger of salmonella poisoning. To provide the best insurance against salmonella, eggs should be kept refrigerated at all times in temperatures of 4° C (40 F) or lower and should be as fresh as possible.

Campbell, Dawn L. *The Tea Book*. Gretna, LA: Pelican, 1995.

McGee, Harold. *On Food and Cooking*. New York: Scribner, 2004.

Schmidt, William. *The Flowing Bowl*. New York: Webster, 1892.

Audrey Saunders

egg still is another name for the Chinese still, a distinct style of internal-condensation pot still. See also STILL, POT.

elder refers to any one of several species of flowering shrubs or trees in the *Sambucus* genus found in temperate and subtropical zones around the world. Both the fragrant white elderflowers and the deep purple-black elderberries (especially of *S. nigra*) are used as drink ingredients. Recently, elderflower-flavored syrups and liqueurs, exemplified by St-Germain, have become popular cocktail ingredients. The berries have been used for centuries to darken the color and increase the fruit flavor of certain wines, most famously ports. By the 1840s, elderberry use was so widespread in Portugal that the prominent winemaker Baron Forrester railed against them in a famous screed titled "A Word or Two about Port." Though mid-twentieth-century Ports can be found that betray their use, the practice seems finally to have passed by the wayside.

See also ADULTERATION.

Mayson, Richard. *Port and the Douro*. Oxford: Infinite Ideas, 2012.

Read, Jan. *The Wines of Portugal*. London: Faber & Faber, 1982.

Doug Frost

El Diablo is a tequila variation on a Rum Buck. In 1940 it first appeared in a drink book called *The How and When* as the "Diablo." Seven years later, Trader Vic ran the recipe in his *Bartender's Guide*, swapping 30 ml (1 oz) of tequila for the rum and calling it a "Mexican El Diablo," which he shortened to "El Diablo" in his revised 1972 *Guide*. This incarnation has since become popular on cocktail menus as a tequila-based alternative to the ubiquitous Margarita.

Recipe: Mix 45 ml white rum and 15 ml each lime juice and crème de cassis with shaved ice in a tall glass and top with ginger ale.

See also BERGERON, VICTOR "TRADER VIC"; BUCK; CRÈME DE CASSIS; and MARGARITA.

Bergeron, Trader Vic. *Bartender's Guide*. New York: Garden City, 1947.

Bergeron, Victor J. *Trader Vic's Bartender's Guide, Revised*. New York: Doubleday, 1972.

Gayle, Hyman, and Gerald F. Marco. *The How and When*. Chicago: Marco Importing, 1940.

Jeff Berry

élevage, or "nurturing," is a term sometimes used to encompass the unique, extraordinarily complex, and closely held system of maturation employed in making cognac and some other French spirits, such as Armagnac and calvados. The deliberate aging of brandy in oak barrels is a French, and specifically Cognacais, innovation of the seventeenth century, and French blenders and cellarmasters have spent the succeeding centuries perfecting the process.

Élevage is a slow and gradual process, as is all maturation in wood, but unlike the practice that prevails when aging many spirits, where the new spirit goes into the barrel and sits undisturbed in a warehouse until mature, it is also a dynamic one, involving strategic choices and interventions throughout the aging cycle and even before.

The process begins with choosing the characteristics of the casks: the type of oak used for the staves, the level of their toasting or charring, and the age of the casks—are they new or old? Depending on the style desired for the finished product, the cellarmaster will opt for fine-grained staves (annual growth of the tree lower than 2 mm) or looser-grained ones (annual growth greater than

3 mm), for the nature of the tannins will vary between these, as will the oxidation rate of the spirit. The heating of the barrel (toasting or charring), a technique also known as "bousinage," is practiced in cooperages, which enables the extraction of the aromatic compounds of the wood (e.g., vanillin) responsible for the "toasted" aromas of spirits.

Evaluation

Élevage itself begins with evaluation. When it comes off the still, each batch of new eau-de-vie brings with it its own nuances of flavor, texture, and structure. These nuances bring with them different aging potentials, which must be detected so that the spirit can reach its full development. This detection of potential can only be done by taste, and indeed the ability to project the development of a new spirit many years into the future is at the heart of the master blender's craft. It is the fruit of very long training and apprenticeship and much experience.

By tasting, the blender will determine, for instance, that a certain batch will reach its fullness of expression quickly. Conversely, another one will present a *brioché* (basically, "rich like a brioche") character, a mouth structure that indicates a predisposition to aging. It will be routed to a longer aging, either alone or in an intermediate blend with other batches, to take advantage of its exceptional character.

The First Year in the Barrel

The first year of aging is a crucial phase for the future of the spirits. For the élevage technique, it is generally believed that a period spent in new barrels is decisive for the future maturation of the spirit. This period can vary from three months or so to a year, with different types of barrels used for spirits on different aging paths. A spirit intended to be sold fairly young will generally go into a barrel made from the relatively porous, high-tannin oak from the Limousin forest, while one intended for longer aging will go into one made from the tighter-pored, less tannic oaks of the Tronçais forest. For such spirits, the period of contact with new oak is usually on the shorter side, and indeed some producers use no new oak at all for spirits destined for maximum aging, lest the wood rise up to overpower the flavors of fruit and terroir in the spirit when it has become concentrated through evaporation.

After its time in new oak, the spirit will be moved to older, already-used barrels (called *fûts roux*, "red casks," in cognac production), from which much of the tannins and other wood compounds have already been extracted.

The élevage technique also includes specific techniques for micromanaging the barrels, such as *redouellage*, or "restaving," which involves changing one or a few staves or the head of an old barrel to bring a delicate touch of newer wood to the spirits, or the use of grooved staves in a new barrel to increase the surface area of the oak in contact with the spirit.

Wet Cellar, Dry Cellar?

Once the spirit's initial contact with wood is over and it has been rebarreled, it enters its oxidative aging phase, characterized by slow-acting physical and chemical exchanges between the spirit, the wood, and the air admitted by the porosity of the barrel. This is where the atmosphere of the cellar, its temperature, and humidity, come into play. Wet cellars, where the humidity means that more alcohol evaporates from the spirit than water, bring roundness and mouthfeel. Dry cellars, favoring the evaporation of water, will confer a certain tannic brightness as well as elegance and finesse. A considered alternation decided by the cellarmaster between the two types of "breathing" will give a spirit the subtlety required for a fine brandy. Some fine cognac houses have cellars with up to six levels of humidity to achieve a perfect aging.

Contrary to popular imagery of spirits "forgotten" in a dark cellar, élevage is anything but static. Unlike a simple aging, where a spirit is left to age undisturbed until maturity, élevage involves a series of actions and transfers based on regular assessments by the cellarmaster. The spirits can change barrel and cellar several times; indeed, many are blended with other batches several times during the process, creating preliminary blends, or "coupes," that are the building blocks of the final ones. All of this requires enough storage space and proper cellars of different types. The storage of spirits is highly capital-intensive, demanding the means to build the necessary cellars and buy casks. Assuming both are available, storage decisions are based on the regular tasting of the spirits. The fear of the cellarmaster is that the early potential of the spirit is lost through inadequate aging, and gold will turn into lead.

Full Maturity

When, after three, six, ten, fifteen, twenty, or fifty years (depending on its properties and aging potential), a cognac reaches its full maturity, it will be incorporated into a final blend (very, very few cognacs are sold unblended). The blending of spirits of different ages and from different barrels represents the final stage of élevage—unless, that is, the spirit is destined for preservation in the firm's *paradis*, or "paradise," where it will be preserved alongside other exceptional cognacs in glass demijohns for special use. For the rest, the blending represents its own process of nurturing. The best practice has it taking place over several months or, better, several years, so that different spirits can marry perfectly and show a perfect integration (a quality also referred to as *fondu*, "melted"). This holds true for other components that go into the blend besides brandy: the caramel coloring, the permissible amount of sugar syrup, if any, and even the very water used to reduce the spirit to proof. The best practice is to barrel age each of these components on their own, blended with some eau-de-vie to act as a preservative and make it blend more easily.

See also ARMAGNAC; BLENDING; CALVADOS; COGNAC; and MATURATION.

Faith, Nicholas. *Cognac.* London: Mitchell Beazley, 2004.

Alexandre Gabriel and David Wondrich

ellagic acid is a phenol in whisky, derived from barrels as well as possibly created when water-soluble tannins in barley break down into glucose and either gallic or ellagic acids, both of which are aromatic compounds typical of malt whisky. As an antioxidant, it may ameliorate some negative effects of drinking alcohol.

See also PHENOLS.

Iino, T., K. Nakahara, W. Miki, Y. Kiso, Y. Ogawa, S. Kato, and K. Takeuchi. "Less Damaging Effect of Whisky in Rat Stomachs in Comparison with Pure Ethanol: Role of Ellagic Acid, the Nonalcoholic Component." *Digestion* 64, no. 4 (2001): 214–221.

Doug Frost

ellagic tannins comprise a category of phenols, including such common compounds as castalagin, grandinin, roburin D and E, and vescalagin. For distillers, the critical issue is that the extraction of these compounds is not wholly water soluble but is also affected by heat, time, and pH. Moreover these factors may also speed the degradation and oxidation of ellagic tannins and ellagic acid, a process that can lead to the development of secondary aromas, flavors, and textures.

See also PHENOLS.

Jordão, A. M., J. M. Ricardo-da-Silva, and O. Laureano. "Extraction of Some Ellagic Tannins and Ellagic Acid from Oak Wood Chips in Model Wine Solutions: Effect of Time, pH, Temperature and Alcoholic Content." *South Africa Journal of Viticulture and Enology* 26, no. 2. (2005): 83–89.

McPhail, Donald B., Peter T. Gardner, Garry G. Duthie, Gordon M. Steele, and Kenneth Reid. "Assessment of the Antioxidant Potential of Scotch Whiskeys by Electron Spin Resonance Spectroscopy: Relationship to Hydroxyl-Containing Aromatic Components." *Journal of Agricultural and Food Chemistry* 47, no. 5 (1999): 1937–1941.

Doug Frost

El Presidente is a Cuban cocktail combining rum, vermouth, and dashes of curaçao and grenadine. Introduced in the mid-1910s, it rapidly achieved widespread popularity both in its homeland and abroad. The drink, complex and lightly sweet, was particularly popular among the Cubans themselves, as was demonstrated by Gerardo Machado, the country's president, when he served it at a 1928 state banquet in honor of his American counterpart, Calvin Coolidge (Coolidge, although personally opposed to Prohibition, adhered to the national policy and refused the drink). See PROHIBITION AND TEMPERANCE IN AMERICA.

The Presidente first appears in print in the 1915 *Manual del cantinero* published in Havana by a bartender at the Hotel Inglaterra, John B. Escalante, a Spaniard who had worked for years in New York. It is, however, quite possible that it was actually invented by Constantino Ribalaigua of the Floridita bar: it was at least directly attributed to him in a 1937 article about him, an article he repeatedly reprinted in the bar's promotional cocktail booklets, and he was not known to be a vain or boastful man (the claim published that same year that it was invented by a Chicago bartender in 1912 cannot be corroborated—or disproved). See RIBALAIGUA Y VERT, CONSTANTE; and FLORIDITA. Whoever created it, it must have been christened in honor of Mario Garcia Menocal, president of Cuba from 1913 to 1921 and a man known to enjoy a cocktail.

The Presidente made it out of Cuba in the late 1920s, turning up in international bar guides and American speakeasies. In the next decade, it would appear occasionally in Europe and surprisingly often in the United States—perhaps not a first-rank cocktail like the Sidecar, but not far behind. See SIDECAR. Unfortunately, in its journey from Cuba, one key piece of information regarding its composition was lost: the vermouth in the original was a white, semi-sweet French "vermouth de Chambery." See VERMOUTH. Most of the recipes published for it, however, called simply for "French"—that is, dry—vermouth (this is perhaps due to the fact that Bacardi rum and Noilly Prat vermouth shared the same importer, and the drink was advertised with those brands). See BACARDI and NOILLY PRAT. The resulting drink is awkwardly balanced, driving conscientious mixologists to overemphasize the curaçao or the grenadine or switch to a heavier red vermouth, losing in the process the delicacy that was a large part of the Presidente's original appeal. In any case, its popularity did not outlast the 1950s, although recent years have seen a cautious El Presidente revival.

Recipe: 45 ml each white Cuban rum and sweet, white vermouth and 5 ml each orange curaçao and grenadine. Stir, strain, up. Garnish with orange twist and cherry.

Cuddy, Jack. "Cuban's [sic] Cocktail King Tells Cuddy Daiquiri Recipe." Rome (NY) Sentinel, March 5, 1937.
Escalante, John B. Manual del cantinero. Havana: Imprenta Moderna, 1915.
Lane, French. "They Pay the Freight." Chicago Tribune, March 11, 1937, 19.

David Wondrich

El Tesoro is a traditionally produced, 100 percent agave tequila made by the Camarena family in their La Alteña distillery, near the town of Arandas in the Los Altos region of Jalisco, Mexico. Don Felipe Camarena began producing the family's own tequila in 1937, after having farmed agave for many

years prior. In 1990, at a time when most tequila in the United States was *mixto* and consumed in margaritas, Don Felipe Camarena (the son of the founder) and visionary tequila importers Robert Denton and Marilyn Smith created the brand El Tesoro de Don Felipe. El Tesoro Silver (now called Platinum) quickly became a benchmark tequila for agave aficionados and helped to kick-start the modern premium tequila movement in the United States. See MIXTO. The reposado and añejo are equally well-respected amongst cognoscenti, and it was the Muy Añejo, a cult favorite of the 1990s, and the Paradiso, created with the assistance of cognac legend Alain Royer and aged in French oak barrels, that helped to spawn the extra añejo category that became law several years later. See REPOSADO and AÑEJO.

Don Felipe's son Carlos now manages the family company, which makes El Tesoro under contract for Beam Suntory. La Alteña can still proudly claim to use (mostly) estate-grown agaves, which are baked slowly in adobe *hornos* (ovens), milled in a traditional *tahona*, and fermented in open-top wood tanks with ambient yeasts. El Tesoro is still distilled to proof (40 percent ABV) in relatively small copper alembic stills, and the Platinum version is always bottled immediately to capture freshness and aromatics.

La Alteña also produces the Tapatio brand. Long a cult tequila in Mexico and Europe, Tapatio bears a strong family resemblance to El Tesoro, although the distillery's tahona is apparently reserved by contract for El Tesoro. Tapatio has recently been introduced to the American market, for which it is distilled to a higher 50 percent ABV.

See also AGAVE; TEQUILA; and TAHONA.

Cutler, Lance. The Tequila Lover's Guide to Mexico: Everything There Is to Know About Tequila . . . Including How to Get There. Sonoma, CA: Wine Patrol, 1998.
Estes, Tomas. The Tequila Ambassador. London: Diffordsguide, 2012.
Martineau, Chantal. How the Gringos Stole Tequila: The Modern Age of Mexico's Most Traditional Spirit. Chicago: Chicago Review Press, 2015.
Valenzuela, Ana, and Gary Paul Nabhan. Tequila: A Natural and Cultural History. Tuscon: University of Arizona Press, 2004.

Steven Olson

Embury, David A. (1886–1960), was the author of *The Fine Art of Mixing Drinks*, which was originally published in 1948 and has served for many decades as the seminal work on cocktails and mixology for countless bartenders and cocktail enthusiasts. A descendant of one of the founders of the Methodist church in America and a lawyer by trade, Embury never worked in the beverage or restaurant industry. By his own admission, the New York tax attorney gained his mixological expertise "entirely as a consumer and as a shaker-upper of drinks for the delectation of my guests."

In *The Fine Art of Mixing Drinks*, Embury begins with the declaration "Anyone can make good cocktails," and then puts forth his philosophies and advice on how this is done. He stresses that cocktails are intended as before-dinner drinks and therefore should never have more than a hint of sweetness to them. He details the importance of only using quality spirits, liqueurs, and other ingredients, as well as using plenty of ice. Prior to covering a variety of recipes, he goes into detail on what he refers to as the six basic drinks; namely, the Martini, Manhattan, Old-Fashioned, Daiquiri, Sidecar, and Jack Rose. See MARTINI; MANHATTAN; OLD-FASHIONED COCKTAIL; DAIQUIRI; SIDECAR; and JACK ROSE.

Unlike most other cocktail tomes, *The Fine Art of Mixing Drinks* is less a collection of countless bare-bones recipes and more of a discussion of the process and concepts behind the drinks. Throughout his book Embury includes a fair number of recipes, but in addition to a simple recipe, you will find his thoughtful, and sometimes disparaging, comments about the drinks to help the reader better understand each drink and its construction.

In 1946 and 1947, Embury was the attorney for the National Interfraternity Council and outspokenly led that organization's efforts to prevent the racial integration of American college fraternities. Some argue that that same rigidity and lack of generosity carries over into Embury's mixology, which admittedly can be austere. But nonetheless he remains the preeminent theorist of the cocktail, and his work provides an indispensable framework for discussing them.

Embury, David. *The Fine Art of Mixing Drinks.* New York: Mud Puddle, 1948.

"Sorority 'Explains' Position." *Pittsburgh Courier*, May 4, 1946, 1.

Audrey Saunders and Robert Hess

Employees Only is a cocktail bar with a speakeasy aesthetic and art deco decor in the New York City neighborhood of Greenwich Village. Opened in 2004, it was an early entry in the city's then-aborning craft cocktail scene. See CRAFT COCKTAIL. The bar was founded by five partners—Billy Gilroy, Igor Hadzismajlovic, Jason Kosmas, Henry LaFargue, and Dushan Zaric—all of whom had worked at Pravda or Schiller's Liquor Bar, Manhattan bars run by restaurateur Keith McNally. Employees Only stood apart from other early New York cocktail bars in several respects. The hierarchical bartender apprentice system, in which bar employees slowly move up the company ladder; the formal, white bartender jackets; and the overwhelmingly male bartending staff were all throwbacks to Old World service traditions. While other serious cocktail bars used jiggers, Employees Only continued to free-pour their drinks. See JIGGER and FREE POURING. Also in contrast to other cocktail bars, food was served, including a famous chicken soup ladled out free each night at closing time. Cocktails were largely frothy, fruit, and shaken, using simple infusions and not eschewing vodka, as other New York cocktails bars of that era did. The bartenders' sense of fun and camaraderie attracted a young and lively clientele, and the bar quickly established itself as a party spot. Zaric and Kosmas were among the first of the modern breed of mixologists to publish a cocktail book, *Speakeasy*, released in 2010. Beginning in 2016, the bar began to expand its brand, opening branches in Miami and Singapore.

See also SPEAKEASY (NEW).

Simonson, Robert. *A Proper Drink: How a Band of Bartenders Saved the Civilized World.* New York: Ten Speed, 2016.

Robert Simonson

Engel, Leo (1844–1893), did not introduce American drinks and the American way of bartending to London, but he certainly popularized it and cemented it as a part of the city's culture. Little is known of his early life beyond the fact

Leo Engel, from the 1880 edition of his book. Wellcome Collection.

that he was born in Germany and emigrated to America by 1867 (he became an American citizen in 1874). He may have begun his working life as a soap maker, but by the early 1870s he was tending bar at the popular Ridgewood Shades in Brooklyn, New York; at some point, by his own account, he also worked for Jerry Thomas. See THOMAS, JEREMIAH P. "JERRY." In late 1874, Felix Spiers and Christopher Pond hired Engel to run the American bar in the Criterion, the new theater-restaurant complex in Piccadilly. There Engel offered the full range of American drinks, or at least ones that sounded American (some American visitors were not convinced). Such a thing had been done before in London, but never at such a scale or in such a fashionable venue. The drinks were a sensation, as was "Professor" Engel.

In 1878, Engel codified his craft with the publication of *American and Other Drinks,* to that date the most comprehensive treatment of the new American style of mixed drinks to be published in the United Kingdom. No matter if the great majority of the drinks were plagiarized verbatim, or nearly so, from Thomas; there were also fourteen of "Leo's specialties" and a number of small adjustments to British conditions. The book was a popular one and became a cornerstone of British mixology.

Engel left the Criterion in 1882 to open his own bar, Leo's Desideratum, in Haymarket. When that failed in 1884, he tried his hand as a theatrical agent and manager and then went back to barkeeping, briefly running bars in Leicester Square and St James Square. After the death of his wife in 1888,

Engel moved to France, where he ran the New York Bar at 10 Place de la Madeleine in Paris and then followed in Ciro Capozzi's footsteps as manager of the American bar attached to the Hotel de Paris in Monte Carlo, a position he held until his death. The American bar at the Criterion never got back the popularity it had when Leo was behind it.

See also CIRO'S and CRITERION.

Bailey, James Montgomery. *England from a Back-Window*. Boston: Lee & Shepard, 1879, 260.
"Music Hall Gossip." *The Era*, February 11, 1893, 17.
"On the Lookout." *Brooklyn Eagle*, July 2, 1902, 5.
"On the Riviera." *New York Herald*, Paris ed., March 17, 1892, 1.
Richardson, Leander P. "Queer Things in London." *Chicago Tribune*, March 22, 1882, 5.

David Wondrich

England has done more than perhaps any other country to shape the worlds of distilled spirits and the drinks mixed with them. This is ironic, since it came to distilling late and, for the most part, abandoned it early.

In the 1400s, when the art of distilling spirits from grain swept through northern Europe from Ireland to the Urals, it left England basically unmarked. It was not for want of knowledge: Geoffrey Chaucer's "Canon's Yeoman's Tale," written around 1400, mentions "alambikes" along with "berme" (yeast), "wort," and "fermentacioun" as parts of the alchemist's stock-in-trade. And indeed medicinal spirits were distilled in the abbeys and great houses (where distilling was the province of the mistress of the house), but spirits did not enter recreational use, as they did in Scotland and Ireland. See SCOTLAND AND IRELAND.

This is strange, given that, as the playwright Thomas Dekker wrote in 1623, "an English man is a horse that drinks of all waters." Beers from Hamburg and Rotterdam, wines from Spain, Italy, and even Persia were readily available, particularly in London, but for whatever reason—aristocratic conservatism, island-nation xenophobia, lack of exposure—through the middle of the seventeenth century spirits were confined mostly to nautical use. There, the fact that they took up much less space than beer or wine and did not spoil made them a fixture. But it was only with the restoration of the monarchy in

1660 that spirits drinking began to spread widely among the general run of English drinkers.

At first, it was French brandy that dominated the market; the fact that France was a perpetual enemy did not seem to affect the trade, which grew with incredible rapidity. In 1689, however, England and France went to war, and King William III cut off the supply. In exchange, Parliament passed, with royal encouragement, "an act for encouraging the distilling of brandy and spirits from corn [i.e., grain]," in the hope of encouraging improvement in the notoriously poor quality of English grain spirits (William was Dutch, and he knew grain spirits). See GENEVER. This did in fact lead to a remarkable rise in English grain distilling, although the brandy trade had to be restored for revenue purposes. At the same time, English traders were bringing in increasing amounts of arrack from India and Indonesia and rum—an English elaboration of the raw sugar-cane spirits so common in the New World—from the new colonies in the British Caribbean. See ARRACK and RUM. By the 1720s, England was awash in spirits: "geneva," or simply "gin" for the poor, indifferently distilled from whatever grain could be scraped up that had escaped the brewers and bakers, and the finest imported spirits for the rich. Drunkenness was rampant.

The English solution to the problem of "Gin Lane" (as William Hogarth dubbed his famous portrayal of the desperate alcoholism that gripped London's extensive slums) was already largely in place, in the form of the British excise system. Excise taxes on spirits were of course nothing new, but England approached them with an unusual attention to detail and an iron determination to see them enforced. See EXCISE, TAXES, AND DISTILLATION. In a series of acts beginning in the 1730s, Parliament imposed a tax structure on the freewheeling distilling industry that made it very difficult and very expensive to make spirit from scratch and relatively easy to buy it from one of the firms that had the capital to distill. This divided the industry into "malt distillers" and "rectifiers," who redistilled their purchased spirit into gin. See GIN and RECTIFIER. Around the margins, there were also some who made spirit from imported molasses, which was often blended with imported rum, and others who made cider brandy.

Between 1750 and 1764, English spirits consumption declined from a brutal 25 liters per capita annually to eight liters (today it fluctuates around four liters). At the same time, the quality of what was manufactured increased greatly. So did the quality of what was imported, as English merchants learned to let their stocks mature in oak in the soft, moist climate of the London, Bristol, and Liverpool docklands. See MATURATION. Gradually, spirits around the world began to adapt themselves to the preferences of the large and discerning English market. In the nineteenth century, scotch and Irish whiskies underwent the same treatment that Jamaican rum and even French brandy had gone through, and local products were grown into worldwide brands. See BEEFEATER; PLYMOUTH GIN; and TANQUERAY GORDON & CO.

Today, the eighteenth-century structure still more or less applies: England makes a lot of gin and imports a lot of everything else (now including such formerly exotic things such as vodka, American rye whisky, and Mexican tequila and mezcal), although the micro-distilling movement has spawned a number of new whisky and cider brandy distilleries. See CRAFT DISTILLING.

England's role in the history of mixology is equally important. Whether English sailors adopted punch from India or invented it there, they certainly saw to its global spread, the first mixed drink based on spirits to gain worldwide popularity. See PUNCH. In the mid-nineteenth century, England was also one of the early adopters of the new, American school of mixing drinks, and London has a correspondingly long history of cocktail bars (although perhaps not quite so long as Paris), and of famous bartenders to serve behind them. See CALABRESE, SALVATORE; COLEMAN, ADA; DORELLI, GIAMPIERO "PETER"; ENGEL, LEO; and SAVOY. Another London bartender, Dick Bradsell, was in the vanguard of the twenty-first-century cocktail renaissance, which has seen a long list of bars in the city celebrated for the wild creativity they bring to inventing and presenting drinks. See BRADSELL, DICK; and COCKTAIL RENAISSANCE.

See also DIAGEO and SPIRITS TRADE, HISTORY OF.

Harper, William T. *Origins and Rise of the British Distillery*. Lewiston, NY: Edwin Mellen, 1999.
Mendelsohn, Oscar A. *Drinking with Pepys*. London: Macmillan, 1963.
Wondrich, David. *Punch*. New York: Perigee, 2010.

David Wondrich

Ensslin, Hugo Richard (1878–1929), was a German-American bartender whose 1916 book *Recipes for Mixed Drinks* is one of the most important of its kind from the years just before Prohibition. After early training in Wurttemberg as a painter and a photographer during which he displayed a good deal of promise, Ensslin left Germany for New York at sixteen. He worked there as a cashier for some years and then spent some time in Ohio and back in Germany. Somewhere along the way he learned to tend bar. By the early 1910s, he was settled back in New York and behind the bar of the Hotel Wallick, in Times Square, where he remained at least until Prohibition. In 1925, he followed the manager of the Wallick to Wilkes Barre, Pennsylvania, where he managed the restaurant of the Hotel Sterling. He shot himself in 1929, either due to ill health or over a failed relationship (contemporary accounts differ).

Recipes for Mixed Drinks, which received an expanded second edition in 1917, is a rare book; it was not a popular success in its day, nor was its author one of New York's celebrated bartenders. It is nonetheless an important one: it contains the earliest recipes for a number of drinks that went on to enjoy long careers, including the Aviation, the Blue Moon, and the September Morn, and it details better than any other book precisely what was customarily drunk along New York's cocktail route, the most extensive and sophisticated in the world. See AVIATION COCKTAIL; BLUE MOON; and COCKTAIL ROUTE. It also served as one of the chief sources for Harry Craddock, who plundered it wholesale for his 1930 *Savoy Cocktail Book*. See CRADDOCK, HARRY. Indeed, many of his most memorable drinks, from the Phoebe Snow to the Raymond Hitchcocktail, were originally Ensslin's—or, it must be conceded, were first published by Ensslin: with no personal reminiscence of his bartending or mixology available, we cannot say whether the drinks peculiar to his book were actually created by him.

Ensslin, Hugo. *Recipes for Mixed Drinks*. New York: Mud Puddle, 1916.
"'Hugo' Kills Self." *Wilkes-Barre Evening News*, January 2, 1929, 1.

David Wondrich

The **environmental impact of distillation** is multifaceted, occurring in all stages of spirits production, from raw material growth and extraction through processing, manufacture, distribution, and disposal.

Raw Materials

Distilled spirits are produced from various agricultural products grown all over the world, in diverse conditions with widely varying attention to the environmental impact of the agricultural practices employed. When improperly managed, activities from working farms can negatively affect water quality through sediment and nutrient pollution, air quality through burning or poor management of byproducts, and biodiversity through the increased use of genetically uniform varieties.

According the US Environmental Protection Agency, nutrient pollution is one of America's most widespread, costly, and challenging environmental problems. In the 2000 National Water Quality Inventory, states reported that agricultural nonpoint source (NPS) pollution was the leading source of water-quality impacts on surveyed rivers and lakes, the second largest source of impairments to wetlands, and a major contributor to contamination of surveyed estuaries and groundwater. Agricultural activities that cause NPS pollution include plowing too often or at the wrong time, as well as improper, excessive, or poorly timed application of pesticides, irrigation water, and fertilizer.

The Food and Agriculture Organization of the United Nations has reported that since the 1900s, some 75 percent of genetic diversity has been lost in agricultural crops as farmers worldwide have replaced local varieties with genetically uniform, high-yielding ones. The Harvard School of Public Health has stated that protecting biodiversity in the ecosystems that support food production and fresh water and preserving genetic diversity in our crops are both critical to ensuring our ability to produce food with ever-shrinking terrestrial and aquatic resources. Corn, one of the most common grains used to make spirits, is particularly susceptible to this type of pressure due to the size and competitive nature of its market. See CORN. Agave, with its lengthy maturation period, is also vulnerable to a loss of genetic diversity. See AGAVE.

Raw-material processing and handling present additional potential for environmental impact. Dust from the processing of grain and sugar (including field burns common in the sugar-cane industry) impact air quality and present a hazard to worker safety. See SUGAR and SUGAR CANE. According to the US Occupational Safety and Health Administration, the grain-handling industry is a high-hazard industry where workers can be exposed to numerous serious and life threatening hazards. These hazards include fires and explosions from grain dust accumulation, suffocation from engulfment and entrapment in grain bins, falls from heights, and crushing injuries and amputations from grain handling equipment. In 2010, fifty-one workers in the United States were engulfed by grain stored in bins, and twenty-six died—the highest number on record.

The agricultural products used to produce the vast majority of distilled spirits (grain, sugar cane, agave, and fruit) are all subject to these issues in varying degrees. The larger the scale of the distilling operation, the greater the complexity of the supply chain and the more challenging it is to ensure that all suppliers are employing responsible practices. These concerns can be mitigated through the thoughtful, direct selection of farming partners employing sustainable practices.

Spirits Production

The production of distilled spirits is an energy-intensive process, requiring the precise heating and cooling of large amounts of water and alcohol throughout the process.

The most prevalent sources of energy used for this are carbon-based fuels, either burned in a boiler at the distillery to produce the steam that is used for heating or consumed in the form of electricity, most commonly generated from coal or natural gas, to run compressors that drive the cooling process. Depending on the distilleries' location and available resources, other sources of heating and cooling energy may be available.

Large-scale rum production facilities are often able to integrate sugar-cane processing into the spirits production facilities and use the bagasse (the fibrous part of the sugar cane that remains behind after the cane juice is extracted) to generate high-quality heat and power on site. Agave bagasse may also be used in this way, although it is not yet common practice.

Distilleries located in very wet regions, such as Scotland and parts of the United States, often have an abundance of cold water available that can be used for process cooling, held temporarily in a cooling pond, and then reintroduced back into the environment with minimal impact.

Some distilleries have opted to develop and utilize technology to make their distilleries more energy efficient, reducing the overall need for energy to produce the spirits and lowering the carbon usage per bottle of spirit produced. The scotch whisky industry in particular, driven partially by strong government incentives in the form of taxes and grants, strong financial incentives in the form of expensive fuel costs, and a prevailing sense of responsibility to the land, has invested many resources in developing, testing, and implementing innovative strategies to improve their efficiency, such as mechanical or thermal vapor recompression (MVR/TVR), an advanced method of recovering energy from the distillate. See WHISKY, SCOTCH.

The push to improve energy efficiency can be more powerful for larger producers, where small gains in efficiency can lead to significant financial gains due to the scale of their processes. For small distilleries, although the financial incentives may be less, the smaller scale of the demands and the increased process flexibility can lower the barrier for implementing more creative or innovative efficiencies.

Byproducts of Spirits Production

Spirits production generates many byproducts: spent grain, fruit fibers or pits, pot ale, solvents, carbon dioxide, and others. These byproducts are unavoidable, inherent to the spirits production process, and have the potential to cause significant environmental harm when handled irresponsibly. However, many can find a useful life in other industries when handled conscientiously.

For example, carbon dioxide is a byproduct of all alcohol fermentation. See FERMENTATION. For every pound of ethanol produced for our drinking pleasure, approximately 9/10 of a pound of carbon dioxide is generated by the yeast. Carbon dioxide (from many different sources) is a major culprit in driving global warming. Some large-scale spirits producers capture, compress, and sell the carbon

dioxide generated in their fermentation tanks, thus preventing it from being released into the atmosphere and providing beneficial use for other applications, such as beverage carbonation. See CARBONATION. While carbon dioxide release is certainly undesirable, alcohol fermentation is not a major global contributor of greenhouse gas emissions. The liquid and solid byproducts of spirits production, left behind after mashing and/or distillation in the form of spent wash, spent grain, or spent mash, are often of more immediate concern. See MASH.

The production of malt whisky generates approximately 17.5–20 pounds of spent grain per gallon of proof spirit and 4.5–6 gallons of pot ale per gallon of proof spirit. Grain whisky production is more efficient, with 5–6.5 pounds of spent grain produced per gallon proof spirit and 9–12 gallons of spent wash. See WHISKY, GRAIN. Bourbon and rye whisky production resides in between the two, but the spent grain and pot ale are generally combined in one byproduct stream, called the "spent mash." See WHISKY, BOURBON and WHISKY, RYE. Rum and tequila generate 1.5–2 gallons of spent wash per gallon of absolute alcohol. See RUM and TEQUILA. These byproducts have very high pollution values with a very high biochemical oxygen demand if untreated.

Biochemical oxygen demand (BOD) measures the amount of oxygen required or consumed for the microbiological decomposition (oxidation) of organic material in water. See OXIDATION. The release of products with high BOD into existing waterways poses a potential threat to a variety of aquatic organisms by stimulating algae growth, which uses up the oxygen in the water and essentially suffocates the other aquatic creatures. Severe algal growth also blocks light that is needed for water plants to grow. When the algae and seagrass die, they decay. In the process of decay, more oxygen in the water is used up, and this, in turn, can continue to kill fish, crabs, oysters, and other aquatic animals. Algal growth also makes water unsuitable for human consumption or for use in agriculture. According to the US EPA, this type of pollution is one of America's most widespread, costly, and challenging environmental problems.

Pot ale will typically have 25,000–35,000 ppm BOD out of the still, and spent lees 1,000–2,000 ppm BOD. These byproducts can be reused as high-value animal feed. Depending on the scale of the operation, additional treatment (such as drying) may be necessary to preserve the animal feed for distribution.

This has the benefit of keeping the byproducts out of the watersheds, but the processing requires additional energy. The byproducts can also be treated on site to reduce the BOD via the use of digesters, which are effective and have the added benefit of producing methane that can potentially be used as a supplementary boiler fuel, but they are costly to install and require skilled operators. The draff (solids) can also be burned directly, but with a relatively low efficiency and a high particulate emission.

Sugar-cane- and agave-based washes typically have 5,000–8,000 ppm BOD and chemical oxygen demand (COD) of 25,000–30,000 ppm (similar to BOD). These washes are not useful as animal feed, but if treated properly they can be utilized effectively as fertilizer. Some large-scale producers use "common plants" to handle the byproducts of multiple distilleries at a scale that makes such treatment both environmentally and economically efficient. The byproducts could also be treated off site by third parties, either paid treatment specialists or municipal treatment plants if they are of sufficient scale to handle such waste.

As long as producers are attentive to the environmental risks posed by these byproducts, the threat to the surrounding environment can be minimized. The problems result from inattentive or unconcerned producers with frequent leaks, spills, or intentional releases. Developing nations with lax environmental regulations or limited enforcement capabilities are particularly vulnerable to these types of abuses and often lack the infrastructure to collect or treat this type of emission.

Global Shipping

The rich sensory experience of a bar offering spirits from every corner of the globe is not without consequences. From the farmer's field to a consumer's glass there are many miles of travel required, each mile with an environmental cost. Common environmental impacts of the global shipping industry include the release of oil and chemicals through accidental spills and operational discharges, the transfer of invasive alien species through ballast water and on ship hulls, dumping of garbage and sewage, and air pollution through emissions of sulfur dioxide, nitrogen oxides, and carbon dioxide.

In the United States alone, the transportation industry releases several million tons of gases each year into the atmosphere, containing lead, carbon monoxide, carbon dioxide, methane, nitrogen oxides, and particulate matter. Better engine technology and stringent standards enforced in developed nations have reduced the amount of pollutants released substantially over the last thirty years, but the transportation industry remains one of the largest contributors of greenhouse gas worldwide. The lack of a global framework for addressing the environmental impacts of international shipping and difficulties in monitoring and enforcing presents significant challenges to curbing these impacts.

While many producers are making an effort to prioritize local sourcing of raw materials to significantly reduce their footprint, the loss of local sources for manufactured products like glass bottles presents a serious challenge in this regard. Trends in the spirits industry toward an increasingly global marketplace featuring heavy and irregularly shaped bottles exacerbates this problem.

Packaging

The choice of packaging in which spirits are distributed and marketed to the consumer presents another opportunity for producers to consider the environmental impact of their products. Spirits are most commonly packaged in glass bottles. Glass manufacture is an energy-intensive process, requiring high temperatures reached through the combustion of fuel with its resulting emissions. Glass is a commonly recycled material, although detailed life-cycle analyses on recycled goods have illuminated the complexity of these benefits. When compared with the amount of energy required to send the same goods to landfills or incinerators and make new products from scratch, the results vary dramatically, but recycled glass generally uses about 20 percent less energy to produce than virgin glass. Minimizing the amount of glass per package (thinner bottoms, efficient shaping) reduces the resultant emissions from both the manufacture and shipping of the glass. See GLASSWARE.

Choosing minimally processed, recycled paper labels and water- or vegetable-based inks with no VOC adhesives is another way a spirits producer can minimize the environmental impact of their packaging. Other types of labels, such as transfer labels and screen-printing, utilize potentially hazardous solvents and require additional energy to execute.

Closures are yet another opportunity for producers to make environmentally responsible choices. Independent studies have indicated that the use of natural cork stoppers, as compared to aluminum or plastic, can have a strong beneficial impact.

Water

It is no coincidence that distilleries have historically been located in areas with abundant natural water supplies. It takes more than 30 gallons of water to produce one gallon of finished spirit. In regions with copious natural water supplies there is minimal appreciable impact of a distillery's usage, but the expansion of distilleries into areas with low or unpredictable water supplies can strain already taxed water systems. This impact can be reduced by implementing closed cooling systems that continuously recycle cooling water, although there is a price to be paid in electrical usage for such a system. In a world of increasingly extreme, unpredictable weather and drought events, attention must be paid to conservation in many parts of the world.

"Agriculture." Water.epa.gov. http://water.epa.gov/polwaste/nps/agriculture.cfm (accessed October 19, 2015).

"Agriculture Facts." Water.epa.gov. http://water.epa.gov/polwaste/nps/agriculture_facts.cfm (accessed October 19, 2015).

"Biochemical Oxygen Demand in Water Bodies." UN.org. http://www.un.org/esa/sustdev/natlinfo/indicators/methodology_sheets/freshwater/biochemical_oxygen_demand.pdf (accessed March 3, 2021).

"Biodiversity and Agriculture." Chgehavard.org. http://www.chgeharvard.org/topic/biodiversity-and-agriculture (accessed November 6, 2015).

"Common Impacts of the Shipping Industry." WWF website. http://www.wwf.org.au/our_work/saving_the_natural_world/oceans_and_marine/marine_threats/commercial_shipping/impacts/ (accessed October 25, 2015).

Jain, Radha, and S. Srivastava. "Nutrient Composition of Spent Wash and Its Impact on Sugarcane Growth and Biochemical Attributes." *Physiology and Molecular Biology of Plants* 18, no. 1 (2012): 95–99.

"Nitrogen and Phosphorus." Cbf.org. http://www.cbf.org/about-the-bay/issues/dead-zones/nitrogen-phosphorus (accessed October 12, 2015).

"Nutrient Pollution: The Issue." EPA. http://www2.epa.gov/nutrientpollution/problem (accessed March 3, 2021).

OECD. *Environmental Impacts of International Shipping: The Role of Ports.* Paris: OECD, 2011.

Oñiguez, C. G., C. J. J. Bernal, M. W. Ramírez, and N. J. Villalvazo. "Recycling Agave Bagasse of the Tequila Industry." *Advances in Chemical Engineering and Science* 4 (2014): 135–142.

Piggott, J. R. *The Science and Technology of Whiskies.* Harlow, UK: Longman Scientific & Technical, 1989.

Russell, Inge. *Whisky Technology, Production and Marketing.* Amsterdam: Academic Press, 2003.

"What Is Nutrient Pollution?" NOAA.gov. http://oceanservice.noaa.gov/facts/nutpollution.html (accessed March 3, 2021).

Nicole Austin

enzymes are a class of proteins that catalyze the conversion of a substrate from one form to another without themselves being destroyed. Almost all metabolic processes and reactions within living cells are mediated by enzymes. A typical cell has several thousand kinds of enzymes that carry out its functions. One of the most important features of an enzyme is its active site, where a cluster of amino acids is folded together to create a pocket or a groove where the catalytic event occurs. This pocket is very specific and selective. Researchers often suggest a lock-and-key analogy with enzymes. Recent evidence, however, suggests the effect is more like a baseball glove: the glove is the enzyme that folds around the substrate. Because of this precise attraction of an active site to a substrate, enzymes are highly effective at binding and creating very fast reactions, much more so than an inorganic catalyst like a metal ion. Initial contact between an active site and a potential substrate is a random collision. The two are held together by hydrogen or ionic bonds to amino acids that carry a mild charge. Protons and electrons (energy) will be either donated or accepted between enzyme and substrate. In response, the substrate is either broken apart or joined with another substrate. The enzyme then detaches and repeats the process.

Because they can be sensitive to external pressures, the environment in which enzymes conduct their activities is important. Scientists devote careers to the study of optimizing enzyme performance, known as enzyme kinetics. The two most important parameters of enzyme activity they study are temperature and pH. See pH. Temperature increases within limits often increase reaction rates between enzymes and substrates. As biological material, however, enzymes will denature when exposed to sufficiently high temperatures. Enzymes are unique, and each will deactivate at its own specific temperature. Enzymes that can function at higher temperatures are called thermotolerant. Likewise, the pH of the surrounding environment can affect the ionic charges either on the substrate or on the enzyme, thus affecting the binding process. A third factor enzyme scientists consider is the concentration of either enzyme or substrate. Increasing the concentration of enzyme to substrate will increase the reaction rate, but the effect is not linear. When the enzyme concentrate becomes saturated, reaction rates only marginally improve.

To a brewer this is important for cooking and fermentation processes. The most important objective is to convert starch, a large molecule that can be up to ten thousand molecules of sugar attached together, into the individual sugar units. Yeast consumes sugar but not starch. It has to be cut into pieces before yeast consumes the sugar. Brewers use commercially purchased enzymes or enzymes from the malting process to break apart starch. Typical enzymes used or found in the malt include glucoamylases, alpha-amylases, beta-amylases, glucanases, and proteases. Each enzyme has its own unique temperature, pH, and level of activity. It is up to a brewer to optimize the timing of conversion of starch into sugar during the cooking process. Various temperature ranges may be used in the cooking process, and the mash or wort may be held at specific temperatures for specific lengths of time. Each brewery or distillery designs its own mash bills (proportion of grain to malt or enzyme) based on the size of its equipment. See MASH BILL.

Becker, W. M., and D. W. Deamer. *The World of the Cell*, 2nd ed. Redwood City, CA: Benjamin/Cummings, 1991.

Kelsall, D. R., and T. P. and Lyons. *The Alcohol Textbook*, 3rd ed. Nottingham: Nottingham University Press, 1999.

Palmer, G. H. *Malting, Wort Production and Fermentation*. London: Institute of Brewing, 1990.

Don Livermore

Espresso Martini is a vodka and coffee cocktail created in the 1980s by the British bartender Dick Bradsell that remains one of the most popular and widely recognized classics of modern times. While not technically a Martini, it is a variation for which even purists will often make an exception.

The original recipe was created by Bradsell at London's Soho Brasserie in 1983 for a famous model who asked for something to "wake me up and then fuck me up" (Bradsell has never disclosed who the model was). The choice of coffee was inspired by the fact that the restaurant had recently installed an Illy espresso machine next to the bar.

The recipe has had several incarnations in its lifetime. The latter-day Espresso Martini is typically served "up," but it was originally served on the rocks, when it was known as the Vodka Espresso. This recipe subsequently evolved into the Pharmaceutical Stimulant during Bradsell's time behind the bar at the Pharmacy in Notting Hill. It was only when Bradsell opened Match EC1 with Jonathan Downey in 1997 that he reworked, and renamed, the drink a third time to create the Espresso Martini, which became a mainstay of cocktail lists around the world.

Recipe: Combine 50 ml vodka, 25 ml of very strong espresso, 15 ml Kahlua, 10 ml Tia Maria, and 5 ml sugar syrup (2:1 formula), shake hard with ice, strain into a cocktail glass, and garnish with three coffee beans.

See also BRADSELL, DICK; and DOWNEY, JONATHAN.

"Our Favourite Bartenders: Dick Bradsell." *The Cocktail Lovers*, November 11, 2013. www.thecocktaillovers. com. https://thecocktaillovers.com/our-favourite-bartenders-dick-bradsell/ (accessed March 3, 2021).

Alice Lascelles

essential oils (EOs) are the concentrated essences of botanicals that are soluble in alcohol. Essential oils represent the highly volatile liquids within the plant that carry their scent and contribute a large part of their flavor as well. EOs provide us with the medicinal benefits of botanicals as well as playing a major role in what we taste and smell.

EOs can be extracted from a variety of natural materials: fruit rind, roots (as in the case of orris root from the iris or the root of angelica), grass, woody stems, bark, leaves, seeds, and flower petals. The EOs are extracted from these botanicals through the process of distillation. Different distillation methods can be employed to extract essential oils. The best known in the world of spirits is alcoholic distillation, as for example in the manufacture of gin, where various botanicals such as juniper, angelica, orris, and lemon peel (along with many others) are macerated in neutral grain spirits and then distilled. The botanicals release their essential oils into the alcohol vapor, which then condenses as gin, with the flavors carried by the EOs transferred into the final product.

Another distillation method uses water instead of alcohol. In this method, plant material can either be boiled in the still or placed in a secondary chamber into which steam from the still flows. Hot water and/or steam will soften the cellular walls of the plant material, and its essential oils are then released into the steam. The steam then flows through a condenser coil, just as with alcohol distillation. Once the steam is cooled, the liquid settles and the EO floats to the top.

Post-production, essential oils are used in a variety of ways. They can be employed singularly as flavoring components and added to spirits and liqueurs to produce a desired flavor; one example is crème de menthe. See CRÈME DE MENTHE. Blending juniper along with other essential oils into a neutral spirit without distillation will produce a "compound gin." Behind the bar, food-grade essential oils can be tinctured and then utilized in a mixed drink, or blended together to produce compound bitters.

See also BOTANICAL and GIN.

Aftel, Mandy. *Essence and Alchemy: A Book of Perfume.* New York: North Point Press, 2001.
Arctander, Steffen. *Perfume and Flavor Materials of Natural Origin.* Carol Stream, IL: Allured, 2008.

Audrey Saunders

esters are compounds produced by the chemical reaction between acids and alcohol. In wine and spirit production, they occur mainly as a result of fermentation and aging in a process called esterification. Esters formed during fermentation are influenced by many factors, including base ingredient (grain, fruit, molasses, etc.), fermentation temperature and length, yeast strain(s) used, climate, and other factors, and they can be classified into two groups: acetate esters (acetate plus alcohol) and ethyl esters (ethanol plus fatty acid).

A distilled spirit typically contains hundreds of esters in its makeup, which help create its aroma. The most abundant esters include ethyl hexanoate, with an aroma commonly described as apple, and ethyl acetate, which can contribute both fruity and nail-polish aromas. Other examples of esters and their aromas include ethyl lactate (butter and cream), ethyl cinnamate (cinnamon), isoamyl acetate (banana and pear), and isobutyl acetate (cherry and berries). See AROMA.

Many of the lighter esters from fermentation are removed during distillation. The amount of reflux and the size of the cuts made during distillation will affect the amount of esters left in the resulting spirit, as does the acidity of the type of alcohol; highly acidified cognac, bourbon, and many rums are typically high in esters. See REFLUX and CUT.

Barrel aging also contributes esters, transforming acids into simple esters and simple fruity esters into those with notes that include honey and spice. The spicey and cinnamony ethyl ferrulate is a typical result of barrel aging. Generally speaking, the longer a spirit is in a barrel, the more esters it will have.

See also FERMENTATION and YEAST.

Fromm, James Richard. "Introduction to Esters." http://www.3rd1000.com/chem301/chem301v.htm (accessed March 3, 2021).

Jack Robertiello

Estes, Tomas (1945–2021), was a restaurateur and co-owner of the tequila brand Ocho. A tireless agave spirits advocate, he was known as the tequila ambassador to Europe. Raised in the predominantly Mexican neighborhood of East Los Angeles, Estes (born Thomas; he was actually of British descent) became fascinated with Mexican culture early on. He opened his first restaurant, Café Pacifico, in Amsterdam in 1976 and went on to launch sixteen more establishments, all Mexican in concept, across Europe and Australia over the next four decades. The more he learned about tequila and Mexico's other spirits, the more he strove to share his discoveries, conducting bartender training sessions, writing for trade publications, and accepting speaking engagements. Mexico's National Chamber for the Tequila Industry took note of his efforts and in 2003 named him the spirit's official ambassador to the European Union.

Intrigued by the subtleties of terroir, Estes had another great love, burgundy wine. When Carlos Camarena, who made some of Estes's favorite tequilas, asked him to create a new brand, Estes envisioned a terroir-driven tequila. Ocho is the first major brand to offer single-rancho expressions, designed to showcase agave from a specific field.

See also TEQUILA.

Estes, Tomas. *The Tequila Ambassador*. London: Diffordsguide, 2012.

Chantal Martineau

ethanol, or ethyl alcohol, is the second simplest compound in the family of hydrocarbons known as alcohols, which are defined by the suffix OH. An ethyl group attached to a hydroxyl group, ethanol is written chemically as C_2H_5OH. As the most commonly used alcohol, ethanol is commonly known simply as "alcohol." Ethanol can be produced through several methods, but the most common is fermentation, which is the metabolization by yeast of sugars, usually sucrose and fructose, into ethanol and carbon dioxide. The only method of ethanol production that occurs naturally, fermentation is the source of all ingested ethanol, though further concentration of ethanol in water occurs through fortification or distillation. In addition to its use as an intoxicant due to its psychoactive effects, ethanol has other domestic and industrial uses, most notably as a solvent, an antiseptic, and engine fuel. At room temperature it is a colorless liquid.

The intoxicating properties of ethanol, or at least of compounds where it is present, have been known for at least nine thousand years, and the fermentation of alcoholic beverages out of grains and fruits is generally considered to be the first controlled chemical reaction of any ancient civilization. Evidence of the concentration of ethanol through distillation goes back at least 2,500 years, to India. See DISTILLATION, HISTORY. Due to the azeotropic nature of the bond it forms with water, pure ethanol cannot be isolated by distillation without chemical adjuncts and it was only first isolated by Raymond Lull in the thirteenth century. The composition and formula for ethanol were determined, respectively, by the French chemists Antoine Lavoisier and Nicolas-Theodore de Saussure, in 1781 and 1808. See AZEOTROPE.

The human body responds to the effects of ethanol progressively, as increased consumption leads to displays of excitement, followed by loss of inhibitions and decreased coordination—the expression of these being to a significant degree affected by societal norms surrounding alcohol consumption—and ultimately stupor, which is universal. Ethanol behaves as a depressant, as the compound is transferred from the blood to the brain, where alcohol inhibits the proper functioning of neurotransmitters, the chemical messengers that bridge the synapse between nerve endings. Normal communication between neurons depends on a natural equilibrium of excitatory and inhibitory neurotransmitters. Although these interactions are complex, it appears in the short term primarily that ethanol increases inhibitory neurotransmission and decreases excitatory neurotransmission. The body's attempt to compensate for these actions over time lead to some of the effects of long-term alcohol consumption, such as tolerance, withdrawal symptoms, and possibly addiction. See HEALTH AND SPIRITS.

Ethanol is metabolized in the liver by the enzyme alcohol dehydrogenase. Pharmacological sensitivity to ethanol is not limited to humans or even vertebrates as a whole; sensitivity to ethanol, made evident by impaired motor control, has been observed and studied in insects. Indeed, the study of alcoholic sensitivity in the fruit fly, *Drosophila melanogaster*, has led to the creation of several mutations known (among others) as barfly, tipsy, and cheapdate. These gene sequences are evolutionarily related to genes that code for neurological pathways in vertebrates.

In addition to its intoxicating effects, several other properties of the ethanol compound are significant within the context of spirits and cocktails. Its complete miscibility (ability to dissolve completely with water in any proportion) to form a homogenous and transparent solution permits its storage at any concentration. This property, which holds true with alcohol and many organic substances in addition to water, as well as its related ability to dissolve both polar and non-polar substances, such as ionic salts, essential oils, flavoring, and coloring agents, allows for the integration of complex flavors into potable spirits. Put simply, the diverse and complex flavors attainable in alcoholic beverages are a function of ethanol's ability to dissolve and hold other molecules easily in suspension at any temperature over a wide range of alcoholic concentrations.

Ethanol's boiling point of 78° C allows for the relatively simple distillation from water solutions. And because ethanol has a freezing point of −114° C, alcoholic beverages can be produced, stored, and served below the freezing point of water. As an antiseptic it can be used to preserve organic material and be used for infusions. Ethanol is flammable, and a 40 percent alcohol to water solution will ignite at 26° C when a flame is put to it.

See also FERMENTATION and DISTILLATION, PROCESS.

Heberlein, Ulrike. Genetics of Alcohol-Induced Behaviors in *Drosophila*. *Alcohol Health and Research* 24 (November 2000): 185–188.

Morrison, Robert Thornton, and Robert Neilson Boyd. *Organic Chemistry*. Boston: Allyn & Bacon, 1987.

Valenzuela, C. Fernando. "Alcohol and Neurotransmitter Interactions." *Alcohol Health and Research* 21 (November 1997): 144–148.

Eben Klemm

eugenol (and **isoeugenol**) is a colorless or pale yellow liquid with the smell of cloves. It is extracted from essential oils of spices such as clove, nutmeg, and cinnamon as well as from heated lignin, itself a polyphenol found in oak and other woods. See ESSENTIAL OILS. Poorly mixable in water, eugenol is highly soluble in higher-proof solutions of alcohol and water and hence often imparts its spicy and balsamic aromas to oak-aged spirits such as whisky, rum, and brandy.

See also BARREL and PHENOLS.

"Eugenol." American Chemical Society. https://www.acs.org/content/acs/en/molecule-of-the-week/archive/e/eugenol.html (accessed April 21, 2021).

Doug Frost

Everclear is a brand of neutral spirits distilled from grain established at the beginning of Prohibition by the American Distilling Co. of Chicago (for "medical" use) and now owned by Luxco, a spirits manufacturer and importer based in St. Louis, Missouri. At 95 percent ABV (190 proof), it is the highest-proof spirit available—water and ethanol form an azeotrope slightly above this concentration, meaning that distillation cannot produce anything higher proof. (A 151-proof version of Everclear is also available, sold in US states whose laws limit alcohol content in spirits.) Because its high alcohol content can very efficiently leach flavors from fruits, spices, and other ingredients, Everclear is well suited to serving as the base for infusions like limoncello, compound gin, and bitters. See LIMONCELLO and BITTERS. It is often also used as a base spirit for fraternity-party punches and other similar large-format drinks. See BASE.

See also ETHANOL.

Everclear website. http://www.makeityourown.com/ (accessed March 3, 2021).

Jason Horn

excise, taxes, and distillation. Excise duty or tax on consumer goods is usually paid by the manufacturer or, with some exceptions, the retailer. "Excise" originates from the Dutch *excijs*, from the Latin, *accensum*, to tax. The Dutch in Amsterdam were the first in Europe to also levy a customs duty on imported spirits, in 1498. As with most excise taxes, this was calculated according to the strength of the spirit. Other taxes can also be levied on spirits, from tariffs and ad valorem duty to regional and even district sales taxes under different countries' jurisdictions. There are also licensing fees and duties on raw materials, manufacturing, and retailing. Spirits have traditionally been the most heavily regulated and taxed category of consumer goods, due to the revenue they generate and the way taxation can directly influence the public's consumption behavior. These taxes directly affect the economics of the spirits business at every level, from product portfolios to production output, the construction and layout of distillery premises, size and type of stills, bond warehousing, and even the time and place for purchase and consumption.

The first known excise system comes from Song dynasty China, which established "alcohol and vinegar bureaus" in northern China in 1231–1232 CE. This was intended as a state monopoly on the manufacture and sale of spirits, but when that proved unworkable, it incorporated a complex series of controls and taxes on private production. A modified system continued when the Song yielded to the Yuan dynasty in 1271.

In the West, the most elaborate and influential excise system was created by Britain, beginning in the seventeenth century, and we shall focus on that. Excise and customs on alcoholic products were a primary source of income for Britain and the English-speaking world until the mid-twentieth century, led by the United States, Scotland, Canada, Ireland, and Australia. The commencement of excise and most of the major duty rate increases were introduced to fund military campaigns, a relationship with a long historical nexus. In the United Kingdom, the first excise law was enacted to fund the English Civil War (1642–1651). Every significant duty increase and most revenue-raising regulations had motivations in funding further military expenditures: War of Grand Alliances (1689–1697), Seven Years War (1756–1763), Napoleonic Wars (1803–1815), and Crimean War (1853–1856), followed by the First and Second World Wars. In the United States, the first Federal excise laws were enacted to pay foreign debtors for their Revolutionary War loans (1791–1802). Excise was reintroduced due to the War of 1812 (1814–1817), then again to finance the American Civil War (1862–1865). Excise remained in place after the Civil War, with significant rate increases during the First and Second World Wars (1917 Lever Act).

With the introduction of personal and corporate income taxes in the early twentieth century, the share of government revenue supplied by excise and customs revenue began a slide that continued through the twentieth century. Liquor and tobacco, known as stimulant or sin taxes, generated 80 percent of the government's revenue in these whisky-distilling countries during the second half of the nineteenth century. In 1913, before the advent of the First World War, liquor excise duties, with whisky the dominant spirit, constituted 23 percent of US revenue, 26 percent of revenue in the United Kingdom, 13 percent in Canada, and 23 percent in Australia. By the mid-twentieth century, the introduction of new taxes and increased rates in personal and corporate taxes significantly reduced excise revenue. In 2016, spirits revenue had shrunk to 0.3 percent of total United States income, 0.4 percent in the United Kingdom, and 2 percent in Australia.

The first British excise laws for liquor came into effect in 1663 for "beer, ale, cider and perry." "Aqua vitae and strong waters" were also included when the Scottish Parliament enacted their version of the law in 1664. See STRONG WATER. Ten years after its introduction, the excise rate doubled, then doubled again four years later. Governments now had a lever to extract revenue from their citizens, and they used and abused this with increasing frequency. In 1660,

Parliament created gaugers, or inspectors, who had the right to enter premises and measure prepared liquors (much as the Song had in China). As well as taxing spirits, the government began introducing license fees for manufacturing and retailing. These mounting statutes found consolidation under the 1662 Customs and Excise Act and the first Distillery Act in 1668.

The first laws to oversee product quality standards arrived with the 1696 Prevention of Fraud and Abuses Act. The spirits industry was given another competitive enhancement with the 1729 Act of Laying Down Duty upon Compounded Waters and Spirits, and Upon the Retailer of Spirituous Liquor in 1733. The category targeted was flavored malt spirit, especially gin, whose annual consumption skyrocketed (mainly in London) to thirty-one million liters in 1743. The demand for cheap malt spirit to rectify and compound into gin and British brandy helped commercialize the nascent Scottish distilling industry, as Lowland distilleries became a major supplier of malt and low wines to English rectifiers in the late eighteenth century.

After 1707, Great Britain comprised four polities: England, Wales, Scotland, and Ireland. Britain also administered the thirteen colonies of North America, adding Canada in 1763 and Australia in 1788. Each of these countries and colonies possessed differing levels of self-government, resulting in innumerable local laws and regulations, extending down to districts and towns with varying excise rates and distilling bylaws. They also incurred constant volatility due to regulatory changes. All shared strong cultural roots, comparable liquor consumption habits, and legal precedents for formulating their spirit laws from the British Parliament. To ensure compliance, governments needed to account for every drop of alcohol, whether locally manufactured or imported. Fines and penalties became additional sources of revenue and restraint of the trade and commerce, from still registration to smuggling. The first colony in America to enact excise was Connecticut in 1650, followed by Canada in 1780 and New South Wales in 1819. As colonies gained independence, they enacted new national excise, customs, and distilling laws: the United States in March 1791, Canada in July 1867, and Australia in January 1901.

Until the second half of the eighteenth century, a significant drawback was the inability to measure alcoholic strength precisely in order to extract duties from different liquors accurately. The introduction of the hydrometer (which could measure the proof of a spirit quickly and with good accuracy) in the eighteenth century and its eventual adoption by the government was an important step that also aided new manufacturing practices, such as allowing continuous distillation to be licensed.

As Irish and Scotch whisky emerged as fledgling industries from the 1770s, the proliferation of small, provincial stills necessitated the British government to measure a still's gallon capacity and forecast yearly volume output as an alternative taxation method. The 1786 Licence Wash Act set annual fees for the cubic capacity and doubled excise rates. In 1787, the Distillery Act calculated that a still could be discharged about four times a week. Lowland distillers, with regional tax concessions, were motivated to invent shallow stills that permitted rapid distillation, circumnavigating the act. By 1797, distillers were discharging a 150-liter still every three minutes, twenty-four hours a day. The government responded by increasing the still's capacity licensing fee from £1.5 per gallon (3.8 liters) in 1786 to £162 by 1802. This proved untenable. The 1814 Excise Act and 1816 Small Stills Act led to the landmark 1823 Excise Act, which set the regulatory framework and operational legacy that characterizes the industry standards for excise today.

In the United States, the cost of importing British copper, the recent invention of the steam engine, and different grain mashes led to the invention of wooden chambered steam stills in the 1790s. See STILL, THREE-CHAMBER. By 1816, the federal government registered 650 steam boiler stills (these were also used by Canadian distilleries). The American Commissioner of Excise expressed concern of the inequalities between the ubiquitous common pot stills and these new wooden steam stills. Steam and the invention of continuous stills was also an issue to the British Board of Excise since 1801, which led to the rejection of many patent still submissions until the 1823 Excise Act. They alleged that high proof, high volume continuous patent stills did not conform with the government's batch standards of measurement and risked illicit production and smuggling. Aeneas Coffey, inspector general of excise in Ireland until 1824, patented the most efficient continuous still in 1830, setting the stage for the growth of scotch and Irish blended whiskies under the 1823 Excise Act. See STILL, CONTINUOUS.

In the late nineteenth century, the political influence of the temperance movement and abolitionists radically changed the social and regulatory landscapes in whisky countries. Restrictions and taxations on the public's access to liquor were abundant, and in some instances the manufacture and sale of alcohol was banned outright. Notable incidents of national prohibitions were in Russia (1914–1924), Norway (1916–1927), Canada (1918–1920), and the United States (1920–1933). Other countries used local options to prohibit liquor manufacture and sale at regional and district levels. The consequences of prohibiting liquor sales to governments resulted in heavy financial deficits from the loss of excise revenue and high expenditures in policing and prosecuting illicit activities. By the mid-twentieth century, the political sentiment in liberal democracies shifted from controlling the trade to individual responsibility. The United Kingdom introduced breath testing in the 1967 Road Safety Act, establishing a maximum legal alcohol level; by the 1980s, most Western countries passed roadside breathalyzer tests.

Whisky excise per liter of alcohol in 2018 (100 percent ABV) is US$27.00 per gallon in the United States; £28.74 a liter in the the United Kingdom; CA$12.11 in Canada; €42.57 in Ireland; and AU$84.51 in Australia. While excise may be relatively high in some countries, it no longer serves as a major contributor to the national treasuries. Governments are increasingly being lobbied by organizations to raise duties to prevent or minimize harmful health effects from excessive long-term and dangerous episodic alcohol consumption.

Brander, Michael. *The Original Scotch*. New York: Clarkson Potter, 1975.

Craig, H. Charles. *The Scotch Whisky Industry Record*. Dumbarton, UK: Index, 1994.

De Kergommeaux, Davin. *Canadian Whisky, Second Edition: The New Portable Expert*. Vancouver: Appetite by Random House, 2017.

House of Commons, Committee on the Distilleries in Scotland. *Report Respecting the Distilleries in Scotland &c., &c.*, London: 1799.

McGuire, E. B. *Irish Whisky*. Dublin: Gill & MacMillan, 1973.

Park, Hyunhee. *Soju: A Global History*. Cambridge: Cambridge University Press, 2021.

Ice tools and squeezers. Back row (L-R): citrus squeezer (mid 19th c.), cast iron ice scraper with tinned bowl (late 19th c.); "Lewis" bag (modern); hardwood ice mallet (early 19th c.). Middle row: wood and steel ice fork (late 19th c.); cast iron, ceramic, and wooden citrus squeezer (late 19th c.). Front row: cast iron ice fork (early 20th c.); spring-loaded chrome-plated steel ice crusher (1940s); stainless steel ice scoop (modern); silver-plated ice tongs (1950s). Wondrich Collection. Photograph by Eric Medsker.

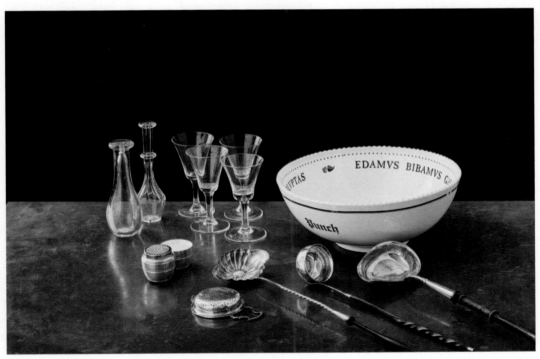

Punch gear. Back row (L-R): Toddy lifter and Punch lifter (British, 19th c.); Punch glasses (modern); Punch bowl (modern). Middle row: nutmeg grater (modern); Punch ladles (French, 20th c., British, 18th c., German, 19th c.). Front row: Punch strainer (British, 20th c.). Wondrich Collection. Photograph by Eric Medsker.

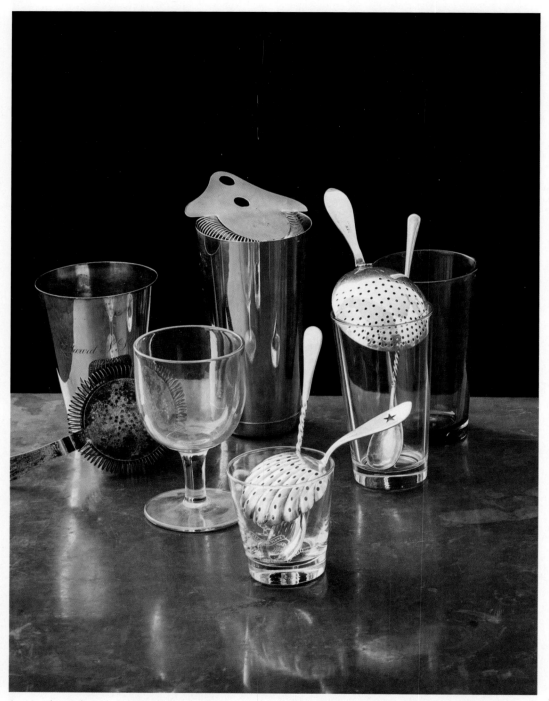

American bar tools. Back row (L-R): silverplate mixing tin (property of Edward S. Stokes, Hoffman House, New York, 1900); stainless steel mixing tin (1919) and Hawthorne-style strainer (1930s); pint mixing glass (modern). Middle row: silverplate Hawthorne strainer (1892); Hoffman House stemmed mixing glass (ca. 1910); large bar glass (modern) with silverplate teardrop barspoon (ca. 1910) and large Julep strainer (1890s). Front row: Pendennis Club small bar glass/Old-Fashioned glass (modern), with silverplate medium barspoon (ca. 1880) and small Julep strainer (1870s). Wondrich Collection. Photograph by Eric Medsker.

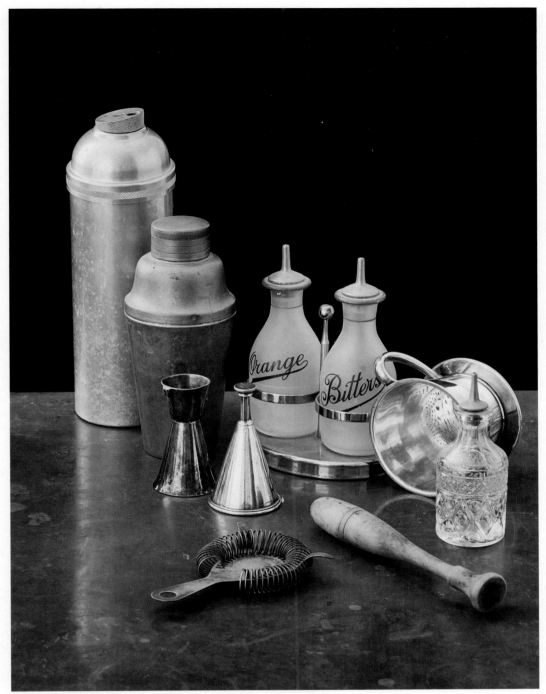

American bar tools, continued. Back row (L-R): pressed aluminum Meshberg/Emson Products patent 3-piece cocktail shaker (1946); brass Hauck patent 3-piece shaker (1884); chrome-plated steel and frosted glass bitters bottle set (1940s); silverplate cup strainer (1860s). Middle row: silverplate Shriner's fez double jigger (1952); silverplate single jigger (1870s); molded glass bitters bottle (1910s). Front row: silverplate Pick-Lashar patent "Handy" Hawthorne-style strainer (1907); wooden ("treen") muddler (ca. 1890). Wondrich Collection. Photograph by Eric Medsker.

European bar tools. Back row (L-R): German silverplate WMF "Parisian" shaker (1920s); British pewter "baluster" 1-gill measure (1890s); French pewter double deciliter measure (ca. 1900); Dutch pewter 1-deciliter measure (ca. 1920). Middle row: Dutch silverplate Concordia "Boston" shaker (ca. 1930s); British Royal Navy copper ½ gill measure (1890s); Spanish pewter centiliter measure (ca. 1900). Front Row: French Christofle lemon-throttler (ca. 1910); Italian Cinzano barspoon (1950s); French Christofle barspoon (ca. 1930s); British Asprey strainer (1930s); French Christofle barspoon (ca. 1910s); all silverplate. Wondrich Collection. Photograph by Eric Medsker.

European, Caribbean, and Japanese bar tools. Back row (L-R): Spanish cocktail-throwing glass (modern); Japanese mixing glass and chrome-plated steel strainer (1960s); 2-piece British silverplate Farrow & Jackson "Boston" shaker (1890s). Middle row: Japanese chrome-plated steel jigger (1960s); British silverplate "3-out" jigger (1920s). Front row: 2 Martinique wooden swizzle-sticks (modern); Trinidadian wooden and steel swizzle stick (modern). Wondrich Collection. Photograph by Eric Medsker.

DRY MARTINI
1/5 French vermouth, 4/5 dry gin, stir with cracked ice, strain. Serve with olive or pearl onion.

MANHATTAN
1/4 Italian vermouth, 3/4 rye, dash of bitters. Stir with cracked ice, strain. Serve with cherry. Dry Manhattan: Use Fr. vermouth, lemon peel.

OLD FASHIONED
Muddle lump sugar in dash of bitters, soda. Add 1 jigger whiskey, 2 ice cubes, fruit, twist of lemon peel.

PINK LADY
1/2 oz. lemon or lime juice, 1/2 oz. grenadine, 3/4 oz. heavy cream, 1¼ oz. gin. Shake with cracked ice, strain.

DAIQUIRI
Juice 1/2 lime or lemon, 1 tsp. sugar. Shake with cracked ice. Add 1½ oz white rum, shake until shaker frosts, strain.

BACARDI
1/2 oz. lemon or lime juice, 1 tsp. sugar, 1 dash grenadine. Shake with cracked ice. Add 1 jigger Bacardi rum, shake well, strain.

ALEXANDER
1/3 jigger crème de cacao, 1/3 jigger heavy cream, 1/3 jigger dry gin. Shake with cracked ice, strain.

CLOVER CLUB
1/2 jigger lemon juice, white of 1 egg, dash of grenadine, 1 jigger dry gin. Shake with cracked ice and strain.

BETWEEN THE SHEETS
Juice of 1/2 lemon, 3/4 oz. rum, 3/4 oz. brandy 3/4 oz. Cointreau. Shake with cracked ice, strain.

DUBONNET
1/3 jigger dry gin, 2/3 jigger Dubonnet, stir with cracked ice, strain. Serve with twist of lemon peel.

BOURBON TODDY
Muddle 1 lump sugar with dash of bitters in 1 oz. water. Add 2 oz bourbon, ice and twist of lemon peel.

BAMBOO
2 oz. dry sherry, 3/4 oz. Italian vermouth. Stir with cracked ice, strain.

Classic Cocktails remain classic; these 25 examples, photographed by Edgar de Evia and published in *Esquire*, August 1948,

SIDECAR

1/3 jigger lime juice, 1/3 jigger Triple Sec or Cointreau, 1/3 jigger brandy. Add shaved ice, shake and strain.

ROB ROY

1/2 jigger Italian vermouth, 2 dashes of bitters, 1/2 jigger Scotch whisky, cracked ice, stir, strain Add twist of lemon peel.

STINGER

1/2 jigger brandy, 1/2 jigger white crème de menthe. Shake with cracked ice until shaker frosts. Strain.

BRONX

Juice of 1/4 orange, 1/4 jigger Italian vermouth, 1/4 jigger Fr. vermouth, 1/2 jigger dry gin. Shake with cracked ice, strain.

SAZARAC

Muddle 1 lump sugar in 1 dash each Angostura, Peychaud's bitters, water. Add jigger bourbon, ice. Stir, strain into glass rinsed with Pernod. Twist of lemon peel.

PRESIDENTE

2 dashes orange curaçao. 1 dash grenadine, 1/2 jigger Fr. vermouth, 1 jigger rum. Add ice, shake and strain.

WHISKEY SOUR

1/2 jigger lemon and lime juice, 1 tsp. pwd. sugar, 1 jigger whiskey. Shake with cracked ice and strain.

WHITE LADY

Juice of 1/2 lemon, white of one egg, 3/4 oz. Cointreau, 1½ oz. gin. Shake with ice, strain.

JACK ROSE

Juice 1/2 lime, white of 1 egg, 1 tsp. grenadine, 1 jigger applejack. Shake with cracked ice, strain.

FRISCO

3/4 oz. Benedictine, 2 oz. bourbon. Stir with cracked ice, strain. Add twist of lemon peel.

CREME DE MENTHE FRAPPE

Nearly fill glass of fine ice with white crème de menthe. Tilt glass. Over back of inserted spoon, slowly pour 1 oz. brandy.

NEW YORKER

Juice of 1/2 lime, dash of grenadine, 2 oz. rye. Shake with cracked ice, strain. Add twist of lemon peel.

CHAMPAGNE

Saturate lump of sugar with dash of bitters. Add ice cube and fill with chilled champagne. Twist of lemon peel.

would look much the same today, although a few of the chosen drinks might be different. Used with permission.

Glassware, all modern unless indicated. Back row (L-R): Wood's Rum Toddy mug (1970s); Pat O'Brien's Hurricane glass (1960s); absinthe glass; Latitude 29 Tiki mug; Collins glass; Highball glass. Second row from back: Glencairn whisky-tasting glass; genever glass; Cocktail or Martini glass; Cocktail coupe (ca. 1960); "Nick and Nora" glass. Third row from back: copper Cock 'n' Bull Moscow Mule mug (1940s); milk glass Tom and Jerry mug (1950s); stemmed pony or liqueur glass; cognac tasting glass; Old Crow cocktail glass (1960s); Mai-Tai glass. Front Row: Kweichow Moutai baijiu glass; shot glass; vodka glass; whisky glass (1960s). Wondrich Collection. Photograph by Eric Medsker.

Royal Commission on Whiskey and Other Potable Spirits. *Interim Report*. London: HM Stationery Office, 1908.

Schottenhammer, Angela. "Distillation and Distilleries in Mongol Yuan China." *Crossroads* 14 (October 2016): 143–160.

Chris Middleton

expositions and world's fairs and other such national and international gatherings were— prior to the age of jet travel and, much later, the internet—the primary avenues by which countries could showcase their national identities and flex their commercial muscles, showing off such things as recent inventions, manufacturing highlights, and agricultural specialties. Wine, spirits, bitters, and cocktails played a significant role in many national displays.

London's Great Exhibition (May 1–October 15, 1851) is considered the first large-scale international fair of its sort. An elaborate "crystal palace" constructed from enormous panes of glass on a prefabricated cast iron structure featured numerous national pavilions, visited by six million people over a six-month period. Unlike certain subsequent fairs, London's 1851 fair was profitable—and the city hosted another World's Fair in 1862.

Paris was a frequent host city during the nineteenth century, with fairs in 1855, 1867, 1878, and 1889—the last fair's Eiffel Tower still stands. Other notable cities included Vienna (Weltausstellung 1873 Wien), Barcelona (Exposición Universal de Barcelona, 1888), and Brussels (Brussels International Exposition, 1897). The United States, seeking to project its ascendant technological and manufacturing prowess, hosted world's fairs in Philadelphia (Centennial Exhibition, 1876), New Orleans (World's Industrial and Cotton Centennial Exposition, 1884), and Chicago (World Columbian Exposition, 1893).

Notable early twentieth-century fairs included Paris (Paris International, 1900), St. Louis (Louisiana Purchase, 1904), San Francisco (Panama–Pacific International Exposition, 1915), Chicago (Century of Progress, 1933–1934), and New York (New York World's Fair, 1939–1940).

Each world's fair was an enormous undertaking, with host cities constructing massive exhibition halls and civic centerpieces; Philadelphia's 1876 exhibition, for example, featured thirty thousand exhibitions across two hundred buildings. Countries spared no expense in creating elaborate pavilions showcasing their nation's best, including wide-ranging offerings such as the telephone, Buffalo Bill and Annie Oakley, the Ferris wheel, motion pictures, and the escalator.

With so many products on hand, competitions were a natural part of the proceedings, judged by international panels of experts across multiple fields. Long before today's crowdsourced reviews and ratings, awards granted by these judges, typically in the form of medals, were highly sought-after endorsements. Winners at the 1876 Centennial Exhibition included a surprising number of names still found on modern bars, including Bacardi rum, Jameson Irish whisky, Smirnov vodka (then a Russian brand), Dolin vermouth, and liqueurs from Marie Brizard, Combier, Luxardo, and Peter Heering. See BACARDI; CHERRY BRANDY; MARASCHINO; SMIRNOFF; and WHISKY, IRISH.

Winning brands frequently emblazoned their product labels with medal representations, often lined in a row. Today's Bacardi, Dewar's, and Angostura labels are among modern labels still featuring the image of medals won a century before.

The fairs also helped brands gain a foothold outside their home countries: Angostura bitters' big break came after winning a medal at London's 1862 fair, which led to much wider international distribution. See ANGOSTURA BITTERS. Jamaica's J. Wray & Nephew won three golds at the same show. See APPLETON ESTATE. Cointreau got a boost after medal wins in Paris (1889) and Chicago (1893). See COINTREAU. Sauza's "mezcal brandy" similarly turned heads at the same 1893 exhibition. See SAUZA. The gold medal win for Jack Daniel's Tennessee whisky in St. Louis (1904) is credited as a major turning point for the brand. See JACK DANIEL'S. Other medal winners from that year include Bacardi and Rhum Barbancourt.

Cocktails were another vehicle by which participating countries promoted themselves to the world, beginning with the dueling "American bars" run by the London catering firms of Spiers & Pond and Bertram & Roberts at the 1867 Paris International Exhibition. These won the two firms enough acclaim back home to allow them to divide the London cocktail bar business between them for a generation—even if at the exhibition itself they were both eclipsed by the bar run by J. M. Van Winkle, an actual American, and its Sherry Cobblers. On one hot day, the bar went through some five hundred bottles of sherry, numbers that caused the planners of subsequent exhibitions to take note.

The coverage generated by the equally popular American bar at the 1873 Vienna Weltausstellung had another effect when it prompted the *New York Sun* to publish a long article on American bartenders and their work. This article was so widely reprinted that it spawned a host of similar articles, and indeed launched the modern field of drinks writing. See MIXOGRAPHY.

International exhibitions proved to be launching pads for drinks to reach new popularity. In 1887, Manhattan Cocktails were introduced to London at the bar run by Buffalo Bill's Wild West Show at the American Exhibition. In 1924, the Planter's Punches mixed by Jamaican bartender E. C. Pinnock at the British Empire Exhibition at Wembley proved immensely popular (and it was the West Indies Pavilion's other featured drink, the Trinidadian Green Swizzle, that so delighted P. G. Wodehouse's Bertie Wooster that he declared, "If ever I marry and have a son, *Green Swizzle Wooster* is the name that will go down in the register"). In 1939, the Zombie, which the New York café impresario Monte Proser pirated from Don the Beachcomber, was served— and served, and served—at the New York World's Fair. And these examples are only three of many. See GREEN SWIZZLE; MANHATTAN COCKTAIL; PLANTER'S PUNCH; and ZOMBIE.

After World War II, World's Fairs and international exhibitions resumed, but with an impact greatly lessened by the rise of mass tourism, which meant that if people wished to learn about French culture, they would do it in France, not at the French pavilion, and of electronic media, which meant that they had already seen James Bond drinking that new cocktail. Today they mostly survive in the form of murkily printed medallions on liquor labels.

Ingram, J. S. *The Centennial Exposition, Described and Illustrated.* Philadelphia: Hubbard Bros., 1876.

Walker, Frances A., ed. *International Exhibition, 1876.* Vol. 4, *Reports and Awards.* Philadelphia: Lippincott, 1880.

Wodehouse, P. G. "The Rummy Affair of Old Biffy." *Saturday Evening Post,* September 27, 1924, 8.

"World's Fairs and Their Legacies." *New York Times* (international edition), May 4, 2015.

Matt Pietrek and David Wondrich

Faith, Nicholas (1933–2018), was an award-winning British journalist and author who wrote over twenty-five books on a wide range of subjects, from railroads to Bordeaux. However, he is best known for his writing on cognac and other spirits, drawing from experience gained during an extensive career covering business at some of the top papers and magazines in England such as the *Economist*, *London's Sunday Times*, and *Financial Times*. He is the author of the 1986 *Cognac: The Story of the World's Greatest Brandy, Nicholas Faith's Guide to Cognac*, and the definitive 2004 *Cognac*, and was considered one of the world's top experts on cognac. He was also a founder of the International Spirits Challenge and was the first recipient of the Bureau National Interprofessional de Cognac's (BNIC) Lifetime Achievement Award. Nicholas Faith championed cognac as a world-class spirit and a base spirit in cocktails, arguing that both British and American traditions are more likely to dictate mixing cognac in a highball with soda.

Faith, Nicholas. *Cognac*. London: Mitchell Beazley, 2004.

Jacki. "Interview with Nicholas Faith on His New Book: *Cognac*." *Cognac Expert Blog*, December 12, 2013. https://blog.cognac-expert.com/nicholas-faith-cognac-book (accessed February 5, 2021).

"Nicholas *Faith*." *Infinite Ideas* (website), http://www.infideas.com/authors/nicholas-faith (accessed February 5, 2021).

Derek Brown

falca is a particularly simple variety of pot still used in Peru and formerly in parts of Chile. See PISCO. To make a Peruvian falca, a sheet of copper is hammered into a simple, wide-mouthed kettle (the *paila*). This is then encased tightly in stucco-covered brick, with a firebox underneath, and covered with a brick dome whose inside is finished with plaster impregnated with a mix of various traditional sealants, among them tar, egg white, burnt sugar, and oil. A hole is made in the top of the dome for

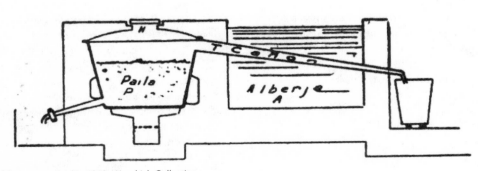

The falca, anatomized in 1942. Wondrich Collection.

filling the still and provided with a simple copper or earthenware lid, and another sheet of copper, rolled into a very long, tapered tube (the *cañon*) is set into the brick just where the dome starts. This tube runs straight through a large, deep tank of water (the *alberja*) and out the other side, where the spirit is collected. See STILL, POT.

The falca is very old: the first record of a still in Peru, owned by a Greek named Pedro Manuel in 1613, describes it simply as a "caldera grande . . . con su tapa e canon"—a "large kettle, with its lid and tube." Some light on its possible origin, and that of distilling in South America in general, can be cast by examining the somewhat more primitive version that was used in Chile. This was described in 1826 by John Meiers, who encountered it in Aconcagua, in the center of the country just north of Santiago. It followed the same general design and terminology but was rather less substantial in construction, with a shallow, removable wooden head that incorporated the cañon, which is laid in a trough of running water. This still bears a strong resemblance to the stills used to this day in the Cape Verde islands to make *grogue*, the local cane spirit, particularly in the cooling arrangement, and it must be noted that the African Atlantic islands were an important staging area for Iberian colonization of the Americas.

The falca has the important advantage of using much less copper than a standard alembic and largely dispensing with the skilled metalwork needed to make still heads and condensing coils (the version Clements Markham encountered in the Peruvian jungle in 1860 is even more frugal, being made out of a clay pot, the broken bottom of another one, and some bamboo tubes). In places where resources are scarce, the advantage is decisive, meaning the difference between distilling and not distilling. On the other hand, its design allows for very little of the purifying reflux alembic-style still heads provide, and distillation must be managed very carefully if one wishes to extract a clean spirit from it. See REFLUX.

The falca is still used in Peru, and when used well it yields an intensely aromatic spirit.

See also HACIENDA LA CARAVEDO.

Markham, Clements. *Travels in Peru and India.* London: 1862.

Miers, John. *Travels in Chile and La Plata*, vol. 2. London: 1826.

Ricome, P. *Industria Peruana de los aguardientes de uva.* Lima: Sección técnica de propaganda agropecuaria, 1942.

David Wondrich

falernum is a traditional liqueur from Barbados. Though recipes vary, falernum is historically rum-, sugar-, and lime-based, with the addition of Caribbean spices such as cloves, ginger, and nutmeg. Almonds are sometimes added. Rum traders in Barbados in the early twentieth century often bottled their own falernum alongside their rum brands. In addition to its use in Planter's Punches and other drinks such as the traditional Corn 'n' Oil (rum, falernum, and bitters) and Green Swizzle (rum, lime, falernum, and wormwood bitters), falernum is also used in baking and other cooking. See GREEN SWIZZLE. Falernum is a key ingredient in many exotic cocktails, including historical examples from the 1930s and 1940s such as the Three Dots and a Dash and the Test Pilot, and is a mainstay in modern tiki bars.

See also PLANTER'S PUNCH; TIKI; and TROPICAL DRINK.

"News of Food; Israeli Red Wine Arriving for Passover— Falernum Syrup Good in Drinks, Meals." *New York Times*, March 15, 1954.

Pariser, Harry S. *Explore Barbados*, San Francisco: Manatee, 2000.

Swizzle Stick [pseud.]. Letter, "The Green Swizzle of the Tropics." *New York Sun*, October 26, 1903, 4.

Martin Cate

fat washing refers to a process for infusing alcohol with flavorful fats, which takes advantage of the fact that most fat-soluble aromatic compounds are also soluble in alcohol. Although fat washing is relatively new in the context of spirits and cocktails, it is inspired by a technique of considerable antiquity known as *enfleurage*, in which odorless fat is infused with the scent of fragrant botanical material such as flowers and subsequently exposed to alcohol in order to transfer the aromatic molecules from the fat to the liquid. See INFUSION.

In the context of spirits and cocktails the fat washing technique allows bartenders to achieve flavors that otherwise would not be possible. In order to produce a fat washed spirit, liquid and/or liquefied fat is combined with the spirit and allowed to infuse for a brief period of time, after which the fat is removed either by chilling the mixture sufficiently to solidify the fat or by using a separatory funnel or other device to separate the liquids by density.

Although fat-washed spirits have come to be more frequently used, they have most notably been employed in so-called molecular mixology cocktails by such bartenders as Eben Freeman, Don Lee, Sam Mason and Tony Palomino. The most widely known cocktail using a fat-washed spirit is the Benton's Old Fashioned developed in 2008 by Don Lee for PDT, the pioneering New York City neo-speakeasy, which uses bourbon that has been fat washed with bacon fat as the base spirit. See SPEAKEASY (NEW).

See also COCKTAIL RENAISSANCE and MOLECULAR MIXOLOGY.

Arnold, Dave. *Liquid Intelligence*. New York: Norton, 2014.

Samuel Lloyd Kinsey

feni (or **fenny**, or **fenim**), one of the only spirits that can rival baijiu in pungency, is made in the Indian state of Goa from the fruit of the cashew tree, *Anacardium occidentale*. It is generally distilled in copper or clay pot stills and rests briefly in miriwood tanks before bottling. In a remarkable example of technological conservatism, the clay stills are essentially identical in design to the ones used in India over two thousand years ago. See DISTILLATION, HISTORY.

Originally, *feni* was a grade of spirit, not a type. The Portuguese colonial government that ruled Goa from 1510 to 1961 (and found the natives already drinking distilled spirits when they arrived) recognized three grades of spirit, making no distinction whether they were made from cashew apples or palm wine, which was also popular: *urraca*, distilled once; *fechado*, distilled twice; and *feni*, distilled three times and thus of appreciably higher proof and purity. By the twentieth century, however, the strongest grade had eclipsed the other two. and the cashew spirit eclipsed the palm one, and thus the name "feni" was awarded to the strong (or at least relatively so) cashew spirit that is still consumed today, although now it is only distilled twice. Indeed, since 2009 Goan feni has been protected by a government

geographical indicator (the only spirit India protects thus), forbidding it to be made elsewhere in India or from anything other than cashew fruit.

Numerous brands of feni are still sold in Goa (and practically nowhere else), although an estimated 75 percent of what is produced goes straight from small-scale local distilleries (some four thousand of which are estimated to be in operation) to bars and retailers without ever seeing a label. Of the bottled brands, Big Boss, PVV, and Madame Rosa, controlled by the Vaz family, are sourced from various of those small producers in a negociant system and are the most traditional in production and style. The most modern, Kazkar, is lighter and less pungent and is exported as a mixing spirit to America and Europe, albeit as yet in small quantities. Even at its least aromatic, feni is a taste that takes some acquiring.

Negocios externos. Lisbon: Imprensa Nacional, 1879.
Zuzarte, Joseph. "The Heady Rise of Cashew Fenni," *Goa Streets*, March 14, 2013. http://goastreets.com/the-heady-rise-of-cashew-feni/ (accessed March 19, 2021).

David Wondrich

fermentation is the biotransformation of organic substances via enzymes by microorganisms such as yeast and bacteria. It is widely recognized that the practice of fermentation is as old as civilization itself, but it is also divided into the epochs of pre- and post-Pasteur, after the French microbiologist, Louis Pasteur (1822–1895), who, assisted by a host of other names in the mid-nineteenth century, started elucidating the science of fermentation, which had been previously approached only empirically. Originally, Pasteur narrowly defined fermentation as an anaerobic process, but since then broader definitions have been accepted that also account for aerobic processes and are more helpful to understanding the breadth of spirits production. Arguably, the most important fermentation process in this context is of course the transformation of sugar to ethanol, but myriad other processes are observed that have significant bearing on both spirit quality and economy.

In 1883, Emile Christian Hansen was the first to isolate a pure yeast cell, *Saccharomyces carlsbergensis*, famously used in lager beers. Rapidly following that achievement, yeasts and other microorganisms were collected and cataloged from around the world. *Saccharomyces* budding yeasts (which reproduce by forming buds that detach and grow into new cells) represent the most commonly found yeast used in alcoholic beverages, having a high frequency of occurrence in nature relative to other yeast species, but even at the birth of the field, non-*Saccharomyces* yeasts were being discovered in ferments that produced some of the most highly regarded spirits of the day. In 1893, Percival Greig of Jamaica, a student of Hansen's, isolated a fission yeast, *Schizosaccharomyces pombe*, which was responsible for the unique character of Jamaica rum (fission yeasts reproduce by dividing themselves in two). In 1894, the Dutch microbiologist Christiaan Eijkman isolated another fission yeast as the active organism in Batavia arrack. See ARRACK, BATAVIA. Fission yeasts have a low frequency of occurrence in nature but can become dominant in distilling material when either density or volatile acidity is abnormally high.

Not all raw materials used in spirits production have readily fermentable sugars, and in the case of grains the process of saccharification must take place in which starch is broken down into fermentable sugars. See SACCHARIFICATION. In the Western tradition, this is facilitated by enzymes in malt, while the Eastern tradition has for centuries also employed the amylo process of starch hydrolysis performed as a type of fermentation itself, using the enzymatic action of molds like koji, also contained in *qu*. See QU. The amylo process has seen some limited use in American whisky production, starting as early as 1914. Widespread adoption has been hindered by the tendency such ferments have to emit aromas not congruent with whisky and a general lack of modern exploration outside of purified enzymes.

Alcoholic fermentation sees the yeast cells eating any available sugar and excreting primarily liquid ethanol and CO_2 gas, but there are many additional congeners that are byproducts of yeast metabolism. Yeast is capable of producing aldehydes, various acids, esters, and higher alcohols, among others, with each species having its own propensity. See ALDEHYDES. Under narrow conditions, select yeast strains are capable of releasing extremely high-value aroma derived from carotene but bound as glycosides, such as the rose ketone β-Damascenone.

Understanding this aroma, which is only present in the minutest quantities but extremely odor active, is at the forefront of the art.

Except under the strictest of pure culture conditions, bacteria are also present alongside yeast, and their own fermentation may have significant influence on flavor. Bacteria are capable of being either aroma-beneficial or detrimental spoilage organisms and may produce substantial congeners like nonvolatile lactic acid at the expense of potential alcohol. Other types may produce volatile propionic or butyric acid from a variety of inputs, which have the potential to become pleasant-smelling esters under narrow conditions but are off-putting in their free state. If vinegar fermentation by aerobic bacteria is allowed to take hold, ethanol is broken down to acetic acid, decreasing yield. Byproducts of bacterial fermentation may help select for a yeast type in open-culture conditions or even halt alcoholic fermentation altogether, as many budding yeasts are sensitive to volatile acids.

Fermentation may be initiated via inoculation with pure cultures of yeast and bacteria under strict sanitary conditions or by varying degrees of open-culture technique, which is generally associated with finer spirits and traditional processes. Pure culture technique often requires antibiotics, which come with the risk of bacterial adaptation rendering them no longer effective, while fully open-culture techniques termed *spontaneous* often rely on either a high natural yeast load such as with fruit or high acid conditions created by recycling stillage where bacteria are mostly inhibited to a degree they cannot suppress alcoholic fermentation. See DUNDER. Muck may also be added because it contributes acids inhibitory to spoilage organisms but not to the desired yeast. Baijiu production often features a solid-state fermentation phase before the water content is increased to harness particular bacteria and yeast that may only be active at a particular level of free water. See RUM, JAMAICA; and; BAIJIU.

Open-culture ferments embrace gradual change and adaptation, while pure cultures are often strictly serialized so there is less opportunity for genetic mutations to cause a drift in the flavor. Eastern fermentation techniques revolving around starting a fermentation with qu are holistic and open culture, while the overwhelming impact of Pasteur was for Western technique during the twentieth century to gradually be dominated by single organisms in overly sanitary conditions. Currently, the spirits industry is seeing a return to open-culture techniques guided by better understanding of the complex mechanisms as well as the breeding of designer *Saccharomyces* yeast strains for pure-culture ferments.

As a rule of thumb, a longer fermentation duration produces more aroma and is typically distilled in a way to take advantage of it. This duration before a spirit is distilled mostly encompasses alcoholic fermentation, but it may also come after a production stage where bacteria were used for biotransformation such as the souring of grains in the sour mash whisky process, or amylo process saccharification. As alcoholic fermentation drags on, risk escalates, bacterial fermentation processes gain in activity, and either aroma improves to offset the change in economy or off aromas develop.

Bourbon ferments may last anywhere between 72 and 120 hours, while cognac may have a duration between two and three weeks. Rum and baijiu see the most varied duration. Light rums can ferment as quickly as twenty-four hours, while the heaviest rum ferments last multiple weeks and justify slow-batch distillation by pot still. Baijiu has durations as short as five days, while some are reported to last multiple months. The chief method of manipulating alcoholic fermentation duration is altering the quantity of yeast present followed by the amount of sugar to be fermented and then other potential stressors.

Ferments for neutral spirits are inoculated with specially selected pure cultures and conducted in closed vessels to limit foreign yeasts and bacteria that may harm economy. Bourbon employs a pure yeast, while its lactic acid bacteria culture is either pure or sometimes open culture. Bourbon is typically fermented in open wooden vats that allow very slight opportunity for adventitious microorganisms despite the swift pace of fermentation. Fruits, employed in brandy making, arrive covered in native yeasts and bacteria, which can quickly start vigorous spontaneous fermentation; however, depending on the demands of economy and risk, pure-culture yeasts may be added to reduce the fermentation duration. Many rum ferments are conducted similarly to neutral spirits, while the heaviest rums are known to encourage any yeasts or bacteria that can tolerate the inhibitory conditions that develop in the various pre-fermented segments that compose the main ferment. Heavy rums typically encourage open culture, but rarely do the raw materials have a yeast load comparative to fruit to truly start spontaneously, and instead each subsequent ferment is seeded with a portion of the last.

The diversity of practices is vast, and many stretch the bounds of what many would think possible. Citrus rinds have been used to create starters at the beginning of the cachaça season, possibly accelerating yeast growth, while the early bourbon donas were reported to use ample amounts of hops as an antibacterial. Some Jamaican distillers deliberately add cane-juice vinegar to heavy-rum ferments to help maintain the dominance of fission yeasts, which can metabolize a portion of the acetic acid. Sea water is added to create a particular rum mark in Barbados, which distinctly influences the congener profile. Some of the most modernist ferments immobilize yeast in alginate beads to protect them from stress and facilitate continuous fermentation.

Fermentation organisms may be just as much an avenue for terroir as the raw materials themselves. Production decisions may help promote local voices that otherwise would never get to express themselves because they have a low frequency of occurrence in nature. Narrow fermentation conditions of which only certain yeasts are capable may also show the uniqueness of raw materials where much aroma needs to be unlocked by a biotransformation, and this is most apparent with carotene-derived aroma. Due to the nature of volatility, the fate of extraordinary terroir-related aroma is tied to ordinary congeners like fusel oil and cannot be captured in the final distillate if excess fusel oil is not kept to the minimum.

Fermentation has a profound impact on aroma and spirit economy, which will influence subsequent production decisions. Not all ferments are fit for batch distillation, which is far less efficient than continuous distillation; the character of the ferment must justify it. A spirit worthy of barrel maturation is a product just as much of fermentation and which microorganisms were allowed to develop as of how it was distilled.

Amerine, M. A. *The Technology of Wine Making*. 4th ed. Westport, CT: AVI, 1980.

Arroyo, Rafael *Studies on Rum*. Agriculture Experiment Station Puerto-Rico, Research Bull. no. 5, 1945.

Greg, Percival H. *The Jamaica Yeasts*. Bulletin Botanical Department, Jamaica (2) II, 157–160, 1895.

Huang, H. T., and D. Phil. *Science and Civilization in China*, vol. 6, *Biology and Biological Technology*, Part 5, *Fermentation and Food Science*. Cambridge: Cambridge University Press, 2000.

Kervegant, D. *Rhums et eaux-de-vie de canne*. Vannes: Ed. du Golf, 1946.

de Kruyff, E. *De fabricatie van Batavia-arak*. Archief voor de suikerindustrie 151, 1909.

Willkie, H, and J. Prochaska. *Fundamentals of Distillery Practice*. Division of Education, Joseph E. Seagram & Sons, 1943.

Stephen Shellenberger

fern bars emerged in the mid-1960s, when the women's movement and the environmental movement converged to transform barrooms from smoky, dimly lit male preserves to bright, cheery greenhouses where both sexes could mingle on equal terms. Although many fern bars were categorized—not unfairly—as pickup joints, they can take credit for bringing America's saloon culture back from the dead by attracting a new generation of young urban professionals who had largely forsaken recreational drinking for recreational drugs.

This new leaf was turned over not only by feminists and ecologists but by nostalgists: fern bars reflected the swinging sixties obsession with retro camp by hanging their houseplants in rooms decorated like gay '90s parlors, complete with Tiffany lamps, brass fittings, and striped awnings, while bar names referenced barber shop quartets and old-timey soda fountains (Bobby McGee's Conglomeration, Shenanigans, Rosie O'Grady's Good Time Emporium).

Fern-bar flirting and networking was fueled largely by Chablis and imported beer. Cocktails, when patrons did order them, tended toward simple constructs like the Tequila Sunrise, Kamikaze, or Harvey Wallbanger. See TEQUILA SUNRISE; KAMIKAZE; and HARVEY WALLBANGER. When fern bars hit their hedonistic peak in the 1970s, frozen "disco drinks" also became popular serves, from Strawberry Daiquiris and Piña Coladas to alcoholic milkshakes with names like Screaming Banana Banshee or Big Fat Schooner of Love, whose calories were meant to be burned off on the dance floor.

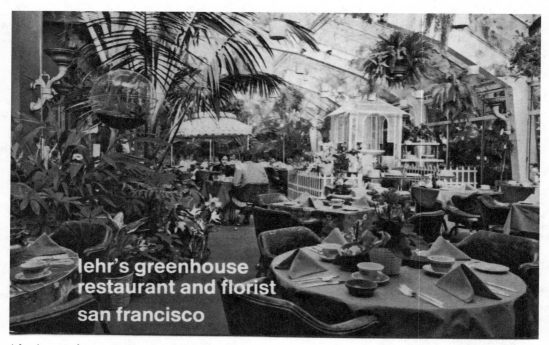

lehr's greenhouse restaurant and florist san francisco

A fern bar at its ferniest, San Francisco (Lehr's Greenhouse was on Sutter Street and lasted from 1972 to 1987). Courtesy of Jeff Berry.

While one of the original fern bars, TGI Friday's, is now an international chain, most of them died on the vine in the Reagan era, victims of the AIDS crisis and the yuppie shift from happy hour to nouvelle cuisine. See TGI FRIDAY'S.

Playboy Clubs International, ed. *Benson and Hedges 100's Presents Drink Recipes from 100 of the Greatest Bars.* N.P.: Philip Morris Incorporated, 1979.

Walker, Judy. "Tales of the Cocktail 'Fern Bars' Seminar is a Trip Down memory Lane." *New Orleans Times-Picayune*, July 22, 2010.

Jeff Berry

fernet is an ill-defined style of Italian bitter digestive. Although widely considered to belong to the amaro family, some argue it forms a category of its own. See AMARO. Known for their strong flavors, fernets are traditionally made with grape spirit and are unsweetened (although they owe their characteristically dark color to burnt sugar), explaining in part their particularly bitter taste.

Perception of fernets has been significantly impacted by the dominance of one brand, Branca, from Milan. It is credited with launching the category in 1845, although Vittone, another producer, has recently worked hard to substantiate claims that they had done so three years earlier.

Branca used to claim that their founder, Bernardino, had invented the formula with a Swedish doctor called Fernet. This is highly unlikely: Fernet (or variations of the name) was a mythical figure said to have lived over a hundred years thanks to an elixir of his invention. In the early eighteenth century, many pharmacists and liquor makers told the tale to sell their own elixirs. Those elixirs were clearly Fernet's forebears: available recipes feature the characteristic ingredients of modern fernets, such as saffron, aloe, quinine, or white agaric. See FRATELLI BRANCA.

Originally thought to cure cholera, fernets were sold in pharmacies well into the twentieth century. That may be why they were little used in classic cocktails—the Hanky Panky being a notable exception. See HANKY PANKY. However, they proved popular with Italian migrants, especially in Argentina, where they are commonly mixed with cola. In recent years, they've found favor with mixologists, both as an insider's drink and as a cocktail ingredient. This has led to a renaissance of the category, with local Italian brands now exported abroad and countries such as the United States producing their own.

See also APERITIF AND DIGESTIVE.

Anon. [attributed to Pons-Augustin Alletz]. *L'Albert Moderne: ou Nouveaux secrets éprouvés et licites.* Basel: Jean Schweighauser, 1770.

Branca di Romanico, Niccolo. *Branca: A Spirited Italian Icon.* New York: Rizzoli, 2015.

Mantegazza, Paolo. *Quadri della natura umana*, vol. 2. Milan: Gaetano Brigola, 1871.

François Monti

Feuerzangenbowle (literally "fire-tongs bowl") is a flaming bowl of sweetened, booze-spiked spiced wine that shows up in Germany at Weihnachten and Silvester (Christmas and New Year's Eve). A derivative of the earlier German student's and soldier's drink Crambambuli (flaming sugar and rum), it dates back at least to the early nineteenth century. Its popularity was boosted by Heinrich Spoerl's 1933 comic novel of the same name and, especially, by the 1944 film based on it, which diverted attention from Germany's increasing setbacks in World War II. Though fire tongs of old have been replaced in recent years with a special brace that fits over a fireproof punch bowl, the function remains the same. Either the tongs or brace supports a sugar cone (*Zuckerhut* in German, or "sugar hat") above heated wine laced with citrus and spices such as cinnamon, cardamom, and cloves (this is for the dominant "Mecklenburg style" Feuerzangenbowle; others add the wine later). The sugar cone is then soaked with high-proof rum or arrack and set alight. The sugar begins to melt, caramelize, and drip into the spiced wine as some alcohol burns off while more spirit is ladled over it. When the sugar is all melted, the punch master serves this hot drink—in heatproof mugs—flaming or not. For safety, however, celebrants should always extinguish cups of flaming Feuerzangenbowle before imbibing.

See also ARRACK; GLÖGG; and PUNCH.

Ruschin, Lilo. *Feuerzangenbowle: historien und rezeptbüchlein.* Berlin: Stapp Verlag, 1967.

Matthew Rowley

Actor Heinz Rühmann (1902–1994) tending the titular drink in the 1944 German film *Die Feuerzangenbowle*. Getty Images.

Field, Colin Peter (1961–), has been the head bartender of the legendary Bar Hemingway at the Ritz Paris hotel since its revival in 1994. Born in Rugby, England, Field came to Paris in 1981 to study at the Ferrandi hotel school and worked at several bars and restaurants in the city before settling in at the Ritz. He has created many well-regarded cocktails, two of the most iconic being the Picasso Martini and the Serendipity. During his tenure at the Ritz, Field has been named the world's best bartender several times by prominent magazines and has proved a worthy successor to Frank Meier, being an authentic hotel bartender of the old style. See MEIER, FRANK.

Field, Colin Peter. *The Cocktails of the Ritz Paris*. New York: Simon & Schuster, 2003.

Fernando Castellon

film, spirits and cocktails in. The very first film of an alcoholic beverage seems to have been shown by the Lumière brothers in Paris in 1895, the first public screening in the history of film. In *Baby's Meal*, two bottles (whether wine or spirits is hard to say) sit in the foreground of the table while a baby eats. Just like that, simply because it was part of life, alcohol entered cinematic stories.

The Universal Language

In Hitchcock's *Foreign Correspondent* (1940), John Jones counts on the interruption of "the universal language" (a tray of Martinis) to rescue him from a conversation in a foreign language. Some directors have made trademarks out of drinking characters like these, whose conversation is fueled by alcohol consumption, and often close-ups of the drink being poured act as an indicator that the liquor enables the plot. Examples include American directors John Cassavetes, who portrays stumbling, often lonely characters who need to drink to go on and Whit Stillman, who depicts the social gatherings and drinking habits of urban haute bourgeoisie

Americans; and Korean director Hong Sang-Soo, in whose films drinking soju leads to a higher form of truth. *The Thin Man* (1934), a humorous take on a detective story, takes things further by making drinking cocktails crucial to unmasking the culprit. In this film, Nick and Nora Charles (William Powell and Myrna Loy) are a couple of rich, happy drunks who enjoy spirits even in bed, the frenetic pace of their drinking enabled, but also somewhat mitigated, by the smaller cocktail glasses of the time. See GLASSWARE. This is representative of the golden age of Hollywood, particularly the Depression era, when viewers enjoyed seeing rich characters hopping from one elegant party to another. We first encounter Nick in a bar where he shares his philosophy about shaking different classic cocktails (the Manhattan, the Bronx, and the dry Martini) to music (there is a proper rhythm for each). The end of the film is a classic dinner reveal, but the camera makes a reveal of its own: the many empty glasses suddenly filling the frame remind us that cocktails were Nick's best weapon in exposing the murderer. Finally, in *Some Like It Hot* (1959), a batch of Manhattans is gradually assembled in the sleeping compartment of a train, with each element hilariously coming from a different source—the shaker is a hot water bottle. The protagonists bond during this improvised cocktail party.

Alcoholic Storylines

When alcohol explicitly takes the center of the plot, two main storylines exist. The happy drunk enjoys life and makes things fun for others; the lost soul drowns his or her despair in alcohol and disconnects from society. It is notable that female characters belong mostly to the second category, with only a few exceptions, such as the carefree character in *Auntie Mame* (1958). In cinematic stories, drinking women always seem to be "broken" and pose a problem to society. In any case, both comic and serious narrative arcs were represented early on. Silent films of the 1910s and 1920s staged drunks whose exaggerated gestures and off timing worked well in burlesque comedies: Charlie Chaplin and Max Linder, among others, exemplify such characters. The alcoholic downfall of doomed working-class characters could be seen in D. W. Griffiths's *Broken Blossoms* (1919) or in *L'Assommoir* (1909), an adaptation of Émile Zola's nineteenth-century naturalistic novel.

Overall, Hollywood seems to be more interested than others in considering the dangers of alcohol, with a taste for redemption stories. However, comedies prevailed for a long time, and critics usually agree on dating the real emergence of a more socially conscious genre after World War II, with films such as *The Lost Weekend* (1945) and *Days of Wine and Roses* (1962) being landmarks in their representation of addiction.

Moreover, the distorted visions and obsessions of the drunken mind allowed filmmakers to experiment very early on with an array of cinematic techniques and strategies: blurred focus, swirling cameras, cut to dream sequences, and superimposition to name a few. *The Small Back Room* (1949) opts for a surrealist rendition of a man's obsession for a bottle of scotch that he is trying to resist. To the ticking of a clock, perceptions are gradually altered; the desired beverage becomes a motif on the wallpaper, then an object of giant proportions.

The Rough Liquor

The Spirit of the Land

Metaphorically playing off of alcohol being the transformed product of the soil, some films construct a mythology that unites the land, its inhabitants, and their local liquor. For example, Western movies, which in many ways work as American origin stories, often associate long shots of the inhospitable reddish landscapes with close-ups of the glass of rye, bourbon, or other whisky ordered at the saloon. On the same note, the comedy *Whisky Galore* (1949) features a small Scottish island "in mourning for a departed spirit," meaning that they are faced with a wartime whisky shortage. The opening sequence establishes the relationship of the inhabitants to their island by use of a voice-over and a montage of landscapes, fishermen, and farmers. When catastrophe hits, it is filmed as a deep crisis of identity that will only be resolved when every niche and cave is filled with the liquor.

This rings very similar to a scene in *The Public Enemy* (1931), when a frenzied Chicago stacks liquor in any container at hand on the eve of Prohibition. Prohibition films participate in the American myth and are a genre of their own with speakeasies, bootlegger gangsters (*Scarface*, 1932), and bathtub gin made in actual bathtubs (*The Roaring Twenties*, 1939). Ironically, historians generally note how wet the films of the Volstead era were.

Hard Characters, Hard Liquors

In the cinematic imagination, bootleg liquor is the drink of the working class, the countryman, or the gangster. Being put to the trial of the moonshine works as some sort of test of manhood. In *Jaws* (1975), Captain Quint, a seasoned shark hunter who negotiates apricot brandy as part of his payment, offers shots of homemade liquor to oceanographer Hopper and police chief Brody, who spits it out. Hopper is in constant opposition with Quint (they compare their scars, and Quint makes fun of Hopper's city hands and college education). In *Jaws*, this stereotypical rivalry is complicated by the fact that Quint is revealed, in a stunning drunken monologue, to have survived the horrific torpedoing of the USS *Indianapolis* during World War II. In fact, war veterans often consume rotgut alcohol in film, as if to remind us of the internal trauma that consumes them. Freddy, a veteran who is skilled at making liquor with anything at hand in *The Master* (2012), is a good example of this.

French cinema, although typically more focused on wine, has its share of memorable eau-de-vie scenes. In the cult film *Les tontons flingueurs* (1963), old school gangsters drink an especially strong "vitriol" that, as we learn, had to be retired due to having caused blindness. In the popular comedy *Les bronzés font du ski* (1979), a group of tourists lost in the mountains has to politely endure some toad-infused shallot brandy, a fictional play on the real vipérine, an alcohol made with vipers.

In cinema, such strong drinks are often a man's affair, although some films represent women who can hold their liquor. Portrayed as the opposite of damsels in distress, they often have to display a form of virility to make it in a man's world. This can be seen in *Raiders of the Lost Ark* (1981). We encounter Marion Ravenwood as the tough owner of a Nepalese tavern where the petite young woman, surrounded by men, is winning a drinking contest against an imposing local. A more refined version of this could be Scarlett O'Hara in *Gone with the Wind* (1939). This character of rare strength and strong attachment to her land (who is casually reminded by Rhett Butler that she is "no lady") is caught several times drinking brandy in secret.

Tailored Drinks as a Screenwriting Device

Ordering or serving a drink is a good way to introduce a character in a script. The first sentence Greta Garbo ever said on film (*Anna Christie*, 1930) was to a bartender: "Give me a whisky, ginger ale on the side, and don't be stingy, baby!" What one orders helps define who one is; it sometimes moves the plot and unlocks poetic associations.

The Personality Drink

As the most represented cocktail in film (the most represented liquor is whisky), the Martini often works as a "neutral" drink, to the point where the main protagonist of *The Hudsucker Proxy* (1994) is told that it is for "squares." However, because of the many variations in a cocktail recipe, tailoring it to one's taste works as an affirmation of singularity. See MARTINI.

The James Bond films are a good example of this. We see Bond having his emblematic cocktail for the first time in *Dr. No* (1962). The villain makes a point of knowing the tastes of Bond, his prisoner, and serves him a medium-dry vodka Martini with lemon peel "shaken, not stirred." In *Casino Royale* (2006), the spy confirms his expertise by inventing the Vesper. See VESPER. That James Bond is such a cocktail connoisseur is important for a character who often has to mix with (and outsmart) an elite crowd, including the self-proclaimed superior minds of the criminal network SPECTRE.

Groundhog Day (1993) comically exploits this trope. Phil Connors inexplicably has to relive the same day every day. He makes the most of it and tries to win the heart of Rita by pretending that "his" drink is the same as hers, a sweet vermouth on the rocks with a twist (in a previous scene, we understood his drink to actually be Jim Beam with water and ice).

The Character Type

Sometimes a cocktail allows poetic associations that reinforce a character type. In the film noir *The Big Sleep* (1946), the femme fatale Vivian orders a Scotch Mist in a textural scene where her shiny jacket makes her stand out amidst the soft black and whites of the bar. The name of the drink is an appropriate match for this enigmatic character who dangerously blurs detective Marlowe's insight. *Rosemary's Baby* (1968) features an unusual cocktail, the Vodka Blush. Satanic cult leader Roman Castevet strategically uses it to impress failed actor Guy Woodhouse by displaying his expertise of the world and its ways (he discovered the drink in Australia). The Belgian dark comedy *C'est arrivé près de chez vous* (1992) makes the most of pairing a character to a cocktail. In this cult mockumentary, the serial killer Ben invents a cocktail named Petit Grégory after a famous French child murder case. In his variation on the Martini, an olive attached to a sugar cube mimics the victim's body being dumped in the water.

A Stage of Life

Spirits can offer small indications about the stage of life of the drinker. In Judd Apatow's comedy *Superbad* (2007), the underage protagonists desperately try to purchase raspberry vodka and Goldslick vodka (a fictional twist on Goldschläger, which contains golden flakes) for their girlfriends. See ORO OR GOLD LIQUEURS. Both drinks match the mainstream imagination of inexperienced teenage drinkers. In Whit Stillman's *The Last Days of Disco* (1998), recent college graduate Alice is shocked when she realizes that ordering Vodka Tonics makes her a bit of a cliché and ends up ordering a Whisky Sour.

A play on these age expectations can be found in the cream-based cocktail. In *The Big Lebowski* (1998), we first encounter the hero buying half and half at the supermarket. The Dude, as he likes to be called, famously drinks White Russians (he also calls them Caucasians) that he sloppily mixes. See WHITE RUSSIAN. This choice of beverage is interesting for a character who is in many ways stuck in a form of adolescence (he does not work and mainly goes bowling with his friends). Another example of a deceptively innocent cocktail can be seen in *Days of Wine and Roses*, where the teetotaler Kirsten is persuaded to taste her first cocktail, a Brandy Alexander, because of her love of chocolate. See BRANDY ALEXANDER. The innocence of this first sip contrasts with the severe degree of her addiction at the end. Finally, the fictional Moloko Plus in Stanley Kubrick's *Clockwork Orange* (1971) operates an interesting reversal of the symbolism of milk. This dairy cocktail is laced with unspecified spirits and opiates, poured from the plastic breast of a statue. The film stages a stark contrast between the innocence of young men drinking milk and their subsequent violent behavior, this being reinforced by the ambiguous role of the state acting as a sort of perverted mother in this dystopian fiction.

The Signature Drink

Sometimes an odd drink choice can be a director's trademark. In Tarantino's *Death Proof* (2007), the bartender (played by the director himself) serves shots of the French liquor Chartreuse. Tarantino was looking for a relatively unknown drink and even had a neon Chartreuse sign made especially for the film. Such unusual choice is common for a director who had a nineteenth century slave master from Mississippi order the anachronistic Polynesian Pearl Diver in *Django Unchained* (2012), probably an homage to Fritz Lang's *The Blue Gardenia* (1953).

Lost Spirits

Finally, bars are a common presence in film, as they function as a microcosm of society. A variation on the bartender type can be seen in the film *Cocktail* (1988) and its flashy take on flair bartending. However, probably no film has so efficiently represented the complex poetry of liquor in its relation to the human mind than Kubrick's masterpiece *The Shining* (1980). Indeed, all spirits break loose when failed writer Jack Torrance walks into the empty bar of the Overlook Hotel and sells his soul to the enigmatic bartender Lloyd for a bourbon on the rocks.

Cornes, Judy. *Alcohol in the Movies, 1898–1962: A Critical History*. Jefferson, NC: McFarland, 2006.

Denzin, Norman K. *Hollywood Shot by Shot: Alcoholism in American Cinema*. New York: A. de Gruyter, 1991.

Good, Howard. *The Drunken Journalist*. Lanham, MD: Scarecrow, 2000.

James, Nick. "I for Intoxication." *Sight and Sound* 7 (1997): 26–28.

Kanner, Melinda. "That's Why the Lady Is a Drunk: Women, Alcoholism and Popular Culture." In *Sexual Politics and Popular Culture*, ed. Diane Raymond, 183–198. Bowling Green, OK: Bowling Green State University Popular Press, 1990.

Lachaud, Maxime. *Redneck Movies*. Pertuis: Rouge Profond, 2014.

Okrent, Daniel. *Last Call: The Rise and Fall of Prohibition.* New York: Scribner, 2011.

Virginie Lauret

filtration is an important, though less visible, aspect of spirit production in which unwanted compounds are removed to improve a spirit's appearance or flavor. Indeed, along with oxidative maturation and fractional distillation, filtration is one of the chief methods of taming raw spirit and rendering it pleasant to drink.

Most spirits undergo a simple mechanical filtration to remove particulate matter, especially if they have been stored in wood. Some undergo additional mechanical or chemical filtration to remove unwanted organic compounds or color from the liquid. Finally, some spirits are filtered to remove compounds that come out of precipitation at low temperatures, as when ice is added, and cause them to become hazy.

There are many types of filtration media. The most common are cloth, paper, and other fibers such as cellulose, followed by sand or other granular materials (such as diatomaceous earth and limestone), and precious metals such as gold, silver, and platinum. There are also adsorption filters, such as activated carbon and zeolites, that remove unwanted compounds at the molecular level and membrane filters that have specific pore sizes.

The most basic method of filtration is to pass a liquid through a woven material, such as cheesecloth or muslin, to remove coarse materials. This is often done when producing bitters or infused spirits. These coarse methods of filtration are a starting point for further filtration because they are relatively fast and help prevent finer filtration systems from being clogged with the coarser material.

Pressure or vacuum filtration is used to improve speed and maximize the efficiency of the filter. Gravity-based filtration is a slow method, especially when filtering small particulate through microscopic filtration media. The addition of pressure or a vacuum to push or pull the liquid through the filter significantly improves the efficiency of the operation. It also maximizes the life of a filter. As a filter removes materials from the filtrate, it also becomes more efficient as particles clog its pores, making it harder for the liquid to pass through but also capturing even smaller particles. Those in turn make it yet more difficult for the liquid to pass through. The use of pressure or a vacuum forces the filter to work for longer, but eventually the filter will become encumbered and need to be replaced. These physical methods of filtration have limited effect on the flavor of spirits and are done for production or cosmetic purposes.

Activated carbon or charcoal filtration is a method that is used to remove organic compounds from a liquid. This is done to improve the taste or color of a spirit. Its use dates back to at least the seventeenth century, when it was employed in eastern Europe in making vodka; by the end of the eighteenth century, it was also used in western Europe for rectifying spirits. See RECTIFICATION and VODKA.

Carbon filtration works through a method called adsorption where molecules, like congeners, adhere to the carbon surface, removing them from the liquid. Filtering through carbon or charcoal is an extreme form of filtration that removes flavor compounds as well as color from a distillate. It is often used in products that are targeting consumers who want a smooth-tasting product, such as vodka and white rum. See BACARDI. It can also be performed on distillate before it is placed in barrels to age, as Jack Daniels and George Dickel do with the Lincoln County process, which involves slowly passing the fresh distillate through a large quantity of sugar maple charcoal to remove impurities (many American whiskies used charcoal filtration in the nineteenth century). See LINCOLN COUNTY PROCESS.

Membrane filters are a specialized filter made from polymers that have a specific pore size. They are commonly used to filter the water that is used to dilute and mix spirits. The filters are found in reverse osmosis filtration systems. The key benefit of membrane filters is that they can filter dissolved minerals from water. Previously, removing minerals required distilling the water, which was a more expensive and time-consuming method.

Because of the specific pore size of membrane filters, there is some interest in this as a method of separating alcohol from water. This would be akin to the distillation and production of grain neutral spirits without the distillery.

In some cases, filtration can refer to the practice of using a material like a limestone (calcium carbonate) to remove iron from water. Iron compounds impart an unpleasant bitter and metallic taste to a spirit and may affect the color of the final product. Many distillers prefer to remove iron from their water source, bourbon distillers in particular. Other filtration methods have difficulty removing specific minerals, but limestone makes the water slightly alkaline and causes iron to precipitate out. The use of limestone also adds trace amounts of calcium carbonate to the water, which can improve its taste.

Molecular sieve technology is a specialized form of filtration that uses zeolites, which are microporous, aluminosilicate minerals. The only notable use in spirit production would be to produce 100 percent ethanol.

Originally a Russian technique first used in making vodka, precious metal filtration—usually done by forcing the spirit through silver- or platinum-impregnated charcoal—can soften a spirit and give it a creamy texture due to their catalytic effect on the ethanol/water mix, helping to break congeners down into esters and pull some minerals out of the water. Gold, however, mostly does its work in the press release.

Vodka, the most highly filtered of spirits, often uses multiple filtrations—such as charcoal, quartz sand, and silver, each designed to remove different impurities. The same vodka, filtered differently, can taste remarkably different.

See also CHILL FILTRATION.

Augustine, Cindy. "Why Filtration Matters When Distilling Vodka." *Liquor.com*, August 16, 2016. https://www.liquor.com/articles/vodka-filtration/ (accessed February 5, 2021).

English, Camper. "Filtration in Spirits." *Alcademics*, August 14, 2012. https://www.alcademics.com/2012/08/filtration-in-spirits-a-primer-.html (accessed February 5, 2021).

"Method for Treatment of Vodka 'Platinum Filtration.'" *RussianPatents.com*. https://russianpatents.com/patent/236/2366694.html (accessed February 5, 2021).

Darcy O'Neil

Fine à l'Eau is simply one part cognac and one to three parts water, served with the brandy in a small stemmed glass and the water, sometimes iced, on the side, to be added as desired. See COGNAC. The drink enjoyed broad popularity in French cafes from the end of the nineteenth century through the middle of the twentieth but has since been supplanted by other, less austere beverages. The name comes from *fine champagne*, a designation for cognac blended from eaux de vie from both the Grand Champagne and Petit Champagne regions.

David Wondrich

Fish House Punch is a classic eighteenth-century combination of lemons, sugar, and a "mixture" of rum, brandy, and peach brandy. Still commonly made in the twenty-first century, it is one of the oldest drinks in circulation. The punch began its long career as the house drink of the Colony in Schuylkill, a club of wealthy and prominent Philadelphians that, beginning in 1732, met regularly at their "fish house" on the Schuylkill river, just outside of town, to fish, eat, and drink. It was the club's particular conceit that it was a sovereign colony of its own. After the American Revolution, it changed its name to the State in Schuylkill, keeping up the pretense that it was its own state—a pretense it maintains to this day.

Among the club's peculiar traditions is its reliance entirely on the members and their guests to perform all of the labor associated with preparing its banquets, from shelling peas to mixing punch, each clad, in the club's heyday, in "a straw hat, of ample dimensions, and [a] large white apron, the badges of membership." (The aprons had big fish painted on them.) These guests have included at least two sitting United States presidents—George Washington and Chester Arthur—and numerous other dignitaries, including the Marquis de Lafayette, all of whom partook of the punch. See WASHINGTON, GEORGE. Although the club is a secretive one and has never officially published the formula for that punch, members of the club have repeatedly allowed it to escape into the wild, since at least 1850. It was first published by Jerry Thomas in 1862. See THOMAS, JEREMIAH P. "JERRY".

It has often been claimed that the punch dates back to the club's founding. This is unlikely, since mixed-spirit punches had not yet come into fashion in 1732, and at that time peach brandy had yet to acquire its reputation as a luxury spirit. Around 1900, two recipes for it were published that claimed to be transcripts of documents held in the club's archive, one from 1793 and the other from 1795. These, which agree in all but detail (and may indeed be based on the same document), suggest a much more likely period for the famous formula's origin,

Five veteran "citizens" of Philadelphia's State in Schuylkill, pictured ca. 1890 with their characteristic white aprons and straw hats. Dr. William Camac (1829–1900), author of one of the more authoritative recipes for Fish House Punch, is at the *left*. Courtesy of the Free Library of Philadelphia.

although there can be little doubt that the club served punch of some kind since its inception. The recipes also help to demonstrate a remarkable consistency in the drink's composition over the years; indeed, later versions leaked by club members differ only in a more restrained use of sugar and a shrinking proportion of the increasingly difficult-to-find peach brandy in the mixture, from 25 percent to 4 percent.

Once its formula was in broad circulation, Fish House Punch became not just a Philadelphia specialty but a national one. In the process, it gained—in some hands, at least—various extraneous ingredients, from Madeira and champagne to curaçao and even cucumber. See CURAÇAO. The disappearance of true peach brandy in the twentieth century led to further changes, including the use of the syrupy, peach-flavored liqueur sold as "peach brandy" and the substitution of whisky for the brandy (as an 1896 newspaper article observed about this switch, until the Civil War "whisky was looked upon as the drink of a groom and not of a gentleman"). In the twenty-first century, however, the cocktail revolution brought Fish House Punch back from the wilderness of whisky and white rum, while the micro-distillers supplied the true peach brandy.

Recipe: Dissolve 250 ml sugar in 250 ml lemon juice. Add 250 ml peach brandy, 250 ml cognac, and 500 ml Jamaican rum. Pour into bowl half-filled with ice and let sit for 30 minutes. Stir, grate nutmeg on top, and, if necessary, adjust proof with up to 1 liter cold water.

See also PEACH BRANDY.

Chambers, Julius. "Walks and Talks." *Brooklyn Eagle,* January 16, 1905, 3.
"Fish-House Punch." *New York Sun,* June 28, 1896, 2.

David Wondrich

The **fix** is an American class of drinks from the mid-nineteenth century with lemon juice, sugar, and spirits, served on ice with a fruit garnish. First appearing in print in 1841 in the form of a Gin Fix (always the most popular version), it is the earliest of the American variations on punch to be served in the "small bar glass," the same glass in which the cocktail was originally served. See GLASSWARE. As such, it is the harbinger of the fusion between punch and the cocktail that would occur at the end of the nineteenth century.

Originally the only difference between a fix and a sour was that the sour lacked the fix's fruit garnish (usually orange slices and berries). See SOUR. Indeed, many considered them the same drink. By the 1880s, however, the sour was customarily strained off the ice, thus creating one point of differentiation between the drinks. Another was the flavored syrup or liqueur that some mixologists at that time had begun using to sweeten their fixes. By then, however, the fix was on its way out: as a bar drink, it did not survive the nineteenth century, although it would pad out bartenders' guides for decades beyond. The fix is one of the few nineteenth-century drink categories that has not profited from the modern cocktail revival, at least not by name: the Bramble, one of the undisputed modern classics, is in fact a fix in everything but name. See BRAMBLE.

Recipe (Gin Fix): Stir 5 ml sugar with 15 ml lemon juice; add 60 ml genever, shake, and strain into ice-filled glass; garnish with half orange wheel and berries in season.

See also COCKTAIL and PUNCH.

"A Meeting at Washington, between Fuller and a Whig from Michigan, One Week after the Election." *Detroit Free Press*, November 25, 1841, 2.
Johnson, Harry. *New and Improved Bartender's Manual.* New York: Harry Johnson, 1882.
Thomas, Jerry. *How to Mix Drinks.* New York: Dick & Fitzgerald, 1862.

David Wondrich

The **fizz**, which in its basic form combines spirits with citrus juice, sugar, and sparkling water, is one of the most important members of the cohort of new drinks that transformed American mixology in the 1870s and 1880s. See also MANHATTAN COCKTAIL and MARTINI. Considering that far and away the most popular iteration of the drink was the Gin Fizz, it is likely that the drink is in some way derived from the Collins, another drink with citrus and soda water and English-style gin, then new in America. See COLLINS and GIN. But the fizz bears the same relation to the Collins that the smash does to the julep: shorter, quicker, faster (unlike the Collins, it originally had no ice in the glass and was meant to be drunk quickly, not sipped over time). See SMASH and JULEP. Its name, of course, is a simple acknowledgment of the sparkling or "fizz" water that is its distinguishing feature.

The fizz first appears in print in 1876, in the second edition of Jerry Thomas's *The Bar-Tender's Guide*, although it may pre-date that: the American journalist Julius Chambers later recalled master lobbyist Sam Ward making one for him on the occasion of their first meeting, in 1875. See THOMAS, JEREMIAH P. "JERRY". Ward, a New Yorker, was a noted bon vivant and boulevardier, and if he set his hand to popularizing a drink it would be popular. In any case, the drink seems to have come from that city; all of the earliest references to it are from there and it shares most of its DNA with the Daisy, whose origins in that city are well documented. See DAISY.

It took until the summers of 1879 and 1880 for the fizz to catch on as the latest thing in thirst-quenching. By 1882, it was firmly enthroned as, to quote the *New York World*, the "ordinary indulgence" in the summer months ("It is cooling and it is good"). In the 1880s and 1890s, the fizz also had a year-round secondary role as a light, effervescent hangover cure. For that, there were several dedicated variations, some of which achieved wide popularity.

In fact, the fizz spawned an unusual number of popular variations. As early as 1882 Harry Johnson was already able to list, along with the standard gin, whisky, and brandy versions, the Silver (with gin and egg white), Golden (with egg yolk), and Morning Glory Fizzes. See JOHNSON, HARRY. The latter, with scotch whisky (rarely used in American drinks of the period), absinthe, and egg white, was apparently Johnson's own creation. It saw wide and enduring service as one of those hangover cures, as its name implies, although not so wide as the Silver Fizz or as enduring as another variation, the famous, and famously delightful, Ramos Fizz. See RAMOS GIN FIZZ. Others included the Bird of Paradise Fizz (a Silver Fizz with a hint of raspberry); the Cream Fizz, which like the Ramos Fizz showed the influence of the soda fountain on this particular wing of mixology; and William Schmidt's Imperial Fizz, which dispensed with the soda water in favor of champagne. See SCHMIDT, WILLIAM.

If the 1890s saw the Gin Fizz yield its primacy as a summer cooler to the Gin Rickey, it nevertheless soldiered on as one of the flagship drinks for English-style gin in America and around the world (by the mid-1880s it was being served in London and Paris, with all the other stops on the international cocktail route soon to follow). See GIN RICKEY. The introduction of sloe gin to the American market in the early 1900s inevitably led to the Sloe Gin Fizz, the final canonical fizz variation, in circulation by 1904. See SLOE GIN. Prohibition did not help the fizz in America: a mild and pleasant drink that required a certain finesse in its preparation, it was at odds with the demands of the time. Meanwhile, in Europe and elsewhere, it continued to be carried on in the books but was never in the first rank of mixed drinks as it had been in America. By the 1950s, it was an antique. When it was made at all, it was usually done with ice in the glass, making it nothing more than a small Collins. New Orleans's Ramos Fizz was one exception, retaining a certain currency in its native city and wherever fancy brunch was served, while the 1970s saw the revival of the Sloe Gin Fizz as a disco drink.

Recent years have seen some renewed interest in the fizz, but not enough that one can consider it fully revived. In part, that is because its two main functions have been rendered obsolete, heat relief by air conditioning and hangover relief by Alka-Seltzer and ibuprofen. Nonetheless, made properly, the Fizz fills a unique position in the world of mixed drinks and one that still has considerable room for exploration.

Recipe: Stir 5 ml sugar into 15 ml lemon juice. Add 60 ml spirits and shake well with ice. Strain into a narrow, 180–240 ml glass and top off with 60 ml chilled sparkling water. For a Silver Fizz add 10 ml egg white before shaking.

Chambers, Julius. "Walks and Talks." *Brooklyn Eagle*, November 29, 1919, 15.
"Local Miscellany: The Barkeeper." *Chicago Tribune*, November 25, 1883, 11.
"Summer Drinks." *New York World*, August 1, 1882, 7.

David Wondrich

A **flag** garnish usually consists of a half slice of orange and a maraschino cherry pinned together with a toothpick and positioned on top of a sour cocktail, often a Collins or specialty cocktail. Extravagant fruit displays date back to the kitchens of Catherine de' Medici, who brought haute cuisine to France in the 1500s, and American bartenders (as shown in Jerry Thomas's seminal 1862 book, *How to Mix Drinks*) have long relied on "fruits of the season" to add visual appeal to their creations. The flag garnish, however, is of fairly recent vintage: while cherries and orange slices were among the popular garnishes for Old-Fashioneds and sours in the 1930s and 1940s, the pinned "flag" doesn't migrate to the Collinses until the early 1950s; the name came a generation after that. See THOMAS, JEREMIAH P. "JERRY".

The flag is still widely used in many bars, but less so among the more modern ones, where there is a growing movement toward featuring more exotic and culinary garnishes.

Lombardo, Erik. "Four Ways to Up Your Garnish Game." *Food 52*, August 21, 2014. http://food52.com/blog/11146-4-ways-to-up-your-garnish-game (accessed February 8, 2021).

Dale DeGroff

flair bartending is a style of bartending that employs the addition of semi-acrobatic maneuvers or tricks to entertain and impress the guest while making a drink. Moves can range from subtle to flashy and are used almost exclusively during drink preparation. The term is commonly used to encompass all manner of skills not strictly required to construct a drink, from quick hand embellishments or juggling and flipping bottles and tools to the use of open flame.

There are two styles of flair bartending that dominate the field: working flair and exhibition flair. Working flair focuses on the preparation of precise cocktails while engaging the guest with visual panache. While the quality of the cocktail is relatively unimportant with exhibition flair, there is nothing about working flair that is in direct competition with the outcome of the drink. Exhibition flair is what one would expect to see at a flair bartending competition, or at flair-centric bars such as Carnival Court in Las Vegas. During an exhibition flair performance, judges evaluate bartenders less on the quality of the cocktail being prepared than on technical ability, precision, showmanship, and the difficulty of the individual aspects of the routine. Performances are often set to music.

Flair bartending can be traced to nineteenth-century American bartender Jerry Thomas, who was well known for his flashy cocktail preparation. As an example, "Professor" Thomas's original creation the Blue Blazer involved pouring flaming whisky in theatrical gestures repeatedly from one vessel into another. The drink is important in the history of bartending, as the fire has little to no effect on the taste of the cocktail; it is purely done for show. See BLUE BLAZER and THOMAS, JEREMIAH P. "JERRY".

The restaurant chain TGI Friday's helped popularize and spread flair bartending. Management in the Marina Del Rey, California, store took notice of employee John Mescall's habit of juggling while making drinks and encouraged other bartenders to adopt the practice, most likely through an in-house competition in 1985. By 1987, the chain had sponsored its first national competition for flair bartending. The competition went global in 1991 and still remains active today. See TGI FRIDAY'S.

Flair bartending hit its zenith in 1988, with the release of the movie *Cocktail*. In it, Bryan Brown's character, an older, more experienced bartender, teaches young Tom Cruise the tricks of the trade, most of which center around flair bartending. Incidentally, the two actors were trained by John "J. B." Bandy, winner of TGI Friday's 1987 flair bartending competition. The movie, a moderate commercial success, remains synonymous with flair bartending for the majority of the public to this day. See FILM, SPIRITS AND COCKTAILS IN.

With the cocktail renaissance beginning in the late 1990s, flair bartending has slowly become relegated to nightclubs and Las Vegas bars, as bartenders and guests began to focus more seriously on fresh ingredients, classic recipes, and culinary techniques and less on theatrics and tricks. At the same time, some prominent modern cocktail bartenders have been using bits of working flair—"throwing" drinks, setting drinks on fire, elaborate styles of shaking—to distinguish themselves from their peers and telegraph their expertise. See COCKTAIL RENAISSANCE.

"About." TGI Friday's World Bartenders Championship. http://www.worldbtc.com/about (accessed May 5, 2021).

Jeffrey Morgenthaler

The **Flame of Love Martini** was the signature drink of Chasen's, the famous Hollywood hangout, which closed in 1995 after almost sixty years in business. It was invented for the establishment's regular guest Dean Martin by long-time bartender Pepe Ruiz after Martin inquired one night why as a regular and member of the infamous Rat Pack he didn't have a drink of his own. The next time Martin came in, Ruiz was ready, having peeled an orange, cut the peel into a number of large strips, and soaked them in brandy.

As Martin watched, Ruiz went into full show business mode, rinsing a chilled champagne coupe with La Iña sherry, then squeezing all but one of the strips of orange peel through the flame of a match into the glass, producing large balls of fire each time and coating the inside of the glass with the roasted citrus oil. Then he shook some gin or Stolichnaya vodka (accounts differ) with ice, poured it into the glass, and flamed a final orange peel over the top. That was in 1970, give or take a year. Ruiz, who started at Chasen's in 1960, continued to make the drink until the restaurant's closing (over time, the drink became exclusively a vodka one, and Ruiz stopped marinating the peels). It remains one of the quintessential Los Angeles cocktails. See FLAMING A TWIST.

Lore has it when Frank Sinatra saw the drink on Chasen's menu at a party there, he got so excited that he ordered sixty-five of them. It remains a show-stopper.

Recipe: Rinse chilled coupe with 10–15 ml chilled fino sherry, flame 3 or 4 orange twists over the glass, shake 90 ml vodka with ice, strain, and flame orange peel over the top. (Some recent variations call for pouring the sherry into the cocktail shaker with the vodka.)

"Flame of Love." *Imbibe Magazine* website, February 11, 2015. http://imbimemagazine.com/flame-of-love/ (accessed February 8, 2021).

Gonzales, Donald J. "Crisis at the Cocktail Hour." *Saturday Review*, November 15, 1975, 46–48.

"The Proper Pour with Charlotte Voisey: Flame of Love Cocktail." *Daily Motion* website. https://www.dailymotion.com/video/x2115wy (accessed April 20, 2021).

Dale DeGroff and David Wondrich

flaming a twist is a highly theatrical technique employed by bartenders and waiters to finish off a cocktail or accent a cup of espresso. Squeezing a small piece of lemon or orange peel will release the fruit's wonderfully aromatic oils, which are also flammable and when lit will produce a small burst of flame and a pleasant scent.

The method is easily (and fairly safely) reproduced: choose a fresh thick-skinned orange or lemon with plenty of oil in the rind. Cut the peel into small coin shapes the size of a quarter but avoid cutting deeply into the fruit—you want just the skin and not the underlying pith. Light a wooden match and allow the sulfur to burn off; pick up the piece of zest with a light touch to avoid bending and prematurely expelling the oils. Holding the zest by its sides gently between your forefinger and thumb, face the skin side down into the drink about five inches above its surface. Position the lit match between the zest and the surface of the drink about four inches above the glass. Snap the twist sharply, propelling the oil through the lit match with velocity onto the surface of the drink; the oils will flame up dramatically. Hold zest far enough above the drink to avoid getting a smoky film on the glass or on the surface of the drink. If the effect doesn't work, the fruit may be too old or dried out. Alkaloids and tannins are also present in the zest, and if overused or if the zest is too large, they will make the drink bitter.

Some young craft bartenders have decided the zest needs warming or roasting, and they hold it over the match for a short time before flaming it. Don't do this. The element of surprise is the key to this effect especially in a darkened bar setting. It should happen quickly before your guests even realize what is happening. The burst of flame is the moment they should be aware. If you turn the effect into a science project, you will confuse and confound your guests, when the idea is to delight.

See also FLAIR BARTENDING.

DeGroff, Dale. *The Craft of the Cocktail.* New York: Clarkson Potter, 2002.

Dietsch, Michael. "Cocktail 101: How to Flame an Orange Twist." *Serious Eats*, February 17, 2011. https://drinks.seriouseats.com/2011/02/cocktail-101-how-to-flame-an-orange-twist-garnish-drink-flaming-peel.html (accessed March 19, 2021).

Dale DeGroff

flaming drinks are a family of cocktails that are either prepared or served on fire for dramatic effect. Flamed drinks are produced either by floating high-strength alcohol on top of the cocktail and setting fire to it, by firing a "jet" of burning alcohol over the surface of the drink, or via flambé of the drink in its entirety. Even 40 percent ABV liquor will burn readily if warmed above 28° C, and spirits of 55 percent ABV and over will burn just fine at room temperature.

History tells us that for as long as humans have been distilling spirits, we have been setting fire to them, and flaming bowls of punch were common in Europe from the eighteenth century on. See FEUERZANGENBOWLE and PUNCH. But it was Jerry Thomas's Blue Blazer, which involves pouring an arc of flaming whisky back and forth between two mugs, that was the first cocktail to harness alcohol's flammable disposition for the betterment of bar room spectacle. See BLUE BLAZER and THOMAS, JEREMIAH P. "JERRY". A century later, the Tiki movement gleefully adopted fire as its ally; cocktails like the Volcano Bowl, with a flaming float of overproof rum, proved popular in the 1970s along with further riffs on punches and the Zombie cocktail, often garnished with a hollowed-out passion fruit (or lime) shell filled with a shot of flaming liquor. See TIKI.

The sense of drama and apprehension that fire presented also made it an obvious choice for the flair bartending community, who in the closing decades of the twentieth century integrated the hot stuff into their performances. The period also saw the rise of the Flaming Ferrari (and subsequent twist Flaming Lamborghini), which was invented by Thai Dang at the London celebrity hangout Nam Long Le Shaker. The Flaming Ferrari is a layered drink comprised of, in order, grenadine, Galliano, black sambuca, and green Chartreuse. The (high-proof) Chartreuse is set on fire and the lucky patron instructed to drink the liquid continuously through a straw as fresh shots of Grand Marnier Cordon Rouge and overproof rum are poured in to keep the flames burning See FLAIR BARTENDING.

Berry, Jeff. *Beach Bum Berry Remixed.* San Jose, CA: SLG, 2009.

Wondrich, David. *Punch.* New York: Perigee, 2010.

Tristan Stephenson

Flanagan, Betty, or **Betsy,** is the mythical inventor of the cocktail, as identified by the early American novelist James Fenimore Cooper (1789–1851) in his 1821 Revolutionary War tale, *The Spy,* where he describes one Elizabeth Flanagan as keeping a "house of entertainment for man and beast" in the village of Four Corners, New York (modern Elmsford), in the "neutral ground" that separated the British forces in New York City and the American forces further up the Hudson River. This is, of course, fiction, but there may be a grain of truth in it.

In the 1870s, a local tradition from the town of Lewiston, New York, on the Niagara River at the state's western border, came to the attention of the American press to the effect that Cooper had based Flanagan on Catherine "Kitty" Hustler, who kept a tavern there at which he had stayed while he was writing the book. Catherine Cherry was born in Britain, apparently of Irish stock, in 1762. She was in Philadelphia by 1777, when she married Thomas Hustler there. A sergeant in the Continental Army, Hustler served through the war and remained in the service until 1802. Around that time he and his wife helped found the town of Lewiston, opening an inn and tavern there. Cooper would have stayed there not while he was writing *The Spy* but in 1809 when he was a midshipman in the navy and accompanied Captain M. T. Woolsey on a small-boat exploration of the southern shores of Lake Ontario, including "some time in and about the Niagara," as he recalled in 1846.

Unfortunately, there is no record of what Kitty Hustler did between 1777 and 1802. It is certainly possible she kept a tavern in Four Corners; it is doubtful that she would have remained in Philadelphia when the British occupied it in 1778 and would have probably followed the army north. What's more, there is much that Cooper got right in his passage about the cocktail: he placed it in the Hudson Valley, where indeed most of the earliest references to it originate; although the mint he had Flanagan putting in the cocktail was not present in its classic iterations, the earliest descriptions display a much wider latitude (plus he correctly identified the Mint Julep as a Virginia drink); the presence of women behind the bar was much more common in eighteenth-century America, when the British model of drinking prevailed, than in the early nineteenth. In short, Catherine Hustler's role in, if not creating, then naming and propagating the cocktail cannot be ruled out.

See also COCK-TAIL and JULEP.

"About Lewiston." *Niagara Falls Gazette,* February 23, 1876, 3.

Cooper, James Fenimore. *Lives of Distinguished American Naval Officers.* Auburn, NY: 1846.

Cooper, James Fenimore. *The Spy.* 1821; repr. New York: Penguin, 1997.

David Wondrich

flavor can be described basically as a combination of taste sensations that happen within the mouth and smell sensations collected in the nose. Certainly enjoying food or drink despite a stuffy nose can be a challenge; the two senses seem to be distinct. We put food and drink into our mouths, mix it with our saliva, and then "taste" it, though we may be more informed by the aromas we sense than the so-called primary flavors of sweet, sour, salt, bitter, and umami. Yet other senses also come into play when we describe "flavor" more comprehensively. The body collects data about food and drink from the look of it and seeks certainty of its provenance and safety by evaluating its texture (*should this be mushy?*); even sound is important for the appreciation of many crunchy foods (snap! crackle! and pop! indeed). Flavor is more and more acknowledged as the collection of all possible sensory responses to food and drink.

Taste describes the collection of sensory information via physiochemical receptors in the mouth, but also the throat, esophagus, stomach and even, some think, the intestines. Fungiform, foliate, and circumvallate papillae, however, provide the greater part of the flavor information our mouths provide us. These are assisted by taste buds, groups of taste receptors composed of microvilli, tiny nerve fibers strung out from the receptor's membrane. These react to certain chemicals (like salt or sugar) or chemical properties (like bitterness, tartness, umami, or acidity). Things then get murky. Perhaps sugar and bitterness are received by the same receptors; what about salty and sour foods? Regardless of how it's collected, this information is bundled, then sent to the medulla and thalamus and on to the cortex.

Tactile perceptions of food and drink in the mouth are just as important to flavor as aromas and specific tastes. The density of a whisky or the silkiness of a Martini inform the taster's preference; our mouths provide such information through the sense of touch, but it is also known that the human gut is responsive to fats and other important food and drink compounds.

Adapting to flavors and aromas affects perceptions as well; eating a sweet dessert will tamp down sweetness receptors' reactivity. A moderately sweet drink, for example, will seem sour next to it; the drink's sweetness has not changed, but it is less perceived, while its sourness is highlighted by its immediate and novel difference from the sweetness.

And most curiously, humans seem to be the only creatures who crave spicy foods; capsaicin (the compound that provides the heat) is sufficient to turn off most other animals.

In the West, our deep-seated notion of four basic tastes is not as old as many think. And some scientists remain hostile to the notion of the so-called fifth flavor, described first by Dr. Kikunae Ikeda in 1919 as *umami*, or deliciousness. This proposed fifth primary flavor stirs controversy because not all scientists believe the mouth contains specific glutamate receptors (though it's agreed the gut holds some). Nonetheless, popular wisdom and contemporary culinary thought accept umami's influence even if there is little agreement upon its impact in food and drink. Dominant umami flavors have been shown to react with bitterness and/or astringency in some tasters, for instance, leaving them with a metallic taste. Young cabernet and raw oysters is a good example of this phenomenon, though the response is by no means universal.

Umami is most often described as savory, though some writers and educators will wax poetic, describing it as "harmony" or "balance." If it is a specific flavor, as many believe, it need not represent some greater qualitative assessment. Those seeking a good representation of umami can taste raw broccoli and then sip the broth from a pan of cooked broccoli. Tomatoes, braised meats—there are many other distinct representations of umami. The question as to whether or not umami is present in spirits is still unsettled, though it is increasingly hypothesized that aged whiskies, agave spirits, and some rums and cachaças can exhibit this same brothy umami flavor.

Beauchamp, Gary K., and Linda Bartoshuk, eds. *Tasting and Smelling*, 2nd ed. San Diego: Academic, 1997.

Wolfe, Jeremy M., Keith R. Kluender, and Dennis M. Levi. *Sensation and Perception*, 3rd ed. Sunderland, MA: Sinauer, 2012.

Kawamura, Yojiro, and Morley R. Kare, eds. *Umami, a Basic Taste*. New York: Dekker, 1987.

Doug Frost

flavored syrup is typically a sugar-based syrup that has had a flavoring added to it. In an alcoholic drink, a flavored syrup will generally replace simple syrup to add complexity, while in a nonalcoholic drink (mocktail) it will be used to provide not only the obvious sweetness but an additional layer of flavor to help compensate for the lack of alcohol and provide some interest as well. See MOCKTAIL.

Grenadine is perhaps the most commonly available flavored syrup, where pomegranate is the flavoring ingredient. For homemade grenadine, you can prepare a standard simple syrup and replace the water with pomegranate juice. Another option is to simmer a cup of pomegranate seeds in two cups of simple syrup for approximately fifteen minutes or until the syrup attains a light brick-red color and has the intensity of flavor that you are looking for. See GRENADINE.

Over the last few decades, the coffee industry brought about an increased demand for flavored sugar syrups (and consequently a wide array of flavors), so it is now possible to find a variety of flavors at many major grocery stores, in varying degrees of quality.

Another commonly used flavored syrup is orgeat, an almond-based syrup that appears most famously in Trader Vic's Mai Tai and Jerry Thomas's Japanese Cocktail. See JAPANESE COCKTAIL and MAI TAI. Much of the modern day commercial orgeat is little more than artificial almond flavoring added to sugar syrup (sometimes with a hint of orange flower water). Dissatisfied with the quality of these existing products, a growing number of bartenders are taking on the task of preparing their own orgeat and experimenting with producing other nut-based syrups as well. Due to this renewed interest for good ingredients, bartenders are seeing an increase in artisanal brands of flavored syrups on the market. See ORGEAT.

There are a number of ways to prepare flavored syrups. One of the easiest is simply to add the flavoring component of your choice directly into simple syrup and let it infuse for a period of time. See INFUSION. Depending on the intended flavoring and ingredient, consideration should be given to the maceration temperature. For example, when working with citrus peel, it's best to refrigerate the infusion during the maceration process so as to preserve the clean, sharp flavors from its essential oil while it infuses into the syrup. It should be stored under refrigeration for the very same reasons. Warming volatile citrus oils will cause them to oxidize, reducing their brightness and fresh aromatics. See MACERATION.

Yet sometimes a cold or room-temperature maceration isn't quite enough to extract the essential oil from a particular material, as in the case of woodier ingredients (such as cinnamon), and it becomes necessary to apply heat to the maceration in order to obtain good flavor extraction.

Of the greatest importance is preparing the ingredient properly. With citrus, for example, it's best to utilize only the zest of the skin; the pith will add bitter notes.

Flavored syrups can also be made by adding either a tincture, a couple of drops of essential oil, or store-bought flavorings extracts to simple syrup. Yet whatever the medium of choice is, always ensure that any ingredient out of the ordinary is food-grade before using.

Arnold, Dave. *Liquid Intelligence*. New York: W. W. Norton, 2014.

Abou-Ganim, Tony, with Mary Elizabeth Faulkner. *The Modern Mixologist: Contemporary Classic Cocktails*. Chicago: Surrey, 2010.

Audrey Saunders

flavorings comprise all tangible, measurable ingredients added to spirits that alter their aromas and flavors. Broadly, the term encompasses those spices, herbs, fruits, seeds, essential oils, oleoresins, essences, extracts, blends, infusions, wines, sweeteners, and other natural and synthetic ingredients added after (and, in the case of some botanicals, during) distillation. The foundation of a spirit's flavors is shaped by factors such as its substrate or base material (barley or molasses, for example), yeast strain, still design, a distiller's cuts during distillation, and barrel selection and management. Building upon that base, flavorings allow distillers, bottlers, rectifiers, and blenders additional levels of control, of both artistry and artifice.

Where flavoring ends and adulteration begins is sometimes a subjective line. Small quantities of flavorings undeclared on the label may be used to adjust, finesse, or subtly finish a product to prepare it for sale. Alternately, they may strongly imbue a spirit with a new flavor, thus fundamentally altering its character. An admixture of synthetic vanillin, for example, may amplify a whisky's existing vanilla notes. See VANILLIN. Other flavorings may transform neutral spirits into candy-flavored schnapps and ersatz brandy. Others still lie at the heart of elegant cordials, gins, and absinthes. The use of flavorings is apparent in well-stocked liquor stores: whiskies flavored with peanut butter, mint extracts, cinnamon and cassia oils, and honey; vodkas with the taste and aroma of chiles, bison grass, hemp, extracts of pear and lime, and pitch-perfect strawberry pavlova; spiced rums; liqueurs made with natural and artificial flavors for banana, orange, ginger, melon, coffee, watermelon, and more; brandies flavored with apricot, blackberry, and apple. The possibilities are almost limitless.

Flavorings have been used for millennia in drinks, but around the middle of the nineteenth century, organic chemists began to analyze spirits systematically to determine their precise chemical composition. Using that research, compounders and rectifiers subsequently created ersatz brandies, rye whiskies, and other beverages. The intent was not necessarily fraud. Among scientists, the thinking was that if all the components of genuine spirits could be determined, recreating those spirits at considerable profit was a simple matter of combining those same compounds with less expensive base spirits. In practice, the widespread adoption of essences, extracts, essential oils, and other flavor compounds invited chiselers and cheats to create such blatant, low-grade fakes that the United States passed the Bottled-in-Bond Act of 1897. See BOTTLED IN BOND and ESSENTIAL OILS.

While flavorings are technically forbidden for a number of spirits, such as straight American whiskies, they are not in and of themselves a cheat or fraud. Many elegant cognacs, for instance, use an oak extract called boisé to finish their brandies. See BOISÉ. In fact, flavorings are required to make numerous spirits, including gin. Whole botanicals (in the form of juniper berries plus citrus, orris root, licorice, angelica, coriander, and other botanicals), extracts, and essences or a combination of them may contribute the classic flavors. See BOTANICAL. Likewise, absinthe relies on a trio of anise, fennel, and grand wormwood with other herbs to achieve its characteristic taste and color. See ABSINTHE and WORMWOOD. Italian amari, Alpine *Kräuterliköre*, Polish *krupnik*, monastic liqueurs like Chartreuse, English sloe gin, Tennessee apple pie moonshine, and countless other spirits rely upon flavorings. See CHARTREUSE; HONEY LIQUEURS; and SLOE GIN.

Flavorings are not restricted to plant matter and its concentrates or derivatives. For centuries distillers deployed meats such as beef, mutton, horse, snails, cured ham, deer, iguana, and others in spirits, although they have become rare in the modern age. An eighteenth-century manuscript at the University of Pennsylvania presents a detailed recipe for Cock Water made from a barnyard fowl distilled with wine, herbs, and fruit. The practice continues: Del Maguey now sells Pechuga, a mezcal distilled in a traditional manner with a chicken breast suspended within the still. See DEL MAGUEY MEZCAL.

Though more properly the domain of blending, small additions of spirits such as brandies or rum in some circumstances act as flavorings. Wines, including but not limited to port, Madeira, and sweet vermouth, are also used. Whiskies may be "finished" in barrels that previously held sherry or other wines to impart a degree of wine character to the bottled spirit. Some, however, are blended with wine. So-called Kansas City–style whisky, a pre-Prohibition style resurrected by J. Rieger & Co., blends various straight whiskies with a small addition of sherry to temper the spirits.

Modern regulations dictate that spirits flavorings may not be harmful in the quantities used, though what is permitted varies by country. In the United States, all added flavorings for commercial spirits must be approved by the Food and Drug Administration, designated as GRAS ("generally recognized as safe"), or affirmed by the maker as GRAS with no FDA objection. The use of calamus, Virginia snakeroot, lead, and other ingredients of the past now understood to be problematic has been discontinued in many countries.

It behooves the modern distiller, bartender, or home enthusiast recreating old recipes to research ingredients thoroughly and follow best practices for their use in drinks.

See also ADULTERATION; AGING; AMARO; AROMA; BLENDING; COMPOUNDING; CORDIALS, DISTILLATION; GIN; INFUSION; and RECTIFICATION.

Beverage Alcohol Manual. https://www.ttb.gov/images/pdfs/spirits_bam/chapter7.pdf (accessed March 19, 2021).

Burns, E. *Bad Whisky: The Scandal That Created the World's Most Successful Spirit.* Glasgow: Neil Wilson. 2011.

Difford, Simon. *Diffordsguide Gin,* 2nd ed. London: Odd Firm of Sin, 2013.

Goldfarb, Aaron. *Hacking Whiskey: Smoking, Blending, Fat Washing, and Other Whiskey Experiments.* Brooklyn: Dovetail, 2018.

Rowley, Matthew. *Lost Recipes of Prohibition: Notes from a Bootlegger's Manual.* New York: Countryman, 2015.

Rowley, Matthew. "Rock Out with Your Cock Ale." Rowley's Whiskey Forge (blog), December 26, 2008. http://matthew-rowley.blogspot.com/2008/12/rock-out-with-your-cock-ale.html (accessed March 19, 2021).

Stewart, Amy. *The Drunken Botanist: The Plants that Create the World's Great Drinks.* Chapel Hill, NC: Algonquin, 2013.

Matthew Rowley

flip generally refers to one of two drinks bearing this name. An early variation, by origin apparently a sailor's drink but also popular in colonial North America, was made by mixing ale, spirit, and sweetener in a pitcher, which was heated by immersing into it a red-hot iron rod. A version more commonly consumed in the nineteenth and early twentieth century was served either warm or chilled and made with ale, spirit, sugar, and a whole egg.

Colonial-Era Flip

Flip was first referred to in print in the 1690s, both in England, where it was defined as a "sea drink of small beer and brandy, sweetened and spiced upon occasion," and in the North American colonies, where it was soon among the most popular of drinks. In the

December 1704 issue of the *New England Almanac*, this short bit of doggerel paid tribute to it:

> The days are short, the weather's cold,
> By tavern fires tales are told.
> Some ask for dram when first come in.
> Others with flip and bounce begin.

Flip's ingredients were described succinctly by Rev. Jedidiah Morse in 1792 as "rum mixed with small beer, and muscovado sugar," although any beer and sweetener could be used. Flip was commonly made in a sizable pitcher rather than an individual tankard, making it a social drink consumed with companions and akin to punch. No definitive recipe exists, but it typically would involve a pitcher of beer into which rum and molasses were added. Cider or spruce beer was at times substituted for the ale, and sugar or dried pumpkin replaced the molasses as sweetener. (A workable ratio for recreating the drink is 24 ounces of ale, 8 ounces of rum, and 4 ounces of molasses.) See BLACK STRAP.

The iron used to heat the drinks was called a loggerhead, originally a tool used by shipbuilders to keep tar pliable in cool weather. In taverns, it was heated in a fireplace until it glowed, then plunged into the pitcher. This would cause the contents to foam up noisily and often overflow the container. The red-hot metal altered the flavor by caramelizing the sugars and toasting the grain in the beer. When it is well made, few of the constituent ingredients may be detected individually.

Flip remained popular throughout the eighteenth century. The poet John Trumbull (1750–1831) saw in the "inspiring flip" "the quintessence of public spirit" as a drink that passed "each patriot lip." Following the American Revolution, ale flip faded in popularity as individually prepared drinks emerged ascendant. Some modern craft bars have concocted variations of flip, including Booker & Dax in Manhattan, which employs an electric loggerhead that heats to 1,500 degrees.

Nineteenth- and Twentieth-Century Flip

As the colonial-era loggerhead flip passed into memory, another drink referred to as flip arose and persisted throughout the nineteenth and early twentieth century.

This variation of flip is more closely related to eggnog, a tipple that by rights should be extinct but arises from the crypt each holiday season. See EGGNOG. The hallmark of the later flip is the inclusion of a whole egg in the mixing. No loggerhead is involved; the drink's vaunted creaminess was made, as described by bartender Jerry Thomas in 1862, "by repeated pouring back and forth between two vessels." See LOGGERHEAD. Thomas's recipe for "rum flip" called for ale warmed on a fire, then mixed with beaten eggs, sugar, nutmeg or ginger, and rum. See THOMAS, JEREMIAH P. "JERRY".

But this was a transitional drink. The flip's final form was first documented in 1874, in an otherwise entirely unoriginal drinks book curated by Ed Simmons of French's Hotel in New York: a whole egg, sugar, and spirits, shaken up with ice and strained into a cocktail or fizz glass. By 1895, George Kappeler's *Modern American Drinks* could do away with the warmed flip altogether, listing instead a dozen flip recipes, all iced. See KAPPELER, GEORGE J.

The latter-day flip saw some revival after Prohibition but soon faded. Modern mixologists have no problem incorporating egg whites into their drinks, but whole eggs are another matter entirely, and the flip, delightful as it may be, is only encountered rarely.

See also EGGS.

Recipe (Brandy Flip, new style): Shake well with ice 60 ml brandy, 15 ml simple syrup, and 1 whole raw egg. Strain into a chilled cocktail glass and grate nutmeg on top.

The American Bar-Tender, New York: Hurst, 1874.

B. E. *A New Dictionary of the Terms Ancient and Modern of the Canting Crew*. London: 1699.

Field, Edward. *The Colonial Tavern: A Glimpse of New England Town Life in the Seventeenth and Eighteenth Centuries*. 1897. Reprint, Bowie, MD: Heritage, 1989.

Thomas, Jerry. *How to Mix Drinks*. New York: Dick & Fitzgerald, 1862.

Wayne Curtis

To **float** a cocktail ingredient is to layer it on top of a drink as the crowning touch, usually by pouring it slowly and carefully over the back of a spoon onto

Wine floats on a trio of New York Sours. Wondrich Collection.

the surface. The Pousse Café, which appears in Jerry Thomas's 1862 *Bon Vivant's Companion, or How to Mix Drinks*, is the earliest example of a floated drink—and the most extreme, as it is composed entirely of floats, each layered atop the other according to its relative density (starting with the heaviest ingredient at bottom and ending with the lightest on top). See POUSSE CAFÉ. Most floated drinks, however, have only one layer.

Some floats are strictly cosmetic, such as the layer of dark rum floated on tall tropical punches; these drinks are usually served with a straw or stir stick, indicating that the drinker should not sip the top layer of straight hard liquor directly but instead mix it into the drink. This type of float may be visually appealing, but it pits the drink's palette against the drinker's palate. Other floats are integral to the flavor of a drink, which is enhanced by sipping the drink through the intact top layer. Chief among these is the Irish Coffee, with its floated layer of dairy cream. The New York Sour's red wine float is another tasty example: the wine's alcohol content is low enough to imbibe directly, and its flavor compliments the bourbon-lemon-sugar blend below as this blend is sipped through the float. See IRISH COFFEE and NEW YORK SOUR.

Thomas, Jerry. *How to Mix Drinks*. New York: Dick & Fitzgerald, 1862.

Jeff Berry

Floc de Gascogne is a French mistelle or "vin de mutage"—either white or rosé—where grape juice in its first stage of fermentation is mixed with Armagnac (just as cognac makes its pineau des charentes), resulting in something that is akin to a fortified wine, with an alcohol content of some 18–20 percent. See MISTELLE. Both the juice and the Armagnac must come from the legally defined areas of Armagnac production. See ARMAGNAC. Approximately 2,300 acres of grapevines provide the juice. Within any particular holding, white grapes must by law include at least 70 percent Colombard, gros manseng, and ugni blanc (cognac's dominant grape), and no more than 30 percent can be comprised of folle blanche, mauzac, petit manseng, sauvignon blanc, sauvignon gris, baroque, and sémillon. For red wine holdings, no more than 50 percent can be Tannat, while cabernet franc, cabernet sauvignon, malbec (called cot in this region), fer servadou, and merlot are not limited by law.

Typically, Floc is made from two-thirds to three-quarters grape juice and one-third to one-quarter Armagnac (at least 52 percent alcohol by volume), often coming from the same property, and slowly added over several days or more. The Armagnac is very young and not influenced by new oak maturation but has been stored in stainless steel or in older barrels. This new Floc de Gascogne cannot be bottled or sold until March 15 every year. It carries no vintage date (indeed, Flocs may be blended from more than one vintage of Armagnac). Sometimes it is barrel aged.

Floc de Gascogne was first known as Pineau (like its sibling in cognac) but was only a trifle in 1977 when it received official status (as a VQPRD), with perhaps only a few hundred cases produced annually. From there on it grew quickly and gained its AOC status in 1990; 2009 saw Floc receive POD status (Protected Designation of Origin). Its name, coined only in 1954, derives from "Lou Floc" which in the Occitan language means "bouquet of flowers." Producers will often describe the unfermented juice as redolent of violets, roses, and plum blossoms.

Production today totals about one million liters from 120 or so producers, representing about 15 percent of the region's total wine production, of which about a third is sold at the cellar door, mostly for local consumption, and another third is sold in French stores.

Styles can vary from bright and fruity to more pungent and austere, the difference sometimes being a function of barrel aging and sometimes of the choice of grapes (gros manseng tends to have more color and floral aromas). Floc is typically served cool or cold (4.5–7° C; 40–45° F) and is increasingly viewed as a cocktail enhancer, though most is still consumed on the rocks.

Comité Interprofessionnel du Floc-de-Gascogne. *Floc de Gascogne*. http://flocdegascogne.fr (accessed February 9, 2021).

Neal, Charles. *Armagnac*. San Francisco: Flame Grape, 1998.

Doug Frost

floor malting refers to the traditional—indeed ancient—method of malting grain on a stone or cement floor. It is still practiced by a handful of old distilleries in Scotland and new micro-distilleries elsewhere. After the grain is steeped in water to activate the enzymatic process that initiates the sprout growth, it is then spread onto a floor in a layer approximately 15–30 cm (6–12 in) thick. This layer is turned over by shovel every few hours to prevent rootlets from clinging together en masse (a phenomenon sometimes called "felting"), release heat generated by germination, and dissipate carbon dioxide buildup. After approximately four to six days on the floor, maltmen transfer the grain to a kiln for drying. Many single malt scotch distilleries and independent malt producers celebrate floor malting to score points with consumers for whom the idea of folksy alcohol production methods resonates positively, and also to honor the past. However, floor malting is labor-intensive and inefficient, and scotch malt distilleries began moving away from it as early as 1910. Temperature changes, injury, time, mold, rodents, and dirt are just a few floor malting concerns. Consequently, even the few scotch distilleries that do floor malt obtain about 85–90 percent of their malt from producers who use large-scale and industrial equipment.

See also BARLEY; MALTING; and MONKEY SHOULDER.

Bruce-Gardyne, Tom. "Think Tank: Floor Maltings." *Unfiltered*, May 2019. https://www.smws.com.au/think-tank-floor-maltings/ (accessed February 9, 2021).

Heather Greene

The **Floridita** cocktail, with rum, vermouth, crème de cacao, and lime juice, is perhaps the most creative of the many Daiquiri variations created by the mid-twentieth-century master of Daiquiri variations, Constantino Ribalaigua Vert of Havana's Bar La Florida, aka the Floridita. For reasons unknown this delicious cocktail does not appear in any edition of the souvenir Floridita recipe booklets Constantino published between 1935 and 1948. It would have been lost to time if Victor "Trader Vic" Bergeron hadn't encountered it on a 1938 visit to the Floridita, put it on the inaugural menu at Trader Vic's, and eventually published it in his 1972 *Bar Guide*.

Recipe: Combine juice of one lime, 30 ml white Cuban or Puerto Rican rum, 15 ml red vermouth, 7.5 ml white crème de cacao, and one teaspoon each orange curaçao and grenadine; shake with ice and strain into a cocktail coupe. Garnish with an orange peel twist.

See also BERGERON, VICTOR "TRADER VIC"; CRÈME DE CACAO; DAIQUIRI; and RIBALAIGUA Y VERT, CONSTANTE.

Bergeron, Victor J. *Trader Vic's Bartender's Guide, Revised*. New York: Doubleday, 1972.

Jeff Berry

flower-based spirits—that is, spirits distilled from fermented flowers—are exceedingly rare, but because floral flavors are very popular in cocktails, there are a number of spirits, both historical and modern, that are flavored with flowers. Flowers such as rose, lavender, and chamomile are common ingredients in amari, vermouths, and other types of aromatized wines. See AMARO; VERMOUTH; and WINES, FORTIFIED. (In fact, vermouth maker Noilly Prat allegedly uses more than half of France's total annual chamomile crop in its products.) See NOILLY PRAT. Wormwood, used often in both vermouth and absinthe, can be considered a floral ingredient as well—some producers use the plant's flowers as well as its leaves. See WORMWOOD and ABSINTHE.

There are also many different types of flower-based liqueurs. Perhaps the best known of these is crème de violette, a purple liqueur made with violet petals that was popular in the early 1900s in cocktails such as the Aviation and the Blue Moon, and which saw a revival during the twenty-first-century cocktail boom. See AVIATION COCKTAIL; BLUE MOON; and CRÈME DE VIOLETTE. Rose is another common liqueur ingredient as well: parfait amour, often flavored with rose, berries, and citrus, was popular in the 1800s and early 1900s, as was crème de roses, both little seen these days, and rose petals are sometimes used in the category of rosolio, an Italian cordial originally flavored with sundew flowers that dates to the Renaissance. See PARFAIT AMOUR and ROSOLIO.

A modern creation flavored with elderflowers, St-Germain is another flower-based liqueur that has become very popular in the early twenty-first century and has inspired a number of imitators. See COOPER SPIRITS. In addition to these, distilleries around the world make liqueurs and other spirits flavored with honeysuckle, rose geranium, hibiscus, marigold, poppy, iris, and other flowers. (Even artichoke-based amari like Cynar fall into this category, as the edible portion of the artichoke is botanically an immature flower.)

But these are all spirits flavored with flowers. The main spirit distilled from them is an Indian specialty, mahua, made from the flowers of the mahua tree (*Bassia latifolia*). When dried, these blossoms are as much as 40 percent fermentable sugars, but they are also rich in a glucoside that causes diarrhea. This compound persists in wine made from the flowers but does not pass through the still. Mahua has been made in parts of India since at least the 1400s, and it may go back to antiquity.

Brown, Jared. "Noilly Prat Ambre Vermouth." *The Historians* (blog), March 20, 2009. http://thehistorians-jaredbrown.blogspot.com/2009/03/noilly-prat-ambre-vermouth.html (accessed March 19, 2021).

Mahdihassan, S. "The Earliest Distillation Units: Pottery in Indo-Pakistan." *Pakistan Archaeology* 8 (1972): 159–168.

Regan, Gaz. "The Cocktailian: Creme de Violette Lifts Aviation to the Moon." *San Francisco Chronicle*, September 27, 2007. https://www.sfgate.com/wine/article/The-Cocktailian-Creme-de-violette-lifts-Aviation-2520581.php (accessed March 19, 2021).

Jason Horn

foams, as used in cocktails, are complex airy structures composed mostly of gas and liquid: bubbles valiantly holding their own against gravity and time. Foams provide textural variety, soften the bite of rough spirits, and may add additional taste and aroma to drinks. They may be coarse or fine, flowing or set, delicate or quite thick. Wine, beer, fruit and vegetable juices, diluted liqueurs and spirits, and other liquids may be turned into cocktail foams through manual shaking and whisking or with tools including stand mixers, immersion blenders, espresso machine steam wands, and pressurized whipping siphons, all of which incorporate air or gas into liquids. Some culinary foams are evanescent structures that cling to existence for mere minutes, while heat-set foams, such as marshmallows or meringue, may endure for months. That stability depends upon the methods and ingredients used to create them. Bartenders traditionally have used eggs, dairy, and sometimes pineapple juice to create a top layer of fine foam upon drinks. See EGGS. Fresh egg whites, despite an aroma occasionally likened to wet dog, are a venerable favorite for creating supple foam atop classic shaken drinks as the Pisco Sour and Ramos Fizz, while an Irish Coffee is incomplete without its blanket of whipped cream. See WHISKY, IRISH; PISCO SOUR; and RAMOS GIN FIZZ. Drinkers with a modernist bent deploy a wider range of foaming agents that fall broadly into six categories: fats, gelling agents, proteins, starches, surfactants, and solids, some of which are acceptable for drinkers with restricted diets. Aquafaba, the residuum of chickpea cooking water, for instance, is suitable for vegans. Like egg whites, however, it can release a strong and, to some, disagreeable odor. Other foaming agents include agar, gelatin, gum arabic, xanthan gum, pectins, sodium alginate, maltodextrin, methylcellulose, and powdered soy lecithin. See AGAR; GELATIN; and GUM SYRUP. Commercial cocktail foaming agents include Fee Foam, Versawhip, Foam Magic, Wonderfoam, and Instafoam (with *Quillaja*, or soap bark, extract).

See also DAIRY; DRY SHAKE; NITROGEN, LIQUID; and TEXTURE AND MOUTHFEEL.

Arnold, D. *Liquid Intelligence: The Art and Science of the Perfect Cocktail*. New York: W. W. Norton, 2014.

Jaworska, M. "Science Your Way to a Texturally Complex Cocktail." *Punch*, June 27, 2017. https://punchdrink.com/articles/science-your-way-to-texturally-complex-cocktail-aquafaba-soy-lecithin-drink-recipe/ (accessed March 19, 2021).

McGee, H. *On Food and Cooking: The Science and Lore of the Kitchen.* New York: Simon & Schuster, 2007.

Myhrvold, N., C. Young, and M. Bilet. *Modernist Cuisine*, vol 4, *Ingredients and Preparations.* Bellevue, WA: Cooking Lab, 2011.

Matthew Rowley

Fog Cutter, with rum, brandy, gin, sherry, and various juices, is a popular faux-Polynesian punch invented by "Trader Vic" Bergeron by 1940, notable for its unusual mixture of three base spirits and because it was the first "tiki" drink served in a bespoke ceramic mug designed specifically for it (initiating a trend still followed by tiki bars today). Its name is derived from a generic American term for a morning drink ("eye-opener" is another) that dates back at least to the 1840s.

Vic first printed the recipe in his 1946 *Book of Food and Drink.* "You can get pretty stinking on these, no fooling," wrote Vic, who only served two to a customer at his Trader Vic's restaurants. By the late 1940s he'd scaled down the Fog Cutter to a lighter, electrically blended version, which he rechristened the Samoan Fog Cutter (to make one, cut down the rum to 45 ml and the brandy to 15 ml, then blend everything except sherry with one cup crushed ice; serve as below).

By the mid-1950s, hundreds of tiki-themed restaurants and bars had appropriated the Fog Cutter. Even non-tiki cocktail menus featured it, often modified to fit a restaurant's theme; Seattle's Norselander, to take one example, swapped aquavit for the sherry and called the drink a Viking Fog Cutter.

Recipe: Combine 60 ml each lemon juice and light Puerto Rican rum, 30 ml each orange juice and brandy, and 15 ml each orgeat syrup and gin, shake with ice and pour unstrained into a tall glass or Fog Cutter mug. Top with a sherry float and garnish with mint.

See also BERGERON, VICTOR "TRADER VIC"; PUNCH; and TIKI.

Bergeron, Victor J. *Trader Vic's Bartender's Guide, Revised.* New York: Doubleday, 1972.
Bergeron, Victor J. *Trader Vic's Book of Food and Drink.* New York: Doubleday, 1946.

Jeff Berry

Foley, Ray (1943–) is the founder and editor of *Bartender* magazine, which he launched on a whim in 1979 and has since grown to a circulation of more than 250,000. His service industry roots were planted at the Manor in West Orange, New Jersey, where he tended bar at the Terrace Lounge. In the decades since, he has earned a reputation as an advocate for bartenders, having founded the Bartender Hall of Fame and the nonprofit Bartender's Foundation Incorporated and authored more than a dozen books on cocktails and bartending, including *Bartending for Dummies* (2010). His advocacy, however, has not generally extended to the new-old style of bartending characteristic of the twenty-first century, for which he has expressed frequent and public disdain. Foley is a notable collector of vintage drink books and is credited with creating the Fuzzy Navel cocktail to promote then-new-to-market DeKuyper Peachtree Schnapps.

See also DE KUYPER.

Bartender. https://bartender.com (accessed February 9, 2021).
Genovese, Peter. "Raising the Bar: Fuzzy Navel Inventor/ 'Bartending for Dummies' Author and His Liquid Empire." *NJ.com*, June 25, 2012. http://www.nj.com/entertainment/dining/index.ssf/2012/06/raising_the_bar_-_the_fuzzy_na.html (accessed February 9, 2021).

Lauren Viera

Ford, Simon (1972–), is one of the catalysts of the modern cocktail renaissance. A bartender and a bon vivant turned brand ambassador and finally liquor company cofounder, Ford was born in Hastings, England, and raised in Bath. While working for Plymouth Gin starting in the late 1990s, and later at Pernod-Ricard after its acquisition of Plymouth in 2009, Ford pioneered the role of brand ambassador, especially in the area of brand education. See PLYMOUTH GIN. Realizing that bringing bartenders together for travel, spirits education, encounters with distillery personnel, and professional networking among themselves would extend both the influence of the sponsoring brands as well as the education and professional standing of the invited bartenders, Ford convinced his employers to pay for a series of distillery visits, boozy historical walking tours, celebrations of bars and individual classic cocktails, and such that were as entertaining as they were educational. This developed into a brand education model that was copied and employed across the liquor and bar industries. Ford's reputation as an industry icon was burnished by his long-standing role as host of the Spirited Awards show during the annual Tales of the Cocktail event in New Orleans. After departing Pernod Ricard, Ford went on to become a cofounder of the 86 Company liquor concern in 2012, which included the well-regarded Fords Gin in its portfolio. In 2019, Fords Gin was purchased by the Brown-Forman corporation.

See also BROWN-FORMAN; PERNOD-RICARD; and TALES OF THE COCKTAIL.

"Simon Ford: Co-Founder, the 86 Co." *Punch Magazine*. https://punchdrink.com/lookbook/simon-ford-co-founder-the-86-company-spirits/ (accessed March 19, 2021).
Text message exchange with Simon Ford, July 6, 2020.
Tuennerman, Ann. "A Chat with Ann Tuennerman and Simon Ford." Tales of the Cocktail Foundation, May 23, 2017. http://3.16.131.86/people/chat-ann-tuennerman-and-simon-ford (accessed March 19, 2021).

David Moo

A **forgotten classic** is a cocktail or other alcoholic mixed drink that enjoyed popularity, albeit limited, at the time of its creation or in the years following. Its fame was not necessarily international or national. Instead, it may have been regional, or even confined to a single bar. Unlike the Martini, Old-Fashioned, Negroni, Margarita, and similar well-known drinks that maintained their appeal over the years, forgotten classics fell into disuse or obscurity. Some, such as the Last Word, have been rediscovered and embraced by the international cocktail crowd. Others remain in hiding yet to be revived.

Certain recipes fell from favor due to the discontinuation of key ingredients or died with their creators, while others were consigned to obscurity without apparent reason, even though they are "still grand," as cocktail historian Ted Haigh observes, "and full of potential." Examples include the Corpse Reviver no. 1 (long overshadowed by the Corpse Reviver no. 2), a mixture of cognac, calvados, and sweet vermouth that appears in Harry Craddock's 1930 *Savoy Cocktail Book*; Cameron's Kick, a whisky sour built on a base of scotch and Irish whisky and sweetened with orgeat that first appeared in Harry McElhone's 1922 *ABC of Mixing Cocktails*; the Saratoga Cocktail, a Jerry Thomas original; and, from the Savoy, the blend of Chartreuse, gin, apple brandy, and sweet vermouth known as Warday's Cocktail. As discontinued ingredients are reintroduced and once-unobtainable bartender's guides get reprinted or posted online, modern bartenders become advocates, and some of these classics are forgotten no more.

See also CORPSE REVIVER; CRADDOCK, HARRY LAWSON; HAIGH, TED; LAST WORD; McELHONE, HENRY "HARRY"; and THOMAS, JEREMIAH P. "JERRY."

Caiafa, Frank. *The Waldorf Astoria Bar Book*. New York: Penguin, 2016.
Haigh, Ted. *Vintage Spirits and Forgotten Cocktails*. Gloucester, MA: Quarry, 2009.
Wondrich, David, "Six Forgotten Cocktails That Deserve to Be Revived." *Telegraph*, March 13, 2015. https://www.telegraph.co.uk/foodanddrink/foodanddrinkadvice/11464235/Six-forgotten-cocktails-that-deserve-to-be-revived.html (accessed January 5, 2020).

Chloe Frechette

Forsyths Ltd., coppersmiths and metalworkers, of Rothes, Scotland, is the United Kingdom's leading manufacturer of equipment for the whisky industry. The company is family-owned and was founded by Alexander Forsyth (1873–1955). He served an apprenticeship at a brass and copperworks in Rothes, Speyside, during the 1890s, acquiring the business in 1933 and renaming it A. Forsyth & Son.

The son was Ernest—better known as "Toot" (1918–1983)—and after war service he took over the firm, soon introducing new welding techniques to replace traditional riveting. In the late 1960s he was joined by his sons, Richard and William, and the former became managing director in the mid-1970s, renaming the company Forsyths Ltd. Richard was succeeded as managing director in 2009 by his son, Richard Ernest.

Until the 1980s, the company's focus was entirely on hand-beaten copper pot stills and condensers. The slump in the whisky industry at that time encouraged diversification into the fabrication of equipment for the paper, oil and gas, and pharmaceutical industries. But the company's core business remains coppersmithing for distilleries all over the world.

See also STILL, POT.

Gray, John R. *Rothes Past and Present: A History of the Town and Parish and of Lodge St. John (Operative) no.193, Ancient Free and Accepted Masons of Scotland.* Stirling, UK: E. Mackay, 1954.

"Our History." Forsyths website. http://www.forsyths.com/about-us/our-history/ (accessed February 9, 2021).

Charles MacLean

Fougner, G. Selmer (1884–1941), was a cosmopolitan bon vivant who wrote the daily wine and spirits column for the *New York Sun* from its

G. Selmer Fougner, from a 1940 magazine advertisement. Wondrich Collection.

inception in 1933 until his untimely death, and in the process essentially created modern drinks writing. Born in Chicago to an intellectual French-Norwegian family that moved to France when he was nine, Fougner was educated at the Sorbonne before returning to America, where he worked at a number of New York newspapers, sometimes returning to France in their service: he was, for a time, the society editor of the legendary Paris edition of the *New York Herald* and, during World War I, reported on the fighting in that country for the *Sun* with skill and courage. After a few years working for the US Treasury Department, he rejoined the *Sun*, there to remain for the rest of his days. Somewhere along the way, Fougner's easy acquaintance with the good things in life (and perhaps his well-upholstered figure) earned him the nickname "Baron."

In 1933, with the repeal of Prohibition looming, Baron Fougner was the natural person for the *Sun* to assign to write a twenty-five-part series to help readers navigate the unfamiliar waters of legal wines and spirits. The column, a daily one, made its debut on October 20 of that year. By the time Prohibition was actually repealed Fougner was well into his second series. After that, the column was a fixture of the paper and ran until his death. By March 1934, Along the Wine Trail, as it was called, had assumed the form it would retain right up to the end. After a brief epigraph—a bible verse, a few lines of poetry—Fougner would typically use the first part of the two half columns he was allotted to weigh in on some topic that was on his mind. Before his column, wine writing tended to be high-toned and mystifying, while cocktail writing was jocular and even aggressively vulgar. Fougner was neither. As Lucius Beebe noted, he was "the arch-foe of pretentiousness and ritualism in drinking," but neither was he boorish or particularly humorous. See BEEBE, LUCIUS. While wine was his specialty, he genuinely liked cocktails and beer and did not condescend to those who drank them, nor did he assume that everything imported was ipso facto better than what was produced in the United States (indeed, he was an early and influential advocate of American wines). He covered unusual spirits such as vodka and tequila, in those days little known in America, and he knew his whisky.

The second half of his column was generally devoted to readers' questions, which he answered with patience, no matter how stupid (the one asking whether all scotch whisky was actually made in Australia comes to mind). When he didn't know the answer, he threw the question open to his readers. His was a broad net: the *Sun* had wide distribution, and his audience was nationwide. For the modern cocktail historian, this is the most valuable part of the column, as many of those readers had firsthand knowledge of the origins of various famous drinks (his column seems to have been particularly popular with former bartenders). Indeed, of just the drinks in this volume, their testimony has helped illuminate the history of, among others, the Cohasset Punch, the Daiquiri, the Rob Roy, the Singapore Sling, and the Ward Eight. See COHASSET PUNCH; DAIQUIRI; ROB ROY; SINGAPORE SLING; and WARD EIGHT.

Fougner was a busy man. Besides his *Sun* column and the books that were woven together from excerpts from it, he wrote a column for *Scribner's Magazine* and guides to New York restaurants and gourmet dinners; founded and led Les Amis d'Escoffier, a fine dining society; judged cocktail competitions; toured wine regions; and other such things too numerous to mention. But it is for his column and the patient, informed, skeptical way he guided readers toward the good things to drink and gently (usually) shepherded them away from the bad that he will be remembered. Baron Fougner is the Jerry Thomas of drinks writers. See THOMAS, JEREMIAH P. "JERRY".

Beebe, Lucius. "This New York." *Oakland Tribune*, April 15, 1961, 21.

Fougner, G. Selmer. *Along the Wine Trail.* Boston: Stratford, 1935.

David Wondrich

Fouquet, Louis Émile (1872–1905), a Parisian restaurateur, was one of the early French advocates of the American school of mixed drinks. Born in Paris to parents who owned the Grande Épicerie Rivoli, a fine grocery, at twenty-three years old he opened the Criterion bar and buffet in front of the Saint-Lazare station, where American and English travelers arrived to Paris. The year after, in 1896, he published *Bariana*, the second French cocktail book, and in 1899 he opened the Criterion-Fouquet's Bar on the Champs-Élysées. After his premature death of typhoid fever, his friend Leopold Mourier, a famed restaurateur, became the tutor of Fouquet's two sons and built Fouquet's Bar into one of the most famous and fashionable in Paris.

"Fouquet." *Journal officiel de l'alimentation*, July 15, 1916, 17.

Fouquet, Louis. *Bariana*. Paris: 1896.

"Nouvelle création." *Le temps*, September 24, 1898, 3.

"Une bonne nouvelle." *Le journal*, October 15, 1896, 1.

Fernando Castellon

Fox, Richard K. (1846–1922), was the influential publisher of the *National Police Gazette*, a sensational newspaper that also did much to advance the craft of bartending. Born in Belfast, Ireland, where he began his newspaper career as messenger for an advertising department, Fox arrived in New York in 1874, married and penniless. Less than three months later he was business manager of the *New York Police Gazette*, which three years later he bought, changing "New York" to "National." Remaking his acquisition to target the sporting youth of its day, Fox mixed its staple tabloid crime journalism with sports and entertainment news, turning it into the first nationally successful men's lifestyle periodical.

The spiritual ancestor of reality media, Fox attempted to elevate average people into stars through *Gazette*-sponsored competitions. One of these, starting in May 1899, was the world's first bartender's contest, which ran for at least seventeen years, with thousands of recipes from contestants across the globe. See COCKTAIL CONTESTS. Drinks from this contest were featured in Charley Mahoney's *Hoffman House Bartender's Guide*, which Fox published (it was the first bartender's guide to be illustrated with photographs) and included the Commodore, Ping Pong, Modern, Mountain, Fanciulli, and Du Barry Cocktails, all of which received some acclaim, and the Dizzy Sour. See HOFFMAN HOUSE. A different bartender was spotlighted each week, such as Frank J. May, who in the April 22, 1905, issue was acclaimed as inventor of the Jack Rose (he probably wasn't). See JACK ROSE.

Mahoney, Charles S. *The Hoffman House Bartender's Guide*. New York: Richard K. Fox, 1905.

Doug Stailey

fractional distillation is a process of separating and isolating compounds within a mixture, based on their specific volatility and boiling points in a continuous distillation process. In principle, simple distillation, as done by a pot still, is very similar, but in practice it is not an effective means of separating and isolating compounds that have relatively close boiling points—for example, ethanol and water, the two compounds of greatest concentration in an alcoholic fermented substrate (i.e., beer or wine). Therefore, to achieve separation, a column fitted with perforated trays is utilized, the trays serving as partial barriers dividing the column into stages. On each tray, vapor is forced to mix with a thin layer of liquid enriching the volatile content throughout the column. This causes each stage to have a slightly different chemical makeup; in relation to ethanol, more volatile compounds will concentrate at the top of the column and less volatile toward the bottom—hence, fractionation. During a steady-state operation, draws can be made and condensed off these trays based on the gradients within the column. The same theory can be applied to a packed column (i.e., with ceramic beads); however, the transition in volatility is streamlined versus a stage-wise shift.

An industrial example of fractional distillation is the side-stream collection of fusel oils, which are primarily collected to limit their presence in the final spirit. Since the compounds present within this fraction are less volatile than ethanol (although in close range), they can be removed on trays in a lower section of the column below the spirit collection tray.

See also COLUMN STILL; DISTILLATION, PROCESS; and FUSEL OIL.

Madson, P. W. "Ethanol Distillation: The Fundamentals." In *The Alcohol Textbook: A Reference for the Beverage, Fuel and Industrial Alcohol Industries*, 4th ed., by W. M. Ingledew, 319–336. Nottingham, UK: Nottingham University Press, 2009.

Elizabeth Rhoades

France produces the world's best-known and most valuable grape brandies (see ARMAGNAC and COGNAC), the world's best-known apple brandy (see CALVADOS), many of the world's most respected liqueurs (see BÉNÉDICTINE; CHARTREUSE; COINTREAU; and GRAND MARNIER), and a host of aperitifs, digestifs, and fortified wines (see PICON; DUBONNET COCKTAIL; and SUZE) essential to the cocktail. Spirit and liqueur production is so entwined with France that even in non-Francophone countries, generic liqueurs are often known by their French names, such as crème de cacao, crème de cassis, crème de menthe, triple sec, and many others.

The export value of French spirits is enormous—in 2019, the country shipped 53 million nine-liter cases of spirits valued at more than €4.66 billion. Currently, twenty-two French regions are granted the French geographical designation "appellation d'origine contrôlée" (AOC) on their spirit labels, with most of them variants of cognac (9) and Armagnac (5), although the list also includes the island of Martinique for rum. See RHUM AGRICOLE.

Distillation is said to have entered France in the late 1200s, when the Catalan alchemist Arnold de Vilanova [also known as Arnaud de Villeneuve (1238–1311)] is thought to have been the first to distill French wines. It was certainly there by 1310, when Vital du Four (1260–1327), the Franciscan prior of Eauze (in the heart of the modern Armagnac region), recorded instructions for its manufacture and detailed its medicinal and social virtues.

As trade routes opened, spices and ingredients including ginger, orange, and chocolate made their way into liqueurs, with prosperous households installing their own stills. They became more fashionable after Catherine De Medici (1519–1589) married Henry II of France and introduced the culture of liqueur drinking to the French court. Spirits were employed regularly as anesthetics and as digestive aids.

The European trade of spirits is thought to have commenced around 1517 when a "barrique d'eau ardent" was shipped from Bordeaux—presumably, it was distilled from wine made in or around what is today the Cognac region. The growing interest among Dutch and English traders in French wine contributed to the commercialization of brandy—wine that spoiled during shipping led them to promote distillation as a preservative of the desirable alcohol. See SPIRITS TRADE, HISTORY OF.

Until the mid-twentieth century, traveling distillers were a common sight in the French countryside as farmers looked to benefit from excess fruit. Many of those stills are to be found at distilleries in the Armagnac and Calvados regions, though they no longer travel.

While invented in Switzerland, absinthe has a deep cultural connection to the French as the infamous high-proof wormwood- and anise-flavored beverage garnered enormous popularity in Belle Epoque Paris of the late nineteenth and early twentieth centuries until it was banned (from 1915 until the early twenty-first century). See ABSINTHE. Absinthe's departure helped lead to the rise of other anise-flavored spirits, generically known as pastis—Pernod and Ricard are the best known. See PASTIS and PERNOD-RICARD.

Chartreuse was developed in 1840 by Carthusian monks in the French Alps using a 1605 formula as a starting point. Bénédictine was first produced in 1863, following—as the company maintained—a 1510 monastic formula. Other French spirits worth noting include the pomace-based marc; the blend of grape juice, grape must, and cognac called pineau des Charentes; the mainly Alsatian eau-de-vie kirschwasser, as well as eaux-de-vie poire Williams, framboise, and fraise. See EAU-DE-VIE; KIRSCHWASSER; MARC; and PINEAU DES CHARENTES. France has since the late twentieth century also become a major force in vodka production, with brands including Grey Goose and Cîroc important internationally.

The French were the first Europeans to accept the American school of mixology—or rather, the Parisians were. See LEFEUVRE, ÉMILE. American-style bars have operated in that city from the 1840s on, and it still hosts some of the world's leading cocktail bars. See HARRY'S NEW YORK BAR. France's major contributions to cocktails include the 1900s Rose (the Chatham Bar in Paris), the 1920s Mimosa (the Ritz Bar, Paris), the Sidecar (although that is disputed), and Dijon's Kir, popularized in the 1960s. See KIR; MIMOSA; ROSE; and SIDECAR.

Faith, Nicholas. *Cognac.* London: Mitchel Beazley, 2005.

"First Distillation of the French Wines." L'encyclopédie du Cognac. https://www.pediacognac.com/en/la-distillation-dela-distillation-enla-distillation/gegin-der-destillation-derfranzosischen-weinenfirst-distillation-of-the-french-winesdebut-de-la-distillation-des-vins-francais/ (accessed March 19, 2021).

Furno, Vitalis de. *Liber selectiorum remediorum pro conservanda sanitate.* Mainz: 1531.

Mattsson, Henrik. *Calvados: The World's Premier Apple Brandy.* Malmo, Sweden: Flavourrider.com, 2005.

Jack Robertiello

Francis, Richard "Dick" (1827–1888), was a Washington, DC, bartender known for his long service at one of that city's most beloved old watering holes and his many friendships with members of the United States' governing class. Francis was born to free black parents in Surry County, Virginia. When he was twenty-one, he began working at Andrew Hancock's saloon, a quaint, curio-filled establishment on Pennsylvania Avenue near the White House. He would remain there for thirty-six years, most of them as head bartender.

Among the regular customers with whom Francis was, as the *Washington Post* noted in his obituary, "on terms of friendly intimacy" were such major political figures of the late antebellum years as Daniel Webster, Henry Clay, and John C. Calhoun. Indeed, that same obituary posited that Francis "had probably known more of the men famous in American history and had had a better opportunity of observing them" than any person of his race in the country.

Of course, Francis wouldn't have met all of those celebrities if his characteristic humor and courtly manners weren't accompanied by superior skills as a mixologist. Under his administration, the bar at Hancock's became famous for its strictly-according-to-Hoyle Mint Julep, its Flowerpot Punch (an elaborately garnished single-serving punch), its sugar-rimmed Hell and Blazes Cocktail, its Hot Buttered Rum, and a few other specialties. See MINT JULEP; PUNCH; and HOT BUTTERED RUM. Add the excellent fried chicken dinner served in the back room, and the loyalty of Francis's customers is easily understood.

In 1885, Francis left Hancock's when one of his regulars, a senator, secured him the management of the Senate's bar and restaurant. He died three years later, leaving behind a more than modest fortune earned through his extensive and canny investments in Washington real estate. Although Francis apparently never learned to read or write, his son, John R. Francis, became a medical doctor and an educator and a pioneer of the civil rights movement. Hancock's soldiered on until 1914, when Prohibitionist fervor cost it its liquor license. See PROHIBITION AND TEMPERANCE IN AMERICA. The quaint little building it occupied was demolished in 1931.

"A Famous Bartender Dead." *Washington Post,* November 6, 1888, p2.

"Hancock's Once Famous Resort Bites Dust before Modern Progress." *Washington Post*, August 16, 1931.

David Wondrich

Frank, Sidney (1919–2006), born in hard circumstances in Montville, Connecticut, went on to parlay a genius for marketing spirits into a fortune worth billions, changing the landscape of the spirits business in the process. Frank claimed that his family was so poor that he slept on old burlap sacks. Although he was nonetheless able to gain admission to the prestigious Brown University, he was forced to drop out after his first year because he had run out of money for tuition. Through his classmate Edward Sarnoff (son of David Sarnoff, the founder of RCA), he met Louise Rosenstiel (1923–1973), the daughter of Lewis Rosenstiel, the head of Schenley, at the time one of the largest spirits companies in the world. See ROSENSTIEL, LEWIS.

After working during the Second World War for Pratt and Whitney, the airplane engine maker, as a troubleshooter for alcohol-injection systems for high-altitude flight, Frank married Louise Rosenstiel and soon went to work for Schenley. His promotions came rapidly, until he became president of the company's distilling wing in 1955 and of the parent company in 1960. His tenure was not smooth, though, and eventually he was forced out of the company. For a time he ran an art gallery and then, in 1972, founded the Sidney Frank Importing Co. At first, his offerings were underwhelming: a Japanese sake, John Crabbie light blended scotch whisky, a Liebfraumilch named Grey Goose. In the late 1970s, however, he acquired the rights to import Jägermeister, Germany's most popular liqueur. See JÄGERMEISTER.

The bitter herbal liqueur had already been developing a cult following in New Orleans, and when in a 1985 article the *Baton Rouge Advocate* attributed that to the perception that the liqueur was like "liquid Valium," Frank capitalized on that in marketing it—at least until one of his distributors got investigated when they accidentally used some of the marketing materials in an advertisement. That was in 1990. The next year he tried something different, assembling a crew of female models, whom he called Jägerettes, and later a crew of male models, Jägerdudes, to promote the liqueur around America.

He also created a bar-top machine to chill the liqueur and make it more quaffable.

While Jägermeister was a smash hit, his biggest success came when he took the Grey Goose name and applied it to a super-premium vodka, which he later sold to Bacardi for more than $2 billion. Other entrepreneurs tried to copy his success, creating dozens of other brands using Frank's Grey Goose marketing plan. See GREY GOOSE.

After Grey Goose's sale he donated more than $100 million to Brown University for financial aid for needy students and for a new building. Sidney Frank Importing continued for a number of years after its founder's death until the parent company of Jägermeister, Mast-Jägermeister, bought out Frank's heirs for the company's name and intellectual property.

Clifford, Stefanie. "Q&A: Sidney Frank." *Inc.*, September 2005.
Demmons, Douglas. "Latest Liquor Craze Sweeps into Baton Rouge." *Baton Rouge Advocate*, May 12, 1985, B-1.
Martin, Douglas. "Sidney Frank, 86, Dies." *New York Times*, January 12, 2006.
Rothbaum, Noah. *The Business of Spirits*. New York: Kaplan, 2007.
Schneider, Doug. "Liqueur Ad Prompts Investigation." *Syracuse Post-Standard*, October 23, 1990, B-1.

Noah Rothbaum

frappe, or more properly *frappé(e)*, is a somewhat slippery term (from the French *frapper*, "to strike") found in bartender's guides from around the turn of the twentieth century, originally meaning that a drink is to be served poured over finely cracked ice (i.e., ice that has been struck) or shaved ice, as in the "Vermouth Frappee" found in the 1884 *Modern Bartender* by O. H. Byron.

The term was most commonly associated with a pair of so-called dude's drinks, the Absinthe Frappé (first attested to in 1873 and popular across America by 1885) and the Crème de Menthe Frappé (popular by 1894). Since these drinks were often shaken with ice, by 1900 to "frappe" a drink also came to mean "to shake it with ice." Thus Harry Johnson instructs that crème de menthe should be served on fine ice, but "if you are asked for a Crème de Menthe frappé," the liqueur must be shaken with fine ice and strained into the glass. Is this confusing? Yes, it is. Our only consolation is that it was then too.

See ABSINTHE FRAPPÉ; CRÈME DE MENTHE; and JOHNSON, HARRY.

"Hope Springs Eternal." *San Francisco Chronicle,* January 31, 1873, 3.

Johnson, Harry. *New and Improved Bartender's Manual.* New York: Harry Johnson, 1900.

"What It Costs to Drink." *Nashville Tennessean,* June 1, 1885, 7.

David Wondrich

Fratelli Branca is the Milan-based company known worldwide for its Fernet-Branca. See FERNET. The notoriously bitter herbal spirit was created in 1845 by Bernardino Branca (1802–1886), a self-taught apothecary, perhaps as an anti-cholera tonic. His fernet became the archetype for a class of amari: strongly bitter, herbal, without much sugar, and with a relatively high alcohol content.

As Fernet-Branca's popularity grew, his three sons—Luigi, Giuseppe, and Stefano—joined him in business. The home creation became a commercial enterprise and was named Fratelli Branca ("Branca Brothers"). The family showed a quick grasp for marketing, linking the brand to bold artwork on promotional calendars and posters. The brand spread through the world's cities and became a standard in many bars.

When the global prohibition movement took hold, the company returned to its roots, promoting Fernet-Branca as a medicinal herbal tonic. That kept them steadily in business until the last years of World War II, when the Allied bombing campaign leveled much of industrial Milan. The company was quick to rebuild, but the brand slowed through the 1950s.

The cocktail revival brought new interest to the brand in the early 2000s, and the company brought brands like Punt e Mes and Carpano Classic into the portfolio through the acquisition of Carpano (of Turin) in 2001. Sales and the company profile increased through the 2010s.

The company is still family-controlled, run by Niccolò Branca (1957–), the sixth generation of Brancas to operate the company. They maintain the company motto: Novare Serbando, or "Renew, but conserve," a simultaneous tip of the hat to innovation and tradition.

"Fratelli Branca." Wikipedia. https://en.wikipedia.org/wiki/Fratelli_Branca (accessed March 19, 2021).

Fratelli Branca company website. https://www.brancadistillerie.com/en/the-company/ (accessed March 19, 2021).

"Fratelli Branca Distillerie S.r.l." *Difford's Guide.* https://www.diffordsguide.com/producers/22/fratelli-branca-distillerie-srl/history (accessed March 19, 2021).

Lew Bryson

free pouring is a mental system of volume measurement used when making cocktails. Other than an unrestricted pour spout (called a "speed pourer") that fits in the neck of a bottle, no special measuring tools such as jiggers are required during the actual drink-making process when free pouring. Instead, bartenders judge the volume poured either by observing the levels of liquid in the mixing glass or, more frequently, by a system of "counts." Such counts are precisely timed numbers noted silently in the bartender's mind while pouring that correspond to fractions of an ounce.

In order to free pour properly, professional bartenders undergo rigorous training, usually at regular intervals, to maintain accuracy and consistency. An empty bottle may be filled with water, for example, and fitted with a speed pourer; then tests are conducted blind. Testing kits, such as that made by Exacto-Pour, gauge accuracy to within the nearest sixteenth of an ounce.

See also JIGGER and POUR SPOUT.

Morgenthaler, Jeffrey, *The Bar Book: Elements of Cocktail Technique.* San Francisco: Chronicle Books, 2014.

Jeffrey Morgenthaler

freeze distillation, or ice distillation, is a term for the ancient practice of fractional freezing, which is also known as freeze concentration. At the heart of distillation is the separation of components by evaporation and condensation. The process works because of the different boiling points of alcohol and water. But their melting points—the points at which they go from solid to liquid—differ as well (for various reasons it is easier to reliably measure a substance's melting point than its freezing point, at which it goes from liquid to solid). The melting point of ethanol is −114° C, and the melting point of water is 0° C. Ice distillation uses that fact to isolate the alcohol through successive freezing and thawing. Once the temperature of a fermented beverage is lowered beyond the melting point of water, the water begins to freeze, and the remaining liquid has a higher concentration of ethanol. This allows the distiller to strain out the water from the ethanol-rich mixture. This process, commonly referred to as "jacking," has been used for centuries. It is often credited as the origin of both vodka and, in colonial America, the apple brandy spirit applejack. However, concentration by freezing is less efficient than distillation and leaves many undesirable compounds, like methanol and fusel oils, in the resulting liquid. Therefore, it is no longer widely used in the production of alcoholic beverages. However, some products like Eisbock beers are still made using the fractional freezing method.

See also APPLEJACK; DISTILLATION, PROCESS; and VODKA.

Pokhlebkin, William. *A History of Vodka.* Translated Renfrey Clarke. London: Verso, 1991.

Rowley, Matthew B. *The Joy of Moonshine.* New York: Lark, 2007.

Jason Grizzanti

The **French Martini**, neither French nor a Martini, is a mix of vodka, Chambord liqueur, and pineapple juice that was one of the most popular drinks of the 1990s. The drink's precise origin is difficult to pin down, but it had to be before 1995, when it first appears in print, and after 1979, when Chambord was first "imported, prepared and bottled" by a Philadelphia liqueur maker (although the maker claimed it is an ancient French formula, its raspberry-blackberry flavor goes against the French tradition of single-fruit infusions). Much as the Cosmopolitan is essentially a Martini-glass variation on the Kamikaze, the French Martini is a Martini-glass variation on the 1980s Sex on the Beach (vodka, Chambord, pineapple juice, and either peach schnapps, Midori melon liqueur, or 7-Up). See COSMOPOLITAN.

The name "French Martini" had already been used in the 1970s by Seagram's gin to promote a Dry Martini with a couple of drops of cognac in it and in the 1980s for a mixture of gin and Lillet. Once the Chambord version became popular, they were forgotten. That popularization was greatly aided by the drink's appearance in early 1996 on the opening menu of New York's iconic Martini bar, Pravda. See EMPLOYEES ONLY.

Recipe: Shake with ice: 45 ml vodka, 45 ml fresh or canned pineapple juice and 15 ml Chambord. Garnish with a small piece of pineapple on the edge of the glass.

"Chambord: Liqueur Royale de France." Advertisement, *Los Angeles Times Home Magazine*, October 21, 1979, 59.

Tillotson, Kristin. "Couth, Conversation and Cocktails, Anyone?" *Minneapolis Star tribune*, December 7, 1995, E-1.

Fernando Castellon and David Wondrich

The **French 75**, with gin or brandy, lemon juice, sugar, and champagne—essentially, a Champagne or "Imperial" Tom Collins—is one of the few mixed drinks to rise to prominence during the United States' fourteen years of Prohibition. It is also reputed, not inaccurately, to be one of the most intoxicating mixed drinks in standard usage and commands a healthy respect among cocktail aficionados.

The drink's formula and its name first appear together in 1927, in *Here's How!*, a Prohibition-defying little book put out by a New York humor magazine, although some drinkers recalled them being found together in America at least since the beginning of Prohibition and among Americans in France during the war years immediately preceding. Both, however, had been in use before. When Charles Dickens entertained visitors to his suite in Boston's Parker House hotel in 1867, it was with "Tom gin and champagne cups"; that mixture was apparently also a favorite with the Prince of Wales and King Kalakaua of Hawaii, either with or without the lemon juice and sugar. As for the name, in 1915, the popular Broadway columnist O. O. "Odd" McIntyre reported that war correspondent E. Alexander Powell had "brought back from the front" a cocktail named the

"Soixante-Quinze—the French Seventy-five." This one, however, consisted of gin and calvados (or applejack) with grenadine and sometimes a dash of absinthe or lemon juice. While it enjoyed some currency in Europe, it was entirely eclipsed by the American drink that usurped its name.

That name, a reference to the "canon de 75 modèle 1897," the standard French field gun of World War I, is also a clue to the drink's origin: only the Americans, who adopted the gun in 1917 and used it in large numbers, called it the "French 75," to distinguish it from the inferior, American-designed 3-inch (76.2 mm) M1902 gun. The French gun's reputation for having excellent accuracy and a high rate of fire carried over into American service and was the basis for the name's attachment to the hard-hitting Champagne Collins.

The drink achieved a certain transatlantic notoriety after Harry Craddock included it in the widely popular *Savoy Cocktail Book* in 1930. See CRADDOCK, HARRY LAWSON. It was the perfect embodiment of the Jazz Age: heady, extravagant, and irresponsible. Some aficionados, such as the American actress Tallulah Bankhead, preferred theirs with cognac instead of gin, whether due to the taste or because it eliminated the anomaly of having a "French" drink based on an English spirit.

The French 75 retained some popularity during the Dark Ages of mixology and came roaring back with the cocktail renaissance, along with the arguments surrounding it: gin or cognac, up or on ice, flute or highball glass. See COCKTAIL RENAISSANCE. Indeed, one of the stations of the cross of the modern cocktail cult is partaking of its namesake at Arnaud's French 75 bar in New Orleans, where the drink is made with cognac and served up, in a flute—all three counter to the original recipe, yet in this case accepted by even the staunchest traditionalist.

Recipe (traditional): Stir 5 ml sugar into 15 ml lemon juice. Add 60 ml London dry gin, shake, and strain into a highball glass filled with cracked ice. Top off with chilled champagne.

Arnaud's version (recipe by former head bartender Chris Hannah): Shake 37 ml VSOP cognac, 7 ml lemon juice, and 7 ml simple syrup; strain into chilled champagne flute, and top off with 75 ml chilled brut champagne.

"Notable Apartments." *New Haven Register*, March 22, 1885, 3.

Judge Jr. *Here's How!* New York: John Day, 1927.

David Wondrich

Frozen Daiquiri is a blended variation of the Daiquiri, originally popularized by Constantino Ribalaigua at Havana's Floridita bar. See also DAIQUIRI; FLORIDITA; and RIBALAIGUA Y VERT, CONSTANTE.

frozen drinks, blender drinks, are alcoholic beverages made by grinding the ingredients and ice together in an electric blender. In the first edition of his seminal *Bartender's Guide*, Victor "Trader Vic" Bergeron, erstwhile champion of the faux-Polynesian beverage revolution, renders the following judgment: "The use of mechanical mixers is varied and in many cases abused. Most cocktails, as mentioned before, are best stirred or shaken. Putting them in a mechanical mixer dilutes them to a sickly mess. Waring blenders and other mechanical mixers are indispensable, however, for . . . Daiquirís, and drinks where snow ice is required." See BERGERON, VICTOR "TRADER VIC."

In 1910, Fred Osius formed the Hamilton Beach Manufacturing Co. in Racine, Wisconsin, naming it after a pair of his employees. In the mid-1920s, he set out to reimagine the electric mixer patented in 1922 by Stephen J. Poplawski (also of Racine) to make malted milkshakes (another Wisconsin invention). In 1933, Osius talked the popular bandleader Fred Waring into funding and championing his patented Miracle Mixer, released to the American public in 1933. It has since come to be recognized as the first true electric blender. In 1937, however, after tinkering with the design himself, Waring released an improved version, the Waring Blendor (spelled with an "o"). It was this version that became the classic.

The legendary Constantino Ribailagua Vert of the Floridita bar in Havana, Cuba, was among the first barmen to adopt the blender as a standard tool for drink making, inspiring many of the great bartenders of the 1930s and beyond to follow suit. According to legend, Ribailagua made more than ten million Daiquiris in his time. There is much dispute about his precise technique, but for many drinks he seems to have used the blender much in the same way that the modern bartender employs a cocktail shaker, pulsing the ingredients just long enough to chill them, but not so long as to turn the drink to slush. Rumor has it that "Constante" favored a Waring as his blender of choice. He was known for then filtering out even the tiniest shards of ice with a fine mesh sieve.

Ribalaigua was perhaps the most influential mixologist of the twentieth century, and soon many others were following his lead, at first in Havana and then throughout the Caribbean. In 1954, guests at the Varadero Internacional hotel in Havana were greeted with a "frozen banana Daiquiri"; soon after, the (frozen) Piña Colada served a similar function in San Juan. See DAIQUIRI; PIÑA COLADA; and RIBALAIGUA Y VERT, CONSTANTE.

By the early 1960s, some were turning the Margarita into a blender drink. When Texan Mariano Martinez introduced the frozen Margarita machine in 1973, that completed the transformation of the frozen drink from expert bartender's product to anything-goes crowd pleaser. Just splash some white rum, mixto tequila, or whatever into the blender, add some sour mix, and throw in whatever fruit you've got handy. Add ice, grind it all together, and pour it out into an oversized, stemmed glass. Done.

Come the twenty-first-century cocktail revival, outside of tiki bars, where blenders are still an essential tool, it was as if every freshly minted new "mixologist" was handed a plaque reading "No Blenders" to hang behind his or her bar. That is beginning to change, as cocktail culture begins to relax. In fact, one of the hot drinks of 2017 was the blender-friendly Frosé (for "frozen rosé"), and there are signs that other such light, friendly frozen drinks are attracting new fans.

See MARGARITA.

Bergeron, Victor. *Bartender's Guide*. Garden City, NY: Doubleday, 1947.

Berry, Jeff. *Beachbum Berry's Potions of the Caribbean*. New York: Cocktail Kingdom, 2014.

Foley, Ray. *The Ultimate Little Frozen Drinks Book*. Naperville, IL: Sourcebooks, 2001.

Poplawski, Stephen J. Beverage mixer. US Patent 1,480,914, granted January 15, 1924.

"Varadero Beach Is West Indies Riviera," *Boston Herald*, December 5, 1954, sec. 4, 14.

Richard Boccato

fruit juice has long been an essential component for mixing drinks, starting in the seventeenth century with punch and blooming in the mid-1800s with the advent of cobblers, sours, slings, and rickeys. At the turn of the twentieth century, the orange juice in the Bronx Cocktail took the cocktail from the saloon into the home. During Prohibition, fruit juice gained even more traction as a way to disguise the taste of bootleg liquor; after Repeal, consumers continued gravitating from boozy to fruity drinks (in a 1953 *Collier's* magazine cartoon, a hostess serving cocktails to her guests assures them, "I kept the rum down, so as not to spoil the taste of the fruit juice"). See PROHIBITION AND TEMPERANCE IN AMERICA. In the 1990s, the cranberry- and lime-juice-driven Cosmopolitan brought the cocktail back from the brink of extinction. And while the twenty-first-century cocktail renaissance has returned spirit-forward drinks to center stage, fruit juice still plays an important role in contemporary mixology, if more as supporting actor than headliner. See COCKTAIL RENAISSANCE.

While one would be hard-pressed to name a fruit that hasn't found its way into a mixed drink, some fruits are harder to press than others: apple, pear, cherry, and apricot, for example, are so labor-intensive to juice that they're most often deployed as drink ingredients in the form of fruit-flavored liqueurs. The following fruit types are likelier to be juiced into today's drinks.

Lime and lemon are the most cocktail-friendly members of the citrus family, because their acidity makes an ideal counterbalance to any sweetening agent. See CITRIC ACID. Entire drink categories would cease to exist without this symbiosis, particularly punches and sours. Use only fresh fruit; commercially bottled lime and lemon juice always results in an inferior drink (the sole exception is the Gimlet). See GIMLET. Grapefruit juice is another matter; pink and ruby red grapefruit lack the bitterness of the more elusive yellow grapefruit, bitterness that most mixed drink recipes require. In the absence of fresh yellow grapefruit, choose bottled yellow over fresh pink or red. Some orange varieties are also better than others for mixology; given the choice, opt for Valencias over the less flavorful navels. To juice citrus fruit, use a standard kitchen reamer with a ribbed dome and seed trap; in high-volume situations, scale up to a lever-operated citrus press.

Strawberries, raspberries, blackberries, and blueberries lend a welcome additional flavor layer to cocktails, cobblers, and sours. Because they're too small for juice reamers, fresh berries are usually integrated into drinks by muddling the fruit in the mixing glass, as you would express mint in a Mojito or lime in a Caipirinha. In fact, these two particular drinks are ideal vehicles for berries (yes, Blackberry Mojitos have become a cliché, but that doesn't make them any less tasty). See MOJITO and CAIPIRINHA. In the eighteenth and nineteenth centuries, berries were often preserved in vinegar-based syrups, which resulted in strongly flavored beverages called shrubs, a practice that today's craft cocktail bartenders have revived. See MUDDLER and SHRUBS.

Banana, mango, papaya, lychee, and their ilk lend exotic interest to frozen fruit daiquiris, margaritas, coladas, and batidas. Juicing these dense, fibrous fruits is well-nigh impossible with a reamer or muddler. Purée them in a food processor, or simply toss the diced fruit directly into a blender with your other frozen-drink-recipe ingredients. Passion fruit and guava, both common in tiki drinks, are not commonly available fresh; in a pinch, purchase them in the form of frozen 100 percent fruit pulp. Fresh pineapples are easy to find but not easy to liquefy; store-bought unsweetened pineapple juice is a perfectly reasonable alternative for the casual drinker who is disinclined to skin, dice, and pummel a fresh pineapple for a thimble full of juice—no matter how much more delicious that thimble may be. See FROZEN DRINKS, BLENDER DRINKS; and TIKI.

Like pineapples, extracting juice from tomatoes (essential to the Bloody Mary) and cranberries (de rigueur for the Cosmopolitan) is a chore better left to professionals; opt for unsweetened, organic bottlings. See BLOODY MARY and COSMOPOLITAN. So too with pomegranate juice, which plays a crucial role in mixology when combined with sugar into a pomegranate syrup called grenadine. See GRENADINE.

See also GIMLET and PUNCH.

Clarke, Paul. *The Cocktail Chronicles*. Nashville, TN: Spring House, 2015.
Regan, Gary. *The Joy of Mixology*. New York: Clarkson Potter, 2003.
Schumann, Charles. *Tropical Bar Book: Drinks and Stories*. New York: Stewart, Tabori & Chang, 1989.

Jeff Berry

Fundo los Nichos is the oldest operating *pisquera*, or pisco distillery, in Chile and serves as something like a living museum of the Chilean version of the spirit. Located deep in the Andes in the arid hills between Pisco Elqui and Horcon, the picturesque distillery's cellars were built in 1868 by José Dolores Rodríguez Callejas (1842–1904), and distilling began shortly afterward. It was carried on after his death by his seventh son, Rigoberto Rodríguez Rodríguez (1879–1945), who in the 1930s also founded the still-popular Tres Erres ("Three Rs") brand of pisco, with its own distillery in Pisco Elqui. The original lenticular-headed alembics were replaced in the 1950s by German hybrid stills, but Fundo los Nichos still distills from a mix of aromatic (moscatel rosada; moscatel de Alejandría) and non-aromatic (Pedro Jiménez; moscatel de Austria) grapes to around 55 percent ABV and rests the spirit for one to three years in generations-old tanks made from indigenous *rauli* wood (*Nothofagus alpina*, a species of southern beech). Some goes on to age in oak casks. The resulting spirit, made in very small quantities, is highly prized within Chile. It is not exported.

See also ANDEAN SOUTH AMERICA and PISCO.

Herrera, Galvarino Peralta. *Destilería Fundo los Nichos*. Pisco Elqui, Chile: Vitivinícola Fundo los Nichos, N.d.
Olmedo, Claudia. *40 grados*. Santiago: Emporio Creativo, 2011.

David Wondrich

furfural ($C_5H_4O_2$) is a heterocyclic aldehyde found in many spirits, produced from the breakdown of sugars when heated with acids, as are found in many distillers' washes. A colorless or pale yellow oily liquid with the aroma of bitter almonds and even caramel or cherry (it is recognizable as a component of vanilla), it slowly turns reddish-brown with oxidation. See OXIDATION. A heavy molecule with a high boiling point, furfural tends to be found much more in pot-still products than in column-still ones, where it is easy to exclude. Its low volatility means that it is generally not noticeably diminished by barrel aging. In fact, since it can be produced in oak when it is charred or toasted, furfural levels sometimes increase during the aging process, through both concentration and leaching. Toxic in large quantities, furfural has often been one of the compounds blamed for producing hangovers.

"Furfural." American Chemical Society. https://www.acs.org/content/acs/en/molecule-of-the-week/archive/f/furfural.html (accessed April 21, 2021).

"Compound Summary: Furfural." *PubChem*. https://pubchem.ncbi.nlm.nih.gov/compound/7362 (accessed February 9, 2021).

Thorpe, T. E. *A Dictionary of Applied Chemistry*. London: Longmans, Green, 1912–1916.

Doug Frost

fusel oil is a category of organic compounds that are byproducts of alcoholic fermentation. These include secondary alcohols like methanol, propanol, and amyl alcohol as well as higher alcohols that have boiling points higher than ethanol. When present in small amounts they provide flavor to spirits like rum, brandy, and whisky. In excess, they can have a negative impact, producing a hot, solvent-like flavor. Fusel oils are known to have adverse health effects that lead to more severe hangovers. The more volatile compounds in fusel oil tend to dissipate during barrel aging, but many remain in the spirit.

See also METHANOL and ETHANOL.

Herstein, Karl M., and Morris Jacobs. *Chemistry and Technology of Wines and Liquors*. New York: D. Van Nostrand, 1948.

Darcy O'Neill

Gaige, Crosby (1882–1949), started from humble beginnings as the son of the postmaster of Skunk Hollow, New York, and went on to make millions as one of the premier Broadway producers of the early twentieth century. In 1912, Gaige partnered with the Selwyn brothers for his first hit, *Within the Law*, launching a twenty-five-year career encompassing 150 plays. Yet Gaige's true passions—collecting fine vintages and cooking—lay outside the theater. After the crash of 1929, he looked to these interests for livelihood, contributing the monthly Cellar and Pantry column to *Country Life*, along with other magazine assignments. In 1937, NBC broadcast his daily radio program, *Kitchen Cavalcade*. He edited several cookbooks and wrote two cocktail manuals. *Crosby Gaige's Cocktail Guide and Ladies' Companion* (1941) displays his noted wit and features celebrity contributions, a forward by Lucius Beebe, illustrations by Rea Irvin, and original recipes, including "Let's Slide Downstairs," and "Madame, Can You Walk?" It is also notable for being one of the vectors through which the Bloody Mary spread. The straight-faced, spiral-bound *Standard Cocktail Guide* followed in 1944. See Beebe, Lucius; and Bloody Mary.

"Crosby Gaige, Noted Play Producer, Tells How to Live a Life." *Peekskill Evening Star*, May 20, 1936, 2.

Gaige, Crosby. *Crosby Gaige's Cocktail Guide and Ladies Companion*. New York: M. Barrows, 1941.

Gaige, Crosby. *Footlights and Highlights*. New York: E. P. Dutton, 1948.

"New Shows Ahead." *Radio Daily*, September 16, 1937, 6.

Doug Stailey

Galliano is a sweet herbal liqueur first created in Livorno, Italy. It is easily recognized by its bright yellow color and distinctive long-necked bottle. (The latter has occasionally come in handy as an impromptu weapon for bartenders to use against unruly patrons.) Tasting prominently of vanilla and anise, the liqueur was known for many years primarily as an aperitif or digestive. However, it truly came into its own in the 1970s as a defining ingredient in such popular cocktails as the Harvey Wallbanger and Golden Cadillac. During that decade, it was the top-selling imported liqueur in the United States.

Galliano was invented in 1896 by the Italian distiller Arturo Vaccari of Livorno, who named the liqueur to commemorate Giuseppe Galliano, a military hero killed that year at the battle of Adowa during the First Italo-Ethiopian War. Vaccari was one of the few Italian liqueur manufacturers to court a global export market at the time, with Galliano reaching North and South America and even Japan by 1906. The vicissitudes of the twentieth century, however, prevented it from reaching its sales potential until the late 1960s. In 2010, owner Lucas Bols, who had bought the brand from Remy Cointreau, reintroduced what it said was Galliano's original formula in a bid to recapture the interest of serious bartenders. The new product, named Galliano l'Autentico, replaced a weaker, more syrupy iteration that was introduced in 1979. Galliano also makes a coffee liqueur called Ristretto. Both are made in the Netherlands.

See also Harvey Wallbanger.

Grimes, Williams. *Straight Up or On the Rocks*, 2nd ed. New York: North Point, 2001.

Robert Simonson

gallic acid is a type of phenol and antioxidant created when water-soluble ellagic tannins break down into glucose and either gallic acid or ellagic acid. Both gallic and ellagic acids give woody aromas and flavors to barrel-aged spirits, though gallic acid is more abundant in uncharred woods. Its presence in a spirit is in fact one of the prime guarantors that that spirit has been aged the traditional way, by leaving it in an oak barrel for a number of years.

Gallic acid's name reflects the traditional use of oak "galls"—abnormal, tumor-like growths on oak trees caused by the larvae of parasitic wasps—for the easy collection of tannic acid.

See also ELLAGIC ACID; ELLAGIC TANNINS; and PHENOLS.

"Gallic Acid." American Chemical Society. https://www. acs.org/content/acs/en/molecule-of-the-week/archive/g/gallic-acid.html (accessed April 21, 2021).

Lee, K. Y. Monica, Alistair Paterson, John R. Piggott, and Graeme D. Richardson. "Origins of Flavour in Whiskies and a Revised Flavour Wheel: A Review." *Journal of The Institute of Brewing* 107, no. 5 (2001): 287–313.

Doug Frost

Gandharan still is an ancient form of clay pot still, developed in what is now Pakistan, in which the alcohol vapor is drawn off through a tube from the bulbous still head to condense in a cooled receiver. It survived into the twentieth century in some parts of India. See also DISTILLATION, HISTORY; and ARRACK, COCONUT.

garnish is the final touch on a drink, an added bit of embellishment that can enhance the visual character of the drink and differentiate it from otherwise similar drinks. Its choice may be related to the drink's components in terms of flavor or origin (as, for example, a strip of orange peel decorating a drink that uses curaçao), but a simple contrast of colors between the drink and the garnish may be just as appealing.

There are two types of garnishes: functional and visual.

Functional garnishes, such as citrus twists, may utilize essential oils to change the texture of the drink and to play an important aromatic role, with lemon peel offering fruit aromas and freshness, lime peel giving complex aromas and bitterness, orange peel showing orange flavors and greater or lesser freshness (dependent upon the variety), and grapefruit peel generating a lightly fruity and very elegant nose.

To fulfill this role, all citrus must be fresh, with the skin firm and glossy. Today there are many new

A. b. is the alembic and capital luted together. D. e. a refrigeratory and receiver of one piece, and the latter connected with the head by a bamboo, c.

A traditional Sri Lankan arrack still, in the Gandharan style. Wondrich Collection.

citrus varieties, with the only obstacle the cost. See TWIST.

Aromatic leaves such as mint, basil, or kaffir lime belong in this group as well, even if the impact is only on the nose. Techniques include muddling or shaking these leaves in the shaker or slapping them in your hands; each can release the essential oils on the leaf's surface. Dried spices such as star anise, cinnamon stick, vanilla bean, and pimento can lend a visual impact to the drink, in addition to their taste influence.

The same happens with a salt rim (whether white or colored) or a sugar rim (regardless of its type): there is both a visual enhancement and an increased mouth feel, influenced by the size of the grains (typically, the smaller the better so that the garnish flavoring and the cocktail are harmonious).

Visual garnishes include berries (strawberries, raspberries, blueberries, cranberries, etc.), pineapple (leaves or slices), citrus wedges (which give the consumer the option of turning them into a functional garnish by squeezing them in the drink), vegetables (celery stalks and such), and edible flowers (rose petals and orchids).

The quality of the garnish is crucial, whether the olive of a Dry Martini, the onion in a Gibson, or the amarena cherry in an Old-Fashioned (often dried to limit the taste impact in the drink). With citrus and vegetables, the variety and even the cut can offer an individual touch, requiring little extra time.

Even a simple straw can be considered as part of a drink's garnish, particularly if it is unusual in size or color (clear straws are of course the most neutral, ideal for clear drinks, while white straws are better options for the fruitier drinks). The use of accessories such as umbrellas, flags, and swizzle sticks are sometimes requirements of the venue (such as in tiki bars, known for their elaborate, even architectural garnishes) or honor a specific date on the calendar, but these don't define great drinks. Neither do stunt garnishes, such as mini hamburgers or slices of pizza impaled on skewers and stuck into Bloody Marys.

Castellon, Fernando. *Larousse des cocktails*. Paris: Larousse, 2004.

DeGroff, Dale. *Craft of the Cocktail*. New York: Clarkson Potter, 2002.

Fernando Castellon

Garrick Club Punch, a mix of genever or gin, sugar, lemon peel, lemon juice, and maraschino liqueur, chilled with iced soda water, is one of the main vectors by which American-style iced drinks gained a foothold in Britain. See GENEVER and GIN. The drink was introduced to London's exclusive Garrick Club—which opened in 1832 as a place for the wealthy and aristocratic to rub shoulders with the literary and bohemian—by the club's first manager, the brash, even vulgar, American theatrical impresario Stephen Price (1782–1840). Price was a hard-drinking New Yorker who consumed what was later described as "gin and water" (it could very well have been this punch) in such quantities that his theatrical friends in New York once presented him with a special quart goblet for it.

Price's Punch escaped the precincts of the Garrick when the irrepressible Theodore Hook, the leading wit of his day, stopped in there one warm afternoon in July 1835 and complained of his thirst. Price personally made him a jug of the punch. Hook liked it so much that he finished it and, "with the accompaniment of some chops," five more to boot. He became the drink's evangelist.

While a novelty in London, Price's drink appears to have been nothing more than a slight variation on the "treacherous" (as a Boston paper labeled it in 1828) American creation "Soda Punch," attested to in New York and Boston since at least 1822 and one of the beverages that would end up on Peter Bent Brigham's iconic and influential 1842 Boston drinks list. See BRIGHAM, PETER BENT. In Britain, the recipe would spread far and wide, helped by the fact that it was written on the inside cover of the Garrick's members' book and thus available to a high percentage of sporting London. Before long, its defining feature, the iced soda water, was adopted by London's aristocratic and sporty Limmer's Hotel, where it would become associated with John Collin, the hotel's headwaiter. It also served as the basis for the British school of sling-making, yielding among others the Singapore Gin Sling. See COLLINS; SINGAPORE SLING; and GIN SLING.

Although the original recipe simply specifies "gin," evidence suggests that that meant "Holland gin," or genever, although it may profitably also be made with Old Tom or London dry gin. See OLD TOM GIN and LONDON DRY GIN.

Recipe: In a 2-liter pitcher, muddle the spiral-cut peel of 1 lemon in 300 ml genever. Stir 60 ml sugar into 60 ml lemon juice and add to pitcher, along with 60 ml maraschino liqueur. Stir well and add 300 ml chilled soda water and 750 ml cold water (original) or 750 grams ice (better).

"For the Evening Gazette." *Boston Evening Gazette*, April 12, 1828, 1.

"The Garrick." *Harrisburg (PA) Telegraph*, July 29, 1873, 1.

Review of *The Original*, by Thomas Walker. *London Quarterly Review*, February, 1836, 256.

David Wondrich

gelatin is the final result obtained from boiling down collagen sources such as the skin, bones, tendons, ligaments, and hooves of cows or pigs; it is sold in either powdered or sheet form. Reconstituted into a flavorless, clear liquid, this fining agent or solidifier was a popular ingredient during the nineteenth and twentieth centuries for making jellies, mixed drinks, and some ales. The "calves-feet jelly" specified in the recipes for Oxford Punch, Lawn Sleeves, White Wine Negus, Restorative Punch, and Egg Punch contained in the pioneering *Oxford Night-Caps* was a fining agent, capturing proteins and other particulates as the jelly solidified, thereby speeding up the clarification process when the mixture was strained before service.

London celebrity chef Alexis Soyer prescribed a way to make jelly stock in 1851, placing two calves' feet in three quarts of water and simmering the mixture for five hours. The resulting base was combined the next day with Rum Punch to make a spirituous dessert jelly. The same principle was adapted by Jerry "the Professor" Thomas in his Punch Jelly, a sherbet-cum-cognac and Jamaican rum concoction, appearing in his 1862 *The Bar-Tender's Guide*. See THOMAS, JEREMIAH P. "JERRY".

The techniques for employing gelatin as a fining agent or as a solidifier for mixed drinks rarely appeared after the turn of the twentieth century until they were rediscovered and revived at the turn of the twenty-first: Barcelona's Dry Martini Cocktail Bar included jellified versions of a gin and tonic and a Negroni on its menu that followed Soyer and Thomas's techniques, while London's Hawksmoor steak restaurant featured a revival of the Victorian-era Criterion Milk Punch that was fined with gelatin.

Oxford Night Caps. Oxford: Henry Slater, 1827.

Soyer, Alexis Benoit. *The Modern Housewife*. New York: D. Appleton, 1851.

Soyer, Alexis Benoit. *A Shilling Cookery for the People*. London: George Routledge, 1854.

Thomas, Jerry. *The Bar-Tender's Guide*. New York: Dick & Fitzgerald, 1862.

Anistatia R. Miller and Jared M. Brown

genever—from the French *baie de genièvre*, meaning juniper berry—is a botanical grain spirit containing juniper. It is spelled *jenever* (yuh-NAY-vur) in the modern-day Dutch language and is the national drink of both the Netherlands and Belgium, both of which possess distinct and

The back of a promotional playing card for Hertekamp Oude Genever, ca. 1960, showing the traditional broad-shouldered, square case bottle. Wondrich Collection.

legitimate genever-making traditions, and which collectively consume the largest share of the world genever market. *Jonge* genever is typically consumed as a chilled shot with a small beer on the side (the combination is named a *kopstoot*, or headbutt) or as a vodka substitute mixed with soda or juice, while *oude* genever is typically consumed neat or in cocktails. See KOPSTOOT. Although it is often trumpeted as the ancestor of gin, juniper is not traditionally dominant in genever's aroma and flavor, and genever typically uses far fewer, and a far smaller amount of, botanicals. Taste-wise, *jonge* genever is closest to vodka, while *oude* genever is closest in flavor to a whisky.

Origins

The origins of genever lie in the spirit-based medicines that were created with the awakening, or reawakening, of European distilling in the twelfth century. See DISTILLATION, HISTORY. At first, the spirit used was grape-based, whether wine was produced in the distiller's region or not. Belgian priest and academic Thomas van Cantimpré's *Liber de Natura Rerum* encyclopedia (completed in 1245) mentions juniper berries being cooked in rainwater or in wine as a stomach medicine; van Cantimpré's countryman Jacob van Maerlant translated this book into middle Dutch, expanded it, and published it as *Der Naturen Bloeme* in 1269, the oldest known printed mention of distilling in the Netherlands. Van Maerlant mentioned juniper constantly—juniper was clearly a benchmark medicine at the time, an aid to digestion, aches, and pains, as well as a flavoring and preservative.

History

A plague epidemic in the Netherlands that began in 1349 led to widespread medicinal use of both juniper (as disinfectant; plague doctors packed their "bird nose" masks with it) and distilled medicinal alcohol; a 1351 text by the Belgian Johannes van Aalter describes making wine-based aqua vitae, a medicinal distillate. See HEALTH AND SPIRITS.

In 1495, an unknown but clearly wealthy individual in the Arnhem/Apeldoorn region of the Netherlands self-published a lavish single edition of a cookbook featuring a recipe titled "Gebrande Wyn Te Maken" (Making burned wine), which is now part of the Sloane Manuscripts in the British Library. This recipe, in among the food recipes, has a very similar method to distilling French wine to van Aalter's but features in addition, as botanicals, a huge array of what were at the time the most fantastically expensive spices in the world: nutmeg, cloves, galangal, ginger, grains of paradise, and cinnamon, to name but a few. In fact, juniper is one of the least expensive ingredients. This 1495 recipe is seen as the very first mention of a recreational juniper spirit, but since by 1497 distilled alcohol was being taxed in Amsterdam, we must assume that drinking distilled spirits for fun started earlier than 1495 but later than 1350 or so. Initially, French wine as a base was recommended for medicinal distillates and for higher quality in general, but by 1588, as the German/Dutch Casper Janszoon Coolhaes wrote in his influential distilling manual *Van seeckere seer costelijcke wateren*, grain had replaced grapes as the base for making recreational alcohol. See COOLHAES, CASPAR JANSZOON. Genever became the national drink of the Netherlands and was a mainstay during the Golden Age of Dutch wealth and influence in the 1600s, accompanying their navy and the ships of the Dutch East India Company as they attained dominance of the seas and trade.

When England gained a Dutch king, Willem of Orange in 1688, trade links between the Netherlands and England—already very strong—led to huge demand for genever in England. Based on cheap, high-quality barley and rye secured through the Netherlands's excellent trading relationship with the northern European Hanseatic League and made by the most experienced distillers in Europe, Dutch genever was a rich spirit tasting mostly of the grain from which it was made. English distillers, trying to copy it, lacked the raw materials and often the skill to do so; instead, they rectified their grain spirit by redistillation and other means and made up the missing flavor by adding vastly more botanicals and sugar, creating a stripped-down version of genever to which they gave a stripped-down name: gin. See GIN.

Distilling back in the Netherlands had become such big business that it posed hygiene and safety issues, and cities ruled that distillation be moved to satellite towns such as Weesp (the satellite of Amsterdam) and Schiedam (the satellite of

Rotterdam). Schiedam grew to have almost four hundred distilleries of one sort or another by the late 1800s, each of them privately owned but utilizing standardized mash bills, fermenters, and stills to make a product—*moutwijn*; see the section "Production"—that was greatly uniform from distiller to distiller. By that time, maize had been added to the spirit's mash bill, taking a roughly equal share with malted barley and rye; triple distillation (in pot stills) was standard; and the amount of juniper and other botanicals added varied according to the intended market: very little for Britain, a lot for the United States.

The United States was a major market. Genever reigned supreme there during the first golden age of cocktails of the mid-1800s, making up by far the bulk of imported gin. It was hit hard in the late 1800s by the rise of lighter, drier drinks such as the Dry Martini (dry vermouth and genever do not mix well), followed rapidly by a world war, Prohibition, and another war. Post-1945, Dutch distillers began experimenting with using less *moutwijn*, leading to the birth of the wildly successful (not to mention profitable) *jonge* style, which came to dominate the market domestically and virtually killed off the *oude* style. Vicious price wars in the 1970s coupled with changing tastes led to a huge decline in genever sales in Belgium and the Netherlands, and the category as a whole still suffers major reductions in sales year-on-year in those countries.

Happily, the resurgence in popularity of classic cocktails since the 1990s has ensured that *oude*-style genever is once more on the radar of serious mixologists. Its signature classic cocktails can be said to be the Improved Holland Gin Cock-Tail, the Collins, and the Martinez. See COLLINS and MARTINEZ.

Production

The heart of all genever is *moutwijn* (malt wine), a grain distillate distilled at least three times. Made from what is usually a multigrain mash fermented from rye, corn, and malted barley, the first distillate from a short stripping column is called *ruwnat*, the second (from a pot still) *enkelnat*, and the third (also pot still) *bestnat*, or *moutwijn*; *moutwijn* must be between 46 percent and 48 percent alcohol by volume. See TRIPLE DISTILLATION (FULL AND PARTIAL).

Optionally, this *moutwijn* can then be distilled a fourth time to make what is known as *korenwijn* (literally, "grainwine," but not to be confused with korenwijn/korenwyn/corenwyn). Formerly, the *moutwijn*, usually purchased from brokers, was redistilled with botanicals to make genever; now, it is more commonly blended with neutral spirits that have been distilled with botanicals including juniper berries or juniper aroma. These neutral spirits may be from sugar beets or (for better quality brands) grain.

Jonge (young) style genever must contain a minimum of 1.5 percent and a maximum of 15 percent *moutwijn* (most stay close to the minimum), be at least 35 percent ABV, contain no more than 10 grams of sugar per liter, and be made in the Netherlands or Belgium. *Jonge* is by far the best-selling style of genever—currently 25 percent of the total Dutch liquor market is genever, 98 percent of which is *jonge*.

Oude (old) style genever must contain a minimum of 15 percent *moutwijn* (most contain about 17 percent), be a minimum of 35 percent ABV, contain no more than 20 g sugar per liter, and be made in the Netherlands or Belgium. *Oude* is what most people outside the Netherlands and Belgium expect genever to be.

Korenwijn/korenwyn/corenwyn is a Netherlands-only luxury *oude*-style genever that must contain a minimum of 51 percent *moutwijn* (most brands contain about 53 percent), be a minimum of 38 percent ABV, and contain no more than 20 g sugar per liter.

There is no requirement to age any genever regardless of the name, but if aging is mentioned on the label, it must be for a minimum of one year in barrels no larger than a seven-hundred-liter capacity. Genever may legally be made anywhere in the Netherlands, Belgium, the Nordrhein-Westfalen and Niedersachsen regions of Germany, and the Nord and Pas de Calais regions of France. Other styles of genever not legally regulated by the above categories include 100 percent malt-wine genever (regulated by the voluntary Seal of Schiedam), fruit genevers (which typically don't contain *moutwijn*), and cream genevers (ditto).

See KORENWIJN and MOUTWIJN.

Jansen, Herman. In *Minutes of Evidence Taken by the Royal Commission on Whiskey and Other Potable Spirits*, vol. 2. London: HMSO, 55–57.

van Schoonenberghe, Eric. *Jenever in de Lage Landen* [Genever in the Low Countries]. Oostkamp, Belgium, Stichting Kunstboek, 1996.

European Union Regulation 2019/787 on the Definition, Description, Presentation and Labelling of Spirit Drinks. https://eur-lex.europa.eu/legal-content/EN/TXT/?uri=celex%3A32019R0787 (accessed July 30, 2021).

Netherlands Spirits Producers Association. "Regulations on Naming Distilled- and Weak-Distilled Spirits, 2009, Netherlands (lapsed)." https://www.spiritsnl.nl (accessed February 9, 2021).

Philip Duff

Geographical Indication (GI) and Protected Designation of Origin (PDO) are legal frameworks that protect and promote spirits identified as originating from a specific town, region, or country. The most comprehensive list of protected spirit drinks is supplied by Regulation no. 110/2008 of the European Parliament, a 2008 update of a 1989 law. (The regulations for aromatized wines and aromatized-wine-based drinks are set out in a separate no. 1601/91.) The purpose of geographical indication in general is to maintain the integrity of association between countries and regions and the food and drink that they produce, but a protected status also helps to preserve the practices of what are often long-established artisanal producers, as well as protecting premium products from counterfeit and non-genuine competitors.

A PDO product must be manufactured entirely in the area indicated, while a product with a GI requires that only some stages of the production take place in the indicated country or region. Spirits tend to fall under the GI category, as it is relatively uncommon for a distiller to conduct every stage of production—from growing to distilling to blending or other processing to bottling and packaging—in the same region, particularly when it comes to the larger firms and more popular spirits. Neither PDO nor GI should be confused with an indication of source—for example "made in China"—where there need not be any definable characteristic that derives from its place of origin.

The European GI/PDO system first came into effect in 1992, but similar systems have existed for much longer. In France, for example, the *appellation d'origine contrôlée* (AOC) has its origins in the fifteenth century, when a parliamentary decree granted Roquefort cheese protection from imitators. France also passed the first modern law for the protection of place in 1919 and today includes Armagnac, calvados, cognac, and Martinique rhum among its list of protected spirits.

The EU's current list of GI spirits includes many spirit subcategories that originate from certain regions or countries, but also spirits, liqueurs, and aperitifs that have "acquired their character and definitive qualities" from a specific area and its associated production methods. In total, there are forty spirit categories and hundreds of registered European GIs. The majority of the spirits featured are fruit- and wine-based. Some are household names, such as cognac and calvados, but most, such as Medronheira do Algarve (a Portuguese spirit made in the Algarve region and distilled from the fermented fruit of the *Arbutus unedo* tree) are far less familiar, and some—black-muscat-raisin spirit, German *Hefebrand* (wine-lees brandy)— are positively archaic. There are, however, some grain spirits covered, including several juniper-flavored ones, such as gin de Mahón (from the Spanish island of Minorca) and Balegemse jenever (farmhouse Belgian genever), as well as caraway spirits such as Dansk akvavit. Also covered are various anise-flavored spirits and a wide range of liqueurs, including everything from cassis de Dijon to Irish cream. See CREAM LIQUEURS and CRÈME DE CASSIS.

In the United States there are only a handful of GI spirits, namely, Kentucky bourbon and Tennessee whisky, although "bourbon" must itself be produced in the United States. See WHISKY, BOURBON. Mexico protects tequila and various other regional varieties of mezcal, plus Michoacán's cane-based charanda. See CHARANDA. A number of Caribbean nations have established the Authentic Caribbean Rum (ACR) designation, although it is a loose one when it comes to dictating production norms. See RUM. Pisco is protected in both Peru and Chile, although neither country recognizes the other's regulations. See PISCO.

Where products are exported to other countries, there are often international agreements in place that protect spirits at both ends of the trade. One example of this is the 1997 Agreement between the European Community and the United Mexican States on the Mutual Recognition and Protection of Designations for Spirit Drinks, which ensures the rules concerning tequila labeling are consistent on both sides of the Atlantic.

Furthermore, the Trade-Related Aspects of Intellectual Property Rights (TRIPS) Agreement administered by the World Trade Organization sets down minimum standards for intellectual property that includes strict provisions for spirits. Article 23 of the agreement states that members are required to provide remedies against spirits that do not actually originate in the place indicated by the GI, even where the true place of origin is indicated or where the GI is used in translation or in conjunction with "kind," "type," "style," "imitation" or "the like." (An example of this would be "Italian-style grappa made in Loughton.")

While GIs often specify some broad characteristics of the covered spirits, such as source materials, distillation and bottling proofs, and sweetening, they tend not to control the specific methods of production used to make a spirit. So while EU law requires that whisky labeled "scotch whisky" must be from Scotland, the rules regarding exactly how "whisky" must be made are covered in a separate section of the legislation, and much of the detail is in fact left up to the individual countries to define.

The GI/PDO framework has been the subject of some degree of criticism since its inception. Most critics have focused on the issue of self-regulation, where areas awarded a protected GI, if left unchecked, could have potential issues with product price fixing, labor control, and profit channeling. A GI can also prove difficult to obtain for some, since locating a distillery within a designated geographical area may be price prohibitive—not a problem if you're handed acres of grape-growing farmland in Cognac's Grande Champagne region but a disadvantage for a talented cellar master lacking the capital to buy property in the region. Another point of contention is the consumer's assumption that a product with a PDO is ascribed a value of being inherently "good" or at the very least better than a similar product made outside of the PDO, although the designation in fact has nothing to say about production standards.

Authentic Caribbean Rum website. https://acr-rum.com/en/ (accessed March 30, 2021).

"Regulation (EC) No 110/2008 of the European Parliament and of the Council of 15 January 2008." *Official Journal of the European Union*, February 2, 2008, L 39/16-54.

Tristan Stephenson

Germain-Robin, considered by many the premium producer of California brandies, was born of a chance encounter in California's Mendocino County in 1981, when professor-cum-rancher Ansley Coale picked up a hitchhiker who turned out to be Hubert Germain-Robin (1950–), the ninth-generation scion of a legendary cognac-making family. The two men hatched a plan to produce artisanal brandy from local wines on Coale's ranch, drawing on Germain-Robin's extensive distilling expertise. Germain-Robin returned to his native France to procure a vintage *alambic Charentais* cognac still, and soon he was distilling brandy for his eponymous label from wine made with locally-sourced pinot noir and other high-quality wine grape varieties. (In contrast, cognac is made mostly from ugni blanc, a grape that yields undistinguished wines.) Aged in French oak barrels, the inaugural 1982 vintage was released five years later. Though acclaim for Germain-Robin's brandy wasn't immediate, its enthusiastic embrace by Ronald Reagan and subsequent US presidents soon helped to solidify its reputation as America's answer to fine cognac.

Hubert Germain-Robin left the company in 2006 to pursue a consulting career, turning over the production reins to his assistant, Joe Corley. In 2017, Germain-Robin was purchased by E. & J. Gallo, and production was subsequently transferred to the historic McCall distillery near Fresno. There the brandy is distilled in traditional cognac stills installed by Suntory in the early 1990s and recently refurbished by Gallo—under the direction of none other than Hubert Germain-Robin.

See also BRANDY and COGNAC.

Boyd, Gerald. D. "French Twist." *San Francisco Chronicle*, November 25, 2001.
Prial, Frank J. "A Choice Encounter." *New York Times Magazine*, September 4, 1988.

David Mahoney

Germany, Switzerland, and Austria share a common history, with the strong trade routes between the countries and the frequent shifting of the borders between them ensuring much overlap in their drinking traditions. Yet there are also significant historical differences, particularly when it comes to Germany: in the north, spirit was primarily made from grain and later from potatoes, while in the south there are strong traditions of distilling alcohol from fruit and even in some areas roots.

In the twelfth century, when the practice of distilling spirits began spreading throughout southern Europe, Switzerland, Austria, and most of Germany were part of the Holy Roman Empire, along with large areas of what is today Italy. It is not overly speculative to assume that the knowledge of distillation spread north, probably via monks and monasteries. In any case, distillation was firmly established in the region by the 1400s. In the year 1507 grain brandy was mentioned for the first time in documents in the city of Nordhausen. See KORN. The first potato distillery was built in the Palatinate in 1750. In 1810, distilling was generally permitted, previously only allowed to gentry and brewers (this restriction was not always followed). In the years 1810–1887 many more grain and potato distilleries were established, especially in the German north. Already in 1831 there were approximately seventeen thousand potato distilleries.

This diversity of small distillers is a feature of the industry in all three countries: there is no multinational "big player" from the region, and most producers are small or middle-sized. Only a few products have an international distribution. One exception is the herbal liqueur Jägermeister, which is the most successful German spirit, being in the top 100 worldwide. See JÄGERMEISTER. Korn, though widespread in the region, is virtually unknown outside of it, although it was quite influential on the early development of the United States' rye whisky. See WHISKY, RYE.

Two spirits that have found export markets, if specialized ones, are a pair of eaux-de-vie, kirschwasser and poire Williams. See KIRSCHWASSER and POIRE WILLIAMS. Nowadays the Williams pear has around 1,500 varieties worldwide, of which there are over seven hundred cultivated varieties in Germany alone. But in the south basically every type of fruit is distilled, with many regional specialties and even strictly local ones, where small producers have spirits made of ingredients that grow only in that locale. See EAU-DE-VIE; OBSTLER; and SCHNAPPS.

Recent developments show a big investment in whisky distillation in all the three countries, with many fruit distillers moving into grain distillation. The best known of them outside the region, Hans Reisetbauer of Austria, began making apple schnapps in 1994 and whisky in 1996, and today makes a wide variety of innovative spirits. Currently Germany has more whisky distillers than Scotland, if considerably smaller ones. The same is true for the big seller early twenty-first century, gin. Switzerland forbade the distillation of potatoes or grain during World War I, to protect the nation's food supply.

The Christian Beltz kornbranntwein distillery in Nordhausen, Germany, as portrayed on a 1902 invoice. Note the mashing/still room *top center*, with its twin brick-jacketed pot stills and the coopers preparing barrels for shipping *bottom right*. Wondrich Collection.

This prohibition was only lifted for potatoes in 1997 and for grain in 1999. In Austria it was possible to use grain, but it is uncommon.

Cocktail culture in the region is quite old: Germany, in particular, had a long tradition of mixing drinks and was one of the early adopters of punch, which was common there by the early 1700s. German punch makers had no problem coming up with their own variations. See FEUERZANGENBOWLE. This experience meant that many German bartenders were highly successful in America. See ENSSLIN, HUGO RICHARD; JOHNSON, HARRY; and SCHMIDT, WILLIAM. Some German American bartenders returned to their home country and influenced the drink culture there. In Germany the Verein der Barmixer (bartenders' union) was founded in 1909 and published the first bartending magazine in Europe, the *American Bar Journal*. The first German bar book, *Lexicon der getränke*, by Hans Schönfeld and John Leybold, followed in 1913. In Austria, the first bartenders' union was established 1926, and in Switzerland it started in Zürich in 1927. All three were suspended or abolished during the world wars but were able to re-establish themselves in the 1950s. Even in the former East Germany bars continued to be found in hotels, and there was even a cocktail book, *Wir mixen,* published in 1958. The leading figure in the field of bartending and mixology in the three German-speaking countries was the Swiss J. H. "Harry" Schraemli (1904–1995); he published the first manual at the Hotelfachschule Luzern. His book *Das große Lehrbuch der Bar* is today a collector's item. (The inventive Swiss-Italian mixologist Elvzio Grassi must also be mentioned, who as bartender at the Bar Argentino in Lugano published *Mille misture* (1936), one of the most inventive cocktail books ever written.)

Until the 1980s, cocktails in the three countries were served mainly in hotel bars: the "American bar" as a solo establishment was a rarity, although there were exceptions, such as Kruger's American Bar in Vienna, which dates back to the 1920s. Other types of bars existed, of course, but there the leisure and pleasure factor was more important than the quality of mixed drinks. The first wave of new cocktail bars started in the early 1980s and got a real boost at the beginning of the 2000s. From 2007 on, an important impulse was provided by the first bar show on the continent, Bar Convent Berlin (BCB). At first just for the so-called GSA countries (Germany, Switzerland, and Austria), it evolved into the world's leading high-end bar trade show, spreading to other countries (e.g., Bar Convent Brooklyn, launched in 2018) or inspiring them to create their own.

All three countries nowadays have a vivid cocktail scene, mainly concentrated in the bigger cities. In Austria, Vienna is dominant; in Switzerland, it is stronger in the German-speaking part, and particularly in Zurich (where the Kronenhalle Bar is an institution), Basel, and Berne; but Geneva, in the French part, also has a modern bar scene. In Germany, Munich has the most prominent bar internationally with the legendary Schumann's, followed by Le Lion in Hamburg. After becoming the capital again, Berlin is also an excellent place for mixed drinks. But in every significant city the sophisticated drinker will find a decent spot for a mixed drink.

Bundesverband der Spirituosen Industrie. https://www.spirituosen-verband.de/ (accessed March 22, 2021).

Henseler, Udo, and Bernhard Weichsel. *Wir mixen.* Leipzig: Fachbuchverlag Leipzig, 1958.

Schäfer, Bernhard. *Gin*. Munich: Gräfe und Unzer Verlag, 2016.

Schraemli, Harry. *Das grosse Lehrbuch der Bar*. Luzern: Fachbücherverl. Union Helvetica, 1949.

Siegel, Simon, et al. *Handlexikon der Getränke*. Linz: Rudolf Trauner, 1985.

Bernhard Schäfer

gibberellins are a family of plant hormones that are responsible for stimulating growth and seed germination, which includes gibberellic acid (GA). Gibberellins play an integral role during plant development, and therefore they have an overall effect on plant-based spirit and cocktail raw-material quality from mint to barley. Their role in the biochemical and structural degradation (modification) of the cereal grain endosperm (i.e., rye, wheat, and barley) and hydrolytic enzyme synthesis during malting is what makes it of particular interest to distillers and brewers alike.

The synthesis of gibberellins begins in the embryo after its carbohydrate reserves have been depleted. They then migrate into the aleurone, where they stimulate the production of hydrolytic enzymes for modification upon the start of germination. These enzymes, in addition to those from other plant tissues, are key to malting, as well as beer and whisky production; during mashing, they allow the starch in the endosperm to be solubilized and further degraded into fermentable sugars for the yeast to convert to alcohol.

Exogenous forms (GA) have found use in malting as an additive to the water in which the grain is initially steeped, in a process called "gibbing," which helps to ensure an efficient and homogeneous modification. With the gibbing process, grains are abraded gently to damage the kernel, which allows for more rapid and increased hydration. See KERNEL. The supplemental GA increases the rate of starch and protein-degrading enzyme production, which accelerates modification and leads to lower malting losses. Gibbing is often practiced in the production of malt for use with mash bills that are mostly comprised of non-malted cereals, such as corn, wheat, and/or rye (e.g., in American bourbon and rye whisky and in scotch and Irish grain whisky; additives, including GA, are prohibited in malt production for scotch whisky). The increased levels of starch-degrading enzymes are desired, as they are absent in non-malted grains.

See also MALTING.

Briggs, D. E., J. S. Hough, R. Stevens, and T. W. Young. "The Biochemistry of Malting Grain." In *Malting and Brewing Science*, vol. 1, *Malt and Sweet Wort*, 2d ed., 57–107. Kluwer Academic / Plenum, 1981.

Dolan, Timothy C. S. "Malt Whiskies: Raw Materials and Processing." In *Whisky Technology, Production, and Marketing*, ed. Inge Russell, Charlie Bamforth, and Graham Stewart, 44–55. San Diego, CA: Elsevier, 2003.

Gupta, Ramwant, and S. K. Chakrabarty. "Gibberellic Acid in Plant: Still a Mystery Unresolved." *Plant Signaling and Behavior* 8, no. 9 (2013): E25504-1-25504-5.

Elizabeth Rhoades

Gibson is a variation of the classic dry Martini, created at San Francisco's Bohemian Club in 1898 and named for either illustrator Charles Dana Gibson, creator of the Gibson Girl drawings, or socialite Walder D. K. Gibson, both members. See MARTINI. Originally, it was simply a Dry Martini without orange bitters, but once that drink lost the bitters, its distinguishing mark became its garnish: a pickled onion. See ONION.

A **Gimlet** is a simple cocktail with a difficult explanation. Traditionally composed of gin and preserved lime juice (Rose's Lime Juice was the standard for around a century), originally with the common addition of soda water, the Gimlet also has a vodka-based version, as well as variations made with fresh lime juice and sugar or with homemade lime cordial in lieu of Rose's.

The Gimlet's genesis began with the passage of the Merchant Shipping Act of 1867, which mandated that British merchant ships stock rations of lime juice to prevent scurvy; the same year, Lauchlan Rose (1829–1885) of Edinburgh patented an alcohol-free process of preserving lime juice, and Rose's Lime Juice Cordial was soon widely distributed. By the 1870s, Rose & Co. was advertising its product as a "delicious drink agreeable in all seasons" when combined with spirits. In 1900, the company even went so far as to launch a bottled mix of its lime juice and ten-year-old scotch whisky. However, by then gin had already begun to assert itself as the natural complement to the preserved juice.

The first time the combination has a name attached is in 1917, with the somewhat garbled "Gillette Cocktail, Chicago Style" recorded by Tom Bullock, which has fresh lime juice and Old Tom gin (the "Chicago style" remains unexplained). Both the current name and the Rose's appear in 1922 in *Harry's ABC of Cocktails*; there, equal parts Rose's and Plymouth gin are called for (the latter being the appropriate choice for a drink identified as "a very popular beverage in the Navy"). See BULLOCK, TOM (THOMAS WASHINGTON); and McELHONE, HENRY "HARRY."

The cocktail's ratio dried out considerably in coming decades, and as with the Martini, vodka eventually supplanted gin in many late-twentieth-century Gimlets (with that, the soda water, which had helped to cut the lime cordial's sweetness, disappeared from the drink). A sordid staple in literature—Ernest Hemingway, David Mamet, and Raymond Chandler all put Gimlets in the hands of fictional characters, typically predators or their prey—the Gimlet is frequently freshened up in twenty-first-century bars, with fresh lime juice and simple syrup replacing the mass-market cordial. Bartenders including Toby Cecchini in New York and Todd Appel in Chicago devised fresh lime cordial recipes to replace Rose's, and Jennifer Colliau prepared a complex Navy Gimlet for the Interval at Long Now bar in San Francisco, using lime oleo-saccharum and clarified lime juice in a base of navy-strength gin.

Recipe: Shake 60 ml gin (London dry or Plymouth) and 20 ml lime cordial with ice, and strain into chilled cocktail glass. Top with 30 ml chilled sparkling water, if desired.

Note: This recipe is adapted from the listing for the Gimblet in the *Savoy Cocktail Guide*, 1930. That book also lists a recipe for the Gimlet, listed as an equal-parts composition of gin and lime cordial served on the rocks, but the Gimblet listing more closely resembles the traditional serving of a Gimlet.

Clarke, Paul. "History and Character of the Gimlet." *Mixologist: The Journal of the American Cocktail* 1 (2005): 59–74.

Cecchini, Toby. "Raw Lime Cordial." *New York Times,* 2011 http://cooking.nytimes.com/recipes/1015312-raw-lime-cordial (accessed September 30, 2016).

McElhone, Harry. *Harry's ABC of Cocktails.* London: Odhams, [1922].

Paul Clarke

gin, one of the most historically and commercially important spirit categories, is made by flavoring neutral spirits with juniper berries and other botanicals, chiefly through distillation, but sometimes by infusion or compounding. See INFUSION and COMPOUNDING. Originating at the end of the seventeenth century as a British imitation of Dutch genever, gin has become a global spirit, manufactured and sold in just about every region. See GENEVER. Its history, a matchlessly complex one, can be divided into four distinct phases.

The Gin Craze (1690–1760)

The history of gin has been shaped more by government regulation and taxation than that of any other spirit. See EXCISE, TAXES, AND DISTILLATION. Indeed, gin was born from an act of British Parliament, the 1690 "Act for Encouraging the Distilling of Brandy and Spirits from Corn," passed at the instigation of King William. In the 1670s and 1680s the habit of drinking spirits recreationally had finally reached England. See PUNCH. England, however, did not have a developed distilling industry, so the market was supplied mostly from her on-again, off-again enemy France. William officially banned this trade. The 1690 act was intended to develop a grain-distilling industry like the one in his native Netherlands and assist British agriculture.

Unfortunately, the act, which abolished the Worshipful Company of Distillers' monopoly on distilling and lowered the tax on low wines made from British grain from 12 pence a gallon to 1 penny, worked both too well and not well enough: by the first decade of the new century, domestic "geneva" (as the English pronounced *jenever*), or "gin" for short, was everywhere, with literally thousands of new entrants in the distilling trade. See LOW WINES. From half a million gallons in 1690, English distillery output rose to two million gallons in 1713 and, by a low estimate, 4.3 million in 1729. The new tax meant that barriers to entering the market

Silver-plated Gordon's gin promotional barspoon, bearing the brand's famous boar's head logo, ca. 1950. Wondrich Collection.

were low. It also, however, meant that competition was plentiful. The result was a race to the bottom, as grocers, publicans, and other new distillers fought to supply the increasingly crowded slums of London with cheap spirit. Far from the wholesome, artisanal barley- and rye-malt Dutch original, much of the new English corn spirit was hastily distilled from such things as beer lees and raw, salt-water-damaged grain with just enough malt to allow it to ferment. The juniper flavoring often came not from real juniper berries, as used in Holland, but from turpentine and worse. While genuine Dutch "Hollands" sold for high prices—thus monopolizing the high end of the market—London gin was sold at prices even the poorest could afford.

This is not the place to go into the sordid details of the social disaster known as the "gin craze." It should, however, be pointed out that much of what was vilified as gin was not in fact technically gin: there was a good deal of cheap spirit made in England, and while much of it was grain-based imitation genever, much was also grain- or molasses-spirit adulterated into a nasty reflection of French brandy or turned into "aniseed water," "peppermint water" or some other cordial. (Like "rum" in late nineteenth-century America, "gin" was often used not as a technical term but as a moral one, denoting any spirit consumed by those one looks down on.)

Nor was the social dysfunction confined to the poor: all classes of English society binged on spirits in the eighteenth century, whether it was in a bowl of punch, used to fortify a bottle of wine (English vintners customarily added spirit to almost every category of imported wine before bottling it), or drunk by the quartern-measure (120 ml) in the back alleys of London.

It should also be noted that the problem was not unique to England: as Didier Nouraisson has observed, massive and disruptive rises in spirit consumption are closely tied to industrialization, as occurred in France and the United States in the early nineteenth century. In England, it just happened earlier.

The Rise of the Rectifiers (1760–1880)

Throughout the first half of the eighteenth century, Parliament made spasmodic attempts to put the cat at least partway back in the bag, including raising taxes, tightening licensing requirements, and various kinds of de jure and de facto prohibition. Eventually, it hit on the right combination with a dizzyingly complex and ever-shifting set of excise laws that tightly governed the spirits trade. Its main pillars were a strict separation between distilling spirits and selling them to the general public, a tax and regulatory structure that favored large firms over small ones, particularly when it came to distilling, and a tight control of distillation and rectification proofs based on hydrometer testing, first mandated in 1765. See HYDROMETER.

Under this system, gin began as "raw spirit," a double-distilled grain spirit that was essentially unaged whisky, made from malt by a small cartel of very large-scale "malt distillers" in England and, after 1826, Scotland and Ireland (these did not always use pure malt, particularly in England, although they were enjoined from fermenting non-grain sugars). These firms were only allowed to sell their product wholesale and only at a single, legally mandated strength, the equivalent of 61 percent ABV.

To become gin, the raw spirit required flavoring with juniper (often supplemented or replaced entirely by a cheaper substitute, turpentine) and other botanicals, and it required reducing in proof and sweetening—unsweetened gin was sold, but only so that the customers could sweeten it themselves. See BOTANICAL. By law, "compound spirits" such as gin could not be sold to the public at above a certain proof: until 1818, 44.6 percent ABV; after that, 47.4 percent. Usually, the proof was considerably lower: an 1855 analysis for the *Lancet* of thirty-eight samples of gin purchased in London found the strengths ranging between a high of 48.8 percent ABV (and hence illegal) and a low of 22.4 percent, with an average of 36.5 percent. The sugar content in the thirty-six sweetened gins ranged from 20.6 to 83 grams per liter. (To put that in context, today the EU requires a minimum of 100 grams per liter for most liqueurs, while a Swedish government test of twenty-eight rums found an average of 16 grams per liter of added sugar.)

Some retailers—public houses and wine and spirits merchants—did the flavoring, reducing, and sweetening themselves, pocketing the profit made on the difference in purchase proof and sale proof. But malt distillers only dealt in large quantities, and without distillation the resulting product was palpably inferior. Most retailers therefore bought their gin from rectifiers, who redistilled the raw spirit once or twice with their proprietary botanical blends and reduced it to compound-spirit proof. See RECTIFIER (OCCUPATION). If desired, they could also sweeten it and further reduce it, but most retailers preferred to do that themselves—why give the rectifiers the extra profit? Many retailers also added a "doctor" to give the gin the impression of being stronger than it was. Cayenne pepper and grains of paradise were the most innocuous ingredients found in these. Others included sulfuric acid, oil of almonds, and quicklime. Each retailer usually had gin available at three or four different prices, depending on the degree of reduction, from unsweetened, which was straight from the rectifier, to various grades of "cordial," or sweetened gin, from "Old Tom" or "cream of the valley," only lightly reduced and sweetened and generally undoctored, to the quite sweet, dilute, and doctored "common gin." See OLD TOM GIN.

These excise regulations and the practices they fostered decisively pulled British gin away from its original Dutch model, particularly after the malt distillers adopted continuous stills in the 1830s (the rectifiers generally stuck with pot stills). See STILL, CONTINUOUS. While genever remained primarily a distiller's spirit, reliant on its grain base for most of its flavor, gin had become a rectifier's one, where the base spirit was as neutral as possible and the flavor came from added botanicals. Indeed, in 1789 when George Bishop, who had studied distilling in the Netherlands, wanted to make Dutch-style gin in Maidstone, Kent, he had to get a special act of Parliament to allow it (Original Maidstone Hollands Gin, as it was called, enjoyed a high reputation for quality and was made, on and off, under various owners for another century or so; it has recently been revived).

Another dissenter from the predominant style was Coates & Co's Plymouth gin, made in that town since at least 1800. Unsweetened (although reduced in proof) and lightly inflected with botanicals, it still retained some of the malty character of its base spirit and was considered an intermediary between London and Dutch styles of gin. See PLYMOUTH GIN.

England's former colony the United States also took its own path. As one American distiller wrote in 1907, "There are really only two kinds of gin": Holland gin and English gin, with the former being "known by the simple name of gin." This reversal of British practice had deep roots, genever having been made in the Dutch colony that became New York as early as 1640. Without the strictures of the British excise system and with plenty of cheap grain available, beginning in the years after independence some American distillers, "actuated by a laudable desire to equal the Holland gin, justly deemed superior to that of any other part of the world" (as Pennsylvania distiller Harrison Hall wrote in 1813), focused their energies on making a heavier, grain-forward product, often by redistilling raw whisky, of which there was an abundance, with gin botanicals. As far as can be determined, the resulting spirit wasn't pre-sweetened, in the British style. Since British excise made it almost impossible to export gin until the law changed in 1850, the only models American distillers had to measure themselves against were Dutch. Only at the end of the nineteenth century did they begin working in the British style.

In the London of 1760, gin was still the liquid crack of the urban poor. But over the next century, as a number of distillers established reputations for making a superior product and found retailers who would keep their adulteration within reasonable bounds, gin found a place for itself. Never elegant, gin became at least traditional, something a working person could drink by the dram and a gentleman could have as the motivating force in a bowl of punch.

The Great Brands (1880–2000)

In 1879, the British government set 37 percent ABV as a minimum proof at which the retailers could sell their gin to the public. At a stroke, this removed much of the incentive for retailers to do their own reduction. At the same time, largely because of widespread concerns about adulteration (fanned in no small part by temperance advocates), distillers and rectifiers in Britain and elsewhere were moving toward bottling their own spirits so that retailers would have to sell or dispense from factory-sealed, labeled containers. One of the effects of this change was that those distillers and rectifiers became not just suppliers but brands. Some London rectifiers, to be sure, had already gone a long way toward that, but after 1879 the trend accelerated. Firms such as Gordon's, Booth's, Seager and Evans, Tanqueray, Nicholson, Coates, and Burnett managed to establish their brands as commercial icons, not just locally but throughout the vast British Empire, and in the United States as well.

While plenty of cordial gin was still bottled, generally as the lightly sweetened Old Tom gin, by the 1890s it was being sidelined by unsweetened gin. The public taste in England and especially in America, a fast-growing market, was for lighter, dryer drinks, and "dry" gin fit right in (the term dates back to at least 1833, although it was at first a relative term and was only fixed to unsweetened gin when that began to be consumed in its own right). At the same time, gin was becoming more homogenous. The base spirit was now in most cases completely neutral, which removed one source of difference. The lack of sweetening removed another. Finally, gin makers had reached a general consensus on the botanicals that supplied the spirit's flavor. Juniper berries, of course (turpentine was a thing of the past); angelica, which boosts the juniper; coriander, for its lemony notes; orris root, to fix the other botanicals. Some used licorice, others orange peel, cardamom, almonds, and caraway seeds. But even the ones who used the more exotic flavorings did it in small amounts, accenting the flavor, not changing it.

This style of gin remained remarkably stable throughout the twentieth century, not just in Britain but globally. Because it was based on neutral spirits, London dry gin was much easier to imitate than earlier versions of gin, even if grain was a scarcity. With the reach of the British Empire, imitations sprang up on every continent save Antarctica, some of them quite popular (in 2012, the sugar-cane-based San Miguel gin, made in the Philippines since the nineteenth century, became the largest-selling gin in the world).

American distillers had adopted the new style by the end of the nineteenth century, largely abandoning the older, Dutch-style gins they had been making. In 1904, the Wilson Distilling Co. even went so far as to buy the equipment and formulae of the Camberwell Distilling Co. of London (established 1797) and transport them to Baltimore, where they used them to make the popular El Bart dry gin. Such domestic brands received a boost during World War I, only to be cut off at the knees by Prohibition in 1919. (About the thirteen years that followed, during which—in a throwback to eighteenth-century London—gin was compounded from raw spirit and juniper syrup—there is little to

say.) The major British brands, in the meanwhile, weathered that war, American Prohibition, the Great Depression, and the next war, only to run into a much bigger problem in the postwar years: vodka. See VODKA.

The niche London dry gin occupied in the spirits market from the 1880s through World War II was the one for the lightest, cleanest spirit commercially available. Many drinkers liked it in mixed drinks for just that reason: compared to whisky, brandy, or the heavier rums of the day, it blended right in. Vodka, however, was even lighter, being entirely purged of aromatic elements. Many drinkers found they preferred that. By 1954, vodka, a commercially insignificant spirit before the war, was outselling gin in some parts of the American market. In 1969 it outsold gin nationwide. The picture was little better in the United Kingdom.

The last two decades of the twentieth century saw the old gin brands struggle with consolidation, drops in price and proof, and declining market share. Like rye whisky, it was a spirit of the past.

The Gin Insurgency (2000–Present)

The new millennium brought a dramatic change in gin's fortunes. The cocktail renaissance, focused on reviving forgotten knowledge, was at first largely fueled by gin. See COCKTAIL RENAISSANCE. Old-line brands such as Plymouth, Beefeater, and Tanqueray suddenly found themselves in vogue, if not widely then deeply. Some of the larger producers cautiously essayed new bottlings, such as Bombay Sapphire (launched in 1987 to capitalize on an uptick in interest in the classic Martini), Hendrick's, and Tanqueray no. 10 (both launched in 2000). See HENDRICK'S GIN. But now there was a new factor: in 1996, the Anchor Distilling Co. of San Francisco, a then-tiny offshoot of the brewing company of the same name, launched Junipero gin. This was the pebble that starts the avalanche. Over the next twenty years, Junipero would be joined by literally hundreds of other small-producer gins. At first, this movement was confined to the United States, but by 2010 it was spreading worldwide.

It is difficult to generalize about the gin these small distilleries are making or to assign a style to it—indeed, among their many products one finds are true, rectified Old Tom, revisionist Old Tom, American genever (aged and unaged), eighteenth-century-style Dutch pot-still genever, and classic London Dry gin, along with a myriad of gins using nontraditional base spirits; unusual, often local, botanicals; or both. While it's true that the vast majority of these fall more or less in the English style, with a neutral base spirit that is rectified with botanicals, there are numerous examples where the base spirit is anything but neutral, and many of the English-style ones don't taste remotely like traditional London dry gin. Any category that can contain them all must be so loosely defined as to be meaningless.

Eventually, these new gins will sort themselves into consistent new categories or align themselves with older ones. In the meanwhile, as Mao Zedong said, "Let a hundred flowers bloom."

Dillon, Patrick. *The Much-Lamented Death of Madam Geneva*. London: Review, 2002.

Harper, William T. *Origins and Rise of the British Distillery*. Lewiston, NY: Edwin Mellen, 1999.

Hassall, Arthur Hill. *Food and Its Adulterations; Comprising the Reports of the Analytical Sanitary Commission of "The Lancet" for the Years 1851 to 1854*. London: Longman, Brown, Green & Longmans, 1855.

Montefiore, Joshua. *A Commercial Dictionary*. London: 1803.

Mr. Seager and Mr. Evans: The Story of a Great Partnership. London: Seager & Evans, 1964.

Smyth, William A. *The Publican's Guide, or, Key to the Distill-House*. London: 1781.

David Wondrich

Mixology

Gin is alone among the major spirits categories in being mostly consumed in mixed drinks. That was not always the case: during the gin craze, it was almost invariably drunk by the dram, neat. By the 1730s, however, references to "Gin Punch" begin to appear in England. By the early nineteenth century, this high-low combination had evolved into Gin Twist (a short, impromptu punch) and would become known as the Collins. See COLLINS. The combination of gin and bitters, which in America would evolve into Cock-Tail, is of a similar antiquity. See COCK-TAIL. The introduction of English gin to the United States in the mid-nineteenth century helped to revolutionize the American art of the bar: drinks such as the Gin Fizz, the Martini, the Gin Rickey, all based on Old Tom, Plymouth, or London dry gin, were among the most popular of their day. See GIN FIZZ; MARTINI; and GIN RICKEY. By the turn of the twentieth century, the ascendancy of the Dry Martini ensured that London dry gin would dominate the whole category, thrusting the other English gins and Dutch genever into the background. The cocktail renaissance has seen that process reversed, with new gin drinks being created as new styles appear or old ones are resurrected.

See also BUCHU BRANDY AND BUCHU GIN; CARTER-HEAD STILL; and SLOE GIN.

Ashworth, William J. *Customs and Excise: Trade, Production, and Consumption in England, 1640–1845*. Oxford: Oxford University Press, 2003.

The **Gin and Tonic** is a member of the highball category of drink, combining a spirit (typically London dry gin) with a carbonated, nonalcoholic mixer (in this case tonic or quinine water), and served on ice in a highball glass. See HIGHBALL. The drink dates back to the latter part of the nineteenth century, from most accounts in British colonial India, with British soldiers mixing gin with their antimalarial quinine water. While a great many cocktail origin stories don't hold up to factual scrutiny, the Gin and Tonic's might just be accurate: it first appears in print in an 1868 description of the races at Sealkote (now Sialkot), near Lahore, and as early as 1881 it is referred to as "the drink most patronised in India."

Quinine is an extract from the bark of the cinchona tree, native to South America. See TONIC WATER. It was identified by the indigenous peoples of that continent, as well as French and Italian researchers, as being of use in treating chills, fever, and malaria, all common in tropical climes. On May 28, 1858, Britain's Erasmus Bond patented the first "aerated tonic liquid," soda water spiked with quinine (an extract of South American chinchona bark)—in other words, tonic water. It was first sold only in India and other British possessions in the tropics, and indeed was rather a rarity elsewhere until the 1920s.

Traditionally, the Gin and Tonic is made with twice as much tonic water as gin, with a garnish of either a wedge of lime (most common) or lemon (more popular in the United Kingdom and

Commonwealth nations). The drink only made it to America in the mid-1930s, but it rapidly became a summertime classic. It is featured in Charles H. Baker Jr.'s seminal 1939 book, *The Gentleman's Companion*, in which Baker noted that the drink was "originated to combat fevers, real or alleged" and "became accepted over here by American hosts who wanted to impress folk with having combed the Orient." Baker also observed that "Americans, and some Britishers not so hidebound as to insist on brassy, half-warm drinks, added 2 lumps of ice, and a twist of lime peel." In his 1948 book *The Fine Art of Mixing Drinks*, David Embury agreed, noting that "four to five cubes is none too much for a 14- to 16- ounce Collins glass. There is nothing more insipid than a lukewarm drink." See EMBURY, DAVID A. As to quantity, Baker offered the following warning to "those who embrace this drink to remember it is a medicine and not primarily a stimulant only. . . . We suggest from 2 to 4 drinks of gin and tonic as being plenty for any one sitting." By the 1950s, the Gin and Tonic had become one of the identifying marks of the northeastern white, Anglo-Saxon Protestant—basically, the summer adjunct to the Dry Martini.

In popular culture, Ernest Hemingway featured the drink in his 1938 short story "The Denunciation," set at Chicote's Bar in Madrid during the Spanish Civil War, and he later offered his own variation on the Gin and Tonic in his novel *Islands in the Stream*, set in Bimini and Cuba, in which the character Thomas Hudson enjoyed the drink "with a piece of lime peel in the glass and a few drops of Angostura in the drink."

Additionally, Ian Fleming featured the drink in his 1958 James Bond novel *Dr. No*, featuring the drink (a double) being made of the juice of "one whole green lime."

Today, the Gin and Tonic is enjoying a renaissance, particularly in Spain, where craft bartenders are creating variations on the drink using a variety of additional ingredients, ranging from amaro to bitters to aperitif to herbs and botanicals to vermouth and other fortified wines, not to mention the burgeoning range of artisanal and craft gins on the market. Further, the arrival of premium and artisanal brands of tonic water, as well as the implementation of improved delivery systems in bars and restaurants (featuring house-made tonic waters using tonic syrup and charged water), has greatly improved the quality and variety of contemporary offerings.

Recipe: Combine 30 ml gin and 60 ml tonic water in a highball glass, and garnish with a lime wedge.

See also BAKER, CHARLES HENRY, JR.

Anglo Indian [pseud.]. "Tonic." *London Sporting Times*, May 14, 1881, 2.

Baker, Charles H., Jr. *The Gentleman's Companion—Being an Exotic Drinking Book or, Around the World with Jigger, Beaker and Flask*. New York: Crown, 1946.

"Sealkote Races." *Oriental Sporting Magazine*, November 16, 1868, 1838.

Philip Greene

Gin Buck, a variation of the refreshing long drink known as the Buck, combines gin with citrus juice and ginger ale. See also BUCK; GIN; and LONG DRINK.

The **Gin Fizz**, with gin, lemon juice, sugar, and soda water, is first recorded in 1876. Ever since, it has been the most popular of the fizzes, both unmodified and with various additions, such as egg whites (for a Silver Fizz) or fresh berries. See FIZZ and RAMOS GIN FIZZ.

Recipe: In a cocktail shaker, stir 5 ml sugar and 15 ml lemon juice; add 60 ml gin (London dry or Old Tom) and shake well with ice. Strain into a chilled tall glass (240–300 ml) and top with chilled sparkling water. Stir briefly.

David Wondrich

ginger ale and ginger beer are very similar beverages that at one time were the same but have evolved to represent slightly different products. Ginger has for centuries been used as a medicinal compound as well as a beverage flavor. The earliest ginger concoctions were fermented like beers and wine to produce ginger beer that had a light alcohol content of 2–3 percent, with recipes being handed down through the generations. Many recipes for the fermented version were published in books, and advertisements for bottled ginger beer appear in the early 1800s as one of the first carbonated mineral waters to add a flavor.

In the 1800s, the terms ginger ale and ginger beer were interchangeable, but eventually they became somewhat distinct products. Ginger beer became associated with the fermented beverage and was targeted by the temperance movement because of its alcohol content. Ginger ale became associated with the nonalcoholic, artificially carbonated version.

Ginger ale was used as a mixer in highballs in the 1800s, and recipes can be found in books from that period. In William Schmidt's book *The Flowing Bowl*, ginger beer is used in a number of drinks including the Bridge Brace and the Easter Crocus.

Belfast ginger ale was often described in publications as the finest ginger ale available. The key ingredient that made Belfast ginger ale popular was capsaicin from hot peppers. The capsaicin was used to duplicate the spicy zing of fresh ginger because the compound in ginger that give it its kick, gingerol, rapidly breaks down in the presence of water, creating zingerone. Zingerone is far less pungent than gingerol, hence the need to add an approximate replacement. Today, ginger beers still use capsaicin to boost their flavor profile, giving it a distinctly spicy quality.

A typical ginger ale formulation would be made using fresh ginger or ginger extract, capsaicin tincture, sugar, and citric acid, as well as flavoring compounds like lemon or orange oil and sometimes caramel coloring. This mixture is prepared either as a syrup or bottled with carbonated water but could also be mixed with water and fermented.

Nowadays the key difference between ginger ale and ginger beer is that modern ginger ale is a much milder product that lacks the spicy punch of its sibling. Ginger ale should not contain capsaicin tincture, though there are no regulations that control this, and some brands may contain capsaicin.

One of the modern inventors of modern ginger ale was John McLaughlin, a graduate of the University of Toronto pharmacy program, who patented a formula for "Dry Pale Ginger Ale." This product is still sold worldwide today as Canada Dry Ginger Ale.

Ginger ale is a very popular mixer at bars. The most common combinations of ginger ale are with basic whisky or blended scotch. The Vodka and Ginger is a simple take on the Moscow Mule, which uses spicy ginger beer, lime juice, and vodka and is served in a copper mug. There are many popular cocktails made with ginger beer such as the aforementioned Moscow Mule and others like the Dark and Stormy, Horse's Neck, Kentucky Buck, and the Gin-Gin Mule. See GIN-GIN MULE.

Donovan, Tristan. *Fizz: How Soda Shook Up the World*. Chicago: Chicago Review Press, 2013.
O'Neil, Darcy. *Fix the Pumps*. N.p.: Art of Drink, 2009.

Darcy O'Neil

The **Gin-Gin Mule** is a long drink created by Audrey Saunders (1962–) in 2000 for Beacon Restaurant in New York City and was featured on the menu of her seminal New York City bar, Pegu Club. Inspired by the Moscow Mule and Mojito, it is considered a modern classic and one of the most influential cocktails of the twenty-first century. The Gin-Gin Mule is composed of London dry gin, muddled mint, sugar, lime juice, and an uncarbonated fresh ginger infusion, which Ms. Saunders has described as "non-negotiable" and essential to the character of the drink.

The Mojito was just starting to become popular in New York City in 1999 when Dale DeGroff taught Saunders how to make the drink at their short-lived restaurant bar Blackbird, and it quickly became one of her favorites. This was the first time Saunders had experienced the use of fresh herbs in a cocktail, and, desiring to incorporate the Mojito's fresh mint flavor into her burgeoning exploration of gin, she replaced the Mojito's white rum with gin. Further experimentation led Saunders to seek an ingredient that would enhance the gin's botanicals, and for this she turned to a ginger beer she had already developed for use in a drink at Beacon named the Jamaican Firefly. Spicy fresh ginger tempered by cooling mint proved a winning combination with London dry gin's juniper-forward botanicals, and the drink was born.

Recipe: Combine 22.5 ml fresh lime juice, 30 ml simple syrup, and 6 sprigs of mint in mixing glass and muddle. Add 45 ml gin, 30 ml ginger beer, and ice, and shake well. Strain into a highball glass filled with ice, and garnish with mint leaves.

See also SAUNDERS, AUDREY; and DEGROFF, DALE.

DeGroff, Dale. *The Craft of the Cocktail*. New York: Clarkson Potter, 2002.

Samuel Lloyd Kinsey

The **Gin Rickey**, with gin, lime juice, and sparkling water, is a cooling highball that is the official Cocktail of Washington, DC. It is a variation on the original Rickey, which was made with bourbon whisky, and is first found in print in 1893. See RICKEY.

Recipe: In a tall glass (240–300 ml), combine 45 ml gin (London dry or Old Tom) and the juice of half a lime. Add ice cubes and the squeezed-out lime shell and top with chilled sparkling water. Stir briefly.

"Gin Rickey and Joe Rickey." *Buffalo (NY) Courier*, August 9, 1893, 3.

Derek Brown

Gin Sling was the most popular variation of the sling—and, in fact, one of the most popular drinks of any kind—in post-Revolutionary America. See GENEVER and SLING.

glass, cocktail, also known as a "Martini glass," is more than an item of glassware; it is a worldwide icon that wherever its image—the inverted right triangle, the slender stem, the halfhearted stabilizing base—is displayed proclaims "drinks served here." Ironically, it was never intended as a cocktail glass at all.

In the early nineteenth century, when the cocktail was still "Cock-Tail," a specific drink, not a broad class of them, it was served in the standard unstemmed, heavy-bottomed "small bar glass"—what we know today as an "Old-Fashioned glass." See COCK-TAIL and GLASSWARE. Small, stemmed glasses were known and used—and even small, stemmed conical glasses—but as wine glasses and dram glasses, not for American mixed drinks. See DRAM. But the original Cock-Tail was made either without ice or with a small lump or two in the glass. Once bartenders began stirring or tossing the drink with ice and then straining it, a stemmed glass was required so that the chilled drink would not be warmed by the heat of the drinker's hand. See TOSSING. At first, as one finds in bartender's guides from the 1860s, wine glasses were used, either plain or "fancy." These usually had a rounded bowl, curving inwards at the top. By the early 1870s, however, one begins to see recipes calling specifically for a "cocktail glass," and before long these begin to appear in glassware catalogues. The bowl is still rounded, but the glass has dispensed with the incurving rim (perhaps to make it easier to strain the cocktail into it from the height

The typical cocktail glass, ca. 1910, *left*, and post-1930, *right*. Wondrich Collection.

at which bartenders usually performed that action), but the sides are higher than those of a proper champagne coupe.

By the end of the century, a type of conical glass had come into use for cocktails, but its cone was narrower than that on the iconic one and was truncated at the bottom, creating a flat part where it met the stem, which was often ornamented. In 1925, however, the Austrian J & L Lobmeyr crystal firm included a line of glassware designed by the Austrian architect Oswald Haerdtl (1899–1959) among its numerous entries in the Paris Exposition Internationale des Arts Décoratifs, the first major international design showcase after the First World War (and the birthplace of art deco). The exposition's rules stipulated that all items exhibited must be of entirely new design, a challenge Haerdtl's "Ambassador" line met with, among other things, a champagne coupe that had an unprecedentedly wide, conical bowl, just short of a right triangle, with slightly flared sides that merged seamlessly into a tall, slender stem.

Haerdtl's design was an immediate hit and was quickly imitated by other designers, many of them straightening out the slight flare and making it strictly geometrical. At first these glasses were indeed used for champagne, as one sees in several Hollywood movies from the late 1920s. By 1933, however, when America repealed Prohibition, the style was the last word in cocktail glasses. It did not hurt that its simplified outline made it a natural choice for portraying in neon.

The early cocktail glasses were very small, holding from 75 to 90 ml. Haerdtl's design, although elegant, was quite prone to spillage if filled anywhere close to the rim, yet if the "wash line" was too low, customers would think they were being cheated. See TENSION LINE. That led to bigger glasses—which the customers then expected to be filled. By 1939 this vicious circle had led to the "double Martini glass," which held from 180 to 240 ml. After the Second World War, the glass kept growing. By the 1970s, a double Martini glass might hold as much as 480 ml, a paralyzing amount of liquid given the ultradry Martinis of the day, or really any Martini, no matter how you mix it. With the cocktail renaissance of the twenty-first century, sanity reasserted itself and the standard size was closer to 150 ml. Indeed, the sanity even went beyond that, in resurrecting the use of parallel-sided or even incurved coupes and "Nick and Nora" glasses—just as elegant

as Haerdtl's design and far less likely to spill. See COCKTAIL RENAISSANCE.

See also EXPOSITIONS AND WORLD'S FAIRS.

"American Fancy Drinks." *New York Sun*, August 22, 1873, 3.

Fiederer, Luke. "AD Classics: Exposition Internationale des Arts Décoratifs et Industriels Modernes." *ArchDaily*, August 19, 2016. www.archdaily.com/793367/ad-classics-exposition-internationale-des-arts-decoratifs-et-industriels-modernes (accessed April 11, 2021).

Wondrich, David. *Imbibe!*, 2nd ed. New York: Perigee, 2015.

David Wondrich

glass, Martini, is a name commonly used for the classic stemmed cocktail glass with the inverted-cone bowl—a usage that has led to drinks served in such a glass but bearing no resemblance to an actual Martini falling under its rubric on cocktail menus. See also GLASS, COCKTAIL; GLASSWARE; and MARTINI.

glass, Old-Fashioned, is a short, heavy-bottomed tumbler used to serve its namesake cocktail and other mixed drinks, also used for straight spirits with ice (hence, its alias: a rocks glass). In the nineteenth century, it was known as the "small bar glass." See also OLD-FASHIONED COCKTAIL and ROCKS.

glassware is not an easy topic to address concisely: over the thousand-odd years during which there has been a well-documented spirits industry at least in one part of the world or another, people have poured those spirits, mixed or unmixed, into a dizzying array of glasses: dram glasses, punch glasses, rummers, tiffs, chimneys, tulips—the list goes on and on. The 1913–1914 Albert Pick & Co. hotel- and restaurant-supply catalogue features sixty pages of glasses, illustrated to the tune of some thirty to the page. And that's just the standard American stuff. There are more kinds today even in America, and once one factors in the rest of the world—15-ml Chinese baijiu glasses, 50-ml Serbian *čokanj* flasks (for rakija), copitas for mezcal, absinthe glasses, tiki mugs, the huge stemmed goblets they serve the Negroni Sbagliato in at Bar Basso in Milan, on and on—there is no hope of covering even a representative sample of them all. Given that, it seems wise to focus on the few basic types that serve as the backbone of modern bar service.

Originally, which is to say at from the mid-eighteenth century to the beginning of the nineteenth, British and American bars—the most direct progenitors of the modern bar—had only a handful of glass types for spirits and mixed drinks. They had wine glasses, which were small and stemmed and generally v-shaped, which were also used for punch (a "wine glass" was in fact a standard measure and was two ounces, or 60 ml). They had dram glasses, which were a little sturdier and perhaps a little smaller. The rummer, a footed glass with a large bowl, varied widely in size but held at least six ounces (180 ml) and sometimes two or three times that.

The American bar of the early nineteenth century, with its novel devotion to the ins and outs of iced drinks, changed this around slightly. For one thing, Americans didn't like stems as much as the British did: early American glasses tended to sit right on the bar, foregoing the commanding elevation a stem gives. The dram glass became a whisky or brandy glass, which held some two ounces (60 ml) and maybe a little more and had a heavy bottom, in part to give it the illusion that it held still more. After Prohibition, this shrank into the one-and-a-half to two-ounce (45–60 ml) shot glass, with the same heavy bottom.

Next in size was the "small bar glass." Heavy-bottomed and slant-sided, this glass held five or six ounces (150–180 ml) and was used both for mixing and for serving cocktails and other "short drinks." In his 1862 *The Bar-Tender's Guide*, Jerry Thomas specifies it for smashes, slings, toddies, spirit-based sangarees, fixes, skins, the Knickerbocker, the Blue Blazer, and of course the various cocktails—"short drinks," as they called them in Europe. See THOMAS, JEREMIAH P. "JERRY." By the 1880s, its mixing use had fallen by the wayside, and it was used mainly for the Old-Fashioned (basically, a whisky cocktail as it had been made before syrup, straining, and stemware) and related drinks, such as New Orleans's Sazerac Cocktail, for which it is still used. See COCKTAIL and SAZERAC COCKTAIL. In the 1930s and 1940s, the size of the glass began creeping up as Old-Fashioneds gained bulky fruit garnishes; by

the end of the 1940s eight- or nine-ounce (240 or 270 ml) versions were common, followed rapidly by the 12- to 16-ounce (360–480 ml) Double Old-Fashioned, aka "bucket," glass. Eventually this edged out the single glass. By the end of the century, a preference for straight sides rather than slanted ones had turned the glass into a squat, heavy-bottomed cylinder. Nowadays, the bucket glass is used for straight spirits, spirits on ice and rocks, and drinks such as Old-Fashioneds, Caipirinhas, and Margaritas; the single glass is only found holding Sazeracs, and even that is rare.

Just as there was a small bar glass, there was also a large bar glass. This was a tall, slant-sided affair that held 12–16 ounces (360–480 ml). As with the small glass, this was both a mixing glass and a serving one, since the custom was to mix drinks in the glass in which they were served. With the introduction of the shaker tin in the 1840s, that did not change. Punches, guleps (often shaken at the time), beer- and wine-based sangarees, eggnogs, and other "long drinks" (as the Europeans dubbed them) were all built, shaken, and served in the glass.

As glassware became more specialized, it became far less common to use the large bar glass as a service glass or the small one as a mixing glass. By 1900, a bartender might serve the occasional Mint Julep in the large glass or mix a Sazerac in the small one (that was the nostalgic ritual that the Sazerac House came up with for the drink), but usually the large glass was strictly for mixing and the small one strictly for serving drinks in. This usage lasted throughout the twentieth century, although with the craft beer movement of the 1970s the pint mixing glass got drafted to serve as the American pint beer glass (Americans had not previously made much use of pints for beer, so these were the only pint glasses that most bars had).

Nowadays, since bars are very well stocked with pint glasses, they are also used for large rocks drinks such as the Bloody Mary and often take the place of the Collins glass. Many bartenders, however, prefer to shake drinks in all-metal shakers and stir their drinks in cylindrical Japanese-style spouted glasses (the parallel sides make stirring much easier, as the ice has more room to move).

Once bartenders were stirring their cocktails with ice and then straining them off it (as Jerry Thomas detailed for his "fancy" cocktails), the drink demanded a stemmed glass, so that the patron's hand would not be chilled by the drink and his drink not warmed by his hand. For the cocktail glass, the answer to this problem, see GLASS, COCKTAIL.

When, in the 1850s, the sour was a new drink, it went into the same small bar glass as socktails and other short drinks. But once the cocktail got its own stemmed glass, there was a problem. All the ingredients that went into a cocktail were supposed to add up to one two-ounce (60 ml) jigger, give or take a spoonful here and a dash there. Sours, however, began with a jigger of booze and then added citrus juice and a sweetener, and often a red wine float. This meant that they wouldn't fit into the standard cocktail glass. Enter the narrowish, tapered, footed five- or six-ounce (150–180 ml) sour glass. Without the foot, it was a "Delmonico" glass, named after the famous New York restaurant. By the twentieth century, the standard sour glass often took on aspects of the champagne flute, with a short stem and sides that gently curved in at the top, although the older, slant-sided version was—and is—still common. When cocktail glasses got bigger, sours could be served in them, too, and the sour glass began falling away. See SOUR.

The fizz glass and the Collins glass round out the traditional suite of barroom glasses. Both were introduced in the 1870s, both were cylindrical, and both were narrow, so that the carbonated drinks they were meant to hold would stay that way. The Fizz glass, however, held about six ounces (180 ml), while the Collins glass, meant to hold ice as well as citrus and gin, held two to four times that. With the introduction of the highball in the 1890s, it went first into the fizz glass, and then an intermediate 8- to 12-ounce (240–360 ml) glass bridged the distance between the fizz and the Collins glasses. See COLLINS; FIZZ; and HIGHBALL.

One could go on, through champagne coupes (sometimes used for cocktails) and flutes (also used, although less commonly), to the specialized glasses demanded by various nitpicky drinks such as the Pousse Café, the Irish Coffee, the Hurricane (a huge glass modeled on the hurricane-lamp chimney glass), the Moscow Mule (a copper mug, because why not), and on to tiny cordial glasses, enormous brandy snifters, and so forth. But it is always worth remembering the immensely popular bar the late Gary Regan worked at on New York's Upper East Side during the 1970s, which stocked only one kind of glass. Whatever you ordered, it went into a white wine glass. Nobody complained. See REGAN, GARY.

Albert Pick & Co. *General Catalog 1913–4*. 1913; repr., n.p. Ross Bolton: 2008.

DeGroff, Dale. *The New Craft of the Cocktail*, rev. ed. New York: Clarkson Potter, 2020.

Hartshorne, Albert. *Antique Drinking Glasses*. New York: Brussel & Brussel, 1968.

Johnson, Byron A., and Sharon P. Johnson. *Wild West Bartender's Bible*. Austin: Texas Monthly Press, 1986.

Morgenthaler, Jeffrey. *The Bar Book*. San Francisco: Chronicle, 2014.

Wondrich, David. *Imbibe!*, 2nd ed. New York: Perigee, 2015.

David Wondrich

The **Glenfiddich** distillery in Dufftown (in the Speyside region) is the core business of William Grant & Sons, Scotland's largest independent, family-owned whisky distiller. The original distillery was built by William Grant (1839–1923) and his family in 1887, and the first whisky was distilled on Christmas Day of that year. Descendants of the family still own the company. See SCOTLAND AND IRELAND.

This is a huge facility, with a capacity of 14 million liters a year, making it the second-largest malt distillery in Scotland, eclipsed only by the Macallan, which after its recent expansion makes 15 million liters a year. See MACALLAN. The twenty-eight pot stills are maintained by in-house coppersmiths, and a staff of coopers build and repair casks, work that has largely been outsourced at other distilleries.

Glenfiddich was a pioneer in marketing and exporting single malt whisky, beginning in the early 1960s, using their signature triangular bottle, introduced in 1956. They were also the first to open their doors to tourists, in 1969.

The flagship expression is twelve years old. The Glenfiddich brand was the world's best-selling single malt until 2015, when rival Glenlivet inched ahead.

Though large, the distillery continues to experiment with wood finishes and special bottlings. The standard fifteen-year-old expression is a product of the distillery's "solera vat," a unique system where mature whiskies from different types of casks are mingled in a large wooden vat. Half of the vat is drawn off and bottled, then it is filled again; it never fully empties, so the whisky is a mingling of all the casks ever poured into it.

See also WHISKY, SINGLE-MALT, GLOBAL.

Broom, Dave. *The World Atlas of Whisky*, rev. ed. London: Mitchell Beazley, 2014.
Glenfiddich website. http://www.glenfiddich.com/ (accessed February 11, 2021).

Lew Bryson

The **Glenlivet** is a whisky distillery in the Speyside district of Highland Scotland—the first in that region to take out a distilling license, in 1824. The founder was George Smith (1792–1871), a tenant of the Duke of Gordon. The duke was largely responsible for promoting the Excise Act of 1823, which encouraged illicit distillers to "go legal." Smith had been making whisky illegally since at least 1815, and when—urged by his landlord—he applied for a license, his former colleagues threatened to, in his words, "burn the distillery to the ground, and me at the heart of it. The laird of Aberlour presented me with a pair of hair-trigger pistols worth ten guineas, and they were never out of my belt for ten years." Today these pistols are displayed in the distillery's visitor center.

The illicit spirit from Glenlivet already had a high reputation: when King George IV visited Edinburgh in 1822, he reportedly "drank nothing else." Andrew Usher & Co, of Edinburgh, were offering it for sale in 1821 and were sole agents for the make by 1844 and were offering "the Real Glenlivet Whisky" for sale in London (the first scotch to be promoted there). In 1853 they used it in the first ever branded scotch whisky, Usher's Old Vatted Glenlivet.

In 1840, George Smith was able to lease another farm nearby and open a second, small, distillery. In 1859 he moved his operations to the present site at Minmore, half a mile from his original distillery. He was succeeded by his son, John Gordon Smith, in 1871. By the 1880s the name Glenlivet had become synonymous with quality: thirty distilleries, some of them miles from the glen itself, attached it to their own. This gave rise to Glenlivet being described as "the longest glen in Scotland." In 1884, J. G. Smith obtained a court order that only his whisky could be described as "The Glenlivet."

As soon as Prohibition was lifted in America, George Smith's great-grandson went there to promote his whisky, the first single malt ever seen in the United States. It caused such a stir that he made it onto the front page of *Time* magazine, with the line: "The heart of Great Britain's export trade is the Scotch whisky industry. The heart of the Scotch industry is The Glenlivet." Now owned by Chivas Brothers, the scotch whisky division of Pernod-Ricard, the Glenlivet is the second-bestselling single malt in the world. See PERNOD-RICARD. Capacity was increased by 75 percent at the distillery in 2010 (to 10.5 million liters of pure alcohol), and there are plans for further substantial expansion in the near future. The Glenlivet's signature expression, a twelve-year-old malt made without influence of peat or sherry, is a subtle, even delicate whisky that is considered one of the benchmarks of the category.

See also SINGLE MALT.

Francis, Edward. *The Glenlivet: Spirit of the Place*. Whitley, UK: Good Books, 1997.
Glenlivet: Where Romance and Business Meet. Ballindalloch, UK: Glenlivet Distillery, 1959.
Grant, Elizabeth. *Memoirs of a Highland Lady*. Edinburgh: Cannongate, 1898.
MacLean, Charles. *Scotch Whisky: A Liquid History*. London: Cassell, 1997.
Wilson, Ross. *Scotch: Its History and Romance*. Newton Abbot, UK: David & Charles, 1973.

Charles MacLean

Glenmorangie is a historic, well-respected single malt scotch distillery celebrated for its boundary-pushing wood maturation program and for its towering copper pot stills. Located in the town of Tain, Scotland, about forty miles south of Inverness, the distillery is considered to be in the northern Highlands.

Production started in 1849, five years after a gentleman named William Matheson (ca. 1805–1862) applied for a distilling license for an old brewery at Morangie, near Tain. It wasn't until 1887, however, that the Glenmorangie Distillery Company Ltd was formed, making whisky in well-used old gin stills brought north from London. Exact replicas of these unique and sinewy stills—an unusual architecture for scotch whisky pot stills—continue to lend the distillery's hallmark top notes of fruits, florals, and heather.

The brand's reputation blossomed under the helm of "whisky creator" Dr. Bill Lumsden in the 1990s, when he released a slew of what are now commonly called "finished" whiskies. The term, quite possibly popularized by his team, refers to the process of transferring whisky out of one cask and "finishing" it for flavor in another type of cask. The distillery released Madeira- and cherry-finished whiskies in 1996, and by the end of the millennium, they had also released whiskies aged in Sauternes, port, and cognac casks.

When luxury-goods titan Louis Vuitton Moet Hennessy (LVMH) purchased the brand in 2004, tensions between scotch whisky loyalists and LVMH reverberated in the media: some thought that the new packaging and label introduced in 2007 was too French. LVMH still owns Glenmorangie, and auld-alliance tensions have since settled, even if fans continue to mispronounce their popular releases such as the Nectar D'or, the Quinta Ruban, and the Lasanta.

See also SINGLE MALT and STILL, POT.

Craig, Charles H. *The Scotch Whisky Industry Record.* Glasgow: Index, 1994.
Roskrow, Dominic, Gavin D. Smith, Juergen Diebel, and Davin de Kergommeaux. *Whisky Opus: The World's Greatest Distilleries and Their Whiskey.* New York: DK, 2012.

Heather Greene

glögg is a variety of Swedish hot mulled wine akin to Austrian Glühwein, German Feuerzangenbowle, British negus, Dutch bisschopswijn, and French vin chaud and cousin to the ypocras of medieval physicians. See FEUERZANGENBOWLE and NEGUS. In Finland and Denmark, the same concoction is glögi and gløgg, respectively. Across Scandinavia, these mulled wines are traditional accompaniments to Yuletide celebrations. Known—at least in general form—to ancient Greeks and Romans, such spiced wines have been made in Scandinavia since the seventeenth century. By the mid-1900s, consumers could purchase prepared versions to heat at their leisure.

In Nordic countries, modern retailers sell alcoholic and non-alcoholic versions. Glögg can be made with *brännvin* (unflavored spirits), *saft* (fruit juice), *rödvin* (red wine), and other beverages or mixtures thereof. Typical botanicals include cinnamon, cardamom, citrus peel, and ginger. It is almost always sweetened with sugar. As with Feuerzangenbowle, that sugar is sometimes perched on a rack above the surface of wine gently simmering in a fireproof bowl or pot, soaked with spirits, and set ablaze. When about half-melted, it may be stirred into the mix. Makers often include raisins and almonds; each drinker scoops a few of each into his or her cup, drink and snack all in one.

See also MULLED DRINKS and SCANDINAVIA.

Fredrikson, Karin. *The Great Scandinavian Cook Book.* New York: Crown, 1967.
Meehan, Thomas. "Yma Dream." *New Yorker*, February 24, 1962.
Nilsson, Magnus. *The Nordic Cookbook.* New York: Phaidon, 2015.

Matthew Rowley

glycerin, also known as glycerol ($C_3H_8O_3$), is a nontoxic sugar alcohol that occurs naturally in food and is soluble in both alcohol and water. It is an excellent solvent and is often used to increase the solubility of organic compounds in water for products with low alcohol content. It can also be added to spirits to increase viscosity, body, or mouthfeel and add sweetness. Glycerin has been used to smooth out the harsh characteristics of poorly distilled spirits and mask flaws in those products (it is commonly found in cheap vodkas). See TEXTURE AND MOUTHFEEL.

O'Neil, Darcy. "Glycerol in Vodka Results." *Art of Drink*, February 27, 2011. https://www.artofdrink.com/science/glycerol-in-vodka-results (accessed February 11, 2021).

Darcy O'Neil

gomme syrup is the quasi-French term for gum syrup, a rich sugar syrup ostensibly thickened with gum arabic that was favored by nineteenth-century bartenders, although many of them quietly omitted the actual gum. See GUM SYRUP.

Gooderham & Worts, the pioneering Canadian whisky maker, traces its beginnings to what is now Toronto in 1837, when William Gooderham

(1790–1881), a Norfolk-born miller, built a small distillery to dispose of waste wheat and barley. In 1845, his nephew, James Gooderham Worts (1818–1882), installed copper pot stills to supplant the existing wooden one and added rye to the recipe to satisfy consumer demand for more flavor. See STILL, THREE-CHAMBER. In 1859, the company invested $200,000 in a new five-story stone distillery. By the 1860s, the *Montreal Gazette* reported it was the largest distillery in the world, producing 11.4 million liters (3 million US gallons) of whisky annually, making it the largest taxpayer in British North America. Rising prohibition sentiments in the family's Protestant faith dampened their enthusiasm, and their distillery languished. Entrepreneur Harry Hatch purchased it in 1923, selling the whisky to rumrunners. Commercial success enabled him, in 1926, to purchase Hiram Walker's distillery in Windsor, and he began moving production there. By 1957, whisky making stopped at Gooderham & Worts, and the distillery switched to making antifreeze. Today the converted distillery complex is a housing, shopping, and entertainment district, although the brand has recently been revived by Pernod-Ricard for a four-grain whisky made at the company's Corby distillery in Windsor, Ontario.

See also HIRAM WALKER AND SONS; and WHISKY, CANADIAN.

De Kergommeaux, Davin. *Canadian Whisky, Second Edition: The New Portable Expert.* Vancouver: Appetite by Random House, 2017.

Davin de Kergommeaux

Gordon's is a venerable brand of London dry gin. See LONDON DRY GIN. Founded by Alexander Gordon (1742–1821) in 1769 and family-owned until 1877, it is currently owned by Diageo and is the bestselling gin in the world. See also DIAGEO and TANQUERAY GORDON & CO.

grain-based spirits encompass a vast array of the world's distilled beverages, including spirits as disparate as scotch whisky and Korean soju. Their unifying trait is that they are all distilled from the dry fruit of cultivated grasses—otherwise known as cereal grain, or simply grain. Unlike spirits distilled from fruit, sugar cane, or agave, which all contain sugar, grain-based spirits must rely on saccharification to convert a grain's starch into sugar before it can undergo fermentation and thereby produce the ethanol (ethyl alcohol) that is subsequently concentrated by distillation. See SACCHARIFICATION; FERMENTATION; and ETHANOL.

In the Western world, whisky is perhaps the spirit most closely associated with grain, if only because all whiskies are made from grain. See WHISKY. Malted barley serves as the traditional cornerstone for most of the whisky made in Scotland and Ireland (as well as in Japan and India), though grain whisky distilled in column stills from other grains makes up the lion's share of most blends. See BARLEY and WHISKY, GRAIN. Scotland's single malt whisky is distilled in pot stills entirely from unmalted barley, while Ireland's pot still whisky is made from a blend of malted and unmalted barley. See SCOTLAND AND IRELAND and SINGLE MALT.

Corn (or maize) is the basic building block of many of the whiskies made in the United States and Canada. See CORN and UNITED STATES AND CANADA. Although Canadian whisky is often referred to as rye, corn is usually the predominant grain in blends. See RYE. American whisky labeled "corn whisky" is made from a mash containing at least 80 percent corn. See MASH. Both bourbon and Tennessee whisky are made from a mash containing at least 51 percent corn, with malted barley and either wheat or rye making up the remainder. The proportions of rye and corn are reversed in American rye whisky; likewise for wheat and corn in wheat whisky. American craft distillers have also experimented with whiskies made predominantly from other grains, such as spelt and triticale (a rye/wheat hybrid). Corn is also used extensively in Africa for a variety of spirits. Some are industrialized, but most are unbranded and made by small-scale pot distillation for local sale. Often the corn is combined with millet or cassava chips. See CENTRAL AND EAST AFRICA and KWETE.

Although there is a common misperception that vodka is typically made from potatoes, most vodka is actually made from grain—particularly wheat, but also rye, corn, and barley. See VODKA. The same holds true for gin (which is essentially a juniper-flavored vodka). See GIN. It's not uncommon for producers of vodka and gin to purchase grain neutral spirits that they then redistill and dilute before bottling. See NEUTRAL SPIRITS. Contemporary versions of genever, the precursor to gin, are made by blending neutral spirits with malt wine, a whisky-like spirit typically made from any combination of rye, corn, wheat, and malted barley. See GENEVER. And while aquavit is often made from potatoes, it can also be made from grain, as can a number of other spirits that call for neutral spirits. See AQUAVIT.

China's national spirit, baijiu, is typically made mostly from sorghum, often mixed with wheat, though some baijiu is made from rice or other grains. See BAIJIU; SORGHUM; and RICE. Rice is also the traditional foundation for Korean soju and Japanese shochu. See SOJU and SHOCHU. In the Himalayan nations of Nepal and Tibet, millet is the basis for most raksi, a sort of moonshine made in rustic stills.

LaVilla, Joseph. "Grain-Based Spirits." In The Wine, Beer, and Spirits Handbook, 359–370. Hoboken, NJ: John Wiley, 2010.

David Mahoney

The **Grand Hotel** was a renowned establishment in Yokohama, Japan. In 1890, the hotel put in a new bar, bringing in Louis Eppinger from Oregon to run it. See BAMBOO COCKTAIL. Under his skilled management, the bar gained an international reputation (particularly for its Dry Martinis) and introduced modern American drink mixing to Japan, which embraced the art and made it its own. See DRY.

David Wondrich

Grand Marnier, a proprietary brand of curaçao made in France from bitter oranges and cognac, has long been one of the most prestigious liqueurs on the market. Its roots date to 1827, when the Lapostolle family founded a cognac distillery in Neauphle-le-Château. In 1876, Julia Lapostolle married Louis-Alexandre Marnier. Soon after, the family founded the House of Marnier Lapostolle. In 1891, Marnier created a premium curaçao for the famous Café Royal in London, replacing the neutral spirit customarily used for a final infusion of orange peels with aged cognac purchased by the café. Soon after, he repeated the process for restaurateur Louis Auguste Paillard in Paris, who suggested Marnier distinguish the bottle of his "Curaçao Royal" with a red ribbon and then sued him (unsuccessfully) when the brand, which Marnier was now selling to the general public, became successful. By 1899, it had become so successful that Marnier changed its name to Grand Marnier, to avoid comparison with ordinary curaçaos.

Marnier's original formula, which according to the family remains unchanged, uses peels of the *bigarade*, or Seville orange, which are both distilled and infused in young cognac to make the standard Cordon Rouge. There is also a Cordon Jaune, based entirely on neutral spirits, and a number of rarer expressions, such as the rarified Quintessence, which features a blend of cognacs that are up to a century old.

The Mimosa, the staple of brunch and daytime drinking, is believed to have been invented at the Paris Ritz in 1898; the original version combined champagne with orange juice and Grand Marnier. See MIMOSA.

Grand Marnier was served on the Titanic, where passengers would have been offered a sip of the liqueur at the end of their meals. An unopened bottle recovered from the Titanic's crash site is now on display at the Titanic Belfast museum.

More recently, the popularity of AMC's *Mad Men* put a spotlight on nuclear-era cocktails. The B-52, named after the US long-range bombers, is a mix of Grand Marnier, Kahlua, and Bailey's Irish Cream.

See also COGNAC.

Clarkson, Janet. Food History Almanac: Over 1,300 Years of World Culinary History, Culture, and Social Influence. Lanham, MD: Rowman & Littlefield, 2014.
Gelman, Judy, and Peter Zheutlin. The Unofficial Mad Men Cookbook: Inside the Kitchens, Bars, and Restaurants of Mad Men. Dallas: BenBella, 2011
Pouillet, E., et al., eds., Annales de la propriété industrielle, vol. 44. Paris: Arthur Rousseau, 1898.

Elva Ramirez

grapes provide the basis for a wealth of distilled spirits the world over. They are most common in wine-growing regions, where distillation can add value in two main situations: an abundance of grapes unfit for quality wine production, or an abundance of grape marc—the skins, seeds, and other leftover solids from winemaking. Like any fruit distillates or wine itself, the best grape spirits capture the inherent qualities of their ingredients with clarity, precision, and deliciousness.

Grape distillates fall under the category of brandy, a term used to describe a distillate of any sort of fruit. When used alone, however, it always implies a grape spirit. They can be produced from fermented grape juice (wine) or pomace—the skins, seeds, stems, and other solids left over from wine production.

History

Along with various cereal grains, palm sap, sugar cane, and agave, grapes are one of the most anciently and widely used materials for distillation of spirits. To the degree that distillation was practiced in Greco-Roman antiquity, it was based on grape wine, and there is some evidence that grape wine was distilled in China in the first millennium CE. Certainly, when medieval Europe discovered, or rediscovered, the art, it was grape wine that was the first and preferred distillation material. It was also the earliest base material to support a European spirits industry, with the development of brandy distilling in southern France, the Iberian Peninsula, and Greece and liqueur-making in Italy. See AMARO and ARMAGNAC.

The human urge to wring out the maximum amount of usefulness from any given material meant that wine distilling was often accompanied by a secondary effort to recover alcohol from the leftovers and waste from winemaking. The resulting pomace spirits were historically not well regarded, often with reason. Consider the description Pierre Duplais gives in his 1871 *Treatise on the Manufacture and Distillation of Alcoholic Liquors* of the "very objectionable" method common among French vintners: "The marc [i.e., pomace], on leaving the press, is borne to a deep pit dug in the earth and sometimes plastered with clay, in which it is packed and pressed as it is brought. When the press is full, it is covered with straw, vine leaves, and twigs, over which is thrown a thick bed of earth to prevent contact with the air. The whole is left to ferment for about six weeks." It's not hard to imagine the quality of distillate produced from the resulting fermented muck. Fortunately, conditions have improved since.

Methods

The best wine-based distillates tend to come from regions not associated with quality wine production. That's because distillation requires grapes that are more acidic and less ripe than would make a pleasant wine. Cognac may be the most famous example, made mostly from the rather dull-tasting ugni blanc. While it and the region's other local grapes will never make a head-turning wine in cognac's cold Atlantic clime, their high acidity allows for the grapes to remain pristine from vineyard to still, without the use of sulfur dioxide (a commonly used preservative in winemaking that's banned in cognac). These sharp-tasting grapes are first fermented into wine; distillation then further concentrates the wine's aromatic compounds. In order to be considered a brandy, the EU decrees that wine-based distillates be aged in wooden receptacles for at least six months. Many spend far longer than that in barrels, where oxidation as well as compounds present in the wood mellow the spirit, bringing to it warm notes of caramel, vanilla, and spice. In other parts of the world, grape distillates are not customarily aged.

Distillates made from grape pomace are more common, and they can be made either by fermenting the moist pomace directly or mixing it with water. When pomace has not had a chance to ferment—as with the pomace of many white wines, where the skins are separated from the juice early in the winemaking process—it needs to be fermented before distillation.

The resulting marc is most often presented as a white spirit, without barrel aging, the flavors focused on the aromatic compounds concentrated in the grape skins. In many places, grape marcs are varietally labeled, offering a unique window into the nature of the grape used.

Regional Distillates

While the Dutch take credit for the name "brandy," a corruption of *brandewijn*, or "burnt wine," the French are most closely associated with the spirit, with more than thirty-five legally protected brandy appellations. Cognac, named for the region along the Atlantic just north of Bordeaux, is the most famous, followed by Armagnac, a single-distilled brandy made in Gascony from a similar blend of ugni blanc, folle blanch, and Colombard with baco 22A, bottled at 50 percent ABV. Regions more known for wine, such as Burgundy, often have their own unique eau-de-vie de vin or fine, distillates made from wine, or marc, distilled from grape pomace. Grape distillates are also key to making many of France's famed for-tified wines, mistelles or vins de liqueur such as macvin, pineau de Charentes, and ratafia: the addition of distilled grape spirit kills off any sugar-eating yeasts in the wine or must, resulting in a stable, sweet, grape-based drink traditionally served as an aperitif or digestive.

Italy produces brandy but is far better known for grappa, a clear distillate made from pomace. The name comes from Bassano del Grappa, a town in Veneto where Bortolo Nardini began producing grappa in the late 1700s. The north remains most closely associated with grappa, although it's made everywhere; Sicily and Marsala claim two of the country's nine grappa geographical indications (GIs, officially recognized and defined areas of production).

Spain out-distills both countries with brandy. The country's celebrated brandy de Jerez is rather confusingly made from grapes grown and distilled in La Mancha, in central Spain, and then aged in Jerez. It's in this hot, humid southern region where the brandy takes on its characteristic flavors, the result of long aging in used sherry casks with regular circulation through a solera system, whereby younger and older brandies are slowly blended together. Brandy del Penèdes, grown and distilled in northeastern Spain, sometimes employs a solera system as well but tends to be lighter and leaner in flavors. Spain also has a long history of pomace-based spirits; the first known documented evidence of "licor de orujo" dates to 1693. While it's found all over the country, Galicia claims the most esteemed version, supported by a GI as well as a yearly festival in Potes.

In nearby Portugal, the locals produce aguardente vínica, a grape-based brandy used mainly to fortify port wines, although sometimes it's aged in oak and bottled as aguardente vínica velha. More popular is aguardente bagaçeira, distilled from pomace.

The Spanish conquistadors exported their knowledge of winegrowing and distillation to South America after arriving in the 1500s. Their vines grew particularly well in Peru, where pisco, a wine distillate, is considered the national spirit, supported by a GI; however, Chile also claims pisco to be its own. Bolivia focuses on singani, a clear distillation of the fragrant muscat of Alexandria grape, while Mexico excels with wood-aged brandies. The Spanish influence continues right up the coast into California, where brandy production dates to the 1800s. At least one California company also distills vodka from grapes.

The Dutch also played a part in spreading distilling knowledge around the world, most notably in South Africa. The country remains a power-house in the production of brandy, which they call brandewijn.

Germany and Austria have their own version of grape-based brandy called Weinbrand; Asbach, Germany's best-known company, claims that founder Hugo Asbach coined the term after the Treaty of Versailles outlawed the use of cognac outside of France. (Asbach was clearly a savvy marketer: he is also said to have introduced the liquor-filled chocolate truffle in the 1920s, targeted at women, who weren't supposed to be drinking in public.)

Eastern Europe is also rich in grape-based spirits, notably pálinka in Hungary and pálenka in Czechia; Romanian vinars (brandy); and an array of grape-based spirits that fall under variations of the word rakia/rakya that turn up from Albania, Macedonia, Serbia, Bulgaria, Montenegro, and Croatia. Go south and rakia turns into raki in the Mediterranean countries and tsipouro and tsikoudia in Greece and Cyprus, and it is often flavored with herbs and spices, especially licorice-flavored ones such as anise and fennel. See OUZO.

See also POMACE BRANDY; MARC; EAU-DE-VIE; and BRANDY, GRAPE.

Bamforth, Charles W., and Robert E. Ward, eds. *The Oxford Handbook of Food Fermentations*. Oxford: Oxford University Press, 2014.

"Brandewijn." *etymologiebank.nl*. http://www.etymologiebank.nl/trefwoord/brandewijn (accessed February 12, 2021).

Bureau National Interprofessionnel du Cognac. *L'Encyclopédie du Cognac*. http://www.pediacognac.com/ (accessed February 12, 2021).

European Commission. *E-Spirit Drinks*. http://ec.europa.eu/agriculture/spirits/index.cfm (accessed June 15, 2017).

Official Journal of the European Union. Regulation (ec) No 110/2008 of the European Parliament and of the Council. http://eur-lex.europa.eu/LexUriServ/LexUriServ.do?uri=OJ:L:2008:039:0016:0054:EN:PDF (accessed February 12, 2021).

Ridgewell, Mark. *Spirits Distilled*. Oxford: Infinite Ideas, 2014.

Tara Q. Thomas

grappa is an Italian pomace brandy, the equivalent to France's marc, and is protected by European Union and Italian law. The pomace—skins, stems, seeds, and other solid matter remaining after grapes are pressed to make wine, called *vinaccia* in Italian—must come from grapes grown and vinified in Italy and can be distilled anywhere in the country, though most grappa comes from the northern provinces. It can be distilled to a maximum of 86 percent ABV. Continuous stills are primarily used by the major industrial producers who account for the majority of grappa produced, while pot stills are mainly used in artisanal production. There are currently around 130 grappa producers in the country. It is estimated that more than 60 percent of the distilleries are in the northeast and about 20 percent in the northwest. About a third are located in the Veneto. Several of the most important ones are based in the town of Bassano del Grappa in Vicenza, the historic home of the drink and the source of the spirit's current name, which until the 1950s was as likely to be called "aquavite" or "acqua vitae." By tradition, grappa was known as "cot" in Piemonte and "sgnapa" or "graspa" in Triveneto.

By Italian law, there are a variety of defined grappas: *giovane* or *bianco*, aged a minimum of six months, usually in stainless steel or glass; *affinata in legno*, aged in wood six to twelve months; *invecchiata*, aged in wood at least twelve months; and *riserva* or *stravecchia*, aged in wood at least eighteen months. When aged in wood, some grappa sees oak, but cherry, acacia, chestnut, and other woods are used as well.

There are also grappas granted geographical names—for example, grappa di Barolo, grappa Friuli, and the like; grappa monovitigno, coming at least 85 percent from a single grape variety; and grappa aromatizzata, containing herbs, spices, or fruits like basil, chamomile, gentian, juniper, licorice, lemon balm, nettle, pine, rhubarb, or rue. Grappas called aromatica are simply made from aromatic grapes like moscato or sauvignon blanc, and they can be bottled giovane, affinata, or riserva. Regardless of the many categories, most grappa by far is unoaked and minimally aged.

To be sold, grappa must have an alcoholic content of not less than 37.5 percent ABV (40 percent for those with geographic indications) and can be as high as 60 percent. Muscat, chardonnay, cabernet sauvignon, pinot nero, and prosecco are the most used varietals.

Three varieties of vinaccia, depending on the degree of their fermentation, are used: unfermented, usually from white wines; half-fermented, usually from rosé wines; and fully fermented, from red wine. The vinaccia is then distilled in its solid form, as Italian law prohibits adding water, and is heated until the alcohol begins to evaporate and is then captured, cooled, and condensed into a liquid.

After distillation, producers are allowed to add water, as well as 2 percent sugar and 3 percent natural additives (fruits, herbs, flavors, aromas, and natural coloring) per liter of undiluted grappa. Regulations require that these additives not affect the grappaws sensory profile, but none of these additions need to be stated on the label.

The best grappa comes from fresh vinaccia, which usually has a higher residual sugar content thanks to light crushing. Single-grape-varietal grappas are usually considered more flavorful and refined, aromatically rich while retaining the earthy and sometimes petrol-like quality of more rustic grappas. They are also pricier. The single varietals from northern regions are particularly prized, since they're made with red grapes that are grown in a cool climate and possess the high acidity needed to produce finer spirits.

Grappa is traditionally consumed with espresso in a drink known as *caffé coretto*, or "corrected coffee"—espresso served with a side of grappa, some of which is added to the coffee immediately, with the remaining grappa swirled into the coffee cup after the coffee is consumed. While it is sometimes served in the morning, the practice likely developed as a result of both being presented after meals. The Instituto Nazionale Grappa recommends serving grappa in small tulip-shaped glasses with open rims, rather than balloons or narrow glasses.

Until the early 1990s, grappa was much ridiculed outside of Italy as a fiery, rough Italian moonshine, a workingman's drink made from the dregs of the winemaking process. The transformation from a rustic peasant tipple into a premium drink began in the early 1970s with producers like Giannola Nonino, who had inherited the Nonino distillery and launched the first super-premium grappa, a single varietal made from the native Friulian grape picolit using only freshly and lightly pressed pomace. Other producers, like Romano Levi, developed a cult following for rare grappas, and savvy Italian marketers began to package the spirit in elaborate hand-blown Murano glass bottles.

With the rise of northern Italian cooking internationally, grappa began to be discovered by international spirit fans. Still, annual production has stayed relatively flat, around 45 million 700 ml bottles per year, with most consumed in Italy; Germany by far is the largest export market. Today Nonino and Poli are among the best-known artisanal producers, while Bonollo, Nardini, and Stock are the major industrial producers.

See also POMACE BRANDY.

Behrendt, Axel, and Bibiana Behrendt. *Grappa: A Guide to the Best*. New York: Abbeville, 1999.

Bodin, Ove. *Grappa: Italy Bottled*. Stockholm: Stockholm Text, 2012.

Instituto Nazionale Grappa. http://www.istitutograppa.org/ita/le-domande-sulla-grappa.html (accessed February 12, 2021).

Jack Robertiello

The **Grasshopper** is a sweet, mint-flavored cocktail, typically served after dinner. It emerged in the middle of the twentieth century as a species of Pousse Café made with equal parts crème de menthe, crème de cacao, and cream.

The drink's name and its two alcoholic ingredients were already wedded together in 1908, when San Francisco bartender "Cocktail Bill" Boothby included a Grasshopper (with equal parts cacao and menthe layered in a pony or Pousse Café glass) in his *World's Drinks and How to Mix Them*. He attributed it to Harry O'Brien, "late of the Palace Hotel" in that city. That version appeared occasionally in American and European bartenders' guides through the 1930s. See BOOTHBY, WILLIAM T. "COCKTAIL BILL."

It is unknown precisely when the layered two-ingredient Grasshopper Pousse Café became the shaken (or sometimes blended) three-ingredient Grasshopper cocktail. New Orleans legend has it that the drink was invented in 1928 or thereabouts by Philip Guichet, owner of Tujague's Restaurant there, for a cocktail contest in New York City. The Grasshopper is one of Tujague's signature cocktails today, but no documentary evidence substantiates the claim that Guichet was the creator.

The printed record, instead, points to the Midwest as the most likely place of origin and the years just after World War II as the time. The first known printed reference to the Grasshopper as a cocktail appeared in Neal O'Hara's column for *Boston Traveler* in February 1950, which noted, "Currently popular in the midwest is the Grasshopper Cocktail." The following month, Clementine Paddleford of the *New York Herald-Tribune* attributed the cocktail's creation to Fazio's Towne Room in Milwaukee, though a reader subsequently wrote to insist that it first appeared at Charlie's Café Exceptionale in Minneapolis. In July of that year, Louis Sobol, a New York journalist, found it popular in Rapid City, South Dakota; he had not previously heard of it.

The Grasshopper enjoyed a surge of popularity in the 1950s as many Americans were abandoning whisky-heavy drinks in favor of lighter and sweeter cocktails, but the drink's vogue was short-lived. By 1961, the *New York Times* was reporting that "a drink like the grasshopper . . . catches on for a while and then fades out." It persisted most stubbornly in the Midwest, which embraced a blended variant in which the regular cream is replaced by ice cream—more an alcoholic milkshake than a cocktail. Cocktail enthusiasts have tended to treat the Grasshopper with disdain, lumping it in with White Russians and other heavy, sweet, cream-laden drinks. See WHITE RUSSIAN. David Embury, in the third edition of *The Fine Art of Mixing Drinks*, provides a short gloss of the Grasshopper and a variant with blackberry brandy added and notes, "With or without the blackberry, as a cocktail it is strictly vile." See EMBURY, DAVID A. In recent years, though, bartenders have started rediscovering this mid-twentieth-century dessert drink, and it lives on today as a standard if minor part of the American cocktail canon. It helps greatly if one follows Tujague's lead and adds an equal part of cognac to the mix (a fix already suggested in 1951 by the mixologists at the Columbia restaurant in Tampa, Florida).

Recipe: Combine 30 ml each of crème de menthe, crème de cacao, and heavy cream in a cocktail shaker filled with shaved ice. Shake vigorously until the mixture is silky, and strain into a chilled cocktail glass. Optional: add 30 ml VSOP-grade cognac to the other ingredients and proceed as above.

See also POUSSE CAFÉ.

DeJesus, Erin. "It's Not Easy Being Green: The Weird History of the Grasshopper." Eater, October 23, 2014. http://www.eater.com/2014/10/23/7036159/

a-brief-history-of-the-grasshopper (accessed February 12, 2021).

Paddleford, Clementine. "Grasshopper Cocktail." *Baltimore Sun*, September 8, 1950, 14.

Robert F. Moss

Gray, "Colonel" Jim (1855–1914), was the second-most famous bartender in New York during the first golden age of the cocktail, yielding only to William Schmidt, although his approach to the craft of mixing drinks was the antithesis of Schmidt's. See SCHMIDT, WILLIAM. James W. Gray was a native New Yorker who began working behind the bar at fifteen. In 1882, he was at the Astor House when he was recruited by the Fifth Avenue Hotel, New York's most prestigious (it was where sitting presidents stayed, as well as the prince of Wales). See ASTOR HOUSE. Gray remained there until a few weeks before the hotel's closing in 1908. The hotel was a home away from home for the Republican party, and Gray (ironically, a Democrat) entertained among his regular customers presidents Ulysses S. Grant, who "seldom drank anything except ale or porter," and Chester A. Arthur, "a very sociable, pleasant customer" who liked a Tom Collins, along with a parade of other Republican officeholders. See TOM COLLINS.

Gray was famous as a mixer of drinks, but more for their quality than their variety: his specialties were Medford Rum Punch, made by the glass, and the Old-Fashioned, which he claimed to have invented in 1881 (his version cannot be considered orthodox, as it was shaken and omitted the bitters). See OLD-FASHIONED COCKTAIL. But Gray was as renowned for his hospitality, gentlemanly demeanor, and rectitude as for his drinks. He was also known for his gaudy vests, a personal trademark: he changed them several times a day, and his prominent customers made it a game to see who could bring him the loudest fabric.

With the demise of the Fifth Avenue, Gray moved north one block to the Hotel Albemarle and then next door to the Hoffman House, where he took over Charley Mahoney's old job as bar manager. See HOFFMAN HOUSE. At his welcoming reception, attended by Buffalo Bill Cody and a host of other celebrities of the day, "to demonstrate that he was still a spring chicken" Gray "mixed 35 punches in 45 minutes, talking the while." The closing of the Hoffman House in 1911 basically put an end to his career as the dean of Fifth Avenue bartenders and, symbolically, to the first era of the bartender as celebrity.

"Gloom in Fifth Avenue Bar." *New York Sun*, April 7, 1908, 7.

"Grief at Razing of Fifth-Avenue Hotel." *New York Herald*, March 29, 1908, 9.

"Col. Jim Gray Jogs North." *New York Sun*, April 11, 1910, 7.

David Wondrich

Greece may be best known for ouzo when it comes to spirits, but it offers much more than the anise-scented liquor. Given the country's widespread cultivation of grapevines for wine production, this should come as no surprise—something good has to come of all the muck of grape skins, pulp, and dead yeast left over from the process. The Greeks may even have been the first to apply distillation to the production of potable beverages: While that credit often goes to the Indians, thanks to the discovery of alcohol-producing stills dating to 150 BCE in what is now Pakistan, the fact that they were in an Indo-Greek site raises the question of whether the Greeks brought the process to India or took it home with them. Some researchers examining pithoi, large earthenware jars excavated in Crete, have even suggested that the Minoans were distilling alcohol as early as the middle Minoan period (ca. 1900 to 1700 BCE). See DISTILLATION, HISTORY.

It was many more centuries, however, until materials were refined enough to make alcoholic distillation commonplace. Byzantine coppersmiths perfected the alembic, a word that comes from the Greek *ambix*; this became *al-ʿanbīk* in Arabic, referring specifically to the vase-like vessel used in distillation. The Venetians brought their glass-making skills to Greece during their colonization of the Ionian Islands in the mid-fourteenth to late eighteenth centuries; as glass conducts heat much better than the glazed earthenware stills that were common, they were able to produce purer, more potent distillates. Meanwhile, the restrictions placed on the production of alcohol during the Turkish occupation of Greece (1453–1821) did little to diminish the Greek's reputation for high-quality distillates: as some interpretations of the Qur'an allow for distillates, the Greeks maintained a thriving industry distilling wine castoffs into raki—so much so that the "rakitzides" became a privileged caste. See RAKI.

After the fall of the Ottoman Empire, grape marc distillation lost some of its shine, as anyone who made a little wine could distill the leftover pomace and even sell off some of the resulting *apóstagma* (distillate). See MARC. Popularly called *tsipouro* across northern Greece, *tsikoudia* in Crete, and *zivania* in Cyprus, these unaged, unflavored grape distillates remain integral to Greek culture, shared at every social event, even as they remain unknown to most outsiders. It's not for lack of quality—like Italian grappa, tsipouro comes in a range of variations, including sophisticated single-varietal and barrel-aged versions. See GRAPPA. Rather, the situation stems from a law in 1917 that allowed only grape growers to distill grape marc, while professional distillers were allowed to distill anything, and in industrial quantities. Spirits such as ouzo, by that time distilled with molasses or other non-grape spirits, took over the marketplace. This ruling did not change until 1989; it would take another nineteen years for the EU to declare tsipouro unique to Greece, with specific geographical indications for versions produced in Macedonia, Thessaly, and Tirnavos as well.

Outside of ouzo, Greece's best-known spirit is most likely Metaxa, which Spyros Metaxa (1843–1909) launched in 1888 with a blend of aged wine distillates, fresh muscat wines from Samos and Limnos, rose petals, and herbs; the company is now owned by drinks giant Rémy Cointreau. But Greece offers much more to the drinks enthusiast, with over two hundred licensed distillers in 2015 and nineteen spirits that carry a PGI—a Protected Geographical Indication, an EU-administered label intended to safeguard traditional products and growing methods for products particular to a place. Masticha of Chios is one of the country's most unique, flavored with the resin of the mastic tree indigenous to this northern Aegean island. Like ouzo, masticha is drunk cold, with the addition of water, which makes the spirit louche (turn cloudy).

Kumquats provide the flavoring for the Koum Kouat of Corfu, where the fruit of the diminutive citrus trees has earned its own PGI; on Naxos in the Cyclades, the leaves of the citron tree, along with the citrus stems and peels, are distilled for Kitro of Naxos, a spirit that dates to at least the early 1800s. Cinnamon and clove provide the primary flavorings for Tentura, a dark, sweet liqueur that seems to have originated in the port city of Patras as a low-cost alternative to Chartreuse, Bénédictine, and other imported liqueurs, but now has its own PGI. (Distillers on Kythira produce a similarly spiced spirit they call fatourda, but it has no PGI.)

These are just the officially defined spirits; wherever there is a fruit, herb, spice, bark, or nut with an interesting flavor, it's likely that someone in this country has created a distillate with it. And given the renewed interest in artisan spirits that's followed the country's wine renaissance, the list is growing longer quickly.

See also OUZO and METAXA.

Aines, Ethan D. "Carousing with the Ancients: The Archeology of Alcohol: A Review of Literature." https://www.slideshare.net/eaines/carousing-with-the-ancients-the-archaeology-of-wine-and-beer-in-the-fertile-crescent-and-mediterranean-region (accessed April 4, 2021).

Greek Federation of Spirits Producers. SEAOP. http://www.seaop.gr/ (accessed February 12, 2021).

Official Journal of the European Union. Regulation (Ec) No 110/2008 of the European Parliament and of the Council of 15 January 2008 on the Definition, Description, Presentation, Labelling and the Protection of Geographical Indications of Spirit Drinks and Repealing Council Regulation (EEC) No 1576/89. http://eur-lex.europa.eu/LexUriServ/LexUriServ.do?uri=OJ:L:2008:039:0016:0054:EN:PDF (accessed February 12, 2021).

Smaragidis, Andreas. *Tsikoudia: Spirit of Crete*. Crete: Dokimakis Editions, 2010.

Tara Q. Thomas

Green Swizzle is a traditional Caribbean drink made famous in P. G. Wodehouse's 1925 short story "The Rummy Affair of Old Biffy," in which, after a lifesaving encounter with the drink at the British Empire Exhibition, Bertie Wooster promises that should he eventually have a son, "Green Swizzle Wooster is the name that will go down in the register." The drink was long believed to be fictional, but the modern availability of newspaper databases has revealed that it was not only real but for a time quite popular, at least in its native region, and has even turned up a handful of recipes. Although these differ in detail, they agree that the essential ingredients were gin or rum, Falernum (or, in Trinidad, the Angostura company's equivalent, Carypton), wormwood bitters (a simple infusion of wormwood and strong rum), and ice. See FALERNUM. The pool of other ingredients included lime juice, sugar, Angostura bitters, and soda water.

There were two competing bastions of Green Swizzling: the Bridgetown Club, in Barbados, the drink's probable place of origin, and the Queen's Park Hotel, in Port of Spain, Trinidad. As far as can be determined, it was invented around 1900. The original Green Swizzle's star seems to have faded by the late 1920s, although a Falernum-less Green Swizzle incorporating green crème de menthe popped up at the Floridita bar in Havana at the end of the next decade and was passed around for a time. It is one of the few drinks that Constante Ribalaigua did not improve. Properly made, the original Green Swizzle is a complex, refreshing, and intriguing drink, and one well worth reviving.

See also SWIZZLE.

Recipe: Fill a tall glass half full with shaved ice, 60 ml good white rum or gin, 30 ml Falernum, and 5 ml wormwood bitters. Twirl a swizzle stick rapidly until the ice is melted and the drink is almost a frappe. Add a straw. Optional adjuncts: 22 ml lime juice, 30 ml soda water, and 8 dashes of Angostura bitters added as a float.

"A Note on West Indian Drinks." *Times from London*, May 24, 1910, 37.

Bridgetown Club [pseudonym]. "Green Swizzle Formula." *New York Herald*, October 19, 1907, 8.

Schoff, Wilfred H. "Cinderellas of the Caribbean." *Los Angeles Times* January 8, 1917.

"Sure of the Swizzle." *New York Herald Magazine*, August 19, 1908, 2.

Darcy O'Neill and David Wondrich

grenadine syrup was originally a pomegranate syrup employed by French apothecaries to hide the taste of medicines, but by the turn of the nineteenth century, the *limonadiers* of Paris (who prepared the fancy drinks in that city) knew of it. It quickly became popular throughout France, and in *Le confiseur moderne* (1803), confectioner J.-J. Machet relates that "in Languedoc [pomegranate juice] is made into a syrup or a kind of lemonade by mixing sugar therein; it is considered cordial and astringent, and it is drunk with pleasure."

On October 5, 1869, Victor Rillet, a recent French immigrant, obtained a patent for the first grenadine syrup produced in the United States. Rillet used real pomegranates, pressed and fermented, with a few natural additives. In May 1870, Rillet advertised for "active, pushing young men, of good address, to sell Grenadine Syrup . . . far superior to any other summer beverage known." Rillet's product immediately drew competitors, many of whom used artificial ingredients. By July 1891, the *Druggist's Circular* complained of "vile imitation," and recipes from the late nineteenth century rarely contain any pomegranate.

After Repeal, commercial grenadine in the United States was an imitation, much to the displeasure of American gourmets, who had been enjoying the genuine product in the American bars of Paris. In June 1936, *New York Sun* drinks columnist G. Selmer Fougner wrote of "innumerable products masquerading under that name," and claimed that all reputable French producers used real pomegranate juice. This took some decades to sink in, but today, both pomegranate-based and artificial variants are widely available, and making one's own grenadine is a minor rite of passage for the aspiring mixologist. See FOUGNER, G. SELMER.

Grenadine syrup was used in mixed drinks as early as November 1894, when a recipe for a "Grenadine Fiz" appeared in newsprint, and the next year, George Kapeller's *Modern American Drinks* claimed that a Grenadine Cocktail is any cocktail that used it. But Grenadine's real popularity as an ingredient began by 1905, with the rise to popularity of the Jack Rose Cocktail. By 1907, when the Royal Smile was first formulated at the Waldorf Astoria, grenadine syrup was an established mixer. See JACK ROSE. It has been used since as a combination sweetener and coloring agent, lending such drinks as the Bacardi Cocktail, the Tequila Sunrise, and the nonalcoholic Shirley Temple their characteristic rosy hues. See TEQUILA SUNRISE.

Fougner, G. Selmer. "Along the Wine Trail." *New York Sun*, June 26, 1936, 14.

Morgenthaler, Jeffrey. "How to Make Your Own Grenadine." *Jeffreymorgenthaler.com*, December 10, 2009. "https://jeffreymorgenthaler.com/how-to-make-your-own-grenadine/" (accessed January 25, 2021).

Doug Stailey

Grey Goose vodka was created by veteran spirits executive Sidney Frank (1919–2006) in 1997. With Grey Goose, Frank, who had run the international liquor conglomerate Schenley and had turned the bitter German liqueur Jägermeister into a sensation, started the super-premium vodka craze that ushered in the twenty-first century.

Frank already had used the name Grey Goose for a wine, which had been unsuccessful. He had better luck with the wheat-based vodka, which he had distilled in central France but bottled in Cognac, a region famous around the world for luxury brandy; that gave Grey Goose an immediate, and marketable, cachet. See COGNAC.

The strategy Frank adopted for making his vodka a best seller was simple. He first doubled the suggested retail price of the popular Swedish import Absolut Vodka (Grey Goose debuted at $30; Absolut was selling for about $15). See ABSOLUT. He then submitted his brand to the Beverage Testing Institute for ranking, which named it the best-tasting vodka in the world.

In the late 1990s there were relatively few spirits competitions, and Frank capitalized on the accolade in an extensive advertising campaign. Consumers were impressed by the high price of Grey Goose. When they asked a bartender or store clerk about why it was so much, they were told it was just named the world's best vodka, which, naturally, sealed many sales.

Frank supposedly preferred producing vodka over whisky or even Jägermeister, since as he told *Inc.* magazine, "you make it today, you sell it tomorrow." He sold the brand in 2006 for more than $2 billion to Bacardi, which continues to produce and sell Grey Goose. See BACARDI.

See also FRANK, SIDNEY.

Clifford, Stephanie. "How I Did It: Sidney Frank," *Inc.*, September 2005. https://www.inc.com/magazine/20050901/qa.html (accessed February 12, 2021).
Martin, Douglas. "Sidney Frank, 86, Dies." *New York Times*, January 12, 2006.

Rothbaum, Noah. *The Business of Spirits*. New York: Kaplan, 2007.

Noah Rothbaum

Grimes, William "Biff" (1950–), is an American journalist and the author of the influential *Straight Up or on the Rocks: The Story of the American Cocktail* (1993, 2002), the first accurate history of the American school of drinking, and three other books on food and drink. Since 1989, he has worked for the *New York Times* as a magazine writer, culture reporter, theater columnist, restaurant critic, book reviewer, and, most recently, obituary writer. Former *New York Times* executive editor Bill Keller said that Grimes's byline "carries a signature, a blend (or call it a cocktail—Biff wrote a book about drinks) of gentle wit, graceful style and wide-ranging erudition."

Grimes, William. *Straight Up or on the Rocks: The Story of the American Cocktail*. Rev. ed. New York: North Point, 2001.
Koblin, John. "William Grimes Is New Obit Writer for the Times." *Observer*, March 7, 2008. http://observer.com/2008/03/william-grimes-is-new-obit-writer-for-the-itimesi/ (accessed February 12, 2021).

Lauren Clark

grog, when defined most narrowly, is rum diluted with water. Although it has roots in the seafaring life during the first half of the eighteenth century, the word later came to be used more generically to refer to any and all types of alcoholic beverage.

"Grog" was first introduced to the British Navy in 1740 by Admiral Edward Vernon. Spirits had long been part of a seaman's daily rations in the British Navy (as well as many others), and Vernon took note of the "pernicious custom of the seamen drinking their allowance of rum in drams, and often at once." Given that among the tasks of seamen was to scramble high aloft in the rigging to furl and unfurl sails, alcohol-fueled instability was a liability. Vernon announced that henceforth the daily spirits ration would be issued diluted with four parts of water to every part of rum, and it would be split and served twice daily, rather than all at once (the proportion of water to rum varied over time; from 1937 until the ration was discontinued in 1970, it was a more reasonable two parts water to one of rum).

As to the name, Vernon reportedly favored an overcoat made of a woven fabric waterproofed with gum, a type of fabric call "grogram." His nickname was thus Old Grogram, and so a truncated version was applied to the diluted rum.

Like the term "rum," grog became a broad-brush term for any sort of liquor, and references crop up to grog shops, grog bowls, and the like. An 1898 article in the *Overland Monthly and Out West* magazine noted of US presidents Polk, Hayes, and Harrison that "all three knew good grog when they tasted it." Later still, Donn "Don the Beachcomber" Beach appropriated the name for his Navy Grog (first found in print in 1942), a rum, grapefruit, and honey drink that became one of the great tiki classics, even if it is in fact a punch and not a grog at all. See BEACH, DONN; and PUNCH.

Recipe: With all due ceremony, combine two to four parts water with one part 54.5 percent ABV rum. See NAVY-STRENGTH.

Pack, James. *Nelson's Blood: The Story of Naval Rum*. Stroud, UK: Sutton, 1982.

Wayne Curtis

Grohusko, Jacob Abraham "Jack" (1876–1943), was a New York City bartender and the author of *Jack's Manual*, a valuable bartender's guide that saw four editions between 1908 and 1934. Grohusko was born to a Russian Jewish family in England and was brought to New York at an early age. By 1900, perhaps after working for a stretch in the wine department at the Plaza Hotel, he was tending bar at Baracca's, a popular Italian restaurant in downtown New York, where he developed a reputation as a mixologist; "One trial" of his drinks there, a journalist opined, "will convince the most skeptical." It was there he published the first edition of his *Jack's Manual*, which in its early editions (1908, 1910, 1916) is an excellent snapshot of the first golden age of the cocktail. It also marks the first appearance of the Brooklyn Cocktail (Grohusko never lived in Brooklyn, but Victor Baracca, the owner of the restaurant, did). In 1910, Grohusko teamed up with Italian chef Bruto Garcelli to open Bruto & Jack's, an eatery also in downtown New York,

which ran well into the Prohibition years. Grohusko also developed and marketed barware, including a well-designed julep strainer. In 1934, he published a greatly-expanded Repeal edition of his book; that is the last we hear of him.

See also BROOKLYN COCKTAIL and COCKTAIL STRAINER.

Grohusko, Jack. *Jack's Manual*. New York: J. A. Grohusko, 1908.

"Notes." *Bonfort's Wine and Spirit Circular*, May 10, 1909, 9.

David Wondrich

guaro is a distilled alcoholic drink from Central America. It is a variety of aguardiente, a general name in the Spanish Caribbean for distilled spirits made from sugar-cane juice and the byproducts of sugar making. See AGUARDIENTE AND AGUARDENTE and CARIBBEAN. Guaro probably began as a variety of illicitly made "bush" rums used to meet the alcoholic demands of African and Indigenous laborers. Today, guaro production is more regulated, especially in Costa Rica, where it is distilled in column stills to a neutral spirit and then diluted with water upon reaching markets. Elsewhere, it is frequently found as a pot-distilled moonshine, often flavored with local fruits. While guaro is a distilled drink today, the name probably has its origins in the fermented sugar-cane-based drinks of the past. Its name probably descends from the cognate terms *guarapo*, *guacapo*, *grippo*, and *grappe*, used in the early colonial era in many parts of the Spanish, British, and French Caribbean for fermented drinks made from sugar-cane juice. The drink was primarily associated with enslaved Africans, who produced them on sugar plantations. They made these drinks to recreate as closely as possible the fermented beers and palm wines that were traditionally consumed throughout much of the West African homelands of enslaved peoples in the Caribbean. See SUGAR CANE.

See also CENTRAL AMERICA.

Smith, Frederick H. *Caribbean Rum: A Social and Economic History*. Gainesville: University Press of Florida, 2005.

Frederick H. Smith

Guilin Sanhua is a rice-aroma-style baijiu distillery. Situated in the fabled rocky landscape of

Guilin, in the north of the coastal Guanxi province not far from the Guizhou border, it is the foremost exemplar of southeast China's centuries-old *sanhua* ("three flowers") liquor style. All of its baijiu uses rice fermented with small *qu* made of rice and medicinal herbs. See XIAO ("SMALL") QU. Unlike most baijiu distilleries, Guilin Sanhua steams its grains three times, ferments them in a semisolid state, and employs continuous distillation. Its premium spirits are aged in caves tucked into the side of limestone hills, or karst. The Chinese government founded Guilin Sanhua in 1952 from several smaller distilleries and named its products first among "small-qu liquors" in 1957.

See also RICE-AROMA-STYLE BAIJIU.

Huang Faxin, David Tiande Cai, and Wai-Kit Nip. "Chinese Wines: Jiu." In *Handbook of Food Science, Technology, and Engineering*, vol. 4, ed. Yiu H. Hui. Boca Raton, FL: CRC, 2005.

Derek Sandhaus

gum syrup, sometimes *gomme* and often shortened to *gum*, has been a bartenders' staple since the nineteenth century. Multiple syrups parade under this name. Classically, however, gum syrup is rich simple syrup made luxe by the addition of powdered gum arabic. See RICH SIMPLE SYRUP. Also known as GA or acacia gum, gum arabic is an exudate, the hardened sap of *Acacia senegal, A. seyal*, and closely related trees that grow wild in sub-Saharan Africa and in parts of India. It is termed arabic after Arab traders who once brought the raw material to Europe, but it has been known since the second millennium BCE. Added to sugar syrup, this hydrocolloid contributes a silken mouthfeel to cocktails, a weighty unctuousness that is especially pleasing in spirituous drinks. Perhaps because they found it difficult to use, corner-cutting bartenders jettisoned powdered gum long ago yet retained the names *gomme* or *gum* for their gumless syrups. Ratios of sugar to water in old recipes range from equal parts to quadruple the sugar. Although heavy syrups must be heated to dissolve the sugar, gum arabic itself requires no heating to hydrate. Pioneering mixographer Charles H. Baker clarified his version with egg whites, a move largely obviated by the purity of modern refined sugar, but which results in a particularly limpid syrup. Modernist bartenders have experimented with other thickening and emulsification agents in their gum syrups, including xanthan gum and powdered egg white, to replace or act in concert with gum arabic. Jeffrey Morgenthaler's proportions yield excellent results with the classic ingredients.

Recipe: In a small container, combine 55 g gum arabic and 60 ml water. Stir to blend, then cover the mix. When the gum arabic is completely dissolved (after approximately 48 hours), heat 340 g superfine sugar and 120 ml water in a small saucepan. Heat gently until the sugar begins to dissolve, then fold in the hydrated gum arabic mixture. Remove from heat immediately and let cool. Bottle the syrup and store in the refrigerator indefinitely.

See also BAKER, CHARLES HENRY, JR.; SUGAR; and SYRUP.

Montenegro, M. A., M. L. Boiero, L. Valle, and C. D. Borsarell. "Gum Arabic: More Than an Edible Emulsifier." *Products and Applications of Biopolymers* 51 (2012): 953–978.
Morgenthaler, J. *The Bar Book: Elements of Cocktail Technique*. San Francisco: Chronicle Books, 2014.
Myhrvold, N., C. Young, and M. Bilet. *Modernist Cuisine*, vol 4, *Ingredients and Preparations*. Bellevue, WA: Cooking Lab, 2011.
Patel, S., and A. Goyal. "Applications of Natural Polymer Gum Arabic: A Review." *International Journal of Food Properties* 18, no. 5 (2015): 986–998.

Matthew Rowley

habanero is an aged aguardiente from the Mexican state of Tabasco that is blended with small amounts of sherry or other sweet wines to create what is essentially a cane-based version of Spanish brandy. The most plausible of the several uncorroborated stories for the spirit's origin has one Juan Ruiz, a Tabasco sugar hacienda owner, importing some aguardiente from Havana to have something to sell after a flood destroyed his crop. "The aguardiente was placed in wooden kegs and barrels that had previously held muscatel and sherry wines" from Spain, which, after "Gulf hurricanes and storms" stretched a voyage of three or four days to "six months," transformed the raw spirit into something smooth and delightful. Perhaps a more likely story is that habanero was a conscious attempt to imitate the smooth, well-aged Cuban rums made by Bacardi and others. In any case, the leading brands, those of Berreteaga y Cia. and Juan Pizá y Cia., were established in 1865 and 1884, respectively. During the spirit's heyday, which ran from the early 1900s until the 1950s, there were a number of other, much smaller companies making habanero as well.

Habanero enjoyed a good reputation, for the most part, with foreign visitors to Mexico, particularly as a base for cocktails and other mixed drinks, and several attempts were made to establish a market for it in the United States. The most ambitious came after Repeal in 1933, when the Mexican-American Habanero Company sought to capitalize on the increased familiarity with Mexican spirits that Prohibition had engendered and began importing both Berreteaga and Pizá. It went bankrupt a year later. Other attempts followed, particularly during World War II, when the American liquor supply was again restricted, but none took. Some Habanero is still made and sold locally in Tabasco, but it is not generally exported.

See also AGUARDIENTE AND AGUARDENTE and CHINGUIRITO.

Fougner, G. Selmer. "Along the Wine Trail." *New York Sun*, May 5, 1934, 6, and March 24, 1938, 11.
"Piza habanero añejo." undated booklet (post-1934).

David Wondrich

Brochure for Piza Habanero, ca. 1925. Wondrich Collection.

Hacienda la Caravedo is the oldest pisco distillery in Peru and perhaps the oldest working distillery in the western hemisphere. Located in the Ica valley, the center of the Peruvian pisco industry, it dates back to 1684 and comprises a large estate with its own vineyards and a landmarked orange-stucco colonial-style great house. After some ups and downs in the early and mid-twentieth century, under the direction of the Peruvian-born but Napa Valley–trained Rodrigo Peschiera Mifflin, who bought the estate with his father in the mid-1990s, the estate was rededicated to producing pisco in the most traditional style, with modern biodynamic touches. Fortunately, it still had its *falcas*, the indigenous style of pot still, and they were still wood-fired and set in the traditional gravity-fed system whereby grapes were pressed at the top of a hill, fermented a little lower down, and distilled near the bottom. See FALCA.

In 2010, the Peschieras sold the property to William Kallop, a Texas oilman, his son Brent, and Johnny Schuler, a Bolivian-born Lima restaurateur and pisco and wine expert (he was a founding member of the National Tasters Guild of Peru). The new owners built a second distillery, across the courtyard from the old falcas, featuring modern steam-jacketed alembics (later they also added a suite of Charentais-style cognac stills elsewhere on the property). With this large capacity and Schuler as master distiller, Pisco Portón, their new brand, was able to offer a wide range of high-quality piscos, including the rare mosto verde, and became an award winner and an export leader, selling pisco even in Chile. See PISCO.

Dicum, Gregory. *The Pisco Book*. San Francisco: ClearGrape, 2011.

English, Camper. "A Visit to La Caravedo." *Alcademics*, January 6, 2015. https://www.alcademics.com/2015/01/a-visit-to-la-caravedo-home-of-pisco-porton-in-ica-peru-.html (accessed May 3, 2021).

David Wondrich

Haigh, Ted (1956–), known in the cocktail realm as "Dr. Cocktail," is a cocktail historian, writer, and collector of vintage spirits and cocktail arcana who was one of the midwives of the modern cocktail renaissance. See COCKTAIL RENAISSANCE. A graphic designer and art director for motion pictures and television based in Burbank, California, Haigh is also the author of *Vintage Spirits and Forgotten Cocktails*, a guide to long-neglected cocktail recipes that upon its publication in 2004 helped fan the flames of the then-smoldering cocktail renaissance. A lifelong obsessive collector—in addition to vintage spirits and cocktail guides, his collections have included antique automobiles, World War II–era neckwear, and more than three thousand 78 rpm records—Haigh began diligently researching cocktails starting in the 1980s. He introduced his Dr. Cocktail persona on AOL when he began hosting the spirit boards in 1995 and has maintained it through his cocktail career: as cofounder (with Martin Doudoroff) of the CocktailDB.com database (relaunched in 2004), as a cofounder of the Museum of the American Cocktail in 2005, and as a speaker during the formative years of Tales of the Cocktail. See MUSEUM OF THE AMERICAN COCKTAIL and TALES OF THE COCKTAIL. In his 2004 book and as a regular columnist for *Imbibe* magazine starting in 2006, Haigh reintroduced long-obscure recipes back into the cocktail lexicon, including those for the Boulevardier and the Corpse Reviver no. 2. See CORPSE REVIVER.

Clarke, Paul. "Characters: Ted Haigh." *Imbibe*, May 22, 2006, http://imbibemagazine.com/doctor-cocktail-ted-haigh/ (accessed February 12, 2021).

Haigh, Ted. *Vintage Spirits and Forgotten Cocktails*. Beverly, MA: Quarry Books, 2004.

Hodgman, John. "All Shaken Up." *New York Times*, October 17, 2004, http://www.nytimes.com/2004/10/17/magazine/all-shaken-up.html (accessed February 12, 2021).

Paul Clarke

The **Hailstorm**, or Hail-Storm, is a popular American drink of the early nineteenth century whose general makeup—spirits, sugar, ice—is as clear as its precise details are elusive. The first printed recipe for it came only in 1913, a good eighty years after its first known appearance, in an 1833 newspaper. There, it is presented as a potent Virginian eye-opener, but no further detail is given, nor are the other contemporary sources much more helpful.

There were, we can nonetheless say, two schools of thought as to the Hailstorm's composition. One considered it synonymous with iced Mint Julep. Thus the correspondent to the *Baltimore Sun* who in 1860 extolled the joys of " 'hail storm,' yclept 'mint julep,' which comes to you congealed in its own frostwork—the icicles hanging pendant from its rim in the most tempting manner, with just mint and good brandy enough to make one, like Oliver Twist, constantly sigh for 'more,' after the accustomed sized goblet has been drained."

Others, however, imply that there was some difference between the drinks, for example, the Irish actor Tyrone Power, who in 1836 dubbed the New York innkeeper Cato Alexander "foremost among cullers of mint, whether for *julep* or *hail-storm*." See ALEXANDER, CATO. On the other hand, the 1913 recipe suggests the distinction is that the Hailstorm is made like a julep, but without mint. In any case, the drink was not recorded by Jerry Thomas or any of the other important nineteenth century mixographers, and by the end of the century it had joined its contemporaries the Pig and Whistle, Moral Suasion, and Tip and Ty in the file of curiosities and mysteries.

See also JULEP and MIXOLOGY, THE HISTORY OF.

"Our Staunton Correspondence." *New York Family Herald*, September 26, 1860, 7.
Power, Tyrone, *Impressions of America*. London: R. Bentley, 1836.
"Virginia Hospitality." *Alexandria (VA) Gazette*, July 16, 1833, 5.
Williams, Martha McCulloch. *Dishes and Beverages of the Old South*. New York: McBride, Nast, 1913.

David Wondrich

Haimo, Oscar (1904–1982), author of *Cocktail and Wine Digest: The Barmen's Bible*, published annually from 1943 through 1977 [first published as *Cocktail and Wine Digest (from Private Notes)*]. Born into poverty in the Passage Bullourde, then a Jewish ghetto in Paris, he rose to be maître de bar of the Hotel Pierre in Manhattan and president of the International Bar Managers Association. Too young to serve in World War I, he took the opportunity provided him by wartime labor shortages to wait tables at quality Parisian venues. In the early 1920s, he was trained as bartender at the Paris Ritz by Frank Meier, author of *The Artistry of Mixing Drinks*. See MEIER, FRANK; and RITZ BAR. After stints as an army officer and a ship's steward, the ever-resourceful Haimo worked

at the Royalty Bar and the Casino in Monaco before emigrating to New York in 1929, where he slung drinks in Prohibition-era speakeasies. See SPEAKEASY (OLD). In 1939, his Parisian credentials led to a bartending gig at the Belgian Pavilion of the New York World's Fair. From there, he went on to manage the six bars of the Hotel Pierre. His self-published *Cocktail Digest* became popular, and celebrity columnists praised his creations. Haimo was also known for his free program teaching bartending skills to World War II veterans in need of work.

Haimo, Oscar. *Cocktail and Wine Digest (from Private Notes)*. New York: Comet Press, 1943.
Haimo, Oscar. *Nothing Lasts Forever: An Autobiography*. New York: International Cocktail, Wine & Spirits Digest, 1953.
Winchell, Walter. "By Walter Winchell, the Man on Broadway." *Syracuse Herald-Journal*, February 25, 1942.

Doug Stailey

Hamilton, Edward "Ed" (1954–), is an American rum authority who has researched, written about, and imported West Indian rums since the 1980s. In 1984, the "minister of rum," a Florida native, lived aboard a 38-foot sailboat in the Caribbean while engaged in inter-island rum arbitrage (read: smuggling). His research led to a broader interest in the spirit, and in 1995 he published his first guide to rum. In 2003 he acquired an importer's license and began to introduce Martinique rums into the United States. In 2014 he started importing high-ester rums from Jamaica (as well as rums from other islands) under his Ministry of Rum Collection label.

See also CARIBBEAN and RUM.

Hamilton, Edward. *The Complete Guide to Rum: The Authoritative Guide to Rums of the World*. Chicago: Triumph, 1997.

Wayne Curtis

The **Hanky Panky** cocktail—half dry gin, half sweet vermouth, and two dashes of Fernet Branca—is the first canonical cocktail definitively attributed to a female bartender. See MILK PUNCH and SHERRY COBBLER. It was created by Ada "Coley" Coleman (1875–1966) when she was the head bartender at the American Bar at London's Savoy Hotel. See COLEMAN, ADA. There are two more or less contemporary accounts of the circumstances, published in London newspapers as 1925 turned into 1926, which agree in their broad details: a few years prior, the actor and impresario Sir Charles Hawtrey (1858–1923), a mentor of young Noël Coward and one of Coleman's many special customers, came into the bar complaining of fatigue from overwork ("Coley, I'm half dead; what can you do to make me quite alive?," the *Sphere* has him asking). "I spent hours experimenting," Coleman told the *People*, "until I invented a new cocktail." Hawtrey either dubbed the resulting drink "the real hanky panky" on the spot, or came in the next day asking for "that hanky panky stuff." In any case, the name stuck. (At the time, "hanky panky" was a phrase more associated with magic than sexual shenanigans—a relative of "hocus-pocus.")

A likely date for the drink's creation was in mid-1921, when Hawtrey was, despite his failing health, both producing and starring in *Ambrose Applejohn's Adventure* at the Savoy Theatre, next door to the hotel. Hawtrey was busy in 1921; before that production, he was the producer of multiple shows including Basil McDonald Hastings's 1919 farce, *Hanky Panky John*, whose title character is "nicknamed Hanky Panky because he had invented a cocktail so-called."

The Hanky Panky is the only one of Coleman's drinks known to survive—although it is possible that a number of drinks in the 1930 Savoy Cocktail Book, written by Harry Craddock, who pushed her out of her job in 1926, are actually hers. See CRADDOCK, HARRY LAWSON. A simple variation on the Martini, it is one of the first cocktails to make use of Fernet Branca (available in Britain since at least 1887), which in the small quantity Coleman used brings a surprising richness and depth to it without making it overtly bitter.

Recipe: Stir with ice 60 ml London dry gin, 30 ml sweet vermouth, and 5–10 ml Fernet Branca; strain into a chilled cocktail class and twist orange peel over the top.

"Cocktails as a Guide to Character." *People*, December 20, 1925, 2.

Haigh, Ted. *Vintage Spirits and Forgotten Cocktails-Deluxe Edition.* Gloucester, MA: Quarry, 2009.

Regan, Gary. "Masters of Mixology: Ada Coleman." *Liquor.com.* http://www.liquor.com/articles/masters-of-mixology-ada-coleman/#gs.TsvbZVA (accessed February 15, 2021).

"Thumbnail Interviews with the Great: The Cocktail Queen." *Sphere*, January 2, 1926, 28.

West-Ender. "Things Theatrical." *Sporting Times*, February 5, 1921, 3.

Dinah Sanders and David Wondrich

Hansell, John (1960–), is the founder and editor of *Whisky Advocate*, a leading magazine covering the whisky industry. Like many early players in the whisky renaissance, Hansell came to the field indirectly: while working as an environmental chemist for Pennsylvania Power and Light (the forerunner of PPL Corp.) in the early 1990s, he developed an interest in off-beat beers and parlayed that into a beer-sharing club with an accompanying newsletter called *On Tap*. As his interests spread to include whisky, Hansell changed the name of the newsletter to *Malt Advocate* in 1994, and the following year switched its focus almost entirely to whisky, while also expanding to a magazine format, with distribution, full color, and glossy print. Hansell soon added staff and contributors, including some of the leading names in whisky writing, like Michael Jackson, Jim Murray, and Lew Bryson. In 1998 he launched WhiskyFest in New York, one of the first high-profile whisky-tasting events in the United States, and later expanded it to Chicago, San Francisco, and Washington. In 2010 M. Shanken Communications purchased *Malt Advocate* and the following year renamed it *Whisky Advocate*, keeping Hansell at the helm.

See JACKSON, MICHAEL; MURRAY, JIM; and SPIRITS WRITING.

"News." *Whisky Advocate.* https://www.whiskyadvocate.com/news/ (accessed June 10, 2021).

Clay Risen

The **hard shake** is a style of shaking a cocktail or other drink. It does not simply mean to shake hard, but rather is an elaborate style of shaking developed by the Japanese bartender Kazuo Uyeda (1944–) whereby the ice in the shaker travels in a triangle rather than the usual back-and-forth oscillation. See UYEDA, KAZUO. This is achieved by fluctuating the vertical level of the shaker, typically in descending steps, followed by a twisting motion, all with quick snaps of the wrists.

The hard shake's proponents claim it produces superior aeration and frothiness in cocktails and results in fewer shattered ice cubes, which in theory minimizes the risk of over-dilution. A perfectly executed hard shake will have the ice circulating around the edges of a shaker rather than crashing from end to end, resulting in a shaker full of whole cubes with rounded edges.

Though its alluring visual flair is admired, many believe that the hard shake does not actually deliver any meaningful benefits in cocktails. Notably, Dave Arnold, who has conducted extensive experiments on shaking styles, concluded that "from a technical standpoint, your shaking technique doesn't matter at all. As long as you shake for between 8 and 12 seconds, your cocktails will be the same no matter what you do." On the subject of aeration he adds that he was "not able to detect any appreciable difference in the texture of drinks shaking with different styles."

On the other hand, Japanese American bartender Kenta Goto (owner of Bar Goto in New York) posits that the hard shake may be advantageous in Japan because most bartenders there use the smaller cobbler shakers and block ice, which is very hard. He says this "may contribute finer aeration when using . . . an airtight container like a cobbler shaker." See COCKTAIL SHAKER. It should be noted the hard shake is not the status quo in Japan and is practiced habitually by only a handful of bartenders.

When it comes to shaking with the spacious two-piece Boston shaker, the choice of most cocktail bartenders around the world, and large ice cubes from a machine such as a Kold Draft, there appears to be a consensus that the hard shake will not have any impact on the cocktail, save for a presentational one.

Arnold, David. *Liquid Intelligence*. New York: Norton, 2015.

Cisneros, Frank (former bartender at the Mandarin Oriental in Tokyo), in discussion with the author, August 2018.

Goto, Kenta (owner of Bar Goto), in discussion.

Uyeda, Kazuo. *Cocktail Techniques*. New York: Mud Puddle, 2010.

Tom Macy

Harrington, Paul (1967–), is one of the pioneers of the twenty-first-century cocktail renaissance. A native of Bellevue, Washington, he tended bar at Enrico's in San Francisco and the Townhouse Bar & Grill in nearby Emeryville, which he had helped to make famous for its cocktails. In 1995, he was recruited by HotWired (the pioneering new website for *Wired* magazine) to provide cocktail recipes and content for the CocktailTime part of the site. Before long this led to a column, the Alchemist, which provided weekly recipes for often classic cocktails and discussed their histories. The column was enormously influential, introducing many bartenders and home mixologists to what a properly made cocktail should be. The content of the site was repackaged and slightly updated in 1998 in the book *Cocktail: The Drinks Bible for the 21st Century*, which he wrote along with Laura Moorhead, his editor at HotWired. It is one of the foundational texts of the cocktail movement that followed.

Soon after, Harrington quit bartending to work as an architect, returning in 2012 to set up the bar program at the well-regarded Clover restaurant in Spokane, Washington. One of Harrington's signature drinks is the Jasmine. He created it in 1990 while working at the Townhouse as a riff on the Pegu Club cocktail. It is made from gin, Cointreau, Campari, and lemon juice (inspired by a Charles Schumann book, Harrington only used fresh juices; that was unusual at the time). The Jasmine is often used as a drink to introduce people to gin or Campari, or both. See SCHUMANN, CHARLES.

See also COCKTAIL RENAISSANCE; JASMINE; and PEGU CLUB COCKTAIL.

Farrell, Shanna. "The West Coast Cocktail Revival Started in Emeryville Thanks to This Man." *Berkeleyside Nosh*, September 15, 2017. https://www.berkeleyside.com/2017/09/15/west-coast-cocktail-revival-started-emeryville-thanks-man (accessed March 22, 2021).

Harrington, Paul, and Laura Moorhead. *Cocktail: The Drinks Bible for the 21st Century*. New York: Viking, 1998.

Robert Hess

Harry's New York Bar, in Paris, is one of the most famous and oldest cocktail bars still in operation. From the 1920s, American tourists were famously instructed to tell cab drivers to bring them to "Sank Roo Doe Noo" (5 rue Daunou, the bar's address) and made it their first port of call when they were eager for a reminder of home. At Harry's, they could eat "chiens chauds" (hot dogs) and drink good beer (a rarity in the France of old) at its mahogany bar—said to have been imported from the States—surrounded by sports and college memorabilia hanging from the wood-paneled walls. And, of course, there were cocktails.

The bar owes its current name to legendary bartender and owner Harry McElhone. If Harry's has been made famous by high-profile clients such as Ernest Hemingway (who is said to have once drunk twenty Whisky Sours at the bar), F. Scott Fitzgerald, or George Gershwin, it was already a haven for Americans, famous or not, before Scotsman McElhone took over in 1923.

The New York Bar, as it was then called, was opened by retired jockey Tod Sloan in 1911 and fast became a magnet for sportsmen and journalists. An inveterate gambler and poor manager, he quickly sold his interest to another jockey, Milton Henry. Henry sold off during World War I, but in 1920, Nell Henry, his by then ex-wife, bought it back. She managed to attract a new crowd, in particular thanks to the basement's cabaret. Offering a revolving lineup of good American musicians with no cover charge, it was one of the very few places open between dinner time and the opening of the dance clubs where patrons were not forced to order champagne or harassed by bar girls.

When McElhone, a renowned bartender with international experience, bought the place (and added his name to that of the bar), he built on this solid foundation. A congenial character, he got on famously with the great sportsmen, journalists, and artists of the lost generation who patronized his bar. Harry's became the place to see and be seen for the increasing number of US tourists attracted by Paris for its romance—and its (legal) bars.

McElhone's keen marketing instinct also helped out. His team would regularly come up with drinks to celebrate world events (or mock prohibition: the Scofflaw, for instance), organize beer drinking contests, or spread fantastic stories about patrons visiting with strange pets such as lions and panthers. The bar was also the founding "trap" of the International Bar Flies, a drinkers' association, in 1924, and to this day organizes straw polls for each US presidential election. Friends in the press would relay each initiative and create more publicity.

During World War II, McElhone fled to London, and the authorities seized the bar. After Paris's liberation, Harry's found a growing French clientele, among which were the likes of Jean-Paul Sartre. When McElhone died in 1958, his son Andy took over. He was followed in 1989 by McElhone's grandson Duncan. Today, Harry's is run by the latter's wife and their son.

According to bar lore, Harry's is also the birthplace of legendary cocktails such as the Bloody Mary, the Sidecar, the White Lady, and the French 75. See BLOODY MARY; SIDECAR; WHITE LADY; and FRENCH 75. These mostly bogus claims only came up after McElhone's death in 1958. Some are particularly surprising: for instance, back in 1922 McElhone himself had attributed the Sidecar to bartender Malachi McGarry of Buck's Club in London.

This insistence to claim drinks they didn't create is all the more confusing since the truth would barely make a dent in the bar's reputation: it is for its antiquated charms and the legendary figures who drank (and made drinks) there that tourists keep on flocking through its famed revolving doors, not for the drinks that were supposedly invented there.

See also McELHONE, HENRY "HARRY."

Cleveland Plain Dealer, August 12, 1962.

Reynolds, Bruce. *Paris with the Lid Lifted*. New York: A. L. Burt, 1927.

Woon, Basil. *The Paris That's Not in the Guidebooks*. New York: Robert M. McBride, 1931.

François Monti

Harvey Wallbanger

Harvey Wallbanger is a Screwdriver—vodka and orange juice—lent a dash of exoticism by a float of the Italian liqueur Galliano. This simple highball enjoyed a popularity in the 1970s equaled by few other postwar drinks. During the peak of its popularity, it inspired bottled versions and cake mixes. Much of the hype surrounding the drink was due to a marketing campaign hatched by George Bednar, who worked for McKesson Imports, Galliano's importer at the time, featuring a dopey-looking cartoon surfer mascot (the eponymous Harvey) created by New York marketer Bill Young, and a racy catchphrase ("My name is Harvey Wallbanger and I can be made"). The drink itself was likely the work of bartender Donato "Duke" Antone, who may have created it as early as the early 1950s at the Hollywood bar Black Watch, calling it the Duke Screwdriver. See ANTONE, DONATO "DUKE." How it acquired its new and now famous label is not known. Bednar encountered the drink under that name while on a scouting trip in Los Angeles, California, in the late 1960s, investigating wide consumption of Galliano there. McKesson adopted the cocktail and built a marketing campaign around it in 1969, offering free merchandise to anyone who threw a Wallbanger party or event; thousands did. Later, McKesson enlisted Antone to promote the drink, an early instance of a corporate-mixologist collaboration, and one of the most successful.

See also SCREWDRIVER and GALLIANO.

Recipe: Combine in a tall glass full of ice 45 ml vodka and 120 ml orange juice. Float 22 ml Galliano on top and add a straw and a maraschino cherry.

Simonson, Robert. "Banging My Head against a Wall." *Lucky Peach* 12 (August 2014), 96–99.

Robert Simonson

Haus Alpenz is an American specialty wine-and-spirits importer based in Edina, Minnesota. Founded in 2005 by Eric Seed (1969–), the company initially focused on importing esoteric Austrian spirits such as zirbenschnaps (sold as Zirbenz Stone Pine Liqueur of the Alps, a liqueur flavored with the fruit of the arolla pine), owing to Seed's early interest in rustic alpine liqueurs borne from his time spent in Vienna as a student. But in response to demands from bartenders and other customers, Alpenz began importing spirits and liqueurs long absent from the American market, including crème de violette (under the Rothman & Winter name), allspice liqueur, and Batavia arrack, along with aperitif wines including the Dolin line of Chambery vermouths, Cocchi's Vermouth di Torino and Aperitivo Americano, and Byrrh Grand Quinquina. See CRÈME DE VIOLETTE and ARRACK, BATAVIA. The company also specializes in spirits that lack mass-market appeal but are highly desired in cocktail circles, such as an Old Tom gin and a navy-strength gin from venerable London producer Hayman's, the potently aromatic Smith & Cross Jamaican rum, and a range of aperitifs and digestives including Cappelletti Vino Aperitivo Americano Rosso. See OLD TOM GIN and NAVY-STRENGTH. By focusing on such esoteric products and on their utility in a cocktail environment, and by emphasizing authenticity of flavor and an appreciation of culinary traditions, Haus Alpenz developed a dedicated audience during the early twenty-first century cocktail renaissance, with its vermouths, liqueurs, and other products reaching the status of near necessity in serious cocktail bars. See COCKTAIL RENAISSANCE.

Felten, Eric. "Alpine Liqueur Comes to Aspen." *Wall Street Journal*, April 8–9, 2006.
Haus Alpenz website. https://alpenz.com (accessed February 15, 2021).

Paul Clarke

Havana Club is a popular brand of Cuban rums distributed globally (except in the United States) by the French Pernod-Ricard company. The brand grew out of a distillery founded by the Arechabala family in Cardenas, Cuba, in 1878. The Havana Club brand was created in 1934, following the repeal of US Prohibition, as a light, crisp rum targeted at the American market. The family left Cuba for Spain with the rise of Fidel Castro, who nationalized the distillery in 1960.

The Arechabala family allowed its trademark registration to lapse in 1973, believing it had no further value. Cubaexport, an enterprise owned by the Cuban government, registered the lapsed mark in the United States in 1976 and sold limited quantities in Cuba and some Eastern European countries. In 1993, Pernod-Ricard formed a joint venture with the government of Cuba to expand global distribution and marketing. Havana Club, like all Cuban goods, was blocked from sales in the United States by a blanket embargo. Nonetheless, by 1998, Havana Club was among the fastest-growing rums in the world, producing more than one million cases annually (both in previously existing distilleries and in ones built expressly for the brand) and gaining adherents in Italy, England, Canada, and elsewhere. As is the Cuban style, Havana Club is a blend of column-distilled molasses-based rums, some quite rich, that are aged and charcoal-filtered before bottling or further aging.

In 1997, the Bacardi family, which by and large had been unchallenged in rum sales globally, purchased from the Arechabala family the claim to any remaining rights in the lapsed trademark. Bacardi then launched a years-long battle over the trademark in the United States, claiming in part that it had been seized illegally. The legal battle has yet to conclude. Both Pernod Ricard and Bacardi currently produce versions of Havana Club, although Bacardi's two versions (Havana Club Puerto Rican Rum) are sold only in the United States. For the rest of the world, the Cuban Havana Club remains the flagship for that country's rum industry. In 2018, it sold some 4.6 million cases, making it the world's fifth-largest rum brand.

See also BACARDI and RUM.

Gjelten, Tom. *Bacardi and the Long Fight for Cuba: The Biography of a Cause.* New York: Viking, 2008.

Wayne Curtis

heads are the volatile compounds such as methanol and acetaldehyde that are removed at the beginning of a distillation run. See also CUT.

health and spirits. The effect of alcoholic drinks on the brain and body has simultaneously worried, impressed, and downright mystified us ever since we learned of their existence. Over the centuries, the opinion on alcohol has swung between healthful, hurtful, and everything in between. But one line of thought has remained constant for hundreds of years: if you drink, drink in moderation, because any positive health benefit from drinking a little alcohol will be watered down by the negative aspects of drinking a lot of it.

Hope in a Bottle: The Early Years

From the beginning of distillation through the eighteenth century, distilled spirits were one of the most concentrated and effective medicines known to humanity, and indeed, at most times and places where they were known, they were an important part of the physician's pharmacopoeia, however that profession was construed. See DISTILLATION, HISTORY. The stimulant properties of concentrated alcohol were noted early on, particularly in Europe. In the 1200s, the author of a treatise attributed to Ramon Llull "admired the smell and flavor of . . . distilled spirit and presciently suggested that it might be an excellent stimulant for soldiers before they went into battle," writes Rod Phillips in *Alcohol: A History*. Llull's colleague, fixated on finding youth-preserving potions, believed spirits held a key to those, too. The excellent extractive and preservative properties of spirits assisted in this belief, as alcoholized extracts of medicinal herbs were easily prepared and once prepared appeared incorruptible, remaining fresh for as long as they could be kept on the shelf.

While different infusions and botanical distillations were applied to different diseases (juniper spirits, for instance, were held to be a remedy for kidney problems), there was a great deal of leeway in their prescription. Indeed, that same juniper spirit was enlisted to perk up weary soldiers, but also to fight wound infection and a hundred other things. By the 1600s, European physicians were even prescribing spirits preventatively, with a half spoonful a day prescribed to maintain general overall health. By then, physicians considered distilled beverages a fixit for everything from forgetfulness to heart disease.

Growing Concerns

As the popularity of spirits widened, it became hard to draw the line between when spirits could be helpful and when they may be harmful. And even as physicians continued to prescribe them, alcohol's health halo began to fade. The dangers of excess grew more apparent, particularly in the seventeenth century, when new spirits, such as rum and whisky, also entered the fray. More people imbibing meant more frequent outbreaks of drunken behavior, prompting worries over not only the effect of spirits on overall wellness but also its threat to social order and public peace.

What doctors didn't know then, which we are understanding increasingly better now, is that the ethanol in alcoholic beverages lessens (and, in higher doses, deactivates) the brain-circuit activity that allows us to feel anxious and afraid. And depending on the dose, it can hinder the ability to control behavior and make judgments, whether it's buying items in a store or correctly reading another person's body language. Without realizing that hard liquor contains a higher concentration of alcohol by volume compared to fermented beverages, early drinkers would imbibe in the same amounts and succumb to more reckless behavior than with the former. By definition, a typical 45-ml shot of 40 percent ABV liquor contains almost 20 ml of pure ethanol, which is the same amount of alcohol as 350 ml of beer (5 percent ABV) or 150 ml of wine (12 percent ABV). See ETHANOL.

In 1917, the American Medical Association drew up a resolution declaring that it "opposes the use of alcohol as a beverage" and that "the use of alcohol as a therapeutic agent should be discouraged." True, some doctors continued to prescribe spirits even through Prohibition—a loophole for drinking—but advances in medical science meant there was finally an explanation for the strange behaviors and failing health associated for centuries with drinking too much. See PROHIBITION AND TEMPERANCE IN AMERICA.

In 1969, a hallmark paper published in the *New England Journal of Medicine* secured the association between heavy drinking and liver damage. Heavy drinking is now defined as more than three drinks a day or more than seven per week for women; it's more than four drinks a day or more than 14 per week for men. According to the National Institute of Alcohol Abuse and Alcoholism (NIAAA), about 20 percent of heavy drinkers develop an enlarged liver, known as fatty liver disease. The condition is reduced or disappears when drinking is stopped, but continued overdrinking can lead to more serious problems, such as alcoholic hepatitis, where the cells in the liver can get inflamed. All this can eventually lead to a condition called cirrhosis, where scar tissue replaces normal liver tissue, blood flow is disrupted, and the organ ultimately shuts down.

A 1973 article in *The Lancet*, a British medical journal, introduced the term "fetal alcohol syndrome." When a pregnant woman drinks an alcoholic beverage, the alcohol passes from her bloodstream and into the placenta and the fetus. Alcohol present in a developing baby's bloodstream can then interfere with the development of the brain and other critical organs, as well as their structures and how they function. This can result in stunted growth, reduced muscle tone and coordination, delayed cognitive development, heart defects, and facial deformities. Scientists now theorize that this may stem from alcohol's tendency to prevent the absorption of folate, an important nutrient for fetal development. The greatest risk for severe problems occurs when a woman binge-drinks or is a regular heavy drinker, though even lesser amounts can cause damage. According to the US Department of Health and Human Services, there is no known safe level of alcohol consumption during pregnancy.

Besides chronic overdrinking, binge-drinking carries with it its own dangers. The NIAAA defines it as a pattern of drinking alcohol that brings blood alcohol concentration (BAC) to 0.08g/dl or above—which is typically five or more drinks consecutively in males or four or more in females over the course of about two hours. Most binge drinkers are not, in fact, alcohol dependent, and they're most commonly between the ages of eighteen and thirty-four years old. A 2011 *Journal of Substance Use* paper reported that underage drinkers were more likely to binge on spirits, particularly vodka, than wine or beer. Besides impaired driving (and the potential tragedies that can arise from it), extreme cases of binge drinking can lead to alcohol poisoning—a condition in which there is so much alcohol in the bloodstream that areas of the brain controlling basic life-support functions begin to shut down. Symptoms include confusion; difficulty remaining conscious; vomiting; seizures; trouble with breathing; slow heart rate; clammy skin; dulled responses, such as no gag reflex; and extremely low body temperature.

New Health Worries

More recently, scientists have investigated the effect of alcohol on the immune system. In a 2011 *British Journal of Pharmacology* study on mice, alcohol caused an immune response in the brain, and the researchers believe that it is these changes that underlie the more obvious symptoms of too much alcohol, such as slurred speech and stumbling. When drugs were used to block certain immune receptors in the mice, the alcoholic effects were reduced. In a 2015 University of Maryland study, when healthy subjects guzzled enough alcohol in twenty minutes or so that a breathalyzer test registered 0.1 percent, two to five hours later their blood showed a decrease in the levels of disease-fighting cells—the same kinds that appear in the bloodstream when you have an infection or get a cut—and a reduction in their ability to function. These changes suggest that even a single binge episode could weaken our ability to recover.

So convincing is the evidence linking alcohol to certain forms of cancer that the US Department of Health and Human Services National Toxicology Program lists alcohol as a known human carcinogen. The higher the intake—particularly over a consistent period of time—the higher the risk. For head and neck cancer (including the oral cavity, except for lips), throat, and larynx, those who consumed more than three and a half drinks per day (50 grams) had at least two to three times greater risk of developing these cancers than nondrinkers. For esophageal cancer, there's an increased risk for squamous-cell carcinoma, particularly if the drinker happens to have inherited a faulty alcohol metabolism gene. Alcohol is a primary cause of liver cancer.

For breast cancer, more than 100 epidemiological studies suggest that the more you drink, the greater the risk. As the *British Journal of Cancer* reports: "For every 10 grams of alcohol consumed per day (slightly less than one drink) researchers observed a small (7 percent) increase in breast cancer risk." The increased risk was 7 percent for every 10 grams for colorectal cancer. It appears that the compounds produced when alcohol is broken down (notably, the toxin acetaldehyde) can damage DNA and proteins. Alcohol also seems to interfere with the absorption of nutrients and increases the levels of estrogen, which in itself has been linked to increased breast cancer risks.

For reasons unknown, alcohol is associated with *decreased* risk of kidney cancer and non-Hodgkin lymphoma.

A New Positive Spin

The news on alcohol took a surprising positive turn in 1996, when Morley Safer on *60 Minutes* reported on a possible explanation for the "French paradox," the phenomenon in which fewer French suffer from heart disease despite their fattier diets. As the theory goes, it's because they imbibe in more wine than Americans, and wine, particularly red wine, contains resveratrol, a powerful antioxidant found in the skin of dark grapes. But it later turned out that the alcohol itself—whether in wine, beer, or spirits—had its own healthful benefits.

Although wine has garnered much of the attention for its heart-health connection since that 1996 report, the revival of alcohol as a healthful (or at least not harmful) drink began many years before. A 1996 *British Medical Journal* paper that reviewed twenty-five of those earlier studies—which, together, covered a range of alcoholic drinks (including wine, spirits, and beer) in relation to lower risks for coronary heart disease—reported that none of the drink categories had a stronger association than the other. More than 100 prospective studies have linked moderate alcohol intake to lower rates of various types of disease and cardiovascular-related deaths.

With moderate drinking, the molecules of alcohol seem, over time, to increase the concentration of high density lipoprotein (HDL) cholesterol, often called the "good" cholesterol, in the blood; HDL helps keep the inner wall of blood vessels healthy. Sam Zakhari, head of the office of scientific affairs at the Distilled Spirits Council of the United States, reports that moderate doses of alcohol also seem to prevent blood platelets from sticking together and improve other factors that affect blood clotting.

When consumed in moderation, alcohol may cut diabetes risks. In a 2011 *American Journal of Clinical Nutrition* paper, women who consumed a diet high in refined carbohydrates but also moderate levels of alcohol (about two drinks a week) had a 30 percent lower chance of developing type 2 diabetes than women with similar diets who refrained from alcohol. However, heavy drinking did not offset risks for diabetes. A 2013 *Annals of Epidemiology* paper suggests that alcohol's ability to increase levels of HDL may help decrease the chances of diabetes. While the verdict is still out as to the details of how alcohol lowers diabetes risks, researchers believe that it can enhance the levels of anti-inflammatory molecules, as well as proteins (ghrelin, adiponectin) associated with insulin resistance.

While heavy drinking can cause cumulative damage to the brain in the long term, including shrinkage and learning and memory problems, several studies have also linked moderate alcohol consumption to some improved aspects of cognition, at least among older adults. A 2015 *American Journal of Alzheimer's Disease and Other Dementias* paper reported that adults aged sixty or over who drank alcohol in moderation had a larger hippocampal volume and better episodic memory (the ability to recall past autobiographical events and experiences) than those who refrained. No difference was seen with respect to the amount of alcohol that participants consumed during middle age. Scientists believe that light to moderate amounts of alcohol may promote the generation of nerve cells in the hippocampus as well as the levels of brain chemicals associated with memory. It's worth noting, however, that while this research suggests moderate alcohol consumption may be beneficial to the brain during old age, consuming even small amounts of alcohol can be harmful to older adults with certain medical conditions or who are taking certain medications.

For both old and young people, alcohol remains potentially addictive and destructive when consumed in excess. As a result, medical experts stress that it's best to consider its possible advantages simply as a bonus when enjoying the occasional drink and, instead, count on reaping your health benefits primarily from a good diet and frequent exercise.

American Liver Foundation. "Alcohol Related Disease." https://liverfoundation.org/alcohol-related-liver-disease/ (accessed April 22, 2021).

"Drinking Red Wine for Heart Health? Read This Before You Toast." American Heart Association, May 24, 2019. https://www.heart.org/en/news/2019/05/24/drinking-red-wine-for-heart-health-read-this-before-you-toast (accessed April 22, 2021).

Foster, Gerald S., and Benjamin Castleman. "Case-30-1969: Liver Disease Associated with Positive L.E.-Cell Test and Positive Rheumatoid Factor; Case Records of the Massachusetts General Hospital." New England Journal of Medicine 281 (1969): 206–213. https://www.nejm.org/doi/full/10.1056/NEJM196907242810408 (accessed April 22, 2021).

"How Morley Safer Convinced Americans to Drink More Wine." CBS News, August 28, 2016, https://www.cbsnews.com/news/how-morley-safer-convinced-americans-to-drink-more-wine/ (accessed April 22, 2021).

National Cancer Institute. "Alcohol and Cancer Risk Fact Sheet." https://www.cancer.gov/about-cancer/causes-prevention/risk/alcohol/alcohol-fact-sheet (accessed April 22, 2021).

National Institute on Alcohol Abuse and Alcoholism. "Alcohol and Your Health: Research-Based Information on Drinking and its Impact." https://www.niaaa.nih.gov/alcohol-health (accessed April 22, 2021).

Phillips, Rod. Alcohol: A History. Chapel Hill: University of North Carolina Press, 2014.

Room, Robin. "Fetal Alcohol Syndrome: A Biography of a Diagnosis." The Lancet, June 11, 2005. https://www.thelancet.com/journals/lancet/article/PIIS0140-6736(05)66681-0/fulltext (accessed April 22, 2021).

Joanne Chen

heart is the desirable portion of a distillation run that comes off a still after the heads and before the tails. See also CUT.

heat exchangers are designed to transfer energy, in the form of heat, from one substance to another. Effective and efficient control of temperature being essential to every stage of spirits production, distilleries use many different types of them, from ones as simple as a pipe that carries hot vapor through a vat of cold wine to intricate and highly engineered pieces of equipment capable of heating or cooling hundreds of gallons of fluid every minute. They are used to heat and cool the mash, remove the heat of fermentation, drive the distillation process, and then condense and cool the distillate. Even the still itself acts as a heat exchanger, transferring heat from the vapors inside the still to the air in the room. Heat exchangers can also be used to make a distillery more energy efficient, by recovering waste heat and transferring it to parts of the process where the heat is needed.

See also CHAUFFE-VIN; DISTILLATE; DISTILLATION, PROCESS; FERMENTATION; and MASH.

McCabe, Warren L., and Julian C. Smith. Unit Operations of Chemical Engineering. 6th ed. Boston: McGraw Hill, 2001.

Nicole Austin

Heaven Hill Brands, located near Bardstown, Kentucky, is one of the biggest liquor companies in the United States. Founded shortly after Prohibition by the Shapira family and outside investors, the company took its name from William Heavenhill, a farmer who, more than a century earlier, had worked the land where the company was located. A newcomer to the whisky industry, Heaven Hill hired distillers from the Beam family to oversee production. This line of

Beams, from the same extended family as the name-sake competitor (now Beam-Suntory), have held key positions at Heaven Hill ever since.

Hungry for revenue in an industry where products often age for lengthy periods, Heaven Hill sold its first whiskies and other spirits to outside distributors who aged and branded them however they saw fit. As is common for new distilleries, some of Heaven Hill's own early brands, such as Bourbon Falls, were relatively young (about two years old) and were eventually discontinued. As the company matured and developed more of its own brands, however, it was able to provide older products, including Evan Williams and Elijah Craig bourbons, both named after Kentucky settlers. Over the years, it also acquired brands of whisky, rum, gin, vodka, and various liqueurs from its competitors, including Rittenhouse Rye, Dubonnet, Admiral Nelson's, and Hpnotiq, among others. By the 1970s, the Shapira family had bought out its various partners and took full control of the company.

In the early 2000s, as the American whisky market picked up, a number of the company's miscellaneous old whisky brands, such as Rittenhouse rye and Mellow Corn corn whisky, suddenly began generating a good deal of interest, and its extensive stocks of long-aged bourbon and rye proved to be invaluable. As of 2019, it remained the largest independent, family-owned distillery in the United States.

See also WHISKY, BOURBON.

Zoeller, Chester. *Bourbon in Kentucky: A History of Distilleries in Kentucky.* Louisville, KY: Butler, 2010.

Cecil, Sam K. *Bourbon: The Evolution of Kentucky Whiskey.* New York: Turner, 2010.

Cowdery, Charles K. *Bourbon, Straight: The Uncut and Unfiltered Story of American Whiskey.* Chicago: Made and Bottled in Kentucky, 2004.

Veach, Michael. *Kentucky Bourbon Whiskey, an American Heritage.* Lexington: University Press of Kentucky, 2013.

Reid Mitenbuler

Hellenistic still is an ancient form of pot still in which alcohol vapor condenses on the inner surface of a large concave or pointed head and runs down into a circular gutter before draining through a pipe into a receiver. See DISTILLATION, HISTORY.

Hemingway Daiquiri, which adds a barspoon each of white grapefruit juice and maraschino liqueur to the traditional Daiquiri recipe and omits the sugar, is a version of the Daiquiri no. 3 from Havana's Floridita bar, named for the bibulous writer who downed them in impressive volume there. These days, most people leave the sugar in. See also DAIQUIRI and FLORIDITA.

Hendrick's Gin has carved out a singular and substantial niche in the gin market since its launch at the dawn of this century. See GIN. Flavored with cucumber and rose essences and packaged in squat bottles reminiscent of Victorian apothecary jars, the gin has led growth in the premium gin category, with annual sales that have rocketed past the million-case mark.

Developed in the late 1990s for Scottish spirits company William Grant & Sons by in-house chemist Lesley Gracie (1956–), who still oversees its distillation, Hendrick's was reportedly inspired by two quintessential fixtures of British summers: cucumber sandwiches and rose gardens. After much experimentation, Gracie settled on a blend of gins made on two antique stills that Charles Gordon, great-grandson of the company's founder, bought at auction in 1966: a pot still dating back to 1860 and a Carter-head still made in 1948. See CARTER-HEAD STILL. Juniper and ten other botanicals are boiled directly in the pot still's kettle, whereas in the Carter head they are placed in a vapor infusion chamber in the still's lyne arm, creating a more delicate distillate. See JUNIPER and BOTANICAL. Because the cucumber and rose essences are added after distillation and blending, Hendrick's cannot be labeled as a London dry gin. See LONDON DRY GIN.

In 2018, William Grant built a Victorian-inspired "gin palace" for Hendrick's to replace its original modest quarters at the massive Girvan distillery in the Scottish Lowlands. The newer facility is equipped with six stills, including four exact replicas of the original stills.

See also STILL, POT.

Gin Cooperative. *A History of Hendrick's.* https://thegincooperative.com (accessed March 22, 2021).

David Mahoney

Hennessy, a part of the international luxury-goods conglomerate LVMH Moët Hennessy Louis Vuitton since 1987, is the largest cognac producer in the world, with over 40 percent of the market. Its iconic label, bearing the family's coat of arms and a grapevine wreath, hints at a rich heritage. The house dates back to 1765, when Irishman Richard Hennessy (1727–1800) launched a brandy exporting business. By the mid-1800s, it was the leading cognac producer, a status it has never lost. In 1852, it alone was responsible for nearly 25 percent of all cognac sold. It was also one of the pioneers in the move from sales by the cask to by the bottle, a process that was accelerated in the 1870s by the collapse of the bulk brandy business due to phylloxera. In the 1870s, Hennessy was, with Martell, one of the pioneers in classifying its products by the number of stars on the label, with one star meaning six years old, two stars nine and three stars twelve (Hennessy claims to have invented the system, but evidence is contradictory). With degradation of the ages over time, this system became the industry standard until the 1960s, when it was replaced by the current system of VS, VSOP, XO, and the like. In fact, the designation XO was a Hennessy one as well, introduced in 1870 for an "extra old" blend of one hundred eaux-de-vie aged over forty years. See XO.

In the modern era, the brand has taken a decidedly hip and urban turn, organizing traveling photo exhibitions, partnering with artists such as Shepard Fairey to create limited-edition bottles, and collaborating with hip-hop stars like the Roots, Nas, and Mobb Deep. And while its entry-level cognacs have declined in age since the nineteenth century, as have those of its competitors, the company still bottles a number of very well-regarded, and expensive, older blends, produced under the supervision of the Fillioux family, its master blenders since 1800. While the company does some of its own distilling, it functions primarily as a negociant, buying raw or partially matured spirits from hundreds of winegrower-distillers and finishing and blending them in its own vast warehouses.

See also COGNAC; COURVOISIER; EAU-DE-VIE; MARTELL; and RÉMY MARTIN.

Faith, Nicholas. *Cognac*. London: Mitchell Beazley, 2004.
"Hennessy Legacy." Hennessy website. http://www.hennessy.com/us/250/ (accessed on February 15, 2021).
"Some Very Interesting Information Showing How the Seven Ages of Hennessy's Brandy Can Be Employed" (advertisement). *London Times*, December 1, 1906, 13.

Alia Akkam

Henry Africa's was the most famous West Coast exemplar of the 1970s "singles bar." In contrast to the dark, clubby, male-dominated saloons that preceded the sexual revolution, singles bars were well-lit, airy, female-friendly "meet markets" that arose when second-wave feminism collided with cocktail culture. Not without irony, many singles bars were decorated like 1890s Gilded Age lounges, which had often banned unescorted women. They fancifully resurrected the era's brass rails, Tiffany lamps, and potted plants—so many plants, in so many places, that those singles bars also came to be called fern bars. See FERN BARS.

When Norman Jay Hobday (1933–2011) opened Henry Africa's in San Francisco in 1969, it wasn't the first leafy coed hotspot in the Bay Area (three years earlier the Kingston Trio had bankrolled the Trident in Sausalito). But it was the funkiest. In addition to the usual Gay Nineties indoor garden look, Hobday decorated with electric trains, mounted taxidermy heads, and whimsical Victorian knickknacks. It somehow managed to suggest both innocent fun and a Barbary Coast bordello: the perfect combination for his newly "liberated" clientele. The drinks also played naughty and nice: the Lemon Drop, Hobday's most enduring original cocktail, recreated the taste of the eponymous children's candy to mask the presence of two full shots of vodka. See LEMON DROP.

Hobday loved his bar as much as his customers did, legally changing his name to Henry Africa a few years before it closed in 1986. He then opened an even more elaborate fern bar called Capt. Eddie Rickenbacker's, but he remained Henry Africa until his dying day in 2011.

Whiting, Sam. "Henry Africa—Fern Bar Creator—Dies." *San Francisco Chronicle*, March 2, 2011.

Jeff Berry

Henry's Bar was the premiere American bar in Paris from the 1890s until the 1920s and still retained a fashionable clientele until it closed in 1938. It was

Henry's Bar in 1907, with Henry Tepé, *center*. Wondrich Collection.

opened by Henry Tépé (ca. 1856–1918), a German whose sole experience with the United States was as a ship's boy, when he spent an afternoon walking around Hoboken, New Jersey, between sailings. After that he spent some time in England and then at the Hotel Chatham in Paris, popular with Americans, where he ended up in charge of the new American bar. In 1889, he opened his own bar at 11 Rue Volney, around the corner from the Chatham. Almost immediately, it became the refuge for the homesick American of sporting inclinations. Dark and intimate, the bar was a place, as an 1893 article described it, where "15 or 20 well-dressed and well-to-do Americans and Englishmen . . . sit or stand talking in the cozy room. Whiskey Sours, Gin Fizzes, . . . [and] a real free lunch mingle with a real barkeeper and a real bar and the good old American language." Over the whole thing presided the trim, elegant figure of Tépé, at least when he wasn't at the races (he was a pillar of the Paris turf).

Tépé's head barkeeper at the turn of the century, Otto, had a reputation as a mixologist, and indeed Henry's seems to have been the vector for the new, vermouth-heavy school of American mixology to colonize Paris. It certainly retained a reputation

as having the best cocktails in town well into the 1920s, when it was eclipsed by Harry's New York Bar, around the corner on Rue Daunou. See Harry's New York Bar. Tépé, perhaps suffering from dementia, committed suicide in 1918. The bar continued, but more as an exclusive old-timers' club than the lively place it had been. It closed just short of its fiftieth anniversary.

"Paris the Disappointing." *New York Sun*. July 30, 1893, 5.
"What Three Members of the Brooklyn Club Saw Abroad." *Brooklyn Daily Eagle*, August 8, 1909, 3.
Woon, Basil. *The Paris That's Not in the Guide Books*. New York: R. M. McBride, 1931.

David Wondrich

herbal liqueur is a sweetened alcoholic beverage with flavors derived from herbs and spices. These liqueurs are typically made by steeping herbs, roots, leaves, flowers, citrus peels, or other botanical ingredients in alcohol. Typical herbs and spices used in these liqueurs include angelica, anise, cardamom, cinnamon, clove, coriander, fennel, gentian, hyssop, iris, juniper, lemon balm, marjoram, mint, oregano, peppermint, star anise, thyme, and turmeric.

Herbal liqueurs are made using a variety of production methods and base spirits. The French liqueur Bigallet Thym, for example, is made by macerating and then distilling thyme sprigs in a neutral alcohol made of sugar beets. Another French liqueur, Giffard's Vanille de Madagascar, uses grape neutral alcohol flavored with vanilla extract and sweetened with cane sugar; other vanilla liqueurs, however (such as Gabriel Boudier Vanille au Cognac and the now-discontinued Navan, from Grand Marnier) are built on a cognac base. Mexico's Ancho Reyes is made by steeping ancho chiles in neutral alcohol for six months. Sugar syrup is added to balance the flavors and provide body to the liqueur. Many herbal liqueurs were originally used medicinally, as an herbal remedy or tonic and as a digestive aid. See HEALTH AND SPIRITS.

Common brands of herbal liqueurs include Bénédictine, Chartreuse, Jägermeister, Liquore Strega, and Galliano. See BÉNÉDICTINE; CHARTREUSE; and GALLIANO. Strega is a yellow Italian herbal liqueur that derives its color from saffron; other flavors come from mint, juniper, and fennel. Herbal liqueurs include such subcategories as amari and fernets.

See also AMARO and FERNET.

McCart, Melissa. "Dine: The Lure and Lore of Herbal Liqueurs." *Pittsburgh Post-Gazette*, March 17, 2013. http://www.post-gazette.com/libations/2013/03/17/Dine-The-lure-and-lore-of-herbal-liqueurs/stories/201303170144 (accessed February 15, 2021).

Michael Dietsch

herbs, in culinary terms, are the leafy green parts of a plant, often used as a flavoring in cuisine. In cooking, they can be utilized either fresh or dried, but for cocktail preparation they are best used fresh, when their essential oils are the sharpest and fully concentrated.

Many herbs have a history of medicinal attributes associated to them, with a multitude of health benefits from their essential oils. Such herbs have been used as both medicinal and flavoring components in such prepared beverage products as gin, vermouth, and absinthe and in proprietary products such as Campari and Chartreuse. See GIN; VERMOUTH; ABSINTHE; CAMPARI;

and CHARTREUSE. Initially, these products were often intended to be consumed either straight or mixed with water in order to enjoy their benefits. Gradually over time, though, various drinks were created which made use of their unique and specific flavor profiles in both alcoholic and nonalcoholic beverages.

In modern-day cocktail preparation, we are witnessing an expansion of the use of herbs not only as muddled ingredients but as decorative garnish or frozen artfully into ice cubes. See GARNISH. Herbs such as rosemary, basil, and thyme are increasingly making appearances in mixed drinks; the most common among them is mint. Alongside its historical prominence in the Mojito, the Mint Julep, and the Southside, mint also plays a role as an aromatic garnish in the Mai Tai. See MOJITO; MINT JULEP; SOUTHSIDE; and MAI TAI.

Herbs can be utilized in spirituous infusions as well as in flavored syrups. See INFUSION and FLAVORED SYRUP. In most of these products, a single herb is utilized rather than a blend. Alcohol (which acts as a solvent) extracts the herb's essential oil and, after being strained, is used to flavor a cocktail. In the absence of alcohol (if creating a rosemary-flavored simple syrup, for instance) it may be necessary to employ heat to break down the woody structure of the herb and provide ideal extraction.

To use herbs *á la minute* in cocktails, it is common for bartenders to add a fresh sprig of herb into the mixing tin and "muddle" it to quickly infuse its essential oils into the drink. Many herbs (such as mint) store their essential oils on the surface of their leaves in small cells (known as sessile secretory glands), which are essentially like microscopic balloons that are easily ruptured during the muddling process to release their oils.

Depending on the degree (or lack) of woodiness of an herb, muddling can provide a much more efficient way to extract the essence of an herb rather than macerating it in syrup. A syrup may weigh heavily on the sharp flavor of the herb and suppress its crisp, clean flavor profile. Yet even with muddling's efficient flavor extraction, caution should always be used. Aggressive muddling will break down the plant matter itself and release unwanted compounds into the drink (such as chlorophyll), offering an undesirable bitter flavor.

As an aromatic garnish, it has become standard to slap the sprig between one's hands, releasing its aroma into the air around it and thus increasing the cocktail's aromatic intensity.

Proper storage plays an important role in preserving an herb's essential oils and aromas. A good method is to place only the very bottoms of trimmed stems into a cup containing a shallow ice-water bath, which will allow the leaves to remain plump and hydrated.

Stewart, Amy. *The Drunken Botanist*. Chapel Hill, NC: Algonquin, 2013.

Stobart, Tom. *Herbs, Spices and Flavorings*. Woodstock, NY: Overlook, 1970.

Audrey Saunders

Herradura is a tequila distillery in Amatitán, Jalisco, founded in 1870 by Félix López (ca. 1825–1878) on a hacienda formerly owned by Feliciano Romo, a Catholic priest (it is likely the property had been producing mezcal for several generations before that). The distillery trademarked its horseshoe logo (*herradura* is Spanish for "horseshoe") in 1928. Herradura bottles only 100 percent blue agave tequila, eschewing blended *mixtos*. American entertainers Bing Crosby and Phil Harris began importing the brand to the United States in 1955 after discovering it on a trip to Mexico, and for a time Herradura was the only 100 percent agave tequila available in the United States. The company claims it introduced the now ubiquitous reposado category in 1974. The reposado category, however, was already being discussed in tequila industry circles in 1970, and Sauza's lightly-aged Hornitos expression, a reposado in all but name, dates back to the early 1960s. See REPOSADO.

The Herradura brand became popular with modern mixologists after Julio Bermejo, owner of the influential Tommy's Mexican Restaurant in San Francisco made it his well tequila, using it in his famous Tommy's Margarita. In 1994, Herradura introduced the El Jimador brand, which became the top-selling tequila in Mexico. After more than a century in family hands, the company was sold in 2007 to the US-based company Brown-Forman. These days, Tommy's uses Luna Azul reposado in the well.

See also BROWN-FORMAN; MARGARITA; and TEQUILA.

Martineau, Chantal. *How the Gringos Stole Tequila*. Chicago: Chicago Review Press, 2015.

Robert Simonson

herrengedeck, or "gentleman's setup," is the German name for a shot of korn with a beer chaser, a drink generally associated with older, traditional-minded drinkers. See also KORN and BOILERMAKER.

Hess, Robert (1959–), is a technology professional and cocktail evangelist near Seattle, Washington. The son of a Methodist minister, Hess was a technical evangelist at Microsoft and worked for the company from 1988 to 2012.

In 1998, marrying his computer expertise with a lifelong interest in cocktails, Hess launched DrinkBoy, a website and web forum that soon became a major focal point of the then-nascent cocktail renaissance, attracting a global audience of bartenders and cocktail enthusiasts. (After Microsoft shuttered MSN Groups—the platform upon which the DrinkBoy forum was based—Hess launched a related site, the Chanticleer Society, in 2008, in collaboration with a group of other cocktail enthusiasts.) In 2007, Hess began hosting an online video series, *The Cocktail Spirit with Robert Hess*, on the Small Screen Network, covering cocktail recipes, history, and technique.

A cofounder of the Museum of the American Cocktail, Hess first encountered Audrey Saunders, a New York bartender and major figure in the twenty-first-century cocktail renaissance, in 2002, at Bemelmans Bar, where Saunders worked prior to opening her seminal establishment, Pegu Club, in 2005. See PEGU CLUB. Hess and Saunders married in 2011, conducting two ceremonies—the first, on July 4, a private wedding for friends and family near Hess's family home in Washington State and the second a public ceremony for bartenders and cocktail enthusiasts, at Tales of the Cocktail in New Orleans. See TALES OF THE COCKTAIL. Hess and Saunders plan to launch an education program aimed at career bartenders from their home in Duvall, Washington.

See also DRINKBOY FORUM; MUSEUM OF THE AMERICAN COCKTAIL; and SAUNDERS, AUDREY.

Channel 9 Team. "Robert Hess—What Is a Technology Evangelist?" *Channel 9*, June 1, 2004. https://channel9.msdn.com/Blogs/TheChannel9Team/Robert-Hess-What-is-a-technology-evangelist (accessed February 15, 2021).

Chanticleer Society website. http://chanticleersociety.org/ (accessed February 15, 2021).

The Cocktail Spirit with Robert Hess. Small Screen Cocktails, YouTube, https://www.youtube.com/channel/UCArqex7-NK9TIUpTd5_-rmw (accessed April 22, 2021).

DrinkBoy website. http://www.drinkboy.com (accessed February 15, 2021).

Simonson, Robert. "Audrey Saunders and Robert Hess." *New York Times*, July 29, 2011. http://www.nytimes.com/2011/07/31/fashion/weddings/audrey-saunders-and-robert-hess-vows.html (accessed February 15, 2021).

Tsong, Nicole. "Robert Hess / Raises Toasts to the Art of the Cocktail." *Seattle Times*, November 12, 2006. http://www.seattletimes.com/pacific-nw-magazine/robert-hess-raises-toasts-to-the-art-of-the-cocktail/ (accessed February 15, 2021).

Paul Clarke

The **Highball** is a resolutely simple drink: spirits, sparkling water, and ice. Its roots go back to the Austrian Spritzer—white wine and soda-water—and George Gordon, Lord Byron, who popularized it in the first part of his work *Don Juan*, where, in a stanza widely excerpted by the British press when the poem's first cantos were published in 1819, he extolled the virtues of "hock [i.e., German white wine] and soda-water" (2.180) as a hangover cure. (He had probably been exposed to the drink while wintering in Venice, then under Austrian control.) If in Venice it was a summer cooler, in Britain it was mostly taken as Byron suggested, often while invoking his name.

By the 1830s, British hangover sufferers had found a way to rectify the Spritzer's main defect, want of strength, by replacing the wine with brandy. Brandy and Soda became one of the most popular drinks of the mid-nineteenth century, both as a morning drink and as something for gentlemen to sip at their clubs. A decade later it had spread from London to New York, where it was much affected by the fast-living Broadway swells.

Yet while its popularity in England stretched to the end of the century, in America it was soon replaced by other, more recondite beverages—fizzes, rickeys, coolers, and the like. See FIZZ; RICKEY; and COOLER.

With the rise in popularity—and evolution in quality—of scotch and Irish whiskies, British drinkers began mixing those with soda too (the practice seems to have gained its first firm foothold in Ireland). Once the oidium and then phylloxera epidemics of the second half of the century began biting into the cognac supply, Whisky and Soda became the standard. Eventually, the drink jumped the Atlantic, but it took a while—Americans traditionally looked more to Paris than to London for their fashions, in clothes and otherwise. Besides, the only scotch whisky imported was heavy malt whisky, used exclusively in Hot Toddies, while Irish whisky was usually drunk in punch, and domestic whiskies were generally consumed neat or in cocktails and sours. See TODDY; COCKTAIL; and SOUR. One comes across the occasional pocket of Rye and Soda or Bourbon and Soda drinkers, but there were not many.

American Francophilia began to yield to Anglophilia in the 1870s, in drinks as well as elsewhere. The (British) Collins began to take off, and with it Old Tom gin. See COLLINS and OLD TOM GIN. By the late 1880s, the British Whisky and Soda was beginning to appear in fashionable New York bars, complete with the blended scotch whisky that made it so palatable in Britain. At first, it was merely, as a Pittsburgh newspaper dubbed it in 1891, "the latest drink among the ultra-fashionable young men in the Fifth Avenue clubs," making it a symbol of the "dude," the effeminate, Londonized New York dandy. By 1895, though, it was rapidly edging into the mainstream, pushed in large part by the craze for another Scottish creation, golf. It also gained an American name, "Scotch Highball."

The etymology of "Highball" has been much debated. In America, the word was used in baseball, poker, and railroads, in each to mean a different thing. In Ireland, whence a great many of New York's bartenders hailed, a "ball" was a short glass of whisky. The name could have come from any of these; no Rosetta Stone has been found to tell us which, but the preponderance of the evidence points to the tall glass theory: as a Pennsylvania newspaper put it in

1892, "A 'high ball,' in the lingo of the bar-keeper, is above four fingers" (i.e., a drink higher in the glass than the width of four fingers).

Before long, the Scotch Highball opened the door for the rye and bourbon versions. By the 1910s, ginger ale began taking the place of the soda water, particularly with rye, and there was even an attempt to promote a Coca-Cola version, at first glance very far indeed from the original conception of the drink. See CUBA LIBRE. During American Prohibition, however, it was these sweetened versions, such as the Gin Buck, that proved the most popular. That popularity continued through the 1930s and 1940s and soon spread to encompass Latin America (see BATANGA) and beyond. By the 1950s, the Highball was one of the dominant forms in which spirits were consumed worldwide, both in its dry original version and in its sweeter variants such as the Gin and Tonic and the 7 and 7 (Seagram's 7 Crowns blended whisky and the lemon-lime-flavored 7-Up). See GIN AND TONIC and SEAGRAM COMPANY LTD. That has not changed, although the late 2010s saw a movement in the more artistic bars to upgrade the drink in both its ingredients and its techniques (conspicuous in the latter is the use of the Japanese Suntory highball machine, which pre-chills the liquor and hyper-carbonates the water).

Recipe: Pour 45–60 ml spirits into a tall, ice-filled glass. Add 60–90 ml chilled sparkling water or other carbonated beverage. Stir lightly.

"A Little Off Once a Year." *New York Sun*, March 9, 1890, 16.

"Girls Who Want Husbands." *Pittsburgh Daily Post*, March 7, 1891, 9.

"Hot Weather (a Rhapsody)." *Dublin Evening Packet*, June 16, 1835, 3.

"Quaker City Notes." *Harrisburg (PA) Telegraph*, December 12, 1892, 2.

"The 'Scotch High Ball.'" *Wilkes-Barre (PA) Weekly Dollar News*, May 23, 1896, 8.

David Wondrich

high wines is a term used to designate the higher-alcohol distillate that emerges from the second run of a double distillation (commonly referred to as white dog in bourbon whisky production). See DOUBLE DISTILLATION; HOLANDAS; LOW WINES; WHISKY, BOURBON; and WHITE DOG.

himbeeressig (German: raspberry vinegar) is a sweetened raspberry vinegar syrup that was popular in cocktails as well as soda fountain drinks in the pre-Prohibition era, especially in New Orleans.

Himbeeressig entered the beverage world via the apothecary, and formulae for compounding raspberry vinegar and raspberry vinegar syrup appear frequently in nineteenth-century handbooks for pharmacists and chemists. While according to the 1887 edition of the *National Dispensatory*, plain raspberry syrup has "no special medicinal virtues" but instead "forms an agreeable addition to mixtures, and with water a pleasant drink for febrile affections [that is, conditions accompanied by fever]," the raspberry version at least would add the astringent properties of vinegar without unduly impairing the drink's pleasantness.

The pharmacy and the bar were closely related in the nineteenth century, and raspberry vinegar syrup soon found its way into cocktails. In *How to Mix Drinks* (1862), Jerry Thomas includes three recipes for raspberry vinegar syrup, all of which call for macerating raspberries in vinegar for days then straining and sweetening with various amounts of sugar. See THOMAS, JEREMIAH P. "JERRY".

Raspberry vinegar syrup was particularly popular in New Orleans, which had a large German American community, and there it was commonly referred to by its German name, *Himbeeressig*. As early as the 1870s, the Loubat Glassware and Cork Company included himbeeressig among its line of products, and in the 1920s, it was still advertising it as one of the fourteen flavors of Loubat's Syrups, which sold to soda fountains in one-gallon jugs for $1.50 apiece.

In *Famous New Orleans Drinks and How to Mix 'Em* (1937), Stanley Clisby Arthur misspelled the syrup's name in his treatment of the Roffignac cocktail, noting that the original version of the drink was made with "red Hembarig . . . a popular syrup when old New Orleans was young." That misspelling has confused numerous cocktail enthusiasts who've tried to track down this elusive ingredient to make an authentic Roffignac, but it is merely himbeeressig—raspberry vinegar syrup—that they need. See ARTHUR, STANLEY CLISBY.

Recipe: Put 350 g raspberries and 750 ml vinegar in a large plastic container and let them soak for eight days. Strain through a sieve, mashing and pressing the raspberries to extract all their juice. Put the liquid in a saucepan along with 1 kg sugar, bring to a boil over high heat, stirring to dissolve the sugar. Let it simmer a minute or two, then cool and bottle.

Arthur, Stanley Clisby. *New Orleans Drinks and How to Mix 'Em.* New Orleans: Harmanson, 1937.
Stillé, Alfred, and John Michael Maisch. *The National Dispensatory,* 3rd ed. Philadelphia: Henry C. Leas's Son, 1884, 1481.

Robert F. Moss

Hine of Jarnac, France, has long specialized in selling cognacs made from grapes grown and distilled in the Grande and Petite Champagne regions, with an emphasis on minimal wood impact. A favorite in the English market, Hine developed a reputation for "early-landed, late-bottled" cognacs—single-vintage brandies sent to England for further aging in casks stored in waterside bonded warehouses in Bristol and other cities where low temperatures and high humidity slowed evaporation and created particularly light and fruity spirits. In exceptional years, the house sets aside a few casks of Grande Champagne cognacs to be aged and sold as single vintages.

The house of Hine began after English merchant Thomas Hine sent his sixteen-year-old namesake son to France in 1791 to learn to make cognac. The young Hine met and married the daughter of a cognac négociant named Delamain in 1796 and expanded the business into a major source of bespoke cognacs for English wine merchants. In 1817, it became Thomas Hine & Co. and in 1821 became one of the first houses to ship glass containers of cognac to England, long before bottling had become the norm. In 1962, Hine was appointed official cognac supplier to Queen Elizabeth II of England. As a Royal Warrant holder, Hine may display the royal arms and the legend "by appointment" on products and advertising. Hine also is one of the larger cognac firms still owning significant vineyards, and recently, in response to growing demand for a cocktail-friendly cognac, Eric Forget, Hine's cellarmaster, collaborated with the French Bartenders Association to create H by HINE. The company is currently owned by the closely held French company EDV SAS.

See also COGNAC.

Broom, Dave. "Pale Beauties That Thrive in the Dark." *Telegraph,* December 15, 2001.
Faith, Nicholas. *Cognac.* London: Mitchell Beazley, 2005.

Jack Robertiello

Hiram Walker and Sons, with an annual capacity exceeding 55 million liters of absolute alcohol, is the largest producer of beverage alcohol in North America. Founder Hiram Walker (1816–1899) was a Detroit grocer and sixth-generation American.

Walker first sold whisky in his grocery store in 1849. By 1854, he had started making whisky by rectifying spirits distilled by others. In 1858, temperance sentiments in the United States led him across the Detroit River to Windsor, Ontario, to build a distillery on 190 hectares. Using a wooden continuous still and copper doubler, the distillery made 3,200 liters of whisky daily.

Walker is considered the first Canadian distiller to blend base whisky made from corn with flavoring whisky distilled from rye, and the first to sell whisky in bottles. He lived in Canada only four years and then commuted on the ferry that he owned from Hamtramck, Michigan. He built houses for his workers on the edge of Windsor, which quickly grew into a small town: Walkerville.

In 1867 Walker began exporting beyond North America, eventually reaching some 155 countries. As the temperance movement resurged, Walker's heirs became concerned, and in 1926 they sold the distillery to entrepreneur Harry Hatch for half its estimated value. Hatch made it a bootlegging hub, one of the rare profitable Canadian distilleries during Prohibition. Nevertheless, sales to rumrunners rarely matched pre-Prohibition volumes. When the American stock market crashed in 1929, sales plummeted, and the distillery was said to be losing more alcohol by evaporation than sales.

In 1987, Hatch's son, Clifford, sold the distillery to Allied Lyons (later Allied Domecq). Pernod Ricard took over ownership in 2005, while management was turned over to a Pernod Ricard subsidiary,

Corby Distillers of Canada. In an unusual arrangement, while making a wide range of whiskies (including the rare malted rye) and other spirits for Pernod Ricard's various brands, including Corby and Wiser's, the distillery also continues to make Walker's original Canadian Club brand, which had been sold separately and is now owned by Beam Suntory.

See also CANADIAN CLUB.

De Kergommeaux, Davin. *Canadian Whisky, Second Edition: The New Portable Expert*. Vancouver: Appetite by Random House, 2017.

Davin de Kergommeaux

The **Hoffman House** hotel's bar in New York, on then-fashionable Madison Square, enjoyed an international reputation as the city's, and hence quite possibly the world's, finest drinking establishment. Between 1883 and its final closing in 1911, to drink there was to rub elbows with a dazzling crowd of Broadway swells, high-living sporting men, and celebrities of every type, from William Randolph Hearst to Buffalo Bill Cody.

To have tended bar at the Hoffman House was enough to set a man up in his own saloon or qualify him to work at any bar in the world; among its many alumni were Frank Meier and Harry Craddock, along with a remarkable number of bartenders of local prominence in New York. See MEIER, FRANK; and CRADDOCK, HARRY LAWSON. The bar was considered one of New York's temples of mixology, and its employees invented a great many drinks of their own. Few of these, however, achieved lasting popularity (the Adonis, with sherry and vermouth, is probably the best known of them). See BAMBOO COCKTAIL. Nonetheless, the bar was instrumental in popularizing many classic drinks, including the fizz, the Martini (in both its sweet and dry incarnations), and the Collins. See FIZZ; MARTINI; and COLLINS.

The Hoffman House opened in 1864. For its first eighteen years, the bar was well regarded, but not in the city's first rank. Its first head bartender, Fred Eberlin, saw much greater success when he left to open his own bar in 1872. See DAISY. His successor, Frederick Loud, ran things quietly for the next ten years. Then, in 1881, Cassius H. Read, the hotel's owner, brought in a partner, placing him in charge of the bar. Edward S. Stokes (1841–1901) was notorious for shooting the ruthless financier James "Big Jim" Fisk to death on the steps of the Grand Central hotel in 1872, but he also knew what it took to make an impression.

In 1882, when the bar reopened after Stokes's extensive renovation, it caused a sensation. "There is nothing cheap here," wrote the New York correspondent for the *Cleveland Leader*, "and few kings have taken their toddy in better quarters." The windows were stained glass; the bar and the

THE FAMOUS HOFFMAN HOUSE BAR, NEW YORK CITY.

Charles Mahoney at the bar of the Hoffman House, 1905. Wondrich Collection.

wall-paneling were all carved mahogany—"no shoddy and no veneering"—and the mosaic floor was marble. The walls were hung with paintings, including a Turner, a Narcissus shakily attributed to Correggio, and the bar's centerpiece, the immense *Nymphs and Satyr* by William-Adolphe Boguereau, which featured great expanses of pink female flesh and cost $10,000. There was a Gobelin tapestry that had belonged to Napoleon III (a party of visitors from the West once sat in front of it waiting for it to go up until it was explained to them that they were in a bar, not a theater). The bric-a-brac scattered thickly around the room was old and expensive.

The sixteen bartenders were led by Joseph McKone, who had a wide reputation as the handsomest in the city; William F. "Billy" Mulhall (1858–1941), who was (as the *New York Herald* put it) "good at making whiskey sours"; and John F. Irish, who would go on to run the famous bar at the Manhattan Club. See MANHATTAN COCKTAIL. After McKone and Irish moved on, Mulhall came into his own. By 1887, as the *Evening World* reported, he had gained a reputation as "the most proficient artist in his line in the metropolis." Two years later, when Stokes opened a branch of the bar downtown, Mulhall was in charge, his position at the Madison Square bar being taken by Billy Dugay, another fine mixologist. Besides mixed drinks, the bar offered such rarities as American rye whisky bottled in 1826 and "an old Hennessy more than fifty years in bottle," as Mulhall later recalled. This cost a dollar a drink, an unheard-of price at the time.

Despite its popularity, the bar and hotel fell into financial difficulties in the mid-1890s. As part of a renovation aimed at restoring the hotel's fortunes, in 1896 the bar was closed, replaced by a smaller one in the building's new annex. Gone were the paintings, the statues, the suits of armor, and other objets d'art, and gone, soon, was Stokes.

With the new bar came a new head bartender, Charley Mahoney (1858–1923), an alumnus of Clark's, a "blatant, flagrant and unblushing" Tenderloin dive, and a thoroughgoing sporting man. Under his tutelage, the bar regained its popularity, although its clientele ran more to high-stakes gamblers than dignitaries. Indeed, Mahoney was as famous for being a stakeholder for large bets as he was for mixing drinks. He was, however, one of the popularizers of the Dry Martini (under the name "Mahoney Cocktail") and, in 1905, published the seminal *Hoffman House Bartender's Guide*, with a notable number of unique recipes, including the excellent Modern Cocktail.

In 1910, with the hotel faltering, Mahoney retired and was replaced in his role as bar manager and host by the popular Jim Gray, formerly of the Fifth Avenue Hotel. See GRAY, "COLONEL" JIM. The hotel closed the next year and was torn down for development soon after. It lived on in the city's culture for several decades more, however, as the ultimate example of the fancy New York bar.

"A Palace of Sin." *Jamestown (NY) Evening Journal*, August 29, 1883.

De Fontain, F. G. *The Hoffman House: Its Attractions.* New York: Edward S. Stokes, 1895.

"Fine Fancies in Drinks." *New York Evening World*, October 10, 1887, 4.

Mahoney, Charles S. *The Hoffman House Bartender's Guide.* New York: Richard K. Fox, 1905.

Mulhall, William F. "The Golden Age of Booze." In *Valentine's Manual of Old New York*, 126–135. New York: Valentine's Manual, 1923.

David Wondrich

hogo is an English rum merchants' term of the eighteenth and nineteenth centuries denoting the sharp, sulfurous, meaty "funk" peculiar to raw sugarcane spirits. The term is derived from the French *haut goût*, "high taste" (like that which is produced in game birds by hanging them for some days before eating them), and was originally used chiefly to describe either that "flesh somewhat tainted" (as Francis Grose defined it in 1785) or the odor of the unwashed human body.

The term made it into the world of rum in 1708 when John Oldmixon, in his study of Britain's American colonies, wrote that the rum made in Jamaica had "a certain Twang or Hogo that it receives from the Juice of the Cane" that kept it from reaching the perfection of French brandy. In 1740, we find Charles Leslie noting that the cane juice was itself "without any ill Taste or Hogo"; in 1788, it is James Newport of Philadelphia advertising that the rum he was making was "very well flavoured, and free from hogo"; in 1886, it is the novelist Grant Allen having a Trinidadian planter define it as "the strong and somewhat offensive molasses-like flavour of new rum." After that it crops up, albeit infrequently, until the 1920s, when Laurence Green heard it used in Mauritius.

Leslie's observation is key to understanding hogo's source: it is only when alcohol is introduced through long fermentation in a bacteria-rich environment that sugar-cane juice and its derivatives develop the esters that convey hogo, and only with distillation that they become concentrated enough to be truly aromatic. See ESTERS. Long aging will break up some of these molecules, but if they are present in sufficient concentration, as in certain high-ester Jamaican rums, not even that will eliminate them.

As can be deduced from the above examples, those aromas have not always been considered desirable. Indeed, with the work of Rafael Arroyo and others making it all too easy to remove them, the last half of the twentieth century saw cleaner fermentation, column distillation, and long barrel aging make hogo largely a thing of the past in sugar-cane spirits, although there were holdouts: rhum agricole, cachaça, Batavia arrack, and a few examples of Jamaica rum and demerara rum still exhibited the quality to varying degree. See ARROYO VALDESPINO, RAFAEL; RHUM AGRICOLE; CACHAÇA; ARRACK, BATAVIA; RUM, JAMAICA; and RUM, DEMERARA. The story, however, does not end there: with the cocktail renaissance, some consumers wanted more from their rum, particularly for punch and tiki drinks, operating on the old Norman principle that andouillette—chitterling sausage—"doit sentir un peu la merde, mais pas trop" (must smell a bit like excrement but not too much). See COCKTAIL RENAISSANCE; PUNCH; and TIKI. Too much, and one cannot dispel thoughts of tainted meat and unwashed bodies. A little hogo, however, makes rum interesting and keeps it from being a mere sugar-cane vodka or brandy; it is what makes rum rum. Since 2010, not only has the term been revived, but increasing numbers of rums on the market display some hogo—a few of them even perhaps too much.

Allen, Grant. *In All Shades*, vol. 3. London: Chatto & Windus, 1886.

Green, Lawrence G. *Harbours of Memory*. Cape Town: Howard Timmins, 1969.

Leslie, Charles. *A New and Exact Account of Jamaica*. London: 1740.

Oldmixon, John. *The British Empire in America*, vol. 2. London: 1708.

Wondrich, David. *Punch*. New York: Perigee, 2010.

David Wondrich

hogshead is a type of large oak cask traditionally used in aging wine but also frequently used to age whisky in Scotland, where distillers often create hogsheads from the disassembled staves of multiple bourbon barrels. Its standard capacity is 238 liters (63 gallons). See also WHISKY, BOURBON; MATURATION; BARREL; and WHISKY, SCOTCH.

hokonui is a moonshine whisky distilled secretively in the Hokonui Mountains of New Zealand's Southland region. It is made from malted barley, sugar, liquid malt, yeast, and water, distilled in a copper pot still, and mixed with honey for a hint of color. The tradition began in the late 1800s when experienced distiller and widow Mary McRae and her children moved to New Zealand from Scotland and soon began making moonshine. As the drink gained popularity, more and more stills popped up across the region to fill the void created by lackluster, often diluted imports and growing temperance and prohibition movements. Those movements were able to enact laws, and indeed parts of the region were legally dry for most of the first half of the twentieth century, but thanks to hokonui's enthusiastic fan base those laws never managed to stop the illicit distilling. Today, hokonui is available to purchase legally from commercial distilleries. See MOONSHINE.

Wolfe, Kerry. "Hokonui Moonshine Museum." *Atlas Obscura*. https://www.atlasobscura.com/places/hokonui-moonshine-museum (accessed February 16, 2021).

Anna Archibald

holandas, the Spanish term for high wines (the word points to the Dutch influence in Iberian distilling), is applied to the pot-still distillate that constitutes the highest-quality component in the blending of brandy de Jerez. See also BRANDY DE JEREZ; DISTILLATE; HIGH WINES; and STILL, POT.

Holland gin and **Hollands** are archaic English names for genever, the Dutch ancestor of gin. See GENEVER and GIN.

home distilling varies greatly as a status and practice around the world. The reasons people practice distillation break down into three overarching categories:

1. Cultural or traditional practices, common in many locations, a focus on using excess agricultural products, personal consumption, or for income (especially in developing countries).
2. Economic savings, primarily in countries with high tax rates on spirits. Such distillers tend to be concerned more with cost rather than with producing high-quality spirits.
3. Hobby and experimentation, focused on quality and/or novel products.

One of these reasons for distilling often drives a distiller's choice of still design, with simple pot stills found where traditional products are commonly made, reflux stills where the primary aim is high proof and relatively neutral spirits, and compound stills in use where distillers desire the ability to control the distillation process fully and thereby make a wide variety of products.

While all of these motivations can be found anywhere in the world, one usually predominates. In very broad strokes:

In the United States and Canada, unlicensed distillation of beverage alcohol is illegal, but in both countries distillation of high-proof ethanol for fuel use is permitted and even encouraged. See UNITED STATES AND CANADA.

In eastern and southern Europe, where home distillation is widely practiced, such activity is legal, lightly regulated, or even ignored by the government. In general, these countries are low-tax environments. Most home distillation is done on farms or small villas, using fermented local fruits. The stills are simple pot stills, which often may be found for sale at local markets.

In some central European countries, home distillation is legal, but stills must be licensed, and authorities collect a tax on the products. Quite a few people make eau-de-vie under these regimes. See EAU-DE-VIE.

In the developing world (much of Asia, Africa, India, and Latin America), home distillation is either legal or a very low priority for governments with more pressing issues. In remote areas, often a few home distillers will produce local traditional products for sale, but using small-scale equipment. I visited such a distillery in southern Ethiopia, where the fermentations took place in 20-liter fuel cans and the ceramic pot still had a capacity of about 12 liters.

In Scandinavia, where taxes on spirits are universally high, home distillation is prohibited but widely practiced. (I once sat next to a Swedish man on a long flight, and when he found that I manufacture stills, he said, "Two things you have to know. First, it is illegal. Second, everyone does it.") The predominant product made is high-proof flavorless ethanol (most commonly made from a wash of fermented table sugar), which is diluted and mixed with a wide range of flavor essences to create facsimiles of standard products. Since the practice is illegal, Scandinavian home distillers favor compact, easily hidden stills. From Norway to Finland, there is significant interest in, and experimentation around, the development of automatic stills that can operate in a closet without intervention while producing the desired product. These stills tend to be fairly technically advanced reflux/compound stills. See SCANDINAVIA.

In western Europe north of Iberia, home distillation is generally prohibited. That does not prevent distillers from practicing in secret. The primary drivers are hobbyist experimentation and economic considerations.

In Australia, home distillation is illegal but common due to the high tax regime. Widespread experimentation followed New Zealand's legalization of private, noncommercial distillation in 1996. From that liberalization of law came the subsequent experimentation and development of new generations of small but high-quality distillation equipment and novel techniques. See AUSTRALIA AND NEW ZEALAND.

In South Africa, home distillation is legal if distillers meet certain requirements. The most commonly produced product is *mampoer*, often called peach brandy, although it can be made with apricots, plums, figs, pineapples, or other fruits. See PEACH BRANDY and SOUTH AFRICA.

In most of the Islamic world, where alcohol is officially forbidden, home distillation is illegal. In some countries (e.g., Saudi Arabia) the penalties are truly dire. Nevertheless, some people (especially expatriate workers) have long practiced it clandestinely. Still designs and raw materials are similar to Scandinavian practice but may include raisins, dates, and other dried fruits. A basic distilling manual called *The Blue Flame* circulated at least since the 1970s among expatriate American workers for the Aramco oil company in Saudi Arabia. The underground classic often was mimeographed and passed on to new arrivals by experienced engineers and other employees who, if they were leaving the country, might even pass on compact little stills. See MIDDLE EAST.

See also MOONSHINE; and STILL, TYPES OF.

Howard, Kathleen, and Norman Gilbat. *The Lore of Still Building*. Fostoria, OH: Noguska, 1999.

Pavliuchuk, Volodimir. *Cordial Waters: A Compleat Guide to Ardent Spirits of the World*. Seattle: Amphora Society. 2008.

Nixon, Michael, and Michael McCaw. *The Compleat Distiller*, 2nd ed. Seattle: Amphora Society, 2010.

Rowley, Matthew. *Moonshine!* Ashville, NC: Lark, 2007.

Smiley, Ian. *Making Pure Corn Whiskey*, 2nd ed. Seattle: Amphora Society, 2003.

Zymurgy Bob [pseud.]. *Making Fine Spirits Using Simple, Easy-to-Build Gear*. Seattle: Amphora Society, 2011.

Mike McCaw

honey liqueurs have roots that stretch back at least to Cleopatra's time, when the Hellenistic Greeks would infuse wine with spices and sweeten it with honey; while this isn't quite what we call a liqueur today, it shows the use of honey in a liqueur-style drink. Honey itself was the staple sweetener for drinks in most of the world until the 1500s brought an explosion in sugar-cane cultivation and processing.

During the thirteenth and fourteenth centuries, in Europe we see the amalgamation of distilled spirit, spices from ever-expanding trade routes, and honey to form medicinal drams, touted as remedies for everything from gout to the common cold. At first, the honey was added before distillation, which meant that it would contribute little more than its aroma to the final distillate. By the beginning of

the sixteenth century, however, as recreational, or at least prophylactic, uses of distilled spirits outstripped purely therapeutic ones, one finds honey being used to sweeten the end product, as in the recipe recorded by Caterina Sforza in around 1500, where aqua vitae is infused with gentian and tormentil (both quite bitter) and two other botanicals and then sweetened with clarified honey. The result can be considered the ancestor of the modern Italian amaro. See AQUA VITAE and APERITIF AND DIGESTIVE.

Even though the 1600s saw it largely displaced by the cheaper and more neutral-flavored cane sugar, honey would continue to be used to flavor some herbal liqueurs. In fact, a number of perennial favorites rely on honey for their sweetness, including yellow Chartreuse, Bénédictine, Drambuie, and Irish Mist. See BÉNÉDICTINE and CHARTREUSE.

In those formulae, the honey takes a backseat to the herbs. There is, however, another approach to using honey in liqueurs, one that treats it as a flavoring ingredient in its own right. We see this in Hieronymus Brunschwig's pioneering 1500 book on distillation, where he details a "honey water" made from fermented and distilled honey. Honey-flavored liqueurs would go on to become a specialty of the southern Baltic region, with the East Prussian *Bärenfäng* ("bear trap," so called after the practice of trapping bears with honey mixed with grain spirit; today this is marketed internationally as Bärenjäger) and the Polish and Lithuanian *krupnik*, a mix of vodka with locally sourced herbs and spices and clover honey. (Lithuanian legend holds that the drink dates to the early fourteenth century, when one of the Grand Duke Gediminas's knights used it to cure him of a deathly bout with the flu.) Served hot, krupnik is a wintertime favorite that was traditionally made by grandparents at Christmastime to be enjoyed at end of year celebrations. Commercially available examples are mostly aimed at the domestic markets in Poland and Lithuania, but they are also sometimes exported.

Another stronghold of honey-flavored liqueurs is the United States, beginning with "peach and honey," a mixture—either made to order or pre-bottled—of aged peach brandy and honey that was popular until the end of the nineteenth century. See PEACH BRANDY. In 1975, Jimmy Russell of the Wild Turkey distillery revived the practice, after a fashion, with Wild Turkey Liqueur, bourbon-based and honey flavored. While the product was not a runaway success, it paved the way for a plethora of honey-bourbon liqueurs in the 2000s, most of them quite successful.

Andreae, Illa. *Alle schnäpse dieser welt.* Zurich: Transitbooks AG, 1973.

Brunschwig, Hieronymus. *The vertuose boke of distyllacyon.* Translated by Laurence Andrew. London: 1527.

Leinböck, Johann Georg. *Der aechte Waidmann: Neustes handbuch für jäger und jagdfreunde,* vol. 2. Vienna: 1831.

Pasolini, Pier Desiderio. *Caterina Sforza,* vol. 3. Rome: Loescher, 1893.

Shawn Soole and David Wondrich

hong qu ("red qu" or "red yeast rice") is rice that has been cultured with the red mold *Monascus purpureus* and dried. It is used in the traditional manufacture of soy sauce, rice wine, and Batavia arrack. See ARRACK, BATAVIA.

hops, the flower cones of the hop plant, *Humulus lupulus*, are widely used as a flavoring and bittering addition to beers, but they also have several uses in distillation.

One such use has little to do with the flavor or bitterness of hops, but rather with the antibacterial properties of the so-called alpha and beta acids they contain. This is of particular utility in distilled spirits, because the mash is often not brought to a microbe-killing boil before going to fermentation. Adding hops to the mash helps prevent wild yeasts and bacteria from growing in the wort and creating unwanted flavors and aromas. See FERMENTATION.

Hops were also used in this way in the "dona jug" method of yeast propagation used in American whisky making. A small amount of hops would be added to keep the liquid clear of bacteria and allow the yeast to grow unhindered. In both of these cases, only small amounts of hops are used, and yet their pungency ensures that they will have some effect on the flavor of the final spirit.

Some distillers who have seen the popularity of strongly hopped IPA beers have also made hopped whiskies. The hops can be introduced in the distillation to bring flavor and bitterness, but the more volatile aroma compounds would have to be added after distillation or they would be lost.

Hops are traditionally part of the botanical charge of genever. Bols Genever, for instance, has used hops in their botanicals mixture since 1664: a small, balanced amount to add a touch of bitterness to the sweeter flavors of juniper, licorice, and angelica root. See GENEVER.

There is a tradition of hop schnapps in the hop-growing areas of southern Germany. These are essentially a hop eau-de-vie, infused with fresh green hops, and largely a curiosity.

See also SCHNAPPS; FERMENTATION; and MASH.

Interviews with distillers/blenders: Dr. Donald Livermore (of Corby Spirit & Wine) and Conor O'Driscoll (Heaven Hill).
Personal communication with Lucas Bols NV.

Lew Bryson

hors d'age is a French term meaning "beyond age." Although it has been used informally to describe exceptionally old spirits since at least the 1870s, it was only formalized in the mid-twentieth century. Today it is a legally recognized term in the three appellation d'origine contrôlée (AOC) designations for spirits in France: Armagnac, calvados, and cognac. The aging requirements for these three appellations differ; in Armagnac, the hors d'age term refers to spirits whose youngest eau-de-vie is at least ten years old, while in calvados and cognac it is a minimum of six years, the same as XO. In practice all three appellations exceed the minimum legal requirements. Outside of France, while the term is sometimes seen on AOC Martinique Rhum Agricole labels, it is not a legally defined designation.

Faith, Nicholas. *Cognac.* Oxford: Infinite Ideas, 2014.
"Lettre d' un libre . . . baigneur." *L' avenir d' Arachon,* September 1, 1872, 1.

May Matta-Aliah

hot buttered rum is a colonial-era drink once favored for being medicinal, warming, and chock-full of calories. It remains popular today in certain precincts owing to its richness and tastiness, particularly during winter.

Initially prescribed for its medicinal value in aiding hoarseness of voice, the drink was agreeable enough to be consumed recreationally. Recipes vary, but the ingredients are usually consistent: rum, butter, sugar, spices, and hot water. One early recipe called for "butter the size of a black walnut" and "maple sugar the size of a large hickory nut," mixed with boiling water, rum, and "nutmeg for the ladies."

The twentieth-century revival of the drink can in large part be attributed to the historic fiction of novelist Kenneth Roberts. In his 1937 bestseller *Northwest Passage* he wrote, "After a man's had two-three drinks of hot buttered rum, he don't shoot a catamount. All he's got to do is walk up to him and kiss him just once, then put him in his bag, all limp."

One who was not convinced was David Embury, author of the 1948 *Fine Art of Mixing Drinks*. "The lump of butter is the final insult," he wrote. "It blends with the hot rum just about as satisfactorily as warm olive oil blends with champagne." He noted that hot buttered rum should be "permitted only in the Northwest Passage and, even there, only by highly imaginative and overenthusiastic novelists."

Embury has a point; the butter often leaves a slick. This can be remedied to a degree by preparing a batter with butter, sugar, and spices, then using this to mix with rum and hot water.

Recipe: Blend one cup softened, salted butter with 2 cups brown sugar, 1 teaspoon cinnamon, 1/2 teaspoon nutmeg. Store in refrigerator until needed. In mug, add one teaspoon of batter and 60 ml dark rum; fill with hot water. Stir and serve.

Roberts, Kenneth. *Northwest Passage*. New York: Doubleday Doran, 1937.

Wayne Curtis

The **Hotel Adlon** opened in October 1907 with the backing of Kaiser Wilhelm II at imperial Berlin's most fashionable address: Unter den Linden 1. Hotelier Lorenz Adlon modeled his magnificent Adlon on modern American hotels. It attracted a mix of nobles, diplomats, spies, titans of industry, kings, film stars, and presidents. It was considered *the* place to stay; in fact, the kaiser routinely housed guests there instead of his old, drafty palace. Most of the original hotel burned down in 1945 when, some claim, Soviet soldiers drunk on looted wine torched it.

From the beginning, Americans clamored for cocktails at the hotel bar rather than for beer or wine. Because his German staff could not satisfy American thirsts, Lorenz Adlon traveled to New York and Chicago in 1911 to learn the secrets of cocktails. By the time Prohibition went into effect nine years later, the hotel's bar had become a Mecca for heavy-drinking Americans. There, the staff, under the direction of Fred Bielmann, the learned head bartender from the mid-1920s until at least the mid-1930s, mixed Manhattans, Scofflaws, Golden and Claret Fizzes, Brandy Flips, and other American-style libations at all hours of the day—and for a fraction of the cost in the United States. Despite occasional counterfeit Hamburg spirits sneaking in, the liquors were high quality. See Manhattan Cocktail; fizz; and flip. Loitering journalists drank at the bar, traded gossip, and kept tabs on arriving notables such as Marlene Dietrich, Charlie Chaplin, the king and queen of Siam, Albert Einstein, and Theodore Roosevelt. In 1930, the actress Lillian Harvey won the first "internationalen Cocktail-Konkurrenz" at the Adlon with her Hocus Pocus. See cocktail contests. In 1997, the Kempinski hotel group opened the hotel, finally rebuilt after the 1945 conflagration.

Grothe, Solveig. "Hotel Adlon: Deutschlands erste Adresse." *Der Spiegel*, October 21, 2007. http://www.spiegel.de/einestages/100-jahre-hotel-adlon-a-948049.html (accessed February 17, 2021).

"Old Broadway in New Berlin." *New York Times*, November 12, 1922.

"Wanted: Cocktail Mixer." *Evening World*, January 28, 1911.

Zitzlsperger, Ulrike C. "Reading Across Cultures: Global Narratives, Hotels and Railway Stations." *Fudan Journal of the Humanities and Social Sciences* 9, no. 2 (June 2016): 193–211.

Matthew Rowley

Hotel Nacional was the house drink at the Hotel Nacional de Cuba, Havana's grandest luxury resort when it opened in 1930. In his 1936 book *The Barman's Mentor*, veteran Prohibition-era Havana bartender Eddie Woelke claimed authorship of what he simply called the "Nacional." His recipe was 1/2 jigger each white rum and pineapple juice plus 2 dashes each lime juice and apricot brandy, shaken with ice and strained into a coupe. In 1939, mixographer Charles

Baker referred to the same drink in his *Gentleman's Companion* as the "Hotel Nacional Special" and attributed it to Wil P. Taylor, the hotel's manager from 1931 to 1933; Taylor's recipe (same ingredients, different ratio) lacks the balance of Woelke's.

While the drink, a pleasant and refreshing one, is not seen often in modern bars, it is sometimes found in tiki bars and bars with a tropical cast.

Recipe: Shake with ice 45 ml white rum, 45 ml pineapple juice (fresh or canned), 7 ml fresh lime juice, and 7 ml apricot brandy. Strain into cocktail glass and add cherry.

See also BAKER, CHARLES HENRY, JR.

Baker, Charles. *The Gentleman's Companion*. 1939; repr. New York: Crown.
Woelke, Eddie, and Stafford Brothers. *The Barman's Mentor*. New York: Stafford Brothers, 1936.

Jeff Berry

hot sauce / hot pepper has been used to spice up mixed drinks at least since the early days of the Cock-Tail, where it sometimes took the place of the bitters. See COCK-TAIL. It was not, however, a mainstream ingredient until the Bloody Mary made it so. See BLOODY MARY. In modern mixology, it is not uncommon to find a dash or two of hot sauce in a drink or a pinch of dried hot pepper sprinkled on top as a garnish. Hot pepper was also used by unscrupulous rectifiers to give a bit of bite to underproof spirits until food-purity laws put an end to such shenanigans. See also RECTIFICATION.

hot whisky, a favorite libation of the Emerald Isle, is essentially a hot toddy made with Irish whisky, sugar, and boiling water and garnished with a clove-studded slice of lemon. See also TODDY.

Hudson is an American craft whisky brand created by the Tuthilltown Spirits company, which was founded in 2003 by Ralph Erenzo and Brian Lee. In 2001, Erenzo purchased the old Tuthilltown Gristmill, which had been in operation near Gardiner, New York, for over two hundred years, where he hoped to run a campground for climbers visiting the Shawangunk Ridge. His neighbors, however, objected to this plan, and research led Ralph to recognize the opportunities afforded by new legislation allowing small distilleries in New York State. Tuthilltown became the first distillery in New York to obtain the new class of license and the first whisky distillery to operate in the state since prohibition (there were once well over a thousand). Tuthilltown's first product was a vodka made from New York apples. In 2007, they released Hudson Manhattan Rye, a 92-proof whisky made from 100 percent New York rye. The Hudson brand soon grew to include an unaged New York corn whisky and a 100 percent corn Baby Bourbon aged in small barrels. They also make a Four Grain Bourbon and a single malt whisky, as well as various short-run specialty bottles. In 2010, Tuthilltown formed a partnership with UK-based William Grant and Sons for production and worldwide distribution of the Hudson Whiskey brand, marking one of the first major deals struck between a large spirits company and a small-scale distiller.

See also CRAFT DISTILLING.

Reid Mitenbuler. *Bourbon Empire; The Past and Future of America's Whiskey*. New York: Viking, 2015.
Rodewald, James. *American Spirit; An Exploration of the Craft Distilling Revolution*. New York: Sterling Epicure, 2014.

Max Watman

The **hue/color** of a spirit is indicative of changes made post-distillation. The distillation process creates a clear, almost colorless liquid. Color can come from flavoring materials added to the spirit, then allowed to steep for varying lengths of time. These infusions and macerations may include fruits, herbs and grasses, roots, leaves, bark, coffee beans, vanilla pods, or other materials. See INFUSION and MACERATION. Alcohol's solvent action leaches color and flavor from the material.

The hue of an aged spirit (e.g., whisky, rum, brandy) derives from aging in barrels or casks, where the color is absorbed from the wood. See AGING and BARREL. Darker color may indicate more age, but using new wood gives more color faster than aging in used barrels. Smaller barrels put a higher ratio of liquid in direct contact with the wood, also adding color faster.

Natural or artificial colors may also be added directly; use of caramel color is common in some types of whisky, while brandies may be adjusted for market with the addition of *boisé*. See CARAMEL and BOISÉ.

See also OAK; WOOD CHEMISTRY; and WOOD/ BARREL FINISHING.

Bryson, Lew. *Tasting Whiskey: An Insider's Guide to the Unique Pleasures of the World's Finest Spirits*. North Adams, MA: Storey, 2014.

Lew Bryson

The **Hurricane**, a hefty slug of dark rum mixed with citrus and passion fruit juices, served in a glass shaped like the chimney of an old hurricane lantern, has been a wildly popular staple of New Orleans drinking since its introduction at Pat O'Brien's bar on St Peter Street (Benson Harrison "Pat" O'Brien and his partner Charlie Cantrell converted their French Quarter speakeasy to a public bar on December 3, 1933—two days before Prohibition officially ended). Head bartender Louis Culligan is credited with the drink's creation; O'Brien claimed that occurred during World War II, when whisky allocation was such that it was only available if one bought large amounts of rum. In a recipe he shared with *Cabaret Quarterly* in 1956, Culligan specified 120 ml gold rum to 60 ml each "red passion fruit mix" and "the juice of two lemons." (Various red-colored "passion fruit" punch mixes and cordials emerged in the 1920s; many remain available today.)

Against this story, one must balance the recipe for "Hurricane Punch" found in *The Rum Connoisseur*, a 1941 booklet published by the Ronrico Corp. of San Juan, Puerto Rico: 120 ml rum, 60 ml "Passion Fruit syrup," and 30 ml each of lemon and lime juice, served in a "special blue glass." (The drink may have been related to the short-lived Hurricane Club, open on Broadway in New York from 1940 to 1941.)

Whether Culligan invented the drink or copied it from a promotion booklet doesn't matter: the Hurricane Punch was just another recipe in a book; Pat O'Brien's Hurricane was a sensation. "Pat O's" became wildly popular with locals, who enjoyed the neighborhood vibe of the main bar, the dueling pianos in the piano bar, and the beautiful courtyard patio bar with its flaming fountain. From the 1950s on its popularity with tourists grew enormously, as did the popularity of its signature drink; it began appearing at bars all over the city. Another ten years, and it was nationwide.

The Hurricane's popularity led to the bar's introduction, in around 1980, of a prepackaged mix both bottled and in powder, which is sold along with the drink's signature glassware. Other preparations use a fresh-ingredient approach, following the original recipe but with the substitution of passion fruit syrup, or a 1:1 mixture of passion fruit pulp and simple syrup. The drink is traditionally garnished with an orange-cherry flag. See FLAG.

Recipe: Shake or blend 120 ml gold rum, 60 ml red passion fruit mix, and 60 ml lemon juice (or 30 ml lemon juice and 30 ml lime juice) with ice. Pour unstrained into Hurricane glass. Add a straw and garnish with an orange-cherry flag.

See also PAT O'BRIEN'S.

Berry, Jeff. *Beachbum Berry Remixed: A Gallery of Tiki Drinks*. San Jose, CA: Club Tiki/SLG, 2009.
East, Charles. "New Orleans." *Cabaret Quarterly* 5 (1956): 33.

Chuck Taggart

hydrometer, which measures the densities of liquids, is an ancient invention that has been used to gauge the alcoholic strength of spirits since the eighteenth century. Like distillation itself, the hydrometer (or, to be precise, alcoholometer) relies on the difference in density between ethanol and water. Since ethanol is lighter than water, the lower a spirit's density, the higher its proof and the deeper a weighted float will sink into it—the principle behind the device.

The first practical hydrometer for gauging the strength of spirits was invented and marketed by John Clarke, a London instrument maker, in the mid-1720s. It took the form of a hollow copper or brass globe with a long, flat graduated stem protruding from it and, opposite the stem, a spur onto which one of a set of calibrated weights was screwed, chosen according to the liquid's temperature (which affects the density of the liquid) and range of expected proof. With the right weight, the surface level of the spirit falls in the (narrow) range marked on the stem and can be measured.

After decades of informal use, Clarke's device was officially mandated in 1787. It was not entirely satisfactory, however, as it required at least thirty-four and (eventually) as many as three hundred different weights and used an archaic mode of calibration, displaying its results as the proportion of water one had to add to, or remove from, the spirit being measured to bring it to proof (50 percent alcohol, by weight). In 1817, Clarke's hydrometer was replaced by a streamlined version developed by the master exciseman Bartholomew Sikes (1731–1803), which used only nine weights and was accompanied by an exhaustive book of tables that, accounting for temperature, enabled the gauger to precisely determine the percentage of alcohol by which a spirit was over or under proof. In Britain, Sikes's hydrometer remained in use until the 1970s, its little wooden cases—each containing the brass hydrometer; its precisely cut, neatly arrayed brass weights; and a thermometer—becoming common fixtures wherever spirits were distilled, bottled, or wholesaled.

While Britain relied on the variable-weight brass hydrometer and the system of measuring alcohol by weight, most other countries, including France, Germany, and the United States, preferred to use the "constant weight hydrometer." This came in the form of a small set of glass hydrometers with much longer stems, allowing each to measure a much broader range of proofs than the short-stemmed British ones. Coupled with them were similar tables to Sikes's, except these went one step further and converted the percentage of alcohol by weight to the percentage by volume according to the French Gay-Lussac or Cartier or German Tralles systems, which differ only in detail. These are still in use today, although they have been partly supplanted by electronic refractometers.

It should be noted that all buoyancy-based hydrometers will yield false readings if the spirit has been sweetened or had its density otherwise manipulated; this is known as "obscuration." Such a spirit must be distilled down to its components to determine its precise proof.

See also PROOF.

Ashworth, William J. "Between the Trader and the Public: British Alcohol Standards and the Proof of Good Governance." *Technology and Culture*, January, 2001, 27–50.

Crandall, E. R. *Hydrometers and Hydrometry*. Detroit: E. R. Crandall, 1954.

Tate, Francis G. H. *Alcoholometry*. London: HMSO, 1930.

David Wondrich

hydrosol is the water-based byproduct of distillation for essential oil. In early history, distilled plant waters were in widespread use for their medicinal value long before essential oils as we know them today. Hydrosols were primarily used for health benefits, as they retain the nutrients of the plants that they were extracted from. Distilled plant waters contain volatile hydrophilic compounds from a plant, yet not the tannic acid and bitter substances. Their fragrance is reminiscent of their partner essential oils, although not as strong. Sometimes the aroma is different and not as pleasant as the essential oil from the same plant. The most commonly utilized hydrosols in mixed drinks are orange blossom water and rose water. See ORANGE FLOWER WATER and RAMOS GIN FIZZ. Today, however, these are often not true hydrosols, but rather water to which oils and/or artificial flavorings have been added. They are heavily concentrated and should be using sparingly.

See also ESSENTIAL OILS.

Price, Len, and Shirley Price. *Understanding Hydrolats: The Specific Hydrosols for Aromatherapy*. Edinburgh, NY: Churchill Livingstone, 2004.

Audrey Saunders

IBA (International Bartenders Association)

is an organization that counts bartenders in sixty-four countries and territories as members and represents bartending as a profession. The IBA was founded in 1951 at the Grand Hotel in Torquay, England, by bartenders from Denmark, France, Italy, the Netherlands, Sweden, Switzerland, and the United Kingdom, which provided its first president, W. J. "Billy" Tarling. See TARLING, WILLIAM JAMES "BILLY". Its presence is primarily felt in Europe and Asia. The IBA holds an annual contest called the World Cocktail Competition (originally called the International Cocktail Competition), which began in 1955 and is held in a different country each year. The association has become best known, perhaps, for its list of sanctioned, "official" cocktails, the standardized recipes for which are often consulted by media and bartenders alike.

See UNITED KINGDOM BARTENDERS GUILD (UKBG) and UNITED STATES BARTENDERS' GUILD (USBG).

IBA website. https://www.iba-world.com (accessed February 17, 2021).

Robert Simonson

The **Iberian Peninsula** comprises two primary countries: Spain and Portugal, both of which have centuries-long distillation industries. They have become especially important as spirit manufacturers only since the late nineteenth century as their traditional fortified wine manufacturers have evolved and as decreasing sales of fortified wines have led to a surplus of spirit.

The renowned alchemist and physician Arnaud de Villanova (then residing in Madrid) is often credited with pioneering the distillation of alcohol in Europe in the thirteenth century when he distilled grape spirit with various botanicals for medicinal purposes. Nonetheless, the Portuguese and Spanish historically preferred wines to spirits, for both cultural reasons and political ones. That said, Iberians have a long tradition of turning local wines, and the pomace resulting from their production, into brandy, much of it used for fortifying wine. Since the nineteenth century, Spain in particular has also shown an interest in imported rum (not too surprising given the long history of sugar production in its former Caribbean colonies) and, more recently, gin, both imported and domestic (in fact, the Balearic Islands, a former haven for the British Navy, have been producing the latter since the eighteenth century). Spain also has a narrow but deep history of top-notch cocktail bars run by star mixologists dating back to the late nineteenth century.

Spain's most famous spirit is brandy de Jerez, made in the Jerez region of Andalusia. Although domestic sales are sagging, exports of brandy de Jerez are strong as it has developed a good reputation in foreign markets. The favored liqueur remains pacharán, a neutral spirit flavored with anise and sloe berries and sold at 25–35 percent ABV. The recipe for pacharán first appeared in print in 1441. There is both a general classification for Spanish pacharán and a separate protected designation of origin for pacharán navarro (1988). Other legally designated spirits and liqueurs in Spain include palo de Mallorca, brandy de Penedés, ratafia Catalana, cantueso Alacantino, licor café de Galicia, licor hierbas de Galicia, aguardente de hierbas de Galicia, aperitivo café de Alcoy, herbero de la Sierra de Mariola, Orujo de Galicia, aguardiente de sidra de Asturias, and two "honey rums" ronmiel and ronmiel de Canarias, and (as is common among Mediterranean countries) several anise-flavored spirits, anís Paloma Monforte del Cid, anís Espanol, hierbas Ibicencas, hierbas Mallorcas, cazalla, chinchón, Ojén, and rute.

Portugal has historically been more abstemious than Spain when it comes to alcohol, and its history with distillation has been debated (see WINES, FORTIFIED), but it is indisputable that after the Methuen Treaty of 1703, which gave Portuguese wines preferential trade status in Britain, large quantities of port were being made for that market by the addition of grape spirit to fermenting must. The island of Madeira had codified the use of grape spirit for the same purposes long before then, suggesting that in Portugal distilled spirits were originally and primarily employed as an adjunct for the island's famous wine. Port and Madeira were also widely sought after in the British American colonies, largely supplanting the Canary and sack from the Spanish Atlantic islands that had been popular in the early Atlantic world of the fifteenth through seventeenth centuries.

Portugal's well known spirits include anis Português, Évora anisada, licor de Singeverga, poncha da Madeira, medronho do Buçaco, medronho do Algarve, aguardente de pêra da Lousã (a pear distillate), and the ubiquitous cherry liqueur, ginjinha portuguesa, as well as no fewer than six different PDO (protected designation of origin) aguardentes and four such aguardente bagaceiras.

See also AGUARDIENTE AND AGUARDENTE; BOADAS, MIGUEL; and CHICOTE, PEDRO "PERICO".

Doug Frost

ice, history of its use. The art of preserving ice formed in winter so that it can be used to cool drinks in the heat of summer is almost as old as civilization itself: it was already old in 1780 BCE, when Zimri-Lim, king of the Mesopotamian city of Mari, claimed to have built the world's first dedicated ice house, where blocks of it were stored under an insulating layer of tamarisk branches. The use of snow and ice to cool wine was a feature of Greek and Roman civilization, to the point that it was sold in the marketplaces. Iced drinks were well known

in Persia and China and Mughal India. In Europe, the great specialists in iced drinks were the Italians, going back at least to the Renaissance. And indeed, it was Italian *limonadiers*—specialists in Italian iced sherbets—in France who first seem to have united ice and distilled spirits when they began making delicate iced punches (attested to as early as 1765). See PUNCH. That got the French finally to appreciate punch, a drink they had previously rejected as crude and English.

It took Americans, however, to make the combination of ice and spirits not just known but customary. Already in 1784, just as the Parisian limonadiers were perfecting their punches, one Archibald McElroy was advertising "Ice Punch" in the Philadelphia newspapers. By 1810, when the *Almanach des gourmands* was advising its Parisian readers that the best "Punch glacé" in town was to be found at the Café Tortoni, Ice Punch was being sold in New York and Boston (where it was a specialty of Othello Pollard, a pioneering African American caterer), and taverns in Virginia were selling iced Mint Juleps.

It is true that one could sometimes find iced punch in London too, either at the Prince Regent's residence (he was a devotee) or at the occasional grand public banquet, such as the one at Vauxhall gardens in 1813 where 1,300 people sat down to a dinner accompanied by wines and "iced punch." See REGENT'S PUNCH. In Europe, however, iced drinks were a luxury. In America, they were an everyday thing. (There were already technical differences between American iced drinks and European ones: the latter were usually bottled and then iced, preventing the drink from having direct contact with the ice, which was often of dubious quality; in America, drinks were built right on the ice, so that in a bowl of punch it would provide both chilling and dilution.)

The modern ice trade began in 1806 when Frederic Tudor (1783–1864), a visionary and persistent Yankee merchant, shipped a cargo of Boston ice to Martinique. By the 1820s, Tudor was regularly supplying ice to New Orleans, Charleston, Savannah, and a number of Caribbean ports. His competitors, of whom there would be many, took care of New York, Philadelphia, Baltimore, and the other sweltering cities of the Mid-Atlantic States. Between them, Tudor and the others created the necessary technology—from horse-drawn ice cutters to steam-powered block hoists—to harvest the thick, clean ice with which the frigid New England winters covered every pond and river and ship the heavy, half-meter square blocks as far away as Calcutta. For every step of their journey they traveled under insulation, from harvest to deposit in the customer's new "refrigerator."

The ever-increasing availability of ice completely changed American drinking. One of Tudor's practices appears to have been to supply a prominent bar in each market he entered with free ice for a year, with the proviso that the establishment not raise its prices. "A single conspicuous bar keeper . . . selling steadily his liquors all cold without an increase in price [will] render it absolutely necessary that the others come to it or lose their customers," as he wrote in an undated paper. Beginning in the 1830s, American bartenders began not just using ice but lavishing it about. In Virginia, the African American bartenders, both free and enslaved, who mixed most of the "fancy drinks" there turned the Mint Julep into the "Hail-Storm Julep," where the drink was cooled not by a mere lump of ice but by having the glass packed with finely cracked ice and then having more molded around its outside. In New York, the Sherry Cobbler was shaken up with a glassful of ice pebbles. By the 1840s, the swells in New Orleans were drinking their brandy on ice, and those in New York were even putting it in their Cock-Tails, a drink that had up to that point been drunk at room temperature. See COBBLER; COCK-TAIL; and JULEP.

The 1840s also saw this new-model American bar exported, with examples appearing in Paris and London. That of course required unusual amounts of ice, at least by European standards. In Britain, those were largely sourced from Wenham Lake in Massachusetts and Rockland Lake in New York, at least until Norwegian entrepreneurs set up American-style ice harvesting outside of Oslo.

Natural ice was not without its problems. The source could be polluted, increasingly common as the United States industrialized. Worse, the supply could fail entirely, whether from a warm winter (such as the one of 1828, which saw Tudor scrambling and one of his ship captains hack up a floating Arctic iceberg to fulfill his Martinique contracts), an extra-hot summer, or some fault in the chain of transmission.

Beginning in the 1860s, the massive American natural-ice industry, which had spread from coast to coast, began to receive competition from steam-driven artificial ice makers. As the technology of artificial ice improved, it gradually displaced natural ice, without changing the business much from the consumer end: ice was still delivered in large blocks well into the twentieth century. Bartenders still had to know how to break down the blocks, and they still had the ability to cut ice in different sizes to go with different drinks. Only after the Second World War did it become standard for bars (and home mixologists, for that matter) to make their own ice. At first, this came in cold, hard cubes. By the 1960s, however, machines had been introduced that made ice in cloudy chips or elongated rings, shapes that froze quickly and filled a glass easily, but also melted in no time and had little appeal to the eye. See ICE MACHINE. Gresham's law saw to it that by the 1980s this style of ice had come to dominate the marketplace, in the United States and—since the postwar years had seen much of the rest of the world adapt to using ice, if not on an American level, then at least to a far greater one than before—practically everywhere else as well, with the admirable exception of Japan. See JAPAN.

One of the core tenets of the twenty-first-century cocktail renaissance was that ice was important—that one could not make good drinks without good ice. This led, among other things, to a revival of the fortunes of the Kold Draft company, maker of (admittedly temperamental) ice machines that supplied the large, cold, and hard cubes of yore. Some bartenders and mixologists made ice their special study, working with full-scale blocks and learning anew how to break them down to produce ice of any desired size and shape. In 2010, Richard Boccato, a Milk & Honey alumnus and owner of the highly regarded Queens, New York, bar Dutch Kills, went so far as to install a full-scale Clinebell ice-block maker in the basement of Weather Up, a Manhattan bar he was working with. He was the first to do so, but he would not be the last. See CLINEBELL ICE MACHINE and MILK & HONEY. It is only a matter of time before horse ploughs are once again quartering the frozen ponds of Massachusetts.

See also COCKTAIL and ICE CARVING.

David, Elizabeth. *Harvest of the Cold Months*. New York: Viking, 1994.

Smith, Philip Chadwick Foster. *Crystal Blocks of Yankee Coldness*. Wenham, MA: Wenham Historical Association and Museum, 1962.

Weightman, Gavin. *The Frozen Water Trade.* New York: Hyperion, 2003.

Wondrich, David. *Imbibe!*, 2nd. ed. New York: Perigee, 2015.

David Wondrich

ice, science of its use. For an understanding of how to most efficiently use ice to control temperature and dilution in beverages, and of how clear ice is produced both at home and in ice machines, we will look at the science of freezing water and melting ice. For simplicity's sake, we will assume the typical conditions of freezer-temperature ice submerged in room-temperature beverages, rather than all possible situations.

The cooling of beverages with ice is due mostly to its melting, which results in the dilution of the beverage with water. Ice melts thus: first the solid ice will warm up to its melting temperature of 0° C, then change its state by melting from solid into liquid, and then the liquid water, which is still at 0° C, can warm further. Only one-half calorie of energy is required to warm 1 g of ice by 1° C, and one full calorie is needed to warm 1 g of water by 1° C, but the change of state requires that a relatively huge 80 calories be expended before 1g of ice at 0° C becomes 1 g of water at 0° C. So from a typical freezer temperature of −18° C, to warm up 1 g of ice to its melting temperature requires only 9 calories of energy but another 80 calories to melt it.

This energy needed to melt the ice is taken from its surrounding environment: the beverage in which the ice is placed. As the beverage loses energy, its temperature decreases. A little of that energy stolen from the beverage goes toward warming up ice, and a lot toward melting it, so we can simply round up to say that the chilling of an iced beverage is the result of ice melting, and also that the chilling of an iced beverage results in dilution. For iced drinks, chilling and dilution are critically linked.

Rate of Chilling and Dilution

Ice melts at its surface, so the greater the surface area of ice in a beverage, the more melting that can take place at a given time. For a given total volume (or weight) of ice, smaller pieces will have a greater combined surface area than a single large piece. For example, a single, large cube of ice 10 cm square has a volume of 1,000 cm³ and a surface area of 600 cm², while that same cube split into eight 5-cm cubes will have the same combined volume of 1,000 cm³ but double the surface area at 1,200 cm². Thus the smaller group of cubes with their larger total surface area can chill a beverage at a faster rate than a single large cube.

However if both the larger and smaller cubes melt completely into a beverage, they will chill the drink to the same final temperature (and dilution), since the same amount of energy is required to melt the same volume of ice. In other words, the volume (or weight) of ice we add to a drink determines how much it can chill, while the surface area of the ice determines how quickly it can chill. In the real world we use more ice than is necessary to chill a drink, and it will reach an equilibrium temperature with no significant additional chilling or dilution from ice. But unless we are holding the beverage in a perfectly insulated container, additional dilution will occur over time in response to heat gain from ambient temperature.

If we want to chill (and therefore dilute) a drink with ice at the slowest rate possible, as may be desired for whisky on the rocks, we can use one large ice sphere, because spheres have the lowest surface-area-to-volume ratio of any shape. Conversely, small chips of ice will chill a drink faster than big cubes.

To further increase the rate of chilling, we stir or shake drinks, moving more of the warm beverage over the surfaces of the ice. This sweeps away the just-melted surface water on the ice so that the warmer beverage can continue to be in contact with the ice's surface (again, most of the cooling of the drink comes from ice melting). Shaking with ice hastens this process and also increases the ice's surface area by shattering it into smaller pieces, thus speeding chilling even more. Shaking cocktails reduces their temperature faster than stirring (assuming roughly the same size ice), but it also adds texture via air bubbles.

Wet, glossy-appearing ice (such as ice kept out in an ice bowl) has newly melted water clinging to its surfaces. When we add wet ice to a drink, we are adding both ice that is very effective at cooling and water that is not. The water will still dilute the drink without the payoff of chilling it much, so if we want to chill drinks most effectively, we should use non-wet ice. Ice can be strained or toweled off to remove some of its surface water.

Freezing and Clear Ice

Ice is unusual in that it floats on its liquid form, water, rather than sinks. When water freezes, its molecules arrange into a hexagonal lattice pattern repeated in all directions to form an ice crystal. The spacious arrangement of atoms in the crystal results in ice being less dense than its liquid water form.

Pure water (pure H_2O) chilled to 0° C does not spontaneously crystallize into ice; it needs a nucleus to grow from. Pure water can become supercooled: the condition of remaining in the liquid state below its freezing point. Supercooled pure water will eventually self-nucleate at cold enough temperatures, but in any real-world situation water is not 100 percent H_2O, and a foreign particle like a speck of dust or a grain of salt in it will act as a starting point for crystallization at just below water's freezing temperature.

In a natural setting like a lake, ice crystals grow in a thin layer across the surface and then thicken downward. Ice thickens at a slower and slower rate over time, as the energy from the environment needed to freeze the water must conduct through the existing ice at the surface first.

When ice crystals grow slowly, they reject incorporating impurities including trapped air, minerals, and anything else not pure H_2O, which don't fit into their neat crystal lattice. The pure ice is perfectly clear, and impurities are pushed away from the growing crystal. In a typical freezer, the cold environment surrounds an ice cube tray on all sides, so ice forms not only on the surface but also on the inner walls and thickens in toward the middle. The first part to freeze is typically clear, and the last part to freeze is where the impurities and air are concentrated, forming a cloudy core. (This is easier to see by freezing water in a single container like a plastic cup instead of a tray of cubes.) Additionally, because water expands as it becomes a solid and the last part to freeze is in the center of a cube, the ice will often shatter or crack when fully frozen, increasing perceived cloudiness.

Water can also form cloudy ice when it freezes quickly, as multiple fast-growing crystals surround and trap impurities and air, rather than pushing them away.

Clear ice can be produced at home or in machines by encouraging the water to freeze in one direction only (sometimes called "directional freezing"), rather than forming from the outside in toward the center. A simple way to accomplish this is by filling an insulated container with no top (such as a hard-sided beer cooler with the top off) with water and leaving this in a freezer. The insulation on the sides and bottom of the container prevents or at least slows ice forming on those sides, encouraging the ice to thicken only from the top toward the bottom.

The final part of the block to freeze, the bottom section, will be cloudy, much like the core of a standard ice cube. To harvest only clear ice, the slab of ice can be removed from the insulated container before it has fully frozen to the bottom, leaving behind water. Alternately, if left to freeze all the way, the cloudy bottom of the fully frozen block can be cut off to retain only the clear section. Most recently available clear-ice-producing trays for home use employ directional freezing with insulated containers and clear/cloudy section separators.

Various techniques have been reported to increase ice clarity, whether in a typical ice cube tray or within the directional freezing system. Most are attempts at slowing the rate of freezing, minimizing minerals and other impurities, and/or minimizing gases in the water. Boiling water before freezing it, a much-promoted (but usually ineffective) technique, is meant to capitalize on reducing gases in water.

Many ice sculpture block machines also freeze water in one direction, but from the bottom toward the top. A cold plate is located on the bottom of a large, water-filled container, and a water pump closer to the surface circulates water to prevent ice from freezing over at the top. The block forms from the bottom up, and then the remaining surface water (which would have been cloudy ice if allowed to freeze) is discarded. Other clear-ice-producing machines, typically those that make smaller shapes, pump or spray water over a cold plate and continually discard the runoff, so that only clear ice forms. See CLINEBELL ICE MACHINE.

How Ice Is Used in Modern Mixology

While ice cube machines and the shape and sizes of ice they produce vary in different parts of the world, very few models produce large, clear ice cubes bigger than 32 mm (1.25″) square as of this writing. In recent years larger sizes of clear ice have been desired by bartenders in order to serve cocktails and spirits on a single cube or sphere. Clear ice is largely an aesthetic choice over cloudy ice, but it should also contain fewer minerals/impurities and melt at a slower rate. As cloudy ice's bubble pockets melt, more surface area is exposed and the melting rate can increase; additionally, cloudy ice tends to crack more readily due to the way it was formed.

Seeking to offer large, clear cubes and other shapes, bartenders began to cut cocktail ice out of very large (136 kg [300 pound]) clear blocks made in sculpture block ice machines. In 2010, the bar Weather Up in the Tribeca neighborhood of Manhattan installed an in-house sculpture ice machine for cocktail ice use, probably the first bar to do so. Weather Up partner and bartender Richard Boccato then launched Hundredweight Ice with other partners in 2011 adjacent to his bar Dutch Kills, to produce and deliver specialty cocktail ice to other bars as well.

This model of cutting sculpture ice blocks into glass-sized smaller cubes was replicated around the United States and in other countries. Blocks are typically cut using power tools (inducing electric chainsaws and band saws) and hand tools to reduce them to desired shapes and sizes. Common sizes of ice produced in this method include large cubes and single tall "spears" to fit Collins glasses, though everything from large spheres to ice punchbowls are cut down from these large blocks. See ICE CARVING.

Beverages can be chilled by methods other than adding ice to liquid—whether the purpose of this is to specifically avoid dilution or not—with varying degrees of effectiveness. Liquid ingredients, bar tools, and glassware can be chilled in refrigerators or freezers, or they can be chilled with ice that is not incorporated into the drink. Frozen objects such as stones and metal and plastic cubes can be added to the beverage in the glass. In specialty freezers, ice can be kept at extremely cold temperatures and used to minimize dilution (more cooling power comes from ice warming up to its melting point). Dry ice (solid carbon dioxide) and liquid nitrogen are sometimes used to chill glassware or are added to drinks, though these require special safety training and handling.

Arnold, Dave. *Liquid Intelligence: The Art and Science of the Perfect Cocktail*, New York: W. W. Norton, 2014.

English, Camper. "Index of Ice Experiments on Alcademics." https://www.alcademics.com/index-of-ice-experiments-on-alcademics.html (accessed March 23, 2021).

Gosnell, Mariana: *Ice: The Nature, History, and Uses of This Astonishing Substance*. Chicago: University of Chicago Press, 2007.

Simonson, Robert. "TriBeCa bar Will Have Its Own Iceworks." *New York Times*, October 12, 2010. https://dinersjournal.blogs.nytimes.com/2010/10/12/tribeca-bar-will-have-its-own-iceworks/ (accessed March 23, 2021).

Camper English

ice carving in a bar context is not the art of chainsawing and chiseling swans and salmon-fishing bears out of large blocks of ice, but rather the craft of breaking those blocks down into pieces small enough and uniform enough to be used for chilling drinks for service. In the nineteenth and early twentieth centuries, this was part of every American bartender's competence, at least if he or she was working in a bar that served mixed drinks. For something so central to American bartending, however, there is very little detailed information to be found on the topic in bartender's guides or in the many newspaper articles from the time devoted to bartenders and their craft. See ICE, HISTORY OF ITS USE.

According to the 1887 posthumous edition of Jerry Thomas's *The Bar-Tender's Guide*, the bartender should always have shaved ice ready for drinks that are mostly spirits, and "small lumps of ice" for the others. To these one can add the larger blocks that would be needed for punches and cups. Some bars went beyond that: as described in a widely reprinted 1899 article in the *Chicago Chronicle*, not "content to break up ice in irregular shapes, making pieces about as big as a toy rubber ball" (this was for an Old-Fashioned), they carefully carved ice "into perfect cubes about two inches [5 cm] on a side, so that every cocktail gets just as much ice as every other one." If bartenders were doing this in Chicago, they were no doubt doing it elsewhere as well (although it is a Chicago bartender, John Applegreen, who specified that "lump ice" for drinks should be "about the size of an egg, but cut square or diamond shape"). See OLD-FASHIONED COCKTAIL.

By the 1840s, at any rate, the bartender's kit included ice saws, axes, and chisels for reducing the large blocks to more manageable size, plus ice picks, mallets, and knives for the finer work of producing pieces that will fit in a glass and the kind of finely cracked ice that went into a Mint Julep. See JULEP. Eventually it would include tools for the even finer work that those Chicago bartenders were turning out, and patent ice shavers that could be dragged across the top of an ice block to get a drink's worth of ice, fresh-shaved. See ICE MALLET.

After Prohibition, bars quickly moved to making their own ice, which came pre-cubed for service. It would be a long time before some bartenders went back to breaking down blocks. But when Milan's elegant and popular Bar Basso was reimagined under new ownership in 1967, Mirko Stocchetto (the bar's proprietor and longtime head barman) opted to source large blocks of ice from a local factory to execute and cool his cocktails. Although this may not appear to have been an entirely unprecedented maneuver from the perspective of the modern bartender, it must be understood that these events were transpiring at a time when the techniques and protocol of the European "American bar" that had flourished from the late nineteenth century until the Second World War were altogether waning in lieu of contrived faux-Polynesian antics and careless entertaining with commercially bottled mixers at the home bar.

Even more astounding were the ways in which the bar staff at Bar Basso chose to cut down their factory ice by hand, using various saws and other sharp implements, in order to fit their custom "bicchieroni" (large cocktail glasses). When necessity became the mother of invention yet again after their local ice factory shut down, Stocchetto and his staff began freezing their own ice at the bar in plastic molds to suit the needs of their burgeoning cocktail program.

Legend has it that one fateful evening at Bar Basso back in 1967, Stocchetto reached for a bottle of gin to complete a Negroni (commonly equal parts Campari, sweet vermouth, and gin), yet he inexplicably found a bottle of prosecco in his hand. Thankfully he did not resist the urge to defy tradition, and the joyous outcome of his now-infamous "mistake" was the Negroni Sbagliato (*sbagliato* translates from Italian as "erroneous," "wrong," or "mistaken"), which Stocchetto has been faithfully

serving over large cubes of ice at Bar Basso for half a century. See CIRO'S; ITALY; and NEGRONI.

Another place that ice carving continued unabated was in Japan. However, it took a trip through New York City for this painstakingly maintained skill to edge back into the spotlight. Some thirty-three years after Stocchetto instituted his idiosyncratic ice program and several thousand miles away, the concept of "big ice" in bars would arrive at the forefront of the cocktail world when Sasha Petraske and Toby Maloney of New York City's Milk & Honey first embraced the idea of freezing large blocks of ice in-house, which they also cut by hand into various shapes and forms—each intended for specific drinks within the wide scope of their largely classic cocktail repertoire. See MILK & HONEY; and PETRASKE, SASHA.

Petraske admitted that he drew much of his inspiration for the ice program at Milk & Honey from his observations and experiences at New York City's Angel's Share, a well-hidden East Village cocktail haunt whose entrance is easily overlooked within the Japanese restaurant in which it is housed: "We got the idea from Angel's Share. Although some American bars never stopped using the big ice, I believe that the Japanese can be credited for the current craze for large format ice. Even if Angel's Share hadn't been around, eventually we would have bumped into Tokyo bartenders."

For in the Tokyo cocktail bar scene, where Angel's Share's bartenders had trained, a meticulous understanding of the importance of ice as it contributes to a drink has been a fundamental aspect of many heralded bar programs—most notably that of Kazuo Uyeda at his bar, simply known as Tender. His unwavering attention to detail in every facet of cocktail preparation has always included a particular focus on the effects of varying gradations of ice as they relate to specific drink-making techniques. Uyeda's principles regarding the contributions and effects of hand-cut ice upon the modern interpretation of the classic cocktail is quite possibly the indirect foundation for the Western bartender's current appreciation of large-format frozen water in our drinks. See TENDER BAR and UYEDA, KAZUO.

With Milk & Honey setting the example, many modern bars instituted block ice programs, even going so far as installing massive Clinebell ice machines, capable of making it one large block at a time. Today, it is once again expected of a top-level bartender that he or she will be able to take one of those blocks and deftly reduce it to usable parts, each sized and shaped according to the glass in which it will do its work. That is progress. See CLINEBELL ICE MACHINE.

Applegreen, John. *Applegreen's Barkeeper's Guide*, 2nd ed. Chicago: Hotel Monthly, 1904.

Gosnell, Mariana. *Ice: The Nature, the History, and the Uses of an Astonishing Substance*. Chicago: University of Chicago Press, 2007.

Marling, Karal Ann. *Ice: Great Moments in the History of Hard, Cold Water*. St. Paul, Minnesota: Borealis, 2008.

Uyeda, Kazuo. *Cocktail Techniques*. New York: Mud Puddle, 2010.

Wondrich, David, *Imbibe!*, 2nd ed. New York: Perigee, 2015.

Richard Boccato and David Wondrich

ice cream and sorbets drifted into the bartender's arsenal from the soda fountain in the late nineteenth century with the Couperee (brandy, liqueur, and vanilla ice cream with soda water), first recorded in 1887. The addition of ice cream to a fancy drink was also a favorite gambit of William "The Only William" Schmidt, the most celebrated mixologist of the age. See SCHMIDT, WILLIAM. The popularity of ice cream drinks has ebbed and flowed since, but such drinks have never quite disappeared. Ice cream, blended or used as scoops, may be used in place of milk, cream, or half-and-half in "frozen" versions of classic dessert drinks such as the Grasshopper, Brandy Alexander, and Golden Cadillac (all three particularly popular in the 1970s, when ice cream drinks were very much in style), while fruit sorbets may stand in for some or all of the ice in others. See GRASSHOPPER and ALEXANDER COCKTAIL. A scoop of ice cream or sorbet can also top an alcoholic beverage such as Guinness Stout, sparkling wine, or even a mixed cocktail.

See also TGI FRIDAY'S.

Schmidt, William. *The Flowing Bowl*. New York: Charles L. Webster, 1892.

Thomas, Jerry. *The Bar-Tender's Guide*. New York: Dick & Fitzgerald, 1887.

Jason Horn

The **ice machine** is an essential tool of the cocktail craft. The early era of the cocktail relied on the wide-reaching ice trade (headed most prominently by Frederic Tudor, Boston's "Ice King"), which harvested ice from lakes and ponds in winter, then stored and distributed the ice to hotels, bars, restaurants, and other ventures. While artificial refrigeration was developed as early as 1748 (as demonstrated by William Cullen at the University of Glasgow), the first documented production of "artificial" ice was in 1844, when John Gorrie, a Florida-based physician, experimented with ice production while searching for ways to cool the rooms of patients suffering from yellow fever. Gorrie was granted a patent in 1851 for a machine that produces ice, but attempts to commercialize the project were crushed by Tudor. In 1853, Alexander Twining gained a patent for an ice-making machine, and a similar patent was granted in Australia to James Harrison in 1855. The first artificial-ice plants in the United States appeared in 1860, and by 1909 there were around two thousand in operation; these plants produced ice in 200-pound blocks, made by submerging containers filled with fresh water into tanks of salt water (which freezes at a lower temperature) cooled to below 0° C. The first machine to produce edible, tube-shaped ice was introduced in 1929 by Jurgen Hans, who in 1932 founded Külinda in Frankfurt; the company is still involved in refrigeration technology.

Today's ice machines function largely in a similar manner to the earliest machines. A low-pressure refrigerant vapor is pressurized by a compressor; a condenser converts this vapor into a high-pressure liquid, which is drained out through a throttle valve. This process depressurizes the liquid, which is conducted to an evaporator, where heat exchange occurs, dropping the temperature. Commercial icemakers operate by running water across a stainless-steel evaporator cooled below the freezing point; horizontal evaporators wash more air and dissolved solids away as the water cools, resulting in harder, clearer, cleaner ice, whereas vertical evaporators may operate faster but can produce softer, "wetter" ice.

Home icemakers typically use vertical evaporators to produce cubes or half-moons of ice. Bars and restaurants use commercial machines from producers including Manitowoc, Ice-O-Matic, and Scotsman, and the most widely utilized machines produce either pebble ice or dimpled cubes for use in soft drinks. With the early twenty-first-century cocktail renaissance, bartenders began to turn their attention to different styles of ice production and different types of ice machines. While some bars tap nineteenth-century technology by purchasing large blocks of ice (or producing them in-house with machines such as the cult favorite Clinebell model) and then cutting or crushing the ice for service, others have turned to horizontal-evaporator machines for the colder, clearer ice they produce.

Beginning in 1955, Pennsylvania-based Kold-Draft has produced ice machines that utilize a distinctive "upside down" horizontal evaporator and water-plate system. This approach pumps water up into the machine's ice-cube cells, circulating the water as the ice freezes from the cube's exterior inward, washing away dissolved solids and resulting in hard, clear cubes that became favorites of craft-cocktail bartenders. Founded in Nagoya, Japan, in 1947, Hoshizaki gained a similar reputation among cocktail bartenders for machines that produce clear, 1-1/4-inch cubes and pellet-size "cubelets." Bars that use large quantities of crushed or pebble-size ice sometimes utilize special ice machines such as the Clawson Hail Queen, a stainless-steel box with moving blades that can crush thirty pounds of ice in a minute.

See also ICE, SCIENCE OF ITS USE; and ICE, HISTORY OF ITS USE.

Chapel, George. "Gorrie's Fridge." http://www.phys.ufl. edu/~ihas/gorrie/fridge.htm (accessed February 17, 2021).

Parker, Ian. "The Emperor of Ice." *New Yorker*, February 12, 2001. http://www.newyorker.com/magazine/ 2001/02/12/the-emperor-of-ice-2 (accessed February 17, 2021).

Scherlinder Morse, Minna. "Chilly Reception." *Smithsonian*, July 2002. http://www.smithsonianmag.com/ history/chilly-reception-66099329/?no-ist (accessed February 17, 2021).

Paul Clarke

The **ice mallet**, a large, heavy, one-handed hardwood maul or hand sledge used to crack ice into fine fragments or even powder, has been a part of the bartender's toolkit on and off for nearly two hundred

An early nineteenth-century American hardwood ice mallet. Wondrich Collection.

years, perhaps longer. The earliest known reference to its use in making drinks is found in the 1847 fourth edition of *Oxford Night Caps*, as the recipe for both the Sherry Cobbler and Julep called for powdered ice: "Pound a small quantity of ice quite fine, by wrapping it in a coarse cloth, and beating it with a mallet or rolling pin." This book also recommended the use of ice imported from the Wenham Lake Ice Co., of Massachusetts, which had become a luxury item in England. See MIXOGRAPHY.

By the 1840s in America, ice in drinks had become a staple, not a luxury, and the annual arrival of the hot weather saw the newspapers full of advertisements for ice mallets and ice picks. (In place of the coarse cloth, many American bartenders used canvas coin sacks.) As a standard bar tool, the mallets were simple, sturdy things, although the 1846 edition of *The American Home Cook Book* mentioned an "ice mallet with pick that slides into the handle" as being "requisite" in "furnishing a kitchen." (The earliest known US patent on a mallet was no. 52,696, granted to Albert C. Eddy on February 20, 1866.)

But if bartender Harry Johnson included the mallet among the "List of the Utensils in Complete

Form Used in Saloons, Etc." in the various editions of his iconic *Bartender's Manual*, it was another thing that didn't survive Prohibition. See JOHNSON, HARRY. With the decline of the Mint Julep, that much fine ice simply wasn't needed. See JULEP. After Repeal, bartenders were reduced to cracking ice with little tappers or tiny patent metal hammers with bottle openers in the handles.

In recent years, though, the ice mallet has enjoyed something of a renaissance, due in large part to its use by the legendary New Orleans bartender Chris McMillian. See MCMILLIAN, CHRIS. McMillian recalls that he began experimenting with the mallet around 2000 while working at the Ritz-Carlton's Library Lounge, and while reading the 1963 book *The Social History of Bourbon*, by Gerald Carson. Mr. McMillian originally began using the mallet to crush ice for his Mint Juleps and Mojitos. The hammers he and his earliest disciples used were true ice mallets, impressive in their size and heft. As the technique became more popular, the market has been flooded with new, purpose-made ice mallets, all too many of them puny, light affairs that require far more effort than the original ones did.

An American Woman [pseud.]. *The American Home Cook Book*. New York: Dick & Fitzgerald, 1854.
"Ice cream Frozen in Thirty Minutes." *New York Evening Post*, June 26, 1849, 3.
Johnson, Harry. *New and Improved Bartender's Manual*. New York: Samisch & Goldmann, 1882.
McMillian, Chris. Interview, February 2, 2020.

Philip Greene

India and Central Asia are crucial to the early history of distillation, although today their participation in the global spirits trade rather belies their importance. There is a good deal of archaeological evidence and even some textual evidence to suggest that the Indian subcontinent was one of the earliest centers of distillation and was perhaps even the first place to develop the practice on something approaching an industrial scale.

The archeological record covers a period from 100 BCE (and perhaps earlier) to 200 CE and an area stretching from Gandhara in the north (present-day northwest Pakistan and southern Afghanistan) to Mysore in the far south. It is not unambiguous: the people doing the digging, in the mid-twentieth century, were not looking specifically for evidence of distillation, and even if there were sufficient interest in pursuing some of the most promising findings, around Taxila in the old Gandharan kingdom, present conditions in the region make such a dig unlikely. But combined with evidence from various Ayurvedic texts (admittedly also ambiguous) that suggest the term *surā*, normally taken to mean a fermented drink, actually means a distilled one, and from the less-ambiguous *Arthashastra*, an administrative manual attributed to Kautilya and completed by the third century CE, which notes that "householders should be free to manufacture white liquor on festive occasions," there is a strong case for early distillation in India. Indeed, the Gandharan excavations appear to show combined distillery-taverns, where spirits were made in the back and served in the front. See DISTILLATION, HISTORY.

In any case, by the late 1200s, as Baranî, the historian of the Delhi Sultanate (the predecessor to the Mughal Empire), records, there was a lively trade in cane spirits in Delhi and northern India. See RUM. At the same time, southern and western India made large amounts of palm-sap arrack. See ARRACK and PALMSAP. These spirits were full-fledged articles of commerce, at a time when the European spirits trade was just beginning. See SPIRITS TRADE, HISTORY OF. These were not the only spirits made in India; mahua flowers were distilled in central India; the southwest saw cashew fruits were made into the spirit that would eventually be called *feni*; and jaggery, or palm sugar, was widely distilled, often with various botanicals (sometimes including cannabis). See FENI and MAHUA.

The arrival of European colonizers in the late 1400s did little to change the subcontinent's drinkways, at least at first. Indeed, it was the Europeans who adopted Indian drinks. The Portuguese, unable to get wine, took to distilling raisins in palm arrack to make a (strong) facsimile. The English made an artificial wine of arrack, citrus juice, sugar, and water, either following an Indian model or at the very least adopting Indian ingredients wholesale. This punch, as they called it, became the first globally popular drink based on spirits, and did more than anything else to normalize spirits drinking. See PUNCH.

Eventually, however, European, and specifically English, influences took root. It wasn't just the punch houses and London-style taverns that began popping up wherever the English settled (e.g., the famous Harmonic Tavern in Calcutta, whose bo-hemian patronage in the 1780s would have been considered fast company even in London). It was also things like Bengal rum (which had been known as Bengal arrack before the rise of the British rum trade), which developed along lines first laid out in the British Caribbean (e.g., barrel aging) and was widely exported throughout Asia and the East Indies. The explosive growth of the British whisky in-dustry in the nineteenth century took full advantage of the huge export market that India represented, but already by the end of the 1820s the inevitable had happened, and India had started making its own whisky, at Kasauli in the western Himalayas where the cool climate resembles that of Scotland. Today, India's whisky industry is one of the largest in the world, although the bulk of what it makes are blends of scotch malt and grain whiskies and local spirit, either grain- or molasses-based; several of these are among the largest-selling whisky brands in the world. See BAGPIPER. That said, the Amrut dis-tillery, founded by J. N. Radhakrishna Rao Jagdale in Bangalore in 1948, makes some world-class award-winning malts, and other Indian distilleries have followed.

Amrut is made from grain grown in the Punjab and elsewhere in northern India. Today, however, other than the whisky still made at Kasauli, the re-gion is not the distilling center it once was. In the 1700s, for instance, one would have found cane-spirit drinkers in Delhi, and if one had continued north, Nepal would perhaps have yielded some more cane spirit (it certainly makes that now) and Kashmir would have yielded grape brandy, as would Afghanistan, if you knew whom to talk to (wines and spirits were made in small quantities there by members of the Jewish and Armenian Christian communities, as was common throughout the re-gion). In the northern parts of Afghanistan, one would have been likely to encounter the true spirit of Central Asia, *arajhi*. This distilled kumiss (fermented mare's milk) was the preferred drink of the Mongols, and its manufacture dates back to at least the 1100s CE. This at least can still be found in the region: in Kyrgyzstan, for instance, it is sold as *chagirmak* (although vodka is much easier to find there, thanks to the state-of-the-art former Soviet vodka distillery maintained at Tokmok). It is some-what easier to find in Mongolia, where it is called *arkhi*. This is one of the oldest distilling traditions on earth. The product, however, is not exported. See ARRACK.

Allchin, F. R. "India: The Ancient Home of Distillation?" *Man*, March 1979, 55–63.

Hobbs, H. *John Barleycorn Bahadur*. Calcutta: Thacker, Spink, 1944.

Mahdihassan, S. "The Earliest Distillation Units: Pot-tery in Indo-Pakistan." *Pakistan Archaeology* 8 (197): 159–168.

Oort, Marianne S. "Surā in the Paippalāda Samhitā of the *Atharvaveda*." *Journal of the American Oriental Society*, April-June 2002, pp. 355-60.

Park, Hyunhee. *Soju: A Global History*. Cambridge: Cam-bridge University Press, 2021.

Prakash Sangar, Satya. *Food and Drinks in Mughhal India*. New Delhi: Reliance, 1999.

Wondrich, David. *Punch!* New York: Perigee, 2010.

David Wondrich

Indonesia, a country in Southeast Asia comprised of more than 1,700 islands, was at the center of pro-longed and often brutal colonial expeditions by European powers. Early attempts at colonization were made by both the Portuguese and the English, but control was eventually secured by the Dutch.

The production of spirits in Indonesia reflects its multicultural heritage. Alcohol was welcomed by Hindu, Buddhist, Chinese, and European populations on the islands. Islam, however, eventu-ally became the dominant religion, and Indonesia is now home to the largest population of Muslims in the world, creating tension surrounding the consumption of spirited drinks. Despite Muslim proscriptions against alcohol, Europeans arriving in Indonesia found that the enjoyment of spirits was widespread. Dutch colonists landing on their first mission there in 1596 reported that the local Chinese community produced "much aqua vitae of rice and Cocus [coconut sap], which the Iauars [Javans] by night come to buy, and drinke it secretly, for by Mahomets law it is forbidden to them."

Locally produced drinks include beer, rice wine, palm wine known as *tuak*, a distilled spirit made from tuak called *sopi*, and *ciu*, a rum made from mo-lasses. Much of this rum is illegally distilled in small improvised stills, diverted from the legal produc-tion of industrial alcohol. There is also a significant amount of *arak beras*, "rice spirit," made mostly on

Bali. Much of this is essentially neutral spirit that has been flavored with fruits and berries, similarly to what is done with lambanog in the neighboring Philippines, but there is also an *arak beras ketan*, "pure rice spirit," which is unflavored and lightly aromatic. There is even a low-proof (14.7 percent ABV), rice-based "jenever" from West Java, about which the less said the better.

By far the most famous spirit produced in Indonesia is the rum relative Batavia arrack, made in Java from local molasses and rice. This was one of the world's major spirits from the 1600s well into the 1900s. It is still produced in small quantities, but the export market for it is not large, and the domestic market is shrinking fast.

In fact, today the nation's Muslim majority increasingly seeks to restrict alcohol, succeeding recently in banning its sale in small stores. High-profile cases of poisonings from poorly distilled black market spirits have also led to warnings to tourists to avoid drinking illicit drams. Yet the tourism business, especially in Hindu-majority Bali, remains a strong opposing force to the contemporary prohibition efforts.

Martin, Scott C., ed. *The SAGE Encyclopedia of Alcohol.* Thousand Oaks, CA: SAGE, 2014.

Owens, David J., ed. *Indigenous Fermented Foods of Southeast Asia.* Boca Raton, FL: CRC, 2014.

Wondrich, David. *Punch: The Delights (and Dangers) of the Flowing Bowl.* New York: Perigee, 2010.

Jacob Grier and David Wondrich

infusion is the process of extracting flavor compounds from materials such as herbs and spices using a solvent such as water, ethanol, or glycerin. See ETHANOL and GLYCERIN. Infusion is typically a quick technique used to prepare a drink or tincture for immediate use, as opposed to maceration, which is a longer and sometimes more complex process. A simple example of an infusion is the preparation of coffee or tea.

The most basic infusion is soaking a spice in water for a few minutes to extract some of the flavor compounds. Increasing the temperature of the water during the process is an excellent way to shorten the infusion time and extract more flavor compounds. Using a combination of water and ethanol, like vodka, can extract different flavors as some compounds may only be soluble in alcohol but not water.

Many liqueurs and spirits start as infusions that are then distilled to capture the aromatic flavors. A common example is gin, where the botanicals are infused into high-proof alcohol and then distilled to extract the aromatics. An innovative rapid infusion method used by many modern mixologists combines botanicals and a solvent—water or a spirit—in a soda siphon, which is then pressurized with capsules of nitrous oxide, an inert gas. This forces the liquid into the plant materials' cell walls and extracts the flavor compounds. What previously took a few hours or longer can be accomplished in a few minutes. One of the unique benefits of this method is that infused cocktails can be prepared fresh.

Natural colors for cocktails can be created using infusion techniques. See HUE/COLOR. Absinthe gets its green color from an infusion process that extracts chlorophyll from herbs like hyssop and melissa. A brilliant yellow color can be made by infusing turmeric or saffron in alcohol. Red colors can be made using cherries, elderberries, or cochineal.

With all methods of infusion, there are a few caveats that need to be mentioned. Increased temperature or pressure can speed up the process, but these methods can also extract undesirable compounds. For example, preparing infusions using hot water may extract more flavor compounds in a short period of time, but as the liquid cools, a haziness may form in the final products because some compounds are only soluble at the higher temperature. Also, higher infusion temperatures can create "cooked" flavors or cause aromatics to vaporize, causing a loss of flavor. Performing a taste test and standardizing methods is the best way to get consistent results with infusions.

Malle, Bettina, and Helge Schmickl. *The Artisan's Guide to Crafting Distilled Spirits.* Southport, NC: Spikehorn, 2015.

Morgenthaler, Jeffrey. "Infusions, Tinctures, and Bitters." In *The Bar Book: Elements of Cocktail Technique,* 119–130. San Francisco: Chronicle Books, 2014.

Darcy O'Neil

The **International Wine and Spirit Competition (IWSC)** is an annual competition recognizing excellence in spirits and wine production worldwide. Launched in London in 1969, it attracts thousands of entries from more than ninety countries, across hundreds of product categories. Producers pay a fee to enter their products, and judging is undertaken by more than three hundred industry experts, including master blenders, distillers, Masters of Wine, buyers, and journalists, who taste and score entries out of 100 using the double-blind method to ensure complete impartiality. Entries are also submitted to chemical analysis to ensure that they are free from faults, contaminants, or illegal additives, a step that makes the IWSC unusually rigorous in the world of drinks competitions. The IWSC awards medals in five categories ranging from Bronze to Gold Outstanding, with any Gold Outstanding products going forward to compete for one of the IWSC trophies. The awards are presented each year at a ceremony in London's Guildhall.

See also COCKTAIL CONTESTS.

International Wine and Spirit Competition website. https://www.iwsc.net (accessed February 17, 2021).

Alice Lascelles

Irish Coffee is one of the world's most popular and lasting drinks, equally famous as a morning cocktail, a hot cocktail, and a coffee cocktail. It is a relatively simple drink, made of hot coffee, sugar or simple syrup, and Irish whisky, topped with a head of whipped cream, but it requires some brio and dexterity to construct properly. It was created in late 1944 or early 1945 at the flying boat station at Foynes, Ireland, when chef Joe Sheridan (1909–1962) was asked to come up with something special with which to greet a group of dignitaries touring the facilities there and at the new airport being built across the Shannon. Ireland had reached an agreement with the American Civil Aviation Board that all American commercial air traffic to and from Europe would stop at the new facility. (The competing story that it was invented at the Dolphin Hotel in Dublin is unsupported, although it should be noted that Sheridan came to Foynes from there.)

By 1947, Sheridan's "Gaelic Coffee," as it was originally known, was being offered to all travelers deplaning at Shannon. The drink got a strong endorsement from the American journalist Temple Fielding's pioneering guidebooks to postwar European travel and began appearing at bars here and there across America.

In 1953, travel writer Stanton Delaplane, who had had the drink at Shannon, brought it to Jack Koeppler (1909–1970), the owner of the Buena Vista Café in San Francisco, and they managed to reverse-engineer it. Although the Buena Vista wasn't the first to introduce the drink to the United States, the concoction rapidly became an institution

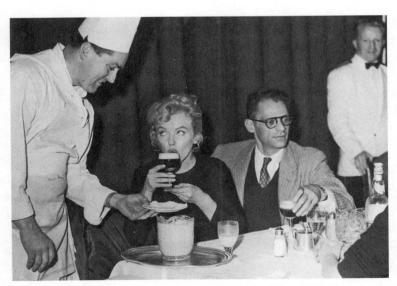

Marilyn Monroe sips an Irish Coffee at Shannon Airport as Arthur Miller ponders following suit, November, 1956. Courtesy of Shannon Airport.

there—by 1955, the bar was going through thirty-six bottles of Irish whisky a day—and thereafter spread in renown.

With fame came adulteration: syrup replaced the original sugar cubes; glasses got bigger (the original footed glass goblet held a restrained 180 ml), which meant the drink was drowned in coffee. Canned whipped cream replaced the fresh. Sometimes it was green. Fortunately, the original formula has seen something of a resurgence in recent years, with bars such as New York's famous Dead Rabbit priding themselves on making the drink the way Sheridan did.

Recipe: Whip 30 ml heavy cream in a cold mixing bowl until it doubles in volume. Warm a 180-ml Irish coffee glass or mug with hot water, then drain. Put 2 sugar cubes (preferably brown or demerara) in warmed glass, then 45 ml Irish whisky and 75 ml fresh, hot coffee. Stir. Gently spoon cream onto the top of the drink.

See also WHISKY, IRISH.

"Airport Inspected." *Dublin Evening Press*, September 23, 1944, 3.

Delaplane, Stanton. "A Postcard from Stan Delaplane." *Reno Journal-gazette*, March 17, 1955, 4.

Fielding, Temple. *Fielding's New Travel Guide to Europe*. New York: William Sloane, 1948.

"U.S. Airlines Pact with Eire." *Dundee (Scotland) Evening Telegraph*, February 2, 1945, 2.

Wondrich, David. "The Five Most Influential Irish Bars in America." *Daily Beast*, March 11, 2019, https://www.thedailybeast.com/for-st-patricks-day-the-five-most-influential-irish-bars-in-america (accessed February 17, 2021).

Robert Simonson and David Wondrich

Irish Distillers Limited (IDL) is the leading distiller in Ireland, and indeed was for a period the only one. Known chiefly for its Jameson and Powers blended whiskies, it also makes an extensive range of single pot still whiskies, along with Cork dry gin and Huzzar vodka. The company was created as a desperate, last-ditch attempt to save the Irish Republic's whisky industry. See WHISKY, IRISH. The twentieth century had been brutal for Irish whisky, and in the 1960s, after two world wars, the Irish Rebellion, American Prohibition, and the Great

The three massive, 80,000-liter pot stills added to Irish Distillers' Midleton distillery in 2013. Courtesy of Irish Distillers Ltd.

Depression, Irish whisky exports were a shambles, and domestic consumption, based on a population of fewer than three million people, was not enough upon which to base a thriving industry. The eighteen working distilleries Alfred Barnard had found in the republic's territory in 1887 were reduced to three (the ten in Northern Ireland were down to two). See BARNARD, ALFRED. Even installing column stills and supplanting the pure pot still whisky that was the Irish trademark with blends, as, for example, John Power & Son was forced to do in the mid-1950s, did not help.

In 1966, therefore, the directors of John Power & Son (founded in 1796), John Jameson & Son (1810), and Cork Distilleries Co. (1867) decided to radically cut their costs by joining forces as Irish Distillers Limited. In 1972, Irish Distillers reached across the border and bought Bushmills, the last distillers in Northern Ireland. Then there was only one distilling company on the whole island. In 1975, Power's and Jameson had closed their Dublin distilleries, and all the firm's distilling was conducted at a new distillery built next to CDC's old facility at Midleton, in County Cork. The New Midleton Distillery was designed to be able to duplicate each of the three firms' characteristic whiskies. It had three enormous pot stills and three column stills, enabling it to make triple-distilled pot still whisky and column-distilled grain whisky (it made no malt whisky). In the distillery's early years, the vast majority of its production went to pot still–grain blended whiskies, chiefly Jameson (for export) and Power's (for the domestic market). For Tullamore and Paddy, both pot still–malt-grain blends, the malt whisky was sourced from Bushmills. IDL did also keep one pure pot still bottling, Redbreast 12, as a link to the company's heritage. See SINGLE POT STILL.

Yet the company was dedicated not just to preserving Irish whisky but to reviving it. Thus in the late 1980s, when it was still struggling with export sales, it embarked on an ambitious program of upgrading its cooperage, replacing tired old barrels as they were emptied rather than reusing them. In 1988, however, the English Grand Metropolitan company, a minority stockholder, tendered a bid to buy the company, with the intent of breaking it up and disposing of some of its brands and assets. IDL resisted, reaching out to the French Pernod-Ricard company for help. Although the French company's bid was lower, it guaranteed the integrity of the company, and it was accepted. See PERNOD-RICARD.

Pernod, after extensive study, made Jameson one of its core brands and moved to market it not as a traditional Irish whisky but as a lifestyle brand for young adults, much in the way vodka was marketed. This strategy was enormously successful—so successful that Pernod's divestment of Bushmills in 2005, Tullamore Dew a couple of years later, and Paddy in 2016 were not seen as threats to Irish Distillers' integrity. By the early 2010s, the company was selling four times as much whisky in America as it had ten years before. At the same time, the investment in better cooperage was paying off as the company released award-winning whisky after award-winning whisky, including a new line of revived pot still whiskies and some superior old blends. In 2013, it added three more huge pot stills to the Midleton facility. Today some 20 percent of the pot still whisky made there is destined to be bottled unblended.

In recent years, IDL's success with Jameson and pot still whiskies such as Yellow Spot and Power's John's Lane, along with prestige blends such as Midleton Very Rare, have in large part inspired a new boom in distilling in Ireland. It is a far cry from the sad days of 1966.

See also Crockett, Barry; and SPIRITS TRADE, HISTORY OF.

Greenhouse, Steven. "Pernod in Friendly Offer for Irish Distillers." *New York Times*, September 6, 1988.

McGuire, E. B. *Irish Whisky* Dublin: Gill & MacMillan, 1973.

"Pernod-Ricard Bid Prevails in Battle for Irish Distillers." *New York Times*, November 25, 1988.

Wondrich, David. Author's notes, marketing presentation, Irish Distillers. Dublin, October, 2001.

David Wondrich

Italia is an archaic name for pisco, derived from the name of the principal variety of aromatic grape used in that spirit's manufacture. See PISCO.

Italy is paradoxically both a major spirits producer, both in volume and in historical importance, and a country of resolutely moderate spirits consumption. It has long produced some of the world's most innovative bartenders, but their greatest impact has generally been felt in other countries.

It is a common orthodoxy that distillation of alcohol was not an ancient Roman competence and that it only came to Italy during the so-called twelfth-century Renaissance, when it was introduced by alchemists influenced by Arab scientific texts. As with much orthodoxy surrounding the history of distillation, there is some evidence that the reality may have been more complex than that; distillation might have been used by some pagan and then Christian Gnostic mystery cults in their rituals and even perhaps to fortify some wines. Thus the documented "discovery" of distillation during the "twelfth-century Renaissance" (the renaissance before the Renaissance) may have been more a case of feeding oxygen to a banked fire than of lighting one from scratch. Certainly Michele Savonarola, who thoroughly investigated the state of distillation in Italy in the 1440s, believed that the two kinds of still he found in use (internal-condensation alembic and external condensation with condensing coil) and the process of making spirit with them dated to antiquity. See STILL, POT.

In any case, by the late Middle Ages, distillation flourished widely throughout the Italian peninsula, with Taddeo Alderotti of Florence (ca. 1220–1295) writing the first detailed treatise on the art in around 1280. In Savonarola's day cheap grape spirit was being made on a quasi-industrial scale and sold in the marketplaces in the north, while costly and complex medicinal liqueurs were being exported as far as England and France. See ROSOLIO.

From the 1500s through the 1800s Italian distillers refined and streamlined those liqueurs into a library of traditional formulae that would form the stock in trade of the *distillatore-liquorista*, the distiller and liqueur maker, a common fixture in Italian towns. Each would make his, or sometimes her, own versions of these formulae—including, for example, maraschino, vermouth, aperitif bitters such as Stoughton's, and digestive ones such as Fernet—and serve them both over the counter and in bottled form. Production was small and distribution local. See APERITIF AND DIGESTIVE and VERMOUTH.

During the nineteenth century, as happened elsewhere, many of these local producers turned their variations on traditional recipes into proprietary brands and began exporting them, including such household names as Martini & Rossi, Campari, and Averna. See AVERNA; CAMPARI; and MARTINI & ROSSI. Eventually, each region, and in some areas each town, had its own preferred brand of amaro, or digestive bitter. Italian brandies and grappe—pomace brandies—did less well on the world market, although these products, mostly from the north, built markets elsewhere in Italy. The end of the twentieth century saw artisanal distillers turn grappa into a world-class sipping spirit, while the modern cocktail renaissance has turned many of the various amari into international cult favorites. See ARZENTE and GRAPPA.

The nineteenth century also saw the "American bar," with its iced drinks made to order, invade Italy—although it arrived there in the 1860s, a generation later than in England and France. (The first American bar in Italy appears to have been the one Leopoldo Bomboni added to his Florence beer bar in 1869.) But the Italian peninsula's combination of a hot climate and a spine of high, cool mountains meant that Italy had a long experience with iced drinks, dating back to Roman times. It also had its own way with mixed drinks, which were traditionally pre-bottled by the *liquorista* rather than mixed to order. Ultimately, the peninsula found its own accommodation with American-style mixology. The cocktail bar gave rise to the cocktail hour, when cafés, restaurants, even pastry shops and confectioners, would suddenly break out the shaker, every drink coming with a bite or two of food. Drinks were mixed to order, but they tended to be lighter in alcohol than their American equivalents, emphasizing refreshment over impact. See AMERICANO; APEROL SPRITZ; and NEGRONI.

At the same time, Italy gave birth to a bartending culture that values precision and elegance, a culture that has produced some of the world's most celebrated bartenders, from Ciro Capozzi, who taught the European aristocracy to drink cocktails, to Peter Dorelli and Salvatore Calabrese. Ironically, most of them have made their mark in the profession outside of Italy; while there are and long have been true, full-scale cocktail bars in Italy, they are relatively few in number, and their influence has traditionally been limited, although the twenty-first century has seen that change: indeed, any list of the world's best cocktail bars would be incomplete without establishments such as Nottingham Forest in Milan and the Jerry Thomas Project in Rome. See CALABRESE, SALVATORE; CIRO'S; and DORELLI, GIAMPIERO "PETER".

Cendali, Antonio, and Luigi Marinatto, eds. *Il barman e i suoi cocktails*, 2nd ed. Milan: Selepress, 1974.

Savonarola, Michele. *Excellentisimi medici Michaelis Savonarolae libellus singularis de arte conficiendi aquam vitae*. Grossenhain: 1532.

Vicario, Renato. *Italian Liqueurs*. N.p.: Aboca: 2014.

"The Week." *Anglo-American Times* (London), March 27, 1869, 10.

Wilson, C. Anne. *Water of Life*. Totnes, UK: Prospect, 2006.

David Wondrich

Jack Daniel's is the leading brand of Tennessee whisky, and indeed its iconic black-label bottling is the bestselling American whisky in the world. See WHISKY, TENNESSEE. The brand is named after its founder, Jasper Newton "Jack" Daniel (1849–1911). Some disagreement exists over his birthdate (the 1849 date was established by author Peter Krass in 2004), but after his father perished in the Civil War, Daniel left home and, it is believed, worked for a local whisky maker named Dan Call. Daniel learned the craft from Call's newly emancipated African American head distiller, Nathan "Nearest" Green (1820–?) before eventually joining Call as a partner. While author Ben Green described the Nearest Green connection already in 1967, it was only in 2016 that the distillery began sharing the story.

When Daniel and Call started the business is debated; the whisky's label states 1866 as the founding year of the distillery, but an 1896 article in the *Nashville American* fixes it as 1874, a 1904 article in *Bonfort's Wine and Spirit Circular* gives 1872, and Krass has a starting date of 1875. Daniel—Call succumbed to temperance-movement pressure and sold out in 1882—made sour-mash whisky from local grain and filtered it through charcoal before barreling it, as was popular in Tennessee. See LINCOLN COUNTY PROCESS and SOUR MASH. His "Old No. 7" brand was a regional success in its part of Tennessee (the distillery was originally registered as no. 7 in its district; when the government renumbered it as no. 16, Daniel, resistant to change as always, stuck with the old one). In 1883, Daniel's distillery was the tenth-largest of the seventy distilleries in its revenue district, making some 400 liters of whisky a day (this was, however, less than a tenth of what the largest, Nelson's Greenbrier, was making). But Daniel kept expanding the business, all the while sticking to his old-fashioned procedures and his locally grown grain. By the early 1890s, he was distilling three times what he had a

Old time sour mash whisky. The purest in Tennessee. The records : !ashington D. C. Show this Distill has been in operation longer Than any in the United States.

JACK DANIEL
LYNCHBURG, TENN.

Advertisement for Jack Daniel's whisky, 1896. Wondrich Collection.

decade before. That plus the cattle he raised on the spent mash made him rich.

In 1908, however, his health deteriorating, Daniel passed the business over to his nephew, Lem Motlow (1869–1947), who had been working for him since he was eighteen. Motlow was an ambitious man, and a good businessman. When Tennessee outlawed the production of alcoholic beverages in 1909, he picked up the whole operation and moved it to Missouri, where he ran the operation until national Prohibition came in 1920. But he was also hotheaded, and in 1924 he shot two railroad employees in a drunken rage, wounding the black porter whose attempt to get him to behave had set him off and killing the white conductor who had come to the porter's aid.

That disgraceful affair, for which he was acquitted by an all-white jury on grounds of self-defense, did not prevent Motlow from getting elected to the Tennessee legislature a few years later, a position he used to tirelessly lobby for the return of distilling to the state, which it had chosen to keep suppressed after Repeal. Finally, he was able to get a state permit in 1938, although Moore County, where the distillery was located, remained—and remains—dry. Once again, Motlow was making sour-mash, charcoal-mellowed whisky, using old-fashioned pot- or three-chamber stills (it appears that this was because the government forced the distillery to shut down during World War II, as it did every distillery that couldn't make neutral spirit for munitions). See STILL, THREE-CHAMBER. Until the war, he also made apple and peach brandies and was probably the last person to legally make the latter until the 2010s. See PEACH BRANDY. In 1956, his heirs sold the brand, a relatively small but highly regarded one, to Kentucky's Brown-Forman company. See BROWN-FORMAN.

Brown-Forman took the brand's small-town, old-school, "authentic" image and, with canny marketing, turned Jack Daniel's into the whisky of the counterculture: the rock and roll whisky. To a degree, this image has remained.

Green, Ben. *Jack Daniel's Legacy.* Shelbyville, TN: n.p., 1967.

Krass, Peter. *Blood and Whiskey: The Life and Times of Jack Daniel.* Hoboken, NJ: John Wiley & Sons, 2004.

"Lynchburg and Moore County." *Nashville American,* March 8, 1896, 18.

"Remorse Grips Distiller Who Killed Conductor." *St. Louis Post-Dispatch,* March 19, 1924, 3.

"Tennessee whiskey." *Bonfort's Wine and Liquor Circular,* June 25, 1904, 174.

Doug Frost and David Wondrich

The **Jack Rose**, a mix of applejack, lime juice, and grenadine, is (along with the Bronx and the Clover Club) one of the triad of popular drinks that, in the first decade of the twentieth century, made it permissible for a cocktail to include citrus juice. See APPLEJACK; GRENADINE; BRONX COCKTAIL; CLOVER CLUB; and COCKTAIL. It also served, for much of the twentieth century, as applejack's toehold in the bar: it was the last applejack cocktail standing.

The creation of the Jack Rose was variously attributed in its day, including to "Bald Jack" Rose, a New York gambler at the heart of the sensational 1912 Becker-Rosenthal murder case; Frank "Jack Rose" May, a Jersey City, New Jersey, bartender and wrestling aficionado; John Coleman, steward of Philadelphia's august Union League Club; and Martin Curry, steward of the tony Tuxedo Club in Tuxedo, New York. There is one more attribution, however, which is both older and better supported than any of those. In 1899, a reporter for the *New York Press* noted, in an item on what bartender Frank Haas was mixing for the city's stockbrokers at Fred Eberlin's downtown bar, that the Whisky Daisy was popular there, but that "the jack-rose is the pet of many connoisseurs." Indeed, Eberlin's was famous for the drink, and in 1913 the long-serving Haas (he had been at the bar since the 1870s) gave his recipe for it: applejack, raspberry syrup, and lemon and orange juices; in other words, a Whisky Daisy with applejack. (This is practically identical to the version printed by Jack Grohusko in his 1908 *Jack's Manual;* his bar was near Eberlin's and drew on the same clientele.) See GROHUSKO, JACOB ABRAHAM "JACK". The name was apparently derived from the Général Jacqueminot, or "Jack" rose, a then-popular hybrid that the drink resembles in color.

By 1913, however, the drink had escaped the narrow confines of downtown New York, getting an update in the process. Gone was the delicate combination of citrus juices; now, it was straight lemon juice or the trendier lime juice. The old-fashioned raspberry syrup was, as was common at the time, replaced with grenadine, also trendy. There were even those who splashed some gin and/or vermouth in the drink (those, too, being trendy ingredients), or threw in an egg white. But it was the simple, three-ingredient version that survived the twentieth century, barely, and made it to revival in the twenty-first. While not one of the standard-bearers of the cocktail renaissance, the Jack Rose is nonetheless a foot soldier in good standing: a solid classic that has its adherents (indeed, in the renaissance's early days Boston even had a Jack Rose Society, comprised of most of the city's top bartenders). See COCKTAIL RENAISSANCE.

Recipe: Shake with ice 60 ml applejack, 15 ml lime juice, and 15 ml grenadine. Strain into chilled cocktail glass.

"A New-Old Drink." *New York Press*, April 28, 1899, 10.
"Cocktail War Divides Brokers into Four Hostile Camps over Bartenders." *New York Evening Telegram*, January 26, 1913, 9.
Grohusko, Jack. *Jack's Manual.* New York: J. A. Grohusko, 1908.

David Wondrich

Jackson, Michael (1942–2007), an English journalist, can justly be considered the father of both whisky and beer writing in the modern era. While he wrote numerous books on whisky and beer, his *The World Guide to Beer* (1977) and *The World Guide to Whisky* (1987) were truly seminal works that have influenced the study of these subjects through the current day. Jackson's memory is most celebrated in America as a beer writer, but his global reputation is arguably more based on his writings on whisky.

Jackson was born in Yorkshire, of Lithuanian Jewish parents (the family name Jakowitz was Anglicized to Jackson when his father emigrated to the United Kingdom). He often contrasted his career with the predispositions of his ancestry, recalling that his parents drank infrequently, and usually sweet wines. Jackson, however, was introduced to beer as a young journalist and began writing a series of pieces called This Is Your Pub for weekly papers in West Yorkshire at the age of sixteen. A job in Edinburgh led to similar musings about malt whisky.

Publication of *The World Guide to Beer* in 1977 was notable for its thorough and serious approach to beer and for introducing the idea of beer "styles," the groupings and relationships of beers such as pale ale, porter, pilsner, bock, and India pale ale. Ten years later, *The World Guide to Whisky* would similarly lay a foundation for a new way of looking at whiskies, showing the relationships among the world whisky types. His follow-on book, *Michael Jackson's Complete Guide to Single Malt Scotch* (1990), rated every single malt brand he could find on a 1–100 scale, along with descriptive notes on each distillery. It was the most complete catalog of scotch whisky since Alfred Barnard's *The Whisky Distilleries of the United Kingdom* in 1887, and it has been regularly updated by noted whisky writers such as Gavin D. Smith and Dominic Roskrow.

That the format and content of these books, unique in their day, seem common and obvious today is perhaps the greatest tribute to Jackson's influence on writers, readers, and drinkers. His influence on distillers and brewers was similarly large, with many counting him as a mentor, an inspiration, or simply a friend.

Jackson's awards and accolades were many. Among others, he was a master of the quaich, a knight of the Ridderschap van de Roerstok, a 2006 James Beard Award winner, noted for lifetime achievement by both *Whisky* and *Whisky Advocate* magazines, and a winner of the Glenfiddich Trophy.

Jackson struggled with diabetes and Parkinson's disease, something he sometimes said was brought on by a freak sporting accident in his younger years. The progress of his disease led to sometimes rambling speech, rocking motion, and growing lack of balance in his gait.

"Understandably, people think I am drunk, especially given my profession. I am not," Jackson assured members of the Michael Jackson Rare Beer Club in December of 2006. "My writing has always fostered the notion of tasting more and drinking less, and I am true to that philosophy. The Gods have a sense of irony in making me look drunk when my intake of alcohol is at its most modest." He planned, he said, to write an autobiography titled *I Am Not Drunk*.

The book never was written. Jackson died of a heart attack brought on by Parkinson's less than a year later, at the age of sixty-five. Tributes included a memorial dinner in London, a Festschrift entitled *Beer Hunter, Whisky Chaser* (Jackson's self-applied *noms de l'alcool*), and a variety of memorial awards and scholarships. His collection of books on whisky and beer, plus his research files and notebooks, was donated to the Oxford Brookes University Library.

See also BEER and WHISKY.

Brooks, Jay. "Michael Jackson Reveals His Battle with Parkinson's." *Brookston Beer Bulletin* (blog), December 18, 2006 (accessed February 17, 2021).

Buxton, Iain, ed. *Beer Hunter, Whisky Chaser: New Writing on Beer and Whisky in Honour of Michael Jackson.* New York: Neil Wilson, 2009.

"Michael Jackson, 65, Beer Critic and Author, Is Dead." *New York Times*, September 3, 2007.

Lew Bryson

Jägermeister, a bittersweet 35 percent ABV *Krauterlikör* that fits roughly in the digestive category, is the top-selling German spirit brand. In 1878, Wilhelm Mast founded the firm today known as Mast-Jägermeister in Wolfenbüttel, Germany. Originally a vinegar manufactory, the firm later began making liqueurs. Wilhelm's son Curt (1897–1970) introduced Jägermeister in 1935. Literally "master of the hunt" in German and known colloquially as Jäger, the barrel-aged drink sold 8.5 million nine-liter cases globally in 2019. Other Mast liqueurs such as kümmel were discontinued, leaving the eponymous liqueur, a small number of brand extensions, and Schlehenfeuer, a sloe gin. See KÜMMEL and SLOE GIN.

In the 1970s Curt Mast's nephew Günter Mast (1927–2011) aggressively expanded the brand by steering Jägermeister to younger consumers. In 1973, for instance, the company was the first to sponsor a German Bundesliga football team, Eintracht Braunschweig. Mast also spearheaded the cheeky "Einer für alle" ("One for all") campaign, which featured everyday Germans offering spurious reasons for drinking Jägermeister. American sales, however, totaled little more than five hundred cases annually through the early 1970s. Although older German-born immigrants and German Americans were Jägermeister's primary consumers, Baton Rouge and New Orleans held pockets of broader interest. Jägermeister achieved a degree of infamy in spots such as the Bourbon Pub, a French Quarter gay bar, and nearby Fritzel's European Jazz Pub, where German-born owner Gunter "Dutch"

Seutter (1929–2003) poured shots for those in the know.

When entrepreneur Sidney Frank spotted a patron drinking the medicinal-tasting liqueur, he sensed opportunity. By 1975, he had secured exclusive American rights. Sales of room-temperature Jägermeister, however, especially in the sometimes hot, humid American southeast where he first acquired rights, remained sluggish. Then came the Valium.

Liquid Valium, Hermann Göring, and the Jägerettes

In 1982 socialite Claus von Bülow was convicted for the attempted murder of his wife, Sunny. At trial, a witness testified that the then-comatose Sunny had advocated using liquid Valium to ease tension. Newspapers reported the sensational testimony, giving the phrase "liquid Valium" a foothold in the American vernacular. Three years later, the *Baton Rouge Advocate* reported, a regular at Fritzel's described a frosted shot of Jägermeister as "liquid Valium. . . . It'll get you totally wiped out." College students could not get enough of it. At the Bourbon Pub, student bartender Andrew Pear enthused, "We call it party syrup back at the dorm. . . . It gets you in a great mood real quick." The article, while clarifying that they were false, reported rumors that the liqueur contained opium, methaqualone, or other substances that got drinkers high or caused hallucinations, and that it might even be banned. Further, it cemented the idea that Jägermeister be served cold. Sidney Frank had millions of copies made. That, combined with relentless guerrilla promotions that included the Jägermeister Tap Machine, a countertop freezer that assured prominent visibility, and hundreds of attractive young women Frank dubbed the Jägerettes (joined later by Jägerdudes) who provided samples at bars and events, sent sales skyrocketing.

Yet rumors persisted. That the drink contained deer's blood was easily disprovable; talk of its presumed Nazi origins, less so. In 1935, the Reichsjägergesetz was enacted, a hunting law that established regional German hunting societies, each headed by its own Jägermeister. By law, German hunters were required to be members of these societies. Hunting enthusiast Hermann Göring, later Reichsmarschall and second only to Adolf Hitler, took the title Reichsjägermeister for himself, the Reich's hunt master. By then, Mast had already registered the liqueur.

The brand's logo has a further seeming Nazi connection. On the cover of *Time* magazine (April 1, 1940) Göring wore a gold and emerald collar pin featuring a stag's head with a swastika rendered in sapphires between its antlers. The emblem bears a striking resemblance to historic and modern Jägermeister labels, which feature a Christian cross in place of the swastika.

Both the brand and the Reichsjägermeister, however, derived the stag design from the legend of Saint Hubertus, a seventh-century hunter who converted to Christianity when seized by a vision of a great stag with a cross between its antlers. Such stag badges were treasured emblems in German hunting societies long before the Nazis. "Hubertusbitter" in fact had been floated as a brand name. Rumors that hunter Curt Mast was friends with Göring remain that: rumors. No proof has surfaced that the two knew each other. The connection between the brand and the Reichsmarschall were so strong in the popular imagination during World War II, however, that German soldiers gave Jägermeister the joking nickname "Göring-schnaps."

Göring-schnaps has given way to frozen shots, shooters such as Jäger Bombs (Jägermeister and Red Bull), and more complex cocktails such as the Jägerita (a Margarita variant invented by bartender David Cordoba) that appeal to an older, more sophisticated crowd. See MARGARITA. Other products include Jägermeister Cold Brew Coffee; Jägermeister Scharf, with additional ginger and galangal; and Manifest, an oaky, luxe 38 percent ABV expression.

See also: AMARO; FRANK, SIDNEY; GERMANY, SWITZERLAND, AND AUSTRIA; GREY GOOSE; KRÄUTERLIKÖR; and LIQUEURS.

"Kaiserabzeichen der Jäger 1911." Ehrnzeichen—Orden.de. ehrenzeichen-orden.de/kaiserreich/kaiserabzeichen-der-jager-1911.html (accessed March 23, 2021).

Kapalschinski. Christoph. "Jägermeister Family: A Dark, Bittersweet Legacy." *Handelsblatt*, September 10, 2015. https://www.handelsblatt.com/english/companies/jaegermeister-family-a-dark-bittersweet-legacy/23506588.html?ticket=ST-5690270-xx9kWWCDXpK4EQ1RhTIr-ap6 (accessed March 23, 2021).

Kelly, James. "How Jägermeister Changed the World of Corporate Shirt Sponsorships." *These Football Times*, May 27, 2020. thesefootballtimes.co/2020/05/27/how-jagermeister-changed-the-world-of-corporate-shirt-sponsorships/ (accessed March 23, 2021).

Kumlehn, Jürgen. *Curt Mast aus Wolfenbüttel: Eine vorläufige biografische Aufhellung.* 2011.

Matthew Rowley

Japan is a mountainous archipelago of more than 6,800 islands, more than 126 million people, and, it can seem, almost that many types of shochu, the country's indigenous distilled spirit. Japan is also a significant producer of whisky and has been for over a century, and it has a sophisticated cocktail culture even older than the whisky one. Indeed, it boasts of some of the most respected cocktail bars on earth.

Although Japan has an abundance of high-quality soft water, less than 12 percent of the country is classified as arable land. Despite or perhaps because of that, it makes an extraordinary variety of alcoholic beverages, from its myriad types and grades of *nihonshu* painstakingly fermented from rice according to ancient traditions (this is of course known to the world as "sake," a term which in Japan is generic for all alcohol), to macro- and microbrewed beer, shochu, malt and blended whiskies, liqueurs and cordials, and even micro-distilled gins. Many of these products enjoy international reputations for quality.

While Japan is probably best known internationally for its nihonshu, the rice wine is outsold domestically by shochu and the closely related *awamori* made in the southernmost island prefecture of Okinawa. Surprisingly, the so-called Scotland of Japan, Kyushu Island in the country's western region, is not known for making whisky at all. More than 250 distilleries in the island's seven prefectures mostly produce shochu, Japan's indigenous spirit, from a dizzying range of raw materials including things as conventional as rice, barley, and sugar cane to unique materials such as carrots and sweet potatoes. Shochu distillers seem to have used just about every plant with fermentable sugar or convertible starch that grows in Japan. See SHOCHU. Both premium shochu and awamori are distilled once in a pot still, often vacuum-assisted, and normally bottled at 25 percent ABV for the former and 30 percent for the latter. Valued for their characteristic aromas and complex flavors, premium shochus have seen their domestic sales triple between 2002 and 2010, demand that delayed the drink's journey to most markets outside Japan. See AWAMORI and SINGLE POT STILL.

Aside from Midori melon liqueur (a disco-era staple), Japan's most recent contribution to world drinking culture is its whisky. Heavily informed by Scottish distilling practices, Japanese single malts have won copious medals, capped by whisky expert and writer Jim Murray crowning Suntory's Yamazaki Single Malt Sherry Cask 2013 number one in the 2015 edition of his annual whisky guide. Yamazaki also happens to be Japan's oldest whisky distillery, founded in 1924. Nikka's Yoichi Distillery, on the northern island of Hokkaido, is the only other whisky distillery in Japan established before World War II. See SUNTORY; WHISKY, JAPANESE; and WHISKY, SCOTCH.

Japan's introduction to the American art of mixing drinks came through the port of Yokohama, with the opening of the International Hotel in 1874 and the installation of former San Francisco saloonkeeper Louis Eppinger as manager of the Grand Hotel in 1890. Eppinger employed Japanese bartenders, and by 1910 they were opening their own bars, this time in Tokyo and aimed at a domestic audience. Today that city supports some of the most renowned cocktail bars on the planet, and the independent tradition of cocktail bartending developed in Japan, with its high-quality tools, its emphasis on precision, and its elaborate treatment of ice, is widely influential abroad.

Alt, Matt. "Good Libations: Examining the Evolution of Japan's Rich Cocktail Culture." *Japan Times*, March 24, 2018. https://www.japantimes.co.jp/life/2018/03/24/food/good-libations-examining-evolution-japans-rich-cocktail-culture (accessed February 17, 2021).

Bunting, Chris. *Drinking Japan*. Tokyo: Tuttle, 2011.

Murray, Jim. *Jim Murray's Whisky Bible 2015*, 12th ed. Florence, AL: Whitman, 2014.

United States Department of Agriculture. *Economic Research Service: Japan*. http://www.ers.usda.gov/topics/international-markets-trade/countries-regions/japan.aspx (accessed February 17, 2021).

Christopher Pellegrini

The **Japanese Cocktail**, a rich but simple combination of brandy, orgeat syrup, and bitters, is among the recipes found in Jerry Thomas's 1862 *The Bar-Tender's Guide*. See THOMAS, JEREMIAH P. "JERRY". It is first mentioned, albeit fleetingly, in print in 1860 as an example of the popular excitement that accompanied the first Japanese mission to the United States and its tour of the country. It is also one of the earliest cocktails whose name is not simply a statement of its main ingredient, and the first such cocktail to have a recipe printed (it should be noted that nothing in the drink is Japanese in any way).

The drink's origins are uncertain, but it is quite possible that it was one of Thomas's original creations. The first solid mention of it is in an 1861 composite portrait of the typical American hotel bar, based primarily on two New York hotels, one of them the Metropolitan, where the Japanese emissaries, several of whom greatly enjoyed American drinks, stayed—and where Thomas was head bartender. (Of all the drinks the author tasted, he declared "the 'Japanese' the most dangerous.")

While the Japanese Cocktail was never widely popular, it nonetheless kept popping up (sometimes as the "Mikado Cocktail") until Prohibition and was part of every serious bartender's repertoire. It has not been successfully revived since. Perhaps it is too much a product of its time: too sweet and rich for those who like their drinks boozy, too boozy and not fruity enough (or at all) for those who like them sweet.

Recipe: Half-fill small tumbler with cracked ice. Add 60 ml brandy, 30 ml orgeat syrup, and 3 ml aromatic bitters. Stir well; lemon twist.

"American Hotels and American Food." *Temple Bar*, June 1860, 353.

Thomas, Jerry. *How to Mix Drinks*. New York: Dick & Fitzgerald, 1862.

David Wondrich

The **Jasmine** is a cocktail composed of gin, lemon juice, Campari, and Cointreau, served up. The drink was developed by Paul Harrington at Townhouse Bar & Grill in Emeryville, California, in the mid-1990s, for a customer—Matt Jasmin (years later, Harrington discovered he'd misspelled Jasmin's name when christening the drink)—who stopped by the bar after a shift at Chez Panisse, and

Harrington chose to prepare a riff on the classic Pegu Club Cocktail. See PEGU CLUB COCKTAIL. Harrington substituted lemon juice for lime and used Campari in place of the Pegu Club's two types of bitters. The second person to sample the Jasmine was Evan Shively, a chef and acquaintance, who told Harrington, "Congratulations—you've invented grapefruit juice."

Recipe: Shake 45 ml gin, 22.5 ml fresh lemon juice, 7.5 ml. Cointreau, and 7.5 ml Campari with ice to chill, and strain into chilled cocktail glass. Garnish with a lemon twist.

See also HARRINGTON, PAUL.

Email communication with Paul Harrington, March 4, 2015.
Email communication with Paul Harrington, September 12, 2016.
Harrington, Paul. *Cocktail: The Drinks Bible for the 21st Century*. New York: Viking, 1998.

Paul Clarke

Jelínek is a venerable Czech brand of slivovitz that has been important in international markets since before the Second World War and is now the world's largest producer of the spirit. In the eighteenth century, an abundance of plum trees surrounding Vizovice, in what was then the Austro-Hungarian province of Moravia, garnered the area a nickname "the Valley of Plums." This plethora of fruit led to the production of slivovitz, the characteristic plum brandy of southeastern Europe. See SLIVOVITZ.

One man intrigued by the distillation process was Jakub Jelínek, who in 1882 rented the grain and fruit distillery operated in Vizovice by a fellow Jew, Aron Eichen, and put his son Zikmund (1859–1936) in charge. Thus was born a four-generation spirits empire.

In 1891, Zikmund Jelínek established a second distillery of his own, which specialized in slivovitz. By 1900, Vizovice had become a substantial distilling center. When Zikmund retired in 1919, having seen Moravia become a part of the new Czechoslovakia, his two sons, Rudolf and Vladimir, took over the family business and began acquiring other local distilleries. In 1926, they parted ways, with Rudolf remaining in charge of the largest of their distilleries. The R. Jelínek company began exporting Kosher slivovitz to the United States after repeal, gaining considerable success in the New York market. In 1938, however, the Nazi occupation of Czechoslovakia put a halt to that. Rudolf was murdered at Auschwitz in 1944.

Rudolf's sons survived the war and restarted the company in 1945, only to see it nationalized three years later. Under state ownership, the R. Jelínek brand, a part of the portfolio of Moravian Distilleries, nonetheless managed to return to the US market in a limited way. In 1994, Jelínek returned to private hands when grandnephew Andre Lenard acquired a role on the advisory board. That year R. Jelínek USA launched stateside, and today it flaunts a wide distribution network throughout the country.

The small export portfolio of R. Jelínek is anchored by thrice-distilled Silver Slivovitz, which embraces a centuries-old recipe. There is also a triple-distilled five-year-old Kosher Slivovitz. Additionally, there is a triple-distilled ten-year-old Gold Slivovitz crafted from mature, late-harvested plums, as well as apricot and poire Williams brandies. The company also produces Bohemia Honey (aged plum brandy and honey), Jelínek Fernet, and a bitter amaro, as well as a potato vodka that is sold both plain and lightly plum-flavored.

See also APRICOT BRANDY and KOSHER SPIRITS.

"Gimbels Famous Liquor Store" (advertisement). *New York Daily News*, March 27, 1936, 26.
R. Jelínek USA. "Our Story." https://rjelinek.us/our-story/ (accessed March 23, 2021).
"Rudolf Jelínek." Holocaust.cz. https://www.holocaust.cz/en/database-of-victims/victim/96231-rudolf-jelinek/ (accessed September 10, 2020).

Alia Akkam

jenever is the Dutch spelling of genever, the juniper-flavored grain spirit that is the ancestor of gin. See GENEVER and GIN.

Jeppson's Malört is a bitter wormwood-based liqueur based on bask brännvin, a Swedish schnapps popular in the early 1900s. After Skåne County native Carl Jeppson reportedly proffered his absinthe-like "two-fisted liquor" as a medicinal alcohol from a cigar shop in Prohibition-era Chicago, Jeppson's Malört spent the latter half of the twentieth century as a dive-bar rite of passage for any local or unsuspecting out-of-towner willing to tolerate its notoriously punitive aftertaste. Due to a recent social media–powered resurgence, Jeppson's Malört (now produced by Chicago's CH distillery) has transcended its provincial inside-joke origins to become a hip cocktail ingredient in scattered American cities—sometimes even unironically.

See also Prohibition and Temperance in America and Wormwood.

Hernandez, Joseph. "In Chicago, a Spirit Rises Despite Bitter Reviews." *Wall Street Journal*, November 20, 2012.
Peters, Mark. "Malort's Meteoric Rise." *Wine Enthusiast*, February 2015.
This Story Will Never End: The Story of Jeppson's Malört (film) Marc Pearlman, dir., (Fire Engine Red Films, 2014).

Jeff Ruby

jigger is a small and handy liquid measure used in constructing mixed drinks, as opposed to the measures used in retailing spirits. See SPIRITS MEASURE. The name, also spelled "gigger," is an Americanism for "a new device that otherwise lacks a name" (it is related to "thingamajig"). The first purpose-made jiggers appeared in the 1870s to replace the sherry glasses and liqueur glasses that had been used previously with silver-plated metal cones. These were provided with stems for easier handling, and in the hands of a skilled bartender they could be used practically as fast as free-pouring. Their nominal capacity was a wineglass—two ounces, or 60 ml—but the surviving examples that have been measured are usually significantly smaller. Originally, a cocktail was sized so that the total volume of its major components was one jigger, and many cocktail recipes were stated in fractions of that jigger.

By the end of the nineteenth century in the United States the jigger had evolved into a double affair with a large and a small cone (wineglass and one-ounce "pony") joined at their apexes. Meanwhile, bars in the United Kingdom had adopted jiggers of their own. These were sized according to the "out" system, where, for example, a "three-out" jigger held a third of a gill (50 ml) and a "six-out" jigger held a sixth of one (25 ml). These were distinct from the government-regulated measures used for straight

spirits. In the 1970s, they were replaced by metric spirits measures. Elsewhere, jiggers were rarely used, or at least rarely standardized, with the significant exception of Japan.

The twentieth century saw the prevailing jigger size in America (where drink size is not regulated) slip from two ounces to an ounce and a half to, often, an ounce and a quarter. This decline was reversed by the Cocktail Renaissance, which brought back the two-ounce jigger, although the total volume of the major components of a cocktail is generally three or even four ounces (90 or 120 ml).

See also COCKTAIL PROPORTIONS and COCKTAIL RECIPES.

McElhone, Harry. *ABC of Mixing Cocktails*. London: Odhams, 1922.
Rogers, Smith & Co.'s Illustrated Catalogue and Price List of Electro Silver Plate N.p., 1878.

David Wondrich

Jim Beam is both the best-selling brand of bourbon and the pivotal character in the family saga that created that success.

Jim Beam the man was James Beauregard Beam, born in 1864 into a family that was already established in the bourbon distilling business. The Beam family had been making whisky since the 1790s, shortly after the arrival in Kentucky of Jacob Beam (who was born Jacob Boehm, most likely in southeastern Pennsylvania). He was of German descent, as were many of the distillers in Pennsylvania and Maryland. Jacob moved west and made whisky from corn, which grew well in Kentucky's rich soil. See CORN.

Jacob's son David, and his son, David M. Beam, made bourbon at their Old Tub distillery, and the Old Tub name gained some distinction through the late 1800s. Jim Beam was David M.'s son. He took over the operation of Old Tub in 1892, along with his brother-in-law. Jim's son T. Jeremiah Beam joined the company in 1913, getting in about six years of experience before Prohibition arrived and shut everything down. See PROHIBITION AND TEMPERANCE IN AMERICA.

When Repeal arrived in late 1933, Jim Beam, still spry at age sixty-nine, gathered his family—his brother Park, Park's sons Carl and Earl, and T. Jeremiah—and family tradition recalls him saying, "Boys, time for us to get back to work." By the following August, he had raised sufficient capital from the Blum family of Chicago and their National Brokerage Co. and started construction; the Beams would manage operations, the Blums would own the business. Distillation began 120 days later. To Jim's chagrin, he learned that he had lost the rights to the Old Tub name, so the whisky became Colonel James B. Beam Whiskey, soon to become the familiar "Jim Beam."

When Jim retired in 1944, his nephew Carl joined T. Jeremiah in running operations. After the end of World War II, Jim Beam the company would step up production substantially, on the way to its current dominance. In 1967, Harry Blum, the company's chairman, sold it to the American Tobacco Co. (later American Brands and then Fortune Brands). Meanwhile, in 1954, Jim Beam's grandson (and T. Jeremiah's nephew) Booker Noe had joined the company, soon becoming the same kind of larger-than-life character as his grandfather.

Booker was master distiller at Jim Beam through four decades. He created several new expressions of whisky, including the Beam Small Batch collection in 1992. This was inspired by the Beam Christmas gift to top accounts: bottles of Booker's own special selection, uncut, unfiltered, just the way he liked it himself. "Booker's Bourbon" was a hit, and was soon for sale, along with three more Booker-selected whiskys as the Beam Small Batch Collection.

Booker not only developed these whiskys; he promoted them. His gravelly voice, plus-size presence, and absolute authenticity were solid support for Jim Beam whiskys. After he retired, his son, Fred Noe, stepped into his big shoes and has grown into the ambassador job. Beam whiskys led the growth of bourbon in the early 2000s, more so after the company acquired the fast-growing Maker's Mark brand (and distillery) in 2005 (the company had already acquired the National Distillers Co. portfolio, including the historic Old Overholt and Old Grand-Dad brands, in 1987). See MAKER'S MARK and OLD OVERHOLT.

The Jim Beam story took a major turn in 2014, when Japanese whisky maker Suntory bought the company, creating Beam Suntory Inc., a company that owns and produces whiskys in all the major regions: Japan, America, Canada (Alberta Distillers Ltd.), Ireland (Kilbeggan, Connemara, and others),

and Scotland (Teacher's, Bowmore, Laphroaig, and others).

Jim Beam Kentucky Straight Bourbon Whiskey, a four-year-old 80-proof whisky in an iconic square bottle with a white label, remains the best-selling bourbon. Other Jim Beam brand whiskys include the Black (extra-aged, 86 proof), Bonded (gold label, 100 proof), Devil's Cut (90 proof, "extracted" from the barrel), Rye (green label), and a changing variety of flavored bottlings.

See also BOOKER NOE II, FREDERICK; SUNTORY; and WHISKY, BOURBON.

Beam Suntory website. https://www.beamsuntory.com/ (accessed February 17, 2021).

Pacult, F. Paul. *American Still Life: The Jim Beam Story and the Making of the World's #1 Bourbon*. Hoboken, NJ: Wiley, 2003.

Regan, Gary, and Mardee Haidin Regan. *The Book of Bourbon and Other Fine American Whiskeys*. Shelburne, VT: Chapters, 1995.

Rothbaum, Noah. "The Jews Who Made American Whiskey." *Daily Beast*, December 16, 2015. https://www.thedailybeast.com/the-jews-who-made-american-whisky-1 (accessed February 17, 2021).

Lew Bryson

Jinro is South Korea's leading producer of soju, a spirit often likened to a low-proof vodka (around 20 percent ABV), and is arguably the world's most popular spirits brand. See SOJU. The company claims Koreans imbibe almost two billion little green 360-ml bottles of it a year, and its success mirrors the country's rise from poverty to prosperity.

Founded in 1924 during the colonial era, when Japanese firms dominated the spirits industry, Jinro was entirely Korean-funded, a source of national pride. Originally located in Yonggang in present-day North Korea, with the outbreak of the Korean War Jinro fled to Pusan (now Busan) in 1951 and in 1954, after the war, to Seoul. It later navigated the Korean government's 1965 ban on distilling rice, which extended to 1999. In 2005, Jinro merged with Hite, the country's foremost beer brewer, creating a Korean beverage powerhouse.

Jinro's flagship soju, Chamisul, is distilled in column stills from rice, barley, sweet potatoes, tapioca, and sugar cane. Sweetened with fructose, but not overtly sweet, it is filtered through bamboo charcoal. Other sojus in the family include Jinro 24, Ilpoom Jinro, and Jinro Otsu. Domestically, it is typically consumed chilled as shots or mixed into beer but has been making cocktail inroads internationally. In addition to its fervent following in South Korea, the company boasts that it can be found in sixty countries. No doubt its marketing efforts have been helped by the use of K-pop stars like Psy of "Gangnam Style" fame.

Jinro exemplifies Korea's approach to its national spirit, which has been engineered to be highly drinkable, food-friendly, and affordable.

See also SOUTH KOREA.

Ye, Jong-Suk. "World's Best Selling Distilled Liquor." *Koreana*, Winter 2013, http://www.koreana.or.kr/months/news_view.asp?b_idx=3177&lang=en&page_type=list (accessed October 28, 2015).

Michael Anstendig

jiu qu refers to the type of qu, a solid-state fermentation starter, used in the production of alcoholic beverages such as baijiu in China. See QU; BAIJIU; and CHINA.

John Collins, a tall, genever-based single-glass punch, has been eclipsed in popularity by its younger brother Tom Collins, though it has been around considerably longer. See also COLLINS; GENEVER; LONG DRINK; and TOM COLLINS.

Johnnie Walker is perennially the world's largest-selling brand of whisky. It was born in 1820 when the young John Walker (1805–1857) used his inheritance to buy a small but prosperous "Italian grocery" (i.e., grocery, wine, and spirits shop) in

Kilmarnock, 50 km southwest of Glasgow, and began selling whisky. Walker's whisky was transformed into a true brand by his son Alexander (1837–1889), a man of steely determination and forceful language. By the mid-1860s, Alexander had trademarked the firm's principal product, Old Highland Whisky, a blend that was sold in both round and square bottles with a distinctive slanting label. See WHISKY, SCOTCH.

Setting up an office in London around 1871 was a key step in taking Walker's whisky to the world: between 1865 and 1880 the business increased fourfold, but from 1880 it exploded. "It seems that my business doubles itself every year," Alexander wrote in 1885, "and I feel sometimes as if I could almost wish it would double itself back because it is really more than one head can carry."

The formation of a limited company in 1886 brought long-standing employees into the business along with Alexander's sons. Quality was at its heart: they invested heavily in whisky stocks to ensure continuity of character of their blends, and also in primary production, purchasing Cardhu distillery in 1893. As the Whisky and Soda age took over from toddy drinking, heralding a lighter style of blend, the company introduced an age-differentiated range in 1906, with White, Red, and Black Label. See HIGHBALL.

"Quality will stand on its merit," Alexander wrote, and advertising was eschewed. Into the vacuum this created in the 1880s and 1890s stepped the nickname "Johnny Walker," celebrated in popular culture but disdained by the Walker family, who felt it was disrespectful to the founder. It took marketing director James Stevenson to persuade the business otherwise, resulting in the creation in 1908 of the famous striding "Johnnie Walker" figure, which rewrote the semiotics of whisky advertising at a stroke.

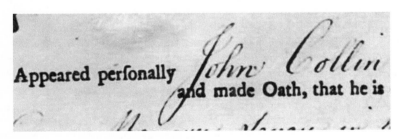

John Collin(s)'s signature, from 1790. Wondrich Collection.

A burgeoning business with the United States was brought to an abrupt end by World War I and Prohibition, but Walker's reputation in the United States was only enhanced during the fourteen "dry years," during which it was a popular illegal import. In 1924 Walker's merged with the Distiller's Company, along with rivals Dewar's and Buchanan's, but retained a large degree of independence, in large part due to the influence of Alexander Walker II (1869–1950), as strong a character as his father. See DISTILLERS COMPANY LTD (DCL). During and after World War II the export of scotch whisky to hard-currency markets was an imperative; the United States, with a particular taste for Black Label, was the most important. Growth was remarkable, with sales going from around one million nine-liter cases in 1955 to ten million in 1975. Oil-rich South American markets and the recovering European economies contributed to this, with Asia also becoming increasingly important. The withdrawal of over a million cases of Red Label from the UK market after a dispute with the EEC in 1978 coincided with the slump in demand that followed the oil crisis. Under new corporate ownership, first United Distillers and then Diageo, the brand clawed its way back to growth (partly due to inspired innovations such as the ultra-premium Blue Label, introduced in 1992), until the reinvention of the "Striding Man" character with the "Keep Walking" campaign saw it pass twenty million cases in 2018.

Morgan, Nicholas. *A Long Stride: The Story of the World's No. 1 Scotch Whisky*. Edinburgh: Canongate, 2020.

Weir, R. B. *The History of the Distiller's Company, 1877–1939*. Oxford: Oxford University Press, 1995.

Nicholas Morgan

Johnson, Harry (1845–1930), was a Prussian-born American bartender and the author of one of the most important early bartender's guides. Dubbed "Dean Emeritus" of his profession by the *New York Sun* in 1910, Johnson reached the height of his career in the late 1800s. A sailor, Johnson was left behind in San Francisco in 1862 to recover from injuries sustained in a shipboard accident. There, he worked his way through restaurant and hotel jobs before he moved to Chicago. He opened his first bar there in 1868 and a year later wrote his first book, the *Bartenders' Manual*, which sold ten thousand

Harry Johnson, from his 1888 *Bartender's Manual*. Courtesy of Cocktail Kingdom.

copies—or so he claimed. Johnson was not always the most reliable chronicler of his own life, and no surviving book tallies perfectly with his description. (Some think this book might be the anonymous *Steward and Barkeeper's Manual* published in 1869 by the Jesse Haney Co. of New York.) The Great Chicago Fire of 1871 put an end to Johnson's business. He may have returned to San Francisco for a time, but he was back in Chicago by 1875, where he married and became an American citizen. He moved to Philadelphia in 1876, to manage a large bar staff at the Grand Exposition Hotel.

Two years later, Johnson moved to New York, where he worked behind the bar at Delmonico's—the favorite haunt of Manhattan luminaries including Diamond Jim Brady, Lillian Russell, and William R. Grace, the city's first Irish mayor—before taking over his own place on the Bowery, the first of several he ran in the city. In 1881 the International News Company asked Johnson to revise and enlarge his *Bartenders' Manual*, printing fifty thousand copies the following year. The 1888 revised and expanded edition presented not only recipes but complete instructions for the operation of a bar. Johnson moved from bars to hotel ownership, opening the Pabst Grand Central Hotel at Columbus Circle in 1902, where he taught his nephew Paul Henckel Jr. the food and beverage business before returning to Germany. Henckel went on to become president of the New York Restaurant Association. Divorced and remarried, Johnson died in Berlin in 1930.

Johnson's 1882 *New and Improved Bartenders' Manual*, with twenty-four pages on how to manage and operate a bar, is the first work of its kind (by the 1900 edition, this section would swell to 157 pages). Johnson was also a talented mixologist, and several of his recipes are still in use today.

Miller, Anistatia, and Jared Brown. *The Deans of Drink* Cheltenham, UK: Mixellany, 2013.
Sharp, R. S. Report on Harry Johnson passport application, April 5, 1920, United States Consular Records, New York.

Anistatia R. Miller and Jared M. Brown

Jose Cuervo is the best-selling brand of tequila in the world. With roots that stretch back to the eighteenth century, it is also the oldest existing tequila producer and is still owned by descendants of the founding family.

José Antonio Cuervo began cultivating agave on land granted to him in 1758 by King Ferdinand VI of Spain in the town of Tequila in the Mexican state of Jalisco. In 1795, Cuervo's son, José María Guadalupe Cuervo, received the first license from King Carlos IV to produce *vino mezcal de Tequila* after a royal ban on commercial production of the agave-based spirit was lifted. Upon José María's death in 1812, his son-in-law, Vicente Albino Rojas, renamed the family distillery La Rojeña, as the older of Cuervo's two distilleries is still known. The tequila brand acquired its current name after Jose Cuervo Labastida assumed control of the company in 1900. Jose Cuervo is currently owned by the Beckmann family, further descendants of José Antonio Cuervo, who also took over ownership of the Bushmills Irish whisky brand in 2015.

Jose Cuervo established itself as the leading global tequila brand beginning with its aggressive, advertising-driven courting of the United States market in the mid-1950s; its early promotion of the Margarita helped to establish the drink, which in turn opened more markets for the tequila. See MARGARITA. Cuervo solidified its position as the leading tequila brand in the 1970s with the explosion in popularity of Cuervo Especial—better known as Cuervo Gold. A *mixto* tequila colored with caramel, it became the favored fuel for spring breaks and fraternity parties. Since then, Cuervo has extended its *mixto* line with silver and cinnamon-flavored versions. Other products sold under the Jose Cuervo label include 100 percent agave tequilas distilled at La Rojeña, such as the Tradicional silver and reposado and the Reserva de la Familia extra anejo.

See also TEQUILA and MIXTO.

Martineau, Chantal. *How the Gringos Stole Tequila: The Modern Age of Mexico's Most Traditional Spirit*. Chicago: Chicago Review, 2015.

David Mahoney

A **juicer**, for cocktail purposes, usually refers specifically to a citrus juicer. Citrus juice, particularly lemon or lime, is one of the most common cocktail ingredients, and the citrus juicer is one of the oldest and most common bar tools. Juicers range from simple hand tools to large (and expensive) countertop machines.

Hand juicers come in a variety of styles. By far the most common for cocktail use is the citrus squeezer, aka hand press or "Mexican elbow." It has two handles connected by a hinge. The bottom handle is attached to a small bowl that is perforated with holes. The top handle is affixed to a bowl of its own that fits neatly into the bottom half. The citrus is sliced in half and placed in the bottom bowl cut-side down, the handles are squeezed together, and the extracted juice streams through the holes. This design, which dates at least to the mid-nineteenth century, allows pressure to be applied onto the fruit in two directions, reducing strain on the one doing the juicing. The juicers come in varying sizes but are best for lemons, limes, and smaller oranges. These are ideal for home bartenders and some low-volume bars, although in skilled hands they can be worked at an astonishing speed.

The largest scale of hand juicer—often also called a stand juicer—stands on a countertop and has a lever that brings a press down onto the fruit.

This is much easier on one's hands and forearms and accommodates fruits of all sizes, making it the most volume-friendly of the manual juicer family. See RA CHAND. Both hand presses and stand juicers can be used to make juice to order.

Generally, high-volume bars will use an electric juicer, working out of the customer's sight. This type has a spinning knob that rapidly extracts and partially—but not entirely—strains the juice before sending it flowing neatly out a spout. In addition to their convenience, electric juicers tend to yield slightly more juice than hand citrus juicers. The horsepower of these varies greatly and their price with it. The most powerful, and durable, models (such as the widely used Sunkist J1) can cost as much as $750.

There is some speculation, notably by Dave Arnold, that juice made with a hand juicer tastes brighter, cleaner, and altogether better than juice made with an electric juicer. One theory is that the added juice extracted by the electric juicer includes some bitter pith or oil from the rind, which gives the juice a sharper and more astringent flavor. But the difference in the cocktails the juice makes seems to be negligible enough that there hasn't been any sign of a movement away from electric juicers.

Arnold, David. "Fresh Lime Juice: WTF?" *Cooking Issues* (blog), October 1, 2010. http://www.cookingissues. com/index.html%3Fp=4601.html (accessed February 17, 2021).

Morganthaler, Jeffery. *The Bar Book*. San Francisco: Chronicle, 2015.

Tom Macy

The **julep** or Mint Julep, with spirits, sugar, water, mint, and ice, is the oldest of the canonical American mixed drinks and is the recipe that more than any other spread the gospel of iced drinks in the country. The drink's name is older than the drink itself: originally, a julep—the name is ultimately derived from *gûl-ab*, the Persian word for rosewater—was a medicinal mixture of water and an infused syrup. Occasionally, these also tasted good, but eighteenth-century British medical books abound in examples involving such profoundly untasty things as camphor syrup. There are also examples of "mint julep," some of them containing small amounts of mint-flavored

MINT JULEP.

Jerry Thomas's (brandy-based) Mint Julep, with slices of citrus and berries lurking in the forest of mint, from his 1862 book. Wondrich Collection.

spirit, although it is generally supplemented by things such as salt and syrup of balsam.

In Britain's American colonies, however, "julep" began to take on a new meaning. In 1770, a Williamsburg, Virginia, newspaper printed a poem on foxhunting by one "S. X.," with the couplet "The sportsmen ready, and the julep o'er, / Which doctors storm at, and which some adore." Clearly, this is not a medicinal drink. Descriptions of just what the Virginians meant by a julep begin to appear in the 1780s. It was a rather more spirituous affair than the English medicinal juleps: "water, sugar, rum, and mint," as a 1787 ode to the drink defined it (under its alternate, more technical, name, Mint Sling); generally, the rum outweighed the water by a considerable amount. See SLING. The preponderance of the evidence points to a Virginia origin for the drink, but there is a 1721 item in a Boston newspaper that mentions "a dram of rum and mint-water" without further explanation, as if it were a known drink (it is likely that the "mint-water" here is in fact a distilled cordial). Whatever the drink's ultimate roots, though, it is with Virginia that it was most closely associated.

It is also in Virginia that the drink's most important addition is first attested to, in 1807: ice. Iced, the julep became a supremely cooling beverage, perfect for the hot summers encountered in North America. In 1817, according to one who knew him, Orsamus Willard of New York's City Hotel, the premiere hotel in the country, was taught to make iced julep by a patron from Virginia. See WILLARD, ORSAMUS. By then, ice was increasingly available in American bars, and the iced julep spread rapidly throughout the country and then the world, bringing all the techniques and possibilities of iced drinks in its wake. See ICE, HISTORY OF ITS USE.

By the 1820s, rum was out of fashion for juleps except as a float for aroma. See FLOAT. French brandy; domestic peach brandy; Spanish, French, and Portuguese wines; Dutch gin; citrus, pineapple, and all kinds of berries in season rapidly found their way into the drink, particularly when it was being concocted by African American bartenders such as John Dabney. See PEACH BRANDY. The one spirit rarely encountered was whisky, considered déclassé for what was perceived as an elegant, even aristocratic drink (albeit a stiff one). Even as late as 1862, when Jerry Thomas included the julep in his pioneering *Bar-Tender's Guide* he assigned the title "Mint Julep" to the brandy version, with the Whisky Julep appearing among the drink's variations. The United States Civil War, however, reversed that relationship: from the 1870s on, Mint Julep increasingly was understood as a whisky drink, and a plain one at that: gone was the rum float, the bits of fruit, and the wines and brandies. It was also increasingly understood as a purely southern drink: what had been a universally popular bar drink became a ritual of southern identity, complete with plantation trappings such as white gloves and silver cups. Whatever popular currency it had left was destroyed by Prohibition. In 1938, after Repeal, Churchill Downs, home of the Kentucky Derby, made a longstanding tradition explicit by naming the bourbon Mint Julep its official drink. From then on, the drink was condemned to be trotted out once a year on Derby day, a fate from which not even the cocktail renaissance has liberated it. See COCKTAIL RENAISSANCE.

Recipe: Stir 10 ml sugar and 15 ml water in a tall glass. Add 6 mint leaves and press lightly with muddler. Pack glass with finely cracked ice. Add 90 ml brandy or bourbon or rye whisky. Stir, add more ice to counter shrinkage, and add 3-4 sprigs of mint. Add straw. Optional: float 15 ml aromatic Jamaican rum on top.

"Brief Notes of the Metropolis." *Buffalo Daily Courier*, June 18, 1851, 2.

"Epistle to Mr. M—k—e." *Philadelphia Independent Gazetteer*, March 17, 1787, 3.

"Fire Works." *Norfolk Gazetteer and Publick Ledger*, May 4, 1807, 3.

Modern Practice of the London Hospital. London: 1764.

S. X. "A Short Poem on Hunting." *Virginia Gazette*, January 11, 1770, 2.

"To the Readers of the Courant in New Hampshire." *New-England Courant*, December 18, 1721, 3.

David Wondrich

juniper is a small, bushy, coniferous shrub with short, prickly needles. Although there are a number of different species of *Juniperus*, it is *Juniperus communis* that is most important to the beverage industry, as its fruit is required in the production of gin. Juniper berries are frequently used in northern Europe and Scandinavia to flavor meats, especially game, and are best utilized when fresh.

Juniper berries in fact are not berries at all but instead soft cones (similar to a pine cone) of the juniper plant. Yet instead of these cones having a tough and woody exterior, they remain slightly moist and fleshy. The essential oils of juniper berries are rich in the monoterpene compounds pinene, germacrene, and myrcene, which provide fresh, sweet, light yet warm, piney-camphorous notes. See ESSENTIAL OILS.

While juniper grows in most regions of the northern hemisphere, the best juniper berries for gin production come from the hot, Mediterranean regions in and around Italy. A juniper berry can take from one to three years to mature, eventually reaching a rich bluish black. Both green and the riper bluish berries can both be found on the same plant and are harvested traditionally by whacking the branches of the shrub with a stick.

Historically, juniper was employed commonly as a medicinal herb. The earliest recorded use of juniper was from an Egyptian papyrus from 1500 BCE, which listed it in a recipe to cure tapeworm infestation. Later, juniper would be utilized by the Romans for various stomach ailments. See HEALTH AND SPIRITS.

It was because of the myriad health-related benefits that juniper offered that the Dutch first created jenever (genever) in the 1500s. Some of the great benefits of juniper are its antiseptic and diuretic properties, which help aid in the removal of waste and acidic toxins from the body. Juniper also helps to increase the flow of digestive fluids, improving digestion and eliminating gas and stomach cramping. It was also employed to treat gout; various infections within the bladder, kidneys, urinary tract, and prostrate; and during times of war to help protect wounds from becoming septic.

Dutch genever was originally intended to be of high medicinal value, but it wouldn't be long before those values were overshadowed by its more intoxicating ones. It is believed that the British first encountered genever while fighting alongside the Dutch during the Eighty Years' War (or Dutch War of Independence, 1568–1648), where it was nicknamed "Dutch courage." The British soon began producing their own version, calling it "gin."

Although it is now severely threatened there, juniper used to grow prolifically in the Scottish Highlands, and during the nineteenth century its berries were collected by local farmers and delivered to the markets in Inverness and Aberdeen for exportation to the Dutch genever distillers. Also during this time Scottish juniper berries were sometimes redistilled with local whiskies to make gin. See WHISKY, SCOTCH. With the modern return to small-scale distilling, such local sources of juniper are once again being exploited to make gin, both in Europe and in the Americas.

See also GENEVER and GIN.

Arctander, Steffen. *Perfume and Flavor Materials of Natural Origin*. Carol Stream, IL: Allured, 2008.

Gin Foundry. "Juniper Defines Gin." Gin Foundry, March 12, 2014. http://www.ginfoundry.com/botanicals/juniper/ (accessed February 17, 2021).

McGee, Harold. *On Food and Cooking: The Science and Lore of the Kitchen*. New York: Scribner, 2004.

Taylor, Alfred Swaine. *A Manual of Medical Jurisprudence*. Philadelphia: Henry C. Lea's Son. 1880.

Audrey Saunders

kachasu, the native spirit of Zambia, Zimbabwe, Malawi, and parts of the Democratic Republic of Congo, is primarily made from malted maize and sugar (occasionally other raw materials are used, such as bananas). The resulting beer is usually single-distilled in pot stills of local design (some are earthenware and wood, while others are made from old oil drums), yielding a spirit that is about 20–30 percent ABV. If double-distilled, as is sometimes done, that figure can reach as high as 70 percent. While kachasu is legal to drink, it is generally illegal to make it or sell it, although its production, generally in the hands of women, is widespread, and enforcement is spotty.

See MOONSHINE.

Mukala, Chola. "In Defence of the Kachasu Industry." *Zambian Economist*, June 10, 2008. http://www.zambian-economist.com/2008/06/in-defence-of-kachasu-industry.html (accessed March 23, 2021).

David Wondrich

Kahlúa, the world's most popular coffee liqueur, has been made in Mexico since 1936. See MEXICO. The brand's name is derived from *kahwa*, the Arabic word for coffee. Originally made by Pedro Domecq, it is now owned by Pernod Ricard. Kahlúa is produced in Mexico City from coffee and a distillate of sugar cane, both grown in the state of Veracruz, as well as rum, vanilla, and caramel. Traditionally bottled at 26.5 percent ABV, its alcohol content was reduced to 20 percent in 2003.

Kahlúa began to make huge strides in sales in the 1960s after its US distribution rights were acquired by Los Angeles entrepreneur Jules Berman, who used antiquities from his pre-Columbian art collection to aggressively promote the brand in magazine ads. It received another shot in the arm in the late 1990s with the release of the cult film classic *The Big Lebowski*, in which the protagonist consumes a steady diet of White Russian cocktails, made with Kahlúa, vodka, and cream. (The creamless Black Russian is another mainstay of Kahlúa cocktails.) See FILM, SPIRITS AND COCKTAILS IN; and WHITE RUSSIAN.

In recent years, Kahlúa has added a number of additional products to its portfolio, including Especial, bottled at 35 percent ABV, and several iterations that include additional flavorings, such as Salted Caramel and French Vanilla.

See also COFFEE LIQUEURS; HABANERO; and PERNOD-RICARD.

Kahlúa website. https://www.Kahlua.com (accessed February 17, 2021).

David Mahoney

Kamikaze is a drink made of vodka, curaçao, and lime juice, usually the preserved kind. It was typically thrown back as a shot, though later on it would be served as often as a cocktail. The ingredients are measured in equal parts, though some increase the vodka component (but delicacy of execution was never the hallmark of this drink). However, some early accounts of the shot have it consisting of only vodka and Rose's lime juice, making it a close relative to the Gimlet. The drink emerged in the United States during the mid-1970s, during the early years of the disco era. Its more lasting fame may be as the progenitor of the more sophisticated Cosmopolitan, which added cranberry juice to the mix. As to the provocative name, the writer Gary Regan recalled one 1970s New York bartender observing, "You don't feel like killing yourself after a Gimlet." See REGAN, GARY.

Recipe: Shake 30 ml each of vodka, triple sec, and lime juice with ice, and strain into a cocktail glass.

See also COSMOPOLITAN and GIMLET.

Gould, Heywood. *Cocktail.* New York: St. Martin's, 1984.

Robert Simonson

kao liang, **kaoliang**, or **gaoliang** is a type of strong unflavored baijiu made by twice distilling sorghum that has been fermented with wheat *qu* and combining the distillations (*gaoliang* is the Chinese word for sorghum). See BAIJIU and QU. It originated in Tianjin (in northern China east of Beijing) during the Ming dynasty (1368–1684), and there are still plenty of mainland producers, but kaoliang is chiefly known because it has become a staple in Taiwan, where its production was brought when the Kuomintang retreated there after the Chinese Civil War. It is a particular specialty of the Taiwanese island of Kinmen, just off the mainland, where it was introduced in 1952. It is also a popular drink in Korea. While it is typically an unflavored spirit, producers often age kaoliang to achieve varying expressions. Common brands include Kinmen Kaoliang Liquor and Yushan Kaoliang Chiew, both from Taiwan.

Needham, Joseph, Ho Ping-Yu, Lu Gwei-Djen, and Nathan Sivin. "Chemical Technique." In *Science and Civilisation in China*, vol. 5, *Chemistry and Chemical Technology*, part 4, *Spagyrical Discovery and Invention: Apparatus, Theories and Gifts*, 114–115. Cambridge: Cambridge University Press, 1980.
Osborne, Lawrence. "Author Lawrence Osborne on Kinmen Kaoliang Liquor." *Wall Street Journal*, July 11, 2014. https://www.wsj.com/articles/author-lawrence-osborne-on-kinmen-kaoliang-liquor-1405108496 (accessed February 17, 2021).

Anna Archibald

Kappeler, George J. (fl. 1895), is the author of *Modern American Drinks*, published in New York in 1895 and one of the best regarded of all classic bartenders' guides for its sensible, balanced recipes. Unfortunately, nothing is known about Kappeler himself: although his publishers identified him as "head barkeeper at the Holland House," one of New York's most modern and elegant hotels, other than a single appearance in the New York city directory he remains a complete cipher. Any press mentions of him add no information beyond what appears in his book. Whatever his background, his publisher's 1916 claim that *Modern American Drinks* was "a standard work because of its reliability" is as accurate in the present cocktail renaissance as it was then. See COCKTAIL RENAISSANCE.

Kappeler, George J. *Modern American Drinks.* New York: Merriam, 1895.

David Wondrich

ketone is an organic compound characterized by a carbonyl group attached to alkyl or aryl groups. Ketones can be produced by the oxidation of secondary alcohols (such compounds include aldehydes, esters, and other flavoring and aromatic compounds). See OXIDATION. Some in Cognac believe that ketones are partly responsible for many characteristic aromas of *rancio* in cognac.

Particular ketones found primarily in very old aged cognacs are now linked to specific aromas and flavors such as green banana and fruitiness (2-butanone); coconut and herbs (2-nonanone); rose, iris, and pineapple (2-undecanone); and mushrooms, coconut, and chicken fat (2-tridecanone).

There is much that is not yet understood about these characteristics and even the sources of these ketones: current thinking is that fatty acids may be altered during fermentation to provide conditions for ketone development. There has been little comparable research among other aged spirit industries, though it may be that similar compounds develop in similar ways in other aged spirits such as whisky or rum.

See also COGNAC and RANCIO.

American Chemical Society website. https://www.acs.org (accessed April 18, 2016).

Doug Frost

kilning is the final part of the malting process, which removes moisture from the germinated grain. It also stops biological activity, preserving the enzymes needed for conversion, and allows the malt to be stored at low temperatures. Drying the malt also generates flavor compounds and allows easier milling. (Kiln-drying is also used to extract moisture from barrel staves to speed up their seasoning, although the process leaves more tannins in the wood than long air-drying outdoors.)

The grain kiln itself is a large chamber with a perforated floor onto which the green malt (at around 35 percent moisture content) is spread. Initially the external moisture is driven off; then as the temperature rises, the water moves from inside to outside of the grain, further lowering moisture. A final period of air-drying drops the moisture down to between 4 and 6 percent.

Today most kilns use hot air to dry the malt, but smoke can be used at the start of the process to impart specific aromas to the grain. The most commonly used fuel for this is peat, but other smokes such as wood can also be used.

As an excessively high kilning temperature will break down the amylolytic enzymes contained in the grain, it is kept at around 72° C. In malt destined for grain whisky this is lower (around 50° C), as higher enzymatic activity is required. During the process the grain will develop color and flavor compounds such as furan, pyrroles, and diketones, which can add smoky chocolate-like aromas. In addition, compounds such as hexanal (which makes a grassy aroma) are produced.

See also BARLEY; MALTING; and PEAT.

Buxton, Ian, and Paul S. Hughes. *The Science and Commerce of Whisky*. Cambridge: Royal Society of Chemistry, 2014.

Lea, Andrew G. H., and John Raymond Piggott, eds. *Fermented Beverage Production*. New York: Kluwer, 2003.

Russell, Inge, and Graham G. Stewart, eds. *Whisky Technology, Production and Marketing*, 2nd ed. Amsterdam: Elsevier, 2014.

Dave Broom

Kir is one of France's most popular traditional aperitifs and one of the few to have gained an international following. Named after Félix Kir (1876–1968), the priest who served as mayor of Dijon between 1945 and 1968, it is made with local ingredients: white Burgundy wine and crème de cassis. The latter has been inextricably linked with Burgundy ever since the phylloxera crisis pushed some wine producers to grow black currants, which were then made into liqueurs.

At the end of the nineteenth century, crème de cassis was a staple of French cafés and an essential ingredient of many mixed drinks. The Vermouth Cassis, for instance, was probably one of the most popular drinks of its time, but cassis was also mixed with Byrrh, gentian-based aperitifs, cognac, or white wine—the last being known as the Blanc Cassis.

It is often claimed that the Blanc Cassis was invented in 1904 in a Dijon café for mayor Henri Barabant. The recipe was probably older, but Barabant made the Blanc Cassis the official drink at the city's receptions. Blanc Cassis was extremely popular all over France in the 1930s, but it took the election of highly respected French resistance veteran Kir for the drink to take its current name. Kir's death in 1968 came at the very beginning of a two-decade period during which the drink named after him was in vogue internationally as a brunch drink and aperitif (the influential American food writer James Beard pronounced it the "favorite aperitif").

Although the Blanc Cassis was probably initially made with any dry white wine, a standard Kir is built with cold Bourgogne aligoté wine. The Kir Royale is a variant made with crémant de Bourgogne, a local sparkling wine, or champagne. Outside of France, of course, the choices of wines used are rather more relaxed.

Recipe: Pour 15 ml crème de cassis into a wine glass, followed by 100 ml cold Bourgogne aligoté.

See also CRÈME DE CASSIS; FRANCE; and VERMOUTH-CASSIS.

Beard, James. "New Tastings Give Tasteful Offerings to Wine Drinkers." *Philadelphia Inquirer*, September 13, 1970, Food Guide, 2.

Gérard, Gaston. *Le miroir du coin et du temps*. Dijon: Edition des Etats Généraux de la Gastronomie française, 1959.

Pitte, Jean-Robert. *Dictionnaire amoureux de la Bourgogne*. Paris: Plon, 2015.

François Monti

kirschwasser, or simply **kirsch**, is an eau-de-vie distilled from cherries and their pits that has a significance unlike many others in the German-speaking part of Europe. Different fruit distillates may play a bigger role locally, but it is kirsch that gained and maintained its reputation as a premium spirit also outside its heartland. From Mount Rigi in the center of Switzerland, where kirsch has played a key role for ages with commercial distilleries and brands dating back to the mid-nineteenth century, through the northern cantons of Aargau, Solothurn, and Basel, to the Schwarzwald in the south of Germany and across the Rhine into Alsace, it is the cherry tree whose white blossoms are the messengers of spring.

Even though many distilleries disappeared and the number of cherry trees in the region—and with that the volume of kirsch produced—decreased dramatically over the last century, kirsch has kept its place and constantly manages to reinvent itself. It is not only sipped as a digestif but also eaten in confectionery and desserts such as the black forest cake, Zuger kirschtorte, or Basler läckerli. Kirsch is also essential in the traditional cheese fondue—both as ingredient and as a delicious companion. It is also of course the base, or one of them, for some classic drinks, including the Café Brulôt and the signature Parisian drink, the Rose (Giovanni Mitta, the Rose's inventor, was from northern Italy near the Swiss border). See Café Brûlot and Rose. With modern bartenders constantly searching for authentic, regional ingredients, kirsch has re-entered the world of cocktails with its fruity and almond-like flavors.

Until the 1990s, most producers generally sold their kirsch in two different qualities: standard and reserve, the latter of which is made from select fruit and rested for three or four years in stainless steel tanks or glass demijohns. Only during an exceptional year do some distilleries go on to produce a *Jahrgangskirsch*. This vintage bottling, usually an assemblage of different cherry varieties and a cuvée of the most sophisticated eaux-de-vie, will reflect this year's harvest, weather, and the distillation style of that era. Of the approximately eight hundred cherry varieties known in Switzerland alone, some are better suited for distillation and some for table use. Whereas the latter come in the size you know from the supermarket, those for distilling tend to be smaller, with wild cherries being even tinier.

The mechanization of the harvest, modern stills with rectification columns, and controlled fermentation would eventually change the taste of kirsch from the late twentieth century onward. Also, the effect of ongoing research and growing knowledge of the different cherry varieties and what each them will bring to an eau-de-vie cannot be underestimated. Today, many producers offer single-variety kirsch like Lauerzer, Dolleseppler, Basler Langstiel, or Steinweichsel, just to name a few. Whereas kirsch is generally aged in glass or steel, some producers have started experimenting with barrel-aging, adding completely new aromas to this already diverse category.

See CHERRY BRANDY; EAU-DE-VIE; and MARASCHINO.

Andreae, Illa. *Alle Schnäpse dieser Welt*. Zurich: Transitbooks, 1973.
Dominé, André. *The World of Spirits and Cocktails*. Bonn: Tandem-Verlag, 2008.

Kaspar Keller

Knickebein, or "knee bend," is a German, and German American, variant of the Pousse Café involving an unbroken egg yolk taken in a regimented four-step process. See POUSSE CAFÉ. Leo Engel, a German American expatriate tending bar at the American Bar in London's Criterion restaurant first detailed this layered cocktail ceremony in 1878, although it had apparently been in circulation for at least a decade before that. See CRITERION; and ENGEL, LEO. His version was equal parts of curaçao, crème de noyaux, and maraschino liqueur, filling the bottom two-thirds of a port glass. Next, an unbroken egg yolk was floated, and the whole drink was topped with whipped egg whites garnished with a few drops of Angostura bitters. Later variations used different liqueurs and occasionally included a spirit layer to separate the yolk and white layers; as a 1913 German bar book noted, "One can produce this drink in many variations," going on to list fourteen of them. Any combination works if the liqueur layers are denser than yolk (approximately 1.025 g/ml). In the literature, some books erroneously have the ingredients shaken like a flip and represent the flavors but not the concept of the drink. See FLIP. William Boothby declared, "This famous Teutonic beverage is little known in America, and few bartenders have ever acquired the art of compounding one. It is an after-dinner drink, and in order to be fully appreciated, it must be partaken of according to the following directions, as four different sensations are experienced by the drinker. Therefore, the duty of the presiding mixologist is to thoroughly explain to the uninitiated the modus operandi, etc." See BOOTHBY, WILLIAM T. "COCKTAIL BILL". Engel described the ceremony:

1. Pass the glass under the *Nostrils* and *Inhale the Flavour.*—Pause.
2. Hold the glass *perpendicularly*, close under your mouth, open it *wide*, and suck the froth by drawing a *Deep Breath.*—Pause again.
3. *Point* the lips and take *one-third* of the *liquid contents* remaining in the glass without *touching the yolk.*—Pause once more.
4. Straighten the body, throw the *head backward*, swallow the contents remaining in the glass *all at once*, at the same time *breaking the yolk* in your mouth.

Recipe (Leo's Knickebein): Separate an egg and whip the white. Pour into a 60-ml, conical, stemmed sherry glass 15 ml each of maraschino, crème de noyaux, and orange curaçao (these may be mixed together or floated in layers, in the order listed). Carefully add the egg yolk and spoon the egg white on top. Dash with Angostura bitters. Sip as above.

See also ANGOSTURA BITTERS; EGGS; and ENGEL, LEO.

Boothby, William T. *The World's Drinks and How to Mix Them.* San Francisco: Pacific Buffet, 1908.

Engel, Leo. *American and Other Drinks.* London: Tinsley Brothers, 1878.

"Knickebein" (saloon advertisement). *San Francisco Bulletin*, March 30, 1869, 4.

Leybold, John, and Hans Schönfeld. *Lexicon der getränke.* Cologne: Verlag von Leybold & Schönfeld, 1913.

Frederic Yarm

The **Knickerbocker** (alias Knickerbocker Punch), a single-serving punch generally based on rum and orange curaçao, is one of the oldest American "fancy drinks" on record. Although we do not know its precise origins—"Knickerbocker" is a nickname for New Yorker—its first known appearance is in 1843 on the iconic list of drinks Peter Brigham offered at the Concert Hall in Boston. See BRIGHAM, PETER BENT. Brigham's list was widely imitated, and by the 1850s Knickerbockers of one sort or another were served all over the United States, plus in Canada, London, and even Paris, where it is documented in 1859 (and was probably being served a decade before that). However, since Brigham never published any recipes or even descriptions of the drinks, these versions were all likely to be a word-of-mouth interpretations or pure improvisations.

That is reflected in the diversity of the earliest published recipes, from the 1860s. The first was published by Jerry Thomas in 1862; Thomas gave no source, and his travels had been wide. See THOMAS, JEREMIAH P. "JERRY". His version was a fairly conventional rum punch, although it used lime juice, a rarity at the time, and the curaçao that sweetened it was reinforced with raspberry syrup, a decidedly fancy touch. Four more recipes came out before the end of the decade. Only one of them even resembles Thomas's. The others include ingredients such as Rhine wine, brandy, port, arrack, and various fruits and exclude the rum, the curaçao, the lime juice, or all three. There is no way of establishing which recipe, if any, is closest to Brigham's.

Eventually, Thomas's recipe became the basis for further variations until the end of the nineteenth century, when the drink, sweet and rummy, fell out of fashion. However, in the 1930s its shaved ice, flavors of rum and lime and fruit, and rustic squeezed-out lime shell garnish all made the Knickerbocker one of the harbingers of a new mixological style; one that would come to be called tiki. See TIKI.

Recipe: Shake with ice 60 ml aged, non-Jamaican rum, 30 ml orange curaçao, 15 ml raspberry syrup, and 15 ml lime juice. Strain into Old-Fashioned glass full of fine ice and garnish with lime shell, pineapple chunks, and raspberries.

Campbell, Charles B. *The American Barkeeper.* San Francisco: Mullin, Mahon, 1867.

"The Contrast." *Boston Christian Reflector*, February 1, 1843, 1.

Lennox, J. *Fast Life: An Autobiography*, London: G. Vickers, 1859.

Thomas, Jerry. *How to Mix Drinks*. New York: Dick & Fitzgerald, 1862.

David Wondrich

koji is the Japanese term for grain or other starchy material that has been treated with *koji-kin*, a mold used in Japanese, Chinese, and Korean culture to ferment soybeans and make alcoholic beverages. See QU. In Japan, those beverages include sake and the spirits shochu and awamori. The mold is typically cultured on rice, from which both sake and awamori are made (awamori, native to Okinawa, is made from Thai rice), but it can also be cultured on barley, sweet potatoes, or buckwheat, the primary raw ingredients of shochu. To make koji for sake, for example, koji-kin is distributed over steamed rice in a hot, humid room called a *koji muro*. For two to three days, the mold is cultivated to grow evenly on the rice. In a process called saccharification, the koji-kin releases enzymes that convert the starches in the rice to sugars, which are then converted to alcohol by yeast during fermentation. See SACCHARIFICATION. Koji also contributes various flavor compounds to the finished beverage, as well as to fermented foods such as miso or soy sauce; one important compound is glutamate, an amino acid that imparts umami, a savoriness or depth of flavor. Koji can be classified according to the color of the mold spores that produced it (shiro/white, kuro/black, or ki/yellow), its raw material (komi/rice, muji/barley), or its end product (shoyu/soy sauce, sake). Typically, sake is made with yellow koji, shochu with black or white koji, and awamori with black koji.

See also AWAMORI and SHOCHU.

Samuels, Monica. "Sake School: Koji, the Miracle Mold." *Serious Eats*, February 1, 2011. http://drinks.seriouseats.com/2011/02/koji-the-miracle-mold-how-sake-is-made.html (accessed February 18, 2021).

"Understanding Shochu." Japan Sake and Shochu Makers Association website. http://www.honkakushochu-awamori.jp/english/understanding-shochu/ (accessed February 18, 2021).

Lauren Clark

Kopstoot, or "head-butt" (often found in the diminutive, Kopstootje), has been the Dutch name for a shot of chilled genever accompanied by a beer chaser since at least the 1940s. See GENEVER. The genever is served in a small, tulip-shaped glass, filled to the very top, and the first sip is taken by bending from the waist with one's hands behind one's back. See also BOILERMAKER.

korenwijn, also known as korenwyn (or according to the spelling of the best-selling brand, Bols Corenwyn), is a deluxe version of *oude*-style genever that has been marketed in the Netherlands since World War II; it is not currently exported. It must contain a minimum of 51 percent malt wine, be at least 38 percent alcohol by volume, and contain no more than twenty grams of sugar per liter,

A double coaster for the tulip glass of genever and the short beer that make up a Kopstoot. Wondrich Collection.

compared to *oude*-style genever's minimum 15 percent malt wine, 35 percent ABV, and maximum 20g sugar/liter. As with regular genever, there is no requirement to age korenwijn, but if it is aged, it must be for a minimum of one year, in an oak barrel with a capacity no larger than 700 liters.

Korenwijn is a tiny percentage of all genever sales and is strongly associated with the herring parties that overtake the Netherlands in late May, when the first catches of herring are landed to be eaten raw and chased with a glass of korenwijn. Heavy advertising for korenwijn has ensured most people serve it chilled. Korenwijn should not be confused with *korenwijn*, which is the name for the optional fourth distillation of the mash during genever production, the first three being *ruwnat*, *enkelnat*, and *bestnat*.

See also GENEVER.

Philip Duff

korn is a grain spirit made in northern Germany since at least 1507, when a grain distillery was established in Nordhausen. In German, as with "corn" in archaic English, *Korn* refers to grain more broadly, rather than to the grain that Americans have come to know as corn (*Zea mays*). See CORN. Oats, buckwheat, and wheat are permitted by law since 1909, but the spirit korn is generally distilled from rye

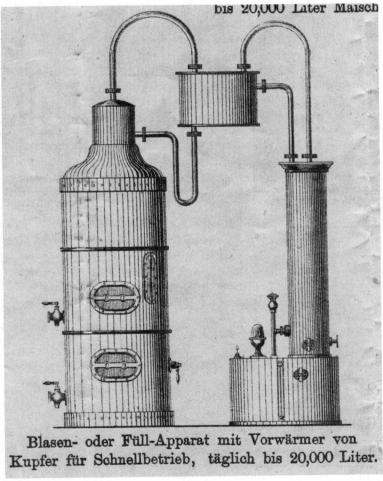

A *Blasenapparat*, or three-chamber still, for making korn, along with its wash heater (*center*) and condenser (*right*). From a brochure for the F. R. Rath company, Neuhandensleben, Saxony, ca. 1890. Wondrich Collection.

with an adjunct of malted barley, although some varieties are made from barley malt alone. In 1789, the Council of Nordhausen adopted a purity law that dictated that at least two-thirds of rye or wheat and no more than one-third barley or malt be used in authentic korn. See also RYE; WHEAT; MALTING; and BARLEY.

Although korn is regarded in Germany as being rather archaic, it was enormously popular until World War II. It also had a strong influence on the early American distilling industry, through the many German distillers who settled in the mid-Atlantic region. The industries shared several key practices, including the heavy use of rye, distilling with the draff in the wash, raising animals on the spent wash, and the use of the *Blasenapparat* or three-chamber still. See STILL, THREE-CHAMBER; and WHISKY, RYE.

In Germany today two types are available: *Korn*, 32 percent ABV, and *Dopplekorn* (sometimes called *Kornbrand*), at 38 percent ABV. If aged in oak barrels, the spirit may be called *Edelkorn or Altkorn* (such aging is usually brief, in well-used cooperage). When cut with glacier meltwater, the resulting spirit is sometimes called *Eiskorn*. Several brands founded in the nineteenth century, such as Hullman, Büre, Büchter, Sallandt, and Schmittmann, remain active, and the Bremen firm Mackenstedter has been producing korn since 1750. *Obstler* (brandies made from fruits such as apple, pear, plums, or blends thereof) are favored in southern Germany, but korn remains popular in the north. See OBSTLER.

The nose and taste of these schnapps are clearly cereal, akin to grain moonshine or white dog. See WHITE DOG. A shot of chilled korn, served either alongside a glass of beer or mixed into it, is known as a *Herrengedeck*, a sort of Teutonic boilermaker. See BOILERMAKER and HERRENGEDECK. In Lower Saxony, such a shot on the side of a beer is a *Lütte Lage*. Drinkers also spike coffee with the Nordhäuser specialty to keep out the cold, wind down a dinner, or face the morning. The *Löffeltrunk* drinking game in northwest Germany involves two drinkers facing each other, each holding a metal spoon of korn in the left hand. After a ritual mutual greeting in the local dialect to demonstrate their relative sobriety ("*Ick seh di!* / I see you!"—"*Dat freit mi* / I am glad!"), each drinks the korn, licks the spoon, and turns it over. Should even a single drop fall to the table, the loser buys the next round.

See also GERMANY, SWITZERLAND, AND AUSTRIA.

Gerlach, Thomas. "Die letzten Hüter des Doppelkorns." *Die Welt*, November 14, 2007. http://www.welt.de/wirtschaft/article1361367/Die-letzten-Hueter-des-Doppelkorns.html (accessed February 18, 2021).

Kreipe, H. *Technologie der Getreide-und Kartoffelbrennerei*. Nuremberg: Carl, 1972.

Lichine, Alexis. *Alexis Lichine's New Encyclopedia of Wines and Spirits*, 5th ed. New York: Alfred A. Knopf, 1987.

Metzger, C., R. Stempell, C. Büschel, and A. Bell. *Culinaria Germany*. Cologne: Könemann, 2007.

Werther, Hans-Dieter, Paul-Ludwig Schierholz, and Steffen Iffland. *500 jahre Nordhäuser Brennereitradition*. Nordhausen-Salza: Steffen Iffland, 2007.

Matthew Rowley

kosher spirits are ones that are made in accordance with traditional Jewish dietary laws (*kashruth*). To ensure that the liquor is kosher, historically, Jews have produced or overseen its production. While there are very strict rules for making wine, since it is used in religious ceremonies, there are fewer rules for distilling spirits. Essentially, all the ingredients must be kosher, which for most spirits is not a particularly difficult standard to meet (kashruth largely applies to animal products, which are rarely used in spirits production), and the stills and other equipment must also be inspected and approved by a kosher certification authority. A spirit aged in a used wine, port, or sherry barrel that has held non-kosher alcohol cannot be kosher. There are a number of organizations, including the Orthodox Union and the London Beth Din, which will certify a spirit as kosher.

See also BOUKHA; JELÍNEK; and SHERRY.

"Steps for Kosher Certification." OU Kosher website. https://oukosher.org/kosher-overview/steps-to-kosher-certification/ (accessed April 27 2021).

Noah Rothbaum

Kräuterlikör is the German term for herbal liqueurs, such as Jägermeister, usually served as a digestive. See also APERITIF AND DIGESTIVE; HERBAL LIQUEUR; and GERMANY, SWITZERLAND, AND AUSTRIA.

kümmel is an herbal liqueur of southern Baltic origin, primarily flavored with caraway seed. It was formerly renowned as an ingredient in cocktails, punches, and drinks short and tall—most famously the Silver Bullet, from the 1930 *Savoy Cocktail Book*. It also has traditional culinary uses in desserts, sauces, and sauerkraut.

Caraway seeds are a traditional Baltic "cover," or basic botanical for flavoring spirits (like aniseed around the Mediterranean and juniper berries along the Rhine), although the time and place of their initial use remains obscure. See AQUAVIT and GENEVER. By the seventeenth century, however, "spiritus carvi," or "caraway spirit," was common in medical texts. The spirit soon made the jump to recreational use. In 1768, a German manual for merchants mentioned caraway as a flavoring for brandy, and a recipe for doppel-kümmel shows up in a German distillers' manual in 1823. In that year, Wilhelm Von Blanckenhagen (1761–1840) commenced commercial production in Allasch, then a Baltic-German region in Latvia. Van Blanckenhagen's Allasch Kümmel, thick with sugar and 40 percent ABV, achieved international recognition at the Leipzig Trade Fair in 1830.

Several Latvian-German distillers soon followed suit, including noted Riga distiller Albert Wolfschmidt (1816–1895), whose kümmel dates to 1847. Eckau Kümmel, originally distilled by another Latvian noble family, Von Pahlen, was an even more potent and slightly less sugary recipe, which, according to its producers, dated to 1805. It was often imitated and sometimes sold in bear figurine bottles, which Ernest Hemingway described in *A Farewell to Arms*. Founded in 1850, the Gilka brand typified the Berlin style of kümmel, somewhat dryer but not as potent.

Allasch Kümmel's popularity spread to Britain in 1851, when Ludwig Mentzendorff contracted with the Van Blankenhagens for distribution there. In 1920, the Van Blanckenhagens fled the Soviet Revolution to northern Germany, where they continued production of the Mentzendorff Kümmel until 1939, when distillation moved to Amsterdam. Today, Mentzendorff Kümmel is distilled by the French Combier company, who also make a doppel-kümmel for US distribution.

Kümmel's heyday as a cocktail ingredient stretched from the 1910s through the 1930s; with the Second World War devastating its home region and the public taste running toward drier, simpler drinks, it had little chance to recover. The cocktail renaissance has so far not proven itself to be kümmel-inflected, although the liqueur does have its adherents (not surprisingly, it mixes well with rye whisky).

See also: GERMANY, SWITZERLAND, AND AUSTRIA; LIQUEURS; and RUSSIA AND EASTERN EUROPE.

"Le kummel du Domaine Eckau du Comte de Pahlen." *Journal officiel de l'alimentation*, June 20, 1916, 9–10.

Miller, Anistatia, and Jared Brown. "Lost Ingredients: Kümmel." *The Historians*, June 20, 2014. http://thehistorians-jaredbrown.blogspot.com/2014/06/lost-ingredients-kummel.html (accessed January 31, 2021).

Ray, Cyril, "Try Kummel on Ice." *The Observer*, May 29, 1966, 19.

Schmidt, Carl Wilhelm. *Das Ganze der Destillirkunst.* Königsberg: Gebrüder Bornträger, 1823.

Doug Stailey

Kweichow Moutai (sometimes transcribed Maotai) is China's most revered and expensive brand of baijiu, a clear spirit whose flagship expression is bottled at 53% ABV. Kweichow Moutai became the most valuable single brand of spirit in the world in 2011, and in 2017 the publicly-traded, partially state-owned Kweichow Moutai Company passed Diageo to become the most valuable spirits company in the world. Produced in Guizhou province (Guizhou was formerly transliterated as "Kweichow") in southern China, this spirit has existed in its current state since the Qing dynasty, in the mid-seventeenth century, and is quite possibly very much older than that. See BAIJIU.

Moutai offers numerous expressions, but its original and most important one is the classic sauce-aroma baijiu, made from wheat *qu*, sorghum, and water through the process of solid-state fermentation. See SAUCE-AROMA-STYLE BAIJIU. To form qu, a koji-like starter, wheat is mashed with water from the Chishui river, molded into bricks, and allowed to ferment in a hot, moist chamber for a month or more to propagate cultures of yeast, fungi, and bacteria. See QU. Eventually, the qu is dried, ground, and mixed with water and red sorghum. This solid mash is buried in underground pits and covered to allow the conversion of starches to sugar and sugar to alcohol to occur simultaneously over a month. The mash is then unearthed, strained, and subjected to steam distillation. The resulting spirit is reserved, while the used mash is fortified with fresh grain and buried again. This process is repeated eight times, and the resulting distillates are then blended to achieve a raw spirit of the desired strength and character. The liquor is then aged in large, semiporous earthenware amphorae from three to twenty years or more; these allow some oxidative aging and concentration without the extraction found in barrel maturation. See MATURATION. Finally, experts blend hundreds of components of varying ages to achieve the final product.

Moutai is constantly in high demand, fetching prices in the hundreds of US dollars per 500-ml bottle. This is due to scarcity, because Moutai is a true spirit of terroir, dependent on the particulars of water, airflow, soil, and microbiology present at the Guizhou distillery, located low in a valley along the banks of the Chishui River. Efforts to increase production—even producing the spirit on nearby stretches of the Chishui—have failed to replicate Moutai's unique flavor, with its pungent redolence of umami-rich foods such as soy sauce and mushrooms, along with fermenting or rotting tropical fruit, as well as savory, herbal, and nutty aromas. All told, over three hundred distinct aromas are recognized in it by Moutai's technicians.

Moutai's reputation as China's premier spirit was solidified in the twentieth century. Famously, it was used by Red Army soldiers to sterilize wounds during the Chinese civil war. It also became known as the "drink of diplomacy" when Richard Nixon toasted with it during his groundbreaking visit in 1972. Traditionally, Maotai is consumed in small 10-ml glasses at meals and accompanying food.

Following a toast, the shot is swallowed all at once, and glasses are refilled. Once a new bottle has been opened, the expectation is that it will be finished on the same occasion.

Mileham, Arabella. "Kweichow Moutai Overtakes Diageo as World's Most Valuable Distiller." *The Drinks Business*, April 11, 2017, https://www.thedrinksbusiness.com/2017/04/kweichow-moutai-overtakes-diageo-as-worlds-most-valuable-distiller/ (accessed February 18, 2021).

Sandhaus, Derek. *Baijiu*. New York: Viking, 2015.

Jordan Mackay

kwete, **enguli**, or **waragi** (Uganda), **ngbako** (Central African Republic), and **lotoko** or **lutuku** (Democratic Republic of the Congo) is a family of spirits distilled from the cloudy, sweet-sour beer (also called *kwete*) made from maize, dried cassava, or both, along with yeast, water, and sometimes malted millet. Reclaimed oil drums are commonly used for fermentation and for constructing the pot stills used, although these can also be made of clay. Production, which is often illicit, is usually in the hands of women. It is not standardized, and distribution is strictly local, but in some locations it is quite extensive. Proofs vary; some lotoko is triple-distilled and quite strong. See MOONSHINE.

Huetz de Lemps, Alain. *Boissons et civilizations en Afrique*. Pessac, France: Presses Universitaires de Bordeaux, 2001.

Muyanja, Charles, and Brenda Shenute. "Traditional Processing, Microbiological, Physiochemical and Sensory Characteristics of Kwete, a Ugandan Fermented Maize Based Beverage." *African Journal of Food Agriculture Nutrition and Development* 9, no. 4 (2009): 1046–1059.

Anna Archibald and David Wondrich

Lactart was created by Alan Avery Claflin (1873–1954), a chemist, at the Avery Lactart Company in 1881 as an alternative to citrus juice and acid phosphate for use in drinks. It was promoted as a wholesome beverage created from the "acid of milk," also known as lactic acid. Lactart was produced by a chemical method, and no dairy products were used in its creation. However, it did have the aroma of sour milk.

Lactart was marketed into the early twentieth century but never achieved a significant market share. Many recipes calling for Lactart can be found in soda fountain books from 1890 to the 1920s but never gained popularity in cocktails until the twenty-first century.

See also CITRUS and ACID PHOSPHATE.

O'Neil, Darcy. *Fix the Pumps*. N.p.: Art of Drink, 2009.

Darcy O'Neil

lactobacillus (LAB) is a large grouping of bacteria, all of which produce lactic acid. They can be derived from the raw material used for fermentation (they are naturally present in many such materials) but in distilleries tend to be in highest concentration within pipes and fermenting vessels. Research has shown that each distillery has its own fingerprint of LAB, created by its particular operating regime; these bacteria colonies can help create an individual character in the distillery's product. LAB's role within flavor creation comes during fermentation. Which flavor compounds are produced depends on a number of factors, primarily the specific LAB colony within the distillery and the length of the fermentation. See FERMENTATION.

As yeast cells die, autolysis starts and LAB start to multiply. The dead yeast cells contain high levels of fatty acids. These are changed (hydroxylated) into lactones, which produce aromatic compounds identified as soft orchard and tropical fruits. See LACTONES.

The acidity of the fermenting liquid also continues to rise, which in turn helps to trigger other LAB. The combination of LAB metabolization of lactates and acetates, alcohol, and higher acidity helps to produce the grouping known as esters. LAB can also reduce smoky (phenolic) aromas. See ESTERS and PHENOLS.

The cleanliness of a distillery also plays a part in lactobacillus generation. Fermenting vessels made of stainless steel (which can be more efficiently cleaned) will have lower LAB levels. Wooden fermenters, conversely, will contain higher levels. Distillers who use stainless steel fermenters but wish to run longer fermentations to produce specific flavors will clean but not sterilize the vessels in order to preserve the LAB colony.

Priest, Fergus G. "Lactic Acid Bacteria: The Uninvited but Generally Welcome Participants in Malt Whisky Fermentation." *Microbiology Today*, February, 2004, 16–18.

Dave Broom

lactones are a group of phenols derived from oak that create many aromas, flavors, and textures in barrel-aged spirits. These include complex milky or coconut notes, vanilla, balsam, wood, pastries, earthiness, apricot, peach, leather, spices, green walnuts, and fresh herbs.

The impact of phenols includes their transformation during barrel heating and/or burning, as well as the interactions with spirit in the presence of oxygen. Thus phenol effects can include "browning," or oxygenation of the phenols; Maillard reactions, in which sugars and amino acids react or transform due to heat; methyloctalactones, or "whisky lactones," including toast or coconut aromas; cyclotene, or maple syrup, grilled, and roasted licorice aromas; maltoland isomaltol, giving aromas of burnt sugar and caramel (both cyclotene and maltol are at least partly responsible for the "toast" aroma in pastries and spirits); furanic aldehydes, with aromas of roasted almonds; furfurals, including aromas of sawdust, maple syrup, toast, toasted almonds, coffee, and caramel; and 5-methyl-furfural, which also offers roasted almond smells. Vanilla is a phenol aldehyde, which is another transformed phenol compound.

As much as phenolic influences can be altered during barrel aging by the condition of the wood and its heating, burning, and such, differing woods (including species of oak) offer differing phenolic and other compounds. American oak is described as containing two or three times more coconut than European oaks (as well as more cocoa and caramel), but some of this (especially the cocoa and caramel) is due to differences in barrel production methods.

See also PHENOL.

"Whiskey Lactone." American Chemical Society. https://www.acs.org/content/acs/en/molecule-of-the-week/archive/w/whiskey-lactone.html (accessed March 27, 2021).

Doug Frost

Laird's, the pioneering American distillers of applejack and apple brandy, is owned by the Laird family: descendants of William Laird of County Fife in Scotland, who in 1698 settled in Monmouth County, New Jersey, then a rich agricultural area across Lower New York Bay from New York City. Although documentation is scarce, Laird family tradition holds that by 1700 William had already drawn on the distilling skills he brought from his homeland

Half-gallon (1.9 liter) bottle for Laird's straight apple brandy, 1930s. Courtesy of Lisa Laird Dunn.

and the abundance of apple orchards in the area to make apple brandy, if initially just for personal use. This was by no means uncommon in that time and place. Some branches of the family continued to produce relatively small quantities of the spirit for local sale. See APPLEJACK.

The current company's origins can be traced to the cider mill a branch of Laird's descendants operated in Scobeyville, an out-of-the-way corner of the county. In 1851, they apparently added a small distillery to the operation, which was taken over by Robert Laird (1835–1912) just after the Civil

War. Laird made improvements to the distillery on numerous occasions, including rebuilding it from scratch in 1871 and again after it burned down in 1875, but it appears to have remained very much a sideline to his cider and apple-butter business, and he appears to have sold largely to the local market until around 1900, although there is a record of him selling some barrels to Park & Tilford, the prominent New York City liquor dealers, in the 1870s.

By this point, applejack was in vogue in the huge New York City market, driven by the popularity of such drinks as the Star Cocktail (an applejack Manhattan), the Widow's Kiss, and the Jack Rose. See JACK ROSE and WIDOW'S KISS. Laird was not the biggest applejack distiller—that was probably the Sayre Bros., in nearby Orange County, New York—or the best known, which was Capt. David Walling, another Monmouth County distiller. But Laird was able to get a premium price for his product, probably because while many of his competitors made their applejack in whole or in part from the "cheese," or pomace left over from cider-pressing, he insisted on making a pure cider brandy from the free-run juice of English redstreak cider apples, most likely using the wooden three-chamber still that was the local industry standard. See STILL, THREE-CHAMBER.

The company survived Laird's death and not only endured Prohibition but thrived by switching production to sweet cider and applesauce, among several other resourceful products. It started distilling again in 1933 when, with Repeal looming, two of Robert Laird's nephews were awarded not only the state's first new distilling permit (making the Scobeyville facility New Jersey DSP 1) but also a federal contract for one million gallons of "medicinal" spirit to help keep the United States supplied until more distilleries could be restarted. From then on, Laird's was far and away the leading applejack distiller in America.

As agricultural land, including orchards for apples and other fruits, slowly dwindled in northern New Jersey, Laird's sought out a more stable source of apples and ultimately shifted distilling operations near Virginia's Shenandoah Valley, which was rich in American history and orchards. Laird's continues to produce its range of apple brandies there to this day, sourcing all of its apples from Virginia. The aging, blending, and bottling still take place in New Jersey.

While Laird & Company has diversified into a range of products for international distribution, their constant focus on heritage helped preserve the Laird's Applejack brand and tradition. The cocktail renaissance of the early twenty-first century saw interest in Laird's applejack awakened from a decades-long slumber as bartenders around the world began to investigate America's distilling and cocktail origins. See COCKTAIL RENAISSANCE. The contemporary focus remains on Laird's Straight Apple Brandy and Bottled-in-Bond Applejack, the latter of which has become a darling of the mixology community. Rarer still are aged apple brandies included in a regular set of limited release offerings. (The entry-level Laird's applejack is a blended product, where straight apple brandy is mixed with neutral spirit; it was introduced in 1972.)

There were once several hundred applejack distilleries; now there is a re-emergence of American craft distilleries producing the spirit today. While the fortunes of applejack have oscillated, Laird's has become synonymous with the category, with over three hundred years dedicated to the family business.

"Jersey Lightning." *Jersey City News*, November 23, 1892, 3.
"A Million Gallons of Apple Brandy." *Red Bank (NJ) Daily Register*, October 4, 1933, 1.
"Monmouth County's Cider Mills." *Red Bank (NJ) Daily Standard*, December 13, 1929, 3.
"Robert Laird's Funeral." *Long Branch (NJ) Daily Record*, March 2, 1912, 1.
"Scobeyville and Vicinity." *Monmouth (NJ) Democrat*, June 8, 1871, 3.
Weiss, Harry B. *The History of Applejack or Apple Brandy in New Jersey*. Trenton: New Jersey Agricultural Society, 1954.

Allen Katz

lambanog, sometimes called lamba or alak ("alcohol"), is a distilled spirit from the Philippines, traditionally made from the sap of nipa or coconut palms. See ARRACK, COCONUT; NIPA; and PHILIPPINES.

It is made primarily in Quezon, a province on Luzon Island southeast of Manila. Though referred to as "coconut vodka" or "coconut wine," lambanog is neither. Rather, it is closer to Goan arrack—and

American moonshine. To make lambanog, plantation workers called *mangagarit* (sickle handlers) scale trees or their surrounding scaffolding to prune flowers from one or more of several palm species. The next day, they collect the resulting sap. Producers either ferment that sap into a popular coconut wine or toddy called *tuba*, which they may sell as-is, or distill into lambanog in direct-fire pot stills, which are often fueled by scrap wood or coconut husks. See STILL, POT.

Commercial brands have existed since the late nineteenth century, but much lambanog continues to be illicitly distilled for domestic markets. Customers often bring their own containers when buying lamba. While coconut flower sap is the traditional substrate, licit and illicit distillers alike may use cane sugar to make their wash.

As with American bootleggers who adulterate moonshine to stretch product and profit, roadside vendors are notorious for cutting and spiking the product, especially the farther they operate from its source. Most production occurs in February and May (the dry season). Its consumption is year-round but rises greatly during fiestas, birthdays, and other special occasions. It may be consumed new, aged, or flavored with spices and seasonal fruits such as mango, jackfruit, grapes, raisins, chico (sapodilla), and mangosteen.

See also ARRACK and MOONSHINE.

Sanchez, P. C. *Philippine Fermented Foods: Principles and Technology*. Honolulu: University of Hawai'i Press, 2008.
Velasco, R. M. "Gender Responsive Value Chain Analysis of the Lambanog Industry in the Philippines." *International Journal of Business and Economic Development* 1. no. 2 (2013).

Matthew Rowley

lao lao is a Laotian whisky distilled from sticky rice and bottled clear and unaged. It is widely regarded as the world's least expensive distilled spirit; full-size bottles can be purchased in Laos for the equivalent of well under a dollar (US). The name "lao lao" is actually two different Laotian words (the language is tonal, so the difference cannot be captured using English spelling) that mean "alcohol" and "Laotian." Most lao lao is produced in small, home-based operations using clay jars for fermentation and distilling

in metal drums over an open flame. See HOME DISTILLING.

Lao lao is typically made during the dry season, January through May, after the year's rice planting and harvest are complete. Steamed rice is mixed with patties of a dough made from pounded dried rice and water called *peng lao* and allowed to ferment for about two weeks before distillation.

Though the spirit can be found in bars throughout the country, many tourists to Laos encounter lao lao production in the village of Ban Xang Hai, also known as "whisky village," near the popular backpacker destination of Luang Prabang. The village is noted for lao lao distillation and sells a variety of bottles, including ones containing snakes, scorpions, and even bear paws.

See also WHISKY, RICE.

Delang, Claudio O. "Keeping the Spirit Alive: Rice Whiskey Production in Northern Lao P.D.R." *Ethnobotany Research and Applications* 6 (2008): 459–470.
Fan, Cindy "Ban Xang Hai." Travelfish.org. http://www.travelfish.org/sight_profile/laos/northern_laos/luang_prabang/luang_prabang/259 (accessed February 18, 2021).

Jason Horn

The **Last Word** is a pre-Prohibition-era concoction composed of equal parts dry gin, maraschino liqueur, Chartreuse, and lime juice. The drink first appears in print in an issue of the *Detroit Athletic Club News* in 1916, where it is listed on a menu, selling for (a high) 35 cents. The recipe was published forty-five years later in Ted Saucier's racy cocktail book *Bottoms Up!* (1951), where an unnamed source from the Detroit Athletic Club writes: "This cocktail was introduced around here about thirty years ago by Frank Fogarty, who was very well known in vaudeville. He was called the 'Dublin Minstrel,' and was a very fine monologue artist." See SAUCIER, TED. Fogarty could have introduced the drink to the area when he performed in Detroit in 1915, just after the club was opened to the public, but there is no other print source linking Fogarty to the Last Word.

The Last Word was largely forgotten until 2003, when bartender Murray Stenson included the drink on the menu at the Zig Zag Cafe in Seattle, Washington. See STENSON, MURRAY. Over the next few years, the Last Word spread across the country and around the world; knowledge of the drink (and its then-obscure ingredients, maraschino liqueur and Chartreuse) signified a serious interest in the mixological arts. The drink is remarkable for its pleasing four-part symmetry and the unexpected harmony of its assertive ingredients. Its formula has inspired scores of new cocktail recipes, notably the Final Ward by Phil Ward and the Naked and Famous by Joaquin Simo.

Recipe: Shake 30 ml each dry gin, maraschino liqueur, Chartreuse, and lime juice with ice, and strain into a stemmed cocktail glass.

See also CHARTREUSE; GIN; and MARASCHINO.

Saucier, Ted. *Bottoms Up*. New York: Greystone, 1951.

St. John Frizell

laudanum is a tincture of opium, that is, an extract of opium made by dissolving it in alcohol. Its principal uses are medicinal, but the concoction was also consumed with recreational abandon by a variety of people in the nineteenth century, most famously the English Romantic writers Thomas de Quincey and Samuel Taylor Coleridge.

The word "laudanum" was first used by the Swiss-German alchemist Paracelsus in the sixteenth century, although it is unclear whether the formula at the time contained opium. The London physician Thomas Sydenham likely made the first recognizable tincture in the 1660s; his recipe is as follows: "One pint of sherry wine, two ounces of good quality Indian or Egyptian opium, one of saffron, a cinnamon stick and a clove, both powdered. Mix and simmer over a vapor bath for two or three days." Later recipes simplified this considerably, macerating the opium in boiling water before adding alcohol. And despite Sydenham's recipe, opium was mostly sourced from Turkey and India. In the latter part of the seventeenth century and throughout the eighteenth and nineteenth centuries, laudanum production and sale proliferated around Europe and North America in the form of a bewildering variety of cordials and preparations to which everything from licorice to pearls to henbane were added. See CORDIALS. (Paregoric, a milder, camphorated tincture of opium, is probably the most famous of these mixtures.) It was sold to the poor and royalty alike,

and given to adults and children alike too. Praised as a panacea, it also killed people if taken in too high a dose. Famous public figures from Thomas Jefferson to Samuel Johnson to Pope Pius VII extolled its virtues.

Apparently the taste was rather bitter. Dosage was measured by the drop, but in the hands of those excessively familiar with it, drops could become glasses. Evidently there was a blurry area between medicinal and recreational use of laudanum. There was also the matter of its addictive potential; however, until the mid-nineteenth century, these issues were little commented on. It was Thomas De Quincey, in his *Confessions of an English Opium Eater* (1822), who gleefully extolled the wonders of a decanter of "ruby red" laudanum, drunk by the wine glass, "warm, and without sugar," with a book of German metaphysics on the table in his Lake Country cottage. He was not alone: Coleridge, Keats, Shelley, Balzac, Baudelaire, Thoreau, Poe, and Novalis all noted the dreamy powers of the beverage. In the process, recreational drug use with its associations of art and youth culture was born.

Although many in the nineteenth century were first exposed to laudanum for medical reasons, and the chemist/druggist shop was likely to be the place of purchase, laudanum was also for sale in grocery stores and via booksellers and traveling peddlers. We are told that in the English Fenlands it was mixed with beer, sometimes by the brewer himself. Nonetheless, its explicit use as an intoxicant was apparently rare—gin remaining considerably cheaper.

The first laws regulating the use of psychoactive substances (the 1868 Poisons and Pharmacy Act in the United Kingdom; the Harrison Narcotic Act of 1914 in the United States) came into being in part because of the excessive unregulated sale and use of opiate-based tonics and beverages such as laudanum. The late nineteenth-century Orientalist vogue for opium smoking, the invention of the hypodermic syringe, and the production of increasingly strong opiates such as morphine and heroin also played a role in the end of the age of the opium drinker. Nonetheless, laudanum is still available by prescription.

Today the ambiguous place of laudanum as a tipple has been taken over by codeine-cough-syrup-based beverages such as purple drank (also known as lean, sizzurp, and Texas tea), a cocktail of codeine and promethazine, mixed with soft drinks such as

Sprite and ice cubes, served in a Styrofoam cup, first popularized by hip-hop artists in Houston, Texas, in the early 1990s.

See also GIN and HEALTH AND SPIRITS.

Booth, Martin. *Opium: A History*. New York: St. Martin's, 1998.

De Quincey, Thomas. *Confessions of an English Opium Eater*. Harmondsworth, UK: Penguin, 1971.

Dormandy, Thomas. *Opium: Reality's Dark Dream*. New Haven, CT: Yale University Press, 2012.

Marcus Boon

layering is a technique that produces a colorful, rainbow-like effect in a tall cocktail or shooter glass. Shooters like the Pousse Café and B-52 are classic examples of this technique, but almost any drink can be layered. See POUSSE CAFÉ.

Layering exploits the varying densities or specific gravities and viscosities of the liquids, which generally depend on their sugar, alcohol, and water content, with the sweetest liqueurs being the densest (heavy cream, a common Pousse Café ingredient, is a special case). The denser liquids will sink to the bottom of the glass while the lighter liquids float on top. Distilled spirits with no added sugar, such as brandy and vodka, have the lowest density because of their high alcohol content; this makes them prone to miscibility and difficult to layer, and they are generally reserved for use as the top layer. Sweetened spirits—liqueurs and cordials—as a category have widely varying sugar levels, which makes them ideal for layering.

There are multiple ways to layer a drink, with some methods calling for the liqueurs to be poured over the back of a spoon and down the wall of the glass, starting with the densest liquid first. Other methods start by pouring the lightest elements first and then streaming the next densest liquid down the middle of the layers, sometimes with the help of special gadgets; this effectively pushes the other liquids on top. Both methods work well and produce visually appealing drinks.

See also POUSSE CAFÉ and SHOOTER.

Regan, Gary. *The Joy of Mixology*. New York: Clarkson Potter, 2003.

Darcy O'Neil

Lefeuvre, Émile (1847–1891), published the first French book dedicated to mixing drinks in the American style and thus stands at the head of the long and fertile tradition of French cocktail books. Born Amedée-Cyril Lefeuvre at Grivesnes, 100 km north of Paris, he left his hometown sometime after his 1872 marriage there and went to work in Paris as a *limonadier*, or coffeehouse keeper. By 1878, he was running a place on his own at 14 boulevard des Batignolles in the Seventeenth Arrondissement, behind Montmartre. In 1882, however, he was back working for others, at the large, two-hundred-seat Café de la Céramique, located at 20 rue du Paradis in the more centrally located Tenth Arrondissement. Lefeuvre tried again to open a new place with a partner in 1887 (at 34 boulevard de Clichy in Pigalle), but it went bankrupt the following year. In 1889, after over a decade in the business, Lefeuvre had considerable experience with an international clientele, had learned to speak English, and had mastered the suite of drinks and techniques belonging to the so-called American bar. Using these accomplishments, in April of that year he published "*Méthode de composer soi-même les boissons Américaines, Anglaises, Italiennes, etc.*" (roughly, "How to mix American, English, Italian and other drinks"), identifying himself on the title page as a "Chef de Bar Cosmopolite" ("cosmopolitan head bartender"). In France, a "bar cosmopolite" was one that made international drinks as well as the standard French ones. The book was timed to come out before that year's Exposition Universelle (for which the Eiffel Tower was built), to welcome the foreigners and help his professional peers to be able to prepare and serve the most popular drinks and bar snacks from America, Denmark, England, Italy, Norway, Russia, and so forth. In addition to the 130-odd recipes for mixed drinks, including most of the American standards (but not the Manhattan or the Martini), there are serving instructions for Russian vodka, Scandinavian aquavit, and other such national drinks (including a "Vermuth di Torino au Fernet-Branca" the first known appearance of the classic Italian combination of vermouth and a bitter aperitif or digestive, which would give rise to the Americano and the Negroni). See AMERICANO and NEGRONI. There are also fifteen recipes for sandwiches and such from various European countries and America and an extensive French-English vocabulary and phrasebook for bars and restaurants.

After publishing the book, Lefeuvre tried to set up an association to help employers to find staff looking for opportunities to work in Paris and make it easier for both parties. Then, at the end of 1890, he went back to his hometown, where he died on February 10 of the next year. Nonetheless, Lefeuvre was a true pioneer, particularly in the international orientation he gave his book, something not found in, for example, Leo Engel's 1878 *American and Other Drinks*, the first English cocktail book. See Engel, Leo. In that, Lefeuvre would set the tone for subsequent European books of its kind.

Annuaire-almanach du commerce, de l'industrie, de la magistrature et de l'administration. Paris: Firmin Didot et Bottin réunis, 1878–1893.
"Jugements du 6 Mars." *Le soleil* (Paris), March 15, 1888, 4.
Lefeuvre, Émile. *Méthode pour composer soi-même les boissons Américaines, Anglaises, Italiennes, etc.* Paris: Lefeuvre, 1889.
"Vérifications et affirmations." *La loi* (Paris), August 12, 1882, 4.

Fernando Castellon

legs (or **tears**) refer to the trail of liquid left by a spirit on the inside of a glass when it is tilted or swirled. Observing the quality of the legs as a determinant of body is a common step in the initial visual assessment of a liquor during a tasting session. Thick, slow-moving legs indicate greater viscosity, which may be a function of more advanced age, higher alcohol, or added sugar.

McGhee, Harold. *On Food and Cooking: The Science and Lore of the Kitchen*, rev. ed. New York: Scribner, 2004.

David Mahoney

Lemon Drop is a cocktail that falls under the family of mixed drinks invented in the Tiffany-lamp and greenery-filled world of the 1970s fern bar, drinks that include blended Daiquiris, wine spritzers, and the Harvey Wallbanger. The Lemon Drop was invented in San Francisco by Norman Hobday, owner of Henry Africa's—arguably the first, and certainly one of the quintessential, genre-defining fern bars of the day.

Henry Africa, aka Norman Hobday, in Henry Africa's, home of the Lemon Drop, in 1983. Courtesy of the *San Francisco Chronicle*.

Though later devolving to a simple chilled vodka shot served with a sugar-coated lemon wedge, the original Lemon Drop was a more elegant affair, served up in a sugar-rimmed cocktail glass. Henry Africa's distinguished itself by using premium spirits and fresh juices to order, meaning that the lemon drops served there would have undoubtedly included freshly squeezed lemon juice. The Lemon Drop later became a staple of the legendary bar Harry Denton's Starlight Room in San Francisco, owned by former Henry Africa's bartender Harry Denton.

Recipe: Shake 60 ml vodka (or citrus vodka), 30 ml simple syrup, and 45 ml fresh lemon juice with ice and strain into a sugar-rimmed cocktail coupe.

See also Henry Africa's and Fern Bars.

Hobday, Norman and Denton, Harry. Interviews, 2010.

McDonnell, Duggan. *Drinking the Devil's Acre: A Love Letter from San Francisco and Her Cocktails.* San Francisco: Chronicle Books, 2015.

Walker, Judy. "Tales of the Cocktail of 'Fern Bars' Seminar is a Trip down Memory Lane." *Times-Picayune*, July 26, 2010. http://www.nola.com/food/index. ssf/2010/07/fern_bars_seminar_is_a_trip_do.html (accessed February 18, 2021).

Whiting, Sam. "Henry Africa—Dies." *San Francisco Chronicle*, March 2, 2011.

Martin Cate

Lewis bag is the modern term for the stout sack, usually made of canvas, used to hold ice so that it may be cracked with a bat or mallet. Ice bag-and-mallet sets were a common household item in 1920s America, ostensibly for use in ice cream making, which requires large quantities of cracked ice. Of course, so does mixing drinks, then illegal due to Prohibition, and one may assume that many of these sets at least did double duty.

Usually these sets consisted of a largish bag of perhaps 10 by 15 inches (25 by 37.5 cm) with a good-sized wooden mallet of conventional construction. By the 1940s, smaller sets began appearing that were more adapted to making a round or two of drinks than a tub of ice cream. Some of these replaced the mallet with a turned wooden bat, handier if less efficient. One such set bore on its box the verse

> With this small mallet gently whack
> Some chunks of ice inside the sack
> And with no bother, in a trice
> You'll have some cleanly broken ice.

Such bar niceties faded away in the 1970s, perhaps hastened by the rise of the blender and the decline of stirred drinks, the main style that requires cracked ice. However, in the late 1990s, just in time for the cocktail renaissance, an item called "The Lewis—Authentic 1940s Ice Bag" began appearing in stores, with the bag accompanied by a standard wooden muddler in place of the bat and a little booklet of classic cocktails. Before long, bartenders and cocktail enthusiasts began making their own bags, for which "Lewis bag" had become (de facto, anyway) the generic name.

The Lewis bag is still the best way of producing the very finely cracked ice demanded by drinks such as the Mint Julep: with a large, heavy mallet, it is quick and thorough, and the canvas wicks away excess moisture. See ICE MALLET and MINT JULEP.

Wondrich, David. *Esquire Drinks*. New York: Hearst, 2002.

David Wondrich

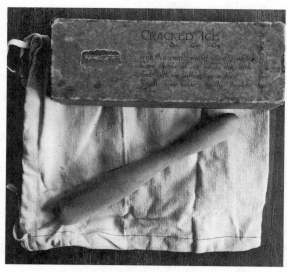

The 1930s precursor to the Lewis bag and "mallet." Wondrich Collection.

light-aroma-style baijiu is a spirit made from sorghum. Traditionally the grain is fermented in pots placed just below ground level to maintain a steady temperature, though today it is sometimes fermented in stone or stainless steel pits to increase yields. The style originated in northern China, and its name refers to the relative mildness of flavor rather than its strength, as it is frequently bottled at an eye-watering excess of 60 percent ABV. Of the many baijiu varieties, light-aroma's production process is one of the cheapest and least labor-intensive; thus it has become a ubiquitous mainstay of working class Chinese.

There are two principal subdivisions of the light-aroma style: *erguotou* and *fenjiu*. Erguotou, best exemplified by leading brands Red Star and Niulanshan, is Beijing's signature baijiu. Its name, which means "second pot head," refers to a distilling method pioneered by the Zhao brothers in the late seventeenth century. Traditional Chinese pot stills used a condenser filled and refilled with pots of cold water, and the Zhaos determined that the spirit made during the second of the three necessary fillings—what a Western distiller would call the "heart"—was of the finest quality. See CHINESE STILL. Following the Communist Revolution of 1949, erguotou followed Chiang Kai-shek's Nationalist government to Taiwan, where with only slight production differences it became known as *kaoliang*, or "sorghum" spirit. Other characteristics typical of modern erguotou include the use of bran-based big qu as its fermentation agent, short fermentation cycles performed in small pits, and the use of neutral spirits in the blending process. See QU.

Fenjiu is named after Fenzhou (modern-day Fenyang, Shanxi Province), whose Xinghuacun Distillery invented the style. It is considered a more refined light-aroma, with greater complexity of flavors. Fenjiu is generally fermented in clay pots using big qu made from barley and peas. Following distillation, rice husks and more qu are added to the sorghum mash, which is fermented and distilled a second time.

Both styles are aged in ceramic or stainless steel jars, erguotou for at least six months, fenjiu for at least a year.

See also BAIJIU; RED STAR; and SORGHUM.

Huang Faxin, David Tiande Cai, and Wai-Kit Nip. "Chinese Wines: Jiu." In *Handbook of Food Science, Technology, and Engineering*, vol. 4 by Yiu H. Hui: 173-1–52. Boca Raton, FL: CRC Press, 2005.

Derek Sandhaus

lignin is a complex organic polymer that gives vascular plants their fibrous, woody character. Lignin is a major component of wood (between 15 and 35 percent of the dry material), supplying the material for the rigid tubular systems (xylem and phloem) that are necessary for the distribution of water and nutrient fluids (sap) throughout the plant. When altered by heat or fire, lignins offer aromas of vanilla, eugenol (clove), and 4-methylguaiacol (or vanilla/spicy/smoky aromas). See AROMA.

"Lignin." American Chemical Society. https://www.acs.org/content/acs/en/molecule-of-the-week/archive/1/lignin.html (accessed February 9, 2021).

Doug Frost

limoncello is a lemon liqueur traditionally produced in Southern Italy, especially along the Sorrentine Peninsula. (The region's lemon growers even have a protected designation for their Sorrento or oval lemon.) Today, other citrus-growing regions of the world, such as the United States' California, also produce limoncello, a reflection of the spirit's growing popularity, which has taken it from Italian specialty to global staple. Although it is not known exactly where or when it was first produced, with accounts of limoncello dating back at least a century, it remained almost exclusively a local specialty until the 1990s. The basic recipe has remained more or less unchanged: lemon peel, free of pith, is steeped in a clear, neutral spirit, such as grappa or vodka, and sweetened with sugar. See GRAPPA and VODKA.

Andrews, Betsy. "One Good Bottle: Limoncello." *Saveur*, May 24, 2010, https://www.saveur.com/article/Wine-and-Drink/One-Good-Bottle-1000083177/ (accessed February 18, 2021).

Clarke, Paul. "Homemade Limoncello." *Imbibe Magazine*, July 10, 2014.

Gulick, Amy. "Limoncello Sorbet." *Italy Magazine*, July 7, 2015.

Rebecca Rothbaum

The **Lincoln County process** is a method of filtering new whisky through hardwood charcoal—typically maple—before it is put in the barrel. This step is associated with Tennessee whisky, although it was not a requirement until 2013 (because there were no requirements for Tennessee whisky until then). Prichard's Tennessee Whisky does not charcoal-filter its distillate before putting it into the barrel and was exempted from the new regulation. Jack Daniels and George Dickel, the two largest producers of Tennessee whisky, both filter their product. George Dickel chills theirs first.

The Lincoln County process is so named because the Jack Daniels distillery was in Lincoln County until the county lines were redrawn. There is no distillery employing the Lincoln County process in Lincoln County at this time. Adding to the irony, the county that Jack Daniels found itself in is dry.

To filter fresh whisky, sugar maple is converted to charcoal and put in vats, which are subsequently filled with fresh distillate. The distillate can be trickled through the charcoal, as it is at Jack Daniels, or the distiller can fill up the vat before the spirit is drained, as it is at George Dickel. The idea of filtering whisky through charcoal before aging it is nothing new: a 1908 study of American whisky found four out of thirty-four bourbon and rye distilleries studied ran their raw distillate through charcoal-packed "leach tubes" prior to barreling.

There is some mythology about the process. Some believe, falsely, that it disqualifies Tennessee whisky from being bourbon. It doesn't. The only reason Tennessee whisky isn't called bourbon is because it is called Tennessee whisky. (Some bourbons are in fact filtered in a similar manner, though none of them would call it the Lincoln County process, for reasons that should be obvious.) Some believe that the process of filtering the whisky through maple charcoal before it enters the barrel removes substantial flavor from the spirit, although others insist that it does not. Inarguably, the Lincoln County process grants the aging of the whisky a head start.

See also WHISKY, TENNESSEE; and JACK DANIEL'S.

Camacho, LeNell. "Chalk One Up for the Charcoal". *The Alcohol Professor*, May 13, 2013. https://www.alcoholprofessor.com/blog-posts/blog/2013/05/13/chalk-one-up-for-the-charcoal (accessed March 24, 2021).

Crampton, C. A., and L. M. Tolman. "A Study of the Changes Taking Place in Whiskey Stored in Wood." *Journal of the American Chemical Society* 30 (January 1908): 98–136.

Max Watman

linie aquavit is a style of Norwegian aquavit double distilled from a base of potatoes. The initial base spirit is distilled in a column still to 96 percent ABV. The second distillation adds a variety of flavoring botanicals in a pot still. Caraway is the signature flavoring botanical, while dill, anise, fennel, and coriander are often included in the botanical mix.

Stylistically, Linie aquavits have a unique form of maturation, as the spirit is placed in 500-liter Spanish oloroso sherry casks for twelve months in a warehouse, before being sent out for four to six months at sea, crossing the equator twice as deck cargo on ships from Norway to Australia and back again. The constant rolling motion of the ship and the fluctuating temperatures during the journey help to mature the spirit during its journey. The name *linie* is the Norwegian word for "line," referencing the two trips that are made across the equator while the spirit matures.

The first linie-style aquavit was created by accident. In 1805 Jorgen B. Lysholms (1796–1843), a merchant from Trondheim, Norway, sent a shipment of aquavit in barrels to Indonesia. Several of the barrels went unsold and were returned to Norway two years later, having been mellowed by the transoceanic journey. Stylistically, linie aquavit has a more mellow caraway character, with the sherry-butt influence adding candied fruit and vanilla notes. The major Norwegian producers of linie aquavits are Arcus Gruppen (Lysholm) and Loiten.

See also: ABV; AGING; AQUAVIT; CARAWAY; COLUMN STILL; KUMMEL; SHERRY; COLUMN STILL; and STILL, POT.

Lexi. "Snaps Visa: Norway's Equatorial Aquavit." *Norwegian American Weekly*, April 8, 2016. https://www.norwegianamerican.com/food/snaps-visa-norways-equatorial-aquavit/ (accessed February 18, 2021).

"Lysholm." *Throndjhems Aquavit Club*. http://www.aquavitclub.no/om-aquavit/lysholm/ (accessed February 18, 2021).

Lance J. Mayhew

liqueurs are spirits that have been flavored and heavily sweetened. See CORDIALS. "Liqueur" was also formerly used as an adjective, attached to "brandy" or "whisky," denoting that the spirit so described was old and rich and could be sipped like a liqueur. See BRANDY and WHISKY.

Llull, Ramon (1232–1316), also known as Raymond Lull, was a Catalan philosopher and theologian of the Franciscan order who made important contributions to the development of formal logic and Medieval literature. He is often incorrectly described as an alchemist and pioneer of alcohol distillation. The confusion arises from anonymous authors who published works under his name. These imposter writings are known as the pseudo-Llull corpus. This situation is quite common in the history of alchemy: alchemy writers often used the names of famous wise men to give their writings greater authority, and to avoid being condemned as charlatans or heretics. The real Ramon Llull opposed the practice of alchemy.

The key pseudo-Llull text concerning alcohol is the *Testament*, published in 1332. *Testament* describes the process of distilling alcohol from wine and claims this process was known to "the ancients" but kept secret. The *Testament* contains the earliest known expression of the concept of pure alcohol ("aqua ardens"), as a distinct substance that is separated from water by means of distillation.

Ultimately 143 texts would falsely claim Llull as their author. A whole mythos grew around the "alchemist" Ramon Llull. According to one story he traveled to England and offered to turn lead into gold for King Edward, on condition that Edward use it to finance a crusade. Llull produced the gold, but the king locked him away and invaded France instead.

The life of the real Ramon Llull was even more impressive than the myth. He was the son of a wealthy Palma family who took up a troubadour life until he had a "come to Jesus moment." According to his autobiography, he was composing a "vulgar tongued" love song one night when Christ appeared to him, floating in midair on the cross. Ramon woke the next morning thinking it had all been a bad dream, but he saw the vision five more times. Finally he gave up his sinful ways and joined the Third Order of Saint Francis.

He believed his divine mission was to convert Muslims to Christianity using rational arguments and logic rather than violent coercion (the preferred method of the day). He learned Arabic (from a Muslim slave), read Arabic philosophy, and developed a system of logic that was a very early precursor to computer science. He also wrote one of the first European novels, *Blanquerna*, and pioneered the mathematical theory of elections. His fans dubbed him "Doctor Illuminatus."

At the age of eighty-two, his zeal to convert the "unbelievers" did him in. He traveled to Béjaïa (in modern day Algeria), where an angry crowd, uninterested in his rational arguments, stoned him to death.

See DISTILLATION, HISTORY.

Forbes, R. J. *Short History of the Art of Distillation*. Leiden: E. J. Brill, 1948.

Llull, Ramon. *Doctor Illuminatus: A Ramon Llull Reader*. Edited and translated by Anthony Bonner. Princeton, NJ: Princeton University Press, 1993.

Principe, Lawrence M. *The Secrets of Alchemy*. Chicago: University of Chicago Press, 2013.

Sam Eilertsen

loggerhead was an iron rod used in the making of flip, a popular colonial-era heated beverage. The rod ranged in length from approximately 50–125 cm (eighteen inches to four feet), and in form it resembled a fireplace poker. The working end was often thicker than the shaft and at times featured a small, bulbous head resembling a small onion.

The loggerhead was initially employed by early shipbuilders to keep the tar used for seam sealing warm and pliable; the rod was placed in a fire until red-hot and then used to stir the tar. Via an uncertain route, the loggerhead made its way into taverns, where it was employed in the heating of drinks. Tavern historian Alice Morse Earle wrote that loggerheads were "as much a part of the chimney furniture of an old time New England tavern and farmhouse as the bellows or andirons." Flip was among the most popular drinks made with loggerheads and typically consisted of rum, beer, and molasses. In

1868 the poet James Lowell celebrated the sound of the loggerhead as it performed its duties:

> Here dozed a fire of beechen logs, that bred
> Strange fancies in its embers golden-red,
> And nursed the loggerhead whose hissing dip,
> Timed by nice instinct, creamed the mug
> of flip.

When tavern discussions became overly animated, tavern-goers would at times grab the loggerheads and employ them as cudgels. As such, these implements live on in a somewhat feral fashion in the oft-used but little understood term "at loggerheads."

Other names for the loggerhead include flip iron, flip dog, and hottle.

See also FLIP.

Earle, Alice Morse. *Stage-Coach and Tavern Days.* New York: Macmillan, 1900.

Wayne Curtis

log still is an unusual form of steam still made from one or more hollowed-out logs. The original design was patented by an American inventor named Robert Gillespie in the early nineteenth century. Variations on the theme were used by some early rye whisky and bourbon distillers, and the name was retained in industry usage to describe the large, wooden three-chamber stills used by many American distillers until Prohibition. See STILL, TYPES OF; WHISKY, RYE; and WHISKY, BOURBON.

London dry gin, characterized by its lack of sweetening and its crisp, juniper-led botanical blend, became the predominant style of gin at the beginning of the twentieth century and still remains so, although its hegemony is weakening with the twenty-first century's interest in innovation in the category. See GIN and BOTANICAL. Despite the geographic specificity of its name, it can be made anywhere in the world.

long drink is a category of mixed drink served in a highball or Collins glass, often over ice. As a technical term of mixology, "long drink" is chiefly British and European. It began, however, as a bit of early nineteenth-century American slang, applied to any tall, refreshing drink. In the 1870s, British bartenders began pairing it with "short drinks" in a binary classification of the new, American-style iced mixed drinks then coming into vogue. Among the American families of drinks

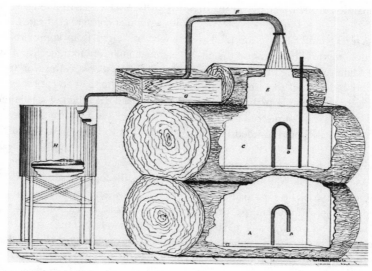

The two-chamber steam still built by Richard E. Wathen of Marion County, Kentucky, out of poplar logs. Wondrich Collection.

that were lumped together under it were cobblers, coolers, fizzes, and juleps. This binary system became standard in Europe but never caught on in the United States.

Long drinks typically are lower in ABV than short drinks, due to the amount of ice and mixers involved—often soda water or fruit juice of some kind. See SODA WATER and FRUIT JUICE. Because they have an overall reputation as being light and refreshing, long drinks proliferate in warm-weather months. The archetypal long drink is the Tom Collins. See TOM COLLINS. Other classic examples include the Pimm's Cup, Dark and Stormy, Gin and Tonic, Cuba Libre, and any number of simple highballs. See PIMM'S CUP; DARK AND STORMY; GIN AND TONIC; CUBA LIBRE; and HIGHBALL.

See also GLASSWARE.

Grimes, William. *Straight Up or On the Rocks*, 2nd ed. New York: North Point Press, 2001.

Robert Simonson

The **Long Island Iced Tea**, notorious for its innocent-tasting potency, is served worldwide and has spawned numerous alcoholic beverages with "tea" in their name. Its most-cited origin story is that bartender Robert "Rosebud" Butt (1947–2014) created the drink for a cocktail contest among the bartenders at the popular Oak Beach Inn in Oak Beach, New York, on Long Island in 1972. His winning recipe was equal parts rum, vodka, gin, tequila (all the white spirits in his well), and triple sec, with splashes of sour mix and cola, served over ice. In his 1998 book, *Scandal at the Oak Bach Inn*, Robert Matheson, the bar's owner, confirms Butt's claim but cites 1973 as the year of the drink's creation. In a PBS Digital Studios profile of Butt in 2013 and on a website Butt created about the drink, he dismisses an anecdote (from a 2006 book) that the Long Island Iced Tea derives from a Prohibition-era drink called the Old Man Bishop, and indeed that claim is completely undocumented. (Another widely repeated claim, by Long Island bartender Craig Weisman, that he and his coworkers created the drink at the popular catering hall Leonard's of Great Neck founders on the fact that the drink was already well known on Long Island when he began working there in 1976.) TGI Friday's, which started in New York City in 1965, also claims to have invented the drink, again without documentation. In any case, the drink first surfaced in 1976 when a Long Island newspaper identified it as a "currently popular, brain-destroying discotheque fad drink." Within five years, it had spread to the rest of America, and soon after to the rest of the world.

Ladies' Night drink ticket from the Oak Beach Inn East, Hampton Bays, New York—the home of the Long Island Iced Tea, 1981. Wondrich Collection.

Recipe: 30 ml each of rum, vodka, gin, tequila, and triple sec with splashes of sour mix and cola. Serve over ice.

See also TGI FRIDAY'S.

DeGroff, Dale. *The Essential Cocktail: The Art of Mixing Perfect Drinks*. New York: Clarkson Potter, 2008.
"Long Island Iced Tea." *Inventors*, February 21, 2013. https://www.youtube.com/watch?v=NRwCjlfyNGQ (accessed February 18, 2021).
"Long Island Iced Tea." OED Appeals, April 21, 2013, citations. http://public.oed.com/appeals/long-island-iced-tea/ (accessed February 18, 2021).
Lowe, Ed. "Practicing before the Bar." *Newsday*, October 7, 1976, 1A.

Lauren Clark

louche is a French term meaning cloudy, disturbed (as in silty water), shadowy, and—by extension—disreputable. It is used to describe the clouding effect in absinthe upon adding water. It is also known as the "ouzo effect."

Absinthe is rich in anethole, the essential oil derived from aniseed, star anise, and fennel seed that is responsible for absinthe's licorice-like flavor. This oil dissolves readily in high-proof alcohol but is insoluble in water. During dilution, when the water-to-absinthe ratio reaches a certain point, the anethole drops out of solution and forms a suspension of microscopic oil droplets in the water—a microemulsion or colloid—creating the attractive, opalescent, cloudy effect known as the louche.

A proper louche is among the characteristics used to evaluate fine absinthe, not merely for its visual aesthetic but as a gauge of flavor balance and finesse in craftsmanship. The louche of a properly prepared glass of absinthe should be opalescent, translucent, and glowing. It is best observed in natural daylight. It should not be either too opaque or too transparent, indicating the absinthe contains either too much or not enough aniseed, respectively. A thick, milk-like, opaque louche will present an overpowering aniseed character, more like ouzo or sambuca, numbing the tongue and obscuring the finer nuances of the more delicate herbs. A thin louche will provide an insipid and watery drink with little character. Some faux absinthes, common to central and eastern Europe, avoid the aniseed flavor (which is why they are categorized as faux absinthe). These often contain gums and resins or other oil-rich spices to obtain the expected louche. This shortcut was a hallmark of an improperly made absinthe in the nineteenth century, just as it is today.

See also ABSINTHE and OUZO.

Nathan-Maister, David. *The Absinthe Encyclopedia*. Burgess Hill, UK: Oxygenee Press, 2009.
Wormwood Society Absinthe Association website. https://www.wormwoodsociety.org (accessed February 18, 2021).

Gwydion Stone

low-pressure distillation, or vacuum distillation, is a high-efficiency alternative to traditional distilling. Distillation at normal atmospheric temperatures is an energy-intensive process. Under normal pressure at sea level, ethanol boils at 78.4° C, but if one lowers the pressure by 50 percent (to half an atmosphere), ethanol will boil at 63° C. This means less energy is required to achieve the same goal, making production more affordable and environmentally friendly. See ENVIRONMENTAL IMPACT OF DISTILLATION.

In a low-pressure distillation setup, the system is sealed, and a pump is used to reduce the internal pressure. The distillation system operates in the same manner as a normal atmospheric still, just at a lower temperature and pressure.

An added benefit of a low-pressure distillation unit is the capability of improved fractionation to produce a purer distillate. The heavier organic compounds found in fusel oils, like propanol and amyl alcohol, are not as volatile as ethanol. The boiling point of these fusel compounds at half an atmosphere requires slightly more energy than normal to boil, resulting in easier fractionation. These slight changes in the volatility of the fusel oils may seem insignificant, but over the course of a long distillation run this makes a significant improvement in the purity of the distillate. The lower heat required also serves to preserve some delicate aromatic compounds that break down at higher temperatures, making it useful for botanically derived or flavored spirits.

Because of the complex nature of low-pressure distillation, it is best suited for large-scale spirit production (although the countertop Rotovap vacuum still is used by many high-end cocktail bars to produce small quantities of unique ingredients;

see ROTARY EVAPORATOR). Despite its obvious advantages for certain types of spirit, the only one for which it is in widespread use is Japanese shochu, although some American distilleries did experiment with it in the mid-twentieth century. See SHOCHU.

See also FUSEL OIL.

McGee, Harold. "A Chill at the Still to Keep Flavors Fresh." *New York Times*, December 1, 2009.
Willkie, Herman F., and Joseph A. Prochaska. *Fundamentals of Distillery Practice*. Louisville, KY: Jos. E. Seagram & Sons, 1943.

Darcy O'Neil

low wines is a term used to designate the relatively low-alcohol distillate that emerges from the first distillation run of a double distillation. See DISTILLATE; DOUBLE DISTILLATION; and HIGH WINES.

Luxardo, based in Torreglia in the Veneto region of Italy, is a leader in the liqueur industry, with products distributed worldwide. Its flagship liqueur, Luxardo Maraschino, is made from marasca cherries and is an ingredient in numerous classic cocktails. See AVIATION COCKTAIL; LAST WORD; and MARASCHINO. The company also produces its own brands of sambuca, amaretto, fernet, limoncello and grappa, among other products. See SAMBUCA; FERNET; LIMONCELLO; and GRAPPA. A second product line includes confectionary liqueurs, maraschino cherries, jams, and fruit syrups. Girolamo Luxardo of Genoa, Italy, established the company in 1821 in Dalmatia (part of Croatia), which was then part of the Austrian Empire. Its facilities were heavily damaged during World War II, and the company moved to its present location in 1947.

Luxardo website http://www.luxardo.it/ (accessed February 18, 2021).

Lauren Clark

Luzhou Laojiao is a strong-aroma-style baijiu distillery based in Luzhou, a city in southwestern

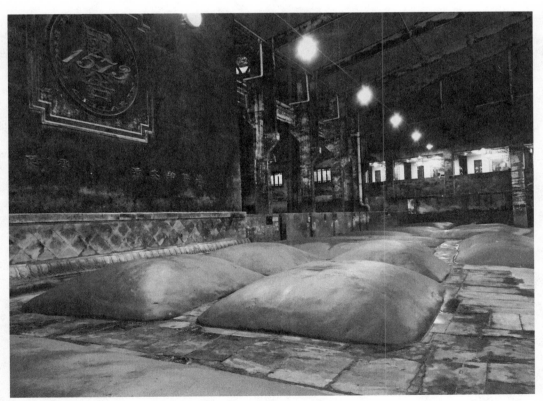

The oldest fermenting pits in Luzhou (*center*), capped with river clay. They date back to 1573. Courtesy of Derek Sandhaus.

China's Sichuan Province. Luzhou's winemaking tradition spans about two thousand years and boasts such luminaries as Guo Huaiyu, alleged creator of big-qu baijiu in the fourteenth century, and Shi Jinzhang, who invented pit-fermented baijiu in the fifteenth century. See DA QU. The Luzhou Laojiao Distillery was founded in 1951, when the Chinese government merged dozens of local distilleries into a state-run entity.

Luzhou Laojiao is best known as the pioneer of the "thousand-year pit, ten-thousand-year mash" production method. This involves fermenting a grain mash in large earthen pits, the walls of which absorb yeasts and other microorganisms from the fermentation cycle over time. After a mash is distilled, one quarter is discarded and replaced with fresh grains and qu to begin fermentation anew. A mash is always returned to the same pit, creating an unending cycle that ensures continuity of flavor.

Conventional wisdom suggests that the longer a fermentation pit is used, the greater the complexity of the resulting baijiu. To be fully mature, an "old pit" has to have been in continuous use for at least thirty years. Luzhou Laojiao currently operates 1,600 old pits, more than a thousand of which are at least a century old. It also owns the most ancient baijiu pits in continuous operation, dating from 1573.

In 1959 the Chinese government commissioned the distillery to write the first technical manual for modern baijiu production, *Luzhou Laojiao big qu baijiu*. It remains an industry leader, particularly for its single-grain strong-aroma-style baijiu, and currently has a stated annual production capacity of 100 million liters.

See also CHINA and STRONG-AROMA-STYLE BAIJIU.

Wang Wen. "High-End Chinese Brands Coming Soon." *Xinhua*, May 1, 2012.

Yang Chen, ed. *Lu Zhou Lao Jiao: Zhong Guo Rong Yao* 泸州老窖：中国荣耀. Chengdu: Qiyuan Zhiban 启源制版, 2010.

Derek Sandhaus

M

The **Macallan** is a single malt scotch whisky first made in 1824 by tenant farmer and former school-teacher Alexander Reid (1782–1847) at Easter Elchies in the heart of Speyside, Scotland. From its humble beginnings, the Macallan has exploded both in size and reputation, to the point where it serves for many as the embodiment of scotch luxury: fans have tagged it the "Rolls-Royce of whisky" and the "Dom Perignon of scotch." In 2014, a Macallan bottling—called simply M—sold for a whopping world-record price of $604,205 to a Hong Kong collector at auction. So strong, in fact, is the collectors' market for older expressions of the brand that it has been plagued by a rash of counterfeit bottlings.

While the whisky made at Easter Elchies always had a reputation for quality even as the distillery passed through several hands after the death of Reid's son in 1848, its survival, like that of many

Pot stills and their heat exchangers at the Macallan distillery, Craigellachie, Scotland. Courtesy of Edrington.

single malt Scotch whiskies, originally depended on supplying liquid for blending houses to sell under brand names such as the Famous Grouse. It wasn't until the latter half of the twentieth century that the distillery—owned by the Kemp family since 1892 when distiller Roderick Kemp (1838–1909) bought it, modernized it, and renamed it the Macallan-Glenlivet after the stream on which it was situated—would release its range of distinctive malt whiskies, which are classically characterized by flavors born of mashing Golden Promise barley, distilling in squat pot stills, and maturing in Spanish sherry oak casks. (The Kemps sold the brand to Highland distillers in 1996.)

By the turn of the millennium, increased whisky demand meant big changes for the Macallan. Sherry butts became increasingly expensive and rare. The Macallan responded to these outside forces by introducing the Fine Oak range in 2004, a collection that was largely aged in bourbon casks, with much less sherry-cask influence.

The Macallan was bought by the Edrington Group (now simply Edrington) in 1999, which markets and bottles the Fine Oak range, the Sherry Oak range, the 1824 series, and the Fine and Rare series, along with limited editions. See EDRINGTON. The Macallan ranks consistently as both a best-selling and top investment-grade brand of Scotch.

In 2018, the Macallan opened a striking new state-of-the-art combined distillery and visitors' center that uses a flowing, grass-covered roof to blend into the landscape. Its stillroom, with thirty-six new pot stills, is designed to be easily expanded, should the brand's sales continue to swell.

See also SINGLE MALT.

Bruce-Gardyne, Tom. "The Macallan: A Brand History." *Spirits Business*, December 2018.

Heather Greene

MacDonald, Aeneas, was the pseudonym of George Malcolm Thomson, publisher of the Porpoise Press, which was at the heart of the early twentieth-century Scottish literary renaissance. His book *Whisky*, published in 1930, is by turns a hard-eyed look at and lyrical evocation of scotch whisky's history, production, and methods of consumption. It is also one of the earliest paeans to single malt whisky and is widely recognized as one of the finest

publications on the subject. It has been reprinted several times in recent years.

MacDonald, Aeneas. *Whisky*. Edited by Ian Buxton. London: Birlinn, 2016.

Dave Broom

maceration is a method of extracting the oils and flavor compounds from a given amount of herbs and spices in a suitable medium such as alcohol, water, glycerin, or combinations of different solvents; it is used for making bitters and syrups and as part of the process in making absinthe and many liqueurs. The most basic method of maceration is to mix the compounds with a solvent in a suitable vessel and allow the mixture to sit for a period, with occasional agitation but without heating, as in infusion. See INFUSION. The mixture is then separated by decanting or filtration and the liquid portion retained.

More complex methods of maceration use precise quantities of solvents as well as exact time requirement to produce an extract with a known potency and to provide a level of consistency from batch to batch. This method was employed by early pharmacists using an apparatus known as a percolator.

A percolator is a large glass cylinder with a stopcock at the bottom. The herbs and spices are packed into the cylinder, and then the solvent is added; the mixture is then macerated for a specific period, and the extract collected using the stopcock. Depending on the method or materials, different solvents like ethanol and water can be used in succession to isolate specific compounds or remove unwanted compounds like bitter alkaloids.

Because maceration is a gentle process, it is used to extract volatile flavors and delicate ones. Certain liqueurs employ it in parallel with distillation, so that an ingredient such as, for example, orange peels will be both distilled in alcohol and macerated in it, with the two liquids blended to make the final product. Maceration is also often used with ingredients that impart color to a liquid, as colors do not survive distillation and are often degraded by heat.

See also ABSINTHE; BITTERS; and GRAND MARNIER.

Rack, John. *The French Wine and Liquor Manufacturer*. New York: Dick & Fitzgerald, 1868.

Darcy O'Neill

mahia ("water of life" in Arabic) is the traditional spirit of Morocco and is made from figs or dates. See AQUA VITAE. Unlike European brandies, which are usually made from fresh ingredients, mahia is traditionally produced from dried fruit, which is moistened, mashed, fermented, and distilled. The resulting spirit is not aged.

In Morocco, as elsewhere in Islamic North Africa, most of the distillation, which dates to well before European colonization, was performed by members of the country's Jewish community, the largest in the region. See BOUKHA. (While the Islamic prohibition of alcohol was often violated, that violation did not generally extend to production.) The resulting products were mostly rustic affairs and sold in general stores or homes, which would become informal taverns; meeting places for both Jews and Muslims to develop friendships. Between 1948 and 1967, however, most of the country's Jews emigrated to Israel or elsewhere, and little mahia is made today.

While mahia is often called a liqueur, it is not actually one, being unsweetened. Instead it is a spirit with fruity and anise notes. In Morocco it is often served at holiday and family gatherings. Traditionally the liquor was also used as a folk remedy; it is considered especially good for earaches when administered with an eyedropper.

Mahia is not widely available in the United States, but Nahmias et Fils, a new distillery in Yonkers, New York, is trying to broaden its appeal with a domestic product.

Huetz de Lemps, Alain. *Boissons et civilizations en Afrique.* Pessac, France: Presses Universitaires de Bordeaux, 2001.

Alice Feiring

mahua is a spirit distilled throughout a broad swath of central India from the dried flowers of the evergreen mahua tree, *Madhuca longifolia*, which are rich in sugar. Indeed, it is the world's only traditional spirit that is produced from flowers. The white blossoms are hand-picked, dried, and then fermented in large clay vessels for up to six days before receiving a single distillation in pot stills. Often referred to as arrack, the centuries-old clear liquor is traditionally made in home stills by the women of the Adivasis tribal groups, though commercial distillation has become commonplace as official regulation increases. Its flavor is floral and deeply pungent; some outsiders have likened its aroma to the smell of mice. See ARRACK.

Deogharia, Jaideep. "High Time to Make Most of Mahua." *Times of India*, April 23, 2013. https://timesofindia.indiatimes.com/city/ranchi/high-time-to-make-most-of-mahua/articleshow/19687715.cms (accessed February 18, 2021).

Froerer, Peggy. "Liquor Disputes and the Communalization of Local Tensions." In *Religious Division and Social Conflict: The Emergence of Hindu Nationalism in Rural India.* New York: Berghahn, 2007.

Anna Archibald

The **Mai Tai** is a rum sour accented with orgeat (almond syrup). In the first half of the tiki era's 1930s–1970s heyday, the most famous faux-Polynesian punch was the Zombie; second place belonged to the Mai Tai, which not only eclipsed the Zombie but outlived the tiki era to become a standard call in mainstream bars and restaurants. The Mai Tai owes little of this success to the fact that it's a great drink—which it is, in the rare cases when it is made correctly. Rather, the Mai Tai's longevity comes from its association with Hawaii; like the Piña Colada, the Mai Tai is as much a symbol as a drink. It's a getaway in a glass.

Selling the drink / selling the dream, ca. 1960. Courtesy of Jeff Berry.

Victor "Trader Vic" Bergeron is generally acknowledged as the Mai Tai's inventor. "In 1944, after success with several exotic rum drinks, I felt a new drink was needed," he wrote in his 1972 *Bar Guide*. In the service bar of his Oakland restaurant, Vic settled on a mix of seventeen-year Wray & Nephew Jamaican rum, lime juice, curaçao, and orgeat and rock candy syrups, which he shook with shaved ice, poured into a double old-fashioned glass, and garnished with mint and a spent lime shell. Vic offered this new creation to Carrie Guild, a friend from Tahiti. She pronounced the drink *maita'i*, Tahitian for "good."

Guild later confirmed this story in a signed affidavit. It went unchallenged until 2002, when Phoebe Beach—the widow of Donn "the Beachcomber" Beach—wrote in her book *Hawaii Tropical Rum Drinks and Cuisine by Don the Beachcomber* that her late husband had created a Mai Tai in 1933. There's no reason to doubt this claim but good reason to doubt that Vic copied Donn's Mai Tai, both because it had disappeared from Don the Beachcomber's menu by the time Vic first visited in 1937 and because Donn's Mai Tai, a blended drink combining Jamaican and Cuban rums with grapefruit and lime juices, Cointreau, falernum, and dashes of Pernod and Angostura bitters, tastes almost nothing like Vic's. See BEACH, DONN.

At any rate, it was Vic's formula that rose to prominence. But not overnight. In fact, the Mai Tai appears to have been a fairly obscure menu item at Trader Vic's restaurant chain until early 1953, when it finally made it into print after Vic included it on the revised drinks list he created for the Royal Hawaiian Hotel on Waikiki Beach (although there was a Trader Vic's operating nearby at the time, Vic had severed his connection with it only months after it opened in 1940). Despite telling the *Honolulu Star-Bulletin* that the Mai Tai was his favorite of the new drinks, he placed it near the bottom of the menu, well below the Zombie and even that old warhorse the Planter's Punch. Nonetheless, it rapidly gained traction with travel writers, and soon the Matson Line, the Royal Hawaiian's owner, began featuring it on its ships and at its other hotels. By 1955 the drink had spread virally through the islands. Or, rather, the name had: Vic's recipe was a trade secret, so rival hotels simply mixed rum with pineapple juice or orange juice, sweetened it with grenadine, and called it a Mai Tai. With Hawaiian statehood in 1959, and the massive influx of tourists who encountered the Mai Tai at hotel luaus, Vic suddenly found his drink the biggest seller at his own mainland restaurants, which by the 1960s he was calling "the home of the Mai Tai."

Ironically, even though the Mai Tai had become an iconic vacation drink by the 1970s, the only place making it properly was Trader Vic's; other boîtes generally did as Hawaii did and served random combinations of rum and fruit juice. Today this is still largely the case, although craft cocktail bars have come to embrace Vic's original formula as the elegant, layered, timeless construct that it is.

Recipe: 60 ml seventeen-year Wray & Nephew Jamaican rum (long defunct: substitute the oldest Jamaican available), the juice of one lime, 15 ml each curaçao and orgeat syrup, and 7.5 ml sugar syrup; shake with shaved ice, pour into a double Old-Fashioned glass, and garnish with mint and a spent lime shell.

See also BERGERON, VICTOR "TRADER VIC"; ORGEAT; PLANTER'S PUNCH; SOUR; and ZOMBIE.

Bergeron, Victor. *Trader Vic's Bartender's Guide, Revised*. New York: Doubleday, 1972.

Berry, Jeff. *Beachbum Berry Remixed*. San Jose, CA: Club Tiki, 2010.

Delaplane, Stanton. "Around the World with Delaplane." *Long Beach (CA) Independent Press-Telegram*, October 2, 1955, 148.

"Something About an Island." *Honolulu Star-Bulletin*, February 4, 1953, 30.

Trader Vic's. "Let's Get the Record Straight on the Mai Tai." Trader Vic's press release, San Francisco, 1970.

Jeff Berry

maître de chai, the French term for "cellarmaster," is commonly used to refer to the person who oversees the aging and blending of brandies such as cognac and Armagnac. See AGING; ARMAGNAC; BLENDING; CELLARMASTER; and COGNAC.

Maker's Mark is a wheated bourbon whisky sold in square bottles and sealed with a distinctive red wax. It is the bestselling premium bourbon in America and yet is also viewed as an important precursor by many of today's small, independent distillers.

The distillery was founded in 1953 in Loretto, Kentucky, by T. William Samuels (it released its first whisky in 1958) and remained in the hands of the Samuels family until 1981. It has had several owners since (it is currently a part of Beam-Suntory), but production has always been overseen by Bill Samuels Jr. (until 2011) or his son, Rob Samuels, and until recently the distillery's product only came in one expression.

The Samuels family began distilling whisky in America in 1779, when Robert Samuels was an officer in the Pennsylvania Militia during the America Revolution. Samuels migrated to Kentucky in 1784, and made whisky as a farmer-distiller with his son William. In 1884, William's son, Taylor William Samuels, started the family's first commercial distillery in Deatsville, Kentucky. Although controlling interest of that distillery was bought by the Starr Distilling Company of Cincinnati in 1909, the Samuels family remained in charge and were partial owners until the plant was closed due to Prohibition. In 1933, the distillery was reorganized and reopened. T. William Samuels began work there as a manager after graduating from the Speed School of Engineering.

T. William, known as Bill, continued at the T. W. Samuels Distillery Co. until 1943, when he left the industry.

In the early 1950s, Bill Samuels returned to the whisky trade. Working in the family kitchen, Bill Samuels is said to have baked and eaten bread to study the flavors inherent in different grains, and to have thereby settled upon the use of wheat as the secondary flavor grain instead of the more common rye. The mash bill for Maker's Mark is 70 percent corn, 16 percent soft red winter wheat, and 14 percent malted barley. Although probably apocryphal, the story has it that Bill Samuels burned his family's original recipe for whisky after coming up with his own.

In 2010, the brand broke with tradition and launched a second expression, Maker's 46, finished with staves of French oak in the barrel and bottled at 46 percent ABV rather than the standard 45 percent. While not a sensation, it was greeted far better than the brand's 2013 attempt to meet unanticipated demand by lowering its ABV to 42 percent. In the face of consumer outrage, that was abandoned. Better no Maker's Mark than a watered-down Maker's Mark.

See also WHISKY, BOURBON.

Zoeller, Chester. *Bourbon in Kentucky: A History of Distilleries in Kentucky*. Louisville, KY: Butler, 2010.

Max Watman

Malibu, the pioneer of the large and lucrative modern spirits category of flavored rum, is a sweet, low-proof blend of Barbados rum, coconut flavoring, and (at least originally) neutral spirits, generally consumed on ice or mixed with pineapple juice to make a sort of instant Piña Colada. See PIÑA COLADA. Developed by the South African affiliate of the International Distillers & Vintners company in the late 1970s, it was originally based—in part, anyway—on Jamaican rum (the Barbados rum came in 1985). See DIAGEO. Launched in the United Kingdom in 1980 and America in 1983, with the slogan "Anything rum can do, Malibu can do better," Malibu was aimed at the type of young, casual drinker attracted to the leisurely Southern California lifestyle then epitomized by Malibu Beach, after which it was named. First bottled at 28 percent ABV ("Low proof is where the market is going these days," its American distributor remarked), it was lowered to 24 percent in 1987 and its current proof, 21 percent, in 2001. That same year, Diageo was forced to sell the brand, and it was acquired by Pernod-Ricard in 2005. See PERNOD-RICARD. Pernod only intensified the brand's emphasis on advertising and promotion to drive sales, sponsoring extensive annual summer ad campaigns, which by 2009 included a twenty-four-hour "Maliboom Boom" online radio station. In 2014 Malibu became the no. 3 biggest-selling rum-based product in the world, with an 8 percent share of the total rum market. Pernod-Ricard now sells nineteen different Malibu products in bottles, cans, and plastic squeeze bags, ranging from the chocolate ice cream–flavored Malibu Sundae to a Malibu Peach Sparkler and Malibu Caribbean Cosmo.

Dougherty, Philip H. " 'Rum,' Sort of, by Paddington." *New York Times*, May 18, 1983.
Espey, James, "The Truth Behind the Truth of Malibu Rum." *International Opulence*. http://www.internationalopulence.com/malibu-rum/ (accessed July 20, 2018).
Schultz, E. J. "In Rum Battle, Malibu Speeds Things Up as Cruzan Goes Slow." *Advertising Age*, May 16, 2014.

Jeff Berry

malting, in which grain is allowed to germinate (thus releasing enzymes that convert its starches to sugars) and then heated to stop further growth, is an essential part of the brewing and distilling process. The saccharification of the grain's starches allows fermentation to occur when the malt is combined with water and yeast. See FERMENTATION and SACCHARIFICATION. Malt, the result of the malting process, is most commonly produced from barley. However, malt is also made from oats, rye, wheat, and maize. For the purpose of this discussion, the malting of barley serves as the primary focus.

Since the mid-twentieth century, the greatest portion of grain that is turned into malt is purchased and accepted for processing between August and September. Bulk storage requires the grain to be "sweated," or dried from an initial moisture content of about 19 percent to approximately 12 percent before it can be stored after it is carefully selected; cleaned of dust, dirt, awns (the spikes or bristles that grow from the seed head), and other undesirable elements; and graded. Newly harvested grain is inspected to confirm the bran is soft to the touch and that there is ample starchy endosperm to nourish the kernel's germ. Henry Stopes, in 1885, itemized the flaws that disqualified grain from selection: any crop that is more than three years old; grain showing signs of mold, insect, or vermin infestation; and a crop with visible damage from reaping, threshing, hummeling, dressing, or stacking.

Grain that meets these quality assurances is then tested to ensure the germ is alive and therefore viable. One old method involved placing a few kernels on a red-hot cinder. If the kernels danced around, they were assumed to be alive. Those that burnt on impact were of no value. Another test involved slowly dropping kernels into a tumbler of water. Kernels that quickly and steadily dropped to the bottom and lay flat were viable. Those that floated or stood up upon descent were unhealthy. Yet another test involved soaking one or two hundred kernels for twenty-four hours in a piece of flannel laying on a plate. The sample was then drained and allowed to sprout for thirty-six to fifty hours at a temperature above 13° C (56° F). By the nineteenth century, a handful of patented devices sped up this testing stage, an improvement over the concurrent acid test that involved splitting a kernel lengthwise and

Turning the barley at the floor maltings in the Bowmore distillery, Islay, Scotland. Courtesy of Beam-Suntory.

applying a drop of concentrated, pure sulfuric acid. If after a few minutes the kernel core turned black or brown, the grain was considered to be useless. Grain that passed any such tests is then sweated before it is stored for about six weeks to avert dormancy of the live kernel, an environmental adaptation found in most cereal grain.

The actual malting process then ensues. The grain is steeped in water at least two or three times over the course of two or three days, bringing the water content to almost 50 percent, thereby encouraging the kernels to sprout. In earlier methods, the grain was then spread onto the malting floor to about 12 cm thick, where it was allowed to germinate while it was repeatedly turned by the shovelful for about six days to prevent heat buildup from the energy exerted by sprouting kernels as it air-dried. See FLOOR MALTING. Modern, large-scale malting operations employ a mechanical turning device to accomplish this same step. The "green malt" is then dried in an oven to terminate germination and encourage caramelization. In Scotland and parts of Ireland, it was traditional to use peat for the fuel and let the smoke rise through a perforated floor to surround the malt, but drying malt over (much less smoky) coke fires was in common practice as early as 1662. See PEAT. Cheaper than toasting over wood fire and less noxious than processing over coal, the resulting "malt" can range in color from pale to amber to dark chocolate with a moisture content of about 4 percent, depending upon the preferences of the individual distiller or brewer. The finished product is then ready to be milled and mashed with water to produce the wort that is combined with yeast to make beer and subsequently distilled spirits.

Findlay, W. P. K. *Modern Brewing Technology*. London: Macmillan, 1971.

Hornsey, Ian S. *A History of Beer and Brewing*. Cambridge: RSC Paperbacks, 2003.

Macey, Alan. 'New Method of Sweating Malting Barley in Bulk.' *Journal of the Institute of Brewing* 58 (1952): 25.

Stopes, Henry. *Malt and Malting*. London: Lyon, 1885.

Anistatia R. Miller and Jared M. Brown

Mamie Taylor is a highball made with scotch whisky, ginger beer, and lime juice, created in 1898 by "an obscure bartender at Ontario Beach," near Rochester, New York, as tribute to an actress of that name who was appearing there. See HIGHBALL and GINGER ALE AND GINGER BEER. The drink enjoyed enormous popularity from 1900 until Prohibition.

See also PRESBYTERIAN; MOSCOW MULE; and WHISKY, SCOTCH.

"Origin of the 'Mamie Taylor.'" *New York Morning Telegram*, July 12, 1900.

Manhattan Cocktail, a mixture of American whisky, bitters, and vermouth, is believed to be the first "modern" cocktail, in that it added an aromatized, fortified wine to the classic Whisky Cocktail, thus appreciably reducing the amount of alcohol in it without diminishing its concentration of flavor or thinning its silky texture. See COCK-TAIL and OLD-FASHIONED COCKTAIL. The Manhattan's creation in the 1870s or early 1880s was something of a watershed moment in bartending, as it was the progenitor of other classic drinks relying on the platform of spirits, vermouth, and bitters, notably the Martini, Rob Roy, Brooklyn, and a host of other spinoffs. See BROOKLYN COCKTAIL; MARTINI; and ROB ROY. "Make no mistake about it," Lucius Beebe wrote in 1946, "the Manhattan was the archetypal short mixed drink and blazed a trail for all others to follow." To Gary Regan, the Manhattan's greatest modern champion, it was "the drink that changed the face of cocktails." See BEEBE, LUCIUS; and REGAN, GARY.

The Manhattan was likely invented in its namesake borough of New York City, with the most commonly known origin story pacing it at the Manhattan Club, a prestigious men's club with strongly Democratic leanings. Modern folklore holds that the circumstances were roughly these, first printed in 1945 by barman-columnist Patrick Murphy, who got them from veteran bar-industry journalist Ed Gibbs and his "research department" (one is entitled to wonder): the drink was invented "on a memorable December 29, 1874 evening at the Manhattan Club," at which "a testimonial dinner was held in honor of Samuel J. Tilden. . . . Official notes on the banquet alluded to declare that the dinner was preceded by a drink made of 'American Whisky, Italian Vermouth and Angostura Bitters.' It proved so popular that club members asked for it again and again, hence [it] became known as the Manhattan Cocktail." Once the story was picked up by Walter Winchell's popular column in 1950—now

The barroom at the Manhattan Club when it was in the Jerome Mansion on Madison Square, New York City, ca. 1901. Library of Congress.

with the added flourish that the Manhattan Club was formerly the home of Jennie Jerome, Winston Churchill's mother—it took root so deeply that it has proved impossible to dislodge. What's more, over the years Ms. Jerome's role has been expanded form first being present at the creation to being its inspiration.

The story, however, is simply not true. While multiple news reports confirm there was in fact a reception honoring Tilden at the Manhattan Club on that date, no mention of the drink's debut, or Ms. Jerome's role in its creation, is found within these stories. Furthermore, in 1874, the club was located in the old Benkard mansion on Fifth Avenue, not the old Jerome mansion on Madison Square, which it wouldn't occupy until 1899. Finally, as David Wondrich has pointed out, Ms. Jerome was not in

New York at the time of the reception, as she had given birth to her Mr. Churchill less than a month before, in Oxfordshire, England.

But while that particular story is false, that does not mean that the cocktail wasn't created at the Manhattan Club. Indeed, the club's official history claimed ownership, and that was the most popular theory at the time. In 1889, a "Boston bartender" went on record to the effect that "the Manhattan cocktail originated in the mind of the drink mixer at the Manhattan Club's rooms in New York." The *New York Sun*, a newspaper that paid unusual attention to matters mixological, concurred, writing in 1891 that "the famous Manhattan cocktail was invented at the club." See ROCK AND RYE. Finally, in 1902, the With the Clubmen column in the *New York Times* succinctly stated that, according to "legend," "the Manhattan Club . . . first gave birth to the Manhattan Cocktail."

There were, and are, numerous competing stories, most of them either easily disproved or slenderly documented and impossible to prove. Perhaps the most viable of them is found in a 1922 article penned by William F. Mulhall, who in the 1880s had been head barkeeper at the legendary Hoffman House, an impeccable credential for one writing about the drinks of the time. See HOFFMAN HOUSE. He stated that "the Manhattan cocktail was invented by a man named Black, who kept a place ten doors below Houston Street on Broadway," back in the 1860s.

While alone in its claim that Black was the drink's inventor, Mulhall's story is plausible. Indeed, Wondrich has located an 1881 sale notice in the *New York Journal* for "the popular lunch and sample room [i.e., bar] formerly owned and conducted by George Black, known as the Manhattan Inn, No. 493 Broadway" (Black had died earlier that year). While the address was indeed on Broadway, it was not exactly "ten doors below Houston Street," but it was close enough, especially when recalled after forty-one years.

Irrespective of where the drink was invented, the earliest known reference to the Manhattan cocktail is found in an 1882 Gotham Gossip column that was syndicated among several small-town American newspapers. It noted that "it is but a short time ago that a mixture of whisky, vermouth and bitters came into vogue. It went under various names: Manhattan cocktail, Turf Club cocktail, and Jockey Club cocktail. Bartenders at first were sorely puzzled what was wanted when it was demanded. But now they are fully cognizant of its various aliases and no difficulty is encountered." Further praise for the Manhattan came the following year in the *Boston Herald*, which called the drink "about as good as anything that can be manufactured." And, in 1884, the Manhattan appeared in not one but three cocktail books, in O. H. Byron's *Modern Bartenders' Guide*, George Winters's *How to Mix Drinks*, and J. W. Gibson's *Scientific Bar-Keeping*. By the end of the decade, it had spread to Vienna and London and Monte Carlo, and from there to the world. See CIRO'S.

While today the standard ratio of whisky to vermouth in the drink tends to be 2:1, in recipes found in these and other books of the 1880s and 1890s, the ratio was often 1:1, or in some cases 1:2, in favor of vermouth. As to the question of whether rye or bourbon was found in the "original" Manhattan, you'll find references to both. The *Boston Herald* described the drink as "the ordinary vermouth cocktail with a foundation of first-rate Bourbon whiskey." Harry Johnson, however, and the editor of the posthumous 1887 edition of Jerry Thomas's *Bar-Tender's Guide* called for rye. See JOHNSON, HARRY; and THOMAS, JEREMIAH P. "JERRY". As to the garnish, a lemon peel was used in the earliest known recipes, with the now-standard cherry not appearing until 1891. See MARASCHINO CHERRIES.

The Manhattan fell on hard times in the 1960s, when straight whisky was replaced by blended and drinks of its ilk came to be served on the rocks, rather than strained into a cocktail glass, thus destroying the silky texture that forms a considerable part of their appeal. Worse, untrained bartenders, reasoning that the Manhattan was like its cousin the Martini, took to skimping on the vermouth, adding only a tiny splash. While gin is light enough to be transformed by such a splash, whisky is not, and the resulting drink managed to spoil the whisky without turning it into a cocktail. The bartender's solution was to add a splash of the unnatural syrup from the maraschino cherry jar. This left the drink ripe for rediscovery, and it was perhaps the first drink that the twenty-first-century cocktail renaissance hauled forth from the mire and refurbished.

Recipe: Stir well with cracked ice 60 ml straight rye or bourbon whisky (preferably bonded), 30 ml Italian red vermouth, and 2–3 dashes Angostura bitters. Strain into a chilled cocktail glass and twist lemon peel over the top. Add a cherry if desired.

"A Cherry in Your Cocktail." *Kansas City Times*, March 15, 1891, 16.

"Gotham Gossip." *Lyndon (KS) Leader*, August 31, 1882, 4.

Greene, Philip. *The Manhattan*. New York: Sterling Epicure, 2016.

"Howard's Letter." *Boston Sunday Herald*, December 9, 1883, 13.

Lait, Jack. "Walter Winchell on Broadway." *Richmond (VA) Times-Dispatch*, August 19, 1950, 7.

Mulhall, William F. "The Golden Age of Booze." In *Valentine's Manual of Old New York*, ed. Henry Collins Brown, 126–137. New York: Valentine's, 1922.

Murphy, Patrick. "The Barman's Corner." *Buckeye Tavern*, March 19, 1945, 6.

Wondrich, David, *Imbibe!*, 2nd ed. New York: Perigee, 2015.

Philip Greene

maple syrup is made by reducing the sap that is collected from tapping maple trees in the beginning of spring, when it naturally flows inside the trees as the days warm. The sap is then evaporated over heat until 40 liters of maple water are reduced to one liter of pure maple syrup. Maple syrup grades are based on the time of the season that the maple sap is harvested; the beginning of the season gathers the highly prized light grade A, while later in the season, the much darker, more traditional grade B is gathered.

Before Prohibition, maple syrup saw some use as a substitute for sugar syrup in mixed drinks, although it does not appear to have been common. For example, it was not among the nine syrups Harry Johnson suggested a bar should stock in his 1888 *Bartender's Manual*. It turns up occasionally in the decades after that in drinks such as the Prohibition-era Applejack Rabbit, with applejack and citrus juices, and David Embury's Canadian Cocktail, with Canadian whisky, bitters, and curaçao. See EMBURY, DAVID A. As with many formerly rare ingredients, the recent cocktail renaissance has seen maple syrup used more often than in years past. Maple syrup's flavor, although subtle, is quite penetrating, and if not deployed carefully, it can dominate a drink. When used properly, though, the syrup can bring a richness and depth of flavor that can be quite appealing.

Embury, David. *The Fine Art of Mixing Drinks*. Garden City, NY: Doubleday, 1948.

Judge Jr. [pseud.]. *Here's How*. New York: John Day, 1928.

Shawn Soole

maraschino is a traditional cherry liqueur and a staple ingredient for bartenders since the late nineteenth century. Unlike cherry brandies, for which the fruit is usually infused and not distilled, maraschinos are clear, colorless distilled liqueurs. Whole marascas, the small, sour, and slightly bitter cherries to which the liqueur owes its name (*Prunus cerasus acidior*), macerate in neutral spirit, crushed pit and leaves included, before being distilled. The resulting spirit is then diluted and sweetened with sugar to produce the final liqueur.

This particular variety of cherry is indigenous to Dalmatia, in Croatia. It is thought the liqueur was first distilled in local monasteries, as "rosolio di Marasca." See ROSOLIO. The industry's growth started in the eighteenth century, when the region was under Venetian domination. Francesco Drioli (1738–1808), a Venetian distiller, is credited with its development in the town of Zadar (then called Zara). Dates are disputed: in the 1930s, the Drioli company claimed to have been founded in 1759, although 1768 or 1769 had been used in all official communications until then, perhaps because it was then that Drioli quit his day job (so to speak) as a merchant to concentrate on distilling. Drioli did not invent the process of making maraschino, though; that distinction belongs to another Zadar-based Venetian distiller, Giuseppe Carceniga, who had perfected the process in 1730 and successfully commercialized it. Carceniga may have been the first producer to export maraschino in its iconic straw-lined bottles—the straw was meant to protect the fragile Murano glass during transportation. It was described in writing as early as 1766, and Drioli didn't start using it until the early 1800s.

Drioli's brand was nevertheless the first to gain wider international recognition. Many distillers soon tried to follow in its footsteps. Most famous among them is Luxardo, the current worldwide leader, set up in 1821 in Zadar. The destruction of the family's distillery by Allied bombing and the murder of two family members by Yugoslav partisans during World War II led to the relocation of the business to Padova, Italy. Other producers, including Drioli, whose distillery was also razed, followed, and after the conflict the Yugoslavian government set up Maraska, Zadar's only remaining maraschino producer, in the ruins of the Luxardo facility. Drioli closed in 1980.

Traditionally drunk on its own in a small liqueur glass as a digestive, maraschino seduced French and Italian upper classes in the late seventeenth and early eighteenth centuries. It made the jump to Britain at the beginning of the nineteenth century and was one of the ingredients in the influential Regent's Punch, the favorite beverage of the prince regent. See REGENT'S PUNCH. It reached the

United States at roughly the same time but only became part of the American bartender's repertoire in the 1860s, with the liqueur first appearing in a couple of European recipes in Charles Campbell's 1867 *American Barkeeper* (a work apparently plagiarized from Jerry Thomas's lost second book). See THOMAS, JEREMIAH P. "JERRY". Mixologists initially used maraschino as cocktail "seasoning": much like bitters, it was called for in small doses in fancy cocktails and vermouth concoctions to enhance the flavor of the main ingredients—the early "Martinez" version of the Martini provides a perfect example of this use. See MARTINI.

Maraschino was also an essential ingredient for Cuban bartenders in the 1920s and 1930s. It plays a key role in the Mary Pickford and the Daiquiri no. 4, the blended Daiquiri with a touch of maraschino that made the Floridita famous. The liqueur was also called upon for the Daiquiri no. 3, now better known as the Hemingway Daiquiri.

After World War II, its offbeat flavor profile—neither sweet nor fruity enough—did not endear it to the new generation of drinkers, and much like classical mixology, maraschino went into decline. This changed with the cocktail renaissance, when bartenders returned to canonical recipes. The most important drink for the liqueur's resurgence was the then little-known Last Word. Unusual in that it called for a whole ounce of maraschino, it was popularized by bartender Murray Stenson in 2004. Now ubiquitous in cocktail bars worldwide, it cemented maraschino's place as an essential cocktail ingredient for today's bartenders. See LAST WORD.

Appiotti, Mirella. "Luxardo, il desaparecido di Zara." *La stampa*, November 21, "Maraschino." *Saperbere*. http://www.saperebere.com/liquori/liquori-m/ (accessed February 19, 2021).

"Marasco." *Annuario Dalmatico*, 1884, 280–282.

Teja, Antonio. *La fabbrica di Maraschino Francesco Drioli all'epoca del suo fondatore (1759–1808).* Genoa: self-published, 1938.

Sother Teague

maraschino cherries are an iconic cocktail garnish, usually encountered in heavily processed form, where the cherries have been steeped in a chemical brine, dyed with artificial colors, and bottled in a thick, artificially flavored sugar syrup. That process was developed by Oregon horticulturist Ernest Wiegand in 1925, ostensibly as a substitute for the traditional process, originating on the Croatian coast, whereby marasca cherries were brined in seawater and then bottled in maraschino liqueur. See MARASCHINO.

More accurately, Wiegand's imitation was a substitute for the French imitation of the Croatian process, which would have had two defects from his point of view: it didn't use Oregon cherries, and it used alcohol (in 1925, Prohibition was the law of the land). The French process was pioneered by the Fils de Charles Teyssonneau company of Bordeaux, who took local bigarreau cherries, bleached, brined, and dyed them, and then packed them in an alcohol solution. Some were packed with their kernels to achieve a maraschino flavor; others used benzaldehyde, extracted from bitter almonds. These were available throughout the United States by 1888 and found their way into drinks almost immediately: in November 1889, an article in the *St. Louis Globe-Democrat* first described a "whiskey and cherry" cocktail with an "imported stoneless French cherry, preserved in French cordial," and claimed it was "the greatest drink at present in St. Louis. . . . Everybody seems to have gone mad after this drink."

In March 1891, a *Kansas City Times* article first prescribed adding a cherry to a Manhattan, and later the same month, the *New York Herald* described the fad actually reaching Manhattan. Popularity, along with tariffs, drove up the price, raising complaints from bar owners. Then the fad passed, and in November 1897, a widely syndicated article in the *Herald* claimed, "Cocktails no longer contain a cherry at the bottom of the glass. . . . Cherries are going out, along with other sweeteners in drinks." Starting in 1904, concerns about toxic coal tar dyes further doomed the cherry.

Modern American Drinks (1895), by George Kappeler, was the first bartender's guide to use maraschino cherries, optional in his Manhattan and Sweet Martini, although that same year, C. F. Lawlor's *The Mixicologist* includes an "imported cherry" in its Martinez. Subsequent manuals up to Repeal rarely called for cherries in those drinks, even provisionally. The cocktail cherry's revival occurred during Prohibition in "American bars" throughout Europe. Most 1920s-era European cocktail books made heavy use of cherries, which the authors considered a standard Manhattan ingredient.

Impressionable Americans drinking abroad began to reconsider the cherry. Nonalcoholic maraschino cherries remained available in the United States throughout Prohibition, and after Repeal they resumed their place in American cocktails, their former unpopularity now forgotten. While the modern cocktail renaissance has brought back real maraschino cherries, such as the ones made by the Italian Luxardo company, the bright-red, plump, and celluloid-like Wiegand-process cherries remain ubiquitous.

"A Cherry in Your Cocktail." *Kansas City Times*, March 15, 1891, 16.

"Cocktails and Punches." *St. Louis Globe-Democrat*, November 17, 1889, 20.

"New Things in Tipples." *New York Herald*, November 21, 1897, sec. 5, 8.

Rehak, Melanie. "Who Made That Cherry?" *New York Times*, September 19, 2014. https://www.nytimes.com/2014/09/21/magazine/who-made-that-maraschino-cherry.html (accessed March 24, 2021).

Doug Stailey

marc (or more correctly **eau-de-vie de marc**), is a pomace brandy distilled widely in France since at least the eighteenth century from the "marc," or pomace, of grapes left over from winemaking. It must be bottled at no less than 37.5 percent ABV (and rarely exceeding 54 percent) and may be aged in oak (the barrels used are customarily old ones), sometimes for a considerable period. No flavoring or additional alcohol can be added.

Types of marc legally accepted and demarcated within the EU include Marc de Champagne, marc d'Aquitaine, marc de Bourgogne, marc du Centre-Est, marc de Franche-Comté, marc du Bugey, marc de Savoie, marc des Côteaux de la Loire, marc des Côtes du Rhône, marc de Provence, marc du Languedoc, marc d'Alsace gewürztraminer (a single variety AOP), marc de Lorraine, marc d'Auvergne, and marc du Jura. Each of these is also allowed to be labeled as " eau-de-vie de marc . . . ," as in eau-de-vie de marc de Champagne or eau-de-vie de originaire marc d'Aquitaine.

These French AOPs require that pomace rather than wine is used; each one has its own protected designation for wine-based spirit (such as eau-de-vie de la Marne for the Champagne region or eau-de-vie de vin originaire d'Aquitaine for the Bordeaux region).

See also POMACE BRANDY.

Doug Frost

The **Margarita** cocktail, classically made with tequila, lime juice, and triple sec curaçao, has become one of the world's favorite mixed drinks, in the process taking tequila from an often poorly regarded Mexican specialty to a global spirit. See TEQUILA; TRIPLE SEC; and CURAÇAO. The Margarita's journey from exotic novelty drink to icon of middle-class hedonism was one of the bright spots in the Dark Ages of mixology that preceded the cocktail renaissance, even if the promise of Jimmy Buffett's 1977 hit song "Margaritaville," where the drink is a symbol of a bohemian life beyond everyday responsibilities, faded away as tequila became big business and Margaritaville just another casual-dining restaurant

The newspaper advertisement that spread the Margarita across America, 1956. Wondrich Collection.

chain. See COCKTAIL RENAISSANCE. At the same time, what it lost in symbolism, the Margarita gained in quality; the popularity of 100 percent agave tequila and the return of precision bartending have meant that in recent years, on average, better Margaritas are being poured than ever before.

The precise origins of the Margarita are one of cocktail history's most notorious swamps and remain resistant to even the most diligent investigation. It is a case not of too little information but too much; even putting aside the open question of the drink's relation to the Tequila Daisy (*margarita* is Spanish for "daisy"), there are at least half a dozen plausible individual claimants to having invented the drink, none of them without problems. See TEQUILA DAISY. They are, in order of their claimed dates of creation and with the year each claim first surfaced:

1936 (1973). David Daniel "Danny" Negrete (1911–1996), at the Garci Crespo Spa, Tehuacan, Mexico.

1937 (1955). John Durlesser (1911–1971), at McHenry's Tail o' the Cock restaurant, Los Angeles.

1942 (1974). Francisco "Pancho" Morales (1918–1996), at Tommy's Place in Ciudad Juarez, Mexico.

1947 (1987). Carlos Daniel "Danny" Herrera (1901–1992), at Rancho La Gloria, Rosarito Beach, Mexico (1987).

1948 (1963). Santos Cruz (1924–2005), at the Studio Lounge, Galveston, Texas.

1948 (1978). Margarita Miller Sames 1911–2009), at her house in Acapulco.

In cases like this it is best to stick to the timeline—the documented evidence as it appears. The timeline starts off with a pair of wild cards. The combination of tequila, lime juice, and Cointreau—the traditional brand of triple sec curaçao used in the drink—is first documented in 1937, in London (of all places), when William J. Tarling of the popular Café Royal included it, under the name Picador, in that institution's cocktail book. See TARLING, WILLIAM JAMES "BILLY". This can be dismissed as a "typing monkey" case of parallel development, a fairly obvious tequila variation on the popular Sidecar, with the more-Mexican lime juice replacing the Sidecar's lemon. See SIDECAR. Not so easily dismissed, however, is the Tequila Sour found in the 1939 drink

booklet that Charlie Connolly (1879–1969), long-time bartender of New York's Players' Club, put together for that city's famous Cotton Club: it has the tequila and the Cointreau and the lime juice, but now it is served in a salt-rimmed cocktail glass with a wedge of lime.

In September, 1953, the recipe finally appeared under the name it bears today when a California newspaper columnist describes the Margarita as he encountered it in Ensenada, Mexico, salt rim and all; this item was rapidly followed by an appearance in *Esquire* magazine, complete with detailed recipe and the tagline "She's from Mexico, Señores, and her name is the Margarita Cocktail—and she is lovely to look at, exciting and provocative." A year later, *Los Angeles Times* columnist Gene Sherman ran into it at Rosarito Beach, Baja (one wonders if it was at Herrera's Rancho la Gloria) and, inquiring as to its origin, was told that it was "belted hard by the international set at Acapulco." A few weeks after that, the *Valley News*, another Los Angeles newspaper, corrected Sherman, explaining that the "Marguerita" was actually invented by Johnny Durlesser, longtime head barman of the Tail o' the Cock, a tony Los Angeles steakhouse, "way back in 1937, when tequila first appeared here" (actually, it would have had to be in 1939, when the restaurant opened). Durlesser was a widely known figure and one of the most respected barmen in the city, by both his customers and his peers, and while his story might not be completely accurate, it is unlikely to have been completely fabricated either.

At the same time, early 1955, Vernon Underwood of Young's Market, the Los Angeles distributor for José Cuervo tequila, noticed that the Tail o' the Cock was suddenly selling a great deal of the stuff and persuaded his employers to enter into an agreement with Cuervo to distribute the brand nationally. Young's promptly launched the first national advertising campaign for tequila, featuring a series of different drink recipes, among them the Margarita, which attracted the lion's share of attention. From then on, the name "Margarita" and the tequila-Cointreau-lime formula were indissolubly joined.

Taking a step back, it's possible to make at least some sense out of all this. It is clear that, in the late 1930s, there was a tequila-based variation on the Sidecar, incorporating the lime juice and salt generally served with tequila at the time, circulating in Southern California and the places in northern Mexico frequented by prosperous Americans. It is not impossible that this was first mixed by Negrete, who had worked behind the famous bar at the Agua Caliente resort in Tijuana, although his claim is somewhat undermined by its first surfacing in 1973 under the aegis of the Sauza company, to be used as a counterweight to the prevailing Cuervo story featuring Durlesser. See TEQUILA SUNRISE.

By 1939, that drink had appeared at Durlesser's bar (he "was asked to duplicate a drink a lady customer had once tasted in Mexico," as he recalled in 1966) and had traveled to Connolly's bar in New York, an easy trip—the Players had a number of members who worked in both the New York theater and Hollywood films. It is unlikely that the name Margarita had been attached to it by this point: during World War II, it turns up in advertisements as the "Tequila Sidecar," and in the 1946 edition of Oscar Haimo's widely used *Cocktail and Wine Digest*, without the salt rim, as the "Mexicano Cocktail" (this was one of the few American cocktail guides to be also distributed in Spanish). Se HAIMO, OSCAR. As late as 1950, Angelo's Copper Room, in Hollywood, was serving it as the "South of the Border."

At the end of the 1940s, however, the drink was clearly gathering momentum, whether because Sames was serving it to her influential guests in Acapulco and Herrera to his at Rancho La Gloria or simply because tequila had been around enough in the Southern California market to reach a tipping point. Then the Tail o' the Cock started pushing it, and that finally put it over the top. Here, it's worth noting that Shelton Henry, the restaurant's owner, was a friend of Sames's and went to some of her Acapulco parties. It's even possible that she was Durlesser's "lady from Mexico": Underwood claimed in 1974 that the name came well after the drink and that McHenry had something to do with it.

That leaves Morales and Cruz. Both of their versions could very well be tequila Sidecar variations, particularly since neither of them originally had the characteristic salt rim, but by 1942, let alone 1948, the drink had been floating around for some time, so it is debatable what they invented. It's possible that they hit on the Margarita name independently, through the drink's connection to the Daisy. See DAISY. But in all of these cases one is entitled to

be more skeptical of the claims to having first named the drink than of having first mixed it: it is easier to rationalize claiming a name for a drink you know you invented than claiming you invented one you know you did not.

With Cuervo's 1956 advertising campaign, the Margarita quickly became established as *the* tequila drink. At first that did not mean much, but by the 1960s Mexican restaurants took off in popularity in the United States as the public began looking for more interesting culinary choices. As the drink spread, it picked up variations. By the beginning of the 1960s, some were making it in the blender. In 1964, Victor "Trader Vic" Bergeron opened the first restaurant in his Señor Pico's chain of Mexican restaurants, serving the Margaritas in amber Mexican bubble-glass champagne coupes; this would be widely imitated. See BERGERON, VICTOR "TRADER VIC." In 1971, Mariano Martinez (1944–) adapted a soft-serve ice cream machine to making Margaritas and installed it at Mariano's Mexican Cuisine, his Dallas, Texas restaurant. The frozen Margarita machine would soon be a fixture of the age. Its spread was helped by the fact that it was perfectly adapted to the fruit-flavored drinks that were increasingly popular. Strawberry Margaritas, Raspberry Margaritas, Watermelon Margaritas—all had their turn. Tequila, it is safe to say, was not the focus of these drinks (indeed, in the 1980s one large New York City operator was caught using grain alcohol instead of tequila in its frozen Margaritas).

At the same time, the regular Margarita had fallen victim to sour mix and lazy bartending. By the end of the 1970s, the average one was likely to be compounded from tequila, and not too much of it; cheap, low-proof triple sec; and sour mix, and served on the rocks. It was larger than Durlesser's had ever been, but most of the volume was sugar water (unless, as some did, you added Budweiser to the mix). The only real lime that came near it was the thin wheel of it perched on the rim. Yet there was also premiumization: the 1980s saw such developments as the añejo-tequila Margarita, including the "Cadillac Margarita" marketed by the Southern California–based El Torito Grill chain, with Grand Marnier replacing the triple sec.

In 1990, Julio Bermejo, of Tommy's Mexican restaurant in San Francisco, put his foot down, so to speak, and introduced a Margarita that undid most of the damage. Sure, it was on the rocks, but it was shaken, with fresh lime juice and quality, 100 percent agave tequila. Instead of the Cointreau, however, Bermejo increased the agave quotient by using agave syrup. The resulting "Tommy's Margarita" went on to become one of the success stories of the cocktail revolution. In recent years, many bartenders have also returned to the old, 1950s formula, but with mezcal replacing the tequila. Many, on the other hand, are still perfectly content to make the drink with mixto tequila, triple sec, and sour mix; as sales figures demonstrate, there are a great many people who have no objection to that.

Recipe: 45 ml blanco tequila, 22 ml Cointreau, 20 ml lime juice. Shake and strain into salt-rimmed coupe (run a cut lime around the outer rim of the glass and roll in coarse salt).

Connolly, Charlie. *The World Famous Cotton Club: Barman Charlie Conolly's 1939 Book of Mixed Drinks*. New York: 1939.
Cooper, Brad. "The Man Who Invented the Margarita." *Texas Monthly*, October 1974, 76–80.
Demarest, Michael. "Memo from Mike." *Santa Rosa (CA) Press-Democrat*, September 17, 1953, 20.
"Valley Ramblings." *Van Nuys (CA) News*, January 13, 1955, 9-C.
Vilas, James. "In the Land of Tequila." *Town and Country*, November 1980, 220.

David Wondrich

mark or marque is used today to denote a specific formula of unblended rum, chiefly in Jamaica. It is a relic of the old global spirits-trade system whereby each spirits producer had its own code—using letters, symbols, or both—that would be branded into its barrel heads. Some of the Jamaican marks are easily decoded, such as the WB mark denoting the Wedderburn family's Blackheath estate, while others, such as the IWO that represented their Blue Castle estate, are more obscure. After the consolidation of the industry in the twentieth century, many Jamaican distilleries continued making rum in the style of other distilleries that were absorbed, retaining the old marks for identification. See RUM, JAMAICA.

Pietrek, Matt. "Jamaican Rum Marques Roundup." *Cocktail Wonk*. https://cocktailwonk.com/rum-marques (accessed February 19, 2021).

David Wondrich

marmalade and jam are fruit preserves that sometimes find their way into mixed drinks. Marmalade is usually made from citrus fruits and sugar and includes tangible pieces of peel, and jams are made from a wider variety of fruits, notably berries, also with sugar. Deployed as a cocktail ingredient, marmalade or jam simultaneously provides sweetness and flavor (usually of one fruit) to a drink. Epitomized in the Breakfast Martini—a bracing mix of gin, Cointreau, lemon juice, and orange marmalade created by Salvatore Calabrese—this practice can be seen as only fitting, in that the cocktail itself, after all, began as part of the morning routine. See CALABRESE, SALVATORE.

Page, Karen, and Andrew Dornenburg. *The Flavor Bible*. New York: Little, Brown, 2008.
Saunders, Rachel. *The Blue Chair Jam Cookbook*. Kansas City, MO: Andrews McMeel, 2010.

Charlotte Voisey

Martell is a brand of cognac and claims to be "the oldest of the great Cognac houses," with a heritage spanning three centuries. The company was founded in 1715, when English merchant Jean Martell (1694–1753), a native of the island of Jersey in the Channel Islands, arrived in France, leaving his home to start trading eaux-de-vie in Cognac. For nearly forty years, Jean Martell devoted his life to the trade. After his death, his widow, Rachel, took over the business, which at that point was by far the largest exporter to the rapidly developing London market. In 1775, Martell's two sons, Jean and Frédéric, continued the family legacy. Martell's first shipment of cognac arrived in the United States shortly thereafter. The nineteenth century saw Martell cede its dominance to Hennessy, but it remained a major producer and exporter. After being sold to Seagram's in 1988, Martell became part of the Pernod-Ricard portfolio in 2001. It is the second largest of the "big four" cognac houses, after HENNESSY.

The brand is known for using a high percentage of eaux-de-vie from the Borderies region in its blends, much of it distilled in house. Borderies is the smallest of the cognac crus, and its eaux-de-vie are prized for their rich, nutty, and often floral aromatics. In 1912, Édouard Martell created what would become the house's signature cognac, Martell Cordon Bleu.

See also COGNAC and EAU-DE-VIE.

Faith, Nicholas. *Cognac: The Story of the World's Greatest Brandy*. Oxford: Infinite Ideas, 2013.

Martell Cognac website. http://www.martell.com/en-us/ (accessed October 23, 2015).

Kara Newman

Martin, John G. (1905–1986), was a businessman and entrepreneur who was largely responsible for establishing a foothold for vodka in the United States. Vodka had little name recognition and no consumer base in 1939 when Martin, the president of the Hartford-based Heublein Inc., bought the US rights to produce Smirnoff vodka—a Russian legacy brand set adrift by the 1917 revolution—from Rudolph Kunett (1893–1979), a Ukrainian immigrant who had been manufacturing the spirit under license in Bethel, Connecticut, with limited success. He paid $14,000. In 1956, Martin bought the licensor, the Paris branch of the Smirnoff company, thus cornering the global market for the brand. Facing an American public that favored whisky, Heublein pushed vodka's versatility as a mixer. This approach first struck gold when Martin and Jack Morgan, the owner of the Cock 'n Bull restaurant in Los Angeles and a producer of ginger beer, invented the Moscow Mule. Martin followed the success of that cocktail with heavy promotion of the Screwdriver, Bloody Mary, Bull Shot, and other vodka-based drinks. See BLOODY MARY; MOSCOW MULE; and SCREWDRIVER. Heublein also proved adept at advertising the new spirit. Ads from the 1950s used desert imagery to sell the dryness of a Smirnoff Martini. Celebrities such as Woody Allen and Zsa Zsa Gabor were drafted to plug the product. Most famous, and influential, was the ad tagline "It Leaves You Breathless," which promoted the social advantages of vodka being an odorless spirit. All of this led to exponential growth in the brand's sales throughout the 1950s.

Martin was chairman of Heublein from 1961 until 1982, when the company was acquired by R. J. Reynolds Industries. Thereafter, he retired. By then, Smirnoff was the bestselling vodka brand in the world and one of the bestselling spirits overall. Born in England and Cambridge-educated, Martin nonetheless favored the American side of his dual citizenship, and served with distinction in the United States Army in World War II, reaching the rank of lieutenant colonel.

See also SMIRNOFF.

"John G. Martin Dies; Popularizer of Vodka." *New York Times*, May 31, 1986.

Robert Simonson

Martinez was an early moniker for the Martini, first appearing in print in 1884. See MARTINI. Though the cocktail's original recipe is subject to interpretation, contemporary mixographers typically call for Old Tom gin, sweet vermouth, maraschino liqueur, and bitters. See OLD TOM GIN; VERMOUTH; MARASCHINO; and BITTERS.

The **Martini**, with gin or (much later) vodka cut with vermouth in ever-shifting proportions, is the iconic cocktail, the one that stands for all of its tribe, whether to take the blame or receive the credit; whether it's the evils of the three-Martini lunch or the delight of getting out of those wet clothes and into a Dry Martini. No other mixed drink, with the possible exception of punch, has inspired so many poems, so much prose, such a plethora of jokes and witticisms and iconic images. See PUNCH.

The precise origin of the Martini has long been sought; indeed, it is one of the holy grails of cocktail history. Theories abound, some of them presented in intricate detail, yet as of this writing none has proved conclusive, and most are easily disproved. That includes the most hallowed of them, which has the drink invented in Martinez, California, for a thirsty miner on his way to San Francisco from gold country ("Martinez" is one of the early names for the drink). Unfortunately, the person who transmitted the story, John "Toddy" Briones (1874–1967), was an infant at the time the invention supposedly took place, and there is no record of the man it was attributed to.

We shall stick to the known facts. The first mentions of a cocktail combining gin and vermouth come from 1883, in a pair of newspaper articles from Cleveland and Chicago, but in both cases it is identified as a Manhattan cocktail (this is not as strange as it seems today: the graininess and richness of genever, the prevailing style of gin in America, make it easy to mistake for whisky when mixed with something as aromatic as vermouth). See MANHATTAN COCKTAIL and GENEVER. The combination would appear under its own name, or rather names, the next year, in two New York bartender's guides. *The Modern Bartender*, by "O. H. Byron" (apparently a pseudonym), contains two recipes for the Manhattan, one with (dry) French vermouth and one with (sweet) Italian vermouth; after them, it lists the Martinez Cocktail, with the statement that it is "same as Manhattan, only you substitute gin for whisky." The other book, published the G. Winter Brewing Co., specifies "Tom gin" and Italian vermouth and calls the mixture "Turf Club" (a name that was also applied to early versions of the Manhattan; the Turf Club was a short-lived but very gaudy New York gambling and sporting association). To further complicate matters, in 1885 a Boston newspaper listed both a Turf Club and a "Martena" among the popular drinks of the day. By 1886, the name "Martini" was also in play, while knowledgeable New Yorkers tended to call the gin-vermouth combination a "Martine," after either popular sportsman Franklin Martine or Judge Randolph Martine (no relation), to each of whom the drink was attributed at the time. As the drink spread, other spellings included "Martineau" and "Martigny." Names learned only by hearing them across a crowded bar tend to display a good deal of variation.

Faced with this level of confusion, the best one can do is stand back and attempt to discern a pattern. One conclusion emerges: whoever invented it, the practice of lightening a whisky or gin cocktail with vermouth (or, conversely, fortifying a vermouth cocktail with gin or whisky) came to public attention through its association with New York City's clubland, the loose association of the prosperous and the prominent that socialized in the city's exclusive clubs and hotel bars, with the whisky version followed by the gin one. We may never know the precise details, but with prominent clubmen Frank and Randolph Martine, the Manhattan Club (home of the Manhattan Cocktail), and the Turf Club all tied up in the drink's early history, it is the

best explanation we have (there are other links to that milieu space forbids us from considering).

At any rate, if the 1880s was the decade of the Manhattan, the 1890s went to its close sibling the Martini. That of course was the name that finally won out, helped no doubt by the dominant position of in the American market of Martini & Sola's (and later Martini & Rossi's) vermouth, which accounted for two out of three bottles of Italian vermouth sold. This mixture of Old Tom gin and vermouth could not, however, completely displace the genever version, which took over the Turf Club or Turf designation (originally the Turf Club seems to have been with Old Tom and the Martin-*x* with genever, but the rising popularity of Old Tom seems to have pulled it into the better-known drink). The French-vermouth Martini implicit in the *Modern Bartender*'s description was in play as well: in 1890, *New York Herald* editor Richard Blumenthal encountered it on a French transatlantic liner, where the purser was serving it as a preprandial appetizer. In general, the mid-1890s saw a trend for drier drinks in America, and the "Dry Martini" (the name is first recorded in 1896 in New York) benefited greatly. By 1900, it was the dominant version.

Up to this point, the Martini was a normal cocktail, just one of the many mixtures an American bartender was expected to have at his fingertips. During the first two decades of the twentieth century, though, it grew into something greater than that; it became, as Lowell Edmunds noted in his definitive exegesis of the drink and its meanings, "the premiere American cocktail." It was a ubiquitous pillar of the new cocktail cult (e.g., 114 of the 284 cocktails the bartenders at the Waldorf-Astoria recorded in their bar book featured gin and vermouth—a full 40 percent). See WALDORF-ASTORIA. But more than that, the Dry Martini in particular was an icon of modernity itself; the liquid version of jazz, motion pictures, and the comic strip—the American lively arts, as critic Gilbert Seldes dubbed them. It was simple, direct, and strong. There was nothing hiding in it, but at the same time it had nuance and intelligence and verve. It was, as H. L. Mencken pronounced it, "the only American invention as perfect as a sonnet."

And yet Americans were not satisfied. No other drink has spawned as many variations as the Martini—as many attempts to perfect the perfect. Between the 1880s and 1900, the drink evolved from a mix of Tom gin and Italian vermouth, with bitters, syrup, and a cherry, to Tom gin or the drier Plymouth or the even drier still London dry gin with French vermouth, orange bitters, and an olive. In the late 1890s, San Franciscan Walter D. K. Gibson took that Plymouth and dry vermouth and threw out the other two ingredients, creating the minimalist Gibson (the Gibson gained its characteristic onion garnish in the 1920s, once the Martini had lost its orange bitters and there was no longer anything but the garnish to distinguish the drinks). See GIBSON. As the Martini traveled around the world, it also began settling in and giving rise to local variations, chief of them being the San Martin of Argentina and Uruguay. See SAN MARTIN. In 1903, a correspondent even wrote the *New York Sun* to claim that the drink was originally a Parisian one, long before it was known in America.

There were a great many other offshoots, most of them based on such mixological minutiae as different brands of dry gin or the addition of dashes of liqueurs (e.g., San Francisco's popular, and early, Barry Cocktail from 1891, which adds drops of crème de menthe to a standard sweet Martini). But there were also fundamental shifts in the composition of the Martini itself. The first took place in the years before Prohibition. The original formula called for equal parts gin and vermouth, making for a fairly gentle drink. In the late 1890s, versions that are two parts of gin to one of vermouth (French or Italian) begin to appear; by the 1910s, that became the new standard, with some drinkers opting for a much stiffer drink: among the variations in the Waldorf-Astoria bar book are versions that are seven and even nine to one.

The next shift took place during World War II, when the standard Dry Martini (the sweet version having by then fallen by the wayside) was three to one, with four and five to one also common. (President Franklin D. Roosevelt, an avid Martini mixer, frequently went as far as seven to one.) In 1954, the United States Internal Revenue Service adjusted its rules specifying the minimum proportion of vermouth in a bottled Martini from one part to three of gin to one part to five. In this, the government was behind the curve, as it so often is: by 1954, a drinker who ordered a Martini would expect it to be at least five to one, while an order for an Extra Dry Martini generally meant no vermouth at all. Indeed, 1952 saw a fad for jokes based on ways of adding the least possible amount of vermouth to the drink. A typical sample: "Leave a capful of vermouth on the radiator overnight and then open the windows for an hour before pouring your gin into an ice-filled pitcher."

The 1950s saw other changes as well: the Martini on the Rocks began appearing in some places (it was first attested to in 1950); in others it was being flavored with a splash of brine from the olive jar (this practice had been tried in one way or another since at least 1901; in the 1980s it would gain the name "Dirty Martini") and there was of course the increasingly popular Vodka Martini, a 1930s experiment that was as annoying to traditionalist drinkers as it was alluring to others. By this point, the "See-Through" or "Silver Bullet," as the minimal-vermouth Martini was sometimes known, was practically the last true cocktail standing: when Bernard DeVoto wrote, in 1949, that "there are only two cocktails . . . a slug of whiskey and . . . the martini," he was speaking for his generation. Other cocktails existed, to be sure, but (outside of tiki bars) they were in eclipse, and that meant that gin or vodka and vermouth in various combination encroached on the depopulated niches of the cocktail ecosystem. See TIKI.

In the 1960s and 1970s, the Martini continued its lonely vigil. The classic gin version, served up with an olive or a twist, was caught in a protracted rear-guard action against the loose aggregation of highballs, coolers, shooters, and whatnot that defined the disco drink—sweet, brightly colored drinks that hid the taste of the alcohol in them. See HIGHBALL; COOLER; and SHOOTER. But the Martini was not well, either: all too often, it was a birdbath-sized basin of barely stirred or over-shaken (there seemed to be no in between) gin or vodka with a skewer of large, warm olives or a pigtail of pithy lemon peel floating in it. Vermouth was added in homeopathic amounts, if at all. The Martini was deeply unfashionable, and those who drank it were lucky to get one at all. In Europe, the situation was somewhat better, but only if you went to the top hotel bars, where things were done to IBA standard and cost accordingly.

In the mid-1980s, the Martini suddenly found itself in style again, an icon of the newly-minted yuppie class. Unfortunately, it was mostly the glass that people were interested in. Over the next decade and a half, that meant a large number of Chocolate Martinis and Cajun Martinis and other drinks, usually with names ending in "-tini," that were basically disco drinks in v-shaped glasses; at least the most popular of these, the Cosmopolitan, was balanced and well-constructed. See CHOCOLATE MARTINI; COSMOPOLITAN; and -TINI. A great many others were not. But with all that attention came a good deal of investigation into the roots of the bartender's craft and, in time, its revival.

The cocktail renaissance of the twenty-first century affected the Martini in paradoxical ways. See COCKTAIL RENAISSANCE. For the first time since the 1940s, it was back in balance, with a significant proportion of good vermouth in it (ratios went from about five to one all the way down to one to one, or even one part gin to two parts vermouth, as was occasionally seen in the 1880s). The olive was out and the twist was back, now as a broad swatch of thin-cut peel with its oil properly expressed on the surface of the drink. Good, firm ice, cracked to order, along with careful stirring and smaller-sized glasses, meant the drink was cold and silky again. Orange bitters came back, as did the occasional dash of real absinthe, popular in the 1890s and 1900s. See ABSINTHE. One even started seeing the old Sweet Martini, with Italian vermouth and the newly revived Old Tom gin (this is often listed as a Martinez, to distinguish it from the Dry Martini).

In return for all that, all the Martini had to give up was its iconic status; its eighty-year-old position as king of all cocktails. The revival in bartending and mixology meant that there were other long-neglected classics being made just as carefully: Daiquiris, Manhattans, Old-Fashioneds, Clover Clubs—the list goes on. See DAIQUIRI; MANHATTAN COCKTAIL; OLD-FASHIONED COCKTAIL; and CLOVER CLUB. To revive that canon involved a good deal of analysis and re-engineering, and that hard look extended to things such as the v-shaped "Martini" glass, which was replaced by more practical styles. Without the glass and the olive, the Martini was just another cocktail, even if it was a better one than it had been in generations.

Recipes: Martini (1880s): Stir 45 ml Old Tom gin, 45 ml Italian vermouth, and 2 dashes Angostura or other aromatic bitters with cracked ice; strain and add cherry.

Dry Martini (1910): Stir 60 ml London dry or Plymouth gin, 30 ml French vermouth, 2 dashes orange bitters, and (optionally) 1 dash absinthe; strain and add lemon twist.

Extra Dry Martini (1955): Stir 90 ml London dry gin or vodka and 5 ml French vermouth; strain and add olive.

Crockett, Albert Stevens. *The Old Waldorf-Astoria Bar Book*. New York: A. S. Crockett, 1935.

DeVoto, Bernard. "The Easy Chair: For the Wayward and Beguiled." *Harper's*, December 1949, 68.

Edmunds, Lowell. *Martini, Straight Up*, 2nd ed. Baltimore: Johns Hopkins University Press, 1998.

"Set 'Em Up Again, Please!" *Boston Herald*, December 13, 1885 18.

"Very Dry Ruling . . ." *Cincinnati Enquirer*, July 6, 1954, 2.

"What'll You Have." *Cleveland Leader*, March 24, 1883, 6.

David Wondrich

Martini & Rossi is the leading brand of vermouth in the world. The company was originally developed as an offshoot of the Distilleria Nazionale del Spirito di Vino, founded in Turin in 1849 by Carlo Re. Production facilities were initially situated at San Salvatore Monferrato, some 70 kilometers east of the city; after Re retired in 1863 they were moved to Pessione, much closer to the city and with a much better rail connection. That year, the firm acquired three new directors—managing director Alessandro Martini (1824–1905), vintner Luigi Rossi (1828–1892), and accountant Teofilo Sola (1831–1879)—from within the company's own ranks, and the firm was renamed Martini, Sola & Cia.

When the Sola family sold out its shares in 1879, the company changed its name to Martini & Rossi. Its exports of vermouth captured a large part of the nascent American market, and it began focusing on that product, rather than the many other aperitifs, digestives, and liqueurs that it also made. Outside of Italy the term "Martini" became synonymous with the words "Italian vermouth" and "vermouth di Torino." Prussian-born bartender Harry Johnson, one of the first non-Italian barmen to recognize the value of vermouth as an ingredient for mixed drinks, published a recipe incorporating vermouth in a cocktail in 1882, and included it in the list of items he held that a bar must stock. See JOHNSON, HARRY.

Martini & Rossi's second product, Martini Extra Dry Vermouth, was introduced on New Year's Day in 1900 in response to the popularity in the United

States of French vermouth in the dry style. A decade later, the company introduced its Martini Bianco in response to the popularity of Dolin's Vermouth de Chambéry Blanc.

The company continued to be owned and managed by the families until 1977, when it was restructured and renamed General Beverage Corporation. The Martini & Rossi brand was finally acquired by Bacardi in 1993.

See also BACARDI and VERMOUTH.

Interviews with Giuseppe Gallo and the archival staff at Martini & Rossi, Pessione, Italy, January through August 2009.

Orengo, Nico. *Mondo Martini*. Sori d'Alba, Italy: Sori Edizioni, [2006].

Anistatia R. Miller and Jared M. Brown

Mary Pickford is a Prohibition-era cocktail, with Bacardi rum, pineapple juice, and grenadine, named after the silent movie star (1892–1979). According to Basil Woon's 1928 book *When It's Cocktail Time in Cuba*, Hotel Sevilla-Biltmore bartender Fred Kaufman invented the drink to commemorate Pickford's visit to Havana; newspaper accounts confirm that she vacationed there in December 1922, when Kaufman most likely created his drink. Purportedly one of the three most ordered cocktails in Cuba during Prohibition (after the Daiquiri and El Presidente), the Mary Pickford became particularly popular at Constantino Ribalaigua's Bar La Florida, where Woon observed him making six at a time. See DAIQUIRI and EL PRESIDENTE.

Recipe: Shake well with ice 60 ml pineapple juice (preferably fresh), 30 ml white rum, and 5 ml grenadine; strain into chilled cocktail glass.

See also FLORIDITA and RIBALAIGUA Y VERT, CONSTANTE.

Leaves, Holly. "Touring North America: Douglas Fairbanks and Mary Pickford en route to New York and Many Eastern Points." *Hollywood Magazine*, September 29, 1922.

Woon, Basil. *When It's Cocktail Time in Cuba*. New York: Horace Liveright, 1928.

Jeff Berry

mash is the mixture of milled grains and hot water that is created at the beginning of the brewing process that leads to fermentation and distillation. "The mash" can also refer to the "mash bill"—the blend of different grains used in American whisky distilling. Mashing is the carefully controlled cooking of this mixture of grains and water, which chemically converts the starches in the grains into fermentable and unfermentable sugars, an essential step on the way to fermentation. See MASHING.

Mashes differ from country to country and often from distillery to distillery. Mashes made up entirely of malt are the easiest to work with and the oldest. Many distilling traditions, however, use a little malt to start saccharification (15 percent will do) and round the rest out with raw grains. Rye, which is common, and oats, formerly used in Ireland and now enjoying a small revival, are the most challenging to work with, as they are quite glutinous.

To start the mash, the grains are milled to a flour-like consistency in order to expose as much surface area as possible to the water and the enzymes, allowing a full and fast conversion. A successful mash begins with a careful and full hydration of the flour as it goes into the mashing vessel. This wet mix of grain flour and hot water is referred to as the "grist"; only once enzymes, either from included malt or added by the distiller, have converted the starches in the grain to sugars does the thick, starchy, and sticky grist become the much more liquid mash.

Mash can be further refined into "wort" by filtering out the remaining solids; this is the practice in Scotland and Ireland and wherever grain distillers have adopted their model. In Germany, however, the mash is traditionally distilled without filtration, and America has always followed this model. See WORT.

Mashing different grains comes with different challenges. Malted barley is relatively simple and straightforward. See BARLEY. Rye and wheat, on the other hand, have a lot more proteins, which will cause the mash to clump and stick together. See RYE and WHEAT. Careful temperature management and addition of beta-glucanase enzymes will help with this, and will also cut down on the notorious excessive foaming in rye fermentation.

See also ENZYMES; FERMENTATION; and WHISKY.

Bamforth, Charles. *Beer: Tap into the Art and Science of Brewing.* New York: Insight, 1998.

Broom, Dave. *The World Atlas of Whisky*, 2nd ed. London: Mitchell Beazley, 2014.

Buxton, Ian, and Paul S. Hughes. *The Science and Commerce of Whisky.* Cambridge: Royal Society of Chemistry, 2013.

Lew Bryson

mash bill is a term used in the United States whisky industry to describe the combination of Poaceae grains (most notably corn, rye, barley, and wheat) that represent formulas for straight whisky recipes, especially in bourbon and rye whiskies. An accounting term from the mid-twentieth century, "mash bill" originally denoted the prices of different grains in costing out the formulation of whisky recipes for mashing and fermentation. Mixed grain recipes were the convention in colonial American whisky since the beginning of American distilling in the early seventeenth century, although there are notable exceptions. See WHISKY, RYE.

Mash bills—when combined with yeast strains, varying fermentation times and conditions, and different types of distillation plant and practices, as well as the bourbon custom of adjusting acidity by the sour mash method—all affect the flavor of the distillate. Grain is the primary component in the base cost of manufacturing whisky, but as commodities the various grains used can vary in price by season; in the past, this led to some fluctuations in mash bills, which of course influenced the flavor of the finished whisky.

Nonetheless, beginning in 1938 the United States regulated the minimum grain-volume thresholds for labeling of straight whiskies: 51 percent corn for bourbon whisky, 80 percent corn for corn whisky, 51 percent rye or rye malt for rye whiskies, 51 percent wheat for wheat whisky, and 51 percent malted barley for malt whisky. This meant that a distillery's cost of production could vary more from year to year, but it gave the consumer a more consistent, trustworthy product.

Today, each distillery usually has a house or proprietary mash bill for their whisky, and often more than one if they make several brands.

In making mixed-grain spirits, American distillers were of course following a practice that was centuries old in continental Europe and the British Isles. On the Continent, the Dutch made their genever from Baltic and local rye mashed with malted barley for saccharification. See GENEVER. Similarly, Scandinavian, German, and Russian distillers were grain captives to their cold-climate rye and barley, although sometimes wheat was used as well, and in some cases, particularly in Germany, malted rye replaced the barley malt. See AQUAVIT; KORN; and VODKA. Government regulations also impacted grain proportions for mash recipes, particularly in Britain, where a progressively punitive malt tax was enacted in 1697, reached a zenith in 1770, and was only abolished in 1880. This forced distillers to economize by increasingly using unmalted grains to mitigate the duty. By the late eighteenth century, Irish whisky was commonly one-third each green barley, malted barley, and oats or rye. Scotland had similar mash recipes, with local bere (an ancient barley landrace) and black oats the predominant grains. By the mid-nineteenth century, continuous patent stills were in wide use, substituting local cereals with cheap imported maize and wheat, subject to commodity prices. See WHISKY, GRAIN; WHISKY, IRISH; and WHISKY, SCOTCH. For the Asian approach to mixed-grain spirits, see BAIJIU.

Beresford, John. *Observations on . . . the State of the Distilling Trade in Ireland.* Dublin: 1782.

Craig, H. Charles. *The Scotch Whisky Industry Record.* Dumbarton, UK: Index, 1994.

Federal Alcohol Administration Act. 96 Article II of Regulations 5. Washington DC, March 1, 1938.

Hall, Harrison. *The Distiller*, 2nd ed. Philadelphia: 1818.

Royal Commission on Whiskey and Other Potable Spirits. *Interim report.* London: HM Stationery Office, 1908, sections 1768–1941; 14232–14320.

Chris Middleton

mashing is the process of mixing water with milled cereal grains to extract their starch and convert it into sugars assimilable by the chosen yeast strain to produce alcohol. The starch contained within the cereal grain endosperm becomes solubilized when the mash achieves the appropriate temperature to gelatinize it. Then, amylolytic enzymes, either contained within the malted barley (endogenous) or from exogenous sources, convert it into smaller fermentable carbohydrates. Each enzyme has an optimal temperature and pH range; however, 62–65° C and 5.4–5.6, respectively, is an ideal profile for targeting the three major amylolytic endogenous enzymes: α-amylase, β-amylase, and limit-dextrinase.

The water is added at a temperature that varies according to the type of mashing. Scotch distillers, for instance, will add water at about 63° C to the mash; bourbon distillers will add rye or wheat to their cooked corn at around 77° C and slowly drop the temperature to 63° C before adding the malt.

For distillers, the aim is to extract and convert all of the starch into fermentable carbohydrates to maximize the ethanol yield. This is contrary to mashing for beer production, where the aim is to balance fermentable carbohydrate and unfermentable dextrin, as these compounds contribute to mouthfeel and the overall sensory experience. However, with the production of distilled spirits, dextrin (residual extract) is not only a loss of ethanol and profit but can contribute to downstream processing issues as well. Mashing protocols are largely determined by cereal grain used, equipment (hammer mill vs. roller mill, mash mixer vs. jet cooker), and the country of production (Scotland vs. United States). See MASH.

A wide variety of cereals are used in modern distilling; however, corn, rye, wheat, and malted barley are the most common. Each grain has a slightly different gelatinization point and this is due largely to the type and ratio of starch molecules, amylose vs. amylopectin, and the size of starch granules in the grain's endosperm. In general, smaller or more tightly compacted granules require a higher gelatinization point, as is the case with corn.

Aside from starch solubilization and composition, other constituents of cereals, such as proteins, β-glucans, and pentosans, also impact mashing. Rye and wheat have higher protein and pentosan levels than corn, which significantly impacts starch concentration and availability. This is largely due to the structure of the endosperm. The plant cells of the endosperm are enclosed within an inner and outer cell wall composed of β-glucans and pentosans; and within the cell, the starch molecules are dispersed within a proteinaceous matrix. In order to access the starch contained within the endosperm for subsequent hydration and conversion, the cell wall structure and intercellular matrix must be degraded.

Since rye and wheat have higher protein and lower starch levels than corn, yields are lower, and substantial proteolysis must occur for maximum extract to be achieved. This is not the case with malted barley, as the malting process has already degraded the cell walls and intracellular protein matrix, thus making the starch readily available for conversion to fermentable carbohydrates during mashing.

Regulations in the country of production can impact the raw materials and processing used. For example, Scotch whisky regulations stipulate that only endogenous enzymes may be used during mashing, and this dictates the mash bill. Meeting this requirement necessitates a greater inclusion of malt with high diastatic power in addition to any other grains used. American whisky has no such stipulations on enzyme origin, and the use of exogenous enzymes (α-amylase, pullulanase, and α-glucosidase) is commonplace. This correlates to a much lower percentage of malted barley within the mash bill and less conservative time and temperature restrictions, as exogenous enzymes generally are more thermostable and more efficient.

In addition to the conversion of starch into fermentable sugars, the extraction and/or generation of necessary nutrients for the chosen yeast strain is critical to a successful fermentation; these nutrients include free amino nitrogen, B-vitamins, zinc, and many others. There is also the generation/release of materials that will eventually contribute to the flavor profile of the spirit, such as ferulic acid. Rye whisky is known for a quintessentially spicy character, which comes from the conversion of ferulic acid into 4-vinyl guaiacol, a clove-like aroma, by the yeast; therefore release of ferulic acid from the grain is a desired step during mashing.

Briggs, D. E., J. S. Hough, R. Stevens, and T. W. Young. "Adjuncts, Sugars, Wort Syrups, and Industrial Enzymes." In *Malting and Brewing Science*, vol. 1, *Malt and Sweet Wort*, 2nd ed., 222–253. Kluwer Academic / Plenum, 1981.

Briggs, D. E., J. S. Hough, R. Stevens, and T. W. Young. "The Chemistry and Biochemistry of Mashing." In *Malting and Brewing Science*, vol. 1, *Malt and Sweet Wort*, 2nd ed., 254–303. Kluwer Academic / Plenum, 1981.

Dolan, Timothy C. S. "Malt Whiskies: Raw Materials and Processing." In *Whisky Technology, Production, and Marketing*, ed. Inge Russell, Charlie Bamforth, and Graham Stewart, 68–70. San Diego: Elsevier, 2003.

Elizabeth Rhoades

The **master blender** is the individual responsible for deciding what mix and percentage of various barrels make up the final flavor profile of an aged spirit. Most aged spirits are blends of liquid from various barrels with different ages, matured in different areas of a number of warehouses. While master distillers have become known as the characters behind many spirits and are often also responsible for the final blend, in many cases, especially with rum, the master blender is the most important person behind the final product. The word "blended" has specific meanings by custom and law depending on the country, especially referring to whisky. Rum producers particularly focus on the skills of their master blenders, like Appleton's current master blender, Joy Spence, and Zacapa's Lorena Vasquez. About a dozen men and women in Scotland currently are in charge of blended scotch whisky brands, a position earned after a multi-year apprenticeship.

See BLENDING.

Broom, Dave. *Rum*. San Francisco: Wine Appreciation Guild, 2003.

Vora, Shivani. "From Chemist to Cocktails: Meet the Rum Industry's First Female Master Blender." *Fortune*, October 24, 2015. http://fortune.com/2015/10/24/female-master-blender/ (accessed February 19, 2021).

Jack Robertiello

master distiller is a term of art rather than science, bestowed on the person in charge of a distillery's output by its ownership. In general, the master distiller is someone who oversees the entire production and aging process: from sourcing and preparing the raw materials—milling the grain, crushing the cane, selecting the juniper berries—to producing and testing the yeast, to creating and maintaining the mash bill, to guiding the fermentation and distillation processes.

Master distiller has long been used—the term dates back at least to the early nineteenth century—as an acknowledgment of the completion of a long, informal, and sometimes nepotistic apprenticeship process, an honorific title indicating ultimate responsibility for a large, fully operating distillery. Contemporary usage has changed that; in many cases today, the master distiller is as much a traveling brand ambassador and marketer as a hands-on, day-to-day distillery manager. The job's duties now often include presenting a company's spirits to consumers and the trade, speaking at events, and otherwise representing the brand to the world.

There is no certifying organization nor series of tests or tasks needed to earn the title, unlike one finds with the traditional guild distinctions of master carpenter or master electrician. Nor is there any need to study under other experienced practitioners of the craft (as is required to earn the master brewer honorific). Therefore, anyone can be named a master distiller or claim the title. For example, in 2014 the owners of the soon to be reopened Old Taylor bourbon distillery named a twenty-eight-year-old with five total years' experience in the distilling business their master distiller. Usually, though, the title is awarded to someone who manages to combine technical expertise and experience with a colorful turn of phrase and the patience to explain such matters to outsiders.

Jack Robertiello

Match was a pace-setting cocktail bar near London's Oxford Circus, founded by entrepreneur Jonathan Downey in 1997. It was a key link between early mixology efforts of 1990s London and the cocktail boom that followed in the next decade. Downey, a Manchester native and corporate lawyer, opened Match in response to what he considered a wanting London bar scene. His aim was to offer quality cocktails in a relaxed atmosphere. The bar proved the cornerstone of what would become Downey's small empire of cocktail dens. For the drinks program, he hired Dick Bradsell, then the most highly regarded cocktail bartender in London. Match helped spread Bradsell's influence as a bartending mentor and increased his number of protégés. Additionally, the initial menu's Matchnificent Seven cocktail list helped further popularize Bradsell creations such as the Bramble, Russian Spring Punch, and Vodka Espresso. Later on, Downey partnered with the equally notable American bartender Dale DeGroff. Downey's demanding vision for Match encompassed every aspect of the bar, from drinks and food to bartender training and hospitality. The name of the bar evoked his then-innovative idea that the drinks were intended to pair with specific food. An instant success, the bar spawned a second Match in London as well as sister bars in Melbourne and Ibiza.

See also BRADSELL, DICK; DEGROFF, DALE; and DOWNEY, JONATHAN.

Simonson, Robert. *A Proper Drink*. San Francisco: Ten Speed, 2016.

Robert Simonson

maturation is the aging of spirits in order to improve their flavor. In most parts of the world, this is done by putting them in oak or other wooden containers after distillation and leaving them there for a period that can be as short as a few days and as long as forty years or more. See BARREL. Some spirits, however, are aged in semi-porous earthenware jugs, or occasionally even large, loosely sealed glass bottles. Moreover, even those spirits that are not destined for further maturation are generally rested after distillation for at least a week or two in stainless steel tanks or other such nonreactive containers, to let flavors integrate and some of the most volatile compounds break down, evaporate, or get reabsorbed.

Chemically, maturation proper is a highly complex process that is not fully understood, or at least not to the point that spirits can be synthesized that are indistinguishable from traditionally aged ones, a thing that distillers and rectifiers have been trying to do since the eighteenth century. See RECTIFICATION and SPEED-AGING. In fact, maturation involves not one process but three. There is extraction, where the spirit becomes infused with compounds from the wood it is being aged in (obviously, this does not apply when nonreactive containers are used). There is oxidation, where the congeners in the spirit (basically, anything that survives distillation beyond water and ethanol) and any wood extracts react with the oxygen entering the container and with each other, thus breaking down and forming new compounds. See CONGENERS. And there is concentration, where the evaporation of ethanol and water through the pores of the container concentrates the congeners and wood extracts and their breakdown products in the liquid left behind.

Before we discuss these in detail, we must emphasize that how they play out is highly dependent on the spirit that goes into the barrel: on its raw material, on its fermentation, on its distillation proof, on the type of still that was used, and on the proof the spirit was reduced to before barreling. These all govern the type and amount of congeners that will be present, and congeners are the key to maturation: without them, aged spirits would just be wood-flavored vodka. See STARKA. The aging process is also quite sensitive to temperature, like any chemical reaction.

Checking the progress of maturation in a cognac *chai*, or cellar. Courtesy of Maison Ferrand.

Extraction

Extraction is the most visible part of the maturation processes and has the fastest results, particularly when new oak barrels are used. Some woods, such as the îpe-roxo used in Brazil, are relatively nonreactive; oak is not one of them. See CACHAÇA and OAK ALTERNATIVES. With ethanol and water both being powerful solvents, in a matter of days the spirit is on its way to becoming, as the British chemist Peter Shaw (1694–1793) described French brandy in 1731, "a dilute tincture of oak." Among the compounds that leach out of the wood are various phenols, such as ellagic acid, eugenol, and gallic acid, and various lactones. See ELLAGIC ACID; EUGENOL; GALLIC ACID; LACTONES; and PHENOLS. They are joined by things such as lignin and furfural, activated by the toasting or charring of the barrel during its construction (although the latter can also be a product of fermentation and distillation), vanillin, and small amounts of wood sugars. See LIGNIN; VANILLIN; and WOOD CHEMISTRY. These all give the spirit a certain impression of sweetness and roundness. There are also, however, tannins, particularly if the barrel is new. These extract fairly quickly and give the spirit an astringency and underlying bitterness. This can be pleasing, but it needs watching, particularly since tannins and related substances such as gallic acid continue to leach into the spirit for as long as it remains in the barrel. See TANNIN.

Oxidation

Oxidation is the result of storing a spirit in a porous container. The most important reactions involve the esterification of fatty acids with ethanol, producing the flavor-bearing compounds known as esters. See ESTERS. Some fermentation and distillation esters also decay, taking with them their bright, floral new-spirit notes. Other higher congener acids reacting with ethanol also form aldehydes, and acetaldehyde in particular. See ACETALDEHYDE and ALDEHYDES. The eye-watering, peppery acrolein, a bacterial compound sometimes found in grain spirits, breaks down. Sulfur compounds transform into less-pungent ones. Many of these reactions are quite gradual, taking years to play out, but they end up softening the spirit and adding depth of flavor to it. These reactions will also occur in earthenware containers, such as the large jars baijiu is often stored in. Indeed, some baijius are thus aged for as much as fifty years, producing a spirit that is greenish in color, soft, and grassy. See OXIDATION.

Concentration

That fifty-year-old baijiu also has a silky, thick texture on the tongue, the result of the third maturation process, concentration, which is the end result of evaporation. In that case, the clay jar has acted like a wooden barrel, which—as Charles Crampton and Lucius Tolman of the United States Internal Revenue Service described it in their landmark 1908 study of whisky maturation—"acts in many ways like the porous membrane of an osmotic cell and has a very decided selective action on the materials passing through it." Ethanol is highly volatile and water moderately so, making them among the substances that will pass through that barrier and evaporate, leaving the heavier, less-volatile flavor compounds behind (ultimately, the viscosity of a well-aged spirit can end up at three times that of water).

This evaporation means that a barrel of, say, rum or whisky will lose anywhere between 1 or 2 percent and 12 percent or more of its content each year to evaporation, depending on the climate in which it is stored. Producers will lament (and lament) this "angel's share," which can be a greedy one indeed: over the eight years of the Crampton and Tolman study, the ryes and bourbons lost an average of 42 percent of their volume. See ANGEL'S SHARE. But without evaporation there is no oxidation and no concentration, and without concentration there is just woody new spirit. (This was proved anew in the early 2000s by the many small-barrel-aged two-year-old whiskies released by new distilleries, where the barrel size had allowed disproportionate contact with the wood, making for a spirit that was as woody as an older one but not as rich or smooth.) Furthermore, there is a certain disingenuousness to bemoaning the angel's share: while a two-year-old bourbon, for example, might fetch some $15 a liter at retail, an eight-year-old one will get at least $45, more than making up for the lost volume.

Another effect of the climate on evaporation is seen with the proof of the spirit. A barrel stored in a hot and dry climate will lose water faster than it loses ethanol, resulting in a spirit that increases in proof the older it gets. In a moist, cold climate, however, it is the alcohol that leads, and the proof decreases. A good cellarmaster has ways of managing this. See CELLARMASTER. Another thing that requires management is tannin levels: tannins are not volatile, and as ethanol and water evaporate, their concentration increases. At a certain point, they will take over the spirit, making it mouth-puckeringly astringent, bitter, and woody. There are ways of avoiding this—in particular, the French art of managed maturation known as élevage—but it is a constant risk, particularly for spirits stored in new or nearly new oak. See ÉLEVAGE.

There is no one rule for how long a spirit should stay in the barrel. Spirits made from pungent materials that have undergone a long fermentation and are then pot-distilled to relatively low proof will take much longer to mature than spirits from neutral materials that are fermented quickly and distilled in a column still to over 90 percent ABV. Spirits can stay longer in well-used barrels than new ones. Spirits that take twelve years to mature in Scotland or Scandinavia might take four in Jalisco or Queensland. But when maturation is done well, when the three processes are made to work together, it is as Smith wrote in 1731: the spirits' "lying so long, as it were in a state of slow digestion, wonderfully takes off from that hot, acrid, and foul taste, peculiar to all spirits or brandies newly distilled, and gives them a coolness and a softness not easily to be introduced by art."

See also RANCIO.

Alcarde, Andre, et al. "Formation of Volatile and Maturation-Related Congeners during the Aging of Sugarcane Spirit in Oak Barrels." *Journal of the Institute of Brewing and Distilling* 120 (2014): 529–536.

Buxton, Ian, and Paul S. Hughes. *The Science and Commerce of Whisky.* London: RSC, 2015.

Crampton, C. A., and L. M. Tolman. "A Study of the Changes Taking Place in Whiskey Stored in Wood." *Journal of the American Chemical Society* 30 (January 1908): 98–136.

Nykänen, Lalli, and Heikki Suomalainen. *Aroma of Beer, Wine, and Distilled Alcoholic Beverages.* Berlin: Akademie Verlag, 1983.

Shaw, Peter. *Three Essays in Artificial Philosophy.* London: 1731.

David Wondrich

Harry McElhone demonstrating the proper way to pour a cocktail, 1919. Wondrich Collection.

McElhone, Henry "Harry" (1890–1958), a Scot who worked in France and catered largely to Americans, earned his reputation as one of the bar world's defining figures behind the bar at Harry's New York Bar in Paris, which he owned and operated from 1923 until his death. See HARRY'S NEW YORK BAR. McElhone was a talented mixologist, inventing several drinks that enjoyed wide circulation, including the Monkey Gland, the Scofflaw, and an early version of the White Lady. His real importance, however, was as a pioneer of branding: through his tireless and clever use of, among other things, publicity stunts and paper ephemera (including menus and self-deprecating postcards, jocular items such as lapel tags requesting that intoxicated patrons be returned to the bar, and numerous updates to the vest-pocket cocktail book that he had published), he created an identity for his bar as not just one of the American bars in Paris but *the* American bar in Paris. Masters of branding such as Don the Beachcomber, Trader Vic, and Allan Stillman of TGI Friday's followed a path that

McElhone laid out. See BEACH, DONN; BERGERON, VICTOR "TRADER VIC"; and TGI FRIDAY'S.

Born in the rough Hilltown section of Dundee, Scotland, McElhone left school at fourteen and after a brief stint as a mill clerk found work as a busboy and then a billiard "marker," or attendant. In that job, he "met several Frenchmen who seemed to be well on the road to prosperity," as he told a Dundee newspaper in 1922. They convinced him to seek his fortune in France. By 1908 his French was good enough for him to be made a bar boy. According to the detailed autobiography he sketched out to *Town and Country* magazine in 1947, that was at the Hotel Beau Séjour, in Cannes. For the next six years, McElhone would tend bar at various French resorts, ending at the Casino at Enghien-les-Bains, just outside of Paris.

When war broke out in 1914, McElhone's first instinct was to join not the British but the French army (his wife was French). When he learned that he would instead be pressed into the dreaded Foreign Legion, he went instead to New York, where he briefly tended bar at the Plaza Hotel in New York and the Hotel Elton in Waterbury, Connecticut. He returned to Paris in early 1915 and was hired to reopen the shuttered New York Bar on Rue Daonou. Shortly afterward, however, McElhone was recruited to be head bartender at the new Ciro's Club in London. There, he mixed Fourth Degrees, Tipperaries, Chorus Ladies, and thirty other Cocktails, along with thirty-four long drinks, for what was left of London's high society. After a year, he joined the Royal Naval Air Service and served in Flanders as an observer for the duration of the war.

In 1919, McElhone returned to London and helped open several new bars, including the one at Buck's Club, before returning to Ciro's. His time there and at Ciro's summer bar at the resort of Deauville, France, made him famous, and it was as "Harry of Ciro's" that he published his *ABC of Mixing Cocktails* at the end of 1922. This guide would see ten editions during his lifetime.

In 1923, McElhone was able to buy the New York Bar in Paris and promptly attached his name to it. He continued to target Americans, advertising it in Paris's American newspapers with a phonetic spelling of the address, *cinq rue Daunou*, as "Sank Roo Doe Noo," so any American arriving in Paris could get directly there by taxi. Perhaps his greatest stunt was creating the IBF (International Bar Flies)—an organization for serious drinkers—with the New York journalist O. O. "Odd" McIntyre (1884–1938) in 1924. By 1927 there were over five thousand members with posts, or "traps," all over the world, and the organization kept growing for years afterward.

In 1940, with German troops closing in on Paris, McElhone locked his important papers in a safe, buried it outside of Paris, and fled with his family, minus one son who was already a prisoner of war, to London. There, he was nearly killed in March 1941, when the Café de Paris, where he was tending bar, was destroyed by a German bomb with large loss of life.

McElhone returned to Paris after the war and picked up where he left off, running the bar until his death. He was succeeded by his son Andrew (1923–1996), his grandson Duncan (1954–1998), and now his great-grandson Franz-Arthur.

Archives Commerciales de la France, September 22, 1923, 1446.

Goodman, Eckert. "Harry's Sank Roo Doe Noo." *Town and Country*, July 1947, 56ff.

"'Harry of Ciro's' Is a Dundee Man." *Dundee Evening Telegraph*, December 26, 1922, 9.

Sir Affable [pseud.]. "Then—and Now." *Sporting Times*, September 25, 1915, 2.

Woon, Basil. *The Paris That's Not in the Guide Books.* New York: Brentano's, 1926.

Fernando Castellon and David Wondrich

McMillian, Chris (1961–), is a fourth-generation bartender based in New Orleans. *Imbibe Magazine* recognized McMillian in 2010 as one of the top 25 most influential cocktail personalities of the past century.

McMillian was born in northern Louisiana, grew up in California and Hawaii, and traveled widely before settling in New Orleans in 1984. Intrigued by the city's historic cocktail culture, McMillian immersed himself in researching early cocktails and defunct New Orleans bars (particularly antebellum bars), freely sharing what he learned with fellow bartenders and customers before cocktail history arose as a popular pursuit.

McMillian got his start as a banquet bartender before taking a position at the Ritz Carlton in downtown New Orleans. While presiding over the hotel's small Library Bar, McMillian became widely known among craft cocktail bartenders for his resurrection of the traditional Mint Julep. Using a canvas ice bag and oversized mallet, he'd pound the ice in syncopation while reciting Soule Smith's late nineteenth-century "Ode to the Mint Julep." McMillian often advocates for bartenders to focus not on drinks but on hospitality. "Making drinks only comprises 10 percent of what I do as a bartender," he has said. "I'm a host, concierge, tour guide—I do any number of things in addition to making drinks."

After leaving the Ritz Carlton, McMillian worked at several New Orleans restaurant and hotel bars before opening Revel, a small restaurant and bar, in 2016 with his wife, Laura, in New Orleans's Mid-City neighborhood. Also that year, he published *Lift Your Spirits*, a history of cocktail culture in New Orleans, cowritten with the author and food historian Elizabeth Williams.

See also MINT JULEP.

Curtis, Wayne. "Characters: Chris McMillian," *Imbibe Magazine*, May/June 2009.

Williams, Elizabeth M., and Chris McMillian. *Lift Your Spirits*. Baton Rouge: LSU Press, 2016.

Wayne Curtis

Meder's Swan genever, although not the largest or the oldest of Dutch marks, was nonetheless the most widely known and consistently popular Dutch gin in America in the nineteenth century. Johan Jacob Meder (1772–1844) partnered with Herbertus Rahder in 1816 to take over the Swan distillery in Schiedam, built in 1795. In 1824, after Rahder's death, Meder brought his son Johan Christian into the business, and they incorporated as J. J. Meder & Zoon. Swan gin was first brought to the United States by Frederick Gebhard, a New Yorker of Dutch birth. Gebhard and his nephew Frederick Suchard eventually secured the exclusive rights to distribute the brand, passing them down to Ferd. Ruttman & Sons and then W. A. Taylor. By 1834, the "much admired" Swan gin (as a North Carolina newspaper dubbed it) was available throughout the United States, always at a premium price.

Swan remained the best-known brand of genever in America throughout the nineteenth century, the spirit's heyday there. In 1866, the firm produced 6,883 hectoliters of gin at 50 percent ABV (the equivalent of over 900,000 750-ml bottles), of which 1,975 hl were exported, most to the United States. By 1882, Meder's production had risen to 44,000 hl (almost six million bottles), the lion's share of that production going to America. The next decade, however, saw Dutch-style gins eclipsed in the American market in favor of English-style ones, and while the brand soldiered on in the market until World War I, it never recovered its position. J. J. Meder & Zoon continued making genever at the Swan distillery until 1969.

See also GENEVER; GIN.

Grashoff, Hans. *Nederland Is Mederland*. Schiedam: National Jenevermuseum, 2016.

"New Goods." *Newbern (NC) Sentinel*, December 19, 1834, 4.

David Wondrich

Meier, Frank (1884–1947), was born in 1884 at Kirchberg in Tirol, Austria. His family were innkeepers, and he grew up in the business, attending hotel school briefly before going to Paris and London, where he became a bar boy at the Hotel Cecil. In 1903, he went to New York and was able to get a job behind the bar at the Hoffman House hotel, one of the most famous in the world, where he worked for seven months before returning to the Cecil. See HOFFMAN HOUSE. He soon left London, though, working at bars throughout France and Belgium and as far afield as Cairo. In 1908, he returned to Paris and opened the Brunswick Bar on the Rue des Capucines, which he ran until the outbreak of war in 1914. He volunteered for the infantry and then transferred to the Foreign Legion, where he saw a good deal of fighting.

Soon after his discharge in 1920, Meier was asked to open a bar in the Ritz Hotel, Paris. Running the bar, one of the most popular and crowded in Paris, on commission, he rapidly became both respected and, if not wealthy, then close to it. By 1926 his reputation was already such that travel journalist Basil Woon could call him "the man whose friendship is more courted than that of a many a president." Although Meier's role was largely managerial, he also found time to mix and create drinks, including the first luxury cocktail. That came about in 1923, when, as reported by Lucius Beebe, he mixed—and sold—a Sidecar with lemon, Cointreau, and a vintage pre-phylloxera cognac from 1865.

In 1936, Meier published *The Artistry of Mixing Drinks* (in English, although printed in Paris), an elegant volume that is one of the few that can stand next to *The Savoy Cocktail Book* in terms of design. The book contained classics and popular Parisian drinks, but also a large number created by Meier, which he marked with a neat "FM" logo. The most famous are the Bee's Knees, the Olympic and his Corpse Reviver no. 2, which might have inspired Ernest Hemingway's famous champagne-and-absinthe "Death in the Afternoon." Along with the regular print run, Meier issued a lot of three hundred numbered copies for special guests; the full list has not survived, but no. 85 was Kermit Roosevelt, and one can only imagine the rest.

During World War II, he stayed at the Ritz even under Nazi occupation, although he seems to have helped the French Resistance (the record is murky), but once the war was finished, he had troubles with the hotel's management because he asked to some clients to pay their tabs to his private bank account in England. He died in 1947.

Beebe, Lucius. *The Stork Club Bar Book*. New York: Rinehart, 1946.

Graves, Charles. "More Celebrities in Cameo." *The Bystander*, January 20, 1937, 89.

"Paris Barman Here on Holiday." *New York Sun*, September 9, 1933, 6.

Préfecture de police de Paris, dossier no. 96951, Meier, Frank.

Woon, Basil. *The Paris That's Not in the Guide Books*. New York: Brentano's, 1926.

Fernando Castellon

Metaxa is a Greek brandy-based liqueur brand founded by the entrepreneur Spyros Metaxa (1843–1909) in 1888. The amber-hued liqueur, which comes in a bottle bearing the image of an ancient Salamina warrior, is a blend of local brandies with muscat wine and a secret mix of botanicals, including rose petals. See BRANDY and BOTANICAL. It is customarily sipped neat, with a single ice cube, but it is also used in variations of classic cocktails, such as the Sidecar or Mint Julep. The brand offers a range of aged expressions, including 5 Stars, 7 Stars, 12 Stars, and the small-batch Private Reserve. Metaxa also bottles the Honey Shot, which is made with dark honey from ancient Egio. The brand is now owned by the French Remy-Cointreau company.

See also MINT JULEP and SIDECAR.

"The History of Metaxa." https://www.metaxa.com/house-of-metaxa/history/ (accessed April 4, 2021).

Alia Akkam

methanol, also known as wood or methyl alcohol, is a toxic form of alcohol that can cause blindness or even death if ingested in sufficient quantities. See HEALTH AND SPIRITS. Produced in very small amounts during fermentation, methanol, which boils at 64.7° C, is an important part of the heads, the first, toxic, part of the distillate, and must be separated from ethanol (which has a higher boiling point) and other desirable compounds to make safely potable spirits. See DISTILLATION; FERMENTATION; and HEADS. Methanol is also added as a denaturant to industrial ethanol to render it unfit for consumption (and therefore not subject to taxes imposed on alcoholic beverages). In the years leading up to and during Prohibition, it was also frequently added to spirits by unscrupulous producers, often with disastrous effects; in the parts of the world where bootlegged and counterfeit spirits are a problem, methanol poisoning is still common. See MOONSHINE and PROHIBITION AND TEMPERANCE IN AMERICA.

See also ETHANOL.

"Wood Alcohol's Trail." *New York Times*, January 15, 1922.

David Mahoney

methylated spirits, also known as denatured alcohol, is a mixture of ethanol with chemicals designed to discourage people from drinking it, such as the toxic methanol (or "methyl alcohol," which gives the compound its name) and the extremely bitter denatonium benzoate. In most countries, alcohol produced for human consumption is taxed at a higher rate than methylated spirits, which are intended for industrial uses.

During Prohibition in the United States, all alcohol produced for industrial purposes was required to be mixed with methanol, which led to many cases of mass poisonings when bootleggers sold industrial alcohol for illicit consumption; in New York City, denatured alcohol consumption killed more than thirty people during the 1926 Christmas season alone. Today, formulas for denatured alcohol supplement the poisons with bitter or otherwise unpalatable and offensive-smelling chemicals and coloring agents in addition to poisons to prevent this.

There are numerous folk methods for purifying methylated spirits so that they may be drunk, such as filtering it through bread, commonly used by desperate drinkers in the old Soviet Union. These are always risky and rarely completely effective.

See also PROHIBITION AND TEMPERANCE IN AMERICA.

Blum, Deborah. "The Chemist's War." *Slate*, February 19, 2010. http://www.slate.com/articles/health_and_science/medical_examiner/2010/02/the_chemists_war.html (accessed February 19, 2021).

Jason Horn

Mexico has an ancient history of fermentation and alcohol production, as the culture of the Native Americans (Indios) included alcohol beverages for religious ceremony, spiritual enlightenment, and familial celebrations, dating back at least two thousand years, if not longer. These fermented beverages were crafted from the staples of a subsistence lifestyle for early Americans, such as pulque from maguey, or the agave plant, which was a primary source of food and nutrition for at least nine thousand years, and maize, or corn, an invention of the indigenous peoples of the Americas that scientists often still credit as one of the first and perhaps greatest feats of genetic engineering of all time—over six thousand years ago. Although distillation in Mexico focused upon fermented *tepache* or *mosto* from the maguey, the indigenous people of Mexico have throughout history fermented virtually everything they could, with most variations depending predominantly upon geography and availability, including *chicha* (sugar-cane juice), *ciruelas* (plums), *chocohuite* (a bromeliad), *matzaoctli* (pineapple wine in Nahuatl, often referred to today as *tapache*), *coyol* or *taberna* (palm wine), *xocoyolle* (of the sorrel family), beer from maize and mecate bark, and *balche*, or mead (honey with bark).

It is commonly taught that there were no spirits in the Americas until the Columbian exchange and the arrival of the Spanish, who are credited with bringing their alembic stills and teaching the Indios how to distill their "crude fermented beverages" into basic distillates. There is, however, a significant body of new evidence that points to distillation existing in a pre-Hispanic Mexico. Many archaeologists and anthropologists in Mexico now agree that distillation, for the purpose of ritual beverages, may have begun as early as 600–400 BCE.

There are several different types of spirits being distilled in Mexico today from the maguey (or agave), most prominently tequila, which is by far the leading spirit of Mexico and still one of the fastest-growing spirit categories in the United States; mezcal, the most ancient and perhaps still the most artisanal spirit in Mexico, itself a rapidly emerging category; and other distillates of agave (maguey), such as raicilla and bacanora. See RAICILLA and BACANORA. There is also Mexican brandy, distilled from local grapes, and scattered local distillations of corn, tropical fruits such as pineapple, and sugar cane, which has a long history in the country and was formerly made and consumed in very large quantities. See CHARANDA, CHINGUIRITO, and HABANERO. Formerly there was also a significant amount of spirit distilled from palm wine in the southern coastal areas.

Mezcal

Until recently, the term *mezcal* could have been used to describe the category of all distillations of agave throughout the country of Mexico, but in spite of the fact that most producers of agave spirits still refer to their spirit as mezcal, that term is now legal only in certain states, and only from registered producers.

To call an agave distillation mezcal, it must carry a *denominacion de origen* from COMERCOM, the governing body of mezcal, and it must be produced in one of the nine designated states: Oaxaca, Durango, Guerrero, San Luis Potosí, Zacatecas, Tamaulipas, Guanajuato, Michoacán, and the recently added state of Puebla (2016). After many years, mezcal has been established as its own category, finally beginning to garner some of the long overdue recognition that these spirits, and their mostly Native American producers, deserve.

Tequila

Tequila, a particular, legally delimited subvariety of mezcal, is truly a Mexican spirit, yet it is at least partially accurate to describe it as a Spanish invention, or intervention, as it was the Spanish and Mexicans of Spanish descent that first converted this ancient native beverage into a modern industry, applying more modern techniques to the artisan agave spirit, and brought this spirit to the world.

Today, tequila, (formerly mezcal de Tequila) is still produced in Jalisco where it originated, near the town of Tequila, but now it can also be produced outside of the state of Jalisco, in four other states, including Nayarit, Tamaulipas, Guanajuato, and Michoacán.

Tequila's global popularity continues to grow. The Margarita has driven awareness and sales, as the drink formerly known as the Tequila Daisy continues to be one of the most popular and important cocktails in the world. See MARGARITA. But increases in consumption can also be directly correlated to the arrival of artisanal, handcrafted tequila.

The United States is responsible for the direct sale of over 75 percent of the exports of mezcal and tequila, but mezcal represents less than 1 percent of that total.

Other Agave Spirits from Mexico

In addition to Mezcals that can be legally produced from these designated and approved states above, there are other unique spirits distilled from the agave plant in Mexico, including bacanora from Sonora; raicilla, from the area around Puerto Vallarta, in Jalisco and Nayarit; tuxca, from around Tuxcacuesco, Jalisco; and comiteco, from Comitán, in Chiapas. Sotol from Chihuahua is distilled from a different species of plant, dasylirion, until recently believed to be a member of the agave family. See SOTOL. There is evidence of some form of mezcal being created through the local, indigenous distillation of maguey in at least twenty states in Mexico today.

New NORMAs (standards and regulations) for mezcal were approved in July of 2016, with updated rules and classifications to determine how and where mezcal can be distilled and how these spirits can be labeled.

See also AGAVE; MEZCAL; and TEQUILA.

Bruman, Henry J. *Alcohol in Ancient Mexico*. Salt Lake City: University of Utah Press, 2000.

Colunga-García Marin, Patricia, Alfonso Larque Saavedra, Luis E. Eguiarte, Daniel Zizumbo-Villareal. *En lo ancestral hay futuro: Del tequila, los mezcales y otros agaves*. Cuernavaca, Mexico: Instituto Nacional de Salud Pública, Consejo Nacional de Ciencia y Tecnología, 2007.

Mann, Charles C. *1491: New Revelations of the Americas before Columbus*. New York: Knopf, 2005.

Sánchez López, Alberto. *Oaxaca, tierra de maguey y mezcal*. [Oaxaca]: Instituto Tecnológico de Oaxaca, 1989.

Serra Puche, Mari Carmen, and Jesús Carlos Lazcano Arce. *El mezcal, una Bebida Prehispánica: Un estudio etnoarqueológico*. Mexico City: Universidad Nacional Autónoma de México, Instituto de Investigaciones Antropológicas, 2016.

Valenzuela, Ana, and Gary Paul Nabhan. *Tequila: A Natural and Cultural History*. Tucson: University of Arizona Press, 2003.

Steve Olson

mezcal, from the Nahuatl words for agave (*metl*) and oven-roasted (*ixcalli*), was the term formerly used to describe the entire category of spirits, or distillates, created from the roasted heart (*piña*) of the agave plant (*maguey*) made anywhere in Mexico. Tequila was originally a specific type of mezcal that was produced only in the state of Jalisco in the region centered on the town of Tequila. Tequila today is legally produced in Jalisco and four other Mexican states: Guanajuato, Tamaulipas, Nayarit, and Michoacán. See TEQUILA. Bacanora from Sonora; raicilla, from an area around Puerto Vallarta, in both Jalisco and Nayarit; tuxca, from Tuxcacuesco, Jalisco; comiteco, from the area of Comitán, Chiapas; and even sotol from Chihuahua were previously considered types of mezcal. See BACANORA; RAICILLA; and SOTOL. However, as a result of the creation of the denominacion de origen (DO) for

One of the bull's hide fermenters, of a design dating back to at least the seventeenth century, used to make 5 Sentidos mezcal at Santa María Ixcatlán, Oaxaca. Courtesy of Sacred.mx.

mezcal, established in 1995, the word "mezcal" today is used specifically, and solely, to describe the agave spirits of nine Mexican states: Oaxaca, Guerrero, Durango, San Luis Potosí, Zacatecas, Guanajuato, Michoacán, Tamaulipas, and the recently approved Puebla (2016), with the state of Oaxaca producing upwards of 90 percent of the regulated mezcal in Mexico. This in spite of the fact that there are over twenty states producing some sort of agave spirit in Mexico today. The new norma oficial mexicana (NOM) 070 SCFI 2015, passed in July of 2016, further categorizes mezcal into classifications and styles, and will attempt to dictate and regulate production methods and process, as well as key issues for the plant, such as which types of maguey can be used, how they should be named, the maturity of the plants, harvesting and cultivation, and the overall agricultural sustainability of the agave.

History

Mezcal has a very long history and a rich culture that surrounds its ancient, artisanal methods of production. It is a matter of dispute today whether there were spirits such as mezcal in Mexico prior to the arrival of Cristobal Colon and the Spanish. It is often taught that it was the Spanish who introduced distillation to the indigenous peoples of Mexico when they arrived with their alembic stills, but there is an increasing amount of evidence that distillation existed prior to the arrival of the Spanish, and some archaeologists and anthropologists believe that distillation, for the purpose of producing ritual beverage, may have begun as early as 600 BCE. Whether or not the indigenous people of Mexico were actually distilling, it is certain that over two thousand years ago, long before the Spanish conquest, the indigenous people of Mexico consumed pulque, a beer from the heart of the maguey (octli, in Nahuatl) and often referred to by the Spanish as vino de mezcal. This "lightning nectar," so named because of the myth of its origins, was to these Native Americans surely a gift from the gods, and it was consumed for religious ceremonies and usually reserved for the spiritual leaders, except for special occasions. It was consumed only in small quantities, as public drunkenness was frowned upon. These cultures worshipped the goddess Mayahuel, who purportedly originated from the maguey.

Evidence of maguey roasted in stone-lined earthen ovens found in Puebla and also in Chihuahua dates back to long before the Christian era, but the earliest documented evidence of pulque consumption is found on a mural in the pyramid of Cholula and dates to around 200 CE. As far as evidence of distillation, the now famous bean pots of Colima date to several hundred years earlier, which were made "to produce a prestige product for ceremonial purposes, with high social and cultural relevance," and another archaeological excavation in the state of Tlaxcala dates ritual consumption of a distilled spirit back to as early as 400 BCE. See DISTILLATION, HISTORY.

Mezcal has been deemed a bebida bendita, or ritual beverage, by Mexico's indigenous people and remains so for palenqueros and mezcaleros (Mezcal producers), and as such, consumption of Mezcal is traditionally reserved for major holidays such as Semana Santa (Easter), Navidad (Christmas), and Dia de los Muertos (Day of the Dead) or important family fiestas and celebrations, such as baptisms, weddings, and even funerals.

The Maguey

The maguey has always been prized and deeply appreciated by Mexico's Native peoples and they have for centuries used maguey for food and drink, sugar, shoes, soap, construction materials, rope, and medicine.

Agave is not a cactus, despite its appearance as such, but is actually one of a family of succulents with more than two hundred species, with the botanical name Agavaceae (Greek for royal or noble). According to agave expert and PhD Ivan Saldaña, there could be as many as 280 species of Agavaceae growing in the landscape from southern Utah to northern Venezuela. As plants go, agaves are survivors that want and expect very little from the environment, and as such thrive in the worst soils in otherwise impossible growing conditions. The maguey has an ancient and symbiotic relationship with corn, beans, and squash, and they are often planted side by side in Oaxaca and other mezcal-producing states.

Mezcals from the demarcated DOs can be produced from many different magueys; estimates range from twenty to forty different species currently harvested for the production of mezcal. These include espadin (*Agave angustifolia*), the most widely cultivated and utilized for Mezcal production; arroqueno (*A. americanus oaxacencis*), an often cultivated maguey formerly used frequently throughout Oaxaca, which because of its uneven ripening and its recent ascension to cult status among bartenders and aficionados has nearly disappeared; and a number of *silvestres* (wild magueys) such as tepextate (*A. marmorata*), tobaziche, barril, madrecuixe, and cuixe (the *A. karwinskii* species) papolome (*A. cupreata*), and the very rare tobala (*A. potatorum*).

Process

There are many ways to produce mezcal. As mezcal has emerged as a successful category, big business has joined in, bringing diffusers and huge stills to the region and finding industrial methods to produce larger quantities of mezcal. But what separates traditional mezcal is its ancient and artisanal methods of production; handcrafted mezcal is unique in the world and should be recognized and protected. See DIFFUSER.

The first step in the process, after growing and maturing magueys for as few as seven or eight years and up to thirty years for some wild magueys, is harvesting the *corazones* (the heart of the plant) and transporting them to the *palenque* (production area) which is no small task in itself, and is still often carried out with the use of burros, mules, or horses. The corazones, sometimes called piñas, because of their resemblance to pineapples after the *pencas* (broad leaves) have been removed, must be first be baked or roasted to convert the fibrous, wood-like plant to a sugar that can be fermented. Traditionally, mezcal piñas are roasted in a conical earthen or stone-lined pit underground for several days, after which the sugars they contain are caramelized, rendering them fermentable.

Then the roasted hearts need to be shredded or pulverized to release the sugars. This process has traditionally been done by hand or by horse, often employing a *molino*, a large, stone wheel driven by horse or mule around a stone-lined, flat, circular grinding area (the name *palenque* signifies a round place). Other producers use heavy wooden bats or mallets and beat each piece of the maguey heart against a stone or in a hollowed out tree trunk. This ancient process is being replaced in much of the production today by modern *desgarradoras*, or gas-powered shredding machines.

Traditionally the shredded fibers, meat, and juices of the maguey are fermented in open tanks with the addition of local water, allowing ambient yeasts and airborne microbes to react with the sugars to create alcohol. This process might last a week or ten days, and for some producers in certain villages it can take up to a month.

Finally, after brewing the roasted and shredded maguey fibers in these open-top fermenters—which range from oak or pine tanks to clay pots, from animal hides to cow bellies (yes, seriously)—the resulting beer is distilled in small stills, usually between 100 and 350 liters. Many traditional producers will put all of the fermented *tepache* (beer of the maguey) into the vessel to be distilled, including all of the fibers of the fermented maguey.

The stills are often copper, and the locals call them *alambiques*, leading us to believe that they are Spanish in origin, or even Moorish, but indeed the old stills bear little resemblance to those of Spain or France. They are usually quite small and are often more cylindrical than round, like a drum, versus a pot. The closest stills in shape to the alembic pot stills of Europe are not actually similar at all, as they are indeed pots, but are constructed from clay, and utilize local *carrizo* (a grass similar to bamboo). The only copper in this process is a small bowl that seals off the top of the still with cold running water circulating through it to condense the vapors on its underside (the similarity of this to the Chinese pot still raises questions that have yet to be answered; see STILL, POT). These clay stills are often completely encased in adobe or are even underground, and most of the traditional producers using copper or steel stills surround their "pots" with adobe bricks and maguey paste, following the ancient tradition.

The first distillation of the tepache is called *ordinario*. The palenqueros then run the ordinario back through the still, this time usually without fibers, for what they call *refinacion*, or refinement, in a second distillation, reaching peak alcohol levels of 60–70 ABV, although it is usually brought off the still at between 45 and 55 ABV.

One of the foundational tenets of traditional mezcal producers is to distill their elixir "to proof"; water is never added to dilute their pure mezcal to a lower alcoholic strength; instead, distillers add the tails of the distillation run. There is a *dicho*, or saying, among the indigenous producers that goes something like this: "Mezcal con agua no es mezcal!" ("Mezcal with water is not mezcal!").

Mezcal Today

Artisanal mezcal may have existed for hundreds or even thousands of years in Mexico, but it is a recent phenomenon in the rest of the world and even for modern Mexicans. Visionary artist Ron Cooper, while creating art in Oaxaca, discovered palenqueros in the mountains of Oaxaca crafting mezcal in the ancient, traditional process. In 1995 Cooper began selling Del Maguey Single Village Mezcal, in order to share what he considered "liquid art." Del Maguey slowly developed near cult status among bartenders, chefs, sommeliers, and spirits connoisseurs. Meanwhile mezcal has become popular in Mexico, which long had scorned it as moonshine and rotgut alcohol, guaranteed to make you go blind and best left for the poor. See COOPER, RON; and DEL MAGUEY MEZCAL. In the past several years,

mezcal has arisen as a category in and of itself and is one of the fastest growing spirit categories in the world. But, while there are numerous quality, artisanal brands, the potential for the industrialization of mezcal is a real and present danger that requires strict regulation.

Legislation

COMERCAM is the Consejo Regulador, or Mexican Regulatory Council, for the quality of mezcal and as such governs and regulates mezcal production and the cultivation of the source material agave in the nine states recognized by the denominacion de origen (DO). The first NORMAs (rules) governing the producing states of mezcal were passed in 1995. These regulations, along with producer certification, began in 2005. The new NORMA, NOM 070 SCFI 2015, passed in July of 2016, further categorizes mezcal into classifications and styles that did not exist previously, such as *artesanal* and *ancestral*.

This is a historic achievement, as these are the first new NORMA rules for mezcal in over twenty years, and they are meant to help to control and regulate the rapid expansion of this exciting, new, but in actuality very ancient category.

Some of the newly established regulations include:

- All bottles labeled mezcal must be 100 percent agave.
- Producers will now be allowed the use of the words *maguey* or *agave* on the label.
- A law governing the maximum amount of acidity allowed in mezcal production has been eliminated.
- There is no exporting of bulk mezcal allowed.

There are now three categories of mezcal:

1. Mezcal:
   100 percent agave, but "mezcal" can be steamed in large ovens, can be fermented in stainless steel using cultured yeasts, and can be made with diffusers; all types of stills are allowed, and water can be added.
2. Mezcal artesanal:
   100 percent agave, this mezcal can be roasted underground but can also be steamed in large ovens; it can be fermented naturally and traditionally or in stainless steel using cultured yeasts; it can be shredded by hand or by horse,

and desgarradoras are also allowed. But it cannot be made with diffusers; only pot stills are allowed; and water can be added.

3. Mezcal ancestral:
100 percent agave, this mezcal must be made by ancient traditional methods: it must be roasted underground; shredded by hand only; fermented naturally in wood, clay, or animal hides; and distilled in traditional clay pots or wood, and water can be added.

There are also now six classes of mezcal:

1. Joven or blanco (white, unaged, the most traditional and most common)
2. Reposado (aged for a minimum of two months and maximum of one year in wood)
3. Añejo (aged minimum one year in barricas)
4. Madurado en vidrio (aged in glass)
5. Abocado con ("flavored with," as in flavored mezcals where the flavors are added after distillation)
6. Destilado con ("distilled with," as in pechugas, where additional ingredients (such as fruits and nuts) are distilled into the mezcal)

Pending legislation could mandate the scientific name of the agave species on the label and may dictate, for the purpose of sustainability, which types of maguey can be used. A new system of rankings has recently been suggested that, if ratified, could require that all registered producers are rated on a scale of sustainability and conformity. There is another proposition requiring producers selling their mezcal outside their village but not registered in a designated DO to call their mezcal *komil*, an ancient, obscure Nahuatl word loosely translated as "inebriating liquid."

Finally

There is a *dicho*, or saying, in Oaxaca: "Para todo mal, mezcal, y para todo bien, también!": "For everything bad, mezcal, and for everything good, also mezcal!"

See also AGAVE and MEXICO.

Bruman, Henry J. *Alcohol in Ancient Mexico*. Salt Lake City: University of Utah Press, 2000.
Colunga-Garcia Marin, Patricia, Alfonso Larque Saavedra, Luis E. Eguiarte, Daniel Zizumbo-Villareal. *En lo ancestral hay futuro: Del tequila, los mezcales y otros agaves*. Cuernavaca, Mexico: Instituto Nacional de Salud Pública, Consejo Nacional de Ciencia y Tecnología, 2007.
Gortari, Yuri de, and Edmundo Escamilla. *Mezcal, Our Essence*. Mexico City: Consejo Mexicano de Productores de Maguey Mezcal, 2009.
Mann, Charles C. *1491: New Revelations of the Americas before Columbus*. New York: Knopf, 2005.
Saldaña Oyarzábal, Iván. *The Anatomy of Mezcal*, Milton, Delaware: Expressit Media, 2016.
Sánchez López, Alberto. *Oaxaca, tierra de maguey y mezcal*. [Oaxaca]: Instituto Tecnológico de Oaxaca, 1989.
Serra Puche, Mari Carmen, and Jesús Carlos Lazcano Arce. *El mezcal, una Bebida Prehispánica: Un estudio etnoarqueológico*. Mexico City: Universidad Nacional Autónoma de México, Instituto de Investigaciones Antropológicas, 2016.
Stewart, Amy. *The Drunken Botanist: The Plants that Create the World's Great Drinks*. Chapel Hill, NC: Algonquin, 2013.
Torrentera, Ulises. *Mezcalaria: Cultura del mezcal*. Oaxaca: Farolito Ediciones, 2012.
Valenzuela, Ana, and Gary Paul Nabhan. *Tequila: A Natural and Cultural History*. Tucson: University of Arizona Press, 2003.
Valenzuela Zapata, Ana G. *El Agave Tequilero, Cultivo e Industria de Mexico*. Mexico City: Ediciones Mundi-Prensa, 2003.
Vasquez-Garcia, J. Antonio, Miguel de J. Chazaro B., Gerardo Hernandez Vera, Ericka Flores Berrio, and Yalma L. Vargas-Rodriguez. *Agaves del Occidente de Mexico*. Guadalajara: Universidad de Guadalajara, 2007.
Vela, Enrique, ed. "El maguey." Special issue, *Arqueologia Mexicana* 57 (2014).

Steve Olson

Michelada is the name of a popular Mexican mixed drink made with beer, lime juice, and hot sauce. It frequently also includes Worcestershire or soy sauce or the umami-rich liquid wheat-gluten seasoning called Maggi (a popular MSG product found in cuisines around the world) and a salt rim. The origins of the Michelada are murky. One oft-cited account tells of a man named Michel Esper creating the drink at the Club Deportivo Potosino in San Luis Potosí in the 1970s; Esper, a civil engineer, has come forward with details to back up the story. Another plausible theory is that the word Michelada derived from the Spanish words for "my cold blonde": *mi chela helada*; "blonde" in this case referring to a light beer, such as a lager or pilsner. It's also possible that *chelada* is simply a Spanish adaptation of the English word "chilled." In any case, anyone familiar with Mexican cuisine could not be surprised that lime, salt, and salsa picante found their way into beer.

Though popular in Mexico, the Michelada has many regional variations and even more modern twists across the globe. It might be made with a darker beer, a range of different condiments, tomato juice, or even Clamato juice. A popular variation, called the *cubana*, incorporates chile powder. In recent years, several beer brands and other beverage companies have tried to capitalize on the popularity of the Michelada with branded cocktail recipes and the launch of new products, including Tecate Michelada, a canned beer drink made with spices, chili pepper, and lime flavor, and Modelo Especial Chelada, made with tomato, lime, and salt flavors. Even Bud Light has a version called Chelada, made with Clamato juice, salt, and lime flavor.

Recipe (Michel Esper's version): In a pint glass full of ice, put 15 ml lime juice and 5 drops each Mexican hot sauce, Worcestershire sauce, and Maggi seasoning. Add a 330 ml bottle of chilled Mexican beer. (Optional: Salt the rim of the glass.)

Cecchini, Toby. "Case Study: It's Michelada Time." *T Magazine*, July 19, 2010. https://tmagazine.blogs. nytimes.com/2010/07/19/case-study-its-michelada-time/ (accessed February 19, 2021).
Estrella de Mar, Jacobo. "La verdadera historia de la invencion de la Michelada." *Vive*, July 15, 2010, 12–13.
Jasso, Ely Cabrero. "Una bebida con origen azul & oro." *Revista Contorno*, 2014, 9.

Chantal Martineau

Mickey Finn, now part of the general language, began in the 1910s as bartender's slang for either a powder or liquid put into a patron's drink to render him or her incapacitated, or, by extension, the drink containing the incapacitating agent. The use of "knock-out drops" (usually chloral hydrate) to incapacitate intoxicated saloon patrons dates back to the 1890s, if not earlier. Usually, however, it was administered by a third party, with or without the collusion of the bartender, and the victim was the robbed elsewhere. However, Michael "Mickey" Finn (1871–?), who operated the Lone Star Café and Palm Garden in Chicago's notorious Levee District from 1896 to 1903, preferred to administer the drug himself, in his "Mickey Finn Special," and rob the customers in the back room. His bar was closed in 1903, but evidently his dedication to the practice attached his name to it in bartender circles. In 1918, a number of Chicago bartenders and waiters were arrested for putting "Mickey Finn Powder," as the packages read, in their customers' drinks, either to get rid of them or to punish them for perceived misbehavior. This time, the powder was tartar emetic and its operation gastric rather than systemic. This type of Mickey Finn remained in use throughout Prohibition, fading in the years after. Fortunately, it is not one of the pre-Prohibition bartending practices revived in recent years.

Asbury, Herbert. *Gem of the Prairie*. New York: Knopf, 1940.
"Waiters Taken for Drugging Nontippers." *Chicago Tribune*, June 23, 1918, 1.

David Wondrich

Micronesia is home to just one operating distillery, Guam's Own, on the Micronesian island of that name. Distilling is therefore rather a lonely proposition.

Despite the incredible technological advances in nearly all aspects of modern life and commerce, getting much-needed raw base materials for distilling to remote island locations in the South Pacific is practically as slow and costly as ever. Couple this fact with the high cost of obtaining or creating potable water and you have a powerful duo of inherent challenges to distilling spirits. In recent decades, brewing operations on Saipan, Palau, and the Marshall Islands have shuttered as a result of these challenges.

Micronesians had no history of alcohol production or use prior to the arrival of the Spanish in the mid-sixteenth century. Islanders in some parts of Micronesia embraced the narcotic effects of kava, the nonalcoholic drink made from the root of the *Piper methysticum*. From the middle 1500s to the later 1700s Guam and other islands were important

The Chinese-style internal condensation pot still observed by Louis-Claude de Freycinet in Guam in 1819. Wondrich Collection.

layovers for the Manila galleons traversing the Pacific. Spanish sailors introduced wine and other alcoholic beverages to Micronesia, and Micronesians, especially in Guam, eventually began to make fermented varieties of sugar-cane juice and coconut palm sap, which they sold to the Spanish as a necessary provision on their long voyages. Micronesians eventually began distilling these fermented drinks, and a French expedition lead by Louis Freycinet in the 1810s found, and illustrated, a Chinese-style pot still being used by the native Chamorro people in Guam in the 1830s. See STILL, POT. Elsewhere, distilling seems to have been more informal and improvised, as in John Jackson's 1853 account of the still he witnessed operating on the island of Banga, off of Tahiti, which was put together from a large pot, an iron gun barrel nested in a water-filled bamboo trough, and a wooden canoe to hold the mash, which was assembled from bananas and other fruit, sugar cane, and *ti* root.

In Guam, the main spirit produced was "aguayente," or "agi," generally distilled from *tuba*, or palm wine, although it was sometimes based on cane juice. When the Americans gained control of Guam following the Spanish-American War, they attempted to stamp out the production of "devil water." Christian missionaries led these temperance efforts. Distilling on a commercial scale would not occur until the years in between World War I and II.

Guam's Own Distillery, founded in 2009, is locally owned and operated. Guam's Own makes a wide array of products including mango vodka, whisky, a trio of rums, and an aguayente, which is an homage to the style of sugar-cane-based spirit once made on colonial Guam. By all accounts, the rums made at Guam's Own are the most successful in Guam in terms of both sales and consumer preference. In the first years of operation, Guam's Own relied heavily on locally grown sugar-cane juice, but these plantations and processing facilities have since closed. Although they make efforts to use local materials, sugar-cane juice, molasses, and other base materials for distilling must be sourced from other nearby islands. Guam's Own products are not exported and are only available on Guam.

De Freycinet, Louis. *Voyage autour du monde*, vol. 2. Paris: 1829.

Jackson, John. "Feejean Islands." In *Journal of a Cruise among the Islands of the Western Pacific*, by John Elphinstone Erskine, 470. London: John Murray, 1853.

Sean Ludford

micro-oxygenation refers to a technique used in wine production on a large scale since the 1990s and sometimes for spirits in different ways since the end of the nineteenth century. For the present technique, minute amounts of oxygen are percolated through wine or spirits via a tube immersed in the liquid. The oxygen softens and integrates tannins without oxidizing flavors or aromas. So far, when it comes to spirits, the technique has been mostly employed by some of the more experimentally inclined micro-distilleries.

It should be noted that wooden barrels, because of their porosity, allow this natural interaction between oxygen and the spirit contained in the barrel during routine aging, and that the gradual and progressive addition of water that is performed while reducing cask-strength spirits to bottling strength assists the oxygenation process. See ÉLEVAGE; MATURATION; and SPEED-AGING.

Anjos, Ofélia, Ilda Caldeira, Rita Roque, Soraia I. Pedro, Sílvia Lourenço, and Sara Canas. "Screening of Different Ageing Technologies of Wine Spirit." *Processes* 8, no. 6 (2020): 736.

Alexandre Gabriel

The **Middle East**, despite the strictures against consuming alcohol that have prevailed in the region since the coming of Islam in the 600s, has a long and distinguished history of distilling alcohol. It may in fact be the cradle of distilling, as Bronze Age pots capable of producing spirits found in Mesopotamia suggest, although this cannot be proved. In the first and second centuries CE, however, Alexandria, Egypt, was a well-documented center for alchemical research, and that included distillation—the first well-documented appearance of it in the West. While the alchemists doing the experimenting were primarily focused on the creation of essential oils and perfumes and the desalinization of water, and not on producing alcoholic beverages, there was nonetheless some basic work done on distilling wine. It is unknown if this was an independent development or if it was influenced by the tradition of distillation in South Asia. See DISTILLATION, HISTORY.

With the Islamic conquest, the Alexandrian knowledge of distillation then moved eastward to modern-day Iran and Iraq, greatly assisted by Arabic and Syriac translations of Greek scientific works. Cities such as Baghdad and Tabriz became centers of chemical experimentation. In Kufa, the polymath Abu Musa Jabir ibn Hayyan (ca. 721–ca. 815),

known in the West as Geber, and his school did a good deal of work with the pot still; from their name for the still head, *al-ambiq*, we derive "alembic." See STILL, POT. Likewise, the term "alcohol" is derived from the Arab alchemical term, *al-kohl*, used for the most refined essence of a substance. But again, this technology was mainly used for distillation of things such as perfumes and petroleum products.

Islamic prohibitions on the consumption of alcoholic beverages did not completely prevent the rise of a culture of spirits production and drinking in the Middle East. For one thing, the region has never been ethnically or religiously homogenous, and there were plenty of Christians and Jews to whom alcohol was not forbidden. Moreover, not all Muslims have always been strictly observant, just as not all Christians or other believers have been. Indeed, the Hanafi school of Islamic jurisprudence, as followed by the Ottoman Turks and the Mughals of India, made room for moderate use of alcoholic beverages that were not wine, as not being explicitly forbidden by the Qur'an. The "moderate use" part was often interpreted loosely.

By the 1400s we read about 'araq (literally, "sweat" in Arabic) being produced in the region. One of the most protean of spirit terms, in the Middle East 'araq is traditionally applied to a spirit distilled from grapes (sometimes in the form of raisins or pomace) or dates and flavored with local anise. The precise origins of this spirit have not been established, but it was being exported to Venice and Genoa by the 1400s, and in subsequent centuries European travelers in Ottoman lands, which encompassed all but the Persian part of the Middle East, found its production, often by Jews or Christians, widespread, if small in scale, and its consumption an open secret. See ARRACK.

As the region industrialized during the late nineteenth and early twentieth centuries, secularization followed, spirits production increased, and consumption moved into the open. This occurred both in the parts of the region that had been colonized by Europe and the parts, such as Turkey and Iran, that remained independent. By the middle of the twentieth century, Turkey was making large amounts of *raki*, its version of arrack, from grapes and also from beet sugar. It was also making a good deal of vodka, as was Iran—before the Iranian Revolution of 1978, there were eight producers, with brands such as Sultanie, Pirouzeh, and Pakdis (this was not perhaps the best quality spirit available: in 1945, the *New Yorker* magazine both labeled it "sheer popskull" and complained that it "doesn't have enough kick").

Today, while Iranians still make a good deal of bootleg *aragh*, the only countries in the region that produce significant amounts of sprits are Turkey, Israel, and Lebanon. Even as Turkey has grown more religiously conservative, it has seen a proliferation of brands of raki. Israel has seen a boom in its alcohol industry. With Judaism having a long association with fermentation and distillation and Israel so isolated from its neighbors, it has long produced wine, and recently has seen several micro-distilleries being launched, which produce vodka and whisky. The Christian parts of Lebanon and Syria have traditionally produced a high-quality, artisanal arak, pot-distilled from wine and pomace, flavored with local anise (much of the Mediterranean has switched to Chinese star anise) and aged in clay. The Lebanese version, at least, is currently enjoying something of a renaissance. See ARRACK and RAKI.

The Middle East has never been at the epicenter of mixology—arrack is usually drunk mixed with water, or at most water and ice—but the region has seen exceptions. While international hotels in most parts of the region have maintained cocktail bars since the end of the nineteenth century, few have risen to greatness. One shining exception is the bar at Shepheard's Hotel, Cairo, world famous in the first half of the twentieth century; during the Second World War, barman Joe Scialom invented the famous Suffering Bastard there. See SCIALOM, JOSEPH. Another wartime invention was the Screwdriver, made by American oilmen working in the region. See SCREWDRIVER. The modern cocktail renaissance has seen new, cutting-edge bars established in Istanbul, Beirut, and Tel Aviv, while the luxury hotels found in the United Arab Emirates have often drawn their inspiration, and their personnel, from the showiest of new London bars.

Forbes, R. J. *A Short History of the Art of Distillation.* Leiden: Brill, 1948.

Huetz de Lemps, Alain. *Boissons et civilizations en Afrique.* Pessac, France: Presses Universitaires de Bordeaux, 2001.

Morewood, Samuel. *A Philosophical and Statistical History . . . of Inebriating Liquors.* Dublin: 1838.

Angus Winchester and David Wondrich

Milk & Honey was a pioneering cocktail bar, opened by Sasha Petraske (1973–2015) in an unassuming space on Eldridge Street in the Lower East Side of New York City on New Year's Eve in 1999. Out of consideration for his neighbors and landlord, who lived in the building and rented the space to him for $800 with the understanding he'd keep the bar quiet, Petraske decorated the front window like a tailor shop, and operated with a reservations-only policy that employed a constantly changing phone number to discourage a scene from developing within and a noisy line outside of the bar.

At a time when celebrity-studded boîtes such as Lot 61, Bowery Bar, and Asia de Cuba were garnering all the headlines in the New York City media, Petraske and his nattily dressed staff eschewed bottle service, fruit-flavored martinis, and DJs in favor of classic cocktails shaken and stirred to a jazz soundtrack.

The American bar at Istanbul's Pera Palace Hotel, touted in this 1931 advertisement, was one of the great scenes of intrigue and romance of the early twentieth century. Wondrich Collection.

Anachronistic in both style and substance, Milk & Honey operated with posted rules prohibiting name-dropping, shouting, unwanted advances upon women, and a handful of other unchivalrous behaviors common in bars of the time. A business card with the phone number was given to patrons by staff members, who carefully vetted the clientele based on their willingness to abide by the bar's ethos.

While legendary barman Dale DeGroff, who frequented the bar and befriended Petraske in the early days, will always be credited for bringing back the cocktail, Milk & Honey should be recognized for codifying contemporary cocktail service. Instead of offering a menu, the staff walked each guest through their options based on spirit preference, mixers of choice, preparation method, and cocktail format to find the perfect option. All ice was hand-cut, each drink was carefully measured with jiggers, only premium spirits and fresh ingredients were employed, and cocktails were served in retro coupes or frozen glasses with steel straws by the most well-trained bar staff in the city.

Each and every bartender split time behind the bar and on the floor as hosts and servers. Longtime employees who went on to open other bars with him include Joseph Schwartz, Richard Boccato, Christy Pope, Chad Solomon, Eric Alperin, Mike Madrusan, Lucinda Sterling, and T. J. Siegal.

In 2013, Petraske moved the venue uptown to 30 East Twenty-Third Street, turning the old space over to longtime bartenders Sam Ross and Michael McIlroy, who reopened it as Attaboy. The uptown location was more than twice the size and operated without the reservation policy and rules related to maintaining the peace in a residential neighborhood, making the new space feel more like a bar then a temple.

Milk & Honey will always be credited as the first of the modern speakeasies that sparked the modern cocktail renaissance, but Petraske never intended it to be labeled as such. See COCKTAIL RENAISSANCE. He cited a hidden Japanese cocktail lounge near Astor Place in the East Village called Angels' Share as his inspiration for Milk & Honey, which closed for good on Twenty-Third Street in 2014, when the sale of the building voided his lease. A second, equally influential location opened in London in 2002 under Petraske's creative direction by Jonathan Downey of Match Bar Group; it fell victim to the Covid-19 pandemic and closed in 2020.

Milk & Honey's legacy includes the creation of many modern cocktail classics, including the Red Hook, Silver Lining, Greenpoint, East Side, Penicillin, Paper Plane, and Gold Rush.

See DeGroff, Dale; Petraske, Sasha; and SPEAKEASY (NEW).

Chaplin, Julia. "Buzz Off: Secret Bars That Spurn Hype." *New York Times*, May 7, 2000. http://www.nytimes.com/2000/05/07/style/buzz-off-secret-bars-that-spurn-hype.html (accessed February 19, 2021).

Merwin, Hugh. "'He Didn't Follow Trends': How Sasha Petraske Reinvented Cocktail Culture and Created a New Bartending Community." *Grub Street*, August 24, 2015. http://www.grubstreet.com/2015/08/sasha-petraske-obit.html (accessed February 19, 2021).

"Sasha Petraske." *Difford's Guide*. http://www.diffordsguide.com/people/3080/bar-owner/sasha-petraske (accessed February 19, 2021).

Jim Meehan

Milk Punch is a dairy-based drink dating to the late 1600s and early 1700s, served originally as a true punch, from a bowl for group gatherings. See PUNCH. First recorded in William Sacheverell's 1688 travelogue of the Scottish isle of Iona, the drink owes its popularization, and possibly its invention, to the playwright and novelist Aphra Behn (1640–1689). The earliest written recipe comes from a 1711 cookbook by Mary Rockett.

Milk Punch in a bowl and in a bottle are different beverages. In the latter, today called clarified Milk Punch, milk is curdled and strained, leaving behind a smooth and stable beverage so popular in mid-eighteenth century England that young Queen Victoria issued a royal warrant to the company of Nathaniel Whisson as "purveyors of milk punch to Her Majesty." Curdling results through the addition of alcohol or acid, as in a 1763 Benjamin Franklin recipe adding brandy and lemon to hot milk.

The clarification made indefinite storage without refrigeration possible—bottles were found in Charles Dickens's wine cellar after his death in 1870 (his Mr. Pickwick was thrilled to take "a most energetic pull" on a bottle of it).

In the original punch bowl presentation, the appeal lies in the quality and freshness of the dairy, sometimes a mixture of milk and cream, although Jerry Thomas's classic 1862 *Bar-Tender's Guide* recipe includes white sugar, water, cognac, rum, milk, nutmeg, and ice. By the 1850s, Milk Punches such as this were generally made individually by the glass, not the bowl (they were often given to the infirm, as a gentle and strengthening beverage). In nineteenth-century New Orleans, Bourbon or Brandy Milk Punch was extremely popular; it is still served at numerous bars and restaurants there today.

Precursors include posset (wine or beer, cream, sugar, and egg, thickened with bread, biscuits, or oatmeal), syllabub (wine or cider, cream, sugar, and spices) and the medieval Irish scáiltín (whisky, hot milk, melted butter, sugar, honey, spices). See SYLLABUB.

Recipe (Mary Rockett's Milk Punch): Peel 2 lemons in long spirals, put the peels in 2-liter jar, cover with 1 liter VSOP cognac, seal, and let sit for 24 hours. Add 240 ml white sugar and 90 ml lemon juice and stir until sugar has mostly dissolved. Heat 500 ml whole milk until scalding hot, pour into the cognac mixture, and let curdle. Grate in 1 nutmeg and let cool. Strain through fine chinois or clean cloth, carefully strain again through the same curds, bottle, and refrigerate. Serve as liqueur or add hot or cold water to taste.

Dickens, Charles. *The Posthumous Papers of the Pickwick Club*. London: Chapman & Hall, 1837.
Wondrich, David. *Punch*. New York: Perigee, 2010.

Jack Robertiello

Miller, Anistatia (1948–), and Brown, Jared

(1964–), the business partners and spouses behind the England-based Mixellany Limited (a consulting and publishing company specializing in the spirits, cocktails, and distillation industries), are among the pioneers of modern mixography and indeed of the cocktail renaissance in general. See COCKTAIL RENAISSANCE and MIXOGRAPHY.

Working almost exclusively as a duo since 1995, they first came together to collaborate on the self-publication of *Shaken Not Stirred: A Celebration of the Martini*. Brown and Miller have dedicated their careers and lives to the scholarship of the industry, piecing together artifacts, anecdotes, recipes, and lore to organize and share the facts, and dispel the myths in their field. Among the very first to appreciate the power of the internet as a tool for the

historiography of drinks, they brought new sources and perspectives to the histories of spirits and mixed drinks in the more than thirty books that they have written together, tackling topics ranging from Cuban rum to champagne cocktails to the lives of famous bartenders. The coauthors have received numerous accolades, including the prestigious Gourmand World Cookbook Award for Best Drink History, for the two-volume *Spirituous Journey: A History of Drink* (2009–2010).

In addition to their published works and their frequent lectures, Brown and Miller have served seminal roles in preserving the industry's past. In collaboration with Dale and Jill DeGroff, Ted "Dr. Cocktail" Haigh, David Wondrich, and some of the world's most prominent cocktail historians, writers, and experts, the pair helped to found the Museum of the American Cocktail in 2004. See MUSEUM OF THE AMERICAN COCKTAIL. Shortly thereafter, they began an extensive three-year conservation project for the Exposition Universelle des Vins et Spiritueux (EUVS), a so-called permanent exhibition of wines and spirits owned by the Ricard family and housed on the island of Bendor off the French Riviera. See PERNOD-RICARD. Culminating with the museum's fiftieth anniversary in 2008, Brown and Miller collected more than five thousand wine and spirits labels from around the world, as well as scholarly papers on viniculture and distillation, and led the organization and preservation of thousands more relics including menus, photographs, and glassware. Chief among their contributions is editing under the EUVS aegis a searchable and comprehensive virtual library of scanned historical cocktail books dating to the early 1700s, a unique and invaluable resource for the student of drink history

Beyond the pair's contributions to mixography, they have also helped to develop several spirits brands. Most notably, Brown is the master distiller at London-based Sipsmith, founded in 2009 as the first licensed copper-pot distillery in that city in nearly two hundred years (its license was granted after two years of lobbying against the city's 1823 Gin Act, which had outlawed gin still operations under 1,800 liters). Brown has credited Sipsmith's success to extensive research in early eighteenth- and nineteenth-century distilling books and the brand's incorporation of traditional distilling methods and use of only historically accurate botanicals. See GIN.

"*The Cocktail Lovers* Interview: Anistatia Miller and Jared Brown." *The Cocktail Lovers*, May 27, 2013. https://thecocktaillovers.com/the-cocktail-lovers-interview-anistatia-miller-and-jared-brown/?doing_wp_cron=1616701770.3195350170135498046875 (accessed March 25, 2021).

EUVS digital collection. http://euvslibrary.com (accessed March 25, 2021).

Miller, Anistatia, and Jared Brown. *The Deans of Drink.* London: Mixellany, 2013.

Mixellany. http://www.mixellany.com/services.html (accessed March 25, 2021).

Lauren Viera

millet is the preferred raw material for making raksi, a homemade spirit popular in Nepal. It is also used by Chicago's Koval Distillery to make whisky. See HOME DISTILLING; RAKSI; and SORGHUM.

The **Mimosa** (or "Champagne Orange") is a variation on the Buck's Fizz, which was created around 1921 by barman Malachi "Pat" McGarry (1878–ca. 1941) as the signature offering at Buck's Club, a private members' establishment in London. Unlike its predecessor, which uses slightly more champagne than orange juice and might include gin and grenadine, the Mimosa is a simple combination of orange juice and chilled champagne, now usually mixed in equal parts. The drink was reputedly created in 1925 and attributed to Frank Meier, head bartender at the Ritz in Paris. See RITZ. The recipe does appear in Meier's 1936 recipe book *The Artistry of Mixing Drinks*, along with McGarry's Buck's Fizz, but it is printed without the little monogram that Meier attached to recipes he claimed as his own, such as the Kolkure, Alfonso XIII, Blue Bird, and Winter Sport cocktails. (Of the five hundred drink recipes in the book, only just over forty bear the monogram.) In that context, it is worth noting that the Mimosa's first appearance in print was in Nice barman Dominique Migliorero's *L'art du shaker*, published in 1925 or before.

The drink's simplicity struck a chord with Parisian society in the same manner as the Buck's Fizz had a few years earlier among British lovers of this morning drink. Along with the Bloody Mary, the Mimosa has become one of the quintessential brunch drinks in America. See BLOODY MARY. The recipe has been replicated around the world over the past eighty years despite the fact that only one thousand copies of Meier's book were ever printed.

See also FIZZ and MEIER, FRANK.

Recipe (Frank Meier's): Put the juice of half an orange in a champagne flute or small wine glass and fill with chilled champagne.

Meier, Frank. *The Artistry of Mixing Drinks*. Paris: Frayam, 1936, 76.

Migliorero, Dominique. *L'art du shaker*. Nice: n.d., ca. 1925.

Anistatia R. Miller and Jared M. Brown

Mint Julep is the quintessential drink of the American South. The standard contemporary version is made with bourbon, sugar, water, cracked or crushed ice, and, of course, mint. See JULEP.

mirabelle is an eau-de-vie—a clear fruit brandy made from yellow plums known as mirabelle plums. It has been made in France—and in particular in the Alsace and Lorraine regions—since the beginning of the nineteenth century, when it appears to have been perfected, and is noted for its delicacy and fragrance. See AROMA. A small but growing number of American producers are also experimenting with making eau-de-vie from mirabelle plums. Clear Creek, a pioneering microdistillery in Portland, Oregon, that specializes in working with fruit brandies, is noted for its exceptional example.

Mirabelle has also made a small contribution to literature: novelist Christopher Buckley was moved to write the following verse after presumably partaking of a little too much during a vacation on the Caribbean island of Anguilla:

> Last night I had some mirabelle.
> Today I do not feel so swell.
> I think that that is it for me
> With any kind of eau de vie.

See also EAU-DE-VIE and BRANDY.

Apple, R. W. "Eau de Vie: Fruit's Essence Captured in a Bottle." *New York Times*, April 1, 1998. http://www.nytimes.com/1998/04/01/dining/eau-de-vie-fruit-s-essence-captured-in-a-bottle.htm (accessed February 19, 2021).

Cadet de Vaux, Antione-Alexis. "Variétés du Koëtsch-wasser." *La décade philosophique, littééraire et politique*, 10 Fructidor, X [August 29, 1789], 434–438.

Kara Newman

mist is a way of serving a drink in a rocks glass over finely crushed or shaved ice, instead of whole cubes. A mist is typically just a single spirit and not a mixed drink (mixed drinks and liqueurs served in this method are often called frappés). See FRAPPE. In a mist, the crushed ice provides a faster, deeper chill and dilutes the spirits a little further, making the drink more refreshing than just a spirit served neat. While the practice dates back to the early nineteenth century (when a spirit thus served was sometimes known as a hailstorm), it only returned into vogue in the early 1940s with the Scotch Mist, from which the category's name is derived. See HAILSTORM.

Haimo, Oscar. *Cocktail Digest (from Private Notes)*. New York: Oscar Haimo, 1943.

Herbst, Sharon Tyler, and Ron Herbst. *The Ultimate A-to-Z Bar Guide*. New York: Broadway, 1998.

Robert Hess

mistelle is a blend of fresh grape juice or must and spirit. Although not actually made with wine, it is often classified as a fortified wine. Thought to come from the medieval Latin *miscitare* (to mix), the French word "mistelle" and the Spanish "mistela" appeared in the early 1900s to specifically describe blends from Spain.

Mistelles can be white or red. A spirit, traditionally wine-based but often a neutral alcohol of agricultural origin, is added to must or grape juice with high sugar content before the start of the fermentation process (the International Organization of Vine and Wine tolerates up to 1 percent of actual alcohol from fermentation). The alcohol prevents microbial growth and halts fermentation, stabilizing the mistelle. Without fermentation, the natural grape sugars and the aromas of the fruit are preserved; the flavor profile is fresher than other fortified wines, though often less complex. Mistelles have a slightly higher alcohol volume than table wines—between 15 and 22 percent.

Although mistelle is a relatively recent word, it describes a much older product. Historically, wines were unstable and difficult to age and could not withstand travel. The "mutage" process, which consisted of stopping fermentation by the addition of either sulfur or alcohol, was found to help. While it's difficult to credit the process to a specific originator, Catalan alchemist Arnaud de Villeneuve is often quoted as the first writer to recommend the addition of alcohol to wine. However, the real authorship of the numerous manuscripts bearing his name is difficult to ascertain.

The success of fortified wines can be traced back to the Dutch and English demand for wine from the sixteenth century. They were looking for stable wines to sell on their markets and contributed greatly to the creation, modernization, and/or sophistication of fortified wines such as port, sherries, Madeira, and Malaga. In France, fortification gave birth to wines such as banyuls, rivesaltes, or maury. However, although mistelles have been used in the formulation of some of these, they are all primarily based on partially or completely fermented wines and as such should not be mistaken with mistelles.

Mistelles remain traditional Spanish products, especially in the regions of Alicante and Valencia, where they are often drunk as a digestive or dessert wine. In France, one finds many regional mistelles, some of which have obtained AOC (appellation d'origine controlee) protection: macvin (fortified with pomace brandy), floc de Gascogne (with Armagnac), and pineau des Charentes. The last is the only one widely known abroad. It owes its prestige to its area of production: it is made in and around Cognac and is fortified with at least one-year-old cognacs. It is drunk as both an aperitif and a digestive. Some pineaus receive significant barrel aging, spending fifteen years or more in oak.

In addition, some mistelles are used in the production process of other fortified wines. Many French aromatized wines—including Noilly Prat vermouth, Dubonnet, Byrrh, and Bonal—depend on mistelles for sweetness and fortification. Although there are exceptions, the presence of mistelle is indeed one of the defining characteristics of the French aromatized wine trade. Its use was promoted by the French government, which saw it as an ideal way to solve the overproduction problem faced by southern France's vineyards. Since the establishment of the European Single Market, many of these brands source their mistelles abroad, particularly in Spain.

See also WINES, FORTIFIED; FLOC DE GASCOGNE; and PINEAU DES CHARENTES.

International Organisation of Vine and Wine website. http://www.oiv.int (accessed March 25, 2021).

Robinson, Jancis, ed. *The Oxford Companion to Wine*, 4th ed. Oxford: Oxford University Press, 2015.

François Monti

mistrà is an Italian name for anisette, used mostly in the parts of the country that border the Adriatic Sea or were under the sway of the Venetian Empire. In general, the spirit is sweetened lightly, if at all, and is bottled at between 40 percent and 50 percent ABV. Its name, in use since at least the eighteenth century, is apparently derived from the Byzantine Greek city of Mystras, from which the Venetians originally imported their anise. See ANISE SPIRITS.

David Wondrich

A **mixing glass** is the receptacle used to hold a cocktail's ingredients while it is stirred. There are two main types in general use, the cheap, tapered pint glass and the more elaborate parallel-sided Japanese-style mixing glass, usually with a spout and a pattern cut or molded into the glass both for decoration and to aid grip. Some bartenders, however, prefer stirring drinks in small shaker tins, mason jars, or even Pyrex beakers.

When it comes down to it, stirring a drink in any of these vessels will dilute and chill it. But choosing a receptacle is dependent on a few factors: cost, threat of breakage, temperature conduction, personal aesthetics, and size.

Today, Japanese-style mixing glasses tend to be the tool of choice for several reasons. Typically, they are designed with a heavier, wider bottom for stability and feature a pour spout to aid in straining. They come in different sizes, including ones large enough for mixing several drinks at once. The older pint glass is the descendant of the so-called large mixing glass, which held from 12 to 16 ounces (360–480 ml) and was used both for stirring and, with a mixing tin, as part of the cocktail shaker. See MIXING TIN. There was also a similarly-tapered "small bar glass," for stirring short drinks such as cocktails. Today, that usage only survives in making Sazeracs. See SAZERAC COCKTAIL.

With glass, there's always a risk of breakage. Metal mixing glasses in similar patterns have recently become more available, and proponents like author Dave Arnold argue that metal cups chill more quickly, making stirring more efficient. If using metal, one must always measure ingredients with a jigger, as it is impossible to check their levels by eye.

Arnold, Dave. *Liquid Intelligence*. New York: W. W. Norton, 2014.

Uyeda, Kazuo. *Cocktail Techniques*. Translated by Marc Adler. New York: Mud Puddle, 2010.

Clair McLafferty

mixing tin is the metal component of the two-part cocktail mixing apparatus known as a Boston shaker. See also BOSTON SHAKER and MIXING GLASS.

mixography is a neologism for writing about mixed drinks. Hypothetically, it could date to the 1860s, when the term "mixology" first appeared, but there's little evidence of its use prior to the 2000s. Regardless, writing has always been an integral part of mixology, just as it is integral to any lasting discipline. While various mixed drink traditions extend back into history, the circumstances that would collect "mixed drinks" as a distinct writing topic did not really come together until the nineteenth century. See MIXOLOGY, THE HISTORY OF.

While punch recipes had appeared in print here and there in cookbooks and such since the seventeenth century, there was no move to compile and publish dedicated drink-recipe anthologies prior to the appearance of *Oxford Night Caps* in 1827. An unsigned booklet of recipes for punches and cups aimed at students at that university, it would enjoy numerous editions, the last in 1931. For its first thirty-odd years, however, it stood alone. In the 1860s, it was joined in Europe by a handful of other works: Henry Porter and George Roberts's *Cups and Their Customs* (London, 1863), *La véritable manière de faire le Punch* by "Turenne" (Paris, 1866), *Cooling Cups and Dainty Drinks*, by the equally pseudonymous "William Terrington," and the 1871 *Gentleman's Table Guide* by Edward Ricket (a South London caterer) and one C. Thomas. Like *Oxford*

Night Caps, all of these works were aimed at the home entertainer, not the working bartender.

On the other hand, the dissemination of mixed drinks in mid-nineteenth-century America—the single-serving variety in particular—happened within a commercial context: professionals made drinks, and the public consumed them (home bars would not really exist for generations). Professional bartenders and publicans shared information mainly through word of mouth and apprenticeship; literacy was not a given; rivalry and secrecy were frequently a factor. Information moved, but haltingly.

After *Oxford Night Caps*, the first major work of commercial literature that formally concerned mixed drinks was an actual book, Jerry Thomas's 1862 *How to Mix Drinks*, published in New York. See THOMAS, JEREMIAH P. "JERRY". Although dressed as a work of convivial literature for the home celebrant, the book was in fact aimed squarely at the trade, as most other American drink books for the remainder of the century would be. These trade books were quite expensive in their day, generally terse, and served a rapidly expanding industry (bars and restaurants) where, again, full literacy could not be taken for granted, at least not in English. The printing of these trade books was commonly paid for by including advertising from bar suppliers (some volumes were even directly commissioned by them as promotional tools) and, occasionally, early liquor brands. Some of the most successful trade books went on to multiple editions.

Jerry Thomas's book is particularly important not just for being the first anthology in which many drink recipes appear in print but also for categorizing them with a thoughtful typology that would persist, stretched to the breaking point, to the present day. From the 1860s, drink-book publishing gradually expanded, as did the quantity and diversity of novel drink recipes to write about.

Harry Johnson's 1882 *Bartender's Manual* adds extensive essays on bar design, operation, and management. See JOHNSON, HARRY. His was not the first work on bar management, but it was the first significant one in the cocktail context. Other standout books from the era that primarily document explosion of recipes in circulation include Leo Engel's *American and Other Drinks* (London, 1878; Engel had worked for Thomas in New York), the pseudonymous O. H. Byron's *Modern Bartender's Guide* (New York, 1884), the posthumous editions of Jerry Thomas's book updated by his publishers (New York, 1876 and 1887), William "Cocktail Bill" Boothby's *American Bartender* (San Francisco, 1891), and George Kappeler's *Modern American Drinks* (New York, 1895). But there were many others, and as a body they establish a pattern of stultifying redundancy, disregard for attribution, and broad plagiarism that characterizes the genre to this day. On the other hand, they were pragmatic, effective, and successfully built atop each other. See BOOTHBY, WILLIAM T. "COCKTAIL BILL"; and ENGEL, LEO.

The bulk of cocktail books were published in New York and London, because that's where the publishing industries were concentrated—it is not unfair to say that mixography has had a persistent bias toward those cities. However, early and significant books were also published in Cincinnati, Chicago, San Francisco, and other cities around the United States. Moreover, "American drinks" and the "American-style bar" were swiftly disseminated internationally via the media, journeymen bartenders, and the American traveling class, who were all too happy to seek, enjoy, and promote cocktails abroad.

The late nineteenth century brought forth cocktail books in France, Germany, and Austria-Hungary. See LEFEUVRE, ÉMILE. Harry Johnson (a German immigrant) printed his own book in a bilingual edition in the 1880s and exported it back to Germany. Louis Fouquet's *Bariana* (1896) in France both reflected and promoted the general interest there in the American cocktail culture streaming in from ocean liners. See FOUQUET, LOUIS ÉMILE. Meanwhile, the popular press—mainly newspapers—tracked the rise of cocktails and mixed drinks as a social fashion. Initially, bars, bartenders and the odd drink drew scattered mention here and there as part of the growing Belle Époque cosmopolitan fabric. The first major article on mixed drinks appeared, unattributed, in the *New York Sun* in 1873. "American Fancy Drinks," as the piece was titled, was a detailed appreciation of American bartending, complete with recipes from some of New York's top drinks mixers. It was widely reprinted and opened the door for a steady stream of such articles that would appear nationwide until Prohibition and beyond. From this point, mixed drinks became an increasingly normal part of society journalism, and the periodical record has produced a fragmented but invaluable picture of American drinking culture that the books cannot.

Moreover, some bartenders, such as William Schmidt, specifically cultivated their relationship with newspapermen. Schmidt's own, unusually lavish book, *The Flowing Bowl* (New York, 1892), contains numerous original drinks concocted specifically for the journalists that frequented his Manhattan bar, and not coincidentally, *The Flowing Bowl* is one of the first American bar manuals to lean, at least slightly, toward the popular market, not just the trade. See SCHMIDT, WILLIAM. The first American book of any importance explicitly aimed at nonprofessional mixologists is probably *The Cocktail Book: A Sideboard Manual for Gentlemen* (Boston, 1902). It is not coincidental that European publications on mixed drinks were often more consumer-oriented than the coincident American books: cocktails were not part of European pub or café traditions, and instead infiltrated through the hotels, casinos, music clubs, and such that catered to critical masses of American transients.

International mixography accelerated in the first two decades of the twentieth century. Frank Newman's *American Bar* (Paris, 1900) went through multiple editions. Jorge Gasparo's *Guia practica del cantinero* appeared out of Monterrey, Mexico in 1909. A book, *Manual del cantinero o cocktelero perfecto* (by E. Moreno, 1910), was printed in Havana, Mexico, and Buenos Aires, although John Escalante's *Manual del cantinero* (Havana, 1915) is the first in a line of essential Cuban publications. Important American publications in this period include *Applegreen's Barkeeper's Guide* (1899), *Louis' Mixed Drinks* (1906), Jack Grohusko's *Jack's Manual* (1909), Charley Mahoney's *Hoffman House Bartender's Guide* (1905), Jacques Straub's *Drinks* (1914), Tom Bullock's *The Ideal Bartender* (1917), and Hugo Ensslin's *Recipes for Mixed Drinks* (1917). Mahoney's book deserves special mention for its relatively extensive front matter concerning bar management at New York's top bar of the era, while Straub's book is an iconic, compact (unofficial) reference to the drinks of the Big Brass Rail at the (original) Waldorf-Astoria. Bullock's is the first by an African American author. Ensslin's is the last significant American cocktail book prior to Prohibition. See ENSSLIN, HUGO RICHARD; and HOFFMAN HOUSE.

By the time Prohibition (1920) temporarily complicated the bartender's profession in the United States, many dozens of trade books existed—including in other countries and languages—and mixed drinks were a major feature of global cosmopolitan culture. In the United States, Prohibition moved mixology from the bars into the homes, creating a new market for how-to books and articles by and for amateurs, as defiant Americans tried to hold on to their disrupted drinking habits. These Prohibition-era books are often delightfully witty, even if the quality of their information is unreliable. Some were self-published, and a few, such as the tiny, infamous "Judge, Jr." books, employed pseudonyms. One landmark of this era is *Drinks Long and Short* (London, 1925), an entire drink recipe book specifically for home use, by Nina Toye and A. H. Adair, which is an early example of a "foodie" or "lifestyle" drink book (in today's sense), following in the rather less sleek footsteps of Edward Spencer's *The Flowing Bowl* (London, 1903). All these new kinds of drink writing are perhaps best contextualized by the broadly contemporary literature by the likes of Hemingway, Fitzgerald, and company and the similarly urbane stylings of *Vanity Fair* and *The New Yorker*.

During American Prohibition, "American-style" bars flourished in Europe and its colonies and in Latin America, as did trade and consumer literature dedicated to mixed drinks. Veteran American bartenders working in Europe such as Harry McElhone (*Harry's ABC of Mixing Cocktails*) and Harry Craddock (*The Savoy Cocktail Book*) published major anthologies to support their résumés, and European and Caribbean bartenders assumed the mantle. See CRADDOCK, HARRY LAWSON; and McELHONE, HENRY "HARRY". As American Bars themselves became tourist attractions, some produced recipe books as souvenirs and promotional items. This same general idea was widely adopted by liquor producers everywhere, who began commissioning their own books and booklets with recipes that specified their products, a practice that remains de rigueur today.

By the conclusion of American Prohibition, the Western world was experiencing an explosion in mixed drink literature. Indeed, more books, articles, and ephemera concerning alcohol and mixed drinks were published in the 1930s than all prior decades combined. The end of Prohibition even spawned its own temporary genre in the United States of witty musings on the return of public alcohol consumption, such as Gilbert Seldes's *The Future of Drinking* (1930), along with dozens of celebratory recipe anthologies. Patrick Gavin Duffy, a bartender from before Prohibition, published a particularly ambitious example of the latter, his *Official Mixer's Manual* (1934). See DUFFY, PATRICK GAVIN. This era is also where the mythology of cocktails—particularly origin stories—suddenly seemed important, and many writers felt obliged to include (usually tall) tales alongside the recipes.

Despite these efforts, cocktail culture remained more anchored abroad than at home in the United States until World War II. The Club de Cantineros, a bartenders' trade group in Cuba, set themselves up as standard bearers and published guides for their members, beginning with the *Manual del cantinero* (1924). The United Kingdom Bartenders Guild, under Harry Craddock and William Tarling, did much the same, starting with *The Book of Approved Cocktails* (1937). Other notable publications from Europe in this era include the best-selling *Cocktails: How to Mix Them* (1922) by Robert Vermeire, several Spanish books by Pedro Chicote such as *El bar Americano en España* (1927), *L'heure du Cocktail* (Paris, 1927), *Cocktails de Paris* (Paris, 1929), and *Des Herrn Munkepunke Cocktail- und Bowlenbuch* (Berlin, 1929). This is also when the first cocktail books appear in Japan, such as *O'Dell's New Book of Cocktails and Fancy Drinks* (1932), although cocktails would only take serious hold there fourteen years later during the years of American occupation. See CHICOTE, PEDRO "PERICO"; MIXOLOGY, THE HISTORY OF; and VERMEIRE, ROBERT.

From the start, cocktail literature for consumers often mirrored the terseness of the trade books in the recipes themselves but added levity in form of ornamentation, humor, and cartoons (often racy, sexist, and racist, consistent with twentieth-century white, patriarchal, cosmopolitan culture and the popular press that served it). Following World War II, lifestyle magazines, such as *Gourmet*, *Town and Country*, *The New Yorker*, *Esquire*, and ultimately *Playboy*, took over as America's cultural authorities, editorializing on what you drank alongside what you wore or read or the theater you attended. Thus, mixed drinks were equally integrated with the commercial, the literary, and the culinary; as predicted by Seldes, the future of drinking was now in the hands of the drinkers and not the bartenders.

In addition to producing their own cocktail books, *Esquire* (and later *Gourmet*) employed traveling socialite Charles H. Baker Jr., who wrote about drinks (and food) in the hyperbolic style of Victorian adventure writers and yielded two of the most distinctive cocktail books ever: *The Gentleman's Companion* (1946) and *The South American Gentleman's Companion* (1952). See BAKER, CHARLES HENRY, JR. Another essential entry from this era is *The Fine Art of Mixing Drinks* (1947), the first theoretical work on mixed drinks, written by attorney David Embury. See EMBURY, DAVID A. Other ubiquitous writers included Crosby Gaige, a theater promoter, gourmand, and cookbook author, and Lucius Beebe, the "cafe society" journalist, gourmand, and historian. The former penned a few books, most notably his *Cocktail Guide and Ladies' Companion* (1941); the latter wrote the *Stork Club Bar Book* (1946) along with many cocktail book prefaces and countless articles for many of the above magazines and a popular column for the *New York Herald Tribune*. G. Selmer Fougner's groundbreaking daily column Along the Wine Trail—which often addressed spirits and cocktails—ran for years in the *New York Sun* and was influential enough to be anthologized multiple times. See FOUGNER, G. SELMER. Probably the most spectacular Cold War cocktail book was Ted Saucier's 1951 *Bottoms Up*, which combined surprisingly well-curated recipes and pinup art in lavish packaging and sold well. Saucier was a publicist for the Waldorf-Astoria Hotel. See SAUCIER, TED.

Along with mixed drinks as a whole, mixography persisted during the compression of the 1960s, 1970s, and 1980s, but with greatly reduced relevance. The state of drinking from this era is thoroughly documented, but subsequent events have largely isolated this period as aberrant. In 1991, when William Grimes published his groundbreaking *Straight Up or On the Rocks*, an exactingly researched history of the cocktail and its kin, it stood alone, but not for long. Yet books were not the main agents for reviving the cocktail's fortunes. As discussed elsewhere, the revival of interest in mixed drinks in the 1990s and the emergence of the internet are inextricable. See COCKTAIL RENAISSANCE. The internet—writing, pictures, audio, and video—is the avenue through which interest was revived, most information spread, and the history reconstructed at a level of detail that was never available in the past (particularly through digitized archives). See HAIGH, TED; HARRINGTON, PAUL; and HESS, ROBERT.

The other essential component of the current mixographical era is the concurrent, wildly expansive multicultural fascination with globe-spanning cuisine, from which contemporary mixology is nearly inextricable. The vast majority of the mixography of the current era has been executed by amateur enthusiasts and professional writers, rather than bartenders (with notable exceptions such as Dale DeGroff and Gary Regan, whose respective works, *The Craft of the Cocktail* and *The Joy of Mixology*, were foundational), and the crossover between food and drink is ubiquitous. See DeGroff, Dale; and Regan, Gary. As in the twentieth century, the literature is dominated by lifestyle periodicals (and what passes for them) and by book publishers seeking to offer a comprehensive range of consumer products. Almost no publications target the trade exclusively; the German magazine *Mixology* is a notable exception. In some ways, contemporary mixography resembles that of the 1930s in that reconstructing knowledge after a traumatic period is one acute need.

New to the discipline, however, is research and writing executed with something approximating academic rigor. Lowell Edmunds's *Martini, Straight Up* (1998) was perhaps the first example; subsequent examples include *Imbibe!* (2007) and *Punch* (2010) by *Esquire*'s drinks correspondent, David Wondrich, *Sippin' Safari* (2007) and *Potions of the Caribbean* (2013) by Jeff Berry, and *Moonshine!* (2007) and *Lost Recipes of Prohibition* (2015) by Matthew Rowley. Equally rigorous, but in the realm of science rather than history, was Dave Arnold's *Liquid Intelligence* (2014). As a sign of how this approach was received, it is worth noting that the James Beard Foundation gave book awards to Wondrich's *Imbibe!*—the first cocktail book to be so honored—and Arnold's work.

The mid- and late 2010s saw more of the new historicism, most prominently in books from Robert Simonson and Philip Greene, but it also saw a flood of bartender's guides, competently written by practicing professionals, but perhaps no longer groundbreaking. In time, undoubtedly, a smattering of these recent volumes will demonstrate enduring influence. At this writing, it is impossible to say if the Covid-19 pandemic of 2020–2021 will bring this age of mixographical abundance to a close or refocus it to home mixology as during Prohibition.

See also Miller, Anistatia, and Brown, Jared; and Spirits Writing.

"American Fancy Drinks." *New York Sun*, August 22, 1873, 3.

Martin Doudoroff

mixology, the history of, stretches back to antiquity, encompassing things such as the Homeric *kykeōn*, wine mixed with grated goat cheese and barley; the combination of wine, beer, and mead whose residue was found in the tomb of King Midas in central Anatolia; the various medicated wines described by Scribonius Largus, the Roman emperor Claudius's physician; and medieval wine drinks such as the highly spiced hippocras and beer drinks such as the bitter Purl. Modern mixology, however, begins with the rise to popularity of distilled spirits, which gave the art a new urgency. As the Italian physician Michele Savonarola observed in the 1440s, "For some, to take this 'water' even in small quantities is difficult and unpleasant, for which one may mix wine or some other liquid with it." He recommends mixing one part spirits with three parts wine, or if not wine, then water or even beer. This was the first recorded mixed drink based on spirits.

The ultimate development of this "pop-in," as the English would come to call it, came in the form of fortified wines, which had the added advantage of keeping longer and standing up to shipping better than the unfortified wines of the day. See Fortified Wines. But it also opened the door to a vast array of mixed drinks. The first people that we know walked through that door did so in India. India had its own, independent version of pop-in, such as the mix of equal parts palm or Bengal arrack and wine, of which the Mughal emperor Jahangir (1569–1627) drank six cups a day (and that was when he was behaving). See Arrack. Sometime between 1600 and 1630, when the first unambiguous description of it was recorded, English merchants in India began drinking a mixture of local arrack, water, citrus juice, and sugar, presumably in equal parts. Spices could also be added, and often were. As "punch," this drink would in one way or another lay the foundation for all of modern mixology. See Punch.

Punch introduced the basic principles of balance that would govern the art of mixing drinks with spirits from then on: sweet versus sour, strong versus weak, spicy versus subtle, stimulating versus refreshing. As with the Martini and many other drinks at the very top of the cocktail pantheon, there was more than one way to balance punch: an excess of citrus, for example, could be made up for with more sugar, but it could also be corrected by adding more water; a deficiency of arrack or whatever other spirit you were using (it worked well with most) could be fixed by splashing in some wine, and so on.

By the 1660s British sailors had spread punch to Europe, Africa, and the Americas. As it took root, it slowly gathered local mutations. Up to this point, we have had few names to wave around. But now we have Hannah Wooley (ca. 1622–1675), who printed the first formal, written recipe for the drink in 1670. That already uses brandy and Bordeaux wine, rather than arrack, and cuts the lemon juice down to a minimum (in England, lemons were very costly). The playwright and novelist Aphra Behn (1640–1689), the first Englishwoman to make a living with her pen, is credited with the invention of Milk Punch, which would go on to become a staple of British drinking. See MILK PUNCH. In the Americas, rum was the spirit, and limes were often the citrus; in Ireland and Scotland, whisky would come to fuel the drink, which would be generally served hot, with the citrus cut back to lemon peel alone.

Up to this point, punch making was rather a "pro-am" affair, with drinkers often mixing their own, even in punch houses (the ingredients would be brought to the table, and they would have at it). In 1731, however, James Ashley (1698–1776) began serving punch in any quantity desired, from a small "tiff" to a large bowl, at his London Punch House near St. Paul's. He—or rather, his chief barkeeper, Mrs. Gaywood (perhaps Catherine Gaywood, 1708–1775), and the young women who served under her—would assemble the drink in front of the guest, so that the quality of the ingredients could be assured. This was the beginning of modern, mixological bartending: individually portioned drinks mixed to order in front of the guest. See ASHLEY, JAMES.

By the late eighteenth century, punch had finally jumped the English Channel. In France, it was the province of the *limonadiers*, professional sweet- and iced-beverage makers, usually of Italian extraction, who treated the drink prismatically, with each of its main components split among several ingredients. Thus, for instance, the sweet element might be supplied by sugar, capillaire syrup, and orange curaçao. See CAPILLAIRE and CURAÇAO. But that curaçao would also contribute to the citrus element and the spirituous element, blending the colors of the rainbow, as it were. This bedrock principle of mixology was already implicit in Wooley's Punch, with the wine splitting the difference between the spirituous and the aqueous elements, but in the hands of the limonadiers it reached a new level of sophistication. See REGENT'S PUNCH.

Meanwhile, in America barkeeping was becoming an increasingly male affair, particularly after independence. There the status of barkeeper was relatively high, particularly in the new towns where taverns served as focal points for settlement, and that pulled men in. At the same time, there was also significant African American representation behind the bar, both free and enslaved. Indeed, America's first famous professional mixologist, Othello Pollard (1758–ca. 1838), of Philadelphia and Boston, was a free African American whose Ice Punch and erudite newspaper advertisements caused a sensation at the turn of the nineteenth century. Yet we have very little information from the period on American bartenders and their work; it was only when European travelers made much of it in the 1820s and 1830s that Americans began to pay attention. Although, for instance, we know iced Mint Juleps were being served at the Wig Wam Gardens in Norfolk, Virginia, in 1807, we do not know the bartender's name or anything about him—or her. See JULEP.

Fancy Drinks

That use of ice was fast becoming the trademark of American mixology, along with an expanded range of drinks mixed to order: most, such as the julep, the sling, and the Cock-Tail, could—much like punch—be seen with various subtractions or substitutions for the citrus, but there were also (less punch-like) eggnogs and a number of other, more original drinks. See COCK-TAIL; EGGNOG; ICE, HISTORY OF ITS USE; and SLING. To be a successful bartender in a city such as New York, Boston, or New Orleans, one had to master a number of drinks from different regions of the country, which were coalescing into an American school of drinking. In New York City, bartenders such as Cato Alexander, an African American freedman; Orsamus Willard, a Yankee from rural Massachusetts; and Martha King Niblo (1802–1851), daughter of a porterhouse keeper, began to cement the foundations of the American school of mixing drinks. Drinks would be mixed to order with ice, in front of the customer, and with a show of energy and dexterity (indeed, Willard was ambidextrous). See ALEXANDER, CATO; SHERRY COBBLER; and WILLARD, ORSAMUS.

The other shoe dropped in the 1830s, when the Hailstorm Julep, a recent specialty of Virginia, spread to the big cities of the Northeast. Where ordinary juleps used a lump or two of ice, this packed the glass with it, smashed to a fine, gelid powder. Prismatic mixology was in full force as rich wines and fragrant rum floats supplemented the brandy that was the standard julep spirit at the time, and in the hands of a Virginia master such as the enslaved Jim Cook (ca. 1808–1870) or the freedman Jasper Crouch, the whole impression of the drink was one of unbridled luxury (indeed, Cook and his partner would make juleps for the prince of Wales when he visited Richmond on his 1860 American tour). See CROUCH, JASPER. By the 1840s, that luxury had become the norm in American drinking: every town of any size had at least one bar that made iced "fancy drinks." The El Dorado in San Francisco, the leading bar there during the first stage of the Gold Rush, used a golden muddler to mix its drinks (it was stolen in 1851). In 1862, Jerry Thomas, who had perhaps worked at the El Dorado, published the first bartender's guide. See THOMAS, JEREMIAH P. "JERRY".

European Developments

At the same time, this new American mixology began making its way over to Europe. Europe, of course, had its own ideas about mixology and its own drinks. The British had their punch and their cups and bowls (wine-based light punches of German inspiration). The Germans had "Bowlen" and a whole series of what are essentially shooters: short, un-iced mixtures of spirits, bitters, and liqueurs (the Dutch had their own versions). The French had their coffee-and-brandy "Mazagran," and the Italians had a wide range of café drinks—things such as the "Scottum" and the "Se Sa Minga" of Milano. See COFFEE DRINKS. But Italian mixology was back-room mixology, where the *liquorista* premixed and bottled the various creations in advance and merely poured them out over the bar.

American-style bars, such as the Café Leblond in Paris and Van Winkle's in London, catered largely to American expatriates, although Leblond did have a clientele among Paris's bohemian class. American drinks made little progress toward general acceptance in Europe. When the Neapolitans were introduced to the cocktail shaker, their first impulse was to use it for coffee. Meanwhile, in the 1860s one European product filtered back to America and dropped into American mixology like the keystone does into an arch: vermouth. A fairly low-proof beverage that had the texture of a spirit, vermouth made for complex, layered cocktails that were also simple. See MANHATTAN COCKTAIL and MARTINI. At the same time, a significant part of the massive wave of German immigration that reached America during the middle of the century washed up behind the bar, bringing with it the palette of liqueurs, bitters, and syrups that had characterized German mixology. See SCHMIDT, WILLIAM.

The Manhattan, the Martini, and their ilk revolutionized American mixology in the 1880s, spawning literally hundreds of variations and thrusting the cocktail to the fore as the standard-bearer for American drinking. In Europe, however, they were developing their own version of the American bar, which kept the Yankee trappings but had its own range of drinks. "Long drinks" were more important than cocktails, and mixologists such as Charley Paul of London made their livings acting American but mixing English. See CRITERION and ENGEL, LEO. Then a Neapolitan who had perhaps worked for Jerry Thomas briefly in New York turned the wheel. In the 1890s, Ciro Capozzi's little bar in Monte Carlo attracted perhaps the most exclusive clientele of any in the world, with the nobility of Europe gathering to sip unpretentious, New York–style cocktails and dine on impeccable London grill food. When Ciro's opened in Paris, London, and then Berlin, the American cocktail's work was done. It was what sophisticated people drank wherever they gathered, and Prohibition, the Great Depression, and two world wars did nothing to change that. See COCKTAIL; COLEMAN, ADA; and SAVOY HOTEL'S AMERICAN BAR.

This cocktail-forward mixology absorbed all influences. Citrus drinks became cocktails, not punches or sours. See BRONX COCKTAIL; DAIQUIRI; and SIDECAR. The 1930s, however, saw both the cocktail encompass new spirits—vodka, tequila—and a counter-school arise, going garish where the cocktail was elegant, complex where the cocktail was simple, rustic where the cocktail was urban. This was the tiki craze, movement, alternative reality—whatever you wish to call it. See TIKI. In terms of mixology, it was based on an intensely prismatic view of punches, much like that of the limonadiers, only this time the rainbow came out in tropical—or rather "tropical"—colors. From the 1930s through the 1960s, it was the loyal opposition. See TIKI.

Meanwhile, the mainstream cocktail culture was struggling. After those twentieth-century shocks, it ended up being narrowly focused on just a few drinks. The Dry Martini was by far the most important of them. Bartenders and drinkers patrolled the boundaries of the drink, narrowing them obsessively. Meanwhile, more and more people wandered off, drinking dubious things such as the Margarita (what is tequila, anyway?) and the Negroni (it's red!) and paying no attention to the traditions of the bar. See MARGARITA and NEGRONI. The big break came in the 1960s, when a new canon of drinks deposed the moribund old order. The new drinks were silly, sweet, simple, colorful, and unintimidating. They had no baggage and no rules. See BOURBON STREET DRINKS; CALIMOTXO; HARVEY WALLBANGER; LEMON DROP; PALOMA; and LONG ISLAND ICED TEA.

But this new canon—disco drinks, many called them—made for a bar culture that was ultimately unsatisfying. The drinks were things you drank while doing something else, and to break the snootiness and narrow thinking of the "Happiness is a Dry Martini" school of mixology, many people felt that too much had been sacrificed: complexity, balance, elegance, contemplation. With the rise of the internet, these people were able to talk to each other, and by the early 2000s, they had spawned a movement. Its principles, or rather its likes and dislikes, were fairly straightforward: keep the non-traditional bartenders (lots of women behind the bar since the 1970s) and the gender-inclusive bars. Keep the creativity that had spawned, for instance, thousands of new shooters. See SHOOTER. But reach back to before Prohibition to grab hold of the tradition and the craft off mixing drinks— the emphasis on quality ingredients and skilled execution. Surprisingly, it worked. See COCKTAIL RENAISSANCE.

Bazzetta de Vemenia, Nino. *I caffè storici d'Italia*. 1939; repr., Novara, Italy: Interlinea, 2010.

Savonarola, Michele. *Libretto de aqua ardente*. In *I trattati in volgare della peste e dell' acqua ardente*, ed. Luigi Belloni, 92. Rome: Società Italiana di Medicina Interna, 1953.

"Stolen." *Daily Alta California*, January 25, 1851, 3.

Wondrich, David. *Imbibe!*, 2nd ed. New York: Perigee, 2015.

Wondrich, David. "The Lost African-American Bartenders Who Created the Cocktail." *Daily Beast*, March 7, 2020. https://www.thedailybeast.com/the-lost-african-american-bartenders-who-created-the-cocktail (accessed May 13, 2021).

Wondrich, David. *Punch*, New York: Perigee, 2010.

Wondrich, David. "Why Did It Take America So Long to Have Female Bartenders?" *Daily Beast*, March 13, 2018. https://www.thedailybeast.com/why-did-it-take-america-so-long-to-have-female-bartenders (accessed May 13, 2021).

Wooley, Hannah. *The Queene-Like Closet*. London: 1670.

David Wondrich

mixology (how to mix drinks) is the act of mixing cocktails and other drinks and encompasses a set of techniques including shaking, stirring, and muddling. The meaning of the word "mixology" is debated among bar industry professionals, whether it is meant to indicate someone who creates drinks or is synonymous with bartending. However, the term "mixologist" itself originates from a passage in a dialect humor column by Charles G. Leland in *Knickerbocker Magazine* in 1856 in which a character refers to a hotel bartender as "a mixologist of tipulars." The magazine was popular, and readers, finding the term amusing, began adopting it, at first in jest. By 1870, the term had taken on a more serious tone, as can be seen in William Fraser Rae's *Westward by Rail*: "The keeper of the White Pine Saloon at Elko, Nev. informs his patrons that, 'The most delicate fancy drinks are compounded by skilful mixologists in a style that captivates the public and makes them happy.'"

The term has since been used in multiple bartending books and many numerous articles referencing cocktails. Regardless of the historical context, mixology and bartending refer to the same set of techniques, with the distinctions that a bartender is generally employed to use these techniques to service guests (there are bartenders who have nothing to do with mixology), whereas a mixologist need not be employed as a bartender to practice mixology.

The principle techniques used in mixology include building, shaking, and stirring drinks. Each one of these techniques is used to elicit various qualities of the drink recipe much as sautéing, boiling, and baking might be used in cooking different recipes. There are far too many variables to discuss within the context of this article, but we will cover the major techniques and some of their usage.

Building is used in simple mixed drinks such as the highball where the ingredients are easily blended and involves pouring the ingredients directly into the serving vessel. An example is a Gin and Tonic, where both the gin and tonic are poured directly into the glass with ice and served. See GIN AND TONIC. Rolling is also a form of building, in which the drink is built in the glass and then "rolled," that is, poured, into a cheater tin (the smaller end of the shaker) or pint glass and then poured back into the glass it was built in. The Bloody Mary, for example, is rolled. See BLOODY MARY.

A more advanced form of rolling is called throwing and is when the mixologist pours the content of a drink back and forth between two tins or a tin and a glass, often theatrically and from a great height. Throwing is best exemplified in the Blue Blazer, where the contents of the glass are tossed between mugs on fire (fire is not necessary for throwing). The Blue Blazer is pictured in a plate in Jerry Thomas's 1862 edition of *How to Mix Drinks: Or, The Bon-Vivant's Companion*. See THOMAS, JEREMIAH P. "JERRY"; and BLUE BLAZER. This technique was nearly abandoned in the twentieth century, though it was the proto-technique for shaking. Throwing was preserved, however, as a part of Spanish and Cuban bartending and from there has recolonized the international bartending community.

Shaking is done in a shaker, comprising a tin and a glass or two cups—one larger and one smaller, sometimes with a built-in strainer, with the mouth of one pressed down over the mouth of the other, which contains the drink's components. See COCKTAIL SHAKER. Adding the liquid and ice forms a seal where the cups meet. The mixologist will then hold the shaker and thrust it back and forth—artistically, it is hoped—until the ingredients are cooled and integrated, and then generally deploy a strainer to keep the spent ice out of the glass. See COCKTAIL STRAINER. According to Dave Arnold, a food science writer and bar owner, the proper length to shake a cocktail is twelve to fifteen seconds, after which there is no appreciable further gain in terms of temperature or dilution. Shaking is most commonly used to incorporate ingredients of various densities and textures such as eggs, sugar, juice, and cream, as it involves a more explosive movement than either building or stirring, but in some countries and regions of the United States it is the default way of mixing.

Bartenders have developed specific shakes for different drinks, such as the Japanese bartender Kazuo Uyeda, who created the Hard Shake. The Hard Shake is a choreographed shake, involving a specific pattern and movements, which purportedly elicits a different texture than standard practices. It is named the Hard Shake not because of how hard the shaker is shaken but because it is hard to master. See JAPAN and UYEDA, KAZUO.

Mixologists have also created different shaking styles to best incorporate egg whites or their vegan analogue, aqua faba (water from soaked chickpeas), such as the dry shake and reverse dry shake. The dry shake is when the drink is shaken before adding ice, and the reverse dry shake is when the drink is shaken with ice first, then strained to remove the ice and shaken again without it. In both cases, the mixologist is creating a texture similar to a meringue.

Stirring is a way to blend cocktails or mixed drinks that involves using a vessel such as a glass pitcher, pint glass, dedicated mixing glass, or even the larger portion of the shaker and a cocktail spoon and ice. See BAR SPOON. Stirring is principally used when the ingredients are all alcohol based, such as with a Martini. See MARTINI. The mixologist will press the backside of the spoon against the vessel and stir, creating a vortex at the top of the liquids. Stirring is more difficult than building or shaking, and its elegant execution depends upon the skill of the mixologist. Kazuo Uyeda describes stirring as weaving silk. (One secret to making stirring much easier is to use cracked ice rather than cubes; this also makes for a colder drink.)

Muddling is used to press or pulverize ingredients, releasing juice, oils, and/or other aromatic compounds into the mixing vessel. To muddle, mixologists use a muddler—a small wooden, plastic, or metal bat—or the back end of the spoon and twist the muddler or spoon while pressing against the ingredients. See MUDDLER. The Mint Julep uses muddling to press the mint leaves into the sugar syrup in a gentle action, where the mixologist will press just enough to extract the oils and aromatic compounds from the leaves. In other drinks, such as the Caipirinha, the muddler is pressed much harder to extract juice from limes. After the ingredients have been muddled, they are also sometimes shaken or stirred and strained to further combine the ingredients and strain out any matter such as leaves or pulp. See MINT JULEP and CAIPIRINHA.

Swizzling is similar to muddling but does not always press against the solid ingredients. It uses a small tree harvested in the Caribbean, *Quararibea turbinata*, also known as the swizzle stick tree, where the branches have been cut and bark removed. (The swizzle stick is not to be confused with the plastic swizzle sticks that are historically found in hotel and tiki drinks.) Mixologists place the stick between their hands and rub their hands back and forth, creating a whirling motion, blending the ingredients. See SWIZZLE; SWIZZLE STICK; and TIKI.

Layering is a technique used to float a spirit, wine, or other liquid ingredient, either on top of the drink or as a series of layers within the drink such as with the Pousse Café, which can be many layers tall. See FLOAT; LAYERING; and POUSSE CAFÉ.

Once the mixologist creates the drinks, they then serve them with specific designations that are either endogenous to the drink or specified by the guest such as "up" or "on the rocks." The term "up" refers to when a drink is served without ice in a stemmed glass such as a coupe. When it is straight spirits without ice, the term is "neat." There is no corresponding "down"; drinks that are served with ice are referred to as "on the rocks." Drinks served up or on the rocks may also have a salted or sugared rim, where the mixologist uses juice, most commonly lemon or lime, around the top outside edge of the glass and the presses the rim into salt or sugar. Therefore a Margarita, which was originally served on the rocks or with ice, may be served "up" instead with or without a salt rim. See MARGARITA.

What mixology does not necessarily include are aspects of hospitality and customer service. These techniques are the hallmark of a bartender, and thus a bartender must use all three sets of skills— hospitality, customer service, and mixology.

See also MIXOLOGY, THE HISTORY OF.

Arnold, Dave. "Tales of the Cocktail: Science of Shaking II." *Cooking Issues*, July 24, 2009. http://www.cookingissues.com/index.html%3Fp=1527.html (accessed April 23, 2021).

Difford, Simon. "The Hard Shake." *Difford's Guide*. https://www.diffordsguide.com/encyclopedia/492/cocktails/the-hard-shake (accessed April 23, 2021).

Janzen, Emma. "The Return of Throwing Cocktails." *Imbibe Magazine*, July 19, 2018. https://imbibemagazine.com/throwing-cocktails/ (accessed April 23, 2021).

Kamholz, Roger. "Is There a Better Way to Make an Egg White Cocktail?" *Punch*, March 13, 2017. https://punchdrink.com/articles/how-to-make-egg-white-cocktail-reverse-dry-shake-flip/ (accessed April 23, 2021).

Rummel, Rachel. "Tools: Swizzle Sticks." *Atlas Obscura*. https://www.atlasobscura.com/foods/swizzle-sticks-cocktails (accessed April 23, 2021).

Uyeda, Kazuo. *Cocktail Techniques*. New York: Mud Puddle, 2010.

Wondrich, David. *Imbibe!* New York: Perigee, 2007.

Derek Brown

mixto is a type of tequila or mezcal that is made from a mixture of agave and other sugars. The agave component in mixto tequila must comprise at least 51 percent, while the minimum required for mixto mezcal is 80 percent. See AGAVE; MEZCAL; and TEQUILA.

Mizuwari is a Japanese take on a highball, with ritualistic attention paid to the adding and stirring of ice, whisky, and—where it differs from the American highball—uncarbonated mineral water. See HIGHBALL and WHISKY.

mocktail is a term that is often used for a nonalcoholic cocktail; although it appears intermittently beginning in the 1910s, it did not reach wide usage the 1970s, when it was popularized by John Doxat (1914–2002), the British journalist and publicist who was the leading drinks writer of his day. Mocktails are intended to be consumed in lieu of an alcoholic drink and should be a tasty, thoughtful combination of ingredients that offers an enjoyable degree of complexity; additionally, mocktails traditionally use a presentation—color, glassware, garnish—that is designed to recall an alcoholic drink. Many point to the Shirley Temple (ginger ale, grenadine, and sometimes orange juice) as being one of the first examples of the genre, but the concept predates the drink by at least a century.

The popularity of nonalcoholic substitutes for mixed drinks got its start in the 1820s, when the temperance movement began to advocate for moderation (if not total abstinence) in the consumption of alcoholic beverages. One way the movement promoted alcohol-free drinking was to install "temperance fountains" that provided free and safe water for people to drink; but also promoted were tea, coffee, soda water, and ginger beer.

How to Mix Drinks by Jerry Thomas (1862) was the first published mixed drinks book to include recipes for cocktails, but it also offered nonalcoholic options. In fact, one of the thirteen cocktail recipes it offers, the Soda Cocktail, is nonalcoholic, and the book's final chapter offers fifteen more recipes for "temperance drinks," among them such drinks as Lemonade, Orangeade, the Imperial Drink for Families, and Ginger Wine. See THOMAS, JEREMIAH P. "JERRY". Many of the bartending manuals that followed Thomas's book included nonalcoholic drinks as well.

Mocktails are also sometimes known as "virgin" cocktails. Typically, these are well-known cocktails with the alcohol left out. The most popular virgin drink is probably the Virgin Mary, prepared as a standard Bloody Mary but with the vodka omitted. See BLOODY MARY. The recipe works well in this regard, with the combination of spices, bright acidity, and meaty umami flavor from the tomato juice providing a high degree of satisfaction despite the absence of alcohol (in the late 1970s, *New York* magazine repeatedly caught Maxwell's Plum, a wildly popular bar, selling Bloody Marys that had no vodka in them at all; its customers never noticed).

While the temperance movement lost most of its momentum following the repeal of Prohibition, the mocktail found its place not outside the bar world but within it. A thoughtful mocktail is suitable for those who don't want to consume alcohol: pregnant women, designated drivers, and those with alcohol issues can all benefit from an alternative that still fits the pattern and ambiance that accompanies cocktails and other mixed drinks. Modern bartenders frequently seek to round out their cocktail lists with mocktails that display the same unique flavor combinations, complexity, and attractive presentation that their cocktails do.

Finally, it must be noted that there are still many who refuse to use the term "mocktail," regarding it as silly and made up; they have yet to suggest anything better.

See PROHIBITION AND TEMPERANCE MOVEMENTS.

Allen, Frederick. "Bloody Mary Blood Test no. 5: No Booze at Maxwell's Plum." *New York*, March 26, 1979, 9.

Doxat, John. *The World of Drinks and Drinking*. New York: Drake, 1971, 158.

Thomas, Jerry. *How to Mix Drinks*. New York: Dick & Fitzgerald, 1862.

Audrey Saunders

modifier as a term, along with "modifying agent," appears to have first been put forth by David Embury in his 1948 book *The Fine Art of Mixing Drinks*, in an attempt to define the ingredients that when added to a base spirit, create a cocktail or other mixed drink. By Embury's definition, almost anything added to the mixing glass besides the base spirit and ice is a modifier. See EMBURY, DAVID A.

Modifiers take on various roles in a cocktail. They can soften the bite of the base spirit, enhance or accentuate the base, or more precisely balance the flavors of the base spirit. See BASE. Typically, an accent ingredient would then be needed to provide a pop of flavor as a final touch. See ACCENT.

A modifier can bring a subtle, subdued flavor to a drink, as in the use of vermouth, triple sec, or a flavored syrup. Or it can be a bolder, more flavorful ingredient that assertively alters the profile as with Campari, Bénédictine, or a citrus juice. While more than a single modifier can be used in a cocktail, it's generally considered best to adopt a "less is more" attitude. Using too many modifiers may not only throw off overall balance, but it can result in a confusing array of flavors or can undermine the structure of the drink. See BALANCE.

Embury, David. *The Fine Art of Mixing Drinks*. Garden City, NY: Doubleday, 1948.

Audrey Saunders

The **Mojito**, essentially a rum Collins with muddled mint, is an early-twentieth-century Cuban invention that became popular with Americans in Prohibition-era Havana, then for the most part fell off the cocktail map until its resurgence in the 1980s at the hands of Cuban Marielito emigrants in Miami—whence it spread to become second only to the Cosmopolitan in US bars. This refreshing cooler has been a common call ever since, and deservedly so, despite critics who deride it as cliché and bartenders who regard it as too much trouble to make. The first published recipe appears as the Mojo de Ron in *Libro de Cocktail*, a 1929 manual by one Juan A. Lasa: "two or three fingers" of Bacardi rum, the juice of a lime, and a barspoon of sugar, all combined in a tall glass with cracked ice, seltzer, one of the squeezed-out lime halves, and a sprig of mint. Lasa also includes a gin version and a "Criollo," or Creole one, which is the rum one but with half the lime juice and added Angostura bitters. The name "Mojito" appears in print two years later, in the drinks booklet put out by Sloppy Joe's bar in Havana. See SLOPPY JOE'S. Later recipes specified muddling the sugar and lime with mint leaves before adding the other ingredients; this results in a far superior Mojito (as does decreasing the lime juice or increasing the sugar to taste).

Cuban folklore traces the Mojito's origin back to 1586, when Sir Francis Drake's crew cured their fever with a similar mixture called "El Draque" (mint, sugar, lime, aguardiente). Nothing in the historical record supports this. However, there's ample evidence that a similar compound called the "Draquecito" was prescribed to prevent cholera in mid-nineteenth-century Cuba; this could very well have inspired the Mojito. Some Cuban authorities maintain, without further evidence, that inspiration struck an unnamed bartender at one of the bars at la Concha beach near Havana one day in 1910 or thereabouts, and the drink spread from there. It is not impossible, anyway.

Recipe: In a tall glass, stir together 15 ml lime juice and 5 ml sugar. Add 5 or 6 mint leaves and muddle them lightly. Fill the glass with ice, add 45 or 60 ml light, Cuban-style rum (or gin), stir, and top off with chilled soda water. Stir once, add a mint sprig, and finish with a straw.

See also COLLINS.

Berry, Jeff. *Beachbum Berry's Potions of the Caribbean.* New York: Cocktail Kingdom, 2014.

Curtis, Wayne. *And a Bottle of Rum: A History of the New World in Ten Cocktails.* New York: Crown, 2006.

Doudoroff, Martin. *Martin's New and Improved Index of Cocktails & Mixed Drinks from the First Golden Age of the American Bar.* iOS8 app. Version 1.1.3, October 20, 2015 (accessed October 30, 2015).

Lasa, Juan A. *Libro de Cocktail.* [Havana]: n.p., 1929.

Jeff Berry

molasses, a byproduct of sugar refining, is a mineral-rich, pungent, and viscous brown syrup with a high sucrose content; its name is derived from the Latin *mellaceus*, "honeyed," via the Portuguese *melaço*. Its sugar content makes it ideal for fermentation and distillation, which is why, along with another byproduct, "skimmings" or "scum," it became one of the bases for rum making on sugar plantations in the Caribbean in the seventeenth century. In the early colonial era, sugar cane juice was boiled in a series of increasingly smaller copper cauldrons as the impurity-rich foam was skimmed off. The sticky juice from the final cauldron was poured into conical clay sugar molds with a small hole on the bottom to allow the molasses to drain into clay jars known as "drips." See SUGAR CANE. In some places, such as Barbados, planters would cap the sugar molds with wet pads of white clay. This practice, known as "claying," removed more molasses and left a lighter and more refined sugarloaf. The molasses could be sent to the fermentation vats in the distillery or boiled again to extract what little sugar remained. (Blackstrap molasses, for instance, is a dark, rich, bitter, and thick substance that has gone through several boilings and thus has a low sugar content that renders it less than ideal for rum making.)

The use of molasses and skimmings (collectively known as "sweets") for rum making highlights the efficiency of early Caribbean sugar planters. Rather than simply dispose of these things—effectively, their industrial waste—they fermented them and distilled them into rum, which was typically thought to contribute 10–20 percent of plantation revenues.

In 1848, the Jamaican distiller Leonard Wray gave the composition of the wash he made his rum from as 10 percent molasses, 20 percent skimmings, 20 percent water, and 50 percent dunder (the spent wash from a previous distillation). See DUNDER.

While he used more dunder than most, the general composition of his wash was roughly representative of common Caribbean practice from the seventeenth century into the early twentieth.

As a result of pressure from French wine and brandy interests, France restricted the import of French Caribbean rum in 1713. With no home market for rum, sugar planters in the French Caribbean colonies had a lot of leftover molasses. They shipped raw molasses to France, where it was used in making gingerbread, or they sold it to merchants in the New England colonies of North America, where it was distilled into rum, although since it was made without the flavor-rich skimmings, it was generally considered an inferior product. (In fact, eighteenth-century English distillers drew a distinction between this "molasses brandy" and true rum.) A typical formula from which a North American rum was distilled would be 20 percent molasses to 40 percent each of dunder and water.

In the twentieth century, the consolidation and technical evolution of the sugar industry meant that skimmings were no longer available to the vast majority of distilleries, and the sweets used for most rums moved to purely molasses.

Molasses was also widely used in colonial North America to sweeten certain mixed drinks. See BLACK STRAP and FLIP. Today, it sometimes appears in drinks, although most often in the form of so-called black rum or blackstrap rum, a light-bodied, column-distilled rum flavored and colored with molasses after distillation.

See also CARIBBEAN; RUM; and SKIMMINGS.

Byrn, M. La Fayette. *The Complete Practical Distiller*. Philadelphia: Henry Cary Baird, 1868.

Smith, Frederick H. *Caribbean Rum: A Social and Economic History*. Gainesville: University Press of Florida, 2005.

Wray, Leonard. *The Practical Sugar Planter*. London: Smith, Elder, 1848.

Frederick H. Smith

mold is a large family of multicellular fungi that produces challenges as well as, in some cases, opportunities for the distiller and the spirits producer. It is a distiller's axiom that the flavor of mold is, along with that of smoke, one of two flavors that cannot be removed from a spirit by redistillation, filtration,

maturation, or any other known process. In much of the world, raw materials that are moldy are therefore rigorously avoided.

East Asia, however, has traditionally used a different approach: taking advantage of the fact that some molds can break down starches into sugars, distillers in China and Japan and some associated areas have put mold at the center of their spirits-making. See ASPERGILLUS ORYZAE; BAIJIU; KOJI; and QU.

Mold is also a byproduct of the maturation of spirits when it is fed by the "angel's share," the alcohol-rich vapor that rises from the casks. Makers of some spirits, such as scotch whisky and French brandies, not only boast of the vigorous growth of mold in and around their barrel-storage facilities but sometimes even insist that their spirits are favorably altered by the mold's influence, or at least that it is a sign of the wholesomeness of their spirit.

See also BAUDOINIA COMPNIACENSIS.

De-Wei, Li. *Biology of Microfungi*. Cham, Switzerland: Springer, 2016.

Moore, David, Geoffrey Robson, and Anthony Trinci. *21st Century Guidebook to Fungi*. London: Cambridge University Press, 2011.

Doug Frost

molecular mixology is the popular term for the application of modern scientific investigation, knowledge, tools, substances, and processes to the creation and production of cocktails, usually with a goal of creating an effect that is unobtainable or impracticable using traditional means and methods. Depending on the intentions and aesthetic of the creator, cocktails produced by these methods may be whimsical or challenging in form and/or context or may be broadly similar to traditional cocktails.

The name derives from the so-called molecular gastronomy or modernist cuisine culinary movement as investigated, practiced, and documented by Hervé This, Ferran Adrià, Heston Blumenthal, Nathan Myhrvold, and others and frequently utilizes ingredients, equipment, and techniques pioneered in that movement. Some influential bartenders in this style are Dave Arnold, Eben Freeman, and Eben Klemm in New York, Tony Conigliaro in London, and Jamie Boudreau in Seattle, Washington.

Representative tools, techniques, and ingredients used by molecular mixology bartenders include the following:

Additives

Bartenders avail themselves of the full range of food-safe chemicals and other additives to produce specific results unobtainable or impracticable by other means. For example, citric and other acids can be used to adjust the sourness of fruit juices; sodium bisulfite helps to preserve the color of green juices; and liquid-filled spheres are created using sodium citrate, sodium alginate, calcium chloride, calcium lactate, and/or calcium lactate gluconate.

Barrel Aging

A cocktail is created in sufficient volume to fill a wooden cask and subsequently aged for a period of time in it. When the desired result is obtained, the barrel-aged cocktail is decanted into a nonreactive vessel for storage and service. The type of wood, size, age, preparation, and previous use of the cask, as well as the length of aging, all influence the results of the barrel-aging process. This technique is primarily used for cocktails such as the Negroni or Manhattan that have an inherently strong flavor and do not contain fresh ingredients.

Carbonation

Carbon dioxide is dissolved into one or more components of a cocktail at high pressure in order to produce an effervescent beverage. Alternatively, fruit may be infused with carbon dioxide in order to create garnish that effervesces as it is eaten. Carbonation produces a characteristic "prickling" sensation in the mouth as the cocktail is consumed, and the carbon dioxide that is released can have a significant impact on perceived flavor as a result of the way it affects retronasal olfaction, the process in which odor molecules pass upward from the oral cavity to olfactory receptors in the back of the nasal cavity.

Clarification

Ingredients such as fresh juices are clarified to produce transparent and frequently colorless liquids having the desirable flavors and other characteristics of the original ingredient. Common clarification techniques employed in molecular mixology include enzymatic degradation, fining, and centrifuging, often in combination. Another popular process is to add gelatin or agar-agar to a liquid, which is subsequently frozen and thawed, trapping unwanted particulate matter in the semisolid matrix that is left behind. Each method of clarification has a different yield and effect on the resultant clarified liquid and may be better suited to particular liquids or contemplated uses. Decolored clarified liquids allow bartenders to produce cocktails with unexpected flavors due to the absence of familiar visual cues, and the removal of suspended particles makes it possible to carbonate beverages containing clarified fresh juices.

Edible Cocktails

Various methods can be employed to produce a solid food otherwise having the flavors and alcoholic content of a cocktail. Some well-known examples of edible cocktails include marshmallows, sorbets, breakfast cereal, gelatin in various shapes, and vacuum-infused fruits or vegetables such as cucumbers.

Fat Washing

This traditional perfumer's technique takes advantage of the fact that most fat-soluble substances are also soluble in alcohol. An aromatic and flavorful fat is combined with a spirit and allowed to rest; then, after the infusion is complete, the mixture is chilled until the fat solidifies and can be strained off. Fat washing has been used to flavor spirits with bacon fat, brown butter, cheese, extra virgin olive oil, duck fat, peanut butter, and chorizo fat, to name a few well-known examples.

Foams

Flavorful liquids are combined with ingredients such as gelatin, lecithin, agar-agar, egg whites, egg white powder, and gum arabic, and air or gas is incorporated to create bubbles. Depending on the ingredients and techniques employed, the foam can be wet or dry, stiff or loose, and having fine or large bubbles. Foams are not typically complete cocktails in and of themselves but are usually layered over a liquid to contribute a contrasting aroma, flavor, and/or texture component.

Gels and Gums

Spirits and other ingredients are combined with a gelling agent such as gelatin or agar-agar, then allowed to set. The gels can be garnished and consumed as an edible cocktail, or they can be used as a garnish or semisolid component in a liquid cocktail.

Liquid Nitrogen

This super-cold liquid is −195.79° C and is used in a variety of innovative and interesting ways in the production of cocktails. For example, green herbs such as mint or basil can be frozen to a very low temperature with liquid nitrogen, shattered into tiny pieces, and combined with spirits to result in an extra-strong herbal extraction without any of the off-flavors normally associated with enthusiastic muddling and oxidation. Liquid nitrogen can be poured onto the surface of a cocktail to create a frozen layer over which other liquids will be added, or spirits may be mixed with liquid nitrogen in order to produce a frozen "cocktail sorbet." Bartenders with ready access to liquid nitrogen also find it convenient for chilling glassware. Special care must be taken when working with liquid nitrogen, as improper use can lead to tissue damage from freezing, asphyxiation from vaporized nitrogen, and even explosions resulting from pressure buildup in unsuitable storage vessels.

Spherification

Various chemicals and techniques are used to create liquid-filled spheres ranging in size from caviar to egg yolks, which are then served as an edible cocktail or used as a component in a liquid cocktail. As the spheres rupture and release their liquid contents in the mouth, they create "bursts" of flavor that, in a liquid cocktail, enhance, alter, or contrast with the primary flavors. Especially popular as a garnish for champagne, spherification has been one of the most widespread techniques of molecular mixology, to such an extent that the company Rémy Cointreau created a special kit with all the ingredients and equipment for making "Cointreau pearls."

Sous Vide

In molecular mixology this technique is primarily used for infusions and takes advantage of one of the primary techniques and equipment sets of molecular gastronomy. Spirits or other liquids are sealed in a plastic pouch or other airtight container together with a flavoring agent such as tea, fresh or dried herbs or spices, fruits, or vegetables. The container is then placed in a temperature-controlled water bath, heated for a period of time, and then chilled and strained. Sous vide techniques allow for precisely controlled infusions and extraction of flavors that would be impossible or impracticable using traditional means. The chamber vacuum machine, a common piece of equipment employed in sous vide techniques, can also be used to quickly infuse porous fruits and vegetables with spirits or other liquids. Although vacuum packaging for culinary use may be highly scrutinized and tightly regulated in some jurisdictions, a jar or bottle serves as well as a vacuum bag for most applications of this technique that have relevance to molecular mixology.

Vacuum Distillation

A piece of laboratory equipment called a rotary evaporator is used to perform distillations at low temperatures by reducing gas pressure. This technology makes it possible to concentrate flavors, extract essential oils, and produce uniquely flavored liquids with high precision and without altering or damaging fresh flavors with heat. Vacuum distillation has been used to concentrate fruit juices, extract aromas from unlikely substances such as leather or soil, remove oak byproducts from barrel-aged spirits, create chile-flavored spirits without spicy capsaicin and tea-flavored spirits without astringent tannins, produce water-based distillations called hydrosols using delicate flowers or herbs, and in the creation of many other products used by molecular mixologists. Although the alcohol-based products are some of the more dramatic and popular vacuum distillates for demonstration purposes, they are illegal to serve in most countries around the world. It is also illegal in many jurisdictions to possess distilling equipment and/or perform distillations of any kind on-premises without a permit. As a result, drinks containing vacuum-distilled components are rarely encountered in a commercial setting.

Arnold, Dave. *Liquid Intelligence*. New York: Norton, 2014.

Boudreau, Jamie. *The Canon Cocktail Book*. New York: Houghton Mifflin Harcourt, 2016.

Conigliaro, Tony. *The Cocktail Lab*. London: Ten Speed, 2013

Liu, Kevin. *Craft Cocktails at Home*. Kevin Liu, 2013.

Samuel Lloyd Kinsey

Monkey Shoulder is a premium blended malt scotch whisky produced by William Grant and Sons. Developed in 2005 as an antidote to the stodgy image under which the scotch category labored, Monkey Shoulder entices a growing legion of younger fans through its cocktail programming led by dynamic, mixology-oriented brand ambassadors. The blend contains single malts from just three distilleries: Glenfiddich, Balvenie, and Kininvie, all owned by William Grant and Sons. According to legend, Monkey Shoulder was a nickname given to a form of bursitis of the shoulder associated with a repetitive strain injury brought about by continually turning barley on a malting floor. See FLOOR MALTING. It was most likely a term used specifically in Speyside, the region in which some of the Monkey Shoulder malts are distilled.

See also GLENFIDDICH and WHISKY, SCOTCH.

Smith, Gavin D. *The A–Z of Whisky*. Glasgow: Neeil Wilson, 2009.

Heather Greene

moonshine is a general term for illicit, unlicensed, or homemade spirits. The laws governing the production and distribution of distilled spirits are many and strict, and disregard of those regulations is the only legitimate defining characteristic of moonshine. The illegal distillation of alcohol is varied and international, flourishing where alcohol is legally prohibited or highly taxed or where law enforcement is weak; in some parts of Africa and Asia, it is the dominant form of spirits production. In more developed economies, moonshining is often linked with counterfeiting, whereby established, often international brands are copied and undersold. All too often, counterfeit or illegal alcohol is contaminated with methanol or other poisons, and injury and death are a distressingly common result of their consumption; without legal regulation, there is no way of guaranteeing a product's purity.

Moonshining is far from homogenous; indeed, that is its nature. Different patterns of it prevail depending on the region. In large parts of Africa, inland Brazil, and the Balkans, it usually takes the form of unlicensed and home distilling, where its legality is a gray area. In Russia, the distilling of *samogon* is illegal but widespread on a home level. In countries such as Iran, Pakistan, and parts of India, where spirits are forbidden, moonshining is often a business. In Great Britain, these days it usually takes the form of the production of counterfeit, and therefore cheap, vodka. In centuries past, though, it gave us malt whisky. See SAMOGON and WHISKY.

In America, where moonshining has a long and lively history, there were no rules against distillation and no taxes paid on distilled spirits until 1791, when the newly formed federal government, in debt after the American Revolution, levied its first tax on an American product, the excise tax on whisky. This tax was unpopular, to say the least, and mostly went uncollected. On the frontier of Pennsylvania, farmers resisted it, believing that they were continuing the battle against taxation without representation. Thirteen thousand troops marched against them. This was the first expression of federal power, and proof that the laws of the newly centralized government would be enforced. Many of those farmers who resisted the tax drifted southward along the Appalachian Mountains, and they brought their distilling traditions with them. Others quietly continued resisting in place. Although often thought of as "corn liquor," the raw materials fermented to make moonshine were traditionally whatever was closest at hand and familiar to the maker. Italian American immigrants in upstate New York, for instance, tended to make grape brandies, whereas the orchardists of the Shenandoah Valley used groundfall apples.

Today, moonshine in America, which is in all cases illegal, can be classified into two major categories: recreational and commercial. Although there are many more individuals pursuing home distillation for fun than there are professional moonshiners, their output is commercially negligible, and law enforcement generally turns a blind eye to their activities. The vast majority of illegal alcohol is produced by individuals committed to continuing criminal enterprise.

The largest concentration of commercial moonshining in America is in the South. Originally, the industry sprang from a regional rejection of federal dominion after the Civil War. Although the Appalachian mountain man often took the blame for hooch, his people were only a scapegoat for a widespread practice. The ubiquity of moonshine then and now has led to a cultural nullification of the laws against it that make it very difficult to discourage, or indeed prosecute, the production of illegal spirits. Prohibition grew the business a great deal, and bootleggers ran rampant until the advent of two-way radios in police cars. See PROHIBITION AND TEMPERANCE IN AMERICA. Although moonshining as a criminal enterprise has certainly receded from its peak, it is far from extinct. In 1993, agents in Pittsylvania County, Virginia, discovered a moonshine distillery that consisted of thirty-six 800-gallon stills, the largest operation ever discovered.

Although commercial moonshiners produce liquor that is slapdash and dangerous, and usually fermented from white sugar with little regard for its taste or the quality, smaller recreational distillers are more akin to enthusiastic home cooks. The robust world of hobby distillers includes moonshiners of many stripes, from those who strive for maximum efficiency to those cherishing a folkloric tradition. For some, distillation is the next obvious step after they've mastered the production of beer. For others, it is an expression of their libertarian independence. Over time, the word "moonshine" came to be associated with clear spirits, mostly corn based. As interest in distilling grew in the early 2000s and the hobby community thrived, many licensed distilleries began to market products—ostensibly legal versions of an illegal product—that tap into the folklore and outlaw mystique attached to moonshine.

See also EXCISE, TAXES, AND DISTILLATION.

Haworth, Alan and Ronald Simpson, eds. *Moonshine Markets: Issues in Unrecorded Alcohol Beverage Production and Consumption*, New York: Brunner-Routledge, 2004.

Rowley, Matthew. *Moonshine!* New York: Lark Crafts, 2007.

Watman, Max. *Chasing the White Dog: An Amateur Outlaw's Adventures in Moonshine*. New York: Simon & Schuster, 2010.

Max Watman

Morris, Victor Vaughan (1873–1929), popularly known as Vic Morris, operated Morris' Bar in downtown Lima, Peru, from 1916 until his death. He is widely credited with creating and popularizing the Pisco Sour.

Born in Salt Lake City, Utah, Morris was a member of a Mormon Church founding family. He operated a flower shop with his brother, Burton, who was shot to death in 1899. Burton's death and the negative outcome of the murder trial that followed significantly affected Victor. In 1903, he left Salt Lake City to take a clerical job with the Cerro de Pasco Railroad Company, which was building a railway to a 14,000-feet-high copper mine in the Peruvian Andes. He worked there until 1916.

Morris relocated then to Lima and opened the Morris' Bar at 847 Calle Boza Street, in the heart of the city's modern business district. There he made the Pisco Sour famous in Lima and soon, through the many foreign travelers who visited his bar, worldwide. A recipe for a drink that was the Pisco Sour in everything but name was already circulating in Lima in 1903; however, it is equally possible that Morris came up with his version independently, adapting the standard American Sour formula to the prevailing local spirit. See SOUR. Nonetheless, and even though his original Pisco Sour recipe varied slightly from the one prepared today, Morris is still regarded as its originator and the father of Peruvian mixology. He died in Lima from cirrhosis in 1929.

See also PISCO SOUR.

"Farewell to . . ." *Deseret Evening News* (Salt Lake City), July 31, 1902.

"Joins Welby's . . ." *Salt Lake Herald*, June 4, 1903.

Ledesma, S. E. *Nuevo manual de cocina a la criolla: almuerzo*. Lima: Ledesma, 1903.

Morris' Bar Visitors' Register, Morris family private collection.

Toro-Lira, Guillermo. *History of Pisco in San Francisco: A Scrapbook of First Hand Accounts*, Lima, Peru: Creatspace, 2010.

Guillermo L. Toro-Lira

The **Moscow Mule** is a drink composed of vodka, ginger beer, and lime juice, traditionally served highball-style in a copper mug. The drink purportedly originated in 1941 at the Cock 'n Bull pub in

Los Angeles, during a meeting between Heublein president John Martin, who at the time was promoting Smirnoff vodka in the United States, and Cock 'n Bull owner Jack Morgan, who was similarly hoping to improve sales of his branded ginger beer (a competing history has Morgan and Martin devising the drink in New York before bringing it to Los Angeles). One version of the story (possibly apocryphal) notes that the bar also had a stock of copper mugs already on hand, which bartenders used to boost the drink's appeal. In fact, it may have been the Cock 'n Bull's head bartender, Charles Wesley "Wes" Price (1890–1962), who did the actual creating; he certainly claimed he did. According to him, it was first served to actors Broderick Crawford and Rod Cameron. This would have had to be before the end of 1942, when the drink first begins to surface in chronicles of the Hollywood "film colony" (the name had already turned up that summer in New York).

Regardless of the origins, the Moscow Mule became one of the first popular uses of vodka in American bars, with the specially labeled copper mugs it was typically served in becoming practically ubiquitous in postwar cocktail lounges. Smirnoff, America's leading vodka brand, promoted the drink heavily and rode its success (and that of the Bloody Mary) to spectacular growth.

After largely disappearing from use in the latter third of the twentieth century, the drink enjoyed a tremendous revival starting around 2010, when bartenders began adding the drink to cocktail menus, and copper mugs became so ubiquitous as to be available at corner drugstores. The drink's popularity came with a price: many bars serving the drink suffered large levels of theft of the signature copper mugs, and in response some began requiring a credit card be held on file until the mug was returned.

Recipe: Combine in ice-filled copper mule mug or highball glass 60 ml vodka, 15 ml lime juice, and 90 ml ginger beer. Stir.

See also SMIRNOFF.

Gwynn, Edith. "Inside Hollywood." *Albuquerque Journal*, December 13, 1942, 16.

Mosby, Aline. "Inventor Claims 'Moscow Mule' Is Really Art." *Boston Globe*, November 18, 1951, 37.

Simonson, Robert. "At Age 75, the Moscow Mule Gets Its Kick Back." *New York Times*, July 20, 2016. http://www.nytimes.com/2016/07/20/dining/moscow-mule.html (accessed February 21, 2021).

Vinh, Tan. "Seattle Bars Getting Moscow Mule Mugged." *Seattle Times*, May 23, 2013. https://www.seattletimes.com/life/food-drink/seattle-bars-getting-moscow-mule-mugged/ (accessed February 21, 2021).

Paul Clarke

Moskovskaya Osobaya ("Moscow Special")

vodka, now produced by Soyuzplodoimport, is one of Russia's most venerable and celebrated spirits. This rye-based vodka allegedly gets its famous clarity and hint of sweetness from the "soft waters of the Russian rivers." Moskovskaya is often touted for its exceptionally smooth taste, clear finish, and lack of burn and is a popular choice for consumption in the traditional Russian manner: chilled and served neat in a shot glass. Moskovskaya vodka's recipe was famously concocted by Dmitry Mendeleev, creator of the periodic table of elements, who used chemical principles to establish the standard for vodka throughout Imperial Russia. Moskovskaya was the first vodka to be patented, in 1894. The brand, which like all vodka was suspended during the early Soviet years, was resurrected in 1925 and was the premium 40 percent ABV vodka until the introduction of Stolichnaya some fifteen years later (a 1950 Soviet price list has regular vodka at 50 rubles/liter, Moskovskaya Osobaya at 56.60, and Stolichnaya at 61.60). See STOLICHNAYA. Moskovskaya remained a Moscow favorite and was a stalwart performer in the export market, regularly earning prestigious medals and prizes at international competitions.

See also VODKA.

Preiskurant no. 119. Moscow: Ministerstvo Torgovli Soyuza SSR, 1950.

Pokhlebkin, William. *A History of Vodka*. Translated by Refry Clarke. London: Verso, 1992.

Trommelen, Edwin. *Davai! Russians and Their Vodka*. Translated by David Stephenson. Montpelier, VT: Russian Information Services, 2012.

Soyuzplodoimport corporate website (Russian language). http://spimport.ru (accessed February 21, 2021).

Jennifer Eremeeva

ВОДКА МОСКОВСКАЯ ОСОБАЯ

Moscovskaya vodka, from a 1957 Soviet liquor catalog aimed at the domestic market. Wondrich Collection.

Mount Gay is a premier rum of Barbados and its most successful rum export. Founded on a plantation in the northern parish of Saint Lucy, where the earliest record of rum production dates to 1703, Mount Gay claims to be the world's oldest rum.

Barbados is the likely cradle of Caribbean rum making, and plantations on the island were producing rum from molasses and skimmings, the byproducts of sugar making, as early as the 1640s. Nearly every sugar plantation in Barbados in the seventeenth century had a rum distillery, and in all likelihood rum making at Mount Gay plantation began decades earlier than 1703. While it was not the first plantation to produce rum in Barbados, it can certainly claim to be the oldest estate to continuously produce rum. In the mid-seventeenth century, William Sandiford, an early colonist and planter, purchased and consolidated lands around what was known as Mount Gilboa. In 1801, the estate was renamed Mount Gay in honor of Sir John Gay Alleyne, a wealthy and talented planter and political figure in Barbados who oversaw improvements in rum and sugar making in Barbados during the mid to late eighteenth century.

Mount Gay uses its double-retort pot stills and column stills to produce a variety of (mostly blended) rums, including a filtered white rum called Silver, an Extra Old aged eight to fifteen years, a high-proof rum called Black, and a distinct blend of its oldest and finest reserves called 1703. However, Mount Gay Eclipse is the estate's staple brand. Named in 1910 for a total eclipse of the sun that occurred that year, Mount Gay Eclipse was refined under the careful watch of Aubrey Fitz-Osbert Ward, who expanded operations and shaped the popularity of Mount Gay rum throughout the twentieth century. Today, Mount Gay rum is a symbol of national pride and identity in Barbados and a big favorite with those involved in sailing the world over, thanks to the brand's strong support of the sport.

See also RUM and CARIBBEAN.

Smith, Frederick H. *Caribbean Rum: A Social and Economic History*. Gainesville: University Press of Florida, 2005.

Frederick H. Smith

moutwijn (Dutch for "malt wine") is a grain-based distillate of relatively low alcoholic strength that is blended with a flavored neutral spirit to make genever. See GENEVER.

muddler, also known as **toddy stick**, is in its traditional form a five- to ten-inch (125 to 250 mm) hardwood pestle with a rounded handle on one end and a flat-bottomed knob on the other, used in mixing drinks to crush sugar and fruit (modern muddlers can take any number of forms, from severely plain to head-scratchingly fanciful, and they are often made of synthetic materials). Although "toddy stick" is the earlier term, first appearing in print in 1823, "muddler" followed three years later and by the 1850s had eclipsed its predecessor. Whatever it is called, it is one of the earliest uniquely American bar tools, and one of the oldest in the modern mixologist's kit.

The muddler's importance in the nascent American art of mixing drinks is testified to by the facts that one couldn't make a Cock-Tail or a toddy without crushing the lumps in which sugar usually came or a Mint Julep without crushing the sugar or pressing the mint. See COCK-TAIL, JULEP, and TODDY. Indeed, in the early nineteenth century many muddlers had silver handles, while muddling ends made of ivory were also quite common.

Eventually, lump sugar was replaced by sugar syrup, or at least finely granulated sugar, and the muddler was relegated to use for the occasional Old-Fashioned and, by the end of the twentieth century, Caipirinha. See CAIPIRINHA and OLD-FASHIONED COCKTAIL.

Valerius Dukeheart (advertisement). *York (PA) Gazette*, August 1, 1826, 3.

Wondrich, David. *Imbibe!*, 2nd ed. New York: Perigee, 2015.

David Wondrich

Mulata, a Cuban cocktail, is nowadays basically an aged-rum chocolate Daiquiri, with crème de cacao supplying the extra flavor component. See DAIQUIRI. In the early 1940s, however, when the drink was introduced (apparently at the Floridita), that component was supplied by Elíxir Bacardi, the Bacardi company's proprietary 69-proof caramel- and raisin-flavored cordial. See FLORIDITA; BACARDI; and CACAO, CRÈME DE.

mulberry (*Morus* species) is any of various flowering plants that grow in temperate zones around the world. Mulberries may be red, white, or pink, depending upon the species, and have been used for millennia as flavoring for wines and for liqueurs such as the French crème de mûre (an essential component of Dick Bradsell's Bramble Cocktail). See BRADSELL, DICK; and LIQUEURS.

Doug Frost

mulled drinks are hot alcoholic beverages that use sweetener and mulling spices such as cinnamon, allspice, ginger, and black pepper. Mulled drinks are found throughout the world and are often considered medicinal or festive. They are served during fall and winter solstices and during popular winter holidays such as Christmas. Though they may use a range of alcoholic beverages as the base, from beer to fortified wines, mulled drinks generally use wine or cider as the base and incorporate further fortification through spirits such as brandy or aquavit. Often the type of alcoholic beverage and spirits used are culturally determined. For instance, in Brazil, Quentão de Vinho is a mulled drink using Brazilian cachaça as the base. In England, Wassail is made with cider. Some additional examples of mulled drinks include the German Glühwein, Scandinavian Glögg/Gløg, and French Vin Chaud.

Though mulling is thought to originate in the sixteenth century as a dessert beverage, with the term mulling indicating grinding (as in spices), similar mulled drinks date back to the first century, when a Roman gourmand Apicus wrote of "conditum paradoxum," a white wine with honey, saffron, mastica, and black pepper. Other mulled-style drinks date to early medieval times and use the names Hippocras Gyle, Pimen, or Piment. Hippocras is a reference to the straining method used to strain the spices, a large sieve called a *manicum Hippocratum*, or the "sleeve of Hippocrates."

Recipe (Mulled Wine): Tie 1 tsp. (5 ml) crushed star anise pods, 2 tsp. (10 ml) cloves, and 2 cinnamon sticks, broken, together in a cheesecloth, making a spice bag. Bring 1 750-ml bottle of red wine, 1 cup (250 ml) water, 1 orange deseeded and sliced, 1/2 cup (125 ml) turbinado sugar, and the spice bag to a boil; reduce heat and simmer for 20 minutes, stirring occasionally. Optional: remove from heat, add 1 cup (250 ml) dark rum or brandy, stir, and return to heat. Remove the spice bag. Serve warm in handled mug garnished with an orange slice and cinnamon stick. Serves eight.

See also GLÖGG.

Day, Ivan. "More on Hippocras" (1977). *Historic Food.* http://www.historicfood.com/Hippocras%20 Recipes.htm (accessed February 21, 2021).

"Medieval Mulled Wine." Medieval Histories, December 9, 2015. https://www.medieval.eu/medieval-mulled-wine/ (accessed February 21, 2021).

Derek Brown

multiple distillation is synonymous with rectification, the process that occurs in a continuous still during the production of spirits. See also RECTIFICATION and STILL, CONTINUOUS.

Munier, Etienne (1732–1820), was a French engineer and official of the royal administration who penned one of the earliest detailed descriptions of the cognac industry and its distilling techniques.

Originally from the east of France, he was assigned to the Angoumois, an administrative division to which the Cognac region belonged, after graduating from the prestigious Ponts et Chaussées civil engineering school. While his initial assignment was improving the transportation network, he was a follower of the physiocratic School, which held that wealth came exclusively from the land. Consequently, he extensively studied the agricultural practices of the Angoumois, with a view to describe current methods and propose their modernization. In 1770, he published his *Mémoire sur la manière de distiller les vins*, a description of the best practices of Angouleme distillers. His magnum opus, though, is a two-volume study on the Angoumois, published in 1779. In this detailed description of agriculture in the whole region, he wrote what cognac historian Nicholas Faith called "our basic source of information about cognac in the later 18th century." Ever the polymath (he wrote treaties on Jerusalem artichokes and wheelbarrows, and he invented a threshing machine), Munier recommended specific changes to the *charentais* still in order to solve a constant problem facing cognac distillers of the time: the alcohol-rich vapors exited the still through a pipe leading down from the side of the head, low and flat-topped in the Dutch style, allowing undesired elements to spill over toward the *serpentin* (condensing coil). Munier's solution was to raise the head; this led to the development of the swan's neck. He was a constant advocate for the development and improvement of the cognac industry until his death at the age of eighty-eight.

See also COGNAC and DISTILLATION, HISTORY.

Bujeaud, Victor et Jérôme. *La Charente révolutionnaire*, vol. 1. Angoulème: Quèlin Frères, 1866.

Faith, Nicholas. *Cognac: The Story of the World's Greatest Brandy*. Oxford: Infinite Ideas, 2013.

Societé Royal D'Agriculture. *De la fermentation des vins et la mellieure maniere de faire l'eau de vie*. Lyon: 1770.

François Monti

Murray, Jim (1957–), the English-born whisky writer, diverted a newspaper career into full-time whisky writing in the 1990s, publishing six books on the topic between 1994 and 1999. The timing was serendipitous—whisky's popularity was growing as food media increasingly embraced the kind of celebrity culture that had already given the wine world several influential tastemakers. Murray had noticed, however, that similar personalities were absent from the fledgling whisky scene, as he told an interviewer in 2014. Murray trademarked his name and began offering his opinions, both through books such as *Jim Murray's Whisky Bible*, a widely popular ratings guide published annually since 2003, and in private tastings. Although Murray is undoubtedly knowledgeable in both British Isles and American whiskies, his unpredictable choices, particularly the *Whisky Bible*'s yearly "world's best whisky" pick, regularly generate controversy among aficionados. This not only underscores the subjectivity of taste but leaves many critics to wonder just how much of Murray's advice is deliberately engineered to generate publicity for his personal brand. In 2020, Murray found himself entangled in additional controversy after fellow spirits writers publicly objected to the sexist language and antiquated attitudes frequently displayed in his reviews and, it is alleged, tastings. Murray dismissed the accusation as "cancel culture," but several spirits companies distanced themselves from him anyway. Nonetheless, his stamp on a whisky has been known to considerably raise a whisky's profile: indeed, in 2016, when he named the Crown Royal Northern Harvest Rye the world's best, it helped to spark a renewed interest in Canadian whisky in general.

See also SPIRITS WRITING.

Bellwood, Owen. "Industry Condemns 'Sexist' Language in Whisky Bible." *The Spirits Business*, September 21, 2020, https://www.thespiritsbusiness.com/2020/09/industry-condemns-sexist-language-in-whisky-bible/ (accessed March 26, 2021).

Murray, Jim. Interview with Pip Courtney from the Australian Broadcasting Corporation. August 3, 2014.

Risen, Clay. "Jim Murray, a Top Whiskey Critic, Faces Accusations of Sexism." *New York Times*, October 1, 2020. https://www.nytimes.com/2020/10/01/dining/drinks/jim-murray-whisky-sexism.html (accessed March 26, 2021).

Reid Mitenbuler

The **Museum of the American Cocktail** is both a physical entity in New Orleans and an organization devoted to raising awareness of and respect for the history of mixology and those who practice the trade.

MOTAC, as it is known, was founded in 2004 by Dale DeGroff and his wife, Jill, along with other luminaries in the cocktail industry, including Gary Regan, Robert Hess, and historian David Wondrich. The fledgling museum hosted a temporary exhibit in New York in 2005, and in 2006 presented the American Cocktail Awards (also known as "the Olives"), an annual ceremony honoring individuals and establishments in the bartending industry, which continues today. The actual museum opened in New Orleans in 2008, with exhibits spotlighting the cocktail in the context of America's political and cultural history, featuring bartending equipment and memorabilia from throughout the cocktail's two-hundred-plus-year history. MOTAC also hosts traveling exhibitions in cities around the country.

See also DeGroff, Dale; Hess, Robert; and Regan, Gary.

Emails sent to the author by MOTAC from 2005–present. Museum of the American Cocktail website. http://natfab. org/cocktail-museum/ (accessed February 21, 2021).

Tony Sachs

Myers's is a rum brand founded in 1879 by Fred L. Myers and well known historically for its Original Dark and Planter's Punch rums. Family-owned for two generations, the brand was sold in 1954 by Fred Myers's grandson, Eustace Myers, to Seagram's, who sold it to Diageo in 2000. See Seagram Company Ltd. and Diageo.

Myers's Original Dark rum is a molasses-based rum sourced primarily from Clarendon Distillery in Jamaica from a blend of pot and column distillates and aged up to four years in white oak barrels. It is made in the style of a traditional black rum, in which caramel, molasses, or both are added back into a rum after distillation, giving it a distinctively dark appearance—darker than could be achieved through aging alone. See molasses and caramel.

In the 1920s, Myers's formulated and bottled (at eight years old and 48.5 percent ABV) a Planter's Punch Rum, also in the black rum style, for use in the drink of that name, as served at Kingston's Myrtle Bank and Tichfield hotels and popularized internationally at the bar of the West Indies Pavilion at the 1924 British Empire Exhibition at Wembley, London. Though there are Planter's Punches on menus throughout the Caribbean that reflect the local juices, spices, and rums where they are served, Myers's helped spread the word that Jamaican rum was the rum that belonged in a Planter's Punch. See Planter's Punch.

Today Myers's continues to produce Original Dark rum, Myers's Legend (a pot still rum aged for ten years), and Myers's Platinum. It is worth noting that Myers's is one of the most frequently misspelled brands on menus and in print around the world.

See also rum.

Berry, Jeff. *Beachbum Berry's Potions of the Caribbean.* New York: Cocktail Kingdom, 2014.
Cate, Martin, with Rebecca Cate. *Smuggler's Cove: Exotic Cocktails, Rum, and the Cult of Tiki,* Berkeley, CA: Ten Speed, 2016.
"Visit to Court of West Indies, Empire Show." *Kingston Daily Gleaner,* June 18, 1924, 6.

Martin Cate

nalivka is the Russian term for aromatic liqueur made from fruits or berries. A traditional method calls for layering ripe fruit cleaned of all leaves and stems with sugar in a jar, which is then covered with cheesecloth and left to sit in a warm place for three to five days until fermentation begins. Vodka is poured over the fruit, and the jar is transferred to a cool, dark place to age for up to six months, depending on the type of fruit used. Before bottling, the liquid is strained, with care taken not to press down on the fruit and cloud the liqueur.

More often a quicker process is used, in which the ripe berries or fruit are placed in a jar, covered with high-quality vodka, and left to macerate in a sunny spot for as little as six weeks. When the vodka is sufficiently flavored, it is strained. Water and sugar are stirred in, and the mixture is heated just long enough to dissolve the sugar, taking care not to let it boil. The liqueur is then cooled and bottled. With an alcohol content of 11–14 percent, a well-made nalivka keeps for years.

Confusingly, the term nalivka is often used synonymously with *nastoika*, which refers to vodka that has been infused for a shorter time, usually with herbs or spices. Where Russians consider nastoika a tonic, nalivka is pure pleasure. Some favorite flavors carry their own names, such as *vishnevka* (cherry), *slivyanka* (plum), and *kalinovka* (guelder rose).

See also LIQUEURS and VODKA.

Molokhovets, Elena. *Classic Russian Cooking: Elena Molokhovets' A Gift to Young Housewives*. Translated by Joyce Toomre. Bloomington: Indiana University Press, 1991.

Darra Goldstein

Napoleon is a term used to categorize the age of cognac and later other French spirits since the middle of the nineteenth century, both capitalizing on the aura and the name of Napoleon (emperor of France from 1804 to 1815) and implying that the cognac thus labeled had been resting in a barrel since the emperor's time. Today, for French regulated spirits registered as AOC such as cognac and Armagnac, the term "Napoleon" can only be used on the label for distillates that have been aged a minimum of six years in wooden casks. For spirits not governed by a French AOC (appellation d'origine contrôlée) or a geographical indication (GI), the term "Napoleon" is used freely and without minimum age requirement.

Faith, Nicholas. *Cognac*. London: Mitchell Beazley, 2004.

Alexandre Gabriel

navy-strength commonly indicates a gin or rum of 57 percent ABV, although in fact the British Royal Navy actually issued its spirits at 54.5 percent ABV. (The misconception arises from the fact that 57 percent ABV is 50 percent alcohol by weight, the old British government-certified strength for proof spirit.) See GIN; PROOF; and RUM.

Negroni is Italy's most prominent contribution to the cocktail pantheon, a harmonious but far from bland mix of gin, red vermouth, and Campari, usually served on ice and—in Italy, anyway—with a splash of soda water.

The history of the Negroni is clear in its general outline, although there is a rather inconvenient gap

Count Negroni, ca. 1920. Courtesy of Luca Picchi.

in its timeline. It is clear that, sometime between the end of the First World War and October 1920, when the drink is named in a surviving letter, Count Camillo Negroni (1868–1933), a Florentine aristocrat who had spent time in America as a cowboy, a gambler, and a fencing instructor, took to having Fosco Scarselli (1898–1963), the bartender at the Café Casoni, where he regularly drank, stiffen up his Americanos with a splash of gin. See AMERICANO. Yet after that letter the Negroni does not resurface again until 1947, at least not under that name and not in Italy.

In Paris, however, the combination of gin, Italian vermouth, and Campari enjoyed such a vogue in the 1920s and early 1930s that the American humorist Nina Wilcox Putnam could joke in 1933 that "all Gaul was divided into three parts: one part gin, one part vermouth, and one part Italian bitters." See CAMPARI. The combination (usually served straight up and without the soda) traveled under several names, most prominently the "Camparinete," and turned up in New York as well. It is possible that Negroni's creation was the inspiration for these drinks, but it is equally possible that they were thought up independently, the combination being

an obvious one. In any case, rising tensions between France and Italy and then war meant that the Parisian taste for Campari did not survive the 1930s.

Meanwhile, the rise of fascism in Italy with its antipathy to all things foreign and un-martial saw to it that Italian cocktail culture kept a low profile and that the Negroni's circulation was limited to a small circle of Florentine bon vivants. In 1947, however, as Italy took its first steps in shaking off the devastation caused by the Second World War, the Negroni was adopted as a sort of signature drink of the new, *dopoguerra* ("postwar") Italy, and in particular of the cafés on the Via Veneto in Rome where the devotees of *la dolce vita* ("the sweet life") gathered. It was probably introduced there at Café Doney, a branch of the Florence institution of the same name that opened in 1946: the company that owned Doney had taken over Café Casoni in 1932 and would have known the drink well.

Whether in Italy, where its relative strength marked it as daringly American, or in the United States or Britain, where it was the drink's bitterness and gaudy red color that pushed boundaries, over the next few years the Negroni became something of a signifier of cosmopolitan taste. As Campari's American importer put it in a 1956 advertisement, it was the "world connoisseur's cocktail." Its jet-set connections helped the drink weather the disco years, which saw so many other classic cocktails fall by the wayside, and then, as the twentieth century rolled into the twenty-first, the Negroni truly came into its own. Bitter enough to be just a little bit challenging but still easy to drink and—just as importantly—easy to make, it became something of an initiation drink for new converts to the craft cocktail movement. In the process, it spawned too many variations to count: White Negronis, with things like blanc vermouth and (uncolored) French gentian bitters, Mezcal Negronis, barrel-aged Negronis, so on and so forth. Nonetheless, the count's original formula has survived with remarkably little alteration, a testament to its fundamental soundness.

Recipe: Combine in an ice-filled Old-Fashioned glass 30 ml gin, 30 ml red vermouth, and 30 ml Campari. Top with a splash of sparkling water, stir, and garnish with half an orange wheel.

Gandiglio, Amedeo, and Ettore Sottass Jr. *Cocktails Portfolio*. Turin: Orma, 1947.

Picchi, Luca. *Negroni Cocktail, an Italian legend.* Florence: Giunti, 2015.

Visentini, Gino. "Addio 'tintarella.'" *Corriere della sera,* July 8–9, 1948, 2.

Wondrich, David. "How the Negroni Conquered America." *Daily Beast,* June 10, 2019. https://www. thedailybeast.com/the-history-of-how-the-negroni-conquered-america (accessed March 26, 2021).

David Wondrich

Negus began life as an English officer's habit of taking water in wine, to avoid what inevitably ensues if you spend all evening pushing about an undiluted bottle. Francis Negus (ca. 1660–1732) was a socially well-connected gentleman who served under Marlborough, was a member of Parliament, and generally exemplified the perfect modern courtier through his various roles in regal sport, including master of the horse and warden of Windsor Forest.

The earliest mention of his drink comes in a chance bit of marginalia by one of his contemporaries, preserved in an edition of Tacitus and reprinted in the journal *Notes and Queries* in 1854. It was written between around 1725 and Negus's death: "After a morning's walk, half a pint of white wine, made hot and sweetened a little, is recond very good.—Col. Negus, a gentn. of tast, advises it, I have heard say." By the end of the century, this simple drink had taken some of the trappings of punch— lemon juice, spices—and had become above all a port drink. As such, it was one of the staples of mild household drinking on both sides of the Atlantic; just the thing if you're a bit chilled or not as sleepy as you might want to be, or merely need a little something to help you relax. Mrs. Beeton even went so far as to suggest that it should be served to children at their parties. Jerry Thomas recommended it for more mature audiences in his 1862 bar guide.

Beeton, S. O. [Isabella Mary]. *Mrs. Beeton's Dictionary of Every-day Cookery.* London: S. O. Beeton, 1865.

Thomas, Jerry. *How to Mix Drinks.* New York: Dick & Fitzgerald. 1862.

TSBR. "Negus." *Notes and Queries: A Medium of Inter-Communication for Literary Men, Artists, Antiquaries, Genealogists, etc.* 244 (1854): 10.

Dinah Sanders and David Wondrich

Neisson is a highly-regarded, award-winning brand of rum produced in Martinique belonging to the rhum agricole category, so made from fresh, raw sugar cane juice rather than the more commonly used molasses. See MOLASSES and SUGAR CANE. Neisson rums are also among the rums of Martinique that are designated as an appellation d'origine contrôlée (AOC) product, just like champagne and cognac. To earn this AOC designation, Neisson rums must adhere to government regulations surrounding the harvest and pressing of the sugar cane, the fermentation of the sugar-cane juice, and the distillation of the cane. AOC Martinique rhum agricole must be distilled using a single-column still.

Established in 1931, Neisson is the last existing Martinique distillery to have been founded by a person of African descent. The distillery and its brand continue to be independent and family-run, with the founder's daughter Claudine Neisson Vernant (1942–), formerly a medical doctor and AIDS researcher, and grandson Grégory Vernant in charge. Hand-cut sugar cane is pressed and the juice fermented for three days prior to being distilled in a single-column copper still to create various products, which include: Rhum Agricole Blanc (unaged rum available at 100- and 105-proof bottlings, as well as a 140-proof product called L'Esprit), Rhum Élevé Sous Bois (aged eighteen months in French Oak), Rhum Réserve Spéciale (aged up to ten years in new French oak and used bourbon and whisky barrels), and special releases of longer-aged products such as their 15 Year and 18 Year.

Neisson rum is often called for by the locals of Martinique by the nickname "Zépol Karé," which is Creole for "square shoulders," after the unique shape of the bottle, designed by the founders of the brand.

See also RHUM AGRICOLE.

Hamilton, Ed. "Neisson Rhum Blanc." http://ministryofrum.com/rumdetails. php?name+Neisson%20Rhum%20Blanc&r=1213 (accessed April 30, 2021).

Payot, Marianne. "Dr Claudine Neisson-Vernant." *L'Express,* October 30, 2003. https://www.lexpress. fr/informations/dr-claudine-neisson-vernant_ 653491.html (accessed March 4, 2021).

Martin Cate

neutral spirits, also known as rectified alcohol, are the purest ethyl alcohol that can be mass-distilled without the use of specialized laboratory equipment. In practice, this means neutral spirits are approximately 95 percent pure ethyl alcohol, with the rest being water and traces of other substances.

Neutral spirits can be produced from any fermentable sugar and are commonly produced from commodity grains, grapes, sugar beets, or molasses. Neutral spirit distilled from grain is typically referred to as "neutral grain spirit" or "grain neutral spirit"; spirit distilled from grapes is called "grape neutral spirit" or "vinous alcohol," and so forth.

Most gin, absinthe, and aquavit is constructed from neutral spirits, as are many shochus and liqueurs and nearly all vodkas. Other spirits, such as American blended whisky and jonge genever, are produced by blending a neutral spirit with a richer, more flavorful one. Neutral spirits are also used as solvents for producing flavor extracts.

Neutral spirits are the essential product of the continuous still. Prior to the commercialization of continuous-still designs in the mid-1800s, neutral spirits didn't really exist; instead, relative purity was approximated through repeat pot-still distillations and filtration. Consequently, the availability of neutral spirits beginning in the mid-nineteenth century marked a major transformation in the spirits business.

See also GIN; STILL, CONTINUOUS; and VODKA.

Bryce, J. H., and G. G. Stewart, eds. *Distilled Spirits: Tradition and Innovation.* Nottingham: Nottingham University Press, 2004.
Buglass, Alan J. *Handbook of Alcoholic Beverages.* Chichester, UK: Wiley, 2011.

Martin Doudoroff

New York Sour may be but one of several names that have been applied to a Whisky Sour with a float of red wine layered on top, but it is the most enduring one and the one in general use today. See WHISKY SOUR and FLOAT. The drink itself dates to the 1880s and is first attested to Chicago, when a bartender in one of the city's top bars shook up a "pleasant-looking, red-headed" Whisky Sour, explaining to the reporter watching him that the "claret [i.e., red wine] 'snap' . . . makes the drink

look well and . . . gives it a better taste." He did not mention a name for the drink, but elsewhere it was known as a "Southern" or "Continental" Sour. In Boston, however, it was called a "New York" Sour, a name attested there as early as 1885 and perpetuated by two works of Boston mixography, the *Cocktail Book* from 1900 and Leo Cotton's hugely influential 1934 *Old Mr. Boston Official Bar-Tenders' Guide.* The New York Sour is one of the drinks that has benefited from the cocktail renaissance, although many young bartenders diminish the visual impact of the crimson float upon the tawny drink by adding egg white and serving the drink over ice, both of which serve to blur the sharp line that otherwise separates the components. See COCKTAIL RENAISSANCE.

Recipe: Shake with ice 60 ml straight rye whisky, 15 ml lemon juice, 15 ml simple syrup, and (optional but recommended) 7 ml orange juice. Strain into chilled cocktail glass and carefully float 15 ml of dry red wine on top. Gently spin the glass along its axis to firm up the layering and serve.

"Local Miscellany: The Barkeeper." *Chicago Tribune,* November 25, 1883, 11.
"Set Em' Up Again, Please!" *Boston Herald,* December 13, 1885, 18.

David Wondrich

Nichol, Tom (1955–), the master distiller at Tanqueray gin from 2006 until his retirement in 2015, is an important figure in the twenty-first-century revival of gin—a passionate, even irascible advocate for the idea that large-scale distilling does not automatically mean compromised quality. Nichol was born in Tullibody, Scotland, not far from the Cambus Distillery where his father worked. Nichol joined Cambus in 1973, and by 1979 had become a distillery supervisor. When Cambus closed in 1993, he joined the Cameronbridge Distillery in Fife, Scotland (originally the Haig Distillery), producing liquid carbon dioxide and moving into grain whisky and neutral grain spirit distillation in 1996. See WHISKY, GRAIN; and NEUTRAL SPIRITS. In 2005 he joined the white spirits team making gin and vodka there and within a year became Tanqueray's master distiller. See MASTER DISTILLER. During his time, Nichol was credited with developing, recreating, or maintaining the consistent style of a range of gins under the Tanqueray brand name, at first the traditional London Dry and the citrusy No. Ten (created in 2000). While master distiller there, he developed the lime-focused Rangpur (introduced in 2007), oversaw a revival of the lighter Malacca based on an original Tanqueray recipe in 2013, and produced the sweetened Old Tom, also based on Tanqueray's original recipe, in 2014. His Bloomsbury, based on a ca. 1880 recipe that includes winter savory and credited to Charles Waugh Tanqueray, son of founder Charles Tanqueray, was released in limited quantity in 2015. Post-Tanqueray, Nichol became a consulting distiller, with two gins released in late 2015, both to considerable acclaim—Midwestern Dry Gin from the J. Rieger Distillery in Kansas City, Missouri, and Christopher Wren from England's City of London Distillery.

See also LONDON DRY GIN; OLD TOM GIN; TANQUERAY GORDON & CO.; AND GORDON'S.

Jack Robertiello

Nicol, Duncan (1852–1926), was the reserved Scottish-born bartender who ran the Bank Exchange saloon in San Francisco from 1887 until its closing in 1920 and made Pisco Punch famous in the process. Born in Glasgow, Nicol was apprenticed at sixteen as a merchant seaman aboard the three-masted barque *Dunfillan*. When the *Dunfillan* called at San Francisco in the summer of 1869, he promptly jumped ship, as so many had done there before him. See, for example, JOHNSON, HARRY; and THOMAS, JEREMIAH P. "JERRY". By 1871, he had secured employment as a porter—basically, a barback—at Alphonso Vaughan's Crystal Palace saloon, in the heart of the city's business district. He was working as a bartender by 1874, and by 1876 he was behind the bar at the famous Parker House on Portsmouth Square. In 1887, after briefly owning his own bar, he joined George Brown as a partner in the Bank Exchange, formerly the city's finest saloon but then fading. See BANK EXCHANGE.

Under Nicol's administration, the Bank Exchange flourished, especially after he made Pisco Punch a specialty there in the mid-1890s. See PISCO PUNCH. But Nicol's Bank Exchange wasn't just a place to get a trendy drink. Nicol was a taciturn man with little tolerance for nonsense, and he ran the bar as a quiet, gentlemanly place where women could drink as well as men, a rarity at the time. He had his rules: no more than three drinks to a customer (there appear to have been exceptions for the regulars who had established they could handle more), and any unruly behavior would be greeted with instant expulsion. Nicol was not hidebound: he renovated the bar in 1903, installing state-of-the-art electric lighting, and in 1922, at age seventy, he learned to drive ("Young fellows like me can't afford to get rusty" was his comment at the time). However, he was conservative. He insisted on working behind the bar until Prohibition forced it to close its doors, sent his customers off every night at ten o'clock, with an old-fashioned "doch-an-doris," or one for the road, and insisted on mixing the Pisco Punches himself.

In 1912, the journalist Pauline Jacobson captured him at work, "obviously clad in a handsomely frogged, spotless white linen coat, his eyeglasses hung behind one ear like a bookkeeper his pen, his white hair cropped close, his smooth-shaven face pink with health and intent upon his work, with hands trembling with the years, yet measuring with the nicety of an apothecary." Prohibition helped a good many people and hurt a good many. Among the latter were not only the Duncan Nicols, the men who had spent a lifetime mastering their craft, but also the customers and other bartenders who lost their example of how to make a rough business elegant.

Jacobson, Pauline. "A Fire-Defying Landmark," *San Francisco Bulletin*, May 4, 1912.

McDonnell, Duggan. *Drinking the Devil's Acre*. San Francisco: Chronicle, 2015.

UK National Archives. *Registry of Shipping and Seamen: Index of Apprentices*. December 1868.

Wondrich, David. *Imbibe!*, 2nd ed. New York: Perigee, 2015.

Paul Clarke and David Wondrich

Nikka, Japan's second-largest whisky producer, has a history that is intertwined with the life of its founder, Masataka Taketsuru (1894–1979), distiller at Japan's first dedicated whisky distillery, Yamazaki. Unhappy at being moved to run Kotobukiya's brewery in Yokohama, he decided to set up his own whisky firm. See SUNTORY and TAKETSURU, MASATAKA.

In July of 1934, he and his Scottish wife moved to the town of Yoichi on the island of Hokkaido and founded Dai Nippon Kaju company, meaning "the great Japanese juice company" (the name Nikka comes from the first two letters of Nippon and Kaju).

Initially producing apple juice and brandy, in 1936 the firm commenced making whisky, and the first blend, Rare Old Nikka Whisky, was launched in 1940. In 1952, the firm's name was changed to Nikka Whisky Co. In 1963, a grain distillery was built within shareholder Asahi's brewery in Nishinomiya.

In 1969 Nikka, still under Taketsuru's control, built its second distillery, Miyagikyo, which since 1999 has also made grain whisky using the Nishinomiya stills. A decade later, the firm's main grain plant was built in Tochigi, and ten years later it bought Scottish distiller Ben Nevis.

Nikka has been a subsidiary of Asahi since 2001. In that year its Yoichi ten-year old single-cask malt whisky won UK-based *Whisky Magazine*'s "Best of the Best" competition, beating all of its Scottish and American rivals. It is considered to be one of the catalysts that triggered international interest in Japanese whisky.

Broom, Dave. *The Way of Whisky: A Journey around Japanese Whisky*. London: Mitchell Beazley, 2017.

Dave Broom

nipa (*Nypa fruticans*) is, along with the coconut and raffia palms, one of the three main species of palm tree from which spirits are commonly distilled. See ARRACK, COCONUT; and OGOGORO. The nipa palm, which grows in mangrove swamps around the Indian Ocean and the South China Sea, is short and leafy, with its trunk growing underground and only the large leaves showing. As with coconut palms, the fruit stalks are cut, and the sap, which is about 14–17 percent sucrose, collected and fermented. The resulting palm wine is then distilled, usually in pot stills, although in the Philippines *lambanog*, as nipa spirit is generally known, is sometimes made in column stills. See LAMBANOG.

In the absence of a detailed history of distilling in Asia, it is difficult to say when nipa spirit was first made. In 1574, the Spanish colonial official Andres de Mirandaola listed it among the spirits characteristic of the Philippines, while in the 1580s, Jan van Linschoten recorded it being distilled in Burma and shipped around the Andaman Sea and Bay of Bengal in large earthenware "Martaban" jars (so called from the Burmese port of that name, now Mottama). In the Philippines, nipa wine was traditionally distilled in wooden Chinese-style *caua* internal-condensation stills, which may be taken as a clue to the origin of the industry. See STILL, POT.

Today the largest manufacture and market is in the Philippines, where both unbranded local versions and branded, even slick modern versions are popular. The former are frequently adulterated and are generally avoided by the cautious drinker. The latter range from the artisanal and delicately aromatic to the industrial and bland. That blandness makes the industrial versions good bases for making flavored spirits. These tend to the artificial: "bubble gum" is a popular variety.

Blair, Emma H., and James A. Robertson. *The Philippine Islands, 1493–1803*, vol. 3. Cleveland: Arthur H. Clark, 1903.

Gibbs, H. D., and W. C. Holmes. "The Alcohol Industry of the Philippine Islands, Part II." *Philippine Journal of Science*, February 1912, 19–46.

Van Linschoten, Jan. *The Voyage of Jan Huyghen van Linschoten to the East Indies*, vol. 1. London: Hakluyt Society, 1885.

David Wondrich

nitrogen, liquid (LN or LN_2), is liquified nitrogen gas, an extremely cold fluid. Despite the dangers inherent in handling a liquid with a boiling point of −196° C, liquid nitrogen has practical and impressive cocktail applications. Like other cryogenic liquids, LN is typically stored in a Dewar, a vacuum flask (named after its inventor, Scottish chemist and physicist James Dewar) vented to prevent explosions. Improper handling may lead to asphyxiation, grievous bodily harm, and death. Liquid nitrogen must never be consumed directly; as it gasifies, the super-cold liquid expands rapidly to almost seven hundred times its volume. Almost instantly, as little as a tablespoon (15 ml) may expand to over 10 liters of nitrogen gas in a drinker's stomach, a potentially lethal indulgence that has led to case reports of organ ruptures, frostbite, subcutaneous emphysema, and pneumoperitoneum (air or gas within the abdominal cavity). Curiously, despite the potential for severe, disfiguring frostbite from sustained contact with liquid nitrogen and from handling or ingesting items that have been frozen with the liquid gas, it may be poured fleetingly and quite safely over one's hand or other body part because of the Leidenfrost effect: super-cold nitrogen forms a protective layer of vapor over one's relatively hot flesh so that the liquid skitters and dances away much as droplets of water sizzle and scamper across a searing hot skillet. In the bar, a splash and swirl of liquid nitrogen rapidly chills glassware and covers the bowl of a coupe with an alluring mantle of delicate white frost. At the same time, vapor clouds billowing from glasses as they chill are a theatrical vision. Cooling glasses à la minute also frees valuable cooler space in a bar, since glassware does not need to be kept cold. Liquid nitrogen may also be used to create exquisite garnishes such as individual juice vesicles from citrus segments that are frozen, smashed, and thawed. Herbs "cryogenic-muddled" by freezing with LN and then muddling, retain their bright, vibrant colors in a cocktail without enzymatic browning associated with muddling alone.

See also HERBS; MOLECULAR MIXOLOGY; and MUDDLER.

Arnold, D. *Liquid Intelligence: The Art and Science of the Perfect Cocktail.* New York: W. W. Norton, 2014.
Arnold, D. "Drinking with Dave: The Bangkok Daiquiri." *Cooking Issues,* February 27, 2013. https://www. cookingissues.com/index.html%3Fp=5856.html (accessed March 26, 2021).
Zheng, Y., X. Yang, and X. Ni. "Barotrauma after Liquid Nitrogen Ingestion: A Case Report and Literature Review." *Postgraduate Medicine* 130, no. 6 (2018): 511–514.

Matthew Rowley

Noilly Prat is a maker of vermouth based in Marseillan in southern France. Its Original Dry Vermouth was among the first dry vermouths to be exported and is today considered the archetype for dry vermouth.

The company was founded in 1855, when Louis Noilly (1801–1865), a Lyon wine and spirit merchant, made his son-in-law, Claudius Prat (1812–1859), a partner and opened a factory in Marseille to produce absinthe, liqueurs, and vermouth. Louis had already begun exporting vermouth to the United States by 1851, using his father Joseph's

recipe; by 1862, it had reached as far as Australia. Both founders died within ten years of starting the business, but Anne-Rosine Prat (1825–1902), daughter of Louis and widow of Claudius, inherited the company in 1865 and ran it for more than forty years, turning it into an international success.

In the 1950s and 1960s, with the decline of the Dry Martini, the brand fell on hard times and was forced to consolidate all of its operations at its facility in Marseillan, on the Mediterranean coast two hours west of Marseille. In 1971 the Italy-based vermouth maker Martini & Rossi acquired the brand, and in 1992 liquor conglomerate Bacardi Limited bought Martini & Rossi, bringing the Noilly Prat brand under its umbrella.

Using a unique process credited to Louis Noilly's father, Joseph, Noilly Prat's vermouths begin with wines made from picpoul and clairette grapes that are aged in oak casks, some of which are stored outdoors and exposed to the elements until the wine within is well oxidized. These are mixed with various aromatics, depending on the type of vermouth, and a small quantity of muscat mistelle for sweetening. See MISTELLE. The brand makes four vermouths at present: Original Dry, based, it is claimed, on Joseph Noilly's 1813 recipe; Extra Dry, a variation on Original Dry created for the American market in 1955, lighter in color and using less-sweet wines; Rouge (created in 1956), a sweet vermouth (which, despite its name and dark color, is made from white wine); and Ambré (created in 1986), a vermouth whose flavor hovers between traditional sweet and dry vermouth.

See also MARTINI & ROSSI and VERMOUTH.

Almanach Bottin du commerce. Paris: 1856.
"Heritage." https://www.noillyprat.com/heritage/ (accessed June 8, 2021).
Mizaga, Ludovic. Email message to author, August 10, 2016.
Richard, Eliane. *Noilly Prat à Marseille.* Marseille: La Thune, 2005.
Talamon, B. Advertisement. *New Orleans Commercial Bulletin,* December 3, 1851, 1.

Jason Horn

Nolet Distillery was founded by Joannes Nolet (1638–1702) in 1691 in Schiedam, just west of Rotterdam in South Holland. In its eleventh generation steered by the same family, the distillery is now owned by Carolus Nolet (1941–), who developed Ketel One vodka. Released in 1983, the winter wheat vodka is named after the oldest coal-fired copper pot still at the distillery (Distilleerketel no. 1). Consistently one of the top-selling vodkas in the United States, Ketel One combines column-distilled wheat spirit with wheat spirit redistilled in ten copper pot stills, including the old ketel no. 1. Ketel One was not the firm's first foray into North America; from 1902 until Prohibition forced its closure in 1920, Nolet operated a distillery in Baltimore to produce spirits for the American market.

In addition to orange- and lemon-and-lime-flavored Ketel One variants, the firm produces two gins: Nolet's Silver Dry (47.6 percent ABV) flavored with Turkish rose, white peach, and fresh raspberry, and Nolet's Reserve (52.3 percent), a limited annual edition. It also distills two juniper-flavored genevers for the Dutch domestic market: clear Originele Ketel 1 Jonge Ambachtelijke Graanjenever (35 percent) and the straw-colored, oak-aged Ketel 1 Matuur (38.4 percent). Harlem Kruiden Liqueur, named after the Dutch city Haarlem, is a 40 percent ABV herbal cordial ("kruiden" is Dutch for "herbs"). It is the Nolet family's stronger, slightly sweeter, and less bitter answer to Jägermeister.

See also: GENEVER; HERBAL LIQUEUR; STILL, POT; and VODKA.

Elliott, Stuart. "Bond's Martini Will Be Shaken with a Different Vodka." *New York Times*, December 15, 2014.

Ketel One website. https://ketelone.com (accessed March 4, 2021).

Ketel1 website (Netherlands). https://ketel1.nl (accessed March 4, 2021).

Matthew Rowley

North Africa (Egypt, Libya, Tunisia, Algeria, and Morocco) has been a Muslim-majority region for over 1,300 years, which makes the historical record on spirits there sparse. Nevertheless, in pre-colonial North Africa there were all the perquisites for a liquor culture. First, Islamic scientists, in particular al-Razi (854–925 CE), experimented with distillation and advanced the technology associated with it. Second, wine literature, which explored the many resonances of intoxication, was a significant part of the Arabic cultural tradition. Third, since pre-Islamic times, the region was well known for the quality of its grains and grapes. The earliest evidence of a possible liquor culture is found in the Christian and Jewish communities. There, especially among the Jewish communities, we find the production of a fig brandy, variably called *mahia* or *bukha*. This, if anything, can be called the native liquor of North Africa and what North Africans would drink aside from *buza*, a slightly fermented farina-like substance; arak; or wine. Consumption changed after the arrival of colonial powers, who brought their drinks and drinking patterns with them. After the 1800s, there was a proliferation in the variety of spirits, placing the region in line with the rest of the world. However, spirits were and remain a third choice behind beer and wine in North Africa. Nevertheless, even with a growing Islamic trend, there are consumers thirsty for the hard stuff. One need only look at Libya, where alcohol has been banned since 1969 but where hundreds died and thousands more were hospitalized in 2013 due to a bad batch of *bukha*.

See DISTILLATION, HISTORY; MAHIA; and MIDDLE EAST.

"Alcohol Consumption High in Tunisia, Despite Prices." *Al-Monitor*, April 26, 2013. https://www.al-monitor.com/fa/culture/2013/04/alcohol-consumption-increases-tunisia-islamists.html (accessed March 26, 2021).

"Alcohol Poisoning Kills 51 in Libya." *BBC News*, March 11, 2013. http://www.bbc.com/news/world-africa-21747409 (accessed March 26, 2021).

Foda, Omar. "The Pyramid and the Crown: The Egyptian Beer Industry from 1897 to 1963." *International Journal of Middle East Studies* 46, no. 1 (2014): 139–158.

Matthee, Rudi. "Alcohol in the Islamic Middle East: Ambivalence and Ambiguity." *Past and Present* 222 (2014): 100–125.

Omar Foda

The **nose** of a spirit is linked to the human organ of that name only in roundabout fashion. In sensory evaluation, the term loosely describes a particular spirit's diverse volatile compounds as they are perceived through the nose; it is an important, perhaps *the* important, clue to that spirit's quality. While this sensory analysis has been supplemented in recent decades by gas chromatography and other techniques of chemical analysis, it has not been replaced by them: as Nykänen and Suomalainen write in their classic study of aromas in alcoholic beverages, "Certain aroma differences are still relatively easily identified by means of sensory tests, while only in very few cases are they explained by results obtained from chemical analysis."

Sensory evaluations of any spirit will include precise descriptions of its "nose," but not all tasters may be sensitive to all the volatile compounds that create olfactory sensations or have the sensory vocabulary to describe what they are smelling. Nonetheless, professional sensory analysis is expected to define the nose as closely as possible by noting both those odorants that are identifiable—for example, common descriptors such as lemon and black pepper in white (unaged) spirits and vanilla and caramel in barrel aged ones—and those that lie below the identification threshold of some tasters. For more casual tasters, a few descriptors will suffice to describe the nose of a spirit or cocktail. Many experienced tasters cultivate far more elaborate, even impressionistic, vocabularies to express a spirit's nose, particularly if their work is meant to be published.

See also AROMA and SENSORY EVALUATION.

Beauchamp, Gary K., and Linda Bartoshuk. *Tasting and Smelling*, 2nd ed. San Diego: Academic Press, 1997.

Buxton, Ian, and Paul S. Hughes. *The Science and Commerce of Whisky*. Cambridge: Royal Society of Chemistry, 2015.

Nykänen, Lalli, and Heikki Suomalainen. *Aroma of Beer, Wine and Distilled Beverages*, Berlin: Akademie Verlag, 1983.

Wolfe, Jeremy M., Keith R. Kluender, and Dennis M. Levi. *Sensation and Perception*, 3rd ed. Sunderland, MA: Sinauer Associates, 2012.

Doug Frost

nutmeg, the dried seed of the Indonesian *Myristica fragrans* tree, was at one time in Europe the king of spices. Once Europeans sailed into Asian waters it became more common, and the closer one was to its source, the more profligate was its use. Since punch, the ancestor of all modern mixed drinks, was born of the European colonial experience in Asia, it is only natural that it would be spiced with grated nutmeg, and indeed the spice is specified in most of the earliest recipes for that beverage. Nutmeg remained the dominant spice for a bowl of punch well into the nineteenth century. But it was also used in punches mixed by the glass, particularly if they contained rum or brandy (or a mixture of the two) or dairy products. In the Caribbean, where nutmeg trees had been induced to grow by the end of the eighteenth century, it is often found in rum drinks of whatever kind. Nutmeg can be unpleasantly hallucinogenic when taken in large quantity. It is found in various liqueurs and cordials, and has been since the late fifteenth century, but always in small amounts.

See also PUNCH.

Wondrich, David. *Punch*. New York: Perigee, 2010.

David Wondrich

nutmeg grater is a portable piece of silverware used to carry and grate nutmeg that was, along with a knife, a punch ladle, and a strainer, an essential part of the eighteenth-century bartender's toolkit. The earliest examples emerged in England around the mid-seventeenth century, when the possession of nutmeg, a costly new spice from Indonesia, was considered an exotic status symbol. Nutmeg graters peaked in popularity during the eighteenth century, by which time nutmeg was a fashionable flavoring for a variety of food and drinks, and in particular punch, the fashionable social drink of the day. See PUNCH.

While some nutmeg graters were designed to sit on the dining table, most took the form of a small silver box, which would have been carried in the pocket or in a traveling canteen that might also contain cutlery, tumblers, and corkscrews. These portable nutmeg graters typically comprised a chamber for holding between one and three nutmegs and a rasp to grate them with, but the design of the casings varied considerably. Circular, cylindrical, or oval-shaped boxes were common, but as the eighteenth century wore on, improvements in manufacturing techniques, the arrival of cheaper, thinner-gauge silver, and a boom in the market for personal silverware gave rise to more elaborate designs including hearts, shells, melons, and strawberries.

Some early designs were remarkably ornate: the Victoria and Albert Museum in London, for example, houses a nutmeg grater from the 1690s

A quartet of very elegant eighteenth-century silver nutmeg graters, from when such a thing was a common gentleman's pocket accessory. © Wellcome Collection.

fashioned from a cowrie shell encased in a lattice of engraved silverwork.

One famous owner of a nutmeg grater was the writer and punch enthusiast Charles Dickens, who "carried [his] grater on his midnight rambles through the foul-smelling back streets of Shadwell, Ratcliff Highway, and Limehouse to sweeten the air."

See also SPICES.

Hewett, Edward W. *Convivial Dickens: The Drinks of Dickens and His Times.* Athens, OH: Ohio University Press, 1983.

"Nutmeg Grater: ca. 1690 (Made)." Victoria and Albert Museum, LOAN:GILBERT.588-2008. http:// collections.vam.ac.uk/item/O156611/nutmeg-grater-unknown/ (accessed March 5, 2021).

"Nutmeg Grater: 1809–1810 (Hallmarked)." Victoria and Albert Museum, M.930-1927. http://collections. vam.ac.uk/item/O78651/nutmeg-grater-e-robinson-and/ (accessed March 5, 2021).

Wondrich, David. *Punch: The Delights (and Dangers) of the Flowing Bowl.* New York: Penguin, 2010.

Alice Lascelles

oak trees have provided the raw material for barrels in which to store and transport alcoholic beverages since Roman times and perhaps earlier. The beverage industry has adopted oak as its dominant choice for maturation vessels and frequently uses it for fermentation vessels as well. It is prized for its pliability, its strength, and its molecular-level permeability, as well as the (relatively) modest influence it has upon flavors and aromas.

Oak is a member of the Fagaceae family, the beeches, and has two genera, only one of which, the genus *Quercus*, is used in producing spirits; it includes more than 250 different species. For oak barrels, the relevant subgenus is *Euquercus*, for which there are six groups of species. Europe utilizes eight indigenous species of oak for alcohol beverage: the three most important are:

Quercus robur—a relatively open-grained oak, most famously found in France's Limousin forest. Important for aging cognac and (in the guise of the "black oak" harvested in the Monlezun forest in southwestern France) Armagnac. *Q. robur* is also dominant in the forests of the Baltic, which formerly supplied a high percentage of the barrel staves used in Great Britain.

Quercus petraea or *sessiflora*—a somewhat tighter-grained, less tannic oak, most famously found in France's Tronçais forest. Also important for cognac.

Quercus pyrenaica—also sometimes used for aging spirits; it was, however, the species that traditionally provided Portuguese producers with their oak barrels, prior to their late twentieth century adoption of French oak.

North America is reliant upon *Quercus alba*, or American white oak, for its barrels; it has a specific internal structure that allows its staves to be sawn and yet resist leaking. European oak staves are created by splitting along the grain; sawing will cause leaking.

European oaks are generally tight-grained due to slow growth in continental climate. US oaks from cool areas such as Ohio and Montana exhibit tight grain, while a wider grain is found in oaks from warmer areas such as Tennessee and Missouri. Lesser-utilized North American oaks include *Quercus macrocarpa* (in Minnesota and central Canada) and *Quercus garryana* (Oregon).

With oak often bent for shipbuilding in the ancient world, early northern European Celts crafted barrels and other oak containers; their cylindrical shapes offered easier and safer transportation than traditional clay amphorae. The Romans took notice and created oak barrels of their own. When cognac distillers began deliberately barrel aging their spirits, in the seventeenth century, they naturally turned to local oak, although other woods, such as chestnut, were sometimes also used. When it began aging whisky a century or so later, the United Kingdom, lacking France's extensive oak forests, imported its barrel staves first from Memel in the Baltic and then, increasingly, from New Orleans and Quebec, switching to American white oak in the process.

Oak's special characteristics are not merely physical; organoleptic elements leach into beverages in oak containers. Those flavors, aromas, and textures can be influenced by the oak's geographic source and treatment; toasting and charring of barrels will have a profound impact upon those beverages. Elements that may be present in toasted or charred oak include furanes (with characteristics of almonds, grilled nuts), lactones (vanilla, nuts, cocoa, coffee, and raw wood), phenols (smoke, pepper, flowers, clove, and caramel), and aldehyde phenols (vanilla and fruit).

Oak's particular structure holds the key to these traits: it is roughly comprised of cellulose (between 40 percent and 50 percent of the tissue) that is nonreactive with alcohol liquids; hemicellulose (usually between 20 percent and 25 percent) that can be hydrolyzed and interact with liquids; phenolic compounds such as lignins (often between 25 percent and 35 percent), enabling sap to penetrate wood and crucial to oak's sensory contribution to beverage; tannins (between 5 percent and 10 percent) and various micro-elements including sugars, lipids, sterols, phenylcetones, minerals, and lesser but volatile substances.

As oak is transformed from raw wood into barrels, the steaming, heating, firing, and/or charring that are part of the process will affect each of these compounds, with the exception of cellulose, which has little bearing on beverage character, flavor, and texture.

Because **hemicellulose** includes sugars, such as glucose, xylose, rhamnose, mannose, and galactose, as well as some polysaccharides, the application of heat can create Maillard-like reactions. Various chemical chains provide furanes, furfurals, aldehydes, and furfuraldehydes during the toasting, heating, and burning. As carbohydrates break down, available aromatics include almonds, butterscotch, caramel, or cherry.

As **phenols** slowly oxidize during a spirit's barrel maturation, there are numerous potential flavors and aromas that can arise including fruit, vanilla, cinnamon, almond, tonka bean, coffee, smoke, pepper, flowers, clove, sawdust, caramel, brown sugar, walnuts, molasses, candy, spice, eugenol, vanilla, leather, and others.

As **lignins** change in the presence of heat, the aromatics offered include vanilla, eugenol (clove), and 4-methylguaiacol (or vanilla/spicy/smoky aromas).

There are endless types of **tannins**, themselves a subset of polyphenols. But just as tannin acts as a preservative with leather (leather was originally tanned by curing animal skin with the juice of oak galls), it slows oxygen's degradation of fruit character in wine. In spirits, its bitter and astringent characteristics also provide a sense of weight, texture, and mouthfeel; the mouth, throat, and body have their own physiochemical receptors for bitterness.

Tannin also has the ability to bind with saliva's proteins. leading to astringency, dryness, and even increased friction in the mouth, all of which lend to a wine or a spirit's perceived weight.

These characteristics are influenced as well by the source wood and barrel processes:

- Species of oak—American oak generally has fewer tannins and more sweet, nutty coconut notes.
- Origin of the wood—research is ongoing, but climate will impact growth and the oak's constituent elements.
- The seasoning of the wood—some wood is kiln dried and some is air dried for months or even years.
- The grain of the wood and other physical characteristics.
- The toasting and/or burning that is part of the coopering process.

Finally, the wood supplies all these many sensory attributes, but oxygen ingress (mostly through the bung, but also through the grain of the oak) sees the polymerization of tannins and the further development of aldehydes. These will be strongly influenced by the location of the barrels, temperature, humidity, and proximity to influences like ocean air.

Buxton, Ian, and Paul S. Hughes. *The Science and Commerce of Whisky*. London: Royal Society of Chemistry, 2014.

Emen, Jake. "Why and How Oak Matters in Whisky." *Whisky Advocate*, Spring 2017.

Johnson, Hugh. *The World of Trees*. London: Mitchell Beazley, 2016.

Doug Frost

oak alternatives. With the oak barrel being the long-established vessel of choice for the aging of spirits, wine, and beer, the twenty-first-century global explosion in the production of these beverages has created recent barrel shortages. Spirits producers have looked for other choices as occasional scarcity and increasing price pressure have given impetus to finding alternate methods to traditional oak aging.

One of those, of course, is using woods that are not oak. Although recent years have seen North American micro-distillers experimenting with barrels made from hickory (*Carya ovata*) and sugar maple (*Acer saccharum*), this is not a new practice. Among the woods that have been used are those related to oak, such as chestnut (*Castanea sativa*), formerly used for barrels and by some distillers in Cognac and still occasionally used in Italy for grappa vats, and, in Chile, rauli wood (*Nothofagus alpina*), a species of southern beech, still used for the large vats in which some pisco is matured. See PISCO.

Other hardwoods have been used as well, both for barrels and for vats. Batavia arrack, a spirit that rivals cognac in antiquity, was traditionally shipped from Java to the Netherlands in 600-liter *leggers* made of teak (*Tectona grandis*), which proved to be strongly extractive over the many months the spirit spent in transit. To this day, teak is used for the large vats the spirit matures in. In Sri Lanka, palm arrack rests in vats of *halmilla* wood (*Bertya cordifolia*). See ARRACK, BATAVIA.

Nowhere, however, goes farther into non-oak woods for aging than Brazil, which uses a long list of woods of varying degrees of reactivity, from the highly reactive *amburana* (*Amburana cearensis*) to the fairly neutral *ipê roxo* (*Tabebuia heptaphylla*), for aging cachaça, chiefly in vats. Of all the alternative woods used for aging, some of the Brazilian ones move the farthest away from oak in their effect on spirits. See CACHAÇA.

For various reasons, however, including cost, supply and—in the case of hickory—excessive porousness, these woods are impractical for anything more than local use. Sticking with oak itself, however, there are numerous alternatives to the standard 200- or 250-liter barrel; included among them are oak chips, but also smaller-sized and miniature barrels, full inner staves (new staves placed inside barrels), new barrel heads, and oak powder, or pulverized oak. These are legal for most spirit production, the notable exception being bourbon whisky and other straight whiskies in the United States, which must be aged in new, charred-oak barrels. But most spirits producers follow the PR practices of the wine industry by not speaking about or even admitting to the use of oak alternatives. Here is a look at some of the most common of them.

Small Barrels

Small-format (50 liter, 100 liter) barrels do not offer a price savings to distillers, but the increase they offer in the spirits' contact with wood, relative to volume, often provides the more significant advantage of rapid infusion of barrel character, allowing new producers to speed products to market. To that end they are embraced by a significant percentage of new distilleries, particularly small ones. Yet something is lost in the haste. Extraction of wood components, regardless of barrel treatment or level of char, is dependent upon numerous factors: solvent alcohol levels and barrel surface to liquid volume are only two of them. Time and temperature are also critical components of the innumerous series of reactions that is barrel maturation. As industry consultant David Pickerell notes, to accomplish the same set of reactions, "you would have to raise the temperature so high that it's not technically feasible. The reaction would be the same but nobody has figured out how to speed up time. You wind up with a hole in your product." See MATURATION and OXIDATION.

Fruit Wood

Those missing pieces include esters that would otherwise be formed through continuous reactions between wood acids and wood sugars; many of the absent characteristics include fruits and flowers. Distillers often include fruit wood among their adjuncts in an effort to provide similar aromas and flavors.

Wine Barrels

The use of port, sherry, and Madeira barrels has a legacy in the whisky industry, even though the bourbon industry historically planted its flag with new charred oak. The Canadian, scotch, and Irish whisky industries have not labored under such constraints; placing an already-aged spirit for a few months in a used fortified wine barrel provides flavor that can be, and is, used to mask green wood elements that derive from oak alternatives that often require some amelioration.

Additions (such as Innerstaves, Stavettes, Oak Spheres, and Sticks in Barrels and Tanks)

Here too, the wine industry has had success, though as with all oak adjuncts, these processes have not been publicized or even widely discussed. Using barrel staves inside non-oak (usually stainless steel) containers is still infrequent in distilleries, but producers have long employed the insertion of staves into older barrels or, more traditionally, the replacement of portions of older barrels (such as barrel heads) with newer wood. Such activities can be summed up with the phrase "barrel maintenance," and no one thinks less of the producers for doing so. Some distillers find it expedient to "improve" existing barrels by shaving, toasting, or charring a barrel head (or sometimes the entire barrel) or simply inserting new, charred barrel heads. In each case, the wood additions are toasted to the same specifications of any standard barrel and serve to "refresh" any used and depleted barrels.

Oak Chips

These are popular tools within the wine industry. Most wines available in retail stores in the lowest price bracket are fermented with oak chips, if they exhibit oak characteristics at all. Both chips and powder can be easily added to a fermenting vessel, and many winemakers believe that few consumers are able to discern a difference from the sensory notes provided by oak barrels. Longevity seems to be a limiting factor, but wines at such price points are unlikely to be placed in someone's cellar for long aging.

With the explosion in brown spirits production, such adjuncts are more and more common, even if few in the industry are likely to include those tools in a public tour of the distillery, especially when barrels are so photogenic. In truth, many of the early efforts with these products have arguably been ham-fisted. But oak powder is increasingly used to boost familiar if disrupted notes that consumers assume derive from the accustomed 200-liter barrel.

Cognac production regulations of 1921 speak directly to the use of oak chips, demonstrating that they were at least occasionally utilized at that time, while inner staves date back to the mid-nineteenth century and "are quite mastered," according to one

distiller, reflecting the confidence that they are artfully and subtly deployed when perceived as necessary.

Boisé

A traditional and common component of many brandies is this infusion of old oak, and it is legally controlled and defined by French law for use in all French brandies. This extract can mimic a fairly complete barrel expression, including some of the esters that mark the positive benefits of time in barrel, at least to a degree. But the use of *boisé* and "petits eaux" (the barrel-aged water used to reduce the spirit to bottling proof) does not contravene the laws and has demonstrably contributed to the success of the wider French brandy industry. See BOISÉ.

Other Oak Infusions

Today, many micro-distillers are utilizing wood infusions created by pressure-cooking wood chips in spirit; this is being described by traditional producers, fairly, as heavy-handed, creating a new kind of boisé characterized by excess bitterness and imbalance.

The wine industry required years of experimentation before its current successes with such adjuncts as described here, so slow improvement is forgivable as long as it is measured and ongoing. As such alternates can reduce costs significantly, distillers will assuredly continue their efforts and experimentation.

Many critics find spirits utilizing these oak alternatives, particularly those aged in small barrels, as lacking in the same constellation of flavors, aromas, and textures that traditional aging offers. But the larger consumer market may not be so discerning.

See also ÉLEVAGE; MATURATION; and OAK.

Bortoletto, Aline M., and André R. Alcarde. "Congeners in Sugar Cane Spirits Aged in Casks of Different Woods." *Food Chemistry* 139 (2013): 695–701.
Buxton, Ian, and Paul S. Hughes. *The Science and Commerce of Whisky*. Cambridge: RSC, 2015.
Jackson, Ronald. *Wine Science, Principles and Applications*, 4th ed. San Diego: Academic Press Elsevier, 2014.
Jeffrey, David W., et al. *Understanding Wine Chemistry*. Chichester, UK: Wiley, 2016.

Wondrich, David. "The Rebirth of an Essential Cocktail Ingredient." *Daily Beast*, October 7, 2017. https://www.thedailybeast.com/the-rebirth-of-an-essential-cocktail-ingredient (accessed March 26, 2021).

Doug Frost

oak chips. Distillers and rectifiers have long used a variety of shortcuts to simulate oak barrel aging. One of the most common is to infuse the spirit with oak chips or even pulverized oak. This adds more contact with the wood and hence creates greater extraction of color and tannins. But of course, that is only part of what barrel aging does, and the technique has no effect on the oxidation or concentration that are also essential to the process. While oak chips and powders are legal for most spirit production, they are forbidden in bourbon and other American straight whiskies. (Similar to oak chips in effect are such stratagems as putting whole new staves inside the barrel, relining the barrel with new oak, or switching the barrel's heads for ones of new oak.)

See also BOISÉ and MATURATION

Doug Frost

oats are a relatively uncommon grain in the making of distilled spirits, although that was not always the case. They are expensive and, on their own, quite viscous and difficult to work with. However, in a mash with other grains, oats paradoxically can make the mash easier to manipulate, and several distilleries in Scotland and the United States incorporate a small amount of oats in their whisky mashes. This practice is not new: in the early nineteenth century, some scotch whiskies had oats in their mashes, and they were used to supplement the malted and raw barley that went into Irish pure pot-still whiskies until the 1950s, generally making up between 10 percent and 30 percent of the mash (along with smaller amounts of rye and sometimes wheat). See WHISKY, IRISH.

Today, oats are also increasingly popular as an "alt whisky" grain: Beam Suntory and Buffalo Trace have released limited-edition, "oated" bourbons (in which oats replace some or all of the rye as the "small" grain), and some distilleries in the United States, including Koval, Central Standard, and High West, have released whiskies made with pure or predominantly oat mash bills. See BUFFALO TRACE DISTILLERY.

See also MASH.

Bell, Darek. *Alt Whiskeys: Alternative Whiskey Recipes and Distilling Techniques for the Adventurous Craft Distiller.* Nashville: Corsair, 2012.
Interim report of the Royal Commission on Whiskey and Other Potable Spirits, vol. 1. London: HMSO, 1908.

Clay Risen

obstler, or *Obstbrand*, is the EU-defined term for regionally delimited German or Italian spirits distilled from a blend of fruits, limited to a defined group of pears and apple types, as well as cherries, plums (including Damson or Mirabelle), apricots, quince, raspberries, blackberries, peaches, rowanberries, elderberries, juniper berries, and red or black currants. If only one of these fruits provides the base of distillation, then the spirit will be labeled by the name of the base fruit (usually followed by the term -*brand*, "brandy," or -*wasser*, "water"), rather than as obstler. (The EU recognizes other similar fruit-based spirits such as *Schwarzwälder Himbeergeist*—German Black Forest raspberry spirit, a kind of *Obstgeist*, or neutral spirit flavored with fruit.)

These mixed-fruit spirits—the combination of apples and pears being the most common—have a long tradition of production in southern Germany, Austria, and the German-speaking parts of Switzerland and Italy; indeed, they are as traditional there as korn and other grain spirits are in the northern German lands. See KORN. Their production is traditionally small-scale and local, a part of farming, but there are a few larger brands, although few if any that are distributed outside their home territory. There are, however, kindred spirits from neighboring regions. See BARACK PALINKA; CALVADOS; QUETSCH; POIRE WILLIAMS; KIRSCHWASSER; and SLIVOVITZ.

Andreae, Illa. *Alle schnäpse dieser welt*. Zurich: Transitbooks AG, 1973.

Doug Frost

oghi is a spirit made in Armenia and in the Armenian regions of neighboring countries from garden fruits and berries. Most commonly distilled from fermented mulberries or grapes, it can also be made from pears, plums, figs, or apricots, among others. While it's often referred to as "vodka" or "moonshine" (*oghi* simply means "spirit"), Armenian brands such as Sapor and Artsakh market it as a fruit brandy or eau-de-vie, respectively. Though there are a number of small commercial producers throughout Armenia, oghi is traditionally made in the home and enjoyed with meals (in the most traditional homes, it is made in a Mongolian-style internal condensation pot still). See STILL, POT. It is also commonly employed to give guests a warm, spirited welcome, which isn't difficult, as it usually clocks in at or around 60 percent ABV. Oghi is also known as "aragh" or "arak," and indeed it is sometimes flavored with anise like the *arak* of Lebanon and the *raki* of Turkey.

See ARRACK and EAU-DE-VIE.

"Fruit-Distilled Moonshine." The Travel Channel. http://www.travelchannel.com/videos/fruit-distilled-moonshine-0229638 (accessed March 29, 2021).
"Palu—Agriculture (Trees)." Houshamadyan. org. https://www.houshamadyan.org/mapottomanempire/vilayetdiyarbekir/palu/economy/agriculture-trees.html (accessed March 29, 2021).

Anna Archibald

ogogoro, also called *ufofop*, *khaikhai*, and "local gin," among other things, is the national spirit of Nigeria, distilled from the sap of the raffia or oil palm (principally *Raphia vinifera*, but other species of *Raphia* are also used). Unlike in Asia, where palm spirits are of great antiquity, West Africa has no long-established history of distillation, and ogogoro is a fairly recent product. Its origins appear to lie in the early 1930s, when the deepening Great Depression, on top of paternalistic restrictions on cheap foreign spirits imposed by the British colonial power, led to a precipitous drop in spirits imports (Nigerian imports of gin, the preferred spirit around the Gulf of Guinea, fell from some 1.3 million liters in 1930 to 223,000 in 1934).

Popular history in Nigeria has it that the spirit was created—illegally, as the same 1919 treaty that limited cheap imports banned local distillation—by locals who had come back from the United States, where they had learned distillation from Prohibition-evading moonshiners. It must be noted, however, that (as Emmanuel Akyeampong pointed out in 1996) distillation already seems to have been known, if not widely practiced, among Ghanaian palm farmers in the nineteenth century, and if they knew it, Nigerian farmers probably did too. See AKPETESHIE. In any case, by 1932 the Niger Delta regions of southeastern Nigeria were a hotbed of moonshining. Ogogoro making spread widely during World War II and the years that followed, although it remained illegal even after Nigeria became independent in 1960. That finally changed in 1968, when the educator and activist Tai Solarin (1922–1994), a teetotaler, contrived to get himself arrested for possessing the spirit in order to dramatize the injustice of prohibiting a local spirit while allowing foreign ones.

As with many tropical spirits, a good deal of ogogoro production is local and unbranded. Sap is tapped from the raffia palm trunks, fermented in plastic drums for a week with environmental yeasts, and then run twice through clay or oil-drum pot stills (these last often take a unique form, with multiple vapor arms coming out of the same still top and running in parallel through the condensing tub). The resulting product, which generally runs around 50 percent ABV, is often adulterated with things such as methanol and can be lethal. Some of it, however, is further rectified and branded. While there have been attempts to export the spirit since the 1970s, only recently have artisanal versions begun to appear that might appeal to foreign consumers. These can also be viewed as a sign that the Nigerian urban elite is beginning to question its traditional preference for foreign spirits, much as the rise in artisanal cachaça in Brazil has shown in that country.

See also CACHAÇA and WEST AFRICA.

Akyeampong, Emmanuel. "What's in a Drink? Class Struggle, Popular Culture and the Politics of Akpeteshie . . . in Ghana." *Journal of African History* 37 (1996): 215–236.
Korieh, Chima T. "Alcohol and Empire: 'Illicit' Gin Production and Control in Colonial Eastern Nigeria." *African Economic History* 31 (2003): 111–134.
Omojola, Olotunde. "The Magic of Making Ogogoro from Palm Wine," Centenary Project, Google Arts and Culture. https://artsandculture.google.

com/exhibit/the-magic-of-making-ogogoro-from-palm-wine-pan-atlantic-university/4wKSE5EMQ7sTKw?hl=en (accessed March 29, 2021).

"Solarin Freed of Gin Charge." *Lagos Daily Times*, September 14, 1968, 3.

David Wondrich

okolehao is a Hawaiian spirit made from the native *ti* (or *ki*) plant, *Cordyline fruticosa*, and bottled at 40–65 percent ABV. Also known as "Hawaiian moonshine" or simply "oke," it was introduced to the islands in the 1790s by William Stevenson, an Australian fugitive. Traditionally, Hawaiians had roasted the large, tuberous ti stems underground for several days, as is done with agave piñas in Mexico (the plant, whose "roots" weigh some 15–20 kg, is a relative of the agave); this would convert their starches to sugars, from which they brewed a mild, beer-like intoxicant. Stevenson taught distillation, jury-rigging a still from two discarded whaling ship blubber-boiling pots, with a gun barrel to draw off the spirit. The repurposed twin cauldrons resembled human buttocks, hence the spirit's name: *okole* is Hawaiian for "buttocks" or "bottom" and *hao* for "iron."

The natives called oke a "gift from heaven," but Yankee missionaries denounced the ti as "the tree of sin" when they pushed for prohibition of all alcohol upon their 1819 arrival. Periodic government bans dogged oke production into the mid-twentieth century, with island bootleggers—who adulterated their ti mash with rice, taro, or any other cheap fermentable starch at hand—routinely jailed for operating oke stills.

The first attempt at making legal okolehao was in 1907, when entrepreneurs set up the Kona Okolehao Distillery on a ti plantation at Ke'ei, near Kona on the Island of Hawaii, using a batch (i.e., pot or three-chamber) still with a doubler and aging the resulting spirit in charred oak barrels in the American style. See STILL, THREE-CHAMBER. Although the spirit was well received, it struggled to find a market, and the distillery closed well before Prohibition set in. In 1935, after Repeal, two new brands were launched, the oak-aged Royal Hawaiian and Old Ti Root. The former, however, appears to have been made from "corn, cane sugar, malted barley, and malted rice," while the latter may have been redistilled from imported spirit. Both companies were bankrupt by the end of 1940.

The jet-age Hawaiian tourism boom reversed oke's fortunes as visitors created a demand for authentic local products. In the 1960s Hawaiian Distillers, a Honolulu-based company, bottled the spirit in tourist-friendly ceramic souvenir decanters in the shape of King Kamehameha I—ironically, the first government official to ban oke.

Hawaiian Distillers' ersatz okolehao—it was actually Kentucky bourbon infused with ti extract—disappeared in the late 1970s. Only since 2012 have local Hawaiian distilleries begun producing oke again, this time from actual ti root augmented with sugar cane.

Alexander, William De Witt. *A Brief History of the Hawaiian People*. New York: American Book Co., 1891.

Berry, Jeff. *Beachbum Berry's Sippin' Safari*. San Jose, CA: Club Tiki, 2007.

Hoover, Will. "Will New 'Okolehao be Your Cup of Ti?" *Honolulu Advertiser*, June 1, 2003.

Rowley, Matthew. "Okolehao, Historic and Modern." *Rowley's Whiskey Forge*, January 17, 2014. http://matthew-rowley.blogspot.com/2014/01/okolehao-historic-and-modern.html (accessed April 23, 2021).

"Royal Hawaiian Okolehao" (advertisement). *Honolulu Advertiser*, March 22, 1935, 9.

Jeff Berry

"A skirt and a lei with every bottle." Advertisement for Royal Hawaiian Okolehao, 1935. Wondrich Collection.

The **Old Absinthe House**, on Bourbon Street in New Orleans's French Quarter, was considered for most of the twentieth century the most famous bar in the United States. The bar, apparently New Orleans's oldest, has long been swaddled in a nimbus of lore and legend. It is said (on the basis of what nobody seems to know) that Jean Lafitte met here with Andrew Jackson to plot their defense of the city against the British during the War of 1812 (he didn't). Other notables said to have patronized the bar include Oscar Wilde, P. T. Barnum, Mark Twain, Walt Whitman, Franklin D. Roosevelt, and a slew of southern statesmen and Confederate generals. Many of them actually did.

The two-and-a-half-story building was constructed in 1806 as a grocery, with the ground floor converted into to a "coffee house"—New Orleanian for "bar"—in 1836 (the date the bar gave in 1878, although accounts differ). By 1842 it was being managed by members of the Aleix family, Catalonian immigrants like the building's owners. On their watch, while not one of the leading bars in the city, it nonetheless had a certain following among New Orleans's bohemian set. Even then, its specialty was absinthe, judging by the fact that in 1869 Leopold Aleix was advertising it as the "Absinthe House."

In 1870 or thereabouts, Aleix hired away the highly regarded bartender at the French Opera House, one Cayetano Ferrer (ca. 1827–1886), a kinsman who came to the city from his native Barcelona in 1844. He took over the bar three years later. Under his management and that of his heirs, the bar, now billed as the "Old Absinthe Room" or the "Old Absinthe House," was instrumental in the city's transformation from a gritty, working city into a tourist hub. Along with the Sazerac House and Henry Ramos's Imperial Cabinet, it became one of the three iconic New Orleans bars at which visitors were practically obliged to stop in. With its custom-made marble absinthe fountains and its drink specialties, the Absinthe Drip and the Absinthe Frappé, it more than any other bar emphasized the uniqueness of New Orleans's heavily French-influenced culture. (Some claim Cayetano Ferrer invented the latter drink there in 1872; in any case, the bar's location was known as "the corner of absinthe and anisette" after the Frappé's active ingredients.)

When absinthe imports were banned in the United States in 1912, the bar allegedly bought and stored seventeen thousand cases, keeping it supplied until Prohibition in 1920—and possibly beyond. After repeatedly running afoul of regulators during Prohibition, the bar was padlocked for a year. When it reopened in 1928, it was missing its old fixtures, which Pierre Cazebonne, who had bought the bar from the Ferrers in 1913, had dismantled and moved to a nearby soda fountain. (This opened as the Old Absinthe House Bar after Repeal with Cayetano's son Jacinto "Jos" Ferrer behind the bar, leading to some confusion.) Until 1943, the Absinthe House was run primarily as a dance hall, under various managers. The first and most prominent of them was Mary Lee "Mamie" Kelley (1890–1972), owner of the notorious Kelley's Ritz in Panama City, Panama, and immortalized by Cole Porter as "Panama Hattie." She lasted until 1931. It is doubtful that she followed the dry law ("Just say that I never took a rap," she told an interviewer in 1961).

In 1943, the bar became the keystone of another New Orleans family dynasty when it was bought by Owen Brennan (1910–1955), then a whisky salesman. He got rid of the dancing, brought in food and cabaret entertainment, and turned it once again into one of the most popular establishments in the city; the Brennan family sold it in 1963 when business had fallen off.

By 1970, the bar had been acquired by James Jr. and Anthony "Tony" Moran, sons of "Diamond Jim" Moran, a onetime associate of the Marcello organized crime family who later went into the restaurant business. As Bourbon Street slid into exploitation and even prostitution, the Old Absinthe House was sucked down with it. In 2002, by which time it was running as a more or less regular Bourbon Street bar, the Morans sold it to Kuwait-born Daiquiri-bar proprietor Yousef "Jober't" Salem al-Adwan (1965–), who also acquired the original bar and fixtures and reinstalled them in a back room of the building. See BOURBON STREET DRINKS.

Today, the Old Absinthe House remains a raffish, atmospheric destination despite the televisions and lite beer that dominate the barroom and its being under near constant siege by brides-to-be and bachelorettes wearing plastic tiaras. As hallowed ground, it remains worthy of a stop, especially if one can see the original green marble absinthe fountains in the rear bar. Despite its various alterations and reconstructions, it remains the oldest continually operating (more or less) bar in New Orleans and one of the very oldest in America. In late 2018, the old bar and its marble fountains underwent restoration, and plans are now afoot to recapture the establishment's former reputation.

See also ABSINTHE and ABSINTHE FRAPPÉ.

"The Absinthe House." *New Orleans Daily Democrat*, June 20, 1869, 1.

Burke, Michael. "Mob Allegations Based on Innuendo." *Pensacola News-Journal*. March 8, 1983, 2.

Jacobs, Howard. "Death Knell Sounded of Bourbon Bistro." *New Orleans Times-Picayune*, May 1, 1963, 13.

"The Old Absynthe Room." *New Orleans Daily Democrat*, November 16, 1878, 5.

"Seventy Five Years." *New Orleans Times-Democrat*, July 19, 1901, 3.

Williams, Elizabeth C., and Chris McMillian. *Lift Your Spirits: A Celebratory History of Cocktail Culture in New Orleans*. Baton Rouge: Louisiana State University Press, 2016.

Wayne Curtis and David Wondrich

Old Crow is a brand of whisky that was named for Dr. James C. Crow (1789–1856), who perfected the sour mash process for fermenting and distilling bourbon. See SOUR MASH. The first use of the name is unclear, but it is believed to have been applied in the 1830s to whisky made by Crow at the Old Oscar Pepper distillery on Glenn's Creek in Versailles, Kentucky, on the grounds of what is now the Woodford Reserve distillery. After its founder's death, the Old Crow brand continued to be made there. It remained a "small-tub," "old fire copper"-style whisky (that is, mashed in small lots and pot-distilled over a wood fire, both considered marks of quality) until Prohibition.

Old Crow was one of the first American whiskies to become established as a brand, with merchants advertising it by name as early as 1845. It remained a popular and well-regarded whisky even after several changes of ownership. After Prohibition ended in 1933, it went in the large National Distillers portfolio. Although not one of their four flagship whiskies, Old Crow was one of the bestselling bourbons on the market into the 1960s. See OLD OVERHOLT. National would make Old Crow until 1987, when the company's assets, including the Old Crow brand, were sold to James B. Beam Distilling.

Beam, of course, already had a flagship bourbon, so Old Crow has languished somewhat as a bargain-priced bourbon, despite the occasional attempt to revive its fortunes. Currently, it is a three-year-old, 80-proof bottling, made to the same mash bill as Jim Beam. It maintains a cult status in some circles, partly due to its lack of advertising, partly due to its price.

The brand has a number of connections to popular culture. It was a favorite of both the classic American humorist Mark Twain and gonzo journalist Hunter S. Thompson. Old Crow is also the brand most commonly named as General Ulysses S. Grant's favorite.

See also CROW, JAMES C.

Courtenay, W. F. "Old Crow Whiskey." *Vicksburg (MS) Daily Whig*, October 30, 1845, 2.

Cowdery, Charles K. *Bourbon, Straight: The Uncut and Unfiltered Story of American Whiskey*. Chicago: Made and Bottled in Kentucky, 2004.

Johnson, E. Polk. *A History of Kentucky and Kentuckians*, vol. 3. Chicago: Lewis, 1912.

Lew Bryson

The **Old-Fashioned Cocktail**, properly made, with sugar, bitters, ice, and (generally) American whisky, is an example of what the "original" cocktail would have been like: the first known definition of a cocktail (which dates back to 1806) described its ingredients as "spirits of any kind, sugar, water, and bitters." Freeze the water, and there's not a whisker of difference between them. See COCK-TAIL. For many years, cocktails remained only slightly more complicated than this mixture, a simple one indeed. They came with utilitarian names such as "Gin Cocktail," "Whisky Cocktail," "Brandy Cocktail," and sometimes, stretching the boundaries, "Fancy Gin Cocktail," which might differ only in the use of a "fancy" stemmed glass and the addition of a lemon twist.

In the 1850s and 1860s, the cocktail started to evolve as bartenders began experimenting with adding splashes of standard liqueurs to the formula—curaçao, maraschino, and the like. But it was only in the 1870s that this evolution yielded something that stepped outside the original definitions, when bartenders began lightening the drink by replacing half the base liquor with vermouth (then new to most Americans). While this yielded such classics as the Manhattan and the Martini, some drinkers preferred their cocktails made using the tried-and-true

OLD-FASHIONED WHISKEY COCKTAIL.
A photographic demonstration of how this popular drink should be served.

The fancy way to serve an Old-Fashioned, as photographed at the Hoffman House bar, 1905. The patron would pour his own whisky and pour it into the glass with the ice and pre-mixed bitters and sugar. Note the ice water on the side. Wondrich Collection.

formula and consequently would call for an "old-fashioned" cocktail. Based on the recipe books of the day, the most popular of these was the Old-Fashioned Whisky Cocktail, which was soon shortened to just "Old-Fashioned." Other versions were in circulation, however, the most popular of them being the Old-Fashioned Gin Cocktail, with genever or a domestic equivalent, and the Old-Fashioned Brandy Cocktail. This last was particularly popular in Wisconsin, and to this day if anyone orders an Old-Fashioned in the state, it will most likely be made with brandy instead of whisky.

While many accounts put the birthplace of the Old-Fashioned as the Pendennis Club in Louisville, Kentucky, people were ordering Old-Fashioneds in Chicago a year before the Pendennis Club was founded (in 1881) and a full three years before it even had a bar. The Pendennis Club may have popularized the drink, but that would be the most that it could or should claim.

During Prohibition and the World War II years, the Old-Fashioned ran into hard times. While the recipes for many standards, such as the Martini, the Manhattan, and the Daiquiri, managed to escape without much doctoring, the Old-Fashioned was not so fortunate. By the late 1940s, it was all too often turned into an overdiluted mess, topped with more water or club soda then there was spirit in the drink. Worse, it was often oversweetened and made further flaccid with the addition of a muddled orange wheel and the smashed remains of a processed maraschino cherry. (Some say this practice started during Prohibition to mask the taste of bad booze.) These changes to the recipe may account for the severe drop-off in the drink's popularity during the latter half of the twentieth century.

The resurgence of classic cocktails, which began in the late 1990s, would bring a new focus on restoring drink recipes back to their original glory. Thankfully, the classic Old-Fashioned recipe was found and dusted off. Now, a new generation of bartenders was making Old-Fashioneds that their great-grandfathers would have been able to recognize and thoroughly enjoy. But these, it turns out, also appealed mightily to the new bartenders' contemporaries: the new Old-Fashioned is one of the great success stories of the cocktail renaissance and is perennially cited as one of the most popular drinks served in cocktail bars.

See also MANHATTAN COCKTAIL; MARTINEZ; and MARTINI.

Recipe: In a heavy-bottomed glass, muddle 1 sugar cube (or 5 ml sugar), 5 ml water and 2–3 dashes Angostura or other bitters. Fill glass with ice, add 60 ml straight rye or bourbon whisky, stir well, and twist lemon peel (for rye) or orange peel (for bourbon) over the top.

Wondrich, David. *Imbibe!*, 2nd ed. New York: Perigee, 2015.

Robert Hess and David Wondrich

Old Forester bourbon dates back to 1870 and has the distinction of being the first American whisky to be sold exclusively in a bottle sealed by its manufacturer, thus making it an important milestone in the evolution of spirits brands. The spirit was dreamed up by George Garvin Brown (1846–1917), a Louisville pharmaceutical salesman, and his half-brother J. T. S. Brown Jr., a whisky merchant. The duo initially marketed it to doctors, who at the time prescribed alcohol for a range of maladies. Unfortunately, at the time the only way for a sick (or healthy) person to obtain whisky was to go to a bar or grocery store and buy a glass or a bottle that had been filled by the establishment or the wholesaler they bought their whisky from; neither distillers nor non-distillery producers bottled their whisky, selling it only by the barrel. Wholesalers and retailers often adulterated their whisky before bottling, stretching it out with ingredients that might have done more harm than good. The Browns' sealed bottle carried a guarantee of purity, and the brothers refused to sell it unless in that bottle.

When the brand was first introduced, its name was spelled with three r's, "Old Forrester." It was later changed to the modern spelling, Old Forester. There are several theories as to why this was done, but, according to the brand, the third r was dropped after Dr. Forrester, who had endorsed the bourbon when it launched, passed away. In any case, the change was made by 1911.

The Brown brothers' single whisky brand survived Prohibition with a medical license and grew into the large liquor company Brown-Forman, which continues to produce and sell Old Forester (the company's annual issue of their small-batch Old Forester Birthday Bourbon is hotly anticipated among bourbon collectors), in addition to a portfolio of bestsellers that includes Jack Daniel's and Herradura tequila. See JACK DANIEL'S and HERRADURA. In fact, Campbell Brown, George Garvin Brown's great-great-grandson, now runs the brand. Campbell Brown recently oversaw the rebuilding of Old Forester's original headquarters on Whiskey Row in Louisville, which now includes an actual working distillery and visitor center.

See also BROWN-FORMAN and WHISKY, BOURBON.

Rothbaum, Noah. *The Art of American Whiskey.* Berkeley, CA: Ten Speed, 2015.

Washburne, George R., and Stanley Bronner, eds. *Beverages de Luxe.* Louisville, KY: Wine & Spirit Bulletin, 1911.

Noah Rothbaum

Old Overholt is a brand of American rye whisky with a long legacy, but that legacy isn't particularly consistent: although it is the oldest continually maintained brand of American whisky, like many legacy rye and bourbon brands it has passed through the hands of several owners, who have produced it to differing standards at different facilities over the years. It is named after Abraham Overholt (1784–1870), a Pennsylvania weaver and farmer who, around 1810, began distilling spirits full-time at his family's West Overton, Pennsylvania, farm. By the Civil War, he had built a new, modern distillery at nearby Broad Ford, a short rail journey to the commercial hub of Pittsburgh. As was common for the time, the spirits were sold more as a bulk commodity

1917 advertisement for Old Overholt rye whisky. With Prohibition looming, American distillers were clutching at straws, the medical virtues of whisky among them. Wondrich Collection.

than as a brand. Nonetheless, Overholt's whisky was of sufficient quality to have been mentioned by name in advertisements since the 1840s (it appeared frequently in Baltimore newspapers then as "Overholt & Sons' Monongahela Rye Whiskey").

The brand name Old Overholt started appearing regularly during the 1870s, shortly after Abraham passed away, found slumped over in his privy. His obituary in the *Washington Reporter* claimed he had amassed wealth "almost equal in extent and value to the Kingdom of many a German Prince." His grandson Henry Clay Frick (1849–1919) used the fortune to begin his career in the steel industry. In 1881, when Frick was already a rich man, he bought the Overholt company, selling a third of it to his banker, Andrew W. Mellon (1855–1937), and a third to Charles W. Mauk (1864–1938), who ran the business. Mauk, an energetic young man, proved to be a more than able manager and with the help of master distiller Jacob "Daddy" Meyers built the brand into the nation's leading name in rye whisky.

After Frick's death the company went to Mellon, who was then secretary of the treasury and was forced to sell it—this was during Prohibition—to the conglomerate later known as National Distillers. National Distillers, who promoted the brand heavily after Repeal, produced the brand at the Overholt distillery until 1952, when in the face of declining public interest in rye it closed the facility. After that, production was shuttled between a few other Pennsylvania distilleries before settling at the Forks of Elkhorn Distillery near Frankfort, Kentucky. By that point, in the 1970s, it was the last nationally distributed brand of rye whisky left; once exclusively sold as a bonded whisky, it was reduced to 40 percent abv and sold at bottom-shelf prices. After Jim Beam Brands purchased the brand in 1987, that distillery was shuttered too and production was moved to Beam's large distillery at Clermont, Kentucky, where it is currently made using the same recipe as Jim Beam Rye.

In 2018, Beam-Suntory took a step toward restoring this historic whisky's fortunes by releasing a bonded version for the first time since the 1960s.

See also WHISKY, RYE; and JIM BEAM.

Advertisements. *Baltimore American and Commercial Daily Advertiser*, November 3, 1845; January 15, 1846; and October 23, 1846.

Cowdery, Charles K. *Bourbon Strange: Surprising Stories of American Whiskey.* Chicago: Made and Bottled in Kentucky, 2014.

Harvey, George, *Henry Clay Frick: The Man.* New York: Charles Scribner's Sons, 1928.

"J. H. White Promoted." *Connelsville (PA) Weekly Courier*, December 22, 1904.

"Neighborhood news." *Washington (PA) Reporter*, January 26, 1870, 5.

"Park & Tilford Buy Overholt Distillery." *New York Times*, May 26, 1925.

Washington Review and Examiner, September 11, 1872, 3.

Wondrich, David, "The Rise and Fall of America's Oldest Whiskey." *Daily Beast*, September 26, 2016. https://www.thedailybeast.com/the-rise-and-fall-of-americas-oldest-whiskey (accessed March 5, 2021).

Reid Mitenbuler

Old Tom gin is a style of sweetened English gin prevalent in the nineteenth century. Old Tom has been poorly understood, and the name has been applied by modern authorities to all sweetened English gin of the period. In fact, the term denoted only the strongest sweetened gin legally available.

Old Tom was neither a distiller's style nor (in general) a rectifier's one, as it has been presented, but rather a retailer's one. See RECTIFIER (OCCUPATION). Before the rise of distillery bottlings in the late nineteenth century, vintners and publicans bought their gin from the rectifiers unsweetened, at one of two fixed proofs: either 17 or 22 degrees under proof Sikes (47.4 percent or 44.6 percent ABV; these ultimately represented proof spirit—50 percent alcohol by weight—diluted with either one-sixth or one-fifth additional water). This was generally turned into "cordial gin" (a term dating back at least to 1757) by adding water and sugar to it. Each retailer customarily offered cordial gin at several prices, according to which proof it started at and how much it had been reduced. Old Tom began as the stronger base gin and had the least added sugar and water. For a cordial gin, therefore, it was (as it was often advertised) "the strongest allowed to be sold," with a strength of well over 40 percent ABV, where the average for all sweetened gins was around 37 percent, and some were sold as low as 22 percent. Sugar levels for Old Tom seem to have been around 35 grams per liter.

The label of a quarter-pint (120 ml) Tanqueray Old Tom Gin bottle, ca. 1910. Wondrich Collection.

Old Tom is often listed as an eighteenth-century style of gin. It first appears in print, however, only in 1810, when it is mentioned in passing in the sporting pages of a London newspaper as a superior grade of gin. It begins appearing in vintners' advertisements in 1812, although it did not achieve wide usage for another decade or so.

Among the origin stories for Old Tom are a pair of notices from *Notes and Queries* in 1860 and 1868, claiming that its name refers to Thomas Chamberlain, distillery manager for the London rectifier Hodges, who kept a special grade of gin for prize customers, and that it was popularized by one Thomas Norris, an ex-Hodges employee who sold that grade under the name "Old Tom" at his public house in Russell Street, Covent Garden. This story has not received the credence it deserves, as it checks out in almost every respect.

Benjamin Hodges (1749–1827), his son, and his grandson were gin rectifiers in London from 1780 until 1870, and Thomas Chamberlain was in fact a partner in the firm from the late 1790s until his death in around 1814. Their firm was described

in 1859 as the foremost "of its kind in England." The early and widespread association between Hodges and Old Tom is well documented, and indeed the company even went so far as to bottle and export its own version of the gin, something very rarely done until the 1880s. As for Norris, he did indeed sell Hodges's gin at his Antelope tavern (not in Russell Street but just steps away in White Hart Yard), although he did not assume ownership until the late 1810s. It is not known where he was before that.

Old Tom survived the transition to distillery bottling in the 1880s, by which time it had begun securing a reputation in the United States and was used in many new mixed drinks, including the Martini and the Gin Fizz. See MARTINI and GIN FIZZ. The next decade, however, saw a public move toward drier drinks, and its importance began to fade. By the late twentieth century, it was essentially unavailable as a commercial product. It was prominent, however, among the old spirits revived in the cocktail renaissance, with Hayman's Old Tom, from London, reaching market in 2007 and Ransom Old Tom, from Oregon, the next year. See COCKTAIL RENAISSANCE. As of this writing, there are at least a dozen gins on the market worldwide calling themselves "Old Tom," with varying degrees of justification, including an important and accurate one from Tanqueray. See TANQUERAY GORDON & CO. and GORDON'S.

See also GIN.

"The Factories of the South: Hodges Distillery." *Lambeth and Southwark Advertiser*, June 18, 1859, 3.
"Greenwich." *Kentish Chronicle*, April 27, 1810, 2.
"Old Tom." *Notes and Queries*, July 7, 1860, 9.
"Old Tom Gin." *Notes and Queries*, March 28, 1868, 298.

David Wondrich

oleo-saccharum, also known among modern mixologists as "oleo," is a mixture of sugar and the oil from citrus peels that is used primarily as a base for punch. See PUNCH. The term, apothecary's Latin for "sugar-oil," appears to be a Continental one from the seventeenth century. That the sweet, brightly citrusy oil adds body and depth of flavor to a punch or other citrus-based drink has been recognized at least since 1670, when Hannah Woolley included lemon "pill" in her punch-like recipe for "Limonado" (lemon peel is the most commonly used, followed by orange and grapefruit; lime peel is used infrequently due to its bitterness).

From the late eighteenth century on, oleo-saccharum was considered one of the indispensable pillars of proper punch making and was frequently cited as such. With the fading of punch as an everyday drink, oleo-saccharum was one of the master's touches that fell by the wayside. Twentieth-century punch recipes rarely called for it. With the cocktail renaissance, however, there eventually came a reevaluation of punch and a second look at oleo-saccharum. See COCKTAIL RENAISSANCE. Since 2010, it has gradually crept back into the mixologist's trick bag.

There are several ways to extract the citrus oil, including some that do not require sugar: soaking the peels in spirits or boiling water will also work. But extracting the oil with sugar is both simple and effective, and it is the preferred method among experienced punch makers. Originally, when sugar came in dense, conical loaves, it was possible to extract the oil by rubbing the fruit vigorously on the surface of the loaf, thus scraping off all the oil-bearing outer skin. In 1869, however, the British drinks authority writing as "William J. Terrington" suggested that the fruit could also be peeled very thinly, eschewing the white pith, and the peels muddled with sugar. See TERRINGTON, WILLIAM. This is effective, but not as effective as the modern method, pioneered by Jeffery Morgenthaler of Portland, Oregon. This involves simply sealing up the sugar and the peels, preferably cut in long spirals, in a vacuum bag or canning jar or other such container and leaving them alone for 12 hours or so (use 50 ml sugar per lemon peel or 75 ml per orange peel). Sugar being hygroscopic, it pulls the liquid oils out of the peels. If they are fresh, one ends up with a mass of moist, citrus-scented sugar and a layer of viscous, sweet citrus oil floating on top. These may be then combined with citrus juice (usually as much juice as sugar), and the resulting shrub will keep refrigerated for up to ten days. See SHRUBS.

Brookes, Richard. *General Dispensatory.* London: 1773.
Morgenthaler, Jeffrey. "Vacuum Seal Oleo Saccharum." *Jeffrey Morgenthaler* (blog), March 13, 2012. https://www.jeffreymorgenthaler.com/vacuum-seal-oleo-saccharum/ (accessed March 5, 2021).
Terrington, William J. *Cooling Cups and Dainty Drinks.* London: Routledge, 1869.
Woolley, Hannah. *The Queen-Like Closet.* London: 1670.
Wondrich, David. *Punch.* New York: Perigee, 2010.

David Wondrich

The **olive**, as a cocktail garnish, looms large in the popular imagination, even though the vast majority of bar olives are only used in one drink: the Martini. Though the lemon twist is often favored as the proper Martini garnish, a silhouetted Martini glass containing a toothpick-skewered olive may be the most recognized cocktail image in the world.

American bartenders began adding olives to their drinks in the mid-1890s as cutting-edge taste turned away from sweet drinks to dry ones. Labeling it a "recent fad," one Brooklyn, New York, newspaper reassured its readers in 1896 that the practice of substituting an olive for the customary maraschino cherry "sounds rather less inviting that a test will prove" and that "the effect as one tastes the olive after draining the cocktail is pleasing." By 1898, "cocktail olives" were being widely advertised. By then, a general principle had been formulated for their use: "The cherry should go with the sweet drink and the olive with the dry," as one cocktail booklet put it that year. There were nonetheless those mixologists who called for the olive in sweet drinks such as the Rob Roy; their advice was and is rarely followed. See ROB ROY.

By the turn of the twentieth century, the olive as a garnish had made it to Europe and "American" bars worldwide. The height of its popularity was the first decade of the twentieth century (see, for example, *Fox's Bartender's Guide*, from 1902, which calls for it in eight of its twenty-seven cocktails, including such relatively sweet ones as the Bijou. See BIJOU COCKTAIL). By the 1930s, however, the fad had faded, and the olive garnish belonged almost solely to the Martini.

Cocktail olives are typically green, usually Spanish, and sometimes stuffed with pimiento (the pepper-stuffed olive was introduced in 1897 as the "Pim-Ola" or "pimola"). The brine in an olive jar began to assume a supplemental role in bartending with the advent of the Dirty Martini, a vodka-based drink that became popular in the 1990s, wherein the spirit is supplemented with the brine from the olive jar.

See also GARNISH and MARTINI.

Cocktails: How to Make Them. Providence, RI: Livermore & Knight, 1898.

Fox, Richard K. *Fox's Bartender's Guide*. New York: Richard K. Fox, 1902.

"A Recent Fad." *Brooklyn Life*, April 11, 1896, 21.

Robert Simonson

Olson, Steven "Steve" (1959–), is an educator, lecturer, and writer on wine, beer, and spirits and an early proponent of craft cocktails in the restaurant world. Through his long consulting relationships with Vinos de Jerez and with Ron Cooper and the Del Maguey brand, he was also instrumental in bringing sherry back into the cocktail bar and mezcal to the rest of the world. See COOPER, RON; DEL MAGUEY MEZCAL; and SHERRY. Olson founded his consulting company, aka wine geek, in 1992, built upon his decades-long involvement in the restaurant and beverage industries. Focused on beverage education for trade, consumers, and members of the media, aka wine geek was Olson's primary enterprise until its disbandment in 2017. In those twenty-five years a great many of the pioneers in the craft cocktail movement could be seen sporting the black aka wine geek shirt at one event or another.

Olson's experience in the service industry dates back to his midwestern childhood, when he was a soda jerk at his parents' small-town Iowa store. During his teens, he spent a significant amount of time at a neighboring restaurant, left in charge by its owners, who were indisposed due to a family illness. He opened the kitchen in the morning before school and ran the bar at night, completing his schoolwork in between. After high school, Olsen has said that it was a "no-brainer" for him to further his industry experience during college and beyond—first as a waiter, then sommelier, then general manager. Olson eventually consulted on dozens of restaurants, including the ones at the luxurious Connecticut resort Mayflower Inn, New York City's Gramercy Tavern, and the legendary Broadmoor in Colorado Springs. At the same time, Olson spent several years involved with industry-focused television productions,

notably for the Food Network. In 1996, he teamed up with Master of Wine and Master Sommelier Doug Frost to present the Sterling School of Hospitality, a groundbreaking seminar series aimed at teaching bartenders and managers how to evaluate spirits through blind tasting.

Olson is a founding member of the New York–based Beverage Alcohol Resource (BAR), whose mission is to spread "the healthy and responsible use of beverage alcohol products through innovative and comprehensive training programs and seminars." See BEVERAGE ALCOHOL RESOURCE (BAR). In 2017, Olson joined Del Maguey, the company for which he had consulted for so many years, cementing his dedication to traditional Mexican agave spirits and their preservation and propagation.

aka wine geek Facebook page. https://www.facebook.com/pg/akawinegeek/about/ (accessed March 5, 2021).

BAR. "Who We Are." https://beveragealcoholresource.com/who-we-are/ (accessed March 5, 2021).

Sutcliffe, Theodora. "Steve Olson Reflects on 1995 and the Magic of Mezcal for Cherry Heering's 200 Years." *Drinks World*, May 16, 2018. http://drinks.world/steve-olson-reflects-1995-magic-mezcal-cherry-heerings-200-years/ (accessed March 5, 2021).

Lauren Viera

The **onion**, known in its pickled form as a "pearl onion," is, like the olive, a cocktail garnish strongly associated with a single cocktail, in this case the Gibson (though they are occasionally found skewered atop a Bloody Mary). Early recipes for the Gibson, dating back to the turn of the last century, show it as a garnishless drink, simply dry gin and dry vermouth (a Dry Martini was those plus orange bitters and, as garnish, either a lemon twist, an olive, or occasionally a cherry). It is unclear how or precisely when the Gibson acquired the onion, but that acquisition was in place by 1922, when it is mentioned in Belgian bartender Robert Vermeire's *Cocktails—How to Mix Them*. (Ten years before Vermeire, it must be noted, an onion-garnished Martini was popular in Seattle, Washington, as the "Judge Hanford Martini," named after a local sport who liked his drink made thus.)

In any case, the onion provided a point of differentiation between the Gibson and the Dry Martini once the latter had been stripped of its orange bitters. The onion as garnish reached its high water mark in the 1930 *Savoy Cocktail Book*, which had four drinks that used it, only two of them being Dry Martini variants. After that, it stuck to the Gibson.

Until recently, tiny, flavorless, commercially produced onions were considered sufficient to the task. By the twenty-first century, however, some enterprising bartenders began to pickle their own. Todd Thrasher in Alexandria, Virginia, and Nick Mautone in New York City were pioneers on this front.

See also GARNISH and GIBSON.

Craddock, Harry. *Savoy Cocktail Book*. London: Constable, 1930.

"Hanford Cocktail Served with Onion." *San Francisco Call*, July 13, 1912, 11.

Morgenthaler, Jeffrey. *The Bar Book*. San Francisco: Chronicle, 2014.

Simonson, Robert. "In Praise of the Gibson, the Classic Cocktail That's Finally Getting Its Due." *Grub Street*, July 28, 2015. https://www.grubstreet.com/2015/07/in-praise-of-the-gibson.html (accessed March 5, 2021).

Robert Simonson

orange bitters are an alcoholic (usually) tincture of bitter orange peel and other supporting botanicals, including coriander, gentian, and chinchona. Originally a standard apothecary's formula, they were created as a potable, mildly bitter digestive. A Dutch specialty, from the eighteenth century through the mid-twentieth Dutch *oranjebitter* were exported throughout Europe and the Americas and to much of Asia as well. Orange bitters have of late been making a comeback as a cocktail ingredient, a use for which they first became popular in the 1880s, around the same time that vermouth started to make a splash in bars. Although they were most likely the bitters used in the original Manhattan, they achieved their apotheosis as an accent to the Dry Martini and its countless gin-and-vermouth cocktail kin at the dawn of the twentieth century. See MANHATTAN COCKTAIL and MARTINI. But the Manhattan soon switched to other, more biting bitters and as the preferred amount of vermouth in the Martini began to dwindle to a drip in the 1960s, the orange bitters component soon disappeared altogether.

By the time the twenty-first century rolled around, the only commercial brand of orange bitters still in existence was an obscure version made by Fee Brothers of Rochester, New York—though cocktail historian Ted Haigh had been doing his level best to rescue it from obscurity after laboriously tracking it down. Fellow cocktail archaeologist Gary Regan, inspired by Charles H. Baker Jr.'s 1939 recipe published in *The Gentleman's Companion*, started making his own orange bitters, and in 2005 he teamed up with Sazerac Co. to produce Regans' Orange Bitters no. 6. See BAKER, CHARLES HENRY, JR.; HAIGH, TED; REGAN, GARY; and SAZERAC CO.

Since then, several other companies have introduced their own brands of orange bitters, including the venerable Angostura, whose aromatic bitters have dominated that category for a century and a half. Enterprising bartenders have even taken to mixing different brands of orange bitters; the combination of Fee Brothers' and Regans' bitters has become common enough to earn it the sobriquet "Feegan's." See ANGOSTURA BITTERS.

See also COCKTAIL RENAISSANCE.

Parsons, Brad Thomas. *Bitters*. Berkeley: Ten Speed, 2011.

David Mahoney

orange flower water, also known as orange blossom water, originates in the Mediterranean region, where bitter orange trees (*Citrus aurantium*) are abundant. The flower petals of the orange tree are steam-distilled in a process similar to making gin using a Carter-head still: water vapor is passed through the flower petals in a tray suspended in the still head, capturing the aromatics and leaving the bitter compounds behind. As a water-based fragrance, it is commonly used in perfume, but it is equally as popular as an ingredient in food and drink. The aroma of the blossom water is earthy, slightly sweet, and floral, while lacking the sweet, citrus-scent characteristics of the oils found in the fruit. In North Africa, orange flower water has found use as a flavor added to coffee and has also been used to mask off-flavors in water stored in clay vessels.

Its use in cocktails is as an aromatic enhancement dashed or spritzed into a drink. The Ramos Gin Fizz is the cocktail most commonly associated with orange flower water. Though there are only a few cocktails that use orange flower water directly, many cocktails, such as the Mai Tai and the Japanese Cocktail, incorporate it through the use of orgeat, of which it is generally a component.

See also RAMOS GIN FIZZ; MAI TAI; JAPANESE COCKTAIL; and ORGEAT.

Darcy O'Neill

orchard syrup is made by reducing fruit juice—chiefly a mix of apple and pear—to a syrup over heat, sometimes with the addition of cane or beet sugar. Apparently derived from the traditional German *Obstsirup* or *Früchtsirup*, it was a favorite of the great nineteenth-century German American bartender Harry Johnson, who used it in punches, cobblers, and crustas. See PUNCH; COBBLER; and CRUSTA. It appears with some regularity in bartender's guides until the mid-twentieth century, almost always in Johnson's Orchard Punch or in a handful of other drinks lifted from one of his books.

See JOHNSON, HARRY.

Johnson, Harry. *New and Improved Bartender's Manual.* New York: Harry Johnson, 1882.
"Wedding Bells California Orchard Syrup" (advertisement). *Golden Gate Monthly*, July, 1902, p. 150.

David Wondrich

orgeat (pronounced or-zhat) is a sweet, usually nonalcoholic almond syrup flavored with orange flower water. Its taste is often compared to marzipan. It is strongly linked with the world of tiki drinks and is an essential ingredient in one of the world's great cocktails, the Mai Tai. The syrup's history goes back centuries and has roots in many different cultures. The name derives from *orge*, the French word for barley, and early recipes indeed called for barley malt. Its use in cocktails dates back at least to the mid-nineteenth century, beginning with Jerry Thomas's 1862 brandy-based Japanese Cocktail. Innocuous potions like orgeat lemonade were also popular temperance drinks during the 1800s. More recently, artificially flavored products from major producers (made using formulae often absent of actual almonds) came to dominate the market until the twenty-first century, when some bartenders and small-scale producers began making orgeat from scratch, utilizing almonds and other natural ingredients. Some, like Small Hand Foods of California, have substituted apricot pits for the traditional, but potentially toxic, bitter almonds.

See also JAPANESE COCKTAIL and MAI TAI.

Thomas, Jerry. *How to Mix Drinks.* New York: Dick & Fitzgerald, 1862.
Wilson, Jason. "Can Orgeat Become Essential?" *Washington Post*, March 12, 2013.

Robert Simonson

oro or gold liqueurs are liqueurs that contain small amounts of gold flakes floating in the liquid. The nontoxic gold does not affect the flavor of the spirit; it is merely a way to make it seem more luxurious. The oldest of these still in existence is Danziger Goldwasser, an herbal liqueur made in what is now Poland since 1598. The best-known today is Goldschlager, a cinnamon liqueur from Switzerland that was introduced in 1993.

A popular myth states that the gold flakes in these products make small cuts in the mouth and throat to speed up the absorption of alcohol into the drinker's bloodstream. This is untrue; gold flakes are too soft to cause such cuts.

See also LIQUEURS.

Goldwasser, the Original Danziger. *Niche Wine & Spirits.* http://www.ourniche.com/spirit/Goldwasser,-The-Original-Danziger/ (accessed November 9, 2015).
Warner, Fara. "Swiss Liqueur Shoots for Gold." *Brandweek*, March 7, 1994, 8.

Jason Horn

orujo, colloquially called *aguardiente de orujo*, is a term used in Spain to designate a grape pomace spirit. EU regulations have demarcated only one orujo, orujo de Galicia. Any of the legal grapes in Galicia may be used for its production, though the regulated grapes of Rias Baixas (primarily albariño, loureiro, and treixadura) are most often used. Top orujo spirits offer concentrated and pleasing aromas and flavors of their foundational grapes. Like many such pomace spirits, the character and quality vary from producer to producer, but at its best, this can be a marvelous spirit, comparable to the best amongst grappa producers.

See BRANDY and POMACE BRANDY.

Doug Frost

Otard, a brand of cognac brandy founded by Baron Jean-Baptiste Otard (1763–1824) and Jean Dupuy (1756–1831) in 1794, as Otard, Dupuy et Cie. Otard's father was a negociant, who sold his brandy to Augiers and Hennessy. The Dupuys were exporters, among the first to trade with the independent United States. In 1795, Otard purchased the Chateau de Cognac, in the Grand Champagne, and converted it into his warehouse. Within ten years, Otard Dupuy was the third largest cognac house, after Hennessy and Martell. See COGNAC.

In 1807, Otard Dupuy became the first cognac to be mentioned by name in an advertisement, and prior to 1870, their brandy was advertised more often than all the competition combined. The earliest notices came from the American South, where by the 1830s Otard had become practically synonymous with cognac, and would have been included in the more high-class juleps and Brandy Punches of that time. See JULEP and PUNCH. Otard was a topic in two novels by Herman Melville and another cowritten by Mark Twain, and it was mentioned in many other works and memoirs by minor authors. In *American and Other Drinks* (1878), London bartender Leo Engel called for it in his recipe for Crimean Cup. See ENGEL, LEO.

Otard's success ended with the phylloxera epidemic, and by 1871, they represented an increasingly distant third place in terms of total exports, with less than 5 percent of the market. The decline in sales continued until Otard was sold in 1930 to the de Ramefort family, who were able to revive the brand from obscurity, succeeding especially in the 1950s. Around the mid-1960s, Otard began to abandon its export business and focus on the European market, where they remain today as a respected brand, Baron Otard, and have some high-end offerings.

Cullen, L. M. *The Brandy Trade under the Ancien Régime.* Cambridge: Cambridge University Press, 2002.

Faith, Nicholas. *Cognac.* London: Mitchell Beazley, 2004.

Ministère de la Culture, Archives Nationales. Dossier LH/2025/19. http://www2.culture.gouv.fr/LH/LH174/PG/FRDAFAN83_OL2025019V003.htm (accessed March 29, 2021).

Robert, A., G. Cougny, and E. Bourloton. *Dictionnaire des parlementaires français.* Paris: Bourloton, 1891.

Doug Stailey

ouzo is Greece's national drink, an anise-flavored distillate geographically defined and protected under EU law since 2006. Its history goes back far further, although the origins are somewhat cloudy. According to the linguist Achilles Tzartzanos, writing in the 1950s, the name "ouzo" arose in his hometown of Tirnavos in the late 1800s, when a textile trader tasted a friend's anise-scented raki and proclaimed it "uso Massalía"—the designation used to denote the top-quality silkworm cocoons destined for Marseilles. See RAKI. Others, however, believe the word arose from the Turkish üzüm, meaning "grapes," and that it originated in the northern Aegean islands, as did the anise plant.

Originally, ouzo was based on grape-derived spirits; today, the law allows for any plant-based ethyl alcohol, and many producers opt for alcohol derived from grains or molasses, which are less expensive than grape-derived spirit. By law, at least 20 percent of the distillate must be distilled with its aromatic compounds; the best are generally considered those that take their flavor entirely from distillation rather than maceration, and these are labeled "100 percent distilled."

While anise (*Pimpinella anisum*) is widely considered the main flavoring, the law stipulates no minimum amount, and other plants containing anethole such as fennel and star anise may also contribute to the spirit's hallmark flavor. In addition, distillers can add a host of other aromatics, such as angelica, cardamom, coriander, cloves, cinnamon, mastic, mint, and nutmeg. Styles vary according to region as well: in Thrace in northeastern Greece, star anise plays a larger role that in Macedonia, where the local fennel is given precedence; on the island of Lesbos, the areas of Mytilene and Plomari use the anise grown on the coast in Lisvori. European Union law recognizes all four areas, plus Kalamata, with PGIs (protected geographical indications) for ouzo.

After distillation, the ouzo is left to rest for twenty to twenty-five days before adding water to bring the final alcohol content down to 37.5–46 percent. The Greeks traditionally water it down further to serve it, whereupon the liquid louches, or turns cloudy, as the water-phobic anethole forms tiny light-reflecting beads. See LOUCHE. As with whisky, the addition of water often makes it easier to appreciate the spirit's complex aromatics, and also makes it a friendlier companion to food, which always accompanies ouzo in Greece.

See also ANISE SPIRITS; GREECE; MARC; and RAKI.

Hellenic Republic General Chemical State Laboratory of Greece. https://gcsl.academia.edu/ (accessed April 30, 2021).

Piggott, John, ed. *Alcoholic Beverages: Sensory Evaluation and Consumer Research*, Cambridge: Woodhead, 2012.

Tara Q. Thomas

overproof typically refers to rum with a much higher than average alcohol content, or proof. Overproof rums are often used in small amounts in mixed drinks, or as a flammable float in flaming drinks. See FLAMING DRINKS; PROOF; and RUM.

oxidation is one of the three main processes that are responsible for the change in spirits as they are matured, along with extraction—where reactive compounds are leached out of the wood from which barrels are made—and evaporation, where volatile compounds burn off and less volatile flavor compounds are concentrated over time. See MATURATION. Technically, oxidation is narrowly defined as the loss of an electron from one molecule to another; it is inseparable from reduction, which is the gain of that electron; together, the process is known as a "redox" reaction. With spirits, as with food and drink, the redox reaction is the chemical basis for the transformations that occur when they are exposed to oxygen. These affect spirits just as they affect a piece of cheese or head of lettuce carelessly left out on the counter. Colors will darken, aromas will fade; flavors will change. In general, with foods and fermented beverages, these changes are negative. If managed carefully, however, oxidation can be used to remove harsh notes and create pleasant ones in distilled spirits.

Traditionally, distillers have managed this contact by storing their spirit in a watertight but slightly air-permeable container, whether it is the charred bourbon barrel, the ancient Armagnac barrel lying in a humid cellar, or the large, unglazed earthenware jars used to age pisco in Peru and baijiu in China. This process allows only the most volatile compounds to evaporate or to bond with the limited oxygen allowed into the container, forming new flavor compounds. Thus bright, fruity notes yield to ones characteristic of cooked or even dried fruit and nuts. In a wine, this would kill the freshness of the aroma; in a spirit, however, freshness can often translate into rawness. Hotter temperatures will hasten those changes; putting a beverage inside a barrel and sticking it in a hot Kentucky warehouse will really complicate things.

Understanding oxygen's influence is still a work in progress, and while far more is understood today than even a few decades ago, traditional distillers did much right by instinct. Wood compounds are transformed by toasting and burning; the presence of these compounds such as lignins, furanes, phenols, and lactones offer material that in the presence of oxygen can combine with volatile compounds from the distillate to create completely new compounds. Particularly complex are the aldehyde phenols, which can offer a wide variety of flavors and aromas. We know they form in the presence of oxygen inside the barrel, but we're still not sure precisely how it all is happening. It is safe to say, however, that through oxidation flavor compounds are created that are found neither in the wood nor in the spirit as it goes into the barrel, and oxidation can hence be seen as the process that turns the aged spirit into something greater than the sum of its parts.

Likewise, there is not total agreement on whether or not spirit can oxidize once it has been bottled, though traditional wisdom says it will not in a well-sealed bottle. It is generally agreed that open or partial containers will allow the escape of ethanol and particular aroma and flavor compounds through evaporation (once sufficient ethanol has evaporated, what is left in the bottle loses its antibacterial properties and becomes vulnerable to decay). But some spirits, particularly agave-based beverages, sometimes exhibit aromatic changes that cannot be sufficiently described by the loss of character through evaporation. More study will be required. Nonetheless, we are certain that oxygen participates in changes that offer hundreds or more aromas, flavors, and textures in spirits and alcohol beverages.

Buxton, Ian, and Paul S. Hughes. *The Science and Commerce of Whisky*. Cambridge: RSC, 2015.

Waterhouse, Andrew Leo, Gavin L. Sacks, and David W. Jeffrey. *Understanding Wine Chemistry*. Chichester, UK: Wiley, 2016

Doug Frost

pacharán (also spelled **patxaran**) is a sloe liqueur, originally from the north of Spain. This digestive, very popular throughout the country, is the result of the maceration of sloe berries (*Prunus spinosa*) in a sweetened, anise-flavored distillate. A close cousin to sloe gin, it is said to have been first made in the Navarra region, where its production is covered since 1988 by a protected geographical indication. See SLOE GIN. Its governing body claims the first pacharáns date from the fifteenth century. It was initially a homemade liqueur, and it's not until the 1950s that commercial brands appeared and popularized it outside regional confines. See HOME DISTILLING.

See also APERITIF AND DIGESTIVE.

Pacharán Navarro. http://www.pacharannavarro.org (accessed March 5, 2021).

François Monti

Pacult, F. Paul (1949–), is a spirits expert and reviewer who came to wield wide influence in the early years of the spirits and cocktail revivals through his newsletter *Spirit Journal*, his extensive consulting with spirits brands, and his role in the BAR trade educational outfit. Born in Chicago, Pacult attended the University of California at Berkeley in the late 1960s. After graduation he spent the next decade working for Sonoma County winemaker Rodney Strong, who encouraged his writing. He moved to New York City in 1982 and opened a wine school. While conducting wine classes, he was approached by the *New York Times* to write about spirits for the newspaper's Sunday magazine. A lengthy article on scotch whisky and its distilleries led to several other such articles, including a story about cognac. He also spent nearly a decade as a spirits columnist for *Wine Enthusiast*. In 1991, at the urging of the wine critic Robert M. Parker Jr., Pacult and his wife, Sue Woodley, launched *Spirit Journal*, a subscription newsletter in which Pacult offered reviews of a wide variety of spirits. The publication, which did not accept advertising from liquor brands, began with a few dozen subscribers; in 2016, it boasted more than thirty thousand readers.

Beginning in 1997, with *Kindred Spirits*, Pacult began publishing books on spirits, including *A Double Scotch*, a history of Chivas Regal and the Glenlivet, and *American Still Life*, a history of the bourbon-making Beam family. For a time in the late 1990s, Pacult and fellow spirits writer Gary Regan cohosted *The Happy Hour*, a New York radio show that gave early exposure to important bartenders and distillers like Dale DeGroff. In 2005, he joined forces with DeGroff, Doug Frost, Steve Olson, Andy Seymour, and David Wondrich to form BAR (Beverage Alcohol Resource), an organization that presents a yearly immersive, five-day course in spirits tasting and cocktail history and practice. BAR was soon after combined with BarSmarts, a joint program from BAR and the spirits firm Pernod Ricard that trains bartenders for basic competence in modern mixology and tests them in person, in cities across the United States. Pacult is also the force behind the Ultimate Spirits Challenge, a spirits competition;

teaches popular traveling seminars on rum, brandy, and other spirits; and as a consultant has helped to create numerous spirits brands and expressions.

See also BEVERAGE ALCOHOL RESOURCE (BAR) and BARSMARTS.

F. Paul Pacult. Interview December 14, 2016.

Robert Simonson

A **pagoda** is the distinctive slatted, curved-roof tower that decorates many whisky distilleries in Scotland. Originally, these were designed by the Scottish architect Charles Doig (1855–1918). Located above the kiln, they acted as an aid to draw hot air (and smoke) through the bed of barley held within. They were originally known as the "Doig's ventilator," and to be architecturally accurate they are cupolas, not pagodas. Designed in the proportions of the golden ratio, they were an adaptation of existing design used to help airflow in hay barns and replaced the rotating, cone-shaped "Cardinal's hats" used in oast houses.

Pagoda at the Leopold Bros. distillery, Denver, Colorado. Courtesy of Todd Leopold.

The first of Doig's ventilators was installed at the Dailuaine distillery in Speyside in 1889. Although very few distilleries still malt their own barley, most have retained the pagoda/cupola/ventilator as an architectural signifier.

See also KILNING; MALTING; and WHISKY, SCOTCH.

"Charles Chree Doig: Basic Biographical Details." *Dictionary of Scottish Architects*. http://www. scottisharchitects.org.uk/architect_full. php?id=200641 (accessed March 5, 2021).
Wilson, Neil. "Why Distilleries Have Cupolas—Not Pagodas." *Scotch Whisky*, June 2, 2016. https:// scotchwhisky.com/magazine/the-way-i-see-it/9504/ why-distilleries-have-cupolas-not-pagodas/ (accessed March 5, 2021).

Dave Broom

The **Painkiller** (sometimes **Pain Killer**) is a mixed drink, loosely in the tiki mode, made with Pusser's aged rum, orange and pineapple juices, and cream of coconut. It is served on crushed ice and garnished with freshly grated nutmeg. It was created at the Soggy Dollar Bar at the Sandcastle, a tiny, casual resort compound on the island of Jost Van Dyke in the British Virgin Islands.

The bar got its name because when it was built, there were no roads or docks leading to the beach. Therefore, it became commonplace for boats to anchor close to shore and for bar patrons to swim to land, where they would pay for their drinks with wet currency—for which there is a designated clothesline where the soggy dollars are hung up to dry behind the bar.

There is some debate as to when the drink was created and by whom. According to the Pusser's Rum Company (who owns the trademark for the Pusser's Painkiller cocktail), their version of the drink was created in the early 1980s at the Soggy Dollar by Daphne Henderson, and the trademarked recipe was a version that Pusser's owner, Charles Tobias, adapted from Henderson's. Henderson, however, bought the Sandcastle in 1980 from George and Marie Myrick, who built it in 1970 and ran it until then. The Myricks claim they came up with the Painkiller in 1971. It first turns up in print ten years later. In the absence of further evidence, the question of its parentage must remain open.

Recipe (Pusser's Painkiller): Dry shake 45 ml Pusser's dark rum, 45 ml pineapple juice, 22 ml cream of coconut, and 15 ml fresh orange juice. Pour into large snifter, fill with crushed ice, swizzle well, top up with more ice, and generously grate nutmeg over the top.

See also SWIZZLE and TIKI.

Berry, Jeff, and Annene Kaye. *Beachbum Berry's Grog Log.* San Jose, CA: SLG, 1998.

Brown, Doug. "Sailin' Along." *Baltimore Evening Sun,* February 12, 1981, GS 7.

Hamilton, Edward. *The Complete Guide to Rum.* Chicago: Triumph, 1997.

"Pusser's Painkiller." Pusser's Rum Ltd. http://pussersrum.com/the-painkiller/ (accessed March 5, 2021).

Sherwood, John. "Seclusion of Sandcastle." *Washington Times,* February 28, 1983, 50.

Richard Boccato

palm sap is the fluid part of any of several tropical or subtropical trees, shrubs, or vines. Fermented palm-sap beverages can come from any of a number of species of palm, including coconut palm, oil palm, wild date palm, nipa palm, raffia palm, and kithul palm. Harvesting of palm sap varies depending on the species of palm. Some plants must be cut down to harvest the sap; others can be harvested while the palm grows. Still other plants, such as the coconut, have sap in their flower-stems that can be harvested.

The most common palm for spirits making is *Cocos nucifera*, the coconut palm. The flowers, which grow from the crown in clusters on their own branches, are cut off, and the sap, which runs from the cut, is collected. A healthy tree can produce about a liter of sap a day.

The sap is allowed to ferment using wild yeasts found on the plant itself or in the surrounding air, resulting in a beverage known as palm wine. In most areas that produce palm wine, the drink is consumed quickly after fermentation, to avoid spoilage; it rarely lasts more than forty-eight hours.

In West Africa, palm wine is consumed regularly by over ten million people. In Cameroon, it goes by names such as *matango, fitchuk,* and *mbu.* In Burkina Faso, it's known as *bandji.* Ghanaians refer to it as *doka* and *nsafufuo,* whereas Nigerians call it *emu* and *ogogoro.* In Kenya, in East Africa, it's called *mnazi.*

Fermented palm wine provides a certain amount of nutrition: chemical analysis of the wine shows it contains thiamin, riboflavin, pyridoxine, and vitamin B12.

Fermentation alone produces a sweet, mildly effervescent beverage of up to 7 percent alcohol by volume; distilling this fermented product produces a spirit of up to 40 percent alcohol by volume. In Ghana, this distilled product goes by the name *akpeteshie*; in Benin, it is *sodabi* (named after the brothers Gbéhalaton and Bonou Kiti Sodabi, World War I veterans who first distilled the spirit on their return from France). Nigerian *ogogoro* can also be distilled. Throughout West Africa, when palm wine is distilled, it is generally done on a local level, and a great deal of the distillation is unregulated or unregistered. See MOONSHINE.

In Sri Lanka and southern India as well, the palm wine (or, as it's known, "toddy," from the Hindi *tari,* "palm sap") is then distilled into a liquor, known as arrack, coconut arrack, or, historically, Goa arrack, after the center of the South Indian industry. See ARRACK, COCONUT. Indian palm arracks are generally unaged, while some Sri Lankan ones are aged in wooden vats for periods ranging from two to fifteen years, yielding a spirit that is, while relatively light in body, smooth and pleasant.

In the Philippines, a similar beverage, lambanog, is common. Sap is taken from coconut flowers and fermented. The fermented liquid is then distilled and bottled without aging. Traditionally, the beverage was made and consumed at home, like moonshine, though now a few commercial brands are available. Some brands are treated much like soju, in that artificial fruit flavors are common, usually accompanied by garish colors, along with other trendy flavors such as bubble gum. See SOJU. There are, however, also artisanal producers who make an exceptionally clean and pleasant spirit.

See also AKPETESHIE; LAMBANOG; and OGOGORO.

Azam-Ali, Sue. *Technical Brief: Toddy and Palm Wine.* Rugby, UK: Practical Action, 2011. https://www.appropedia.org/Toddy_and_Palm_Wine_(Practical_Action_Technical_Brief) (accessed April 30, 2021).

Fourgeau, Catherine, and Johanna Maula. "Producteurs et productrices d'alcool de palme (Sodabi) dans le sud-est du Bénin." *Cahiers d'outre-mer,* April-June 1998, 201–214.

Mbuagbaw, L., and S. G. Noorduyn. "The Palm Wine Trade: Occupational and health hazards." *International Journal of Occupational and Environmental Medicine* 3 (2012): 157–164. http://www.theijoem.com/ijoem/index.php/ijoem/article/view/177/304 (accessed March 5, 2021).

Miller, Anistatia, and Brown, Jared. "Arrack? What the F*@! Is Arrack?" *Imbibe Magazine.* http://imbibe.com/news-articles/spirits-cocktails/features-arrack-what-f-is-arrack7810/ (accessed July 1, 2016).

Michael Dietsch

The **Paloma**, a refreshing mix of tequila, grapefruit soda, lime juice, and salt, is—as is often said about it—what they drink in Mexico instead of the Margarita. See MARGARITA. A version of the Changuirongo, the ur-mixture of a sweet soda such as Coca-Cola, ginger ale, or Fanta with tequila, the Paloma's roots go back to 1950, when a brochure for Squirt, a U.S.-based grapefruit-flavored soda, suggested mixing it with tequila. It is unknown who adapted the combination to Mexican tastes, but Squirt was launched there in 1955. By the early 1970s the combination was being aggressively advertised in the United States (e.g., "Tequila has appeala with Squirt"); in 1974, there was even a short-lived promotion for a "Cactus Banger," with tequila, Squirt, a Galliano knockoff, and a fat wedge of lime.

It would take another twenty years, however, for the tequila–grapefruit soda combination's popularity to become widespread. The process seems to have begun in Jalisco, where it picked up the lime juice and salt that make it such a peerless refresher and became a sort of signature drink of the many bars in the Parián, the mariachi-filled arcaded square in the Guadalajara suburb of San Pedro Tlaquepaque. Tlaquepaque being a major tourist attraction, it didn't take long for the drink to spread to Southern California, where it began appearing in the late 1990s under the name Paloma, Spanish for "dove." Meanwhile, in 1997, Herradura began selling a canned version in Mexico under the name New Mix.

The Paloma's popularity in Mexico ensured that it wasn't just tourists spreading it around; by the early 2000s it had followed the Mexican American diaspora to all corners of the United States, or at least most of them. With the rise of the craft cocktail movement, many bartenders took to replacing the grapefruit-flavored soda with a mixture of grapefruit juice, sugar, and sparkling water, but purists still prefer theirs the original way. (In Tlaquepaque, however, the drink has further evolved into the Cantarito, which is the same thing but served in an earthenware *cazuela*, or casserole dish.)

Recipe: Juice ½ lime into Collins glass, add shell, 60 ml tequila, and a pinch of salt. Add ice and 60 ml grapefruit soda. Stir.

Jacobson, Max. "O.C. on the Menu." *Los Angeles Times,* February 11, 1999, 60R.

Martínez Limón, Enrique, and Carlos Monsiváis. *Tequila: Tradición y destino.* Mexico City: Revimundo, 1999.

"Tequila Has Appeala with Squirt." *Los Angeles Times,* April 28, 1978, IV 10.

Zaslavsky, Nancy. *A Cook's Tour of Mexico.* New York: St. Martin's Griffin, 1997, 36.

David Wondrich

paojiu and yaojiu, respectively "infused alcohol" and "medicinal alcohol," are closely related and often overlapping subcategories of Chinese alcohol. Paojiu is created by steeping herbs, fruits, spices, or even insects and animals in a Chinese grain wine or liquor. Yaojiu, also called *yingyangjiu* (tonic), is often just a paojiu that has been made with one or more medicinal ingredients, but it can also be made by incorporating medicinal ingredients into the recipe of a *qu* (a fermentation agent) during the alcohol production process. See QU.

According to ancient medical journals, doctors determined that by dissolving a medicine into alcohol, the liquid might absorb its curative properties. As the noted sixteenth-century physician Li Shizhen writes in *Compendium of Medica Materia,* rice alcohol "develops the efficacy of the medicine, causes circulation in the network of vessels, stirs the blood, and sets in motion the air." Some of these medical properties might have scientific backing. The Chinese water snakes used for snake paojiu, for instance, are one of nature's richest sources of omega-3 fatty acids. Moreover the concoctions tasted better than either component part: alcohol diminished the medicine's bitterness, and the medicine smoothed out the alcohol's rougher edges.

Today infused spirits are sold in specialty shops throughout China, though many drinkers still prefer to make their own at home. Common paojiu ingredients include cinnamon, anise, ginseng, goji berries, snakes, and bits of deer antler or member. Recent decades have also seen the emergence of mass-produced paojiu and yaojiu. Jing jiu, infused with cinnamon and various botanicals, is an inexpensive and popular health baijiu. Several varieties of mei kwei lu, a supposedly tension-relieving spirit infused with rose extract, and wu chia bi, a multipurpose ginseng mixture, are popular tonics. Many of China's major distillers produce yaojius, like Xinghuacun Fenjiu's bamboo-leaf-infused Chu Yeh Ching Chiew and Wuliangye's caterpillar-fungus-infused Longhu Jiu. Even Changyu, China's premier grape wine and brandy producer, produces a three-penis wine (seal, deer, and dog).

See HEALTH AND SPIRITS.

Cassel, Susie Lan. *The Chinese in America*. Walnut Creek, CA: AltaMira, 2002.

Liao Yuqun. *Traditional Chinese Medicine*. Singapore: Cambridge University Press, 2010.

Xu Ganrong and Bao Tongfa. *Grandiose Survey of Chinese Alcoholic Drinks and Beverages* (中国酒大观目录, Chinese and English versions). Jiangnan University, 1998.

Derek Sandhaus

paradis (French for "paradise") is the part of a cognac or Armagnac house's cellar where the oldest brandies are stored, often in glass demijohns to arrest further maturation. See ARMAGNAC; COGNAC; and MATURATON.

parfait amour ("perfect love") is a traditional liqueur of French origin dating to the eighteenth century. Although largely forgotten by the middle of the twentieth century, parfait amour was popular between the First and Second World Wars. It was rediscovered thanks to the mixology movement in the 1990s. With its complex taste and beautiful purple color, parfait amour is found in cocktail recipes such as the Jupiter Cocktail and the Blue Paradise. A few French and Dutch liqueur producers such as Marie Brizard and Bols include one in their portfolio.

Originally, parfait amour was simply a "cédra(t) rouge"—a citron-flavored liqueur colored red with cochineal. Eventually, it became a melting pot of different flavors, and by 1900 the color had become not red but purple. While the ingredients vary from one manufacturer to another, in general the flavor is obtained from maceration or infusion of fruits, bark, spices, and flowers in alcohol of agricultural origin. These include citron, of course, but also some combination of coriander seeds, cinnamon, orange and lemon peels, and vanilla, and sometimes even violets, raspberries, rose petals, anise, geraniums, almonds, and other botanicals, all of which meld to create a unified combination of floral and spicy notes on the palate. Like any liqueur, parfait amour must have a minimum sugar content of 100 grams per liter with more than 15 percent alcohol. Parfait amour is usually sold at 24–30 percent alcohol.

See also ABV; BOLS; CRÈME DE VIOLETTE; FRANCE; and LIQUEURS.

Déjean, Antoine. *Traité raisoné de la distillation*. Paris: 1753.

Herstein, Karl M., and Morris B. Jacobs. *Chemistry and Technology of Wines and Liquors*, 2nd ed. New York: Van Nostrand, 1948.

Alexandre Gabriel

pastis is a French aperitif flavored with anise and licorice that became popular as an alternative to the outlawed absinthe. See ABSINTHE; APERITIF AND DIGESTIVE; and FRANCE.

Pat O'Brien's has been a fixture in the French Quarter of New Orleans since 1933. The popular bar is best known as the home of the Hurricane. See HURRICANE.

patent still is one of several names (along with column still and Coffey still) for a continuous still. See COFFEY STILL; COLUMN STILL; and STILL, CONTINUOUS.

Patrón tequila is the best-selling luxury brand of tequila in the world. The brand was born in 1989 when John Paul DeJoria (1944–), cofounder of the bestselling hair care company John Paul Mitchell Systems, commissioned architect Martin Crowley to buy locally made furniture and furnishings in

Drinking pastis in Martigues, outside of Marseilles, 1954. Getty Images.

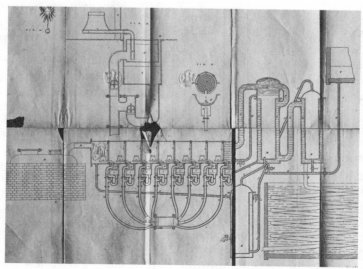

A very rare and very fragile copy of the 1828 patent drawing for Robert Stein's continuous still. The wash flows down from the *top right*, through the three vertical vessels, where it is heated by the vapor from the still or the spent wash moving through their jackets. Then it is fed via a manifold into the eight injectors that spray it into the chambers of the horizontal column, where steam coming from the boiler at *left* strips off the alcohol and passes via woven horsehair membranes from compartment to compartment until it escapes to surround the vertical vessels before going to the condenser, *bottom right*. It's not elegant, but it did work. Wondrich Collection.

Mexico. As an afterthought, DeJoria asked Crowley to bring back a few bottles of high-end tequila. Crowley began visiting distilleries and discovered Siete Leguas. See SIETE LEGUAS.

Impressed with the sample, made from 100 percent Weber blue agave, DeJoria asked Crowley to order ten thousand cases. At the time, nearly all tequila sold in America was the cheaper *mixto* type, a blend of agave- and sugar-cane-based alcohols. See MIXTO. From the outset, DeJoria and Crowley tried to create a luxury tequila market by educating bartenders and drinkers alike about fine tequila. At $37.95 a bottle, Patrón was expensive when it launched. Other tequilas on the American market usually sold for less than half that amount.

The founders, however, were undeterred and started hitting the pavement to promote the brand. Their friends helped promote Patrón: Wolfgang Puck put the distinctive bottle behind the bar at his iconic Hollywood restaurant Spago, and later Clint Eastwood featured it in his film *In the Line of Fire*.

After several years of being produced at the Siete Leguas distillery, Patrón built its own facility in the highlands of Jalisco in 2002. Its master distiller, Francisco Alcaraz, uses traditional methods, including crushing the cooked agave with a giant volcanic stone *tahona* wheel. The brand now includes a range of premium tequilas (and a few tequila-based liqueurs as well), but despite growing exponentially, it still produces much of its base spirit the same way, tahona and all.

Known for its mild agave flavor and smoothness, Patrón built its phenomenal success not so much on an appeal to tequila connoisseurs as on its image as a luxury spirit favored by celebrities. In 2018, the brand was sold to the Bacardi company for $5.1 billion.

See also AGAVE; BACARDI; MEXICO; TAHONA; and TEQUILA.

Rothbaum, Noah. *The Business of Spirits*. New York: Kaplan 2007.
Tickell, Rebecca Harrell, and Josh Tickell, dirs. *Good Fortune*. Ojai, CA: Big Picture Ranch, 2016.

Noah Rothbaum

paxarete is a sherry-based concoction that is used to treat casks destined for aging whisky. It was extensively used in the scotch whisky industry from the late nineteenth century until it was banned in 1990. Its origins lie in Spain, in the Pajarete range of hills between Villamartin and Prado del Rey, forty miles northeast of Jerez. The area is known for its *vino de color*, used as a coloring and flavoring ingredient in the production of sweet sherry styles. It is made by adding reduced grape must to fermenting wine, which is then fortified and aged in solera.

Paxarete is produced by adding this vino de color to a blend of oloroso and PX sherries and some grape must.

Whisky producers in the nineteenth century greatly prized the character given by ex-sherry casks. By the 1870s there was, however, insufficient sherry being imported to Scotland to meet demand. A blender called William Phaup Lowrie is credited with coming up with the solution, making new casks and then treating them with paxarete.

Its use soon became standard practice, either for new casks or for rejuvenating previously filled casks. Cooperages and distillery filling stores would have a cask of "pax" on hand and add the wine to the emptied cask. Some injected it into the empty cask with compressed air. It was also prized as a "secret ingredient" for Christmas puddings.

Its end in scotch came in 1990 when it was decreed to be an additive that affected the flavor of the spirit. It is still used, legally, by distillers in the Americas and East Asia.

Allen, H. W. *Sherry and Port*. London: Constable, 1952.
Buxton, Ian, and Paul S. Hughes. *The Science and Commerce of Whisky*. Cambridge: Royal Society of Chemistry, 2015.

Dave Broom

peach brandy is an American spirit dating back to the early seventeenth century, made by crushing peaches, distilling the fermented liquid that results, and aging the spirit in oak barrels. (In the United States, popular usage also applies the term to sweetened grape brandy flavored with peaches, although United States law insists that this must be called "peach-flavored brandy.") From the mid-eighteenth century to the mid-nineteenth century, peach brandy was the most prestigious and expensive spirit of American manufacture. From the end of World War II through the first decade of the present century, it was no longer made commercially, but its manufacture has since recommenced as part of the boom in micro-distilling.

Americans are not the only people to have made spirit from peaches. Peach spirit has been, and in some cases still is, a common farm-distillery product in parts of France (where it is known as *eau-de-vie de pêche*), Germany (*pfirsich Schnaps*), Hungary (*palinka*), the Balkans (*rakia*), and even Iran (*aragh*) and South Africa (*mampoer*). See EAU-DE-VIE; SCHNAPPS. In none of these places, however, is the spirit an important article of commerce. Indeed, peaches are often combined with other fruits for distillation, and when they are distilled separately, the spirit is made in small quantities. None of these spirits see barrel aging.

The informal nature of their manufacture makes it difficult to trace the history of these spirits or even to determine when they were first made. It is possible that some predate the American peach brandy, but there is no evidence that the English made or knew about peach spirit before colonizing America. Early English distilling manuals discuss "waters" made from the leaves and the flowers of the peach tree, but not from the fruit. Even this was most likely theoretical, as peaches were difficult to grow in England. In North America, quite the opposite was true.

In the early 1600s, when the English started planting colonies in Virginia and the Carolinas, the colonists found peach trees growing wild, descendants of the ones the Spanish planted around Saint Augustine, Florida, in the 1560s. The fruit was so plentiful that the colonists fed their hogs on it, but they also made it into a kind of cider. By the 1640s, this was being distilled. By 1645, Virginia was regulating prices for locally made "aqua vitae or brandy," setting its worth as half that of "English strong waters."

As American distillers gained experience, the valuation of peach brandy, in particular, rose. In 1722, Robert Beverley, in his *History of Virginia*, claimed that peaches yielded "the best spirit next to grapes," and like the best grape spirits, the brandy was beginning to receive significant barrel maturation. By the end of the century, maturation times of six years or more were common, with such a spirit rivaling imported French brandy in price, the only native spirit to come even close to doing so. It was highly prized for use in punches (see FISH HOUSE PUNCH) and other mixed drinks.

The common grade of peach brandy was made by mashing the fruit with wooden pestles in wooden tubs and fermenting the whole mass before straining off the juice for a double distillation. In the early nineteenth century, however, some distillers moved to crushing the peaches between iron gears, thus cracking the pits, and pressing out the juice before fermentation. This made for a cleaner spirit, and the nuttiness of the pits was held to improve the flavor, although it brought a risk of introducing cyanide into the brandy if the distillation was sloppy and run too far into the tails.

Peach brandy was the leading American spirit in quality, if not quantity, through the 1830s, when rye and bourbon whiskies had improved to the point that they could compete. After that, it remained a regional specialty from Maryland south to Georgia, but the inability to manufacture it on an industrial scale doomed it to increasing irrelevance, and by 1900 less than 400,000 liters were produced (most of that in Maryland's Eastern Shore) as opposed to just under 500,000,000 liters of grain spirits. Some peach brandy was made after Repeal (Lem Motlow, of Jack Daniel's, was the best-known producer), but by 1950 the category was dead. The experiments with it starting in the 2010s are still in their early stages, and although they are promising, with at least ten different distilleries making the spirit, it remains to be seen if it can be successfully revived.

Hening, William W. *The Statutes at Large, Being a Collection of the Laws of Virginia*, vol. 1. New York: 1823.

"Old Times Seen Today." *New York Sun*, November 8, 1888, 3.

"Peach brandy," Vicksburg, Mississippi, *Daily Whig*, June 25, 1856, 2.

Wachsmuth, John G. Advertisement. *Philadelphia Federal Gazette*, October 2, 1788, 3.

Wondrich, David. "Is Peach Brandy the Next Hot Spirit?" *Daily Beast*, December 13, 2016. https://www.thedailybeast.com/is-peach-brandy-the-next-hot-spirit (accessed on August 24, 2019).

David Wondrich

peat is, as defined by W. A. Kerr in 1905, "a spongy vegetable substance, composed generally of mosses and aquatic plants in different states of decomposition" that "is in the progressive stage from a vegetable substance to a mineral coal." Because of the waterlogged conditions in peat bogs, there is insufficient oxygen for these organic deposits to be fully decomposed. Instead the plants—not just mosses but also heathers, grasses, and even trees—once dead are layered and pressed by the weight of subsequent generations and turned eventually into a soft, cakey substance without identifiable traces of its component plants, although those are still retained in upper layers of the bog. A peat bog will "grow" approximately 1 mm per year.

Peat is found across northern Europe, Siberia, northern Japan, the United States Pacific Northwest and northern Midwest, and Canada. In the southern hemisphere there are deposits in central Africa, Australia, and New Zealand.

The physical makeup of peat will vary depending on the vegetation that has grown on that spot thousands of years before. Analysis of pollen and fibers from peats cut in different parts of Scotland indicates that each site can be defined by the composition of the peat. In general, peat from mainland Scotland has high levels of lignin from decayed woody material; that from the north, Orkney, and western isles has less lignin and more moss. Orkney has the highest levels of heather. Because of this, it is now believed that the physical makeup of the peat may give different aromatic characteristics to peated malt and, therefore, peated scotch whisky. Anecdotal evidence backs this up, suggesting that peat from the mainland gives off more wood smoke aromas; that from Orkney is more perfumed and heathery; while that from Islay mixes mineral, tarry, and medicinal elements.

In the seventeenth and eighteenth centuries, peat was used extensively in Scotland and in rural Ireland in the production of whisky, as there was no alternative fuel source close to hand for kilning the malted barley. In some locations, peat was also used to fire the stills. The nineteenth century saw the Irish move decisively away from peat as their distilleries consolidated in urban areas, while in Scotland its use became a choice, linked to style more than necessity.

The availability of different fuels for kilning means that today peat is used purely for its aromatic qualities, with barley malt kilned over the fuel giving whisky a distinctive aroma known as "peat reek." This is produced by a series of flavor compounds grouped under the family of phenols. See PHENOLS.

The green malt has a moisture content of between 15 percent and 30 percent. When the smoke from the kiln rises, the phenols adhere to the surface of the still damp barley, imbuing it with their character. It is only at this stage of the kilning process that the phenols have an effect. Once the moisture level of the malted barley drops below 15 percent, any smoke will simply pass across the bed; for that reason, peat is generally only used at the beginning of the kilning process. A peat fire used for kilning will not have any flame but will smolder instead.

A distiller will set a measurement of the phenolic parts per million (PPM) it requires in its malt, with 15 PPM considered light and anything over 30 considered heavy (Ardbeg, the iconic peated single-malt scotch whisky weighs in at 55 PPM, and some experimental bottlings from other distillers range into the 200s). The maltings will then assess how much peat needs to be burned and for how long. It is an inexact science, as the level of smoke will depend of the combustibility of the peat and even the direction and strength of the wind and how it impacts on the draw.

If a lower amount of peatiness is required, then heavily peated malt will be blended with unpeated to meet the correct PPM requirement.

It is mistakenly thought that PPM refers to the smokiness of a mature whisky. Instead it only refers to the malt. Phenols are lost in every part of the process from storage to distillation. Phenols have a high boiling temperature and therefore come across late in the second distillation. The distiller will decide how much of the phenolic section to retain by deciding when to cut from spirit to feints.

An early cut will miss some of the heavier, tarrier components; a later cut will include them. For example, Lagavulin and Caol Ila, both widely respected scotch single malts from Islay, use the same phenolic specification for their malted barley, but their perceived smokiness is very different because of different fermentation regimes, still shapes, and cut points.

Peatiness will also be reduced in maturation, either through evaporation, absorption by the wood of the barrel, or integration into the spirit.

Kerr, W. A. *Peat and Its Products*. Glasgow: Begg, Kennedy & Elder, 1905.

Dave Broom

Pegu Club was an influential New York craft cocktail bar that opened in 2005 in a second-floor space at the border of SoHo and Greenwich Village in Manhattan. See CRAFT COCKTAIL. The bar was named after, and loosely inspired by, the club of the same name in the old British colonial outpost of Rangoon (now Yangon, Myanmar), and its signature cocktail. See PEGU CLUB COCKTAIL. Founded in 1871 and named after the province in which it was located, the original club moved to new, expanded quarters in 1882 in order to receive the prince of Wales, quarters it occupied until the British left the country in 1948; subsequently, it was used by the Myanmar Army before lying vacant for many years. At the time of this writing, plans have been announced to renovate the club's original teak building and incorporate it into a new luxury housing development.

New York's Pegu Club captured some of the exotic, steamship-age glamour associated with the original club without falling into kitsch. Opened by the same team that previously founded the pioneering Flatiron Lounge, with Julie Reiner and the critical addition of beverage director Audrey Saunders, it was the first large bar to fully embrace the craft cocktail esthetic and helped to publicize the movement and ensure its expansion. Saunders, a protégé of Dale DeGroff, brought an exacting drink-building standard to the cocktail list, which featured both pre-Prohibition classics, many of them gin-based (including its namesake cocktail), and notable Saunders originals such as the Gin-Gin Mule and Old Cuban. See DEGROFF, DALE. The opening bartending staff included Phil Ward, Toby Maloney, Chad Solomon, and Jim Meehan, all of whom eventually opened their own, equally influential cocktail bars. Other significant bartenders to have worked there include Brian Miller, Del Pedro, and Kenta Goto. Pegu Club closed its doors in 2020, as much a victim of New York real estate prices as of the coronavirus pandemic.

See also GIN-GIN MULE; REINER, JULIE; and SAUNDERS, AUDREY.

Simonson, Robert. *The Modern Classics*. Berkeley, CA: Ten Speed, 2016.

Robert Simonson

The **Pegu Club Cocktail** is a bracing combination of gin, bitters, lime juice, and orange curaçao. It was the house cocktail of the British officer's club of the same name in what is now Yangon, Myanmar. Precisely when the drink was created and by whom is unknown; the earliest known reference to it is from 1927, in Harry McElhone's *Barflies and Cocktails*. See MCELHONE, HENRY "HARRY". There are, however, references to "red" and "yellow" cocktails being served at another club in Yangon in 1888 (the Pegu Club is a light yellow-orange) and to iced drinks served at the Pegu Club bar the next year, as well as to "ante-tiffin gin cocktails" drunk in Myanmar from 1899, so an early origin for the Pegu Club Cocktail is quite possible.

The drink reached its widest exposure when Harry Craddock reprinted McElhone's recipe for it in the 1930 *Savoy Cocktail Book*, writing that it "has traveled, and is asked for, around the world." See CRADDOCK, HARRY LAWSON. In one respect, however, that recipe has not been generally followed: it specified that the lime juice in it be the preserved and sweetened Rose's, rather than fresh, and limited the amount to 1 teaspoon, implying that this was less than the one-sixth measure of orange curaçao called for (the British habit of giving measures in parts, rather than absolute quantities, and then throwing in some of the latter just for fun, is an eternal source of confusion for the cocktail historian).

However, most modern mixologists follow, wittingly or not, the recipe published earlier that same year by "Jimmy," who had worked at Ciro's in London (just as McElhone had before him); this called for equal parts curaçao and lime juice, presumably fresh, since it did not specify the preserved kind. It is unknown whether Jimmy had an independent source for the recipe or simply modified McElhone's. In any case, his version is a bright, clean, and vibrant drink that would go on to be one of the foundational formulae of the twenty-first century cocktail renaissance.

Recipe (as served at the Pegu Club, New York): 60 ml Tanqueray London dry gin, 22 ml lime juice, 22 ml Marie Brizard orange curaçao, 1 dash Angostura bitters, and 1 dash orange bitters (equal parts Regan's and Fee's). Shake, and strain into a cocktail glass.

See also CURAÇAO; GIN; and PEGU CLUB.

Browne, Edmond Charles. *The Coming of the Great Queen*. London: Harrison & Sons, 1888.
Cocktails by "Jimmy." New York: David McKay, 1930.

Fraser, John Foster. "An Amateur Buddha." *Strand Magazine*, September, 1899, 308.

Audrey Saunders and David Wondrich

peppers (including peppercorns and chile peppers) have long been a staple for adding flavor, spice, and piquancy to alcoholic beverages. Peppercorns, the fruit of the *Piper nigrum* vine, grow in clusters, like berries, and are dried before use. Of South Indian origin, they were brought to Rome in the first century CE, where they were valued for adding flavor to food, of course, but also for their medicinal and mystical properties, as well as a badge of prestige and luxury.

The Romans were the most extravagant users of aromatics in history, using spices lavishly in the kitchen, cosmetics, and elsewhere. Spice-flavored wines were in demand, since spices were supposed to add "heat" to the banquet. Indeed, the first recipe in Marcus Apicius's book, *De re coquinaria* is for "fine spiced wine," a "honey refresher for travelers" spiked with crushed pepper and saffron; this is the first known recipe for a spiced alcoholic beverage.

So important were spices, they famously launched Christopher Columbus around the world, searching for a route to the Indies on behalf of the Spanish monarchy. Although what he found instead was the route to the New World, there were spices there. However, Columbus found the "wrong" spices—not peppercorns, cinnamon, and other Indian spices but allspice berries, vanilla, and fiery chile peppers.

Chile peppers, as the various members of the *Capsicum* genus are known, found their own uses in drinks, particularly in Mexico and in Eastern Europe. In Mexico, bottled chile sauce is a traditional ingredient in Sangrita, the sweet-spicy-fruity drink used as a chaser for shots of tequila. See SANGRITA.

Eastern Europe, and Russia in particular, has added spices and other flavorings to vodka for as long as the spirit has been produced—most experts speculate this was to disguise poorly made home distillations or to make them more palatable. See HOME DISTILLING. Russia's honey- and chile-pepper-infused vodka, known as *pertsovka*, is of particular note. Similarly, the Ukraine's *horilka* is made by steeping chile peppers in vodka. In addition to infusions made at home or produced for consumption in bars or restaurants, a number of commercial bottlings are also available. See also VODKA.

Undoubtedly, these spicy infusions provided inspiration for the pepper-flavored vodkas now available in the United States. Stolichnaya introduced a Pertsovka bottling to the United States in 1962 and rebranded in 2012 as Stoli Hot. See STOLICHNAYA. Meanwhile, Absolut Peppar entered the US market in 1986; the producers claim the brand was intended for use in Bloody Mary cocktails. See ABSOLUT and BLOODY MARY.

In recent decades, as US demographics have shifted, including the sharply growing number of Americans with Latino and/or Asian heritage, tastes have changed too, including a rising acceptance of spicy flavors in food and drink. A growing number of bars now offer one or more spicy cocktails, often flavored with muddled chile peppers, hot sauces like Tabasco or sriracha, or dried spices mixed with salt to rim glasses to give a kick to otherwise familiar Margaritas or other cocktails. See MARGARITA.

Meanwhile, the number of pepper-infused bottlings on liquor store shelves has grown dramatically. In addition to the big brands, a number of smaller US producers offer pepper-flavored vodkas and other spirits. Hangar One Chipotle, made with dried chile peppers (chipotles), debuted in 2007 and had a reputation among chile-heads for being the only spicy liquor around that had actual chile pepper flavor, with a fruity-sweet backbone to support the capsaicin burn. After the Hangar One brand was sold to Proximo Spirits in 2010 (leaving its creator St. George Spirits as an independent entity), the chipotle vodka vanished from store shelves. In 2015, St. George introduced Green Chile Vodka, made with fresh jalapenos, serranos, habaneros, red and yellow bell peppers—but no chipotles. See ST. GEORGE SPIRITS.

It's no longer just vodka anymore, either. Within the past couple of years, chile peppers and peppercorns have been used in commercial bottlings for flavored whiskies, flavored tequilas, and liqueurs, and even as a botanical for gins, not to mention "hellfire" bitters, shrubs, and spicy syrups meant for mixing into cocktails.

Keay, John. *The Spice Route: A History*. Berkeley: University of California Press, 2006.

Kara Newman

percolation, or the filtering of liquid or vapor through a porous object, is one of the essentially five means to flavor a spirit that distillers have at their disposal, along with compounding, maceration, infusion, and distillation. Perhaps most associated with a classic campfire coffee brew or traditional Italian "macchina" for stovetop espresso, the concept of percolation is quite simple: the liquid is heated and either bubbles directly through the substance intended to flavor it or its vapor does. It is most commonly featured in gin production, where botanicals are suspended in a basket or other perforated container (rather than in direct contact with neutral spirit) so that as alcoholic vapors rise in the still, they pass through the botanicals, extracting their essential oils and absorbing flavors and aromatic characteristics as they go. See GIN.

Of note is the type of still employed for percolation: the Carter-head still, where the botanicals are put in a basket contained in an extra chamber that is interposed between the head of a pot still or a rectifying column and its condenser. This was invented in the mid-nineteenth century by a pair of brothers who worked for none other than Aeneas Coffey, inventor of the Coffey still. See COFFEY, AENEAS. The Carter brothers' invention was one of many fanciful developments of the era that fell out of favor by the middle of the twentieth century, until it was revived to make Bombay Sapphire gin in the 1980s.

The technique of percolation results in more delicate flavors and aromas than one gets from adding the botanicals to the still itself. Relatively few gin brands feature percolation or vapor infusion techniques on their own. Rather, is it often utilized in combination with traditional pot still or "one-shot" distillation, the most notable proponent of this style being Hendrick's gin. See HENDRICK'S GIN. Some vodka distillers also use Carter-head stills for percolating their distillate through charcoal. See CHARCOAL FILTRATION.

See also COMPOUNDING; DISTILLATION; INFUSION; and MACERATION.

Allen Katz

A "**Perfect**" Martini or Manhattan is, in the mixologist's lexicon, one whose vermouth quotient is made up of equal parts sweet and dry vermouths. The practice of mixing the vermouths dates back at least to 1901, with the name coming along by the early 1920s. The Perfect Martini fell out of fashion after World War II, but the Perfect Manhattan has retained a small constituency.

See also MANHATTAN COCKTAIL; MARTINI; and VERMOUTH.

"Cocktails, Old and New." *New York Sun*, December 18, 1901, 10.

David Wondrich

Pernod-Ricard is a French-based multinational corporation that is the world's second-largest wine and spirits producer, after Diageo. See DIAGEO. The company was created in 1975 with the fusion of two longstanding rivals of the French aperitif culture: Pernod (founded in 1805) and Ricard (created in 1932). The two leaders, Jean Hémard (1917–1982) and Paul Ricard (1909–1997), joined forces so that they could redirect their energies from competing with each other to competing in the world market with the growing Anglo-American conglomerates such as Seagram's and Grand Metropolitan, even though at the time fully 80 percent of their joint business was in France. By 1979 that was down to 60 percent.

That rapid growth was boosted by the succession of Patrick Ricard (1945–2012), Paul's son, to the helm of the company upon Hémard's retirement in 1978. Over the next thirty years, he pursued an ambitious acquisitions policy that successfully transformed the French business into an international leader in wines and spirits.

The company made its first overseas acquisition in 1980 when it purchased the American whisky brand Wild Turkey. See WILD TURKEY. In 1986, the group started its involvement in Singapore, Japan, China, and other Asian markets. In 1988, it added Irish Distillers to the portfolio in a friendly takeover, bringing the company Jameson, Bushmills, and several other brands, along with Ireland's two operating distilleries. See IRISH DISTILLERS LTD (IDL). The year 1993 saw the company sign a joint development and marketing agreement with the Cuban government, giving it the international marketing rights to Havana Club rum. The company experienced three more major growth spurts with the acquisition in 2001 of a significant portion of Seagram's assets, including the prestigious Martell cognac brand; of Allied Domecq in 2005; and of Absolut vodka in 2008. See ABSOLUT; MARTELL; SEAGRAM COMPANY LTD.; and STOLICHNAYA.

Today, the group employs eighteen thousand people worldwide. Its portfolio also includes such well-known brands as the Glenlivet, Ballantine's, and Chivas Regal Scotch whiskies; Del Maguey mescal, Avion tequila, and Kahlúa coffee liqueur; the Czech herbal liqueur Becherovka; Beefeater and Plymouth gins; G. H. Mumm and Perrier-Jouët champagnes; the French aperitif Suze, the Italian digestive Ramazotti, and Wyborowa Polish vodka. See BEEFEATER; CHIVAS REGAL; DEL MAGUEY MEZCAL; GLENLIVET; PLYMOUTH GIN; and SUZE.

From the late 2000s through the late 2010s, Pernod-Ricard devoted an unusual level of resources to bartender education, including sponsoring the BarSmarts bartender certification program, which tested and certified literally thousands of US bartenders in basic knowledge of spirits and mixology. See BARSMARTS.

See also SPIRITS TRADE, HISTORY OF.

Pernod-Ricard Annual Reports, 1976–2006, https://pernod-ricard.com/en/media/publications-and-reports/publications/archive-annual-reports/ (accessed March 21, 2021).

Fernando Castellon

Petraske, Sasha (1973–2015), was one of the driving forces of modern speakeasy cocktail culture. On New Year's Eve 1999, when he opened the speakeasy-style Milk & Honey (affectionately nicknamed M&H) on the edge of New York City's Chinatown neighborhood, he set the pattern for countless bars that followed. See MILK & HONEY. Sasha—he was universally known by his first name—was an unlikely trendsetter: he was allergic to the stereotype of a speakeasy bar and indeed didn't like to follow trends at all when it came to making drinks and how to enjoy them. He preferred to quietly challenge the status quo. He wore slacks, suspenders, vests, and ties behind the bar before they were industry tropes because that's how he dressed, not because he was playing the role of "speakeasy bartender." Yet independent as he was, Sasha was also a consummate mentor and would go on to open a number of other highly lauded bars in partnership with his former employees.

Sasha was born in New York City and attended the exclusive and challenging Stuyvesant High School, often referred to as the no. 1 public school in the country. Sasha was a promising, straight-edge student, but he dropped out at seventeen and soon joined the United States Army, where he spent nine weeks training as an elite Ranger. The training had a lasting effect on his physical and mental acuity—the way he appeared to be at rest while standing at

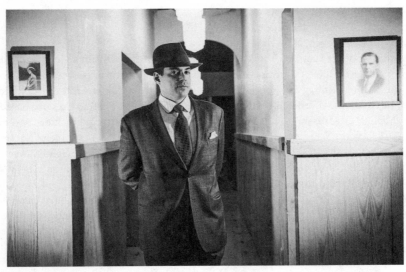

Sasha Petraske at the final incarnation of Milk & Honey, on Twenty-Third Street in Manhattan, ca. 2014. Courtesy of Gabi Porter.

the ready, his ability to stay alert no matter how little sleep he was running on, his aptitude for defusing challenging situations and remaining Buddha-calm under pressure. He was an obsessive note taker and list maker and read the *Economist* every week from cover to cover. At the same time, he had strong ideas about social justice and caring for everyone equally, informed by an old tattered copy of the Communist Manifesto that his grandmother had given him. He loved his cats and was known to feed them sushi-grade tuna.

Sasha trained his bartenders not just in mixing drinks but in etiquette and comportment; to make a priority of cleanliness in everything from their fingernails to their workspace; to stand upright; and above all to be patient. Drinks were to be built in rounds so that all the drinks would be finished and put on the serving tray in a thirty-second window. When brought to the table, they would be served in clockwise order, reflecting how the guests were seated and had ordered.

Sasha's bartenders each became part of a team, almost a tribe, with a shared aesthetic and culture. This idea of a bar team was something new: in 1999, the bartenders at any one place were essentially independent contractors: individualists who each did things their own way and competed more than cooperated with their fellow bartenders.

Sasha's bartenders, however, became a loyal family that opened up other projects with him around the country and globe. In order of their openings after the original Milk & Honey: Milk & Honey, London (2002), with Jonathan Downey; Eastside Company, New York (2005); Little Branch, New York (2005), with Joseph Schwartz; White Star, New York (2008); the Varnish, Los Angeles (2009), with Eric Alperin and Cedd Moses; Dutch Kills, New York (2009), with Richard Boccato; the Everleigh, Melbourne (2011), with Michael Madrusan; Middle Branch, New York (2012), with Schwartz and Lucinda Sterling; Attaboy, New York (2013), with Sam Ross and Mickey McIlroy; Half Step, Austin (2014), with Alperin, Moses, Chris Bostick, and Eric Needleman. See DOWNEY, JONATHAN.

Sasha was Yoda to many young bartending Jedis, and along with the staffs he trained at his bars, he also consulted on various bar projects, extending his codified method of cocktailing beyond his bar family. He was always in search of socially responsible activities

to take part in, and at Bohanan's Prime Steaks and Seafood in San Antonio (one of his consulting gigs), along with the chef, he started an annual cocktail festival—San Antonio Cocktail Conference. The monies raised from the festival were all distributed to various children's charities.

In June of 2015 he was married to Georgette Moger, and the couple fittingly had their honeymoon on the Orient Express. Sasha died of an unexpected heart attack a month after their return. The book he was in the midst of writing was completed by his wife, with the assistance of various members of the Milk & Honey family. *Regarding Cocktails* was published in 2016.

Sasha was uncompromising without arrogance and is remembered for his devotion to doing the important things right. His legacy lives on through many of the top bartenders that trained with him. His attitude to bartending is perhaps best summarized through the following quotation, which was included in the Milk & Honey training compendium:

> Needless to say, the moment any pleasure is taken at demonstrating one's skill at swordsmanship, all possibility of true swordsmanship is lost.
>
> —*Anonymous swordsman, sixteenth-century Japan*

See also COCKTAIL RENAISSANCE.

Petraske, Sasha, and Georgette Moger-Petraske. *Regarding Cocktails*. New York: Phaidon, 2016.

Eric Alperin

Peychaud's Bitters is a popular, bright-red brand of aromatic or cocktail bitters created in New Orleans in the nineteenth century and now made and sold by the Sazerac Co., also based in that city. The proprietary recipe includes several herbs and spices that yield a zesty blend of anise, nutmeg, and clove notes with a slightly sweet, floral taste. Peychaud's Bitters were among the popular brands of the nineteenth century, and one of the few surviving today. They are essential to numerous classic cocktails, such as the Sazerac, the Vieux Carré, the Cocktail à la Louisiane, the Star, the Metropole, and a few early versions of the Manhattan. They are particularly prized by modern mixologists in cocktails with brandy or scotch whisky.

Peychaud's American Aromatic Bitters, as they were originally called (during the Civil War "American" became "Southern American"), were invented by New Orleans pharmacist Antoine Amédée Peychaud (1803–1883). Peychaud was born in the French colony of Saint-Domingue and came to New Orleans as an infant during the slave rebellions (1791–1804) that resulted in the establishment of the independent Republic of Haiti. Peychaud opened his pharmacy in 1834 at 123 Royal Street (now believed to be 437 Royal, near the corner of St. Louis). He introduced his bitters sometime between 1849, when he was still advertising his version of Stoughton's Bitters, and 1857. See COCK-TAIL. In June, 1857, Peychaud advertised in the *New Orleans Bee* that "this cordial has been introduced into general use in the Sazerac House, and other principal Coffee-Houses in this city" (note that in New Orleans "coffee house" was synonymous with "bar"). It is very likely that his bitters were used in making cocktails there, including ones with the Sazerac cognac the bar carried, among other cognacs. See SAZERAC HOUSE. In 1858, to increase sales, Peychaud reduced his product's level of bitterness, and indeed to this day Peychaud's is among the less bitter members of its class.

In 1868, Peychaud was forced to sell the Royal Street building that contained his shop and house; thereafter, he sold or licensed his trademark and formula to a succession of local pharmacists, while also compounding the same formula for Thomas Handy, then proprietor of the Sazerac House, to be sold under the Handy name. This led to a period in the 1890s when three different people in New Orleans were making Peychaud's formula in competition (lawsuits ensued).

Eventually the competitors fell away, and the brand went to the L. E. Jung company, which secured its national distribution in the 1890s and made the bitters until 1940. The brand was acquired a few years later by the Schenley conglomerate, which sold it to the Sazerac Co. in 1970.

According to New Orleans folklore, A. A. Peychaud was the inventor of not only the world's first cocktail but the term itself. In *Old New Orleans* (1936) and *Famous New Orleans Drinks and How to Mix 'Em* (1937), Stanley Clisby Arthur identified that ur-cocktail as a mixture of Sazerac du Forge et Fils cognac, sugar, Peychaud's bitters, and water, served in an hourglass-shaped egg cup (in French,

a *coquetier*, which sounds something like "cocktail") and attributed it to Peychaud himself. According to his obituary, however, Peychaud was eighty years old when he died on June 30, 1883. Inasmuch as the word "cocktail" was first defined in an 1806 newspaper, it seems unlikely that a three-year-old Peychaud could have been a pharmacist, much less invented an iconic drink. But isn't it pretty to think so?

See also SAZERAC CO.

"American Bitter Cordial" (advertisement). *L'abeille de la Nouvelle Orleans*, June 29, 1857, 1.
"Handy v. Commander." *Southern Reporter* 22 (1898): 230–236.
King, Grace. *Creole Families of New Orleans.* New York: Macmillan, 1921.
"Notice—Having Been Informed." *New Orleans Daily Crescent*, June 11, 1858, 6.
"Sazerac Acquires Peychaud's Bitters." *Alexandria (LA) Town Talk*, December 11, 1970, B-10.

Philip Greene

pH is a measure of the hydrogen ion concentration (acidity and alkalinity) of an aqueous solution expressed by a number on a 0–14 scale, for which the value of 7 represents neutrality (pure water registers as 7); lower numbers indicate increasing acidity and higher numbers increasing alkalinity. That neutral 7 can be described as a solution in which hydrogen ions (H+) and hydroxide ions (OH-) are in equal proportion. As the H+ proportion increases (and pH decreases), the solution becomes more acidic. Humans register that decreasing pH as sourness.

In the pH scale, each unit of change represents a tenfold change in acidity or alkalinity, so that the difference between a pH of 6.9 and 7 represents a one-point difference (not one-tenth of a point), measured in hydrogen ions by moles per liter. Thus a beverage that has a pH of 4 can be seen as crisp or tangy while a beverage with a pH of 3 can be frighteningly tart for many people. Solutions with very low pH can damage human tissue.

Pure ethanol is slightly alkaline, with a pH of 7.33. While commercial spirits vary in their pH level, in general a well-made, neutral spirit will have a pH in the 6 to 7 range, although some vodkas register as alkaline due to the water used to reduce them in proof (indeed, this can be seen as one of the hallmarks of the eastern European style of vodka) and others as acidic due to added citric acid (used to mask flaws in distillation). A barrel aged spirit will generally fall somewhere around 4.5, with anything less than 3.5 indicating serious errors in the distillation.

"pH Scale." American Chemical Society. https://www. acs.org/content/acs/en/education/resources/under-graduate/chemistryincontext/interactives/water-eve-rywhere/ph-scale.html.

Valaer, Peter. "Brandy." *Industrial and Engineering Chemistry* 31 (1939): 339–353.

Doug Frost

phenols are a group of volatile aromatic compounds, consisting of a hydroxyl group bonded with an aromatic hydrocarbon group, that give many of the most pungent spirits their characteristic flavor. They perform a number of functions in plants, only one of which is relevant for our purposes: the bitterness they impart discourages feeding by animals (it can even be toxic to insects). In distilled spirits, these useful compounds, when present as congeners, barrel extracts, or components of added botanicals, impart various woody and smoky aromas and flavors. See BOTANICAL; CONGENERS; and MATURATION.

As congeners, phenols are most prominent in Islay scotch whiskies, to which (smoke-derived) guaiacal, furfural, and cresol add the characteristic notes of smoke, and bromophenols (perhaps derived from the island's peaty water) add iodine and seaweed. But (presumably) cane-derived phenols such as dihydroeugenol also have a significant presence in high-ester, pot still Jamaican rums and in Martinique rums. Other spirits heavily influenced by phenols as congeners include pomace brandies, mescal and tequila, and sauce-aroma baijius. See POMACE BRANDY and SAUCE-AROMA-STYLE BAIJIU.

Aging spirits in toasted, heated, or burnt wooden barrels draws out numerous polyphenols—molecules consisting of multiple phenols—that contribute a wide variety of flavors. Phenols and polyphenols may oxidize gradually during barrel maturation, thereby producing flavors and aromas including fruit, vanilla, cinnamon (cinnamic acid), almond (benzoic acid and others), tonka bean (coumarin), coffee, smoke (guaiacol and others), pepper, flowers, clove, sawdust, caramel, brown sugar (maltol), walnuts (phenol aldehyde), and molasses.

Trying to understand the complexity of wood and its influence upon spirits (which can include addition, subtraction, and transformation of compounds) can lead to an alphabet soup of names, including other wood phenols such as 4-methylguaiacol (which gives sweet, candy, eugenol, vanilla, leather, spicy, and smoky aromas), 4-propylguaiacol, 4-ethyl 2, 6-dimethyloxyphenol, and other compounds such as phenyl ketones and aldehydes.

Phenol aldehydes (or phenolic aldehydes), such as vanilla, have properties characteristic of both phenols and aldehydes and are sometimes grouped with phenols. Along with other phenol-derived molecules, the variety of compounds that operate under the term "phenols" combine and interact in so many ways as to justify describing tens of thousands of phenolic compounds and interactions, each potentially contributing to the flavors, aromas, and textures of a wood-aged spirit. See ALDEHYDES.

For botanical-derived phenols, one must look to things such as Italian *amari*, French *apéritifs*, aromatic bitters—all of them rich in bitter phenolics—and, of course, gin: juniper berries are particularly rich in polyphenolic flavonoids. See APERITIF AND DIGESTIVE; BITTERS; and GIN.

See also AROMA and KETONE.

Miller, Gregory H. *Whisky Science* Cham, Switzerland: Springer, 2019.

Nykänen, Lalli, and Heikki Suomalainen. *Aroma of Beer, Wine, and Distilled Alcoholic Beverages*. Berlin: Akademie Verlag, 1983.

Doug Frost

Philippines comprises 7,641 islands in the western Pacific Ocean and is home to approximately 100 million people. After Russia and South Korea, the Philippines have the highest per capita consumption of alcohol in the world. Distilling has been known in the islands since at least 1521, when Ferdinand Magellan and his crew found both palm and rice arrack in use. Of the rice version they encountered on the western island of Palawan (which may have been imported from Southeast China), Antonio Pigafetta, one of the explorers, wrote that it "is as clear as water, but so strong that it intoxicated many of our men." In 1574, a Spanish expedition leader, Andres de Mirandaola, wrote to the king of Spain that natives made distilled "wines" of sugar cane, rice, millet, and various palm species. Over subsequent centuries, that palm arrack, known locally as *lambanog*, was often drunk new, but producers sometimes aged it in wooden barrels. Industrious Manila rectifiers would go on to transform it into a base for imitation spirits and compounded cordials such as anisette, cognac, Chartreuse, whisky, rum, fruit brandies, pineapple gin, genever, maraschino, gin, and more.

At the beginning of the twentieth century, the most widely consumed spirits in the Philippines were domestic compounded gins and various anise-flavored cordials (*anisado, anis, anisette, carabanchel,* and *mallorca*) made with essential oils. They jockeyed for first place with *vino/bino de coco* and *vino de nipa*, the Spanish names for the lambanogs made from coconut- and nipa-palm sap, respectively (about 35 percent ABV).

Today, drinkers throughout the Philippines enjoy brands such as Emperador brandy, Tanduay rum, White Castle whisky, and other distilled spirits, but gin reigns supreme. Filipino gin consumption (1.4 liters per person per year) is the highest in the world and accounts for approximately half of all gin sales globally. The bulk of that gin is made by Ginebra San Miguel, founded in 1834.

See also ARRACK, COCONUT; COMPOUNDING; GIN; LAMBANOG; and NIPA.

"Filipinos 3rd Heaviest Drinkers in the World." *Philippine Star*, February 6, 2014.

Flores, Wilson Lee. "10 Success Secrets of the Philippines' Oldest Distillery." *Philippine Star*, December 21, 2015.

Gibbs, H. D., and W. C. Holmes. "The Alcohol Industry of the Philippine Islands, Part II: Distilled Liquors, Their Consumption and Manufacture." *Philippine Journal of Science* 7A, no. 1 (1912): 19–46.

"High Spirits." *Economist*, June 17, 2013.

Pigafetta, Antonio. *The First Voyage around the World*. Edited and translated by Theodore J. Cachey. New York: Marsilio, 1995.

Matthew Rowley

Picon or **Amer Picon** is a brand of French digestive bitter launched in French Algeria by Gaëtan Picon (1809–1882), a soldier with distilling experience. Born in Genoa when the city was temporarily under French control, Picon was raised in Marseille and apprenticed in distilleries in the south of France. In 1830, he joined the "Armée d'Afrique," which executed the French colonization of Algeria. While in Africa, like many other French soldiers, he contracted a tropical fever, which was treated with quinine-infused wine and other bitters, as was traditional. This experience prompted him in 1837 to try to develop a better-tasting, more effective tonic for African conditions. In 1840, having come up with a formula based on bitter and sweet orange peels augmented with gentian, quinquina, and rhubarb, he quit the army and started a small distillery in the port city of Philippeville (modern Skikda). Soon Picon's Amer Africain was being consumed in quantity throughout French Algeria, and he built two more distilleries.

Yet even though Picon's bitter had won the first of its many international medals at London's Great Exhibition in 1862, it wasn't until the aftermath of the Franco-Prussian war that it gained a foothold in France itself, having been brought there by soldiers from Algeria. In 1872, he built a distillery in in Marseille and renamed his product Amer Picon. By 1909, Amer Picon was being made in four distilleries in France and employing the peels of some three million oranges a year, all from Algeria. It was exported all over Europe and to America and featured in several popular cocktails, including the Brooklyn. See BROOKLYN COCKTAIL.

Its initial proof seems to have been 40 percent ABV. In the 1920s it was reduced to 38 percent, then to 27 percent in the 1970s, and finally, in 1989, to 18 percent. Today the brand is owned by Diageo, the world leading group of spirits and wines. Diageo has yet to revitalize it or fully restore its proof, something that has benefited many other heritage brands, putting its energy instead into marketing Picon Bière, a slightly stronger (21 percent), sweeter offshoot tailored for the popular, if fading, French practice of mixing Amer Picon with beer. As a result, Amer Picon's influence on the cocktail revolution is more as an item of nostalgia than as a living product. In fact, a number of modern mixologists have taken to recreating their own versions of the classic Amer Picon, based on other bitters, neutral spirits, and other ingredients.

Postcard for Amer Picon, with oranges. Ca. 1900. Wondrich Collection.

De Berques, A. "Une grande marque." *La Dépêche coloniale illustrée*, September 31, 1909, 82–87.

Fernando Castellon

Pierre Ferrand is a cognac house based in Ars, France. The brand is unusual in that it controls the entire cognac-making process itself, including growing grapes, fermentation, distillation, and aging. (Most cognac houses buy grapes, wine, and/or brandy from other producers.) The brand's vineyards are located in the so-called Golden Triangle, an area at the center of the Grande Champagne subregion known for the quality of its brandies. Pierre Ferrand eschews the standard naming conventions for cognac, giving each of its bottlings a unique name, ranging from the cocktail-friendly 1840 Original Formula to the long-aged Ancestrale.

The Ferrand family has been producing brandy since the seventeenth century, but the modern brand dates to 1989, when entrepreneur Alexandre Gabriel partnered with Pierre Ferrand to create the eponymous brand with an eye toward export to the United States. Since then Gabriel, who bought out Ferrand upon his retirement in 1993, has created a number of other spirits brands under the Maison Ferrand banner: Citadelle Gin, distilled in small copper pot stills; Mathilde, a line of all-natural fruit liqueurs; Plantation Rum, a set of rums sourced from various distilleries in the Caribbean and South America and aged, at least in part, and blended in France; and Pierre Ferrand Dry Curaçao, an orange liqueur made according to a nineteenth-century recipe with the help of drinks historian David Wondrich.

In 2017, Plantation purchased the West Indies Rum Distillery in Barbados, and along with it a one-third share of National Rum of Jamaica, which owns the iconic Long Pond and Clarendon distilleries. In 2018, Plantation began releasing new rums enabled by this purchase.

Gabriel's activities at Ferrand have caused some eye-rolling and disruption in the staid world of cognac. He has also led primary research into the nature and processes involved in the maturation of spirit, adding to greater understanding of the concept of *rancio*. See ÉLEVAGE and RANCIO. His strong advocacy for the centuries-old tradition of aging and blending Caribbean rums in Europe has proved equally controversial in the world of rum, although the popularity of Plantation's products and the awards they have won have been their own arguments for the practice.

See also COGNAC.

McGrew, G. "Cognac Ferrand — The Father of Artisanal Spirits." Cognac.com, January 2, 2013. http://www.cognac.com/blog/cognac-ferrand-the-father-of-artisanal-spirits/ (accessed March 8, 2021).
Savona, Manuela. Email message to author, August 14, 2016.

Jason Horn

pimento dram (sometimes known as "pimento cordial") is a traditional Jamaican liqueur flavored with berries of the pimento tree (*Pimenta dioica*), commonly known as allspice. Beginning as a folk remedy for diarrhea and cholera, it has been an article of commerce since at least 1850. Pimento dram is made by extracting the lightly fermented, dried berries with a high-proof spirit, most often rum, and adding sugar and lime juice. The resulting liqueur has a flavor reminiscent of cloves, cinnamon, and nutmeg. Traditionally it is enjoyed neat, as a cordial or liqueur, but has found some use in cocktails (such as the Lion's Tail, with bourbon whisky, lime juice, and bitters) due to its unique flavor profile.

See also LIQUEURS.

Darcy O'Neill

Pimm's Cup is a commercially produced bottled cup that bears the name of London oyster seller James Pimm (1798–1866). Customarily served as a tall drink, mixed with fizzy lemonade or soda water, it is traditionally served in Britain as a light, refreshing summer cooler. While there were six varieties marketed under the Pimm's name (each featuring a different base spirit) the most popular has been the "No. 1 Cup," which is essentially a bottled British Gin Sling, minus the citrus and the carbonation. See SLING. Indeed, since being introduced to the United States during the late 1940s, the Pimm's Cup has become a staple summer drink in parts of the United States as well, including New England and, surprisingly, New Orleans.

Married into a Kent-based fishmongering family, James Pimm opened his first oyster bar in 1823 near London's Old Billingsgate Market. Success came quickly; he moved to 7 Lombard Street near the Bank of England, Lloyd's of London, and the Stock Exchange by 1825 and then to a much larger premises by 1835, at 2 Poultry and later 3 Poultry. For a time, Pimm supplied the Royal Family, and his Poultry establishment was depicted in the iconic *Tallis's Street Views of 1840*.

Oysters and other shellfish were frequently accompanied by stout or spirit-based punches and cups. To meet demand, in 1850, Pimm applied for a liquor license but was refused; the following year he was given approval. The establishment was a success, but by 1856 Pimm retreated to his wholesale fish business at Billingsgate, leasing or selling the oyster bar to S. D. Morey, who in turn sold it in 1865 to Frederick Sawyer. Horatio David Davies (1842–1912), the future lord mayor of London, took over the business in 1880, expanding it into a chain that he operated until 1912 when he died.

Capitalizing on gin's popularity, at some point Pimm, one of his employees, or one of their successors blended gin, fruit extracts, liqueurs, bitter herbs, spices, and sugar to make a pre-bottled "cup" (as it was labeled) or "sling" (as it was also advertised), designed to be mixed with lemonade. Only the trademark date of 1912 and its commercial release that same year are confirmed. If there is any documentary evidence that Pimm himself compounded the cup, it has yet to be produced.

The No. 1 cup, a bright red concoction that bears a strong family resemblance to a Singapore Gin Sling, without the lime or soda, was immediately successful and sold widely. It was accompanied at first by a scotch-whisky-based No. 2 and a brandy-based No. 3. Davies' heirs, who owned the brand, eventually added Nos. 4 (rum), 5 (rye whisky), and 6 (vodka) before selling the brand to the Distillers Company in the 1950s. Diageo purchased it in 1997 and has focused on the No. 1 Cup, sometimes adding a seasonal Summer Cup and Winter Cup. See DISTILLERS COMPANY LTD (DCL) and DIAGEO.

"Adjourned Licensing Meetings." London *Era*, March 30, 1851, 14.

Hamey, Baldwin. "James Pimm, London Fishmonger and Confectioner." *London Street Views*, July 8, 2016. https://londonstreetviews.wordpress.com/2016/07/08/james-pimm-fishmonger-and-confectioner/ (accessed March 8, 2021).

Jones, Roger. *What's Who? A Dictionary of Things Named after People and the People They Are Named After*. Leicester, UK: Troubador, 2009.

McConnell, Anita. "Pimm, James (1798–1866)." In *Oxford Dictionary of National Biography*, Oxford: Oxford University Press, 2005.

Post Office London Directory, 1825, 1835, 1841, and 1856.

Anistatia R. Miller and Jared M. Brown

Piña Colada ("strained pineapple") is a frozen drink made of light rum, pineapple, and pre-sweetened coconut cream, first concocted in Puerto

Rico in the mid-1950s or early 1960s. It is considered the signature drink of that island.

Rum had been introduced to pineapple and coconut prior to the 1950s. *Piña colada* was a traditional Cuban drink—strained, sweetened pineapple juice, sometimes with coconut water. Beginning in the 1930s, there were even piña colada stands in cities around the United States, selling a blended version of the drink, made with the richer coconut milk. While both of these were generally nonalcoholic, at least one American journalist suggested the obvious, that the standard pineapple-coconut drink might easily be turned into a "grand rum cocktail" (this was in 1944), and indeed the Cuban version is sometimes found spiked with rum, though always with other added ingredients. But not until the late 1960s did the alcoholic version become the default one, and then it came as a Puerto Rican import.

The drink's creation relied on the introduction in 1949 of Coco Lopez, a canned, sweetened, and emulsified cream of coconut concentrate, developed under the aegis of Puerto Rico's postwar Bootstraps Program for economic development. The Puerto Rican Piña Colada is not documented until sixteen years later, however, which leaves room for two divergent genesis tales. One purports that bartender Ramon Marrero "Monchito" Perez of the Caribe Hilton in San Juan (another Bootstraps project) came up with it in 1954. The other assigns it to the great, and peripatetic, Argentine bartender Ramon Porta Mingot (1905–1974), then working as head bartender at San Juan's Barrachina restaurant, in 1963. Unfortunately, Barrachina is mentioned several times in the press as a new restaurant in 1965. On the other hand, while numerous of the Caribe Hilton's recipes appear in tourism ads and travelers' accounts of the 1950s and early 1960s, some with Coco Lopez, some with pineapple, none put the two together. While this does not invalidate Perez's claim, it does at the very least call the timing into question. See PORTA MINGOT, RAMÓN "RAYMOND".

In any case the new, alcoholic Piña Colada hit big in 1968 and went on to be consumed widely across North America in the 1970s when sweet tropical drinks were ascendant, and then around the world. (Because of its origins in Puerto Rico rather than faux-tropical stateside bars, the Piña Colada is not strictly considered a tiki drink but a close relation that shares a reliance on rum and fruit juices.) Reflecting its popularity, Puerto Rico declared the Piña Colada its national drink in 1978. The Piña Colada experienced another boost in popularity following Rupert Holmes's 1979 musical hit "Escape (The Piña Colada Song)," which included the refrain "If you like Piña Coladas / And getting caught in the rain." The high-calorie drink became less ubiquitous in the more health-conscious 1980s and 1990s but remained on many cocktail lists, where it continues to appeal to drinkers who find small appeal in the assertive taste of hard liquor.

Recipe: Combine in blender: 60 ml white Puerto Rican rum, 120 ml fresh (or at least unsweetened) pineapple juice, 30 ml Coco Lopez or other coconut cream, and 250 ml crushed ice. Blend and serve in tall Collins with cherry garnish. Monchito Perez's recipe from the 1980s calls for 180 ml pineapple juice and adds 30 ml heavy cream.

See also TIKI.

Berry, Jeff. *Potions of the Caribbean*. New York: Cocktail Kingdom, 2014.
"Fancy Rum Refreshers Direct from Famous Restaurants of Puerto Rico," *McAllen (TX) Monitor*, June 9, 1953, 12.
Newman, M. W. "Nathan Leopold: Man with a Past." *Columbia (SC) Record*, March 15, 1965, 6.
Your Guide to Great Rum Drinks. N.p.: Rums of Puerto Rico, [1968].

Wayne Curtis

Pineau des Charentes, a *mistelle* made from fresh-pressed grapes fortified with cognac, has been produced in France's Cognac region for more than four hundred years. Created at the end of the sixteenth century when it was common practice to stabilize wine with spirit, pineau des Charentes has since stayed true to its original method using exclusively local grapes and cognac, which must come from the same farm. Since it was granted an appellation contrôlée (AOC) in 1945, production method is strictly controlled. Pineau des Charentes can be made with white grapes for the white expression and red grapes for the red. It must be barrel aged a minimum of eighteen months before bottling (some are aged for much longer) and have a 16–22 percent ABV.

In France, pineau des Charentes is mostly drunk as an aperitif but is also paired with food such as foie gras or cantaloupe. See APERITIF AND DIGESTIVE.

See also MISTELLE.

Comité National du Pineau des Charentes website. https://www.pineau.fr (accessed March 8, 2021).

Alexandre Gabriel

pinga (Portugese for "drop") is the most popular of the many aliases in Brazil for cachaça, the national spirit. See BRAZIL and CACHAÇA.

Pink Gin, or Gin and Bitters, formerly a great favorite in officers' wardrooms of the British Royal Navy, is as simple as it is historic: English drinkers were combining its two ingredients, gin and bitters, as early as the mid-1700s, and Dutch ones may have been doing something similar even earlier. By the turn of the twentieth century, when the name "Pink Gin" was first applied to the drink, the gin was almost always Plymouth (that town being the location of one of the Royal Navy's most important bases) and the bitters Angostura, but the earliest versions used Stoughton's Bitters and the dilute, sweetened gin that was in universal use in Britain. See PLYMOUTH GIN. This, of course, means that those eighteenth- and early nineteenth-century versions were essentially identical to the American Cock-Tail, which was not customarily iced until the 1840s. See COCK-TAIL.

Pink Gin was in vogue in Britain and North America from World War I through the 1960s. It was favored by military types in the United Kingdom and its colonies and anglophiles in America, where it was one of the few other drinks considered acceptable by Dry Martini cultists. In both places, the addition of ice was common, if not exactly approved.

Recipe: Line the bottom of an Old-Fashioned glass with 5–6 dashes of Angostura. Add 60 ml Plymouth gin and, if necessary 2–3 ice cubes.

See also GIN.

Childers, Erskine. *The Riddle of the Sands.* London: Smith, Elder, 1903.
"An Elegy to the Unlamented Memory of . . . Anti-Sejanus." *London Gazetteer and New Daily Advertiser*, March 17, 1766, 4.

David Wondrich

Pink Lady Cocktail, with gin, grenadine, and, originally, lime juice and applejack, was one of the most popular drinks of the first half of the twentieth century, despite being tarred with a reputation as a so-called ladies' drink—a label attached not so much to drinks that women liked to drink, which were basically the same as the ones men drank, but to drinks that some men believed would make them seem effeminate. Like the Pink Lady, many of those drinks were stronger than the "manly" ones to which they were being compared and no sweeter.

The Pink Lady Cocktail was named after the musical comedy of that name, which opened at New York's New Amsterdam theater in 1911, starring Hazel Dawn (1890–1988), who told a correspondent of drinks historian William Grimes that the drink had been created for a surprise party in her honor at Murray's Roman Gardens on 42nd Street.

Unfortunately, the Pink Lady that was served that evening is probably not the one that ultimately entered the books: the 1911 Pink Lady was a jigger of ojen (a Spanish anisette) shaken up with Peychaud's and Angostura bitters. (In New Orleans, this became known as the "Pink Shimmy.") In 1913, however, Jacques Straub, who drew many of his recipes from the bar book of the Waldorf-Astoria hotel, published the gin-applejack Pink Lady (basically, a Jack Rose with a splash of gin). See JACK ROSE. Although often simplified (the citrus juice was often omitted and the applejack generally replaced by more gin) and augmented with egg white or cream or both, it is this version that entered the canon. By the end of Prohibition, the version encountered in all but the best bars was generally a mix of gin, grenadine, and egg white. It was crude but effective, at least as an intoxicant.

Despite its pedigree, the gin-applejack Pink Lady never quite made it into the cocktail renaissance's list of approved drinks. That is regrettable.

Recipe: Shake well with ice 30 ml gin, 30 ml bonded applejack, 15 ml lime juice, 10 ml grenadine, and 10 ml egg white. Strain into chilled cocktail glass.

See also WALDORF-ASTORIA.

Erhard, Ursinus. "Interesting News from Gotham." *San Francisco Chronicle*, May 28, 1911, 39.
Grimes, William. Personal correspondence, February 22, 2009.
Straub, Jacques. *Straub's Manual of Mixed Drinks.* Chicago: R. Francis Welsh, 1913.

Woelke, Eddie, and Stafford Brothers. *The Barman's Mentor*. New York: Stafford Brothers, 1936.

David Wondrich

pisco is the characteristic grape brandy of Peru and Chile, a descendant of the *aguardiente de uva* made in both places, then parts of the Spanish Viceroyalty of Peru, since the late 1500s that has found an enduring niche worldwide as a cocktail spirit. The Peruvian and Chilean versions of the spirit share a strong family resemblance while differing in detail (as do Bolivia's *singani* and Argentina's *aguardiente de Catamarca*). See ANDEAN SOUTH AMERICA.

Many claims have been made for one sixteenth-century date or another as the beginning of distilling on the west coast of South America, almost all of them colored by the deeply acrimonious dispute between Peru and Chile over pisco's patrimony, in which Peru seeks to ban Chile from calling their national spirit "pisco" (it is as if Ireland sought to prevent Scotland from calling their spirit "whisky"). But this debate is fundamentally a political one and will not be resolved here.

The first stills recorded in the region are in the wills of a pair of wine growers, Maria de Niza, from Santiago, in 1586, and Pedro Manuel, from Peru's Ica valley, in 1613; neither would be the first in its area, and certainly by the early 1600s distilling was common both north and south of the Atacama Desert. The distilling regions have not changed much: the five departments where Peru allows pisco to be made today form a coastal strip running south from Lima, in the country's center, through Ica (the center of the industry, then and now), to Arequipa, Moquegua, and Tacna, on the Chilean border. Eight hundred arid square kilometers of the central Atacama Desert—Peruvian and Bolivian until the 1879 War of the Pacific and Chilean since—interrupt the strip, until it continues with the two Chilean provinces allowed to make pisco, Atacama and Coquimbo, the bulk of the production coming from the latter.

At first, there appears to have been little to differentiate the aguardiente made in the northern region from that made in the south: both were distilled from the mission grape (the Spanish listan prieto varietal); both were mostly used to fortify wine, so that it could survive storage and shipping; both appear to have been stored and shipped primarily in large, semi-porous earthenware *botijas*, not wooden casks (where there are few trees, there are few barrels). Yet even in the sixteenth century there were differences. The 1586 will specifies "un alambique de sacar aguardiente"—"an alembic for drawing off aguardiente." This would have been a valuable piece of specialized equipment, with a still head and a condenser. But such fine metalwork was

The inside of a *falca* still at the El Catador Distillery, Ica, Peru, showing the copper pot, which only reaches partway up the still body, and the bottom of the opening for the canon, or vapor arm, *top right*. Courtesy of Diego Loret de Mola.

common in the south: the Spanish had found extensive copper deposits near Coquimbo, and the region rapidly became known for its coppersmiths. In the north, however, distillers often preferred to make their own stills, using as little of the expensive Chilean copper as possible. In fact, the still that Pedro Manuel left his heirs is described as simply a "caldera grande . . . con su tapa e canon"—a "large kettle, with its lid and tube."

Manuel's is not only the first still recorded on Peruvian territory; it is also the first record of the *falca*, that country's characteristic, simplified version of the pot still. See FALCA. (This still was found in Chile as well, but apparently in the south, not in the north where alembics were made.) In any case, the seventeenth and eighteenth centuries saw the two aguardientes develop along parallel lines. New grapes were introduced—the ancient and highly aromatic "Italia," or moscatel de Alejandría, introduced in the early 1700s; the even older, and also quite aromatic "pastilla" or "moscatel rosada" (muscat blanc à petits grains); the much less aromatic mollar—and were adopted in both regions. Both regions exported a large part of their production to the massive silver mines at Potosí, four thousand meters above sea level in what is now Bolivia, where eventually there were some hundred thousand miners and an insatiable thirst for aguardiente with which to fight the year-round cold and the altitude.

Meanwhile, the vines planted north and south of the desert were hybridizing as they adapted to the different climates: lower in altitude and moister in Peru, where the grapes generally grow in valleys parallel to the coast; much drier and sunnier in the higher-altitude Chilean valleys, which stretch from the crest of the Andes to the coastal plain. There were other differences. In Peru, most of the distilling happened on large estates, many of them run by Catholic monastic orders, and the spirit made was destined for export, largely through the port of Pisco, just to the north of the Ica valley. From there, aguardiente was shipped to ports all over Spanish America (including those in Chile).

South of the Atacama, production was much less centralized, the province of small producers whose aguardiente went largely to the regional market. Like the Peruvian product, it was shipped in clay, but by the late eighteenth or early nineteenth century some producers appear to have begun first resting some of their production in tanks made of the fairly neutral rauli (a type of southern beech) from the forested south of the country. (In Chile's south, producers, of whom there were increasingly many, drew on the country's growing cooperage industry to both store and ship their aguardiente in rauli casks.)

Peru and Chile secured their independence in the 1820s. By then the "aguardiente de Pisco" shipped from that port had begun to gain a reputation, and a market, beyond Latin America—in 1826, a lonely "jar of Pisco de Italia" even made it as far as Liverpool. It is at this point that we first see its name consistently abbreviated to "pisco," mostly by people not from the region. This is almost always confirmable as the Peruvian product. But the tapped "barrel of Pisco" an American woman found in her hotel room in Concepción, in southern Chile, in 1826 gives one pause. It is possible that it was the Peruvian spirit, imported into Chile in a barrel or subsequently racked into one, but the Peruvian industry was not known for using barrels, and there are other early examples of barreled "pisco" associated with Chile. This raises the possibility that, at least as far as foreign travelers were concerned, "pisco" had already become the all-purpose name for the aguardientes distilled on the West Coast of South America.

Then came the California Gold Rush and the huge market for spirits it created: pisco was readily available and became popular in San Francisco and the inland mining regions. What the miners in California liked was Pisco Punch, made with something called "pisco de Italia" (or sometimes "Italian pisco"), which was, as a local newspaper put it in 1864, "a variety of brandy made from grapes in Pisco, Peru" that came in "earthen bottles or jars of an oval form, containing 2 ½ to 3 gallons [10–12 liters] each." See PISCO PUNCH. Yet Chilean aguardiente was also brought into the city, in barrels and jars, although one never finds records of it being actually drunk. By far the majority of what the miners actually drank was no doubt Peruvian, but the situation seems to be like that with Armagnac in America at the time, where shipping records show barrels of it being landed but one only finds "cognac" served in bars. There were no truth-in-labeling laws at the time.

While Peruvian producers such as Don Domingo Elias, who owned most of the vineyards in the plain of Pisco, exported as much pisco as they could, the industry in Chile was in the midst of an agricultural and technological revolution that saw huge amounts of aguardiente being made in the country's central zone, dwarfing what was made in the traditional regions in the north. A good deal of this was made with modern steam distillation, from recently imported European varietals, and aged in barrels, on the French model. See COÑAC. But much of it was aimed at the internal market for clear aguardientes, and indeed some of the producers—all from the central zone—who entered the 1872 Chilean Exposition of Arts and Industries explicitly identified their product as "pisco."

Whether it was this domestic pressure that caused the traditional producers in the north to begin explicitly labeling their product as "pisco" or if it was a reaction to how it was being sold in the United States, by the 1880s the traditional producers in Coquimbo and Atacama were claiming "pisco" as theirs and concertedly bottling their product as such. In 1931, this was made official, with a regulation limiting pisco to those provinces.

Meanwhile, the industry in Peru was under threat as well, as *cañazo*, Peru's local cane spirit—increasingly plentiful and very cheap—ate deeply into its domestic market. See CANE-BASED SPIRITS. American Prohibition added a near-fatal blow when it took away one of the major foreign markets (ironically, the other was in Chile). The late twentieth century was difficult in both countries, with dictatorships, land redistribution, and political unrest. Eventually, due to its overwhelming share of the domestic market, the Chilean industry came out in robust shape, if greatly consolidated. Today, the country's twenty producers make some 35 million liters of pisco a year, compared to the 7.5 million liters made by Peru's four hundred producers. In fact, the Peruvian industry was nearly destroyed in the 1970s but has seen a remarkable recovery in the last twenty years and dominates foreign sales (Peruvian producers such as BarSol, Macchu Pisco, Porton, and Campo de Encanto were early and enthusiastic participants in the modern cocktail renaissance). See COCKTAIL RENAISSANCE.

Today both industries are tightly regulated. Both control the grapes used: Peru allows eight varietals and Chile thirteen (only five are in common use), in each case a mix of aromatic and non-aromatic varietals. Both make piscos from single varietals and ones that are "acholado"—a mix of aromatic and non-aromatic grapes. Both control distillation: in Peru, pisco must be the product of a single distillation in a pot still (mostly alembics are used, although some falcas remain), run into the tails until bottling proof is reached. No water may be added. Chile specifies alembic distillation as well, which must be non-continuous, but in practice allows the pot stills to be connected to short, Armagnac-style rectifying columns that can be used to clean up part of the run. As with most spirits, the result is diluted to bottling proof. Peruvian pisco cannot be aged in wood; Chilean pisco can be but usually isn't. Peru allows a "mosto verde" style, distilled from partially fermented grape must and very aromatic. Chile allows an "artisanal" style, distilled on the crushed grapes and often rested in rauli tanks. The past few years have seen a proliferation of artisanal piscos, many of them from new producers.

Both countries make truly excellent piscos, rich-textured, clean, and headily aromatic. If a Peruvian pisco is disappointing, it is usually because it is hot or roughly distilled. If a Chilean one fails to measure up, it is usually because it is thin and bland. Fortunately, in each case such spirits are easy to avoid.

See also PISCO SOUR.

Angeles Caballero, Cesar. *Peruanidad del pisco*. Lima: Nueva Educacion, 1972.

"Extracts from Letters Written by a Lady in South America. *New-York Spectator*, February 24, 1826, 3.

"Fija reglamento de la denominacion de origen pisco." Ley Chile, December 30, 1999. https://www.bcn.cl/leychile/navegar?idNorma=169561 (accessed April 8, 2020).

Lacoste, Pablo, ed. *El pisco nació en Chile*. Santiago: RIL Editores, 2016.

Olmedo, Claudia. *40 grados*. Santiago: Emporio Creativo, 2011.

"Pisco Is a Variety of Brandy." *Marysville (CA) Daily Appeal*, January 8, 1864, 4.

Ricome, P. *Industria Peruana de los aguardientes de uva*. Lima: Sección técnica de propaganda agropecuaria, 1942.

Toro-Lira, Guillermo. *History of Pisco in San Francisco*. North Charleston, SC: Book Surge, 2010.

Zanutelli Rosas, Manuel, ed. *Crónicas y relaciones que se refireren al origen y virtudes del pisco*. Lima: Banco Latino, 1990.

David Wondrich

Pisco Punch is a much-storied drink, typically composed of pisco, lemon juice, fresh pineapple, and sugar or gum syrup, that is closely linked to San Francisco. The drink is often credited to Duncan Nicol, aka "Pisco John" (1852–1926), who operated the city's Bank Exchange Saloon from 1893 until the onset of Prohibition, although it predates his tenure there: the Bank Exchange opened in 1853 and, as early advertisements show, always stocked pisco, which in San Francisco was almost always consumed in punch. Nonetheless, Nicol's version of the drink became the iconic one. See NICOL, DUNCAN.

Pisco Punch at its most basic is not a San Francisco invention. Punch based on grape-based "aguardiente" was common on the west coast of South America, being recorded in Peru in 1791 and in Chile in 1822. By 1838, "pisco-punch," based presumably on the Peruvian spirit, shipped from the port of Pisco, had gained a foothold in the American community in Honolulu (the Chileans would not begin calling their version "pisco" for another 50 years). See PISCO. Pisco from Peru had been imported to the San Francisco Bay area by 1822, and with the Gold Rush the punch based on it became part of the city's, and the region's, drinking culture. But this was ordinary Pisco Punch: the same sort of punch—cold or hot—that was made with other spirits, but made with pisco. See PUNCH. The drink served by Duncan Nicol was something different (it is unknown precisely when he began serving it: the first document definitively tying the drink to his bar is an advertisement from 1903, but by then the unique qualities of Pisco Punch had been a common topic in the city's newspapers for over a decade).

The Bank Exchange's Pisco Punch enjoyed legendary status for a libation. Those who tried the drink found it extraordinarily exhilarating and "propulsive." Reporter Pauline Jacobson, who visited the bar in 1912, wrote: "One authority claims one punch 'will make a gnat fight an elephant.' Others maintain it floats them in the region of bliss of hasheesh [sic] and absinthe." One of Nicol's obituaries described the punch as an "ambrosial drink" that "softened all asperities, soothed every anguish of the hurt mind, stirred the imagination and seemed to make the whole world kin."

Unfortunately, Nicol worked hard to keep his precise formula secret, stirring (never shaking) each drink from lemon juice squeezed to order, distilled water, and a mix he prepared each morning in the basement of the bar. That mix, and the additional secret ingredient or ingredients it is reputed to have contained, went with him to the grave.

That's not the end of the story, though: in the absence of an "official" recipe, many people have stepped in to offer their versions of the drink. Some of those people had close ties to Nicol. In June 1959, *San Francisco Chronicle* columnist Millie Robbins received a recipe from an "E. J. P. of San Carlos," who claimed to have been a close friend of Nicol, who prepared the punch in his "then new home on Franklin Street in January 1921." E. J. P. (probably Emile J. Pierron, who is listed in the city directory as living on Franklin Street then) also wrote that he was at Nicol's bedside "when he passed away in that Sutter Street hospital in February 1926"; that information, too, checks out, lending credibility to his recipe, which involves marinating pineapple triangles in sugar and pisco and adding them and some of their marinating liquid to a punch stirred up from gum syrup, lime juice, pisco, and water.

This recipe is quite close to the one discovered in 1973 by reporter William Bronson, in a 1941 letter by John Lannes, who had worked for Nicol and managed the Bank Exchange the last year before Prohibition. And in fact both recipes are remarkably similar to the one for "Pisco Punch—Peruvian" printed in 1915, around the height of the drink's popularity, in a cookbook published for the San Francisco Panama Pacific Exposition—and to the one drinks columnist G. Selmer Fougner printed in the *New York Sun* in 1939, found in a Bank Exchange promotional booklet Nicol had given one of Fougner's readers in 1916. See FOUGNER, G. SELMER. If Nicol's exact recipe was lost, then, at least its broad outlines are known.

None of these recipes, however, provides the curious effects described by Pauline Jacobson in 1912, which suggests Nicol's punch may have contained something else. There is an 1864 San Francisco newspaper article that describes the experiences of a man drinking an unidentified "High Toned Drink" in the Bank Exchange Saloon. It describes "exhilarating" symptoms, similar to the ones described by Jacobson, that are compatible with the use of cocaine. Tonics and syrups containing cocaine were very popular from the 1860s to the 1890s; Vin Mariani used coca leaves from Peru in its tonic wine, and Coca-Cola also used them in early production. These concoctions were declared illegal in 1914, and their use in the Pisco Punch may have given Nicol reason to keep the recipe secret until his death.

Recipe (Lannes's): Make a rich simple syrup of 500 g sugar and 250 ml water. Peel and core a pineapple, cut it into rings, cut each ring into 6-8 wedges, and marinate overnight in the syrup. Strain out the chunks and refrigerate. Combine 750 ml Peruvian pisco (Italia style) and 250 ml of the syrup and bottle. To mix, stir with cracked ice 60 ml of the mix, 20 ml lemon or lime juice, and 45 ml water. Strain into large, chilled coupe and add a pineapple chunk.

See also NICOL, DUNCAN; PISCO; and PUNCH.

Bronson, William. "Secrets of Pisco Punch revealed." *California Historical Quarterly*, Fall, 1973, pp. 229–40.

Fougner, G. Selmer. "Along the Wine Trail." *New York Sun*, October 6 and 7, 1939, pp. 36 and 25.

Lafond, Gabriel. *Voyages autour du monde et naufrages celebres*, vol 3. Paris: 1844, p. 211.

Toro-Lira, Guillermo. *History of Pisco in San Francisco: A Scrapbook of First Hand Accounts*. Lima, Peru: Createspace, 2010.

Toro-Lira, Guillermo. *Wings of Cherubs: Saga of the Rediscovery of Pisco Punch*. North Charleston, SC: BookSurge, 2007.

Guillermo L. Toro-Lira and David Wondrich

Pisco Sour is a drink commonly composed of pisco, lemon or lime juice, sugar or simple syrup, egg white, and bitters. It was first served in the Morris' Bar in Lima, Peru, which Victor Morris operated from 1916 to 1929. The first known recipe, and the only one published while Morris' Bar was in operation, appeared in a Lima cookbook in 1924, within an entry for "Whisky Sour," which, translated into English, read: "Whisky Sour. The proportion is for a small glass of whisky, one of water, the juice of a lemon, one spoon of sugar and pieces of ice; put all in a cocktail shaker; shake a lot and serve. The Pisco Sour is prepared the same way." A similar recipe was published in 1930 in Santiago, Chile; neither early recipe includes egg whites or bitters, both common ingredients today. This suggests Morris's original concoction did not have those ingredients, and even in many regions of Chile today, the drink is mixed closer to the basic 1930 formula.

One theory about the change in formula is that Morris's recipe was modified to its present form at the Maury Hotel in Lima by Mario Bruiget, a young pupil of Morris's who later went to work there for fifty years; if so, it must have been before 1928, when an American traveler in Lima encountered the drink made with egg whites. Another theory is that Morris developed his Pisco Sour after reading a Peruvian cookbook published in 1903 that had a "cocktail" recipe calling for shaking an egg white with a cup of pisco, a small spoonful of fine sugar, and drops of lemon juice (no ice or bitters). Also in 1903, *Scientific American* published an encyclopedia of formulas including one for a Silver Sour that is almost identical to the modern Pisco Sour, including ice, but made with gin instead of pisco.

Until the 1960s, the Pisco Sour remained largely a local specialty, albeit one much appreciated by foreign travelers (Charles H. Baker Jr. called it "by far the best drink invention south of the 'Zone'" in 1951). See BAKER, CHARLES HENRY, JR. Only then did it begin to appear with regularity outside of Peru and Chile. In 1960, New York restaurateur Joe Baum included it (as the "Pisco Sawer") on the opening menu for La Fonda del Sol, his extravagant tribute to the cuisines of South America. A few years later, Braniff Airways offered to its passengers on South America–bound flights. It is not until the cocktail renaissance of the early 2000s, though, that the Pisco Sour took its rightful place as one of the indispensable cocktails. See COCKTAIL RENAISSANCE.

The Pisco Sour is one of the few cocktails in the world that has the distinction of having a government-approved day in its tribute. Pisco Sour Day is celebrated in Peru on the first Saturday of February; festivities include a national Pisco Sour mixing contest.

Recipe: Shake with ice: 60 ml pisco, 22 ml lime juice, 22 ml simple syrup, white of 1 egg. Strain into large, chilled coupe and dash the top with Angostura or Peruvian bitters. Note that in Peru this is mixed with lemon juice, but the lemons there fall somewhere between lemons and limes in flavor. Some like to mix the two juices.

See also MORRIS, VICTOR VAUGHAN; and PISCO.

"E. M. A." *El cocinero mundial*. Lima: Imp. Penitenciaría, 1924.

Gonzales, Gustavo. *El Cocktailero internacional*. Santiago: Edición Única, 1930.

Nuevo Manual de cocina a la criolla: Comida. Lima: Imp. Ledesma, 1903.

Titus, E. K. "Hark, tenants!" *Brooklyn Eagle*, April 10, 1928, 5.

Toro-Lira, Guillermo. *History of Pisco in San Francisco: A Scrapbook of First Hand Accounts.* Lima: Createspace, 2010.

Toro-Lira, Guillermo. *Wings of Cherubs: Saga of the Rediscovery of Pisco Punch*, North Charleston, SC: BookSurge, 2007.

Guillermo L. Toro-Lira

pitorro, a member of the rum family, is the Puerto Rican version of moonshine, distilled for the most part illicitly in the countryside from sugar or molasses and typically bottled unaged at over 50 percent ABV, and sometimes as high as 80 percent. See MOONSHINE. There are, however, a handful of legal brands from licensed distilleries, including one in New York City, Port Morris Distillery in the Bronx. Pitorro is popular as a base for Coquito, a Puerto Rican Christmas drink made with coconut milk, eggs, and spices. It is also infused with seasonal fruits to create a liqueur-like drink.

See also RUM.

Zavatto, Amy. "Moonshine around the Globe." *Fox News*, April 25, 2014. http://www.foxnews.com/leisure/2014/04/25/moonshine-around-globe/ (accessed March 8, 2021).

Jason Horn

Planter's Punch has been the unofficial drink of Jamaica since the late nineteenth century, when foreign tourists first encountered this compound of lime juice, sugar, dark Jamaican rum, and water. An old jingle of uncertain origin called out the proportions: "One of sour, two of sweet, three of strong, four of weak." A fifth line sagely advised topping with grated nutmeg, "a touch of spice to make it nice." Variations on this recipe had been noted in the Caribbean as early as 1694, but these rum punches were served in communal bowls. See PUNCH. By 1900, when H. L. Mencken checked into Kingston's Myrtle Bank Hotel and had his first Planter's ("a drink I have esteemed highly ever since"), it had evolved into a single-serving punch, swizzled with crushed ice in a tall tumbler.

Fred L. Myers of the Myers's Rum Company—which sold a Planter's Punch Rum and operated a Planter's Punch Inn on Kingston's wharf—made the drink internationally famous in 1924 when he sent a Myrtle Bank bartender to England to make Planter's Punches for the British Empire Exhibition at Wembley, London, and such notable guests as the Duke and Duchess of York. In 1939 Myers also updated the traditional recipe to "One of sweet, two of sour, three of weak, four of strong." Whether or not his motive was to sell more of his rum, this new ratio greatly improved the drink. See MYERS'S.

Things went downhill from there. In the decades following World War II, Planter's Punch morphed from a drink into a drink category, signifying any rum mixed with any fruit juice. Popular contemporary versions typically call for orange, pineapple, and guava juices, sweetened with grenadine (legendary New York State journalist Hugh W. Robertson, an early dissenter, wrote in 1938 that a bartender who uses grenadine instead of sugar syrup "should be shot at dawn without benefit of clergy").

Recipe (H. W. Robertson, 1938): Shake 60 ml full-bodied, aged rum, 30–60 ml falernum (to taste), 30 ml lime juice; strain into Collins glass with ice, add 60 ml sparkling water, dash with Angostura bitters, and garnish with lemon and orange wheels, mint sprig, and cherry. Simple syrup may be used in place of falernum, although Robertson thought "the man who would do that would steal a dead fly from a blind spider."

See also PUNCH; RUM, JAMAICA; SWIZZLE; and SWIZZLE STICK.

Berry, Jeff. *Potions of the Caribbean.* New York: Cocktail Kingdom, 2014.

Curtis, Wayne. *And a Bottle of Rum: A History of the New World in Ten Cocktails.* New York: Crown, 2006.

Robertson, Hugh W. "In Praise of Planter's Punch." *Yonkers (NY) Herald-Statesman*, July 16, 1938, 4.

Jeff Berry

plums are drupes (stone fruits) related to peaches, cherries, apricots, nectarines, and almonds whose flesh is used to make brandy and pits are used to flavor liqueurs. Plum remains have been found around human settlements as far back as the Neolithic era. Hundreds of varieties across dozens of species exist in a range of colors such as purple, red, green, and yellow. All plums belong to the genus *Prunus* and include Old World or European plums (*P. domestica*), Japanese plums (*P. salicina*), native North American plums (*P. nigra* and others), and *P. simonii*, a Chinese hybrid of *P. salicina* and apricots. The diminutive myrobalan or cherry plum (*P. cerasifera*) is native to Europe and Asia. Gages, both green and yellow, are also plums, but are somewhat smaller and rounder than the oval varieties more commonly cultivated in Europe.

Plum species cross readily, but most plums are high in sugars and yield large amounts of alcohol when fermented. Plum jerkum, a nineteenth-century plum wine from England, was regarded as especially potent. Mirabelles are small yellowish plums used to make a particularly well-regarded French *eau-de-vie*. See MIRABELLE and EAU-DE-VIE. The plum brandy perhaps best known on the United States, however, is eastern European slivovitz. See SLIVOVITZ. Rich, sweet, and astringent damson plums are often grown as hedgerows in the British Isles, where they are sometimes used to create a cordial similar to sloe gin. See SLOE GIN. The pits of plums may be used to make almond-scented noyaux. See CRÈME DE NOYAUX. *Ume*, the fruits steeped in shochu to make *umeshu* or Japanese plum wine, are *Prunus mume*, more closely related to apricots than to plums. See SHOCHU.

See also JELÍNEK; QUETSCH; and SCHNAPPS.

Bennett, Jennifer. *The Harrowsmith Book of Fruit Trees*. Camden East, ON: Camden House, 1991.

"Crowquill's Jottings." *Berrow's Worcester Journal*, October 17, 1891, 5.

Mirel, Elizabeth Post. *Plum Crazy*. New York: Clarkson Potter, 1973.

Spangenberg, Jorge E., Stefanie Jacomet, and Jörg Schibler. "Chemical Analyses of Organic Residues in Archaeological Pottery from Arbon Bleiche." *Journal of Archaeological Science* 33, no. 1 (2006): 1–13.

Matthew Rowley

Plymouth gin is made in the Black Friars distillery in the old English naval port from which the gin takes its name. The business's early years are murky, but it appears to have been founded when the brothers John Clark and William Langmead, of a prominent local brewing family, teamed up with merchant Robert Fuge to take over an old distillery and gin rectifier on Higher Broad Street in the heart of Plymouth. That was in 1800, or at least that's when the partnership's acquisition of the distillery, which had been operating since the 1740s, was announced.

The partnership was an unstable one, however, and went through many changes. In 1814, John Clark and William Langmead got rid of Fuge. Two years later, he bought them out with the help of Thomas Coates (1770–1830), a wealthy London–West India merchant with experience supplying the Royal Navy with rum. From then on, Coates's name would be attached to an ever-shifting list of others— Fox, Williams, Hawker, Griggs, Freedman, May— that seemed to include everyone but Langmead or Fuge. After Coates's death the Plymouth merchant William Henry Hawker (1789–1862) became the dominant partner; the Hawker family would own the brand until 1959.

The years immediately following the end of the Napoleonic Wars were good ones for British gin, which, freed of Dutch competition during the war years, had grown in quality, market share, and price. Before long, the distillery's "rich-flavored Plymouth gin" (as it was described in 1833) had built a dominant position in England's West Country and a reputation for unusual quality.

In 1821 the distillery was moved to larger quarters in a building on South Side Street, some 200 meters to the south, that had been built as a Dominican priory in 1431. The Black Friars Distillery, as it became known, is now Britain's oldest continually operating gin distillery. It is unclear if the firm began as "malt distillers"—that is, distilling their own base spirit from scratch. By 1860, anyway, they were purely "rectifiers," redistilling purchased raw Scottish grain whisky in pot stills with seven botanicals: juniper berry, coriander seed, dried orange peel, dried lemon peel, angelica root, green cardamom, and orris root. The distillery bottled the result, unsweetened, at 44 percent ABV, the lower of the two customary proofs for English gin, and (unusually) mandated that its bulk purchasers do the same. See BOTANICAL and RECTIFIER.

Coates & Co., the name the firm finally settled on in 1842, did a good business with the Royal Navy, as one might expect of the leading, and often the only, working distillery in a city with one of the largest and oldest naval bases in Europe. That business was

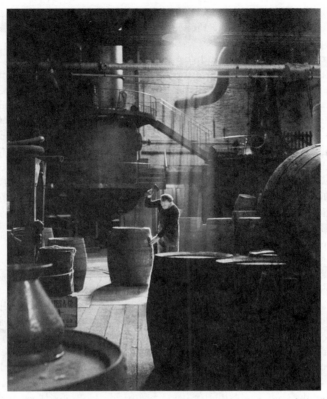

A cooper tightening a barrel band at the Plymouth gin distillery, with a large pot still over his left shoulder, 1954. Getty Images.

not official, though: the only spirit the navy officially bought was rum. See RUM, NAVY. Rather, officers' messes—the groups in which officers were assigned to dine—were given money with which to supplement their rations as they saw fit, including with spirits. By the second half of the nineteenth century, Plymouth gin, often bought directly from the distillery, had become an officers' wardroom fixture, fueling many a Pink Gin and Gimlet. See GIMLET and PINK GIN. In general, the Plymouth being poured was the same bottled, 44 percent stuff that anyone could buy, although during the world wars the distillery may have sometimes made a special bottling available for naval sale at full proof, or 57 percent ABV; this was used for special promotions—the first ships to return from the Falklands in 1983 each got a case—through the 1990s.

The brand was trademarked in 1882 and given a new advertising campaign, claiming it was founded in 1793. That may well be—again, the brand's origins are murky—but the significance of the year

has never been detailed or documented. The gin reached America in the mid-1880s, just in time to catch the Martini as it began its rise to glory, and to get itself in place for the powerful trend toward dry drinks that would sweep the United States in the mid-1890s. See MARTINI. In America, Plymouth gin was a hit. It would continue to be fashionable until Prohibition, providing the base spirit for cocktails such as the Dry Martini and the Gibson. See GIBSON and MARTINI.

Plymouth retained its popularity in Europe, and indeed the seminal 1930 *Savoy Cocktail Book* called specifically for Plymouth in many of its gin recipes (the others simply called for "gin" or "dry gin"). See SAVOY COCKTAIL BOOK. Remarkably, the repeated bombing of Plymouth during World War II—focused on destroying British naval capacity—did not demolish the distillery when much of the city was laid to rubble at the hands of the Nazis, though it did sustain damage. It was the postwar years that were the real challenge. For one thing, the company was sold eight times between 1959 and 2008, when it was acquired by its current owner, the French Pernod-Ricard company. See PERNOD-RICARD. Along the way, its marketing collapsed, and cost-cutting dented its quality. When a group of investors led by brand builders Paul Murphy and Charles Rolls bought the brand from the Allied Domecq group in 1998, the gin was molasses-based and bottled at a stingy 37.5 percent ABV. The first things they did were return it to close to its original proof and switch back to the slightly costlier grain spirit. They also brought the special, full-proof bottling to market as "Plymouth Navy Strength," launching a new gin category in the process.

The brand's revival reconfirmed Plymouth as one of the world's most respected gins. This process was aided greatly by its support for the modern cocktail revival. See COCKTAIL RENAISSANCE and FORD, SIMON. In return, Plymouth gin has been given new life by professionals and gin enthusiasts around the world. Today, the gin, when compared with traditional London dry gin, is both a bit sweeter—the net result of sweet orange and lemony zing—and a bit more earthy, from the rooty angelica and orris. It stands alone in flavor profile both from the recipe and, imperatively, from the unique pot still that has been in use for well over 150 years. A style, a brand, and a place, Plymouth remains steadfast to its long-standing traditions.

See also GIN and OLD TOM GIN.

"The Exeter Annuals." *Exeter and Plymouth Gazette*, December 28, 1833, 2.

"Just the Tonic!" *Liverpool Echo*, February 3, 1983, 7.

"Plymouth—Distillery &c. &c." *Sherborne Mercury*, June 30, 1800, 3.

"Plymouth Distillery." *Royal Cornwall Gazette*, October 19, 1816, 1.

Plymouth gin advertisement. *London Evening Standard*, August 28, 1993, 8.

Royal Commission on Whiskey and Other Potable Spirits. *Interim Report*. London: HM Stationery Office, 1908.

Allen Katz and David Wondrich

Poire Williams is an eau-de-vie, distilled from the Williams Bon Chrétien variety of pears, known as Bartlett in the United States. Made by fermenting crushed fruit and then distilling it in a pot or hybrid still to a relatively low strength, this eau-de-vie is usually colorless, aromatically rich, and distinctive. Produced mainly in Alsace, France, and Switzerland, it requires anywhere between 20 and 60 pounds of pears to make one liter; the spirit is aged in glass or stainless steel containers, for as long as ten years before bottling, with a few brands employing oak as well. Generally bottled between 35 and 45 percent ABV, Poire Williams is sometimes sold with a whole pear inside the bottle, a packaging style known as "prisonnière," accomplished by attaching bottles to fruit buds in the spring and allowing the fruit to grow inside.

See also EAU-DE-VIE.

Jack Robertiello

Poli, Jacopo (1963–), is one of a handful of northern Italian (often Venetian) distillers who have helped to elevate grappa from a rustic and fiery distillate consumed only locally to a highly respected and noble spirit celebrated on the world stage. Poli himself does not claim quite as much, pointing to his predecessors, familial, collegial, and historical. He references Bartolomeo Baglioni's early nineteenth-century invention of a stripping column, as well as Enrico Comboni's creation of steam distillation a few decades later and Tullio Zadra's refinement of the *bagnomaria* (bain-marie, or double boiler) in the 1950s and 1960s. See STILL, CONTINUOUS. Poli's great-grandfather GioBatta Poli (1846–1921) crafted his first still in 1898, in an era when continuous steam distillation had become efficient enough to strip grappa of most character. Subsequent stills at the Poli distillery moved beyond steam copper cauldrons to bain-marie boilers, one of which is a vacuum still installed by Jacopo in 1983.

In the 1970s, Nonino created the first *monovitigno* (single-variety grappa), and Poli and others followed, crafting grappe that were shockingly clean and expressed a purer expression of their source fruit, and began selling their grappe with varietal designations in elaborate and expensive bottles, sometimes hand-blown. Exclusivity helped deliver a message of higher quality and was doubtless a factor in the growth of quality grappa and its often lofty prices. Poli's distillery and home in Schiavon in Veneto is directly across from the Grappa Museum;

Types of Still

The following diagrams, by Don Lee, have been greatly simplified to show the operating principles of the stills.

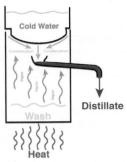

Chinese-style water-cooled internal condensation still. The pot with the wash is sealed with a basin of cold water, which must be refreshed. As the pot is heated, the ethanol vaporizes and then condenses on the cold bottom of the basin. It drips into a cup which has an outflow tube running through the side of the still.

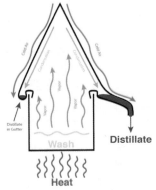

Medieval "alembic" with air-cooled, internal-condensation still head. The head is placed on the pot with the wash. As the pot is (gently) heated, the ethanol vaporizes and rises into the head, where it condenses on the cool surface and runs down the sides into a gutter with an outflow tube.

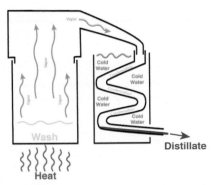

External-condensation still with condensing coil or "worm." As the pot with the wash in it is heated, the ethanol vaporizes and rises into the still head, from which it exits through an outflow pipe that ends in a coil, kept in a tub of constantly-refreshed cold water. As the vapor passes through the coil it condenses and runs out the end as liquid.

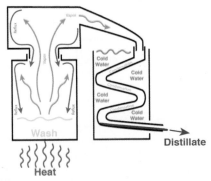

Reflux in operation. As the vapor expands to fill the (cooler) still head, the vapor pressure lessens, and some of the heavier compounds condense (including some water) and fall back down into the pot, increasing the proof and purity of the vapor exiting the still.

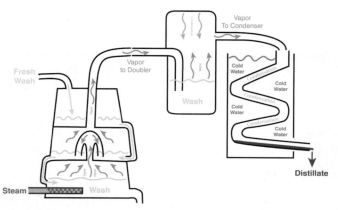

Nineteenth-century three chamber still. (1) The top two chambers of the still (left) are filled with wash and then live steam is run into the bottom chamber. As the steam rises into the middle chamber via a manifold, it is fed into the wash and bubbles up, stripping off the ethanol. The steam/ethanol vapor then passes in a pipe through the top chamber, pre-warming the wash in it, and goes into the doubler. There, the lowered vapor pressure allows water and other, heavier compounds to condense, filling the bottom of the doubler with liquid. The purified ethanol vapor bubbles through this and exits into the condenser. (2) Once the wash in the middle compartment of the still has had most of its alcohol run off, it is dropped through a valve into the bottom compartment and the warmed wash from the top compartment is dropped into the middle compartment. The warmer is refilled, and (3) after this cycle the spent wash in the bottom compartment is drained from the still and replaced by the now-depleted charge from the middle compartment, which is in turn refilled.

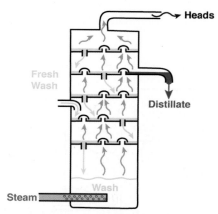

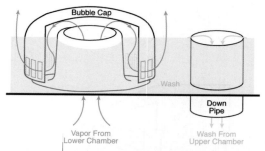

Column still—plate detail. A bubble cap and downpipe, showing how the rising vapor is directed to bubble through the wash.

Continuous or column still. Wash is fed into the side of the column and drips down via a series of perforated plates, slowed by raised rims around the perforations. At the same time, live steam is run into the bottom of the column. As it rises through the perforations, it is directed by bubble-caps to percolate through the pooled wash on the plates, stripping out the ethanol. As the ethanol-enriched steam rises, it leaves water and heavier compounds behind. In the cooler upper reaches of the column, ethanol and other volatile compounds condense. A plate may be sited to catch the ethanol at its condensation and draw it off, while any more volatile compounds can exit the still at the top.

Improvised and Rustic Distilleries

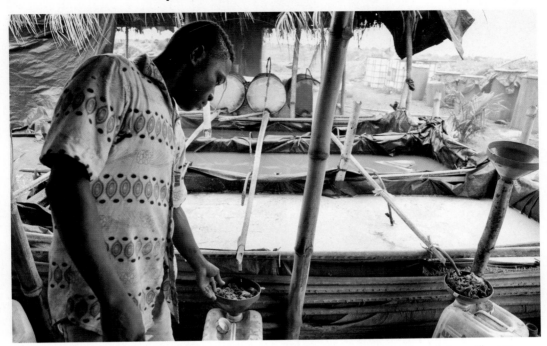

Koutoukou (raffia-palm spirit; see AKPETESHIE and OGOGORO) distillery in Côte d'Ivoire. Note the three oil-drum stills, rear; the vapor passes through three condensing tanks before being filtered through cloth. Photograph by Issouf Sanogo/AFP via Getty Images.

Wood-fired mezcal still at Santo Domingo Albarradas, Oaxaca. Courtesy of Del Maguey.

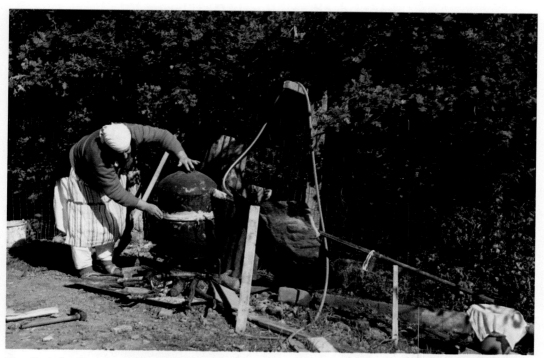

Vitore Vas Lufi making rakia, Fishta, northern Albania. The spirit is condensed by running water from a hose over the long vapor pipe. Photograph by Gent Shkullaku/AFP via Getty Images.

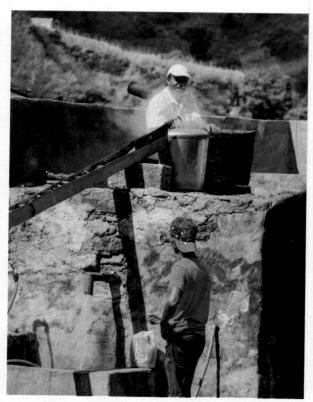

Grogue (cane-juice rum) distillery on Santo Antao, Cape Verde Islands. The still's long vapor arm runs through a trough of running water to condense the spirit. Note the spent wash being evacuated at bottom. Photograph by Martin Zwick/Reda & Co/Universal Images Group via Getty Images.

Traditional Industrial Distilleries

Isabelita Capistrano at her lambanog distillery, Tayabas, Philippines. Note the pot stills behind her. Photograph by Jay Directo/ AFP via Getty Images.

Steam stills at the Kweichow Moutai distillery, Guizhou Province, China. The lids on the two stills, *center* and *right*, are lifted off; the solid-fermented sorghum-wheat mix is shoveled in; the lids are closed; and the stills are connected to the condensers, *left front* and *rear*, with the vapor pipes, *center*. Then steam is run into them, stripping off the ethanol and exiting to the condensers. Wondrich Collection.

Modern Distilleries

The tall column stills at the Monymusk distillery, Jamaica.
Courtesy of Camper English.

The hybrid still and fermenters (*right*) at the New York
Distilling Company, Brooklyn, New York. Such setups are
common in modern craft distilleries. Courtesy of Allen Katz.

The massive, state-of-the-art column stills at the Absolut vodka
distillery, Nöbbelöv, Sweden. Courtesy of Pernod-Ricard.

Fermentation and Rectification

The old open-topped wooden fermenters at the Long Pond distillery, Jamaica. These were consumed by fire in 2018 but have been reconstructed since. Courtesy of Maison Ferrand.

Drawing a sample from one of the covered stainless-steel fermenters at the Hiram Walker Distillery, Windsor, Ontario. Courtesy of Corby Spirit & Wine.

Doubler at the Leopold Bros. distillery, Denver, Colorado. Courtesy of Todd Leopold.

Maturation

One of the rickhouses at the Heaven Hill distillery, Bardstown, Kentucky. Courtesy of Heaven Hill.

Dale DeGroff examines an aging jar, Kweichow Moutai distillery, Guizhou Province, China, 2011. Wondrich Collection.

Paper seal on aging jar, Kweichow Moutai distillery, Guizhou Province, China. Wondrich Collection.

Cognac blending tank. Courtesy of Maison Ferrand.

Poli opened the Poli Grappa Museum in nearby Bassano del Grappa in 2011.

In recent years, the more traditional style of grappa has re-emerged, not to be eclipsed by the greater purity and restraint sought by producers such as Poli, even while Poli continues to expand the range of his distillates to include Sarpa (a blend of cabernet sauvignon and merlot), Chiara, and Taiadéa (grappa and china, or cinchona bark, liqueur). Poli continues to utilize fresh pomace from throughout his home region for his grappe.

Behrendt, Axel, and Bibiana Behrendt. *Grappa: A Guide to the Best*. New York: Abbeville, 2000.
Boudin, Ove. *Grappa: Italy Bottled*. San Francisco: Wine Appreciation, 2008.
Poli, Jacopo. *Grappa: Italian Spirit*. New York: Rizzoli, 2014.

Doug Frost

Policastro, Santiago "Pichín" (1912–2010),

was the dean of Argentine bartenders and the author of the 1955 *Tragos mágicos*, an emblematic cocktail book that advanced modern mixology. Policastro was born in Buenos Aires on September 1, 1912, a son of Italian immigrants. He started his mixology career in the 1930s and by 1935 had created the Clarito, a Dry Martini variation that became one of the most famous Argentine cocktails. He worked at prominent bars in the city, such as Chantecler and Marabú. By the early 1950s he had gained a reputation as a preeminent bartender, an owner of three bars, and the host of a radio program named *Cocktail del Día* (Cocktail of the day); he even appeared in a film, *Vida Nocturna* (Nightlife), in 1955. In 1954, with his cocktail El Pato ("The Duck"), he won the International Cocktail Tournament that was a part of Hospes, the first postwar international hospitality conference, held in in Bern, Switzerland.

On June, 15, 1955, with the support of Argentine president Juan Domingo Perón, he inaugurated a floating beverage fair that was scheduled to travel around the world with the aim of advertising Argentine products. Unfortunately, his trip was canceled three months after its start due to the fall of President Perón. In 1956, with the overthrow of Perón, Pichín fled Argentina for New York City and eventually found himself in exile in Venezuela working with longtime friends and partners at the Pampero rum company.

In addition to being a member and great benefactor of the AMBA (Asociación Mutual de Barmen y Afines de la República Argentina), he founded and sponsored bartender associations throughout Venezuela, Puerto Rico, and Florida. He died on January 16, 2010, in Miami, where he lived during his last years.

"Hospes Berne 1954." *The Swiss Observer*, May 28, 1954, 7388.
Policastro, Santiago. *Tragos Mágicos*. Buenos Aires: Ediciones Riverside, 1955.

Ariel Lombán

Police Gazette Bartender's Medal was an

annual prize awarded to American bartenders in the early years of the twentieth century in one of the country's first cocktail competitions. Sponsored by the *National Police Gazette*, the contest solicited bartenders from around the country to submit their best original recipes for a mixed drink. The creator of the winning recipe received an elaborate gold medallion, while second and third place won a $10 and $5 gold piece, respectively.

The *National Police Gazette* was founded in New York City in 1845 as a sensational crime tabloid, but after Richard Kyle Fox took over as publisher in 1877, it evolved into the country's leading sporting weekly. Blending elements of the sports pages, gossip columns, and girlie magazines, the *Gazette* both reflected and helped shape the rising "bachelor culture" of the late nineteenth and early twentieth centuries. Crime and gossip took a backseat to sporting news, especially boxing and wrestling, and the *Gazette* became the "bible of the barbershop"—and of the barroom too. Both were male havens and prime sources of circulation for the magazine. Fox began running prose portraits of "well-known bartenders" from noted saloons and hotels in the larger American cities, and just before the turn of the century he struck upon what he considered one of his best ideas—the Police Gazette's Bartender's Medal. See FOX, RICHARD K.

The year 1899 appears to be the first one that a medal was awarded, and it went to Philip O. Gross of the Honing Hotel in Cincinnati for the Commodore, a blend of whisky, curaçao, lime juice, and sugar named in honor of Admiral George Dewey, a Spanish-American War naval hero. Gross's prize was a large medallion in the shape of a six-pointed gold star with a glass or mug embossed on each of its points.

The competition was held annually until at least 1909, and thousands of bartenders submitted recipes each year. In addition to the medal itself, which was valued at $100, winning the competition brought fame and career advancement to aspiring mixologists. Peter Sindar, who won the 1901 prize with his rye- and port-based Elk's Fizz, found himself, as one newspaper put it, "in great demand in the fashionable drink emporiums of the East where mixed drinks are the vogue." The influence of the prize, and of the *Police Gazette* itself, faded after World War I, but for a brief period at the turn of the twentieth century it helped establish bartenders' status as admirable figures in American male culture.

See also COCKTAIL CONTESTS.

Chudacoff, Howard P. *The Age of the Bachelor*. Princeton, NJ: Princeton University Press, 1999.

Reel, Guy. *The National Police Gazette and the Making of the Modern American Man*. New York: Palgrave McMillan, 2006.

Robert F. Moss

pomace brandy is a spirit made by distilling the mass of skins, seeds, pulp, and often stems left over after grapes have been crushed so that their juice can be drawn off for fermentation into wine ("pomace" is also sometimes applied to the leftovers of cider making, which are equally distillable). Wine lees and water are also sometimes added to the pomace. Pomace brandies are generally pot-distilled.

Farmers and winemakers have been distilling their pomace since at least the eighteenth century. The resulting spirit, a product of thrift and necessity, has generally had the reputation of being rather rough and fiery; a "country" spirit, rather than a city one (in 1787, the French distiller and physician Pierre-François Nicolas dubbed it "ordinarily disagreeable, with a scorched aroma"). In part this is no doubt due to its production by people who were not primarily distillers, but the nature of the raw materials—with less sugars and more oils, tannins, and other complex organic compounds than in the pure juice—must have something to do with that as well, along with the traditional practice of burying the pomace until the winemaking season was over and only then distilling it.

The majority of pomace brandies are made in Europe, although apple pomace brandy was formerly made in the eastern United States as well. European versions include *bagaceira* (Portugal), *orujo* (Spain), marc (France), grappa (Italy), *Treberschnaps* and *Testerbrand* (Germany), *trepinovec* (Slovenia), *törkölypálinka* (Hungary), some kinds of *rakija* (Serbia), and *tsipouro* (Greece). They are also found in Georgia, as *chacha*, and as far east as Kyrgyzstan. They are also made by a number of craft distillers in the United States. See BAGAÇEIRA; CHACHA; and ORUJO.

Modern pomace brandy making is generally more sanitary and less rough and ready than in years past, with many examples being carefully distilled and well aged. Italy in particular has brought its grappa to a high level of sophistication. See GRAPPA. In general, EU regulations require that pomace spirit be distilled to no higher than 86 percent ABV and bottled at no less than 37.5 percent alcohol by volume (and rarely exceeding 54 percent). No flavoring or additional alcohol can be added. Some countries, such as Italy, add further regulations.

The EU also allows for "fruit marc spirits," which are pomace brandies made with the leftover pulp and such of other fruits, either individually or combined. Stone fruits are the most common, but apple pomace is also distilled (as it was formerly in the United States). Fruit marc spirits can be high in methanol, urethane, and other toxic compounds, particularly if the pomace incudes the cracked pits of the fruit.

Nicolas, Pierre-François. *Manuel du distillateur d'eau de vie*. Excerpted in *Journal de médecine, de chirurgie, et de pharmacie*, March 1787, 531–532.

Owens, Bill, Alan Dikty, and Andrew Faulkner, eds. *The Art of Distilling*, rev. ed. Beverly, MA: Quarto, 2019.

Doug Frost

ponche, Spanish for "punch," lends its name to a number of concoctions from the Caribbean, most of them celebratory beverages with loosely defined formulae. Ponche Navideño in Mexico is the best known, a hot fruit punch served around Christmastime made in countless variations, with most including *tejocote*, the crab-apple-like hawthorn fruit, oranges, apples, dried fruits, brown sugar, spices, and rum or brandy. Ponche de Ron is a Christmas and New Year's tradition in the Dominican Republic and Puerto Rico—an eggnog made with sweetened condensed milk, evaporated milk, egg yolks, cinnamon, and rum. Ponche Crema is a bottled Venezuelan liqueur made with eggs and cream, and there are other commercial beverages bearing the name, including Ponche de Kuba.

See PUNCH.

Hutson, Lucinda. *Viva Tequila*. Austin: University of Texas Press, 2013.

McWilliams, Mark, ed. *Celebration: Proceedings of the Oxford Symposium on Food and Cookery 2011*. Blackawton, UK: Prospect, 2011.

Jack Robertiello

pony glass is a designation for glassware of various volumes, all noted for their relatively diminutive sizes (hence the name). Although the term may be older as a general descriptor for a small glass, in mid-nineteenth-century America it came to mean the smallest glass in which liquor was customarily served. In American bars, this meant a narrow, stemmed glass with a slightly flared rim that held anywhere from two thirds of an ounce (20 ml) to an ounce (30 ml). This was used for liqueur or cordial service (it was also known as a "cordial glass"), as well as serving as a measuring tool for mixing drinks. Once jiggers were adopted, later in the century, the pony came to be defined as half a jigger—thus either three-quarters of an ounce (22.5 ml) or an ounce, depending on whether the jigger's nominal capacity was one and a half ounces or two. But quantities in American bars were never legally defined, and there has always been a great deal of variation in the sizes of various glasses, which means that—confusingly—a pony glass may occasionally measure up to as much as three ounces (90 ml). On a standard two-sided jiggering tool, however, the smaller cone is traditionally called a pony.

See also JIGGER.

Curtis, Wayne. "Mixopedia: The Pony Glass." Imbibe, September 26, 2018. https://imbibemagazine.com/pony-glass-mixopedia/ (accessed March 31, 2021).

David Moo

Porta Mingot, Ramón "Raymond" (1905–1974) was a Spanish bartender, born January 27, 1905. He lived in France, the United States, Chile, and many other countries. In the 1930s, Porta Mingot resided in Buenos Aires, Argentina, where he became a prominent bartender at the illustrious Copper Kettle. With support from the bar's owners, in 1936 Porta Mingot published his book *Gran manual de Cocktails*. This celebrated book contained over 1,200 recipes that showcased the breadth and creativity of Argentine mixology. It was published in Buenos Aires, a city that opened up many bartending opportunities for Porta Mingot and fed his deep passion for soccer. His fondness for the sport was so strong that he dedicated several cocktails recipes to the most popular teams in the country. He received his membership to the AMBA (Asociación Mutual de Barmen y Afines de la República Argentina)—the only association for bartenders in the country—in March 1942. One of his most notable cocktails was El Diamante ("The Diamond"): 1/3 scotch whisky, 1/3 dry sherry, 1/3 Dubonnet rouge, and 1 dash of Angostura bitters, shaken and served in a cocktail glass. It is also widely claimed that Porta Mingot was the inventor of the world famous Piña Colada at the restaurant Barrachina in San Juan, Puerto Rico, in 1963, although this is unlikely. See PIÑA COLADA. Nonetheless, Porta Mingot was a renowned barman and a talented mixologist who shared his knowledge, skills, and art with the world. Although a naturalized American citizen, Ramón Porta Mingot had recently moved back to Buenos Aires when he died.

Porta Mingot, Raymond. *Gran manual de Cocktails*. Buenos Aires: n.p., 1936.

Ariel Lombán

A **posset** is a drink made from curdled milk or cream and wine, fortified wine (such as sack), or ale, the mixture being warmed, sweetened, and frequently thickened by the addition of eggs or egg yolks, bread, oats or barley, or pounded almonds. Left to set, the posset separates into layers—the light and foamy "grace" rising to the top, a custard-like middle layer, and the alcohol below. The upper layers can be eaten custard-fashion with a spoon, leaving a bottom layer of warmed, spiced, or sweetened drink. See LAYERING. Posset originated in medieval Europe as a quasi-medicinal beverage, and its construction became more formalized by the sixteenth and seventeenth centuries. "Posset pots" of this period—typically of earthenware or metal—came with a built-in straw that allowed the liquid layer to be sipped from underneath the topping. This cream-on-top/liquor-below arrangement suggests that the posset is a close cousin to the unheated Syllabub, if plainer, although it is undoubtedly fancier than another cousin, the gruel-and-ale caudle.

The precise definition of the posset proves mutable and nearly infinite in variation. The English cavalier and natural philosopher Sir Kenelm Digby's 1669 recipe for "Sack Posset" is particularly dependent on eggs for body, calling on "half a pint of Sack, and as much Rhenish wine" to be sweetened with sugar, beaten with no fewer than ten egg yolks and eight egg whites, and heated with cinnamon, not to boil but to thicken. Three pints of sweetened cream are boiled and added to the wine and eggs, then the whole is heated, with lemon juice sprinkled atop, and "if you will, you may strew Powder of Cinnamon and Sugar, or Ambergreece upon it."

As late as 1750, the posset in its plainest variation can take the form of a workingman's meal, as in Hertfordshire farmer William Ellis's "palatable supper" of a posset "crum'd with bread" in combination with stale beer and fresh milk. In Shakespeare, posset is largely a pre-bedtime drink or nightcap; in *Macbeth*, Duncan's guards have theirs "drugged" by Lady Macbeth, while in *The Merry Wives of Windsor*, Mistress Quickly promises to make Jack Rugby a posset "soon at night, in faith, at the latter end of a sea-coal fire." Yet posset could also be a fashionable drink served with ceremony: Queen Mary I and her husband, Philip II, received an elaborate crystal posset serving set as a betrothal gift in 1554.

The posset was effectively obsolete by 1800 and, unlike many other such drinks, has not been successfully revived by modern mixologists.

See also WINES, FORTIFIED.

Ellis, William. *The Country Housewife's Family Companion*. London: James Hodges and B. Collins, 1750.
Macdonell, Anne, ed. *The Closet of Sir Kenelm Digby Knight Opened*. London: Philip Lee Warner, 1910.
Pennell, Elizabeth Robins. *My Cookery Book*. New York: Houghton Mifflin, 1903.

William Tipper

potatoes (*Solanum tuberosum*) are edible tubers and the world's fourth-largest field crop (following maize, wheat, and rice). In distillation, potatoes are used mainly in the production of vodka and aquavit, though only a small percentage of these spirits are produced from potatoes; most vodka and aquavit is made from grain.

Because potatoes contain starch and not sugar, distillers must use either enzymes or malted grain (typically barley) to convert the starch into sugar for fermentation. The mash of potatoes, barley (or enzymes), and water is then strained out. Yeast is added to the liquid, which then ferments. The fermented liquid is then distilled.

Historically, vodka was first produced from grain. The potato, a South American crop, reached Europe no earlier than the mid-1500s, and vodka production predated that period. Potatoes became the ingredient of choice in the late 1700s, when the price of potatoes was far lower than the price of grain.

Potato spirit from Germany was used to stretch out cognac stocks during the phylloxera crisis of the late 1800s, which did nothing to help its reputation. There are, however, still a few well-regarded brands of vodka made from potatoes, chiefly from Poland (e.g., Chopin and Luksusowa), but also from Sweden (Karlsson's) and parts of the United States (Woody Creek and Boyd & Blair).

English, Camper. "When Vodka Was Made from Potatoes." Alcademics, September 18, 2014. http://www.alcademics.com/2014/09/when-vodka-was-made-from-potatoes.html (accessed March 8, 2021).

Michael Dietsch

pour spout, or "speed pourer," is commonly employed in bars to facilitate the pouring of frequently used spirits and other drink ingredients. Fitted snugly into the neck of a bottle, a pour spout allows for a steady, predictable flow of liquid when the bottle is upended, which is particularly helpful when free pouring. See FREE POURING. Typical pour spouts are made of stainless steel with a rubber seal (originally, in the late nineteenth century, the seal was cork) or, alternatively, entirely of plastic. Some come equipped with a flap or a screen to keep out insects and debris. A specialized type of spout known as a ball pourer utilizes a floating ball bearing to automatically cut off the flow of liquid after a desired amount has been poured.

Farrow & Jackson Ltd. *The Centenary Catalogue 1898*, facsimile ed. Shepton Beauchamp, UK: Richard Dennis, 1997.

Shelley, Brie. "What's the Best Type of Pour Spout?" BevSpot. https://bevspot.com/whats-the-best-type-of-pour-spout/ (accessed March 8, 2021).

David Mahoney

Pousse Café is an after-dinner drink made with colored cordials and liqueurs poured one atop another in multicolored layers. See LAYER. Bartenders typically build the layers by pouring each ingredient carefully over the back of an inverted bar spoon so that each ingredient settles lightly on top of the one beneath it, creating a layer no thicker than a pencil. Those layers are kept separate by the differing specific gravities of each ingredient, so the heaviest liquid is added first, the next heaviest second, and so on, with the creams and liqueurs, which are denser due to their sugars, typically being added before the spirits.

Originally *pousse café*—literally, in French, "push coffee"—meant simply liqueurs or spirits served after dinner; that is, a drink that pushed or chased the coffee course, a usage that dates back to at least the late eighteenth century in Paris (it is sometimes found as *chasse café*). The term became popular in the United States in the 1850s, particularly in New Orleans and New York City. It is unclear, however, when it began to denote a compound, layered drink. There seems to have been an intermediate stage when it applied to a drink formed of cordials mixed together. It is possible that this shift was influenced by the large number of German immigrants who had begun to enter the bartending profession, as Germany had a long tradition of layering liqueurs.

Jerry Thomas's pioneering *How to Mix Drinks* was published in 1862, just as the shift was underway, and includes recipes for a compound Pousse Café from Paris, plus one from Joseph Santini of New Orleans (1818–1874) and one from François Faivre (1819–?), who ran a saloon on William Street in New York, none of them explicitly described as layered drinks. Thomas does however include a similar "Pousse l'Amour" with an accompanying diagram showing

that it is indeed layered. (Begin with a small wine glass half-filled with maraschino, add the yolk of an egg, surround it with vanilla cordial, then top it with a dash of cognac.) See THOMAS, JEREMIAH P. "JERRY".

In France, *pousse café* remained a more generic term for an after-dinner drink as late as 1889; Albert Barrère defined it as "a small glass of brandy or liqueur drunk after taking coffee." In America, bartenders began to standardize layered versions similar to Thomas's recipes, which were repeated in numerous bartender manuals in the latter half of the nineteenth century. The ingredients in these recipes remain relatively standard, and there were typically three to six colorful layers composed of some combination of maraschino, Chartreuse (either yellow or green), kümmel, curaçao, raspberry syrup, Bénédictine, and brandy. Some instructions call for flaming the top layer of brandy.

In the early twentieth century, the Pousse Café took on more variations, colors, and layers, with six- and seven-layer concoctions becoming par for the course, although one hears of them with as many as eleven and fourteen, constructed as showpieces for the bartender's steady hand. Where nineteenth-century guides call for a small wine glass to be used, by 1903 *Daly's Bartender's Encyclopedia* instructs one to use what was fast becoming a standard piece of barware, a "Pousse Café glass" (a small, tightly flared, stemmed glass of about 45 ml capacity).

Prohibition largely halted the enjoyment of the Pousse Café, but after Repeal it resumed its place as a mainstay of the American bar. Charles Baker included "these pretty rainbow-hued drinks" in his *Gentleman's Companion* (1939), noting that a proper Pousse Café should have seven, five, or three different colored layers. See BAKER, CHARLES HENRY, JR. Additional liqueurs such as crème de violette, crème de menthe, and crème de cacao started being incorporated into a broadening number of variations, including several "angel"-themed versions like the Angel's Kiss (crème de cacao, crème Yvette, prunelle, and sweet cream) and the Angel's Tit (crème de cacao, maraschino, and sweet cream). See CRÈME DE CACAO; CRÈME DE MENTHE; and CRÈME DE VIOLETTE.

In the decades following World War II, the Pousse Café began a slow slide into obscurity. In 1972, a correspondent to Amy Vanderbilt's etiquette column inquired, "I remember when bars used to serve a fascinating drink called a Pousse-cafe. . . . You never see them any more. What happened?" In her response, Vanderbilt quoted the proprietor of New York's Le Mistral, who observed, "Today these drinks are being shaken before being served either straight or over the rocks in an Old Fashioned glass." See OLD-FASHIONED COCKTAIL. The classic Pousse Café was still honored in New Orleans, though, where bartender Nick Castro-giovannoni (1893–1979) of Nick's Big Train Bar enjoyed local fame for making dozens nightly and achieving as many as thirty-four layers.

The legacy of the Pousse Café lives on in layered shots like the B-52, composed of Kahlúa, Bailey's Irish Cream, and Grand Marnier, but the ornate multicolored rainbows are now largely a relic of an earlier time. See KAHLÚA and GRAND MARNIER. "If you want to stump your favorite bartender," the *Washington Evening Star* advised in 1980, "ask him or her to make a pousse cafe. . . . It is unlikely he or she has made a Pousse Café in a long time, if ever." Although there are exceptions—the Anvil Bar, in Houston, Texas, serves some thirty Pousse Cafés a week—the drink has not been embraced by the modern cocktail revival, whether because, as G. Selmer Fougner observed in 1940, "no one has ever pretended that the Pousse Café is ever consumed for its palatability; the drink owes its success only to its appeal to the eye," or because it is difficult to recreate classic examples due to the change in specific gravities of various ingredients over the decades.

Sample recipe: slowly pour 8 ml crème de cassis into a 2- or 3-ounce Pousse Café glass, then insert a barspoon into the glass with the convex part of the spoon's bowl facing upward and the tip touching one side of the glass just above the level of the liquid. Add, in the following order, 8 ml each crème de menthe (Get), Campari, blue curaçao (Senior), Galliano, cognac (40 percent ABV), green Chartreuse, white overproof rum (Wray & Nephew), and Centerba cordial (70 percent ABV), pouring each additional ingredient slowly and steadily over the back of the spoon so that each flows down the side of the glass and settles gently on the layer beneath. Note that due to variations in specific gravities of the ingredients, each Pousse Café recipe must be tested. Gravities may be lightened with vodka.

See also CORDIALS and LIQUEURS.

Barrère, Albert. *Argot and Slang: A New French and English Dictionary*. London: Chuswick, 1887.

"Famed Mixologist 'Mr. Nick' Is Dead." *New Orleans Times-Picayune*, November 8, 1979, 20.

Fougner, G. Selmer. "Along the Wine Trail." *New York Sun*, August 3, 1940, 6.

Frechette, Chloe. "Who Orders a Pousse Café, Anyway?" *Punch*, May 31, 2016, https://punchdrink.com/articles/who-orders-a-pousse-cafe-anyway/ (accessed March 8, 2021).

Hearn, Lafcadio. *La cuisine creole*, 2nd ed. New Orleans: F. F. Hansell & Bro., 1885.

Robert F. Moss

Presbyterian, also known as a Press, is a more Calvinist approach to the Mamie Taylor, made with scotch whisky, ginger ale, and sometimes club soda, without the luxury of lime juice. The Vodka Press is a modern devolution often found in nightclubs. See also GINGER ALE AND GINGER BEER; HIGHBALL; MAMIE TAYLOR; and WHISKY, SCOTCH.

pressure infusion is a process for rapidly infusing flavors from a solid into a liquid and is one of several techniques that can be used to introduce new flavors into a spirit. In pressure infusion, ingredients are placed into a sealed container that is pressurized using a gas—usually nitrogen or nitrous oxide—with low solubility in the liquid at atmospheric pressure. The increased pressure causes the gas to dissolve into the liquid and forces the liquid into the solid material. When the container is subsequently decompressed and the gas quickly comes out of solution, the expanding bubbles rupture the cells of the solid material, and a rapid infusion into the liquid is obtained. This technique can result in a near-instantaneous infusion in contrast to traditional methods that might require multiple hours or weeks, and thus can be particularly useful in preserving "bright" herbaceous and "green" flavors that ordinarily would become dull or muddy over the course of a lengthy traditional infusion. See INFUSION.

Notwithstanding these advantages, pressure infusion is generally used more in bars or at home than for industrial spirits production. While it is fast and thus useful for making *à la minute* the sorts of infusions that are common in the more advanced, technically oriented modern bars, compared to long-term infusion techniques, it is less efficient at extracting flavor components, and larger quantities of the solid ingredient are required to achieve results of comparable intensity. In addition, some flavor components are less readily extracted via pressure infusion, which may result in different flavor characteristics than those produced by more traditional methods.

See also COCKTAIL RENAISSANCE and MOLECULAR MIXOLOGY.

Arnold, Dave. *Liquid Intelligence*. New York: Norton, 2014.

Simpson, Richard J. "Disruption of Cultured Cells by Nitrogen Cavitation." *Cold Spring Harbor Protocols*, 2010.

Samuel Lloyd Kinsey

Prince of Wales cocktail, like Albert Edward (1841–1910), the man who bore the title for sixty years as Victoria's son, exemplifies the conspicuous consumption of the Gilded Age. There are several very different recipes bearing this name, some for punch and some for individual cocktails, but they all have refined and expensive ingredients in common. One nearly lost recipe, however, best demonstrates how a gentleman at the top of sporting society rolled in those champagne days. It is found in a July 1887 item in the *London Evening Telegraph*, describing the drink the prince concocted for the royal patrons of "The Prince of Wales' Own Room" at the London American Exhibition: "rye whisky, powdered sugar, ice, a small piece of pine apple, some Angostura bitters, a little lemon peel, a few drops of Maraschino, and a dash of champagne." This "short drink" blends ingredients from around the world, including the then-extraordinarily-costly pineapple, and requires a freshly opened bottle of champagne, of which perhaps an ounce will be needed per drink (the "dash" here was an unusually flexible measure). As a demonstration of fiscal power, it excels. Fortunately— as the cocktail world rediscovered when David Wondrich spotted the recipe above and began spreading the word in his 2007 book *Imbibe!*—it is also extraordinarily delicious.

It is not, however, the only Prince of Wales cocktail: there was also a French one, based on Madeira; a German one that was merely a watered-down Champagne Cocktail; an English version (a Sidecar

topped off with champagne); and one from Monte Carlo with gin, pineapple juice, and egg white. The prince's is still the best.

Recipe: Stir 5 ml sugar with a dash of Angostura bitters and 3 ml water in a mixing glass until it has dissolved. Add 45 ml rye whisky, 2 ml maraschino, and a small square of pineapple. Fill two-thirds of the glass with crushed ice and shake to crush the pineapple. Strain into a chilled cocktail glass and add 30 ml champagne and a lemon twist.

"A 'Short Drink.' " *London Evening Telegraph*, July 21st, 1887, 2.

Fouquet, Louis. *Bariana*. Paris: Emile Duvoye, 1896.

Seutter, Carl A. *Der mixologist*. Leipzig: P. M. Blühers Verlag, 1909.

Wondrich, David. *Imbibe!*, rev. ed. New York: Perigee, 2015.

Dinah Sanders

Prohibition and Temperance in America. Organized efforts to stop or restrain the consumption of alcohol have existed in the United States for as long as its consumption has been part of American life. These movements, coming in successive waves from the late eighteenth century into the early twentieth century, dedicated themselves to regulating the sale of alcohol, combating alcohol abuse, and addressing the social and medical problems stemming from it. They drew support from a surprising cross section of society, but relied most heavily on evangelical Christians and women as their most steadfast supporters. At their most moderate, they advocated voluntary abstinence from drinking, especially distilled spirits; at their most extreme, they called for the complete prohibition of all alcoholic beverages, a goal ultimately attained in 1920 when the United States adopted Prohibition.

The most notable person in the early American temperance movement was undoubtedly Dr. Benjamin Rush (1746–1813), the Philadelphia-based physician and first surgeon general of the United States. A leading figure in the "American Enlightenment," Rush expressed concern about the growing influence of "ardent spirits" in the newly independent United States. Consumption of alcohol, Rush argued, promoted crime, fostered diseases of the stomach, liver, and nerves, and ultimately led to madness and death. His 1790 treatise, *An Inquiry into the Effects of Spirituous Liquors on the Human Body and the Mind*, warned, "A people corrupted with strong drink cannot long be a free people." (As many early temperance advocates did, Rush drew a distinction between distilled spirits and beer, cider, and wine, which he believed could be consumed in moderation.) Rush's warnings fostered calls for the taxation of distilled spirits and the regulation of taverns in the post-Revolutionary period. His "Moral and Physical Thermometer of Intemperance," which outlined the deleterious effects of alcohol on the American citizen, became one of the most widely reproduced pieces of temperance propaganda in the early republic.

The emergence in the early nineteenth century of the evangelical revival known as the Second Great Awakening gave temperance advocates a new boost. As the young nation expanded, alcohol in all forms became a mainstay of American life. (In 1810, one historian estimates, Americans consumed 21 million gallons of absolute alcohol, suggesting a per capita consumption of 7 gallons a year.) Alcoholism reached "epidemic" proportions, giving the temperance movement a greater sense of urgency. Filled with religious conviction and the desire to improve society, temperance activists formed new associations to promote abstinence from alcohol. Among the most well known was the American Society for the Promotion of Temperance, founded in Boston in 1826 by the minister Lyman Beecher. Later known simply as the American Temperance Society (ATS), the organization grew to include eight thousand local chapters and 1.5 million members nationally by 1836.

The ATS used lectures and "temperance plays," published temperance literature, and promoted voluntary abstinence to curb the growing appetite for alcohol in the United States. It encouraged followers to "take the pledge" by publicly declaring their intent to abstain from alcohol. (One such pledge read "We, the undersigned do hereby promise to abstain from all intoxicating drinks, and in all suitable ways to discountenance their use.") Citizens would line up to sign pledge books; those who pledged total abstinence from alcohol by writing a T next to their name signifying "total abstinence" became known as teetotalers; others simply swore off distilled spirits. Through these efforts, the ATS became the most prominent temperance organization of the period,

but other temperance groups reflected the cause's appeal to a diverse range of Americans. The Knights of Father Matthew, started by Irish Catholics and named after Ireland's great temperance crusader, claimed half a million pledges; the International Order of Good Templars distinguished itself by its willingness to admit women and African Americans. The Washingtonians, begun by a group of reformed "drunkards" in Baltimore in 1840, preached sobriety and guided drinkers to abstinence through mutual support. Within a decade, the group grew 600,000 strong.

Before the outbreak of the Civil War, temperance advocates began shifting their emphasis from abstinence to the need for legislative reform. The greatest milestone here was the passage of the landmark Maine Liquor Law of 1851. Engineered by Neal Dow (1804–1897), the mayor of Portland and an adamant temperance advocate, Maine adopted a complete prohibition of the sale of all alcoholic beverages. Soon, eleven other states passed similar laws (though several were struck down as unconstitutional). As the 1850s came to a close, however, the nation's focus shifted to the issues of slavery, secession, and the Civil War. The Maine Law was repealed in 1856, and the temperance movement lost its hold.

During the Gilded Age (1870–1900), the temperance movement experienced a new resurgence with the rise of the Prohibition Party, the Woman's Christian Temperance Union, and the Anti-Saloon League. Each of these organizations embodied a key characteristic of the temperance activism of the era. The Prohibition Party, founded in 1869, pushed the movement further into the political arena. It fielded candidates in every presidential election after 1872 and consistently threatened to play the spoiler in local elections by mobilizing "dry" voters. Though it had no ambition (or chance) to win the presidency, it kept Prohibition on the national political agenda. (The party also gave a prominent place to women, allowing them to serve as delegates when no other political party did.)

The Woman's Christian Temperance Union (WCTU), founded in Ohio in 1873, emerged from the period as the most well-known temperance organization in American history. While the Prohibition Party worked in the realm of politics, the WCTU took a broader approach to reform. Under the dynamic leadership of Frances Willard (1839–1898), the WCTU advocated not only for prohibition but for also women's suffrage, child labor laws, prison reform, public health laws, and a host of moral and social reform causes. Willard's motto, "Do Everything," reflected both the broad agenda of the WCTU and its methods, as members engaged in lobbying, circulating petitions, publishing, and educational activities to promote temperance. At its peak, the WCTU claimed over 300,000 members, but its influence far exceeded its numerical strength. It gave American women a visible platform in politics, reached millions of Americans through its outreach efforts, and made temperance a key political issue of the era.

Though less well known than the WCTU, the Anti-Saloon League (ASL), founded in 1893, would lead the final push for an amendment to ban the alcohol trade in the United States permanently. Forgoing the WCTU's broad-based approach, the ASL functioned as a lobbying organization, using lawyers and public relations experts to promote local, state, and federal legislation to outlaw the sale of alcohol and the saloon. Its political tactics were ruthless and effective, and it took pride in its well-organized and well-funded political campaigns, which systematically passed "dry" laws and removed "wet" politicians from office.

Together, the WCTU and ASL cast the American alcohol industry as the problem, not the drinker. In this way, the distilling and brewing industries, the saloon trade, and the network of "wet" officials who supported them became the main targets of a coordinated dry campaign that would ultimately result in Prohibition. In the context of the Progressive Era, when reformers fought corruption and monopolies in the meat, pharmaceutical, and oil industries, the distilling and brewing industries made fitting targets. The Distilling Company of America, for example, controlled 90 percent of American distilleries at the turn of the twentieth century; the U. Brewer's Association and the National Wholesale Liquor Dealers Association flooded American politics with money to protect their interests. Even Americans who doubted the wisdom of Prohibition had good reason to express concern about the power and influence of these industries.

A half century of temperance activism by the WCTU and ASL finally culminated in the ratification of the Eighteenth Amendment in 1919, which banned the manufacture, sale, and transportation

of alcoholic beverages. However, the temperance movement owed its final success more to the US entry into World War I than anything else. Americans were swayed by the argument that the nation should sacrifice drinking for the sake of the war effort. This effectively silenced prohibition's opponents, especially German American brewers, and gave Americans new reasons to support Prohibition when they might have opposed it under different circumstances.

When Prohibition took effect in January 1920, it immediately proved unenforceable. The United States was not equipped to impose a complete ban on alcohol, and enforcement efforts fell short due to chronic underfunding and a poorly administered Bureau of Prohibition. As the "noble experiment" faltered, temperance advocates came to be caricatured by a society that quickly decided that Prohibition had been an unrealistic goal and a mistake.

A final irony is found in the arguments that emerged for the repeal of Prohibition in the late 1920s. In response to the excesses of the era, the Women's Organization for Prohibition Reform (WONPR) called for "true temperance" in the United States. Noting that prohibition had only produced crime, public drunkenness, and increased deaths from alcoholism, it called for the repeal of Prohibition in order to end excessive drinking and to protect children from the pervasive presence of alcohol. Their call was similar to the one that had rallied Americans to temperance in the first place.

The repeal of Prohibition in 1933 brought an end to most temperance activism in the United States. After Repeal, temperance organizations failed to attract any sizable support, and their ideology gave way to new thinking about alcohol abuse as a medical and therapeutic issue. Alcoholics Anonymous, founded in 1935, presented a new way of treating problem drinking through group support. (The approach was similar to the one espoused by the Washingtonians a century earlier.) With temperance ideology effectively a relic of the past, since the 1930s, efforts to regulate alcohol have relied primarily on the regulation of alcohol sales, establishing a legal drinking age, drunk driving laws, and taxation.

Blocker, Jack S. *American Temperance Movements: Cycles of Reform*. Boston: Twayne, 1989.

Bordin, Ruth. *Woman and Temperance: The Quest for Power and Liberty, 1873–1900*. Philadelphia: Temple University Press, 1981.

Kerr, K. Austin. *Organized for Prohibition: A New History of the Anti-Saloon League*. New York: Oxford University Press, 1985.

Rorabaugh, W. J. *The Alcoholic Republic: An American Tradition*. New York: Oxford University Press, 1981.

Timberlake, James H. *Prohibition and the Progressive Movement, 1900–1920*. Cambridge, MA: Harvard University Press, 1983.

Michael A. Lerner

proof, in modern usage, is the amount of pure alcohol in a spirit or other alcoholic beverage, stated as a percentage of the total volume of that beverage; when written, that percentage is usually followed by the abbreviation ABV, for "alcohol by volume."

Originally, however, proof was a threshold, a strength at or above which a spirit was acceptable for certain uses. From that, it evolved into a benchmark figure, usually 50 percent alcohol, with the strengths of spirits expressed as a percentage of or other relation to that figure, as in "80 proof," for 80 percent of proof (or 40 percent alcohol), or "10 (degrees) under proof" (also 40 percent alcohol). It was a short step from there to discarding the benchmark strength and simply expressing the strength or "proof" of a spirit as its percentage of alcohol.

Before the invention of the hydrometer, it was impossible to determine the exact strength of a distilled spirit. See HYDROMETER. The earliest methods of which we have record date back to the seventeenth century, with "proof spirit" being first mentioned in 1639. Some tests were simple, binary ones: when you rubbed the spirit between your hands, either it all evaporated or it didn't; when you dipped a piece of paper in it, either the moisture spread (a sign of weak spirit) or it didn't; if you soaked a piece of cloth or a spoonful of gunpowder with it, either it burned or it didn't. Others required more interpretation: if you ignited the spirit and measured how much was left when the flame went out, you would have a rough measure of strength. Or you could raise bubbles in it, whether by blowing into it with a reed or shaking it in a glass vial. The size and duration of the "bead"—the cap of bubbles—gave a fairly good idea of the strength. This last method, in the hands of an experienced user, can yield surprisingly accurate results, within a fairly narrow band of possible proofs (beyond those the bubbles will not properly form). Unfortunately, it is only reliable with spirits straight off the still, as it is easily tricked by adulterants. Nonetheless, this writer has witnessed a veteran *palenquero* at Santa Maria Albarradas in Oaxaca come within a degree or two of hydrometer proof with it.

In his 1690 *Medicina hydrostatica*, Robert Boyle suggested a method of measuring the alcoholic contents of liquids based on their density. This led to a good deal of experimentation with hydrometers, particularly in England, where the excise system demanded a more accurate way of measuring the strength of spirits. In 1762, British Parliament did something revolutionary and established a proof for alcohol: henceforward, proof spirit would have a specific gravity of 0.916, measured at 60° F (the different densities of alcohol and water mean that the ratio between their volumes changes with the temperature of their solution). This translates to 50 percent alcohol, but measured not by volume but by weight (alcohol being lighter than water, that works out to 57 percent ABV). It also adopted the hydrometer John Clarke had been working on since the 1720s to measure where a spirit stood in respect to this proof.

Clarke's device was crude. We need not go into all the details here, but one aspect has stuck with us to this day. It showed its results as proportions: for overproof spirits, the number was how many gallons of the spirit one gallon of water would reduce to proof (the lower the number the stronger the spirit); for underproof ones, it was how many gallons of the spirit would resolve up to proof if you could extract one gallon of water (here, the higher the number, the stronger the spirit). See OVERPROOF. Some of these proportions are still with us, such as the "one in six" underproof, which imported brandy, rum, and arrack could not legally sink below nor domestic gin rise above. Translated into modern proof, that is 47.4 percent ABV, a strength at which a number of London dry gins are still bottled.

Clarke's system was, of course, perfectly mad, and the British government commissioned Charles Blagden and George Gilpin to find a better way. Their detailed findings, which pointed toward a simple ABV-based system, were published in 1794, but the government did not accept them. Instead, in 1818 it adopted a hydrometer by Bartholomew

Sikes (1731–1803), which measured alcohol strictly by weight; at least it had a straight numeric scale. Rather than rejigger all the various proofs enshrined in law, the law simply translated those into the new scale. Thus one in six became "17 degrees under proof," or 41.5 percent alcohol (83 percent of 50 percent). The Sikes system lasted in the United Kingdom and its Commonwealth until 1980.

Meanwhile, other countries developed their own systems of proof. In 1790, the United States adopted a system that measured alcohol also by weight but charged duties based on ranges, rather than exact figures: thus, for example, "first proof" was anything 20 percent or more below proof (50 percent ABV), and "fourth proof" was anything between proof and 20 percent over proof. This, too, was long considered unsatisfactory but ground on with small modifications until 1850, when it was replaced by the system the German Johann Georg Tralles developed based on the calculations of Blagden and Gilpin. This measured alcohol by volume, expressed in percentage of proof (50 percent ABV); thus, an 80-proof spirit was actually 80 percent of 50 percent, or 40 percent ABV. By then, France had adopted an even simpler alcohol-by-volume system, developed by Joseph Louis Gay-Lussac, which dispensed with the idea of a reference proof entirely; the spirit was simply labeled with its percentage of alcohol (this was sometimes stated as a number followed by "GL"). This has become the global standard; the United States, one of the last to adopt it, finally capitulated in 1988. It is now defined as the number of milliliters of pure ethanol contained in 100 ml of liquid, tested at 20° C. It is measured by weighing the liquid and then indexing the weight on a standard chart of densities. (Note that for this to work, the spirit must not be sweetened, which affects its density and "obscures" some of the alcohol contained in it.)

Spirits are marketed at a wide range of proofs—indeed, the same spirit can be sold at different proofs in different countries. Some of these are determined strictly by law: for example, straight spirits in the United States cannot be sold below 40 percent ABV, so a great many are bottled at that proof; where the minimum is 37 percent, many of them will be found at that strength. Others follow tradition: some rums and gins are bottled at 57 percent ABV, which is the old British "proof" (50 percent ABW; some of these are labeled as "navy strength," although in fact the

Royal Navy bought its sprits at 5.5 degrees under proof, or 54.5 percent ABV). See NAVY-STRENGTH. Similarly, spirits at 43 percent ABV and 63 percent ABV are at 75 percent and 110 percent of that British proof, respectively. As another artifact of the old Sikes system, spirits are generally not labeled "overproof" unless they are over 57 percent.

Other spirits have their proofs set for reasons of taste or marketing. The same spirit, diluted to different proofs, can taste subtly, and sometimes not so subtly, different at each one, as different esters are emphasized. Conversely, in the modern cocktail world, higher proofs are often preferred, as they better resist the dilution that is part of drink mixing, so many new spirits are launched at 45–55 percent ABV. Spirits labeled at "cask strength," unless they are also single-barrel, are bottled at an artificial composite proof that suggests the "normal" barrel strength for their category.

Déjean, Antoine. *Traité raisoné de la distillation.* Paris: 1753.

[De Mayerne, Theodore]. *The Distiller of London.* London: 1639.

McCulloh, R. S. *Report . . . on Hydrometers.* Washington, DC: US Department of the Treasury, 1845.

Smith, George. *A Compleat Body of Distilling,* 2nd ed. London: 1731.

Tate, Francis G. H. *Alcolometry.* London: HM Stationery Office, 1930.

David Wondrich

A **proof gallon**, also called a "tax gallon," is the measurable unit used for determining taxation, but the calculation varies per country. A proof gallon is one US gallon at 50 percent alcohol by volume. Thus a gallon of 151-proof rum is 1.51 proof gallons, while a gallon of, say, Bénédictine, at 40 percent ABV, is 0.8 proof gallons. For the United Kingdom and Canada, a proof gallon was formerly an imperial gallon of 4546 cm³ (277.4 cubic inches) at 50 percent alcohol by weight, or 57.1 percent alcohol by volume. At present, however, taxation in those countries is "per liter of absolute alcohol"—in other words, on just the alcohol contained in the beverage.

In 2017, the US excise tax was $13.50 per proof gallon.

See also EXCISE, TAXES, AND DISTILLATION; and PROOF.

John Wiley and Sons. *Kirk-Othmer Food and Feed Technology*. Hoboken, NJ: Wiley, 2008.

Tax and Trade Bureau FAQs on Proof Gallons. https://www.ttb.gov/images/forms_tutorials/f511040/faq_instructions.html (accessed March 8, 2021).

Fred Minnick

prunelle is the French word for the sloe berry, the fruit of the blackthorn bush (*Prunus spinosa*), traditionally collected by hand. The sloes are skinned and dried before producers macerate the core of the fruit in neutral spirits or grape brandy for as long as a year and then sweeten and age the spirit, which is surprisingly almond-like in aroma and flavor. A particular specialty of Burgundy, where many brands of liqueur prunelle de Bourgogne are produced, it is usually served neat in a frosted glass or as a substitute for cassis in a Kir or Kir Royale.

See also KIR.

Jack Robertiello

prune wine was a common additive used by nineteenth-century rectifiers to tame the rawness of young whisky and other callow spirits. See also RECTIFICATION AND RECTIFIER (OCCUPATION).

The **puff** is an archaic and seldom-spotted family of mixed drinks wherein a spirit is mixed with milk or cream, lengthened with soda water, and served on ice. Its first known appearance in print was at the end of 1882, when a bartender described it in the pages of the *New York Sun* as "a seductive, effervescent, creamy sort of throat-cooler, made out of gin, seltzer water, milk, and sugar. You puff it by shaking it up." By 1895 it had made it into cocktails books but either minus the sugar, as in George Kaeppler's iconic *Modern American Drinks*, or with added egg white, as in Herbert Green's *Mixed Drinks*.

The puff's exact origin is not known, but it is one of a large class of drinks that appeared in the 1880s and were influenced by soda-fountain drinks; among the others are the Gin Fizz, the Silver Gin Fizz, the Cream Puff (a rum-based drink), and even the redoubtable Ramos Gin Fizz. See FIZZ and RAMOS GIN FIZZ.

The earliest versions of the puff all appear to be based on gin (when specified, it is the English Old Tom version), but whisky and brandy versions appear by 1889, although they are at first rare. By the early twentieth century, however, the puff had spread internationally, being mentioned in Continental bartending books such as the German *Lexicon der getränke*, by Hans Schönfeld and John Leybold (1913), and the Swiss *Barkeeper's Golden Book*, by Otto Blunier (1935). There, it had transmogrified into a true family with rum, brandy, and whisky versions mentioned.

Unfortunately for the puff, the modern mixology revival has generally spurned cream- and milk-based drinks, so this family has declined and these days is infrequently spotted and even less frequently appreciated. However, recently versions of the drink have reappeared in the United States under the new name "lifts," popularized by the San Francisco bartender Jennifer Colliau.

"Delicatessen." *Aspen (CO) Evening Chronicle*, December 11, 1889, 2.

"Kinnickabine Bake." *New York Sun*, November 19, 1882, 3.

Willett, Andrew. *Elemental Mixology*. Portland, OR: Lulu.com, 2011.

Angus Winchester

punch, a mixture of spirits, citrus juice, sugar, and water, often with the addition of spices, is the foundational drink of modern mixology and the first mixed drink based on spirits to gain global popularity. Its descendants—including the Daiquiri, the Cosmopolitan, and the Margarita—remain at the peak of popularity today. And yet punch's origins cannot be established with any precision or certainty.

The first mention of punch by name was found well over a century ago in the papers of the English East India Company, which was established in 1600, began trading with India the next year, and maintained trading posts there from 1614. In a 1632 letter, one of the company's men at arms writes one to of its merchants who was in the small trading post of Petapoli on India's southeast coast, about to sail up to Bengal as part of the company's first trade mission to that rich province of the Mughal Empire. "I hop you will keep good house," the soldier wrote,

Thomas Rowlandson's *The Pretty Barr Maid*, 1795. The barkeeper squeezes lemons while the besotted gent with the black hat holds her sugar tongs at the ready. Wondrich Collection.

"and drincke punch by no allowanc." Now, "by no allowanc" here can mean either "not at all" or "not limited by ration." Either meaning suggests that the English found this "punch" strongly alluring. But what was it, and where did it come from?

The first question was answered in 1638, by Johan Albrecht de Mandelslo, a young German adventurer who found the British in Surat, on the Arabian Sea north of Mumbai, drinking "Palepuntz" (his phonetic rendering of "bowl o' punch"), which he defined as "a kind of drink consisting of aqua vitae, rose-water, juice of citrons and sugar." This is suspiciously like the English drink George Gascoine had detailed in 1576, "wine [with] . . . Sugar, Limons and sundry sortes of Spices . . . drowned therein," with the water and the aqua vitae—in this case, local palm arrack—uniting to play the role of the wine. But it is even more like the drink that the English merchant Peter Mundy, who was in Surat from 1628 to 1630, noted was "sometimes used" by the English traders there. This was "a Composition of Racke [i.e., arrack], water, sugar, and Juice of Lymes."

Mundy gives the name of this composition not as punch but as "Charebockhra," which is a rendering of the Hindi *chaar bakhra*, or "four shares." Mundy's little-known passage dovetails with the a much better known one from another English traveler to India, John Fryer, who in 1676 wrote home about the "enervating Liquor called *Paunch*" he found the

English drinking there. The name, he explained, was "*Indostan* for Five, from Five Ingredients" (the fifth ingredient was spices, whether Mandelslo's rose-water or the more common nutmeg, mace, cloves, or cinnamon). See SPICES (FOR PUNCH). Along with Mundy's testimony, this strongly suggests that punch was an Indian drink. But unfortunately nothing yet has been found to corroborate that in Indian literature: we know of mixtures of citrus, sugar, and water and mixtures of spirits and water or spirits and wine, but not the full panoply. And "punch" is also an English word, used for something squat and round like the bowls in which punch was served (e.g., the gilded "paunche pot" recorded in an English will from 1600). It is an easy step from the "punch" in "punch bowl" describing its form to describing its function. Until further evidence turns up, the only thing we can say with certainty is that punch was a drink that the English made in India with local ingredients.

It was most assuredly the English who brought punch to the rest of the world, though. Early on, it was adopted by sailors, who could get the citrus at any port of call in the tropics or Mediterranean. The sugar and spirits would keep well even on the longest voyage, unlike beer or even wine, and they always had the water necessary for mixing it (if they didn't, not being able to make punch was the least of their problems). By the 1660s, punch was the staple drink of the Caribbean and North America and had even colonized the British Isles, where it would quickly become the recreational drink of choice, and had begun seeping into the other countries of Europe and South America. The long century and a half between the 1670s and the 1840s was the great age of punch, when a shared bowl of punch of some sort—cold in the summer, hot or even flaming in the winter—was the drink of choice for an impressive chunk of the world. See MIXOLOGY, THE HISTORY OF; ARRACK PUNCH; COBBLER'S PUNCH, FEUERZANGENBOWLE; FISH HOUSE PUNCH; GARRICK CLUB PUNCH; PUNCH BOWLS AND PUNCH PARAPHERNALIA; and SWEDISH PUNCH.

By the middle of the nineteenth century, a great deal had been learned about making punch even more seductive than it already was. Tricks such as the use of "oleo-saccharum" (the oil from citrus peels extracted into sugar) and a premixed "shrub" (citrus and sugar) for depth of flavor and efficiency, of milk or even calf's-foot jelly for smoothness, of tea rather than water for spice, of still or sparkling (or even fortified) wine rather than water for potency (this was known as "Punch Royal"), and a dozen other little things turned a basic sailor's drink into an epicurean one. See OLEO-SACCHARUM and SHRUB. But at the same time the ritual of gathering around the flowing bowl was increasingly out of step with modern life. It was too time consuming and ultimately too intoxicating to sit around and see off a bowl of punch with one's companions, be they the Society of Steaks or the Ladies' Punch Club (to name a pair of London institutions). Punch became a treat for special occasions, trotted out to impress or intoxicate, but not an everyday drink. See CHATHAM ARTILLERY PUNCH.

As punch was made less and less often, that body of experience relating to its construction faded away and the drink became, for the most part, a slapdash assemblage of cheap ingredients geared to intoxicating the most people for the least money. Only in the 2010s did it get a serious second look, with books written about its history and mixologists—such as Nick Strangeway of London and Erick Castro of San Francisco—bringing it back, tricks and all, as an efficient way of getting a well-mixed drink into the hands of a crowd as quickly as possible. See COCKTAIL RENAISSANCE and STRANGEWAY, NICK.

See also ENGLAND and INDIA AND CENTRAL ASIA.

Recipe (Basic Brandy Punch): Peel 4 lemons in long spirals. Put the peels and 180 ml of sugar in a 1-liter jar, seal it, and let it sit overnight. To the resulting oleo-saccharum, add 180 ml strained lemon juice and shake until sugar has dissolved. Pour the contents of the jar, peels and all, into a 4-liter bowl over a 1-liter block of ice. Add 750 ml VSOP-grade cognac or Armagnac and 1 liter cold water. Stir well, grate nutmeg over the top, and ladle out in 90 ml servings. Makes 20+ servings.

Carnac, Richard, ed. *The Travels of Peter Mundy in Europe and Asia, 1608-1667*, vol. 2. Cambridge: Hakluyt Society, 1914.

[Cook, Richard]. *Oxford Night-Caps*. Oxford: 1827.

Turenne [pseud.]. *La véritable manière de faire le Punch*. Paris: 1866.

Wondrich, David. *Punch: The Delights and Dangers of the Flowing Bowl*. New York: Perigee, 2010.

David Wondrich

punch bowls and punch paraphernalia were historically part of the British ritual of punch drinking. A punch bowl is a hemispherical vessel in which punch is made and served. Beginning in the second quarter of the seventeenth century, punch bowls were made from a variety of materials, including glass, pewter, silver, and wood. But by far the most common punch bowls of the seventeenth and eighteenth centuries were ceramic, and these were principally made of British delftware, creamware, pearlware, porcelain, and various stonewares, as well as fine Chinese export porcelain. Inexpensive glass punch bowls became increasingly more common from 1800 until the Victorian era, when punch drinking declined. Punch bowls and the ladles that accompany them are still used today but have become dissociated from their historic context.

Traditional punch bowls came in several sizes, ranging from a half pint to a gallon. Large punch bowls typically measured from 25 to 30 cm in diameter, though some colossal communal bowls that were meant to be the centerpieces of elaborate punch parties were upwards of 50 cm in diameter and could contain over 80 l of punch. What made such large punch bowl potent status symbols was not only their size, material, and quality of workmanship but also the cost of the exotic ingredients mixed within them.

"Sneakers"—as they were called—were the small and commonplace punch bowls that were imbibed from by individuals or, in convivial settings, passed from man to man (or woman to woman—punch drinking observed no gender restrictions). These portable and personal-sized punch bowls were the mass-consumer versions of large, unwieldy, and high-end bowls. They were common at both plebeian and privileged gatherings throughout the Atlantic world and are often found in archaeological excavations of houses, drinking establishments, shipwrecks, and far-off campsites. No matter its size, the ubiquitous punch bowl with its intoxicating content was the magnetic and ritual focal point of early modern British masculine sociability at home; in taverns, social clubs, and guilds; and aboard ships.

Ceramic punch bowls were oftentimes vibrantly hand-painted on the exterior, displaying exotic Chinese porcelain–inspired themes and landscapes, stylized foliage, geometric designs, animals, and a vast array of other scenes. These colorful and eye-catching punch bowls decorated with such fashionable foreign motifs were potent metaphors of the far-reaching tentacles of the expanding mercantilist system of the British Empire.

Inscriptions were often written on the interior of ceramic punch bowls and these became visible as the bowl was emptied. These included pithy exhortations such as "Drink Fair / Dont Swear," calls to conviviality ("One Bowl More & then"), dedications or invitations to toast such as "Success to Trade," and patriotic slogans such as "Success to the British Arms." Punch bowls were also commissioned by individuals as testimonials of business friendships and to commemorate births, marriages, and important political events.

Punch drinking involved a sundry assemblage of paraphernalia. The alcoholic contents of larger bowls were ladled out into glass stemware and tumblers. Punch ladles could be made of silver, pewter, and wood and had deep bowls and long and slender upward-turning handles; these were usually made of whale baleen or wood, so that one could leave the ladle resting in a bowl of hot punch without burning the ladler's hand. Often these handles were twisted, for rubbing between the hands to stir the punch. More expensive ladles had hammered gold or silver coins set in the bottom, while some curios even had coconut-shell bowls, elaborately set in silver.

Circular silver or pewter punch strainers with long "ears" that rested on punch bowl rims were used to filter out the pulp and seeds of the requisite citrus fruit squeezed into them. Nutmeg graters, often made of silver or silver gilt, came in an assortment of sizes and were little pocketable boxes that were used to grate and store a nutmeg seed. See NUTMEG GRATER. Other paraphernalia that accompanied the punch ritual included sugar bowls and sugar dredgers, crushers, nippers and hatchets to cut sugar cones, knives to peel citrus fruit, decanters, wine funnels, bowls for cooling glasses in ice, and cut-glass punch or toddy lifters, a hollow bulb with a hole in the bottom and a long, hollow stem on top; one would sink the bulb in the punch, place one's finger over the hole in the stem, and lift out a serving of punch.

While punch bowls continued to be made through the twentieth century at all price levels, the cheap ones tended to be flimsy and the expensive ones frilly and impractical. Only in recent years has serious attention begun to be paid again to the paraphernalia of punch.

See also PUNCH.

Connell, Neville. "Punch Drinking and Its Accessories." *Journal of the Barbados Museum and Historical Society* 25, no. 1 (1957): 1–17.

Grigsby, Leslie. "'Drink Fair, Don't Swear': Winterthur's Punch Bowls and Punch Drinking in America." *Magazine Antiques* 161, no. 1 (2002): 176–183.

Harvey, Karen. "Ritual Encounters: Punch Parties and Masculinity in the Eighteenth Century." *Past and Present* 124, no. 1 (2012): 165–203.

Konrad A. Antczak

punsch, an ingredient in many pre-Prohibition cocktails, is an arrack-based Swedish and Finnish liqueur. See also ARRACK and SWEDISH PUNCH.

purl is an English drink of the seventeenth century made by infusing ale or, for Purl Royal, wine with wormwood and often other botanicals. See WORMWOOD and BOTANICAL. A form of simple digestive, it was often taken in the morning to combat hangovers. In the nineteenth century, the name was applied to warm ale stiffened with gin.

See also APERITIF AND DIGESTIVE.

Dave Wondrich

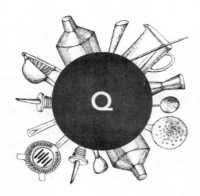

qu, pronounced similarly to the English "chew," is a compound of mashed grains containing molds, yeasts, bacteria, and other naturally occurring microorganisms that is used in the production of fermented Chinese foods and beverages. Qu has no ready equivalent in Western winemaking tradition, let alone the English language, but it is the single most important innovation in East Asian winemaking and the distillation that is derived from it.

Qu can be thought of as an all-in-one Chinese alcohol starter kit. Creation of Western grain alcohol relies on a two-step process of converting starches to sugars (saccharification) and then adding yeast to convert sugar to ethanol (fermentation). See SACCHARIFICATION and FERMENTATION. Qu allows Chinese winemakers to simplify the process to a single step: mixing qu directly with steamed grains kicks off simultaneous saccharification and fermentation, creating a fermented beverage known as *huangjiu* ("yellow wine"), or, in distilled form, *baijiu* ("white wine"; like most Western languages before the eighteenth century, Chinese uses "wine" to cover spirits as well). See BAIJIU.

To produce qu, moistened grains are mashed into a paste, which is then formed into a clump or pressed in a mold and allowed to incubate in a carefully manipulated environment—typically a dark, dank room. The process takes up to a month from start to finish and results in a solid grain mass, saturated with fungi, enzymes, and all manner of airborne microorganisms, which is then dried. Before qu is mixed with steamed grains to initiate fermentation, it is crushed into a fine powder.

Because each qu is essentially an ecosystem unto itself, no two qus are alike. The specific admixture of microorganisms that qu harvests from the air depends on geography and climate, so qu lends to Chinese winemaking something akin to the Western notion of terroir: even a slight difference in scenery can produce surprisingly unique results. See TERROIR.

Qu production has changed little over the years, but the full-scale industrialization of the Chinese alcohol industry in the twentieth century has introduced a few modern twists, the most important of which is the inoculation of grains. By taking samples of the previous batch of mature qu and adding it to the fresh qu during the production process, baijiu distillers are able to ensure greater consistency of flavor over time. As a result, qu recipes are among the most closely guarded trade secrets in the baijiu industry. Visitors to Chinese distilleries will seldom be allowed anywhere near the qu production facilities for fear that a sample of the meticulously cultivated culture might be replicated in a competitor's laboratory.

History

The earliest historical reference to qu comes from the *Book of Records*, compiled around the fifth century BCE, which states that in prehistoric times there were two popular strains of Chinese alcohol. One was a type of beer made with sprouted grains known as *li*, and the other was a rice wine made with qu known as *jiu*. Though we know precious little about these primitive brews, later historians would note that the qu-based drinks were more potent and flavorful, and thus they quickly rendered their competitors obsolete. This is plain enough from the fact that all modern Chinese alcoholic drinks are fermented with qu and that today *jiu* simply means "alcoholic beverage" in Mandarin Chinese.

Qu became an essential element not only of Chinese winemaking but of the greater Chinese culinary tradition, used in the creation of all-important staples like rice vinegar and soy sauce. As the technique for qu fermentation spread throughout the empire and beyond, it became the basis of winemaking traditions in Japan, Korea, Vietnam, Thailand, and other East Asian lands.

In its most primitive form, qu is believed to have been little more than grain that had been left untended and spoiled. By the time China was unified in the third century BCE, manufactured wheat qu was already widely in use, and rice-based qu appeared in southern China no later than the third century CE. By the sixth century CE, there were at least nine distinct types of qu. A thousand years later, during the Ming dynasty, there were hundreds, if not thousands, of varieties. The primary reason for this profusion can be attributed to the popularity at that time of so-called medicinal qu.

Medicinal qu is qu that incorporates ingredients used in traditional Chinese medicine—herbs, spices, and more exotic additions like deer antlers—into its recipe. This is thought to add depth of flavor and complexity to the resulting alcohol while imparting various holistic benefits upon the tippler. The technique is still used by some contemporary brewers and distillers. Leading rice-baijiu distillery Guilin Sanhua uses a qu that contains a secret medicinal ingredient, and Dongjiu, the innovative distillery behind so-called medicine-aroma baijiu, employs as many as a hundred in its qu recipe. See HEALTH AND SPIRITS.

Today qu is divided into countless categories and subcategories depending on raw ingredients and production techniques, but there are two principle types: small qu and big qu.

Small Qu

Small qu is a fermentation agent molded into tiny balls or cakes. It can be made from long-grain rice, glutinous rice, or rice flour. Often herbs and spices are added to small qu to enhance an alcohol's flavor or holistic benefits. It is commonly used as a starter for *huangjiu* and other rice-based Chinese wines and spirits.

The older of the two principle qus, rice-based small qu was first mentioned in the fourth century horticultural guide *Nanfang Caomu Zhuang*. It is produced by mashing rice into a paste, forming the paste into balls or cakes, and allowing them to dry on a bamboo sieve. Sometimes qu powder from an earlier batch is added to the surface to further inoculate a strain. See XIAO ("SMALL") QU.

Big Qu

Big qu is a solid-state fermentation agent formed into large bricks. Most big qu is wheat-based, though it can also be made from wheat bran or a combination of wheat, barley, and peas. It is the preferred starter for most popular styles of baijiu.

Mass production of big qu, the last major qu milestone, is believed to have occurred within the last five centuries. To make it, laborers poured grain paste into wooden molds and used their feet to stamp them into dense bricks. Today this is sometimes simulated using a machine press, though some distilleries still employ the classic method. The bricks are partially dried in the sun before being moved into a dark incubation room, where they will be stacked on straw mats with some room left between bricks to encourage growth of microorganisms. Workers will also regularly adjust the moisture levels and position of the bricks to ensure that the growth is evenly distributed. During this incubation period the core temperature of these bricks will rise rapidly, peaking at around 46° C (115° F) to 63° C (145° F), depending on the variety of big qu, which are sometimes classified by core temperature. After some weeks the qu begins to cool down and is allowed to fully dry into its mature form. It is then stored separately for at least a few months to further develop flavor. See DA QU.

See also CHINA.

Dudgeon, John. *The Beverages of the Chinese.* Tianjin: Tientsin Press, 1895.

Huang Faxin, David Tiande Cai, and Wai-Kit Nip. "Chinese Wines: Jiu." In *Handbook of Food Science, Technology, and Engineering*, vol. 4, by Yiu H. Hui, 173-1–52. Boca Raton, FL: CRC, 2005.

Huang Shusheng 黄书声. *Lun Jiu* 论酒. Beijing: Zhongguo Shidai Jingji Chuban She 中国时代经济出版社, 2012.

Xu Ganrong and Bao Tongfa. *Grandiose Survey of Chinese Alcoholic Drinks and Beverages* (中国酒大观目录, Chinese and English versions). Jiangnan University, 1998.

Zhang Wenxue 张文学 and Xie Ming 谢明, eds. *Zhong Guo Jiu Ji Jiu Wen Hua Gai Lu* 中国酒及酒文化概论. Chengdu: Sichuan Daxue Chuban She 四川大学出版社, 2010.

Derek Sandhaus

Queen's Park Swizzle is a high-octane cousin of the Mojito, with rum, mint, sugar, and bitters, that was long a staple of the Trader Vic's bars and is now considered a tiki standard. It first saw print in the 1946 *Trader Vic's Book of Food and Drink* as "a world-famous drink from the Queen's Park Hotel in Trinidad." Since Vic would have encountered the drink on his one and only stay there in 1938 and it didn't appear in the hotel's 1932 souvenir recipe booklet, its creation was likely between 1933 and 1938. It is also quite possible that Vic created the recipe himself, in loose homage to the swizzle served at the Queen's Park Hotel, since that establishment's characteristic drink was a Green Swizzle. See GREEN SWIZZLE. This was made with no mint, and with Carypton (a local spiced rum unavailable in the United States after Prohibition) instead of rum, which was characteristic of the swizzle, but as made not in Trinidad but in Jamaica (it was, for instance, in the famous Myrtlebank Hotel's swizzle).

Recipe: Combine 90 ml demerara rum, 15 ml sugar syrup, the juice of 1/2 lime, two dashes Angostura bitters, mint leaves, and crushed ice in a tall glass and swizzle.

See also MOJITO; SWIZZLE; SWIZZLE STICK; and BERGERON, VICTOR "TRADER VIC."

Bergeron, Victor. *Trader Vic's Book of Food and Drink.* New York: Doubleday, 1946.
Marshall, Hugh D. *Trinidad and Other Cocktails.* Port of Spain, Trinidad: Queen's Park Hotel, 1932.

Jeff Berry

quetsch is a type of highly aromatic black plum also known as switzen that originated in Asia and gives its name to a plum eau-de-vie made mainly in Alsace, France, but also in Germany, where it is known as zwetschenwasser, and in eastern Europe. See PLUMS and EAU-DE-VIE. A potent and colorless fruit brandy with a complex aroma of plums and nuts, quetsch is usually pot distilled, routinely aged (in glass) up to ten years, and consumed like most eaux-de-vie, neat as an after-dinner digestive.

See also BRANDY and APERITIF AND DIGESTIVE.

Jack Robertiello

QUEEN'S PARK HOTEL, TRINIDAD B.W.I

Foto-Litho Millard & Co. Amsterdam (Holland.)

The well-verandaed Queen's Park Hotel, Port of Spain, Trinidad, ca. 1905. The hotel was demolished in 1996, one year short of its one hundredth anniversary. Wondrich Collection.

Ra Chand Products is a US-based company best known in the cocktail and bar industries for its lever-action countertop citrus juicers (also known as "press" juicers). The company was founded in the mid-1970s by American Keith Siegalkoff (1950–) after extended travels in Mexico. While on that journey, Siegalkoff identified a need for an efficient and durable press juicer for fast production of orange juice and created a design based on a cast-iron version from the 1930s that he had seen. Siegalkoff found a factory in Mexico to produce his designs and began the manufacture of cast-aluminum juicers and tortilla presses, later expanding his product line to other cast-aluminum kitchen wares. The factories used have changed over the years but continue to be in Mexico. The company was incorporated in the United States, first in California and later in Arizona, and was given the name Ra Chand after the mystical universal force described in Seamus Cullen's 1976 erotic science-fantasy novel *Astra and Flondrix*.

Ra Chand juicers found their way into many post-revival cocktail bars and are prized for their durability and speed (unlike most press juicers they use no gears to retard the action) and their simplicity of design, with no internal parts. The Ra Chand juicer's graceful curves give it a sculptural quality, and as such they are often prominently displayed in bars. Noted bartender and cocktail writer Toby Cecchini kept a Ra Chand juicer front and center at his New York bar Passerby. He recalls that it "both knocked out a ton of fresh citrus juice, signaling to the customers the quality of drinks they'd receive, but also stood as a kind of Art Deco piece in the middle of my bar."

See also JUICER.

Cecchini, Toby. Conversation, October 5, 2018.

Siegalkoff, Keith. Telephone conversation, September 10, 2018.

David Moo

Rack Punch is shorthand for Arrack Punch. See ARRACK PUNCH. The antiquated, eighteenth-century colloquialism crops up in Thackeray's *Vanity Fair* as well as in Jerry Thomas's *How to Mix Drinks*. See also THOMAS, JEREMIAH P. "JERRY."

Raffles Long Bar, in Singapore's venerable Raffles Hotel, has long been associated with the Singapore Sling, although its claim to have invented the drink doesn't quite square with the historical record. See SINGAPORE SLING.

raicilla is an agave distillate produced in thirty-two municipalities in four primary regions of western Jalisco and Nayarit, Mexico: the Sierra Occidental, the Sierra de Amula, the Costa Sur, and the Costa Norte. Raicilla can be produced from any variety of agave that grows within these four regions. *Agave maximiliana*, *A. inaequedens*, and *A. valencia* are more common in the mountainous regions, while *A. angustifolia* and *A. rhodacantha* are prevalent along the coast. That diversity in base materials infuses the category: raicillas can be intense and pungent, smoky, earthy, or floral and almost, but not quite, delicate.

As with other agave distillates in Mexico, production entails harvesting and roasting the plants, milling, fermentation, and distillation. Throughout the region, however, diverse production methods reign. Roasting may be in earthen ovens or aboveground masonry ovens. Milling may be by hand in hollowed tree trunks or in stone vats, or by tahona.

Fermentation occurs by natural yeasts with or without the fibers from the hearts included (the fibers mean more labor, but also more flavor). Raicillas may be once- or twice-distilled using the Chinese-style internal condensation stills introduced to Mexico by Filipino sailors in the 1500s, incorporating wooden or clay condensers with copper or stainless pots.

Although raicilla is not protected by a denomination of origin, producers organized into a collective mark in 2000, thereby setting in motion the possibility of becoming an official DO in the future. In 2014, La Venenosa Raicilla became the first on the global market, with four offerings that celebrate the diversity of styles and agaves of the raicilla region. Unlike Oaxacan mezcal, raicilla has yet to be adopted wholesale by the international bartending community; most of it is still sold locally and drunk straight.

See also AGAVE; BACANORA; MEZCAL; and TAHONA.

Valenzuela Zapata, Ana G., and Marie Sarita Gaytán. "Sustaining Biological and Cultural Diversity." *Revue d'ethnoécologie* 2 (2012). http://ethnoecologie.revues.org/990 (accessed April 26, 2021).

Misty Kalkofen

The **Rainbow Room bar**, or the Promenade Bar, as it was officially known, opened in 1987 as part of a grand renovation of the art deco landmark Rainbow Room nightclub, atop New York City's Rockefeller Center. It rapidly became the headquarters of a revolution in cocktail making. Desiring a classic bar that would match the space, Joe Baum (1920–1998), the legendary restaurant impresario who was the Rainbow Room's owner, directed his head bartender, Dale DeGroff (1948–), to take his inspiration from nineteenth-century bartender Jerry Thomas and his 1862 *Bar-Tender's Guide*. After some difficulty procuring a copy of the book, long out of print, DeGroff took inspiration from it as he reintroduced classic techniques for mixing drinks, revived many pre-Prohibition and deco-era cocktails, and set new standards for the American-style bar. A host of devotees went on to adopt these standards and apply them in bars, nightclubs, and restaurants around the world. See DEGROFF, DALE; and THOMAS, JEREMIAH P. "JERRY."

Baum insisted on fresh fruit juices, top-quality spirits and liqueurs, fine glassware, and showmanship. Gone were the soda guns and prefab mixers that had depressed cocktail quality at countless bars over the years. The Rainbow Room became known for bespoke cocktails, assembled painstakingly and presented with a flourish. When the recipe called for an orange or lemon, DeGroff—employing a trick he had seen bartenders at Chasen's in Los Angeles use to make the "Flame of Love" martini—lit a match to ignite the volatile oils in the peel as he squeezed, setting off a small burst of fireworks. See FLAME OF LOVE MARTINI. There were no jiggers; bartenders learned to pour accurately, by eye. See JIGGER.

Cocktails were listed on their own menu, a revival of another old custom that soon became a standard feature at better bars. The early menus, with twenty or more cocktails, were edited down to a more manageable dozen or so, which included familiar classics like the Manhattan, the Old-Fashioned, the Margarita, and the Martini; neglected classics like the Sidecar, the Jack Rose, and the Bronx; and antiquarian cocktails known only to devotees: the Between the Sheets, the Ramos Fizz, the Sazerac, the Stork Club, the Peach Cobbler. See MANHATTAN COCKTAIL; OLD-FASHIONED COCKTAIL; MARGARITA; MARTINI; SIDECAR; JACK ROSE; BRONX COCKTAIL; BETWEEN THE SHEETS; RAMOS GIN FIZZ; SAZERAC COCKTAIL; and STORK CLUB.

The surroundings were elegant. Designed by Hugh Hardy of the firm of Hardy Holzman Pfeiffer Associates, who worked with Baum and the graphic designer Milton Glaser, the bar was intimate in scale, with plush, deco-inspired carpeting and upholstery, a curved mahogany bar, and, suspended from the ceiling, just above DeGroff and his bartending team, a red and black model of a streamlined ocean liner designed by Norman Bel Geddes. Perched on the sixty-fifth floor of the RCA Building in Rockefeller Center, the Promenade Bar resembled a 1930s Hollywood stage set, with the twinkling lights of Manhattan's skyscrapers visible through the windows.

It was a place of relentless experiment. DeGroff, with a nod to the bartenders of yore, made a point of introducing his own inventions, many of them tributes to the great drinks of the past. His signatures included the Ritz, a cognac-based take on the champagne cocktail; the Fitzgerald, a summer gin drink; and the Millennium, a tropical cognac cocktail served in a Martini glass. See RITZ BAR.

The press took notice, as did professionals in the food and drink industry. From his base at the Rainbow Room, DeGroff disseminated his philosophy through seminars, workshops, and walking tours of innovative bars ("cocktail safaris") that caught the attention of aspiring New York bartenders, notably Audrey Saunders (the Pegu Club) and Sasha Petraske (Milk & Honey), who helped spark a cocktail renaissance. See SAUNDERS, AUDREY; PEGU CLUB; PETRASKE, SASHA; and MILK & HONEY. The Promenade Bar closed in 1998 when the Cipriani family took over the operations of the Rainbow Room after Baum's death.

See also DEGROFF, DALE; and COCKTAIL RENAISSANCE.

DeGroff, Dale. *The Craft of the Cocktail*. New York: Clarkson Potter, 2002.
Goldberger, Paul. "The New Rainbow Room: S'Wonderful!" *New York Times*, December 20, 1987.
Grimes, William. "A Bartender Who Stirs and Shakes but Allows No New Twists." *New York Times*, March 27, 1991.

William Grimes

rake or **rummager** is a set of arms that rotate inside a direct-fired pot still; the arms are connected to copper chains or mats that agitate the liquid inside and preventing solids (which can make up 8 percent of the wash) from settling on the bottom where they might burn, creating off flavors and potentially damaging the still. Rummagers also help distribute heat more evenly across the bottom surface of the still. Direct-fired stills, which involve the application of open flames directly underneath, were once ubiquitous but are now found in only a handful of distilleries, including Glenfarclas, Glenfiddich, and the Macallan in Scotland and the Nikka distillery in Japan. (These are generally of otherwise conventional form, but in Ireland in particular a lopsided style of direct-fired still used to be in common use where the neck was displaced to the side of the pot so that the rummager mechanism could be centrally located.) The adoption of steam-coil heating for pot stills rendered rummagers unnecessary.

See also STILL, POT; WHISKY, IRISH; and WHISKY, SCOTCH.

Schidrowitz, Philip. "Spirits." In *Encyclopaedia Britannica*, 11th ed, 700. New York: Encyclopaedia Britannica, 1911.

Clay Risen

raki is an aniseed-flavored spirit, typically distilled from grapes, that is popular in Turkey and the surrounding region. See also ANISE SPIRITS; DISTILLATION, HISTORY; and MIDDLE EAST.

rakija is a brandy made from various kinds of fruit that is popular throughout the Balkan region, in both its commercially produced and homemade forms. See also BRANDY and HOME DISTILLATION.

raksi is a traditional Himalayan distilled spirit from Nepal and Tibet most commonly made from fermented kodo millet, rice, or other grains. It is distilled over a flame—which is continually fed with firewood for the two to three hours the process takes—in a slightly updated version of the ancient internal-condensation still, where the alcoholic vapors rise through the still, condense on the bottom of a metal bowl that seals the still and is kept full of cold water, and are captured in a smaller bowl placed beneath that. Commonly produced in the home or in small countryside operations, raksi is routinely imbibed during celebrations, meals, and social events. In Nepal, raksi's popularity has inspired temperance movements, but as it is offered in a number of religious ceremonies as a gift to the gods, efforts to ban the drink remain largely unsuccessful.

See also STILL, POT.

Tamang, Jyoti Prakash. "Ethnic Starters and Alcoholic Beverages." In *Himalayan Fermented Foods: Microbiology, Nutrition, and Ethnic Values*, by Jyoti Prakash Tamang, 212–215. N.p.: CRC, 2009.

Anna Archibald

Ramos, Henry Charles (1856–1928), was born in Vincennes, Indiana, on August 7, 1856, the son of Prussian immigrants. By 1870, the family was settled in New Orleans, where his father was working at the Navy Yard. In 1874, the younger Ramos began working at Eugene Krost's popular lager beer saloon on Exchange Place, across the street from the Sazerac House. See SAZERAC HOUSE. In 1876, after a stint at another such establishment, which was operated by Hugo Redwitz on Common Street (it's unknown if Ramos was working there on Mardi Gras that year, when the bar served an epic seven thousand glasses of beer), he moved to Baton Rouge, Louisiana. Ramos would remain there for more than a decade.

Ramos's first job in the new city was at the Sumter House, Baton Rouge's leading saloon

Henry Carl Ramos in 1895, just as his eponymous Gin Fizz was beginning to lift him to fame and fortune. Wondrich Collection.

and a full-service, American-style bar, where the bartenders had to also be mixologists. Ramos evidently learned more than just the rudiments of the art there. In 1880, when he struck out on his own to open the Capitol Saloon, the local paper observed that "what he doesn't understand about mixing good drinks ain't worth knowing." The Capitol soon took its place among the leading saloons in town. A large, modern establishment, it offered billiards, coin-operated games, and all the popular barroom amusements of the day.

After selling his interest in the Capitol Saloon at the end of 1886, Ramos took over Pat Moran's Imperial Cabinet saloon at the corner of Carondelet and Gravier streets, in New Orleans's central business district. That was in May 1887. By 1891, he was being described as "genial and universally-popular" and a man who was "born in Mixerville," where all the good mixologists come from. By 1895, the *New Orleans Times-Democrat* was describing the Imperial Cabinet as probably the "one place in New Orleans" best known "among men of the world throughout the United States."

What made it so was, of course, the Ramos Gin Fizz. A simple Silver Fizz cushioned with cream, rendered mysterious with orange flower water, and shaken until all the ice was incorporated, this sweet, lightly alcoholic drink made Ramos world-famous and very prosperous. See RAMOS GIN FIZZ and SILVER FIZZ. By 1899 Ramos's Fizz was being mentioned in newspapers all around the United States, sometimes under the name "New Orleans Fizz." The next year, the *Kansas City Star* dubbed the Imperial Cabinet "the most famous gin fizz saloon in the world." Any visitor to New Orleans, male or female, made his saloon, one of the few in America considered civilized enough for women to be admitted, one of their first stops.

While Ramos made other drinks besides fizzes, only two or three of them have come down to us—a Creole Cocktail that is essentially a Sazerac, a Taft Cocktail (the same thing in a glass with a sugared rim), and a complex take on the Sherry Flip that was flavored with "squee-gee," a house mix of liqueurs. But it was the fizz that brought in the customers, in ever-increasing number.

Ramos' saloon was always busy, but, of course, on Mardi Gras it was almost a frenzy. A crew of bartenders, ranging from eight in 1899 to as many as fifteen ten years later would stand behind the bar, each with one or two "shaker boys"—young black men whose job was to strenuously shake the drinks that the bartenders mixed, for as long as five minutes and more, until all the ice was melted into the drink. The saloon would make some three thousand fizzes a day—so many that Ramos made a second specialty of those flips, which used egg yolks, served egg-yolk omelets on his free-lunch buffet, and still did a thriving business selling the rest of the yolks to bakers. In 1899, *Leslie's Weekly* noted that "he has the largest hennery in the country."

By then, Ramos was a fixture in New Orleans. (In 1903, when the local *Times-Picayune* ran a picture of him taken from behind and asked its readers to guess who it was, several hundred readers guessed correctly.) Operating what was widely regarded as the most gentlemanly saloon in the city, Ramos tolerated no rowdyism at any time, usually kept the place closed on Sundays, and indeed rarely stayed open past eight on other nights. His saloon was considered so respectable that, as Alderman Sidney Story wrote in 1913, "it is not an unusual sight in the winter months, and when the Carnival is on in New Orleans, to find this palatial resort . . . packed not only with men but ladies who have just left the fashionable ball-rooms or the French Opera." It did not hurt that Ramos was active in local politics, club life, and Masonry and served on civic commissions. When Prohibition sentiment began to coalesce in New Orleans, his fellow saloonkeepers deemed him the natural choice to lead the opposition. It helped greatly that, unlike many of his peers, Ramos was abstemious in his personal habits and a good businessman, investing widely in real estate and other businesses. (When, in 1907, a rent increase forced him to move around the corner to Storyville kingpin Thomas Anderson's Stag Saloon on Gravier Street, he and his partners, his younger brother William and head bartender Paul Alpuente, were soon able to buy the building.)

When Prohibition took effect, he closed his saloon, freely gave out his recipe, and went into the paint business (his brand: "Jin Phiz"). His death, in 1928, was national news. Even after his death, he and his saloon were often used as contrasts to the violent, rough speakeasies where Americans did their drinking during Prohibition. To this day, the Ramos Gin Fizz is in most serious bartenders' repertoires. Not even Jerry Thomas could get his name permanently attached to a popular drink. In that achievement, Ramos stands alone.

See also: SCHMIDT, WILLIAM; and THOMAS, JEREMIAH P. "JERRY."

"A Famous Mixologist." *New Orleans Times-Democrat*, September 1, 1895, 28.

"How Late H. C. Ramos Made His World Famous Gin Fizz." *New Orleans Item-Tribune*, September 23, 1928.

"The Man Who Remembers His Friends." *Louisiana Review*, December 30, 1891, 4.

"People Talked About." *Leslie's Illustrated Weekly*, January 19, 1899, 43.

Ramos, Paul H. Letter, *New Orleans Times-Picayune*, April 27, 1981, 14.

David Wondrich

The **Ramos Gin Fizz**, a Silver Gin Fizz cushioned with cream, rendered mysterious with orange flower water, and shaken to a delicate froth, is—along with the Sazerac Cocktail—one of New Orleans's signature drinks, and is the only one of the great classics of mixology to commemorate the bartender who created it in its name. See SAZERAC COCKTAIL and SILVER FIZZ. Henry C. Ramos (1856–1928), the New Orleans bartender in question, parlayed his sweet, subtle, lightly alcoholic creation into fame and fortune in his lifetime, and to this day it remains an object of delight and a well-known test of a bartender's skill. See RAMOS, HENRY CHARLES.

Unfortunately, the drink's precise origins are unknown. The earliest definite notice of it in print is from 1895, when it is both described in an article about Ramos in the *New Orleans Times-Democrat* and provided with a recipe, as the "New Orleans Fizz," in George Kappeler's well-regarded *Modern American Drinks*, published in New York, although Kappeler's recipe lacks the orange flower water. Its precursors certainly include the Cream Lemonade, a nonalcoholic drink with citrus, sugar, cream, egg white, and sparkling water that first starts appearing in the 1880s. Significantly, Cream Lemonade was one of Ramos's specialties in the mid-1880s, when he was keeping a saloon in Baton Rouge, Louisiana.

The drink's precursors must also include the version of a Silver Fizz attributed to "one of the most distinguished Crescent City barkeepers" by the *New Orleans Times-Democrat* in 1890, which was flavored with orange flower water, apparently the first time that ingredient was included in a Gin Fizz. By that point, Ramos was back in New Orleans and well known for his skill mixing drinks, and it is quite possible that he was the bartender in question. On the other hand, the way the anonymous bartender assembled his Silver Fizz is quite different from how Ramos built his eponymous drink, and for bartenders such matters can be like signatures.

But even if Ramos was not the first to add orange flower water to a Silver Fizz, as far as can be determined the idea of combining that drink and a Cream Lemonade was his, as was the characteristic way he made the resulting fizz, which involved shaking it for several minutes, with the sparkling water already added, until the ice was completely dissolved. Certainly his claim to the drink, which was enormously famous, was unchallenged during his lifetime. It cannot be stated precisely when he shook the first one, but the most likely period is between 1892 and 1894. By 1895, his Imperial Cabinet saloon was known as the "Gin Fizz place."

By 1900, the "One and Only One," as Ramos called his fizz, was a New Orleans fixture, one of the boxes a tourist had to check off if he or she visited the city (the drink was considered gentle enough, and Ramos's saloon genteel enough, for ladies). The drink's fame soon spread nationwide, aided by the fact that Ramos had no problem giving out his recipe. Prohibition only increased that fame, as the

Ramos Gin Fizz became a symbol of the delights that the dry law had taken away.

The Ramos Gin Fizz came back with Repeal, given a boost by Huey Long, the flamboyantly populist governor of Louisiana. In 1935, the governor brought to New York the head bartender from New Orleans's Roosevelt Hotel, which had bought the exclusive rights to market the drink from Ramos's heirs, in order to make Ramos Fizzes for the press while Long attacked President Franklin Roosevelt's New Deal. Even through the dark ages of mixology, in the last quarter of the twentieth century, Ramos's creation hung on as something decadently luxurious to have with Sunday brunch. The cocktail renaissance meant only that far more bartenders now had to know how to make a "Ramos." With the revival of the mixer's art, a great deal of attention has been paid to the techniques that go into the drink, with innovations such as "dry shaking," paint-can shakers, and pressurized nitrogen applied to its execution. See DRY SHAKE. Despite all that attention, though, Henry Carl Ramos's basic formula still works just fine.

Recipe: Stir together in shaker 15 ml lemon juice, 15 ml lime juice, and 10 ml sugar; add 45 ml Old Tom gin, 15 ml egg white, 30 ml heavy cream, and 3 or 4 drops orange flower water. Shake thoroughly with ice and strain into chilled highball glass with 30 ml chilled sparkling water first added.

"A Famous Mixologist." *New Orleans Times-Democrat,* September 1, 1895, 28.

"How Late H. C. Ramos Made His World Famous Gin Fizz." New Orleans *Item-Tribune,* September 23, 1928.

"Questions and Answers." *New Orleans Times-Democrat,* January 6, 1890, 3.

David Wondrich

rancio, also sometimes known as "rancio Charentais," is a difficult-to-define characteristic long noted in some very old cognacs: a set of aromas not obviously derived from the grapes it is distilled from or the oak it is aged in that have been described as reminiscent of truffle or cheese or nut oils. Rancio has also been identified in other spirits, although the idea will divide a room full of spirits tasters the way terroir or minerality will divide wine tasters.

Ten or twenty years ago, to apply this very French term to a whisky seemed precious, even absurd, but malt heads such as Gary Regan, an early adopter of the term for whisky, have found that it applies to some of the oldest and most evanescent drams. See REGAN, GARY. Use the word to describe a tequila, however, and its producer could well take deep offense, though that too may change with time.

As with most such terms, ask ten drinkers what rancio means and you will get ten different answers—at least. Alexandre Gabriel of Cognac Ferrand and Jean-Paul Vidal of the French Union nationale des groupements de distillateurs d'alcool have studied the development of rancio and its identification. See PIERRE FERRAND.

Gabriel suggests that ketones are the primary precursors responsible for rancio development (others suggest that the principal one responsible is 2-heptanone, but it is always accompanied by others). See KETONE. His research reflects experience and scientific rigor, but each cognac and Armagnac producer seems to parse these ephemeral matters rather differently. Gabriel differentiates four periods of primary rancio development, all in the barrel:

- 0–5 years, when almond, nougat, and port aromas are developing
- 15–20 years, when jasmine, narcissus, and Roquefort-cheese aromas develop and methyl ketones first appear
- 25–30 years, when a balsam character arises, leached from the wood
- 30+ years, fourth and final period, until the cognac gets too tannic to drink, with silky textures and increasing fruits, along with pepper, coconut, and other aromas, as well as a concentration of heavy esters

Other tasters speak of the same characteristics but appearing in a differing order, so either considerable subjectivity is at work, or there are differing directions of developments for differing producers. Unquestionably, grape-based spirits develop differently than apple-based spirits or grain-based spirits.

Interestingly, in wine circles, the lactone sotolon (which smells of maple syrup and fenugreek) is identified as a sole agent for rancio development, but it is likely that a reductivist mindset is at work when a single compound is considered the origin of so many different aromatic, flavor, and textured compounds. See LACTONES.

Buxton, Ian, and Paul S. Hughes. *The Science and Commerce of Whisky*. Cambridge: Royal Society of Chemistry, 2015.
Waterhouse, Andrew Leo, Gavin L Sacks, and David W. Jeffery. *Understanding Wine Chemistry*. New York: Wiley, 2016.

Doug Frost

ratafia is a homemade cordial popular in parts of France, Spain, and Italy, made by infusing brandy or other spirits with nuts, fruits, herbs, and spices. See BRANDY and CORDIAL.

Ray, Cyril (1908–1991), was one of the most influential wine and spirits writers of the late twentieth century, with a direct and wry style that rendered the musty, mandarin pretensions prevailing in the field instantly obsolete. The son of a Jewish optician from Lancashire, Ray worked a number of improbable jobs, including a brief stint in the Royal Air Force's Balloon Corps, before ending up in 1939 as a war correspondent for the *Manchester Guardian* and then the BBC. In 1943, while covering the brutal battle of Ortona in Italy, Ray (a noncombatant) was forced to assume command of a leaderless Canadian platoon and lead them to safety, earning a coveted mention in dispatches.

In 1956, Ray became the editor of the *Compleat Imbiber*, an annual hardcover anthology of the best in drink writing published by the Gilbey's gin company. Ray's years as a foreign correspondent, including postings in Rome and Moscow, equipped him to appreciate a broad spectrum of drinks, without snobbishness. While he was primarily a wine writer, he also wrote knowledgably and well about spirits (including a book on cognac and a concise but accurate guide to the world's distillates), cocktails, and beer. His 1967 drink memoir, *In a Glass Lightly*, displays both his knowledge and his pugnacious wit (Ray was a committed socialist and an expert on the good things in life).

See also SPIRITS WRITING.

Knightley, Phillip. *The First Casualty*. 1975; repr., New York: Harvest, 1976.
Ray, Cyril. *The Complete Book of Spirits and Liqueurs*. New York: Macmillan, 1977.
Ray, Cyril. *In a Glass Lightly*. London: Methuen, 1967.

David Wondrich

Rea, Brian (1927–2021), a pioneering American bartender, collector, and historian of the bartender's craft, had a huge impact on the world of cocktails for more than five decades. Born in Brooklyn, New York, Rea was a foster child and attended high school briefly before joining the Merchant Marine during World War II.

Rea landed his first bar job in 1947, but his career began in earnest when he was hired at the historic 21 Club in midtown Manhattan. Jerry Berns (1907–2006), who founded the establishment along with his brother Charlie and cousin Jerome Kreindler, was the father that Rea never had. Berns schooled the enthusiastic student in the bar and restaurant business. Rea worked his way up to the head bartender position at a time when 21 was arguably the most famous bar in the world. After his stint at 21, Rea went to work for Billy Reed at the legendary Little Club, where Doris Day started her career as a lounge singer accompanied by a young Cy Coleman.

In the 1960s Rea relocated to the West Coast and worked at Ken Hansen's Scandia on Sunset Boulevard in West Hollywood, the Playboy Club, and Jack Weiser's Frascati Restaurant.

In 1969, Rea dreamed up a new hospitality position, beverage director, which would separate bar and beverage operations from food operations. He spoke with six major hospitality corporations, and one, Host International, was willing to take a chance on the concept and appointed Rea as director of beverage services. Rea managed bar and beverage operations in a number of airports, hotels, restaurants, and airline clubs for Host.

In 1977, Rea left Host and embarked on a consulting career. His clients included Marriott Hotels, Victoria Station, General Mills, Sheraton Hotels, Canteen Corporation, TGI Friday's, and the US Department of Defense and its military clubs, as well as a number of airlines, breweries, distilleries, and wineries. See TGI FRIDAY'S.

Rea authored two books, now out of print, *Brian's Booze Guide* (1976) and *Brian's Bartender Guide* (1978), both displaying his characteristic mix of good-natured humor, common sense, and strong technique. He was also a frequent source for journalists writing about beverages and contributed articles to a number of publications, including *Imbibe*, the *Wall Street Journal*, the *New York Times*, and the *San Francisco Chronicle*.

Rea was owner and so-called barchivist of one of the world's largest collections of drinks related books and ephemera. Rea's third book, *B.A.S.T.A.R.D.S.: Bars and Saloons, Taverns and Related Drink Stories*, was published in 2017.

Rea, Brian. *B.A.S.T.A.R.D.S.: Bars and Saloons, Taverns and Related Drink Stories*. N.p.: CreateSpace, 2017.

Dale DeGroff

rectification is the process of removing congeners from a spirit by redistillation, filtration, or precipitation or of masking their flavor with other compounds. See CONGENERS. Some rectification is integral to the process of making most spirits: in the double distillation that is used for so many pot-stilled spirits, the second distillation can be viewed as process of rectification, and it is worth noting that of the two columns that made up Aeneas Coffey's revolutionary continuous still, the second was identified as the "rectifier." See COFFEY, AENEAS; DISTILLATION, PROCESS; and STILL, CONTINUOUS. But rectification also has a tradition outside the primary distillery, with independent rectifiers reworking spirits to meet market needs as they perceive them. As the English rectifier William Betts testified before a parliamentary commission in 1848, "The grain distiller manufactures the spirit, and the rectifier purchases it from him, to render it fit for the public."

We shall return to that "fit for the public," but let us first examine the various means of rectification. The first is straight redistillation, where the rectifier takes a fairly low-proof spirit, full of impurities, and distills it again, making it purer, stronger, and—for better or worse—less flavorful. Sometimes that redistillation includes adding botanicals, as in the manufacture of gin, aquavit, or anise spirits. See ANISE SPIRITS; AQUAVIT; BOTANICAL; and GIN. Here the redistillation both removes flavors from the original distillation and adds new ones from the botanicals.

Filtration, usually with charcoal, also removes impurities (and in particular oils) and can be used on its own or combined with redistillation for a very pure product—indeed, they give us modern vodka, which represents the commercial triumph of rectified spirit. See CHARCOAL FILTRATION; FILTRATION; and VODKA. There are also chemical means of rectification, including passing the spirit through petroleum byproducts, which will absorb many of the impurities and are easily separable from the spirit, or using various chemicals to imitate the flavor of some other spirit. Some of these chemical methods of rectification were rather frightening, which brings us to that rendering of the spirit "fit for the public."

Rectification was a particularly large and important part of the spirits market in Britain, which from the 1730s used the excise laws to keep original distillers and rectifiers strictly separate (as William Betts detailed). Those who fermented and distilled grain were not allowed to also retail it, while rectifiers were allowed to buy and sell spirits but not distill them from scratch. See EXCISE, TAXES, AND DISTILLATION. At best, this system yielded high-quality gins such as those sold by Philip Booth & Sons or Benjamin Hodges & Son. See OLD TOM GIN. But it also yielded other "compound spirits," including things such as "British brandy," which was the same Scottish or English grain spirit that was rectified into gin but artificially flavored and colored to present some resemblance to French brandy. This was used to meet the market needs of those who could not afford real brandy from the early eighteenth century until the early twentieth. Britain was not alone in making such things: in the United States, there was "Duffy's Pure Malt" whisky, which was merely rectified American grain spirit, neither pure nor made from malt.

Legislation such as the American Pure Food and Drug Act of 1906 put an end to the worst of these products, but flavored neutral spirits are still with us. We no longer hear much about petroleum-byproduct rectification and the like, but neither are those processes necessary: using modern, multiple-column fractional distillation and charcoal filtration, it is possible to make a spirit that has virtually no congeners—that is perfectly rectified, being merely ethanol and water, and precious little of the latter. See AZEOTROPE.

See also DISTILLATION, HISTORY, and SPIRITS TRADE, HISTORY OF.

Nettleton, J. A. *The Manufacture of Spirit at the Various Distilleries of the United Kingdom.* London: Marcus Ward, 1893.

Royal Commission on Whiskey and Other Potable Spirits. *Interim Report.* London: HM Stationery Office, 1908.

Select Committee on Sugar and Coffee Planting. *Sixth Report.* London, HM Stationery Office, 1848.

David Wondrich

rectifier (device) is a general name given to any device that works to purify a spirit during or after distillation. Some rectifiers rely on reflux and are thus built into the distillation process. Of the two columns that constitute the Coffey still, the ancestor of most modern continuous or column stills, one is the "analyzer," where the wash drips down over perforated plates as steam rises through them and strips off the alcohol. The other column is the "rectifier," where that alcohol-rich vapor rises over a descending serpentine pipe carrying the cold wash to the analyzer; in the process, the vapor is cooled to the point that the heavier compounds condense and drop out. See COFFEY, AENEAS; REFLUX; and STILL, CONTINUOUS.

Other rectifiers use chemical means to purify the spirit; these are generally deployed post-distillation. The oldest, most reliable, and by far the safest of these filter the spirit through a layer of charcoal, which will remove some of the heavier, oilier congeners and render a lighter, cleaner spirit. Charcoal rectifiers go back at least to the beginning of the nineteenth century. In 1809, Samuel McHarry, a Pennsylvania distiller, described a simple rectifier made from a wooden barrel with a perforated false bottom inside that was covered with two inches (5 cm) of "ground maple charcoal and burnt brick dust, made to the consistence of mortar with whisky." The rectified spirit would be drawn off at the bottom. By the end of the century, numerous variations of this simple device had been patented, and charcoal rectification was a common part of distilling, particularly for Russian vodka and some types of American whisky and Caribbean rum. Of the twenty-eight anonymous whiskies analyzed in the landmark 1908 study of whisky production and maturation by Charles Crampton and Lucius Tolman of the United States Bureau of Internal Revenue, all three of the corn whiskies and one of the fourteen ryes were run through in charcoal "leach tubs"—rectifiers—after distillation. One of those corn whiskies was most likely from Jack Daniel's, which called its product a corn whisky at the time. The distillery still rectifies its new-make spirit before barreling it. See JACK DANIEL'S.

For most modern spirit rectification, gravity rectifiers have been replaced by pressure filters, but the bulk of these are still filled with "activated carbon" (basically, charcoal).

See also VODKA.

Crampton, C. A., and L. M. Tolman. "A Study of the Changes Taking Place in Whiskey Stored in Wood." *Journal of the American Chemical Society* 30 (January 1908): 98–136.

McHarry, Samuel. *The Practical Distiller*, Harrisburg, PA: 1809.

David Wondrich

rectifier (occupation) is a term with meanings both vague and specific, all of which shift over time and space but nonetheless share the common thread of referring to those who purchase bulk beverage alcohol for resale. In the United States, the 1935 Federal Alcohol Administration Act uses "rectifier" and related terms but does not specifically define them. Because the federal rectification tax was repealed in 1980, Internal Revenue Code regulations no longer define the term. However, the occupation, understood in general terms, dates to the earliest days of commercial distilling. In broad strokes, alcohol rectifiers buy distilled spirits (or wines) from other producers, change them in some way, and sell the resulting product under new labels. Such changes may include re-distilling and purifying those spirits (especially if they are lower proof, are of inconsistent quality, or carry distinctive aromas and taste deemed undesirable); making infusions, macerations, or compounded beverages with them; and creating new blends to package and resell under new labels. In modern parlance, rectifiers may be known as non-distilling producers (NDPs), merchant bottlers, or independent bottlers.

Rectifying as an industry began in Britain in the early eighteenth century, with the establishment of a three-tier system that would persist in some form for over two hundred years. "Malt distillers" made a double-distilled spirit from malted barley (and, later, other grains) and sold it to "rectifiers" (the term is first attested to in 1725). The rectifiers cleaned up the raw spirit by redistillation (either on its own or with botanicals), sometimes along with filtration or chemical adjustment. The resulting spirits—mainly gin or "cologne spirits" (the trade name for neutral alcohol)—were sold in turn to vintners and publicans, who further adulterated them and retailed them to the public. By the middle of the century this system, in place since the 1720s, was enshrined in law. See GIN.

The introduction of the column still in the 1830s, with its ability to produce odorless, nearly pure ethanol out of any sort of grain, fruit, cane, or other fermentable material, revolutionized the rectifier's art. In Britain, the business was tightly controlled. Elsewhere, it was not, and as a result the latter half of the nineteenth century saw the heyday of compounding manuals, such as M. F. Malpeyre's 1868 *Nouveau manuel complet du distillateur-liquoriste*, published in Paris, or Joseph Fleischman's 1885 *The Art of Blending and Compounding Liquors and Wines* from New York, which instructed readers in how to make countless ersatz spirits, wines, and cordials with rectified spirits. At the same time, commercial flavorists such as Fritzsche Brothers, also of New York, published recipes and provided wholesale essences, extracts, colorants, and oils for emulating genuine beverages using such "velvet" or "silent" spirits. American rectifiers in particular soon earned reputations for producing inferior wet goods that deployed acids, oils, extracts, colorants, and glycerin to smooth over raw spirits and mimic properly aged ones. A large percentage of the spirits Americans drank toward the end of the nineteenth century was made up of rectified (nearly neutral) spirits flavored and colored to resemble genuine whisky, brandy, and the like. The Bottled-in-Bond Act of 1897 was enacted precisely to stem the flow of such inferior, ersatz whiskies. See BOTTLED-IN-BOND. Most countries today prohibit the worst excesses of rectification, but there are exceptions.

Some modern-day, tightly regulated rectifiers have still come under fire for dishonest marketing, particularly ones selling whisky and, recently, some rums. Critics argue that these "brands without stills" are frauds and their owners con artists, selling mystery spirits of unknown origins to gullible buyers while pretending to be the actual distiller. Whisky writer Chuck Cowdery coined the term "Potemkin distilleries" to refer to such brands for their disingenuous pose. See COWDERY, CHARLES K. While it's true that some brands are little more than marketing departments with deep pockets that buy, repackage, and sell spirits they've purchased in bulk, there is nothing inherently dishonest with the profession. Many well-known brands began—and some remain—as products bought by rectifiers, blended, and packaged as new labels without ever revealing their origins. Those rectifiers include Paul Jones, who created Four Roses; George Garvin Brown, whose Old Forester blended whiskies from three distilleries; I. W. Bernheim, who made I W Harper with purchased bourbon; W. L. Weller, who owned a still to make gin and redistill whisky purchased elsewhere; and S. C. Herbst, who aged Old Fitzgerald bourbon in Milwaukee that he had purchased in Kentucky. More recently, Compass Box (and other scotch and rum bottlers), High West, Redemption Rye, WhistlePig, Bulleit, Michter's, St. George Spirits, and others have either purchased spirits from others or had spirits distilled to their specifications by others. A great deal of award-winning American whisky, for example, comes from MGP Ingredients industrial distillery (formerly known as Lawrenceburg Distillers Indiana, or LDI), a distiller in Indiana that provides noteworthy spirits to distillers and rectifiers who may age or flavor them further before bottling.

See also COMPOUNDING and RECTIFICATION.

Cowdery, Chuck. "Potemkin Craft Distilleries." *The Chuck Cowdery Blog*, February 11, 2010. http://chuckcowdery.blogspot.com/2010/02/potemkin-craft-distilleries.html (accessed March 9, 2021).

Fleischman, Joseph. *The Art of Blending and Compounding Liquors and Wines.* New York: Dick & Fitzgerald, 1885.

Fritzsche, Schimmel & Co. *Practical Directions, Receipts and Processes for the Production of Various Kinds and Qualities of Brandies, Gins, Whiskeys, Rums, Pictures, Cordials and All Other Liquors by the Application and Use of Essential Oils and Essences.* New York: Fritzsche, Schimmel, 1875.

Shaw, Peter. *Three Essays in Artificial Philosophy.* London: 1731.

Title 26 IRC, sections 5025, 5082, and 5083.

Ury, Steve. "The Complete List of American Whiskey Distilleries and Brands." *Sku's Recent Eats* (blog), May 6, 2017. http://recenteats.blogspot.com/

p/the-complete-list-of-american-whiskey.
html#Independents (accessed March 9, 2021).

Veach, Michael. "History of Rectifiers or 'Non-Distilling
Producers.'" *Bourbonveach*.com, May 16 2016.
https://bourbonveach.com/2016/05/16/history-
of-rectifiers-or-non-distilling-producers/ (accessed
March 9, 2021).

Matthew Rowley

The **Red Hook** is a modern classic cocktail with rye whisky, Punt e Mes, and maraschino liqueur, created by Vincenzo Errico at the New York bar Milk & Honey in 2004. Errico, a Neapolitan who had worked in London, named the drink for a neighborhood in the New York City borough of Brooklyn, thus paying homage to a pair of pre-Prohibition rye-based cocktails named for New York boroughs, the Manhattan and the Brooklyn. The Red Hook inspired a number of additional rye-based drinks named after New York neighborhoods from bartenders in New York and elsewhere. These include the Bensonhurst, the Bushwick, the Carroll Gardens, the Cobble Hill, the Greenpoint, the Little Italy, and the Slope. In the process, the Red Hook prompted bartenders to explore alternatives to vermouth and different kinds of bitters (the Punt e Mes in the drink plays the role of both vermouth and bittering component) and, more importantly, helped to usher in a renaissance of stirred aromatic cocktails in general.

Recipe: Stir with ice 60 ml straight rye whisky, 15 ml Punt e Mes, and 15 ml maraschino liqueur. Strain into a cocktail glass, and add a maraschino cherry.

See also MILK & HONEY.

Chad Solomon

Red Snapper is the more genteel name given to the ur-version of the Bloody Mary served since 1934 at the St. Regis hotel's King Cole Bar in New York. See BLOODY MARY.

Red Star, also known as Hongxing, is a distillery in Beijing best known for its ubiquitous and inexpensive light-aroma-style baijiu. Its signature *erguotou* baijiu uses a sorghum mash, fermented in stone pits and pots with wheat-bran-based big qu.

Red Star traces its origins back to the Yuan Sheng Hao grain depot, whose proprietors, the Zhao brothers, developed the erguotou style in the late seventeenth century. They discovered that the liquor produced during the second phase of distillation—the second pot head, or *erguotou*—was of the highest quality. Other distillers followed the Zhaos' lead, and the style became synonymous with Beijing spirits.

When Red Star was founded in April 1949, it became the first Beijing business licensed for operation in the People's Republic of China. The government created the distillery by merging a dozen private distilleries into a state-run operation tasked with creating baijiu for the new nation's inaugural ceremony on October 1, when Chairman Mao famously proclaimed, "The people of China have stood up." It met the needs of the proletariat then, and it has continued meeting them in the intervening decades. The distillery currently has a production capacity of thirty thousand bottles an hour, most of it priced to give water a run for its money.

See also LIGHT-AROMA-STYLE BAIJIU.

Huang Faxin, David Tiande Cai, and Wai-Kit Nip.
"Chinese Wines: Jiu." In *Handbook of Food Science,
Technology, and Engineering*, vol. 4, by Yiu H. Hui, 173-
1–52. Boca Raton, FL: CRC, 2005.

Wang Kai 王恺, ed. *San Lian Sheng Huo Zhou Kan*
三联生活周刊 675. March 26, 2012.

Derek Sandhaus

reduction is the process by which the alcoholic content of a spirit is lowered to its bottling proof. When a distillate is fresh out of the still, it usually contains 70–96 percent alcohol. When barrel aged, depending on the climate, a spirit typically loses some of its alcohol through the wood, generally 1 percent per year. See ANGEL'S SHARE.

Ideally, the proof, or the percentage of alcohol at which a spirit is bottled and sold, is defined by the master blender, who chooses the perfect proof at which a spirit will show its best organoleptic characteristics, although often taxes, marketing, and tradition also figure into or even drive the choice.

Generally, a spirit is sold between 40 percent and 50 percent alcohol. To reach this point or to adjust it to the perfect proof, the master blender uses a method called "reduction" or "hydration," a process by which a certain quantity of water is added to the spirit in order to lower its percentage of alcohol to the desired proof. Ideally, this is done incrementally in several stages—a process called "progressive reduction"—to avoid "shocking" the spirit.

The water used for the reduction must be totally pure, that is to say, rid of all the molecules that would create turpitude and bad taste. Also, it is known that minerals will harden the taste of a spirit.

Until the nineteenth century, producers used rainwater or distilled water for the reduction. Nowadays, most use water that has been purified through reverse osmosis.

As for ageing, time is the best friend of a good reduction. A very progressive reduction will result in a fully integrated spirit, an essential taste and mouthfeel characteristic referred to as *le fondu* by the cognac master blenders.

In the Cognac region, where reduction is practiced in its most developed, elaborate form, it is usually done in a minimum of three to four stages, starting at least six months before bottling and ideally years before. This being said, each house has its own reduction method, some of them fine-tuned for centuries. Some prefer to hold their spirit at full proof as long as possible, thus also saving much space and time in the process. Others prefer to start their progressive reduction early on. Also, the reduction can be applied to individual lots or the pre-blended ones known as "coupes." See ÉLEVAGE. Some combine these two methods.

Old master blenders will explain that there is a rhythm to reduction, every three months or six months or every year. The first reductions can be more substantial (dropping the alcohol by as much as 10 percent at once) and more spaced in time. However, as bottling time approaches, the reduction steps must be done in smaller steps of no more than 3–4 percent alcohol reduction at a time. Otherwise it would "drown" the spirit, which would lose its most interesting organoleptic characteristics and be aggressive on the palate.

Often a reduction step is done right after a small chosen blending step assembling a few matching barrels in a bigger vat. It is also a time at which a master blender can decide to take a spirit from a drier to a more humid cellar or the other way around, depending on the desired style. Once "married," the resulting spirit is re-dispatched in barrels for further maturation.

The resting time (*temps de marriage*) between two reductions is extremely important. If the time between two progressive reduction steps is not sufficient, it is said that the spirit smells like "fresh blend," a feeling of unsettlement, aggressiveness, and wateriness.

Once the reduction is done, the master blender will often homogenize and oxygenize the spirit with a slow pump that is used as a closed circuit in the reduction vat.

The last step of the reduction occurs generally when the spirit is 2 percent alcohol above the desired bottling proof. This is when a slight filtration or chill filtration is done. Then the spirit is adjusted one last time to be at the final bottle proof.

An ancient reduction method in cognac called *la méthode des petites eaux* (literally "the small-waters method") requires the master blender to mature pure water in used cognac barrels for several months, thus seasoning the water before using it for a progressive reduction. Indeed, with time, the used barrel will impart some of the cognac and tannic elements of the wood to the pure water, preparing it to be integrated into the spirit that will be diluted. This time—and space—consuming method is now only used by a handful of small producers worldwide.

Admittedly, the system used for cognac is reduction at its most elaborate. Elsewhere, some spirits producers will use parts of this system—many of the most carefully made whiskies, for instance, are reduced in stages—while other producers, and in particular the ones working with highly filtered or rectified spirits, have found it acceptable to dispense with the whole system.

Alexandre Gabriel

Reed, Ben (1972–), one of London's best-known bartenders, helped pioneer the role of cocktail consultant in the United Kingdom. Reed rose to prominence as manager of Met Bar, which replaced the Atlantic Bar & Grill as the highest-profile cocktail venue in late 1990s London. His cocktail column for the *Times'* magazine and *Shaker Maker* series for BBC TV helped bring turn-of-the-century cocktail culture to a wider British audience. In 1999, Reed cofounded International Playboy Bartenders (IPBartenders), the United Kingdom's first cocktail consultancy. The author of fourteen books, including *Cool Cocktails*, Reed continues to train bartenders and consult for brands.

See also ATLANTIC BAR & GRILL.

Reed, Ben, and William Lingwood. *Cool Cocktails*. London: Ryland Peters & Small, 2000.

Theodora Sutcliffe

reflux is the part of the distillation process where some of the heavier compounds in the alcohol-rich vapor rising from the heated wash condense out of the vapor and fall back into the wash before the rest of the vapor is drawn off or collected for condensation. Distillers generally consider reflux a desirable thing, as it yields a cleaner, stronger spirit, although how much it is facilitated varies greatly according to the type of still used and the spirit being made.

All stills produce some reflux. In pot stills, this can be manipulated in several ways. The most common is by placing a narrow neck in between the pot and the still head. When the vapor passing out of the neck expands to fill the head, it loses pressure, and as a result some of the heavier compounds—water, fuel oils, and other high-boiling-point compounds—fall out of suspension. The same thing happens if the head of the still is made very tall or drawn up into a point, with the vapor exiting from the top. Cooling the still head with water has a similar effect.

Nonetheless, in a basic pot still the ability to separate ethanol from the other organic components and water is limited; for some spirits, such as cognac and malt whisky, the resulting higher levels of congeners and fusel oils in the final distillate are desirable, and that outweighs the still's inefficiency and the lower distillation proof. On the other hand, distillation equipment that incorporates a rectification column, sometimes referred to as a continuous still, has the capability to produce a product free of extraneous fusel oils and excess water by the amplification of reflux. Accomplishing the same level of purity in a pot still requires the distillate to pass through the distillation process multiple times, which is inefficient.

Schematically, the reflux process in a column still is simple: the still uses the vapor rising through the column from the boiling, mostly spent wash that has collected at the bottom to strip the ethanol from the relatively cool fresh wash, which is fed in at the top and trickles down, in the process condensing the higher-boiling-point compounds in the rising vapor. Inside of the rectifier column, there is insufficient heat for higher-boiling-point components to return to a vapor phase once they have condensed, so they fall back into the boiler. Inside the boiler, there is sufficient energy to convert the water and fusel oils back into a vapor, but they must work their way back up the column before they can make it into the final distillate. The continuous cascade of reflux pushes the fusel oils and water vapor back down into the boiler.

The key to beneficial reflux is the creation of an equilibrium where the fusel oils and water concentrate in the bottom half of the rectifier and the ethanol proceeds to the top. Once the majority of the ethanol is removed from the boiler, the temperature will begin to rise above the boiling point of ethanol, allowing the feints or tails (phenol compounds) to rise inside the rectifier column. This signals the end of the distillation.

Though it is difficult to remove all the fusel oils and water from a distillate, due to things like chemical bonding and the azeotrope effect, a proper rectifying system with steady reflux can attain a nearly pure ethanol concentration of more than 95 percent. See AZEOTROPE. Purification of ethanol beyond that point requires specialized methods.

See also DISTILLATION, PROCESS; and COLUMN STILL.

Hengstebeck, R. J. *Distillation Principles and Design Procedures*. New York: Reinhold, 1961.

Miller, Gregory H. *Whisky Science: A Condensed Distillation*. Cham, Switzerland: Springer Nature Switzerland AG, 2019.

Smith, Gavin. *The A–Z of Whisky*. Glasgow: Angels' Share, 2009.

Darcy O'Neill

refractometer is a device used to measure the alcohol potential of a wort prior to fermentation. See FERMENTATION and WORT.

Regan, Gary (1951–2019), was an author, self-described "bartender emeritus," and the namesake creator of Regans' Orange Bitters no. 6. From around 2010 Regan began publishing under the moniker

Gary Regan goes full bartender at the Slow Food Tribute to Jerry Thomas, held in the Oak Room (formerly the Men's Bar) at the Plaza Hotel, New York, March, 2003. Photograph by Zak Pelaccio.

"gaz regan" and adopted what became a signature streak of eyeliner under his right eye.

Born to pub owners in the county of Lancashire in western England, Regan began tending bar at the age of fourteen at his parents' pub, the Prince Rupert, and dropped out of school shortly thereafter.

In the early 1970s, Regan moved to New York City, where he got a job at Drake's Drum, a popular Upper East Side Irish bar, and continued to work various service-industry jobs through the 1980s. He quit in the early 1990s to pursue writing, landing a drinks column for newly launched glossy *Food Arts* magazine; his big break came when he was pegged to write *The Bartender's Bible* (HarperTorch, 1993), which included 1,001 cocktail recipes and prescriptive bartending advice. He went on to write more than a dozen books, including five volumes of *Gaz Regan's 101 Best New Cocktails* and *The Negroni* (Ten Speed, 2015). His best-known book is the encyclopedic 2003 tome *The Joy of Mixology* (Clarkson Potter), which helped to jumpstart the cocktail renaissance and, with its attention to the social aspects of bartending, provided something of a counterweight to many of the more technically focused bartending books published in the 2000s; it received a revised edition in 2018.

Throughout his career, Regan underscored that a successful bar relies primarily on one variable: the happiness of its patrons. He spread that message through his e-newsletter *Potent Quotables* and bartending masterclasses.

Ford, Simon. "Gary 'Gaz' Regan Knows More about the Culture of Drink Than Basically Anybody." *Food Republic*, May 30, 2013. http://www.foodrepublic.com/2013/05/30/gary-gaz-regan-knows-more-about-the-culture-of-drink-than-basically-anybody/ (accessed March 9, 2021).

Gaz Regan website. http://www.gazregan.com (accessed September 5, 2017).

Maier, Kathryn. "A Conversation with One of the Most Influential Bartenders of Our Time." *Robb Report*, May 26, 2016. http://robbreport.com/food-drink/spirits/conversation-one-most-influential-bartenders-our-time-qa-231875/ (accessed March 9, 2021).

Regan, Gary. *Gaz Regan's Annual Manual for Bartenders, 2011*. London: Mixellany, 2011.

Ventiera, Sara. "Let Gary 'Gaz' Regan Give You a Negroni Lesson." *Village Voice*, May 14, 2015. https://www.villagevoice.com/2015/05/14/let-gary-gaz-regan-give-you-a-negroni-lesson/ (accessed March 9, 2021).

Lauren Viera

Regent's Punch, a rich elaboration on Punch Royal, combining brandy, Batavia arrack, various liqueurs, citrus, green tea, and champagne, served on ice, takes its name from being the preferred evening drink of George Augustus Frederick, prince regent of Great Britain. See ARRACK, BATAVIA; and PUNCH. The prince (1762–1830) was a connoisseur in these matters, perhaps to a fault, and the punch, first recorded in 1817, rapidly found favor beyond the royal household: it was the fashionable drink of the 1820s, both in England and in North America, where its fame spread early, followed quickly by its adoption.

The Regency-era memoirist Captain Gronow, not the most inaccurate of observers, suggested that the punch was created by "Mr. Maddison," the prince's majordomo. Unfortunately, of the many surviving recipes, none appears to be his. There are three, however, that claim some connection to the prince's circles. The earliest, from 1819, is purportedly from "a gentleman who . . . figures high in the upper circles of fashion," and it has several features outside the mainstream of recipes, including the addition of soda water and other wines besides champagne. The other two agree much more closely, differing only in proportion and a few secondary ingredients. The first was printed in 1845 and claims to be from "a person who made the punch daily for the prince's table, at Carlton palace, for six months." The last-printed one is from 1869 and comes with a name: it is "by P. Watier [*sic*], Royal Lodge, 1820: *original*." The "William Terrington" who printed it is probably a pseudonym, but his recipe attributions have proven accurate when they can be checked, and indeed Philippe Wattier was assistant confectioner in the prince's household from 1813 to 1820, and punch making was a recognized part of the confectioner's art. What's more, he lived until 1866, so he could well have given Terrington his old recipe.

It is also worth noting that Wattier was from Metz, since Regent's Punch displays many of the prismatic characteristics of French and German punch making of the late eighteenth century, where the sweet, sour, strong, and weak elements of punch are each divided between several ingredients. Indeed, Regent's Punch acted as a vector for such ideas, and for ingredients such as curaçao, maraschino, and champagne to enter British and American mixology. See CURAÇAO and MARASCHINO. In fact, it enjoyed a longer career in America than it did in Britain, where it quickly faded in the face of Queen Victoria's disapproval of the heavy-drinking ways of her predecessors and their cronies, although it was still occasionally sold as a pre-bottled specialty through the 1880s. In New York, on the other hand, Regent's Punch was particularly appreciated. In the 1820s, William Niblo's rendition of the drink helped him to become the city's leading caterer. Later in the century, the New York State Legislature in Albany, the state capitol, adopted the drink, serving it liberally at all social occasions through the rest of the nineteenth century and until Prohibition. Recent years have seen the formula dusted off again as part of the renewed interest in punch.

Recipe: Infuse the peels of 1 Valencia orange, 1 Seville orange, and 1 lemon in 375 ml cognac for 1 hour. Juice the citrus and add strained juices, 75 ml Batavia arrack, 75 ml old Jamaican rum, 60 ml maraschino or orange curaçao, 75 ml pineapple syrup, and 500 ml cold green tea (made with 10 ml tea leaves). Refrigerate and before serving add 1 bottle chilled champagne. Adjust sweetness to taste with simple syrup.

See also PUNCH.

Acton, Eliza. *Modern Cookery*, 2nd ed. London: Longman, Green, Brown, & Longmans, 1845.

Gabay, Elizabeth. "Champagne Punches and Cocktails." *A History of the World through a Bowl of Punch* (blog), December 17, 2016. https://punchstory.com/2016/12/17/champagne-punches-and-cocktails/ (accessed March 9, 2021).

"Hand in Hand Fancy Dress Ball." *Chester Chronicle*, January 22, 1819, 4.

Terrington, William J. *Cooling Cups and Dainty Drinks*. London: Routledge, 1869.

Wondrich, David. *Punch: The Delights and Dangers of the Flowing Bowl*. New York: Perigee, 2010.

David Wondrich

regulating bodies for spirits and alcohol include governmental agencies at the national and local levels, trade consortiums and associations, and nonprofit organizations. They have been involved with the trade since its very beginning: in Germany, local governments were already regulating distilling and the sale of spirits in the 1400s, when the trade was in its infancy. By the eighteenth century, Britain had a complex and comprehensive system of regulations in place that would have an enormous influence on the development of the spirits business, one that is still felt today. See EXCISE, TAXES, AND DISTILLATION; and GIN.

The United States

The spirits trade in the United States is regulated by agencies at state and federal levels as well as nonprofits. As a result, and owing in large part to the lingering legacy of Prohibition, individual states may have conflicting or contradictory laws for spirits with respect to those of their neighbors.

At the federal level, the Treasury Department manages the Alcohol and Tobacco Tax and Trade Bureau, or TTB for short. The TTB oversees the regulation and enforcement of multiple spirits laws, including the labeling and advertising of distilled spirits; sales and bottling of spirits; and importation and exportation. There are even regulations spelling out the rules of the manufacturing and use of "volatile fruit-flavor concentrate (essence)." The TTB also collects taxes on alcohol, tobacco, firearms, and ammunition sales. The TTB is a relatively new organization, having been founded in January 2003. Its previous incarnation, the Bureau of Alcohol,

Tobacco, and Firearms, or ATF, was reorganized following the passing of the Homeland Security Act of 2002.

Although the names of the departments may change, the history of the United States' spirit regulating bodies illustrates a short history of the nation itself.

After the United States won its independence from the British, the young country found itself saddled with the war's debt. In 1791, Congress passed the first set of laws to collect taxes from its citizens, among them, the Distilled Spirits Tax.

The tax was unpopular with some farmers, and from the start, collecting the tax proved difficult for US regulators. Some tax collectors were tarred and feathered; others were chased out of their homes. The discontent eventually festered into the Whisky Rebellion of 1794, when rebellious citizens fired upon federal tax collectors. The violence quickly escalated, prompting President George Washington to lead federal troops against the insurgents in September 1794. See WASHINGTON, GEORGE.

The insurrection lasted until mid-November, when a large number of the rebels, including their leaders, were arrested. Most of the rebels would eventually be pardoned, including the only two men convicted of treason.

Although violent opposition to the distilled spirits tax was quashed, lingering political pressure prompted Congress to repeal the distilled tax, and other income taxes, in 1802. This would remain the case until the War of 1812, when rising war costs forced the United States to reinstate taxes on distilled spirits and other sources of income. In 1862, costs related to the Civil War again forced Congress to impose several new tariffs on so-called sin and luxury items, such as jewelry, tobacco, and alcohol.

The Volstead Act, passed on July 22, 1919, ushered in the Prohibition era, which banned the production and distribution of alcoholic beverages. The catching of criminals, rather than the collecting of taxes, brought about the Prohibition Reorganization Act of May 27, 1930. The precursor to the TBB, now called the Bureau of Prohibition, was transferred from the Treasury to the Justice Department. Special Agent Eliot Ness would later gain fame by heading up the Prohibition Bureau, which successfully arrested and prosecuted mobsters such as Al Capone, who were profiting from illegal liquor sales.

The passing of the Twenty-First Amendment repealed Prohibition, and with it, the United States against found itself in need of a body on regulating spirits. The Federal Alcohol Administration Act, passed by the 74th Congress on August 29, 1935, was enacted to "further protect the revenue derived from distilled spirits, wine and malt beverages, to regulate interstate and foreign commerce and enforce the postal laws with respect thereto, to enforce the twenty-first amendment, and for other purposes."

The nascent Federal Alcohol Administration, under the purview of the Treasury Department, was deputized as the country's spirits regulator. The Federal Alcohol Administration, for example, outlined consumer-focused regulations, such as protections against deceptive labeling and detailed limitations on advertising of spirits. A separate entity, the Alcohol Tax Unit, dealt with tariffs; both agencies were merged in 1940.

Within the next few years, the Alcohol Tax Unit took on duties related to explosives, firearms, and tobacco, laying the groundwork for what would become the Bureau of Alcohol, Tobacco, and Firearms. In July 1972, following Treasury Department Order 221, the ATF was officially recognized as an independent agency, reporting to the Treasury. The ATF was later reorganized into the United States' current regulating body, the TBB, in 2003.

In contemporary times, taxation on liquor and distilling still remains a flashpoint for the industry. The United States has benefitted greatly from liquor taxes, and revenues show no sign of a downward trend. In 1977, the United States collected $2.3 billion of alcohol tax revenue. By 2013, that number grew to $6.6 billion, according to analysis by the Tax Policy Center.

State and local taxes paid by the liquor industry added up to just under $54 billion in 2014, according to trade group Wine & Spirits Wholesalers of America. The group estimates that 1.83 million Americans have jobs, many of them in family-owned businesses, linked to the manufacture and sales of liquor and wine.

As a result, some of industry's most recognized lobbying and trade group have taken a stance against higher liquor taxes. The Distilled Spirits Council, or DISCUS, argues that taxes on distilled spirits are much higher than similar taxes on wine and beer. Punitive tariffs, the group argues, punish the hospitality industry and threaten employees nationwide. The sentiment is echoed by the American Beverage Licensees trade group and the Wine & Spirits Wholesalers of America.

International Regulation

Most countries have their own regulating bodies that are not dissimilar to the ones in the United States, although they generally have fewer layers of bureaucracy (few countries impose regulations at the provincial level, although India is a very large exception). In the case of the European Union, its regulations parallel most of those of its member nations, although they often add additional detail, governing things such as regional designations and the like.

Internationally, regulating bodies sometimes operate as consortiums that promote the culture of their products, ensure the quality of their spirits, and provide guidance to producers.

The United Kingdom's Scotch Whisky Association dates back to 1912, when the group that would later become the SWA formed as a way to safeguard the sector against rising taxes. See SCOTLAND AND IRELAND.

In France, the Bureau National Interprofessionnel du Cognac, or BNIC, serves as the gatekeeper of the cognac industry. While privately funded, it serves in the interest of cognac producers and aims to protect and promote the spirit locally and internationally (as does the BNIA for Armagnac). See FRANCE.

Mexico, with its booming agave spirits industry, is home to the Tequila Regulatory Council (Consejo Regulador del Tequila, or CRT). As with its French and Scottish counterparts, the CRT hosts journalists, provides historical and contemporary education on its products, and protects the designation of tequila as a purely Mexican product by origin. See MEXICO.

Across the world, regulating bodies may vary in structure and funding, but they tend to be unified in their focus on their native spirits. Brazil has the Brazilian Institute of Cachaça (IBRAC), which represents the cachaça industry. Japan established the Japan Sake and Shochu Makers Association in 1953. Groups are still being established even in modern times; the Irish Whiskey Association, a subset of the Alcohol Beverage Federation of Ireland, was just established in 2014. See BRAZIL.

Occasionally, two groups may even join forces. In December 2016, the Scotch Whisky Association announced a joint agreement with the Brazilian Institute of Cachaça, in which both industries would collaborate on "the prevention of misleading commercial practices, promotion of responsible consumption of alcoholic beverages, and mutual promotion and protection of the geographical indications (GIs) Scotch Whisky and Cachaça."

See also EXCISE, TAXES, AND DISTILLATION; and PROHIBITION AND TEMPERANCE IN AMERICA.

"The BNIC." Cognac France. https://www.cognac.fr/en/bnic/home/ (accessed April 28, 2021). "The Civil War." Tax History Project, http://www.taxhistory.org/www/website.nsf/web/THM1861?OpenDocument (accessed March 31, 2021).

"Federal Taxes and Regulation Policy for Distilled Spirits." Distilled Spirits Council, http://www.discus.org/policy/taxes/ (accessed March 31, 2021).

"International Protection of the Tequila Designation of Origin." Consejo Regulador del Tequila. https://www.crt.org.mx/index.php/en/pages-2/proteccion-del-tequila-a-nivel-internacional (accessed April 28 2021).Office of the General Counsel. *Legislative History of the Federal Alcohol Administration Act*. Washington, DC: Federal Alcohol Control Administration, 1935. Available online at https://archive.org/details/legislativehisto00unit (accessed March 31, 2021).

"Treasury Department Order 221." https://www.atf.gov/our-history/timeline/treasury-department-order-221 (accessed March 31, 2021).

"The TTB Story." https://www.ttb.gov/about-ttb/history (accessed March 31, 2021).

"Who We Are." Scotch Whisky Association. https://www.scotch-whisky.org.uk/who-we-are/ (accessed April 28, 2021).

Wine & Spirits Wholesalers of America website. http://www.wswa.org/ (accessed March 31, 2021).

Elva Ramirez

Reiner, Julie (1971–), is a world-renowned mixologist and the owner and operator of a handful of successful bars and lounges in New York City. As an advocate for fresh-ingredient cocktails in the sour-mix-soaked early-aughts, Reiner was a pioneer of the twenty-first century's modern mixology movement and a mentor to dozens of bartenders who jumpstarted their careers under her watch.

Reiner began her service industry career at age eighteen, working at the Hot Rod Café in her native Honolulu. She bartended herself through college at Florida State University, where, post-nightshift, she would return to find her dormmates "naked and vomiting in the hallway." As she told one interviewer: "I'd walk past them to my room, throw piles of money on the bed, and stand over $200. I was living nicely."

After graduating, Reiner moved to San Francisco for what transpired to be a false start in marketing; she promptly quit to work at the Red Room, a quirky Nob Hill hotel bar, under nightlife tastemaker Linda Fusco. One drag-bar gig and a serious relationship later, Reiner relocated sight-unseen to New York City and landed at the tiny C3 Lounge in the Washington Square Hotel. It was there that her penchant for fresh juice and infusions—cocktail anomalies at the time—caught the interest of renowned mixologist Dale DeGroff and a growing community of forward-thinking cocktail connoisseurs. See DeGroff, Dale.

Reiner opened her first bar, the Jazz Age–inspired Flatiron Lounge, in Manhattan in 2003 (it closed in 2019); two years later, she and Audrey Saunders opened the hugely influential Pegu Club. See Saunders, Audrey; and Pegu Club. Brooklyn's classics-driven Clover Club followed in 2008, winning "Best New Cocktail Lounge in the World" at the following year's Tales of the Cocktail convention. See Tales of the Cocktail. Upscale tiki lounge Lani Kai opened in 2010 and closed in 2012, and Leyenda, Reiner's Latin American *cocteleria* with decorated mixologist Ivy Mix, opened to critical acclaim in 2015. She has written one book, *The Craft Cocktail Party: Delicious Drinks for Every Occasion* (Grand Central Life & Style, 2015).

Akkam, Alia. "The 10 Cocktails That Made My Career: Julie Reiner," *First We Feast* website, October 5, 2015. https://firstwefeast.com/drink/2015/10/the-10-cocktails-that-made-my-career-julie-reiner (accessed March 9, 2021).

Cameron, Ian. "Julie Reiner." Difford's Guide. https://www.diffordsguide.com/encyclopedia/2692/people/julie-reiner (accessed September 5, 2017).

Regan, Gary. "Raising the Bar: Julie Reiner." Liquor.com, June 1, 2010.

Simonson, Robert. "Cocktail Icon Julie Reiner on Her New Book, Her New Bar, and Advice for Bartenders Opening Their First Business." *Grub Street*, May 4, 2015. https://www.grubstreet.com/2015/05/julie-reiner-book-bar-interview.html (accessed March 9, 2021).

Lauren Viera

Rémy Martin is one of the so-called "big four" cognac brands and is among the oldest cognac brands still in existence today. Its founder, Rémy Martin (1695–1773), grew up on a family vineyard in the Charente region of France and started his namesake brand in 1724. In the early eighteenth century, King Louis XV had banned the planting of new grapevines to keep prices from crashing, but in 1738 Martin was granted a royal charter to expand his vineyards, giving a boost to the fledgling company.

For nearly the next two hundred years, the brand was run by several successive generations of the Martin family, until 1924, when it was purchased in a state of near bankruptcy by Andre Renaud, who gradually rebuilt the brand's fortunes. When Renaud died in 1965, his will split the company between his two daughters. André Hériard-Dubreuil (1917–2002), the husband of Anne Marie, the eldest, proved to be a brilliant businessman and built the company into the commercial powerhouse it is today. Geneviève, the other daughter, married Max Cointreau, whose family owned the eponymous orange liqueur. This led to close ties between the two companies, including the establishment of a joint distribution network in 1969 and later a full merger in 1990–1991, creating the spirits giant Rémy Cointreau.

Rémy Cointreau's cognac is all made from grapes grown in the Grande Champagne and Petite Champagne subregions, the two smallest and most prestigious parts of the Cognac region. In 1874, it introduced Louis XIII, a blend of up to 1,200 eaux-de-vie aged as long as a hundred years and bottled in a blown-crystal decanter that is still one of the most expensive cognac bottlings on the market today. In 1927, Remy Martin launched its VSOP, reviving an eighteenth-century age designation for longer-aged cognac that had fallen into disuse. Under Hériard-Dubreuil's regime, the VSOP would go on to smash sales records and force the firm's competitors to launch their own versions. It is still the brand's best-selling bottling. Of the big four, the brand is in a rough tie for second place in terms of sales with Martell.

See also Cointreau and cognac.

Faith, Nicholas. *Cognac*. London: Mitchell Beazley, 2004.

International Directory of Company Histories, vol. 20. Chicago: St. James Press, 1998.

"Our History." https://www.remy-cointreau.com/en/group/our-history/ (accessed March 10, 2021).

Jason Horn

reposado ("rested," in Spanish) refers to tequila that has been aged in oak vats or barrels from two months to one year, in contrast to blanco (aged less than two months) and añejo (aged longer than one year) tequilas. See AÑEJO. The designation was introduced in the mid-1970s, although resting the new spirit in large oak vats prior to bottling had long been a common industry practice. It was enshrined in the Mexican laws governing tequila by 1982.

Many experts regard tequila aged to this range as ideal for sipping, with the time in oak adding just enough mellow, toasty vanilla notes without obscuring tequila's natural honey-like agave, pepper, or citrus characteristics. In addition, a growing number of bartenders prefer reposado for use in premium cocktails: where añejo would be too expensive and blanco too brash, the honeyed tones of reposado lend affordable finesse to mixed drinks.

The reposado designation also is used with other barrel-rested agave spirits, such as mezcal and sotol. See MEZCAL and SOTOL.

See also TEQUILA.

Williams, Ian. *Tequila: A Global History*. London: Reaktion—Edible, 2015.

Kara Newman

retort is a chamber placed between the still and the condenser that forces the vapor to bubble through liquid (either wash or condensed distillate), thus forcing the heavier compounds it contains to condense and making for a stronger distillate. See DOUBLER, THUMPER, KEG, AND RETORT.

David Wondrich

Rhizopus oryzae is one of the most common and significant molds found in qu, the fermentation starter used to make baijiu. See QU and BAIJIU.

rhum agricole, or "agricultural rum," a product of the French West Indies and (to a small extent) the French island of Reunion in the Indian Ocean, is distilled from sugar-cane juice rather than the much more commonly used molasses. See MOLASSES. While some rum was made from sugar-cane juice on sugar plantations in the French Caribbean as early as the seventeenth century, the rhum agricole style itself emerged commercially in the early twentieth century, and its production gained dominance over molasses-based rum in the French Caribbean over the next several decades. See RUM.

Like other islands in the Caribbean, the islands of the French Caribbean, including Martinique and Guadeloupe, initially grew sugar cane in the seventeenth century in order to produce and export sugar to Europe. They also made rum from the byproduct of that sugar production, molasses. However, even in those early sugar estate days, there was a distinction made between *guildive* (the name is a phonetic rendering of the English "kill-devil"), referring to rum made from *vesou* (sugar-cane juice), and *tafia* or *taffia*, made from molasses and skimmings, a distinction that would grow in importance as their rum production evolved. See SKIMMINGS. By the nineteenth century, tafia was applied exclusively to unaged molasses distillate, while the aged distillate became *rhum*—at least, these were the technical terms; as Xavier Rocques pointed out in 1913, "In France, in commerce at the retail level, any spirits from sugar cane or its derivatives are almost always labeled 'rhum.'"

Compared to the rum industries in British colonies such as Barbados and Jamaica, those in the French colonies remained small and technologically backward well into the nineteenth century, due to France's interest in protecting its extensive wine and brandy industries (something Britain lacked entirely); what sugar-cane distilling occurred was almost entirely for local consumption, although a great deal of molasses was exported.

In the mid-nineteenth century, a confluence of events led to an increase and refinement of French Caribbean rum production. Vineyards in France were ravaged by two blights, which devastated wine production and led the French government to lift duties on French Caribbean rum imports. Over this same period, fermentation and distillation methods also improved, and there was increased use of continuous stills, especially in the large industrial distilleries making rum from molasses and DUNDER, primarily centered in the town of Saint-Pierre in Martinique. By the end of the century, the French

Caribbean had transitioned from being primarily a molasses exporter to being a rum exporter, with a large number of distilleries producing molasses-based "rhum industriel" (also commonly referred to as "rhum traditionnel"). In 1900, Martinique was the largest rum exporter in the world.

However, at the same time, the European sugar beet industry emerged, and France largely abandoned cane sugar for beet sugar, thus leaving many of the smaller sugar producers on Martinique and other French islands struggling. Without a market for their sugar, and therefore no molasses byproduct, these smaller producers began to focus on producing rum directly from the fresh juice of the sugar cane, distilling it to low proof (ca. 55 percent ABV) in pot stills. Initially, this *rhum agricole* or *rhum d'habitant* ("locals' rhum," although that term also encompassed rum made from cane syrup) was "exclusively reserved for local consumption," even though—as one observer noted in 1903—it was "certainly superior" to the rhum industriel. See CANE SYRUP.

In 1902, Martinique's Mount Pelée volcano erupted, killing over forty thousand residents of Saint-Pierre and destroying the bulk of the large rhum industriel distilleries. This gave smaller distilleries the opportunity to expand their production of rhum agricole to fill the void in rum production, as did the French army's great demand for rum during World War I. Eventually, French consumers learned to appreciate the once-unfamiliar style; by the 1930s, it was highly prized. In order to protect their wine and brandy production, however, France had implemented import quotas on rum from the islands in the 1920s, and these continued throughout the decades that followed, resulting in the closure of many distilleries in the second half of the century. Just eight distilleries remain today, all but one of them producing rhum agricole, although all now use continuous stills. These survivors are notable for their use of now-antique steam engines to crush the cane and using the residue, or bagasse, to fire their boilers.

In 1996 Martinique received a designation for rhum agricole as an appellation d'origine contrôlée (AOC) product just like champagne and cognac (labeled Appellation d'Origine Contrôlée Martinique Rhum Agricole). To earn this designation, the rhum agricole must be made from the fresh juice of sugar cane and adhere to strict rules of production, some of which are listed here. The cane itself is limited to particular species and volume per hectare and can only be irrigated four months a year to prevent overproduction, and it must be harvested between January and August. The cane juice must only be extracted using grinding or pressing the cane, and must have a minimum sugar content ($> 14°$ Bx) and a minimum pH (> 4.7). Fermentation is restricted to only yeast of the genus *Saccharomyces* and must not exceed 72 hours or a temperature greater than $38.5°$ C, and continuous and closed fermentation is prohibited. Distillation is restricted to continuous distillation using a single-column still restricted to particular parameters (heated by vapor injection, using five to nine rectifying plates, using at least fifteen stripping plates that are between 0.7 and 2 meters in diameter, and reflux chauffe-vins or copper water condensers), and no secondary distillation is allowed. The AOC requires bottling at a minimum of 40 percent ABV (50 percent is the customary proof) and designates three aging categories: *rhum blanc* (rested at least three months after distillation); *élevé sous bois*, meaning rested under wood (aged a minimum of one year on oak), and *rhum vieux* (aged a minimum of three years in oak).

Herve, Joseph. "Il y a rhum et rhum comme il y a fagots et fagots." *Revue internationale des produits coloniaux*, September 1931, 484–488.

Pairault, E. A. *Le rhum et sa fabrication*. Paris: Gauthier-Villars, 1902.

Rhum Agricole website. https://www.rhum-agricole.net/site/en/ (accessed April 30, 2021).

Rocques, Xavier. *Eaux de vie*. Paris: Librairie Polytechnique Ch. Béranger, 1913.

Smith, Frederick H. *Caribbean Rum: A Social and Economic History*. Gainesville: University Press of Florida, 2005.

                                    Martin Cate and David Wondrich

Rhum Barbancourt, one of the world's premier rums, is the only Haitian rum to penetrate international spirits markets. Founded in 1862 by Dupré Barbancourt, a Frenchman who migrated to Haiti, Rhum Barbancourt is among the Caribbean's oldest rum distilleries.

Haiti occupies the western third of the island of Hispaniola, colonized by French settlers in the 1650s and ceded by Spain to France in 1697. In the eighteenth century, French sugar planters in Saint-Domingue, as the colony was known, produced enormous amounts of sugar, which left a lot of molasses available for rum distilling. However, in 1713, French wine and brandy interests had successfully petitioned to close metropolitan markets to French Caribbean rum, thus stifling the development of rum distilling in Saint-Domingue. What rum was produced on sugar estates was given to enslaved workers as part of their weekly rations. In 1791, enslaved peoples and free people of color in Saint-Domingue rose up against French colonial rule and by 1804 had established the independent nation of Haiti.

Dupré Barbancourt (ca. 1837–1907) arrived in Haiti more than a half century after the start of the Haitian Revolution. He was from the Charente region of France, which is known for its fine cognacs. See COGNAC. It is possible that Barbancourt perfected his distilling skills in France and brought them Haiti where he applied them to rum making. His arrival in Haiti coincides with the oidium and phylloxera blights, which devastated grape vineyards in France. Harsh import duties on French Caribbean rum were suspended to help meet the dwindling availability of spirits. Perhaps Barbancourt sought to capitalize on the devastation of French vineyards by making rum for the French market. By 1900, he was the leading distiller in the country (just edging out Sèneque Pierre), and his rhum, based on sugar-cane juice, as was universal in Haiti, had won several international awards.

In the mid-twentieth century, distillers at Barbancourt refined their product and continued winning awards. Yet political upheaval and environmental disasters challenged the success of the company. In 1991, the United Nations imposed a trade embargo that sought to end the military coup that led to the ouster of democratically elected president Jean-Bertrand Aristide. The embargo closed markets to Barbancourt rum, including its largest market in the United States. On January 12, 2010, Haiti was rocked by a devastating earthquake. The storehouse at Rhum Barbancourt suffered serious damage. As much as 30 percent of its stores were damaged, including rums that had been aging for fifteen years. Despite these setbacks, Rhum Barbancourt has remained a strong competitor in the world rum market. Its fifteen-year-old Réserve du domaine is considered one of the finest rums, comparable to the finest cognac. Rhum Barbancourt remains the most internationally recognized rum of Haiti.

See also RUM and CARIBBEAN.

Simpson, J. Montague. *Six months in Port au Prince*. Philadelphia: G. S. Ferguson, 1905.

Smith, Frederick H. *Caribbean Rum: A Social and Economic History*. Gainesville: University Press of Florida, 2005.

Frederick H. Smith

Ribalaigua y Vert, Constante (1888–1952),

the presiding genius of the Floridita bar in Havana, was the dean of Cuban bartenders and unquestionably the most influential mixologist of the twentieth century. As with most bartenders, the details of his early life and career are fragmentary and often contradictory. He was born in Lloret de Mar, near Barcelona, and moved to Havana with his family when he was still quite young. That much is certain. In 1935, Ribalaigua told Thomas Sugrue, an American journalist, that he attended the "English Academy" in Havana and that when he was sixteen his father, a bartender at the old Piña de Plata café at the corner of Obispo and Monserrate in the center of the city "asked him if he wished to learn barkeeping." He did.

We don't know where Ribalaigua began his career behind the bar. At some point between 1898 and 1907 the Piña de Plata was remodeled and renamed the Café Restaurant la Florida. Ribalaigua began working there in either 1912 or 1914 (accounts differ), staying on after the Sala Pareda family, also from Lloret de Mar, purchased the bar in 1918. (Miguel Boadas, a relative of the owners, worked alongside Ribalaigua until 1922.) See BOADAS BAR. Over the next few years, as travel writer Basil Woon noted in 1928, "the bar . . . sprang into vogue." Woon attributed this to "the remarkable talents of the head of the head barman, *Constantino*, a saturnine individual whose peculiar gift consists in his accurate, though seemingly casual, measurements of drinks." By the mid-1930s, Ribalaigua was acknowledged by all—locals, tourists, eventually even his competitors—as the king of Cuban drink makers. In 1935, he bought the bar.

Ribalaigua was an unprepossessing man, quiet and reserved in his demeanor. Even though by the late 1930s he had attained wealth and a degree of international celebrity, he still donned the white jacket every morning and got behind the bar to mix drinks. He was a master of all of the traditional skills—accurate free pouring, stirring, shaking. See FREE POURING; STIRRING; and SHAKE. He was also adept at the "old technique" (as one American dubbed it) of throwing a drink, "pouring from one [glass] to the other at a constantly increasing distance apart." See THROWING (INC. TOSSING). He squeezed all his limes by hand, using his fingers only. At the same time, he was a pioneer in using electric cocktail mixers at his bar and mixed with a far wider range of spirits, including such exotics as scotch whisky, tequila, pisco, and Campari, than his competitors. See CAMPARI.

Ribalaigua's reputation was cemented as much by his creativity as by his skill. It was his practice, as he told Sugrue, to invent a new drink every day "as self discipline." Among his lasting creations are the Daiquiri no. 3, alias "Hemingway Special," with a spoonful each of maraschino and grapefruit juice; the Floridita; and, most likely, the El Presidente. See DAIQUIRI; FLORIDITA; and EL PRESIDENTE. His influence, however, extends far beyond his actual creations, or, for that matter, his celebrity clientele (besides Ernest Hemingway, who was a fixture at the bar, his regulars included everyone from Leopold Stokowski to Marlene Dietrich). As the leading ambassador, as it were, for the tropical drink, he set the bar high: his cocktails were elegant, subtle, balanced, and unfailingly delicious. Their focus on rum and fresh fruit juices proved enormously influential on the American tiki movement—indeed, Trader Vic studied his bar and his drinks closely. See TIKI and BERGERON, VICTOR "TRADER VIC".

In 1950, ill health forced Ribalaigua to step out from behind the bar, although he continued to supervise his establishment, now remodeled yet again, with the traditional open arches closed up and air-conditioning installed. Two years later, he was dead. His heirs ran the bar until 1960, when it was nationalized. It is still open today.

Campoamor, Fernando. *El Floridita de Hemingway.* Havana: Cubaexport, n.d.

Constante Ribalaigua behind the bar at the Floridita, ca. 1935. Courtesy of the Amargura Cultura Collection.

Cuddy, Jack. "Cuban's Cocktail King Tells Cuddy Daiquiri Recipe." *Rome (NY) Daily Sentinel*, March 5, 1937, 12.

McCormick, Henry J. "No Foolin'." *Wisconsin State Journal*, May 17, 1938, 17.

Ramírez-Rosell, Reinaldo. "Constante Ribalaigua, rey del Daiquiri." *Diario de la marina* (Havana), December 7, 1952, 55.

[Ribalaigua, Constante]. *Cocktails—Bar la Florida.* Havana: [1939].

Sugrue, Thomas. "High Sun." *American Magazine*, February 1935, 140.

David Wondrich

rice (*Oryza sativa*) is a cereal grain in the grass family used to make fermented foods and beverages since prehistoric times and distilled spirits since at least the thirteenth century CE. See CEREALS. Cooked rice serves as both a starch and a culture for harvesting yeast and other airborne microorganisms in East Asia, where rice alcohol is ubiquitous. These drinks vary greatly in complexity, ranging from mellow and floral to rich and fruity. The earliest instance of rice alcohol appeared in northern China around 7000 BCE and spread throughout the region. Many ancient rice beers like Chinese *huangjiu*, Japanese sake, and Korean *cheongju* later became the basis for their distilled counterparts: baijiu, shochu, and soju. As rice was a coveted food source, Asian governments often sought to tax and restrict its use in alcohol production. Consequently, other starches have largely supplanted rice as the primary ingredient in most Asian liquors, but it can still be found in some mash bills. See BAIJIU; CHINA; SHOCHU; and SOJU.

McGovern, Patrick E. *Uncorking the Past: The Quest for Wine, Beer, and Other Alcoholic Beverages.* Berkeley: University of California Press, 2009.

Latham, A. J. H. *Rice: The Primary Commodity.* New York: Routledge, 1998.

Derek Sandhaus

rice-aroma-style baijiu is a rice-based spirit closely associated with the folk rice wine (*mijiu*) tradition of southeastern China. Rice baijiu presents a bit of a paradox to outside observers: it is by far the most accessible Chinese spirit to the foreign palate, but it enjoys little prestige in China's domestic market. This is probably attributable to a widespread national preference for bold, aggressive flavors not found in rice spirits, which tend toward a mellow, floral flavor profile similar to Japanese sake and more in line with global preferences.

In terms of production, rice aroma differs from other baijiu styles in several crucial aspects, most obviously in the use of rice and sticky rice instead of sorghum as its primary ingredient. Distillers of rice baijiu typically steam rice three times prior to fermentation. Unlike other categories, rice baijiu performs saccharification and fermentation in separate steps, undertaking the former in small jars with rice-based small qu and the latter in larger jars to which additional water and qu have been added. See SACCHARIFICATION; FERMENTATION; and QU. Rice baijiu is also sometimes made in continuous stills, as opposed to more traditional Chinese pot stills. The raw distillate averages around 58 percent ABV prior to blending and often has a slight yellowish tint.

Different distilleries have also added their own twists. Guilin Sanhua in Guangxi Province—China's most famous rice aroma producer—adds Chinese medicine (its ingredients are a company secret) to its qu, triple-steams its grain, and triple-distills its spirits. Shiwan in Guangdong Province infuses its aged spirits with pork fat. Rice baijiu is the most commonly infused spirit in China and easily takes on the flavor of various traditional herbs and spices.

See also BAIJIU and CHINA.

Huang Faxin, David Tiande Cai, and Wai-Kit Nip. "Chinese Wines: Jiu." In *Handbook of Food Science, Technology, and Engineering*, vol. 4, by Yiu H. Hui, 173-1–52. Boca Raton, FL: CRC, 2005.

Wang Kai 王恺, ed. *San Lian Sheng Huo Zhou Kan* 三联生活周刊 675. March 26, 2012.

Derek Sandhaus

rich simple syrup is a solution of sugar and water, prepared in a ratio of two parts sugar to one part water. The "rich" in the syrup's name is shorthand for the higher sugar-to-water ratio than that found in simple syrup (commonly mixed in a 1:1 ratio), and many choose to use a full-flavored raw sugar such as turbinado or demerara when preparing it, lending additional weight to the descriptor. Rich simple syrup adds slightly less dilution to a drink than simple syrup and is more resistant to spoilage. The term was occasionally used in the nineteenth century and was revived in 2003 by drinks historian David Wondrich specifically to describe the version with raw sugar.

See also SIMPLE SYRUP.

Wondrich, David. *Killer Cocktails.* New York: HarperResource, 2005.

Paul Clarke

The **Rickey** is a highball made from any liquor (though traditionally bourbon, rye, or gin), half of a lime squeezed and dropped in the glass, and carbonated water. No sugar is added to the classic Rickey, though occasionally variations are found with a scant amount of sweetener. By proclamation of the city council in 2011, it is the official cocktail of Washington, DC, where it was popularized in the late 1880s at Shoomaker's bar by Colonel Joseph Kerr "Joe" Rickey (1842–1903), a lobbyist from Missouri, and bartender George Williamson (1849–1915).

COL. RICKEY'S RECIPE FOR A "RICKEY."
(Prepared by Request In His Own Handwriting.)

Joe Rickey's handwritten recipe for the drink that bore his name, 1895: "Large glass—Ice—/whiskey or Gin—/Lime Juice/Carbonated watter/Dont Drink too Many/JK Rickey." Wondrich Collection.

As Rickey told the *New York Herald* in 1893, he "was not the author" of the drink, but "merely its introducer to the East." He went on to give a detailed account of its origins, the first of at least three that were published during his lifetime. According to Rickey, the drink stems from the answer his St. Louis friend Enno Sander (1822–1911), a Prussian-born physician and chemist, gave him when the colonel asked him why he never drank beer. Sander replied that "a drink that contained carbonated water was more exhilarating, refreshing, and at the same time less intoxicating" and "explained what constituted a proper drink": whisky, carbonated water, and ice (it should be noted that Sanders was in the carbonated water business). Rickey "thought his argument forceful and logical" and adopted the drink. See HIGHBALL. His preferred whisky was reportedly Belle of Nelson bourbon, and his preferred water Apollinaris.

To this, Rickey took to adding lemon juice, in an effort to make the drink even more healthful. One day in the late 1880s he ordered one of these drinks over the bar at Shoomaker's, the Washington, DC, politicians' hangout that he frequented, and had even owned for a couple of years after Major Shoomaker's death in 1883. His drink began catching on with the crowd at "Shoo's," as the bar was known—only with lime juice, which Rickey disliked, instead of lemon. Rickey attributed the change to one of the bartenders there. That bartender was more than likely George Williamson, who was the "president" and principal barkeep at the bar and who would have a long association with the Rickey. See SHOOMAKER'S.

Indeed, Washington political writer George Rothwell Brown named Williamson as the Rickey's actual inventor, relating the story that an unknown stranger discussed with Williamson how drinks in the Caribbean were prepared using half of a lime, gave Williamson some limes, and asked him to substitute rye whisky for rum. See SWIZZLE. The following morning Williamson was said to have made one of these for Col. Rickey, who approved.

But whether it was the Prussian doctor who didn't like beer, the man from the Caribbean with the limes, or Joe Rickey himself who invented the drink, and whether Rickey actually drank it or not, his friends certainly drank it and associated it with him. The name itself is attributed to both Rep. William Henry Hatch and Fred Mussey, who were said to be present at Shoomaker's when the drink was created and later came in asking for a "Joe Rickey drink" or saying, "I'll have a Joe Rickey." In any case, both the drink and the name were circulating by the end of 1889 and became widespread in Washington the next summer and the rest of America shortly thereafter.

The "Joe Rickey" may have started as a bourbon drink, but by the mid-1890s it was the Gin Rickey that was the best-known version. Brown argues that the gin version owed its popularity to a joke circulating at the Chicago exposition of 1893, where the *jinrikusha*, or rickshaw, was introduced from Japan. (The joke was already circulating in Washington in 1891: "The first thing a toper asks for in Japan is a gin-ricksha," as the Washington *Star* phrased it.)

Whatever its precise origin, the peerlessly refreshing Gin Rickey became a true sensation, gaining such wide notoriety in the 1890s and 1900s that a 1907 article from the *Los Angeles Herald* could state: "Now let the warm weather come and let the siphons hiss, because the limes are here ready for the gin rickeys. Three hundred cases of rickeys, or to be more explicit, 2,000,000 junior lemons—for, to be sure, they lacked the carbonic water and gin—arrived today from the West Indies on the steamship Pretoria."

The Rickey's popularity waned, of course, and by the 1900s newspapers were already suggesting that the scotch highball and Mamie Taylor were more popular than the once all-conquering Gin Rickey. It never really recovered in the twentieth century, and even its modern revival has extended only fitfully beyond the borders of its hometown.

Recipe: Squeeze half a lime into an ice-filled highball glass and drop in the lime shell. Add 45 ml bourbon or gin and fill with carbonated water.

Brown, George Rothwell. *Washington: A Not Too Serious History*. Baltimore: Norman, 1930.
"Col. Rickey on Mixed Drinks." *New York Sunday Telegraph*, October 6, 1900, pt. 2, 1.
"*DC Councilmember to Declare the Rickey as Washington's Native Cocktail.*" *Washington Post*, July 14, 2011.
Felten, Eric. "A Lobbyist of Special Interest." *Wall Street Journal*, April 19, 2008. http://www.wsj.com/articles/SB120855043970227091 (accessed March 10, 2021).
"He Invented Rickeys." *Syracuse Sunday Herald*, October 6, 1895, 19.
"Inventor of the Gin Rickey." *Washington Post*, October 1, 1911.
"'Rickey' Philosophy." *New York Herald*, December 3, 1893, sec. 4, 4.

Derek Brown

rickhouse, a term frequently used to refer to a warehouse for aging bourbon and other American whisky, is derived from "rick," the name for the wooden structure that supports the barrels of aging spirits. See BARREL; MATURATION; and WHISKY, BOURBON.

Ritz Bar, in the legendary Paris hotel of the same name, was a favorite watering hole for literary luminaries like Ernest Hemingway and F. Scott Fitzgerald. Its most famous bartender was Frank Meier, a specialist in the Sidecar. See MEIER, FRANK; and SIDECAR.

The **Rob Roy**, with sweet vermouth, bitters, and scotch whisky, may be nothing more than a scotch Manhattan, but it is nevertheless a legitimate classic and indeed the premiere cocktail with that spirit. See MANHATTAN COCKTAIL.

As usual in these matters, there are several claims to its creation, the most creditable of which comes from a 1941 letter to G. Selmer Fougner's Along the Wine Trail column in the *New York Sun*, describing how the writer's brother was tending bar at the popular Duke's House, across from the New York ferry in Hoboken, New Jersey, when a representative of the newly introduced Usher's blended scotch whisky came in. See FOUGNER, G. SELMER. The representative wanted a cocktail, but with his whisky. Since at the time scotch was not generally used in cocktails, Henry August Orphal, the bartender, was forced to invent something, which the appreciative salesman and his friends christened the Rob Roy (most likely after the popular Broadway show of the time). According to his brother, Orphal won $10 from the *Police Gazette* for his cocktail; this has not been confirmed, but Orphal's employment in the area as a bartender is well-attested, and other circumstances check out. In any case, the cocktail was in circulation by the end of 1895 and in bar books from the turn of the century. (Orphal's was not the first recorded Rob Roy cocktail; that belonged to well-known

New York bartender Edward F. Barry [1844–1920], who dictated it to a reporter from the *New York Sun* in 1873; unfortunately, in his article the reporter garbled the recipe, and it's unknown if it, too, was a scotch cocktail.)

The Rob Roy's simplicity and harmoniousness (one of the few scotch cocktails to possess that quality) earned it an enduring spot in the cocktail canon, one that it still occupies. It might be reductive to say that it is not a scotch cocktail, but rather *the* scotch cocktail. But it is not wrong.

Recipe: Stir well with ice 60 ml blended scotch whisky, 30 ml sweet vermouth, and 2 dashes Angostura bitters. Strain into cocktail glass. Add cherry or orange twist. Note that early versions called for equal parts whisky and vermouth and used orange bitters, while some modern drinkers prefer Peychaud's Bitters.

Fougner, G. Selmer. "Along the Wine Trail." *New York Sun*, March 24, 1941, 16.

Walker, Dunton. "Gossip of the Nation." *Philadelphia Inquirer*, May 15, 1948, 11.

David Wondrich

rock and rye is an American liqueur and, depending on the bottling proof, can also be classified as a flavored whisky. Comprised of rye whisky and rock candy or rock candy syrup, rock and rye can be traced to the early 1800s, when it was used as a pharmaceutical to treat the common cold, and most likely also to smooth the rough edges off of young rye whisky. It first came to market as a proprietary cordial in the late 1870s, after the *New York Sun* printed an anecdote about the New York political orator Ellis B. Schnabel (1813–1900), where he recommended "rock candy and whisky" as an infallible remedy for tuberculosis and gave himself as proof. The *Sun*'s article was widely reprinted, and the newspaper was deluged with requests for the article. Brands sprang up immediately to capitalize on the public interest. Proprietary rock and rye formulas sold as nostrum medicines at pharmacies proliferated through the rest of the 1800s. Although its medicinal reputation endured well into the twentieth century, at least on a folk level, a reclassification of the rate at which it was taxed from the low "proprietary medicine" rate to the higher "beverage" one

in 1883 laid the foundation for its evolution as a recreational beverage, although American bartenders continued to "prescribe" it for sore throats and coughs.

The beginning of the twentieth century saw the addition of modifying flavors, and over time various branded bottlings for rock and rye have included any number of the following ingredients: large pieces of rock candy in the bottle, honey, horehound, balsam of tolu, cinnamon, citrus, stone fruit, and pineapple. Rock and rye almost disappeared at the end of the twentieth century. The beginning of the twenty-first has, however, brought some signs of its revival, primarily as ready-to-drink pre-mixed cocktail, not a cold remedy.

See also LIQUEURS and WHISKY, RYE.

"Fighting over Rock and Rye." *New York Sun*, February 3, 1879, 1.

"A Lecture in a Horse Car." *New York Sun*, December 23, 1877, 3.

"Rock-and-Rye." *Ogden (UT) Standard*, July 13, 1883, 2.

Chad Solomon

rocks is a bartending term for ice. Customers asking for a drink "on the rocks" wish for it to be served over ice, and those wanting a single cube of ice in their spirit may request "one rock." Because they are generally used to serve spirits on the rocks, Old-Fashioned or lowball glasses are often termed "rocks glasses."

Though the similarity between hard cubes of ice and rocks is readily apparent, the term actually derived from the name of a specific drink: "scotch on the rocks." In 1947, Earl Wilson reported in his It Happened Last Night syndicated column that the current "fad drinks" at New York's 21 Club included "scotch on the rocks," which he explained was "scotch over ice cubes." The term moved quickly into nationwide usage, and by 1950 it had become shorthand for a distinctively American type of drink. ("The average American," noted the *Rockford (IL) Register-Republic* in 1950, is brought up on "a simple and Spartan diet of double Martinis, bloody Marys, and Scotch on the rocks.")

Nor did it take long for the term "on the rocks" to be applied to any straight liquor served over ice rather than neat. In 1948, David Embury included "Gin on the Rocks" in his seminal *Fine Art of Mixing*

Drinks. See EMBURY, DAVID. By 1950, the term had spread to include mixed drinks, the latest thing being the "Martini on the Rocks." Eleven years later, according to the *New York Times*, it was now "vodka on the rocks" that drinkers considered to be "the ultimate in sophistication." Around the same time, Old-Fashioned or lowball glasses—short, sturdy glasses with a wide mouth and straight or rounded sides holding between four and nine ounces—began to be called "on-the-rocks glasses." By the mid-1970s the term was shortened to just "rocks glasses," and it is now the standard way to refer to that particular piece of glassware.

See also GLASS, OLD-FASHIONED; ICE, HISTORY OF ITS USE; and ICE, SCIENCE OF ITS USE.

Felten, Eric. "A Chill to Scotch Purists' Hearts." *Wall Street Journal*, May 16, 2009.

Hamil, Erb. "Rex Reaches Bar." *New Orleans Times-Picayune*, February 19, 1950, section 3, 7.

Robert F. Moss

rolling and **tossing** are both techniques employed by a bartender to mix, aerate, and/or chill drinks.

Rolling is very simple: one simply pours the liquid, ice and all, back and forth between two halves of a Boston shaker or other two-part shaker, held next to each other. This cools and mixes the liquid without aerating it and is traditionally used when pineapple or especially tomato juice is in the mix, because hard shaking breaks down the integrity of the juice, causing it to foam up so much that the texture loses its weight on the tongue. See BLOODY MARY.

Tossing, or "throwing" a drink, as Jerry Thomas refers to it in his seminal book, *How to Mix Drinks, or The Bon-Vivant's Companion*, requires some skill and practice. The technique requires a two-part cocktail shaker—a Boston shaker or the like. Both parts must be large enough to hold the ingredients to be mixed with plenty of room left over. The process begins once all the ingredients, plus ice, are assembled in one half of the shaker set and it is topped with a strainer. The two containers start out very close together, the container with the liquid on top and ready to pour. The bartender begins pouring the liquid from the top container into the empty one below while quickly pulling the top container up and away from the bottom one. This move gives the appearance of a ribbon of liquid connecting the two vessels. Some practitioners add an extra bit of flair by turning their bodies in an arc or even spinning totally around while pouring. Once the original container is almost empty, the bartender quickly brings the two containers together again, pouring the liquid back through the strainer into the original container. He or she will repeat the process four or five times for full effect.

Modern craft bartenders have resurrected and mastered this technique, once almost lost. While its origin is American, the last place it was being practiced was Barcelona, where Miguel Boadas had brought it from Cuba, where the bartenders had originally learned the "swinging movement that can be acquired only by long practice" (as one observer put it in 1899) it from Americans. See BOADAS, MIGUEL; and RIBALAIGUA Y VERT, CONSTANTE.

There is a traditional variant of the process where mugs are used instead of cocktail shakers. The technique is similar to rolling, but the liquid being tossed from one container to the other is hot and on fire. It gives "the appearance of a continued stream of liquid fire," to quote Thomas, its evangelist. He unfortunately provides little guidance as to how to pull off this feat but makes one salient observation: "To become proficient in throwing the liquid from one mug to another, it will be necessary to practice for some time with cold water."

If you want to make Thomas's signature Blue Blazer cocktail, you'll need to master the art of throwing. In the 1862 edition of his book, he includes an illustration depicting a bartender fixing the drink and demonstrating the death-defying act, which is probably the first time it was shown in print. See BLUE BLAZER.

Some nineteenth-century barflies wrote enthusiastic descriptions of American bartenders who could toss a flaming liquid in an arc over their heads. Frankly, that defies the rules of gravity, and the enthusiasm of the scribes who documented that move may have been related to the number of drinks they imbibed while enjoying the spectacle.

See also THOMAS, JEREMIAH P. "JERRY", and BOSTON SHAKER.

Dietsch, Michael. "10 Bartending Terms You Might Not Know." *Serious Eats*, December 12, 2013. http://drinks.seriouseats.com/2013/12/bartending-terms-glossary-behind-the-stick-buyback-bartender-slang.html (accessed March 31, 2021).

"How To Roll a Bloody Mary—Speakeasy Cocktails." YouTube, December 4, 2012. https://www.youtube.com/watch?v=yK_ML-RX83U (accessed March 31, 2021).

Ward, Fannie Brigham. "Many Odd Things in Cuban Cities." *Washington Times*, February 5, 1899, 3.

Dale DeGroff

root-based spirits encompass two kinds of spirits. First are spirits distilled with sugar beet or, rarely, other roots as the basis of the spirit—for example, a vodka made of sugar-beet neutral spirit. The other type includes liquors and liqueurs made by steeping roots or rhizomes in another, usually neutral, spirit. In agricultural and culinary use, the word "root" often denotes true botanical roots, but also rhizomes and tubers. See TUBER-BASED SPIRITS.

True roots that are fermented and distilled are rare. Among them are the carrot, used in Japan to make shochu, and the yellow gentian, used in the German Alps to make *Enzian*. By far the most common, however, is the sugar beet. This is used for *tuzemak*, a rum-like spirit from the Czech Republic and Slovakia, and some craft distillers, such as Brooklyn's Industry City, are also now using sugar beets to make vodka. Sugar-beet alcohol, in fact, is used in variety of products—including as a base for other flavored spirits, such as absinthe, gin, and a great many liqueurs and cocktail bitters.

Most roots used in spirits making are however used to flavor other spirits. Gentian, another true root, is used to add a deeply bitter flavor to cocktail bitters, aperitifs, digestives, vermouths, and especially gentian liqueurs, made by steeping the root and other botanicals in grain alcohol. It was one of the components of Stoughton's Bitters, the first cocktail bitters, and is an important component of their linear descendant Campari. See CAMPARI and STOUGHTON'S BITTERS. Gentian-flavored aperitifs, and liqueurs include Salers, Suze, Bonal, Perigord, and Deribaucourt, most of them products of the Alpine region between France and Italy. See APERITIF AND DIGESTIVE and SUZE.

Another true root, ginseng, provides the base flavoring agent in ginseng root liqueur, common in Korea. Ginseng has long been thought to have therapeutic properties, including regulating blood pressure and increasing blood circulation. See SOUTH KOREA.

The licorice plant is a legume, and its roots are used to flavor candies and sweeteners, as well as Italian liqueurs such as Anima Nera and Liquirizia.

A rhizome is a plant stem that grows underground, sending out roots and shoots. Galangal and calamus are among the rhizomes that have been made into liqueurs, but the most common rhizome liqueur is made from ginger. Examples include the French Domain De Canton ginger liqueur; the King's Ginger, from the United Kingdom; Barrow's Intense, from New York City; and Sikkim Pearl of Himalayas, from India.

See also CORDIALS.

Gentian Research Network. http://gentian.rutgers.edu (accessed April 26, 2021).

Michael Dietsch

The **Rose** cocktail, originally with kirschwasser, French vermouth, and *sirop de groseille* (red currant syrup), was effectively the signature drink of Paris from the early 1900s until World War II. Created by Giovanni "Johnny" Mitta (ca. 1877–?), the diminutive Italian head bartender at the Chatham Bar (on Rue Daunou in the city's American quarter), the drink first appears in print in 1910. Johnny was probably inspired by the most popular perfume of the time, La Rose Jacqueminot, which was so successful that it made its Corsican creator, François Coty (1874–1934), a millionaire.

With the Rose's popularity came an unusual degree of variation in its recipe: from the early 1900s, one finds many different versions, with some cocktail books offering one, some another, and others compiling all the known variants. Judging from these recipes, it seems that not only did each bartender in Paris have his own version, but even each bartender of the Chatham did, with Albert adding cherry brandy and Santos adding gin (this version became the most widespread). Johnny's original version, however, is a uniquely lovely drink, delicate, subtle, and intriguing.

Recipe: Stir with ice 60 ml French dry vermouth, 30 ml kirschwasser, and 5 ml red currant or raspberry syrup or grenadine. Garnish with maraschino cherry. For Albert's version, use 45 ml kirsch, 30 ml vermouth, and 15 ml cherry brandy; for Santos's, use 30 ml each kirsch, gin, and dry vermouth, with

2 dashes crème de cassis and a dash of strawberry liqueur or syrup.

Cappiello, Leonetto. "La Rose Jacqueminot" (Coty poster). 1901.

Chef de Partie. "Rivieriana." *Sporting Times*, March 16, 1912, 10.

Gros, Bernard. "Aux Capucines." *Le Figaro*, April 27, 1910, 5.

Lupoiu, Jean. *370 recettes de Cocktails*. Saigon: Albert Portail, 1927.

Fernando Castellon

Rosenstiel, Lewis (1891–1976), was a whisky baron who ruled with an iron fist. For most of his life Rosenstiel ran Schenley Industries, which through a number of shrewd moves he turned into a giant spirits company that owned brands located around the world, including I. W. Harper and Ancient Age bourbons and Dewar's scotch whisky. "A prodigious worker," according to his obituary in the *New York Times*, "Rosenstiel thought nothing of calling his associates at any hour, day or night, to discuss business." The paper also called him "at one time the most powerful figure in the distilled spirits business." Born in Cincinnati, Rosenstiel was entirely a self-made man, having left school at sixteen and begun in the liquor business soon after.

It was none other than Winston Churchill who, in a chance encounter in 1922 along the French Rivera, inspired him to buy his distilleries. Churchill, according to reports, tipped him off that alcohol would soon be legal once again in America. Rosenstiel purchased several distilleries that were mothballed during Prohibition as well as a stock of whisky. One of his acquisitions was in Schenley, Pennsylvania, which would become the name of his overall company. After the repeal of Prohibition, the company was the second-largest whisky seller, and he enlisted Lehman Brothers to take Schenley public. At the time, the investment house valued his company at $3 million. By 1935, it had sales of $63 million and earnings of $8 million.

"A domineering man with a quick temper" (as the *Times* characterized him), Rosenstiel enjoyed an epic rivalry with the Bronfman family, who owned his main competitor, Seagram's. The two companies battled each other for brands to acquire, market share, shelf space, and, of course, drinkers. See Bronfman family and Seagram Company Ltd.

Rosenstiel famously tried to profit off the Korean War. He figured that, like during World War II, the distilleries would have to shut down to make war goods, which would create a shortage of aged whisky and boost its value. To prepare for this spike in demand, he ramped up production. It was a great plan, except the Korean War didn't last long enough to require a distilling freeze, and Schenley was stuck with warehouses full of barrels. Not a terrible problem, but after the liquor aged for eight years, he would owe the IRS $10.50 in taxes on every last gallon. Rosenstiel convinced the government to extend the period that whisky could age before taxes are due, thus saving Schenley millions and creating a whole new aged-whisky category. To boost sales he also began aggressively marketing older whiskies to drinkers. This strategy eventually bore fruit, but Rosenstiel did not live to see it. Ironically, one of the main reasons for that is the price war in the bourbon industry that was triggered by his overproduction, which created a perception that the whisky was a cheap, low-quality product. This drove a generation's worth of status-conscious drinkers to scotch and Canadian whiskies.

Rosenstiel retired in 1968 and sold his controlling interest in the company. It had been run for a number of years by Sidney Frank, husband to Elizabeth, Rosenstiel's daughter from the second of his five marriages, but Rosenstiel had chased him out of the company, and his shares went to corporate raider Meshulam Riklis. See Frank, Sidney.

See also Dewar's.

Mitenbuler, Reid. *Bourbon Empire*. New York: Viking, 2015.

Rothbaum, Noah. *The Art of American Whiskey*. New York: Ten Speed, 2015.

Sloane, Leonard. "Lewis Rosenstiel, Founder of Schenley Empire, Dies." *New York Times*, January 22, 1976, 37.

Veach, Michael. "Overproduction Issues in Whiskey." *bourbonveachdotcom*, May 19, 2019. https://bourbonveach.com/2019/05/13/overproduction-issues-in-whiskey/ (accessed March 10, 2021).

Noah Rothbaum

rosolio is one of the oldest herbal liqueurs, dating back to the 1400s and, in Italy, still being made today. Originally, its botanical mix was centered on the sundew (*ros solis* in Latin), a name applied to several related members of the *Drosera* genus of car- nivorous marsh plants. The mucilaginous "dew" that clings to the plants leaves is an irritant, which caused the plant to be considered an aphrodisiac, much like the cantharis beetle ("Spanish fly").

Rosolio was being made in northeastern Italy by the mid-1400s, when it was being regularly shipped from Venice (as *aqua ruoxa* in the local dialect) to the Duke of Burgundy and the court of Edward IV of England. It soon became one of the standard for- mulae drawn on by European distillers. Over the centuries, however, that formula changed greatly. The *Drosera* were out, replaced by saffron, which gave the same golden color to the liqueur but was much easier to handle, and the many botanicals used tended toward the spice end of the spectrum. Eventually, the term became a generic one in Italian distilling (elsewhere it had died out entirely). It was, as the *liquorista* Pietro Valsecchi noted in 1857, ap- plied to any mild, sugary liqueur. Citrus was the most popular genus of flavoring, and most of the more pungent spices—the cinnamons, nutmegs, and such—were reduced to mere accents, replaced by things such as fennel and rose petals.

For most of the twentieth century, Rosolio was considered the sort of thing your grandmother sipped. And yet small distillers in Turin and in Sicily and southern Italy continued to make it, in small quantities. With the twenty-first-century revival in interest in traditional spirits, it was inevitable that rosolio would get another look. In 2016, the Amalfi- born international barman Giuseppe Gallo (1980–) launched the Italicus brand of bergamot-flavored ro- solio, to immediate acclaim.

Difford, Simon. "Rosolio: The Italian Liqueur." *Difford's Guide*. https://www.diffordsguide.com/beer-wine- spirits/category/1194/bergamot-liqueurs (accessed March 31, 2021).
Valsecchi, Pietro. *Nuovo ed unico manuale completo del distillatore-liquorista*. Milan: Sanvito, 1857.
Vicario, Renato. *Italian Liqueurs*. N.p.: Aboca, 2014.

David Wondrich

rotary evaporator (rotovap) is a laboratory- grade instrument that uses a vacuum to distill a sol- vent. A rotary evaporator has an evaporation flask, water bath, condenser, vacuum pump, and collecting vessel. Each part contributes to precise and controlled evaporation and condensation. This, and their relative expense, is why rotovaps are usually found in science and medical labs, where they are used to separate dan- gerous compounds from a given solvent.

With the spread of molecular gastronomy and experimental bartending since the beginning of the twenty-first century, chefs and bartenders have harnessed the power of rotary evaporators to im- part flavor to liquids. A rotovap's vacuum allows liquids to be evaporated at lower boiling points be- cause evaporation occurs through pressure at lower temperatures. This is useful to those working with flavor, because heat can damage or pull apart delicate volatiles. The rotating evaporating flask, immersed in a heated water bath, increases the surface area of the solvent, gently speeding up distillation. Through forced convection, the mixture is combined and heated evenly to promote stable evaporation. The resulting gas is then condensed into a liquid and col- lected in a separate vessel. Each component of the solvent is separated based on its specific volatility, while the parts of the original solvent that continue to distill remain in the evaporating flask. This pro- cess separates a solvent according to a strict control of temperature, air pressure, and rotation.

A chiller can reduce the temperature of the coils in the rotovap distillation in order to condense the evaporating liquid more efficiently. The lower the temperature, the better the condensation— otherwise liquid begins to evaporate out. The best results are yielded when small molecules are not allowed to escape. This way, distillates preserve a fuller aroma and flavor spectrum.

Altering the pressure alters the boiling point of the liquid inside the evaporation flask. When the pressure is lowered, the liquid in the evaporation flask more readily evaporates because less pressure compresses it. The vacuum pump and its controller come into play. A vacuum controller stops and starts the pump so that a specific pressure, and therefore boiling point, can be preset by the operator. Since most liquids contain compounds with a variety of different boiling points, common practice is to lower pressure gradually over time, so that different layers of the liquid are stripped individually.

A peristaltic pump may also be used to cut the heads and tails from the rotovap vacuum still without breaking the seal and thereby losing an enormous amount of volatiles. This allows for parts of the liquid to be pulled off to see where the best concentration of flavors is, without compromising the final flavor of the distillation.

Once the correct balance has been ascertained and a formula created, precise distillations are easy to execute and can be replicated repeatedly.

The rotovap can be used to create infusions, concentrations, and hydrosols and also to clarify liquids for bespoke ingredients for cocktails in bars. Beyond producing ingredients that are not available commercially, the rotovap is most useful for protecting the integrity and intensity of an ingredient's flavor, allowing its delicacy to be respected. Beverage alcohol is an excellent medium for carrying flavor and more volatile aromas. The purest and freshest flavors can be extracted from ingredients by removing the water and replacing it with a solvent like alcohol, gently and at low temperatures. Hydrosols can be made by adding solid ingredients into the evaporation flask with water. This makes the most of delicate ingredients, such as herbs and flowers. A rotovap can also strip an aged spirit of the compounds responsible for its barrel notes; these can then be added to a different spirit, giving the impression of aging and "de-aging" spirits. Removing alcohol and water from a given spirit will leave it with only its most flavorful essence, which can then be added to other spirits or ingredients to overhaul their flavor profile.

See MOLECULAR MIXOLOGY.

Arnold, Dave. *Liquid Intelligence*. New York: W. W. Norton, 2014.

Tony Conigliaro

Roux, Michel (1940–2019), revolutionized the marketing of spirits. Every now and then, exceptional people mark their field. This is the case with Roux, who was behind some of the most remarkable success stories in the world of spirits.

Born in the Cognac region of France, Michel Pierre Roux made his career in the United States, where he resided until his death. "I had nothing to lose, everything to gain" he said, explaining his emigration from France to America in 1964 after the war in Algeria, where he was a lieutenant in the paratroops. A graduate of the University of Strasbourg with a degree in hotel management and oenology, he got his start in America working in the catering business in Houston, Texas. Beginning in 1965, he opened a string of restaurants in that state. The Table Royal in Corpus Christi, billed as the city's "only Café Society restaurant," gives an idea of the style of these.

In 1970, Roux was hired as the first salesperson for Carillon Importers Ltd., a wine and spirits importing and distribution subsidiary of Grand Metropolitan (which later became Diageo). At first, Roux focused on wine, even writing a guide to burgundy and one to Bordeaux. In 1979, however, the Swedish state-owned Vin & Sprit partnered with Carillon and Roux to launch its Absolut vodka brand in the United States, and Roux took responsibility for its marketing.

Although the country was in the throes of a recession, Roux and his team decided to position Absolut at the top of the pyramid, with a price 25 percent above its competitors, making it the first "super-premium" vodka in modern history. To help market the brand, Roux hired Andy Warhol to interpret the distinctive round-shouldered, tubby Absolut bottle (Roux was always an avid art collector). Under the direction of the TBWA agency, creative advertising campaigns kept coming, drawing on the contributions of many artists, musicians, and graphic designers to turn the Absolut bottle into a modern icon. The immediate success of his efforts propelled Roux to the head of Carillon in 1982. In 1993, Absolut smashed sales records with 4 million cases sold in the United States within one year.

Other successes marking Michel Roux's career include taking over Grand Marnier liqueur in the United States in the mid-1970s, when it only sold 12,000 cases a year, and repositioning it upmarket; this turned it into a symbol of affordable luxury and increased sales to 470,000 cases a year by 1993. Bombay Sapphire gin's blue bottle was also his idea. With its juniper-light flavor and enticing, modern packaging, Sapphire enticed a new generation of consumers to rediscover gin. And when Roux assumed control of marketing Stolichnaya vodka in the United States, he launched a whole range of flavorings; this was years before other brands' flavored versions invaded liquor store shelves.

Roux left Carillon and Absolut in 1998, having built the vodka from 100,000 cases a year to 4.5 million in the US alone, and founded his own firm, Crillon Importers. Crillon continues to handle a portfolio of boutique brands, including Barbancourt rum and Wyborova vodka. In the twilight of his life, Michel Roux remained convinced that one must pursue "learning all the time" (because "energy lies there") and that "spirits are wonderful products—they tell the story of the world."

Roux received many awards, from the prestigious French Legion of Honor, given to him by President François Mitterrand in 1988, to the Commander of the North Pole medal he received from King Gustav of Sweden in 1991, to an honorary doctorate of humanities from Brandeis University in Massachusetts and distinctions from ten other universities, including Harvard.

See also ABSOLUT; GRAND MARNIER; and STOLICHNAYA.

Lewis, Jack. "Importer Likes Our 'Tastes.'" *Scrantonian*, October 30, 1983, 3–4.
Roux, Michel, with Jay Cheshes and Sheri de Borchgrave. *My Absolut Life*. N.p.: Absolut Co., 2014.

Alexandre Gabriel

royal or **royale** (sometimes even exaggerated into **imperial**) designates, in the lexicon of mixed drinks, an existing drink that has been enhanced by adding wine, and particularly champagne, to it.

See CHAMPAGNE COCKTAILS and PUNCH.

Wondrich, David. *Punch, or The Delights and Dangers of the Flowing Bowl*. New York: Perigee, 2010.

David Wondrich

rum is general term for any distilled alcoholic beverage made from sugar cane (*Saccharum officinalis*), whether it is from the juice of the cane, the sugar crystallized from it, or the byproducts of sugar making, including cane syrup (the juice boiled down almost to the point where the sugar in it crystallizes), skimmings (the impurity-rich froth skimmed off the juice as it boils down), or molasses (the concentrated, uncrystallizable syrup that drains off the sugar). Sugar cane's high sucrose content (12–16 percent) makes it an ideal source for alcohol production, and rum making has emerged in nearly every area of the world where sugar cane grows.

Asian Origins

The early history of cane spirits is very murky indeed. Contrary to popular belief, rum was already old when it began to be made in the Caribbean. According to the Indian historian Ziauddin Barani (1285–1358), "arrack" distilled from raw sugar was widely traded in the Delhi Sultanate at the turn of the fourteenth century, to the point where Sultan 'Ala'uddin Khalji (1266–1316) made a decree prohibiting distillation, which he later had to

Thomas Rowlandson's 1810 print of the West India Docks, the center of Britain's rum trade. Wondrich Collection.

reverse. Details of how the spirit was produced are recorded in the *Ain-i-Akbari*, the meticulous administrative survey of the Moghul Empire completed in 1590 by Grand Vizier Abu al-Fazl Mubarak Al 'Allami (1551–1602). It was made from cane juice or cane juice plus raw sugar; it often had spices and botanicals added; it was distilled once or twice in either external-or internal-condensation pot stills (three types are described); the double-distilled version, called "duátashah," or "twice burnt," was "very strong." By the mid-1600s this spirit, a specialty of Bengal, had entered the European-driven colonial economy of Asia as "Bengal arrack" (a Portuguese trading post was established in Bengal as early as 1528). Eventually, as "Bengal rum," it would lay the foundation for the modern Indian rum industry.

In the absence of a comprehensive history of distillation in Asia, we do not know the origins of this spirit. They are quite possibly very old: from about 200 BCE to 200 CE, the Gandharan kingdom, at the headwaters off the Indus river in modern Pakistan and Afghanistan, appears to have maintained an active distilling industry. It was also one of the pioneers in crystallizing sugar. Were those two technologies combined? We cannot say: as sugar-historian J. H. Galloway notes, "There are lacunae in our knowledge of almost every aspect of activity of this ancient industry," and they are probably unfillable.

Latin America

The Spanish had sugar cane growing in Hispaniola by 1500 and the Portuguese in Brazil by 1520. This was not the first experience with the plant for either: cane had been grown in southern Spain and (Spanish-controlled) Sicily since the tenth century, albeit poorly, and in the Canary Islands, the Cape Verde Islands, Madeira, and São Tomé—the Atlantic islands colonized by the two countries and on whose sugar industry the American one was modeled—since 1425. While the islands all eventually developed rum industries, as did Spain and Sicily (to a much lesser extent), there is no evidence that any of them were distilling cane spirits before the late 1600s. In fact, the first firm evidence we have of cane distillation in the Atlantic world comes only in the 1630s, from Latin America: in 1635, the viceroy of Nueva España—modern Mexico—put out an order banning distillation in general and the spirits

being distilled from cane juice or cane syrups in particular (as well as those distilled from agave). See MEZCAL. That same year, the Brazilian state of Bahia also banned distilling from cane, as did the rest of Brazil (or at least the parts that weren't under Dutch occupation at the time) in 1636. Clearly, these prohibitions were not the beginning of cane spirits in the Americas. As the viceroy noted in 1631, "These drinks have been made for many years."

For their early years, we only have circumstantial evidence. It is possible that cane products were being distilled in the Americas as early as the 1520s, when Bartolomé de las Casas bemoaned how the enslaved Africans working on the sugar plantations in Hispaniola would "draw death and pestilence" from the "beverages that they make from the syrups of the cane and drink." Of course, those drinks could have been fermented only, but the especially deleterious effects of raw cane spirits were frequently noted, and there are other things to suggest that the sugar-plantation workers—enslaved Africans, indigenous Americans, and lower-caste Europeans—had found a way to turn the *cachaza*, or skimmings (the unwanted industrial waste from sugar making) to their advantage through distillation. See SKIMMINGS. In any case, by 1643, there were, as a Cuban official detailed, two kinds of cane *aguardiente*—"burning water," the term used—being made in the region, one from cachaza and the other, less common one from fresh cane juice (which could be produced on small farms by people who didn't have access to a mill). Unlike sugar, or even molasses, which had a market in Europe and was reserved for the plantation owners, rum was originally made by and for the working people.

Certainly, making these spirits for private consumption took no specialized equipment, as the simplified *falca* still used in Peru to make grape aguardiente showed. See PISCO. The knowhow could have come from Europe with the workers, or from Asia, just as the revolutionary vertical-roller sugar-cane mill did, which was evidently brought to Peru from China in the late 1500s by the Jesuits and from there spread throughout the region. But the resulting spirit was made and trafficked in the shadows and made no money for the grandees back home in Spain and Portugal. Only once it spread to the British Caribbean did it become a source of profit to the planters and investors and an article of international commerce.

Caribbean Rum

The British colony of Barbados and the French colony of Martinique were the cradles, if not the birthplaces, of Caribbean rum making. In the 1640s, Dutch migrants and planters from sugar-cane-growing regions in Pernambuco, Brazil, taught the Barbadians and Martiniquans how to cultivate sugar cane and produce sugar. They introduced sugar-cane plants, sugar-making equipment, and capital into Barbados and Martinique, which spurred the rise of sugar production in those two colonies. While in Brazil, the Dutch may have experimented with rum distilling and disseminated that knowledge to planters in Barbados and Martinique, to date there is no clear evidence to support such claims.

Numerous terms have been used for alcoholic beverages made from sugar cane. In the French Caribbean, *tafia*, *eau-de-vie de canne*, and *clarin* all refer to alcoholic beverages made from sugar cane. In the Spanish Americas, *aguardiente de caña*, *guaro*, and *chinguirito* have been used. *Kill devil* referred to distilled sugar-cane-based alcoholic beverages in the early British Caribbean, and this name transferred to the French as *guildive*. Rum became the most common term for a distilled sugar-cane-based alcoholic beverage in the Caribbean. It originated in Barbados in the seventeenth century and derived from the English word "rumbullion." In 1651, Giles Silvester, a sugar planter in Barbados, wrote, "The chiefe fudling they make in the Iland is Rumbullion, als Kill-Divill, and this is made of suggar cones distilled a hott hellish and terrible liquor." Rumbullion was a word commonly used in Devonshire, England, to mean "a great tumult," and its origin probably reflects the volatile effects rum had on the large number of West Country English who settled Barbados in the early seventeenth century. By the mid-1650s, rumbullion was shortened to "rum," much like the English shortened genever to "gin," *uiscebeatha* to "whisky," and *brandewijn* to "brandy." Sugar planters in the French and Spanish Caribbean adopted rum as the term for a distilled sugar-cane-based alcoholic beverage, translating it to *rhum* and *ron*, respectively, although at first these terms were generally restricted to the drink when it was made with molasses and aged in the English style.

In the seventeenth century, Barbados and Martinique initially developed the most advanced rum industries. At first, distillers in these islands made their rum from skimmings in the Latin American style. By the late seventeenth century, however, the Barbadians and the Jamaicans, who had quickly come to rival them, began supplementing the skimmings with molasses, recognizing the greater profit that could be made from rum than from selling the molasses (the practice is first recorded in 1687). By the middle of the next century, they were commonly supplementing the skimmings and molasses with "dunder," the spent wash from the stills, a technique that was known as early as 1690. As the Jamaican planter Leonard Wray wrote in 1848, "Rum is the spirit which is made on sugar estates from the molasses and skimmings resulting from the manufacture of sugar . . . and, together with them, the exhausted wash commonly named dunder." This triumvirate of ingredients would represent the industry's best practices until well into the twentieth century, producing a rum rich in texture and with a certain inimitable "hogo," or funk, to it. See HOGO.

With distillation a developing art in the seventeenth century, the capacity of early Caribbean stills was small, perhaps 100–300 gallons. Yet, despite their small size, by the end of the seventeenth century Barbados was extracting about one million gallons of rum from them annually, and Martinique was probably producing about half that amount.

In the Caribbean, rum making was largely confined to sugar plantations. Rum making had emerged to meet the alcoholic needs of Caribbean colonists, the high cost and limited availability of imported European alcoholic beverages having led colonists to the search for local alternatives. Early settlers in Barbados and Martinique produced a wide variety of alcoholic beverages from local resources, especially cassava and sweet potatoes, and turned to rum making at the start of the sugar revolution in the 1640s. Sugar production provided an enormous amount of waste material, which colonists distilled into rum. Sugar planters doled out huge amounts of rum to the indentured servants and enslaved peoples on their estates. It was given as part of weekly rations, as a prophylactic against colds, and as part of a rewards system.

By the 1650s, however, Barbados had moved beyond local consumption and was exporting its rum to England's North American colonies, and in quantity; indeed, in 1654 Connecticut moved to ban "Berbados Liquors, commonly called Rum,

Kill Devill, or the like." Sugar planters, preoccupied with the profitability of their estates, pursued rum making to supplement plantation revenues. Rum distillation, therefore, highlights the resourcefulness of sugar planters and the efficiency of an industry that turned its waste products into a highly profitable alcoholic commodity, no matter what the human cost.

The early rum trade also catered to markets at the margins of the emerging Atlantic world. British and French Caribbean planters exported rum to non-sugar-cane-growing regions of the Spanish Americas and sold it to Carib Indians in the Lesser Antilles. Caribbean merchants also kept growing their trade with colonists in British and French North America, where rum was exchanged for plantation supplies, especially grain, lumber, and fish. Ireland also received its share of Caribbean rum in exchange for goods needed on sugar estates. And by the end of the seventeenth century, Caribbean rum began to penetrate the West and Central African Coasts. African chiefs and traders valued the novelty of rum, and it became a central item in the gift-giving ceremonies that preceded trade negotiations. See WEST AFRICA. In the late eighteenth and early nineteenth centuries, abolitionists in Europe and North America (many of whom were also temperance advocates) evoked the profane use of demon rum to amplify the insidiousness of the slave trade. While rum was certainly important in the aforementioned ceremonies, and a significant secondary item of trade (along with cloth and iron), it was rarely the sole or primary item of trade. See TRIANGLE TRADE.

The growth of the Atlantic maritime trades also helped to fuel the expansion of rum making in the Caribbean. In early modern Europe, seamen considered alcohol a necessary provision on trading ventures; indeed, a supply of it was customary and considered theirs by right. While wine and brandy filled the hulls of ships departing Europe, sugar planters in Barbados and Martinique exploited the maritime demand for alcohol on the other side of the Atlantic and sold rum to traders for the return voyage. In 1655, the British Royal Navy began issuing rum to some of its sailors, making it an official ration for ships on long voyages in 1731.

In the eighteenth century, mercantilism shaped the growth of Caribbean rum industries. In 1713, Louis XIV of France followed the lead of Spain and Portugal, both of whom did everything possible to discourage the rum trade, and issued a royal decree that prohibited, except for ports in Normandy, the import of French Caribbean rum into France. The declaration specifically argued that rum was pernicious to health and threatened to compete with French wine and brandy. French Caribbean sugar planters, who had no home market for rum, had plenty of cheap rum for North American traders. They also had plenty of molasses, which they sold to New England distillers who used it to make their own rum. In contrast to the French, British officials embraced British Caribbean rum as an ally in their war against foreign spirits that had drained England of capital for centuries. They opened the home market to British Caribbean rum and offered incentives to rum makers, including low import duties.

In the nineteenth century, competition in the distilled spirits industries and the growing global demand for alcohol spurred technological advances in rum making. While the introduction of the continuous still in Europe led to great improvements in the efficiency of distilling, at first it was resisted in the Caribbean, and few sugar estates installed such devices, instead turning to things such as increasing the size of their pot stills and adding retorts or doublers to them to increase efficiency. See DOUBLER. Meanwhile, by the middle of the century the rise of government subsidized beet sugar industries in Europe had glutted world sugar markets. The profitability of Caribbean sugar production declined, and some planters chased greater and greater consolidation and efficiency to achieve economies of scale in sugar production, while others turned increasingly to rum making to help keep their sugar plantations solvent.

These responses were largely antithetical: the more sugar that was extracted from the cane, the less there was for molasses and skimmings, and the more centralized sugar production became, the less access distillers had to things like skimmings and cane juice. European and North American distillers had long made spirit from molasses and water alone. In England, this had been labeled "molasses brandy," to distinguish it from true rum (with which unscrupulous merchants had been blending it since at least the 1720s); in New England, it was "Medford rum" or "Boston particular," and its reputation was a villainous one. See RUM, MEDFORD. Now, distillers everywhere (or everywhere but Jamaica, which stuck stubbornly to the old ways) were adapting to the new realities and making pure molasses rums, and even beginning to turn to continuous stills to do it. See RHUM AGRICOLE; RUM, JAMAICA; and STILL, CONTINUOUS.

In the mid-nineteenth century, the serial, and devastating, attacks of the oidium fungus and phylloxera aphid upon European vineyards greatly reduced wine and brandy production. France was hit especially hard. In 1854, Napoleon III suspended the duty on French Caribbean rum imports in order to replenish alcohol supplies. The move helped introduce rum to the French public on a wider scale. During this time, French Caribbean planters began to distinguish between *rhum agricole* made from pure sugar-cane juice and *rhum industriel* made from molasses. By the end of the century, Martinique was the world's leading rum producer, while Jamaica was being displaced among British holdings by the Demerara region of Guyana and its column-stilled molasses rums.

Rum making also followed the expansion of sugar production in Cuba in the nineteenth century. In 1830, Facundo Bacardi, a Catalonian immigrant, migrated to Cuba and settled in Santiago de Cuba. In 1862, Bacardi, with financial backing from his brother José, purchased a distillery and started what was to become a rum empire. See BACARDI. Cuban rum making expanded in the early twentieth century, and Cuban rum found a strong market in the United States. In order to stimulate the Cuban economy after the Spanish-American War, Cuban goods, including rum, received favored trade status in the United States. Between 1898 and 1902, US forces stationed in Cuba were introduced to Cuban rum and the specialty rum-based drink known as the Daiquiri, named after the southern port town of the same name. During Prohibition (1920–1933) thousands of American tourists flocked to Cuba to indulge their alcoholic desires. As with US troops two decades earlier, they brought back a taste for Cuban rum. Smuggled Cuban rum was one of the spirits most available during prohibition.

In 1898, Puerto Rico was ceded to the United States, and American corporations quickly financed the expansion of sugar-cane cultivation in the island. The new interest in sugar production fueled the growth of Puerto Rican rum making, which challenged Cuba for control of the North American rum market. The Cuban Revolution (1959) closed trade between the United States and Cuba and further spurred the growth of Puerto Rican rum making.

By the 1960s, with the end of colonial status, producers in the emerging countries of the Caribbean had to do their own aging, blending, bottling, branding, and marketing—functions that previously had for the most part been done in Europe. With the further consolidation of the sugar industry, most distillers had to abandon skimmings for good, if they still used them, and buy their molasses as a commodity. What's more, they had to buckle down and install column stills: the market in America and Europe had shifted decisively toward light, "clean" rums, ones where the barrel was more influential on their flavor than the cane, and rum makers had no choice but to follow. Even Jamaica, which had built its reputation on huge, full-flavored pot still rums, had to adapt.

At the beginning of the twenty-first century, rum, which comprises about 11 percent of the world's spirits market, continues to foster economic growth in a number of sugar-cane-growing regions of the world. After three or four decades of retrenchment, when the most popular varieties of rum were the least flavorful, the 2010s brought a renewed interest in the spirit and its history and saw new attention paid to the more traditional, fuller-flavored varieties of rum.

See also CANE-BASED SPIRITS; SPIRITS TRADE, HISTORY OF; and SUGAR CANE.

Al Allami, Abū al-Fazzl ibn Mubārak. *Ain I Akbari*, vol. 1. Translated by H. Blochmann. Calcutta: Baptist Mission Press, 1873

Armendares, Teresa Lozano. *El chinguirito vindicado*. Mexico City: Universitad Nacional Autónoma de México, 2005.

Chez Checo, José. *El ron en la historia Dominicana*. Santo Domingo, Dominican Republic: Centario de Brugal y Compania, 1988.

Davis, N. Darnell. "The Etymology of the Word Rum." *Journal of the Royal Agricultural and Commercial Society of British Guiana* 4 (1885): 76–81.

de las Casas, Bartolomé. *Historia de las Indias*, vol. 5. Madrid: 1876.

Galloway, J. H. *The Sugar-Cane Industry: An Historical Geography*. Cambridge: Cambridge University Press, 1989.

Habib, Irfan. *The Economic History of Medieval India, 1200–1500*. History of Science, Philosophy and

Culture in Indian Civilization 8, part 1. New Delhi: Pearson-Longman, 2011.

Huetz de Lemps, Alain. *Histoire du rhum*. Paris: Editiones Desjonquéres, 1997.

Smith, Frederick H. *Caribbean Rum: A Social and Economic History*. Gainesville: University Press of Florida, 2005.

Smith, Frederick H. *The Archaeology of Alcohol and Drinking*. Gainesville: University Press of Florida, 2008.

Wondrich, David. "Forget the Caribbean: Was Rum Invented in India?" *Daily Beast*, July 9, 2018. https://www.thedailybeast.com/forget-the-caribbean-was-rum-invented-in-india (accessed April 26, 2021).

Frederick H. Smith and David Wondrich

rum, demerara, is rum distilled in Guyana, a small country between Venezuela and Suriname on the Caribbean coast of South America but associated with the Caribbean due to its history as a Dutch and English colony. See CARIBBEAN. Distilled from fermented molasses, the rum is heavy-bodied and rich, with significant molasses character and a moderate degree of fermentation flavors (funk). See MOLASSES. Production follows fermentation in large vats, followed by distillation to varying proofs using a diverse variety of stills. Most demerara rum for export is aged in well-charred, used bourbon barrels, which adds moderate wood/vanillin and char flavors to the flavor profile. Some demerara rum is stripped of color (and some flavor) for bottling as clear rum, but most is left brown and tweaked with caramel color for consistency. Younger blended demerara rums are often heavily darkened with caramel to produce black rums, some of which are bottled as 151-proof rum (particularly prized in tiki drinks) or blended into a navy rum (useful in certain punches). See RUM, NAVY.

Rum production on sugar plantations in the Demerara colonies dates to the 1650s, and sugar production remains a primary industry in Guyana today. From the mid-1800s, Guyana supplied much of the rum for the English navy. By the eighteenth century, Guyana had hundreds of plantation distilleries, but during the nineteenth and twentieth centuries, these distilleries gradually consolidated; as they consolidated, they moved toward greater production efficiencies and became the first distillers in the British Caribbean to embrace column distillation and making rum from molasses and water only, rather than the mixture of skimmings, molasses, and dunder that had been the consensus model in the region. See RUM. As of 1998, all demerara rum is produced by the government-owned Demerara Distillers Ltd (DDL) at a lone distillery: Diamond Estate.

DDL claims to produce twenty different styles of rum at Diamond, employing nine different stills, of both pot- and continuous-still designs. See STILL, POT and STILL, CONTINUOUS. Diamond's are among the oldest operating stills in the world, having been relocated and maintained in service from other facilities. At least two of the stills are made of wood.

Demerara rum is either bottled in-house under the El Dorado brand, which includes several age-statement bottlings, or is exported—as it has been for centuries—for use by blenders. The Wood's, Lamb's, and Lemon Hart brands are longstanding examples of blender rum that is overtly based on demerara rum.

Barty-King, Hugh, and Anton Massel. *Rum Yesterday and Today*. London: Heinemann, 1983.

Demerara Distillers Ltd. http://demeraradistillers.com (accessed April 1, 2021).

Martin Doudoroff

rum, Jamaica. Jamaica has been one of the leading rum producers in the Caribbean since the eighteenth century. The Spanish settled the island in 1494, though it remained a sparsely settled colony consisting largely of cattle ranches until the English took control of the island in 1655; a little sugar was made there, however, and—according to Francisco Morales Padron, the historian of Spanish Jamaica—some "raw spirit." The capture of Jamaica from the Spanish was part of Cromwell's plan to develop British interests in the Caribbean. Many of the troops that participated in the capture of Jamaica were from Barbados, where sugar production had emerged a decade earlier. These Barbadians shaped Jamaica's sugar industry and, therefore, its rum industry. The first governor of Jamaica was Colonel Thomas Modiford, who was a Barbadian plantation owner. Modiford's plantation had one of the first alembics in Barbados. Another Barbadian involved in the capture of Jamaica was Francis Dickenson, who was the original owner of the property that

1904 stereopticon picture of a pot still with double retorts at the Mona estate, the last operating sugar estate in Saint Andrew Parish, Jamaica (it would cease operations by 1910). Library of Congress.

would later become the Appleton Estate, which is one of the oldest rum companies in the world and known today for its premier dark rum. Rum making developed quickly on the island, and indeed the first mention of the use of molasses to supplement the fermented skimmings from which the earliest rum was distilled comes from Jamaica in 1687. See RUM.

In the eighteenth century, rum making in Jamaica soared alongside its expanding sugar industry. Jamaica produced an enormous amount of sugar in the eighteenth century, which generated a great deal of molasses and skimmings for distilling. See MOLASSES and SKIMMINGS. Jamaicans were not the most efficient rum producers in the Caribbean. Unlike Barbadian sugar planters, Jamaicans exported lower grades of semi-refined muscovado sugar, which contained a high amount of molasses that Jamaicans could have distilled into rum. They did, however, distill their rum to a higher alcohol content than many other Caribbean distillers, which reduced shipping costs. In the first two decades of the eighteenth century, Jamaicans exported an annual average of about 100,000 gallons of rum to the British market. By the 1770s, exports reached more than two million gallons annually, and rum from Jamaica represented nearly 90 percent of all rum imports into the British market. British merchants appreciated Jamaican rum for its high alcohol content, which they adulterated with water once it reached British ports. Jamaican rum made its way to North America, where it was exchanged for provisions and plantation supplies. An illegal rum trade also existed between the Jamaicans and the Spanish colonists in Cuba, which supplied

Jamaica with livestock. And perhaps most importantly, Jamaican rum became a staple in the British Royal Navy. Although sugar generated the greatest wealth for Jamaican planters in the eighteenth century, rum often contributed 10–20 percent of plantation revenues.

Rum took a more prominent role in the Jamaican economy in the nineteenth century. The abolition of the slave trade in 1807 and the emancipation of enslaved peoples in the British colonies in 1834 devastated Jamaican sugar production and raised the economic importance of rum. Competition from new sugar-cane-growing regions, especially India, Mauritius, and Cuba lowered the value of sugar on the British market and put many Jamaican planters out of business. The declining output of sugar meant a decrease in rum production. Jamaican rum exports dropped from 13.25 million liters per year in 1830 to about 5.7 million liters a decade later (today the figure is about 20 million).

Such market fluctuations became a theme in Jamaican distilling. In the 1890s, a hefty import tax on rum levied by Germany prompted Jamaican distillers (there were 148 of them in 1893) to develop a "Continental rum," whose fermentation drew in part on a "muck pit" full of cane refuse to produce very high levels of esters. See ESTERS. This rum brought a high price in Germany, where it would be diluted with neutral spirit and sold as "rum verschnitt." See RUM and VERSCHNITT. On the other hand, at some point in the early twentieth century, the Royal Navy stopped buying Jamaican rum: not only was it too expensive, but the sailors found it too pungent for their tastes.

By 1901, Jamaica was down to 110 distilleries. Although it was universally recognized as, essentially, the best rum in the world, good Jamaican rum was expensive to make, and the demand for it was limited. Yet Jamaican distillers refused to abandon their traditions. As the distiller at the legendary Vale Royal estate wrote in 1882, "The chief vehicle of flavour is supposed to be the skimmings and other refuse added to the mixing cistern, as rum made with pure . . . molasses is nearly always devoid of anything like flavour" (the Demerara distillers considered using skimmings "primitive," as one of them testified to the Royal Commission on Whiskey and Other Potable Spirits in 1908). Only after World War II did they change. With distilleries down to forty-eight and falling fast, the survivors added column stills, moved to pure-molasses distilling (with sugar making further consolidated, skimmings were increasingly unavailable), and focused on lighter rums and blends. Independence, which came in 1962, only intensified these trends.

Today there are but six operating distilleries in Jamaica; J. Wray & Co.'s Appleton and New Yarmouth (ultimately owned by Gruppo Campari) together account for some 60 percent of the island's production. National Rums of Jamaica—an equal partnership between the Jamaican state, Demerara Distillers of Guyana, and the French Pierre Ferrand cognac company—owns Clarendon/Monymusk and Long Pond and accounts for much of the rest. See PIERRE FERRAND and RUM, DEMERARA. The historic Hampden Estate and Worthy Park are both well-regarded independents. Despite the ups and downs, Jamaica remains one of the top rum producers in the world, exporting such brands as Appleton Estate rum and Myers's rum. See APPLETON ESTATE and MYERS'S. What's more, after many years of relative inertia, Jamaican pot still rums have recently seen a surge of interest and are beginning to regain their former status in the world of rum.

See also CARIBBEAN.

"A Jamaica Distiller," "Rum Manufacture." *The Sugar Cane*, April 1, 1882, 189–193.

Padron, Francisco Morales. *Jamaica española*. Seville: Escuela de Estudios Hispano-Americanos, 1952.

Pietrek, Matt. "Jamaican Rum Distillery Cheat Sheet." *Cocktail Wonk*, February 26, 2016 https://cocktailwonk.com/2016/02/jamaican-rum-distillery-cheat-sheet.html (accessed April 26, 2021).

Smith, Frederick H. *Caribbean Rum: A Social and Economic History*. Gainesville: University Press of Florida, 2005.

Taylor, John. *Jamaica in 1687*. Edited by D. Buisseret. Kingston: University of the West Indies Press, 2008.

Frederick H. Smith

rum, Medford, was made in the town of Medford, Massachusetts, starting in the early eighteenth century. The town's rum had a reputation for quality and was among the first American spirits "branded" by a connection to a location.

Rum distilling arose in coastal Massachusetts fairly early in the colonial era; molasses was an inexpensive product that served as ballast on return trips during trade missions to the sugar colonies of the West Indies. John Hall opened the first distillery in Medford, about five miles north of Boston, sometime around 1720; others soon followed.

Medford rum's quality remains a matter of speculation, but its producers had a reputation for making better rum than most producers in New England. (It is possible that its marketing may have outstripped the actual quality of the product.) It was also associated with Paul Revere's famous ride: the noted messenger may or may not have sipped a dram with distiller Isaac Hall, John's grandson, during his ride. Later claims were also made that Medford rum was always shipped across the ocean and back again for aging prior to being sold. (The claim is spurious.)

Although Medford was a known distilling center, it was not until the 1830s, when Daniel Lawrence (1797–1879) began widely advertising his "Medford N[ew] E[ngland] Rum," and later just "Medford Rum," that the town's name was associated with its product. Indeed, so successful was Lawrence that the title became associated with all New England rum. The Lawrence company eventually trademarked the phrase in 1871, but by then it was in common usage. Lawrence and Sons produced their rum, which enjoyed a much higher reputation for quality than the category in general, until 1905, when Daniel's sons finally implemented the clause in their father's will that specified that the distillery be closed and its stocks of rum sold within three years of his death. It was the last one in town, and those extra twenty-three years of operation had seen its product—distilled to a high purity in a three-chamber still and generally aged until it was "high flavored, ripe and mellow," as an 1881 citation described it—become a benchmark American spirits brand.

Published bartending guides called for Medford rum as early as Harry Johnson's 1882 Bartender's manual, and mixed drinks with names such as the Medford Rum Sour and Medford Rum Smash appeared with some frequency in later guides, including the posthumous 1887 edition of Jerry Thomas's *Bar-Tender's Guide* and George Kappeler's *Modern American Drinks* (1895). See Johnson, Harry; and Thomas, Jeremiah P. "Jerry".

It is one of history's ironies that New England rum's mixed reputation for quality is most likely due to the fact that it was distilled from molasses alone, rather than molasses and skimmings or cane juice as in the Caribbean, which made for a fruitier, more complex spirit. Today the vast majority of rums are made from molasses alone, and skimmings are almost unknown.

See RUM.

Brooks, Charles. *History of the Town of Medford, Middlesex County, Massachusetts*. Boston: James M. Usher, 1855.

"End of a Medford Distillery." *Carlisle (PA) Sentinel*, May 29, 1882, 1.

Fourteenth Exhibition of the Massachusetts Charitable Mechanic Assoc. Boston: Mudge & Son, 1881.

"Knell of Medford Rum." *Boston Journal*, June 16, 1905, 3–4.

Wayne Curtis

rum, navy, is a style of rum that is traditionally robustly flavored and high-proof. Its origins stem from the British colonization of parts of the Caribbean in the mid-seventeenth century, which required frequent and long voyages by sea. Rum soon became an acceptable way to keep up morale and discipline on board under what were typically terrible conditions. A spirits ration became part of official British naval regulations in 1731 (as an alternative to the traditional daily gallon of beer per man), and in 1775 rum became integral to those rations through a Parliamentary act.

By the end of the eighteenth century, rum had become a commodity stored and aged in warehouses on the London docks and traded by brokers who also blended stocks to create their own brands. The British Royal Navy was one of the largest rum customers in the world and required a high volume of consistent product. For nearly 190 years (1784–1970), a single broker, ED & F Man, sourced most of the rums used, providing a mix of different styles and ages from several British colonies (including Barbados, Guyana, Jamaica, and Trinidad), and delivered it to the Navy's supply depot at Deptford, in the London docklands. There it would spend two years aging and blending in a sort of solera of massive, open-topped wooden tanks. The final result was shipped out at 4.5 degrees under proof (54.5 percent ABV), following an 1866 regulation. Although its composition changed over the years, moving from an entirely pot-stilled blend heavy on Jamaican rum to one whose backbone was column-distilled demerara rum, the final product was always strong enough and richly flavored enough to stand up to the water with which naval regulations insisted it had to be mixed on issue.

During this era, sailors were getting as much as a half pint a day (240 ml) as their daily rum ration (or "tot"). Though this amount would be cut in 1824 to a gill or quarter-pint (150 ml in the new Imperial

Issuing the daily rum ration in the Royal Navy, 1937. It has already been mixed in the large, brass-fixtured tub with twice its volume of water to make grog. Wondrich Collection.

system of measures) and again to a half-gill (75 ml) in 1851, the daily tot, invariably mixed into "grog" (rum and water), was still part of a formal ritual that continued for centuries on board Royal Navy ships, announced daily by the bosun's call of "Up spirits!" However, as ships became more technologically complex and armed with nuclear weapons, it was determined that the rum ration should be abolished. The last day of the ration, July 31, 1970, was nicknamed Black Tot Day, complete with mock burials at sea and sailors wearing black armbands.

While the daily ration may have ended, the style of rum remained popular primarily in the United Kingdom and eastern Canada, and variations of this style are still sold today as "navy style" rums.

See RUM and SPIRITS IN THE MILITARY.

Pack, A. J. Nelson's Blood: The Story of Naval Rum. Emsworth, UK: Kenneth Mason, 1982.
Pietrek, Matt. "Setting the Record Straight on Navy Rum." Cocktail Wonk, December 5, 2019. https://cocktailwonk.com/2019/12/setting-record-straight-british-navy-rum.html (accessed April 1, 2021).

Martin Cate

Rum Punch was one of the earliest and most popular versions of punch. See PUNCH. For centuries, it found great favor with everyone from English aristocrats to Caribbean pirates.

Rupf, Jörg (b. 1944), is a California-based distiller and the founder of St. George Spirits. Born in the town of Colmar in Alsace (then part of Germany, now France), Rupf moved with his family to Freiburg in the Black Forest, eventually settling near Lake Constance. After studying law and receiving his PhD, Rupf became a court system judge in Munich before joining the Ministry of Internal Affairs and, later, the Ministry of Culture. In the mid-1970s, Rupf came to California to pursue postgraduate studies at the University of California, Berkeley; while there, he decided to leave the legal profession and instead distill fruit eau-de-vie, as his family had in Germany. After initially working in Emeryville, California, under the auspices of Veedercrest Vineyards, Rupf founded St. George Spirits in 1982. St. George was the first modern artisanal or craft distillery in the United States, distilling eau-de-vie from fruits

such as pears, cherries, and raspberries, using a 65-gallon Holstein pot still. See ST. GEORGE SPIRITS. Experimenting with fermentation techniques, Rupf tweaked the quality and style of St. George's eau-de-vie, while also mentoring and working with other distillers (including Steve McCarthy, founder of Clear Creek Distillery in Portland, Oregon). In 2001, Rupf teamed up with Ansley Coale, a partner in the Germain-Robin brandy distillery, to create Hangar One, a brand predicated on applying craft distilling techniques to flavored vodka. The project was a great success, both artistically and commercially. The recipient of a Lifetime Achievement Award from the American Distilling Institute and a five-time nominee for the James Beard Foundation for Outstanding Wine and Spirits Professional, Rupf retired from St. George Spirits in 2010.

See also EAU-DE-VIE.

"Founder: Jörg Rupf." St. George Spirits website. http://www.stgeorgespirits.com/story/cast-of-characters/jorg-rupf/ (accessed March 10, 2021).
Rupf, Jörg. "Jörg Rupf: A Distiller's Perspective on Contemporary Cocktail Culture." Interview conducted by Shanna Farrell in 2014 and 2015, Oral History Center of the Bancroft Library, University of California, Berkeley, 2016.

Paul Clarke

Russia and Eastern Europe form an extensive region that is home to a number of distinct but related distilling and drinking cultures. Largely, but not entirely, Slavic, they can be roughly divided into the grain-distilling cultures in the north (Poland, the Baltic States, Belarus, Ukraine, Moldova, and Russia) and the fruit-distilling cultures in the south (the Balkans, the Czech Republic, Slovakia, Hungary, Romania, and Bulgaria); into the zone influenced by the Russian Empire and Prussia and the zone influenced by the Habsburg and Ottoman Empires.

Distilling seems to have come into the region in the fourteenth and fifteenth centuries, although it is possible that it was previously introduced by the Mongols as they swept through in the thirteenth century. There is a multiplicity of routes it could have followed, and it seems to have taken them all: moving up the Dnieper and Volga rivers into Ukraine and Russia; spreading inland into the Balkans from the Venetian towns of the eastern

Adriatic and the Turkish trading posts of the Black Sea and into Poland and Belarus from the trading cities of the eastern Baltic; and diffusing into the Czech and Slovak lands and Hungary from the German-speaking principalities to the west. Already by the 1500s "Hungary water," a rosemary-infused medicinal spirit supposedly created by the queen of that land, was known throughout Europe, and the extensive glass industry in the Czech province of Bohemia was turning out highly regarded alembics and other distilling equipment.

In the seemingly limitless grainlands of the north, stretching from the North German Plain in the west through the vast Russian Plain to the Ural Mountains in the east, distillers naturally turned to grain, just as they had throughout the rest of northern Europe. See GENEVER; KORN; VODKA; and WHISKY. By the 1520s, Polish distillers were making *gorzałka*, their ancestor of vodka, and members of the Russian court were regularly drinking spirits (most likely locally made from grain) before meals. In 1553, Ivan the Terrible of Russia limited the spirits trade to a network of state-owned taverns. State control, sometimes tighter, sometimes looser, would remain a feature of Russian distilling through the twentieth century.

Small molded-glass pre-Revolutionary Smirnoff vodka bottle. Wondrich Collection.

Although distilling is an excellent, and profitable, way of preserving grain and transporting it, raw grain spirits have always been considered challenging to drink. In western Europe, strategies for taming them focused on flavoring, as with genever and aquavit, or (following the lead of French brandy) barrel maturation, as in Scotch and Irish whisky. In Poland and Russia, however, the focus was on rectification: distilling them to as high proof as possible and heavily filtering the result. See FILTRATION and RECTIFICATION. By the nineteenth century, this rectified spirit was occasionally also barrel aged, yielding *starka*. See STARKA. It was also commonly flavored, either before distillation or after (preparing homemade infusions was and remains a popular practice). Some of the most common botanicals used include bison grass (*żubrówka*), hot peppers (*pertsovka*), and lemon peel. Fresh-fruit infusions (*nalivkas*) are also popular. These are often sweetened, as are some of the botanical spirits, yielding local specialties such as the Baltic *krupnik* and the caraway-flavored kümmel. See HONEY LIQUEURS; KÜMMEL; and NALIVKA.

For the most part, however, plain vodka is the drink and has been for a very long time. Following the old adage "Distillation follows industrialization," its manufacture was brought to a great state of technical perfection in the late nineteenth century, and there it has remained, through the brutal years of war that characterized the twentieth century and under the heavy hand of communist rule. Most vodka is made from wheat or rye, but the nineteenth century saw potato spirits introduced in quantity, and Poland in particular makes a number of high-quality potato vodkas. See MOSKOVSKAYA OSOBAYA; RUSSIAN STANDARD; SMIRNOFF; and STOLICHNAYA.

In the Habsburg and Ottoman south of the region, the frequently mountainous terrain tended to limit the amount of grain that could be practically grown, and thus the excess capacity that lent itself to distillation. Fruit trees, however, did particularly well, and distilling proved to be an excellent way of preserving the harvest. Fruit eaux-de-vie became a regional specialty, made by farmers throughout the area. Slivovitz, Hungarian pálinka, Serbian rakija, and Rumanian țuică are all modern descendants of these medieval spirits and are still often made on the village or individual farm level. There they are pot stilled; on the industrial level, where they are also made, hybrid stills or even continuous stills can be used. See BARACK PÁLINKA, EAU-DE-VIE, RAKIJA, SLIVOVITZ, and ȚUICĂ.

In parts of the old Austro-Hungarian Empire, distillation increased with industrialization. In the nineteenth century, the Czech lands, Galicia to their east, and parts of Hungary all developed modern industries making spirit from beet molasses, potatoes, and maize. Inevitably, these spirits found their way into such local drinks as *borovička*, the Czechoslovak version of gin, various liqueurs, and the cheap blends with imported spirits known as *verschnitt*, or "cut," spirits. See RUM and VERSCHNITT.

To balance out this industrial production, there is another characteristic of the region: there is an unusual level of home distilling throughout the area, north and south. In the Balkans, this is mostly legal and is a basic part of farming. In the north, and particularly in Russia and the former parts of the Soviet Union, it is as illegal as it is fantastically persistent. This samogon, as it is called, can be made from anything, with equipment that can range from repurposed kitchen implements to thoroughly professional distillation apparatus. See SAMOGON.

Another distinctive feature of the region is the heavy Jewish involvement in distilling and selling spirits, a profession that was outside the traditional, Christian-only guild system. In tsarist Russia, Jews were often the holders of the local distilling monopolies. In the Baltic countries, they were among the largest distillers. In parts of Hungary, as much as a quarter of the large Jewish population was involved in the distilling trade. In the twentieth century, Nazi genocide and communist nationalization basically put an end to this long tradition, but some brands still survive. See JELÍNEK and KOSHER SPIRITS.

Finally, something must be said about the region's particular spirits-drinking culture. To do it justice would require a book of its own. We may begin by establishing what it is not. Despite the fact that cocktail books were published in Prague and Budapest as early as the 1890s and continued to be published in the region even during Soviet times; despite Slovakia's propensity for producing some of the world's most respected bartenders (e.g., Erik Lorincz, head bartender at London's Savoy Hotel from 2010 until 2017); despite the presence of modern, creative, and highly respected cocktail bars in many of the region's cities, it is not primarily a cocktail culture. See SAVOY HOTEL'S AMERICAN BAR.

Vodka does not need mixing, and for the most part it is not mixed. It is drunk neat, always accompanied by something to nibble on—*zakuski*, which can be as humble as pickles and as luxurious as caviar—and elaborate, heartfelt toasts. What applies to vodka in the north applies to fruit brandies in the south: toasts, food, relentless conviviality. This culture can be, and often is, taken to excess, but there is a majesty to it that can make the more restrained drinking cultures seem wan by comparison.

Erofeev, Venedikt. *Moscow to the End of the Line.* Translated by H. William Tjalsma. New York: Penguin, 1992.

Herlihy, Patricia. *The Alcoholic Empire.* Oxford: Oxford University Press, 2002.

Mew, James, and John Ashton. *Drinks of the World.* London: Leadenhall, 1892.

Schrad, Mark Lawrence. *Vodka Politics.* Oxford: Oxford University Press, 2014.

YIVO Encyclopedia of Jews in Eastern Europe. https://yivoencyclopedia.org/default.aspx (accessed 8 June, 2021).

David Wondrich

Russian Standard, a winter-wheat-based vodka made in St. Petersburg, Russia, was introduced in 1998 by Roust, Inc., the luxury-goods and banking conglomerate controlled by billionaire Roustam Tariko (1962–). The first Russian vodka brand to be developed with the aid of Western marketing expertise (including that of McKinsey, the American consulting giant), Russian Standard rapidly developed a dominant share in the domestic vodka market. In 2009, it represented over 60 percent of the Russian market, although that figure has fallen more recently. Although it is Russia's leading export brand, in 2017 it was only in sixteenth place among vodka brands globally.

Russian Standard was originally made at St. Petersburg's large Liviz distillery, the oldest operating one in Russia (it was founded in 1897), but the brand moved its production to its own new, state-of-the-art distillery in 2006. It is made in several grades, using multiple column distillations whose number increases with the grade, as does the exoticism of the material through which the vodka is filtered. See CHARCOAL FILTRATION. The entry-grade Russian Standard is distilled four times and filtered four times through birch charcoal.

The company's other bottlings include Russian Standard Gold, reportedly inspired by "an ancient Siberian vodka recipe made popular by Peter the Great," which features extracts of Siberian Golden Root (ginseng) for a richer taste; Russian Standard Platinum, which is filtered through silver; and Imperia, marketed as a luxury vodka and filtered through quartz crystal from the Ural Mountains. All of the brand expressions use water from Lake Ladoga, and all are bottled at 40 percent.

See also VODKA.

Panibratov, Andrei. *Russian Multinationals.* New York: Routledge, 2012.

Pasternak, Lois. "Russian Standard Vodka Turns 20." *Travel Markets Insider,* July 20, 2018. http://travelmarketsinsider.net/russian-standard-vodka-turns-20/ (accessed March 10, 2021).

Kara Newman

Rusty Nail is a two-ingredient drink composed of blended scotch and Drambuie. Without a doubt, it is the most famous cocktail to ask for the honeyed Scottish liqueur. Drinks calling for the simple combination sailed under several names before the label Rusty Nail finally stuck (the name, first recorded in 1961, appears to have originated in New York City). Commonplace in postwar America and indicative of the era's hard-drinking ways, the Rusty Nail's adoption by Frank Sinatra's Rat Pack likely spiked its popularity. A drink requiring almost no skill to put together, it was popular with suburban bartenders; its reputation fairly screams "home basement bar." It is typically, though not exclusively, served on the rocks. Classic proportions are two parts scotch, one part Drambuie, but those are frequently adjusted according to the drinker's tastes.

Recipe: Combine 60 ml blended scotch and 30 ml Drambuie in rock glass filled with ice. Stir until chilled.

See also WHISKY, SCOTCH.

Gahagan, Jerry. "Phyllis Back in the Tents." *Philadelphia Daily News,* August 16, 1961, 35.

Wondrich, David. "How to Make a Rusty Nail." *Esquire.* October 26, 2017. https://www.esquire.com/food-drink/drinks/recipes/a3796/rusty-nail-drink-recipe/ (accessed May 26, 2021).

Robert Simonson

rye (*Secale cereale*) is a cereal grain that is used to make spirits, mostly in North America and Europe. Although the largest producers of rye are Germany and Poland, there are only a few rye whiskies in Europe (Zuidam's Millstone from the Netherlands is one). Rye is mostly used for unaged spirits there: vodka or the German korn. Rye's real forte in distillation is North American whiskies. See KORN.

Rye has been used to make whisky in North America since the days of European colonization. German and Bohemian distillers brought their knowledge of rye spirits with them, the knowledge that rye's spicy, oily character adds a zesty thrill of flavor to the sweeter side of other distillates. See WHISKY, RYE.

That spicy, oily character was not so pleasing to Pliny the Elder, the Roman naturalist, who found little good to say about it. His *Natural History* describes it as "a very inferior grain . . . only employed to avert positive famine." He didn't like how it tasted: "Spelt is mixed with this grain to modify its bitterness and even then it is very disagreeable to the stomach."

But rye did have one quality that even Pliny had to acknowledge: "It will grow upon any soil, and yields a hundred-fold; it is employed also as a manure for enriching the land." Rye is tenacious, which brought it out of its birthplace, central and eastern Turkey. Archaeologists have found single grains of rye among stores of other grains in sites across central and eastern Europe, but no stores all of rye grains have been found that date from before about 500 BCE. Rye's tendency to successfully germinate and grow almost anywhere—farmers today call these scattered sproutings "volunteers"—would likely cause it to be considered a weed.

Eventually, the weed was tamed and cultivated, as people of the Iron Age realized that this hardy grass that grew on rocky or peaty soil and shook off snow that would frost other grains was useful, and also palatable. It would continue to travel with Europeans, though central and eastern Europe continues to be its solid home, where breads like pumpernickel, *roggebrood,* and *Knäckebrot* are staple foods.

While small but significant quantities of rye were used in pot-still Irish whiskies until the 1950s and sometimes also in scotch grain whiskies, rye really came into its own as a whisky grain when rooted in the rocky soils of Pennsylvania and the Appalachians. Beginning in the late colonial period, from the Appalachian front to the valleys of the Monongahela River in western Pennsylvania, rye whisky was the spirit of choice, along with apple brandy. It was taxes levied on rye whisky that were the spark for the Whisky Rebellion, and George Washington himself built a commercial distillery at his Mount Vernon estate that made rye whisky. See WASHINGTON, GEORGE. After Prohibition, when rye whisky production largely failed to re-establish itself in this area, production moved to Kentucky, where a style developed using less rye in the formulation and a significant amount of corn. In Canada, too, where the original style of whisky used so much rye that "rye" became generic for whisky, rye use sank throughout the twentieth century, with corn taking its place. Some pure rye was still made as a blending whisky, and in 1946 Distillers Ltd. was started in Calgary to create a market for Alberta-grown rye, and it still uses 100 percent rye in some of its whiskies.

See also WHISKY, IRISH.

Beehre, Karl-Ernst. "The History of Rye Cultivation in Europe." *Vegetation History and Archaeobotany* 1 (1992): 142–156.

Bryson, Lew. *Tasting Whiskey: An Insider's Guide to the Unique Pleasures of the World's Finest Spirits*. North Adams, MA: Storey, 2014.

Kergommeaux, Davin de. *Canadian Whisky*, 2nd ed. N.p.: Appetite, 2017.

Private conversations with Fritz Maytag (Anchor Distilling) and Herman Mihalich (Mountain Laurel Spirits).

Lew Bryson

saccharification is the enzymatic reduction of complex carbohydrates into simple sugars. In the production of alcoholic beverages, ingredients that do not contain sufficient fermentable sugars undergo saccharification in order to break down their starchy components into sugars that can be consumed by the microflora responsible for fermentation. See FERMENTATION and YEAST. Raw materials are prepared by milling and/or cooking, then combined with water to create what is known as the mash, which is where enzymes convert starches into sugars. See MASHING. These enzymes either derive from natural ingredients already present in the mash (primarily malted grain) or are contributed from industrial sources. See MALTING. The mash is then maintained at specific temperatures for various periods of time in order to control the activity of the enzymes, and finally the temperature is raised to denature the enzymes and cease their activity. Following saccharification the mash is fermented and distilled.

The manner in which the unprocessed ingredients are prepared for saccharification; the source, concentration, and type of enzymes present in the mash; and the times and temperatures at which the mash is held all influence the characteristics of the product that is fermented and ultimately distilled. Saccharification is therefore yet another aspect of the distillation process that can be controlled to produce a desired result.

Rogers, Adam. *Proof: The Science of Booze*. New York: Houghton Mifflin Harcourt, 2014.

Samuel Lloyd Kinsey

Saint James is one of the oldest brands of rum and one of the most recognized internationally, having served for over a century as the flagship brand for the French Caribbean. It is produced on the island of Martinique, which in the 1640s was the first French Caribbean colony to produce rum. Like many iconic French brands, its nineteenth-century commercial origins have been obscured by a good deal of supposition and legend. See BÉNÉDICTINE.

In 1882, the Marseilles rum merchant Paulin Lambert (1828–1905), who had been trading in "tafia" (unaged spirit distilled from molasses and skimmings) from Martinique for at least twenty years, decided to launch his own brand, taking that tafia, aging it, and selling it in a proprietary square bottle. "Rhum des Plantations Saint-James," he called his brand, most likely because in France quality rum was viewed as a preserve of the British. The fact that there were no actual Plantations Saint-James was immaterial; people believed there were, and the brand, an immediate success, became a watchword for tradition and authenticity. In 1890, Lambert bought the large and historic Trouvaillant estate, just outside Saint-Pierre (the principal city of Martinique), where cane had been distilled since at least the 1750s, and renamed it the "Plantations Saint-James," thus closing the gap between perception and reality.

In 1902, the eruption of Mount Pelée leveled the town of Saint-Pierre and partially destroyed the Saint James distillery. It nonetheless recovered to produce massive quantities of rum during the First World War and subsequently weather the rise of rhum agricole, selling large amounts of each kind. See RHUM AGRICOLE. The Lambert family sold the business in 1954. In the 1970s, the distillery was moved to Sainte-Marie to centralize production and upgrade distilling operations. The Saint James Rum Museum was built at the new facility, and among the many artifacts it has on display is a conglomeration of twisted and melted Saint James rum bottles from a tavern destroyed during the eruption of Mount Pelée.

See also CARIBBEAN and RUM.

"Archives Rhum Saint-James: histoire administrative." Archives nationales d'outre mer: instruments du recherché en ligne. http://anom.archivesnationales. culture.gouv.fr/ark:/61561/nb754cxp (accessed March 11, 2021).

"Article 2988: Concurrence illicite." *Annales de la propriéte industrielle*, January, 1885, 156–160.

Historique illustré des Plantations Saint-James. Paris: Jules Lévy, n.d.

Smith, Frederick H. *Caribbean Rum: A Social and Economic History*. Gainesville: University Press of Florida, 2005.

Frederick H. Smith

Saintsbury, George Edward Bateman (1845–1933), was an English writer, literary historian, educator, and critic whose lively ideas and writings about wine and, to a lesser but still significant degree, spirits helped form the foundation for modern criticism and description of alcoholic beverages in general.

In *Notes on a Cellar-Book* (1920), his views on drinking, dining, social life, Rum Punch, Whisky Toddy, Holland gin, and the joy and solace that drink can provide brought a genial but thoughtful significance to beverages in an unprecedented manner. The book's whimsy only adds to the sense that drink is fun, at times meaningful, and at other times nothing more (and need be nothing more) than drink. Throughout, he demonstrates that drink is personal, writing, "I have never yet given a second-hand opinion on any thing, or book, or person."

Saintsbury promoted the "proper order" of wines with dinner as well as beverages "after-dinner." He railed against Prohibitionists and maintained that "all fanatics and faddists are dishonest." Nonetheless, he had his firm opinions and preferences: as he wrote, "All alcoholic drinks, rightly used, are good for body and soul alike, but as a restorative of both there is nothing like brandy."

Saintsbury, George. *Notes on a Cellar-Book*. London: Macmillan, 1920.

Doug Frost

salt, or sodium chloride, is a mineral that, in cuisine and in mixed drinks, is not only a primary flavor in itself (along with sweet, sour, and bitter) but also an enhancer and modifier of other flavors.

In cocktails, the most recognized use of salt is in a Margarita, where it is encrusted onto the glass's rim. See MARGARITA. Used in small amounts, salt has the ability to suppress bitter flavors while accentuating sweet, sour, and savory (umami) ones. Some cocktails may be improved by adding small amounts of salt, as in the case of the Bloody Mary. See BLOODY MARY. Working with salt in a drink, it's best to adopt a "less is more" attitude. Once added, it cannot be removed and is almost impossible to remedy. Given this, a very good way to work with salt is to create a conservative saline solution. An easy and restrained recipe: dilute 1 level tablespoon (15ml) into 90 ml of water. Dose this at only a drop or two, and taste.

Salt has historically also been used in various parts of spirits production. It was sometimes used by early distillers to raise the boiling point of the water in a wash, thus raising the proportion of alcohol in the first part of the distilling run. In the eighteenth and nineteenth centuries, some rum distillers in the British Caribbean made a practice of adding salt or salt water to their fermenting wash; in small doses, salt can increase the metabolic activity of yeast. In the nineteenth century, salt was also used by rectifiers for its flavor-enhancing properties in compounding imitations of gin and other spirits. See RECTIFICATION and RUM.

Grainger, James. *The Sugar Cane: A Poem*. London: 1764.
Smith, G. *A Compleat Body of Distilling*. London: 1731.

Audrey Saunders and David Wondrich

A **Salty Dog** is a highball composed of grapefruit juice, salt, and vodka (some recipes call for gin). Many contemporary versions call for the liquid ingredients to be mixed with ice (either in a shaker, then strained into an ice-filled glass, or built directly in the serving glass), and for the drink to be served in a glass with a salted rim (a sugar-salt mix is sometimes used). A relative of the Greyhound (essentially the same drink prepared without salt), the Salty Dog has roots that stretch back to 1916, when American soldiers stationed at Eagle Pass, Texas, during the conflict with Pancho Villa were drinking a mixture of lime juice, salt, and carbonated water under that name. See RICKEY. By the late 1930s, Texans had replaced the lime juice and soda with a healthy slug of white grapefruit juice (usually canned) and stiffened the drink up with a shot of gin. This version soon caught on nationwide, gaining a well-earned reputation as a hot-weather refresher. In the early 1950s, vodka began to edge out the gin, as it was doing in various other drinks. As a vodka drink, the Salty Dog was broadly popular through the 1970s and is still encountered, although usually with the sweeter (and less refreshing) pink grapefruit juice.

Recipe: Combine 60 ml vodka or gin, 120–180 ml grapefruit juice, to taste, and a pinch of kosher salt in an ice-filled highball glass and stir to combine.

See also HIGHBALL.

"El Paso Beer Depot" (advertisement). *El Paso (TX) Herald-Post*, June 24, 1938.

"Have a Salty Dog." *Cincinnati Post*, July 18. 1916, 1.

Knowlton, Andrew. "The Salty Dog." *Bon Appétit* website, June 8, 2010. http://www.bonappetit.com/recipe/the-salty-dog (accessed March 10, 2021).

O'Reilly, Peggy. "Few Here Know a 'Salty Dog' but Texans Use 'Em to Cool Off." *Brooklyn Eagle*, August 26, 1951, 8.

Paul Clarke and David Wondrich

sambuca is a traditional Italian liqueur made with aniseed, star anise, fennel seeds, elderflower, and other herbs and spices macerated in alcohol. It is one of several aniseed-based spirits popular around the Mediterranean, and in Italy in particular, home to many variations on the concept, including *anisetta, anice secco, anesone triduo,* and *mistrà*. Commercial production of sambuca dates to 1851, when Luigi Manzi (1809–1873) from the Neapolitan isle of Ischia started producing the liqueur around the port of Civitavecchia near Rome. The name Sambuca may derive from *sambuchelli*, young boys that used to sell water mixed with green aniseed on Ischia. This concoction is still popular in Palermo, where is called *zammù*, a term derived from the Arab *zammut*, a drink that arrived in Italy from the Middle East. However, the Oxford English Dictionary maintains that the term is derived instead from the Latin word *sambucus*, meaning "elderberry" and which is the genus name of the common elder.

While Sambuca Manzi is still produced, Angelo Molinari started a commercial distribution of his popular sambuca in 1945. Today, other small producers such as Colazingari and Sarandrea make different styles of sambuca. Sarandrea claims to be the only producer who still use elderflower in the recipe.

Sambuca became popular in Italy during the 1950s after the launch of Molinari's version. In Rome it's still typical to eschew sugar in one's espresso in favor of a splash of the anise-flavored liqueur. Around Rome, Sambuca is sipped straight from the freezer, while around the world is usually served "con la mosca" (with the fly): one or three coffee beans inside the cup resembling, with a bit of imagination, a cluster of little houseflies.

See also ANISE SPIRITS; MISTRÀ; and OUZO.

Molinari website. https://www.molinari.it (accessed April 1, 2021).

"Sambuca Manzi, fu un personaggio mitico di Ischia a inventare il célèbre liquore," *L'Isclano*, April 9, 2014. https://www.isclano.com/it/luigi-manzi-da-ischia-inventore-della-sambuca/ (accessed April 1, 2021).

Sarandrea website. https://sarandrea.it (accessed April 1, 2021).

Antonio Parlapiano

samogon, the native illicit spirit of Russia—the Russian form of moonshine—is said to have been first produced in response to Ivan the Terrible's monopolization of wine production in the sixteenth century. Seemingly every Russian government since has attempted to enforce some sort of prohibition, but all have failed. (Samogon is also distilled in Belarus and in Ukraine as *samohon*.)

The word *samogon* means "self-distilled," and like all home brews it is made from whatever happens to be around—fruit, grain, honey, potatoes, beets—and has a reputation for potency that does not reflect the reality. (Ethanol is ethanol, after all, and bootleggers aren't in the business of making it any stronger than it has to be.) It is almost always pot-distilled, in homemade equipment that varies widely in size and sophistication. Ad-hoc, Rube Goldberg assemblies of kitchenware are not unknown, but neither are rectification columns. See RECTIFICATION and STILL, POT.

After distillation, samogon aspires to be a neutral spirit (as with all illicit products, results vary widely) ready for infusion with herbs and spices such as saffron, rosemary, lemon peel, or cardamon; dried fruits; or roasted barley.

Like its counterpart in America, samogon is a predominantly rural tradition, and its production increases in times of economic distress. It is frequently used for bartering and to circumvent low prices for grain.

In the 1970s an economist at Duke University gathered data about food production in the Soviet Union, and by collating the numbers for alcohol and the agricultural products used to produce alcohol (and looking at what was unaccounted for), he deduced that the production of samogon in the second half of the twentieth century increased the total alcohol production in Russia by one-third. In 1988, a survey found that 68 percent of agricultural, 45 percent of industrial, and 24 percent of intellectual workers drank homemade alcoholic beverages. Since the collapse of the Soviet Union, samogon production and consumption have only increased, sometimes to a truly alarming level.

See also MOONSHINE; RUSSIA AND EASTERN EUROPE; and VODKA.

Zaigraev, Grigory. "The Russian Model of Non-commercial Alcohol Consumption." In *Moonshine Markets*, ed. Alan Haworth and Ronald Simpson, 31–40. New York: Brunner Routledge, 2004.

Max Watman

samshoo or **samshu** is the Western name, of dubious etymology, for the rice baijiu sailors and merchants encountered in southeastern China beginning in the seventeenth century. It was both prized and feared. The term, first attested to in William Dampier's 1697 *New voyage Round the World*, fell out of use in the twentieth century, most likely because in many Chinese ports then under colonial rule, Western sailors were able to drink spirits more familiar to them. See BAIJIU.

Sandhaus, Derek. "Don't Drink the Samshoo." *300 Shots at Greatness*, September 18, 2012. https://300shots.wordpress.com/2012/09/18/dont-drink-the-samshu/ (accessed April 1, 2021).

David Wondrich

sangaree is a cold mixed drink consisting of a base ingredient, usually a wine, sweetened, diluted with ice or ice water, and topped with spice or a float of port wine. See FLOAT. It originated as a spiced Madeira punch, referred to as Sang-Gris by the French clergyman and adventurer Jean-Baptiste Labat (1663–1738). According to Labat, it was an English drink, and the translation, "gray blood," was a term in the British horse trade for a variety of gray mare. In 1694, Labat encountered Sang-Gris in Martinique, later describing it as "made from Madeira wine which is placed in a crystal or faience bowl with sugar, lemon juice, a little powdered cinnamon and clove, a lot of nutmeg, and a crust of toasted bread" and then passed through a fine cloth to filter. This wine-based punch's relation to the Spanish Sangria, to which it bears a close resemblance, remains to be established. See PUNCH.

In 1736, new restrictions on the gin trade were imposed in Britain, and at least one hawker of gin punches turned to "a new Punch made of strong Madeira Wine, and called Sangre." This Madeira punch was known as Sangaree by the 1780s and was popular throughout western Europe and the Americas. The definition of Sangaree eventually broadened, and by the late 1820s included mixtures calling for port wine, claret, porter, and stronger spirits. Jerry Thomas included six different Sangarees in his 1862 *Bar-Tender's guide*: two with wine, two with spirits, and two with beer—and none with Madeira. See THOMAS, JEREMIAH P. "JERRY". Mentioned in works by Dickens, Hawthorne, Thackeray, and Kipling, the Sangaree is a mild, refreshing drink, once considered suitable for invalids and the mildly temperate.

Recipe (Port Wine Sangaree): In a cocktail shaker, stir 10 ml of sugar into 90 ml of tawny port, fill with ice, shake well, and strain into tall glass over fresh ice. Grate nutmeg over the top.

Labat, J. Baptiste. *Nouveau voyage aux isles de l'Amerique*. Paris: 1722.
Nichols, J. "Historical Chronicle, 1736, September." *Gentleman's Magazine* 6 (1736): 550–551.

Doug Stailey

sangrita is a popular nonalcoholic accompaniment served with tequila. Many have laid claim to sangrita, but its probable origins lie in the early twentieth century in the resort region of Chapala, Jalisco, where local restaurateur Jose Edmundo Sanchez served house-made agave firewater. To quench the hooch-fueled flames in their patrons' mouths and throats, Don Jose's wife, Doña Guadalupe, prepared plates of sliced oranges sprinkled with chili and salt. As the popularity of her side dish grew, the combination transitioned to a liquid form, which they offered in their restaurant. Known as *sangrita del diabolo*, "little blood of the Devil," it made its debut in 1925.

In 1957, the couple's entrepreneurial son, Edmundo Sanchez Nuño, launched Productos Sane, a company whose first offering was a bottled version of his parents' house beverage spiked with red vegetable dye and labeled Sangrita de la Viuda de Sanchez (Sangrita of the widow Sanchez), a nod to Doña Guadalupe (Jose had died in 1929). The rights to Sangrita de la Viuda were sold to the Cuervo company in 1970, but by then sangrita had taken a different trajectory in Mexican drinking culture. Whether due to the bright red color of the bottled version or its name, the accepted recipe for Sangrita turned toward the nightshades and became a tomato-juice-based shooter resembling a tiny Bloody Mary. Thanks in large part to a yearly sangrita competition hosted by Tequila Ocho, sangrita is returning to its role as a consort of tequila meant to complement and highlight rather than overpower. Though the exact recipe for that first companion may be lost, the following recipe from Portland, Oregon, bartender Jeffrey Morgenthaler is a refreshing homage to Doña Guadalupe's palate-saving offering.

Recipe: Mix 30 ml fresh orange juice, 25 ml fresh lime juice, 15 ml real pomegranate grenadine, and a pinch (approx. 2 ml) pasilla chile powder; chill and serve.

See also AGAVE; JOSE CUERVO; MEXICO; SHOOTER; TEQUILA.

"Gente nuestra: Edmondo Sánchez Nuño."
  Página: semanario de la Ribera de Chapala, December 17, 2016, 14–15.
McCaleb, Kenneth. "Tequila—Mexican Elixir." *Esquire*, September, 1960, 159–162.
Morgenthaler, Jeffrey. "How to Make Sangrita." Jeffrey Morgenthaler website, June 10, 2008. http://www.jeffreymorgenthaler.com/2008/how-to-make-sangrita/ (accessed March 10, 2021).
Potters, Cristina. "From That Little Beginning." *Mexico Cooks* (blog), March 14, 2007. http://mexicocooks.typepad.com/mexico_cooks/2007/03/salsa_cholula.html (accessed March 10, 2021).

Misty Kalkofen

The **San Martín** cocktail, named after Don José de San Martín (1778–1850), the highest hero and liberator of Argentina, Chile, and Peru, was created at the beginning of the twentieth century, although its author is unknown (it is recorded as early as 1907). Apparently, it was the Argentine interpretation of the Martini, and although it was very popular in its first decades of life, both in Argentina and in neighboring Uruguay, today it has somewhat fallen into oblivion. When it is consumed, it is generally the "dry" San Martín that is ordered. Its dominant version is that which appears in the *Manual del bar* by AMBA (Asociación Mutual de Barmen y Afines de la República Argentina): ½ London dry gin, ½ dry vermouth, stirred and served in a cocktail glass, decorated with a twist of lemon.

There are, however, many variations of this cocktail. The earlier ones generally used sweet vermouth and Old Tom gin, such as that by Benito Iglesias, in his pioneering *El arte del cocktelero* (1911). In 1920, José Penedo offered a demisec version in his *Guía del cocktelero*, with dry gin. Some of the early versions were served on the rocks, and many featured dashes of maraschino, cherry brandy, curaçao, or even green or yellow Chartreuse, often in combination. (It is such a version that made it into Harry Craddock's *Savoy Cocktail Book*, under the mangled name "Sand Martin.")

Thanks to its great acceptance by the public of the early twentieth century, there were some brands that created a bottled version such as Tommy's Cocktail by Champagnette Ltd. in 1917 or American Club by Dellepiane & Cía. in 1934. In 1936, Pini Hnos. & Cía. Ltda. also brought the cocktail to home drinkers with its bottled *San Martín*, creating a product ready to drink straight up, on ice, or chilled.

Recipe (1910s version): Stir with ice 45 ml London dry gin, 45 ml sweet vermouth, 2 dashes orange bitters, and 1 dash each of maraschino liqueur and cherry brandy (other liqueurs may be used). Strain into chilled cocktail glass and twist orange peel over the top.

AMBA *Manual del Bar*. Buenos Aires: AMBA, 1953.

Iglesias, Benito. *El Arte del Cocktelero*. Buenos Aires: Librería Americana, 1911.

Penedo, José. *Guía del Cocktelero*. Buenos Aires: Rosario, 1920.

Ariel Lombán

Santa Cruz rum was the commercial name for the rum of Saint Croix in the Danish Virgin Islands, one of the most important spirits in the nineteenth-century American bartender's toolkit. It began appearing in the United States in the 1790s and by the 1820s was, along with Jamaican rum, the leading type of imported rum in the American market, a staple in cold Rum Punches and in so-called fancy drinks such as the Knickerbocker. See RUM, JAMAICAN; RUM PUNCH; and KNICKERBOCKER.

Unfortunately, while the heavy, aromatic Jamaican style of rum is well understood, Santa Cruz rum is one of the spirits world's deeper mysteries. It had a reputation for purity and strength (it was often sold at well over proof), but beyond that precise information on how it was produced is scarce and fragmentary, and detailed descriptions of its characteristics are rare. Modern sampling of rare specimens surviving from the nineteenth century reveals that it tasted nothing like the light, clean, rather anodyne spirit made on the island today: medium-weight, bright and grassy, it had plenty of hogo but also a delicacy not found in the full-throated Jamaican rums of the day. See HOGO.

What evidence we do have about its distillation suggests that this delicacy was due to the exceptional cleanliness of the island's distilleries and their use of only molasses and skimmings for distillation, without the additional dunder used in Jamaica or resorting to the column still as in Guyana. See MO-LASSES; SKIMMINGS; and DUNDER. Both of those things would mean fewer bacterially produced esters in the rum than in Jamaican rum and its imitators. See ESTERS. (The skimmings set it apart, on the other hand, from the pure-molasses Medford rum that dominated the lower end of the American market.) See RUM, MEDFORD. There is also some evidence that, as the island's sugar industry began to struggle in the early twentieth century, its distillers began basing their rum on pure cane juice or cane syrup.

In 1916, the United States purchased Saint Croix and two other islands from Denmark. By then, rum production there was already in decline: the island exported less than 200,000 liters that year rum, half of the figure for 1903. Part of the decline was due to internal reasons, but it was also due to the fading American interest in rum and the diversion of what interest there was to newly introduced Cuban and Puerto Rican rums. Three years later, Prohibition switched the remaining distilleries to making non-potable bay rum. With repeal, distilling was reestablished, but the rum made, now in column stills, had little resemblance to the earlier style. See COLUMN STILL.

An Invalid [pseud.]. *A Winter in the West Indies and Florida*. New York: Wiley & Putnam, 1839.

Burton, R. H. "The Distillation of Rum." *The Sugar Cane*, December 1, 1875, 626.

David Wondrich

The **Saratoga** cocktail, popular from the late 1880s until American Prohibition, is not one drink but two: two competing, very different formulae that shared one name (Saratoga Springs, New York, was famed for its mineral springs, its racecourse, and the high play at its gambling houses). The first drink, a 2:1 Manhattan with half the whisky replaced by brandy, appeared in the 1887 posthumous edition of Jerry Thomas's *Bar-Tenders Guide*; the second, a fancy Brandy Cocktail with a "squirt" of champagne, was published by Harry Johnson the following year. See MANHATTAN and JOHNSON, HARRY. For the next thirty years, mixologists took sides: where one appeared, the other was excluded. Johnson's version, perhaps the most common, frequently saw its expensive champagne replaced by soda water (as was sometimes done in Saratoga Springs, with whisky substituted for the brandy) or omitted entirely, while in Europe the "Jerry Thomas" version saw its American whisky replaced with scotch or Irish versions. Neither version was simple enough to withstand Prohibition mixologists, and by the 1930s the drinks were a mere memory.

Modern mixologists occasionally trot out the Jerry Thomas version as a substitute (and an exceptionally toothsome one it is) for the Manhattan.

Recipe (the Johnson version): Stir with ice 45 ml old cognac, 5 ml maraschino, 5 ml pineapple syrup, 2 dashes aromatic bitters; strain into coupe; add strawberry and 15–30 ml chilled champagne; garnish with a lemon twist.

"The Summer Season." *Baltimore Sun*, August 18, 1892, 3.

Wondrich, David. *Imbibe!*, 2nd ed. New York: Perigee, 2015.

David Wondrich

Satan's Whiskers is a cocktail whose recipe first appeared in print in *The Savoy Cocktail Book* (1930). Equal parts gin, orange juice, and sweet and dry vermouth, with a dash of orange bitters, it took two forms: "curled" had half a part of orange curaçao, while "straight" called for Grand Marnier instead (which is, of course, simply a fancy brand of orange curaçao). A twist on the Bronx, one of the most popular cocktails in 1920s Europe, Satan's Whiskers made its way to the United States in both variations within months of repeal, and both were found in Patrick Gavin Duffy's 1934 *The Official Mixer's Manual*. However, they quickly fell into decline after World War II, until championed as lost classics by Paul Harrington and Ted Haigh at the turn of the twenty-first century. In 2014, a bar named after the drink opened in Bethnal Green, London; it rapidly became one of the city's most popular.

Recipe: Combine 30 ml each of gin, orange juice, sweet vermouth, and dry vermouth with a dash of orange bitters. Add 15 ml orange curaçao or Grand Marnier as desired, shake, and strain.

See also Bronx Cocktail; Harrington, Paul; and Haigh, Ted.

Haigh, Ted. *Vintage Spirits and Forgotten Cocktails*. Beverly, MA: Quarry, 2009.

François Monti

sauce-aroma-style baijiu is a spirit distilled from sorghum that has been fermented in stone-lined pits. It is the costliest variety of baijiu to produce and is prized by baijiu connoisseurs. The style is notable for rich, savory tastes and a lingering fragrance reminiscent of the Chinese culinary staple soy sauce, for which it is named.

Its origins lie in the remote village of Maotai, buried deep in the mountains of southwestern China's Guizhou Province. During the Qing Dynasty (1644–1912), Maotai was strategically positioned along the Chishui River and served as a distribution center for the government's salt monopoly. Though the region had an eclectic folk winemaking tradition, the salt merchants stationed there found local spirits wanting. The merchants recruited northern distillers to improve upon local pit-fermentation methods, and sauce-aroma was the happy result.

The ingredients are simple—wheat-based big qu and sorghum—but the production process is Byzantine. See QU. After qu is added to steamed sorghum, the mash is formed into waist-high mounds and left alone while fermentation begins. Once the distiller determines the grains are ready, the mash is shoveled into large pits lined with stone bricks and sealed with mud to finish fermenting over the course of a month. The mash is unloaded and distilled, then fresh grains are added to the spent mash, and the cycle begins anew. The process is repeated a total of seven times, and a full production cycle lasts about a year. The distillate from each stage is stored and aged separately in large, semipermeable clay jars for at least three years before the master blender combines them.

Sauce-aroma-style baijiu has enjoyed great success due as much to official patronage as to its complex and layered flavor. Kweichow Moutai, the style's most famous brand, was a favorite of Prime Minister Zhou Enlai, who made it the Chinese Communist Party's official banquet baijiu for state dinners in the 1950s. See Kweichow Moutai.

See also baijiu and China.

Moutai: Globalization of a Chinese Icon. Kweichow Moutai, 2012.

Xu Ganrong and Bao Tongfa. *Grandiose Survey of Chinese Alcoholic Drinks and Beverages* (中国酒大观目录, Chinese and English versions). Jiangnan University, 1998.

Derek Sandhaus

Saucier, Ted (1894–1970), is the author of *Bottoms Up* (1951), a volume of cocktail recipes. Punctuated by risqué pinups executed by prominent graphic artists, *Bottoms Up* included the earliest prescription for the Last Word, a cocktail concocted before Prohibition at the Detroit Athletic Club and still popular. In 1930, the Waldorf Astoria hotel appointed Saucier public relations director. The Canadian-born bon vivant made himself the hotel's embodiment and became ubiquitous in society pages. Obliging columnists incorporated his feuilletons touting the hotel's events; *Billboard* voted him top press agent of 1943. Saucier consulted as technical advisor for *Weekend at the Waldorf*, one of the top-grossing films of 1945. In 1950, he founded his own agency with his former employers as clients.

Saucier's book, which received a second, augmented edition in 1962, is a favorite source for historically inclined modern mixologists, as it frequently lists the sources for its recipes, including many famous bars and celebrities of the day.

See also LAST WORD and WALDORF-ASTORIA.

"Behind the Scenes in Hollywood." *Tipton (IN) Daily Tribune*, November 7, 1944, 2.

"Louella G. Parsons Hollywood." *Albany (NY) Times-Union*, March 11, 1950.

"New York's Top PAed Hotels." *Billboard*, September 4, 1943, 17.

Saucier, Ted. *Bottoms Up*. New York: Greystone, 1951

Van Raalte, Joseph. "Bo Broadway." *Binghamton (NY) Press*, July 14, 1930.

Doug Stailey

Saunders, Audrey (1962–), was the operating partner behind New York's seminal cocktail lounge, Pegu Club, on West Houston Street. From the day that its doors opened in the summer of 2005 the bar was celebrated as a center for the emerging "craft cocktail" movement. See CRAFT COCKTAIL. The bar, which closed in 2020, was known for its meticulously prepared specialty cocktails and attentive service. Saunders pioneered the practice of tabletop cocktail condiments, including a selection of small bottles holding simple syrup, fresh juice, and bitters, which allow the guests to add a personal touch to their cocktails.

Saunders trained many of today's top bartenders at Pegu Club, some of whom have opened their own celebrated bars. Standouts among the bar's alumni are Jim Meehan, who started the James Beard award-winning Please Don't Tell (PDT), and Phil Ward, who started tequila-and-mezcal-centric bar Mayahuel.

Audrey Saunders behind the bar at Pegu Club in New York. Courtesy of Audrey Saunders.

Saunders came late to the beverage business, leaving the corporate cleaning business that she cofounded, Contract Services of America, to become a bartender at the Waterfront Alehouse in Brooklyn. She was consumed by the world of bars and restaurants and worked tirelessly to train herself in the industry. It was in this period that Saunders met Dale DeGroff, the head bartender at New York's iconic Rainbow Room. See DEGROFF, DALE. As he recalls,

I was moonlighting as a teacher in the NYU Continuing Education program in the hotel, restaurant, and beverage department. The class was called the Business of the Bar, and I shared the allotted four hours with a financial controller from the B. E. Rock Company, the firm that operated the Rainbow Room in Rockefeller Center, which employed us both.

Saunders was so passionate about the bar world that she approached me after the class and offered to work for free to learn about high-end beverage service. I managed a union shop at the Rainbow, and that wasn't an option. The B. E. Rock Company was an early co-sponsor of the City Meals on Wheels Initiative, and as a group we worked closely with the mayor and other restaurateurs on events to promote the charity as well as events to promote tourism in the city. I needed help—none of the participants are paid, so it wasn't easy to find willing bar staff—I turned to Saunders. She worked regularly on charity events with me for a couple years. Then in 1999, she worked for chef Waldy Malouf as lead bartender at the acclaimed Beacon Restaurant on West Fifty-Sixth Street. After two years there, she took a management position at Tonic, a bar and restaurant in the Chelsea. Tonic closed right after the tragedy of 9/11.

I brought Audrey in as bar manager of Bemelman's Bar in the historic Carlyle Hotel in 2001. I was contracted to redo the beverage service, menus, and training at the bar, but the establishment needed a full-time manager to run the program when my contract expired. Saunders excelled in this job. Beverage sales in the bar and lounge rose by 1,000 percent in the first year. In 2005, she was approached to become the creative talent and the operating partner at Pegu Club.

Today Saunders and her husband, Robert Hess, a former Microsoft project manager and a cocktail pioneer in his own right, are putting finishing touches on the Ravenwood Beverage Institute on their property in rural Washington. See HESS, ROBERT. The institute will be a "retreat" of sorts for talented men and women who are blazing a trail in the new craft bar movement.

See also PEGU CLUB.

"Mixologist Audrey Saunders of Pegu Club—Biography." *Star Chefs*, April 2012. https://www.starchefs.com/cook/chefs/bio/audrey-saunders (accessed May 25, 2021).

Simonson, Robert. "Audrey Saunders and Robert Hess." *New York Times*, July 29, 2011. http://www.nytimes.com/2011/07/31/fashion/weddings/audrey-saunders-and-robert-hess-vows.html (accessed May 25, 2021).

Wells, Pete. "Mixing It Up with a Cocktail Purist." *Food and Wine*, March 31, 2015. http://www.foodandwine.com/articles/mixing-it-up-with-a-cocktail-purist (accessed May 25, 2021).

Dale DeGroff and David Wondrich

Sauza, founded by Cenobio Sauza (1842–1909) in 1873, is the second-largest tequila brand in the world and is sold in seventy-five countries worldwide. Cenobio got his start in the tequila business managing the Cuervo family's hacienda. Having purchased La Antigua Cruz, an old distillery in the town of Tequila, when he was just sixteen, he used the experience gained working for the Cuervos to strike out on his own. He renamed his distillery La Perseverancia (Perseverance) and within decades was Cuervo's biggest competitor. See JOSE CUERVO. In 1893, he submitted his tequila to the World's Columbian Exposition in Chicago and won a gold medal, winning 22 of 25 points for purity, 23 for distillation, 23 for taste, and 24 for "appearance and general condition."

Cenobio died in 1909, leaving the family business to his son, Eladio, who would steer it through the turbulent years of the Mexican Revolution (1910–1920). Eladio promoted his tequila on Guadalajara's first radio station and served it in a nightclub he opened called La Colonial. He also introduced bottling to replace the casks in which the family tequila had previously been sold. By the time of his death in 1946, Tequila Sauza was selling more than one million cases annually. Eladio's son Francisco Javier eventually took over and ran Tequila Sauza for thirty years, during which he transformed it into a global brand, then sold half his shares to Pedro Domecq, a Spanish spirits conglomerate. When he died in 1990, the remaining shares transferred to Pedro Domecq. In 1994, Pedro Domecq merged with Allied Lyons to form Allied Domecq. In 2005, it was acquired by Fortune Brands, which in 2011 was split into two companies, one of which became Beam, Inc. In 2014, Beam was itself acquired by the Japanese brewing and distilling group Suntory. See SUNTORY.

Francisco Javier Sauza's son never had the opportunity to take over the family business. His grandson, however, who was raised in the United States and became interested in tequila on trips to visit family in Mexico, decided to start his own brand. Installing his operation on a property that had remained in his family for generations, he set out to make a 100 percent estate-grown agave tequila using a *tahona*, the ancient stone mill used to crush cooked agave for tequila production. See TAHONA. Barred from using his family name, he was forced to come up with a

Label for Tequila Sauza Añejo, trademarked in 1924. Wondrich Collection.

new name for his brand and chose Los Abuelos, in honor of his grandfather, great-grandfather, and great-great-grandfather Cenobio. Due to a trademark infringement issue involving a rum with a similar name, he was forced to rechristen it Fortaleza. The brand remains unconnected to Tequila Sauza.

Tequila Sauza produces a comprehensive line of tequilas, including *plata* (silver), *joven* (gold) (sweetened with a caramel, which also adds color), *reposado* (rested or slightly aged), and *añejo*. See REPOSADO and AÑEJO. The basic line is made with 51 percent agave distillate and 49 percent other sugars, known as a *mixto* tequila. See MIXTO. A signature line of tequilas is made with 100 percent blue agave. The agave plants used to make all Tequila Sauza products are grown in the valley of Tequila, which has come to be known in the tequila industry as the Lowlands. (The valley sits at about 4,000 feet above sea level, versus the Highlands, which are at some 6,000 feet, but the region can hardly be considered "low.") The agave hearts are processed by diffuser, meaning they are fed raw through industrial shredders and hydrolyzed using steam and chemicals. The extracted sugars are diluted with water and cooked before being fermented and distilled. See DIFFUSER.

Several other brands exist under the company's umbrella, including the luxury brand Tres Generaciones and Hornitos, both of which are 100 percent agave tequilas processed by diffuser.

In 2014, Beam acquired a stake in singer Justin Timberlake's 901 Tequila and rebranded it Sauza 901. Sauza also has a chile- and cucumber-flavored tequila in its lineup.

See also MEXICO and TEQUILA.

Agraz Garcia de Alba, Gabriel. *Historia de la industria tequila Sauza*. Guadalajara: Sauza, 1963.

Bowen, Sarah. *Divided Spirits: Tequila, Mezcal, and the Politics of Production*. Berkeley: University of California Press, 2015.

Gaytán, Marie. *¡Tequila!: Distilling the Spirit of Mexico*. Stanford, CA: Stanford University Press, 2014.

Valenzuela, Ana. *Tequila: A Natural and Cultural History*. Tucson: University of Arizona Press, 2003.

Chantal Martineau

The **Savoy Hotel's American Bar** is both historically important and a current trendsetter for bars and mixology, a status it has maintained for more than a century. The lavish London hotel was opened in 1889, adjacent to the Savoy Theatre, by impresario Richard D'Oyly Carte (1844–1901), who staged the popular operettas of William S. Gilbert and Arthur Sullivan. He, along with a handful of investors including composer Sullivan, set a new benchmark for British luxury hotels. The first British accommodation to sport electrical lighting as well as constant hot and cold running water in every room, the Savoy also offered its elite clientele a remarkable new feature: en-suite marble bathrooms in nearly all of its 268 rooms.

Harvesting the talents of the famed French chef George August Escoffier and hotel manager César Ritz for the hotel's opening, D'Oyly Carte attracted an extravagant roster of guests, including Edward, Prince of Wales; actress Sarah Bernhardt; and whisky baron Sir Thomas Dewar. The hotel did not, however, open with a dedicated bar. Although it is claimed that it added the American Bar in 1893, it did not, as a 1900 appeals court case shows (the Savoy "had no bar or counter for the sale of intoxicating liquors," as the facts of the case stated, and sold them only at tables in its grill room and restaurant). In fact, the first mention of an American Bar in the hotel comes from 1903, which suggests it was only installed when Rupert D'Oyly Carte (1876–1948) restructured the hotel after his father's death. (There was no doubt a service bar before that, where drinks were mixed for the tables as required, and this might explain why the hotel claims that the hotel's first bartender, Frank Wells, had worked there from 1900 to 1903.)

The American Bar—so named because of the style of drinks that it served, which incorporated ice in their preparation, not after the Americans who provided the bulk of its clientele in its early years—was apparently first presided over by Ruth "Kitty" Burgess, whom customers also called Miss B. By the end of 1903, she was joined by Ada Coleman (1874–1966), whom Rupert moved there from the bar at the Savoy's sister hotel, the Claridge.

Coleman brought a head full of new drinks and sterling charisma. She and Burgess became known as Kitty and Coley, even though they did not get along. Customers liked Coley's new cocktail repertoire and bubbling personality. Kitty didn't know how to mix the new drinks; she asked Coley to give her the recipes, and Coley refused. For twenty years, the pair never spoke if they were on the same shift. Despite Kitty's seniority, customers assumed that Coley was the head bartender. Then along came Harry.

Hired to work the Savoy's dispensary bar in 1921, the English-born, American-trained Harry Craddock (1876–1964) used his training and his acquired American accent to turn a new page in the Savoy's history. As Prohibition in the United States unfolded, American tourists flocked to the Savoy. However, Americans felt it was inappropriate for women to work in barrooms. It appears that Rupert D'Oyly Carte bowed to his patrons' whims, retiring Kitty and Coley on December 17, 1925, and placing Craddock at the helm. See CRADDOCK, HARRY LAWSON.

Achieving celebrity status in his own right before he resigned in 1939, in the mere nineteen years he spent there Craddock almost singlehandedly made the American Bar not only famous but peerlessly influential. A large part of that was due to his 1930 compilation *The Savoy Cocktail Book*, which became an instant classic and has been one of the defining works of mixography for going on a hundred years.

Other notable bartenders followed in his legacy. Eddie Clarke (1939–1942) crafted dedicatory drinks for the British navy, army, and air force. See CLARKE, EDWIN "EDDIE" J. Reginald "Johnnie" Johnson (1942–1954) created a drink for Princess Elizabeth's marriage to Prince Philip. Joe Gilmore (1954–1975) celebrated astronaut Neil Armstrong's first walk on the moon with a special creation. Harry "Vic" Vicars (1975–1981) and Victor Gower (1981–1985) saw through the disco years before Peter Dorelli (1985–2000) took to the bar and toasted the end of the twentieth century with his Millennium Cocktail. See DORELLI, GIAMPIERO "PETER". Seeing the American Bar through to its closing for a major refurbishment, Salim Khoury (2003–2010) created the Blushing Monarch, inspired by the late Princess Diana Spencer, which won him, in 1992, UK Barman of the Year. With the reopening of the Savoy, Erik Lorincz took the helm as head bartender, continuing a long-standing tradition for bartending excellence. When he stepped down in 2018, his place was taken by Maxim Schulte. In 2021 it passed to Shannon Tebay, the first American to hold it.

The bar has been rearranged, redecorated, and rebuilt numerous times over the last century, but it has always remained in the first rank of bars, a place of pilgrimage for cocktail drinkers the world over.

See also COLEMAN, ADA, and CRADDOCK, HARRY LAWSON.

Ashburner, F. "Escoffier, Georges Auguste." *Oxford Dictionary of National Biography*.

Jacobs, Arthur. "Carte, Richard D'Oyly." *Oxford Dictionary of National Biography*.

Gilmore, Joe and Dorelli, Peter. Interviews, April 12, 2009, October 23, 2010, and December 21, 2015.

"Police Intelligence: Bow Street." *London Evening Standard*, December 3, 1903, 9.

"Savoy Hotel Company v. London County Council, June 22, 1900." In *The Law Reports, Queen's Bench Division*, 665–670. London: 1900.

Saunders, Minott. "Worked in Silence." *Windsor (ON) Star*, February 16, 1926, 19.

Anistatia R. Miller and Jared M. Brown

Sazerac Co. is an American maker of spirits headquartered in Metairie, Louisiana. Emerging from the New Orleans concern that operated the Sazerac House and popularized the Sazerac cocktail, the Sazerac Company has evolved over the years into a large spirits manufacturer with a stable that includes many of the country's leading whisky brands.

The company traces its roots to the Thomas H. Handy Co., a New Orleans wholesale and retail liquor dealer and operator of the Sazerac House. See SAZERAC HOUSE. After founder Thomas Handy died in 1893, the firm continued under the ownership of Handy's widow and several business associates, including his two head bartenders. In 1900 they trademarked the Sazerac brand and began selling a line of premixed, bottled cocktails, including their famous Whisky Cocktail, which would become "the" Sazerac cocktail. See SAZERAC COCKTAIL.

In 1919, with Prohibition looming, the firm was reorganized as the Sazerac Company, with Christopher O'Reilly (1872–1941), the manager of the Sazerac House, as president. It rode out Prohibition as a grocery wholesaler. Immediately after repeal, the firm resumed its original trade selling wines and imported spirits as well as its namesake Sazerac cocktail. In 1948, the Sazerac Company was purchased by the Magnolia Liquor Company, a New Orleans wine and spirits distributor. By the 1970s, the firm had acquired two classic New Orleans products (and key ingredients in the Sazerac cocktail), Peychaud's American Aromatic Bitters and Herbsaint, an anise-flavored absinthe substitute. See PEYCHAUD'S BITTERS. As the liquor industry as a whole was consolidating in the 1980s, the Sazerac Company took steps to grow from a regional supplier to a national distributor, and it steadily added more brands to its stable.

In the 1990s, amid the market revival of premium bourbons, the Sazerac Company moved aggressively into the whisky market. In 1992 it purchased the old E. H. Taylor distillery in Frankfort, Kentucky and renamed it Buffalo Trace, and in 1999 bought Old Charter from Diageo. See TAYLOR, COL. E. H.; BUFFALO TRACE DISTILLERY; and DIAGEO. In March 2009, the Sazerac Company acquired the Tom Moore distillery in Bardstown and the Glenmore distillery in Owensboro.

The Sazerac Company today distills and distributes more than 250 brands of liquor, including Buffalo Trace, W. L. Weller, Pappy Van Winkle, George T. Stagg, Ancient Age, and Sazerac Rye, along with dozens of vodka, gin, tequila, and rum brands, making it one of the largest privately held distillers in the American market.

"Probers Reveal Lack of Licenses." *New Orleans Times-Picayune*, November 16, 1948.

Quale, Jennifer. "The Drink That Old Orleans Made Famous." *New Orleans Times-Picayune*, October 27, 1974.

Quillen, Kimberly. "Sazerac Company to Expand Operations, Workforce in Kentucky." *New Orleans Times-Picayune*, June 21, 2009.

Robert F. Moss

Sazerac cocktail, an almost mythically alluring mix of rye whisky, sugar, and Peychaud's bitters served in an absinthe-rinsed glass, is an item of New Orleans identity, and indeed in 2008 the Louisiana state legislature declared it the official cocktail of New Orleans. While there is general agreement that the drink was invented at the Sazerac House saloon on Royal Street in New Orleans's French Quarter, when that was and what its original form was are subjects of enduring contention.

The Louisiana-based Sazerac Company—maker of, among other things, Sazerac Rye whisky and Peychaud's Bitters—follows the 1930s historian of New Orleans drinks Stanley Clisby Arthur (1881–1963) in asserting that the first Sazerac was mixed and popularized by Antoine Amedie Peychaud at his pharmacy on Royal Street, using his proprietary bitters and Sazerac de Forge cognac, and that this became the specialty of the Sazerac House (named after the cognac, which it distributed) in the 1850s. See SAZERAC CO. and SAZERAC HOUSE. According to this theory, the drink's base was switched to rye in 1873, and the absinthe added around the same time.

The ❧ Sazerac ❧ Cocktails

Whiskey,   Manhattan,   Martini,   Tom Gin,
Holland Gin,   Vermouth.

Prepared and Bottled by

**Thos. W.
Handy
& Co.**

**NEW
ORLEANS,
LA.**

These Cocktails are made from the best liquors
that can be procured; being mixed in accurate
proportions they will always be found of uniform quality.

**FOR TIRED
WOMEN**   As a tonic, Sazerac Cocktail should be in every
home. They will put
new life into one after a day's hard shopping.
Endless worry of household duties can be done
away with, if the needed tonic is at hand.

**As a Ladies' Drink
The "Sazerac Cocktail"
Has no Equal.**

**FOR TIRED
MEN . . .**   After a busy day, see
that you have at home a
bottle of Sazerac Cock-
tails. As an appetizer and general tonic for
the business man they have no equal.

**FOR SALE BY ALL FANCY GRO-
CERS and on BUFFET TRAINS of
ALL LEADING RAILWAYS : : : :**

"As a ladies' drink the Sazerac Cocktail has no equal."
1902 advertisement for the Sazerac line of bottled cocktails.
Eventually only the Whisky Cocktail remained, as the
Sazerac. Wondrich Collection.

Unfortunately, Arthur's account is undercut by numerous errors, accidental and deliberate, and corroborating evidence for his claims is scarce. See ARTHUR, STANLEY CLISBY. The Sazerac cocktail was first mentioned in print only in 1899 and does not appear in the great many known newspaper articles about the Sazerac House from the 1850s until then, nor in any of its advertisements. The articles do not mention any cocktail specialty at all until 1895, while all the advertisements prove is that the bar carried Sazerac cognac and Peychaud's Bitters. But the newspapers also show that it carried several other types of cognac and bitters as well, including the popular Otard and Boker's brands, and that many other bars in New Orleans and throughout America also carried Sazerac de Forge cognac and Peychaud's Bitters. If the bar was making Sazerac brandy cocktails with Peychaud's, they weren't the only ones it was making, and it wasn't the only place

making them. Indeed, as early as 1843 the *New York Sunday Mercury* was saying (perhaps with some exaggeration) that wherever one ordered a cocktail, one would receive "a beverage compounded of brandy, sugar, absynthe [*sic*], bitters and ice." See COCKTAIL.

The part of the Sazerac cocktail's history that we can document begins in September 1895, when a thousand-word puff piece on the Sazerac House notes that bartender and co-owner Vincent Miret (1847–1899) had a "reputation as the best mixer of whisky cocktails in the City of New Orleans." At some point between that year (as the bar claimed on its trademark application) and 1899, when they first appear in advertisements, the Sazerac House began selling a line of bottled cocktails. There were six, including a plain Whisky Cocktail, but no Sazerac cocktail per se.

Meanwhile, however, the bar's version of its Whisky Cocktail had become widely imitated in the Crescent City. Not the precise formula, which was proprietary (according to a handwritten recipe sheet owned by the grandnephew of Chris O'Reilly, the bar's manager in the 1910s, it only differed from a standard Whisky Cocktail by using a dash of maraschino and both Peychaud's and Angostura bitters), but rather the way the bartenders at the Sazerac had of "dashing . . . absinthe into the glass into which the mixture is to be strained—first, however, throwing the absinthe out of the tumbler so as to leave only the aroma, minus the taste" (thus the *Chicago Inter Ocean* in 1901). The drink is still made the same way today.

By then, with the death of Miret, his partner Billy Wilkinson (1854–1904) had taken over as the bar's Whisky Cocktail specialist, and it was on his watch that the Sazerac Whisky Cocktail became the Sazerac cocktail (indeed, local opinion at the time had it that he was the Sazerac's creator, as the *Times-Picayune* stated in 1902). With the bar's bottled cocktails gaining national distribution and New Orleans rapidly developing as a tourist hub, having a Sazerac at the Sazerac House soon became one of the things a man had to do when he visited the city (the bar did not admit women). By 1910, bartenders around the nation were mixing their versions of the Sazerac, which enjoyed a vogue among the sort of dedicated drinkers who found a Bronx or even a Martini insufficiently boozy, among them the short story writer O. Henry, who had one or more every afternoon at the café next to his New York apartment. See BRONX COCKTAIL. The irony is that, aside from the novel technique for incorporating the absinthe, the Sazerac was virtually identical to Jerry Thomas's 1876 Improved Whisky Cocktail. Its popularity shows how much the American idea of the cocktail had changed in thirty years, from a glass of iced spirits with accents to a harmonious blend of spirits and other, less alcoholic ingredients.

After the repeal of Prohibition, New Orleans embraced the Sazerac cocktail anew, although its birthplace was gone, and one of its key ingredients, absinthe, was illegal. But the Roosevelt Hotel built the drink a new headquarters in 1949 when it opened its Sazerac Bar, and local substitutes such as Herbsaint and Green Opal took the place of the absinthe. The city's bars continued to make the drink for the locals and a few adventurous tourists, even as other, splashier drinks stepped into the spotlight. See BOURBON STREET DRINKS; HURRICANE. In the rest of the world, the drink occupied a space halfway between nostalgia and legend. By the end of the twentieth century, Peychaud's Bitters were practically unavailable outside of New Orleans, and the balance had tilted toward legend. With the cocktail renaissance, all of that would change. Odd bitters, absinthe, and rye whisky were three of the secret handshakes of the new craft-cocktail movement, and the Sazerac rode the renewal of interest in all three back into rude good health. Today it is one of the unassailable classics, a drink that every good bartender is expected to have mastered.

Recipe (Miret-Wilkinson Sazerac): Fill a small Old-Fashioned glass with ice and let it chill. In a second one, combine 5 ml rich simple syrup, 3 ml maraschino liqueur (optional), 2 dashes Peychaud's Bitters, 1 dash Angostura bitters, and 60 ml straight rye whisky. Add ice and stir. Empty the first glass, pour 5 ml absinthe into it, swirl it around and dump it out. Strain the mixed drink into it and twist lemon peel over the top.

"The merchants' Train Home." *New Orleans Picayune*, May 29, 1902, 3.

"The Sazerac." *New Orleans Semi-Weekly Times-Democrat*, September 1, 1895, 16.

"Sazerac Cocktail." Recipe sheet, presumably written by Christopher O'Reilly, ca. 1910, attached to author's correspondence with Stephen Joseph of New Orleans, May 5, 2020.

"Two Features of New Orleans." *Chicago Sunday Inter Ocean*, February 17, 1901, 4.

Wondrich, David. "Is the Sazerac a New Orleans Cocktail?" *Daily Beast*, April 24, 2017. https://www.thedailybeast.com/is-the-sazerac-a-new-orleans-cocktail (accessed March 11, 2021).

David Wondrich

Sazerac House (aka **Sazerac Bar**, **Sazerac Saloon**) was the pioneering New Orleans saloon that introduced the Sazerac cocktail to the world.

In the late 1850s, John B. Schiller took over the old Merchant's Exchange and converted it into the Sazerac Coffee House. A combination saloon and liquor import house occupying two lots stretching between Royal Street and Exchange Place, the business took its name from Sazerac de Forge et Fils, an esteemed brand of imported cognac brandy. In 1871, Schiller's clerk, Thomas B. Handy, took over the business and promptly renamed it Thomas H. Handy & Co., though locals still tended to call it the Sazerac House.

Through a complicated chain of events, a former employee of Handy's named Vincent Micas ended up operating a rival Sazerac House in New Orleans, but it was Handy's saloon—rebuilt from the ground up in 1882—that became one of the city's most noted drinking establishments. In the 1880s and 1890s, one account remembered, the Sazerac House was "the meeting place of all the business and political men of the city. If one had a big business deal the Sazerac offered the logical place for its discussion: foot on rail, one discussed weighty matters while waiting for the cocktail."

The cocktail in question became known as the Sazerac cocktail, but likely not until after Thomas Handy's death in 1893. In 1903, Handy's widow, his clerk, and William Wilkinson, the bar's popular head bartenders, trademarked the word Sazerac and began selling a bottled premixed version of their saloon's famous concoction, which they distributed across the country.

The Sazerac House flourished until the arrival of prohibition, and in 1920 the building was converted into fancy marble-adorned restaurant complete with an orchestra and a French chef.

The only known picture of the Sazerac House, from the background of a Prohibition-era poster. The site is now a hotel garage. Wondrich Collection.

Thomas H. Handy & Co., reorganized as the Sazerac Company, survived the dry years as a grocery wholesaler. After Repeal, its principals relaunched the Sazerac House in a new location at 300 Carondelet street in the Central Business District, replicating the original Royal Street establishment down to the same brass spittoons and some of the old bartenders. Women were prohibited except one day per year—Mardi Gras.

The new Sazerac House lasted until 1948, when the Sazerac Company was purchased by the Magnolia Liquor Company and the saloon shuttered.

See also Sazerac Co. and Sazerac cocktail.

"A City Institution." *New Orleans Times*, April 23, 1876, 12.

Moss, Robert F. "The Unexpurgated History of the Sazerac Cocktail." http://www.robertfmoss.com/p/i-will-warn-you-in-advance-that-this.html (accessed October 30, 2015).

"Opening This Day." *New Orleans Daily Picayune*, October 5, 1882, 2.

Quale, Jennifer. "The Drink that Old Orleans Made Famous." *New Orleans Times-Picayune*, October 27, 1974.

"The Sazerac." *New Orleans Times-Democrat*, September 1, 1895, 16.

Robert F. Moss

Scandinavia refers primarily to Sweden, Norway, and Denmark, three Northern European nations linked by geography, language, and culture, including drinking culture. Scandinavia is part of, and sometimes used as shorthand for, the broader Nordic region that also includes Finland, Iceland, the Faroe Islands, and various territories.

The etymology for distilled spirits in Scandinavian languages has its roots in "burnt wine" (e.g., *brændevin* in Danish), reflecting early use of wine as a base for distillation. Production shifted to grain and potatoes, often flavored with botanicals such as caraway to improve the taste. Distilled spirits had a substantial presence in Scandinavia by the 1500s, when they were allegedly consumed for their medicinal qualities, if often to excess. By the 1600s home distillation was widespread throughout the region. This period has been dubbed "the Great Nordic Intoxication" by historians and resulted in regulatory measures such as taxes and bans on home distillation to reduce consumption. See HOME DISTILLING. Temperance movements swept Scandinavia beginning in the nineteenth century, resulting in further restrictions and, in some countries, total prohibition. Alcohol sales in Nordic countries remain tightly regulated.

Along with Sweden's Absolut vodka, aquavit is the spirit most closely identified with Scandinavia, but the region also specializes in bitter and bittersweet herbal digestives (such as the intensely, even excruciatingly bitter wormwood-flavored *bäska droppar*), and spirits with unique flavorings such as salmiak, birch, and cloudberry. Spirits in Scandinavia are often consumed neat, particularly on holidays and as a companion to food. Cocktail culture and interest in other spirits is rising in Scandinavia, however, and the area is home to highly regarded cocktail bars and producers of spirits such as gin and whisky.

See also ABSOLUT; AQUAVIT; and BRANDY.

Brandt, Tova, ed. *Skål! Scandinavian Spirits.* Elk Horn, IA: Museum of Danish America, 2015.
Snowdon, Christopher. *The Art of Suppression.* Ripon, UK: Little Dice, 2011.

Jacob Grier

Schmidt, William (1850?–1905), nicknamed "the Only William," was the most famous American bartender of the nineteenth century. Arguably, he was also the first cocktail bartender to achieve celebrity for the artistry of his drinks rather than the force of his personality. His 1891 book, *The Flowing Bowl: What and When to Drink*, introduced new patterns, techniques, and ingredients to the bartender's art and a spirit of creativity that, though anomalous in its day, has tendrils that reach deep into the mixology of today. From 1888 almost until his death he was a regular presence in the pages of the New York newspapers and hence, through the practice of syndication, in the national ones. Indeed, such was his fame that he became proverbial: the standard against which all other mixologists were measured.

Schmidt was born in Heide, northwest of Hamburg, Germany. According to his death certificate, that was in 1850, although his photographs suggest a man rather older than that. In any case, he worked for a time in Hamburg before coming to America in 1868. There, he settled first in Chicago, where he ended up as bar manager at the Tivoli Garden, the city's largest, most luxurious beer hall, until it closed in 1882. He next surfaced in New York, on a warm day in May 1888, when a reporter from

the *New York Sun* found himself in George Hillen's Bridge Exchange, a large saloon right next to the Brooklyn Bridge, and witnessed a virtuoso display of bartending and mixology from the elaborately mustachioed German behind the bar. Before the year was out, Schmidt would have seven more major articles devoted to him, in both the *Sun* and the *New York World*. With that, his reputation was made: he was "William of the Bridge," "William the Learned," or, once he left Hillen's, "the Only William."

Schmidt's stock in trade consisted of a theatrical but precise style of bartending, a good deal of imagination in combining ingredients and in naming the combinations, and an ability to describe what he was doing in complete paragraphs of articulate, ornamental speech. All three qualities made him the perfect subject for the press of his day: his descriptions were detailed and amusing, his drinks unusual, and his showy bartending a perfect subject for the engravings and photographs with which American newspapers were beginning to abound.

In November 1889, after a few months in Europe (where he was offered, among other jobs, the directorship of the bar at the new Eiffel Tower), Schmidt opened his own bar in New York, on Broadway just above Park Row. That business failed quickly and had to be sold. Unusually, Schmidt stayed on as head bartender, working there, with the occasional hiatus, until just before his death in 1905. There he poured his drinks in arcs, gave them fanciful names, talked to anyone who would listen (particularly if that person was a journalist), and made himself an institution.

Schmidt's book only cemented his position. *The Flowing Bowl* was the most elaborate bartender's guide to come out since Jerry Thomas's seminal work of 1862. Unlike that work, however, which contained only a handful of drinks original to Thomas, its 229 recipes included over a hundred that were, as well as can be determined, the author's own creations. What's more, ingredients new to the American bar abound, including orange bitters, digestives such as Fernet Branca and Calisaya, and liqueurs such as parfait amour, kümmel, and crèmes de cacao, menthe, vanille, violette, and roses. See ORANGE BITTERS; APERITIF AND DIGESTIVE; FRATELLI BRANCA; PARFAIT AMOUR; and KÜMMEL. There are also a number of soda fountain ingredients, including acid phosphate, various fruit syrups, and ice cream. The drinks' names are just as novel: to cite a few, there are the Angelus, the Broker's Thought, the Weeper's Joy, the Brain-Duster. Ultimately, *The Flowing Bowl* is the first truly personal cocktail book.

For the rest of the 1890s, Schmidt remained the dean of American mixologists. In 1899, the influential and hugely popular *Police Gazette* named him as head judge in its inaugural cocktail contest, which drew hundreds of entries from bartenders nationwide. In 1902, a newspaper article quoting the recipe for Schmidt's "Hohenzollern Punch" was placed before Kaiser Wilhelm. Reportedly, the German ruler wrote in the margin, "Schrecklicher Katzenjammer an Morgen"—"Fearsome hangover in the morning." When news of the imperial judgment reached him, the Only William was not pleased. "I have the highest respect for His Majesty," he told the *World*, "but a Katzenjammer? Never! . . . In the morning you would wake refreshed." And on he went, delving into aesthetics, the theory of punch making, and several other cogent topics and ending with a final eulogy of his creation as "a triumphant, grateful mixture of all that makes life worth living into one soft, sweet, artistic, harmonious whole, fit for prince or plebeian."

With the turn of the new century, however, Schmidt's style of mauve-decade mixology was being eclipsed by a more minimalist aesthetic. He soldiered on nonetheless, until the end of 1904, when, faced with a pay cut, he quit his job. He was dead within three months. His death certificate gave the cause as "senile dementia," but a sentimentalist would no doubt attribute it to heartbreak. He left no survivors and is buried in an unmarked grave on Long Island.

Few, if any, of Schmidt's drinks made it into the canon of drinks that a bartender was expected to know. But if his recipes have faded away, the space he opened for creativity, his expansion of the bartender's palette, and his clever use of publicity and the media permanently changed the culture of mixed drinks.

"He Will Be Missed." *New York Sun,* April 14, 1889, 5.

" 'The Only William' and His Latest Summer Brew."
   New York Sunday Telegraph, June 29, 1902, 2.

" 'The Only William' Is Dead." *New York Sun*, February
   10, 1905.

"William, King of Bartenders." *New York Press*, October
   13, 1889, 1.

David Wondrich

schnapps is, very loosely, a type of distilled spirit, although pinning down a precise definition is challenging. "It is easier to write about the psychology of a woman than to understand a schnapps," the German writer Erich Maria Remarque, best known as the author of *All Quiet on the Western Front*, wrote in a 1924 treatise called "On the Mixing of Delicious Schnapps." As though to clarify his meaning, he added: "Schnapps has a soul."

We should rightly recoil at Remarque's male chauvinism, but we must agree with him that schnapps is difficult to understand. Remarque may have been alluding to what he perceived as an inherently elusive, perhaps even supernatural, quality in the spirit, but the real challenge in getting a handle on schnapps is far more prosaic. The word, which derives from the German word *Schnaps* (a dram of liquor, from the Low German *snappen*, "to snap") is used in Germany to mean strong liquor generally, and is applied to a great multitude of wildly varying spirits.

More narrowly, and especially among English speakers, it is most commonly used to denote two distinct, separate categories of liquor. The first is the traditional, northern European style of schnapps associated most intimately with Austria and Germany: a close kin to eau-de-vie, in which fruit supplies flavor, and no sweeteners or other superfluous ingredients are added. See EAU-DE-VIE. Apples, apricots, cherries, pears, and plums are commonly used fruits for making schnapps—unless, of course, one is in the Netherlands, and the schnapps in question is "Schiedam schnapps," which is a nineteenth-century trade name for ordinary genever. See GENEVER.

The other style might most conveniently be called the artificial style, in which sweetening agents and synthetic flavorings are frequently used, sometimes to create such fanciful concoctions as butterscotch and root beer schnapps, though less outré varieties, such as sour apple and peach, are used more often in the making of cocktails.

It gets still more complicated: in the traditional style, there are two different methods of producing fruit schnapps. One applies to schnapps called *Brand*. The other method applies to a variety called *Geist* (ghost). Brand is the more prevalent of the two, and is made by fermenting fresh fruit and then distilling the resulting mash to obtain a spirit of approximately 65 percent alcohol by volume. It is stored for at least one year in open containers, then diluted with water to achieve a more palatable proportion of alcohol, approximately 40 percent.

To make schnapps of the Geist variety, fruits are added to a neutral alcohol base and left to macerate. See MACERATION. Then, the mixture is redistilled and diluted in the same manner as the Brand style.

The altogether different artificial variety—an American specialty, originally midwestern—comprises a loosely knit family of viscous, sweetened, flavored liqueur that bears little resemblance to its Teutonic progenitor. In drink mixing, the latter sort of schnapps is deployed in numerous cocktails, many of which are associated with the 1970s and 1980s, during which they had their heydays. Peach schnapps features in Sex on the Beach and the Woo Woo. Peppermint schnapps appears in the Golden Eagle and the Hornet. See Sex on the Beach and Woo Woo. The once ubiquitous Apple Martini, or Appletini, of the 1990s relies on the inclusion of electric-green apple, or sour apple, schnapps.

In the musical *Fiddler on the Roof*, Tevye the dairyman celebrates the arrangement of his daughter Tzeitel's marriage to the rich, old butcher Lazar Wolf with a bit of schnapps. "We'll raise a glass / And sip a glass of schnapps," they sing in "To Life."

Tzeitel winds up marrying Motel the tailor instead.

See also Germany, Switzerland, and Austria.

Kochan, Thomas. Discussion with the author, July 4, 2016.

Rosie Schaap

schnapps, Schiedam, is a nineteenth-century moniker for genever, so called because of the scores of gin distilleries located in the Dutch city by that name. See Genever.

Schumann, Charles (1941–), the world's most published author of cocktail books today, could easily be called the godfather of contemporary German bartending. In the mid-1970s, when he began his career in Harry's New York Bar in Munich, cocktails had fallen into disrepute in Germany. See Harry's New York Bar. With very few exceptions, they were uninspired concoctions with ready-made garnishes, drunk by old men in dusty, if not dubious, hotel bars.

Although Schumann was not the only gifted barman in the country at that time, he was responsible for demonstrating that mixing drinks can be a "fine art." By his uncompromising quality standards, his distinctive style, and, not least, his substantial charisma, Schumann became, if not the role model, then a *spiritus rector*, a guiding spirit, for barmen all over the country.

Thus, Schumann is highly responsible for the appreciation cocktails have gained over the last decades.

His own early creations, the notorious Swimming Pool and the Flying Kangaroo, were heavy variations of the Piña Colada and are dissed today by Schumann himself but were very popular in the 1980s. See Piña Colada. Later, he developed mainly rum-based drinks, always mixing white and brown rums together, often pimped with overproof rum and always rather fruity—tiki-style, but sort of Bauhaus-tiki, served without the usual tackiness. This less-is-more attitude is also behind the design of his three bars in Munich. His original Schumann's American Bar, opened in 1982, was renamed and relocated as Schumann's Bar in a larger, more temple-like location in 2003; Schumann's Tagesbar opened in 2001, and Les Fleurs du Mal opened in 2013 on the floor above Schumann's Bar.

International recognition came with the publication of his books: *American Bar* was released 1991 and later published in the United States, the United Kingdom, France, and Japan. The worldwide success of this cocktail compendium may partly be due to the fine artwork of illustrator Günter Mattei, who also designed Schumann's earlier works *Schumann's Barbuch* (1984, translated into Italian, Spanish, and Danish) and *Schumann's Tropical Barbook* (1986, English, Spanish, Italian).

Several decades on, the workaholic still plays host in his three bars. In 2019, he fell into controversy when outcry over strongly negative comments he made in *Schumann's bargespräche*, a 2017 film about him, and elsewhere regarding the role of women in the bar industry caused him to return the Bar Icon award the 50 Best Bars organization had just given him. Whether these were made for the sake of argument as his defenders claim, pointing to his history of mentoring women bartenders and hiring them for some of his bars, or represent deep convictions as his critics say, pointing to his refusal to hire women at his main bar, the episode shows that the bar world has moved beyond the "boys will be boys" attitude that prevailed in Schumann's heyday.

See also Embury, David A.; and Meier, Frank.

"Charles Schumann Faces Allegations of Sexism and Misogyny." *Mixology*, October 14, 2019, https://mixology.eu/en/charles-schumann-sexism-best-bars/ (accessed March 11, 2021).

Stefan Gabányi

Scialom, Joseph (1910–2004), *né* Giuseppe Chalom di fu Isacco, became the most famous bartender of World War II when his drink the Suffering Bastard purportedly helped win the Second Battle of El Alamein.

An Egyptian-born, Paris-educated chemist fluent in eight languages, Scialom abandoned a pharmaceutical career in 1938 to tend bar at Shepheard's Hotel in Cairo. Three years later Shepheard's storied Long Bar became both an officers' club for Britain's Eighth Army and a press club for journalists covering the campaign against Hitler's Afrika Korps. One morning in October 1942, Scialom's Eighth Army regulars were mobilized to El Alamein after a marathon night at the Long Bar. From the front lines they cabled Scialom pleading for his signature hangover cure, the gin- and brandy-based Suffering Bastard: Scialom sent them four gallons in Thermoses via taxi cab; while it's highly unlikely that this turned the tide in what would become the deciding battle of the desert war, Scialom's journalist regulars seized on the story.

Scialom parlayed this press into a career as Hilton International's corporate mixologist, which sent him from San Juan and Havana to London and Rome, followed by a residency in Manhattan that included the Waldorf-Astoria, the Four Seasons, and Windows on the World atop one of the Twin Towers. He retired in 1977 but lived to see the Towers fall on September 11, 2001, from a nursing home TV in Hallandale, Florida. He died there three years later, but his Bastard suffers on in bars around the world.

Recipe (Scialom's Suffering Bastard): Shake well with ice 30 ml each gin and brandy, 15 ml lime cordial, and 2 dashes Angostura bitters; strain into ice-filled Collins glass and top with ginger beer; garnish with orange slice and mint sprig.

See also ANGOSTURA BITTERS and GINGER ALE AND GINGER BEER.

Berry, Jeff. *Beachbum Berry's Potions of the Caribbean.* New York: Cocktail Kingdom, 2014.

Jeff Berry

Scotland and Ireland, separated by less than fifty miles of sea, are surely the homes of whisky. Scotch whisky is what most people in the world mean when they say the word "whisky," and there are places where a bottle of blended Scotch works as well as currency. Irish whisky was once a similarly globe-girdling colossus before falling on hard times in the twentieth century. It may have been down and out, indeed almost dead by the 1970s, but it has staged a stirring comeback with the help of the worldwide Irish pub phenomenon.

Whisky almost certainly originated here as well, most likely in Ireland as medieval monks applied the scientific knowledge they'd gleaned from the best libraries of Europe and beyond to everyday issues, like how to make the essences for which distilling was largely used. Someone had the bright idea of making an essence of beer, and the monks called it *usquebaugh* (also seen as *uisce beatha*), the Gaelic words for the "water of life," or perhaps "lively water." As more people made it and drank it, *usquebaugh*, pronounced (roughly) "ish-ka b'ah" was shortened to "ish-ka" and then twisted a bit to "whisky."

Both regions have rich whisky folklore, often centered on clandestine distilling. In Scotland, making illicit whisky was a profitable if dangerous sideline for many farmers, immortalized in Edwin Landseer's painting *An Illicit Whisky Still in the Highlands.* The unlicensed and untaxed whisky, called "peat-reek" for the redolent fumes from the peat burned to heat the hidden copper pot, the "sma' still," was either consumed nearby or smuggled to towns, often far south into England.

In Ireland the spirit is called *poitín*, a Gaelic diminutive that means, roughly, "dear little pot." Poitín is still made today, and the lore is that you stole out at night to leave money in a well-known local crevice or hollow tree and returned a few days later to find a bottle of poitín, clear, unaged, and of authoritative strength, and you didn't ask questions. See HOME DISTILLATION and MOONSHINE.

Both regions also have thriving legal whisky industries that grew from Industrial Age beginnings. Distilling may have started as a cottage industry, but the Scots and Irish grew it to mighty proportions, helped along by the trading acumen and reach of the British Empire. What's interesting is that in Scotland, it was largely the distillers out in the countryside, who did things the small and old-fashioned way, who succeeded in the long run; Glenlivet, for instance, is still tucked away in a green glen, reached only by a two-lane road. See GLENLIVET. But in Ireland it was the big, urban distillers who did things on a relatively huge scale—big stills, big warehouses—that won out, at least before the crash of Irish whisky in the wake of American Prohibition and the post-independence trade war with the British Empire.

The similarities that connect the different whiskies in their smaller regions also connect Scotch and Irish whiskies to some extent. Both are aged in used barrels, mostly a combination of bourbon and sherry casks. Both are largely barley-based, with other cereals used in the grain whiskies used for blending. See BARLEY and GRAIN. Both rely on blended whisky for the majority of their sales but make premium bottlings of more flavorful whiskies, and both have been experimenting with different wood for aging. See WHISKY, BLENDED.

While there has been a lot of consolidation in the industry in both regions, the most recent years have seen a small surge in new distilleries. It remains to be seen how these will affect the industries, but it shows that even the ancestral homes of whisky still have a lot of life.

The strong whisky cultures in both places have to some degree drawn attention from their traditions of mixing drinks, which are also strong, if somewhat narrowly focused. In both Scotland and Ireland, Whisky Punch was widely popular from the beginning of the eighteenth century through the middle of the nineteenth, and in Ireland it still is, as the Hot Whisky. See HOT WHISKY. Scotland soon learned to do without the citrus component in its punch, yielding toddy, the reigning mixed drink in the country until the late 1800s, when it was displaced by (blended) Whisky and Soda. See HIGHBALL and TODDY. The end of the nineteenth century saw American-style cocktail bars open in Dublin and Belfast and the major Scottish cities; their descendants include Belfast's award-winning Merchant's Hotel and Edinburgh's Bramble. Ironically, the best-known mixed drink from either country was invented not at a smart hotel bar but by a hungover chef at a rural airport. See IRISH COFFEE.

See also WHISKY; WHISKY, IRISH; WHISKY, POT STILL; and WHISKY, SCOTCH.

Broom, Dave. *The World Atlas of Whisky*, 2nd ed. London: Mitchell Beazley, 2014

Bryson, Lew. *Tasting Whiskey*. North Adams, MA: Storey, 2014.

O'Connor, Fionnán. *A Glass Apart: Irish Single Pot Still Whiskey*. Mulgrave, Australia: Images, 2015

Lew Bryson

Screwdriver is a highball composed of orange juice and vodka. The drink is a product of World War II, when American troops and civilian technicians in theaters such as China and Turkey, where whisky and other well-known potables were scarce, took to cutting neutral spirit—whether it was military ethanol or Turkish vodka—with orange juice. The name "Screwdriver" for the practice first turns up in Ankara, Turkey, in 1943, where it was apparently coined by interned American airmen, but its etymology has never been adequately explained. When the Screwdriver drinkers returned home, they brought the drink's recipe with them, and just in time for the nascent vodka boom. The drink enjoyed great popularity in the postwar years as American drinking habits skewed simpler and stronger, and vodka came to be favored. The fact that it was featured prominently in the advertising for Smirnoff, the leading American vodka brand, did not hurt that popularity. In the 1960s, the Screwdriver went on to serve as the foundation of later highballs such as the Harvey Wallbanger and Sloe Comfortable Screw. See HARVEY WALLBANGER. It remains widely popular, although it seldom receives much discussion among cocktail aficionados.

Recipe: Pour 45 ml vodka in highball glass filled with ice. Top with 90 ml orange juice. Garnish with orange slice if desired.

See also HIGHBALL and SMIRNOFF.

"Allied Troops in China Eat Turkey." *Rockford (IL) Morning star*, November 26, 1943.

Cohn, Art. "War Diary." *Long Beach (CA) Independent*, August 1, 1944, 11.

O'Brien, Mrs. Frank. "Friend, Foe Dine in Ankara at Pop Karpic's Restaurant." *Baltimore Sun*, May 23, 1943, 3.

Robert Simonson

The **Seagram Company Ltd.** was one of the most dominant names in the spirits business in the twentieth century. It was led by the Bronfman family, who started out as tobacco farmers in Russia but emigrated to Canada in the late nineteenth century, where they became involved in the mail-order whisky trade. In the early 1920s, led by Samuel (1889–1971), the family established a distillery at LaSalle, in suburban Montreal. On the basis of that, they were able to elicit a $2.5 million investment in their Distillers Corporation Limited from Scotland's mighty DCL (Distillers Company Limited; it is unlikely that the similarity in names was coincidental). See DISTILLERS COMPANY LTD (DCL). That enabled them to buy out another Canadian distillery, owned by Joseph E. Seagram & Sons. Seagram (1841–1920) had made a success of his VO brand, but the business struggled after his death. As "Distillers Corporation-Seagrams Ltd." the Bronfmans' growing firm was initially very successful, with $2.2 million in profits in 1929 (it would change its name again in 1975, to Seagram Company Limited). Reports suggest those profits had a lot to do with Prohibition in the United States; the Bronfmans certainly had no problem selling to bootleggers. "Of course we knew where it went," he would tell a later interviewer.

When Prohibition ended in 1933, the company was also in a good position because Sam Bronfman had stockpiled a considerable amount of aged whisky. Since DCL didn't want to enter the United States market and Seagram did, the Bronfmans were able to buy their partner out and gain complete autonomy. Using that aged whisky, Seagram focused on high-quality blends in the Canadian style, although some of them were made at new distilleries in the United States. Among the brands that the company launched and promoted under its umbrella were Seagram's 7 Crown, an American blend that used aged neutral spirit contrary to American practice, and the Canadian blend Crown Royal (introduced in 1939). See CROWN ROYAL.

The 1940s, 1950s, and 1960s saw the company grow rapidly until it had thirty-nine distilleries in fifteen countries, including thirteen in the United States and seven in Canada. The company's dozens and dozens of brands included Captain Morgan rum, Chivas Regal scotch whisky, and Sandeman ports and sherries. See CHIVAS REGAL. It also owned eighteen wineries and an oil company in Texas. Thanks to an aggressive education and quality-control program, many of the company's brands were among the most respected of their kind (as early as 1940, Seagram had published a company-wide distillers' manual for its production staff, showcasing state-of-the-art techniques and even over-the-horizon ones such as the use of aspergillus fungus as a fermentation starter). See ASPERGILLUS ORYZAE.

Eventually, the company became known for far more than spirits—besides wine and oil, it also invested heavily in chemicals, owning 25 percent of DuPont, and the entertainment business. By then, of course, Samuel Bronfman was long gone, and other members of the Bronfman family were in charge, chiefly his grandson Edgar Bronfman Jr. It was his decision to acquire an 80 percent share in MCA Inc., now Universal Studios Inc. It proved to be a notoriously bad one, and in 2000 Seagram, whose spirits business still made it the world's third-largest liquor company, was forced to sell to the French conglomerate Vivendi SA, for $42 billion. In turn, Vivendi sold off Seagram's spirits brands to Diageo PLC and Pernod-Ricard SA, two other industry heavyweights. See DIAGEO and PERNOD-RICARD. Seagram's history was effectively over, a turn of events that Samuel Bronfman's son, Charles, who rose through the ranks to become Seagram co-chairman, later regretted. "It was a family tragedy," he told Canada's Globe and Mail newspaper in 2013.

See also BRONFMAN FAMILY.

Faith, Nicholas. The Bronfmans: The Rise and Fall of the House of Seagram. London: Thomas Dunne, 2006.

Kapner, Suzanne. "Diageo and Pernod Buy and Divide Up Seagram Beverage Assets." New York Times, December 20, 2000.

Marrus, Michael R. Samuel Bronfman. Hanover, NH: Brandeis University Press, 1991.

Slater, Joanna. "Charles Bronfman Opens Up about Seagram's Demise." Toronto Globe and Mail, April 5, 2013. http://www.theglobeandmail.com/report-on-business/careers/careers-leadership/charles-bronfman-opens-up-about-seagrams-demise-it-is-a-disaster/article10816816/ (accessed April 2, 2021).

Charles Passy

sensory evaluation is the sum of the actions taken to understand a food or beverage in all its organoleptic complexity. While chemical analyses such as gas chromatography can generate a great deal of data about a specific spirit, sensory evaluation still provides a great deal of information otherwise unobtainable, particularly about how a spirit may be received by its consumers—about its quality, in other words. "Tasting" is a shortened description of this activity, but more than mere tasting is involved.

A thorough sensory evaluation includes distinct phases. Sight, smell, and taste are the primary senses used for a full sensory evaluation, but the proprioceptors required for texture analysis as well as hot and cold receptors on the lips and in the mouth and throat come into play. Touch is used even if it is less obviously deployed. Highly sensitive individuals describe the sounds of some foods as painful, irritating, or enjoyable.

The evaluation usually begins with sight. To judge the sight of a spirit, evaluators roll the liquid around the glass to observe its viscosity as the liquid moves inside the glass and runs down its sides. They carefully note color as well. See HUE/COLOR. These can be clues to the spirit's maturity as well as to the presence of added ingredients such as sugar, caramel, or glycerin.

Next, evaluators smell the spirit. There is no single aroma for any spirit, no matter how simple it might be. Alcohol beverages contain hundreds, sometimes thousands, of aromatic compounds. A thoughtful evaluation requires useful glassware (shapes and sizes vary according to the taster's preference and often according to the spirit itself) and a patient evaluator. Aromas can seem to change (or differing aromas present themselves) as the evaluator moves his or her nose around the top and opening of the glass. See AROMA.

Third, tasting a spirit allows for an evaluation of many aspects of the spirit: again, texture is potentially separate from the accepted primary flavors of sweet, sour, salt, bitter, and umami. Each of these has its own specific receptors in the mouth, throat, and even the stomach (some believe that there are in fact intestinal receptors as well).

Temperature receptors indicate heat or cold, but compounds such as capsaicin can mimic heat, while menthol and even mint can stimulate cold receptors. See TEXTURE AND MOUTHFEEL.

Humans are primarily "retro-nasal" smellers (that is, we collect aromatic compounds most readily in the backs of our mouths, throats, and nasal passages) rather than ortho-nasal smellers (as are dogs). Most, therefore, "taste" a great deal more flavors in the mouth than they are able to sense merely by sniffing the spirit in the glass. But like all such matters, everyone is different.

A proper sensory evaluation requires patience throughout, particularly as some spirits continue to generate flavor after the spirit has been swallowed. Many factors are at play, chief among them the fact that enzymes in saliva have begun to catalyze, break down, or otherwise alter the spirit's compounds. Time, especially for very complex spirits, often offers great rewards.

Beauchamp, Gary, and Linda Bartoshuk. *Tasting and Smelling*. Cambridge: Academic Press, 1997.

Wolfe, Jeremy, Keith Kluender, and Dennis Levi. *Sensation and Perception*. Sunderland, MA: Sinauer Associates, 2011.

Doug Frost

serpentine, coupe à la, is a method of increasing the purity of a distillate that belongs to the intermediate period in the history of cognac, when it was already established as a superior-quality product but the procedures for its production had not yet been fully perfected. See COGNAC. In the 1680s, as cognac was establishing itself as an export product, it was generally made by redistilling low wines, often with fresh wine added to them, and diluting them with the *secondes*, or tails. With the *coupe à la serpentine*, the distiller cut the flow of spirits from the condensing coil—the serpentine—before the secondes came through, diverting them to be retained separately and mixed with the next batch of low wines for redistillation. At roughly 60 percent ABV, the spirit thus produced was considerably stronger and cleaner than the alternative, albeit more expensive (although that was partially offset by saving money on shipping). The adoption of this practice began in the mid-1700s and became an industry standard by the 1770s. While the examples of Peruvian piscos and a number of Mexican mezcals and tequilas demonstrate that it is quite possible to make quality spirits that are reduced to bottling proof with the tails, the adoption of the coupe à la serpentine nonetheless can be seen as one of the foundational moments of modern spirit making, with its prioritization on purity and emphasis on efficiency. See MEZCAL; PISCO; and TEQUILA.

Cullen, L. M. *The Brandy Trade under the Ancien Régime*. Cambridge: Cambridge University Press, 1998.

David Wondrich

Sex on the Beach is likely to come to mind first if one is required to summon up the silliest of drink names, even if there are far more ridiculous (and more risqué) ones.

Its origins, which lie in the late 1970s or early 1980s—it first surfaces in 1986—are murky, although it appears to have been popularized by the wildly successful Lucy's Surfeteria bar in

New York City. There is also disagreement as to its components. Vodka and juices (cranberry, orange, pineapple, alone or in combination) always dominate, bolstered by a smaller portion of liqueur (peach schnapps, Chambord, or Midori are the usual culprits). It is invariably a highball, served over ice. What might be considered the standard recipe calls for equal proportions of vodka, cranberry juice, and orange juice, with a third as much peach schnapps—a Woo Woo, with orange juice. See Woo Woo. Ultimately, this is one of those drinks where anything that ends up sweet and juicy with a hidden kick will pass muster.

Recipe: Combine 30 ml vodka, 30 ml cranberry juice, 30 ml orange juice, and 10 ml peach schnapps into a highball glass. Serve over ice.

Croke, Karen. "Surf Bars." *New York Daily News*, March 22, 1987, 12.

Regan, Gary. *The Bartender's Bible.* New York: Harpercollins, 1993.

"Sex on the Breach." CocktailDB. https://www. thecocktaildb.com/drink/12754-Sex-on-the-Beach (accessed March 11, 2021).

Rosie Schaap

To **shake** a cocktail or other mixed drink means to vigorously rock it back in forth in a shaker to blend the ingredients, before straining it into a glass. Together with stirring, it is one of the two primary methods of mixing cocktails. One of the most significant reasons to shake a cocktail is to get the benefits of the ice churning back and forth, which affects a drink in a multitude of ways.

First off, shaking chills and dilutes a cocktail much faster than stirring does because more contact is generated between the liquid and the ice. For this reason, one needs to spend less time shaking—typically 8–12 seconds.

Shaking also alters a cocktail's texture. The ice aerates the cocktail, giving it a lighter and livelier consistency. This is visually evident in a layer of bubbly froth on the cocktail's surface. Finally, perhaps the most significant, if less obvious, impact shaking has on a cocktail is that it emulsifies ingredients into a unified whole, so separate flavors cannot be parsed out as easily. This results in a markedly different texture and mouthfeel than stirring gives.

There are some ingredients that are so resistant to mixing that in practice they can only be blended through the force of shaking, such as eggs, cream, and fruit purees.

History of Shaking

Shaking was developed in the United States and became an established a technique for mixing cocktails by the 1840s, once iced drinks had become commonplace. By the 1850s it was widespread. It evolved from a technique known today as rolling or throwing wherein bartenders would mix a cocktail by pouring it back and forth between two vessels. See ROLLING. Eventually these vessels were wedged together to form what we know today as the shaker. See COCKTAIL SHAKER. A shaker allows cocktails to be mixed more vigorously without the threat of spilling, and this is due to the seal formed between the two parts—when the ice chills the air and liquid within the shaker, they contract, forming a vacuum and further preventing any leakage. (If the shaker is poorly designed, this vacuum, slight as it may be, can make the parts extremely difficult to separate.)

Which Drinks Are Best Shaken

It is generally agreed upon that a cocktail should be shaken if it contains any fresh, nonalcoholic ingredients. Citrus juice is the most frequent example, along with dairy products, fruits, and herbs. Another way to look at it is if it's cloudy, it should be shaken. Drinks with these types of ingredients benefit from the light, aerated texture that shaking provides because they tend to be in the bright, citrusy, and refreshing vein. They are also usually consumed more quickly, so the added chill and dilution is helpful. The Daiquiri, Whisky Sour, and Margarita are all prime examples of classic shaken drinks. See DAIQUIRI; WHISKY SOUR; and MARGARITA.

How to Shake

Regardless of the type of shaker being used, it is best to shake it horizontally: vertically will not get the ice moving properly. It is also advisable to keep a hand, or at least a finger or two, on each end for added support and to prevent it from flying apart should the vacuum fail. With a two-piece shaker, the mouth of the larger tin should be facing the bartender, just in case the seal does come undone, as its contents will end up on them and not the guests.

To shake, thrust the shaker back and forth with purpose. Give it all you've got. Many bartenders have their own variations on how they shake. Some add a rhythm, such as a syncopated maraca beat, while others are wildly animated and physical. In the words of legendary bartender Harry Craddock on shaking a cocktail, "You are trying to wake it up, not send it to sleep!" See CRADDOCK, HARRY LAWSON.

See also STIR.

Arnold, David. *Liquid Intelligence*. New York: W. W. Norton, 2015.

Craddock, Harry. *The Savoy Cocktail Book*. London: Constable, 1930.

Embury, David A. *The Fine Art of Mixing Drinks*. New York: Mud Puddle, 2008.

Uyeda, Kazuo. *Cocktail Techniques*. New York: Mud Puddle, 2010.

Wondrich, David. *Imbibe!*, 2nd ed. New York: Penguin, 2015.

Tom Macy

sherry, a fortified wine with a long history of appearances in cocktails of various sorts, reached its apotheosis in the Sherry Cobbler, an early nineteenth-century creation. See also SHERRY COBBLER and WINES, FORTIFIED.

The **Sherry Cobbler**—a simple mix of sherry, sugar, and citrus peels or slices, shaken or tossed with ice, poured into a tall glass, and garnished with fruit and berries in season and sipped through a straw—was one of the most popular mixed drinks of the nineteenth century and did more than any other to convert the world to taking its warm-weather drinks iced in the American style. The king of the cobbler family, the drink is first recorded in the summer of 1838, when Jane Ellice, a vivacious young Englishwoman traveling in New York State, included a recipe in her diary, pronouncing it "delicious & easy of composition." By September of that year, the *New York Star* was writing about it as if it were too well known to require explanation. (The common claim that it appears with the cocktail and the julep in the 1809 first edition of Washington Irving's *Knickerbocker's History of New York* is erroneous;

the drinks were not introduced until the 1848 revised edition.) See COCKTAIL and JULEP. By 1839 its popularity had spread as far as New Orleans, at least, and before long it was known throughout the United States. Then Charles Dickens came to visit. Spending the first half of 1842 in America, Dickens had plenty of time to try American iced drinks. His *American Notes for General Circulation*, published in October of that year, contained many notices of them, and in particular the julep and the Sherry Cobbler, which he deemed "refreshments never to be thought of afterwards, in summer, by those who would preserve contented minds." This endorsement, coupled with a rapturous description of the drink in his next novel, *Martin Chuzzlewit*, effectively alerted the world to the drink's easy charms.

In 1843, a bar opened in the Strand, London, devoted to American iced drinks (which in practice meant the cobbler and the julep), with others soon following, not only in London but in Dublin, Liverpool, Paris, and even as far afield as Sydney, Australia. At first, the cobbler was restricted to the early adopters—the ones who thirsted for novelties and were willing to try the strange American practice of drinking through a straw. In 1867, however, there was an American bar at the widely attended Paris Universal Exposition. It went through five hundred bottles of sherry a day, all for cobblers. That was the watershed; after it, the cobbler was no longer a novelty. "It is an American invention," as British drinks writer William Terrington wrote in 1869, "but [it] has become an universal favourite."

In its homeland, in the meanwhile, the Sherry Cobbler remained a staple. As master bartender Harry Johnson observed in 1888, it was "without doubt the most popular beverage in the country, with ladies as well as with gentleman." See JOHNSON, HARRY. By then, however, the public taste was already beginning to shift, and within ten years the cobbler's hot-weather primacy would be seriously challenged by a new generation of refreshing, spirits-based drinks, including the highball, the rickey, and various coolers. See HIGHBALL; RICKEY; and COOLER. When the decline came, it was precipitous: as one Chicago drinker noted in 1906, "I don't know as I ever heard of a man ordering a cobbler these days." When he tried, the bartender had to look it up. The imposition of Prohibition hammered in the final nail: sherry was uneconomical for the bootlegger and scofflaw drinkers tended to want their illicit beverages to be as strong as possible; there was little place for a gentle refresher such as the Sherry Cobbler. Even outside America, it fell into disfavor. By the 1960s, it was only found in bartenders' guides, and only the more comprehensive ones at that. The cocktail renaissance has at least given it a little new life, but one cannot in all accuracy call it popular.

Recipe: Stir 10 ml sugar in 120 ml amontillado or oloroso sherry. Add cracked ice and either 2 long ribbons of lemon peel or 1 orange wheel cut in two. Shake well, pour unstrained into a Collins glass, garnish with orange wedge, and add a straw.

See also COBBLER.

"American Drinks." *New Orleans Daily Picayune*, May 28, 1843, 2.

Dickens, Charles. *American Notes for General Circulation.* London: Chapman & Hall, 1842.

"Dickens's Admirers Try Experiments." *Chicago Interocean*, April 15, 1906 7.

Godsell, Patricia, ed. *The Diary of Jane Ellice.* [Toronto]: Oberon, 1975.

Grimes, William. *Straight Up or on the Rocks*, 2nd ed. New York: North Point, 2001.

Johnson, Harry. *New and Improved Illustrated Bartenders' Manual.* New York: 1888.

David Wondrich

shochu is a clear Japanese spirit most often distilled from sweet potatoes (*Ipomoea batatas*), barley, or rice. All shochu is required to use the starch-saccharifying ability of aspergillus molds in the form of koji to power a fermentation process similar to that of Okinawan awamori. See ASPERGILLUS ORYZAE; AWAMORI; and KOJI. Long a drink downed by the working classes in its center of production, Kyushu Island, shochu has enjoyed surging respect and demand across the country since the turn of the twenty-first century.

Somewhat confusingly, shochu can be divided into two major camps. The first is a neutral, column-distilled product (*kōrui*), known as "multiply distilled" shochu. It is generally used as a medium-proof (25 percent ABV) cocktail fuel or the kick in homemade macerations. The more interesting type is *honkaku*, or premium, shochu (also known as "singly distilled shochu"). This is an aromatic and flavorful pot-still liquor (also generally bottled at 25 percent ABV). It has recently found new generations of admirers across Japan, with World Trade Organization regional protection granted to four traditional varieties. A third category is a blend of the previous two, thus necessitating all manner of labeling regulations that clearly list ingredients, still type, region, and in some cases aging and whether the koji is handmade. Much shochu in the US market is erroneously labeled "soju" to allow sale on a beer and wine license in California, a quirk that causes misunderstandings in those markets and consternation by those aware of the immense differences between the two spirits. See SOJU.

History and Production

The particulars of shochu's origins in Kyushu are buried within the overlapping reports of liquor reaching the island by boat from the Okinawa Islands, Korea, and China. Most scholars point to the late fifteenth or early sixteenth century as the likely start of shochu production (there is a 1549 reference to "arrack made of rice" from a European traveler), but 1559 is the earliest explicit reference to the drink. This was uncovered at Koriyama Hachiman Shrine in present-day Kagoshima Prefecture, where two disgruntled carpenters apparently hid some graffiti beneath the roof that read, "The chief Shinto priest of the shrine was so stingy that he never once gave us shochu to drink." See ARRACK. The thirsty craftsmen were likely referring to rice shochu, as sweet potatoes had not yet been widely welcomed on Kagoshima's volcanic shores. Much like with the awamori distilled in Okinawa, rice was the main starch used during the early decades of shochu's spread. The proud rice shochu tradition of southern Kumamoto Prefecture exhibits a complexity that is regionally protected by the WTO as Kuma shochu. Okinawa's rice-based awamori, which is thought to be a direct ancestor of early rice shochu varieties in Kyushu, is recognized by the WTO as Ryukyu awamori. In other parts of the country, it has become common to distill sake lees, a shochu production method that was originally employed to create alcohol-free lees that could then be used as fertilizer. Modern iterations of this genre exhibit strong floral and fruit notes.

Riemon Maeda, a Yamagawa fisherman, is popularly credited with bringing sweet potato tubers to Kyushu from Okinawa in 1705, a move that would quickly see potato crops usurp rice paddies in southern Kyushu's unforgiving, volcanic-ash-laden soil. However, both starch sources would become integral to potato shochu, since rice is the most common koji vehicle used in the starter mash. See MASH. Because shochu does not use malted grains, the enzymatic action of koji is used to convert rice starch to glucose both before and during the mash, a delicate temperature- and humidity-controlled process that takes nearly two days to complete. See MALTING. The most commonly used koji strain used in the premium shochu industry is white (*Aspergillus kawachi*), but products made with yellow (*A. oryzae*) and black (*A. awamori*) are gaining in popularity.

The primary ferment bubbles away for around five days in large earthenware pots as the rice koji and yeast work simultaneously to chop starches into glucose and then metabolize the sugar into alcohol, carbon dioxide, and heat. This unique process, which is also central to awamori and sake brewing and can achieve mash alcohol levels around 18 percent, is termed multiple parallel fermentation. See FERMENTATION. The secondary mash welcomes steamed potatoes, which will be allowed to ferment for one to two weeks before distillation in a pot still (often under a vacuum) and aging in pots, enamel or steel tanks, or wooden casks. The distillate generally carries an alcohol percentage in the high 30s to low 40s (maximum bottling proof is 45 percent for premium shochu, 35 percent for the multiply distilled product). Sweet potato shochu made in Kagoshima Prefecture with local ingredients can carry the WTO regional appellation satsuma shochu. Of the dozens of sweet potato varietals used to make shochu today, the most common is the white-fleshed, starch-rich *koganesengan*.

Alternatively, unmalted two-row barley can be added to the secondary mash, guiding aroma and flavor profiles in entirely new directions. The oldest and most famous barley shochu tradition, which emerged during the rice control policies in Nagasaki Prefecture during the 1700s, is iki shochu, a WTO-protected drink that uses a 2:1 barley-to-rice koji ratio in the mash. As recently as the 1970s, Oita Prefecture reinvented the genre with barley shochu that eschews rice koji in the starter mash and uses a pure barley koji instead. Iichiko, the omnipresent barley shochu brand from Oita, first hit the market in 1979. Oita barley shochu is sometimes bottled at 20 percent ABV rather than the standard 25 percent. According to the industry publication *Shurui sangyō nenkan 2015*, 41.4 percent of premium shochu shipments in 2014 were the barley product, while 44.5 percent were sweet potato.

Another popular variety is the brown-sugar shochu made in Kagoshima's Amami Islands, which in 1953 was exempted from steep rum taxes thanks to the use of rice koji in the mash and the celebratory mood of the authorities upon reversion of the islands from US occupation. (The cane-koji combination it uses is reminiscent of the process used to make Batavia arrack.) See ARRACK, BATAVIA. Buckwheat shochu arrived on the scene in 1973 in the form of a top-selling brand from Miyazaki Prefecture, Unkai. Honkaku shochu has evolved over the years to include more than fifty approved starch ingredients—from chestnuts to carrots—and thousands of brands distilled by well over 450 distilleries nationwide. The most popular categories of premium shochu (particularly sweet potato) have hundreds of labels, most made by artisanal distilleries, encompassing an immense spectrum of aroma and flavor.

Enjoyment

Precious few are the rules governing how to drink premium shochu. Most serving decisions come down to the shochu in question and personal taste. In addition to drinking it neat, many people order their shochu on the rocks, mixed with cool or hot water, or cut with club soda. Cocktails made with multiply distilled shochu and citrus fruit or tea mixers in the *chuhai* style are common convenience store and pub options, but international bartenders are beginning to experiment more with the more robust, complex flavors of honkaku shochu.

Connoisseurs love to sample shochu at a 3:2 ratio with hot water, especially sweet potato shochu during the winter months, because in addition to opening up the drink's rich aroma, umami and sweet notes will become more readily noticeable on the palate. As explained by the Sake School of America, umami is "comprised mainly of palmitic acid, ethyl, and ethyl linoleate," and hot water aids their dissolution and expression in what is called an *oyuwari* mix (hot water is added to the cup first, room-temperature shochu second).

There are also few particulars about drinking vessels. In an effort to head off taxation issues, the authorities have allowed the product an 0.08 or less spectrometer color reading, which precludes lengthy aging in wood and guarantees that shochu will generally not contain hues worthy of admiration. See AGING. As such, even opaque receptacles such as the beautiful ceramics made in Japan can be used as guiltlessly as rocks or wine glasses. Small black-glazed kettles called *kuro joka* are sometimes used in Kagoshima to heat sweet potato shochu that was diluted with water two or three days prior. This tradition, known as *maewari*, can be enjoyed in many specialty shochu bars around Japan and is further evidence of the drink's versatility in serving and food pairing. In April of 2012, the Japanese government officially designated shochu and awamori as Japan's national liquors.

See also BARLEY and RICE.

"Characteristics and Production Methods of the Main Varieties of Honkaku Shōchū and Awamori." http://www.honkakushochu-awamori.jp/english/pdf/no_4.pdf (accessed April 5, 2021).
Pellegrini, Christopher. *The Shochu Handbook: an Introduction to Japan's Indigenous Distilled Drink.* Dublin, OH: Telemachus, 2014.
Sake School of America. *Shochu Adviser Certificate Course.* Los Angeles: Sake School of America, 2015.
Shurui Sangyō Nenkan 2015 [Alcohol industry almanac 2015]. Tokyo: Jōzō Sangyō Shinbunsha, 2015.

Christopher Pellegrini

Shoomaker's was a Washington, DC, bar and liquor distributor opened in the aftermath of the Civil War by German immigrants Captain Robert Otto "Charley" Hertzog (1830–1881) and Major William Shoomaker (1834–1883), who had served together in the New York Infantry. It was located near the National Theatre at 1331 E Street, along a stretch known as Rum Row. Shoomaker's is best known for being the place where the Rickey was invented, a drink named after the bar's later owner, Colonel Joseph "Joe" K. Rickey—a Democratic lobbyist from Missouri—who bought it from William Shoomaker's estate in 1883 and sold it three years later, retaining the real estate. See RICKEY. The bar was run by August Noack (1863–1931), another German American, from the 1880s until its closing

in 1917, much of that time in conjunction with head bartender George Williamson (1849–1915).

Shoomaker's was also well known for its famous clientele, including writers, politicians, and political types, as well as the quality of its whisky and wine, prompting Judge Samuel Cowan of Texas during an investigation by the congressional agricultural committee to declare about Shoomaker's, "I have heard that they sell whisky there of the best quality in Washington."

The bar was located in the back of the store where Shoomaker's distributed spirits and wine and had its own brand of rye whisky, which was commonly used in the whisky version of a Rickey. Shoomaker's was famous for its clients and cocktails but infamous for its decor—having bawdy pictures and dusty tables—and was also affectionately known as "Shoo's" or "Cobweb Hall," the latter because at its first location it was never dusted of cobwebs. An added attraction was, for a time, the presence upstairs from the bar of Darden's gambling room, known as the "boss game" of Rum Row.

On October 31, 1917, the Sheppard Act went into effect, effectively enacting Prohibition in the District. See PROHIBITION AND TEMPERANCE IN AMERICA. Shoomaker's closed their doors at ten that evening, when they ran out of liquor, and guests are purported to have ended the night by singing the then-popular song "Over There."

"Cobwebs and Quality Mark Shoomaker's Wine." *Washington Times*, December 30, 1906.
Faulkner, Virginia. "Last Days Before Prohibition." *Washington Post*, December 10, 1933.
Hubbard, Elbert. *A Little Journey to Shoomaker's: Being an Appreciation and Eye-Opener.* New York: Roycrofters, 1909.

Derek Brown

A **shooter** is a style of mixed drink designed to be consumed in one or two gulps, usually served in a shot glass or similar small-capacity glass. Unlike a straight pour of a single spirit, a shooter is typically composed of multiple ingredients, often including liqueurs or syrups.

The shooter's precursors include drinks such as the Knickebein—a nineteenth century after-dinner drink composed of liqueurs (often maraschino, crème de noyaux, and curaçao), topped with a whole egg yolk and, depending on the recipe, a little cognac or kirschwasser, or a puff of meringue—and the Angel's Tit (or Angel's Tip), an early twentieth-century drink composed of crème de cacao, whipped cream, and a cherry. See KNICKEBEIN. While pousse cafés—multilayered drinks composed in a cordial or shot glass—bear similarities to shooters, early styles of the drink were often designed for sipping. See POUSSE CAFÉ.

The final quarter of the twentieth century was a heyday for shooter-style drinks, and the style remains robust in many bars and clubs, especially those catering to a younger clientele. Starting in the mid-1970s, the Kamikaze opened the path. See KAMIKAZE. Typical of what followed is the B-52 (named either for the type of bomber flown during the Vietnam War or the New Wave band, depending on the origin story), with coffee liqueur, Irish cream liqueur, and curaçao layered together in a glass. The B-52 begat variations such as the B-54 (with amaretto in place of the curaçao) and B-55 (with absinthe). Some shooters follow the questionable-taste nomenclature standard established by the Angel's Tit, such as the Slippery Nipple (sambuca and Irish cream), Redheaded Slut (Jägermeister, peach schnapps, and cranberry juice), and the Duck Fart (layered coffee liqueur, Irish cream, and Canadian whisky), while others are inspired by pop culture, such as the Incredible Hulk (Hpnotiq liqueur and cognac) and the Papa Smurf (blue mint liqueur and Irish cream).

Some drinks enjoy life both as a shooter and as a full cocktail. The Lemon Drop is one such drink, and the Kamikaze itself had a steady run as a popular shot and as a cocktail in the late twentieth century (as the latter, it spawned the mighty Cosmopolitan). See COSMOPOLITAN and LEMON DROP.

A staple of college bars and clubs, the shooter was initially disdained by bartenders during the early years of the twenty-first-century cocktail resurgence, but the style has gradually crept into use. Some shooters are simply classic cocktails mixed in a short form such as the Snaquiri (a shot-size Daiquiri), while others are lightly masqueraded classics, such as the Nolita, a shooter of Punt e Mes, rye whisky, and Angostura bitters. Other shooters reflect the popularity of Italian amari and other bitter flavors in the cocktail realm, with two ingredients often mixed in equal parts: the Hard Start is a combination of Fernet-Branca and Branca Menta; the Ferrari, Fernet-Branca and Campari; and the Maserati, mezcal and Amaro Ramazzotti.

Bohrer, Andrew. *The Best Shots You've Never Tried.* Avon, MA: Adams Media, 2012.
Cole, Jennifer V. "How the 50/50 Became More Than Just a Shot." *Punch,* September 7, 2016, http://punchdrink.com/articles/how-the-ferrari-became-more-than-just-a-shot-amaro-cocktails/ (accessed March 11, 2021).
Difford, Simon. *Difford's Encyclopedia of Cocktails.* Ontario: Firefly, 2009.
Hofmann, Regan. "The Craft Cocktail's Final Frontier: Shooters." *Punch,* October 20, 2015. http://punchdrink.com/articles/craft-cocktail-bars-final-frontier-composed-shooters-and-shots/ (accessed March 11, 2021).
Knockerville, Johnny. "Incredible Hulk." Liquor.com, October 19, 2015. http://www.liquor.com/recipes/incredible-hulk/.
Regan, Gary. *The Joy of Mixology: The Consummate Guide to the Bartender's Craft.* New York: Clarkson Potter, 2003.

Paul Clarke

shrubs are acidified syrups used to make beverages. One variety of shrub blends citrus juice with sugar to make a syrup that's then mixed with rum or brandy. This type of shrub is related to a punch; in fact, spirits writer David Wondrich believes it might have been a prototype for punch. Another variety of shrub is a syrup made of fruit juice (or, in rarer cases, vegetable juice), sugar, and vinegar. See FRUIT JUICE; SUGAR; and VINEGAR.

"Shrub" is derived from the Arabic word *sharāb,* or beverage, from which is also derived the Persian word *sharbat,* which denotes a nonalcoholic beverage that combines sugar and water and is usually flavored with a fruit or spice. Words derived from *sharbat* include the Turkish derivative *sherbet,* the Italian *sorbetto,* and the French *sorbet,* along with the English word *syrup,* which comes via the Latin *siropus.* The drink, which dates back to at least the twelfth century, was first served very cold over ice or snow brought down from the mountains, or it was frozen by placing a vessel of sherbet into a saltpeter bath to chill it.

Western Europeans encountered sherbets and shrubs as early as the mid-sixteenth century. In the

1540s and 1550s, a French botanist named Pierre Belon encountered sherbets made of figs, plums, pears, peaches, apricots, and grapes on the streets of Turkey. The philosopher Francis Bacon wrote of sherbet in 1627, describing it as a type of candied conserve, made of sugar and lemons or sugar and violets or other flowers. As traders from Venice and other mercantile cities did business with Persia, Egypt, and Turkey, they encountered sherbet and eventually brought the beverage home, chiefly in the version that used citrus juice as its flavoring.

By the 1700s, this sherbet had arrived in England and taken the name shrub. Yet there was a difference, as one can see by the first English recipe for it, from the 1705 *Pastry Cook's Vade-Mecum*: there were lemons and sugar and water, to be sure, but there were also two quarts of brandy and a quart of wine. This conception was the common one. In New York, an act of 1732 set a levy on the importation of rum, brandy, other distilled liquor, or shrub. By the mid-1730s, taverns and vintners were offering bottled shrub for sale as, essentially, a sort of bottled punch base, complete with everything but the customary large portion of hot or cold water that diluted punch to wine strength and a scraping of nutmeg. James Ashley, of the famous London Punch House, offered his famous Seville orange shrub—the only kind he would use for making punch—in quantities up to the large barrels known as hogsheads. See PUNCH.

Shrub also found a place aboard ships. In 1747 an anonymous correspondent to the *Gentleman's Magazine* suggests equipping ships with fruit, especially lemons and oranges. Should carrying fruit prove impractical, the writer suggests that "a mixture of lemon juice and rum (shrub as they call it) may be carried in any quantity, as it will keep a long time." Shrub proved to be useful for sailors for an important reason: the citrus in it contained vitamin C, which was later found to prevent scurvy. In fact, the prevalence of scurvy aboard ships prompted the first clinical trials in medicine. James Lind, a Scottish physician who served in the British Royal Navy, found that scurvy killed more British sailors than it did their French and Spanish rivals. Though Lind didn't understand the role or even the existence of vitamins, he suspected that citrus had an antiscorbutic effect and set out to test the theory by giving one group of scorbutic sailors a ration of citrus. (Other groups drank such things as vinegar and cider.) Naval officers were convinced enough by Lind's work that they began mixing citrus juice and sugar into the twice-daily issue of grog (rum and water). See CITRUS.

As more practical and portable sources of vitamin C became available, shrub became less frequently transported aboard ship, but by this time, shrub was popular in England's North American colonies. Around this time, the vinegar version of shrub began to gain popularity in those colonies, and after the United States declared its independence, vinegar shrubs became fairly common in some parts of the country—in no small case because citrus was expensive to import into colonial America, and vinegar was an acceptable substitute. Its use as a citrus substitute in America is attested to as early as 1678, when a ledger preserved among the colonial governor of New York's papers has a line for "3 pints rum 2 lb. sugar and a [quart] vinegar . . . to make punch." Vinegar shrubs of the eighteenth and nineteenth centuries were a simple blend of vinegar, sugar, and fruit, cooked together to form a syrup. The vinegar and sugar acted as preservatives to keep fruit from going bad, thus extending its shelf life. Similar to Persian sharbat, vinegar shrub would be mixed with water to form a sort of soft drink. They were also prescribed for medicinal purposes for various ailments.

Both forms of shrub—vinegar and citrus—declined in popularity toward the end of the nineteenth century. Evolutions in food preservation made shrub's preservative properties unnecessary, as the ability to sell fruit in cans or in frozen form developed, and the eclipse of the shared bowl of punch as an everyday social drink removed it from the bartender's daily work.

The cocktail renaissance of the early 2000s marked a return to form for the shrub, as American bartenders began to rediscover it. See COCKTAIL RENAISSANCE. Currently, the preferred form of shrub in the bar world is the vinegar-based version, though the rum-and-citrus version lives on in bars that serve punch and finds an echo in tiki bars. Vinegar-based shrubs include versions based on any imaginable fruit and also sometimes vegetables such as carrot or celery. Bartenders find that shrub gives them a way to feature bright fruit flavors without also adding a lot of sweetness. They also provide a good base for crafting nonalcoholic cocktails. See MOCKTAIL.

Christoph, Peter R., and Florence A. Christoph, eds. *The Andros Papers: Files of the Provincial Secretary of New York... 1679–1680.* Syracuse, NY: Syracuse University Press, 1989.

Dietsch, Michael. *Shrubs: An Old-Fashioned Drink for Modern Times.* New York: Countryman, 2016.

Jurafsky, Dan. *The Language of Food.* New York: W. W. Norton, 2014.

Lind, James. *A Treatise on the Scurvy.* London: 1757.

Ramadan, Nesta. *Persian Cooking.* Bethesda, MD: Iranbooks, 1997.

Wondrich, David. *Imbibe!*, 2nd ed. New York: Perigee, 2015.

Michael Dietsch

Shui Jing Fang is a strong-aroma-style baijiu producer based in Chengdu, the capital city of southwestern China's Sichuan Province. Its story begins in 1998 when the city's largest distillery, Quanxing, was renovating its facilities on historic Shui Jing Street and discovered the ruins of a fifteenth-century distillery buried underneath. Once archaeologists had unearthed distillation hearths and fermentation pits, Quanxing scientists synthesized the bacteria found in the pit walls. Using this as the basis for a new premium baijiu, Quanxing released the Shui Jing Fang (*fang* meaning workshop or distillery) brand in 2000.

It was around this time that foreign spirits corporations began taking an interest in baijiu. The industry, which had experienced uninterrupted profit growth since the 1980s, presented an attractive target for acquisition, but most of the distilleries were state-owned and protected by policies preventing their sale to foreign entities. British spirits company Diageo sidestepped this obstacle in 2007 by striking an agreement with Quanxing's parent company to splinter Shui Jing Fang off into a new corporation of which Diageo would be a minority shareholder. Over the next several years, at a cost of hundreds of millions of pounds, Diageo increased its share until it became the company's majority shareholder in 2011. See DIAGEO.

Shui Jing Fang had by this point established itself as a leading high-end baijiu brand in China and was beginning to see some success abroad, particularly in South Korea. However, due to the austerity measures imposed in 2013 by new president Xi Jinping that devastated the premium baijiu segment, the company was forced into a period of retrenchment. By the late 2010s, this was essentially over, and Shui Jing Fang resumed its assault on the global luxury market.

See also STRONG-AROMA-STYLE BAIJIU.

"Pouring a Big One." *China Economic Review*, May 1, 2008.

Sonne, Paul, and Laurie Burkitt. "China Approves Diageo Baijiu Bid." *Wall Street Journal*, June 27, 2011.

Derek Sandhaus

The **Sidecar**, with cognac, curaçao triple sec, and lemon juice, is the most iconic of all cognac cocktails, enduring as a symbol of sophisticated drinking for a century. Its recipe first appeared in print in 1922 in two different cocktail books by London bartenders: Robert Vermeire's *Cocktails: How to Mix Them*, published in May, and *Harry's ABC of Mixing Cocktails* by Harry McElhone, which came out at the end of the year. See McELHONE, HENRY "HARRY" and VERMEIRE, ROBERT. McElhone has this to say about the drink: "This cocktail is very popular in France. It was first introduced in London by MacGarry, the celebrated bar-tender of Buck's Club" (it is worth noting that McElhone had worked alongside Malachi "Pat" McGarry at the club in its early days). See MIMOSA. In the French-language edition of his book, published in Brussels in 1938, Vermeire went on to specify the south of France as the drink's home. It could have been invented at the Carlton Hotel in Cannes, but no proof from the period has yet been found, and its exact origin remains unknown. In any case, in a widely copied 1923 article Frank Meir of the Ritz bar in Paris listed it as the second most popular of the nine cocktails that were "new since the war," after (McElhone's) Monkey Gland. See MEIER, FRANK.

The Sidecar found great favor during the 1920s in European bars, but it was also a popular speakeasy drink in New York and elsewhere in America, serving as a symbol of sophisticated, chic drinking. Adding to its cachet was the practice of Meier's (as recorded by Lucius Beebe in 1946) of making a luxury Sidecar that cost five US dollars at that time, using the Ritz's own bottling of a vintage pre-phylloxera cognac from 1865. It has been claimed, not without reason, that this was the beginning of luxury cocktails. (In the early 2000s, when Ritz head bartender Colin Field was exploring the hotel's cellars, he found two bottles of Ritz Cognac Vintage 1865, which, when he looked under the label, turned out to have been produced by Remy Martin.)

There are two main schools of Sidecar mixing, one calling for equal parts of its three ingredients, another for two parts cognac to one each of triple sec and lemon; there are also others that tinker with the proportions in their own ways. Since the 1930s, the drink has often been served in a glass whose rim is frosted with sugar, particularly in the United States.

Recipe: shake well with ice 45 ml cognac, 22 ml Cointreau or other triple sec, and 22 ml fresh lemon juice. In America, a sugar rim is usually added (preferably superfine sugar).

Beebe, Lucius. *The Stork Club Bar Book*. New York: Rinehart, 1946.

McElhone, Harry. *ABC of Mixing Cocktails*. London: Odhams, 1922.

"'Monkey Gland' is in full vogue." *New York Herald* (Paris ed.), April 26, 1923, 5.

Vermeire, Robert. *L'Art du Cocktail*. Bruxelles: Imprimerie de l'Office de Publicité, 1938.

Vermeire, Robert. *Cocktails—How to Mix Them*. London: Herbert Jenkins, 1922.

Fernando Castellon

Siete Leguas is a brand of tequila produced under NOM 1120 in the municipality of Atotonilco al Alto, Jalisco. Founded in 1952 by Don Ignacio González, Siete Leguas is named after the prized horse of General Pancho Villa and references the distance a horse could supposedly travel in one day (seven leagues). The family tradition continues through Juan Fernando González de Anda, the son of Don Ignacio, who currently manages the operations.

Siete Leguas is unique in that the NOM encompasses two distilleries: the original distillery, El Centenario, and La Vencedora, completed in 1984. Using family-owned agave as well as agave purchased to support the local economy, Siete Leguas uses traditional and modern techniques to create its signature flavor. El Centenario uses small brick ovens, a mule-drawn *tahona*, small-vat fermentation with fibers, and double distillation in small copper pot stills, the first

of which includes fibers (the retention of the fibers in both these steps is held to increase the depth of agave flavor in the finished product). La Vencedora incorporates modern techniques using large brick ovens, roller mills, large stainless fermenters without fibers, and a double distillation in large copper pot stills without fibers. Juan Fernando and master distiller Arturo Valle-Salcedo then manually blend the tequila produced from the two distilleries for the final *blanco* product. Siete Leguas is aged in American white oak barrels. Expressions offered include an eight-month-old reposado, a two-year-old añejo, and the five-year-old D'Antaño.

See also TAHONA; TEQUILA.

Martineau, Chantal. *How the Gringos Stole Tequila*. San Antonio, TX: Trinity University Press, 2015.

Misty Kalkofen

Silver Fizz is a variation on the classic Gin Fizz, which brings an extra element of richness (and, reputedly, hangover-reducing properties), thanks to the addition of egg white. See GIN FIZZ.

simple syrup is sugar dissolved in water, used to sweeten cocktails because loaf or granulated sugar dilutes poorly in spirits. It was first called "simple" by pharmacists to differentiate it from compounded syrups, made with medicinal plants. It is also the base of flavored syrups. It can be made by stirring or shaking both ingredients cold or by simmering them on a stove until dissolved. Simple syrup can be made in equal parts (frustratingly, recipes rarely specify whether by weight or by volume), but it is often more concentrated, with two or more parts of sugar to one of water. Exact proportions naturally impact the sweetness of the syrup.

See also FLAVORED SYRUP and GUM SYRUP.

Morgenthaler, Jeffrey. *The Bar Book: Elements of Cocktail Technique*. San Francisco: Chronicle, 2014.

François Monti

singani is an unaged Bolivian brandy made from muscat of Alexandria grapes grown at exceptionally high elevations in the Andes mountains. See ANDEAN SOUTH AMERICA; BRANDY; and PISCO.

The **Singapore Sling**, or Straits Sling, a mixture of gin, liqueurs, fruit juices, and soda water that was a mainstay of mid-twentieth-century tippling, bears one of the most storied and romantic names in the annals of mixed drink. It is not, however, a true sling in the original American style, nor was it exclusive to Singapore even before it achieved global fame.

By the end of the nineteenth century, the American Gin Sling had been reformulated by British drinkers, particularly in Britain's Asian colonies, to include liqueurs and citrus juice. (Already in 1861, Charles Francatelli, the eminent Victorian chef, had included lemon slices in his recipe for the drink; the liqueurs date back at least to 1870, and both combined in 1881.) As a result, as the English mixographer Edward Spencer observed in 1903, "What we call a gin-sling is known in the United States as a John Collins" (a finicky American might rather have labeled it a cooler). See GIN SLING; JOHN COLLINS; and COOLER.

At some point near the end of the nineteenth century, drinkers in Singapore began taking their slings with a splash of cherry brandy in them, a practice first documented in a 1903 reference from a Singapore newspaper to "pink slings for pale people." See CHERRY BRANDY. The first rough recipe for this comes from 1913, in an anecdote about the strategy a member of the Singapore Cricket Club used to get a Sling at the bar there, which considered them vulgar and refused to make them: he simply "ordered one Cherry Brandy, one Domb [i.e., Bénédictine], one Gin, one Lime Juice, some Ice and [soda] water, a few dashes of bitters—and then enjoyed a really decent Sling." See BÉNÉDICTINE.

If the Cricket Club was reluctant to make slings, there were numerous other places in Singapore that weren't. Chief among them in reputation was the bar at the John Little department store, followed by the Long Bar at the Raffles Hotel and the bar at Robinson's department store. Similar slings, however, were also being made elsewhere in the Straits Settlements (the administrative unit to which Singapore belonged), in the surrounding Federated Malay States, in Shanghai and Hong Kong, and indeed throughout British Asia. There was a good deal of latitude in the recipes for these, with the Bénédictine often replaced or supplemented by curaçao and the cherry brandy (either Heering or Bols) by red wine or sloe gin. See BOLS and SLOE GIN.

Nor was the drink confined to its native turf: as early as 1910, the Anglo-American Bar in Salzburg, Austria, was advertising a "Singapore Gin Sling" on its menu. (Willy, the head bartender, spent his winters at the Savoy Hotel in Cairo, where he must have learned the drink from travelers passing through Egypt on their way from Singapore to Britain.) By the mid-1920s, the drink was known around the world. Over the years, it became more and more become closely associated with the Raffles, as that was the leading hotel in the city and the place most tourists first encountered it, and eventually the bar there claimed ownership over the drink.

Until the 1970s, the Raffles version of the sling was little different from the standard one. Then, with business faltering, Roberto Pregarz, the hotel's Trieste-born manager, "'improved' it, keeping the same ingredients but changing the shape of the glass and adding a few other touches to make it more exotic," as he told a reporter in 1986. He might have been a bit disingenuous here: starting in 1974, when he made over the hotel, there was suddenly a lot less of the pricey Bénédictine and Cherry Heering in the drink, and it now had pineapple and orange juices along with the lime—at first only a little of each, but that would change—plus a little splash of Cointreau. What's more, this was touted as the drink's lost "original recipe," found only in the memory of the veteran Raffles barman Ngiam Tong Boon, who had supposedly invented the drink in 1915. All these changes gave the drink a Raffles-linked history and the hotel a drink that, unlike the boozy, rather austere original, was overtly "tropical" and perfectly adapted to the disco drink era. See MIXOLOGY, THE HISTORY OF.

While recent years have seen efforts to extricate the original Singapore Sling from the sweet, rather sticky modern Raffles version, they have not generally been successful.

Recipe (1910s version): Combine in ice-filled highball glass: 45 ml gin, 15 ml lime juice, 15 ml Cherry Heering, 15 ml Bénédictine. Top off with chilled sparkling water, stir, and dash Angostura bitters on top.

See also SLING.

Cawley, Janet. "Dwarfed by Towers, Storied Raffles Still Alive and Slinging." *Chicago Tribune*, December 3, 1986, 24.

Fougner, G. Selmer. "Along the Wine Trail." *New York Sun*, August 21, 1934, 21; September 13, 1934, 32; October 15, 1934, 25; July 14, 1936, 23; November 8, 1937, 24.

"More about Gin Slings." *Singapore Weekly Sun*, September 20, 1913, 7.

David Wondrich

single barrel refers to the use of aged spirits, typically whisky, from a single barrel to fill individual bottles for sale. The effects of aging vary from barrel to barrel, and for that reason distillers usually "dump" a (sometimes very large) number of barrels together to ensure consistency. Single-barrel spirits, on the other hand, will carry all the unique qualities and variations of an individual barrel. Bottlers will often handwrite the barrel number, aging warehouse, and other details on a label to underline the authenticity of the contents, and some consumers will seek out bottles from specific barrels. In the nineteenth century, when spirits were shipped in barrels, most whiskies were single-barrel; the modern practice, however, was pioneered in 1984 by Elmer T. Lee with the Blanton's brand.

See also BLANTON'S.

Chuck Cowdery. "We Like Single Barrel Bourbons. Here's Why." *Chuck Cowdery Blog*, February 7, 2011. http://chuckcowdery.blogspot.com/2011/02/we-like-single-barrel-bourbons-heres.html (accessed April 5, 2021).

Clay Risen

single malt refers to a category of whisky made in a single distillery from a single type of malted grain—usually barley, but rye single malts are also found. Scotland, of course, is famous for producing this type of liquor (formerly known as "self" whisky), but distillers in other countries, including Ireland, Japan, America, India, and Scandinavia, are also now making it. Historically, single malts from different distilleries were mixed together with grain whisky to form smoother blends, but since the early 1960s brands have been bottling single malt on its own. See WHISKY, GRAIN. In the modern era, Glenfiddich was the first to sell and market single malt in the United States. See GLENFIDDICH. It took about thirty years, but the style of whisky has become very popular around the world with drinkers, bartenders, and distillers.

See also BARLEY and WHISKY, SCOTCH.

Smith, Gavin D. *The A–Z of Whisky*. Glasgow: Neil Wilson, 2009.

Noah Rothbaum

single pot still whisky is an Irish specialty, made in pot stills at a single distillery from a mix of malted and unmalted barley (until the 1950s, it also included relatively small proportions of oats and rye or wheat). It became the predominant Irish style when the British government imposed a malt tax in 1785. The economic burden resulting from this tax would have crippled the large Irish distilleries. Mixing malted and unmalted barley avoided this. It also led to the creation of a style regarded as the gold standard in terms of quality in the nineteenth century. On the strength of this rich but smooth style, Irish distillers were able to resist blending with column-still grain whisky until the middle of the twentieth century. See WHISKY, GRAIN. The style almost died in the late twentieth century, only to make a decisive return in the twenty-first.

A single pot still whisky will use a mash bill of 60:40 unmalted to malted barley (there must be by law at least 30 percent of each grain, and no more than 5 percent of any other grain), given a long fermentation, and then double or (usually) triple distilled. The use of unmalted barley adds a fat, unctuous quality to the spirit along with a crisp acidic bite on the back palate. Brands include Redbreast, Green Spot, and Powers John's Lane.

McGuire, E. B. *Irish Whisky*. Dublin: Gill & MacMillan, 1973.

Dave Broom

skimmings, also known as "scum," are the foam skimmed off the top of the cauldrons in which sugar-cane juice was traditionally boiled down until crystallization, along with the water used to wash out the cauldrons and clean the various tools employed in the sugar-making process. In making Caribbean rum, from the seventeenth century until well into the twentieth, these liquids were collected, allowed to settle, and combined with molasses to form the "sweets" that were mixed with water and distilled into rum (this process appears to have been used throughout the region). The skimmings, which are rich in sucrose and minerals, impart a good deal of raw cane flavor (of the sort found in rhum agricole) to rum; however, they are almost never used anymore, due to the consolidation of sugar making into central refineries, rather than at individual plantations. See MOLASSES; RHUM AGRICOLE; and RUM.

Wray, Leonard. *The Practical Sugar Planter*. London: Smith, Elder, 1848.

David Wondrich

The **sling**, a simple, even basic mixture of spirits, sugar, and water, is among the earlier varieties of mixed alcoholic beverage. Of American origin, it became popular at the end of the eighteenth century (it is first recorded to in Maryland in 1778) and remained so well into the nineteenth century and, in the bastardized form of the Singapore Sling, into the twenty-first. With respect to the origin of the name, David Wondrich speculates that it "most likely takes [its name] from the act of 'slinging' one back."

The sling was mentioned, by way of well-established reference, in the oft-cited May 13, 1806, item in the *Hudson (NY) Balance and Columbian Repository*, which first defined the cocktail, noting that "it is vulgarly called bittered sling." See COCK-TAIL. Like the cocktail and the julep, it can be seen as an offshoot of punch, although where the cocktail substitutes bitters for the citrus and a julep mint, the sling leaves that space blank. See JULEP. In that, the sling is identical to the British toddy, although it was typically made with equal parts water and spirit, where the weaker toddy typically used two parts of water to one of spirit.

Popular variations during the nineteenth century included the Rum Sling, Brandy Sling, Gin Sling, and Whisky Sling, all of which were quite popular. In a 1910 story, the late editor and politician Horace Greeley (1811–1872) was quoted as saying that in his youth "a wedding without 'toddy,' 'sling' or 'punch,' with rum undisguised in abundance, would have been deemed a poor, mean affair, even among the penniless." Indeed, according to Wondrich, "the Sling, particularly the gin variety

(first attested to in 1800), soon became one of the iconic American drinks, consumed morning, noon, and night everywhere American was spoken."

Indeed, as the *Antijacobin Review* noted in 1814, "Rum, brandy, or gin sling, is a common beverage for travellers throughout the States; and the stage-coachmen, in the course of a journey, take 'a special good quantity of it.'" By then, as the author added, "Sometimes [the sling] consists only of the liquor and water; but in general it is made of milk with ginger or nutmeg in it." While the milk was perhaps not standard, the nutmeg certainly was, as an 1825 *New-York Evening Post* confirms when it attests that "half a tumbler of gin sling, well covered with powdered nutmeg, proves a speedy and efficacious stop in that dangerous and alarming complaint, a bleeding of the lungs."

Further, in Jerry Thomas's 1862 book, *How to Mix Drinks, or, The Bon-Vivant's Companion*, he noted that the main distinguishing characteristic between a "toddy" (sugar, water, spirit, and ice) and a "sling" was nutmeg, writing that "the brandy sling is made with the same ingredients as the brandy toddy, except you grate a little nutmeg on top." In the posthumous 1887 edition of the book, however, the editor quietly removed the nutmeg requirement; by then, the once-ubiquitous ingredient was beginning to fall out of favor. On the other hand, both the 1882 and 1888 editions of Harry Johnson's *New and Improved Illustrated Bartender's Manual* call for grated nutmeg atop drinks such as the Cold Whisky Sling, the Hot Scotch Whisky Sling, and the Brandy Sling.

The latter half of the nineteenth century and the beginning of the twentieth saw a broadening of the sling's ingredients outside of the United States, particularly in the British realm. The most famous of the British slings, the Singapore Sling, contains citrus, liqueur(s), and other sweeteners. See SINGAPORE SLING.

Recipe (Jerry Thomas's Gin Sling): In an Old-Fashioned glass, stir a barspoon of sugar with 30 ml water until sugar has dissolved. Add 2 or 3 ice cubes and 60 ml genever. Stir well and grate nutmeg over the top.

See also TODDY.

"Lambert's Travels through Canada and the United States." *Antijacobin Review*, July 1814, 552.

"When Everybody Drank—Horace Greeley's Recollections of the Liquor Habit a Century Ago." *Tampa (FL) Tribune*, December 18, 1910, 47.

Wondrich, David. *Imbibe!*, 2nd ed. New York: Perigee, 2015.

Philip Greene

slivovitz is an eau-de-vie made from fermented damson plums. The name comes from the Slavic word for plums—*šljiva, slivka, śliwka, slíva*—and the spirit is often referred to as plum brandy. Most slivovitz is produced and consumed in central and eastern Europe, and a number of countries in that area lay claim to having created it. The European Union's solution to these competing claims is a compromise that recognizes "slivovitz" as a generic name, which allows each country to personalize it (e.g., Serbian slivovitz / Srpska šljivovica). Historically, most slivovitz has been made by home distillers, but today there are great commercially produced craft versions. See HOME DISTILLING.

To make slivovitz, damson plums are harvested when they're fully ripe and have the highest sugar content. The plums are ground coarsely and combined with water. The combination is allowed to ferment and is often exposed to wild yeast for up to two weeks. After the fermentation is complete, the "plum wine" is ready to be distilled in traditional copper pot stills. The first distillation is called "soft brandy" and has an ABV of no more than 30 percent. The soft brandy is then distilled again. The finished slivovitz has an ABV of anywhere between 40 and 60 percent.

After distillation slivovitz can be bottled unaged or can be aged in wooden barrels. However, the unaged variety is in fact generally rested for a month in glass or stainless steel vats. It is then cut with water to reduce its ABV to somewhere between 40–45 percent depending on the producer. Slivovitz can be aged for up to twenty years, usually in an uncharred oak barrel. But casks made from walnut, mulberry, acacia, or ash trees are sometimes used and give slivovitz a great depth of flavor.

People in eastern or central Europe generally drink slivovitz as an aperitif or, in the case of older brandies, as a digestive. When pairing with food, it works well with charcuterie, pâté, both young and aged cheeses, butter, radishes, roasted peppers, and all grain breads. The spirit is traditionally served at room temperature in a sipping serving of no more the 60 ml either in traditional glasses called *čokanjčići*, shot glasses, or a small snifter if the slivovitz is aged.

In winter, slivovitz is often a part of Christmas celebrations and can be offered hot—spiced and sweetened. Some of the better brands available on the market are Stara Sokolova Rakija—Šljivovica, Navip Šljivovica, Maraska Šljivovica, Jelínek Slivovitz, Vilina Trava Šljivovica, and Manastirka Šljivovica.

See also EAU-DE-VIE; JELÍNEK; OAK ALTERNATIVES; and PLUMS.

Ridgwell, Mark. *Spirits Explained*. Cheltenham, UK: Mixellany, 2012.

Šljivovica.net. http://www.sljivovica.net/ (accessed April 5, 2021).

Dushan Zaric

sloe gin is an extremely popular British infusion of blackthorn berries in gin sweetened with sugar. It is traditionally served around the Christmas and New Year holidays. Prepared by numerous rural households since the nineteenth century, sloe gins (along with damson plum gin) were made as a standard harvest-time activity. Mentions of sloe gin in the media make their appearance during the 1830s in publications such as the *Cheltenham Chronicle*. By the end of the nineteenth century, that sloe gin was commercially produced in England is evidenced by legal cases in which trademarks and patents were contested in court cases decided by the House of Lords' Privy Council. By the beginning of the twentieth century, it was being exported to the United States, where it enjoyed a brief vogue as a cocktail ingredient.

After a decline in popularity during the twentieth century and decades of absence from drinks menus (except for a slight mid-twentieth-century rise as a key ingredient in the popular Sloe Gin Fizz), sloe gin has found a resurgence of interest as a digestive. It is currently produced by British commercial gin rectifiers Gordon's, Plymouth, Sipsmith, Hayman's, and others, including several American micro-distillers (Brooklyn's Greenhook distillery makes theirs with the beach plums that grow in the dunes behind Long Island beaches). Within Britain itself, sloe gin continues to be a beverage made from traditional recipes that are handed down within generations of rural families. Wintertime competitions are held in countryside pubs and fairs to determine whose recipe is the best within a given area.

See also GIN.

"Boord and Son v. Huddart." *Law Times*, February 29, 1904, 718–721.
Spencer, Edward. *Cakes and Ale*. London: Grant Richards, 1897.

Anistatia R. Miller and Jared M. Brown

Sloppy Joe's was the most popular bar in Havana for American tourists during Prohibition. For many, their entire Cuban vacation consisted of a cab ride from the cruise ship to Sloppy Joe's, where they drank their fill, then headed directly back to the ship and home. Joe's, which billed itself as "first port of call, out where the wet begins," was literally the only sight they saw on the island. On busy nights customers massed ten-deep at the bar, with eleven bartenders working the same shift and policemen at the door to prevent stampedes.

Why Joe's? For one thing, Cubans didn't drink there; it was strictly a *yanqui* bar, and Yankees were then a largely xenophobic lot. For another, Joe's wasn't a clip joint: prices were low and cocktails were good.

Proprietor José Abeal Y Otero's gold mine began in 1917 as a sleepy bodega called La Victoria. See ABEAL Y OTERO, JOSE "SLOPPY JOE." Legend has it that when a local newspaperman asked José for a loan and he refused, the newsman published an editorial urging the sanitation department to inspect "a place on Zulueta Street which should be called Sloppy Joe's." José was furious, but the name stuck—and made him millions during Prohibition, because the name sounded American to Americans. This also helped the bar survive the lean years of World War II, when US servicemen were the only patrons, but sealed its doom after Castro's revolution kept Americans away, and anti-American sentiment kept locals away. Joe's shuttered in 1965 but reopened on the same spot in 2013—once again, primarily as a tourist attraction.

Sloppy Joe's spawned many imitators, the most famous of them being Sloppy Joe's in Key West, Florida, which officially opened when Prohibition was repealed. Its name was swiped directly from José Abeal's bar, with which it shared some of its clientele. There, however, the connection ended.

See also PROHIBITION AND TEMPERANCE IN AMERICA.

Berry, Jeff. *Beachbum Berry's Potions of the Caribbean*. New York: Cocktail Kingdom, 2014.
Clark, Sydney. *All the Best in Cuba*. New York: Dodd, Mead, 1946.
Orsi, Peter. "Cheers! Havana Original Sloppy Joe's Bar Reopens." *Associated Press*, April 13, 2013.

Jeff Berry

small batch is a marketing term that promotes a common American whisky practice. It typically means that the spirit is produced by vatting and bottling a smaller number of barrels than are usual for a production batch of a particular whisky brand. Since small batch is not a federally defined term, that batch may contain two barrels or two hundred or more. Although batch sizes are rarely disclosed, twenty to fifty barrels seems to be the most common range.

Jim Beam's Booker Noe is considered the pioneer of small batching due to the 1988 release of Booker's, a bottling marketed as being "small batch." By 1994, Beam had folded it into a "Small-Batch Collection," with three other such bottlings. It must be noted, though, that the supposed virtues of "small-batch" production had been a fixture in American food and beverage marketing since the 1930s, when it was applied to everything from soup to candy. By the 1940s, advertisements for YPM blended whisky were boasting that it was made "the small-batch way"; twenty years later, Kentucky River Bourbon said its whisky was small batch because "every step in distilling . . . is taken more slowly," and—perhaps more relevantly—the extensive advertising campaign in the early 1980s for Calvert Extra blended whisky touted it as an example of "small batch distilling."

See BOOKER NOE II, FREDERICK; SINGLE BARREL; and WHISKY, BOURBON.

"Plum Pudding or Whiskey?" *Philadelphia Inquirer*, December 20, 1940, 33.
"The Small Batch Bourbon." *Salisbury (MD) Daily Times*, April 29, 1964, 28.

Fred Minnick

The **smash** or smash-up is one of the families of American drinks recognized by Jerry Thomas in his pioneering 1862 *Bar-Tender's Guide*. Featuring spirits, sugar, mint, and ice, shaken together, it represents the adaptation of the already-venerable julep to a more go-ahead age. See JULEP. As such, this "Julep on a small plan" (as Thomas dubbed it) was, along with the cobbler, the iced cocktail, and the Knickerbocker, one of the standard-bearers of the new American school of drinking. See COBBLER; COCKTAIL; and KNICKERBOCKER.

The smash's origins are obscure, although some during its heyday considered it a southern drink. "Smasher," an American slang term applied to anything exceptional, is first recorded applied to a drink in New Orleans in 1842. See DAISY. It is not clear, however, if that mention denotes a specific formula or is merely an allusion to the effect of a generous drink of spirits, or, if indeed it is a specific formula, what that formula is. To further confuse matters, that same year, a traveler in Arkansas writes of a request for a smasher being answered with a "glass bottle of the 'stuff,' containing several descriptions of roots," which implies a dose of bitters and not the classic smash. See BITTERS.

In 1843, however, there is a "smasher" included on the famous and influential drinks list at Peter Bent Brigham's Oyster Saloon in Boston, which indicates a mixed drink with a specific formula. See BRIGHAM, PETER. An 1848 description of the "cool depths" of a "Brandy Smash" ("smash" had begun replacing "smasher" in the middle of that decade), "clinking with young hail-stones, and an 1849 reference to "fresh mint" as the sine qua non for the drink indicate that it had begun to fall in harmony with the drink as defined by Thomas.

The 1850s were the decade of the smash in general, and in particular the Brandy Smash, far and away the most popular version (it was followed distantly by the Gin Smash and the Whisky Smash). It was the drink of checkered-trousered Broadway swells, of miners laden with gold dust from the "diggings" of California, of gamblers and artists and politicians. Wherever there were sporty Americans, mint, and ice, there were smashes. By the 1860s, however, for whatever reason the smash began fading (perhaps it was too fussy for a short drink). It would live on in bartender's guides, thanks to its prominence in Thomas's book, but one hears more and more infrequently of them being actually served across the bar, and then usually to older drinkers. By 1900, the drink was effectively dead and did not share in the brief renaissance that followed Repeal. In the modern age, it was fortunate to find an advocate in Dale DeGroff, whose Whisky Peach Smash, although not canonical (it contains lemon juice and peach slices), nonetheless begat its own line of modern smashes, which show no sign of dying out. See DEGROFF, DALE.

Recipe: Shake gently with ice: 5–6 mint leaves, 15 ml simple syrup, and 60 ml brandy, genever, or American whisky. Strain into Old-Fashioned glass full of cracked ice and garnish with mint sprigs and berries.

See also BRANDY SMASH and WHISKY SMASH.

"Going into Liquidation." *Madison (WI) Express*, April 2, 1842, 4.
"Meeting of the Police Club." *National Police Gazette*, April 14, 1849, 3.
"Scraps from Old Nick." *Cleveland Weekly Plain Dealer*, October 25, 1848, 3.

David Wondrich

smell, the sense of, is the detection of diverse volatile compounds to which humans are sensitive and is an essential tool for analyzing and enjoying spirits. Understanding how humans collect and register various odorants (the volatile compounds that create olfactory sensations) can help lead to greater appreciation of the nearly limitless variety of descriptors inherent in a spirit, as well as better comprehension of those specific odorants that are crucial to specific spirit categories, although it is important to bear in mind that people differ in their abilities to sense, smell, and identify many compounds, with some of that difference being physical and some experiential. A key, even essential, part of identifying aromas is having a personal library of smells to which one can compare them.

Within the sinus cavity are two olfactory epithelia, each six to twelve square centimeters, one at the top of each nasal passage. They include about twenty million cilia-laden olfactory sensory neurons (a tenth of the number dogs have) that constantly regenerate themselves, although the rate decreases with age. The cilia contain odorant-bonding olfactory receptors, and the information they collect is sent from these olfactory bulbs to the brain.

Fascinatingly, the once prevalent theory that each cilium receives one odorant (the old "lock and key" method) is long discredited. Instead, we have found no fixed code for odorant perception; the manner in which glomeruli in the olfactory bulbs respond to aroma seems more experiential than physiologically predetermined. For the purposes of spirits analysis and description, this means that until you've experienced a particular smell, it's virtually impossible to describe that smell. Though that may seem to be circular logic, imagine trying to describe "artichoke" to someone; all would be best served by simply smelling and tasting artichoke.

Prevalent theories for the sense of smell include the vibration theory, whereby the atomic structure of each odorant vibrates in a unique pattern, interpreted by the olfactory receptors, or the shape-pattern theory, in which odorant molecules are detected by olfactory receptors based upon their molecular shape as captured by the olfactory bulb's numerous glomeruli. Short answer: we don't know. But taking cues from the shape-pattern theory has led to a wealth of artificial smells, some of which are indistinguishable from those of the original compounds.

Olfactory sensations belong to the limbic system, which directly or indirectly encompasses the olfactory cortex, the amygdala, the hippocampus, and other primordial brain structures involved in the formation of memory and emotion. This unmediated and direct linkage is part of the reason why many drugs are designed to be inhaled. But just as interestingly, smells take longer to notice and identify than other sensations (taste, touch, sight, hearing). The words are usually hard to find; the sense of smell doesn't travel through the thalamus like other senses, and the thalamus works with language.

For most tasters and all professionals, the greatest challenge is the disparity between what is often referred to as "detection threshold" and "identification threshold." A smell is constructed in the brain: it is a report generated after the brain has compared a detected volatile compound or set of compounds to its database of identified, half-identified, and even unidentified but retained smells. As Harold McGee puts it, smells are "shaped and presented as simplified conscious perceptions by the actively editing, synthesizing brain." It's frustrating to smell something but to be unable to determine exactly what it is— to get an inconclusive report. While there is debate whether the detection threshold is fixed (it's not), there is general agreement that the identification

threshold responds to experience—that tasters can to some degree train themselves to identify a smell they detect. Members of the wine industry, for example, have trained themselves to smell TCA (2,4,6-trichloroanisole), that moldy newspaper-cork smell, as well as volatile acidity or ethyl acetate. See TCA (2, 4, 6-TRICHLOROANISOLE).

If you struggle finding words to apply to the aromas in spirits and beverages, however, you are normal. Anthropologists maintain that among the world's languages there are fewer words exclusive to the sense of smell than to any other sense. A large part of olfactory training for spirits tasting is cultivating a vocabulary of descriptors that are both consistent and communicable—so that ideally whenever you're presented with a spirit that has been aged in a new American oak barrel, for instance, you have a unique olfactory identifier for that fact on which you can rely, and which you can communicate to others so that they too can identify that fact.

This is not easy. Furthermore, there are barriers for even trained nosers. Some are long-term: as humans age, we lose sensitivity to smell; partly this is because the epithelial pads lose their ability to regenerate olfactory receptors. Most people's sense of taste will not lessen, fascinatingly; but some scientists believe that perhaps half of the population aged 85 or older is anosmic, or unable to detect most smells.

Others are temporary, or at least reversible, but frustrating. For instance, olfactory receptors become unresponsive after continued exposure to certain smells; *adaptation* (some call it olfactory habituation) explains why a smelly room stops being so smelly, but when pet owners return home from a vacation (for instance), they are first struck by how smelly that room "has become." Yet the same phenomenon can happen in only a minute or two of nosing a particular beverage, so tasters find that smelling the same spirit repeatedly provides fewer and fewer descriptors. It's best to switch to something else for at least a few seconds. The brain, as it were, resets quickly and provides a wealth of aromas as if the spirit was poured anew. It can also help to switch nostrils: for some reason, we continuously favor one nostril over the other. No pattern in that preferential use of only one nostril for oxygen as well as aroma detection can be found; and the brain seems to switch from nostril to nostril throughout the day.

Equally, a barrier to the communication of aromas can be posed by generational or geographical differences: people grow up with different smells around them, and the common benchmarks from which we construct our vocabulary of smells can be obscure to people who grew up in another time or place.

See also AROMA and TASTING SPIRITS.

Beauchamp, Gary, and Linda Bartoshuk. *Tasting and Smelling*. Cambridge: Academic Press, 1997.

Classen, Constance, David Howes, and Anthony Synnott. *Aroma: the Cultural History of Smell*. London: Routledge, 1994.

McGee, Harold. *Nose Dive: A Field Guide to the World's Smells*. New York: Penguin, 2020.

Wolfe, Jeremy, Keith Kluender, and Dennis Levi. *Sensation and Perception*. Sunderland, MA: Sinauer Associates, 2011.

Doug Frost

Smirnoff is, as of 2021, the world's bestselling vodka brand, with more than forty different bottlings and flavors available. The modern Smirnoff brand was founded in the United States at the end of Prohibition, but it traces its heritage to Pyotr Arsenievich Smirnov, who opened one of the first vodka distilleries to use a continuous column still in Russia in 1867. Pyotr's son, Vladimir, fled Russia following the country's revolution in 1917 and settled in Constantinople (now Istanbul) and later France, where he changed the spelling of his last name to the more phonetic Smirnoff.

Vladimir Smirnoff made small amounts of vodka himself, but he sold the rights to his name and the insignia of the family's old vodka brand to Rudolph Kunett, a Russian expatriate living in the United States, in 1933. Kunett set up a small distilling operation that was purchased in 1938 by John G. Martin, an executive for Heublein, Inc.

American drinkers were not very familiar with vodka at the time, and Martin sold Smirnoff emphasizing its neutral smell and taste, labeling it "white whiskey." In the early 1940s, Martin teamed up with Jack Morgan, the owner of a Los Angeles pub called the Cock 'n' Bull, which had its own house brand of ginger beer. The pair combined the vodka and ginger beer to create the Moscow Mule cocktail. Martin had engraved copper Moscow Mule mugs made and gave them away to bartenders around the country throughout the 1940s, leading to a massive and sustained burst in the popularity of both Smirnoff in particular and vodka in general. By 1978, Smirnoff was the bestselling distilled spirit in the United States.

Smirnoff's owner Heublein was purchased by R. J. Reynolds in 1982, and then the brand was sold to Grand Metropolitan in 1987, which merged with Guinness to form the liquor giant Diageo in 1997.

See also VODKA; MOSCOW MULE; and MORGAN, JACK.

Himelstein, Linda. *The King of Vodka: the Story of Piotr Smirnov*. New York: Harper Collins, 2009.

Ryan, Bill. "Smirnoff White Whiskey—No Smell, No Taste." *New York Times*, February 19, 1995.

Jason Horn

smoke is sometimes added to a cocktail for visual, aromatic, or flavor appeal. Perhaps the most common way of utilizing smoke is via a handheld smoking gun, in which wood chips or other flavorful flammables (tea, tobacco, herbs, etc.) are ignited, with the smoke directed via a nozzle into a drinking vessel or atop a prepared cocktail. Other methods of adding smoke to cocktails include placing cocktail ingredients (such as fruit or ice) in a traditional cold-smoker before use, igniting an aromatic next to an empty glass or a prepared cocktail and then covering both with an airtight container, or using a smoky spirit such as a peated scotch whisky or mezcal.

Krigbaum, Megan, and Kate Krader. "Smoked Cocktails." *Food and Wine*, last modified June 22, 2017. http://www.foodandwine.com/articles/smoked-cocktails (accessed April 5, 2021).

Small Screen Drinks. "How to Smoke a Cocktail—Raising the Bar with Jamie Boudreau—Small Screen." YouTube. https://www.youtube.com/watch?v=XpO0xdxyUkg (accessed April 5, 2021).

Paul Clarke

smoking is a process whereby the flavor of smoke is picked up by the grains used in fermentation and passed along through the process to the resultant whisky. Although many people use the term "smoke" to describe one of the aromas detected in aged American whisky, this flavor is not actually from smoke but from the lignin in the charred wood on the inside of the barrel in which that whisky was rested. See LIGNIN.

Smoke flavor from actual smoke is most commonly found in scotch whisky. See WHISKY, SCOTCH. Samuel Johnson himself noted upon visiting Scotland that there were no trees left there. Highlanders therefore were forced to use peat as fuel. Peat burns very inefficiently and makes a lot of smoke and little heat, but it was all they had, and they used it to cook over, to heat their homes, and to dry out their malted barley, which retained the flavor of the peat smoke all the way through fermentation and distillation and into the bottle. Over time, this flavor became associated with scotch whisky and when better means of heat became available to distillers there, they added peat to their fires to attain the flavor.

Notable adventures in smoking American whisky include Rick Wasmund's Copper Fox, for which the grains are smoked over apple and cherry wood, and Balcones Brimstone Corn Whisky, to which Chip Tate added the flavors of smoked Texas scrub oak.

Smoke flavors are also found in many mezcals, sometimes quite strongly; these result from the preparation of the *piñas*, or agave hearts, which must be roasted to convert the starches therein into sugars. The traditional method, still used by many village producers, is to roast them over coals in earth-covered pits. In the process, they pick up a good deal of smoke. See MEZCAL.

Some rums also have smoky notes, if much more subdued ones. These notes can result from the flash-burning of the cane in the fields before harvest (to remove vermin) or the use of open fire in the production process, but most are not from smoke itself and come from the interaction between the molasses and the yeasts used to make the rum and the barrels used to age it. Some "smoked" rums, however, have smoke deliberately added to them.

In cocktails and other drinks, smoke notes usually come from scotch or mezcal, but some technologically inclined mixologists add it with electric smoking guns or by burning herbs under a glass and using that to cover the drink.

Bell, Darek. *Fire Water: Experimental Smoked Whiskeys.* Nashville, TN: Corsair Artisan Distillery, 2014.

Max Watman

soda water, aerated water, or carbonated water is the commercial offspring of naturally sparkling spring water. One of its most famous sources was the Selters spring, situated near the town of Neiderselters, Germany. Discovered in 772 CE, these light, effervescent waters were first lauded for their health benefits in 1581 by physician Jakob Theodor, called Tabernaemontanus. A spa was built on the site so royalty and the elite could "take the waters." The village also profited, a century later, from the bottling and shipping of "Selters waters," which commanded a high price and thus inspired scientists to find a way to replicate this miracle cure for indigestion.

Swedish chemistry professor Torbern Bergman was frugal man who could not afford imported aerated waters to cure his digestive problems. Bergman developed a process in 1771 that replicated sparkling spring water by dissolving chalk and sulfuric acid in water to generate carbon dioxide gas. That same year, the British clergyman and natural philosopher Joseph Priestley contrived an alternate method, suspending a bowl of water above a fermenting beer vat. Both men published their methods, yet neither of them pursued commercialization. In 1776, a critic for the *London Review*, commenting on Manchester apothecary Thomas Henry's description of Priestley's aerated water, postulated that it might become as "fashionable as French wine at the fashionable taverns."

The Swiss watchmaker Jean-Jacob Schweppe read both of these accounts and conducted his own experiments. Drawing also on the results achieved in 1777 by French chemist Antoine Lavoisier, he found a viably commercial solution. Schweppe's discovery became a reality in 1783, when he wrote: "I use a compression pump which I named the 'Geneva Machine' because of my origins. In a stirring apparatus, I produce gas with chalk and sulfuric acid; I then purify it with water before heating it with a container full of charcoal. . . . The taste is pretty strong. Maybe I should add natural plant oil."

More interested in gaining certification from the medical community than a profit, Schweppe unfortunately trusted the sales of his water to a friend, who commissioned engineer Nicolas Paul to fashion an aeration device to go into direct competition. (Schweppe's water exceeded the sales of Selter and other spa waters, so it was not surprising that a greedy rivalry emerged.)

The tables turned when Paul made Schweppe's friend a substandard machine and himself a refined one. In retribution, Schweppe went into partnership with Paul and rival pharmacist Henry Albert Gosse in 1790, making a product with distilled water and expanding their offerings and operations to London. From their first factory at 141 Drury Lane, the partnership produced three waters, which were reviewed by industrialist Matthew Boulton and natural philosopher Erasmus Darwin (grandfather of naturalist Charles Darwin): "No. 1 is for common drinking with your dinner. No. 2 is for nephritic patients and No. 3 contains the most alkali given only in more violent cases."

The secret to Schweppe's success was its bottles. Gas commonly escaped around the cork, leaving carbonated water flat within a day. Packaged in strong stoneware bottles with a rounded bottom that required it to be stored on its side, which prevented the cork from drying out and leaking, Schweppe's sparkling water sold for at apothecaries 6s, 6d per dozen, including the bottles. Pressure to construct cheap mineral water machines that were meant to encourage street cart sales fueled the company's 1795 dissolution, but Schweppe persisted and expanded the business, spurred on by a growing customer base. He would see the eighteenth century draw to a close as a wealthy entrepreneur. He retired in 1798, selling 75 percent of his interest to three Channel Island businessmen. Henry William Lauzun, Francis Charles Lauzun, and Robert Charles Brohier continued the soda water business and expanded upon it throughout the nineteenth century.

It wasn't until the 1820s that soda water consistently found its way into mixed drinks, with an assist from George Gordon, Lord Byron, who sang the praises of "hock [Rhine wine] and soda-water" in his poem *Don Juan*, written between 1819 and 1824. By the 1830s, Brandy and Soda had become a common London drink, and that city's Garrick Club was serving a Gin Punch cooled by iced soda water—the invention of its manager, Stephen Price, an American. It took a few years for American drinkers to follow the British lead, but by 1862 Jerry Thomas's groundbreaking *How to Mix Drinks* was listing a number of soda-water drinks, including a "Soda Cocktail" (soda water, sugar, and bitters). See THOMAS, JEREMIAH P. "JERRY".

In the second half of the nineteenth century, soda-water drinks proliferated, with whole classes of them being created and flourishing: coolers and daisies, Collinses and highballs, and spritzes and fizzes and on and on ad infinitum. Soda water assumed the role it maintains today, as a way of diluting a drink without making it uninteresting.

See AMERICANO; APEROL SPRITZ; COOLER; DAISY; FIZZ; HIGHBALL; JOHN COLLINS; RICKEY; and SINGAPORE SLING.

W. Review of *Essays Physical and Chemical by M. Lavoisier* by Thomas Henry. *London Review*, September, 1776, 214.

Wondrich, David. *Imbibe!*, 2nd ed. New York: Perigee, 2015.

Anistatia R. Miller and Jared M. Brown

soju, distilled from grain or other starches, is Korea's revered national spirit and is imbibed in such heroic quantities throughout the country that it is one of the world's top-selling spirits by volume. Indeed, an astonishing 3.63 billion little green bottles of the clear distillate are quaffed annually—around ninety of the 360-ml bottles per person.

Soju divides into two main categories, traditional soju, which is pot-distilled from rice, and diluted soju, which is 95 percent ABV column-distilled alcohol from any number of grains or tubers diluted to around 20 percent ABV with water, then slightly sweetened. While traditional soju is showing signs of revival, it is the diluted style that fills all those little bottles and has come to represent the category overall.

Soju is generally consumed neat as a chilled shot. While somewhat akin to vodka in its simplicity and flavor neutrality, its average ABV of 20 percent makes it much easier to drink and an excellent foil to Korea's robust cuisine. Indeed, the spirit is trending lower in potency as younger generations seek to moderate their alcohol consumption.

Exceedingly affordable, soju is less than two US dollars a bottle at retail in Korea, where it is served at almost every bar and restaurant and is always stocked in supermarkets and corner convenience stores. (Its lower proof also allows soju's US sale in places that can only serve wine and beer, without the necessity of a costly liquor license.)

Soju is ubiquitous in Korea at family meals and special occasions, but its role in business culture cannot be overstated. Deals are concluded over soju, and it is the fuel of obligatory after-work outings designed to build team spirit. Colleagues will go out on the town, visiting at least three spots—restaurants, bars, and *noraebang* (karaoke) parlors. Soju is downed until the wee hours, and everyone still reports for work bright and early. The wear and tear of the practice is evidenced by the fact that senior managers can designate juniors to drink soju on their behalf. While such outings have become less frequent in recent years, they are still a part of corporate life.

Origins and History

Spirits were first produced on the Korean peninsula during the Mongolian invasion in the thirteenth century. Mongol military encampments in Gaegyeong (now Kaesong), Andong, and Jeju Island became centers of distillation, a distinction these regions retain even today. Korea already had an advanced drinks culture, with variations of brewed rice wine made by every family. Alcohol was seen as a means of achieving communion with ancestral and heavenly gods, and soju, first documented in about 1375, quickly captured the national imagination, first among the aristocracy and ultimately regular people.

The process for making traditional soju begins with *nuruk*, a grain cake (traditionally of rice, barley, and wheat) that is inoculated with the *Aspergillus oryzae* fungus, which converts starch into fermentable sugar. See ASPERGILLUS ORYZAE and QU. The cake is then dried and pulverized and mixed with cooked rice, water, and yeast. This mixture ferments for about twelve days to create rice wine, which is then filtered to remove any particles. The clear liquid is distilled in a *soju gori*, a gourd-shaped, water-cooled internal condensation pot still, often made of ceramic, that is peculiar to Korea. See STILL, POT.

By the seventeenth century, soju had become wildly popular, with thousands of distilleries dotting the landscape and many Koreans of means distilling at home, to the point that the government made frequent attempts to prohibit its manufacture, as a means of preserving the peninsula's grain supply. Their very frequency indicates their degree of success.

Immediately following Japan's occupation of Korea in 1910, however, a Liquor Tax Act was enacted that effectively outlawed home brewing and

distilling and forced many traditional drinks handed down over generations into extinction. The rapid industrialization of Korea would also come into play, especially after 1919, when the Japanese began to introduce column stills and the use of sweet potatoes and cassava or tapioca as base materials. Mass production of soju began in 1924 with Jinro, with its marquee spirit clocking in at 35 percent ABV, and an industry consolidation began. See JINRO. Soju's low-proof modern incarnation can be traced to the years after the Korean War, when food shortages were rampant and there were further crackdowns on informal distillation.

In 1965, the Korean government forbade the distillation of rice, the irreplaceable staple grain. In its place, other starchy ingredients, like sweet potatoes and tapioca, gained new prominence. In 1976, the Korean government mandated one distillery per province, further consolidating the industry. The mandate was reversed twenty years later when it was ruled an unconstitutional infringement on market freedom.

Today, the vast majority of soju comes to life via dilution, rather than traditional methods. Soju producers source their alcohol from the Korea Ethanol Supplies Company, where the amounts of production and sales are strictly controlled by law. The very high proof distillate is then diluted with water to bring it to an acceptable proof. Sweeteners, like sugar or stevia, and flavorings, like citric acid, are subtly added to create nuance and differentiation.

While the ban on using rice for distillation was lifted in the 1990s, the diluted style of soju continues to dominate Korea's drinks landscape. With a greater awareness of healthful living and the entry of younger generations into the workforce, soju has become more diluted, with some as low as 17 percent ABV, and fruit-flavored expressions, such as apple, citron, strawberry, peach, and grapefruit, increasingly popular. In fact, Jinro, the largest producer, recently began exporting 16.9 percent ABV to seven overseas markets, including the United States and Japan.

The beauty of soju is that it is a complete solution. Prediluted with no hard edges, it is the equivalent of an RTD, and only a shot glass is required. Soju is also enjoyed as the base of *à la minute* infusions with lemon or cucumber slices, as well as in cocktails. It is especially popular in *somaek*, a boilermaker that combines *soju* with *maekju* (beer).

Soju is nearly always enjoyed in conjunction with food, with popular traditional accompaniments such as *bossam* (steamed pork wrapped in sesame leaves), *dooboo kimchi* (boiled tofu topped with kimchi), *hweh* (raw fish, sashimi-style, served with spicy chili sauce), and *samgyeopsal* (grilled pork belly).

Soju brands, including Jinro's Chamisul and Lotte's Chum Churum, remain ever-popular juggernauts, in both Korea and Koreatowns across America. Hwayo and Andong are reviving the more traditional rice style, as are Tokki and West 32, which originated in New York City (the latter has since relocated to Korea).

Today, there is a growing interest in the artisanal approach, with some trendsetting bars in Seoul exclusively offering curated lists of traditional soju to their guests. However, because of the price differential, force of habit, and massive marketing budgets of the incumbents, it will take time and dedication for traditional soju to impact the billions of little green bottles that have come to represent soju for generations of millions of Koreans.

Andong Soju Traditional Food Museum. "Soju." https://www.andongsoju.com:2033/eng/sub1/sub1.asp (accessed March 15, 2021).

English, Camper. "Getting Nerdy about Soju." *Alcademics*, July 7, 2020. https://www.alcademics.com/2020/07/getting-nerdy-about-soju-production-sticky-rice-nuruk-fermentation-multi-abvs-korean-production.html (accessed March 15, 2021).

Melissa. "The History of Soju and Its Modernization." *10 Magazine*, January 12, 2021. https://10mag.com/the-history-of-soju-and-its-modernization/ (accessed March 15, 2021).

Park, Hyunhee. *Soju: A Global History*. Cambridge: Cambridge University Press, 2021.

Michael Anstendig

solera is a rank of barrels used for maturing wines and spirits where, as liquid is withdrawn from the oldest one (never entirely emptying the barrel), it is replaced by a like quantity from the next oldest, which is replenished from the next one, and so forth. See MATURATION.

sorghum, also known in English as broomcorn or milo, is a drought-tolerant grass of the same subfamily as corn, millet, and sugar cane whose stalks and seeds are both used to make spirits. *Sorghum bicolor* is widely cultivated as a cereal crop in Africa and Asia and used as animal feed in many other regions. It has tall sugar-rich stalks topped with dense clusters of starchy kernels, dark red or yellowish white in color.

Pressing sorghum stalks and boiling its juice creates syrup, which can be distilled into so-called sorghum whisky. Though it is actually closer to rum in character, lack of sugar cane in the production process prevents its official classification as such. Historically, sorghum rum was made in places as far afield as Australia and Sicily, but its current heartland is the southern United States (although it must be labeled "whisky," "rum" being legally limited to sugar cane products).

In Africa, sorghum is malted and brewed to create several traditional beers, and elsewhere sorghum beer is gaining traction as a gluten-free product. Though sorghum behaves much like barley in malting, it has higher gelatinization temperatures, and its tannins can interfere with starch breakdown if not neutralized.

The sorghum kernel is most frequently distilled in China, where as much as 90 percent of domestic sorghum—and much more imported from elsewhere—is used in baijiu production. Baijiu distillers pulverize and steam sorghum kernels to aid gelatinization before initiating fermentation with naturally harvested yeast cultures, or *qu*. See QU. Distillers work with several species of sorghum: non-waxy varieties have more protein and starch, but waxy varieties gelatinize more readily and yield more alcohol. Following distillation, baijiu mash is recycled for further fermentation, sometimes with the addition of fresh grain, or used as animal feed. Sorghum has a naturally bitter taste, but once distilled it becomes fruitier with a complex, somewhat nutty aroma.

See also BAIJIU; RUM.

Smith, Wayne C., and Richard A. Fredericksen, eds. *Sorghum: Origin, History, Technology, and Production*. New York: John Wiley & Sons, 2006.

Taylor, John R. N., Tilman J. Schober, and Scott R. Bean. "Novel Food and Non-food Uses for Sorghum and Millets." *Journal of Cereal Science* 44 (2006): 252–271.

Derek Sandhaus

sotol is an alcoholic beverage distilled in Mexico from the cooked and fermented heads of several species of plants of the genus *Dasylirion*, commonly known as *sotol* or *desert spoon*. Dasylirion plants are native to, and most abundantly found in, the Chihuahuan Desert, which straddles northern Mexico and parts of the American Southwest. Once classified in the same family as agave, dasylirion is now recognized under a separate family, Nolinaceae. Sotol is protected by a Mexican denomination of origin established in 2002 that allows production in the states of Chihuahua, Durango, and Coahuila, a large region that includes forests, prairies, and deserts.

When the plants are approximately fifteen years old, workers harvest them and take them to a *vinata*, or distillery, where the production process is similar to that of agave distillates. See AGAVE. The plants are cooked, milled, fermented, and distilled. Sotol producers range from artisanal (earth pit roasting, ambient fermentation, and small copper stills) to modern (large concrete ovens, commercial yeasts, and column stills). By law sotol must contain a minimum of 51 percent fermentable sugars from dasylirion. Further, it can be aged using acacia, ash, beech, chestnut, or oak barrels. Given such environmental diversity and aging options, sotol exhibits a range of flavors. See OAK ALTERNATIVES.

Sotol is gaining wider acclaim as global interest in Mexican spirits grows. Don Cuco and Hacienda de Chihuahua are the most prominent producers; however, smaller brands such as Ocho Cientos and Sotol por Siempre are starting to make marks on the international drinking scene.

See also MEXICO.

Gardea, Alfonso A., Lloyd T. Finley, J. Antonio Orozco-Avitia, Noemi Bañuelos, Martín Esqueda, and Travis H. Huxman. "Bacanora and Sotol: So Far, So Close." *Estudios Sociales* 2 (2012): 153–68.

Misty Kalkofen

The **sour**, a short, single-serving punch-offshoot with spirits, citrus juice, and a sweetening agent, served up, is one of the most important classes of modern drinks. See PUNCH. Indeed, many of the most popular cocktails are in fact sours. See MARGARITA; DAIQUIRI; COSMOPOLITAN; and SIDECAR.

The sour is an American drink of the 1850s, appearing at roughly the same time as its close cousin the fix and the julep-derived smash (the sour's first appearance in print is a casual reference in the *New York Times* from 1857). See FIX; SMASH. All of these can be viewed as short adaptations of drinks traditionally served long, designed to make them quicker to consume and less intoxicating: Jerry Thomas's individual Brandy Punch, for example, has over 200 ml of liquid, 90 of that being spirits, while his sour cuts the spirits down to 60 ml and the total volume to a little over 100. See LONG DRINK and THOMAS, JEREMIAH P. "JERRY". There is, however, another, more evolutionary way of looking at the drink's origin, as illuminated in an 1826 article from a Cincinnati newspaper on the many ways Americans took their spirits, using whisky as an example. Among the twenty-two different varieties of whisky and whisky drinks listed are "whisky sweet and sour" and "whisky sour and sweet." This, an early instance of the American propensity for customizing one's drinks, might have begun as an ad hoc preference when ordering a glass of punch, but by Thomas's day each way had become its own drink. "Sweet and sour" went down the path of the fancy drink and became the fix, with fruit garnish and the only souring agent being a slice of lemon stirred in, while the "sour and sweet" became the rather more austere sour, which Thomas describes as the same as a fix but "omitting all fruits except a small piece of lemon, the juice of which must be pressed in the glass." In any case, the sour rapidly became one of the most important classes of American drink. As the *Atlanta Daily Constitution* put it in 1879, "When American meets American then comes the Whisky Sour."

The most popular spirits for sours were originally, in rough order, brandy, Santa Cruz rum, Holland gin or genever, and American whisky. See RUM; SANTA CRUZ RUM; and GENEVER. By the 1870s, whisky had moved into first place, and would stay there. At the same time, bartenders had taken to straining the sour into a separate glass rather than serving it in the glass it was mixed in. This required the adoption of a new glass. Like the cocktail glass that was then coming into vogue, the sour glass was stemmed (to keep the hand from warming it), but it was larger—some 150 ml, versus the cocktail glass's 90 ml—in order to accommodate the citrus juice and the water used to dissolve the sugar that went into the drink (both drinks were based on a 2-ounce, or 60-ml, jigger of spirits).

As long as they were straining the sour into its own glass, mixologists began experimenting with it in other ways both small and large, from replacing the granulated sugar with simple syrup (the most exacting ones always resisted that shortcut, preferring to stir the sugar into the juice before adding the other ingredients) or importing the fruit garnish from the fix to putting the whisky version in a large goblet and topping it off with soda water (this, basically a fizz, was known as a "Hari Kari"), or incorporating egg white into it and serving it in a sugar-rimmed glass. See FIZZ. In 1883, Rochester, New York, bartender Patsy McDonough (1850–1893) called that last one a "Frosted Sour"; minus the sugar rim, it would become the default sour, particularly in Europe and Latin America. See PISCO SOUR. The ne plus ultra was to float a layer of dry red wine on top of a regular sour; also first attested to in 1883, this went through several names before settling on New York Sour. See NEW YORK SOUR. Some of these variations even became their own categories of drinks, with the requisite variations of their own; note, for example, the Daisy, which incorporated syrups or liqueurs for sweetening. See DAISY.

The creativity that went into the sour got diverted in the first decade of the twentieth century, when the popularity of drinks such as the Bronx made it acceptable for citrus juice to be used in a cocktail. See BRONX COCKTAIL. Aside from a few fossilized expressions—the Whisky Sour; the Stone Sour (with orange juice added to the lemon)—new citrus drinks served straight up were henceforth generally pulled into the cocktail category due to its increasing gravitational power as it became the stand-in in popular iconography for all mixed drinks. (As a late counterbalance, there is the whole tangled world of tiki drinks, almost every one of them a punch or a sour at heart. See TIKI.)

Even worse for the sour was another development of the twentieth century, "sour mix," a bottled (or, God help us, powdered) blend of citric acid, sugar, artificial or real lemon or lime flavor (or often both), and a foaming agent (to give the appearance of egg white). This was found occasionally in New York bars before Prohibition, was widespread after Repeal, and was nearly universal from the 1960s through the 1980s. Fortunately, in recent years such shortcuts have become unfashionable, and, in the best establishments, at least, the sour has returned to its pristine excellence.

Recipe: Stir 7 ml sugar in 15 ml lemon juice; add 60 ml spirits and (optionally) 15 ml egg white; shake, strain into large cocktail glass, and garnish with cherry and orange slice.

"Coffee." *Natchez Newspaper and Public Advertiser*, November 29, 1826, 3 (from the *Cincinnati Western Tiller*).
McDonough, Patsy. *McDonough's Bar-Keeper's Guide*. Rochester, NY: 1883.
"Peeps behind the Political Curtain." *New York Times*, June 23, 1857, 1.
"When American Meets American." *Atlanta Daily Constitution*, February 20, 1879, 2.
Wondrich, David. *Imbibe!*, 2nd ed. New York: Perigee, 2015.

David Wondrich

sour mash is spent stillage—mash that has had all the alcohol distilled out of it—that is added to a subsequent batch of mash before it is distilled. Many spirits incorporate souring processes in mashing and fermentation, but the "sour mash" process is most often associated with the American bourbons and Tennessee whiskies. Spirits consumers are generally familiar with the term because most large American whisky brands identify their products as "sour mash." The largest-selling bottling of them all proclaims it right on the front label: "Jack Daniel's Old No. 7 Brand Tennessee Sour Mash Whiskey."

Credit for the modern sour mashing process using backset stillage is often given to Dr. James C. Crow, an early industry legend known for applying a scientific approach to whisky making, but the process certainly predates the 1830s, when Crow became active in American whisky distilling. By the 1750s, rum distillers in the British Caribbean were mixing "dunder"—spent stillage—in with the skimmings and molasses from which they made their rum. See DUNDER and RUM. The process was being recommended by American distillers' manuals by the 1810s but doesn't appear to have become widespread until the middle of the century, when it became a selling point for bourbons and Tennessee whiskies (eastern ryes stayed with the sweet-mash process). See WHISKY, BOURBON; WHISKY, RYE; and WHISKY, TENNESSEE.

Today the most common practice in sour mashing is to return some portion of stillage to subsequent mash cooks. Whole stillage is what remains after distillation separates the new whisky from the fermented beer. Large, insoluble grain solids can be separated from the dissolved, thin stillage fraction by centrifugation or by running over gravity screens. This thin stillage, called backset, is added to the mash cooker along with water and fresh grain meal. The proportion of backset in the mash varies but typically ranges from 10 percent to 25 percent of the fresh mash by volume.

Backset stillage performs several functions in helping to optimize grain conversion and yeast performance in mashing and fermentation. The primary benefits are due to the recycled yeast cells (killed by the heat of distillation) and recycled organic acids. The recycled yeast cells serve as an ideal nutrient source for yeast in the next fermentation cycle, and the recycled organic acids act to lower the pH of the mash. That increased acidity in the mash suppresses the growth of ever-present spoilage bacteria, thus giving live yeast a competitive advantage in the fermenter. Targeting a lower pH throughout the mashing cycle and in the early stages of fermentation improves enzymatic conversion of grain starch to fermentable sugars and accelerates initial yeast activity.

A second component of sour mashing that is a very traditional but less well known is the use of a lactic bacteria soured yeast mash. In this process, lactic bacteria are inoculated into a secondary mash stream used to condition and scale up the yeast at the distillery. These "lactics" produce lactic acid and lower the pH, acidifying the yeast mash. The two components of sour mashing, backset stillage and lactic soured yeast mash, work together to optimize pH balance throughout mashing and fermentation cycles. See LACTOBACILLUS.

Sour mashing practices vary across the industry, and the process is not strictly defined. The process has evolved over several centuries. It could be argued that the early practice of holding over fermented beer from a finished fermenter to provide active yeast to subsequent fermentation could provide some of the same nutritional and acidification benefits as backset stillage. However, that approach was not a best practice for yeast maintenance, and distillers learned to cultivate and inoculate a fresh, active yeast to start fermentation.

Bryson, Lew. *Whiskey Master Class*. Beverly, MA: Quarto, 2020.

Veach, Michael. "Early Sour Mash." *Bourbonveachdotcom*, July 9, 2017. https://bourbonveach.com/2018/07/09/early-sour-mash/ (accessed March 29, 2021).

Kevin Smith

sour mix is a packaged mixture of sweet (sugar) and sour (lemon and/or lime juice, or an artificial equivalent), designed to provide a more convenient and consistent way of incorporating those ingredients than squeezing fresh juice and sweetening it to order. See SOUR. There are many brands of prepackaged sour mix (aka sweet-and-sour mix, margarita mix, daiquiri mix, etc.) commercially available, most of which tend to be laden with chemicals and preservatives. A fresh version of sour mix can be made by mixing equal parts of simple syrup and lemon and/or lime juice. (For a "margarita mix," some orange juice may be added as well.) Some bars list "homemade" or "house sour mix" on their menus as an ingredient to indicate they aren't using a commercial mix. See SIMPLE SYRUP.

Rose's Lime Juice (known as Rose's Lime Cordial in the United Kingdom) could be considered the first sour mix. Patented in 1867, it was not specifically designed as a cocktail ingredient but was soon thereafter advertised for use in mixed drinks and would become the defining ingredient in the Gimlet. See GIMLET. By the beginning of the twentieth century, many American bars, at least, were using a prepackaged mix. In the days before the Pure Food and Drug Act, this was often highly suspect. As the American journalist Julius Chambers noted in 1904, "At all cheap bars there is a fluid bought by the gallon and compounded of acetic acid and syrup" with "white of egg" (which in small quantities would foam slightly when shaken, as real lemon juice does). By 1911, even many respectable hotel bars had graduated from fresh juice to Lemos, a somewhat better grade of sour mix sold by the C. M. Brooke company of Melbourne, Australia, and Brooklyn, New York.

The use of commercial sour mix in place of fresh juices would get a boost during Prohibition, for both commercial bars and home use. Holland House marketed a variety of cocktail mixes, along with sour mix, to the general public in the 1940s. They were seen as a quick and easy way to make cocktails without "mess or guess." It wouldn't be until the late 1980s when the use of fresh-squeezed juices would gradually start to return. Dale DeGroff is famous for promoting fresh juices when he worked at the Rainbow Room in New York's Rockefeller Center and in his many consulting jobs. One of the ways he converted bars and hotels to fresh juice was by demonstrating that, contrary to what its makers claimed, sour mix was actually more expensive than fresh juice—not unit for unit, where sour mix enjoyed a slight edge, but in total, since a greater volume of the mix was required per drink. See DeGroff, Dale, and Rainbow Room bar. While it was slow to catch on, by the late 1990s we begin to see the emergence of the craft cocktail movement, which would finally bring fresh juices back in fashion.

The intent of using a sour mix is to simplify the process of making a mixed drink by replacing the need of adding two ingredients (simple syrup, then fresh lemon juice or lime juice) with that of simply adding a single ingredient (sour mix). Using premade sour mix presents challenges, as well: the type of citrus required or the ratio of sweet to sour can vary widely among different drinks and recipes, and fresh-made sour mix has a shorter lifespan.

Chambers, Julius. "Walks and Talks with Men and Women of the Hour." *Chicago Tribune*, June 22, 1904, 6.

DeGroff, Dale. *The Craft of the Cocktail*. New York: Clarkson Potter, 2002.

"A Public Benefactor." *New York Hotel Record*, October 14, 1913, 8.

Regan, Gary. *The Joy of Mixology*. New York: Clarkson Potter, 2003.

"Rose's" (advertisement). In *London and Suburban Licensed Victuallers'... Directory*, ed. Henry Downes Miles, iii. London: Miles, 1874.

Robert Hess

South Africa has been a significant producer of grape brandy, more or less in the European style, since it was settled by Dutch colonists in the seventeenth century, although the production and use of fermented alcoholic drinks was widespread in South African tribal societies long before the Dutch arrived. The Xhosa, for example, made (and continue to make) traditional grain-based beers, which are central to their social and spiritual life. Europeans introduced viticulture in the seventeenth century, and wine making expanded in the nineteenth century as European vineyards were being ravaged by the oidium, peronospera, and phylloxera epidemics. South African wines helped replenish the dwindling availability of wine in Europe, though those diseases and pests eventually devastated South African vineyards too.

The country's alcohol industry was continuously warped by its colonial station, with favorable export status (always to the United Kingdom) ending abruptly in 1861. Its importance to the Crown lurched about as diamonds (1867) and gold (1884) were discovered, commensurate with strife and wars (the Anglo-Zulu War of 1879 and the Boer Wars of 1880 and 1889). Alcohol became not only an economic weapon but a tool for social control as well. The *dop*, the nineteenth-century strategy of labor control by which workers were paid in tots (whether wine, beer, or spirits), created generations of impoverished alcoholics. See dop. Even today, estimates of continuing worker exploitation through the dop range between 2 percent and 20 percent in the agricultural sector, and fetal alcohol syndrome is estimated to affect 5 percent of births.

Well into the twentieth century, the alcohol industry struggled haphazardly to respond to the dictates of empire. By 1895, 1.5 million gallons of brandy were being produced, equal to 25 percent of the volume of wine production, due as much to a plummeting export market as to some inherent need for more spirit.

The Ko-operatieve Wijnbouwers Vereniging van Zuid-Afrika (KWV) was created in 1918 amid a collapsing, dire market. With broad control over the production, sale, and export of wine and spirits, this government-owned virtual monopoly ruled the industry until the end of apartheid. Though illegal, home brew and distillate became a hidden feature of the landscape throughout this vast country. From the 1930s, brewers were making *skomfani skokiaan*, from sugar, yeast, and water. Others made *isiqataviku* ("kill-quick"), *babaton*, and *chechisa* ("hurry-up") or *isishimeyane*, made from sugar cane, yeast, cooked potatoes, and brandy. *Mampoer* or *witblits* ("white lightning") was a farm product, distilled from peaches and carrying a reputation for potency. Under apartheid, only whites were allowed to make or drink alcoholic drinks; speak-easies and shebeen culture in the black townships remain a harmful legacy to this day. While domestic sales were denied to the KWV by its charter until recently, it historically supplied spirit to merchants and estates, each prohibited from distilling at all or at least constrained from maturing and marketing spirit.

Since democracy's flowering in 1994, South African wines have become widely heralded around the globe; the country's spirits remain less celebrated, at least partly due to their past ubiquity as low-quality dop. Unsurprisingly, only the KWV has older spirits stocks from which to draw its brandy components. KWV brandies remain dominant in the domestic market; very few consumers are fortunate enough to taste their oldest and finest brandies. They are worth seeking out, as is the company's Van Der Hum ("what's-his-name"), a brandy-based curaçao flavored with local *naartjes* tangerines that has been a South African specialty since at least the late nineteenth century.

Since 1981 South African brandy must contain a minimum 30 percent pot-still brandy (the remainder is neutral wine spirit); 1990 saw the minimum alcohol level reduced from 43 percent to 38 percent ABV. A new category was launched as well: pot-still brandy, with a minimum of 90 percent pot-still spirit.

The old problems remain: Euromonitor estimates that nearly one-quarter of all spirits consumed in South Africa are illegal home brews, which are unregulated and sometimes lethal. With brandy sales little more than half what they were a few decades ago, whisky consumption in South Africa has rapidly increased (sixth highest in the world). Domestic whisky production is also on the rise, led primarily by the giant Distell Corporation. The country's best-known liqueur is Amarula, the world's no. 2 cream liqueur.

See also CENTRAL AND EAST AFRICA.

Gossage, J. Phillip. *Alcohol Use, Working Conditions, Job Benefits, and the Legacy of; the "Dop" System among Farm Workers in the Western Cape Province, South Africa: Hope Despite High Levels of Risky Drinking.* Bethesda, MD: US National Library of Medicine, National Institutes of Health, 2014.

Department of Community Health. *The 'Dop' System, Alcohol Abuse and Social Control amongst Farm Workers in South Africa: A Public Health Challenge.* Rondebosch, South Africa: University of Cape Town Medical School, 1999.

Doug Frost

Southeast Asia, with regard to its spirits and cocktails, remains relatively unknown in the West. The history of distillation there has also yet to be fully uncovered, although there are hints of Chinese influence in the still designs employed on Southeast Asian islands. European explorers arriving in the region encountered spirits distilled from rice wine, palm wine, sugar cane, and coconut sap, all of which are still produced today. These go by a variety of names, often falling under the generic "arrack," and are sometimes marketed as "whisky" despite their different means of production. See ARRACK.

The consumption of alcohol in the region reflects not only native traditions but also influences from China and Japan, the European colonial era, a loosening of attitudes driven by modern tourism, and restrictions imposed by nominally dry Muslims. In Malaysia, for example, a dual legal system governs alcohol among the Islamic Malay majority and the assorted Chinese, Indians, and indigenous peoples, resulting in competing aims in regulation; consumption figures suggest substantial tippling among many of those who claim to abstain.

European-style lager beers, such as Singapore's famous Tiger, are locally produced and very popular throughout Southeast Asia. In Vietnam, the Portuguese and French spurred demand for European wine. Rice distillates are widely and informally produced as part of household cottage industries. The typical process for making these, as is well documented in Vietnam, involves a two-step fermentation process using starters known as *ciu*. These dough-like masses are made from ground rice or cassava, sometimes with herbs and spices added, which are inoculated and allowed to grow mold. These dried starters are added to rice, which turns the starches into sugar. Yeasts turn these sugars into fermented alcohol, which can be distilled to high proof or simply fortified with additional spirits. See BAIJIU and QU.

Two cocktails that originated in Southeast Asia have taken on prominent status in the cocktail canon, both of them developed in hotels and clubs catering to Western visitors. The Singapore Sling, a gin-based cocktail that has taken on a variety of incarnations, is credited, probably erroneously, to the Raffles Hotel in Singapore and was popularized by the likes of W. Somerset Maugham, Noel Coward, and Ernest Hemingway. See SINGAPORE

SLING. The Pegu Club, the eponymous cocktail of a club built for British officers and administrators in 1882 in Yangon, Myanmar, was also recorded by European bartenders and appeared in the *Savoy Cocktail Book*, and has enjoyed a revival with the renaissance in classic cocktails. See PEGU CLUB COCKTAIL. In recent years, bars making contemporary cocktails have also begun to proliferate in Southeast Asian countries, leading to a young but vibrant cocktail culture.

See also ARRACK, BATAVIA; INDONESIA; and QU.

Martin, Scott C., ed. *The SAGE Encyclopedia of Alcohol.* Thousand Oaks, CA: SAGE, 2014.

Owens, David J., ed. *Indigenous Fermented Foods of Southeast Asia.* Boca Raton, FL: CRC, 2014.

Jacob Grier

South Korea comprises the southern half of the mountainous and forested Korean Peninsula, which it shares precariously with North Korea. Home to 51.2 million people and five thousand years of uninterrupted history, South Korea is one of the world's largest spirits manufacturers and consumers and has both a thriving traditional pub culture and, in the country's sophisticated, 24/7 capital, Seoul, a burgeoning craft cocktail scene.

The need to preserve foods to be eaten during long, bitter winters led Koreans to master fermentation. Kimchi, Korea's pickled vegetables, along with countless other dishes like sauces and salted fish, relies on this foundational technique. It is no surprise that Koreans likewise mastered fermentation for beverages. Over the centuries, they created many variations of rice wine (technically beer, as it is grain-based), which became the fuel for communing with nature and the gods and celebrating life's milestones.

In the thirteenth century, the Mongols descended upon Korea en route to Japan. They brought with them the technique of distillation, which Koreans enthusiastically embraced. The result is soju, a ubiquitous, vodka-like clear spirit that is produced and consumed in mind-boggling quantities. Originally an artisanally crafted pot-stilled rice spirit, today it is an industrial juggernaut commonly made of column-distilled sweet potatoes and tapioca and diluted to proof. South Korea produces 3.63 billion bottles of the latter annually, making it one of the most popular spirits categories on the planet

by volume, if not the most. Now, traditional soju is even showing signs of a comeback. In recent years, Western-style cocktail bars staffed by seasoned bartenders have begun to impact the fast-paced nightlife scene of Seoul and win accolades and recognition on the world stage for their very high levels of creativity and execution. The country's intrepid drink slingers have embraced experimenting with indigenous ingredients and sometimes incorporate traditional Korean spirits, liqueurs, and rice wines to excellent effect. See COCKTAIL RENAISSANCE.

In addition, makgeolli, traditionally a bubbly and cloudy rice wine enjoyed by farmers, has been embraced anew by Korean rappers, with artisanal versions increasingly popular and worth seeking out. Beyond soju, Koreans are fond of scotch whisky, both blended and single malt. Prestigious bottles such as Johnnie Walker Blue Label are proudly conferred as gifts when visiting friends and family, with many households displaying such bottles in the equivalent of a trophy cabinet in their living rooms. See JOHNNIE WALKER. In addition, Seoul boasts bars that specialize in scotch whisky and offer an encyclopedic array of bottlings.

In Korea's collectivist culture, group harmony and solidarity are paramount. Drinking has its own rituals that adhere to Confucian hierarchical etiquette. It is highly frowned upon to pour one's own drink, let alone tipple alone, so friends, colleagues, and family members are fast to refill a drained glass. Generally, when an elder pours or accepts a pour from someone younger or less senior, the elder holds the bottle or glass with one hand. But when a junior person does the honors, they hold with two hands. Moreover, the less senior person, when receiving a pour, drinks after turning their face aside to "conceal" their sipping with their hand as a sign of deference and respect.

Koehler, Robert. *Korean Wines and Spirits.* Seoul: Korea Foundation, 2014.

"Mixologists Raise the Bar." *Korea Herald*, March 30, 2010. http://www.koreaherald.com/view.php?ud=20090307000009 (accessed April 5, 2021).

Michael Anstendig

The **Southside**—a tall drink of gin, lemon juice, sugar, mint, and soda, favored by the upper-crusty country-club set—was rumored (incorrectly) to be born in the Prohibition-era speakeasies of Chicago's South Side. See PROHIBITION AND TEMPERANCE IN AMERICA. Instead, the Southside evolved from the Mint Juleps made at Snedecor's Tavern on Long Island, which itself evolved into the Southside Sportsman's Club. It was there where, more than a century ago, New York's plutocrats would go to fish for trout. They picked up a taste for the drink made at the Southside club and started asking for "that Southside drink" at all the country clubs where they did their golfing, swimming, and tennis playing. This is how the Southside came to be known as the essential country-club quaff. It has also for many years been the house drink at New York's 21 Club, the former speakeasy that became one of the traditional places in New York to see corporate executives, politicians, and other such big game in the wild. This has done nothing to change the drink's reputation.

Recipe: Shake 45 ml gin, 30 ml fresh lemon juice, 22.5 ml simple syrup (or ½ tablespoon superfine sugar), and half a dozen fresh mint leaves vigorously with ice. Strain into an ice-filled highball glass. Top with club soda, give a quick stir, and garnish with a sprig of mint. For a more minty Southside, combine a cup of lemon juice with ¾ cup simple syrup and pack the mixture with fresh mint leaves. Let steep in the fridge for two or three days. Strain and use 60 ml of the Southside "mix" in each drink. The country clubs of Maryland's Hunt Country substitute rum for the gin.

Felten, Eric. "A Privilege of the Privileged." *The Wall Street Journal*, August 18, 2007.

Eric Felten

Spanish Coffee, a snifter of flaming brandy, Kahlua, and 151-proof rum that is extinguished with hot coffee, is an elaboration of Pedro Chicote's 1928 flaming Coffee Grog. It was brought to America by Juan Abella (1930–), a Catalan, in 1965 and introduced to instant acclaim at the Five Chateaux restaurant in Cambridge, Massachusetts. In 1968 Abella moved to Miami, Florida, bringing the drink with him. It enjoyed a certain fleeting regional popularity as an after dinner drink in the 1970s but found its true home at the venerable Huber's Café, in Portland, Oregon. Forty years later, Huber's still serves five thousand of its elaborated, perfected Spanish Coffees a week.

Recipe: Rim an Irish Coffee glass with sugar. Add 22 ml Spanish brandy and 22 ml overproof rum. Set liquor on fire and swirl glass to brown the sugar. Add 22 ml Kahlua and 90 ml coffee. Top with unsweetened whipped cream and grate nutmeg on top. Note: Huber's replaces the brandy with triple sec and uses 60 ml Kahlua.

See also CHICOTE, PEDRO "PERICO" and KAHLÚA.

"Flaming Spanish Coffee Ole!" (advertisement). *Boston Herald*, November 12, 1965.
Chicote, Pedro. *Cocktails*. Madrid: Sucesores de Rivadeneyra: 1928.

David Wondrich

spanking for aromatized garnishes is a technique whereby the aroma of aromatic garnishes such as mint is released by a single clap of the garnish between the bartender's hands or by whipping it against the wrist or back of the hand or straw. The technique was pioneered and championed at the New York City bar Milk & Honey by bartender Toby Maloney (1968–), whose intention was to use a showman's flourish to enhance aroma as well as calling attention to the drink. See MILK & HONEY. Other aromatic botanicals that work well with this technique include but are not limited to: lemon verbena, lavender, rosemary, sage, and basil. See BOTANICAL. Care should be taken not to crush, bruise, or tear the garnish, which should be slapped or whipped just hard enough to release the aromatic essential oils. See ESSENTIAL OILS.

See also AROMA.

Chad Solomon

speakeasy (new) is a style of cocktail bar ostensibly modeled on the Prohibition-era speakeasies of the 1920s, typified by a hidden entrance, a secret password or phone number, and, often, posted rules of decorum and a reservations-only policy for admission. Opened in 1999 behind an unmarked door, New York's Milk & Honey was one of the first modern cocktail bars to borrow cues from the traditions of Prohibition-era speakeasies, followed soon after by New York's PDT, which is entered through a phone booth at the rear of a restaurant.

The entrance to the modern speakeasy PDT in New York. Courtesy of Jeff Bell.

See MILK & HONEY. Despite belonging more to the classic saloons of the years before Prohibition than to the original speakeasies, plush interiors, vintage light fixtures, and antique mirrors became signatures of the new speakeasy aesthetic. See SPEAKEASY (OLD). For the first decade of the cocktail revival, these decorative touches came to symbolize the seriousness of the cocktails served within. As the availability of quality cocktails is becoming the rule rather than the exception, the need to signal their presence through a uniform aesthetic is waning.

See also PROHIBITION AND TEMPERANCE IN AMERICA.

Ross, Christopher. "Bar Design in the Post-Speakeasy Era." *Punch*, January 15, 2015. https://punchdrink.com/articles/bar-design-in-the-post-speakeasy-era/ (accessed March 11, 2021).

Cloe Frechette

speakeasy (old) is an illegal business that sells alcoholic beverages. The term, an Irish one, is derived from the need to speak "easily" or softly in an illicit drinking house to avoid drawing the law. It was current in the United States from the 1880s, when it began to replace the earlier terms "blind pig" or "blind tiger" (the establishments would charge admission, ostensibly to view one of the animals in question, but would instead pour the customer a drink once the admission charge was paid and the customer safely inside). "Speakeasy" only became widely used in America during Prohibition (1920–1933), when illegal drinking places became ubiquitous.

Every city had some form of speakeasies, though no city is more associated with the illicit bars than New York, which may have had up to 35,000 speakeasies during Prohibition. Hollywood movies encouraged the myth that these speakeasies were armed with a narrow sliding window at eye level and that consumers had to know a password to get in. The reality was often different. Access was gained through knowing the owner or a regular customer, or by simply swearing that one was not a police officer or a Prohibition Bureau agent.

Speakeasies came in many varieties. At the high end were swanky cocktail bars or jazz clubs such as New York's famed Cotton Club, where Duke Ellington led the band. Others were in dingy cellars or upstairs rooms, hidden in plain sight by a legitimate business, or even in someone's living room. A cigar shop or a lunchroom might have a "little back room" that was only accessible to those in the know. Not all speakeasies were places to get a drink: often it was just a place to buy an illicit bottle for home consumption—say, out of the basement of a candy store.

The saloon was a man's domain before Prohibition, but the speakeasy quickly changed that. American women earned the right to vote in 1920—the same year that Prohibition went into effect—and now that it was illegal to drink, women could break the law in a speakeasy just as equally as men could. Many women owned and operated speakeasies, the best known being Texas Guinan, the brash hostess of the high-end 300 Club in Manhattan, who greeted her well-heeled guests with "Hello, suckers."

Distilled spirits were the drinks of choice at speakeasies, as they offered more concentrated alcohol and thus were more profitable to bootleggers. Gin and whisky of varying quality were served. "Bathtub gin" was often repurposed industrial alcohol cut with water in the bathtub, and to make it more palatable, bartenders added fruit juices or sugary flavorings. See BATHTUB GIN. Whisky could be genuine bourbon, Canadian, or scotch—or it could be grain alcohol with caramel coloring, creosote, and iodine for that peaty flavor. Prohibition-era consumers had no way of knowing what was actually in their glass.

A popular speakeasy drinking arrangement was known as a "setup." A customer would receive a glass of ice and a bottle of ginger ale or soda. Upon request, a waiter would discreetly fetch a bottle of booze. Drinks were sometimes served in a coffee mug or a teacup as a disguise, should the police raid the joint.

The famous Prohibition Bureau agents Izzy Einstein and Moe Smith never carried guns but used countless comical disguises to gain entry to speakeasies, then slapped the cuffs on nearly five thousand people. It was easy to find speakeasies, they discovered: in Baltimore, Izzy wrote, "All I had to do was get on a street car and ask the conductor to let me off at a place where I could get a drink. He pointed one out to me almost the first block."

Speakeasies played a significant role in undermining Prohibition. An anti-Prohibition group, the Crusaders, published maps in 1930 and 1932 of where police raided speakeasies in Washington, DC—all to show how widespread law breaking was among the American public. The 1932 map showed 1,155 raids where alcohol was discovered, including a number at federal offices.

See also PROHIBITION AND TEMPERANCE IN AMERICA; SPEAKEASY (NEW)

Davenport, Walter. "Bartender's Guide to Washington." *Collier's*, February 16, 1929.

Einstein, Izzy. *Prohibition Agent no. 1*. New York: Frederick A. Stokes, 1932.

Gately, Iain. *Drink: A Cultural History of Alcohol.* New York: Gotham, 2008.

Lerner, Michael A. *Dry Manhattan: Prohibition in New York City.* Cambridge, MA: Harvard University Press, 2007.

Peck, Garrett. *Prohibition in Washington, D.C.: How Dry We Weren't.* Charleston, SC: History Press, 2011.

Garrett Peck

speed-aging or rapid-aging is when mechanical, ultrasonic, or chemical methods are employed to reduce the time a spirit must spend maturing in wood. Beverage manufacturers have long attempted to cheat time using rapid-aging techniques. While the Romans first employed rapid-aging techniques in wine, they were not documented in spirits production until the mid-nineteenth century. In 1867, Frenchman M. Cousseilhat used rotatable wooden paddles to agitate the spirit in the barrel like a butter churn. Using a similar concept, the apparatus patented in the United Sates by Josiah Peiffer and Samuel Richards placed barrels on roller slats and agitated them back and forth in a heated room. The inventors claimed this "ripened" whisky within a few weeks. In the late 1800s, several more agitation systems would be created, including an 1879 heat-and-motion device that offered "practical value and utility."

At the turn of the twentieth century, sonic and ultrasonic treatments showed positive effects on wine and would later be tested on spirits. In 1937, inventors used ultrasonic radiation to accelerate esterification, wood extraction, tannin hydrolysis, and aldehyde oxidation. More than a decade later, German researchers reported using sound energy to raise ester content about 120 percent in wine distillate. They also used ultrasound to emphasize ozone in spirits aging.

By the 1960s, rapid aging fell out of fashion and was considered "not very satisfying." Nonetheless, contemporary spirits companies continue to experiment, aging whisky in five-gallon barrels, claiming the smaller size allows more surface contact with wood. They've used bass speakers to push spirits deeper into the wood and brought back agitation systems, ultrasonic energy, chemical reactors, and container pressure, all in an effort to create brown spirits faster.

None of these systems have proved to be entirely successful or satisfying. While many of them can increase extraction (where the spirit pulls compounds out of the wood) and a few can increase oxidation (where the congeners in the spirit break down and their components react with the air in the barrel), they struggle with mimicking the effects of the long, slow evaporation that helps so greatly to give the mature spirit its silky texture.

See also MATURATION.

Peiffer, Josiah. Improvement in Apparatus for Aging Whisky and Other Spirits. US Patent 112,485A, March 7, 1871.

Singelton, V. L. "Aging of Wines and Other Spiritous Products, Acceleration by Physical Treatments." *Hilgardia* 32, no. 7 (May 1962): 77.

"A Whisky-Ageing Apparatus." *Record of the Times*, August 6, 1879.

Fred Minnick

spherification is a technique consisting of shaping liquid into spheres, also known as "direct spherification." By submerging liquid containing sodium alginate into calcium, a thin odorless, colorless, and tasteless membrane forms around the liquid interior, creating an edible sphere that is solid on the outside and liquid on the inside. Originally developed in the 1950s by Unilever, the Dutch-British consumer goods company, as an innovative drug delivery system, the technique was adopted by the culinary world beginning in 2003 with Spain's now-defunct el Bulli restaurant and by the molecular mixology world not long after. Often called "caviar" for their resemblance to roe, the spheres can be created in a variety of sizes and can incorporate solids that become suspended in the liquid, such as mint leaves in a Mojito-flavored sphere. A similar technique known as reverse spherification calls for submerging liquid with a high calcium, acid, or alcohol content into an alginate bath with the same results. The process can also be completed with non-chemical components, such as cold oil.

See also COCKTAIL RENAISSANCE and MIXOLOGY, THE HISTORY OF.

Potter, Jeff. *Cooking for Geeks: Real Science, Great Cooks and Good Food*, 2nd ed. Beijing: O'Reilly, 2016.

Chloe Frechette

spices are one of the canonical five ingredients needed to make punch, along with spirits, citrus juice, sugar, and water. See PUNCH. Of the five, however, they are the only one whose omission does not disqualify the drink from being called punch: without the spirit, it is lemonade; without the citrus, Toddy; without the water, a sour, and without the sugar—without the sugar it is unthinkable. See SOUR and TODDY.

The most important punch spice has always been nutmeg, first attested to in 1653 by the French traveler François De la Boullaye le Gouz (1623–1668?), who found the English in India using it to point up their "Bolleponge," or "Bowl of Punch." It remained the early favorite by a long shot, used in Asia and in Europe, in the Caribbean and North America, and on ships at sea. Nonetheless, mace—nutmeg's protective sibling, as it were—also found early use, as did cloves, cinnamon, rosewater, and even ambergris, alkermes (the vermillion-colored early cordial), and musk.

The eighteenth century saw allspice added to the reserve shelf and tea step to the fore. Punch made with tea is first recorded in 1728 and became common by the 1740s, with green tea originally being preferred. See TEA. By the end of the century, tea had become a staple ingredient and was featured, along with maraschino and curaçao, in Regent's Punch, considered the acme of punch making on both sides of the Atlantic. See REGENT'S PUNCH. By the middle of the nineteenth century, however, tea had rather fallen out of favor as a punch spice, leaving the spice field to various liqueurs and nutmeg. In the twentieth century, even that faded away as punch became an occasional drink at best—except, of course, in tiki bars, which had their own take on things. See TIKI.

The revival of interest in the punch maker's art in the 2010s brought a new perspective to spicing the drink, one derived from the cocktail. Among the things used to provide punch's fifth element were cocktail bitters, vermouths, aperitifs and digestives, herbal liqueurs, herbal teas, spiced syrups, chile peppers, and too many other things to mention. Among all that creativity, though, there were still a good many punch makers who stuck with the almost four-hundred-year-old tradition of using nutmeg.

Wondrich, David. *Punch*. New York: Perigee, 2010.

David Wondrich

spirits are alcoholic beverages created by the distillation of fermented sugar-rich organic material, resulting in a higher concentration of ethanol than is found in the original fermented source. See DISTILLATION; ETHANOL; and FERMENTATION. Spirits typically contain 37–50 percent alcohol by volume, although a few, such as Japanese shochu, are sold at as low as 25 percent, and many, such as the white rum sold in the English-speaking Caribbean, are stronger. See RUM and SHOCHU. While most are unsweetened, others—most notably rum—may harbor additional sweeteners. The English term "spirit" for these beverages was introduced in the mid-seventeenth century, based on the Latin *spiritus*. In modern English, these beverages are often referred to generically as "hard liquor" or simply "liquor." Generic terms in other languages that are frequently encountered include the German *Geist* ("ghost" or "spirit"); the Arabic *arrack* ("dripping" or "distillate"), used throughout Asia and the Middle East; the Spanish and Portuguese *aguardiente/aguardente* ("burning water"); the French *eau-de-vie* ("water of life"), and the Chinese *baijiu* ("white or clear spirit"). See ANDEAN SOUTH AMERICA; ARRACK; BAIJIU; and EAU-DE-VIE.

Spirits are often categorized as white spirits, which are commonly sold un- or minimally aged (such as vodka, most gin, and some tequilas and rums), and brown spirits, typically aged in barrels before bottling (such as whisky and brandy). Not every spirit fits into this dichotomy: baijiu, Peruvian pisco, and Lebanese arrack are often aged in semiporous earthenware containers, which mellow the spirit without coloring it.

The varieties of spirits made around the world are legion. See APPENDIX I: THE WIDE WORLD OF SPIRITS. Practically, though, the vast majority of spirits sold in the world fall under the following broad categories, most of them defined by their base materials: arrack, baijiu, brandy, gin, mezcal, rum, soju, vodka, and the amorphous category that includes liqueurs, cordials, and bitters.

See also AMARO; BITTERS; BRANDY; GIN; LIQUEURS; MEZCAL; SOJU; and VODKA.

David Mahoney

spirit safe is a locked glass-and-metal box through which distillate runs during distillation of whisky. Originally required for tax assessment purposes (in scotch whisky distilleries, the excise office kept the only key to the safe's lock until relatively recently), it is also used by distillers to determine the appropriate time to make a cut. See CUT; DISTILLATION; and WHISKY.

spirits collecting is the practice of systematically seeking out and acquiring bottles of liquor as a hobby. Although some spirits collectors consume their acquisitions, as is overwhelmingly the case in the much larger field of wine collecting, many objectify their bottles. Traditionally collectors gravitated toward brown spirits (whisky, cognac, and rum), with notable exceptions such as miniatures and Chartreuse, but within the last twenty years collecting habits have diversified greatly to encompass virtually all types and brands of spirits. Currently the field of spirits collecting is the largest and most robust that it has ever been, mirroring the rapidly expanding contemporary spirits market. At present, the most sought-after and expensive bottles in spirits collecting are pre-phylloxera cognac (roughly, from before 1860), pre-ban absinthe (before 1914), pre-Prohibition bourbon and rye (before 1920), pre-revolutionary Cuban rum (before 1959), and post–World War II whisky from mothballed scotch malt distilleries, Japan, and Kentucky.

Spirits collecting in its earliest form coincided with the appearance of branded individual bottles and large-scale advertising campaigns, such as those of Martini & Rossi and Johnnie Walker, in the late nineteenth and early twentieth centuries. See MARTINI & ROSSI and JOHNNIE WALKER. But this hobby was not widespread until after the social and political unrest of the two world wars and Prohibition. Primary large-scale popular collecting after World War II was initially of miniature bottles, produced in vast quantities by many brands for marketing and promotional purposes, particularly relating to travel (trains, ships, buses, airplanes, and hotel minibars). Having been successfully indoctrinated, collectors amassed these same brands in full-sized bottles in the 1950s and 1960s. This type of collecting was archaeological and encyclopedic in nature, with the goal of gathering as many examples as possible of a type (blended scotch) or a brand of spirit (Johnnie Walker).

Like art collectors, spirits collectors' first acquisitions are often nationalistic or patriotic: the

Scots and scotch; Americans and American whisky; the French and French bistro drinks such as cognac, vermouths, and various herbal spirits including absinthe, pastis, and Chartreuse; the Italians and grappas or Italian caffè drinks such as brandy, vermouth, amari, and liqueurs. Scotch whisky was collected broadly by type (for example, blends), area (Highland), or vertically by brand (Lagavulin) and cognac broadly across brands and vertically by brand (Hennessy ultimately became the most avidly collected). See HENNESSY. Similarly, collectors then developed emulative international tastes—the American, French, Italians, and Japanese collecting scotch whisky, for example. Bill Pigati, whose family has owned Del Rio, a famous restaurant near Chicago, since the 1920s was an early example of a collector in this classical vein, although he was slightly ahead of his time; he bought blended scotch whisky in the 1940s and early 1950s, which was very popular during the period (his collection was acquired by the Whisky Exchange and has now largely been resold). Beginning in 1960, Valentino Zagatti began to form what would become a three-thousand-bottle collection of Scotch malts (he wrote two books on the subject, and his collection is now housed in Sassenheim, the Netherlands). Stephen Remsberg, now of New Orleans, was inspired to begin his twelve-thousand-bottle collection of rums of the world in 1973 by his regular patronage of the Chicago Trader Vic's and Don the Beachhcomber's.

Other factors, such as historic events, sometimes also define collecting subgroups. Such academic collecting signals that the field has reached a certain maturity and offers brands an opportunity to capitalize on the demand. For example, in an effort to liquidate a glut of Kentucky bourbon during the 1950s, 1960s and 1970s, Jim Beam presented it in ceramic decanters of every imaginable shape, size, and theme. Through creative lighthearted marketing, they successfully sold a lot of their product, rejuvenated the brand, and created a collector's market for novel and occasional decanters as sets that is still active thirty-five years after they launched the last examples. See JIM BEAM. Bell's followed suit and ultimately became more famous and collected with their eponymous packaging for blended scotch whisky.

Today, after several generations of brand reinforcement, the most popular category of collecting is whisky, prompted by the myriad new bottlings from scotch, Kentucky bourbon, and Japanese brands with different barrel finishes, age statements, and barrel strengths (often sold exclusively through duty-free shops). Many collectors of this material view it as an investment, and this speculation has proven accurate. In fact, organized investment instruments for whisky have emerged in the form of the Platinum Whisky Investment Fund in Hong Kong, WhiskyInvestDirect in London, and World Whisky Index in the Netherlands. But the growing large-scale appetite for vintage bottlings in the early twenty-first century signals that buying "dusties" is not merely a resurgent trend but still core to the canon of spirits collecting and appealing to a new generation of collectors.

See also COCKTAIL RENAISSANCE and TIKI.

Bauer, Bryce T. "Inside the Booming Market For Vintage Spirits." *Punch*, January 29, 2016. https://punchdrink. com/articles/inside-the-vintage-liquor-bottles-spirits-market/ (accessed April 5, 2021).

Marshall, Wyatt. "Inside the Dusty World of Vintage Spirits Collectors." *Munchies* (*Vice blog*), December 29, 2016. https://www.vice.com/en/article/vvxq84/inside-the-dusty-world-of-vintage-spirit-collectors (accessed April 5, 2021).

Newton, Mark. "Politics, Mavericks and War: Scotch Advertising in the Early 20th Century." *Whisky Magazine*, July 2016, 23–25.

Pariseau, Leslie. "Cocktails from Another Era at 500 Euros a Pop." *Punch*, November 5, 2013. https://punchdrink.com/articles/cocktails-from-another-era-at-500-euros-a-pop/ (accessed April 5, 2021).

Ross, Christopher. "What Would You Pay for a True Taste of Cocktail History?" *Punch*, December 9, 2016. https://punchdrink.com/articles/taste-of-history-vintage-cocktail-liquor/ (accessed April 5, 2021).

Winding, Elizabeth. "Spirited Away." *Metropolitan*, October 2014, 44–47.

Edgar Harden

spirits in the military. The global spread of distilled spirits in the sixteenth and seventeenth centuries inaugurated a new phase in the long and close relationship between alcoholic beverages and the world's armed forces. There has been a connection between strong drink and the military since antiquity. Going back to the days before Christ, Roman soldiers drank a sour, vinegar-based wine known as *acetum* (when diluted with water it was known as *posca*) and were also known to drink ordinary wine as well as beer. In the days of the ancient Greeks, peace negotiations at the conclusion of war were always accompanied by wine. In fact, as Eric Felten writes, "The plural of the Greek word for 'libation,' *spondai*, is the word for treaty." Historically, in both the military and everyday life, beer or wine was a preferred option over a suspect water supply; it was simply safer to drink. Furthermore, until the nineteenth century recruiting efforts were accompanied in many armies and navies by free-flowing alcohol. (In 1775, for example, Philadelphia's Tun Tavern served as the first recruiting station for America's first marines.) This practice was not only open to abuse; it practically demanded it.

Spirits being both much more easily transportable and almost immune to spoilage, by the seventeenth century they began to supplant or entirely replace fermented beverages in many militaries. Consider, as one example among a great many, the experience of the British Royal Navy. Spirits began appearing in place of its ration of beer (one five-quart "beer gallon" per person per day, at mealtimes) in the mid-1600s. By 1732, as Ian Williams notes, navy regulations specified that in the absence of the beer, which went bad distressingly fast, "a pint of wine or half a pint of 'brandy, rum or arrack' would suffice." The type of spirit depended on what was available in the nearby ports. In 1740, as commander of the Royal Navy's West Indies Station, Admiral Edward Vernon "ordered the daily half a pint of rum diluted with a quart of water" and, when appropriate, served with "extra lime juice and sugar that it be made more palatable" to the sailors. Thus began the tradition of "grog," that name reportedly coming from Vernon's habit of wearing a coat of "grogram" cloth. Vernon's order also specified that the ration "be mixed in a scuttled butt" (a repurposed barrel half) and dispensed openly, so the men could ensure they were "not defrauded of their full allowance of rum." For those who found a four-to-one mix of water and rum somewhat lacking, Vernon suggested that "those that are good husbandmen" supplement it with purchased lime juice and sugar, effectively turning it into punch. The addition of lime or lemon juice also carried health benefits, as the vitamin C in it was a good deterrent to scurvy, and indeed by Nelson's time it was official policy to

issue the rum in the form of punch. See PUNCH and RUM, NAVY.

The Royal Navy is not the only service with its characteristic drinks (besides punch, there were the Pink Gin and the Gimlet). See GIMLET and PINK GIN. There are drinks commemorating particular army units, notably the Sixty-Ninth Regiment Punch and the National Guard Seventh Regiment Punch (both American), the British 32nd Regiment Punch and Bengal Lancers' Punch, the Shanghai Cossack Punch, the coffee-and-cognac Mazagran, popular among the early French forces in Algeria, and the (American) Chatham Artillery Punch. See CHATHAM ARTILLERY PUNCH. There are drinks to honor the various branches of the military, such as the Army Cocktail, Army and Navy Cocktail, the Fortitudine Punch, and the Leatherneck Cocktail (US Marine Corps), and several versions of Navy Grog. All of these are American, but perhaps the most dedicated inventors of military drinks were members the old Imperial German Army. Not only did many of the kaiser's regiments have their own punch recipes, but according to a 1913 compendium, each one had its own mixed shot—all 470 of them.

The Americans, however, are the champions at naming drinks for their military leaders, as will be attested by General Harrison's Eggnog, General Burnside's Favorite, the Old Hickory (named for General Andrew Jackson), the CINCPAC Special (named for Admiral Chester Nimitz, the commander in chief of the Pacific forces during World War II), the Fanciuli Cocktail (named for the director of the marine band in the 1890s), Admiral Schley Punch, and Ernest Hemingway's "Montgomery Martini," made with a 15:1 ratio of gin to vermouth, so named because of Hemingway's belief that British field marshal Bernard Law Montgomery was so cautious he required a 15-to-1 troop advantage before committing them to battle. There are also drinks named for particular weapons, such as the B-52 (named for the American bomber), the Hand Grenade, the Depth Bomb and Depth Charge, the 75 or French 75 (named for the French 75 mm artillery piece), and the Artillery Cocktail.

There are even drinks commemorating particular military campaigns or events, notably the Guadalcanal Cocktail, the Remember the Maine (honoring the destruction of the USS *Maine* in Havana Harbor, which led to the Spanish-American

War), the Cuba Libre (celebrating Cuba's independence from Spain), and the Daiquiri (US forces landed at Daiquiri Beach, Cuba, during the Spanish-American War). Fittingly, the Daiquiri is said to have made its US debut at the Army-Navy Club in Washington, DC, circa 1909.

One should also consider the various drinks consumed by men at war, such as the Soldier's Camping Punch (from the American Civil War), the British military staple "Gunfire" (hot tea laced with rum, dating back to the nineteenth century), the generic term "jungle juice" (applying to any resourceful alcoholic concoction), "torpedo juice" (a drink made from the alcohol found in a torpedo), and the notion that men about to engage in combat might obtain "Dutch courage" from a swig of spirit. When the Italian army went to war in North Africa in 1940, its officers brought with them a stupendous cache of *aperitivi* and *digestivi*, not so much for carousing as to make sure that their rations would sit properly. Lastly, militaries around the world offer ceremonial drinks to celebrate anniversaries, feast days, promotions (sometimes known as "wet downs"), a crewmember's first crossing of the equator (whereby he or she matures from a "pollywog" to a "shellback"), and other events.

There have been varying opinions on alcohol's role in the military. George Washington reasoned that "the benefits arising from the moderate use of strong Liquor have been experienced in All Armies, and are not to be disputed." Echoing that sentiment, Admiral Henry K. Hewitt, the US naval commander in North African waters, argued that sailors be allowed to drink beer while at sea, offering that "nothing would be so good for sailors' morale in wartime as beer." However, in 1914, US navy secretary Josephus Daniels issued General Order no. 99, which decreed that "the use or introduction for drinking purposes of alcoholic liquors on board any naval vessel or within any navy yard or station is strictly prohibited." Similarly, the British Royal Navy served its final daily "grog" ration on July 31, 1970, a day that became known as "Black Tot Day." In general, it's safe to say that, with one or two possible exceptions, today's armed services—at least in the major industrialized countries—are the soberest they have ever been.

Arbuckle, Graeme. *Customs and Traditions of the Canadian Navy*. Halifax: Nimbus, 1984).

Astor, Gerald. *Semper Fi in the Sky: The Marine Air Battles of World War II*. New York: Presidio, 2005.
Beveridge, N. E. [Harold R. Peterson]. *Cups of Valor*. Harrisburg, PA: Stackpole, 1968.
Bowlen und Pünsche zum Manöver- und Feldgebrauch der deutschen Armee. Leipzig: Weber, [1900].
Bronner, Simon J. *Crossing the Line: Violence, Play, and Drama in Naval Equator Traditions*. Amsterdam: Amsterdam University Press, 2006.
Felten, Eric. *How's Your Drink?* Chicago: Surry, 2007.
Hemingway, Ernest. *Across the River and into the Trees*. New York: Charles Scribner's Sons, 1950.
Leybold, John, and Hans Schönfeld. *Lexicon der getränke*. Cologne: Verlag von Leybold & Schönfeld, 1913.
Ranft, B. McL., ed. *The Vernon Papers*. London: Navy Records Society, 1958.
Williams, Ian. *Rum: A Social and Sociable History of the Real Spirit of 1776*. New York: Nation, 2005.

Philip Greene

spirits measure is a government-regulated liquid measure used in retailing spirits. At one point in the early twentieth century, most European countries subscribed to some version of this system, whereby every account that retailed spirits by the drink or in bulk had to use a set of approved measures, which would be periodically inspected and stamped to indicate that they had not been altered.

Most countries followed the French model with their measures, using a graduated set of handled pewter cylinders that were broadly similar in design, although countries differed in the sizes employed (France, for example, used the sequence 10 ml–20 ml–50 ml–100 ml–200 ml–500 ml–1 liter, while Italy replaced the 10-, 20-, and 200-ml measures with 12.5-, 25-, and 250-ml ones). Imperial Russia tended to favor the squat, copper *charka* (in Russian measures), and the United Kingdom used a dizzying variety of different designs, some of them very quaint, in quarter gills, half gills, gills, and various divisions of the pint, the quart, and the gallon.

Today, with all but the smallest quantities of spirits sold in sealed bottles, most of these systems have fallen by the wayside, although the United Kingdom still regulates its measures. Even these have been reduced to simple stainless steel cylinders (metric of course), with the sole remaining eccentricity being the fact that the basic measure is 25 ml in England, Wales, and Northern Ireland and 35 ml in Scotland.

See EXCISE TAXES AND DISTILLATION and JIGGER.

Johnstone, William D. *For Good Measure: A Complete Compendium of International Weights and Measures.* New York: Harper Collins, 1977.

David Wondrich

spirits trade, history of, covers a remarkably diverse, intricate business that is over a millennium old, involves all seven continents (yes, spirits are both distilled and sold in Antarctica), and supplies probably half the ethanol the world consumes every year. Its participants range from the grandmother who runs a batch of palm wine through her oil-drum still every couple of weeks and sells the results to her neighbors, provided they supply their own bottles, to the publicly held corporation with distilleries in

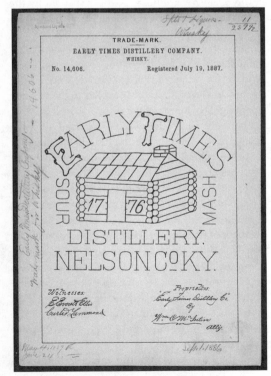

A major step in the evolution of the spirits trade was the introduction of brands with protectable trademarks, such as this 1887 American one for Early Times whisky. Library of Congress.

twelve countries, most of them with visitors' centers and all of them with special bottlings for duty-free.

To chart the trade's history, much of which has not been written, and lay out its current structure would require a volume larger than this one; here, the best we can do is provide a rough outline of its development and a back-of-the-envelope sketch of its organization. This must necessarily be an incomplete view: although in many countries the spirits trade is among the most highly taxed and regulated of businesses, in others it is completely unregulated or run mostly off the books, making it very difficult to diagram. See MOONSHINE.

Structurally, the spirits trade can be divided into three tiers, each of which operates in its own way and yet is also connected to the other two: (1) distillers who make a traditional product and retail it locally or sell it in bulk; (2) négociants or NDPs (non-distiller producers), who do not distill themselves but rather take spirits made by others, prepare them for market (this can include processes such as aging, rectifying, flavoring, or blending), and bottle them for sale under their own names or resell them to other NDPs; and (3) distillers who prepare their own spirits for market, bottle them, and sell them nationally or internationally under their own brands (thus effectively combining the other two tiers).

These tiers are historical, in that the first came before the second and the second before the third. But they are also contemporaneous, as each subsequent stage did not erase the one that preceded it: despite the prevalence of global brands such as Absolut vodka, Johnnie Walker whisky, and the like, the world still holds untold thousands of little distilleries that ferment the produce of their region, distill it, and sell the spirit to their neighbors just as distillers were doing a thousand years ago.

Nor are the tiers exclusive: in this complicated industry, there are many brands that both buy spirit and distill their own, thus bridging tiers two and three (this is the model followed by many cognac and scotch whisky producers). See COGNAC and WHISKY, SCOTCH. Others both sell bulk spirit and bottle and market their own brands, a model common in the rum industry (tiers one and three). It also must be noted that these tiers are not markers of quality, at least not from the consumer's point of view: thanks to tier-two companies such as Del Maguey, which bottles and provides international distribution for mezcals sourced from village distillers, tier-one products can share the same top shelf as tier-three ones. See DEL MAGUEY MEZCAL.

Origin of the Trade

Until the early modern period, we have only the slenderest evidence with which to chart the early progress of the spirits trade, and any history must be a tentative one. That said, the earliest traces we have of it are from the period between 150 BCE and 250 CE, from Gandhara and Taxila in what is now Pakistan and Afghanistan. There, archaeologists have uncovered the remains of several buildings where back-room distilleries, with multiple clay pot stills and numerous condenser/storage jars, are joined to front-room taverns, with stacks of drinking cups. Both cups and condensers are stamped with seals, suggesting some sort of excise system and thus a well-established and lucrative trade. By the 800s CE, in some parts of Asia first-tier producers such as these appear to have already gone into commerce with (second-tier) traders and merchants such as the ones who were shipping palm spirit in large "Martaban" jars from ports in Siam and Burma to destinations around the Andaman Sea and Bay of Bengal.

By the 1200s, the spirits trade in Asia seems to have developed into a complex system of overlapping networks, with sugar-cane arrack being traded all over northern India, grape spirit moving east along the Silk Road from Central Asia to China, and palm arrack still being traded around the Bay of Bengal, now along with other distillates. By the 1400s, we see not only rice spirit being shipped from ports in southern China to the Philippines and Java but Chinese distillers settling in both places and manufacturing the spirit locally. See ARRACK, BATAVIA; and BAIJIU. Unfortunately, in the absence of a detailed history of distillation and spirits in Asia, we have frustratingly little detail on all this activity.

Meanwhile, in western Europe, distillation had moved out of the realms of alchemy and speculative medicine and into the marketplace. Michele Savonarola, whose thorough 1440s survey of the state of distillation in Italy is the earliest truly comprehensive treatment of the subject, found that "aqua ardente" was in such widespread use as to be sold "in the piazzas to the poor and wretched." At the same time, Venetian merchants were exporting a rather higher grade of spirit to the royal courts of England and Burgundy. See ROSOLIO.

At the end of the 1400s, of course, heavily armed European merchant-explorers reached both the Americas and India, upending the trade networks in both hemispheres (among many other things). By the 1510s, the Portuguese were shipping palm arrack back to Lisbon from Goa. At the same time, the Spanish were shipping wine and brandy to their new colonies in the Americas. The rest of the century saw these tenuous threads develop into a new, global trade network uniting Europe, Asia, Africa, and the Americas, with way stations at many of the islands in between.

The 1500s also saw a global boom in distilling, from pisco in the Spanish Viceroyalty of Peru and agave spirits in Mexico, to whisky in Scotland and Ireland, vodka in Russia and the Baltic, brandy in France, genever in Holland, and korn in Germany. See PISCO. Although it is almost entirely undocumented, it also appears that cane spirits began to be distilled first in Brazil and then in Mexico and in the Spanish Caribbean, possibly sparked by the Portuguese experience in Bengal, where sugar-cane arrack was in widespread use. See RUM.

With the spectacular growth in transatlantic traffic that marked the beginning of the seventeenth century, the center of the spirits trade shifted from the Indian Ocean / South China Sea to the Atlantic (marking the triumph of the wooden barrel over the earthenware jar as the world's preferred shipping container for spirits). See BARREL. If the previous century saw breakthroughs in tier-one distilling, the new one was the age of the trader. Led by the Dutch, European merchants learned to mature, blend, and rectify spirits and to use them to fortify wine so that it would survive the long ocean voyages that were the mark of the new age. Dutch traders, it should be noted, also did much to encourage distillation, to the point that they supplied their trading partners in places such as Java, northeastern Brazil, and the Loire region of France with stills and instruction in their use. In 1631 alone, Nantes, the base of the Loire brandy trade, imported 235 copper stills from the Netherlands.

At the same time, governments began to try to control the trade: to channel it, encourage convenient branches, and truncate inconvenient ones. We can see the effect in the American rum trade, a byproduct of the metastasizing American sugar industry, which was swallowing human lives by the hundreds of thousands and making a few families unprecedentedly wealthy. Beginning in the 1650s, the English colony of Barbados began exporting the spirit, first to other English colonies in North America and then, by the end of the century, to the home country and other parts of Europe. In that trade, it was soon joined by Jamaica and England's other Caribbean colonies. (Barbados, too, might have had Dutch instruction in distilling.) See TRIANGLE TRADE.

On the other hand, Spanish, Portuguese, and French America also made enormous quantities of sugar yet exported no rum at all, at least legally. In all three empires, the spirits trade was regulated to benefit European brandy producers, and distillation in their American colonies was banned or tightly restricted. With enforcement of these rules being spotty at best, they did little to stop domestic spirits trades from arising in colonies such as Brazil, Martinique, and Mexico (which had extensive industries making not only rum but also agave, palm, and maize spirits). While ineffective at preventing much of the colonial population from drinking the cheap domestic spirits, the prohibitions did ensure that the trade would remain at a first-tier level—that it would be denied the capital, expertise, and markets needed to compete internationally. Indeed, in the mid-1600s, when Brazilian distillers began illegally shipping their rum to West Africa, their discerning would-be customers ranked it at the very bottom of the list of available spirits. See CACHAÇA.

In the eighteenth century, we see the groundwork laid for third-tier production—for distillers to be in control of their own marketing and distribution and turn production into branding. At first, this took the form of closer integration between distillers and merchants, whether it was James Delamain (1738–1800), the pioneering Dublin-born cognac merchant, setting up his own distilling operation with which to supplement the brandy he purchased or the move by the Wedderburn family, who distilled a very high grade of rum at their numerous Jamaica estates, into the shipping business. See COGNAC and RUM, JAMAICAN.

There were still three important conditions lacking for tier-three production: (1) a way of building consumer demand targeted for the product of one distiller, rather than for a category of spirit, the product of a region, or from one merchant; (2) a

way of reliably getting the product from the distillery to the consumer without passing through the blender's vats; and (3) a way of brushing off the free riders that any success in building a brand would inevitably attract, as George Smith's Glenlivet whisky and Benjamin Hodges's Old Tom gin did in the 1820s. See GLENLIVET and OLD TOM GIN.

The first problem, that of publicity, was solved by the growth in literacy that came with industrialization the nineteenth century and the subsequent rise in journalism and advertising, while late-century developments in bottling technology and the move to factory bottling and tamper-resistant packaging solved the second. See BOTTLES, LABELING, AND PACKAGING. By mid-century, distillers were already supplying retailers, who bought spirits by the barrel and bottled them for the consumer, with branded labels; the vulnerabilities of that system are, and were, obvious. Finally, the mid-century adoption of trademark laws by the major industrialized countries helped would-be brand builders to solve, or at least mitigate, the problem of imitators, although in the early years it often took a great deal of legal wrangling.

By the end of the nineteenth century, not only were spirits booming—"distillation follows industrialization," as the saying has it (in France, e.g., per capita spirits consumption tripled between 1830 and 1900)—but third-tier companies were appearing worldwide, from Scotland's pioneering whisky conglomerate, Distillers Company Ltd., formed in 1877, to the Bacardi company, formed in 1862 after Spain lifted its prohibition on colonial distilling, to the 1901 BAM (Batavia Arrack Maatschappij), which combined the highly regarded KWT (Khow Wan Tjiang) and OGL (Ong Goan Liong) Indonesian arrack distilleries under one Amsterdam-based corporate ownership. See ARRACK, BATAVIA; BACARDI; and DISTILLERS COMPANY LTD (DCL). Although such companies enjoyed the advantages of controlling their own production and eliminating the markups between producer and merchant, as well as certain marketing advantages attendant on the ability to point to a distillery where their product was made, they did not replace tier-one or tier-two companies, which learned to work around the new producers.

The twentieth century brought another wrinkle in the form of state ownership, where a national government becomes the producer, brand owner, and distributor. Such spirits were generally kept for domestic use, but not always, and indeed such iconic brands as Havana Club rum, Stolichnaya vodka, Absolut vodka, and Kweichow Moutai are, or were, entirely or in part state-owned. See KWEICHOW MOUTAI and STOLICHNAYA. The century also saw a number of companies follow DCL's lead and amass large portfolios of disparate brands, particularly in the postwar years, when companies such as the Canadian Seagram's organization realized that developed brands could be bought and sold just like barrels of whisky, facilities and all, and that there was an art to blending a portfolio just like there was to blending a spirit. See SEAGRAM COMPANY LTD.

This century has seen the popularity of micro-distilleries explode, first in the United States and now in places like Ireland, Italy, and England. While many of these upstarts produce what they sell, many others buy spirits from large bulk producers, like Midwest Grain Products of Indiana (MGP) in Lawrenceburg, Indiana, and Distilled Resources, Inc. in Rigby, Idaho—making them second-tier producers masquerading as first-tier ones.

Meanwhile, most modern multinational spirits companies, such as the British Diageo, the French Pernod Ricard, the Japanese-American Beam Suntory, and the Italian Gruppo Campari, maintain diversified collections of brands large and small, including everything from recently purchased tier-one micro-distillers to iconic legacy brands that are produced on a massive scale. The small brands give credibility to the large ones, and the large ones guarantee market access to the small. See CAMPARI; DIAGEO; JIM BEAM; and PERNOD-RICARD. All the while, there are still untold thousands of small distilleries operating—legally or otherwise—around the world, where the owner gets up every morning to check the fermentation, fire up the still, or fill a neighbor's water bottle with new-make spirit. It must be borne in mind that the vast majority of these are essentially invisible to the global trade, which is largely confined to the spirits categories that made up the Atlantic trade in the nineteenth century—brandy, rum, gin, and whisky. Yet the trade is not immutable: the twentieth century saw vodka and tequila globalized, and it is entirely possible that there will be further additions. At present, baijiu is standing in the wings, and it is not impossible that we will see a return of palm spirits to international trade.

Cullen, L. M. *The Brandy Trade under the Ancien Régime.* Cambridge: Cambridge University Press, 1998.

Francis, A. D. *The Wine Trade.* London: A. & C. Black, 1972.

Haworth, Alan, and Ronald Simpson, eds. *Moonshine Markets.* New York: Brunner-Routledge, 2004.

Kops, Henriette de Bruyn. *A Spirited Exchange: The Wine and Brandy Trade between France and the Dutch Republic in Its Atlantic Framework, 1600–1650.* Leiden: E. J. Brill, 2007.

Nourrisson, Didier. *Le buveur du XIXe siècle.* Paris: Albin Michel, 1990.

Royal Commission on Whiskey and Other Potable Spirits. *Interim Report.* London: HM Stationery Office, 1908.

Savonarola, Michele. *I trattati in volgare della peste e dell' acqua ardente.* Edited by Luigi Belloni. Rome: Società Italiana di Medicina Interna, 1953.

Weir, R. B. *The History of the Distillers Company, 1877–1939.* Oxford: Clarendon, 1995.

David Wondrich

spirits writing is the art of writing about spirits—the potable sort, not the ghostly sort, though the very fact that the two share a name points to a similarity: both are vaporous substances that provoke a powerful mix of awe, intrigue, admiration, and fear, inspiring stories, legends, and endless study. But where writing on ghosts tends to excel in the fantastical realm, writing on potable spirits provides a window into our everyday existence. Over time, spirits writing has tracked our growth as civilized (and not-so-civilized) beings, our choices and attitudes shaped by geography, technology, and social structures.

Distillation Manuals

Manual writing may seem a far cry from what we term "spirits writing" today, but early writings provide a window into the power that distillation offered mankind. Distillation was considered alchemy, a wondrous, powerful magic that could free souls, and might it was hoped, lead to immortality. "We call it *aqua vitae*," Arnald of Villanova wrote in the thirteenth century, "and this name is remarkably suitable, since it is really a water of immortality. It prolongs life, clears away ill-humors, revives the heart, and maintains youth." John of Rupescissa, author of *Liber de consideratione quintae essentiae* (ca. 1350), considered alcohol a quasi-divine *quinta essentia*—a "fifth substance" beyond the canonical four (earth, water, air, and fire). Even two hundred years later, the Italian author Giambattista della Porta proposed that distillers were magicians aligned with nature; in *De distillationibus*, he provides drawings of stills shaped like long-necked birds, turtles, bears, and a seven-headed bird, each design reflecting the nature of the thing being distilled.

A new phase of spirits writing came in the 1500s, with the rise of the printing press: the ease of printing, and simultaneous rise in literacy rates, opened the door to the how-to manual, a genre especially suited to distillation. Spirits writing took on a more practical tone as it moved from magic toward medicine. One of the earliest known texts of this sort, *Liber de arte distillandi* by the German surgeon Hieronymus Brunschwig, was terrifically popular, going through sixteen editions between 1500 and 1568. While the term of the day, "medicinal waters," suggests that spirits were seen as a little less otherworldly, Brunschwig's recipes remained near magical in their purported powers, curing maladies ranging from malaria to marital issues.

Still, the arcane nature and danger of distillation kept the process largely to doctors and monks. It would take another two hundred years to fully put control right into the hands of the reader, as Ambrose Cooper did in *The Complete Distiller* (1757). By that time, distillates were already moving from the sickbed to the dining table. "Liquors are among the not-lesser amenities of life, and of dining," François Massialot had written nearly fifty years earlier in his *Nouvelle instruction pour les confitures, les liqueurs et les fruits*; "there are refreshments for spring and summer, and others to strengthen and give warmth in winter." The new books freed the process of their manufacture from the alchemical obfuscation with which it had been veiled. Yet the accessibility that characterized the distillers' manuals published from the late 1600s to the early 1800s would eventually fall victim to the increasing professionalization of the practical arts that followed the Industrial Revolution. Indeed, in 1708 Massialot himself had already warned that to treat of distilled spirits required "particular knowledge of which not everyone is capable," which required an arcane specialized vocabulary. By the late nineteenth century, distillers'

manuals had become technical documents, essentially incomprehensible to the layperson. See DISTILLATION, HISTORY.

Writing for the Consumer

Meanwhile, as people on both sides of the Atlantic became more affluent and alcohol became more widely available, writers began analyzing and explaining the available spirits with an eye to demystifying them for the consumer. The *Almanach des gourmands*, published annually between 1803 and 1812 by the pioneering Parisian culinary writer Alexandre Grimod de la Reynière (1758–1837), contained among its numerous and varied articles on matters of the table items dissecting things such as curaçao, vermouth, and punch for the consumer.

It would, however, be an Irish excise officer who published the first book to survey the vast and generally unexplored world of spirits. *Essay on the Inventions and Customs of Ancient and Modern Nations in the Use of Wine and Other Liquors*, published in 1824 by Samuel Morewood (1772–1851), may have also covered fermented beverages, but it placed a special emphasis on distilled drinks, and indeed included the first comprehensive history of the distillation of alcohol. Global in its scope, the book has some sections that have not been entirely superseded today. Such survey books would go on to be a staple of the genre, with examples such as the English writers James Mew and John Ashton's 1892 *Drinks of the World* and the 1900 *La distillerie dans le monde entier* (issued in conjunction with the Paris Universal Exposition that year) providing prominent early examples. Some surveys were more specialized: in the 1880s, Alfred Barnard, a London Journalist, toured the whisky distilleries of Great Britain and recorded his impressions in a fascinating look at Victorian distilling. See BARNARD, ALFRED.

The nineteenth century also saw the birth of another important genre of drink books, the bartender's guide. See MIXOGRAPHY. By the end of the century, the more sophisticated examples of the genre, such as William Schmidt's *The Flowing Bowl* (1892), contained sections on history, poetry, and measured words on the place of alcohol in a balanced diet—all efforts to show alcohol in a sophisticated light during a time it was increasingly coming under attack. See SCHMIDT, WILLIAM.

The Praises of Rum

The temperance movement and Prohibition may have been the best things that ever happened to drinks writing. The fight for the right to drink only encouraged more people to write about alcohol, in any forum possible, and with emotion. Newspapers were launched to rail against alcohol, like *The Lily* in 1849, in which founder Amelia Bloomer raged against "the great evil of intemperance . . . the cause of so much misery and taxation." Such sermonizing only encouraged drink writers to sing alcohol's praises more artfully, and many took to periodicals to voice their support. "The Praises of Rum," from an 1829 issue of *The Ariel*, a literary gazette out of Philadelphia, begins, "This subject has been treated by an able pen in verse, but so much has lately been said against rum, and the temperance societies are pulling the spigots out of all the barrels which contain this nourishing drink, that we have concluded to take up the pen in its favor, confident of conquering all its opponents. . . . No sooner does this cordial thrill though the blood, than poverty loses its horrors. . . . Rum is a truly republican liquor, for, like death, it is a universal leveler. It brings the judge and the charcoal merchant together in the same cellar."

Although spirits writing in America went into remission during Prohibition, it didn't disappear in the rest of the world. Indeed, the 1920s saw a new genre introduced, the "what to drink" book. The English literary critic George Saintsbury's 1920 *Notes on a Cellar Book* devoted a key three chapters to spirits, running through the categories and describing favorite bottles in each. Ten years later *Whisky*, by "Aeneas MacDonald" (the Scottish journalist George Malcolm Thomson), provided the drinker with a concise education in that seductive spirit, just as Robert Delamain's 1935 *Histoire du cognac* did for that (equally seductive) one. See MACDONALD, AENEAS; and SAINTSBURY, GEORGE EDWARD BATEMAN.

In the United States, the disaster that was Prohibition paradoxically opened the door to writing about drinking in general in newspapers and magazines and upscale literature alike, with authors capitalizing on the danger, intrigue, and glamour of the Jazz Age speakeasy. While F. Scott Fitzgerald was chronicling the lifestyle of bootleggers and the people who loved them in *The Great Gatsby*, Harold Ross, the editor of the *New Yorker*, introduced a nightlife column dedicated in order to attract readers: When Nights Are Bold, launched on April 25, 1925, would become Tables for Two a few months later, a column still in existence today, if less boozy. Over at the *New York Press*, the *New York American*, and later the *Evening Post*, Maury H. B. Paul gained fame as Cholly Knickerbocker, "America's most famous and highly paid ($50,000 a year) Society columnist," according to *Life*.

Despite the perceived sophistication of those who drank throughout Prohibition, the truth is that high-quality spirits were hard to come by. After Repeal, however, writers raced to re-educate readers, among them Alma Whitaker, a reporter for the *Los Angeles Times* who authored *Bacchus Behave! The Lost Art of Polite Drinking* in 1933. "Having been involved for so long with synthetic gin, flapper whiskey, and a varied assortment of friendship-testing home brews, our palates and our manners can scarcely be expected to cope successfully with the niceties of the superior nectars that await our fancy," she opined. "If we are as fussy and fastidious about the quality, quantity and service of our liquor and about the conduct of our guests as we are about the food, the table service and the accouterments of our parties, all will be well."

Knowing your drinks became a marker of worldliness, and popular titles reflected this, whether it was in references penned by famous European barmen or in the pages of *Esquire* magazine, whose iconic Potables column ran from 1933 through World War II. The *New York Sun* had a daily column on drinks run by the estimable G. Selmer Fougner, who fielded readers' queries on the bottles they had or wished to have. See FOUGNER, G. SELMER.

By the end of the 1940s, the idea that a man of the world should know his scotch from his rye and his vodka from his white rum was a settled principle of magazine editing, particularly since bon vivants make ripe targets for advertising. After *Playboy* hired a jet-setting chef named Thomas Mario in 1954 to pen a regular column on wines, spirits, and mixed drinks, publisher Hugh Hefner explained that it provided an opportunity "to include lush, elegant, romantic illustrations . . . depicting the urban male wining and dining alone with a beautiful girl." *Esquire*, *Gentlemen's Quarterly*, and a host of other men's magazines all devoted pages to drink as well, mostly targeting the upwardly mobile, debonair modern man. But women were targeted as well, although more for cocktails—a part of entertaining—than for spirits, but spirits were not entirely ignored in such general-audience magazines as *Gourmet* and *Vanity Fair*, and even in straight women's magazines such as *Cosmopolitan* and *Redbook*.

Yet the 1960s made good-life accessories such as Scotch on the Rocks in the paneled basement or the cart of fine French brandies and eaux-de-vie that the maître d' wheels around after dinner seem stuffy and unfashionable, and even the best spirits writers, such as John Doxat and Cyril Ray in Britain, Henry Crowgey in the United States, and Illa Andreae in Germany (1902–1992; her 1973 *Alle schnäpse dieser welt*, billed as "the international book of liquid pleasures," is an essential guide to the wide and complex field of central European spirits), were to some degree voices crying in the wilderness. See CROWGEY, HENRY GUNDRY; and RAY, CYRIL. Spirits writers were Ella Fitzgeralds in a Janis Joplin world.

The Internet Age

Drinks began earning writers' serious attention once again in the 1990s, spurred to a large extent by the sudden rise to popularity of single-malt scotch whiskies in the previous decade and the return to a sense of craft in mixing drinks, spearheaded by Dale DeGroff at New York's newly reopened Rainbow Room in 1987. The whiskies came in a vast profusion and required a certain expertise to navigate, while DeGroff's drinks were a wake-up call for a generation of drinkers used to canned juices and sour mix, and they inspired a look back at vintage cocktail books and other vintage spirits. These developments exposed the lack of information available on what was already in the market, which writers stepped in to fill.

So did new voices. F. Paul Pacult, who'd been covering California wines in the 1980s, made an important move with his new quarterly *Spirit Journal*. Rather than accept advertising or fees for reviewing products, Pacult's subscription-only newsletter inspired a generation of drinkers to look beyond the ads and labels and actually taste what was in the bottle. Other writers began to take a single-subject approach, drilling down on the history and mechanics of particular spirit to celebrate its complexities and place in time and space. Now, no subject was too esoteric: when Barnaby Conrad III published *Absinthe: History in a Bottle*, in 1988, the spirit was outlawed in the United States, and there was but one

domestic stand-in, New Orleans's Herbsaint. That would change. Other authorities such as Michael Jackson (whisky), Ed Hamilton (rum), and Dave Broom (gin) penned volumes that quickly became classic references. The *Malt Advocate* (later the *Whisky Advocate*) in the United States and *Whisky* magazine in Britain provided specialist forums for those spirits. See HANSELL, JOHN; and PACULT, F. PAUL.

The lifestyle magazines began to revamp their drinks columns, both in print and, eventually, online, and new topics—agave spirits, gin, American whiskies—edged into the spotlight. The internet speeded everything up, providing a way for drinks enthusiasts to share their knowledge, whether by posting their musings or by providing gathering places for the cognoscenti to exchange information and tips. Early sites such as Ted Haigh's drcocktail.com and cocktaildb.com and Robert Hess's Drinkboy.com, launched in 1998, were essential for drawing together people dedicated to the craft of the cocktail. Much of the discussion on these sites centered on the spirits necessary for mixing the classic cocktails being bandied about. And, thanks to the ease of searching databases around the world and back in time via digitized texts, spirits archaeologists not only could now work faster and more thoroughly than ever previously imagined but also now had the ability to check what brands are saying now against what they used to say fifty or a hundred years ago.

There are downsides to the plethora of spirits writing the internet introduced. As spirits writers with real research chops such as Jared Brown and Anistatia Miller and François Monti have found, early texts weren't always accurate or honest, and understanding them requires a thorough knowledge of the language, materials, and techniques used at the time; yesteryear's gin is not today's Tanqueray. See MILLER, ANISTATIA, AND BROWN, JARED.

Nonetheless, the 2010s proved to be a golden age of spirits writing, as a plethora of new, skilled writers addressed topics that had previously only received the most basic treatment. Chantal Martineau and Emma Jantzen wrote in depth about agave spirits, as did Heather Greene, Fred Minnick, and Davin De Kergommeaux about whisky, Derek Sandhaus about baijiu, and Kara Newman about, well, everything. Unfortunately, for every solidly researched, interesting, stylishly written piece on a spirit, there remain at least a dozen others with titles such as "Four New Rums to Pour over Your Pancakes" or other such clickbait. But in the end, there's plenty of good reading, from people who have a respect for drinks and the people who drink them and an interest in the place they hold in the world.

Andreae, Illa. *Alle schnäpse dieser welt*. Zurich: Transitbooks AG, 1973.

Forbes, R. J. *Short History of the Art of Distillation*. Leiden: E. J. Brill, 1948.

Massialot, François. *Nouvelle instruction pour les confitures, les liqueurs, et les fruits*. Paris: 1708.

Nouraisson, Didier. *Le buveur du XIXe siècle*. Paris: Albin Michel, 1990.

Pokhlebkin, Vilyam V. *A History of Vodka*. Translated by Renfrey Clarke. London: Verso, 1992.

Tara Q. Thomas and David Wondrich

spiritus frumenti is apothecary's Latin for "spirit of grain." In nineteenth-century America, it was used in dispensary books to indicate whisky. It would have remained an obscure term were it not for Prohibition, when the only way to get whisky legally was by prescription. Spiritus frumenti was the term physicians used when writing their prescriptions, and—to make sure there was no error in the process—several of the available brands of medicinal whisky incorporated it into their labeling.

David Wondrich

starka is a barrel-aged vodka, typically double-distilled from a rye mash in column stills, with roots dating back to the fifteenth century in eastern Europe (primarily Poland, Lithuania, and Russia). See DOUBLE DISTILLATION and VODKA. Some producers may age the spirit in used wine or whisky barrels. Flavoring botanicals, if used, are imbued into the spirit during barrel aging rather than distillation. (Apple and lime leaves and plum blossoms are common.) Modern starka obtains the majority of its coloring from the interaction of the distillate with the wooden barrel; the length of time in which the interaction occurs can range from a few months to over fifty years.

Modern starka production centers around Poland and the United States, with Polmos Szeczin in Poland producing a range of starkas from ten years to fifty years old (Szecin's production facility in Lithuania no longer makes starka). In the United States, craft distillers in Missouri and Oregon have produced starka that is barrel aged for less than a year but does not contain flavoring botanicals.

Modern apocryphal reports suggest that a father, to celebrate his child's birth, would fill an oak barrel previously used to hold wine with a 75-proof distillate, add flavoring botanicals if desired, seal the barrel with beeswax, and then bury it, not to be dug up until the child's wedding day. Traditionally, starka is consumed as a chilled shot, accompanied by zakuski, the traditional Baltic appetizer of cured meats, hard cheeses, pickled vegetables, and sardines. In the fifteenth-century Polish language, *starka* meant both the style of vodka itself as well as an old woman.

It should be noted that modern starka differs from whisky in that it is distilled to a much higher proof and hence enters the barrel with far fewer congeners than whisky. This results in a much lighter spirit, with most of the flavor coming from extraction from the wood, not oxidation of the congeners.

See also VODKA.

Mayhew, Lance. "Starka: Bridging the Gap Between Vodka and Whiskey." *Chilled Magazine*. https://chilledmagazine.com/starka-bridging-the-gap-between-vodka-and-whiskey (accessed April 6, 2021).

Saint Louis Distillery website. http://www.stldistillery.com/ (accessed April 6, 2021).

Lance J. Mayhew

The **St. Charles Hotel** in New Orleans was, when it opened in 1837, one of America's first grand luxury hotels, along with Boston's Tremont House (1829) and New York's Astor House (1836). It was destroyed twice by fire, in 1851 and again in 1894, and was finally demolished in 1974. In the years before the Civil War its bar was an icon not only of New Orleans drinking but of Southern drinking in general, in ways both inspiring and repugnant.

The hotel's first iteration (1837–1851) was distinguished by the dome over the center of the building, on St. Charles Avenue in the heart of the city's American Quarter. Beneath the dome was the hotel's grand "saloon," airy and round. This was in fact the hotel's lobby, although it had a small bar attached to it, and one could drink and eat at the tables there. The main bar, however, was directly underneath: "The bar-room in the basement was . . . octagonal in shape, seventy feet in diameter and twenty feet high, having an exterior circle of Ionic columns," as one observer described it. There, as New Yorker Oakley Hall wrote in 1842, could "be seen hundreds of steady, conscientious lovers of lunches and liquors going and returning, or clustering by pillar and column in social merriment" enjoying "the juleps, and punches, and nogs" served from the bar in the middle of the room. That lunch was free—in fact, the St. Charles's free lunch, recorded as early as 1840, may be the first on record. The bar was "capable of accommodating from four to five hundred persons without inconvenience."

The bar was known for the skill of its bartenders. As the *Daily Delta* noted in 1850, "Colonel" T. L. Craft, the hotel's head bartender, "discovered a cocktail, which is a compound of incomparable delicacy and richness," while the St. Charles Punch, with port wine, brandy, and lemon, was included in the 1862 first edition of Jerry Thomas's book and went on to be something of a bar staple. See THOMAS, JEREMIAH P. "JERRY". When the hotel was rebuilt after its first fire, the "large and fine" bar was, as *Gleason's Pictorial* magazine reported, "much like its far-famed predecessor." Its marble bar covered three sides of the octagon.

One of the things the bar was famous for was its Saturday night slave auctions, when a pair of auction blocks would be dragged into the room and placed at each end of the marble bar. One was for men and boys, the other for women and girls, who were sold to the highest bidder as the customers drank, commented, and pawed the unfortunate human chattel. Albert Deane Richardson, who witnessed several auctions there in 1861, pronounced them "the most utterly revolting spectacle that I have ever looked upon."

Auctions continued in the bar after the Civil War, but they were of real estate, not human beings. The bar remained one of New Orleans's most prominent, but as the century wore on, it was gradually eclipsed by Santini's, the Sazerac, Henry Ramos's, and the Old Absinthe House. See OLD ABSINTHE HOUSE; RAMOS, HENRY CHARLES; and SAZERAC HOUSE. However, the hotel during this era also featured a bar known as Parlor P, which was "one of the great political centers outside of Washington," and a regular meeting place of social clubs and horse-racing enthusiasts in the latter half of the nineteenth century. In 1889, noted New Orleans bar operator

Leon Lamothe took over the operation of the main bar, restoring it to splendor, but he died in 1891, and the bar burned with the rest of the hotel three years later.

During its third and final iteration, which began in 1896, the hotel boasted many eating and drinking establishments. There was the bar itself, now reduced to a fairly small room in the basement. But there was also the Salon de Danse, which offered beer and highballs, and the Italian Garden, which offered an extensive cocktail list. The St. Charles Bar was refurbished after Repeal; it was described in 1938 as "among the oldest and best-known bars in the city," known for the "wide variety of drinks . . . served, especial pride being taken in its 'Planter's Punch' and 'Old Fashioned' cocktail." Unfortunately, the hotel did not survive to serve them again in the 2000s.

"Exchange Hotel." *New Orleans Daily Picayune*, February 9, 1837, 2.

Goss [pseud.]. "Those Lunches." *New Orleans Daily Picayune*, December 25, 1840, 2.

Hall, A. Oakey. *A Manhattaner in New Orleans*. New York: 1850.

"The New St. Charles Hotel." *Gleason's Pictorial*, July 16, 1853, 1.

Richardson, Albert D. *The Secret Service*. Hartford, CT: 1865.

Richey, Emma Cecilia, and Evelina Prescott Kean. *The New Orleans Book*. New Orleans: Searcy & Pfaff, 1919.

Philip Greene and David Wondrich

Stenson, Murray (1949–), is a Seattle bartender who was instrumental in helping usher in the cocktail renaissance in the Pacific Northwest and around the world. Affectionately nicknamed "Mur the Blur" by his friends and regular guests after a local racehorse, he is known for his speed, hospitality, and almost encyclopedic memory of cocktails.

His career began in the 1970s; he first worked as a bartender in 1976 at Benjamin's in Bellevue, Washington. Throughout the 1970s, 1980s, and 1990s, Stenson worked in numerous Seattle bars and restaurants, most notably at the famed restaurant Il Bistro in Pike Place Market, where he managed the bar for nearly a decade.

In 2001, Ben Dougherty and Kacy Fitch, co-owners of Zig Zag Café, hired Mur the Blur away from Il Bistro to run their bar. While there, Stenson brought international notoriety to the bar as well as to Seattle's burgeoning cocktail culture.

A longtime avid collector of antique cocktail books, Stenson was one of the earliest bartenders to rediscover the obscure *Bottoms Up* by Ted Saucier. See SAUCIER, TED. During his tenure at Zig Zag, Stenson single-handedly revived the Last Word, a house cocktail of the Detroit Athletic Club that was first published in *Bottoms Up*. Thanks to him, the Last Word quickly spread around the world and has become an iconic classic. Murray left Zig Zag Café in 2012 and has since worked on and off at several Seattle bars.

See also LAST WORD.

Clarke, Paul. "Characters: Murray Stenson." *Imbibe Magazine*, October 22, 2012. http://imbibemagazine. com/characters-murray-stenson/ (accessed March 11, 2021).

Vermillion, Allecia. "Zig Zag's the Last Word: An Oral History." *Seattle Met*, December 1, 2014. http://www. seattlemet.com/articles/2014/12/1/zig-zag-the-last-word-an-oral-history-december-2014 (accessed March 11, 2021).

Jeffrey Morgenthaler

St. George Spirits is a distillery based in Alameda, California. Founded in 1982 by the German-born distiller Jörg Rupf (1944–), St. George initially focused on Old World–style eaux-de-vie, made from California-grown fruits including pears, cherries, and raspberries. In 1984, Bill Mannshart joined the distillery as the first official employee; following his retirement in 1996, Rupf hired Lance Winters (1965–), a former navy nuclear engineer, as head distiller. At the time, Winters was working as a brewer at a nearby brewpub in Hayward and brought a bottle of his homemade whisky as a liquid resume to the initial interview with Rupf.

Around this time, St. George began expanding beyond its original brandy roots, barreling its first single-malt whisky in 1997 (the first bottles were released in 2000), creating the Hangar One line of vodkas in 2002, experimenting with spirits made from agave (Agua Azul, a single release in 2008), and, in 2007, introducing St. George Absinthe Vert, the first domestically produced absinthe to be released in the United States in almost a century.

In 2005, St. George added Dave Smith to the distilling team. Following the sale of Hangar One to Proximo Spirits in 2010 (under terms of the sale, St. George continued producing the spirit until 2015), Rupf retired, Winters assumed the title of master distiller, and Smith was named head distiller. Following Rupf's departure, St. George continued expanding its product line, adding the agricole-style Agua Libre rum in 2010 (rebranded in 2013 as

Murray Stenson at the Zig Zag in Seattle, ca. 2010. Photograph by Dan Crawford.

St. George California Agricole Rum), a line of three gins in 2011, a new range of vodkas in 2015, and Bruto Americano aperitif liqueur in 2016.

In addition to its commercial releases, St. George maintains an active and esoteric experimental program, which has produced limited-edition spirits for events, bars, and other institutions, ranging from spirits distilled with Dungeness crab, kombu seaweed, and Winters's family Christmas tree to a popcorn bourbon, carrot eau-de-vie, and custom-designed spirits for San Francisco bars and liquor stores.

See also RUPF, JÖRG, and EAU-DE-VIE.

Pape, Allie. "Hangar One and St. George Spirits Are Parting Ways." *Eater San Francisco*, May 1, 2014. http://sf.eater.com/2014/5/1/6231343/hangar-one-and-st-george-spirits-are-parting-ways (accessed April 6, 2021).

Pape, Allie. "St. George Spirits Launches Three New Solo Vodkas After Hangar One Sale." *Eater San Francisco*, March 4, 2014. http://sf.eater.com/2015/3/4/8148815/st-george-spirits-new-vodkas-chile-citrus-all-purpose-hangar-one (accessed April 6, 2021).

"St. George Spirits Is America's Craftiest Distillery." Food Republic, April 22, 2015. http://www.foodrepublic.com/2015/04/22/st-george-spirits-is-americas-craftiest-distillery/ (accessed April 6, 2021).

St. George Spirits website. https://stgeorgespirits.com (accessed April 6, 2021).

Paul Clarke

still, continuous, also known as the column, patent, or Coffey still, is used to make by far the greatest proportion of the world's distilled spirits, although rather fewer of its luxury spirits. Continuous stills are highly efficient, capable of producing almost pure ethanol at high, and indeed continuous, volume, without having to stop to be charged with wash or emptied of stillage.

There are many small variations on the design, but all follow the same basic design, centered on a tall copper (or stainless steel and copper) column equipped with a number of perforated metal plates that divide the interior into discrete compartments. These plates are designed to capture condensing vapor and allow it to pool around the multiple perforations: each hole has a raised rim around it that

prevents a portion of the condensate from simply dripping back down and is topped with a bubble cap that forces the rising steam to detour back down into the pooled liquid, condensing a portion of it. The contact between the vapor and liquid in the plates helps to strip the vapor of water and fusel oils. This process is called countercurrent reflux. See REFLUX.

During this process, an equilibrium is created where the ascending vapor is continuously enriched with the most volatile components, such as alcohol, while the descending liquid flow brings with it the water and other less-volatile components. The water-enriched liquid in the plates eventually descends back into the boiler, while the most volatile components in the vapor either reach the top of the column and enter into the condenser or, in a taller column, find their separate condensing places at plates high up near the top, where they can be drawn off as liquids.

Obtaining high-purity alcohol from a fermented mash is a complex process that requires separating many components based on their boiling points, volatility, density, and solubilities. In a pot still, this separation is accomplished over time, with the carefully controlled application of heat releasing one compound after another from the mash, so that the most volatile ones will pass through the condenser first and the least volatile ones last. Managed carefully, this can yield a heart of some 60–80 percent ethanol, but the process will take hours. It can be sped up by using very wide, very shallow stills and high heat, as Scottish distillers learned to do in the late eighteenth century when they were taxed upon the volume of their stills (the more charges they could run off in a day, the less tax they paid per gallon). But this came with a loss of quality and purity.

A column still solves this problem by separating the various fractions of the wash not temporally but spatially, so they are all vaporized at the same time, recondensing higher and higher up the column depending on their various condensation temperatures. As these temperatures are known, plates may be placed to catch them, and the chambers thus formed may be individually tapped as desired. Usually, it is only the ethanol compartment that is tapped, with a steady, unvarying stream of up to 95 percent ethanol being drawn off as long as wash continues to be fed into the still. For some spirits, however (chiefly American whiskies) the

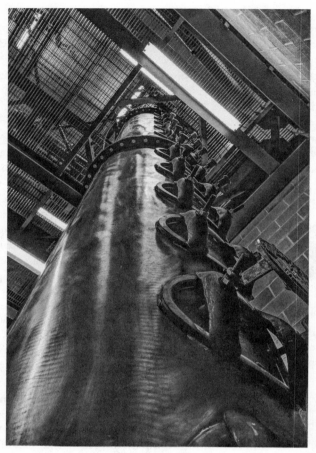

The distilling column at the Michter's whisky distillery, Shively, Kentucky. Courtesy of Michter's.

column is tapped further down, allowing various heavier congeners and more water to be drawn off with the ethanol. See WHISKY, BOURBON.

History

The continuous still is a product of the early nineteenth century, but it is a fairly obvious development of the idea of steam distillation, which was already described and illustrated by the German-Dutch alchemist and distiller Johann Rudolph Glauber in the 1640s in the third part of his treatise on "philosophical furnaces." His still was simple: a copper vessel full of water was heated in a furnace; the steam that generated was funneled through a pipe into the bottom of a wooden barrel containing wash; the vapor that rose from the wash exited the top of the barrel through another pipe and went through a condenser.

His invention, if such it was, seems to have lain dormant for over a century. At the end of the 1700s, though, there was an upsurge in interest in steam distillation, with one S. Thomas Wood receiving a British patent for steam distillation in 1785, the American Alexander Anderson patenting an "improvement in a steam still" in 1794, and Count Rumford suggesting distilling with live steam injection in 1802. In Britain, the excise blocked any practical application of this. In America, however, John Giraud had patented a "Perpetual Steam Still" in 1811; "Patent Steam-Distilled Rye Whiskey" was being sold in Baltimore by 1812; an improvement on Glauber's still was being marketed in Nashville by 1817; and by 1829 steam-distilled whisky was being sold as the "common" grade, with pot-still whisky bringing a premium in price. In the form of the log still and the three-chamber still, live-steam distillation became the American norm until the 1860s, and remained so for rye whisky until World War II. See STILL, THREE-CHAMBER; and WHISKY, RYE. These stills were not continuous, in that they required attention, but neither were they single-batch. If a pot still is a muzzle loader and a modern continuous still a machine gun, they are bolt-action rifles. (As Todd Leopold, one of the very few people alive today who has experience with a three-chamber still, points out, where it can take a typical pot still up to six hours to run off a charge, a three-chamber still will do it in about thirty minutes, at which point another charge is fed into it and the cycle repeats.)

Meanwhile, in France Jean-Édouard Adam and then Jean-Baptiste Cellier-Blumenthal (1768–1840) pursued a still that could run continuously using live-steam injection. It was the latter who first came up with the idea of using a column divided into compartments by permeable horizontal plates, in 1813 (he added the bubble cap two years later). See CELLIER-BLUMENTHAL, JEAN-BAPTISTE. It took a while for Cellier-Blumenthal's still, brilliantly simple and robust, to catch on. In the meanwhile, with excise objections overcome, similar but inferior stills such as those of Jean-Jacques Saintmarc (1826) and Robert Stein (1828) were adopted in Britain, Saintmarc's for gin (when the Nicholson company of London installed one in 1826, it became the largest gin rectifier in Britain, apparently making some 18,000 liters of gin a day) and rum and Stein's for whisky. (For a diagram of Stein's most unlikely still, see PATENT STILL.) Then, in 1828, Aeneas Coffey, an Irish exciseman, patented a column still that was almost as simple as Cellier-Blumenthal's and just as effective. It had the advantage of splitting the column in two, making it much easier to install, with one column—the "analyzer"—dripping the already heated wash through valved plates into steam rising from the bottom, and the other—the "rectifier"—feeding the vapor into the bottom so that it could heat the wash running down through the still in a serpentine tube and collecting any condensate on its own set of plates.

Pros and Cons

By the 1860s, after dozens of patented variations and minor improvements, the technology of continuous distillation was essentially perfected (today's column stills differ only in detail). Column stills were turning out London gin; demerara rum; Glasgow, Belfast, and Ontario grain whisky; French beet spirit, German potato spirit and korn; Russian vodka (beginning in the 1870s); American bourbon; some Dutch genevers and Italian grappas, and a number of other spirits. Their popularity with producers wasn't just because of the impressive cleanliness and purity of the spirits produced; it was also the volume. In 1833, the ten largest distilleries in Scotland used pot stills. By 1846, seven of them had replaced their pots with columns. The ratio of capital expense to output was less than half that of a pot distillery.

And yet a number of spirits, also produced by canny businesspeople, did not switch: cognac and Scottish malt whisky resisted to this day; American rye whisky largely kept its three-chamber stills until World War II; Irish whisky and Jamaican rum only brought in columns in the 1950s. Looking farther afield, tequila, Peruvian pisco, Batavia arrack, and baijiu all stuck to their pot stills as well. It is no coincidence that among these spirits are some of the world's most highly prized: spirits that are considered a cut above in quality and that bring a premium price per liter even fresh off the still. For spirits whose selling point is rich, deep flavor, the quick distillation a column gives seems to release less flavor than long boiling in a pot, even if the column is tapped lower down to catch more congeners. But in 1908, when a British parliamentary commission listened to weeks of testimony to establish whether it should limit the definition of whisky to the pot still product, it decided not to, and rightly so. There is a place for both kinds of spirit, each delicious in its own way.

Forbes, R. J. *Short History of the Art of Distillation.* Leiden: E. J. Brill, 1948.

Gillespie, R. "Steam Still" (advertisement). *Nashville Clarion*, September 9, 1817, 3.

Glauber, Johann Rudolph. *Furnorum philosophicorum pars tertia.* Amsterdam: 1651.

Leopold, Todd. Communication with David Wondrich, May 20, 2021.

"Patent Steam-Distilled Rye Whiskey" (advertisement). *Baltimore American*, January 29, 1812, 3.

Weir, R. B. *The History of the Distillers Company, 1877–1939*, Oxford: Clarendon, 1995.

Willkie, H., and J. Prochaska. *Fundamentals of Distillery Practice.* N.p.: Division of Education, Joseph E. Seagram & Sons, 1943.

David Wondrich and Darcy O'Neil

still, hybrid is a pot still with a rectification column attached to it. See STILL, CONTINUOUS, and STILL, POT. This style of still became very popular with European schnapps producers and later with American craft distillers because of its versatility and its ability to process in small batches. See EAU-DE-VIE and SCHNAPPS. The rectification column allows the distiller to produce a spirit of a very high purity, such as vodka, but the still can also be configured to produce richer, lower-proof spirits. See VODKA.

The action of distillation is the separation of liquids that have different boiling points. The rectification column works to create distinct separation between the vapors of these liquid compounds (chiefly ethanol and water), more than a basic pot still can create. The column's temperature is hottest near the bottom and cooler at the top. This temperature gradient allows lower boiling point compounds to rise to the top (where they can be collected), while those with higher boiling points remain lower in the column.

The most common column design contains a series of copper plates, which allow vapor to pass upward and liquid to condense and reflux down. Though these plates have many styles, they most often contain several bubble caps—a device that allows vapor to rise freely while creating a slight hindrance to liquid refluxing down the column.

During batch distillation, most of the undesirable volatile compounds (such as aldehydes, esters, acetone, and methanol) rise to the top of the column and exit through the condenser before the ethanol, which distillers seek to collect. While ethanol is coming through the still, most of the heavier compounds (including propanol, fusel oils, water, butanol, and amyl alcohol) stay lower in the column. With more plates in the column, a greater degree of separation can be achieved and a purer ethanol distillate can be collected. It takes a large number of plates, or more than one pass through the still, to reach the concentration of ethanol legally required to make vodka.

Most hybrid stills allow a distiller to turn plates on or off to allow a greater or lesser degree of rectification. Some designs allow the column to be bypassed altogether, to create a pure pot-still spirit with more congeners, or flavor-producing compounds. This versatility is especially useful in making whisky because some of the compounds considered impurities in clear spirits are the precursors of desirable flavors in barrel-aged spirits. The versatility of the hybrid still allows distillers to create several different styles of spirits from the same still.

Dikty, Alan, and Bill Owens. "The Distilling Process." In *The Art of Distilling Whiskey and Other Spirits*, 24–39. Beverly, MA: Quarry, 2009.

Murray, Douglas. "Grain Whiskey Distillation." In *Whisky: Technology, Production and Marketing*, 2nd ed, ed. Inge Russell and Graham Stewart, 179–198. Oxford: Elsevier, 2014.

Owens, Bill. "Distillation Principles." In *Craft Whiskey Distilling*, 12–23. Hayward, CA: White Mule, 2008.

Bill Owens and Andrew Faulkner

still, pot, is the oldest and most basic tool for separating and concentrating the alcohol found in a wine, beer, or other fermented alcoholic beverages.

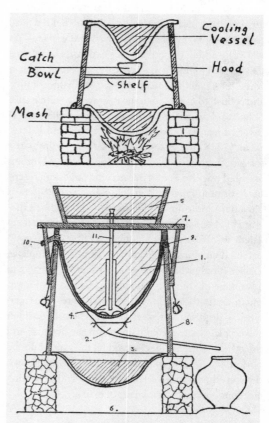

FIG. 210. (Upper) MONGOLIAN STILL. (Lower) CHINESE STILL. (1) Condensing or cooling vessel. (2) Pewter catch basin with conveyer pipe. (3) Cast iron bowl with mash. (4) Pewter funnel. (5) Shallow wooden tub. (6) Fire box. (7) Wooden frame supporting shallow tub. (8) Barrel-shaped hood. (9) Gasket of sewn cloth, filled with sand. (10) Overflow pipe. (11) Wooden pipe with wooden stopper for letting cold water run down into the condensing vessel.

Diagrams of the so-called "Mongolian" and "Chinese" type internal-condensation stills from Rudolf Hommel's classic 1937 *China at Work*. Wondrich Collection.

A Chinese still, photographed by Hommel in the 1920s. Wondrich Collection.

Une des Distilleries de MM. PELLISSON PÈRE & Cⁱᵉ. à COGNAC

One of the distilleries owned by Pelisson Père & Co., in Cognac, with eight alembic Charentais stills arranged in pairs along the right wall, ca. 1900. Wondrich Collection.

See DISTILLATION, HISTORY. That said, it is frustratingly difficult to give a simple description of the device. The Scottish American distiller John McCulloch accurately identified the problem in 1867, when he wrote that "anything is a still that will hold and sustain a continued and uninterrupted boiling of water, and at the same time save for collection and liquefaction the steam that is given off from it." While such a device will often take the shape of the still that is enshrined in popular culture—a copper pot topped with a bulbous head that has a pipe leading from it to a condensing coil—it can and very often does take one of a multitude of other forms, from a tall, coopered wooden cylinder with a tin hat, to a stack of three clay pots, to a couple of old oil drums and some bamboo pipes.

At heart, the pot still must have two components: the pot where the liquid is heated to the point that it steams, and the cover that catches and condenses that steam. A pot is a pot; the covers are where things get complicated. They can be divided into two main types: the ones that condense the steam inside the still and the ones that draw it off to be condensed separately (the copper-pot-with-coil is of course an example of the latter): internal condensation and external condensation.

Both types of still are of great antiquity, although in the absence of a full modern study of the archaeology of distillation, it is impossible to say if they were originally used for distilling alcohol. The oldest form of internal-condensation still, a style of deep clay pot with a spouted gutter around its mouth, was discovered at Tepe Gawra in what is now Iraqi Kurdistan. When fitted with a simple domed lid resting on the outer rim of the gutter, it allows the vapor that passes though the neck of the pot to expand, cool, and condense on the (relatively cool) inside of the lid. The liquid then collects in the gutter and runs out the spout. With the spout and gutter built into the head, this style of still lasted in common use until the eighteenth century. (There is a misconception shared by several twentieth-century historians of distillation that stills of this type could only have been used for perfumes, as they run too hot to condense alcohol. In fact, if the fire is carefully managed, they can produce spirit. Not much spirit, and not particularly good, but spirit nonetheless.) With a water jacket added to the head for much greater efficiency, this style of annular-gutter still remains in use in China and in Portugal and some of its former colonies.

The simplest form of the water-cooled internal condensation still is apparently also very old. Nothing more than a pot with the neck sealed off by a round-bottomed bowl of cold water (the vapor from the boiling wash condenses on the bottom of the bowl and drips into a cup propped up in the pot above the wash level), this most basic device requires no special equipment and is hence is almost invisible to archaeology. Its use has nonetheless been posited in cultures as widely separated as first-millennium BCE India and pre-Columbian Central America, and documented in a belt stretching from Mongolia all the way west to Armenia. See CHERRY BRANDY. Adding an exit spout from the collecting cup running out through the side of the pot, one has the so-called Chinese still that some Oaxacan *palenques* use to make mezcal. See MEZCAL.

The external-condensation still is also of great antiquity. At its most basic, a pot with another pot that fits into its neck and has a tube leading out of the side, it dates at least to 1800 BCE, the posited age of an example found at Pyrgos in Cyprus. In the Pyrgos still, the exit tube leads to a third jug, which is kept in a bowl of cold water; as the vapor leaves the still, it expands into the cold jug and condenses. The same system and still design were used at Shaikhan Dheri in India 1,600 years later, and indeed was documented to be still in use in parts of the subcontinent in the early twentieth century.

More efficient is the version of the external-condensation still that bathes the exit tube in a tub of cold water, generally after it has been bent into a spiral. This innovation—the "worm," as it is known in Scotland—has been attributed to the Italian physician Taddeo Alderotti (ca. 1210–1295), although Michele Savonarola (1385–ca. 1466), who thoroughly explored the matter of distillation in the 1440s, believed that it was traditional knowledge and dated back to antiquity. In any case, this is the version that generally came to dominate European distilling and American distilling.

In the seventeenth century, copper became the primary material for pot stills, at least for commercial distilling, although tin, pewter, and—unfortunately—lead were sometimes used for the condensing coil and other fittings until the nineteenth century. That century saw numerous other innovations, including a mind-bending variety of different still shapes. Some took root: the tall still head, to create more reflux (favored in Scotland); heating by steam coil rather than firebox; the wine warmer used in cognac making; the use of a doubler or retort system. Others, including most of the eccentric shapes, fell by the wayside. See DOUBLER and REFLUX. As distillation spread through the so-called world of villages in the twentieth century, pot stills took new forms and found new materials (the used steel oil drum is particularly popular), but they generally followed the external-condensation, water-cooled model. See CENTRAL AND EAST AFRICA, and OGOGORO. The average seventeenth-century Dutch distiller, after a quick lesson on heating, would have no problem producing spirit in any modern distillery using pot stills.

For a technology that is perhaps five thousand years old to persist, it must do something better than any other alternative. The pot still is far less efficient than the column still or even the three-chamber still at separating ethanol from water and the multitude of other compounds found in a fermented wash, with each style of pot still being inefficient in a slightly different way (no formal comparative study has been made, but personal experience has shown that internal condensation stills make a rounder, more pungent spirit and external ones a cleaner, more spirity one). That very inefficiency leaves room for flavor—for the character of the base material and its fermentation to persist. That can make for a rough or even foul result, but in the hands of an artist it results in beauty.

See also COGNAC; SPIRITS TRADE, HISTORY OF; STILL, THREE-CHAMBER; WHISKY, IRISH; and WHISKY, SCOTCH.

Allchin, F. R. "Stamped Tangas and Condensers: Evidence of Distillation at Shaikhan Dheri." In *South Asian archaeology*, ed. M. Taddei, 755–797. Naples: Istituto Universitario Orientale, 1979.

Butler, Anthony R., and Joseph Needham. "An Experimental Comparison of the East Asian, Hellenistic, and Indian (Gandhāran) Stills." *Ambix*, July 1980, 69–76.

Mahdihassan, S. "The Earliest Distillation Units: Pottery in Indo-Pakistan." *Pakistan Archaeology* 8 (1972): 159–168.

Needham, Joseph, Gwei-Jen Lu, et al. *Science and Civilization in China*, vol. 5, part 4, *Chemistry and Chemical Technology*. Cambridge: Cambridge University Press, 1980.

Samorini, Giorgio. *Distillatori arcaici*. https://samorini.it/archeologia/varie/distillatori-arcaici (accessed April 6, 2021).

Savonarola, Michele. *I trattati in volgare della peste e dell' acqua ardente*. Edited by Luigi Belloni. Rome: Società Italiana di Medicina Interna, 1953.

David Wondrich

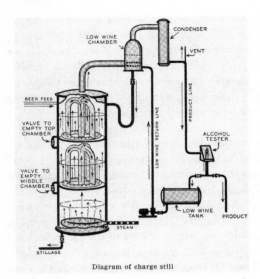

Diagram of charge still

The three-chamber still explained, from a 1943 Joseph E. Seagram & Sons house distillers' manual. In most such stills, the top compartment is merely a pre-warmer for the wash, rather than a full distilling chamber as pictured here. Wondrich Collection.

still, three-chamber, or simply chamber, represents an intermediate stage between a pot still and a continuous or column still. In common use in the United States and Germany during the nineteenth century, it is rarely seen today and until recent years was essentially forgotten, even though it has certain advantages not possessed by either of the other types.

The three-chamber still takes the form of a copper column or, frequently, a wooden one assembled from staves (in the United States, poplar, cypress, and cedar were the preferred woods). This is divided internally by horizontal copper plates into three distinct compartments (some have four, with the middle one repeated). Live steam is piped into the bottom compartment and fresh wash into the top one, which is merely a warmer, with the pipe leading hot vapor out of the still going through it, cooling the vapor and heating the wash in the process. See REFLUX. Once the wash is warmed, it is dropped into the middle compartment through a valve. There, steam rises up from the lower compartment through a pipe that is bent back down almost to the compartment floor, forcing the steam to bubble through the wash and strip off the alcohol within, which exits the still through the warmer. When most of the alcohol has been extracted from the wash in the middle compartment, it is dropped to the bottom one via another valve, and the middle compartment is refilled from the warmer. Once that charge has been run, the bottom compartment is evacuated to make way for it, and the process repeats.

Three-chamber stills are almost invariably connected to doublers, which essentially perform another distillation before sending the vapor to the condenser. See DOUBLER, THUMPER, KEG, OR

RETORT. The resulting distillate, at about 80–85 percent ABV, is generally heavier than a column-still spirit but lighter than a pot-still one. The still is particularly useful for thick (non-filtered) grain mashes, as the grain cooks in the still for far longer than it does in a column still, without the possibility of burning. The long cooking time extracts a wide range of congeners, making for a rich spirit, and also yields a well-cooked spent mash that makes a superior cattle feed. That is no longer the important consideration it was in the nineteenth century, when American and German distilleries often raised cattle.

The basic principle of the three-chamber still—to use steam to strip the alcohol from a wash—is an old one, dating at least to the German-Dutch alchemist and engineer Johann Rudolf Glauber (1604–1670), who in his 1646–1647 *Furni novi philosophici* ("New philosophical furnaces") described and illustrated a still where water is heated in a closed copper vessel and the resulting steam injected into the bottom of a wooden barrel full of wash, exiting at the top to go to a condenser. However, the idea seems to have remained dormant until the late eighteenth century, when European and American distillers started to experiment with steam distillation.

The early steam stills, such as Heinrich Pistorius's influential one from 1817, which became widely used in Germany and functions mechanically like a three-chamber still, were fairly complex, with separate distilling chambers joined by pipes. In America, anyway, the three-chambered wooden column appears to have been introduced in the 1820s or 1830s, although steam distillation with wooden stills was already widespread in the 1810s. It is not known who invented it, but it was an excellent piece of design: simple, cheap to make (particularly in an era when distilleries generally had coopers on staff), easy to operate, and effective. By the middle of the century, as the Scottish American distiller John McCulloch noted in 1867, the wooden three-chamber still had become the default still in America. Although German distillers tended to prefer continuous stills, the "Blasenapparat" ("chamber device") in wood or, more commonly, copper was nonetheless widely used in korn distillation.

In America, continuous stills began replacing three-chamber ones in the 1880s, particularly in Kentucky. See STILL, CONTINUOUS. Yet, according to *Bonfort's Wine and Spirit Circular*, after a decade or so many distillers switched back, finding that the spirit they were making was lacking. The three-chamber still was particularly favored for rye whisky, although some bourbon producers swore by it as well (one major supporter was Solomon Herbst's respected Old Fitzgerald distillery, which used a wooden three-chamber beer still).

In the United States, Prohibition killed off the three-chamber still. The distilleries that either survived the Great Drought or were successfully launched after Repeal had to be ruthlessly efficient: the market was a volume one, not a specialty one. And, as the German distilling authority Max Delbrück's distilling lexicon noted in 1915, continuous stills "use less operating steam and deliver a purer spirit with a higher alcohol content" (this doomed the still in Germany as well). Today only two three-chamber stills are known to be in operation: an old one at the West Indies Rum Distillery in Barbados (although mostly used for grain spirits, the stills were also sometimes used for brandy and rum), and a new one custom-built for the Leopold Brothers distillery in Denver, Colorado, who are using it to make rye whisky.

See also DISTILLATION, HISTORY and WHISKY, RYE.

Delbrück, Max, ed. *Illustriertes brennerei-lexicon.* Berlin: Parey, 1915.

Glauber, John Rudolph. *A Description of New Philosophical Furnaces.* Translated by J[ohn] F[rench]. London: 1651.

McCulloch, J. *Distillation, brewing, and malting.* San Francisco: A. Roman, 1867.

"Our Western Department." *Bonfort's Wine and Spirit Circular,* July 10, 1902, 221–225.

"Steam still." *Nashville Clarion and Tennessee State Gazette,* September 9, 1817, 3.

David Wondrich

still, types of. The designs of devices used to separate ethanol from water are legion, but ultimately the vast majority of them fall into just a handful of categories. The oldest and simplest is the pot still, of which the iconic copper pot with bulbous cap and cooling coil is just one of a great many very diverse types. See STILL, POT. Then there are the continuous still, the column still, the Coffey still, and the patent still, all of which denote the same thing. See STILL, CONTINUOUS. The hybrid still, or Capel still, as it is known in Chile, after the massive cooperative distillery where it is featured, is a pot still with an attached column. See STILL, HYBRID. The three-chamber (or just chamber) still is very rare these days but was formerly quite important in North American distilling. Finally, there is the vacuum still, which comes in large and small sizes, the former being used chiefly in Japan for making shochu and the latter being a fixture of high-end cocktail bars of a certain type. See ROTARY EVAPORATOR (ROTOVAP); SHOCHU; and VACUUM DISTILLATION.

See also RETORT.

David Wondrich

still head, also known as, among many other things, the "onion," is the bulbous top of a pot still, from which the alcohol-rich vapor is drawn off for condensation. See also DISTILLATION; DISTILLATION, HISTORY; and STILL, POT.

stills, heat sources, have taken on many forms throughout history. Early distillers used wood and charcoal as heating sources, boiling the contents of the still over an open flame (gentler methods, such as nestling the still in a pile of warm dung, worked for some kinds of essence extraction but did not provide enough heat to distill alcohol). The Dutch in the seventeenth and eighteenth centuries were the world's leaders in distillation, and also the first to use German Ruhr Valley coal, due to their lack of local fuelwood. The Dutch also made major advances in furnace and flue construction, sealing their stills into brick structures with better control of heat distribution and, equally importantly, lower costs in energy usage. England and Lowland Scotland began to exploit their coal pits to power the steam engine and usher in the Industrial Revolution—and to distill their grain spirits and molasses brandy. See RUM. In the impoverished Scottish Highlands, with only 5 percent of its ancient forests standing by 1600, much of the populace was forced to use local peat to heat its homes, brew its beer, and distill its spirits. (Peat was also employed to dry the malted barley, where the smoky kilns gave Scotch whisky its distinctive "peat reek" flavor. See MALTING.)

The exploitation of steam had major implications for the distilling industry: its use to heat stills, either directly or indirectly, significantly lowered costs, improved distillate quality, and, when injected directly into a continuous still, made a much lighter, purer spirit. By the early nineteenth century, inventors in the British Isles, western Europe, and the United States had patented numerous steam stills for batch distillation. In the United States, this would lead to the greatly simplified, surprisingly effective three-chamber still (later adopted in Germany for korn distillation as the "Blasenapparat"). See STILL, THREE-CHAMBER. At the same time, others in Britain and France were perfecting the continuous or column still. See STILL, CONTINUOUS. Both of these had steam injected directly into the still, where it would strip the alcohol from the wash. As the steam was generated remotely, any energy source could be used to produce the steam, without fear of it burning too hot or producing too much smoke: wood, coal, *bagasse* (the squeezed-out remains of sugar cane), oil, gas—all were acceptable.

By the 1870s, distillers had learned to heat pot stills with steam, which was either sent into the still through a sealed copper coil at the pot still's base or sent into a jacket that covered the bottom half of the still. This prevented the burnt or "empyreumatic" taste caused by naked flame scorching the wash inside the still. Some distillers preferred to continue to use direct-fired stills, but by the second half of the twentieth century they had become increasingly rare, at least in the major industrial countries, with the major exception of France, which requires that cognac be distilled over an open flame; additionally, many Armagnac and calvados distillers still use wood-fired stills. (Of course, untold thousands of wood-fired pot stills also continue to operate in villages around the world.) At the same time, distilleries shifted from coal to on-demand oil and gas as more cost-effective fuels. In the twenty-first century, the industry has embraced renewable resources and biogas generation from waste products to produce the energy required to run a distillery and generate the steam to heat the stills.

See also FRANCE.

Neynaber, A. F. W. "On Distillation." *The Pharmacist*, October 1876, 313–316.

Chris Middleton

The **Stinger**, a notoriously intoxicating mixture of brandy and white crème de menthe, is the king of after-dinner cocktails. It was not an instant sensation. Although it is no longer as fashionable as it was during the twentieth century, it still retains something of its reputation as a top-hat-and-tails drink. It first earned that reputation in the decade before Prohibition. It did not hurt that millionaire playboy Reginald Vanderbilt (1880–1925) always used to shake them up for his friends—always with a dash of absinthe—at the bar in his New York mansion. It is quite unlikely, though, that he invented it, as was claimed in the 1920s: the drink first appears in 1890, when he was ten.

At the end of that year, Herman, the head bartender at New York's Hotel Bartholdi, introduced the Bartholdi Cocktail, made from two fashionable after-dinner tipples, cognac and crème de menthe, shaken together with ice and finished with a spray of lemon oil (his version used green crème de menthe, the white style not yet being widely available in America). The combination was rich and cool, potent and refreshing, and it endured, although the name did not. Over the next two decades, it surfaced under various names: the Judge, the Brant, the Ice Trust Cocktail. Sometimes it had the twist, sometimes bitters, sometimes a dash of absinthe.

In 1913 it finally hit it big, this time as the Stinger, the name most likely taken from a boxing term for a quick jab to the head. With its catchy name and with proponents such as Vanderbilt (it is possible he had something to do with reintroducing it and naming it, although credit for that may also go to James B. Regan of New York's Hotel Knickerbocker), it became quite fashionable, the sort of thing drunk by clubmen and debutantes and their ilk. It retained that cachet for the next fifty or sixty years, finally petering out in the 1980s. By then, it had spawned numerous variations, most of them aimed at replacing the expensive cognac with some other, cheaper spirit. Unfortunately, the success of the drink depends on using an old, deep-flavored, and mellow spirit, for which the other options are practically as expensive as the cognac. The declining ages of affordable cognacs may explain why the Stinger has not flourished in the modern era, although it does have its proponents. See COGNAC.

Unlike most drinks that are made only from spirituous ingredients, the Stinger is always shaken, to ensure maximum coldness and extra dilution. It is also often served frappé, in a cocktail glass full of cracked or crushed ice. Proportions of spirit to liqueur vary, and have always varied, although many believe the ideal is three parts of the former to one of the latter (a proportion first hit on by John Applegreen in 1913). Made thus, the Stinger justifies the dangerous old saying Dale DeGroff is fond of quoting: "What goes with a Stinger? Another Stinger." See DEGROFF, DALE.

Recipe: Shake 60 ml cognac or Armagnac, VSOP or older, and 20 ml white crème de menthe (preferably French) and strain into chilled coupe, which may be filled with finely cracked ice.

Applegreen, John. "The Book of Smiles." *Hotel Monthly*, July 1913, 8.

Bee, John [John Badcock]. *Sportsman's Slang: A New Dictionary*, London: John Bee, 1825, 166.

Converse, Thelma Morgan. "Behind the Curtains with the 400." *Indianapolis Sunday Star Magazine*, July 8, 1923.

"Life in the Hotels." *New York Evening Telegram*, January 15, 1891, 4.

McIntyre, O. O. "New York Day by Day." *Buffalo Evening News*, June 11, 1935, 20.

David Wondrich

stirring a cocktail is one of the two primary methods of mixing, along with shaking. It is typically performed in a mixing glass with a bar spoon. But one can stir a drink in, and with, almost anything. The primary purpose of stirring a cocktail, as opposed to shaking it, is to incorporate the ingredients without agitation so the drink's texture remains smooth and even, and without any air bubbles. Additionally, some believe the ingredients in a stirred cocktail retain more of their distinctiveness, almost as if they were layered on top of one another. Finally, stirring chills and dilutes a drink more slowly than shaking, so more mixing time is required for the process.

History of Stirring

People have been stirring cocktails as long as they have been making them. Back in the late eighteenth century, stirring would have been a simple, straight-forward way of integrating ingredients and dissolving sugar. In those days it was performed with a toddy stick. See MUDDLER. It wasn't until the 1830s and 1840s, when ice became a common bar fixture and the bar spoon came onto the scene that the technique became more refined. See BAR SPOON. Now the technique could be employed as a bona fide alternative to the tossing and shaking that were the fashionable ways of mixing drinks. See ROLLING and SHAKE.

In fact, by the 1870s, stirring had become the most fashionable way of mixing. In the United States, anyway, tossing was on its way out, and in the most stylish bars, shaking was only done when unavoidable. That would reverse after Prohibition, when the flood of untrained bartenders ensured that shaking (much easier to do well that stirring) would be the orthodoxy. For much of the twentieth century in the United States, not much weight was placed on the technique of stirring itself, though in the late twentieth century in Japan, bartenders developed a new style of technique that was both ergonomically and aesthetically superior. What we now refer to as the "Japanese stir" has been adopted by many craft bartenders worldwide.

Which Cocktails Are Best Stirred?

It is generally accepted that stirring is best for cocktails that are comprised of only alcohol-based ingredients, such as spirits, fortified wines, or liqueurs. The appearance of these drinks also benefits, as alcohol-based ingredients are generally clear or translucent. The lack of aeration from stirring preserves their clarity. The Manhattan, Old-Fashioned, and Martini are some principal examples (with apologies to James Bond on the latter). See MANHATTAN COCKTAIL; OLD-FASHIONED COCKTAIL; and MARTINI.

Stylistically, these drinks are more spirit-forward. Stirring helps keep the overall structure of a spirit intact, with its subtleties more perceptible thanks to the even, silky texture. Also, with slightly less dilution and no aeration, a stirred drink will also seem a good bit stiffer than a shaken one, which is ideal for these types of cocktails because they are better when sipped and savored more slowly. As Kazuo Uyeda notes in his *Cocktail Techniques*, "Shaking takes the bite off alcohol, stirring leaves it in." See UYEDA, KAZUO.

How to Stir

Broadly speaking, stirring a cocktail is very much like stirring something in everyday life. The spoon—or whatever apparatus is being used—pushes the ingredients around in a circle, and you try not to make a mess. Of course, for professional bartenders using a Japanese-style stir, it is a bit more involved. The goal of this technique is for the back of the spoon to remain against the inner wall of the mixing glass at all times, never moving into the center (this is much easier in a parallel-sided Japanese mixing glass than in a tapered American one). See MIXING GLASS. This effortlessly pushes the ice around in a gracefully quiet whirlwind. The Japanese-style stir has three major benefits: it allows the bartender to stir faster; it is more fluid, providing better control of chilling and dilution; and—perhaps most importantly—it looks effortless and elegant.

There are various approaches to the Japanese stir. A common one is to hold the top of the bar spoon in place with the thumb and index finger while the middle and ring fingers take turns pushing and pulling it around the glass, sharing the balance of power, as the spoon spins between the top fingers. It helps to keep the bar spoon pressed up against the glass's edge and let the contours guide it around.

As one begins to stir faster, the centrifugal force against the spoon will do most of the work, and the hand will just be the conductor. This takes some practice to master. But keep in mind that while it is fairly important for professional bartenders to learn, it isn't a prerequisite to making good drinks. As long as the cocktail gets chilled and diluted without being shaken, it's a stirring success.

How Long to Stir

Stirring typically takes 15–30 seconds. Variables include the condition of the ice, whether or not the mixing glass is chilled, and stirring speed. Large or dry ice cubes, a cold mixing glass, and slower stirring means more time is needed. Conversely, small or wet ice, a room temperature mixing glass, and faster stirring will need less time. To further expedite the rate of chilling and dilution some bartenders will hand-crack ice cubes to create more surface area; this greatly speeds up chilling and dilution.

See also ICE, SCIENCE OF ITS USE; and SHAKE.

Arnold, David. "Cocktail Science in General: Part 1 of 2." *Cooking Issues* (blog), September 2, 2010. http://www.cookingissues.com/index.html%3Fp=4585.html (accessed April 6, 2021).

Arnold, David. "Cocktail Science in General: Part 2 of 2." *Cooking Issues* (blog), September 8, 2010. http://www.cookingissues.com/index.html%3Fp=4601.html (accessed April 6, 2021).

Arnold, David. *Liquid Intelligence*. New York: W. W. Norton, 2015.

Embury, David A. *The Fine Art of Mixing Drinks*. New York: Mud Puddle, 2008.

Morgenthaler, Jeffrey. *The Bar Book*. San Francisco: Chronicle, 2015.

Oxford Night Caps. Oxford: 1827. Available online at https://euvs-vintage-cocktail-books.cld.bz/1827-Oxford-night-caps-a-collection-of-receipts-for-making-various-beverages-used-in-the-university1/2 (accessed April 6, 2021).

Uyeda, Kazuo. *Cocktail Techniques*. Translated by Marc Adler/Trustforte Language Services, Philip Hanson. New York: Mud Puddle, 2010.

Wondrich, David. *Imbibe!*, 2nd ed. New York City: Perigee, 2015.

Tom Macy

Stock Spirits Group is a multinational spirits producer focused on markets in central and eastern Europe. The company was born in Trieste—then part of the Austro-Hungarian empire—in 1884 with the founding of the Camis & Stock "steam distillery" by Lionello Stock (1866–1948), a Croatian Jew, and Carlo Camis. The company's flagship product was a brandy known as Stock Cognac Medicinal. Camis left the firm in 1906, while Stock proceeded to turn the brandy into a bestseller throughout the empire. Following World War I and the empire's collapse, Trieste, and Stock himself, became Italian. Nonetheless, he acquired distilleries at Božkov in Czechoslovakia and Požega in Croatia as well as in other parts of the former empire. The bitter herbal liqueur Fernet Stock began production at the Božkov distillery in 1927; it remains one of the most popular spirits in what is now the Czech Republic.

Because it was deemed Jewish property, the Božkov distillery was seized by the Nazis during World War II. It was briefly returned to Stock family control after the war, only to be nationalized by the newly formed Communist government the following year. In 1993, the distillery was once again acquired by the Stock company in Trieste. By then, the company offered a wide array of brands in Italy—Stock (spirits, liqueurs, and vermouths), Grappa Julia, Gran Gala (a curaçao), Keglevich (vodkas and fruit brandies)—and throughout central Europe.

A series of mergers and acquisitions beginning in 1995 led to the formation of the Stock Spirits Group in 2008. Based in the United Kingdom, the company owns and operates production facilities in Poland and Germany in addition to the original Božkov distillery. (The Trieste office and distillery were closed in 2009 and 2012, respectively.) With an extensive portfolio that includes a wide range of vodkas and liqueurs as well as rum and other spirits, Stock is the leading spirits producer in both Poland and the Czech Republic.

See also ARZENTE, FERNET.

Archivio Stock S.p.a. https://www.inheritage.it/it/scheda/archivio-stock-s-p-a-.htm (accessed March 12, 2021).

Stock Spirits Group. *Historical Reports*. https://www.stockspirits.com/investors/results_reports_presentations/historical_reports.aspx.

David Mahoney

Stolichnaya is a historic brand of vodka that was the Soviet Union's primary spirits export from the 1950s until the Union's collapse in 1991. Stolichnaya (the name can be translated as "Capital City") would remain the world's largest-selling vodka brand for several years after that. For a celebrated and fairly recent brand, its history is exceptionally murky, in part due to claims advanced by the interested parties in a longstanding dispute over the brand's current ownership.

The one thing everybody seems to agree on is that the brand was created by the noted Soviet engineer Viktor Grigorevich Svirida (1907–ca. 1995).

expensive vodka of the five kinds listed. In the absence of other documentation, it is safest to assign the brand's origin to the immediate postwar years, when the Soviet Union was modernizing its vodka industry; and indeed the brand's now-iconic label, with its drawing of the 1930s Russian Constructivist-style Hotel Moskva, in its original state bore the logo of a Soviet entity that was renamed in 1946.

The use of a pictorial label was unique for a Soviet vodka at the time, and indeed Stolichnaya made use of several other innovations not previously used in Soviet vodka making, including quartz-sand filtration (along with the traditional charcoal filtration) and sweetening (a restrained 2 grams of beet-sugar were added per liter, just enough to smooth the spirit's edge and add a little body to it). It was made from wheat with a little rye and used "live"—i.e., not distilled—water. In the late 1950s, the Soviet government began to test export markets for Stolichnaya, including the United Kingdom (successfully) and the United States (less so).

After trying again in the mid-1960s, the Soviets finally cracked the American market in 1972, with a massive trade deal that had PepsiCo acquire the importing rights to Stolichnaya in an unusual deal that had them trading vodka for cola and then selling the vodka (including the pepper-flavored Pertsovka, launched at Khrushchev's insistence in 1962, and the herb- and honey-flavored Okhotnichaya). The rest of the 1970s were a period of spectacular growth for the brand, with sales jumping from next to nothing to 600,000 cases a year. "Stoli," as it was known, was the leading imported vodka in sales and was also perceived as the best vodka on the market period. No drink in the 1970s was more fashionable.

Then the Soviet Union invaded Afghanistan. The next few years were tough ones for the brand in the US market; years of bottle smashings, consumer boycotts, state boycotts. The Soviet destruction of a Korean airliner in 1983 did nothing to help matters. While Stolichnaya was struggling, another import, Absolut, began eating up its market share, guided by marketing genius Michel Roux. The rest of the 1980s saw the two brands battling it out, with Stoli by far the underdog. New, lighter flavors were introduced, which helped, as did the launch of the super-premium Stolichnaya Cristall in 1989 and a marketing campaign from Roux, who had left Absolut. See ABSOLUT and ROUX, MICHEL.

СТОЛИЧНАЯ ВОДКА

Stolichnaya vodka, from a 1957 Soviet liquor catalog aimed at the domestic market. Wondrich Collection.

Beyond that, the brand's creation has been placed as early as 1938 and as late as 1953, with various dates in between also cited, including four of the five years that the Soviet Union was locked in its desperate struggle with Nazi Germany. No documentation has been brought forward for any of these dates, and it is highly unlikely that, for instance, the Soviet Union created its first brand of luxury vodka in Leningrad while it was under siege, as one story has it. We do know that the brand was in circulation by 1950, because it appears in the price current for spirits the Trade Ministry of the Soviet Union published that year, where (adjusted for proof) it is the most

The fall of the Soviet Union in 1991 threw the brand's legal status in chaos. Although it was the largest vodka brand in the world, nobody knew who actually owned it. After more than a decade of wrangling, during which the US rights passed from PepsiCo to Grand Metropolitan (soon to become Diageo) and then to Allied Domecq, the brand—or at least the export brand—ended up being owned by Yuri Shefler's offshore-based SPI Corp. Domestically, the brand was renationalized by the Russian Federation. SPI and Soyuzplodoimport, the domestic owner, have been fighting over it ever since. At present, the export version is made at Kaliningrad's SPI-RVVK distillery from rectified Russian bulk alcohol.

See also VODKA.

Howarth, Peter, et al., eds. *The Spirit of Russian Vodka*. London: Stolichnaya Brand Organization, [2008].

Katalog likerno-vodochnikh izdelii [Catalog of alcoholic beverages]. Moscow: Prodofromlenie, 1957.

"Preiskurant no. 119." Moscow: Ministerstvo Togrovli Soyuza SSR, 1950.

Trommelen, Edward. *Davai: The Russians and Their Vodka*. Translated by David Stephenson. Montpelier, VT: Russian Life, 2012.

David Wondrich

Stone Fence, otherwise known as Stone Wall or Sampson, is an early North American drink with roots dating to the colonial era; as Sampson, it is recorded as early as 1750. At its most basic, the drink is made of roughly equal portions of spirits (originally rum, and then whisky) and sweet cider (nonalcoholic) or, preferably, hard cider. Applejack was at times substituted where whisky was in short supply or applejack abundant. The drink was sometimes served hot with sugar and occasionally garnished with a lemon peel or an orange peel adorned with whole cloves. See APPLEJACK. Jerry Thomas mentioned the drink in his 1862 bar guide, in which he called for adding "two or three small lumps of ice." See THOMAS, JEREMIAH P. "JERRY". Made in the colonial manner, with hard cider and lots of rum, it is as lethal as the guns at Bunker Hill.

Felten, Eric. "A Rustic Refreshment." *Wall Street Journal*, April 21, 2007.

Folsom, George. *History of Saco and Biddeford*. Saco, ME: 1830.

Wayne Curtis

The **Stork Club** was "New York's New Yorkiest place," famed gossip columnist Walter Winchell once wrote. Established in 1929 and located at 3 East Fifty-Third Street for most of its existence, the bar was a revolving door of mid-twentieth-century icons: Marilyn Monroe, Frank Sinatra, J. Edgar Hoover, and the Kennedys were all regulars. Writers like Winchell treated the club as a gossip bazaar, making it better known for its glitzy clientele than its drinks, although Johnny Brooks and then Nathaniel "Cookie" Cook, the head bartenders, were highly regarded and the bar helped to popularize a number of drinks, including the Bloody Mary, the Blinker, the Salty Dog, and even the Vodka Martini. (The bar and its drinks were lovingly memorialized by *New York Herald Tribune* columnist Lucius Beebe when he penned *The Stork Club Bar Book* in 1946.)

Owner Sherman Billingsley carefully orchestrated the Stork Club's unique atmosphere, deftly steering customers—celebrities and civilians alike—into a complex hierarchy of seating arrangements one could interpret as favors, punishments, or tactics to generate drama for the columns. "Celebrities were the sugar that Billingsley used to swat the fly," recalled the writer John Lahr, who visited the club in his youth. Billingsley himself put it more simply, telling the *New York Times* in 1945, "The out-of-towners come to see the natives who come to see each other."

In 1951, the club's reputation was blemished when the singer Josephine Baker claimed she had been refused service. "The Stork discriminates against everybody," Winchell offered in defense. "It's a snob joint." The crowds shrank after that. By 1963 the club, which had never needed to advertise, began promoting a $1.99 hamburger-and-fries deal. That's when the old-timers probably knew it was over. Add in a spate of union troubles—Billingsley was famously tight with a dollar—and two years later it was shuttered. When the building was demolished, a still was found in a secret basement room that showed signs of having been used far more recently than Repeal. That's one way to keep liquor costs down.

Beebe, Lucius. *The Stork Club Bar Book*. New York: Rinehart, 1946.

Blumenthal, Ralph. *Stork Club: America's Most Famous Nightspot and the Lost World of Cafe Society*. New York: Little, Brown, 2000.

Feinberg, Alexander. "The Why of Night Clubs."
 New York Times, May 20, 1945.

Lahr, John. "Hog Heaven." *New Yorker*, May 8, 2000, 118.

"Stork Club Is Picketed: Negro Group Assails Refusal
 to Serve Josephine Baker." *New York Times*, October
 23, 1951.

Reid Mitenbuler

Stoughton's Bitters, the first product of their kind, were the defining component of the original "Cock-Tail," and the squat, square-shouldered little bottle they came in was a fixture in bars until the mid-nineteenth century. They were the creation of London apothecary Richard Stoughton (1665–1716), who completed his apprenticeship in 1687 and opened his own shop, just south of London Bridge, soon after. In 1690 or thereabouts, he began selling a new creation of his, an alcoholic extract of various bitter barks, roots, and herbs designed to produce instant purl (beer or wine infused with wormwood and other botanicals). See PURL. All one had to do was add a teaspoon or so of his Elixir Magnum Stomachicum ("Great stomachic elixir") to one's glass of ale or Canary wine, and it was done. By the early 1700s, it was also being added to brandy, with gin to follow. See COCK-TAIL.

Stoughton, a pioneer in marketing and one of the most dedicated and prolific advertisers of his age, touted the elixir as a stomach settler and general remedy for everything up to and including the common hangover. Yet it appears to have been the "pleasant, bitterish taste" (as Stoughton described it) of his "bitters," as they were being called by the 1710s, that made them popular, not only in Britain and its colonies but throughout Europe and the Americas. In 1712, Stoughton obtained a royal patent, only the second granted to a medicine. That dissuaded his imitators for a while, but by the 1730s imitations were common, and recipes for recreating the bitters were beginning to see print, although they offered far fewer ingredients than the twenty-two Stoughton had claimed. Nonetheless, by the end of the century the bitters were a standard apothecary's product, with at least three different formulae in circulation. See CAMPARI.

It is probably impossible at this remove to determine what Stoughton's original formula was, but the imitations all agree in using gentian and bitter orange peel in a brandy base, with cochineal to give it its often-described deep red-orange coloring. Other possible ingredients are Virginia snakeroot, germander, aloe, cascarilla, and rhubarb. The first half of the nineteenth century saw Stoughton's gradually eased out of the bar, where they had become a fixture, by a new wave of proprietary bitters, and one rarely hears of them after the 1850s.

See also ANGOSTURA BITTERS, BITTERS, and PEYCHAUD'S BITTERS.

*The Complete Family-Piece and Country Gentleman's and
 Farmer's Best Guide*. London: 1737.

Davies, Raymond E. M. "Dr. Richard Stoughton and
 His Great Cordial Elixir." *Pharmaceutical journal* 240
 (1988): 377–381.

"The Great Cordial Elixir" (advertisement). *Athenian
 Mercury* (London), July 7, 1693.

Rennie, James. *A New Supplement to the Complete
 Pharmacopoeias*, London: 1829.

David Wondrich

Straits Sling is another name for the Singapore Sling, Singapore having been, from 1867 to 1946, a part of the Straits Settlements, a British crown colony. See SINGAPORE SLING.

Strangeway, Nick (1968–), is a celebrated London craft bartender. In 1988, while studying art by day, he began tending bar at Fred's Club, where he met longtime mentor Dick Bradsell. The two went on to work together in other establishments, including the Flamingo, Detroit, and Dick's Bar at the Atlantic Bar & Grill. See ATLANTIC BAR & GRILL and BRADSELL, DICK.

In 1998 Strangeway became bar manager for Che, which won the *Evening Standard*'s Bar of the Year during his tenure. In 2003, he moved to consulting, helping bars and restaurants develop their drinks programs and spirits companies develop their brands. In 2006 he signed on as manager for the opening of Hawksmoor Steakhouse, which won Best New Restaurant Bar that year. In 2008, he won the International Bartender of the Year award at Tales of the Cocktail. Strangeway also established long-term working relationships with a number of high-profile UK chefs, most notably Mark Hix, with whom he collaborated on Mark's Bar in both the Soho Hix restaurant and the Belgraves Hotel.

Strangeway developed a global reputation as both an innovator and a mixed drinks historian. At Hawksmoor, for instance, he reintroduced London to the concept of punch, as well as instituting seasonal menus that often used ingredients for which he would forage. Among other product innovations, Nick is also a co-creator of Hepple Gin, which is produced in Northumberland in the United Kingdom. In 2013, he launched Absolut Craft, a limited edition line of naturally flavored vodkas. See ABSOLUT.

Martin, Richard. "Nick Strangeway Has Bartender Fatigue." *Food Republic*, April 5, 2012. http://www.foodrepublic.com/2012/04/05/nick-strangeway-has-bartender-fatigue/ (accessed March 12, 2021).

"Meet the Team." Strangehill website. http://www.strangehill.co.uk/meet-the-team/ (accessed March 12, 2021).

Audrey Saunders

strong-aroma-style baijiu is a Chinese grain spirit famous for its use of mud-pit fermentation. There are two predominant varieties of strong-aroma: simple grain, distilled entirely from sorghum, and mixed grain, distilled from sorghum and a combination of other grains, usually long-grain rice, sticky rice, wheat, and corn. Aside from ingredients, there is no major distinction between the two varieties in terms of production, and many distilleries produce both.

Strong-aroma baijiu is created by mixing steamed grains with wheat-based qu and burying the grains in large earthen pits. See QU. After the pit is loaded, it is sealed with mud to reduce aeration, and distillers regularly water down the seals or cover them with plastic to maintain high levels of moisture. After fermenting for two to three months, the grains are unloaded and distilled a layer at a time, with the deepest layer producing the finest spirits. The topmost layer of mash is discarded and replaced with fresh grains and more qu, then loaded back in the pits to begin the cycle anew. Spirits are stored and aged separately, then blended together into the final product.

Chinese distillers believe that the quality of a strong-aroma baijiu is connected to the age of the fermentation pit. Over countless fermentation cycles the yeasts and other microorganisms in the qu are absorbed into the walls and floor of the pit, further facilitating fermentation and developing stronger flavors over time. Most believe that a pit must be used for at least three years before it can produce acceptable baijiu, and at least thirty years for high-quality baijiu. Three major strong-aroma distilleries—Luzhou Laojiao, Shui Jing Fang, and Wuliangye—employ fermentation pits first used during the Ming dynasty (1368–1644). See LUZHOU LAOJIAO; SHUI JING FANG; and WULIANGYE.

Owing to its rich, fiery taste, it is the most popular baijiu style in China, accounting for at least two-thirds of the category's production and nearly all of the premium segment. It is closely associated with the humid and fertile Sichuan Province, China's leading baijiu producer, but also has production centers in the eastern provinces of Anhui, Jiangsu, and Shandong.

See also SAUCE-AROMA-STYLE BAIJIU.

Huang Faxin, David Tiande Cai, and Wai-Kit Nip. "Chinese Wines: Jiu." In *Handbook of Food Science, Technology, and Engineering*, vol. 4, by Yiu H. Hui. Boca Raton, FL: CRC, 2005.

Zhang Wenxue 张文学 and Xie Ming 谢明, eds. *Zhong Guo Jiu Ji Jiu Wen Hua Gai Lun* 中国酒及酒文化概论. Chengdu: Sichuan Daxue Chuban She 四川大学出版社, 2010.

Derek Sandhaus

strong water is an early English term for distilled spirit, first attested to in 1590 and essentially obsolete by the middle of the next century. Originally an umbrella term for any clear, reactive liquid, including acids, "strong water" became a popular alternative to the learned *aqua vitae* for describing spirits and was in wide use throughout the seventeenth century. Once English speakers began to differentiate the spirits they drank by type and base material, "strong water" generally gave way to "brandy," "rum," "geneva," "rack," "usquebaugh," and the like, although it is occasionally found in legal documents through the end of the eighteenth century and after that as a deliberate archaism.

See also AQUA VITAE and SPIRITS.

Forman, Simon. *The Autobiography and Personal Diary of Dr. Simon Forman*. Edited by J. O. Halliwell. London: 1849.

Howell, James. *Familiar Letters or Epistolae Ho-elianae*,
vol. 2. London: Dent, 1903.

Wilson, C. Anne. *Water of Life*. Totnes,
UK: Prospect, 2006.

David Wondrich

structure in a cocktail is the interplay of all the components that go into making the drink and how they work together. Understanding the role each of a drink's components plays is a fundamental aspect of being able to understand why one cocktail works and a similar one doesn't.

Discussing the structure of a cocktail can be more challenging than discussing the structure of food. With a piece of fried chicken, it is easier to visualize, identify, and experience the separate functions of a crunchy outer coating, the moist inner flesh, and the hard bone that supports it all. You can also describe the flavor differences between the skin and the meat as well as the savory aroma that fills the room.

With a cocktail, however, the flavors, textures, hues, and aromas are contained in fluids and, though mixed together, still result in a unitary liquid. While this liquid may have discernible components within its overall architecture—a particular flavor, a texture, a perceived brightness, softness, or funk—defining how those pieces work together is challenging. In a Last Word cocktail, with gin, lime juice, maraschino liqueur, and green Chartreuse, it is easy to identify the drink's sweetness as coming from the two liqueurs and its acidity from the lime, but with three pungent, highly flavored spirits in it, untangling its botanical notes is much less straightforward.

A cocktail's structure is the summation of many individual factors. You may have to consider the characteristics of the base spirit, the function of each ingredient and the interplay between them, the ratios contained in the recipe itself, its balance, the roles of any acid or sweet ingredients (are they modifiers, fundamentally changing thee texture and effect of the drink, or are they mere accents?), the function of any chosen counter-modifier, the resultant effect from the layering of flavors, the intensity of any bitterness, the drink's viscosity, overall aroma, and so on.

The best way to understand structure is to analyze the overall architecture of a portfolio of classic drinks, for example, the Manhattan, Martini, Negroni, Old Fashioned, and Daiquiri. See DAIQUIRI; MANHATTAN COCKTAIL; MARTINI; NEGRONI; and OLD-FASHIONED COCKTAIL. Select one recipe, and evaluate each individual component, focusing on how ingredients work with each other and if they blend together. Just because history dictates a specific recipe, that doesn't mean it has to be followed verbatim. Nor does it mean that the recipe structure is appropriate for all choices of ingredients.

The original Sidecar recipe was equal parts of cognac, Cointreau, and lemon juice, but bartenders eventually realized that this 1–1–1 structure wasn't ideal for all; adjustments were needed to achieve proper balance and express the character of the ingredients. See SIDECAR. Likewise, the Negroni is typically described as a recipe of equal parts, but that doesn't mean that there isn't potential to adjust those proportions in order for the ingredients to realize their full potential together.

Approaching the structure of a drink like the Negroni in order to adjust its proportions means looking at the ingredients, as well as the choice of specific brands. While Campari is bitter, it is also sweet; adding equal parts sweet vermouth can make the drink feel heavy on the palate from richness and viscosity. This makes it important to focus on tempering this sweetness with the gin, but which gin— and how much of it to use?

With respect to Campari, would a gin utilizing an orange botanical be a better choice than one without? How would a juniper-forward gin work in the drink, different from one with more delicate juniper notes? Might increasing the amount of gin help cut through some of the Negroni's overall sweetness and provide a little more "spine" to the drink's overall structure? Or is there another way to do that, perhaps with a splash of chilled sparkling water?

As aromatic cocktails are prepared with all clear ingredients and therefore stirred, it would be assumed that the Negroni should be prepared by stirring it. Yet many historical recipes indicate that it is shaken. How does the difference of shaking or stirring affect the texture of the final product given its historical ratio of 1–1–1? Is it better to serve the drink up or on the rocks? Should it be garnished with orange slice or an orange twist?

Developing an intimate understanding of each individual component of a drink recipe and how they affect one another offers the ability to fine-tune the structure of any drink with great precision.

See also TASTING SPIRITS.

Arnold, Dave. *Liquid Intelligence*. New York: W. W. Norton, 2014.

Page, Karen, and Andrew Dornenburg. *The Flavor Bible*. New York: Little, Brown, 2008.

Audrey Saunders

sugar is a sweet, soluble carbohydrate, produced naturally during the process of photosynthesis to provide food and energy to plants. Sugar is also a substance people use to make food and beverages sweeter. Sugar also plays a crucial role in the production of wine, beer, and spirits. The ethanol in beverage alcohol is formed when yeast consumes the natural sugars found in the raw material—for example, to make wine, vintners use yeast to convert fruit sugar into alcohol.

Sugars come in two kinds. Monosaccharides have a single molecule; they include glucose, fructose, and dextrose (all have the formula $C_6H_{12}O_6$, but with different structures). Disaccharides are made of pairs of molecules, either two different monosaccharides or two of the same. Thus sucrose, the sugar found in sugar cane and sugar beets, is a glucose molecule and a fructose one, while malt-derived maltose is two glucose molecules. (Polysaccharides, including starches, are made of several sugar molecules bonded together.) For yeast to be able to consume sugars during fermentation, they must first break disaccharides down into monosaccharides (they must have polysaccharides broken down for them). See FERMENTATION.

Commercial sugar can be dextrose, glucose, fructose, or sucrose, although most refined white sugar is pure sucrose. Commercial sugar is usually found in the form of white or brown crystals or a fine white powder.

Sugar Sources and Production Methods

Sugar cane is one of humanity's oldest food ingredients; a native of Papua New Guinea, it has been domesticated since 8000 BCE. See SUGAR CANE. As far as can be determined, the processing of cane juice to obtain crystallized sugar dates back to the late first millennium BCE, in northern India. Since then, production methods for transforming sugar cane into processed sugar have changed dramatically, but not uniformly: there are still places where the process used would be recognizable to the people who invented it. At this most basic level, sugar cane is chopped and ground, pressed, or pounded to extract its juice. This liquid is then heated in a series of ever-smaller kettles to evaporate the water and concentrate the sugar, causing sugar crystals to appear. The process is labor intensive. Modern technology has brought mechanical cane-cutting, steam mills, diffusers (which use hot water to wash the juice out of the fiber), vacuum pans, centrifuges, and charcoal filtration to the process. See DIFFUSER. To make sugar from beets, the roots are washed, sliced thin, and sent to a diffuser. The juice, like that of cane sugar, is heated to evaporate the water and concentrate the sugars, causing crystals to form. See BEETS.

With these more efficient production methods, modern commercial white sugar (whether from cane or from beets) is more refined than sugar available in the past. Until the late nineteenth century, it took a great deal of processing to make fine-crystaled white sugar, and much of the sugar in use was darker and coarser in grain. Solid loaves of unrefined sugar are sold in Asia as jaggery (also called *gurh*, *gud*, and *gul*) and in Latin America as panela or piloncillo. Other types of sugars are made from fruits such as dates; saps and resins of trees such as palm, coconut, and maple; and grains such as maize and barley.

Types of Sugar

Refined sugars available commercially include granulated sugar, which is the most highly refined form of commercial sugar. It's always white, easy to pour and measure, and made for table use and for cooking and preserving. Granulated sugar does not dissolve well into cocktails, however, and is usually made into simple syrup for cocktail use. See SIMPLE SYRUP. Granulated sugar can also be found in so-called superfine form, which is a more finely grained sugar meant to dissolve quickly in liquids.

Other refined sugars include light and dark brown sugar, which contain molasses. The darker the sugar, the higher the molasses content. Molasses is a byproduct of sugar making. As the juice of sugar cane and sugar beets is boiled down to extract the sugar, the dark syrup that results from the boiling process is molasses. Natural brown sugar has residual molasses that was never cooked out of the sugar, whereas refined brown sugar has molasses added back to refined white sugar. This practice of adding molasses to refined white sugar allows manufacturers to ensure consistency from batch to batch because they can precisely measure the amount of molasses added to the sugar. The color, texture, and flavor of natural brown sugar vary based on how much molasses remains in the product. See MOLASSES.

Some types of unrefined or partially refined brown sugars include muscovado, turbinado, and demerara. Muscovado is made by drying sugar crystals in low heat, sometimes outside in the sun. Turbinado and demerara are both dried in a centrifuge. (The centrifuge resembles a turbine, giving origin to the name *turbinado*.)

Proponents of unrefined sugars claim that these sugars contain minerals that provide some health benefits from consuming them, but research on this shows these claims to be unsupportable; the mineral content of unrefined sugar is simply too low to add nutritive value to the sugar. Nevertheless, unrefined sugars generally have richer and more complex aromas and flavors, making them desirable in certain cocktail applications.

Cocktail Uses

Sugar loaves used in the 1800s were different from any kind of sugar available today. Firstly, they were made of sugar that was refined less than modern sugar is—sometimes much less. Secondly, the loaves were more solid than any sugar loaf commercially available today and required special tools, such as "sugar nippers," to break them down for use. In preparing drinks such as punches, it was common for a bartender to take lemons and rub their peels on a block of sugar, for the purpose of stripping the oils from the peel and transferring their aromas to the sugar block. Modern loaves would crumble if treated that way.

Granulated white sugar, whether in syrup or crystal form, lacks the complexity of those old loaf sugars, but it provides a bright, clean taste and a clear appearance in a drink. See SOUR. Evaporated cane juice, now in common use, is a bit softer in taste and slightly darker in color. Both of these sugars are usually fine-grained enough to dissolve without being made into syrup. (Before Prohibition, master bartenders insisted on granulated sugar in sours and syrup only in drinks such as the original Cock-Tail, where there wasn't enough water to dissolve the sugar.) Brown sugars such as turbinado, muscovado and demerara are usually coarse-grained to the point that they will not dissolve with simple stirring or shaking or be too sticky to pour like white sugar, and must be made into syrups. They will darken an otherwise clear drink but also provide rich flavors from the molasses, reminding the drinker of caramel, honey, and vanilla. Brown sugars, thanks to the molasses content, also have a heavier body in syrup form. Their rich flavors and heavier body mean they pair best with dark spirits such as whisky, brandy, or rum. Dark sugars are especially well suited for tiki and other rum-based drinks. See TIKI.

Similar syrups can be made from sugars such as the Indonesian *gula jawa*, a dark and sticky mix of palm and cane sugars; Indian palm sugar and jaggery; and Latin American panela and piloncillo. These are usually made as high-Brix rich simple syrup, as they are less sweet than granulated sugar and need the concentration. (The sugar content of a given liquid is referred to as "degrees Brix"; 1 degree Brix is equivalent to 1 gram of sucrose in 100 grams of solution. See BRIX.) Jaggery and panela syrups are useful in making drinks such as punches, where the historical antecedent would have used sugars less refined than modern commercial sugars, and the extra flavor they bring won't knock the drinks out of balance.

See also SACCHARIFICATION and SUGAR CANE.

Foster, Kelli. "A Complete Visual Guide to 11 Different Kinds of Sugar." *Kitchn*, December 8, 2014. http://www.thekitchn.com/a-complete-visual-guide-to-sugar-ingredient-intelligence-213715 (accessed April 27, 2021).

Geerligs, H. C. Prinsen. *The World's Cane Sugar Industry: Past and Present.* Altrincham, UK: N. Rodger, 1912.

Solmonson, Leslie Jacobs. "How Sweet It Is: Using Different Sweeteners for Your Cocktails." *Chilled.* http://chilledmagazine.com/how-sweet-it-is-using-different-sweeteners-for-your-cocktails (accessed April 27, 2021).

"Types of Sugar." The Sugar Association. https://www.sugar.org/all-about-sugar/types-of-sugar/ (accessed April 27, 2021).

Michael Dietsch

sugar cane figures prominently in the history of spirits because it has provided the basic sucrose necessary for the fermentation and distillation of a wide variety of alcoholic beverages, most notably rum. The production of fermented and distilled alcoholic beverages made from sugar cane follows the historical migration of sugar cane around the globe. Botanists believe that sugar cane (*Saccharum officinarum*) was first domesticated in New Guinea about eight thousand years ago. It spread throughout the Pacific islands, reaching Hawaii around 600 CE.

From the Pacific, sugar cane spread to India and China, and it is here that we find the earliest evidence for the production of sugar-cane-based alcoholic beverages. In his search for the origins of sugar production, anthropologist Sidney Mintz argued that the earliest datable mention of sugar cane is from Alexander the Great's general Nearchus, during his conquest of the Indus river region in 327 BCE. Nearchus noted, "A reed in India brings forth honey without the help of bees, from which an intoxicating drink is made though the plant bears no fruit." Ironically, the reference is not to sugar but to an alcoholic beverage made from sugar-cane juice. There are numerous other references to the fermentation of sugar-cane juice in ancient India. For example, the laws of Manu, dating to 200 BCE–200 CE, placed restrictions on the use of alcohol among Hindus, including alcoholic drinks made from sugar cane. The *Caraka Samhita*, possibly written as early as 78 CE, identified sugar as one of the nine sources for wine. Ye-lu Ch'u ts'ai, the Chinese minister to Genghis Khan, wrote during his travels to the Indus valley that sugar cane was cultivated and from its juice "people make wine." Fermented sugar drinks were also described in the *Arthashastra of Kautilya*, which may have been written as early as the third century BCE. Thus, the evidence indicates that India developed the earliest tradition of using the juice of sugar cane to produce alcohol.

The Muslim expansion in the 700s spread sugar cane across the Mediterranean, yet its use as an alcoholic beverage failed to take hold in these new territories. By the 900s, sugar making had reached as far west as the island of Sicily and southern Spain, confirming the saying that "sugar followed the Qur'an." The Crusades helped introduce sugar to Europe, and Crusaders themselves became sugar producers in some parts of the conquered Arab world in the 1100s. For almost six hundred years, until the fifteenth century, the supply of sugar to the Muslim and Christian worlds came exclusively from the Levant and Mediterranean sugar industries. There is some evidence that sugar cane was used in the production of alcohol in the Arab world. In 1200, Marco Polo wrote that in Zanzibar "they have no grape vines, but make a sort of wine from rice and sugar, with the addition of some spicy drugs." Yet despite the strength of the Levantine and Mediterranean sugar industries, as well as the knowledge, at least in some parts of the Arab world, that sugar cane could be used to produce alcohol, there is no clear evidence of any concerted effort to advance the production of sugar-cane-based alcoholic beverages. The technological inefficiency of Mediterranean sugar production, the high value of even poorer quality sugar, and the Muslim prohibitions against alcohol drinking probably helped ensure that few Mediterranean sugar producers would turn their sugar-cane juice and the byproducts of sugar making into alcohol.

In the mid-fifteenth century, the production of sugar began in the Atlantic islands off the West African coast. Spanish and Portuguese investors, with the help of Italian merchants and sugar producers, transferred the capital, technology, and knowledge necessary to cultivate sugar cane and produce sugar in the Atlantic islands. The main islands included Madeira, the Canaries, and Sâo Tomé. Madeira, under Portuguese rule, was the earliest and most successful of the Atlantic sugar islands. Sugar producers in the Spanish Canaries began exporting sugar at least as early as 1506, and producers in Sâo Tomé were also producing sugar in the sixteenth century. Yet despite the presence of sugar, the increasing knowledge of alcohol distillation in Europe, and a growing urban population of avid alcohol consumers in Europe, there is no evidence for the commercial or even local production of alcoholic beverages from sugar cane in the Portuguese and Spanish Atlantic islands in the fifteenth and sixteenth centuries.

Christopher Columbus carried sugar cane to the Caribbean on his second voyage in 1493, and a sugar factory was established on Hispaniola ten years later. Small mills produced sugar for export, as well as molasses for local consumption, but it appears that Spanish colonials in Hispaniola had little interest in the byproducts of sugar production. In 1535, Spanish colonial official Gonzalo de Oviedo y Valdes wrote, "The ships that come out from Spain return loaded with sugar of fine quality, and the skimmings and syrup that are wasted on this island or given away would make another great province rich." Although sugar-cane juice and the byproducts of sugar making were readily available in the Spanish Caribbean in the sixteenth century, there is no clear evidence that colonists used these materials to distill rum, nor is there incontrovertible evidence that colonists in the sugar-cane growing regions of Brazil and New Spain (Mexico) distilled rum in the sixteenth century.

If the colonists in the sixteenth-century Caribbean indeed did not distill rum, they did exploit the alcoholic potential of sugar cane. In the sugar-cane-growing regions of the Caribbean, colonists used sugar-cane juice and the byproducts of sugar making to produce fermented alcoholic drinks. The earliest evidence in the Americas for the use of sugar cane in the production of an alcoholic beverage is in Spanish Santo Domingo. In 1550, Spanish Dominican friar Bartolomé de Las Casas, describing the period 1511–1520, reported that enslaved Africans, once in the Spanish colony, died quickly from a variety of factors, including the "beverages they drank made from sugarcane." However, Las Casas does not specify whether this drink was fermented or distilled, nor does he give it a name. This implies that despite the variety of names used to signify fermented and distilled grapes in Europe in the sixteenth century, there was no name for an alcoholic beverage made from sugar-cane juice. The absence of a name suggests that the drink was new and uncommon. However, in 1596, Dr. Layfield, a chaplain on an English privateering voyage, landed in Puerto Rico and reported that the Spanish colonists of the island drank a fermented drink called "guacapo" made of molasses and spices.

Guacapo, or more commonly *guarapo* in the Spanish colonies, was the first specific name for an alcoholic beverage made from sugar-cane juice in the New World, and it was a fermented drink produced on a small scale for local consumption. Regional variations of the name sprang up throughout the Americas. In Brazil, fermented sugar-cane drinks were called *garapa*, and in the French Caribbean they were called *grappe*. In Barbados, enslaved peoples consumed a fermented sugar-cane-based drink called *grippo*, which seems to be analogous to *guarapo*, *garapa*, and *grappe*.

These were fermented alcoholic drinks that should not be confused with distilled rum. Yet it is quite possible that they coexisted with distilled drinks. Certainly such drinks were no novelty, at least in theory. Iberian brandy was common in sixteenth-century Latin America, as was the local version, produced in Peru and shipped (illegally) around the region. Many of the Spanish and Portuguese colonists would have even encountered cane spirits in Asia—both empires featured a good deal of back and forth between their Asian and American holdings. See Pisco.

When the French traveler François Pyard de Laval, who visited Brazil in 1510, wrote that there "they make wine from sugarcane, which is cheap and is only for the slaves and the natives of the place," the word he used for wine, *vin*, is the same one he used for the distilled palm arrack he encountered in Goa, in Portuguese India. And certainly when the viceroy of Mexico prohibited distillation from cane in the 1630s, he noted that it had been practiced "for many years," which means the miners who were recorded selling "vino de azúcar"—"sugar wine" in Taxco in 1600 may have been selling rum (it has often been remarked that one of the biggest obstacles to understanding the early history of distilling is the slow development of a specialized vocabulary). None of this is conclusive, but that may be the best we can hope for; the lives of enslaved African and indentured Native American sugar-mill workers and their lower-class European managers in sixteenth-century Latin America were barely documented to begin with, and the centuries that have passed since then have been turbulent ones and not always conducive to preserving documents.

In any case, enslaved Africans in the Caribbean played a key role in the manufacture of these cane drinks. In Santo Domingo, Las Casas's mid-sixteenth-century reference to alcoholic sugar-cane-based concoctions hinted that Africans were the primary consumers and, perhaps, producers, of these beverages; this is corroborated by Pyard de Laval for Brazil. Enslaved Africans, as with Europeans, sought to reestablish traditional patterns of alcohol use in the Caribbean. In Martinique, at least, some planters allowed their enslaved workers to collect the unwanted skimmings that spilled over the cauldrons during the sugar boiling process, which they then used to ferment (and possibly distill) "intoxicating drinks." Although Europeans recognized the alcoholic potential of sugar cane, Africans also came from societies that produced a wide variety of fermented alcoholic drinks, and they, rather than the Europeans, may have conducted some of the initial experiments with fermented varieties of sugar-cane juice in the Caribbean. As for distillation, the history of its extremely rapid spread in late nineteenth- and early twentieth-century West and Central Africa and the great ingenuity displayed there in making stills from materials at hand show that it need have taken no time at all, historically speaking, for it to spread throughout the enslaved African population in Latin America. See CENTRAL AND EAST AFRICA; WEST AFRICA; and OGOGORO.

Sugar cane spread out of the South Pacific eight thousand years ago and returned as rum in the hulls of the ships of Captain James Cook and other European explorers. Those explorers recorded the widespread presence and cultivation of sugar cane in the Pacific, though Pacific Islanders used sugar cane only as a vegetable plant. In 1788, the British brought its industrial cultivation to Australia, but they were only following what the Dutch had done in Java. See AUSTRALIA AND NEW ZEALAND and ARRACK, BATAVIA. By the early nineteenth century, American firms had built sugar estates in Hawaii that soon began distilling rum. In 1827, the Hawaiian governor Boki sold his sugar factory to a syndicated company that abandoned sugar making for rum distilling. Christian missionaries objected to the distillery and persuaded King Kaahumanu to destroy the plantation. In the 1880s, the French Pacific colonies of Tahiti and New Caledonia also produced rum and even managed to export some twenty thousand gallons a year to France. Today, cane is grown throughout the tropics, and everywhere it is grown rum is made from it.

See also CANE-BASED SPIRITS and CARIBBEAN.

Bretschneider, E. Extracts from the Si Yu Lu (YE-LU CH'U TS'AI). Vol.1 pt. 1: notes on Chinese travelers. In Medieval Researches from Eastern Asiatic Sources. London: K. Paul, Trench, Trubner, and Company, 1967.

Chandra Kaviratna, A., and P. Sharma. Caraka Samhita. Translated by A. Chandra Kaviratna and P. Sharma. 5 vols. Delhi: Sri Satguru, 1996.

Craton, Michael, James Walvin, and David Wright, eds. Slavery, Abolition, and Emancipation: Black Slaves and the British Empire, A Thematic Documentary. London: Longman, 1976.

Deerr, Noel, Cane Sugar: A Text on the Agriculture of Sugar Cane, the Manufacture of Cane Sugar, and the Analysis of Sugar House Products; together with a Chapter on the Fermentation of Molasses. Manchester: Norman Rodger, 1911.

Doniger, Wendy, and Brian Smith, eds. The Laws of Manu. London: Penguin, 1991.

Fernandez-Armesto, Felipe. The Canary Islands after the Conquest: The Making of a Colonial Society in the Early Sixteenth Century. Oxford: Clarendon, 1982.

Galloway, J. H. "The Mediterranean Sugar Industry." Geographical Review 67, no. 2 (1977): 177–192.

Las Casas, Bartolome de. History of the Indies. Translated by A. Collard. New York: Harper & Row, 1971.

Layfield, Dr. "A Large Relation of the Port Ricco Voiage; Written, as Is Reported, by That Learned Man and Reverend Divine Doctor Layfield, His Lordships Chaplaine and Attendant in That Expedition; Very Much Abbreviated." In Hakluytus Postumus or Purchas His Pilgrimes, ed. S. Purchas, 16:44–106. Glasgow: James MacLehose, 1906.

Mintz, Sidney W. Sweetness and Power: The Place of Sugar in Modern History. London: Penguin, 1985.

Schwartz, Stuart B. Sugar Plantations in the Formation of Brazilian Society: Bahia, 1550–1835. Cambridge: Cambridge University Press, 1985.

Smith, Frederick H. Caribbean Rum: A Social and Economic History. Gainesville: University Press of Florida, 2005.

Frederick H. Smith

sugar rim, where the outside of the rim of a glass in which a cocktail or other mixed drink will be served has been moistened and rolled in sugar to create a frosted effect, has been a part of "fancy" mixology at least since the 1850s. That's when Joseph Santini (1817–1874) of New Orleans applied it to his version of the Cock-Tail, which he christened the Crusta, after the crust that the sugar formed when it was left to set. See CRUSTA. After that, it joined the bartender's repertoire, to be deployed when a drink needed a fancy touch. With the trend toward

A sugar rim on an East India Cocktail. Wondrich Collection.

to perform this operation well in advance, letting the glass sit at room temperature for an hour so that the sugar will set. Otherwise, condensation from the cold drink will cause the sugar to run down the glass, creating a sticky mess.

Chapin & Gore. *Manual: What to Use, How to Mix, How to Serve.* Chicago: Chapin & Gore, 1935.

"The Onlooker." *New York Evening Telegram*, April 21, 1908, 8.

David Wondrich

Suntory, the leading Japanese drinks company, was established by Shinjiro Torii (1879–1962), who had started in the wine and spirit business at his uncle Gisuke Konishi's firm in Osaka, making *yoshu*, or imitation foreign-style spirits. See JAPAN. In 1899 he opened his own store, Torii Shoten, and began bottling his own brands including, in 1919, an imported Scotch blend he called Tory's.

He started his production firm Kotobukiya in 1921 and three years later opened the Yamazaki distillery, Japan's first dedicated whisky distillery, with master distiller Masataka Taketsuru, who had learned his trade in Scotland. See TAKETSURU, MASATAKA. In 1929 a blend, Shirofuda ("white label") appeared. Its lack of success resulted in Torii crafting whiskies that better suited Japanese sensibilities. In 1937, the Kakubin blend was launched. It remains Japan's top-selling blend.

In 1952, Torii founded a chain of bars, called Tory's, to tap into the growth of whisky drinking among the emerging Japanese salarymen.

His second son, Keizo Saji, renamed the firm Suntory in 1963 and embarked on a premiumization strategy, introducing brands such as Suntory Royal, Reserve, and Hibiki. The firm's second distillery, Hakushu, opened in 1972 and was for a period the largest single malt distillery in the world. In 1984, Yamazaki became the first Japanese single malt brand. At the same time, Suntory had been steadily diversifying into beer, wine, soft drinks, coffee, health products, and horticulture—it created the world's first blue rose. The firm also invested in Scotch whisky, buying Morrison Bowmore and a stake in Macallan. In 2014 it bought the American firm Jim Beam, becoming the world's third largest distiller. The new firm was renamed BeamSuntory.

drier drinks that came at the turn of the twentieth century, however, it began to seem outdated: as one New York newspaperman snarked in 1908, "In Gananoque [a small town in Ontario, Canada] and other commercial centers they still put sugar around the rim of the glass."

The sugar rim returned to vogue in the 1930s, when American bartenders began applying it to the Sidecar, which did not originally have it (this no doubt influenced the salt rim on the Margarita, which can be viewed as a tequila Sidecar). See MARGARITA and SIDECAR. It is still the default presentation for the Sidecar, but is used infrequently otherwise.

To rim a glass properly with sugar, rub a piece of lemon around the outside rim of the glass, ensuring that a band a centimeter (roughly half an inch) wide is well and consistently moistened. Then roll the glass in sugar, making sure to get a consistent coating. (Although superfine or caster sugar is traditional, different types or even colors of sugar can be used, depending on the effect desired.) It is best

See also WHISKY, JAPANESE.

Broom, Dave. *The Way of Whisky: A Journey around Japanese Whisky.* London: Mitchell Beazley, 2017.

Dave Broom

supertaster is a term originated by sensory analysts Linda Bartoshuk and Katherine Fast to describe individuals with greater sensitivity to certain specific flavors, especially bitterness; this will of course affect the way they taste and appreciate not only foods but also spirits and cocktails. Originally, this sensitivity was attributed to a greater density of sensory fungiform papillae on their tongues. Since Bartoshuk introduced the term in 2005, more has been learned about the physiological differences that exist in the human mouth, but also in other parts of the body where physiochemical "flavor" receptors are found, such as the throat, stomach, and even, some scientists believe, the intestinal tract.

Those with the most numerous fungiform papillae tend to exhibit the most extreme responses to most tastes; studies have shown that extreme supertasters will avoid even slightly bitter vegetables, leading to a disproportionate increase in colon polyps in that population. Many also avoid spirits in general; others gravitate away from the ones rich in tannins (e.g., bourbon, aged rum) and mixed drinks that are high in acidity. Less extreme supertasters can, however, prove to be excellent judges of complex spirits.

See TASTING SPIRITS.

Beauchamp, Gary, and Linda Bartoshuk. *Tasting and Smelling: Handbook of Perception and Cognition,* 2nd ed. Cambridge: Academic Press, 1997.

Wolfe, Jeremy, Keith Kluender, and Dennis Levi. *Sensation and Perception,* 3rd ed. Sunderland, MA: Sinauer Associates, 2012.

Doug Frost

Suze is a proprietary brand of bitter aperitif predominately flavored with gentian root and having a strong yellow-orange color. Although its origins have been claimed to stretch as far back as 1796, its documentable history as a brand extends only to 1898, when the brand was registered by Fernand Moureaux, a Parisian distiller, and his partner, Henri Porte. In 1965 the company was acquired by Pernod and is

A gentian uprooter, from a Suze promotional calendar, 1953. Wondrich Collection.

now part of the Pernod Ricard SA portfolio. It is one of the most popular aperitif beverages in France.

The distinctive Suze bottle was designed by Porte and trademarked in 1913, but the brand was already popular enough to be immortalized by Pablo Picasso in one of his collages, *Verre et bouteille de Suze,* from 1912. Since that time the company has become known for the artistic quality of its publicity materials and has produced a number of limited edition bottles.

The range of Suze products encompasses the flagship product Suze; Suze pour Bière, a formulation including candied citrus and spices that is intended to be mixed with beer; Suze Agrumes, flavored with orange, tangerine, and lemon; Suze Pêche de Vigne & Abricot, flavored with peach and apricot; and Suze Fruits Rouges, flavored with raspberry, blackberry, and blueberry—all of which are bottled at 15 percent ABV. In 2009, to celebrate its 120th anniversary, the company introduced Suze Saveur d'Autrefois ("Taste of yesteryear"), a formulation at 20 percent ABV (the brand was launched at 32 percent, reduced to 20 percent after World War I and 15 percent after World War II), said to be inspired by the original formulation and having a particularly strong flavor of gentian.

Suze is a component of many cocktails from the revival period, but most noteworthy is the White Negroni, created in 2001 by Wayne Collins and consisting of equal parts Plymouth gin, Lillet Blanc, and Suze. This drink is said to have been invented by Collins out of necessity when, finding himself in Bordeaux without Campari to make Negronis, he bought Suze as a substitute and paired it with the equally French Lillet Blanc to create one of the most widely-known and enduring Negroni variations of the cocktail revival. See COLLINS, WAYNE.

Other gentian aperitifs in this style include the French products Avèze, Couderc Gentiane, and Salers Aperitif and, from the United States, Bittermens Amère Sauvage.

In 2017, Suze introduced a line of cocktail bitters including Suze Aromatic, flavored with gentian, cinnamon, and cardamom; Suze Red Aromatic, flavored with gentian, nutmeg, and anise; and Suze Orange, flavored with gentian, orange peel, and bergamot.

Wondrich, David. "The Secret to Drinking Like the French." *Daily Beast*, June 7, 2019. https://www. thedailybeast.com/the-secret-to-drinking-like-the-french-suze (accessed March 12, 2021).

Samuel Lloyd Kinsey

Swedish Punch (*Svensk punsch*) is a highly sweetened, slightly spicy liqueur created in Sweden in the eighteenth century. Swedish Punch is defined by the use of Indonesian Batavia arrack as its base spirit and dominant flavor. See ARRACK, BATAVIA. The liqueur's bold taste and high sugar content evoke thoughts of some kind of unruly rum-punch concentrate, although its alcohol content is usually quite moderate, in the 25 percent range. See PUNCH.

Swedish Punch consumption hit its heyday from the mid-1800s to the early 1900s. Originally made to order and served warm, the punch was best known as an accompaniment to yellow pea soup (ärtsoppa), followed by pancakes with strawberry jam and cream, a traditional Thursday dinner at Swedish universities.

An 1854 article in the *New Monthly Magazine* describes Swedish Punch as "a mixture of arrack, hock [German white wine], sugar, and a little water." (As with many other hot punches, the citrus content is minimal and is provided, if present at all, by the peel rather than juice.) Another English traveler described the punch in 1858 as "a universal evening drink, and one of the most insidious ever invented, despite its agreeable flavor."

By 1845, J. Cederlund Sønner commercialized a bottled version, after which the fashion turned to consuming it well chilled. The earliest known reference to Swedish Punch as an ingredient in mixed drinks comes from the 1905 *Hoffman House Bartender's Guide*, where it is found in a highball. Its best-known uses, however, are in Hugo Ensslin's 1917 Doctor Cocktail, with lime juice, and the excellent Diki Diki, with apple brandy and grapefruit juice, published by Robert Vermeire in 1922. See ENSSLIN, HUGO RICHARD; and VERMEIRE, ROBERT.

The craft cocktail movement of the early twenty-first century (and the associated reexamination of vintage recipes) spawned renewed interest in Swedish Punch. See CRAFT COCKTAIL. In 2011, Henrik Facile and Eric Seed of Haus Alpenz collaborated to create Kronan Swedish Punsch. Although not utilized during the golden age of tiki (1930s–1960s), its rum-forward, sweet and spicy characteristics have inspired modern craft tiki bartenders to use it in numerous recipes. See TIKI.

"A Fortnight in Finnland." *New Monthly Magazine*, January, 1854, 423–431.
"Punsch." Spritmuseum Stockholm. https://spritmuseum.se/kunskap/dryckernas-historia/punsch/ (accessed March 12, 2021).
Simonson, Robert. "How About a Nice Swedish Punsch?" *New York Times*, May 19, 2011. https://dinersjournal.blogs.nytimes.com/2011/05/19/how-about-a-nice-swedish-punsch/ (accessed March 12, 2021).
Taylor, Bernard. *Northern Travel: Summer and Winter Pictures of Sweden, Lapland, and Norway*. London: Sampson Low, Son: 1858.

Matt Pietrek

The **swizzle** is a style of drink defined not by its particular ingredients but instead by the technique used to make it, in which the drink's components are whisked together with crushed ice using a swizzle stick, resulting in a perfectly aerated, chilled, and diluted cocktail. Those components include spirits, of course (rum and gin traditionally being the most common), a sweetener—either sugar syrup or falernum—and bitters, sometimes with the addition of lime juice. See FALERNUM.

The history of the swizzle stick stems back to the 1600s in the West Indies when a small branch was used to stir a molasses and water drink known as a "Switchel." By the late 1800s, along with the newfound presence of ice in the Caribbean, there are print references to cocktails being "frothed" or "frisked into effervescence" by putting a stick into the glass and rubbing it between one's palms, which "imparts to it a rotary motion, constantly increasing, until the foam produced by the whirling twigs reaches the top of the tall glass." One traveler in Trinidad in the late 1800s specifically chronicled a cocktail being "stirred briskly with a swizzle-stick, rubbed rapidly between the hands." See SWIZZLE STICK.

To properly swizzle a drink, add the ingredients to a tall glass you will be serving in, such as a Collins, and fill the glass about three-quarters full with crushed ice. Take the swizzle stick and push the end toward the bottom of the glass, and place the handle between the palms of your hands. Briskly roll the handle between your palms, rotating the end in the drink while raising the stick up and down the length of the glass. Continue until the outside of the glass is well frosted, then top with additional crushed ice.

Two of the most famous historic swizzles are the Queen's Park Swizzle and the Green Swizzle, both of which originate in Trinidad and prominently feature rum and Angostura bitters. Trader Vic wrote, "Most true Swizzles, because of their origin, call for rum, but nearly all punches can be swizzled," a sentiment that is backed up by many a recipe for gin and whisky swizzles.

See also SWIZZLE; SWIZZLE STICK; QUEEN'S PARK SWIZZLE; GREEN SWIZZLE; and ANGOSTURA BITTERS.

Bergeron, Vic. *Trader Vic's Bartender's Guide.* Garden City, NY: Doubleday, 1947.

"Something in Regard to the Ordinary Citizen's Liking for Bitter Waters." *New York Morning Telegraph*, March 26, 1901, 6.

Winder, Lise, ed. *Dictionary of the English/Creole of Trinidad and Tobago: On Historical Principles.* Montreal: McGill-Queen's University Press, 2008.

Wondrich, David. *Imbibe!*, 2nd ed. New York: Perigee, 2015.

Martin Cate

swizzle stick is a slender wooden rod with three to five spokes radiating horizontally from one end (picture a toy airplane propeller affixed to a pencil) used to "swizzle" a drink—as opposed to shaking, stirring, or blending electrically—by whisking the ingredients in a glass or pitcher filled with crushed

ice. Proper swizzling technique involves rapidly rotating the stick between your palms while simultaneously raising and lowering it, until the whirring spokes froth the drink and frost the glass.

Swizzle sticks are often confused with stir sticks, the mass-produced plastic wands used not to make drinks but to decorate them. The traditional wooden swizzle stick has been an artisanal Caribbean product since at least the eighteenth century (when swizzling was first documented by visiting Europeans). Then as now, it begins life as a branch on the trunk of the *Quararibea turbinata* shrub, or swizzlestick tree, which grows wild throughout the West Indies. To make a swizzle stick, snap off a branch with the proper protruding "propeller blade" twigs, then strip off the bark and trim the twigs so that they'll fit inside a tall glass.

The swizzle stick is primarily associated with a specific category of drink called, fittingly enough, the swizzle. A notable exception that falls both within and without the category is the Ti Punch, a swizzle by any other name that's whisked with a *baton-lélé* or *bois-lélé* (what the French-speaking Caribbean islanders call their swizzle sticks).

See also SWIZZLE and TI' PUNCH.

Aspinall, Algernon Edward. *The Pocket Guide to the West Indies.* London: Edward Stanford, 1907.

Grose, Francis. *A Classical Dictionary of the Vulgar Tongue.* London: S. Hooper, 1788.

Jeff Berry

The **syllabub** is an English confection in which cream or fresh milk is blended into wine or cider along with sugar and spices to create a sumptuous, delicate dairy topping resting above the alcohol. Unlike its close relative the posset, the syllabub is not thickened by heating but through whipping or otherwise frothing the dairy element into the airy lightness that is the drink's signature: William King wrote in 1704, "Thy white wine, sugar, milk, together club / To make that gentle viand, syllabub." The syllabub's very name would become synonymous with frivolity, fashion, and ephemeral pleasures.

The "solybubbe" is mentioned as far back as John Heywood's 1537 *Thersytes*, while one of the earliest published recipes for syllabub appears in the 1658 compendium *The Queens Closet Opened* by one "W. M.": "Fill your Sillabub-pot with Syder (for that is the best for a Sillabub) and good store of Sugar and a little Nutmeg; stir it well together, put in as much thick Cream by two or three spoonfuls at a time, as hard as you can, as though you milke it in, then stir it together exceeding softly once about, and let it stand two hours at least ere it is eaten, for the standing makes the Curd."

Although the combination of dairy curds and wine or cider has its roots in the most elemental mixology (some early recipes directed that the cow be milked directly into the cider), the syllabub becomes truly noteworthy in the seventeenth and eighteenth centuries as a stage for ingenuity in display, as the contrast between the wine and froth could be set off in decorative glassware and arrayed for dazzling visual effect. Syllabub appears as a noteworthy treat in Samuel Pepys's diary ("Then to Commissioner Pett's and had a good sullybub and other good things, and merry") and Alexander Pope's letters. In Philip Mercier's ca. 1747 painting *The Sense of Taste*, a silver tray proffers a collection of multicolored syllabubs to the fashionable revelers pictured.

The drinks Mercier represents are likely to be examples of "whipt syllabub," in which whisking of the wine and cream produced prodigious bubbles, which is then left to dry overnight in a sieve. The 1757 cookbook author Hannah Glasse recommends the use of a chocolate mill to rapidly froth an "everlasting syllabub" from a mixture of cream, sack, Rhenish wine, sugar, orange juice, and lemon peel. Purpose-built syllabub churns of metal, not unlike small butter churns, were manufactured through the nineteenth century in both England and the United States as quick-acting syllabub aerators.

As delicate as the foam atop the glass, the fashion for syllabubs receded in the nineteenth and twentieth centuries.

Recipe (Sir Kenelm Digby's Whip Posset): Combine in a nonreactive bowl 500 ml whipping cream, 60 ml fine sugar, the whites of 2 eggs, and 120 ml oloroso sherry. Whip until the mixture begins to froth. Skim off the froth and put it into a deep, footed 1-liter vessel. Repeat until bowl is empty.

Day, Ivan. "Further Musings on Syllabub." *Petits Propos Culinaires* 53 (1996).

Digby, Kenelm. *The Closet of the Eminently Learned Sir Kenelme Digbie, Knight, Opened.* London: 1669.

W. M. *The Queens Closet Opened: Being Incomparable Secrets in Physick, Chyrurgery, Preserving, Candying, and Cookery, and Which Were Presented to the Queen.* London: 1658.

William Tipper

Sylvius, Franciscus (known as **Dr. Sylvius**), is

cited so often and so widely as the inventor of gin that drinks historians have come to despair of ever stripping him of that title, one to which he has no claim. The attribution was injected into the mainstream of drink history by Samuel Morewood, the founder of the field, in his pioneering 1824 *Essay on the Inventions and Customs of Both Ancients and Moderns in the Use of Inebriating Liquors*. See MIXOGRAPHY. In writing about gin, he notes that "Kaempfer attributes the discovery of this spirit to Professor Sylvius of Leiden."

Franz de le Boë (1614–1672) was a German-born physician, chemist, and anatomist who practiced in Holland. (As was customary, he Latinized his name, yielding "Franciscus Sylvius": *sylvius* means "of the forest," as does "de le Boë.") In 1691, when the German physician and traveler Engelbert Kämpfer (1651–1716) found himself being questioned closely by the Japanese shogun about the most effective medicine he knew for prolonging life, he identified it as "a certain spirituous liquor which could . . . comfort the spirit," newly invented. When pressed for its name, he replied "sal volatile oleosum Sylvii," explaining in his journal that the Japanese esteemed "long and high-sounded names."

Morewood took this "Sylvius's oily volatile salt" to be nothing but ordinary genever, probably correctly. But while Kämpfer seems to have been referring to Sylvius's particular formulation of the traditional Dutch spirit (genever dates back at the very least to the late 1400s), Morewood understood that as a paternity claim for the spirit in general, and most nineteenth- and twentieth-century authorities followed him without question. Only recently have drinks historians begun to correct his faulty math. See GENEVER and GIN.

Kämpfer, Engelbert. *History of Japan.* Translated by J. G. Scheuchzer. 1727; repr. Glasgow: MacLehose, 1906.

Morewood, Samuel. *Essay on the Inventions and Customs of Both Ancients and Moderns in the Use of Inebriating Liquors.* Dublin: 1824.

David Wondrich

tafia was the name given to a raw, unaged rum that was made in French colonies in the Caribbean as well as in Louisiana. See CANE-BASED SPIRITS and RUM.

tahona is a type of Mexican roller mill consisting of a large stone wheel fixed on a horizontal axle that is then pulled to rotate the wheel on a circular stone base. Mills similar to the tahona were used in ancient Greek and Roman times for the purpose of grinding grains, as well as in second century CE China for crushing the cinnabar used in vermillion pigment. This style of mill most likely did not come into use in Mexico until the seventeenth century with the arrival of the Spanish, who introduced beasts of burden and a type of mining procedure known as the patio process. The patio process increased silver extraction through fine grinding of ore in an *arrastra*, or drag mill, which consisted of a large irregular stone pulled around a fixed circular surface. Relatively primitive arrastras gave way to the more efficient wide-rimmed tahona.

Today the tahona is most familiar through its use in the production of tequila, mezcal, and other agave distillates. Many producers adopted tahonas to replace the labor-intensive process of crushing roasted agave by hand using large wooden mallets (although this procedure is still used to make a number of mezcals). Further technological advances led to

A tahona (or a "molino," as it is known in Oaxaca) at the palenque of Rogelio Martinez Cruz in Santa Maria Albarradas, Oaxaca. Courtesy of Del Maguey.

even more efficient mechanical crushing methods; today very few horse- or tractor-drawn tahonas are used in tequila production. Tahonas are still common, however, throughout Oaxaca (where it is commonly known as a *molino*) and other regions of Mexico where other agave spirits are produced. The use of a tahona is often considered to be a sort of talisman of artisanal production.

See AGAVE; MEZCAL; and TEQUILA.

Lynch, A. J., and Chester A. Rowland. *The History of Grinding*. Littleton, CO: Society for Mining, Metallurgy, and Exploration, 2005.

Misty Kalkofen

tails, known in Scotland as "feints," are the parts of the distillate that come off a still after a cut is made to separate them from the desirable hearts. Tails are either discarded or redistilled in a later run. See CUT; DISTILLATION, PROCESS; and HEART.

Taketsuru, Masataka (1894–1979), is, with Shinjiro Torii, viewed as one of the two founding fathers of Japanese whisky. See SUNTORY. Born into a sake-brewing family from Takehara, close to Hiroshima, he graduated in chemistry before starting to work for Osaka-based Settsu Shozu, one of a number of firms producing *yoshu* (foreign liquors).

The firm had plans to make whisky in Japan, so in 1918 Taketsuru traveled to Glasgow to study chemistry and gain practical experience in distilleries. In only two years he completed his studies and worked at Longmorn, Bo'ness grain distillery, and, most significantly, Hazelburn in Campbeltown, one of the few distilleries with a laboratory. He also found time to woo and marry his landlady's daughter, Rita Cowan.

In 1920 the couple returned to Japan to discover that Settsu Shuzo was under administration, so plans for the whisky distillery had been put on hold. In 1922 Taketsuru resigned, but the following year was hired as distiller by Shinjiro Torii for his new distillery at Yamazaki. He remained with Torii until 1934 when, slighted by a demotion to the brewery, he resigned. He and Rita headed north to Hokkaido, the location he believed most closely resembled the conditions he had experienced in Scotland. His distillery in the fishing port of Yoichi started operations the same year.

Taketsuru and Rita lived in Hokkaido for the rest of their lives. His company, Nikka, would grow to become Japan's second-largest whisky producer. See NIKKA.

In 2014, the Japanese television station NHK began broadcasting an *asadora* (morning drama) called *Massan* based around Masataka and Rita's love story.

See also WHISKY, JAPANESE.

Broom, Dave. *The Way of Whisky: A Journey around Japanese Whisky*. London: Mitchell Beazley, 2017.

Dave Broom

Tales of the Cocktail is an annual spirited conference in New Orleans, a city that has historically celebrated intoxication and nightlife. Bartenders, bar owners, chefs, distillers, distributors, marketers, spirits writers, and garden-variety hedonists pour in each July for five days of forums and festivities.

Ann Rogers Tuennerman founded Tales, as it is popularly known, on September 19, 2002. Born in 1964, she grew up in New Orleans and pursued a career in public relations, applying that experience to promote the Crescent City. The inaugural event was a walking tour of French Quarter bars and restaurants conducted by Joe Gendusa, a licensed tour guide, and partly inspired by photojournalist Kerri McCaffety's book *Obituary Cocktail: The Great Saloons of New Orleans*. The afternoon integrated lore about the Napoleon House, Tujague's, Arnaud's, the Carousel Bar, and two hometown drinks that had fallen from grace, the Sazerac and the Ramos Gin Fizz. See SAZERAC COCKTAIL and RAMOS GIN FIZZ.

For the first anniversary of the initial Tales, Tuennerman lured in cocktail cognoscenti, expanded the bacchanal to two days, and secured $25,000 in sponsorship from Southern Comfort. Two hundred revelers hobnobbed with cocktail book authors and explored New Orleans's dining, literary, and drinks culture. Among the speakers were Dale DeGroff, Gary Regan, Barnaby Conrad III, Anistatia Miller and Jared Brown, and vintage barware collector Stephen Visakay. The events were free save for set-menu dinners paired with drinks at historic establishments for $75. See DEGROFF, DALE; REGAN, GARY; and MILLER, ANISTATIA, AND BROWN, JARED.

In 2004, Tales was moved up to mid-August, the city's slowest tourism time, to capitalize on cheaper hotel rates. Educational seminars and cocktail clinics were added, and the number of attendees increased to three hundred. Also noted was a climb in humidity, blood alcohol levels, and aspirin sales.

New Orleans's gravitational pull proved even more vital in 2006, the year after Hurricane Katrina's devastation. Tuennerman was determined to not let Tales become one of its casualties and anchored the event in mid-July to avoid the August anniversary of the flooding. Roughly five hundred devotees made the pilgrimage. Until that year all events, save for the dinners, were complimentary.

In 2008, the New Orleans backdrop provided the inspiration for another Tales ritual, the Cocktail Funeral. Anistatia Miller and Jared Brown documented in their 2012 book, *Tales of the Cocktail from A to Z*, that jazz funeral processions were held for the scorned Appletini (2008), Redheaded Slut (2009), Sex on the Beach (2010), and Long Island Iced Tea (2011), "buried with hundreds of reveling mourners in gleeful attendance." See SEX ON THE BEACH and LONG ISLAND ICED TEA.

Also in 2008, the Cocktail Apprentice Program began, giving ambitious bartenders a chance to learn alongside cocktail luminaries. Don Lee, cofounder of Cocktail Kingdom, a comprehensive manufacturer and distributor of bar materials, has overseen the program since its inception. He reported that six hundred applications from as far away as Estonia come in every year for just sixty slots. The international, mixed-gender team works twelve-hour days, in 2015 squeezing 5,510 lemons and 24,200 limes and preparing fifty-three sub-recipes, such as lemon-thyme syrup, for a total of 199,550 drink servings.

Industry professionals have come to rely on the event for networking, learning new tricks, tasting new products, hearing accepted cocktail history debunked, and bumping into friends, colleagues, and fans from curb to curb. Hotel Monteleone on Royal Street is the official headquarters. After hours, night owls traditionally migrate around the corner to the Old Absinthe House on Bourbon Street and to the Alibi on Iberville Street. See OLD ABSINTHE HOUSE.

At the thirteenth annual Tales in 2015 there were sixteen thousand registrants able to choose from 349 events, including eighty seminars, seventy-five dining and drinking extravaganzas, and the Spirited Awards ceremony, the Oscars of the cocktail world. Ticket prices generally ranged from $49 to $250. Revenue of $15.6 million was generated for the city. Since 2003, participants have traveled to New Orleans from thirty-five countries and all continents except Antarctica.

Founder Ann R. Tuennerman, who is white, tendered her resignation in 2017 following the controversy that exploded after she posted a Facebook Live video of herself wearing blackface for the Zulu Mardi Gras parade in New Orleans. While this is traditional for white guests of Zulu, the main African American Mardi Gras Krewe, it served to highlight the lack of diversity that had long been a point of contention among Tales of the Cocktail attendees and led to the airing of other longstanding grievances. Tuennerman and her husband, Paul, sold Tales for an undisclosed sum to prominent local business people, the Solomon family and Neal Bodenheimer, who kept Tales from disintegrating. The organization was converted into a nonprofit foundation in 2018, declaring a renewed commitment to education and trust within the global spirits community.

English, Camper. "8 Lessons from the World's Largest Booze Convention," *Details*, July 23, 2014. https://static1.squarespace.com/static/53e0e276e4b0f775e0590d41/t/559a22b6e4b0edd30ab1b9b4/1436164790937/USA+-+Details+-+Plantation+-+July+2014.jpg (accessed April 28, 2021).

Gendusa, Joe. *History with a Twist: Lemon or Lime*. New Orleans: 2008.

Knapp, Gwendolyn. "What I Learned Working at Tales of the Cocktail," *Eater*, July 2, 2015. http://www.eater.com/2015/7/2/8884877/behind-the-scenes-tales-of-the-cocktail (accessed April 6, 2021).

Simonson, Robert. "Tales of the Cocktail, a Troubled Event, May Have a Savior." *New York Times*, December 22, 2017. https://www.nytimes.com/2017/12/22/dining/drinks/tales-of-the-cocktail-new-orleans.html (accessed April 6, 2021).

Vora, Shivani. "Even Hurricane Katrina Couldn't Shake New Orleans' Cocktail Queen," *Fortune*, August 24, 2015. http://fortune.com/2015/08/24/even-hurricane-katrina-couldnt-shake-new-orleans-cocktail-queen/ (accessed April 6, 2021).

Julie Besonen

Talisker is the only single malt Scotch whisky produced on the wild and hauntingly beautiful Isle of Skye, the largest of the inner Hebridian Islands scattered off the west coast of Scotland. A rich, slightly saline dram with a little fire to it, it is a benchmark of Scottish distilling.

Often referred to as an "Island" whisky, Talisker actually falls under the Scotch Whisky Association's designation as a Highland malt. Diageo currently owns Talisker and often markets the brand as part of its "Classic Malt" collection. See DIAGEO.

In 1829, when brothers Hugh and Kenneth MacAskill signed a lease to work the land that would soon house the Talisker distillery, the demographic of Skye was already beginning to shift. Over the next five decades, between twenty thousand and thirty thousand people would be driven from the island in the mass displacement known as the Clearances. Legend has it that the MacAskill brothers, like many lairds and tacksmen (landholders) of the era, forced tenants out of their ancestral lands to be replaced by sheep, which were certainly less feisty and a more reliable source of income. Alongside the sheep and the grass, unfussed by the din of angry farmers, the brothers began distilling. That was in 1831. In 1833, they got a license for it.

The distillery, one of the few in Scotland that practiced triple distillation, proved such a failure,

though, that the Bank of North Scotland took it over by 1848. Over the next three-quarters of a century, Talisker passed through more hands than there are ghosts roaming Skye's wild moorlands. In 1925, it finally settled down as a part of the DCL empire. See DISTILLERS COMPANY LTD. In 1928, it shifted to double distillation.

A fire ravaged the distillery in 1960, forcing it to close for two years. Exact replicas of the original five pot stills and worm condenser tubs operate today and offer the sixty thousand visitors per year a glimpse into the beauty of distilling in a bygone era. Pot-still lyne arms carry the alcoholic vapor to outside worm tubs—so called because of the coiled pipes submerged within the tank of water. Unusual loops in the lyne arms allow the alcohol vapor to begin condensing even before even reaching the worm tubs.

All water used in Talisker's production process comes from Cnoc nan Spereag (Hawk Hill), which flows over peat. Talisker is considered a medium-peated whisky, with the malted barley shipped in from Glenn Ord. Since 2008, Talisker has expanded its lineup from the ten- and eighteen-year-old malts to a variety of no-age-statement (NAS) whiskies that include the Talisker Storm, 57 North, Dark Storm, and Port Ruighe. It has also long been a key component of the blend used for Johnnie Walker Black Label.

The Talisker distillery, Isle of Skye, Scotland. Courtesy of Diageo.

See JOHNNIE WALKER; WHISKY, SCOTCH; and STILL, POT.

Craig, H. Charles. *The Scotch Whisky Industry Record.* Dumbarton, UK: Index, 1994.

"Talisker Distillery." *Difford's Guide.* https://www.diffordsguide.com/producers/72/talisker-distillery/history (accessed April 6, 2021).

Heather Greene

tannin is a critical structural element in fine red wines and in barrel-aged spirits. It is derived from barrels and any other wood that comes into prolonged contact with a spirit, as well as from wood elements in wine-based spirits such as brandies and pomace brandies, including grape skins, seeds, and stems.

Tannin is a type of polyphenol, and like other polyphenols, it tends to be highly reactive in the mouth and body, as well as in solutions of alcohol. See PHENOLS. When tasted, it creates both bitterness and astringency. Bitterness is a basic taste—the body has its own physiochemical receptors for it, just as it does for sweet, sour, salt, and umami. Astringency is at least partially based upon tannin's ability to bind with saliva's proteins, leading to dryness and even increased friction in the mouth, all of which add to a spirit's perceived weight.

Polyphenolic reactivity also manifests in tannin's complex bonding and re-bonding with various other compounds. While humans are capable of discerning sensory/tactile differences between these differing compounds, the science is still nascent in being able to predict and define the sensory character of them. Tasters will describe tannins as "sharp" or "fruity" or "sandpaper" or "blocky," among many other descriptors, and there are numerous theories as to how and why certain tannins might be so perceived, but there is no consensus. Researchers will talk about tannins, catechins, epicatechins, and the like, and undoubtedly each of those elements contributes to mouthfeel. But discussions of "short-chain tannins" (which were once thought to be more intense but now are believed to leave a softer impression) and "long chain tannins" (which also have flip-flopped their reputation) are still more hypothesis than fact. Says Steven Price of ETS Laboratories, "I don't think we'll ever really be able to analyze tannins in the laboratory as well as we do in our mouths." Discussion of the "number" of tannins seems to be pointless as well; there may be billions of structural isomers possible for a single tannin consisting of thirty monomers, according to wine chemistry.

Nonetheless, spirits producers will choose barrels, wood products, and practices based upon their perception of "which" tannins each will impart to their beverage. Whether or not there is a solid scientific basis for these views, most tasters find at least moderate agreement in describing the character imparted by each choice. American oak barrels are often seen to have more aggressive tannins than European oak, but this is far too general a view to be particularly useful in the distillery or warehouse.

For one, while *Quercus alba* is the primary oak used for American barrel production, there are others, such as Oregon's *Quercus garryana*, that offer a differing tannin "profile". European forests host several species of oak trees: *Quercus robur* is the most common for French oak production, but *Quercus petraea*, with its notably finer grain, seems to provide less overt tannins. And specific forests, by providing divergent growing conditions, may exhibit tighter or looser grains and are perceived to express stronger or smoother tannins as a result.

Barrels from the Alliers, Tronçais, or Vosges forests are most often directed toward wine production. Oaks from the Limousin or Monleuzon forests, both showing looser grains, are more commonly discussed in regard to their appropriateness for brandy (cognac and Armagnac, respectively). Moreover, cognac producers will alternate between barrels sourced from the Limousin and Tronçais forests as they seek to either bolster their brandy for the long haul (with Limousin) or create a softer, perhaps earlier-drinking cognac (with Tronçais).

Tannin uptake is also based upon warehouse conditions (particularly humidity and heat) as well as the size and age of the barrels. American oak tends to give up its tannin more quickly than European oak (though this, too, is a rough generalization). And for coopers, a hotter, faster "toast" of the wood will tend to generate more prominent, grittier tannins, while a slower toast may offer gentler tannins.

With every spirit that is barrel aged, there is a point after which the tannins from the barrel eclipse the base material from which the spirit was distilled, and another beyond which all but the most motivated or tannin-insensitive drinkers will find the spirit too astringent to drink. The warehouse manager must recognize when the first point is approaching and also know just how long it will then take before the spirit hits the second. Right now, this remains an art.

See also BARREL; ÉLEVAGE; MATURATION; POMACE BRANDY and TEXTURE.

Buxton, Ian, and Paul S. Hughes. *The Science and Commerce of Whisky*. London: Royal Society of Chemistry, 2015.

Jackson, Ronald. *Wine Science, Principles and Applications*, 4th ed. Amsterdam: Academic Press, 2014.

Jeffrey, David W., Gavin Sacks, and Andrew Waterhouse. *Understanding Wine Chemistry*. Chichester, UK: Wiley, 2016

Doug Frost

Tanqueray Gordon & Co. was formed by the 1898 merger of two of the leading brands of London dry gin: Gordon's, founded in the eighteenth century, and Tanqueray, founded in the early nineteenth. Today a part of the Diageo conglomerate, the brands, which have remained distinct, are two of the most successful and respected progenitors of the London dry style and have maintained a strong cultural legacy through a combination of savvy product design and marketing acumen.

Alexander Gordon (1742–1823) began selling his eponymous gin in 1769. Initially he sold it as a merchant in St Mary Axe in East London, but by 1776 he had taken a partner and set up a proper distillery on Barnaby Street in Southwark. In 1786 he moved again to Clerkenwell, where many other gin distillers had found access to clean, ideal water. Alexander's son Charles (1774–1849) joined his father as a partner, and by 1817 Gordon and Co. were among the biggest gin rectifiers in London, behind only Phillip Booth. See OLD TOM GIN.

Nearby, Charles Tanqueray (1810–1865) was breaking with three generations of family tradition in the church; his eponymous gin began production in 1830. He opened up on Vine Street in Bloomsbury and worked closely with the Currie family, an established distilling family in London. By the late 1830s, the words "English gin" and "London gin" no longer connoted an inferior product. As Charles Pope wrote, "British gin has now very nearly superseded the use of the foreign article." Charles Tanqueray

distilled gin, with more and more success until he died, passing the distillery on to son Charles Waugh Tanqueray (1848–1931), who would oversee several more decades of expansion, culminating in the merger with Gordon and Co.

Tanqueray, Gordon would be acquired 1922 by the Distillers Company, who began to build distilleries in a few of their biggest markets in order to turn some of their exports into (advantageously taxed) domestic products. Before repeal had even passed in the United States, they laid the foundation for their Linden, New Jersey, distillery. It would begin making Gordon's gin just months after prohibition ended (Tanqueray always remained a British product).

While both gins were commercially successful and won awards at international fairs and exhibitions, they still sought to expand their reach by appealing to a wider audience. They targeted women by marketing their gins as medicine in women's magazines. Gordon's launched variants including lemon-, orange-, and mint-flavored gins in the early twentieth century; in the early twenty-first they launched cucumber and elderflower. Tanqueray's Malacca Gin, an 1839 formula revived in 1997 (and again in 2012 after the previous revival proved premature) would push the envelope in two separate launches, highlighting a more contemporary botanical profile.

While Tanqueray was always respected, Gordon's gin became a cultural touchstone. It was the fuel for novelist Theodore Dreiser's work and took on symbolic importance in Hemingway's, being called out by name on four separate occasions in *Across the River and into the Trees*. In 1951 the gin was the first intentional product placement in film, when Katharine Hepburn threw it overboard in *The African Queen*. James Bond's Vesper was a three-to-one ratio of Gordon's to vodka. Tanqueray was nearly an afterthought among imported gins until the 1950s, but it's since been the downfall of Bruce Springsteen's "Johnny 99" and has been namedropped by the Notorious B.I.G., the Ramones, and Snoop Dogg.

Though the exact recipes of the two gins, similar to the taste, are guarded secrets, their botanical bills are widely purported to contain some or all of the following: Gordon's may include juniper, coriander, licorice, angelica, orris root, orange, and lemon. Tanqueray purportedly features but four botanicals: juniper, coriander, angelica, and licorice.

Many distillers have been inspired by these formulae, and the flavor profile suggested by these botanical bills was the dominant expression in gin up until the start of the twenty-first century.

Both gins are often grouped together for their juniper-forward palates. Gordon's London Dry Gin leads with juniper but has softer lemon and coriander-tinged notes on the palate; Tanqueray London Dry Gin is perceptibly sharper with more pine but segueing into an earthier, richer finish with just a hint of licorice. Even though current owners Diageo moved production entirely to Scotland in 1998, the two brands still represent London. In 2008, the European Union codified London gin descriptively as a dry gin distilled in a fashion that is quite precisely the work Tanqueray and Gordon's have been doing for over a century.

Their success and endurance have led the brands to be seen by some as default; however, their enviable success and strong brand identity have brought them continued success even into the twenty-first century. In 2015, Gordon's was the second-best-selling gin worldwide and Tanqueray the sixth, with combined sales of 6.8 million cases of gin, and Gordon's remains the bestselling gin in the world outside of the Philippines.

Cromwell, Thomas Kitson. *History and Description of the Parish of Clerkenwell.* London: Sherwood, 1828.

Gustafson, Axel. *The Foundation of Death: A Study of the Drink-Question.* Boston: Ginn, Heath, 1885.

The House of Commons. Accounts Relating to Distillation in England, Scotland and Ireland: No 1–11. 1822.

Official Journal of the European Union. Regulation (EC) No 110/2008 of the European Parliament and of the Council of 15 January 2008 on the definition, description, presentation, labelling and the protection of geographical indications of spirit drinks and repealing Council Regulation (EEC) No 1576/89.

Pope, Charles. *The Yearly Journal of Trade, 1837–8 . . . : A Sketch of the Origin and Progress of Trade and Miscellaneous Information Not to Be Found in Any Work Besides.* 17th ed. London: Thorp & Graham, 1838.

Aaron Knoll

Tarling, William James "Billy"

Tarling, William James "Billy" (1904–1998), is one of the lesser-documented legends of British bartending. In 1930, after working at the Leicester cocktail bar Glasshouse St. (near Leicester Square), he joined London's Café Royal as head barman. It was a pivotal point in London bartending: Harry Craddock had just published *The Savoy Cocktail Book,* his compilation of the drinks served at the American Bar at the Savoy Hotel. Three years later, the pair joined to establish the United Kingdom Bartenders Guild. Craddock was elected the guild's first president, but Tarling was concerned that Craddock, rather than the talents of the growing brotherhood of London bartenders, garnered too much personal attention. That year, Tarling instigated the compilation of the UKBG's first drinks book, published as *Approved Drinks.* While employed by the Café Royal Tarling compiled an additional book of mixed drinks, of which one thousand copies were printed in 1937. It has become one of the world's rarer drinks volumes. In 1951, Tarling and his family moved to Harrogate, where he presided over the Prince of Wales Hotel bar until his retirement. That same year, he represented the UKBG at the foundational meeting for the International Bartenders Association and was elected its first president.

See also CRADDOCK, HARRY LAWSON; SAVOY HOTEL'S AMERICAN BAR; and see IBA and UNITED KINGDOM BARTENDERS GUILD (UKBG).

"Happy Evenings Ahead." *Yorkshire Evening Post,* October 12, 1951, 11.

West Yorkshire Electoral Records, 1952.

Anistatia R. Miller and Jared M. Brown

tasting spirits will always be subjective and cannot be treated as an exact science, but it can nonetheless be guided by discipline and informed by practice. To begin with, each person develops different preferences among food and drink, so it should be assumed that each taster is having a slightly different experience, based on a lifetime of experiences that informs his or her preferences.

It is also understood that each individual has greater or lesser sensitivities to an innumerable array of aromas and flavors; for example, "supertasters," as they are known, are highly sensitive to bitterness. See SUPERTASTER. The so-called primary flavors of sweet, sour, salt, bitter, and umami are not universally experienced, and there is no precise norm for any of them.

Equally, there is no one, best tasting method; each person can and ought to approach tasting differently. That said, the method used by the BAR group (Beverage Alcohol Resource) to teach spirits tasting and analysis (based at least in part on some of the concepts also used by the Court of Master Sommeliers) has been proved effective in helping literally hundreds of students to correctly identify spirits in blind tasting. See BEVERAGE ALCOHOL RESOURCE (BAR). These techniques, described below, although necessarily personal and subjective, are based upon the ideas and practices of a great many professionals in the wine and spirits industry—people with long experience blind-tasting spirits in a wide range of categories.

Sensory evaluation relies upon the senses of sight, smell, touch, and taste to identify a spirit's primary characteristics. With wine analysis, the majority of the appropriate descriptors can be gathered via sight and smell; tasting is usually deployed more often to verify than to determine.

Spirits are different, not only because of the variability of their alcoholic strengths but also due to factors such as blending, compounding, and flavoring, which can make a spirit smell like something it's not. Furthermore, taste becomes a critically important measure of sweetness, tartness, bitterness, and perhaps more importantly, alcohol strength and purity. Spirits of 40 percent or 50 percent can all smell powerful, but well-crafted spirits can provide elegance as well, a trait difficult to smell. Tasting the spirit and then, after twenty or thirty seconds, drawing air gently in through the mouth can expose methanol volatility or other impurities. Conversely, very clean spirit will respond to oxygen by stimulating the cold receptors as mint does. Well-crafted spirit may generate a salivary response; spirit with ameliorants or additives may taste thick and sweet in the finish.

As with all beverage analysis, patience can be revealing. A great spirit may offer power; it may offer delicacy. It should linger; it should seem cleaner in equal measure to the length of the finish. It's difficult to put into words what great spirit is, whether it is a vodka, a whisky, a mezcal, a cognac. But each spirit category contains greater and lesser examples. Those that are wanting are typically short in flavor; they may be sweet or off, or smell or taste hotter than their alcohol percentage indicates. Great spirits seem to gather complexity as they linger in the mouth. They ought to embody the most indefinable character of all: balance.

Balance is subjective; this should be admitted at the outset. Yet there is a common thread: balanced spirit has many descriptors but none that dominate. A balanced spirit offers its myriad flavors and aromas an equal opportunity to manifest. Moreover, a balanced spirit often embodies a term the British and Irish have long celebrated: "moreish-ness," the idea that a great spirit makes you want to drink more of it. See BALANCE.

But these qualitative assessments require consistency; and that requires a tasting system. The mistake made by most amateur tasters is to focus only upon the obvious traits; a serious taster takes the time and commits to the discipline required to notice all available descriptors, the obvious and the nuanced.

Always learn what you can from the look of a spirit. Brown spirits offer certain clues. White spirits can do the same. Many rich and powerful vodkas and gins look weighty as they roll around in a glass; they may appear pewter or even grey. Many commercial white spirits with only commercial ambitions look like water; those that have had sugar added to them (a bad idea with gin or vodka) tend to leave a ring around the glass.

Brown spirits are rarely simply brown. Bourbon often has a red cast; actors in old Western movies sometimes used the term "red eye" to describe good whisky. The idea wasn't absurd; whisky barrel makers talk about the "red line" in a barrel, the limit at which the burn and char has saturated the wood. Aging a spirit in a newly charred barrel will give whisky a decidedly red cast. Conversely, spirits aged in used barrels won't offer that red hue. See BARREL.

After evaluating the spirit visually, it is best to proceed to evaluating its aroma. Aromas in great spirits can be overwhelmingly complex, but a systematic approach offers organizing principles that allow cacophony to organize into music.

A good place to begin is with fruit. Does this spirit have fruit aromas? (A spirit does not need to be distilled from fruit to have them; while it may seem counterintuitive, even grain-based spirits show fruity aromas and flavors, courtesy of yeasts and the flavors inherent in the grain.) If so, what kind? Categories of fruit can be broken down into pomme fruits (apples and pears, aromas often found in, for instance, malt whiskies), citrus fruits (oranges, lemons, limes, grapefruits, tangerines, characteristic of white spirits), stone fruits (peaches, apricots, nectarines, quince, found in many brandies), tropical fruits (bananas, pineapples, kiwis, and the like, often associated with cane and agave spirits), dried and concentrated fruits, melons, red fruits, black fruits, on and on. Ask yourself about the condition of those fruits: Are they ripe or unripe, fresh, cooked, or desiccated? In barrel-aged spirits, the longer it has been in the barrel, the farther from fresh the fruit notes tend to be. See AROMA.

Next, check for flowers. Younger spirits are often quite floral, but so are aged Highland malt whiskies. The flowers may be fresh; they may be dried. Then look for herbs, grains, vegetables (tequilas, for instance, can have strong green pepper notes), minerals (although these can be difficult to pick up on the palate, some vodkas have subtle mineral notes, as do some tequilas), and spices. Even though one of these categories is unlikely to be represented, it is always worth consciously checking for it. Spirits are complex, and subsidiary notes can be surprising. Finally, check for "other." That can include the "hogo" found in many rums, the honey found in many barley spirits, peat smoke, and the cheesy, mushroomy notes of rancio. See HOGO; PEAT; and RANCIO.

Only once the spirit's scent has been thoroughly searched into should you proceed to tasting. This will confirm, but also sometimes challenge, the information you pulled out of the nose, while adding information on proof, texture, and finish. The aromas and the flavors you perceive will collectively become that individual spirit's profile, something to stick into your memory for the next time you might encounter it. If you perform similar analyses on multiple expressions from the same category, you will be able to pick out common elements that will form the category's profile, enabling you to see how a particular expression fits into it—and also to reach an informed opinion on its quality.

To see the kind of thinking that goes into making such a determination, let us backtrack and take another look at spices. Notes of various baking spices—cinnamon, clove, allspice, nutmeg—are generally a sign that a spirit has been aged in wood. But so are overtly "woody" flavors, including sawdust, wood ash, old-furniture aromas, and notes of pine resin and cedar.

One of the legitimate queries for any spirits taster—indeed, perhaps the primary one—is "Is this spirit good to drink?" In the case of a barrel-aged

spirit, the question becomes: Is the wood expressed as enhancing spice, or does the bitter, dusty, spicy character of wood aging overwhelm the fresh and even fruity notes of a bright spirit? There is no right or wrong to such a question: we have entered the realm of the subjective.

With brown spirits, barrels have very distinct aromas and flavors. First, they are spicy (cinnamon, clove, allspice, nutmeg, black pepper, and many other spices). Barrels also provide torrefaction aromas: caramel, butterscotch, maple, vanilla, and such. European barrels may present more with vanilla and ginger; American oak barrels will offer notes of vanilla too, but there is often an herbal element, such as dill; American oak also provides more prominent coconut notes than does European oak. American oak doesn't leak when you cut it across the grain; European oak does, so European oak barrels are split along the grain, while American oak barrels are sawn along the quarter grain; they can smell like fresh or charred sawdust as a result, as do the spirits aged within them. These descriptions may seem precious and absurd; if you pay attention to the aromas in spirits, they are not. Spirits that have spent too long in a barrel will lose their balance, with the woody, spicy flavor of the wood (along with bitterness and astringency) overwhelming all other flavors. For some collectors, this is not perceived as a problem; older is better. But assuming that it is considered a problem generally, where is the line between spice and wood? Its placement may be different for you depending on the base spirit, the type of oak, and any number of other factors. This is where system and experience can only take you so far. What you are left with is taste, and, of course, there is no accounting for that. All one can do is try to understand it.

See also FLAVOR and SENSORY EVALUATION.

Beauchamp, Gary, and Linda Bartoshuk. *Tasting and Smelling.* Cambridge: Academic Press, 1997.
Wolfe, Jeremy, Keith Kluender, and Dennis Levi. *Sensation and Perception.* Sunderland, MA: Sinauer Associates, 2011.

Doug Frost

Taylor, Col. E. H. (1830–1923), was one of the seminal forces in bourbon history. He was involved in the creation of the Bottled-in-Bond Act and was the first distillery owner to realize the power of whisky tourism. He served as the mayor of Frankfort, Kentucky, and as a Kentucky state representative. Both the "colonel" and the "Jr.," which he also used in his name sometimes, were honorifics; Taylor never served in the military, and "E. H. Taylor Sr." was his uncle, not his father.

Born in Kentucky, Taylor would eventually go to work for his uncle in a Lexington bank. He saw the money to be made in the whisky business and, after returning from a tour of European distilleries in 1867, opened a distillery. Two years later, he bought a small distillery in Leestown and renamed it the OFC Distillery (the letters stood for either Old Fire Copper, or Old Fashioned-Copper); it is known today as Buffalo Trace. Taylor failed to make OFC profitable, and he sold the distillery to George T. Stagg's firm in the late 1870s; he and Stagg would feud for years over the use of the Taylor name.

Taylor built a new distillery on Glenn's Creek. The Old Taylor distillery was eye-catching, built around a Rhenish-style castle with gleaming limestone walls, turrets, and a massive gate, surrounded by extensive sunken gardens and a key-shaped cistern (water, Taylor said, was the key to good bourbon). The public could visit the distillery, a completely new idea. Old Taylor was a success.

Taylor then took on bottlers of "rectified" whisky, which he considered a threat to quality bourbon. His lobbying would lead to the Bottled-in-Bond Act, the first American food purity law. Unfortunately, Taylor proved unable to prevail against Prohibition. Old Taylor closed for the duration, and he would not live to see it reopen.

See also BOTTLED IN BOND and BUFFALO TRACE DISTILLERY.

Sullivan, Jack. "Col. E. H. Taylor Jr.: The Face and Signature of Kentucky Bourbon." *Those Pre-Pro Whiskey Men!* (blog), January 10, 2015. http://pre-prowhiskeymen.blogspot.com/2015/01/col-e-h-taylor-jr-face-and-signature-of.html (accessed March 12, 2021).

Lew Bryson

TCA (2,4,6-trichloroanisole) is the chemical compound responsible for what is commonly known as "cork taint," where TCA suppresses a wine or spirit's inherent aromas and adds its own musty, wet cardboard aroma, essentially ruining the drink, although it poses no health risk. Created when certain airborne fungi come into contact with the antimicrobial chlorinated phenolic compounds with which wood is commonly treated, TCA can ruin the character and aromas of a wine or spirit in even the tiniest amounts (five or six parts per trillion is a generally accepted threshold for detection by humans, although sensitivity varies widely between individuals). Although cork has been the main offender in conveying TCA into contact with spirits, other vectors can include barrels, labeling, and ambient distillery conditions.

Because spirits are increasingly being bottled with natural cork, the incidence of cork taint has been on the rise for spirits using such closures. Though data for spirits is scarce, in 2000, incidence of TCA was claimed to be as high as 10 percent of all cork-finish wines. The industry has taken action since, including more judicious care of the cork-oak bark processed into corks and the elimination of chlorine bleaching (chlorine is a catalyst for cork taint), and perhaps only 1 percent to 2 percent of cork-finish products may exhibit TCA today. But vigilance on the part of producers and consumers should continue.

See also CLOSURES and CORK.

Jackson, Ron. *Wine Science*. London: Academic Press, 2014.

Takeuchi, Hiroko, Hiroyuki Kato, and Takashi Kurahashi. "2,4,6-Trichloroanisole as a Potent Suppressor of Olfactory Signal Transduction." *Proceedings of the National Academy of Sciences* 110 (October 2013): 16235–16240.

Doug Frost

tea, an infusion of the leaves of *Camellia sinensis* evergreen trees, has been mixed with spirits since at least the early eighteenth century, when it was a common component of punch. The tea tree is native to South and Eastern Asia, where it is a major global cash crop, and its consumption there can be documented back to the third century CE, when it appears in a medical text written by the Chinese physician Hua Tuo (ca. 140–208). Its consumption bears striking similarities to that of distilled spirits, in that both were originally introduced for their medicinal virtues prior to being popularized as recreational drinks. As with spirits, the history of tea is laden with stories, myths, and legends surrounding its origin, and there is very little hard information to counter that. Whatever its origin, tea drinking carries with it long-established rituals and ceremonies, as of course does drinking spirits.

Merchants and priests introduced tea to Europe in the sixteenth century. It became fashionable in London in the mid-seventeenth century, when it was introduced along with coffee, chocolate, and punch. By the 1670s, punch was being served in tea- and coffeehouses. Coffee and spirits do not seem to have been mixed until the mid-nineteenth century. See COFFEE DRINKS. Tea, however, was soon enlisted by punch-makers, with "Tea Punch," which was made with green tea instead of water, appearing in Britain as early as 1728. By the end of the century, it was a staple of British punch making, and indeed punch making everywhere. See REGENT'S PUNCH and SWEDISH PUNCH. In 1840, the London *Magazine of Domestic Economy* gave "using tea instead of water" as one of the bedrock rules for making punch.

Due to the tremendous variety and types of tea, its flavors are vastly varied, including but not limited to astringent, nutty, floral, bitter, cooling, grassy, smoky, and even sweet notes. (If not derived from the tea shrub, similar infusions made from flowers, fruits, or leaves from other plants are called tisanes or herbal infusions and can be consumed in the same manner as traditional tea.) That variety allows tea to blend into cocktails and other mixed drinks in a multitude of ways, adding flavor, aroma, and texture, making it a go-to ingredient for twenty-first-century mixologists. It can be used as dilution, as in punch, or made into syrups, infusions, ice, powder, and even smoke. Ironically, though, the most famous modern tea drink, the Long Island Iced Tea, has no tea in it at all. See LONG ISLAND ICED TEA.

See also MIXOLOGY.

Heiss, Mary Lou, and Robert J. Heiss. *The Story of Tea: A Cultural History and Drinking Guide.* Berkeley: Ten Speed, 2007.

"Miscellaneous Domestic Matters." *Magazine of Domestic Economy,* January 1840, 218–219.

Saberi, Helen. *Tea: A Global History.* London: Reaktion, 2010.

Sother Teague

Tender Bar is an institution in the Ginza neighborhood of Tokyo, Japan, founded by the nattily dressed Kazuo Uyeda (1944–), the originator of the "hard shake." See UYEDA, KAZUO. This distinctively choreographed and ferociously precise mixing style, developed by Uyeda over his more than half a century tending bars in Tokyo, is said to micro-aerate cocktails for a smoother-than-smooth texture. A 2009 public demonstration of the technique at the Hiro Ballroom in New York City propelled Uyeda to international media attention and sparked debates among New York City's most serious mixologists. Proponents call the hard shake a quintessentially Japanese form of cocktail Zen; critics counter it is no more efficacious than the usual vigorous shake. Any doubts quickly evaporate when the white-coated Uyeda presents one with one of his signature drinks, such as a velvety, jade-colored Gimlet, or the M-30 Rain, an almost bioluminescent mixture of vodka, pamplemousse schnapps, lime juice, and blue curaçao.

Though Tender Bar, on the fifth floor of a typical Tokyo elevator building, regularly lands on global best-bar lists, establishments of this sort are not intended for casual tourists or those looking for a wild night. Ginza cocktail bars are the product of a very localized business ecosystem, hushed and contemplative spaces where a drink ordered might take fifteen minutes or more to arrive, the better for a salaryman to quietly seal a deal with a client or sort through the latest office intrigue with a colleague without interruption. Tender Bar, with its line of low-backed stools along the bar, its handful of booths, and its low ceiling and lower lighting, is archetypical.

Tender Bar shut its doors in summer of 2020, a casualty of the COVID-19 pandemic and government-mandated shortened business hours. It has since reopened in a new space nearby, where—Fate willing—Uyeda will be serving up his hard-shaken signatures for the foreseeable future.

Uyeda, Kazuo. *Cocktail Techniques.* New York: Mud Puddle, 2010.

Matt Alt

tension line, or "wash line," refers to the liquid fill level of a measuring device such as a jigger or a piece of glassware. Proper care should be taken when using measuring to achieve accuracy and consistency. To fill "to tension" means that the meniscus forms over the top of the jigger. See JIGGER. This becomes essential when utilizing classic-style jiggers that have no indicator line present. "Wash line" can also refer to liquid fill level in a piece of glassware. The wash line should never reach the lip of the glass but instead have a "collar," or sufficient space from the rim to prevent spilling when carrying the drink.

See also MIXOLOGY.

Morgenthaler, Jeffrey. *The Bar Book: Elements of Cocktail Technique.* San Francisco: Chronicle, 2014.

Chad Solomon

tequila is a regionally-defined type of mezcal obtained through double distillation of fermented carbohydrates extracted from cooked or uncooked blue agave (*Agave tequilana* Weber var. azul), for which the Mexican law NOM 006-2021 defines all the terms of reference. See AGAVE and MEZCAL. Alcohol concentration may vary between 35 percent and 55 percent ABV. It takes its name from the city of Tequila in the western Mexican state of Jalisco. Ideas differ about the meaning of the term *tequila*, but it is originally a Nahuatl word related to *tequio*: "a place where people work" and "a place where people are cutting."

Tequila has been popular from its debut in the seventeenth century. The first and most refined name of the spirit was "vino mezcal de Tequila," but to the people of Mexico it has always been "mezcal" or "mezcal de Tequila." Quickly recognized as an important local product, it never faced persecution or periods of prohibition as was the case for other Mexican agave spirits such as mezcal, *bacanora*, and *raicilla*. Industrial production and export to the United States began in the nineteenth century: it was being sold in San Francisco as early as 1855 and advertised nationwide as "Nature's Own Tonic" by the Tequila Tonic Export Co. of Chicago in 1889. After the Mexican Revolution (1910–1920), tequila became more widely recognized abroad and something of a Mexican icon within the country thanks to Mexican cinema.

In 1972 the Mexican regulatory body Norma Obligatoria Mexicana, or NOM, chose tequila for the first Mexican denomination of origin. Since then the tequila specifications have been updated and new rules and modifications made. All the varied specifications may be found in the current Official Mexican Standard for Tequila, under NOM-006-SCFI-2012. Tequila may only be produced within the NOM-delineated denomination of origin area in Jalisco and other municipalities from Guanajuato, Michoacán, Nayarit, and Tamaulipas. In Jalisco state there are two main agave-growing regions, each with its reputation for the special qualities of the tequila made from agaves grown there: Los Altos (highlands) and El Centro (lowlands). Tequila was first produced in the "lowland" valley of Tequila, but within in the last seventy years production has been extended to the Los Altos highlands area. With six hundred meters of difference in elevation between the two areas, effects of factors such as temperature and local climate influence plant growth rates, physiology, and sugar type and concentration differently. Fermentation rates and distillation technology also differ in the two regions. In the lowland or Tequila region, agave plants produce less sugar, and fermentation takes place in cooled systems. The highlands triangle, a plateau with the highest elevation of Jalisco state, is recognized for the quality of its production. The highest recorded sugars in agave plants occur here, but there is also a risk of freezing and of potential damage to the sensitive plants.

An 1887 reference indicates that at that time at least nine varieties of agave were cultivated for tequila production. Plant conservation studies show clearly that there were traditionally four closely related tequila agave subspecies: azul (blue), sigüín, criollo, and variegated azul.

Agave takes from five to nine years to reach to a maturity and harvestable size, depending on environmental factors, agricultural technique, and the extraction and distillation technology of the producer. Advances in modern agronomy and the exclusive use of agave azul have helped to shorten this cycle with monocultures and diffusers hydrolisation. Tequila has two categories: the 100 percent agave, and *mixto*, which is made from a fermented base of 51 percent agave carbohydrate and 49 percent sugars from other sources that are not required by law to be identified but are usually from sugar cane. See CHINGUIRITO. (In the Mexican law governing tequila passed in 1949, only 100 percent agave tequilas were allowed; after the big export boom of the early 1960s stressed agave supplies, that went down to 70 percent and again to 51 percent in 1970.)

Agave carbohydrates, mainly a structurally distinct form of inulin now called agavin, are prepared for fermentation through two hydrolysis processes. In the traditional craft method, roasting and water vapor are used to extract the starches from the *piñas*, or agave hearts. Since the year 2000 the most common technology employed by the largest distilleries is the diffuser, which treats shredded raw piñas with an acid to separate starch from fresh agave juice. See DIFFUSER.

Tequila producers are under no obligation to indicate the extraction and hydrolysis methods employed, though there are clear qualitative differences. Tequila 100 percent from oven-roasted agave is closest to the original traditional process. Heat from the roasting process and in the subsequent water vapor step sweetens both flavor and aroma. Acid extraction of starches from pressed agave juice does not yield the same results but is a more efficient method for the conversion of the large polysaccharides (agavin) to fermentable sugars.

Today some distilleries have adapted the industrial process to include traditional elements to improve aroma and flavor, such as the *tahona* stone machinery for crushing cooked piñas. See TAHONA.

Tequila is generally double-distilled in stainless steel and copper pot stills, although a few producers use continuous or column stills. The final distillate, at no more than 75 percent ABV and usually considerably lower, is called *tequila ordinario*, which may undergo various steps of filtration, dilution, flavoring, and aging. Sweeteners, glycerin, and oak extracts may be and frequently are used for gold, *reposado*, and aged tequilas. See REPOSADO.

In 2020 tequila was produced in 163 certified distilleries (Consejo Regulador del Tequila) with a total production of 374 million liters and 1,758 brands registered. The primary export market for tequila is the United States (254 million liters in 2020). Less than 20 percent of production is shipped to European countries.

Tequila has a huge range of uses in cocktails, for sipping, and also in shots. In Mexico it is commonly consumed with citrus-fruit cocktails, but also in Margaritas or with tomato sauce and chiles. See MARGARITA and SANGRITA. Older and local people tend to drink it neat, sipping it slowly before meals.

Gaytan, Marie-Sarita. ¡*Tequila!: Distilling the Spirit of Mexico*. Stanford, CA: Stanford University Press, 2014.

Gutiérrez González, Salvador. *Realidad y Mitos del Tequila*. Guadalajara: Editorial Agata, 2001.
Valenzuela-Zapata, Ana G., and Paul G. Nabhan. *Tequila: A Natural and Cultural History*. Tucson: University of Arizona Press, 2003.

Ana G. Valenzuela-Zapata

The **Tequila Daisy** is one of the more puzzling drinks in the canon: the first tequila-based drink to gain a toehold in the mixological canon, it is mentioned in print widely and frequently beginning in 1930 and was popular in both Mexico and the American Southwest, yet no datable recipe for, or detailed description of, it appears in print until 1958. (There are, however, two very similar recipes in a pair of drink booklets collectors have found from rival liquor stores in Monterrey, Mexico; these are undated but probably from the late 1930s or early 1940s.) Henry Madden (1882–1948), an itinerant Kansan who was co-owner of the popular Turf Bar in Tijuana, Mexico, claimed to have invented the drink during Prohibition, when Tijuana was thronged with thirsty Americans. "In mixing a drink," he told a reporter in 1936, "I grabbed the wrong bottle and the customer was so delighted that he called for another and spread the good news far and wide." His bar called itself for years afterwards the "home of and the originators of the famous Tequila Daisy," a claim that appears to have been accepted in Tijuana and has yet to be disproven.

One must assume that that customer ordered a daisy—but what kind? If it was a Jerry Thomas–style, orange-liqueur-sweetened Brandy Daisy, that puts Madden's mistake at the head of the lineage of the Margarita, under which one will find further discussion of that possibility. See THOMAS, JEREMIAH P. "JERRY", and MARGARITA. If, however, it was the turn-of-the-century, grenadine-sweetened Gin Daisy, then what he would have made is something very much like the original Tequila Sunrise: tequila, lime juice, grenadine, and soda water, with ice. See TEQUILA SUNRISE. This is congruent with the 1958 version, and not too different from the ones from Monterrey, which omit the soda and use cherry brandy in place of the grenadine. Eventually, both versions would exist side by side, in a way: *margarita* is the Spanish word for "daisy," and the drink we know under that name is practically identical to a tequila version of Thomas's Daisy. Unfortunately, without further evidence, one cannot say which of these versions was

"Main Street" (Avenida Revolución) in Tijuana, Mexico, in the 1920s. Just to the *left* of the ornate San Francisco Cafe is the Turf Bar, which claimed to be the home of the Tequila Daisy. Wondrich Collection.

first or most circulated. Was it merely the John the Baptist to the Margarita's son of God, as it were, or was in fact an early avatar of the son himself? Perhaps it was both.

With the rise of the Margarita in the early 1950s, the grenadine-sweetened Tequila Daisy fell into eclipse. Despite its historic charms, it has not been revived.

Recipe: Shake 60 ml blanco tequila, 22 ml lime juice, and 15 ml grenadine with ice. Strain into chilled cocktail glass and add 15 ml sparkling water.

See also DAISY.

Brown, Helen Evans. *A Book of Appetizers*. Los Angeles: Ward Richie, 1958.

Graham, James. "Grahams Sightseeing Southern California." *Moville (IA) Mail*, July 23, 1936.

David Wondrich

The **Tequila Sunrise** is not one drink but two, which share a common name and two common ingredients but little else. The earliest one, a variation on the Daisy combining tequila, lime juice, crème de cassis, grenadine, and soda water, was created around 1930 at the Agua Caliente racetrack, hotel, spa, and casino complex in Tijuana, Mexico, where it was promoted as a hangover cure. See also DAISY. The drink made it into the more comprehensive cocktail books and, while not quite popular, was nonetheless one of the better-known tequila drinks.

In 1970, however, Bobby Lozoff, bartender at the wildly popular Trident restaurant in Sausalito, California, did not stick to any of those books when he made his first Tequila Sunrise. As was the custom of the house, he simply created his own version. It shared tequila and grenadine with the Mexican version but rounded them out with (according to the earliest published recipe) a splash of gin and a good deal of orange juice, with the grenadine sunk in the orange-colored drink to create a sunrise effect. In 1972, he served this to Mick Jagger of the Rolling Stones, who liked it. The band adopted it, minus the gin, as semi-official drink for their American tour, then just beginning. By the end of the year, the drink was famous, and indeed became one of the linchpins of 1970s American mixology.

Recipe (Agua Caliente version): Combine 60 ml reposado tequila, juice and shell of ½ lime, 15 ml grenadine, and 5 ml crème de cassis in highball glass.

Recipe (Trident version): Shake with ice 45 ml reposado tequila, 22 ml London dry gin (optional), and 75 ml fresh-squeezed orange juice. Pour into highball glass and add 5–10 ml grenadine, letting it sink to the bottom of the glass.

Bottoms up—y como!, 3rd ed. [Tijuana]: Agua Caliente, n. d.

Burkhart, Jeff. "Just Another Tequila Sunrise." *National Geographic Assignment Blog*, February 17, 2012. http://nationalgeographicassignmentblog.com/2012/02/17/just_another_tequila_sunrise/index.html (accessed March 12, 2021).

Greenfield, Robert. *S.T.P.: A Journey through America with the Rolling Stones.* 1974; repr., New York: Da Capo, 2002.

"People, etc." *Philadelphia Daily News*, September 8, 1972, 44.

David Wondrich

terpenes comprise a large group of hydrocarbons that give many different flowers, trees, fruits, roots, and other plant materials their pungent aromas, many of which find their ways into distilled spirits. The word *terpene* is derived from turpentine, as the resinous aromas of conifers are largely due to terpenes. But so are the complex, intense aromas of hops and cannabis—as well as those of mint and juniper berries and even roses and lemon peel. See HOPS.

Some terpenes can bring very pleasant aromas to beverages (they are largely responsible for the fruity aromas found in brandies); others, such as the terpenes that drive the aroma of *Penicillium roquefortii*—a fungus used to create blue cheeses such as Roquefort, Stilton, and gorgonzola—are rather less welcome. In 1983, Nykänen and Suomalainen compiled a list of at least 92 "terpene . . . compounds and their oxygenated derivatives" found in a limited sampling of chiefly European spirits. An analysis of gin, for instance, turned up—among many others—myrcene, limonene, α- and β-pinene, thujene, geraniol, and bornanone (which gives camphor its flavor). Bornanone and geraniol are also found in cognac, as well as γ-terpineol, damascenone, and a large number of other terpenes. Menthol turns up in Jamaican rum, β-ionone in whisky, and so forth.

Terpenes (or terpenoids, which are terpenes rearranged by oxidation or other chemical actions) are often constituent elements in essential oils and are added to compounded spirits in that form. These are often more faithful representatives of their plant sources than distilled spirits, since terpenes tend to break down with increased temperature and acidity, and the hot, acid environment of the still degrades all but the most volatile ones. This produces a simplified aroma, dominated by the terpenes from the raw material that have the lowest aroma threshold (i.e., the ones that we smell first), without the heavier ones to give them depth. Thus, for example, a crème de menthe made exclusively by distillation will taste like menthol, not fresh mint.

See also ACETALDEHYDE and PHENOLS.

Jackson, Ronald. *Wine Science: Principles and Applications*, 4th ed. San Diego: Academic Press, 2014.

Marais, J. "Terpenes in the Aroma of Grapes and Wines: A Review." *South African Journal of Enology and Viticulture* 4, no. 2 (1983): 49–58.

Nykänen, Lalli, and Heikki Suomalainen. *Aroma of Beer, Wine, and Distilled Alcoholic Beverages.* Berlin: Akademie Verlag, 1983.

Doug Frost

Terrington, William, is the probably pseudonymous author of the 1869 work *Cooling Cups and Dainty Drinks*, one of the pillars of British mixography. Widely and approvingly reviewed when it came out, the book is the best picture we have of what the United Kingdom was drinking in the high Victorian period, as it was moving from its native punches and cups to the American-style iced drinks that were on the cusp of sweeping the world. Unfortunately, we know nothing of its author: public records offer no obvious candidate. There is, however, a note in the *Naval and Military Gazette* that associates the book, and by extension its author, with the Wenham Lake Ice Co. Judging by the amount of attention the book pays to iced drinks, it is possible that it was sponsored by that company and that the author chose to perform his or her work for hire under a pseudonym.

See MIXOGRAPHY.

"Cooling Cups and Dainty Drinks." *Naval and Military Gazette*, July 3, 1869, 10.

Terrington, William. *Cooling Cups and Dainty Drinks.* London: Routledge, 1869.

David Wondrich

terroir—the idea that the flavor of a food or beverage is in some way determined by the place(s) where it is made and its raw materials have been grown—is a concept, much debated within wine circles, whose application to distilled spirits has only recently begun to be explored (the exception being single-malt scotch whisky, which has long been described as reflective of place). It has been greeted with some skepticism: spirits, after all, are the products of a manufacturing process that is much more technologically complex than that used for wines. That said, it can be argued that the terroir concept lies at the heart of Europe's appellation system, in which, for example, a juniper-flavored grain spirit cannot be called "Steinhäger" unless it is distilled in that corner of Germany, south of the Black Forest—even if it is otherwise chemically identical. See Geographical Indication (GI) and Protected Designation of Origin (PDO). The concept of the impact of place can become fusty or mysterious in the voices of some, but simply put, "terroir" is terrain. The factors that can vary with a spirit's place of origin include climate, weather, season, topography, geography, proximity to specific flora, soil, subsoils, and the place and conditions under which these beverages are stored, and even the local traditions and regulations that can affect decisions made by the people who are producing the spirit.

Some spirits, such as Absolut vodka, rely upon locally sourced grains and water from a specific aquifer. See Absolut. It is arguable that the most distinctive flavor characteristics of Absolut are due to the distillery's aquifer-drawn water, a reflection of terroir. Islay single malt is presumed to be smoky and briny because of its location; Islay distillers insist that barrel storage near the ocean is the chief influence. Yet few whisky barrels are actually stored on the island—most are sent to Glasgow. On the other hand, Islay peat is traditionally wetter than peats on the mainland (wet vegetation creates more smoke), which means that any peated malt used that comes from local maltings will tend to be smoked to a greater degree than other malts. The influence of that peat doesn't stop there: the water on Islay is to a significant degree flavored by the peat through which it filters, which means that any whisky made there using the local water will display some peat notes. One could continue with examples of rums, agave spirits, brandies, baijius, and so forth, each displaying influences of terroir, but it should be clear already that the concept will repay further investigation and discussion.

See also baijiu; rum, Jamaica; and whisky, scotch.

Sandhaus, Derek. *Drunk in China*. Lincoln, NE: Potomac, 2019.

Doug Frost

texture and **mouthfeel** are essentially synonymous terms for the tactile properties of a spirit—for the level and quality of its thickness or viscosity. "Weight" is often used in a similar fashion, although it is not strictly synonymous. Texture is the product of several distinct factors, including alcohol levels, glycerol and sugar content, and the presence of tannins and phenols, as well as of trace elements such as polysaccharides, sterols, and other compounds, some of which are not fully understood. Of all these factors, residual or added sugar generally offers the most dramatic (and easily detectible) impact on the mouthfeel of a spirit.

A spirit's alcohol level is also very important in forming its texture. Paradoxically, an aged spirit at 50 percent ABV will carry more perception of weight for most tasters than the same spirit at 30 percent, even though alcohol is physically lighter than water. But alcohol is a sugar and has its own viscosity. Tasters may also differentiate between the mouthfeel of unaged spirits at the same or similar alcohol percentages, whether this is due to perceived quality of spirit or innate compounds. For instance, among vodkas, water used for dilution may be utterly neutral or it may have mineral content that creates a greater palate impression—adding texture and mouthfeel.

With oak-aged spirits, time in barrels can add elements that contribute to texture: tannins, phenols, furans, lactones, glycerols, and various sugars (including arabinose, fructose, glucose, and xylose) often increase with time in barrels due to the processes of extraction and concentration inherent in barrel aging. See maturation. Sterols such as beta-sitosterol also seem to originate during alcohol's sojourn in oak containers; these too can add to mouthfeel and texture.

Tannins will bind with salivary proteins, creating the sensation of dryness, bitterness, friction, and astringency. Somatosensation provides more information through thermoreceptors (for temperature responses), mechanoreceptors (for pressure or viscosity), proprioceptors (which help us identify muscle movements, including those of the tongue), or even nociceptors (pain sensors).

Additionally, some proteins may generate physiochemical responses that can affect textural perception, particularly those associated with the coolness of mint or the heat sensation provided by capsaicin. These may not add directly to a sensation of weight but have a direct impact on texture. Nerves in our mouths contain a protein called TRP-V1 that generally indicates a rise in temperature. Capsaicin, by activating that protein, tricks the brain into believing that something is hot. Conversely another protein, TRPM8, is activated by cold temperatures as well as by menthol, mint, and eucalyptus oil; this cooling sensation may make a spirit seem lighter and crisper than it might be perceived were they not present.

Each of these factors can play a role in the texture of a cocktail as well, depending on the drink: with something simple such as a Dry Martini, the texture of the gin will have a much greater impact than in a Saturn, José "Popo" Galsini's 1967 tiki classic, where the gin has to cohabitate with falernum, orgeat, passionfruit nectar, and sweetened lemon juice. Sparkling wine, egg whites or yolks, honey, agave syrup, milk fat, fruit, coffee or cocoa beans (or their infusions), broth, vinegar, herbs, flowers, bark, grains, nutraceuticals, or any one of the myriad other substances that can find their way into a mixed drink can dominate the mouthfeel of that drink, through either the five so-called primary flavors (sweet, sour, salty, bitter, and umami), somatosensation, viscosity, or other sensory or even mental interactions. Technique, too, holds sway, with the most obvious extremes being the silky texture of a properly stirred Manhattan or the sprightly effervescence of a shaken Daiquiri.

See also TASTING SPIRITS.

Buxton, Ian, and Paul S. Hughes. *The Science and Commerce of Whisky.* London: RSC, 2015.

Jeffrey, David W, Gavin Sacks, and Andrew Waterhouse. *Understanding Wine Chemistry.* Chichester, UK: Wiley, 2016.

Shepard, Gordon M. *Neuroenology.* New York: Columbia University Press, 2016.

Doug Frost

TGI Friday's is a casual-dining conglomerate with more than nine hundred restaurants in sixty countries. The company was founded in 1965 by Alan Stillman (1936), a perfume salesman who bought a neighborhood bar on Manhattan's Upper East Side and spruced up the decor and the menu in hopes of attracting the stewardesses and models who lived nearby. The original TGI Friday's popularized the concept of the singles bar, propitiously, at the dawn of the sexual revolution. At a time when many bars were still mired in the gender-segregated drinking culture of the nineteenth century, Friday's was a sort of domesticated saloon—prettified with Tiffany lamps, bentwood chairs, and potted plants (spawning the nickname "fern bar") and enlivened with bartenders dressed in red-and-white-striped soccer shirts and serving Harvey Wallbangers. See FERN BARS and HARVEY WALLBANGER. It did indeed attract young women, and quickly inspired imitators. It launched its first franchise in Memphis in 1970; restaurants in Nashville and Little Rock soon followed. In 1972, Stillman and franchise partners Dan Scoggin and Walt Henrion opened a large Friday's in Dallas (where the company would be headquartered after its purchase in 1975 by Carlson Companies, Inc.). Scoggin and Henrion ushered in greater organization, tiered seating, and an expanded menu, which popularized casual-dining staples such as loaded potato skins. The bar remained the focal point of Friday's, however, and the chain made "happy hour" an institution. It also paid a great deal of attention to training its bartenders, developing a notably rigorous training program. By the 1980s, the chain's training went beyond learning the classics and the fanciful drinks of the day and into flair bartending, in which Friday's was a pioneer. It was John Bandy, who won Friday's first Bartender Olympics (now the World Bartender Championship), who trained Tom Cruise and Bryan Brown, the stars of the 1988 movie *Cocktail*, in their bottle-throwing and other flair moves. See FILM, SPIRITS AND COCKTAILS IN. Over time, Fridays morphed into a family-friendly beacon of American dining as well as a purveyor of packaged foods inspired by its menu. Carlson Companies sold Fridays to Sentinel Capital Partners and TriArtisan Capital Partners in 2014 for $800 million.

Twilley, Nicola. "How T.G.I. Friday's Helped Invent the Singles Bar." *New Yorker*, July 2, 2015. http://www.newyorker.com/culture/culture-desk/how-t-g-i-fridays-helped-invent-the-singles-bar (accessed March 12, 2021).

Lauren Clark

A **thief** is a traditional tubular tool that is used to extract a spirit sample from a barrel; it was known originally (in the seventeenth century) as a "valentia," which was often corrupted into "valinch," "velincher," and similar words, but that term is now obsolete. A thief is usually made of glass or copper and operates by creating a vacuum. You plunge it through the bunghole of the barrel, and once the hole at the tip is sufficiently submerged, you cover a small hole at the top with your thumb. Once the thief is removed from the cask and positioned over a glass or a pitcher, you release your thumb and the spirit comes rushing out. It is essentially a giant fancy straw. In Scotland, some distillery and warehouse workers use the related "dog," which is like an oversized metal cigar tube on a chain, to take a clandestine sample that can easily be hidden in one's clothing.

See also BARREL.

"Glossary of Bourbon & Whiskey Terms." Kentucky Distillers' Association website. http://kybourbon. com/bourbon_culture-2/glossary_of_bourbon_ whiskey_terms/ (accessed March 12, 2021).

Noah Rothbaum

Thomas, Jeremiah P. "Jerry" (1830–1885),

was a sailor, a gold miner, an artist, a theatrical promoter, and the most famous American bartender of his age. He was also the man who wrote the first bartender's guide to document the unique American way of mixing drinks and, not coincidentally, the first American bartender to make it into the history books. His *How to Mix Drinks, or the Bon-Vivant's Companion*, also known as the *Bar-Tender's Guide*, has been cited as the authoritative early source on the topic ever since it appeared in 1862. Even in the dark days of the 1960s and 1970s his legacy never completely faded away, but it gained new currency with the cocktail renaissance of the twenty-first century, which looked to him and his work as one of its chief inspirations. See COCKTAIL RENAISSANCE.

Thomas was born on October 30, 1830, in Sackets Harbor, New York, on the shores of Lake Ontario, but his family moved to the bustling port city of New Haven when he was still young. There, in the mid-1840s, he began working as a barback at the popular Park House hotel, managed by his older brother David. In 1847 or 1848, however, Thomas did what many young men of his generation were doing and shipped out as a sailor. How many voyages he served on and where they went are subject to conflicting information, but his last voyage, on the bark Ann Smith, is well documented: it left New Haven in March 1849, sailed around Cape Horn, and arrived in San Francisco in November. There, Thomas jumped ship and, as he later recalled, "ran off into the mountains after gold." By the time he left California in 1851, he had $16,000 worth of

Jerry Thomas's Dream, detail, 1864. Thomas was an accomplished artist and this is his self-portrait. Wondrich Collection.

the stuff in his pocket and had been a miner, bartender, theatrical promoter, and who knows what else beside.

The next few years are a jumble. Thomas ran a bar in New York, then one back in New Haven, and also worked in Charleston; New Orleans; Chicago; Keokuk, Iowa; and at the prestigious Planter's House in St. Louis, where he was head bartender. In 1858, he returned to New York to helm the bar at the Metropolitan Hotel, a new and prestigious establishment with an extensive theatrical and sporting clientele. In 1860, he left the Metropolitan to travel to England to witness the first international heavyweight boxing championship, returning to open a bar with his brother George at 622 Broadway in New York. That bar failed by the end of 1861, and Thomas apparently returned to the Metropolitan.

It was while he was there, in June of 1862, that the New York publishing firm of Dick & Fitzgerald published the *Bar-Tender's Guide*. The first book of its kind, it was widely reviewed and sales were high. Through it, Thomas did more than anyone else to establish a canon of American drinks. The drinks he included were distributed into classes, including cobblers, cocktails, fixes, juleps, punches, sours, slings, smashes, and toddies, plus a catchall category of "fancy drinks." At the same time, however, Thomas excluded drinks explicitly associated with his contemporaries, some of them very popular, such as Peter Bent Brigham's Moral Suasion or the Ladies' Blush by Charles W. Geekie, of Baltimore. See BRIGHAM, PETER BENT. Indeed, the only American bartender to whom Thomas credited any drinks is Joseph Santini of New Orleans, at whose Jewel of the South he might have worked during his time in that city. Of his own drinks, as far as can be established Thomas only included two: the Blue Blazer and the Japanese Cocktail. See BLUE BLAZER and JAPANESE COCKTAIL.

Thomas did not own the rights to the *Bar-Tender's Guide*. At the end of 1863, at which point he had moved on first to the Occidental Hotel in San Francisco (under the same ownership as the Metropolitan) and then to the mining boomtown of Virginia City, Nevada, he self-published another book, *The Portrait Gallery of Distinguished Bar-Keepers*. Besides drink recipes, including many not in his previous work, the book contained biographical sketches of other American bartenders and a fairly extensive autobiography, along with illustrations by his own hand (among his many other talents he was a skilled artist). Unfortunately, no copies of this book are known to exist: all we have are a detailed review and a recipe book from 1867, *The American Bar-Keeper*, by the pseudonymous "Charles B. Campbell" of San Francisco, which pirated the recipes and some of the introduction. Were a copy to turn up, its biographies of Thomas's colleagues would prove invaluable.

Thomas returned to New York and the Metropolitan in early 1865. The next year, he and George opened another Broadway bar, this one at Twenty-Second Street. This one proved to be one of the most popular in the city, known as much for its extensive collection of etchings as for the high quality of its drinks. In 1872, the brothers moved a few blocks further up Broadway, to a large space that proved even more popular than the last and cemented Thomas as a national figure—America's bartender. That popularity was due in large part to the bar's amusements: billiard tables, sports betting, bowling lanes, and even a basement shooting gallery. Add double life-sized portraits on the walls of Thomas mixing drinks and a statue near the entrance of the same, and you have the antithesis of the hushed modern speakeasy bar.

In 1876, Dick & Fitzgerald published a second edition of the *Bar-Tender's Guide*, including an appendix of the latest drinks, among them the Collins, the Fizz, and the "Improved" Cocktail, the precursor to the Sazerac (there was also a posthumous third edition in 1887). See COLLINS; FIZZ; and SAZERAC COCKTAIL. By the end of the year, Thomas, who had invested improvidently in the stock market, had left the big bar on Broadway and moved downtown, across from the ASTOR HOUSE. From then on, his fortunes declined, and the string of bars he ran grew less and less ambitious, until he was reduced to working for others. He died on December 14, 1885, and is buried in Woodlawn Cemetery in New York. "Jerry Thomas was the best barkeeper I ever saw," commented Charles Leland, his boss at the Metropolitan, after Thomas's death. "He had no rival in the city."

Yet by 1885, Thomas's outsize, swaggering personality (he once gave an interview with a pair of white rats frolicking on his head and shoulders) was out of fashion among bartenders, with customers preferring the more deferential elegance of a William Schmidt. See SCHMIDT, WILLIAM. Nonetheless, he remained the founding authority, the place one started when investigating the origin and development of American drinks, even when such things were of little interest to drinkers at large. Even as one macho-drinking San Francisco journalist commemorated the hundredth anniversary of Thomas's book by pronouncing it a "frightening treatise" and asserting that the Professor (as Thomas had come to be known, after he was so dubbed by journalist Herbert Asbury in 1928) "knew nothing about the pleasures of alcohol," others were publishing gin advertisements citing his authority (erroneously) for the origin of the Martini. See MARTINI.

In 1988, Joe Baum, the new operator of New York's legendary Rainbow Room, instructed his head bartender, Dale DeGroff, to refer to Thomas's book as he built the new bar program. See DeGROFF, DALE. By then, the strong, elemental drinks Thomas collected came as a revelation, and their influence has permeated the cocktail renaissance—even if it has become fashionable in recent years among some mixologists to regard them as primitive artifacts whose only worth is the basis they provide for creative improvement.

"Jerry Thomas's Career." *New York World*, December 20, 1885, 23.
"Jerry Thomas's Pictures." *New York Sun*, March 28, 1882, 3.
Wondrich, David. *Imbibe!*, 2nd ed. New York: Perigee, 2015.

David Wondrich

three star is a designation of age used on cognac bottles from the 1860s through the 1970s, originally indicating a sipping cognac "well on the road to maturity," as a 1906 Hennessy advertisement put it. With the shift from selling cognac in barrels to selling it in branded bottles in the second half of the nineteenth century, cognac producers needed a way to indicate the approximate ages of the blends they were selling. In the 1860s, Jas. Hennessy & Co. took to marking their bottles with a neck shield bearing one, two, or three stars. Their meaning was somewhat loose: in 1868, three stars was ten years old, but by 1906, when the company took out advertisements detailing the system, it had come to stand for at least twelve years old, with two stars being nine and one being six.

Hennessy did not trademark the stars, and they were rapidly adopted by other producers, most notably Martell. Otard Dupuy, the other market leader at the time, at first used grapes in place of the stars, but eventually its bottles, too, bore the stars. Unfortunately, the star system, which had no legal force behind it, degraded over the years; by the mid-twentieth century, one star had come to mean a mere two years, with three standing for only six. By the 1970s, the one- and two-star grades were essentially defunct, and three-star was replaced by the new VS designation, which required the cognac to be at least two years old.

See also COGNAC.

•

Faith, Nicholas. *Cognac*. Oxford: Infinite Ideas, 2014.
"Cognac Brandy" (advertisement). *Wexford* (Ireland) *People*, December 19, 1868, 5.
"The Seven Ages of Hennessy's Brandy" (advertisement). *London Times*, December 1, 1906, 13.

David Wondrich

tiki is a catch-all term not only for tiki drinks—faux-Polynesian punches and cocktails, mostly rum-based, with exotic flavorings and theatrical garnishes—but for the entire tiki pop culture boom engendered by those drinks, which from its inception in 1934 to its 1960s peak grew to encompass faux-Polynesian music, fashion, dining, interior design, and commercial architecture. This phenomenon is unique in cocktail history: usually a pop culture trend inspires a drink trend (à la *Sex and the City* and the Cosmopolitan cocktail), but in tiki's case the drinks came first.

Where did these drinks originate? From the mind of one man, who single-handedly created the tiki bar and the tiki drink. Just a few weeks after Prohibition ended, a former bootlegger named Ernest Raymond Beaumont Gantt—alias Donn Beach—opened Don the Beachcomber's, a tiny South Seas–themed bar in a Hollywood hotel lobby. See BEACH, DONN; and PROHIBITION AND TEMPERANCE IN AMERICA. In his earlier travels to Jamaica, he'd met his mixological muse: the Planter's Punch, which became the foundation for over sixty of his groundbreaking original recipes, from the Tahitian Punch and the Zombie to the Pearl Diver and the Missionary's Downfall. See PLANTER'S PUNCH and ZOMBIE.

Like most classic Caribbean drinks, such as Cuba's Daiquiri and Martinique's Ti' Punch, the Planter's Punch has only three ingredients: rum, lime, and sugar. See DAIQUIRI and TI' PUNCH. Beach took this simple construct and complicated it. Instead of just lime, he'd add a second or third citrus juice to a recipe; instead of just sugar, he'd mix together multiple sweeteners; and instead of just one rum, he'd combine two or three radically different distillates in the same drink to create a base flavor more compelling than any single expression.

Tiki drinks, then, are essentially Caribbean drinks "squared" or "cubed." With their multiple layers of flavor, their house-made syrups and tinctures, and their fresh fruit, spices, and herbs, Beach's drinks were the first post-Prohibition culinary craft cocktails—sixty years before that terminology existed.

Instead of craft cocktails, Beach called these drinks his "rhum rhapsodies." Over the years they became known in the trade as "exotic cocktails," or "exotics" for short. (Only recently have twenty-first-century cocktail writers reclassified them as "tiki drinks"). By any name, in 1934 this was a new and exciting concept for American drinkers, especially after the devolution of mixology imposed by thirteen years of Prohibition, and in no time Beach's tiny bar was crammed with movie stars and millionaires. In 1937 he opened a larger restaurant across the street from his original location, and its phenomenal success launched the tiki trend that would increasingly come to co-opt American leisure time for the next forty years.

Rival restaurateurs copied Beach's South Seas decor and got his recipes by poaching his bartenders. Beach tried to stop employee theft by encrypting his recipes—replacing ingredient names with numbers that matched the labels on the bottles behind his bar—and by suing rivals who put his drinks on their menus. But by the late 1930s there were over 150 Polynesian-themed bars and restaurants serving his drinks, often changing the names to avoid Beach's lawyers (the Missionary's Downfall, for example, was variously known as the Padre's Pitfall and the Apostle's Breakdown).

Beach's most successful rival refused to resort to thievery. "I didn't know a damn thing about that kind of booze," Victor Jules "Trader Vic" Bergeron wrote in his autobiography, "and I thought I'd like to learn." He traveled to the Caribbean to study the art of tropical mixology, as Beach had before him. When Vic returned to his Oakland restaurant with this new knowledge, he transformed himself from an imitator

to an innovator. He found his own mixological style, creating variations on the Daiquiri in much the same way that Beach had riffed on the Planter's Punch. In short order Vic hatched the Scorpion, the Fog Cutter, and the Mai Tai, three drinks which became as popular as Beach's rhum rhapsodies. See BERGERON, VICTOR "TRADER VIC"; FOG CUTTER; and MAI TAI.

Tiki's growth from a drink trend to a lifestyle trend began with the end of World War II and the return of American servicemen from the actual South Pacific. No matter how horrific their combat experience there, most of them had fond memories of Hawaii, which served as a transshipment center for fresh troops arriving from the mainland and veterans bound for home. To relive their Hawaiian idyll, they flocked to faux-Polynesian restaurants in their home towns, paying for their Pukka Punches with the spoils of the postwar manufacturing boom. When Pacific vet James Michener's *Tales of the South Pacific* became a smash Broadway musical in 1949, new tiki boîtes across the country named themselves after Michener's mythical island, Bali Hai; still more named themselves after Pacific explorer Thor Heyerdahl's bestselling 1957 book *Aku-Aku*. By the time Hawaii became the fiftieth state in 1959, the entire United States was infected with tropical fever. Not just restaurants but bowling alleys (Kona Lanes), amusement parks (Tiki Gardens), hotels and apartment buildings (Outrigger Inn, Aloha Arms), even clothing stores (Boutiki) went tiki as suburbanites dressed in Hawaiian shirts, listened to modern-primitive "exotica" music LPs, and held backyard luaus with drinks made from instant Mai Tai mix bought at their local supermarket.

The ascendancy of Polynesian pop culture encouraged more and more restaurateurs to go tiki, which meant increased competition for customers, which meant ever more elaborate interior decor. To "build a better mousetrap," as Trader Vic put it in an *Oakland Tribune* interview, owners often hired Hollywood art directors to stoke the fantasy that patrons were drinking by moonlight in a South Seas island grotto, complete with indoor waterfalls and dawn-to-dusk lighting changes. The drinks also became increasingly theatrical. In an effort to outshine their rivals, tiki bartenders put their punches in bespoke ceramic tiki mugs and communal bowls, encased them in ice shells, set them aflame, or shrouded them in a dry-ice-induced vapor cloud to suggest a smoking volcano.

Technicolor drinks served in movie-set bars: it sounds gimmicky, and it was. But it was also just what Americans needed to distract them from the stifling middle-class conformity and political paranoia of the Eisenhower era, not to mention the daily reminder of possible nuclear annihilation as the Cold War heated up in the Kennedy years.

In the 1970s, tiki entered its fourth decade of profitability. But the tide was finally beginning to ebb. The specter of the Vietnam War made Polynesian Pop seem culturally naive and politically incorrect; with Saigon falling to the Viet Cong, the last place to go for a fantasy escape from the nightly news was the Saigon Room of the Kon-tiki restaurant chain.

In the early 1980s, the Mai Tai gave way to the Margarita and the Zombie to the Screaming Orgasm. Tiki bartenders scattered to the four winds, taking their secret knowledge with them. But with the current global craft cocktail renaissance, a new generation has rediscovered and embraced tiki's complexity and theatricality. Mai Tais and Zombies are once again popping up on drink menus across the United States and Europe, along with original new tiki concoctions by contemporary mixologists, and tiki bars are once again luring crowds into their artificial paradises.

But faux Polynesia has new rough seas to weather in the twenty-first century. With US sociopolitical divides widened by the Trump administration, tiki has found itself caught in the crossfire of the culture wars. On the left, social justice advocates condemn Polynesian pop for appropriating and exploiting the sacred religious and cultural artifacts of Pasifika peoples. On the right, neo-Nazi activists have in turn appropriated Polynesian pop itself, marching in aloha shirts while brandishing tiki torches along with their automatic rifles and racist placards. Ironically, a tropical cocktail culture founded on escape from the modern world now finds itself smack dab in the middle of it. If there was ever a time for tropaholics to anesthetize with a Zombie or a Painkiller, this is surely it.

See also BERGERON, VICTOR "TRADER VIC"; BEACH, DONN; and CRAFT COCKTAIL.

Bergeron, Victor J. *Frankly Speaking: Trader Vic's Own Story.* New York: Doubleday, 1973.

Berry, Jeff. *Beachbum Berry's Potions of the Caribbean.* New York: Cocktail Kingdom, 2014.

Berry, Jeff. *Beachbum Berry's Sippin' Safari.* San Jose, CA: Club Tiki, 2007.

MacKenzie, Bob. "Trader Vic Bergeron: 'Who Cares About the Past?'" *Oakland Tribune*, September 29, 1976.

Jeff Berry

tincture is a concentrated extract of an herb, spice, or other botanical in alcohol. See BOTANICAL. Historically, tinctures were originally used as medicinal products, but over time they found their way into cuisine as well as beverages. Tinctures can be used similarly to cocktail bitters, but unlike bitters a tincture will only offer a single note of flavor. See BITTERS. They are generally prepared through simple infusion or maceration. See INFUSION and MACERATION. The base alcohol can be anywhere from 40 percent to 96 percent (neutral spirit) ABV, but there is loose agreement that a 50 percent ABV vodka (in other words, a 50 percent aqueous solution of ethanol) is adequate to extract the majority of plant constituents.

There is a similarity between a tincture and a flavored vodka that has been infused by natural means. The biggest difference is the concentration of flavor, with the vodka infusion being much more diluted. See VODKA. The typical method to create a tincture is to add one part of the botanical to approximately five parts of spirit. Briefly agitate daily, allow the mixture to macerate for two weeks, and then strain into a glass bottle and cap to store. During the maceration phase, the volatile components of the base material will be extracted into the spirit, and the resultant liquid will be fairly concentrated.

Once made, store a smaller amount of tincture in a bottle with a dasher top (or eyedropper), in order to allow the addition to cocktails one dash at a time, or in an atomizer/mister. For storage it is best to either store in a cool, dark place or use a darkly tinted glass bottle to limit oxidation, which is accelerated by light. Oxidation will eventually cause a breakdown in the flavor compounds, weakening the concentrate.

Keep in mind the skin and cellular structure of the botanical when choosing the proof of an alcohol to macerate in. Some woodier botanicals such as cinnamon will benefit from higher proof spirit to fully penetrate the botanical's exterior.

In the posthumous 1887 edition of Jerry Thomas's *Bar-Tenders Guide*, there are recipes for the manufacture of several different tinctures. One example is for "cinnamon tincture" which combines 2 pounds of ground cinnamon with 1 gallon of (high-proof) neutral spirit, macerated for eight days. It's strained off, reserving both the liquid and the cinnamon. Then the strained-off cinnamon is mixed with 1 quart of "proof spirit" (essentially, that's 50 percent vodka), strained again, and then combined with the first liquid and filtered through blotting paper (a coffee filter will do). The use of vodka in the second step is an attempt to extract the water-soluble volatiles and might perhaps work best if it too were allowed to rest for a few days. Since cinnamon in stick form is relatively porous, this filtration process would be easier with stick cinnamon instead of ground. Simply allow it to rest for a day or two longer.

The book also includes recipes for lemon, orange, and clove tinctures as well. Additional useful options might include black pepper, cardamom, allspice, nutmeg, coriander, star anise, lavender, or juniper, as only a few examples.

As with bitters, tinctures can also be dashed into a drink (so as to provide a flavor within the drink itself), applied to the top of a drink using a dropper, or sprayed with a mister to provide more of an aromatic garnish. While tinctures of a single botanical maceration don't provide the complexity that bitters do, employing different combinations of them will enable the user to create hundreds of different and unique flavor profiles.

See also GARNISH and MIXOLOGY.

Phillips, Michael, and Nancy Phillips. *The Herbalist's Way: The Art and Practice of Healing with Plant Medicines.* White River Junction, VT: Chelsea Green, 2005

Thomas, Jerry. *The Bar-Tender's Guide.* New York: Dick & Fitzgerald, 1887.

Audrey Saunders

twenty years of people looking elsewhere for their intoxicants. The new cocktail drinkers of the period had little connection with the traditions of mixology and many were interested in the Martini more as a visual symbol of sophistication than as an actual drink. Martinis, after all, consisted mostly of straight gin or vodka, and as such were fairly difficult for novice drinkers to accept. To appeal to this new clientele who desired the allure and sex appeal that accompanied the Martini yet did not like the actual drink itself, bartenders began applying the term "Martini" to any drink served in the ubiquitous V-shaped cocktail glass associated with that drink.

In the 1980s and 1990s, bars would list multiple drinks on their menus categorized as "martinis." Popular drinks included the Lemon Drop Martini (a Vodka Sour) and the Chocolate Martini, which defies categorization. See LEMON DROP and CHOCOLATE MARTINI. It also became common to simply add the "-tini" suffix to many drinks' names, as shorthand that they were mixed drinks served in a cocktail glass; perhaps the most popular example is the Appletini, with the Chocolatini and Flirtini not too far behind. These drinks would typically focus on disguising their base spirit (usually vodka) with various sweet and fruity syrups and flavorings.

As the craft cocktail resurgence of the late 1990s began to evolve, there was a backlash against the "tini-ization" of drinks and a return to the classic Martini. As craft bars began to emerge, their cocktail menus no longer included long lists of "Martinis," and customers would gradually start to rediscover the difference between traditional drink styles. See CRAFT COCKTAIL.

Conrad, Barnaby. *The Martini.* New York: Chronicle, 1995

Miller, Anistatia, and Brown, Jared. *Shaken Not Stirred: A Celebration of the Martini.* New York: Harper Collins, 2013.

Samovar Vodka (advertisement). *Baltimore Evening Sun,* July 2, 1946, 15.

Robert Hess

-tini is a suffix popularly incorporated in a cocktail's name in order to associate the drink with the Martini and its perceived status. While the practice dates to at least the 1940s and the "Vodka-tini," it wasn't fully exploited until the 1980s and the renewed interest in mixed drinks the decade brought after

Ti' Punch is a popular drink in the French West Indies, especially in Martinique. The name is Creole, derived from the French "petit punch," and the drink, which dates back to at least the 1880s, when Lafcadio Hearn encountered it in Martinique,

Postcard, "L'heure du punch," Martinique, 1970s. Note the ice, which some would consider noncanonical in a Ti' Punch. Wondrich Collection.

is served everywhere from fancy hotels to rustic beach bars. It consists of three ingredients—rum, sugar, and a squeeze of lime peel—and is commonly made with cane syrup and 100-proof unaged rhum agricole, a French-style rum with distinctive grassy, vegetal notes.

The drink often involves a small ritual. A bottle of rum is typically placed on the bar or table, along with small bowls of sugar, lime, and occasionally ice (some insist this must never be used, but it has been cited as an integral part of the drink since 1903, and Dr. André Nègre, the great chronicler of the cuisine of the French Antilles, was a proponent of it). Each customer makes a drink to his or her own liking: some incline toward sweet; others prefer only a fleeting hint of lime zest. Claudine Neisson-Vernant, the matriarch of the family behind Martinique's Neisson Rhum, likens the making of Ti' Punch to a Japanese tea ceremony—a moment best shared with friends.

Recipe: Place a small amount of sugar or cane syrup into a tumbler along with a bit of fresh lime—this can be as large as a wedge, but is usually a disc of peel with a little flesh clinging to it, squeezed peel-down into the glass. Add 60 ml white rhum agricole (50 percent ABV is traditional; an aged rhum will yield a "Vieux Punch," which often omits the lime) and stir until the sweetener is dissolved, pressing the lime in the process. Some prefer to swizzle using the

bois lélé, an island plant that forms five branches at each joint and is harvested and trimmed to form a star-shaped stirrer. This is rolled between the palms to frisk the drink into happy effervescence. An ice cube or two for cooling and dilution is optional.

See also RHUM AGRICOLE and SWIZZLE STICK.

Clarke, Paul. "An Introduction to Ti' Punch," *Imbibe Magazine*, July 19, 2015. http://imbibemagazine.com/introduction-ti-punch/ (accessed March 12, 2021).

Hearn, Lafcadio. *Two Years in the French West Indies.* New York: Harper & Brothers, 1890.

Nègre, André. *Antilles et Guyane a travers leur cuisine*, 5th ed. Caen: Le Brun, 1973.

"Notes sur la Martinique." *La réforme sociale*, July 1903, 583.

Wayne Curtis

toasting (barrel) is a process of heating the inside of a barrel to enhance the release of vanillin and other flavor compounds. Toasting is commonly associated with barrels intended to age wine, though American whisky barrels sometimes undergo toasting prior to charring. See also CHARRING, TOASTING (AND RECHARRING); OAK; and VANILLIN.

The **toddy** is a simple drink combining distilled spirits, sugar, and hot or cold water. Its origin is murky, but it does not appear to be linked to the South Asian palm wine of the same name and can best be understood as a simplification of punch, without the often hard-to-get citrus. See PUNCH. It first appears in print in England in 1741 and was already a popular drink in British America in 1750. It was in Scotland, however, where one newspaper noted that "every household has its toddy gods," that the drink and its preparation became an institution, particularly in the hot version.

Toddies are typically composed by adding boiling water to a warmed tumbler or larger vessel that contains the liquor and sugar and stirring until the sugar has dissolved. (Nutmeg, freshly scraped over the finished drink, is a traditional but optional fillip.) If it is composed in larger quantities, portions might be transferred to individual tumblers with a ladle or "toddy lifter," a bulb-shaped glass or crystal device with a long neck and openings at each end that acts much like a pipette. The toddy maker submerges its bulbous end in prepared toddy, allows its chamber to fill with the hot drink, then seals the top aperture with a thumb and carefully transfers a roughly uniform dose to individual tumblers. To assure that the individual hot toddy is indeed hot rather than merely warm when served, American bartender Jeffery Morgenthaler advises using a "bartender's bain-marie," a shaker tin containing the ingredients nestled inside a larger tin partly filled with hot water, before finishing with piping-hot water.

Although most drinkers today know them as "hot" toddies, cold toddies were at one point quite common, both as toddies and under another name: sling. See SLING. Until the widespread use of the muddler, a similar wooden, metal, or sometimes glass rod known as a "toddy stick" was used to crush lumps of sugar in the cold toddy (or sling, julep, or cocktail) and to stir the resulting concoction. Add mint to that cold drink and you have a julep; with bitters, it's a Jefferson-era Cock-Tail. See JULEP and COCK-TAIL. Squeeze a piece of lemon peel over the hot toddy and drop it in the tumbler and you have a skin on your hands. In Ireland, the local product used for the spirit in the combination along with a clove-studded slice of lemon yields a chest-warming soother called a "Hot Whisky." See HOT WHISKY.

Because of the dilution involved, and as a vestige of the hot toddy's therapeutic reputation for flagging constitutions, strongly flavored spirits are preferred in constructing the drink. Nineteenth-century papers in Scotland and England advertised "toddy whisky"—that is, robust malt whisky ideally suited for toddy making (in America, before the 1890s virtually the only way scotch whisky was consumed was in "Hot Scotches," as scotch-whisky toddies were called). Pot-stilled whisky, brandy, and rum (especially Jamaican rum) are toddy stalwarts of ancient renown. Malty genever makes a respectable toddy, while a hot gin toddy (known occasionally as a "Cockroach") has enjoyed some traction in America. Although vodka toddies exist as a theoretical possibility, the relative neutrality of the spirit plays to the strengths of neither the vodka nor the toddy.

The toddy has lent itself to endless other variations over the centuries. Drinkers who may favor one spirit over others or who feel that the drink would be improved adding or substituting ingredients, such as cider for the water, have given rise to national, regional, and idiosyncratic expressions. That this polymorphous concoction remains in circulation under a roster of assumed names and with unorthodox constituents is testament to its enduring popularity. The bare-fisted tripartite toddy exists today alongside modern interpretations that take the concept well beyond its original ingredients to include fruit juices, teas, and spices arguably more at home in juleps and punch. In the eastern United States, especially in Pennsylvania, Maryland, and adjacent areas, a specimen known as Apple Toddy, which includes roasted apple and whisky, rum, or brandy, has been enjoyed for over two hundred years. Twenty-first-century examples may include mezcal or other strongly flavored spirits or even liqueurs such as rock and rye, with sweetness adjusted to taste.

Recipe (Scotch Whisky Toddy): Rinse an earthenware mug with boiling water. Add 1 barspoon (5 ml) demerara sugar and a swatch of thin-cut lemon peel. Add 30 ml boiling water and stir to dissolve the sugar. Add 60 ml single malt scotch and finish with another 30 ml boiling water.

See also ROCK AND RYE.

Aberdeen Journal, and General Advertiser for the North of Scotland, December 20, 1865, 3.

Lloyd's Weekly Newspaper (London), September, 5, 1858, 1.

Morgenthaler, Jeffrey. "Hot Toddies suck—long live the Hot Toddy." Jeffrey Morgenthaler website, February

7, 2014. https://www.jeffreymorgenthaler.com/hot-toddies-suck-long-live-the-hot-toddy/ (accessed June 3, 2021).

"To the Publisher of the *News-Letter*." *New-York Gazette*, July 30, 1750, 2.

"Toddy Lifter." Philadelphia Museum of Art. https://www.philamuseum.org/collections/permanent/106281.html (accessed June 3, 2021).

The Trials of Samuel Goodere, Esq., etc. London: 1741.

Matthew Rowley

Tom and Jerry, the soul-soothing winter warmer combining brandy, rum, and an egg batter with hot water or milk, dates back to long before Tom and Jerry were even cat and mouse. It came into being sometime in the early 1800s and is often said to have been created by the author Pierce Egan in an attempt to promote his 1821 book *Life in London* (whose main characters were Jerry Hawthorn and "Corinthian Tom"), as well as the play based on it, *Tom and Jerry, or Life in London*. Unfortunately, there is no evidence for this theory, or for the drink actually being served in England during the 1820s (the closest thing was the "Tom and Jerry shop," a small, informal alehouse, "Tom and Jerry" being a slang term for ale that predates Egan's book by at least a generation).

The drink was also (and most famously) attributed to Jerry Thomas, which sounds plausible given the similarity between the names of the drink and the celebrated barman, as well as the fact that in his 1862 *Bar-Tender's Guide* he stated that the drink is also sometimes called "Jerry Thomas." Mr. Thomas even made claim to having created the drink, saying that he first concocted it in 1847. See THOMAS, JEREMIAH P. "JERRY".

In fact the earliest known printed reference to the Tom and Jerry, as a drink made of "saleratus [baking soda], eggs, sugar, nutmeg, ginger, allspice and rum," is an 1827 reference from the *Salem (MA) Gazette*; "Professor" Thomas was not born until 1830. Yet while Jerry Thomas might not have created the Tom and Jerry, we can wholeheartedly give him more credit than any other man for popularizing it. And for this, we will be forever grateful.

From the mid-nineteenth century until the mid-twentieth, Tom and Jerry was a cold-weather staple in American bars. The characteristic small, porcelain "shaving mugs" in which it was served came out every November, along with the bowl to hold the batter, and got put away again every March. By the 1950s, however, it had become a regional specialty, popular in the Great Lakes region not as a wintertime bar drink but as something served at home during the year-end holidays. With the cocktail revival of the twenty-first century, it has slowly regained some of its lost territory, although its spread is hampered by its complexity and its highly caloric nature.

In general, Tom and Jerry is made by separating eggs and whipping the whites on their own and the yolks with sugar, spices, and a little rum. These are then folded together into a batter, of which a spoonful is put into a mug along with a mix of brandy and rum and then topped off with boiling water or milk. Some versions of the drink omit the rum from the batter, others use brandy instead. Using rum in the batter and only brandy in the drink is perhaps slightly more authentic from a historical perspective (Thomas gives it as the default but mentions the brandy and rum version as well) but also provides both a gentle and distinct character. Many of the early recipes call for boiling water instead of hot milk to mix the batter in. However, the use of milk provides more body and a delightful texture to the drink, which should be seen as an improvement.

Recipe: Separate the yolks and whites of 12 eggs, beat egg whites to a stiff froth and the yolks until they are well blended. Mix together the yolks and whites and then add 900 g sugar, 30 ml rich Jamaican rum, 1 ½ tsp ground cinnamon, ½ tsp ground allspice, ½ grated nutmeg, and ¼ tsp ground cloves. Stir the mixture well until it is well blended and takes on the consistence of a light batter. Refrigerate immediately until needed and use within four to six hours. For each drink: Using a small, pre-heated coffee mug, combine 30 ml of the above mixture and 30 ml of cognac, and then fill the mug with up to 90 ml of hot milk (or water). Garnish with freshly grated nutmeg.

"At the Police Court in Boston." *Salem (MA) Gazette*, March 20, 1827, 2.

Thomas, Jerry. *How to Mix Drinks*. New York: Dick & Fitzgerald, 1862.

Wondrich, David. *Imbibe!*, 2nd ed. New York: Penguin, 2015.

Audrey Saunders

tomato-based cocktails constitute a category of drinks long dominated by the Bloody Mary and her sanguinary kin, such as the Bloody Caesar and the Bloody Maria, which combine some form of spirit with tomato juice, Worcestershire sauce, and other seasonings. See BLOODY CAESAR and BLOODY MARY. In relatively recent years, however, mixologists have created a variety of tomato-based cocktails that take advantage of the fresh flavors of the fruit just off the vine.

One of the easiest methods of infusing fresh tomato flavors into a cocktail is by muddling tomatoes in a shaker before adding other ingredients. This technique is used, for example, in Julie Reiner's tequila-based Maria Sin Sangre; its recipe starts with muddling half a dozen cherry tomatoes with basil leaves and simple syrup. Scott Baird of San Francisco (1981–) begins his bourbon- and beer-based Spaghetti Western in a similar manner. See REINER, JULIE.

Another commonly employed method to extract tomato essence for use in cocktails is to make tomato water by straining chopped or puréed tomatoes. While Alexandria, Virginia, bartender Todd Thrasher (1969–) wasn't the first mixologist to replace packaged tomato juice with tomato water in the Bloody Mary, he may have done the most to popularize the updated version with his nearly clear Tomato Water Bloody Mary. Chicago bartender Charles Joly (1976–) has also relied on tomato water for the various iterations of his Midnight Mary, the latest of which brought the venerable brunch staple firmly into the twenty-first century with the addition of nitrogen-frozen basil foam.

See also TOMATO JUICE.

David Mahoney

tomato juice started to gain traction as a beverage in the United States during Prohibition. Tomato juice was known prior to the American Civil War, especially as an ingredient in sauces, vinegars, and tomato wine and as a braising liquid. By 1870, cases of French spiced tomato juice were being imported to New Orleans, possibly as a sauce for cooking. What's more, by the 1910s the liquid drained off of canned tomatoes was in common use in American sporting circles as a hangover cure. But in 1917, when Chef Louis Perrin at the French Lick Springs

Hotel in Orange County, Indiana, made a batch for guests to drink after his kitchen ran out of orange juice, it became a hit and led to wide demand. From there, canned tomato juice quickly became a popular mass-produced beverage and by the late 1920s was widely advertised as a breakfast drink in the United States. It also saw service during the Volstead years, either plain or as the "Tomato Juice Cocktail," as an alternative to alcohol for upright citizens (less upright ones who had overdone things the night before sometimes added gin to it). The cocktail, heavily promoted by the tomato juice industry beginning in 1928, was simply the juice, chilled and seasoned with "salt, lemon juice, Tabasco and Worcestershire sauce." See BLOODY MARY. Manufacturers also pushed the canned juice as a panacea for infirm Americans and healthy babies alike. Consisting of pressed tomato juice or tomato paste, often with added salt, the juice can also contained additives such as garlic powder or onion powder. Tomato juice features in a number of mixed drinks besides the Bloody Mary, from some versions of the Michelada to the Red Snapper, to Canada's Bloody Caesar.

See also BLOODY CAESAR; MICHELADA; and RED SNAPPER.

Drowne, Kathleen, and Patrick Huber. *The 1920's.* Westport, CT: Greenwood, 2004.
"Landing from Bark Johanne Marie." *New Orleans Daily Picayune,* February 17, 1870, 6.
McIntyre, O. O. "New York Day by Day." *San Francisco Examiner,* January 19, 1929, 28.
Smith, Andrew. *Pure Ketchup: A History of America's National Condiment.* Columbia: South Carolina University Press, 1996.
"Tomato Cocktails Click." *Johnson City (TN) Staff-News,* October 19, 1928, 10.

Chloe Frechette

Tom Collins is at root simply an extra-large glass of Gin Punch lengthened with soda water and ice. See PUNCH. Considered a humble, undistinguished libation by some, it is nonetheless one of the best known and enduring mixed drinks of all time, as popular in the 1950s as it was in the 1870s. It has lent its name to the long, thin glass (the Collins glass) in which the drink is typically served.

The name is an American contortion of the John Collins, a drink named after John Collin (ca. 1771–1843), the headwaiter and proprietor of Limmer's Old House in London who helped to popularize the potion in punch form. See JOHN COLLINS. By 1864, the drink, along with its signature extra-large glass, had made it to Canada and Australia, and before long it was in the United States, too.

How the John Collins became the Tom Collins is one the best origin stories in the annals of bar culture. American barflies of the 1870s derived much sport from pranking fellow tipplers with the news that a scalawag named Tom Collins had been bad-mouthing them around town and that Collins could be found at a tavern nearby; a wild goose chase and laughs aplenty ensued. In 1874, newspapers were filled with jocular mentions of the elusive Mr. Collins.

One result of this barroom game was that the John Collins became the Tom Collins, most likely with an assist from the fact that, as a new English import, it was generally made with Old Tom gin, another fairly new English import. See OLD TOM GIN. In any case, by the 1880s bartenders' guides were reserving the John Collins name for the version made with Dutch genever or its American imitation. After Prohibition, with Old Tom and genever both all but extinct in America, the Tom Collins was made with London Dry gin and the John Collins with bourbon whisky. See PROHIBITION AND TEMPERANCE IN AMERICA and LONDON DRY GIN. The Tom Collins remained popular enough after Repeal to inspire premixed versions and bottled Tom Collins mixers. By the 1940s, it had become one of the most popular drinks in America—on one summer afternoon in 1843, the bar of the Commodore Hotel in New York City served over 1,100 of them—and a drink often favored by women.

Its ubiquity decreased in the late twentieth century, as older drinks were discarded by younger generations. However, with the return of Old Tom gin in the twenty-first century, many cocktail bars restored the drink to its natural state, and the Tom Collins found renewed relevance.

The drink's formula lends itself nicely to other spirits. The Rum Collins dates to the 1930s, when it was quite popular; it was likely the child of Americans' discovery of Cuba during the dry years. The Vodka Collins began to emerge in the 1930s and became ubiquitous in the 1950s. Though the drink contains citrus, most bartenders insist it should not be shaken but built in the glass and stirred. Refreshing and light in body, the Tom Collins reigns supreme in summer. It is a drink meant to be lingered over, "with reverence and meditation," as David Embury has it. See EMBURY, DAVID A.

Recipe: Combine 45 ml Old Tom Gin, 22 ml lemon juice, and 30 ml simple syrup in a Collins glass filled with ice. Stir well until chilled. Top with soda water and garnish with a lemon wheel.

See also GIN FIZZ and LONG DRINK.

Simonson, Robert. "The Cat's Meow." *Imbibe Magazine*, August 4, 2012. https://imbibemagazine.com/old-tom-gin/ (accessed March 12, 2021).
Wondrich, David. "How the John Collins Became the Tom Collins." *Daily Beast*, July 21, 2017. https://www.thedailybeast.com/how-the-john-collins-became-the-tom-collins (accessed March 12, 2021).

Robert Simonson

tonic water is a brainchild of Schweppe's, the company that first produced commercially viable artificial soda water (the concept had been pioneered by the English physician William Falconer in the late 1770s). In 1790, and in partnership with Nicholas Paul and Henry Albert Gosse when he moved operations to London, former watchmaker Johann-Jacob Schweppe (1740–1821) introduced three different soda waters to the British medical community and public: table soda, soda for kidney patients, and soda for patients with serious digestive complaints. Each differed in the intensity of carbonation and alkali content.

Schweppe focused all of his efforts on those products, making him and his partners wealthy to a point that Schweppe sought retirement. He sold the majority of his interest to a group of British businessmen who continued operations but focused their attentions on beating the growing influx of competitors and supplying increased demand. Consumer popularity proved that no competitor could beat the combination of low price and high quality of Schweppe's waters. In 1824, the partners retired and sold J. Schweppe & Company to majority shareholder and managing director Robert Brohier, his brother R. J. Brohier, and Richard Annesley Sparkes. This partnership had a different vision: one that coupled medical breakthroughs with popular demand and changing palates.

Quinine, a South American extract of cinchona tree bark, was isolated and named by French researchers Pierre Joseph Pelletier and Joseph Caventou in 1820. Traditionally, cinchona was fermented into a beverage by indigenous peoples as a remedy for the chills, a common symptom of malaria. As early as 1631, Italian physicians applied cinchona for the same purpose. But it was Pelletier's and Caventou's study that sparked broader interest and application, especially in 1851, when it took on a very practical and palatable form in the hands of Schweppe's, who immediately began development of a commercial recipe for a bottled chinchona drink.

The Schweppes partners finally patented, in 1858, commercial "Indian tonic water" that combined its successful soda water with quinine and sweetening. Paired with gin and touted as healthful, it already had been adopted as a daily quencher for British subjects living in tropical areas. The commercial distribution of tonic water in the 1870s vaulted the Gin and Tonic toward the top of the drinks menu, standing shoulder to shoulder with the John Collins and the Tom Collins. See GIN AND TONIC; JOHN COLLINS; and TOM COLLINS.

Finally, it should be noted that most modern tonic waters have greatly reduced levels of quinine and greatly augmented levels of sugar compared to the nineteenth-century version.

Miller, Anistatia, and Jared Brown. "The Perfect Mixer." *Mixology Magazine*, special supplement, 2010.
Walker, Kim, and Mark Nesbitt. *Just the Tonic*. Kew, UK: Royal Botanic Gardens, 2019.

Anistatia R. Miller and Jared M. Brown

Maria Dolores Boadas tossing a cocktail behind the bar at Bar Boadas, Barcelona, ca. 1965. Courtesy of Bar Boadas.

tossing, also known as "**rolling**" or "**throwing**," is a cocktail-mixing technique in which the ingredients are poured back and forth from a height between two mixing vessels. See MIXOLOGY, THE HISTORY OF and ROLLING.

tourist drink can refer to any alcoholic beverage intended primarily for consumption by vacationers and generally eschewed by the natives of the region. See also UMBRELLA DRINK.

Trader Vic's is a chain of tiki bars that began in Oakland, California. See TIKI. Its founder, Victor Bergeron, claimed to have invented the Mai Tai. See BERGERON, VICTOR "TRADER VIC"; and MAI TAI.

Treacle, a stirred rum cocktail with an apple juice float, was created by the British bartender Dick Bradsell at London's Flamingo Bar in the late 1990s. The name refers to the caramelized flavor produced by combining apple juice with the rich molasses notes of a dark Jamaican pot-still rum.

According to colleagues, Bradsell was frequently irked by those who insisted on using pressed or cloudy apple juice to make this drink, since he maintained that only clear apple juice, from concentrate, would achieve the desired "treacly" flavor. The drink's success also depends on the use of an aged pot-still rum, preferably one from Jamaica.

Recipe: Stir 25 ml dark rum with 5 ml sugar syrup, 2 dashes of Angostura bitters, and two ice cubes in a rocks glass, before adding another 25 ml dark rum, two more ice cubes, and stirring again. Top glass with ice and finish with an apple juice float and a lemon twist.

The Caribe Hilton's original Piña Colada—the tourist drink of all tourist drinks—as recreated by Annene Kay. Courtesy of Annene Kay.

See also BRADSELL, DICK.

"Our Favourite Bartenders: Dick Bradsell." *The Cocktail Lovers*, November 11, 2013. https://thecocktaillovers.com/our-favourite-bartenders-dick-bradsell/ (accessed April 7, 2021).

Alice Lascelles

The **triangle trade** is a phrase often used to simplify the complex transatlantic trade relations of the eighteenth century and nineteenth century. It typically refers to the three-way trade between Africa, the West Indies, and either North America or Europe, which typically involved rum, molasses, and enslaved human beings.

The North American version of the triangle trade was more narrowly tied to rum. In general outline, it involved traders purchasing men, women, and children on Africa's west coast, then sailing with their human cargo to the West Indies. At the sugar plantations there, the survivors of the brutal Middle Passage were then traded for molasses, which was shipped to New England. See MOLASSES. There it would be made into rum at one of the dozens of coastal distilleries, which would then be shipped to Africa to trade for more people, perpetuating the cycle.

The European variant was similar, although it more typically involved trading humans for sugar, rum, and coffee in the West Indies, which was then shipped to Europe to trade for manufactured goods, which were in turn shipped to Africa.

The idea of New England rum being traded for slaves has deep roots. Nicholas Cresswell, a young man who kept a detailed journal of his travels in North America between 1774 and 1777, wrote that "[New Englanders] import large quantities of molasses from the West Indies, which they distill and sell to Africa and the other Colonies."

Two-way trade was common—between, for instance, Gambia and Barbados, or Boston and Jamaica, or Brazil and Angola—hauling rum or cachaça to trade for enslaved workers or molasses to trade for salt pork and lumber.

But the notion of the North American triangle trade took seed in the mid-nineteenth century, well after the trade had ceased. Several historians drew upon scattered examples of three-legged trade to extrapolate more broadly, eventually claiming that it underpinned New England's economic success. The idea also served politically as the Civil War loomed; Southerners seeking to counteract New Englanders who criticized slavery found it expedient to claim that the north had benefited from slavery early on.

More modern scholarship, however, has found that the North American triangle trade was an idea that was largely overblown. While each leg of the trade could been seen in aggregate, the idea of individual businesses making a fortune running the cycles of the trade as described above—or the region becoming enriched—is more spurious.

Historian Clifford Shipton examined hundreds of New England shipping records yet failed to find "a single example of a ship engaged in such a triangular trade." Another historian looking at the transatlantic

The bar at the original Trader Vic's, Emeryville, California. Courtesy of Jeff Berry.

trade found eighteen Rhode Island boats involved in the slave trade, compared to 352 involved in the coastal trade and 150 in the two-way trade with the West Indies, suggesting it was a relatively small part of the regional economy. Rum historian John McCusker has concluded that "the involvement of the Continental Colonies in the slave trade [during the later colonial period] was insignificant by every measure we can apply but a human one."

The triangle trade has persisted in many history books and popular culture. The *Dictionary of American History* (1940) called triangular trade "the backbone of New England prosperity." The trade was featured most notably in the 1969 Broadway hit musical *1776*, which featured the musical number "Molasses to Rum." ("Molasses to rum to slaves / Oh what a beautiful waltz / You dance with us / We dance with you / Molasses and rum and slaves . . .")

See also CARIBBEAN; NORTH AFRICA; and RUM.

McCusker, John. *Rum and the American Revolution: The Rum Trade and the Balance of Payments of the Thirteen Continental Colonies*. New York: Garland, 1989.

Rawley, James A. *The Transatlantic Slave Trade: A History*. New York & London: W. W. Norton, 1981.

Smith, Frederick H. *Caribbean Rum: A Social and Economic History*. Gainesville, University Press of Florida, 2005.

Wayne Curtis

The **Trident** is a cocktail composed of aquavit, dry sherry, Cynar, and peach bitters, served up with a lemon twist. Developed in 2002 by the pioneering Seattle-based cocktail enthusiast Robert Hess, the Trident is composed along similar lines as the Negroni, in that its primary components are measured in equal parts, and that its flavor skews dry, herbaceous, and bitter. See NEGRONI. The drink first appeared on a cocktail menu at Seattle's Zig Zag Café—where, at one point, the drink's popularity was such that the bar was using more Cynar than all other bars in Washington State combined—and the appeal soon spread to other cities.

Recipe: Stir with cracked ice 30 ml dry amontillado sherry, 30 ml aquavit, 30 ml Cynar, and 1 dash each peach and orange bitters. Strain into chilled cocktail glass and twist lemon peel over the top.

See also HESS, ROBERT.

Hess, Robert. *The Essential Bartender's Guide.*
New York: Mud Puddle, 2008.

Paul Clarke

triple distillation (full and partial), a process in which a spirit (or some component of the finished product) undergoes three distillations, is common practice in whisky distilleries in Ireland, though it is also employed by a few distilleries in Scotland. See also DISTILLATION, PROCESS; SCOTLAND AND IRELAND; and WHISKY.

triple sec has no strict definition but generally connotes a white curaçao, the liqueur originally made from oranges grown on the island of the same name. See CURAÇAO.

tropical drink, to contemporary Western ears, is a generic term for any fruity rum punch or frozen colada. But this is a blinkered view of a much broader drink category that stretches back hundreds of years, crosses many cultural divides, and encompasses a wide variety of alcoholic beverages. These can be divided into two main categories: indigenous drinks made in the tropics before European contact and the hybrid drinks that resulted after the Old World invaded the equatorial regions of the New.

Pre-contact tropical drinks existed almost everywhere that pre-contact tropical peoples did. Equatorial Central and West Africans brewed palm wine, while tropical East Africans fermented millet seeds into a strong, bitter intoxicant called *pombe*. In South America, Amazonian tribes brewed chicha, a low-ABV maize beer, while the Miskito people of Central America fermented bananas into *mishlaw*. The Kalinago of the Caribbean islands chewed cassava bread, spat it into a bowl, and waited for the enzymes in their saliva to ferment it into *ouicou*. In the South Pacific, Vanuatu islanders fermented the kava plant in much the same way, chewing its psychoactive root and then spitting it into coconut milk. In the Philippines, Bataan natives soaked berries in sugar-cane juice, which fermented in large clay jars into *bashee*.

Moving farther east, we encounter not just fermentation but distillation. Throughout Indonesia and the Indian subcontinent, palm sap (and sometimes rice or coconut) was distilled into an aqua vitae called either toddy or arrack. See AQUA VITAE; TODDY; and ARRACK. It was here in Southeast Asia, with the arrival of English and Dutch traders, that the "hybrid" tropical drink template was born. See SOUTHEAST ASIA. By the early 1600s, European traders were mixing the local arrack with local citrus juice and sugar to make what would come to be called punch (historian David Wondrich suggests that Sri Lankan natives may have invented a proto-punch called *vinperle* even before East met West). See PUNCH.

Sailors brought punch back with them to Europe and, more important to the development of the hybrid tropical drink, to Europe's fledgling Caribbean colonies, which conveniently happened to grow the prized tropical produce that went in Southeast Asian punches (courtesy of Columbus, who had introduced both limes and sugar to the West Indies). Here British and French planters folded a new ingredient into punch: rum, which they'd begun distilling from the leftovers of the sugar-making process in the mid-1600s.

By the turn of the twentieth century, the bones of Caribbean punch—rum, lime, and sugar—had also become the spine of the modern, single-serving tropical drink. Jamaica mixed rum, lime, and sugar into Planter's Punch; Martinique swizzled them into Petit (or Ti') Punch; and Cuba shook them into the Daiquiri and Mojito. See DAIQUIRI; MOJITO; PLANTER'S PUNCH; and TI' PUNCH. Prohibition brought these drinks to the attention of the United States, where after Repeal proto-tiki bartenders fleshed out the Caribbean rum-lime-sugar formula with multiple fruit juices and spice-infused syrups. See FRUIT JUICE. These faux-Polynesian concoctions dominated the tropical drink category in the years following World War II, which also saw the rise of two other mainstays of the contemporary tropical drink—pineapple and coconut—courtesy of the Piña Colada, which began life in 1954 at a Puerto Rican hotel bar. See PIÑA COLADA.

Farther south, late twentieth-century tourists also discovered the hybrid tropical drinks of Brazil, where transplanted Southeast Asian punch had evolved over time into the Caipirinha (lime, sugar, and the local sugar-cane distillate cachaça) and the Batida (cachaça blended with mango, papaya, or any other tropical fruit at hand). See CAIPIRINHA and BATIDA.

In the twenty-first century, tropical drink mixology continues to evolve. Thai basil, lemongrass, persimmon, sandalwood, and ever more exotic ingredients now find their way into punches, coladas, and neo-tiki drinks at craft cocktail bars. Meanwhile, in the tropics themselves, indigenous peoples still ferment and consume *pombe*, *chicha*, and kava root, much as they always have.

See also RUM PUNCH and TIKI.

Berry, Jeff. *Potions of the Caribbean*. New York: Cocktail Kingdom, 2015.

Peters, Carl. *New Light on Dark Africa: Being the Narrative of the German Emin Pasha Expedition*. London: Ward, Locke, 1891.

Wondrich, David. *Punch: The Delights (and Dangers) of the Flowing Bowl*. New York: Perigree, 2010.

Jeff Berry

tuber-based spirits are liquors or liqueurs distilled with tubers as the basis of the spirit—for example, a vodka made of potatoes or yams, or a liqueur based on beet-sugar spirit.

Shochu is a Japanese spirit distilled from a variety of possible sources—most often barley or rice, but sometimes sweet potatoes or potatoes. Shochu is traditionally low in proof, about 25 percent alcohol by volume, but some higher-proof products (up to 35 percent alcohol by volume) are available. The lower-proof varieties are usually drunk neat or on the rocks, with the higher-proof versions more suitable for cocktails. See SHOCHU.

Though, as with shochu, most vodka, aquavit, and gin are grain-based, potato vodka is common—mostly in Poland and elsewhere in eastern Europe—and examples of vodkas and occasionally gins distilled from tubers such as yam, sweet potato, and cassava do exist, as does a thriving cottage industry in much of Africa making spirits from cassava and dried cassava chips. See CENTRAL AND EAST AFRICA, and KWETE. Some of these products are distilled multiple times to become as neutral as possible, while others are distilled once and retain some of the flavor of the base ingredient.

In Germany, the Jerusalem artichoke (*Helianthus tuberosus*, also called sunchoke, sunroot, earth apple, or topinambur) is made into a type of brandy called topinambur. In California, the distillery Charbay experimented with a never-released spirit, somewhat akin to tequila, made from Jerusalem artichoke.

In California's Central Valley, the Corbin Cash distillery makes a vodka out of sweet potatoes (*Ipomoea batatas*) and also a sweet-potato liqueur; whereas the vodka is distilled to remove most of the flavor of the sweet potato, the liqueur is designed to keep the flavor in.

Cyclamen (*Cyclamen hederifolium*, also known as sow bread) has historically been used in medicinal liqueurs, where it's blended with other herbs, roots, tubers, and flowers and then mixed with alcohol and sugar to make a potable tonic used against infection.

See also VODKA; AQUAVIT; and GIN.

"Alcoholic Beverage Q&A." National Research Institute of Brewing. http://www.nrib.go.jp/English/sake/esakefaq04.htm (accessed July 1, 2016).

Olmsted, Larry. "The Best Spirit You've (Probably) Never Tasted: Japan's Shochu." *Forbes*. http://www.forbes.com/sites/larryolmsted/2013/08/06/the-best-spirit-youve-probably-never-tasted-japans-shochu/ (accessed April 7, 2021).

Michael Dietsch

tuica is a popular type of plum brandy made in Romania, most often in homes, and served as an aperitif. See APERITIF AND DIGESTIVE; BRANDY; HOME DISTILLING; and SLIVOVITZ.

twist is a strip of citrus zest used as a cocktail garnish. Its name derives from the twisting it receives to express its oils before being dropped into a drink. See ZEST, CITRUS.

Ueno, Hidetsugu (1967–), is a bartender and bar owner and is considered by many to be the de facto global ambassador for Japanese bartending due to extensive world travel and his comfort with lecturing in English. He is also considered one of the "five godfathers" of Japanese bartending. See UYEDA, KAZUO.

Ueno started bartending in 1992, though his rise to prominence started eight years later as opening bartender at the critically revered Star Bar in Tokyo with his friend Hishahi Kishi. This led him in 2008 to open his own bar, Bar High Five, in Tokyo's frenetic Ginza neighborhood. High Five has won numerous international plaudits. Renowned for carving ice into diamond shapes, Ueno San, as he is known, has been a judge for Diageo's World Class Competition since its inception and in 2016 won World's Best Bartender at the Tales of the Cocktail Spirited Awards.

See also ICE CARVING; JAPAN; and TALES OF THE COCKTAIL.

"Hidetsugu Ueno San." Difford's Guide. https://www.diffordsguide.com/people/9307/bartender/hidetsugu-ueno-san (accessed December 12, 2016).
McGoram, Simon. "An Interview with Hidetsugu Ueno." *Australian Bartender*, February 6, 2011. https://australianbartender.com.au/2011/02/06/an-interview-with-hidetsugu-ueno/ (accessed December 12, 2016).

Angus Winchester

ullage has two primary definitions. The first refers to the free space above a liquid in a container such as a barrel, bottle, or tank. It may be intentional—to allow for expansion of a liquid, for instance—or created when a heated product cools and contracts. Ullage may also refer to the loss of liquid from evaporation or leakage (sometimes called "outages" or "angel's share"). See ANGEL'S SHARE. Rates vary with humidity, heat, and barometric pressure, ranging from 2 percent to 20 percent in volume loss per year. In general, the greater the ullage, the faster the evaporation (due to the increased surface area of the liquid relative to the volume); in some hot climates where evaporation is high, cellar masters prefer to control their ullage by combining barrels once it has reached a set level.

Ullage was initially a tax concern; brewers and distillers balked at paying excise on lost alcohol. *The Theory and Practice of Gauging* (1740) published measurement standards for excise officers to account for ullage. Gauger's manuals eventually included complicated equations to measure standing and reposing casks.

See also MATURATION.

Batemen, Joseph. *The Excise Officer's Manual and Improved Gauger*. London: A. Maxwell, 1840.
Shirtcliffe, Robert. *The Theory and Practice of Gauging,* London: H. Woodfall, 1740.

Fred Minnick

umbrella drink is another name for a tiki drink, derived from the ubiquitous paper parasols used as a decorative garnish in the tropical concoctions. See GARNISH and TIKI.

The **United Kingdom Bartenders Guild (UKBG)** is a fraternal organization for professional bartenders in the United Kingdom, with more than four hundred members in four regions of the British Isles as of October 2015.

The UKBG is the world's oldest organization of its kind still in existence, having been founded in 1934 by a group of bartenders who had competed in a European cocktail competition. Harry Craddock of the Savoy American Bar was its first president. See CRADDOCK, HARRY LAWSON. Though based mainly in London, the group included in its early rosters bartenders from much of the current and former British Empire, including in India, New Zealand, Kenya, and Jamaica, as well as aboard transatlantic ocean liners. It was initially famous for maintaining a library of all known cocktail recipes and registry of new ones at its London headquarters, which was almost destroyed by a German incendiary bomb during World War II. The war slowed the organization's growth, but its many members who served in the armed forces received care packages of cigarettes, chocolate, soap, and issues of *Bartender* magazine throughout the war thanks to UKBG fundraising efforts.

After the war, emigrant bartenders set up UKBG chapters in the United States, Canada, Australia, and South Africa that later evolved into those nations' own national bartender guilds. A chapter was founded in southern California in 1949 by Egidio "Angus" Angerosa (1903–1982), a Neapolitan who had assisted Harry Craddock in running the guild in London. See CRADDOCK, HARRY LAWSON. This was very active, sponsoring yearly competitions that were widely publicized. In 1961, it split from the UKBG to become the California Bartenders Guild, from which the United States Bartenders Guild would be formed in 1971. See UNITED STATES BARTENDERS' GUILD (USBG).

In 1951, the UKBG was instrumental in the founding of the International Bartenders Association, with then UKBG president W. J. Tarling serving as the first president of the IBA. See TARLING, WILLIAM JAMES "BILLY." In 1952, the UKBG set up the first formal bartender training course in the United Kingdom, and the following year, it published the first edition of the *UKBG Guide to Drinks*, now called the *UKBG International Guide to Drinks* and currently in its eleventh edition. The guild continues to provide education for its members and organize cocktail contests and other events.

Slavin, Jim. Private email correspondence, November 13, 2015

UKBG International Guide to Drinks, 4th ed. London: UKBG, 1965.

Jason Horn

The **United States and Canada** comprise the former British colonies of North America, along with significant pieces of the American empires of France, Spain, the Netherlands, and Sweden that they absorbed over the years. Their drinking cultures, although divergent in detail, nonetheless share a common DNA and retain a good deal of their British heritage. That heritage is not an abstemious one: the United States is the largest spirits-consuming country in the world by value, if not by absolute volume or per capita, and the largest importer, while both countries are major spirits producers and exporters. The United States is also the birthplace of the so-called American bar, where iced drinks are assembled to order in front of the customer, and it still to a large degree drives global trends in mixology (an American word). See MIXOLOGY, THE HISTORY OF.

Despite its British heritage, American and Canadian drinking culture has some key differences. In the late 1500s and early 1600s, when Britain began establishing colonies in North America, the settlers it sent across the Atlantic found themselves at the end of a long and tenuous supply line. The beer and ale that were their staple daily drink proved challenging to brew and difficult to keep in the hotter climate found in America, and particularly in the South. Likewise, the wine that the upper classes drank could not be made locally (American vines provided an undrinkable product, while European ones fell victim to the phylloxera louse) and was expensive and chancy to import. As a result, the colonists turned to distillation. Spirits would not be widely consumed in England itself until after the Restoration in 1660, while the colonists had been making large amounts of apple brandy, which was known in Britain, and peach brandy, which was not, since the early 1640s. See PEACH BRANDY. They also experimented with other fruit brandies, sometimes successfully, and with distilling spirits from various European grains and the indigenous maize, or Indian corn. See CORN. The development of local spirits was greatly assisted by the absorption of the Dutch colony of New Netherlands, where many were experienced at distilling from grain, and, in the early 1700s, by the arrival in Pennsylvania of large numbers of farmers from the western parts of Germany, where both grain and fruit spirits were common. By the mid-1650s, the colonists were also importing rum from the Caribbean in quantity, and by the end of the century they were making their own, after a fashion, from Caribbean molasses.

By the 1740s, as Britain extended its dominion (French Canada fell to British conquest in 1763), rye whisky was being made in many of the colonies, but particularly in the Middle Atlantic ones. See WHISKY, RYE. Corn whisky soon followed, particularly in the West. With the American Revolution in 1776, the northernmost colonies remained loyal to the English crown. Henceforth, Canadian distillers, who had begun making rum in the 1760s and grain spirits soon after, would draw increasingly on British, and in particular Scottish, expertise, while those in the United States managed things in their own, sometimes peculiar, fashion, which led to such idiosyncrasies as the three-chamber still and aging in charred barrels. See STILL, THREE-CHAMBER; and BARREL.

The United States also diverged from Britain in the way it drank its spirits. Americans made a specialty of mixed drinks. By the end of the eighteenth century, British punch (first found in the American colonies in the 1660s) and toddy had spawned the julep, sling, and Cock-Tail, all drinks with deep British roots but a peculiar American flair. See PUNCH; TODDY; JULEP; SLING; and COCK-TAIL. Over the next generation, these and other single-serving mixed drinks, some of them iced, spread throughout the expanding United States and across the porous Canadian border. Under the influence of star mixologists such as Peter Bent Brigham, Joseph Santini, John Dabney, Jerry Thomas, and William Schmidt, mixing drinks developed into a true American folk art, and by the middle of the nineteenth century an international one. See BRIGHAM, PETER BENT; THOMAS, JEREMIAH P. "JERRY"; and SCHMIDT, WILLIAM. As masses of immigrants poured into the country, new ingredients— vermouth, European liqueurs—were introduced and new drinks created including the Martini, the Manhattan, and the fizz. See VERMOUTH; MARTINI; MANHATTAN COCKTAIL; and FIZZ.

Meanwhile, American whisky came into its own as rye, bourbon, and Tennessee whisky slowly displaced peach and apple brandy as the premiere American spirits. See WHISKY, BOURBON; and WHISKY, TENNESSEE. Canadian whisky too was developing into a national spirit, although there was

still a good deal of cheap rum being distilled in the Maritime provinces. (Like New England's Medford rum, made in large quantities through the nineteenth century, this rum generally had a poor reputation.) See RUM, MEDFORD. Canadian distillers originally made mixed-grain whiskies like those in the United States, but as the nineteenth century rolled into the twentieth, they began following the scotch model, where straight, full-flavored whisky was blended with lighter grain whisky. See WHISKY, GRAIN; and WHISKY, CANADIAN.

The first decades of the twentieth century saw the United States and, briefly, Canada enact Prohibition laws forbidding the sale of spirits (and, in the United States, all other alcoholic beverages) within their respective territories, but only the United States also forbade their manufacture. See PROHIBITION AND TEMPERANCE IN AMERICA. As a result, in 1933, when the American law was repealed after fourteen years, the country's distilling industry was in ruins. Canadian distillers, on the other hand, few in number (there were twenty-five in 1927) but large and technically advanced, were thriving, having supplied much of the United States' illicit whisky during the dry years. By the time it joined World War II, in 1941, the United States had rebuilt its distilling industry, after a fashion: where there had been 6,211 operating distilleries in the country in 1890, in 1943 there were only 238, the largest and most successful of which were operated by the conglomerates known as the "big four": Seton Porter's National Distillers Products, Schenley Distilleries, Hiram Walker & Sons, and Joseph E. Seagram & Sons (the last two being Canadian-owned). See HIRAM WALKER AND SONS and SEAGRAM COMPANY LTD. The decades after the war brought even more consolidation and homogenization (as it did to food industries in general), so that by 1997 there were a mere sixty licensed distillers in the country.

This consolidation was aided in part by the meteoric rise of vodka, a spirit that rewards economies of scale. See VODKA. Indeed, after a meteoric rise in the 1950s and 1960s, in 1976 vodka displaced whisky, which in the 1930s had been 85 percent of the spirits market, as the nation's most popular spirit. Vodka made it there on the back of a new wave of mixology, one relying on simple drinks that could be made with packaged ingredients: the Screwdriver, the Moscow Mule, and the Bloody Mary (and, of course, its Canadian offshoot, the Bloody Caesar). See SCREWDRIVER; MOSCOW MULE; BLOODY

MARY; and BLOODY CAESAR. Joining them in the 1950s was the tequila-based Margarita and a whole lot of rum-based tiki drinks. See MARGARITA and TIKI.

By the 1980s, mixology had in the majority of American and Canadian bars been reduced to its least common denominator, with artificially flavored liquors mixed with prepackaged juices and poured over quick-melting ice chips. A few bartenders, however, saw the potential in reviving the best practices of the craft and were rewarded by a small but enthusiastic and vocal clientele when they did so.

The turn of the twenty-first century saw this clique (and ones like it in Europe) serve as the seeds for a revival in the fine art of mixing drinks. See COCKTAIL RENAISSANCE. It also saw the beginning of a deconsolidation in the distilling industry, as micro-distillers began opening with increasing frequency in the United States and, by the 2010s, in Canada. By 2010, vodka's growth had almost come to a standstill, while whisky began booming, including the almost-extinct rye whisky, now a micro-distillery staple. In general, younger American and Canadian drinkers began to develop a taste for more specialized and even exotic spirits, such as mezcal and Italian aperitifs and digestives, mostly drunk in cocktails. See MEZCAL and APERITIF AND DIGESTIVE. A few decades in to the twenty-first century, this trend shows no signs of abating.

Liquor Industry Hearings. Washington, DC: US General Printing Office, 1944.

Morewood, Samuel. *A Philosophical and Statistical History of the Inventions and Customs of Ancient and Modern Nations in the Manufacture and Use of Inebriating Liquors.* Dublin: 1838.

Steiner, Bernard Christian. *Archives of Maryland XLI.* Baltimore: Maryland Historical Society, 1922.

Trumbull, J. Hammond. *Public Records of the Colony of Connecticut.* Hartford: Brown & Parson, 1850.

United States Tariff Commission. *Whisky.* Washington, DC: United States Tariff Commission, 1958.

Wondrich, David. *Imbibe!*, 2nd ed. New York: Perigee, 2015.

David Wondrich

The **United States Bartenders' Guild (USBG)** is a fraternal organization for American professional bartenders, with more than five thousand members in fifty-two local city and state chapters throughout the United States as of October 2015. It is the United States' only affiliate organization of the International Bartenders Guild. See IBA.

Dedicated to advancing the craft and prestige of bartending as a career, USBG offers a variety of educational and social events for bartenders, as well as group health insurance for its members. It also runs the Master Accreditation Program, a series of exams and education with three levels of certification for bartender expertise, and USBG Pulse, an online social network of bartenders and bar owners.

USBG was founded in 1971 when the California Bartenders' Guild, a successor to the California chapter of the United Kingdom Bartenders' Guild, reorganized as a national nonprofit corporation and adding other city chapters. However, by the 1990s the guild had grown weak and insubstantial and was down to a single branch, when the growing craft cocktail revival gave it a new lease on life.

In 2001, Tony Abou-Ganim helped establish a Las Vegas chapter. A San Francisco chapter soon followed and proved influential in helping the city's aborning cocktail movement to coalesce, counting local rising bartenders Marcovaldo Dionysos, Jacques Bezuidenhout, and David Nepove among its early members. By 2017, the USBG had chapters in more than sixty cities and more than six thousand members. While formally affiliated with the IBA, which acts as an umbrella organization to several bartenders' guilds, the current USBG has grown into a much more modern, activist enterprise, hosting regular meetings, social events, and educational seminars worldwide and acting as a bridge between members and various corporate-sponsored bartending competitions. Forming a new chapter requires a minimum of forty paid members, as well as a few other organizational tasks.

See also ABOU-GANIM, TONY; UNITED KINGDOM BARTENDERS' GUILD (UKBG); and BARTENDING SCHOOLS.

California Bartenders Guild. *Good Taste*, July 1962, 1.

Nepove, David. Interview. June 22, 2017.

United States Bartenders' Guild website. https://www.usbg.org/home (accessed March 12, 2021).

Jason Horn and Robert Simonson

usquebaugh (spelled variously) is the earliest English rendering of the Irish term *uisce beatha* and Scottish Gaelic *uisge beatha*, "water of life," dating at least to the late 1500s; by the mid-1700s it was superseded by "whisky." See AQUA VITAE and WHISKY.

Until the early 1700s, usquebaugh was usually encountered, at least beyond the Scottish Highlands or the Irish countryside, in the form of a malt spirit that had been turned into a cordial (and had the rawness of the spirit masked) by flavoring with licorice and nutmeg and a combination of other spices (e.g., cinnamon, cloves, caraway seeds, and ginger), and sweetening with raisins, dates, and cane sugar. The Irish version was particularly prized—"It cannot be made anywhere [else] in that perfection," the English writer James Howell noted in 1634—and was exported not only to England but to the European continent as well.

On the continent, usquebaugh took on a life of its own, its formula—with brandy replacing the malt spirit, a good-sized dose of saffron for color, and a great latitude among the spices—having been absorbed into the floating corpus of recipes from which distiller-liquorists drew the products with which they stocked their shelves. This "escubac," as the French called it, finally fell out of favor in the mid-nineteenth century. In the United Kingdom, the compound usquebaugh had begun to yield to the (greatly improved) unflavored product in the 1730s and was seldom seen after 1800, although the name lived on as a folkloric synonym for "whisky."

See also CORDIALS.

Company of Distillers of London. *The Distiller of London.* London: 1639.

Déjean [perh. Antoine Hornot]. *Traité raisonné de la distillation*, 4th ed. Paris: 1778.

Howell, James. *Familiar Letters, or Epistolae ho-elianae*, vol. 2. London: Dent, 1903.

David Wondrich

Uyeda, Kazuo (1944–), is a bartender and bar owner who is considered one of the five "grand masters of Japanese bartending," along with Yuichi Hoshi, Hisashi Kishi, Takao Mori, and Hidetsugu Ueno. See UENO, HIDETSUGU. His global claim to fame is as the inventor of the "hard shake," a highly stylized way of employing the three-piece cocktail shaker that he claims rounds off spirit flavors and creates a far colder and smoother cocktail than other shaking styles. See HARD SHAKE.

Uyeda was born in Chanai, Hokkaido. His first bartending job was at Tokyo Kaikan in 1966. Eight years later he moved to Shiseido Parlor and Bar l'Osier, where he was appointed chief bartender and director in 1995. In 1997, Uyeda opened his own bar in Ginza, Tender, where he is still to be found most nights. See TENDER BAR.

Despite a reticent and private demeanor and a lack of English skills, he rose to global visibility via the Slovak bartender Stanislav Vrdrna, who idolized him and organized training sessions for him in Bratislava and New York where he introduced the hard shake to the Western bartending world.

He is the author of several bartending books, including *Cocktail Techniques,* published in 2000, which is one of the very few Japanese bartending books to have been translated into English. His signature drink is the Grasshopper, and he is also credited with the coral garnish whereby salt is applied thickly to the outside of the glass using colored liquors. See GRASSHOPPER. In common with many Japanese bartenders, he pays much more attention to the color and appearance of his drinks than is common in Western bartending.

"Kazuo Uyeda." *Difford's Guide.* https://www.diffordsguide.com/people/51651/bartender/kazuo-uyeda (accessed March 15, 2021).

Tamasaburau. "The Best Tokyo Bars: Meet the Masters." *Time Out Tokyo,* July 8, 2016, https://www.timeout.com/tokyo/bars-and-pubs/the-best-tokyo-bars-masters (accessed March 15, 2021).

Uyeda, Kazuo. *Cocktail Techniques.* New York: Mud Puddle, 2010.

Angus Winchester

vacuum distillation is a method of extracting volatile compounds by creating a vacuum in the system to lower the vapor pressure and boiling point of the volatile liquids while making the process more energy efficient. This is done by attaching a pump to the outflow pipe from the condenser, thus reducing the air pressure in the still. The key benefit of vacuum distillation is the lower temperatures needed to make aroma compounds volatile, which helps preserve heat-sensitive compounds.

When distilling the aroma compounds from delicate sources, like fruits and spices, the high temperatures found in normal atmospheric stills often degrade the compounds, resulting in a "cooked" flavor in the distillate. For example, instead of fresh strawberry aromas you may get cooked jam aromas.

Using a vacuum still allows the aroma compounds to be separated with a very low energy input, generally just warm water, which preserves the delicate flavors and gives a true representation of the fruit or spice.

Although this method of distillation is relatively rare in the production of spirits, it is not new—the British physician Richard Shannon detailed the technique in 1805, and it has long been used in Japan for making shochu. See SHOCHU. It was also occasionally used in the United States for making brandy, and from 1950 until around 1973 the Mr. Boston company sold a "Vacuum Distilled Gin." In 2009, that last idea was revived by the Bacardi company, with their Oxley gin, vacuum-distilled at the Thames distillery outside of London. See BACARDI and GIN.

Vacuum distillation has found use in restaurants and bars where the extraction of unique flavor compounds is used as enhancements for cocktails. Benchtop rotary evaporators, commonly used in laboratories, are the preferred equipment, as they are compact and easy to operate. The key benefit of this method is the concentration of flavors that would normally be too subtle to detect or in the raw form would be inappropriate to add to a drink, like soil and flowers. These distillates capture and amplify the aromas, which can then be used to make a cocktail that is truly unique. See ROTARY EVAPORATOR.

Shannon, Richard. *A Practical Treatise On Brewing, Distillation and Rectification.* London: 1805.

Darcy O'Neil

A **vacuum sealer** has a primary function of removing air before sealing a product inside a plastic bag. It is often comprised of a powerful vacuum pump connected to a basin, lid, and heated seal bar. A product intended to be sealed is placed inside a special plastic bag laid inside the machine. Closing the lid and activating the vacuum pump draws air from the chamber, whereupon the heat bar melts the open edges of the plastic bag together. The process creates an air-free package, extending the shelf life of its contents and limiting or slowing bacterial growth. (An oxygen-free environment presents food safety issues itself, so care must be taken when sealing ingredients that are susceptible to anaerobic bacteria, such as meat.) Unlike other vacuum sealers that pull air through the bag—as opposed to vacating air around and inside the bag—a chamber vacuum sealer has the ability to seal liquids efficiently, making it well suited for culinary and cocktail uses.

Innovative chefs learned to adapt the technique, created for food preservation, to cooking, immersing the bags for many hours in a constant-temperature hot water bath. This "sous vide" technique has been adopted for cocktail use, allowing bartenders to explore the application of heat with sealed infusions (previously difficult due to alcohol's evaporation with applied heat) and in syrup production. Controlled heat acts as an asset in targeting specific flavors. See FLAVORED SYRUP.

A chamber vacuum machine can also be used to rapidly infuse flavors into liquid or garnishes—much like rapid iSi infusions. This process involves placing a shallow pan containing a porous ingredient and an infusing liquid in the vacuum chamber. When the vacuum is activated, the lowered pressure will break air cavities inside the ingredient, thereby allowing liquid to enter. When air is returned into the chamber, the liquid is pulled from the ingredient—and along with it flavor, color, and aroma. Conversely, a liquid can be used to flavor an edible ingredient.

Chamber vacuum sealers are often expensive and, depending on the location of its use, may trigger greater scrutiny from local health department regulators due to heightened food safety concerns when sealing volatile ingredients such as meat.

See also INFUSION.

Arnold, Dave. *Liquid Intelligence*. New York: W. W. Norton, 2014.
"How the Chamber Style Vacuum Sealers Work." *Chef Steps*. https://www.chefsteps.com/activities/how-chamber-style-vacuum-sealers-work (accessed April 7, 2021).
Myhrvold, Nathan, Chris Young, and Maxime Bilet. *Modernist Cuisine: Techniques and Equipment*, vol. 2. Bellevue, WA: Cooking Lab, 2011.

Alexander Paul Day

vanillin, the naturally occurring phenolic aldehyde that gives vanilla beans their principal flavor, is used as a flavoring agent for many foodstuffs, usually in synthetic form; in spirits, however, it is a natural byproduct of barrel aging. It can be leached from raw oak, but the processes of barrel production (during which lignin and tannins are broken down by heat and fire) increases its availability in the wood. Vanillin is alcohol soluble and slightly water soluble and will slowly dissolve into the spirit as it ages, giving aged spirits some of their sweet and rich flavor notes. Over time, vanillin will react with the oxygen in the barrel; as it degrades, its breakdown products react with some of the other compounds in the spirit, adding more flavors.

See also BARREL; CHARRING, TOASTING (AND RECHARRING); MATURATION; and PHENOL.

Buxton, Ian, and Paul S. Hughes. *The Science and Commerce of Whisky*. London: RSC, 2015.
Esposito, Lawrence J., et al. *Kirk-Othmer Encyclopedia of Chemical Technology*, 4th ed. New York: John Wiley & Sons, 1997.
Jackson, Ronald. *Wine Science: Principles and Applications*, 4th ed. Amsterdam: Elsevier, 2014.

Doug Frost

Vecchia Romagna is a Bologna, Italy–based distilling company that traces its roots back to 1820 when Jean Bouton (later Italianized to Buton) left Charente, France, to build a distillery in Ozzano, just outside the city. Its brandy is distilled from trebbiano bianco grapes in Charentais copper stills and was produced for the first time in 1939. Vecchia Romagna is currently the leading Italian brandy in its home market. The distillery employs both pot and continuous stills and ages the distillates separately in Limousin oak prior to bottling. See STILL, POT; and STILL, CONTINUOUS. The most popular line is Vecchia Romagna Etichetta Nera (Black Label), a blend of three-year-old brandies, and the company also markets a ten-year-old reserva, as well as twenty-five- and thirty-five-year-old brandies in very small quantities. (Vecchia Romagna has also produced numerous liqueurs and brandies under the Buton name, some labeled "cognac.") Since 1999, it has been owned by Bologna-based Gruppo Montenegro.

See also BRANDY and LIQUEURS.

Venturini, Nestore, ed. *Enciclopidea delle bevande alcoliche*. Padua: Meb, 1984.

Jack Robertiello

Vendome Copper and Brass Works is a company based in Louisville, Kentucky, that has become the preeminent manufacturer of stills, condensers, and other equipment for the American distilling industry. It is a family business, currently run by the fourth generation of the Sherman family.

The company was founded around 1909 (the company itself is unsure of the actual date) by

W. Elmore Sherman Sr. (1878–1963). Sherman had gained experience in the distillery fabrication business at the Louisville branch of Hoffman, Ahlers & Co., a Cincinnati company. When Hoffman hit a chaotic streak of bad luck, Sherman seized the opportunity and started his own company, picking up a number of Hoffman's customers.

The new company quickly gained contracts in the distilling business, in the local bourbon industry and as far away as Mexico and Burma. The company also made equipment for creosote and turpentine manufacturers.

Prohibition almost ended Vendome. The company found small amounts of work in the wood products niche and tried making boilers and pumps; Sherman took work as a bookkeeper with another firm.

The advent of Repeal saved the company. The boom that followed Repeal brought both refurbishment of old distilleries and construction of new ones. When World War II brought a requirement for production of huge amounts of industrial alcohol as chemical feedstock, Vendome adapted. They adapted again when metallurgical advances from the war made stainless steel an affordable material for distilleries.

This ability to change skills and find new customers outside the beverage alcohol field—pharmaceuticals, dairy, fuel alcohol, chemicals—led Vendome to dominance in their field and preserved the company again during the decline of bourbon in the 1980s. When the craft distilling phenomenon came around, Vendome was ready for that business as well. Their familiar script nameplate continues to be a common sight in American distilleries large and small.

See also STILL, CONTINUOUS; and WHISKY, BOURBON.

Vendome company website. http://vendomecopper.com/ (accessed March 15, 2021).

Lew Bryson

Vermeire, Robert (1891–1976), was a Belgian bartender who made a name for himself in London during World War I and is best remembered for his seminal book, *Cocktails: How to Mix Them* (1922), which introduced some of the earliest recipes for classics such as the Sidecar and the Singapore Sling.

Robert, inventor of cocktails that cure last nights, and author of a book on them

The only known portrait of the elusive Robert Vermeire is this quick 1922 pencil sketch from a London magazine. Wondrich Collection.

Vermeire was born in Knokke, Belgium on May 10, 1891, the son of noted local hoteliers. Sent to London when World War I broke out, he soon became a bartender at the Royal Automobile Club. Before the war's end, Vermeire moved to the Criterion, one of the oldest American bars in the city, where manager Luigi Naintré handpicked him in 1920 for his new venture, the Embassy Club, a member's-only dancing club. See CRITERION. "Kings and princes dine and dance there; so do statesmen and great painter and singers; so do the prettiest actresses," said a 1930 article in the *Evening News*. While at the Embassy, Vermeire wrote *Cocktails: How to Mix Them*, one of the first European mass-market cocktail books. It went on to sell over 150,000 copies and was translated into French and, according to the author, Japanese.

In 1923, he opened Robert's, in his Belgian hometown. Bar, restaurant, and hotel, it became a sensation and even attracted clients from London. The 1929 crash put an end to the party, and Vermeire filed for bankruptcy. It wasn't until 1938 that he got back on his feet and took over the bar of the Albert Ier, one of Brussels's most luxurious hotels. World War II arguably ended his career: both his sons collaborated with the Germans, and the huge fines that followed the end of the war put his family under considerable financial strain. Although he continued to work until 1958, Vermeire did not regain any form of financial stability—a sad end to an otherwise illustrious career.

See also COCKTAIL RECIPES.

Gorissen, Agnès. "Le Castel a créé le Zoute." http://archives.lesoir.be/le-castel-a-cree-le-zoute-sa-disparition-en-brise-l-ame_t-19890923-Z02041.html (accessed February 4, 2016).

"A King of London Clubs." *Evening News*, reprinted in the *Singapore Free Press and Mercantile Advertiser*, June 9, 1930, 8.

François Monti

vermouth is a class of aromatized, fortified aperitif wine with particularly close ties to cocktail culture. "Aromatized" means the wine has been infused with botanicals for flavor and color, and the flavor of vermouth is principally defined by these herbs and spices, not the base wine. "Fortified" means the wine contains added distilled alcohol—usually some sort of grape brandy—and this component can serve multiple purposes, including arresting wine fermentation to preserve sweetness and fresh-fruit flavors, extracting flavors from botanicals, and improving shelf stability. See MISTELLE. "Aperitif" indicates a bittersweet, gastric-stimulating, appetite-enhancing character, largely stemming from the aromatization botanicals—wormwood, in particular, for which vermouth is named and which should play an essential, if nuanced, role in any genuine vermouth. See APERITIF AND DIGESTIVE and WORMWOOD.

Modern vermouth is traditionally assembled from white wine, wormwood (*Artemisia absinthium* and/or *Artemisia pontica*), and some combination of herbs, spices, flowers, roots, sugar, and alcohol. Vermouths can also be flavored, such as Italian red vermouths with added vanilla, quinine, or bitters, a Turinese tradition (originally as *vermouth alla vaniglia*) that survives today. Regulations in the European Union and United States add legal form and weight to some of these attributes, but these regulations are recent and selective in scope.

The modern form of vermouth emerged in the eighteenth century in Piemonte and Savoy—then part of the Kingdom of Sardinia, and today parts of Italy and France. With the botanically rich foothills of the Alps, wine-producing regions, wealth, and access to Ligurian ports and the spice trade, the area bears many attributes that contributed to the formation of vermouth. The direct antecedents of modern vermouth were *Wermut*, *vermut*, or *vermutte* of Hungarian and German origin (wormwood wines); regional wine infusions; wines flavored with distilled botanicals; and spiced wines enjoyed by European aristocracy. Modern vermouth inherits aspects of each.

Vermouth was nominally commercialized in the late 1700s in Torino. A young employee of the Turinese Liquoreria Marendazzo, Antonio

September, 1869: Vermouth meets the cocktail, Knoxville, Tennessee. Wondrich Collection.

Benedetto Carpano (1764–1815), is typically credited with this, although historical verification is problematic. In any case, Carpano's template for the drink was sufficiently refined to become a local favorite. (The vermouth brand named for Carpano that is familiar today appears to have been created some decades later.) Various imitators arose in the early 1800s, including Cinzano and Cora, but these Turinese vermouths remained strictly regional products until the 1830s, when records show vermouths were exported to New World communities with a large Italian population, including Buenos Aires, New Orleans, San Francisco, and New York.

Meanwhile, in the early nineteenth century, the French wine merchant Joseph Noilly began developing a dramatically different concept of vermouth in Lyon, based on wines that had oxidized during shipping. By 1844, Noilly's heirs had commercialized his interpretation of vermouth under the brand Noilly Prat and were exporting some of their product to the United States out of Marseilles. See NOILLY PRAT. Their evolved product was lighter-bodied than Torino vermouth and contained less sugar. More critically, it was built upon Herault wines deliberately oxidized through seaside barrel aging in the Camargue, a practice that dramatically affected the flavor of the product. Marseilles remained the center of both their business and their product's culture for many years—their vermouth became at least as important for cooking as drinking in Provençal cuisine—and spawned local imitators (e.g., Chappaz), very few of which survive today.

Between the late 1830s to the early 1860s, regional wars and political instability inhibited the export of vermouth, although producers like Noilly Prat, Cinzano, and Cora flourished nevertheless. In 1863, the manufacturer Martini, Sola & Cia was established outside Torino (with direct railway access to Piedmontese agricultural regions and the port at Genoa) with the aim of mass-producing vermouth and other wines for export markets; production commenced around 1868. By 1879, the firm had been renamed Martini & Rossi and was on its way to becoming a global market leader in vermouth by volume, a distinction it has held ever since. See MARTINI & ROSSI. More or less concurrently, Noilly Prat also achieved export scale from its base in Marseillan and began shipping to many of the same foreign markets as Martini, eventually achieving a lasting market leadership of their own. For both companies, the Americas were a market capable of fueling enormous growth, with enough residual opportunities to keep many smaller brands busy.

By the 1870s, enough vermouth was reaching American markets to elevate it above an ethnic specialty and into the mainstream. In the United States, vermouth encountered the ascendant cocktail culture and proved such an intriguing and adaptable mixed-drink ingredient that it permanently changed mixology. The United States has remained the single largest vermouth market in the world, the demand driven entirely by cocktails. Italian vermouths also enjoyed extensive popularity as a standalone aperitif in South America and greater Europe.

During this time, it became common to refer to vermouth styles as "Italian" or "French." As proprietary products with complex, secret recipes, there was little to immediately differentiate these products from each other but the brand names, which could be transient, and the countries of origin on the labels, which were less so. Rising demand in the late nineteenth and early twentieth centuries—especially the ascendant popularity of dry vermouth in cocktails—drove many producers to diversify their products into multiple styles. French vermouth producers started offering Torino-style vermouths, and Italian producers such as Martini & Rossi added interpretations of the drier style that Noilly initiated.

Inspired by the relatively obscure, lightly sweet *blanc* style that had emerged in Chambéry, on the French side of the Savoy Alps, in the late nineteenth century, Italian producers also began offering a new *bianco* (white) style. As product lines diversified, caramel or black walnut coloring agents were adopted for some products, and additional labeling terminology emerged, with "rosso," "rouge," "bianco," "blanc," and "dry" appearing on labels. In the United States, where the white style never caught on, "sweet" (for Italian) and "dry" (for French) also became common parlance. Disruption from the world wars combined with the industrial boom in the United States led to major development of American vermouth production. By the late 1940s, New York Harbor–based Vermouth Industries of America and their Tribuno brand were second only to Martini & Rossi in US market share, although they competed on price, not quality. Gallo, in California, also did a large business in cheaper domestic vermouth during the mid-twentieth century.

A particular cultural feature in the postwar United States was a focus on the Dry Martini. See MARTINI. As enthusiasm gave way to obsession, the use of vermouth became associated with dilution (cheapness) and off flavors (contamination) in the drink, and vermouth became something to be minimized. Opportunistic vermouth producers responded by making milder dry vermouths and rendering them colorless via aggressive filtration (so that more could be used, and hence sold, without it showing in the color of the drink), and the demand proved a boon to some Chambéry-based producers, who already offered dry vermouths without the distinctive oxidative character of Noilly Prat. In the early 1960s, Noilly Prat developed a lighter formula to sell exclusively to the US market; this lighter formula remains as Noilly Prat Extra Dry (as opposed to Noilly Prat Original Dry) and may no longer be exclusive to the United States.

Interest in vermouth faded out in the United States in the 1960s and 1970s, and the wine stagnated in a soft global market for three decades. Starting in the 1990s, the cocktail renaissance rekindled interest in vermouth, eventually leading to a renewal of the category. The harbinger was Carpano's introduction of Antica Formula in 2001, a radically richer, vanilla-flavored red vermouth based on an old recipe and marketed as a premium offering. This new vermouth was a revelation to many bartenders, and expectations were rewritten across the board. The subsequent decade saw an accelerated growth of new premium vermouths and upgraded older ones from Italy, France, and elsewhere. The same interest and global marketplace have also dramatically elevated similar wine styles such as quinquina and americano, which, except for Dubonnet, had largely remained regional specialties. Another regional tradition, Spanish vermouth, which dates to at least the late nineteenth century and is heavily influenced by local wine practices (solera aging, for example) also emerged internationally. Boutique winemakers in the United States introduced a second wave of domestic vermouths, although this time, theirs have been consistently high-end offerings, and most are sufficiently idiosyncratic to no longer be recognizable as vermouth, despite their labeling.

Buglass, Alan J. *Handbook of Alcoholic Beverages*. Chichester, UK: Wiley, 2011.

Monti, François. *El gran libro del vermut*. Barcelona: Ediciones B, S. A., 2015.

Strucchi, Arnaldo. *Il vermouth Di Torino*. Casale Monferrato, Italy: C. Cassone, 1907.

Martin Doudoroff

vermouth-based cocktails. Vermouths from Italy and France were available in some American markets as early as the late 1830s, but weren't in wide use until the 1880s, when the wine abruptly appeared as a fully adopted bar ingredient. See VERMOUTH. By the turn of the twentieth century, vermouth was largely defining cocktail culture.

One of the first recorded applications of vermouth was as a base ingredient in the Vermouth Cocktail (vermouth plus bitters, gum syrup, and/or maraschino liqueur); that was in 1868, when it was served at a banquet for the Sorosis Club, a women's literary association, in New York. Also present from the outset were a few variations on the already-common Gin Cocktail, Improved Gin Cocktail, Whisky Cocktail, and Improved Whisky Cocktail—antecedents to the Martini, Martinez, Manhattan, and Saratoga, respectively—by integrating vermouth alongside the given gin or whisky base. See MARTINI; MARTINEZ; MANHATTAN COCKTAIL; and SARATOGA. Theodore Proulx most incisively expressed the logic in 1888: "[The Manhattan] is made the same way as any other cocktail, except that you will use one-half vermouth and one-half whisky in place of all whisky, omitting absinthe," and "[The Martini] is half Old Tom gin and half vermouth made like any other cocktail; no absinthe." In both cases, Proulx was referring to Italian (red) vermouth, but dry vermouth from Marseilles was also available and crops up in other sources, treated similarly.

Over the course of the next forty years and beyond, vermouth would be tried in combination with virtually every other available cocktail ingredient, leaving literally thousands of recipes in the public record. A few, such as the Bronx Cocktail, enjoyed great popularity in their day. See BRONX COCKTAIL. Other celebrated vermouth "classics"—some obscure in their day—include the Negroni, Americano, El Presidente, Saratoga, Bijou, Blood and Sand, Vieux Carré, Blackthorn, and Rose. See

NEGRONI; AMERICANO; EL PRESIDENTE; BIJOU COCKTAIL; BLOOD AND SAND; VIEUX CARRÉ; BLACKTHORN COCKTAIL; and ROSE. (Another once-popular classic, the Dubonnet Cocktail, was based on Dubonnet quinquina, a cousin of vermouth.) See DUBONNET COCKTAIL. Throughout, however, the Martini and Manhattan remained unremittingly popular, spawning many permutations and variations.

Most nineteenth-century vermouth-cocktail recipes refer to just "vermouth," "vino vermouth," or "Italian vermouth" when referencing what we now think of as red, or sweet, vermouth and to "French vermouth" to call out what we now think of as dry vermouth. The basis for this is that in the nineteenth century, vermouth bottle labels were often inscrutable beyond a brand name and the country of origin, and unlike today, brands weren't marketing multiple styles of vermouth—Italian companies made darker-colored, sweeter vermouth, and French companies made drier, lighter-colored vermouths. This situation began to change around the turn of the twentieth century, when market leaders such as Martini & Rossi diversified their product lines, introducing their own interpretations of dry vermouth and white vermouth (also called *bianco* or *blanc* vermouth). See MARTINI & ROSSI. While white vermouth would remain fairly obscure until recently, dry vermouth and sweet vermouth (which meant red vermouth) began appearing on labels and in the literature.

Vermouth is often employed in stronger, stirred cocktails; the combination of vermouth with citrus juice is relatively rare, but not unheard of. See CLOVER CLUB and COHASSET PUNCH. For a time beginning in the 1910s, it was common to refer to cocktails that contained equal portions of red and dry vermouths (among other ingredients) as "perfect" (e.g., the Perfect Martini uses an equal mixture of red and dry vermouths instead of one or the other). See PERFECT. While innumerable cocktails have been invented since the 1910s that draw on vermouth, it is fair to say that by the end of that decade all of the major lines of development that they would follow were explored.

"The Bohemian Banquet to the Sorosisians." *New York Herald*, June 14, 1868, 7.

Byron, O. H. *The Modern Bartender's Guide.* New York: Excelsior, 1884.

Jerry Thomas. *The Bar-Tender's Guide.* New York: Dick & Fitzgerald, 1887.

Proulx, Theodore. *Bartender's Manual.* Chicago: Theodore Proulx, 1888.

Wondrich, David. *Imbibe!*, 2nd ed. New York: Perigee, 2015.

Martin Doudoroff

Vermouth-Cassis, with dry vermouth, crème de cassis, and sparkling water, is the most popular wine-based cocktail in France. It dates back to at least the early 1880s, as it is mentioned in French newspapers as early as 1882. It reached the United States in the 1930s, enjoying a brief vogue there, and remained very popular in France until the late 1960s.

The Vermouth-Cassis is also the progenitor of two important variations, the Blanc-Cassis and Kir Royal. The Blanc-Cassis was invented in 1904, at the Café Georges in the Burgundian city of Beaunes; it is obtained by replacing the dry vermouth with local white wine, generally Bourgogne-aligoté and omitting the sparkling water. It has been a classic in Burgundy since the 1920s, particularly since the crème de cassis, like the aligoté, is a local product.

In the 1950s, Canon Félix Kir (1876–1968), who was mayor of the city of Dijon and also a member of the French National Assembly, was often in Paris, and to promote the Blanc-Cassis while there he made a habit of only drinking that, to the point that the press renamed the drink Kir, as a tribute to him. In the 1970s, the bubbles made their appearance, and the Kir Royal, with champagne or other sparkling wine replacing the aligoté, became a big hit in France and then worldwide. There was even a German television show named after it during the 1980s.

Recipe: Combine in tall glass with ice 60 ml French dry vermouth (Noilly Prat recommended), 22 ml crème de cassis, and 30 ml sparkling water. Garnish with a lemon peel twisted over the drink.

See also KIR.

Courrier des États-Unis, July 11, 1882.

Le Cri des Terriens, April 28, 1925.

Douarche, Léon. *En Marge de la Troisième.* Paris: Éditions Brunier, 1957.

Fernando Castellon

verschnitt, German for "cut," is used in Germany to designate a product that has been blended from an imported spirit (e.g., rum, arrack, genever, or brandy) and locally produced neutral potato or grain spirits. The amount of the imported flavoring spirit can be very low: for rum verschnitt, by far the most popular of these blends, according to EU regulations, the rum can be as little as 5 percent of the whole (for other categories of spirit the minimum begins at 10 percent).

Rum verschnitt owes its origins to a series of tariff increases imposed by the Zollverein, the German Customs Union, in 1889, which made it uneconomical to import Jamaican and other rums for direct consumption. In concert with German marketers (principally Finke & Co., of Bremen and Kingston), Jamaican producers perfected a style of rum with ester levels so high as to be practically non-potable. This "German" or "Continental" rum could be cut with a very high proportion of neutral spirit and still taste like rum. Even though rum verschnitt itself has mostly fallen out of use, the flavoring rums it spawned have become an essential rum blender's tool.

In Germany, verschnitt spirits must be clearly labeled as such. In other countries, the same practice—mixing a little straight spirit with a lot of neutral spirit—also prevails, without the unambiguous labeling; thus in Austria it is *inländer* rum, in the Netherlands *jonge* genever, and in the United States "blended" whisky.

See ARRACK, BATAVIA; BLENDING; and RUM, JAMAICA.

Andreae, Illa. *Alle schnäpse dieser welt.* Zurich: Transitbooks, 1973.

Cousins, H. H. "Jamaica Rum." *Bulletin of the Department of Agriculture, Jamaica,* 1909, 62–65.

Delbruck, Max. "Verschnittbranntweine." In *Illustriertes brennerei-lexicon,* 626. Berlin: Parey, 1915.

David Wondrich

The **Vesper** is a cocktail consisting of gin, vodka, and the French aperitif Lillet (formerly known as Kina Lillet). It was the first cocktail ordered by James Bond in the novel that marked his debut, Ian Fleming's 1953 *Casino Royale*. Bond ordered it thus: "Three measures of Gordon's, one of vodka, half a measure of Kina Lillet. Shake it very well until it's ice-cold, then add a large thin slice of lemon peel." The drink is presented as his original on-the-spot invention and at first has no name, but later Bond "borrows" the name of his colleague (later lover and then revealed as a Russian double agent) Vesper Lynd and christens it the Vesper. After her suicide at the end of the book he never drinks it again.

It has long been believed that the drink was created for Fleming at Dukes Hotel in London by famed London Bartender Gilberto Preti, but this has been debunked, as Preti did not begin working at Dukes until almost twenty years after the author's death (Preti's place in the story is probably due to the fact that he was apparently once consulted by one of the film Bonds on "how to make a proper Martini," as *Country Life* reported in 1995). A much more plausible story is told by Fleming's longtime friend and fellow Jamaica resident and OSS veteran Ivar Bryce, to whom Fleming had inscribed a copy of *Casino Royale* "For Ivar, who mixed the first *Vesper.*" Apparently Fleming pinched the name for the character (and Bryce for the cocktail, which he recalls concocting with Fleming's assistance) from "a curious drink of frozen rum with fruit and herbs," presented to him at a country house in Jamaica with the butler's formal pronouncement that "Vespers are served."

Although Bond was admirably clear on how to make the drink, its construction today is somewhat vexed due to the persistent rumor that when Lillet's maker dropped "Kina" (a French word for "quinine") from the brand's name in 1986, it also significantly reduced the product's quinine content and hence bitterness, making faithful reproduction of the drink impossible with the Lillet that still exists. During the early days of the cocktail renaissance, this led to some often unfortunate experiments with quinine powder. Fortunately, as Olivier Londeix has shown in his detailed 1998 independent history of the brand, the reduction in Lillet's bitterness occurred in 1917, decades before Bryce and Fleming were experimenting with it.

Due to its impeccable pop-culture pedigree, the Vesper still appears on cocktail lists, whether it's made with Lillet or with some other, more bitter aperitif. As "fictional" drinks go it's not bad, and with its split base of gin and vodka it is very au courant.

Recipe: Shake well with ice 75 ml gin, 25 ml vodka, and 12 ml Lillet Blonde. Strain into a chilled cocktail glass and twist lemon peel over the top.

Bryce, Ivar. *You Only Live Once*. 1975; repr., Lanham, MD: University Presses of America, 1984.

Fleming, Ian. *Casino Royale*. London: Jonathan Cape, 1953.

"Gilberto Preti's Country Life Cocktail." *Country Life*, November 2, 1995, 96

Leigh, James. *The Complete Guide to the Drinks of James Bond*, 2nd ed. Raleigh, NC: lulu.com, 2012.

Londeix, Olivier. *Lillet, 1862–1985*. Pessac, France: Presses Universitaires de Bordeaux, 1998.

Angus Winchester and David Wondrich

Vicard, or Groupe Vicard, is a third-generation, family-owned French cooperage company based in Cognac that specializes in barrel production as well as barrel stave aging. Their barrels are used in the production of both wine and spirits, including many notable cognac brands. The Vicard workshop was founded by Paul Vicard in 1925, when it produced less than a dozen barrels daily. Vicard currently produces almost ten times that—some forty thousand barrels a year, of which 70 percent are exported. Their largest markets are in Italy, Spain, the United States, and South American countries.

Vicard uses various sources of oak, predominately French (as well as from bordering countries), but also American and eastern European. The bulk of their wood is harvested from forests in central and northeastern France. They also own a stave yard outside of Cognac in Merrains du Périgord that produces 4,000 cubic meters per year (approximately 141,243 cubic feet).

See also BARREL.

Brown, Derek. Notes from Site Visit to Vicard, Cognac, France, September 12, 2012.

Groupe Vicard website. https://www.groupe-vicard.com/eng/ (accessed April 8, 2021).

Derek Brown

The **Vieux Carré** is a signature cocktail of New Orleans's Monteleone Hotel. A Manhattan variant, it was created in the 1930s by then–head bartender Walter Bergeron (1889–1947), who had worked at the bar before Prohibition and returned upon Repeal. Its recipe first appeared in print in 1937. The Vieux Carré (pronounced "VOO ka-RAY" in local New Orleans parlance) is named for the French Quarter, and the name translates as "old square." Once nearly forgotten locally, even in the hotel where it was born, the Vieux Carré was saved from obscurity by the twenty-first-century cocktail renaissance. Rich, complex, elegant, and evocative, it is typically served on the rocks, but serving it up makes for a lovely presentation. See COCKTAIL RENAISSANCE and MANHATTAN COCKTAIL.

Recipe: Stir 30 ml each of straight rye whisky, cognac, and sweet vermouth, 5 ml Bénédictine DOM liqueur, and 2 dashes each of Angostura bitters and Peychaud's Bitters with ice and strain into a large rocks glass over fresh ice. Garnish with lemon peel and a cherry.

Arthur, Stanley Clisby. *New Orleans Drinks and How to Mix 'Em*. New Orleans: Harmanson, 1937.

Haigh, Ted. *Vintage Spirits and Forgotten Cocktails*. Beverly, MA: Quarry, 2009.

Chuck Taggart

vinegar results from a process in which a beer or wine undergoes a secondary fermentation, transforming ethanol into acetic acid; if left alone in the proper conditions, all fermented beverages will turn to vinegar. Most culinary vinegar is produced from grape wine or fortified wine such as sherry, but such beverages as beer, apple cider, other fruit wines, and rice wine can also be used for vinegar production.

Vinegar is occasionally used in distillation: in Jamaica, for example, some varieties of pot-still rum have cane vinegar (from fermented cane juice) added to the wash, which adjusts the fermentation environment to favor certain strains of yeast and aids in congener formation. See FERMENTATION. Vinegar is also used in mixed drinks, both on its own (in drinks such as the Caribbean Switchel, where it is mixed with molasses and water) and mixed with spirits—it appears as a citrus substitute in punch as early as 1670. See PUNCH and SHRUBS.

McGee, Harold. *On Food and Cooking*. New York: Scribner, 2004.

Michael Dietsch

vodka has ventured from contentious origins in eastern Europe to become the world's most popular,

1934: the first shipment of vodka from the Soviet Union arrives in New York. Unfortunately, the glass the 100%-wheat vodka was bottled in proved too fragile for American commercial use and the "Genuine Imported Russian Vodka" brand was not a success. Getty Images.

bestselling spirit. Vodka's rise to global prominence is based largely on its versatility and ease of manufacture. "Vodka is unlike other forms of alcohol in that there is no justifiable excuse for drinking it," claims Russian writer Viktor Erofeev. "The Frenchman will praise the aroma of cognac, and the Scotsman will laud the flavor of whiskey. Vodka, however, is colorless, odorless, and tasteless. At the same time, it is an acrid and irritating drink." But since it is the outcome rather than the process that is important, Erofeev claims, "You might as well inject vodka into your bloodstream as drink it."

While many prefer to drink vodka "neat"— often, as Erofeev suggests, in one gulp, grimacing and swearing—its versatility as a relatively flavorless, colorless, odorless spirit has made vodka the basis for all manner of cocktails and mixed drinks: Martinis and Bloody Marys, Screwdrivers, Cosmopolitans, Moscow Mules, Black Russians, White Russians, and Vodka Tonics. See BLOODY MARY; COSMOPOLITAN; MARTINI; MOSCOW MULE; and WHITE RUSSIAN. As a product of continuous stills, distilled to very high purity and filtered to even higher, vodka has little to gain from aging in wood. While—pace Erofeev—it does have its nuances, its subtle bouquets, its hints of terroir

and craft, they are but lightly engraved on its surface. With vodka served at room temperature, a trained palate will be able to perceive them; served straight from the freezer, as is common, or stirred up into a Dry Martini, they will be very faint indeed; mixed with tomato juice and lemon juice; Tabasco and Worcestershire, they will all but disappear. In more recent years, vodka manufacturers have found this versatility a virtue, by marketing vodkas with added flavors. Some of these, such as lemon and hot pepper, are traditional: Russians have a long tradition of flavoring their vodka. Others, such as chocolate, donut, bacon, and even salmon, are not.

Traditional vodka is distilled from a fermented mash of rye, wheat, potatoes, or molasses from sugar beets native to eastern Europe and the Baltic region. However, as its popularity has grown, distillers have taken to using any starchy or sugary plant matter: corn, rice, fruit, sorghum, soybeans, or just sugar. Even milk has been used. Whatever the raw material, it is fermented and then distilled in continuous stills to the highest proof that can be practically achieved, generally coming off the still at between 95 and 97 percent pure ethanol, beyond which alcohol cannot easily be separated from water. See AZEOTROPE. This spirit is then filtered through charcoal, silver, or one of a number of other substances. See FILTRATION. It is then watered down to the requisite alcoholic content of between 35 and 50 percent ABV, with 40 percent (80 US proof) being the recognized standard. The European Union has set 37.5 percent as the minimum alcoholic content for a beverage to be classified as vodka. It is often claimed that the "ideal" strength of vodka at 38 percent ABV was established by Dmitry Mendeleev—the nineteenth-century Russian chemist and father of the periodic table of elements—which was then rounded to 40 percent by the Russian imperial vodka monopoly for greater ease in assessing taxes. As with so much of vodka history, this assertion has achieved the status of legend without any actual evidence. However, with the reintroduction of a monopoly on distilled spirits in 1895, the Russian authorities did standardize what we today know as vodka as the product of industrial rectification through modern distillation columns. From that point, the distillation of traditional "polugar" vodka through copper pot stills was outlawed (polugar has been reintroduced in recent years).

Contested Origins

Much of the history of vodka is shrouded in mystery, misinformation, and unverified legend—no more so than the question of vodka's origins. When and where "vodka" originated has become a matter of national pride, especially between Russians and Poles: both lay claim to their "little water": водка in Russian, wódka in Polish. Both view vodka as a defining trait of what it means to be Russian or Polish, and both associate the advent of vodka with the beginnings of the nation itself.

Like many other spiritous beverages, vodka traces its history back to medieval alchemists of the twelfth century who distilled grape wine lees to make medicinal elixirs. But how—and when—did the knowledge of distillation move from the monasteries of pre-Renaissance Italy to the imperial court of Moscow?

The most likely scenario takes a southern route from the Italian city-state of Genoa, beginning around 1290 CE. The seafaring Genoese had a monopoly on commerce in the Black Sea, including the bustling port city of Caffa (present-day Feodosia) on the Crimean Peninsula. When Caffa was sacked by the Mongol Khan Tamerlane in 1395, Genoese merchants, alchemists, and even ambassadors fled

north through Muscovy, bringing medicinal aqua vitae with them. The monasteries of Moscow were fertile grounds for this new practice, as monks quickly transformed this Genoese art of distilling wine into aqua vitae into a product—vodka—that could be distilled from local produce: not grapes but grains (primarily rye and wheat) and soft spring water. Another theory holds that distillation came to Russia through long-established trade routes of the Hanseatic League in Pskov and Novgorod, near the Baltic Sea. Imported wines had been documented along this route as far back as 1436, though no record was made of aqua vitae, much less "vodka" as we know it today. Armchair historians in Russia claim that vodka actually arrived in Novgorod hundreds of years earlier—in the 1250s—because ancient birch-bark documents from that era contain a word that looks vaguely like "vodka" in Russian. Professional archaeologists and linguists have roundly debunked such claims. Others hypothesize that Russians learned distillation independently from the Tatars of Asia in the sixteenth century. One Mongolian technique calls for leaving a fermented mash out in subzero weather: when the water freezes, the ice can be removed, leaving concentrated liquid alcohol. Yet not only were such indigenous experimentations dependent on the season, but they also left highly concentrated fusel oils, which are often fatal. But the Mongols also knew distillation by fire, with the simple but effective "Mongolian still," in which alcoholic vapors from boiling wash condensed on the bottom of a bowl full of cold water and were caught in a cup. See STILL, POT. Through whichever route, anyway, by the early sixteenth century the alchemists' aqua vitae had already taken root in Muscovy as "burnt wine"—the spiritous beverage we might recognize today as polugar, or pot-still vodka. The Polish claim to vodka is only slightly clearer. Beginning in the thirteenth century, a number of Polish physicians studied alchemy in the medical schools of Salerno and Montpellier, before returning to the Kingdom of Poland. By the fourteenth and fifteenth centuries, the curriculum of Jagiellonian University in Krakow included Latin essays on distilling "burning water" (aqua ardente). The term wódka first appeared in Polish court documents in 1405, though likely referring to distilled medicines, whereas gorzałka was first mentioned in Joannes Murmelius's 1528 dictionary, becoming the primary term for all distilled beverages for much of Polish history. By the sixteenth century—both in Poland and in Russia—distilled spirits had become widespread as an acceptable beverage, though not yet an object of widespread consumption, although Sigmund von Heberstein, the Austrian ambassador to Muscovy in the 1510s and 1520s, found that the nobles of the Russian court "at the beginning of the meal always drank aqua vitae." Unfortunately, Heberstein describes this spirit no further. See AQUA VITAE.

Vodka's Rise

Vodka became the national drink of both Poland and the Russian Empire only gradually. In premodern times, Poles and Russian drank fermented beer, wine, ale, mead, and kvas (a low-alcohol drink made from fermented bread), similar to peasants across Europe. The shift away from mildly alcoholic fermented beverages to the more potent distilled vodka has less to do with culture and more with economic and political decisions associated with the expansion of the Muscovite empire, as vodka was the perfect vehicle for indirect taxation.

When, in 1552, Ivan the Terrible (r. 1533–1584) defeated the rival Khanate of Kazan on the Volga River, he was impressed with the system of government-run taverns the Tatars called *kabak* and decreed that Russia should have them too, so that all profits from the liquor trade were funneled into the new tsar's treasury. In *Of the Russe Common Wealth* (1591), English ambassador Giles Fletcher wrote: "In every great towne of his Realme he hath a Caback or drinking house, where is sold aquavitæ (which they cal Russewine) mead, beere, &c. Out of these hee receiveth rent that amounteth to a great summe of money.... You shall have manie there that have drunk all away to the verie skinne, and so walk naked (whom they call Naga.) While they are in the Caback, none may call them foorth whatsoever cause there be, because he hindereth the Emperours revenue." And a significant revenue it was. The Law Code of 1649, which formalized serfdom, also outlawed buying or selling vodka beyond the kabak under penalty of torture. The tavern keepers (or *tselovalniki*: "kissers" who swore an allegiance to the tsar by kissing the Orthodox cross) could not refuse even a habitual drunkard, lest the tsar's revenue be diminished. Since their lucrative positions depended on generating ever more revenue for the

state, tavern keepers and administrators pushed more potent distilled vodkas over fermented beers and meads since the profit margins were so much higher. In time, the tavern became the means by which the Russian state exploited its own people: the sole purveyor of a potent and addictive substance that generated widespread misery for the peasantry but also enormous profits for the state. Within a generation, the traditionally self-sufficient Russian village had been obliterated—replaced with an entire system of gentry distillers, merchants, and government bureaucrats that propagated and profited from the peasants' drunkenness. While the system produced widespread impoverishment, systemic corruption, and entrenched autocratic governance, it was also a boon for the early tsarist empire. As Moscow's capacity to extract resources grew, so too did its capacity to build its military, expand, and ultimately broadcast its power across vast swaths of Eurasia, ultimately becoming the largest empire on earth. Vodka runs like a red thread through the fabric of Russian history. Tsar Peter the Great (r. 1696–1725) had a herculean appetite for vodka and took great pleasure in forcing subordinates and foreign dignitaries to drink for his amusement. The penalty for violating Peter's bacchanalian code of conduct during days-long drunken banquets was the "Great Eagle": a massive, ornate goblet filled with 1.5 liters of vodka, to be consumed on the spot. Revelers often had to be carried home; more than a few died from alcohol poisoning. Empress Catherine the Great (r. 1762–1796) came to power by means of a palace coup, deposing her husband, Peter III, who was a drunken imbecile. It helped that she bribed the military with promises of vodka—something that would become a tradition for aspirants to the throne. Meanwhile, the empire itself became ever more dependent on vodka revenues, becoming the state's single largest source of income by the nineteenth century, comprising nearly one-third of the budget of the mighty Russian Empire. Inspired by American and European temperance efforts, in 1858–1859 peasants in the annexed Polish and Baltic provinces—and later the Russian heartland—began taking pledges of abstinence from vodka. While the taverns emptied and the health of the population improved, the corrupt vodka-tax administrators went bankrupt, imperiling the financial stability of the Russian treasury itself. Eventually, the army had to be called in to suppress the sobriety rebellion, forcing peasants to drink, beating and arresting those who refused.

This absurdity highlighted the eternal conundrum of vodka in Russia: the health and well-being of Russian society was diametrically opposed to the financial interests of the Russian Empire—and the Soviet Union and present-day Russian Federation that followed it. If at any point the majority of Russians suddenly decided to stop drinking vodka, the government would face immediate bankruptcy. So generations of tsarist bureaucrats, communist commissars, and Russian legislators have worked hard to prevent that from happening.

Those efforts could only be overridden by a command from the autocrat himself, which has only happened twice, both times ending in political disaster. In 1914, at the outset of World War I, heavy drinker turned temperance convert Tsar Nicholas II (ruled 1894–1917) decreed a prohibition on vodka to facilitate the war effort, making Russia the world's first prohibition country. Unfortunately, getting rid of the single largest source of revenue during the greatest war the world had yet seen turned out to be a bad idea. They tried to paper over the gaping hole in the budget by simply printing more rubles. The resulting hyperinflation crippled the Russian economy and fanned the flames of social revolution that would consume the empire itself. The same pattern would repeat itself later in the twentieth century. Vladimir Lenin (r. 1917–1924) was a principled prohibitionist who refused to bring back vodka and its concordant economic subjugation, despite widespread homebrewing. See SAMOGON. His successor, the heavy-drinking Joseph Stalin (r. 1924–1953), had no such qualms and in 1925 revived the vodka monopoly as the financial foundation for his totalitarian industrialization. By the 1970s, vodka revenues again constituted a quarter of the revenues of the Soviet superpower. When he came to power in 1985, Mikhail Gorbachev instituted the sweeping reforms of perestroika (economic restructuring) and glasnost (free speech), but only after he initiated an anti-alcohol campaign in the name of labor productivity, once again blowing a massive hole in the state budget. The Soviets tried to paper over the shortfall in vodka revenues by printing more rubles, which exacerbated the hyperinflation and fueled widespread discontent, and soon the Soviet empire itself fell to revolution. The tension between state finance and the welfare of the Russian population has bedeviled the post-Soviet administrations of both Boris Yeltsin (1992–2000) and Vladimir Putin (2000–present).

Vodka as Global Commodity

Vodka's international domination was a relatively recent development. Lenin's Bolshevik Revolution, and the resulting civil war and famines of the 1920s, set many Russian gentry distillers to flight, and they took vodka with them. It was in one community of Russian exiles in France where American cowboy philosopher Will Rogers first encountered vodka, and he struggled to explain it to his fellow Americans: "How they can concentrate so much insensibility into one prescription is almost a chemical wonder," Rogers recounted. "One tiny sip of this Vodka poison and it will do the same amount of material damage to mind and body that an American strives for for hours [sic]."

It was in France that Vladimir Smirnov—exiled son of the former vodka purveyor to the tsars, Pyotr Smirnov—met with the Russian-born American entrepreneur Rudolph Kunett, whose family had supplied grains to the Smirnov distillery in pre-revolutionary Russia. Smirnov sold the American émigré the rights to market vodka in the United States under the name Pierre Smirnoff & Sons, with initial production beginning in Bethel, Connecticut, following the repeal of prohibition. See SMIRNOFF. Yet it was only in the 1950s that Smirnoff vodka sales took off, thanks largely to a slick advertising campaign showcasing Hollywood celebrities. In the first James Bond movie, *Dr. No* (1962), Sean Connery famously ordered a martini "shaken, not stirred" with Smirnoff vodka. Its iconic position in Hollywood propelled Smirnoff into a globally recognized brand by the 1970s, and vodka as a dominant liquor, outselling rum, gin, and bourbon both in the United States and around the world. Smirnoff was joined by Explorer and Absolut from Sweden, which began to be aggressively marketed as vodkas rather than traditional brännvin (burnt wine), harking back to those early European origins. See ABSOLUT. American and European vodkas largely did not have to contend with competition from vodkas produced in the Soviet Union or the countries of the Warsaw Pact, with the exception of Stolichnaya. In 1972, the Pepsi-Cola Company struck a barter deal with the Soviet government to exclusively market "Stoli" in the West, in exchange for making Pepsi the first American consumer product sold widely in the Soviet Union. See STOLICHNAYA. Only with the end of the Cold War in 1989 and the collapse of the Soviet Union (and its vodka monopoly) in 1991 were entrepreneurs of the traditional vodka territories of Russia, Poland, and the rest of eastern Europe free to market their national beverages. Yet they were at a competitive disadvantage trying to penetrate a global liquor marketplace dominated by multinational corporations and well-established brands, often with Russian-sounding names. Nonetheless, the Russian Standard brand has established itself globally, and others, such as Beluga, have gained some traction. See RUSSIAN STANDARD.

See also RUSSIA AND EASTERN EUROPE and STARKA.

Christian, David. *Living Water: Vodka and Russian Society on the Eve of Emancipation*. Oxford: Clarendon, 1990.

Erofeev, Victor. "The Russian God." *New Yorker*, December 16, 2002.

Fletcher, Giles. *Of the Russe Common Wealth*. 1591; repr. Cambridge, MA: Harvard University Press, 1966.

Heberstein, Sigmund von. *Rerum moscoviticarum comentarii*. Amsterdam: 1527.

Himelstein, Linda. *The King of Vodka: The Story of Pyotr Smirnov and the Upheaval of an Empire*. New York: HarperCollins, 2009.

Rodionov, Boris V. *Bol'shoi obman: Pravda i lozh' o russkoi vodke*. Moscow: ACT, 2011.

Rogers, Will. *There's Not a Bathing Suit in Russia and Other Bare Facts*. New York: Albert & Charles Boni, 1927.

Schrad, Mark Lawrence. *Vodka Politics: Alcohol, Autocracy, and the Secret History of the Russian State*. New York: Oxford University Press, 2014.

Simpson, Scott. "History and Mythology of Polish Vodka: 1270–2007." *Food and History* 8, no. 1 (2010): 121–148.

Mark L. Schrad

VS, an abbreviation for "very special," is a common age designation for young cognac and other brandies. For a cognac to be labeled VS (or, alternatively, ***), the youngest eau-de-vie component in the blend must have matured in oak casks for at least two years. Brandy from France's Armagnac region bearing the VS designation must age in oak for at least one year. While brandies produced in the United States may use the VS designation, there is no legally required minimum aging period.

See also COGNAC and THREE STAR.

Bureau National Interprofessionnel du Cognac. *L'encyclopédie du Cognac*. http://www.pediacognac.com (accessed March 15, 2021).

David Mahoney

VSOP is a common midrange age designation for cognac and other brandies. Its use dates back to 1817, when the future King George IV of Great Britain asked the venerable cognac house of Hennessy to create a "very superior old pale cognac" (at the time, "very superior old pale" was a common designation for fine sherries). Any eau-de-vie used in a VSOP cognac must have aged in an oak cask for at least four years. The same is true for brandies from Armagnac and Calvados. Although brandies produced in the United States may bear the VSOP designation, there is no minimum aging requirement associated with it.

See also COGNAC and HENNESSY.

Bromley and Short, auctioneers (advertisement). *London Morning Post*, June 29, 1814, 4.

Bureau National Interprofessionnel du Cognac. *L'encyclopédie du Cognac*. http://www.pediacognac.com (accessed July 6, 2021).

David Mahoney

wacholder is basically a German gin—a mildly juniper-flavored spirit made in a style similar to Dutch genever. See GENEVER; GERMANY, SWITZERLAND, AND AUSTRIA; and GIN.

The **Waldorf-Astoria** hotel in New York had a bar that was one of the most influential in America and the world from the early 1890s until it closed for Prohibition in 1919, and again from Repeal in 1933 until well into the postwar years.

When the large, modern Waldorf hotel opened at the corner of Fifth Avenue and Thirty-Third Street in 1893, it had no traditional, stand-up American-style bar: drinks were served only at tables, in the then-fashionable cafe format. In 1897, however, the Astoria hotel opened next door, occupying the rest of the block up to Thirty-Fourth Street. The hotels were soon joined, forming the Waldorf-Astoria, known by regulars as the "Hyphen." It was the largest hotel in the world, and New York's most advanced. The Astoria part had a real barroom: an extravaganza in brass and mahogany, as was typical of the time, with a rectangular bar occupying the middle and heavy wooden cafe tables on one side. Dominating the central back bar were twin bronze statues of a bull and a bear.

The bar was an instant success. Where Jim Grey's bar at the Fifth-Avenue Hotel drew politicians and the bar at the Hoffman House gamblers and the sporting set, the Waldorf-Astoria bar catered more to industrialists and financiers such as J. P. Morgan, a daily visitor. See HOFFMAN HOUSE. It got its share of celebrities as well, including the Wild West showman William "Buffalo Bill" Cody, a regular, and William Butler Yeats.

Where the Hoffman House's bar showed a strong German influence, the Hyphen's was an Irish bar. Its head bartenders until Prohibition were mostly Irish-born or at least of Irish extraction, among them John E. "Curly" O'Connor, Johnny Solan, Phil Kennedy, Michael Killackey, and Edward Murnane. The bar's mixology may have reflected that distinction; in its bar book (kept by Solan and preserved by the hotel's press agent, Albert Stevens Crockett, who used it as the basis for two books and the unpublished manuscript for a third), there were even a few Irish whisky–based cocktails, a rarity at the time.

The Waldorf-Astoria's bar was cradle to several popular cocktails, including the Bronx, the most popular newcomer of its day, and the Clover Club, invented in Philadelphia but made at the hotel's bar since at least 1901. See BRONX COCKTAIL and CLOVER CLUB. In general, the bar specialized in strong, simple drinks, and indeed was a pioneer in the streamlining of American mixology that occurred in the first two decades of the twentieth century.

During Prohibition, the Waldorf-Astoria moved to Park Avenue and Forty-Ninth Street, leaving the old edifice to be replaced by the Empire State Building. With Repeal, in 1933, the new hotel added a large barroom on the Park Avenue side, presided over by the bull and bear from the old one. O'Connor and a few of the old bartenders were even behind the bar (now an oval), to preserve continuity. To further preserve that continuity, the new bar was for men only. For the next twenty-odd years, it maintained its prestige and influence, but by the mid-1950s it started stumbling. Men were less interested in cocktails and more in women. In 1959, as if admitting defeat, the hotel moved the bar to the less prestigious Lexington Avenue side and began admitting women soon after. The bar persisted, although it was no longer a temple of mixology. At the time of this writing, the Waldorf Astoria, which dropped its hyphen in 2009, is closed for extensive renovation. It is not known what will become of the bar, some of whose fixtures date back to the Waldorf days.

Crockett, Albert Stevens. *Old Waldorf Bar Days.*
    New York: Aventine, 1931.
"Waldorf's Bar Courting Fame." *New York Sun*, December
    11, 1934, 48.

David Wondrich

waragi, supposedly short for "war gin," is a clear Ugandan spirit distilled originally from bananas, either locally or in the form of Uganda Waragi, local spirit rectified, branded, and distributed by the government; Uganda Waragi is now made from imported cane spirit. See CENTRAL AND EAST AFRICA, and BANANAS.

Ward Eight, Boston's best-known cocktail, is a variation on the Whisky Sour—or rather, a variation on a variation on the Whisky Sour, the Hari-Kari. See SOUR. Created sometime around the turn of the twentieth century, it would make regular appearances in drink-mixing manuals for decades thereafter until it was given new recognition by Boston bars in the early twenty-first century. Like the Hari-Kari, which took its final form in the early 1880s, the Ward Eight lengthens the standard sour formula with soda water, but then it goes on to add a pair of then-new and trendy ingredients, grenadine and orange juice. While the orange juice is not in any of the earliest recipes, the grenadine is original: along with the Jack Rose, the Ward Eight is one of the first American cocktails to use the syrup. There is, however, an unusual amount of variation in the extant recipes for the Ward Eight, and examples can be found without the orange juice, of course, but also without the grenadine, the soda, or any combination of the three.

There is also a good deal of variation in the accounts of the Ward Eight's origins. The most widely cited one puts its creation on election eve 1898, at Boston's historic Locke-Ober restaurant, with bartender Tom Hussion concocting it at the request of members of the Hendricks Club—a social club formed by Martin "the Mahatma" Lomasney, the powerful and wily boss of Boston's Eighth Ward—to commemorate what they correctly assumed was their leader's imminent election to the state legislature. That Lomasney, who abstained from alcohol, probably wasn't at the celebration that night is not even the salient point of dispute (it is more damning that Hussion only started at the restaurant in 1900). Other accounts attribute the drink to another Locke-Ober bartender, Billy Kane, as well Charlie Carter of the Puritan Club in 1903. Also, grenadine was rarely used in the United States until the 1910s. Nevertheless, early recipes for the Ward Eight appear in a 1907 *Boston Herald* column referring to "the most talked-of drink in Boston" and the 1913 edition of *The Cocktail Book: A Sideboard Manual for Gentlemen.* The year after Prohibition ended, 1934, *Esquire* named the Ward Eight one of the year's top ten cocktails. By the 1950s, it had fallen out of use, although Locke-Ober continued to make a fairly ghastly rendition of it until it closed in 2012.

Recipe (1907): In shaker, stir 20 ml lemon juice and 5 ml sugar; add 7 ml grenadine and 60 ml rye whisky (or 45 ml rye and 15 ml amontillado sherry, as suggested by an old Boston bartender in 1934). Shake well with ice and strain into stemmed goblet. Add 30 ml chilled sparkling water, orange slice, and berries in season. Optional: add 7 ml orange juice or 5 ml orange curaçao.

"The Fairbanks Cocktail Popular." *Boston Herald*, August
    4, 1907, sec. 2, 12.
Schorow, Stephanie. *Drinking Boston: A History of the City
    and Its Spirits.* Wellesley, MA: Union Park, 2012.
Van Nostrand, Albert D. "The Lomasney Legend." *New
    England Quarterly* 21, no. 4 (1948): 435–458.
Wondrich, David. "The Ward Eight Cocktail History."
    Imbibe, December 13, 2012. http://imbibemagazine.
    com/ward-eight-cocktail-history/ (accessed March
    15, 2021).

Lauren Clark

Washington, George (1732–1799), the commanding general of the Continental Army during the American Revolution and first president of the United States, also owned one of the largest whisky distilleries in early America. He erected a substantial stone still house at his Mount Vernon estate in northern Virginia in 1797, the same year that he stepped down from the presidency. Earlier in that year, Washington's plantation manager, a Scotsman named James Anderson who was also an experienced distiller, had successfully lobbied his employer to invest in the distillery with the promise of quick and easy profits. Two pot stills were set up in an existing building, where they produced six hundred gallons of rye whisky over the course of the year at a substantial gain of £83. See WHISKY, RYE. By that June, Anderson already was convinced of the success of the venture, and he proposed building a stone distillery, outfitted with a total of five copper pot stills and a water boiler.

Before agreeing to the Scotsman's offer, Washington wrote to a knowledgeable friend and local rum distiller, John Fitzgerald, asking his advice on the matter. Fitzgerald assured Washington that there was a ready market, concluding that "as to a sale of the Whisky there can be no doubt if the Quantity was ten times as much as he [Anderson] can make provided it is of good quality." Washington's enslaved workers began constructing the still house in October, and it was completed by the following March. In 1798 Anderson distilled 4,400 gallons of spirits. The next year production leapt to roughly 10,500 gallons, and Washington earned a profit of $1,858 (£600; Washington began using dollars and cents for his financial accounts in 1799), making the distillery the second most profitable activity on the entire Mount Vernon plantation and lifting it into the ranks of the largest whisky producers in the country. Washington's whisky was marketed to the surrounding area, especially the nearby community of Alexandria, where it was sold on consignment by local merchants. After Washington's death in December 1799, the distillery continued to operate for a number of years, until it was destroyed by fire in 1814 and never rebuilt.

See also AGING; DISTILLATION, HISTORY; DISTILLATION, PROCESS; and STILL, POT.

Fitzgerald, John, to George Washington, June 12, 1797. In *Papers of George Washington: Retirement Series*, ed. W. W. Abbot, 1:180–181. Charlottesville: University Press of Virginia, 1998.

Pogue, Dennis J., *Founding Spirits: George Washington and the Beginnings of the American Whiskey Industry*. Buena Vista, VA: Harbour, 2011.

Dennis J. Pogue

water-bath still is a modification of a standard pot still, often used for distilling cordials, in which a separate vessel is placed inside the water-filled still pot (similar, in principle, to a double boiler or bain-marie). See also CORDIALS and STILL, POT.

well or **rail** is the stainless steel rack of liquor bottles kept directly below the bar. It is also known as the "speed well," since these bottles are easy for the bartender to reach, allowing for quicker drink execution. A "well drink" or "rail drink" is a mixed drink made with an inexpensive, generic liquor (the kind usually used in the well) rather than a named or "call" brand. See CALL DRINK. These drinks tend to be cheaper, and some bars offer specials on them to attract and encourage more business. Depending on the establishment, the quality of liquors used in the well may vary widely, with some upscale bars using premium liquors for their well drinks, while dives tend to use generic or value brands.

Chad Solomon

West Africa experienced the spread of distillation in a way that is linked to the distribution of its major religions. Alongside adherents to African traditional religions, the population is split between Christianity and Islam. The area that includes Senegal, Mali, Niger, and the northern parts of Ghana, Ivory Coast, Nigeria, and Cameroon is predominantly Islamic, and the areas to the south, including parts of Sierra Leone, Ivory Coast, Ghana, Togo, Benin, Nigeria, and Cameroon, are largely Christian. Alcohol consumption is significantly higher in the Christian (and African traditional) sectors, and this is also where most distilleries are located. West African distilleries mainly produce local versions of brandy, rum, gin, and bitters by flavoring industrially distilled neutral spirits. These drinks are safe to consume but are not interesting for drinks connoisseurs attracted to artisanal processes and subtle and different flavors.

The technology of distilling was first introduced in West Africa around 1800 by a Danish colonialist who briefly produced liquor on a plantation in the Volta Region of Ghana, but at that time this knowledge did not spread, and Africans made no subsequent attempts at it. In the absence of local distillation West Africans consumed imported liquor: rum, brandy, and gin made up a large proportion of West Africa's maritime trade from the sixteenth century until well into the twentieth century (first as part of the slave trade, later as part of the trade in agricultural produce). See TRIANGLE TRADE.

In the early 1880s, a Jamaican entrepreneur made another attempt at founding a distillery in West Africa, but that too soon closed. In Nigeria, during the first decade of the twentieth century, a profitable liquor industry emerged compounding spirits on the basis of imported alcohol of high strength but was closed down through colonial legislation in 1909. Shortly thereafter, a cottage industry of home distillation emerged in several parts of coastal West Africa but was quickly outlawed by colonial administrations that depended on taxes on imported spirits to cover colonial expenses. During the 1930s, illegal home distillation of *akpeteshie* spread rapidly and greatly reduced the foreign imports. Akpeteshie, made from palm wine, and other home-distilled "local gin" largely replaced foreign imports and in some instances became symbols of colonial resistance. They continue to be widely produced and consumed, and liquor imports into West Africa have never returned to their pre-1930s levels.

The first distilleries in West Africa that produced drinks on an industrial scale that were safe to consume and sold through commercial distribution networks were established around the time that West African countries achieved independence, during the 1950s and 1960s. African governments encouraged local distilling industries as part of development policies based on industrialization to create local substitutes for imported goods. This usually involved technical assistance (at a fee) from an established European company in the design of the distillery, bottling plant, and production processes. The drinks thus produced were similar to those previously imported but could be offered at a lower price. The names and packaging were (and continue to be) designed to resemble the familiar, previously imported European brands. Ghana's GIHOC distillery, for example, has been making Castle Bridge London dry gin, Buccaneer rum,

and Chevalier brandy, each in bottles of a shape and color commonly associated with these popular brands, and with labels to match. See LONDON DRY GIN. One recent marketing innovation concerns the packaging: alongside the existing bottles, distilleries have introduced little sachets containing a single serving of gin, thus placing the purchase of distilled drinks within the reach of those with very small incomes (though this market is also served by home-distilled akpeteshie). These sachets have become enormously popular, in the process creating serious sustainability and environmental issues.

An increasingly popular drink is the herbal bitter, which usually has a name with an African association (such as Mandingo bitters) and is said to have medicinal properties that, among other things, cleanse the system and improve sexual performance. Meanwhile, the category of schnapps gin is associated with its use in African traditions such as the pouring of libation, weddings, outdoorings, and funerals, the payment of shrine priests, and as a customary gift to traditional leaders. In Nigeria, Seaman's Schnapps is marketed as "the original prayer drink." A billboard campaign showing Nigerians from diverse ethnic groups praying with schnapps refers to the unity-in-diversity theme with the slogan "Many Prayers, One Drink," thereby ignoring the large Muslim part of the population. At the same time, the widespread presence of Islam and the rise of born-again Christianity challenge the consumption of distilled liquors in West Africa.

See also AKPETESHIE and HOME DISTILLING.

Akyeampong, Emmanuel. *Drink, Power, and Cultural Change. A Social History of Alcohol in Ghana, c. 1800 to Recent Times*. Portsmouth, NH: Heinemann, 1996.

Heap, Simon. "Before 'Star': The Import Substitution of Western-Style Alcohol in Nigeria, 1870–1970." *African Economic History* 24 (1996): 69–89.

Van den Bersselaar, Dmitri. *The King of Drinks: Schnapps Gin from Modernity to Tradition*. Leiden: Brill, 2007.

Dmitri van den Bersselaar

wheat (*Triticum aestivum* is the dominant variety) is one of the most common grains used in distilled spirits, although its use largely postdates the Industrial Revolution and the improvements in agriculture that followed it. Before that, in many places it was prohibited to distill from wheat, as its supply was allocated to bakers for making bread, a major part of the diet.

Particularly in combination with corn or maize, wheat tends to produce a smooth, sweet distillate, which is one reason it is a popular ingredient in bourbon mash bills. See MASH BILL and WHISKY, BOURBON. Wheat is common in the production of scotch grain whisky and German whiskies such as Owen (*der schwäbische Whisky*). Some American whisky distillers use it in place of rye in their bourbon mash bills to create "wheated bourbons"—popular brands include Maker's Mark, W. L. Weller, Larceny, and the Old Rip Van Winkle line. See MAKER'S MARK. There are also a number of majority-wheat and all-wheat whiskies, most notably Bernheim, from Heaven Hill. While wheat is most often associated with whisky, it is also a common base for vodka (e.g., Grey Goose) and gin (e.g., Death's Door) and is used in making the *qu* that is a major component of some styles of baijiu. See QU.

In general, distillers prefer "soft" varieties of wheat, which have higher yields and lower viscosity, making them easier to work with in a mash (the gluten in wheat means that it must be mashed carefully to avoid it turning into a sticky mess). Note however that buckwheat (*Fagopyrum esculentum*), which is increasingly popular among craft distillers, is not a species of wheat; in fact, it is not a cereal grain at all but a fruit seed, related to sorrel and rhubarb. See CEREALS.

"Der Schwäbische Whisky." Berghof Rabel website. https://www.berghof-rabel.hoffrisch.de/whisky/schwaebischer-whisky.htm (accessed May 4, 2021).

Thomann, G. *Liquor laws of the United States, Part II: Colonial liquor laws*, New York: United States Brewers' Assoc, 1887.

Clay Risen

whisky is one of the major traditional branches of the family tree of distilled spirits, along with brandy, rum, baijiu, and the like. See SPIRITS. Although there is no global legal definition for whisky, it is agreed that the term refers to a cereal-grain-based, non-neutral spirit which is usually aged in wood. Each whisky-producing country will have its own variations on that theme. The legislation for bourbon and Tennessee whisky, for example, is different from that for Scotch or Irish whisky.

While barley and corn (maize) are the most commonly used grains, wheat and rye are widely used, and in recent years distillers have widened the net further, distilling from grains and pseudo-grains such as spelt, emmer, rice, and quinoa. See CEREALS. Whisky has been and is still made in pot stills, continuous stills, hybrid stills, and even the now-rare three-chamber stills. See STILL, TYPES OF. Oak is the most commonly used material for casks, but chestnut has on occasion been coopered.

While its origins are obscure, and much debated, whisky's traditions begin in Scotland and Ireland, and indeed its name is an English mangling of the Gaelic *uisce beatha*, "water of life," much like "brandy" is an English mangling of the Dutch *brandewijn*. See AQUA VITAE. (The convention by which Scotland and Canada spell it "whisky" and Ireland and the United States "whiskey" is of no great antiquity, dating back to the mid-twentieth century, and there are plenty of examples of Scots spelling it "whiskey" and Americans "whisky.") In any case, the first record of a beer being distilled in the British Isles comes in Geoffrey Chaucer's *Canterbury Tales* (1378–1400), where "wort" appears among a list of ingredients used by an alchemist who is being lampooned in "The Canon's Yeoman's Tale." The first record of grain distillation in Scotland comes a century later, although it is unlikely that it was unknown prior to that date. In Ireland, grain distilling doesn't make it into the record until 1556, but when it does, it's in the form of a Parliamentary act acknowledging that it was "now universally throughout the realm made" and banning its traffic and its production to all but the most substantial property owners. That suggests that it was no novelty there either.

It must be borne in mind, though, that this early whisky had little to distinguish itself from the grain spirits that were popping up throughout northern Europe at the time. German distillers had begun distilling from grain by 1507, and German cities were prohibiting it by 1530. By 1551, Russians were beginning their meals with "aqua vitae," presumably distilled from grain. By 1588, Dutch distillers had moved from using French wine as the base for their genever to making their own from barley and rye. All of these spirits were pot-distilled from malt (at least in part), and if they spent any time in a wooden barrel, it was for transportation and storage, not maturation. Any differences would come from flavoring or slight variations in the process due to local conditions (German distillers, for instance, tended to dry their malt over wood fires, while the Scots used peat fires). See AQUA VITAE; GENEVER; KORN; and VODKA.

Early records suggest that the early proto-whiskies were sometimes consumed neat but more commonly compounded with local herbs and roots to make a drink that would become known as "usquebaugh." This would become a noted specialty of Ireland. Over the centuries recipes would become more elaborate, often involving the use of raisins to soften the spirit and saffron to color it. By the end of the seventeenth century, usquebaugh was being exported to England in considerable quantity and was known on the Continent as well. Meanwhile, as equipment improved and knowledge advanced, the unflavored "whisky" (the term is first recorded in 1715) was becoming more and more popular on its home turf.

Distillation of whisky in Scotland and Ireland was mostly rural, with farmers using surplus grain to supplement their income. From the eighteenth century onward, larger distilleries began to be established in cities: after the gin craze that came to a head in the 1730s, the British government moved to heavily restrict distillation through stiff excise taxes that made it almost impossible for any but the largest-scale distilleries to make a profit. In Scotland some of these "malt distillers" (they did not have to use pure malt, although the Scottish ones tended to) began to supply base spirit for the English gin rectifiers.

At the same time, whisky had taken root in America—or rather, a grain spirit that would become known by that name had. Although there had been experiments with grain distilling in the seventeenth century, they did not produce a marketable spirit until the Germans stepped in: a wave of immigration from Germany's western borderlands in the first decades of the eighteenth century brought a number of distillers with experience at distilling rye-based korn to Pennsylvania and Maryland, and by the 1740s the "korn dram" they were making was well established. See WHISKY, RYE. Before long their traditions would become inextricably entangled with those brought by another wave of immigrants, Scotch-Irish from Ulster and Scotland driven into exile by the Highland Clearances and the failure of the Jacobite Rising of 1745. At the same time, many of the distillers who had stayed home in Ireland and

Scotland, without the capital to become licensed malt distillers, continued to make "small still" whisky, but outside the bounds of the law.

A severe drop in revenue forced the government to change course. In 1823 an Excise Act was passed. Among the measures was an easing on the size of still permitted to be used. The modern whisky era in Scotland and Ireland started at that point. The rural distillers in Scotland began to specialize in pot still whiskies made from malted barley—"malt whisky." Prior to this, their whiskies included oats and rye and sometimes unmalted barley. See GLENLIVET and WHISKY, SCOTCH.

The larger urban distilleries in the Lowlands of Scotland and the cities of Ireland also prospered, with the Scottish ones adopting the new continuous/column still to make a newer style of whisky that would become known as "grain." While a wide range of cereals were used, most were wheat-based. See STILL, CONTINUOUS; and WHISKY, GRAIN.

The major Irish distillers adhered to pot still distillation, although the pot stills used were of enormous size. They had the advantage in terms of making a consistent product in volume while their Scots colleagues were struggling. A malt tax then prompted them to distill from a mixed mash of malted and unmalted barley, creating single pot still whisky. This would become hugely popular. See WHISKY, IRISH. The Scots responded in 1853 when Andrew Usher launched a blend of malt and grain whiskies. By the twentieth century, blended scotch would be the world's pre-eminent style. See WHISKY, BLENDED.

At the same time, the American and Canadian whisky industries had become established and were making very different styles. Part of this is down to the grains that grew in the New World. The German-style pure-rye distillates still persisted in Pennsylvania and Maryland, as "eastern rye." West of that, mixed mash bills in the Celtic style prevailed, but with corn (maize) rather than unmalted barley. See MASH BILL. By the 1820s, American distillers had taken to putting their whisky into new, charred oak barrels, at first because it colored the spirit faster but then because American drinkers had learned to like the tang it imparted.

As in the British Isles, the nineteenth century was a time of new technology being adapted. Column stills and charcoal filtration were both used, but the most common setup until the end of the century was the steam-injected three-chamber still, usually made out of wooden staves, coupled with a doubler. See DOUBLER, THUMPER, KEG, AND RETORT; and STILL, THREE-CHAMBER. This made a spirit that was smoother than a pot still one but richer than a column still one. See WHISKY, BOURBON; and WHISKY, TENNESSEE.

The late nineteenth century is also the start of another phenomenon: the brand. Distillers, rectifiers, and blenders began putting their names on bottles or casks of whisky as a guarantee of provenance and quality. Many of the whisky industry's most famous names started to become commercially renowned at this time: the Beam and Samuels families in Kentucky; Jack Daniel in Tennessee; Hiram Walker and Joseph Seagram in Canada; John Jameson and John Power in Dublin; and John Walker, James Buchanan, John Dewar, and the Chivas brothers in Scotland. See CHIVAS REGAL; DEWAR'S; HIRAM WALKER AND SONS; JACK DANIEL'S; JIM BEAM; and JOHNNIE WALKER. All recognized the need for consistency and quality in the product. By the end of the century these family-owned firms—especially the blenders of Scotland—would also become pioneers in the new art of advertising.

Whisky drinks were beginning to diversify. As well as usquebaugh (or scubac, as it also became known), whisky had formed the base for punch, slings, cocktails, and toddies. The late nineteenth century would see the rise of the Whisky Julep and the advent of new whisky cocktails such as the Manhattan, Old-Fashioned, Sazerac, and Rob Roy. See JULEP; MANHATTAN COCKTAIL; OLD-FASHIONED COCKTAIL; ROB ROY; and SAZERAC COCKTAIL. The phylloxera-induced collapse of the French brandy industry in the 1870s had also presented scotch and Irish whisky with an opportunity, with whisky replacing brandy in the then popular middle-class mix of brandy and soda. See BRANDY. It would be the advent of the Whisky Highball that would catapult scotch to dominance. See HIGHBALL.

This dominance was also helped by the imposition of Prohibition in the United States in 1920 and the fallout from Ireland gaining independence. While American whisky distilleries closed down, Ireland found itself cut out of the British Empire market, at that point the largest trading bloc in the world. A refusal to deal with bootleggers, high domestic taxes, and an export ban sealed most Irish whisky distilleries' fate.

One of the consequences of scotch whisky's commercial success was the rise of would-be imitators, or at least acolytes. By 1900, Germany was making a fair amount of whisky—not that that required much of a departure from the korn it had been making for centuries. Japan's industry, however, was entirely new, and became quite large. During the twentieth century, India, Mexico, and a handful of other countries also joined the list. See WHISKY, JAPANESE.

While the American industry restarted in 1933, it largely shut down again during World War II in a conversion to industrial alcohol production for the war effort. Scotland meanwhile continued to produce whisky, albeit in limited amounts. By 1946, blended scotch was in the dominant position in terms of branding and stocks.

Scotch's hegemony would continue through the 1960s and into the 1970s. By then the Irish industry (now down to two distilleries) reformulated Jameson and began to promote a new, lighter style. Bourbon, which had tried to compete with scotch and Canadian whisky in the 1960s by going light, had begun to return to its roots and to explore the premium end of the market. It was still, however, selling less on its home market than Canadian whisky. See WHISKY, CANADIAN.

The late 1970s saw a global decline in whisky sales as a new generation of consumers turned away from spirits that they deemed to be old fashioned. In Scotland, this resulted in the mass closure of distilleries, and elsewhere it stalled the Irish whisky and bourbon revivals. In Japan a buoyant domestic market was devastated.

The seeds of whisky's revival were planted at this low point. In Scotland a fall in sales of blends resulted in distillers beginning to promote the more intense, individualistic single malts. By the end of the twentieth century, this emphasis on provenance and flavor resonated with the demands of a premium-oriented consumer. All the established whisky-producing countries began to emphasize the heritage and flavor of their brands. Single pot still reemerged in Ireland, premium aged bourbon and rye in America, single malt in Scotland and Japan, and rye in Canada.

The craft brewing phenomenon was simultaneously underway in America. In time, a similar model would be applied to a new wave of distillers, small-scale, local, premium, a template that would be taken up by new distillers around the world. Some follow a "Scottish" approach, others a "bourbon" model. All are clear in their intent to make a whisky that speaks of its place by using the cereals native or best adapted to the region or using smoking or brewing techniques using local woods.

There is now a greater diversity of whisky than at any point in its history.

Broom, Dave. *The World Atlas of Whisky*, rev. ed. London: Mitchell Beazley, 2014.

Craig, H. Charles. *The Scotch Whisky Industry Record*, Dumbarton, UK: Index, 1994.

Crowgey, Henry, *Kentucky Bourbon: The Early Years of Whiskeymaking*. Lexington: University Press of Kentucky, 1971.

Harper, William T. *Origins and Rise of the British Distillery*. Lewiston, NY: Edwin Mellen, 1999.

Tlusty, B. Ann. *Bacchus and Civic Order: The Culture of Drink in Early Modern Germany*. Charlottesville: University Press of Virginia, 2001.

Dave Broom and David Wondrich

whisky, blended, is a single term with multiple, confusing meanings. In Scotland and many other countries, blended whisky is made by combining the malt whiskies from two or more distilleries, as well as grain whiskies (i.e., distilled from grains besides malted barley, usually on a column still to produce a light, neutral flavor). See WHISKY, GRAIN; and WHISKY, SINGLE-MALT, GLOBAL. The two components are usually mixed in a ratio of roughly 40 percent malt whisky and 60 percent grain whisky, although that can vary significantly. Flavoring and coloring are also allowed. If the constituent elements are all single malt whiskies, then the final product is called "blended malt whisky" (or, in the past, "vatted malt whisky").

Until the last decades of the twentieth century, almost all Scotch whisky bottled and sold was blended, and many of the most famous whisky brands—Johnnie Walker, Ballantine's, Dewar's, Chivas—are named after the grocers who traditionally bought whiskies from different distilleries and combined them to produce a signature flavor profile. See JOHNNIE WALKER; DEWAR'S; and CHIVAS REGAL. Even today, blended whisky dominates the industry: 90 percent of all whisky sold worldwide is a blend. While many inexpensive brands of blended whisky exist, they also include some of the market's

most prestigious brands, such as Johnnie Walker and Compass Box, and skilled master blenders are highly sought after. See COMPASS BOX.

Blends are also common in Ireland, Canada, and Japan, made along similar lines. In Ireland, it is generally pure pot-still whisky that is blended with the grain whisky, although malt-grain blends and even pot-still–malt-grain blends are also popular. In Canada, the grain whisky is blended with various expressions of rye, corn, and wheat whisky. See WHISKY, CANADIAN; WHISKY, IRISH; and WHISKY, JAPANESE.

In the United States, in contrast, blended whisky is typically made by adding a small amount of straight whisky (by law at least 20 percent, and in practice rarely more than that) to a base of grain neutral spirits. For that reason, blended whisky in the United States has a questionable reputation, and blends tend to occupy the bottom shelf in the liquor store whisky section. However, over the last decade a small number of distillers and bottlers—perhaps most notably High West—have made names for themselves as blenders in the Scottish tradition, buying whisky from different distilleries and then blending them to meet a certain flavor profile. Their products are usually labeled "a blend of straight whiskies," which means that no grain neutral spirits have been added.

See also BLENDING and WHISKY, SCOTCH.

Broom, Dave. *Whiskey: A Connoisseur's Guide*. London: Carlton, 1998.

United States Tax and Trade Bureau. *Beverage Alcohol Manual*, chapter 4, 2007.

Clay Risen

whisky, bourbon, is the characteristic whisky of the United States and can only be made there, although contrary to popular belief it need not be made in the state of Kentucky. However, Kentucky still produces the vast majority of the bourbon made. According to the Kentucky Distillers' Association, the state made two million 200-liter barrels of bourbon each year in 2018 and 2019. As of January 2020, there were 9.3 million barrels of bourbon aging in Kentucky warehouses.

Distillers of the whisky must adhere to tight federal regulations, including the types of grain that are used. According to the Alcohol and Tobacco Tax and

Label for Peach Orchard bourbon, ca. 1873. The illustration shows the old "fire copper" style of bourbon making, with a wood-fired pot still. Attached to the still (in cutaway view) are the worm tub and what appears to be a large charcoal rectifier. Library of Congress.

Trade Bureau (TTB), bourbon needs to be made from at least 51 percent corn (maize). The rest of the mash bill typically includes 5–15 percent malted barley, which helps with the fermentation process, and the rest is rounded out with either wheat or, more commonly, rye. See MASH BILL. The percentages of each grain vary from brand to brand, but almost all bourbons follow one of three recipes: the standard formula (corn, malted barley, and rye); the so-called wheated bourbon (corn, malted barley ,and wheat); and a high-rye version (similar to the standard formula, but with a larger proportion of rye grain; between 20 and 35 percent is considered high rye). Distillers occasionally make a four-grain recipe calling for corn, malted barley, rye, and wheat. (The more rye added, the spicier the whisky.)

Today, the milled grains are mixed together with hot water ("mashed") and fermented to make what is called a "distiller's beer." See MASH. This mixture is then generally pumped unstrained into a column still. See STILL, CONTINUOUS. The size of the still and its configuration vary widely across the industry. Some brands also use what is called a thumper, or a doubler, to distill the spirit a second time. See DOUBLER, THUMPER, KEG, AND RETORT. The twenty-first-century craft-distilling boom has

seen a significant number of small distilleries return to making bourbon in pot stills, which are what the whisky was originally produced in two hundred years ago.

Bourbon cannot be more than 62.5 percent ABV when it comes off the still and must be at least 40 percent ABV—and no more than 80 percent—when it's bottled and sold. Like all spirits, bourbon starts out clear and gets its color and much of its flavor from barrel aging. Federal regulations also stipulate how the spirit can be aged. It must be "stored" in a new oak container, which now generally means an unused barrel made from American oak. This requirement is unique to the United States and does more than anything else to set bourbon (along with rye and Tennessee whiskies) apart from whisky made elsewhere. See WHISKY, RYE; and WHISKY, TENNESSEE. The inside of the container is charred (also a point of uniqueness) and generally has an appearance similar to alligator skin. (American cooperages will char the wood to each brand's specifications, and there are several different levels of char that are generally used.) The charring of the wood helps to caramelize the sugars in the wood, and the charcoal is a natural filter that removes some of the less advantageous compounds from the spirit as well as impurities.

See BARREL; CHARCOAL FILTRATION; CHARRING, TOASTING (AND RECHARRING); and MATURATION.

Every year the barrel ages it loses some of its volume to evaporation. See ANGEL'S SHARE. Given Kentucky's hot, relatively dry summers, bourbon generally gets stronger as it ages, since the water evaporates before the alcohol. After a distillery uses a barrel once, that barrel can't be used again to make bourbon. The industry therefore generates mountains of lightly used surplus barrels every year. A great many of them find a second life around the world, put to work aging everything from Scotch whisky to rum to tequila. (They can also be used to make American whisky, but it cannot be labeled bourbon or rye.) There is no minimum age requirement for bourbon: if it spends just a few days in oak, it can still be called bourbon. Only after two years, however, can it be called "straight" bourbon.

The origins of bourbon are, as is so often the case, obscure. Reverend Elijah Craig (1738–1808) is often credited as Kentucky's first distiller, back in 1789, and hence the grandfather of bourbon (there is a modern brand of whisky owned by Heaven Hill that honors him). However, as Henry Crowgey notes in his landmark history of the spirit, "Any argument as to the identity of Kentucky's first distiller should be considered purely academic." See CROWGEY, HENRY GUNDRY. Settlers had been filtering into Kentucky since the 1770s, founding their first towns in 1774 and 1775. Distilling was a common frontier skill, and it's highly unlikely that they would have let fifteen years elapse before making some whisky from the corn that grew so well in the territory.

There are several elaborate theories about the origins of the name "bourbon," and they have been debated endlessly. But as Gerald Carson writes in *The Social History of Bourbon*, "Perhaps there has been altogether too much emphasis upon who was the first man to make old-fashioned small-tub whisky of the bourbon type, and in what country he did it. Distilling was common work incidental to western pioneer life, as prosaic as building a fodder stack. Let us look back upon the accomplishment of our sturdy grandsirs and agree that there is glory enough for all."

Kentucky corn whisky started out as a spirit made by farmers. It turned a perishable product into a finished and sought-after one. (The spent grain, left over from the distillation process, would be used as feed for cattle. The animal dung would then be used to fertilize the next crop of grains growing. This created a sustainable model of production and limited the amount of waste produced.) The characteristic American practice of distilling a mash, which has the particles of ground-up grain in it, rather than a wash, in which they have been filtered out, can be explained by the fact that this makes a much better animal feed. It is also how *Kornbranntwein* was made in Germany. See KORN.

While German immigrants have been largely written out of bourbon history, many early distillers were in fact German, including the widely influential Beam family, whose contributions to the industry run far and wide. The family traces its history back to Johannes Jakob Boehm, who either arrived in the United States from Germany in the 1750s or was born in southeastern Pennsylvania to parents who had recently come over from the old country. Either way, he ultimately changed his name to Jacob Beam. See JIM BEAM. An influx of Jews from Germany and eastern Europe (who had centuries of distilling and liquor business knowledge) also helped build the industry in the 1800s.

By the 1820s, "bourbon" had become a well-known descriptor and had begun appearing in advertisements, such as the 1827 one by H. I. De Bruin of Maysville, Kentucky, for "3 years old bourbon whisky of superior quality." In 1824, a Pennsylvanian how-to-book writer by the name of Parker noted in his discussion of distilling that "if the inside of a new barrel be charred or burnt black, it will add much to the flavor, and will also give a good color to the liquor." Charring was a well-known technique that had been discussed in European scientific journals since the late 1700s, and had already been used by Jamaican rum-distillers to rectify faulty spirits and by ship provisioners to keep water from spoiling, but this was the first acknowledgment of its use in American whisky making. It rapidly became the standard, for rye and for bourbon as well.

Many of the customers for this original bourbon would buy the whisky from small farm producers and blend them together and/or re-distill the liquor. Some of the bourbon was also shipped to the East Coast to be blended into rye whisky. By the 1840s, however, American drinkers were beginning to appreciate the quality of real Kentucky bourbon. It was particularly popular in Chicago and the big new cities of the Midwest and on the frontier; the thickly settled Northeast and the great port of New Orleans tended to prefer the spicier, leaner rye whisky. See WHISKY, RYE. The American Civil War also disrupted bourbon production, with many of the distillers finding themselves involved in the fighting.

Because of the phylloxera epidemic—which destroyed grape vineyards across Europe in the late 1800s and wrecked cognac, port, and sherry brands—bourbon was also shipped to the East. The implosion of the Irish whisky category shortly after the turn of the century also helped spur bourbon sales. See WHISKY, IRISH. By then, bourbon distillers had largely moved away from the old-fashioned "small-tub, fire-copper" method of making the whisky, where the mashing was done in many individual barrels and hand-stirred and the whisky distilled in copper pot stills. Some still made "bourbon steam" whisky, where mashing was done mechanically in large tubs and distilling in large, wooden three-chamber stills with wooden doublers, but by the 1880s most large bourbon distillers had switched to copper column stills. See STILL, THREE-CHAMBER. These yielded a clean, smooth whisky with a good deal of richness to it.

Unfortunately, like the rest of the American liquor industry, Prohibition destroyed the bourbon category, although some brands were permitted to bottle so-called medicinal whisky. See PROHIBITION AND TEMPERANCE IN AMERICA. After Repeal (in December 1933), the bourbon industry was in disarray. Some brands released whisky made before Prohibition went into effect, which was overpoweringly woody and almost undrinkable. Money poured into the category, with new brands building distilleries and releasing very young whiskies just to get something out. There was also a wave of consolidation. A few large companies, including Seagram's, Schenley, and Brown-Forman, bought up many smaller brands and even more intellectual property. The industry shut down again in the 1940s for World War II, and the distillers made a range of supplies for the armed forces, with the War Production Board helping the ones still using pot and three-chamber stills to switch to column stills. Bourbon became quite scarce during the war.

After World War II ended, there was a renewed race to produce bourbon. Through the 1950s and 1960s, bourbon's popularity continued to grow. In 1964, Congress declared bourbon a "distinctive product of the United States," protecting it from foreign competition. Sales of bourbon in the United States reached an apex in 1970. The good times were short lived and, thanks to a range of factors, including the popularity of vodka and a seismic generational shift, sales of the whisky decreased for roughly the next thirty years.

The rebirth of bourbon is a fairly recent phenomenon. American distillers followed the lead of single malt scotch makers and realized that premium bourbon would attract a crowd of new buyers and change the perception of the whisky. One of the first people to realize that this was the appropriate shift was Elmer T. Lee, who created the groundbreaking single-barrel whisky Blanton's Bourbon. Booker Noe, Jim Beam's grandson, was also clandestinely working on a special project that would later become what we now know as Booker's Bourbon. It was the first release in his Small Batch Bourbon Collection, which would ultimately include Knob Creek, Baker's, and Basil Hayden's. These whiskies helped Beam prosper in the modern era and helped save the American whisky industry. See BOOKER NOE II, FREDERICK.

According to IWSR Drinks Market Analysis, sales of bourbon by volume in the United States have increased by 167 percent from 2000 to 2020. (And drinkers around the world have developed a taste for bourbon, with exports rising steadily until the recent tariff wars disrupted business.) This recent popularity of the whisky has inspired a new generation of brands based in Kentucky and around the country, including New York, Texas, and California. Modern distillers have mined history to create a range of whiskies that attempt to capture the past, while others have pushed boundaries, experimenting with everything from barrel design to the variety of grain to create new versions of the spirit.

Bryson, Lew. "America's First Family of Bourbon: the Beams." *Daily Beast*, January 22, 2020. https://www. thedailybeast.com/the-beams-are-americas-first-family-of-bourbon (accessed May 11, 2021) .

Carson, Gerald. *The Social History of Bourbon*. Lexington: University Press of Kentucky, 1963.

Crowgey, Henry G. *Kentucky Bourbon*. Lexington: University Press of Kentucky, 1971

De Bruin, H. I. Advertisement. *Maysville (KY) Eagle*, November 27, 1827.

"Kentucky Bourbon Quick Shots." Kentucky Distillers' Association. https://kybourbon.com/bourbon_culture-2/key_bourbon_facts/ (accessed May 11, 2021).

"Kentucky Whiskey: The Different Methods of Distillation." *New York Times*, April 4, 1870.

Mitenbuler, Reid. *Bourbon Empire*. New York: Viking, 2015.

Moss, Robert F. "How Bourbon Really Got Its Name." Robert F. Moss website, July 29, 2020. https://www.robertfmoss.com/features/How-Bourbon-Really-Got-Its-Name (accessed May 11, 2021)

Parker, M. *The Arcana of Arts and Sciences, or Farmers' and Mechanics' Manual.* Washington, PA: n.p., 1824.

Rothbaum, Noah. *The Art of American Whiskey.* Berkeley, CA: Ten Speed, 2015.

Noah Rothbaum

whisky, Canadian, is an alcoholic beverage distilled in Canada from fermented grain and aged in new or used oak barrels for at least three years.

When It Began

Early British and French immigrants to Canada brought small stills among their household effects. Using Caribbean molasses and local fruit, they made potable alcohol other than whisky. As settlement reached inland to Ontario, molasses became more difficult to obtain, and grain was used for distilling.

The first record of commercial whisky making in Canada dates to 1821, when Thomas Molson began distilling in Montreal for export to Britain. Major distilleries soon sprang up along Ontario's Great Lakes waterway: in present-day Toronto (Gooderham & Worts), Belleville (Corby), Waterloo (Hespeler & Randall—later Seagram's), Prescott (Wiser), and Windsor (Hiram Walker). See GOODERHAM & WORTS and HIRAM WALKER AND SONS. Commercial distilling west of Ontario did not begin until the mid-twentieth century.

In 1887, Canada became the first country to introduce legislation requiring that whisky be aged. This was intended to force producers to store whisky long enough for revenue officers to find and tax it. Before that legislation was implemented in 1889 and 1890, what was sold as whisky was mostly newly distilled grain spirit, often filtered through charcoal-filled columns. Phased in over two years, this new requirement brought an end to small-scale distillation in Canada.

How It Is Made

Typically, Canadian whisky is made from one or more of corn (maize), wheat, barley, or rye. See CORN; WHEAT; BARLEY; and RYE. Different grains are mashed, fermented, distilled, and matured separately to emphasize their distinct qualities. Two types of spirit are produced: base and flavoring. Base is distilled to high ABV (then diluted for aging), and flavoring to low ABV. Base emphasizes wood, while flavoring emphasizes grain-derived flavors. (The base whisky is analogous to the grain whisky used in blended Scotch whiskies, while the flavoring whiskies are closer to the straight whiskies of the United States.) See WHISKY, GRAIN. When mature, individual whiskies are blended together to create the finished product. Since Canadian distillers generally do not buy or exchange spirits, most Canadian whiskies are appropriately termed single-distillery blends.

Following the Rules

Canada's Food and Drug Act requires that Canadian whisky be: (a) made from a mash of cereal grain or cereal grain products saccharified by malt-derived or other enzymes; (b) fermented by yeast or a mixture of yeast and other microorganisms; (c) aged in wood for not less than three years; (d) of the character, including aroma and taste, generally attributed to Canadian whisky; (e) mashed, distilled, and aged in Canada; and (f) not less than 40 percent alcohol by volume. See SACCHARIFICATION and ENZYMES. It may include caramel coloring and flavoring. See CARAMEL; HUE/COLOR; and FLAVORING.

Names and Grains

The Canadian tradition of calling its whisky "rye" began when wheat was the principal Canadian grain. People preferred wheat whisky flavored with rye grain and began calling it "rye." Since corn produces more alcohol than wheat, some distillers began importing corn from the United States in the mid-to-late nineteenth century. In the 1950s, varieties of corn that could mature in Canada's short growing season were developed, making corn Canada's predominant whisky grain. As with wheat whisky, corn whisky is generally flavored with small amounts of rye. Today, several Canadian distilleries continue to make whisky from grains other than corn.

Who Makes It

From a peak of about two dozen in the 1970s, today just eight large-scale distilleries remain. Three of these are in Alberta (Black Velvet, Highwood, and Alberta Distillers), one in Manitoba (Diageo Global Supply Gimli), three in Ontario (Hiram Walker and Sons, Canadian Mist, and Forty Creek), and one in Quebec (Diageo Global Supply Valleyfield). Canada has no regionally defined whisky styles; each distillery uses specific grain combinations and distinct processes. Recently, some Canadian micro-distillers have begun making small quantities of whisky, though not always in the traditional Canadian whisky style.

Where and How It Is Served

Canadian whisky is commonly thought of as mixing whisky, to be enjoyed with ginger ale or cola in a highball or mixed in a cocktail. See GINGER ALE AND GINGER BEER; COLA; HIGHBALL; and COCKTAIL. Some prefer to drink it straight, in shots. Steep provincial taxes on the value of finished goods have encouraged producers to keep strengths at the legal minimum. Nevertheless, producers are now releasing richly flavored sipping whiskies at higher proofs, to be consumed neat or with ice or a splash of water.

Canadian whisky is the bestselling whisky style in North America and second (behind bourbon) in the United States. Canada bottles 21 million nine-liter cases annually but only 15 percent is consumed there. The United States accounts for 75 percent of sales, with the remaining 10 percent representing Canadian whisky's international reach to approximately 150 countries. Top-selling brands include Crown Royal, Wiser's, Canadian Club, Forty Creek, Gibson's, Black Velvet, Windsor, Seagram's, VO, Canadian Mist, Potter's, Golden Wedding, and Alberta Premium. See CROWN ROYAL; CANADIAN CLUB; GIBSON; and SEAGRAM COMPANY LTD. The number of brands available outside of Canada and the United States is limited.

De Kergommeaux, Davin. *Canadian Whisky, Second Edition: The New Portable Expert.* Vancouver: Appetite by Random House, 2017.
De Kergommeaux, Davin. "A Journalist's Primer on Canadian Whisky." *Canadian Whisky.* https://canadianwhisky.org/blog/news-views/a-journalists-primer-on-canadian-whisky.html (accessed April 9, 2021).

Davin de Kergommeaux

whisky, corn, is an often overlooked and sometimes ridiculed class of American whisky that is, by regulation, made from a mash of at least 80 percent corn (bourbon need only be 51 percent corn). There is no age requirement, but if it is aged, it must be put to rest in used or uncharred oak. The result is a spirited, often "green" drink, with a notably sweet corn-oil taste and lacking the astringent woodiness of bourbon.

Corn whisky has been a southern specialty in the United States from the middle of the eighteenth century. As a widely reprinted 1885 newspaper article put it, only partly facetiously, "It is nearly certain death to offer a drinker from Florida or Georgia any but corn whisky." In the years after Prohibition, however, the style had a hard time getting reestablished, with much of its former constituency going to the more widely available bourbon. By the 1960s, corn whisky had become a rarity.

However, modern craft distillers took a shine to corn whisky, with the Balcones and Berkshire Mountain distilleries releasing notable examples of aged product, which had only been available previously from Heaven Hill in their bottled-in-bond Mellow Corn. See HEAVEN HILL.

Moonshine is often called "corn," "corn whisky," or "corn liquor," but this is more a figure of speech than an accurate representation of any correlation between corn whisky and moonshine, as the producers of bootleg liquor do not abide by the regulations that govern taxed spirit.

See also CORN and MOONSHINE.

"By His Drinks." *Buffalo Commercial Advertiser,* November 30, 1885, 2.
Zhang, Sarah. "Drinking Mellow Corn, a Whiskey That Is Like 'Bourbon on Steroids.'" Gizmodo, January 2, 2015. https://gizmodo.com/drinking-mellow-corn-a-whiskey-that-is-like-bourbon-o-1677050873 (accessed April 9, 2021).

Max Watman

whisky, grain, is the term used to define the high-ABV whisky produced in continuous stills in Scotland, Ireland, and Japan. (In Canada, the style is known as "base whisky," a distinction without a difference.) Grain whisky tends to be made from corn (maize) or soft winter wheat with some high-nitrogen, high-diastase malted barley added for saccharification. SEE SACCHARIFICATION. Some distillers, however, also make grain whisky from mixed mash bills, rye, or 100 percent malted barley.

In terms of process, the main cereal is milled into a fine flour, then cooked in hot water into a slurry to gelatinize the starch. After this, another slurry, this one of malted barley, is added, and conversion takes place. Unlike in malt distilling, there is no separation of liquid from solids. Distillation takes place in column stills of various designs. The maximum strength permissible for grain whisky is 94.8 percent ABV, in order for the spirit to have retained the characteristics of its base ingredient.

Grain whisky as a drink dates back to the 1830s, when continuous stills were first adopted in the Scottish Lowlands to turn out massive quantities of lightly flavored but pure whisky that could be sold very cheaply to urban industrial workers. (Distillation follows industrialization, as the saying goes.) Its acceptance as a distinct category of whisky is due to the 1908 British Royal Commission on Whiskey and Other Potable Spirits, which settled (legally, anyway) the heated debate between the pot-still malt whisky makers and the continuous-still operators about whether this new distillate was whisky at all. Legally, it was—as long as you called it "grain whisky," and not just plain "whisky."

As the distillate is collected at such a high strength, grain whisky will always be lighter in character than malt whisky. It will age more quickly (after twelve years, it tends to taste mostly of the barrel) and on its own easily disappears in a mixed drink. It is, however, most commonly used in making blended whisky, but some 100 percent grain whiskies (either single distillery bottlings or blends of different grain distilleries) are becoming more widely seen.

See also COFFEY STILL; STILL, CONTINUOUS; WHISKY, BLENDED; and WHISKY, CANADIAN.

Buxton, Ian, and Paul S. Hughes. *The Science and Commerce of Whisky*. Cambridge: RSC, 2015.

Lea, A. G. H., and J. Piggott, eds. *Fermented Beverage Production*. New York: Kluwer Academic/Plenum, 2003.

Royal Commission on Whiskey and Other Potable Spirits. *Interim Report*. London: HM Stationery Office, 1908.

Russell, Inge, ed. *Whisky Technology, Production and Marketing*. Amsterdam: Academic Press, 2003.

Dave Broom

whisky, Irish is, along with its cousin scotch whisky, one of the twin roots from which the whole family tree of whisky stems. The question of which of the two roots is older is one that is argued passionately based on very limited original evidence, with no definitive answer. The first unambiguous mention of scotch whisky is earlier, but the first one of Irish whisky indicates wider use. See WHISKY.

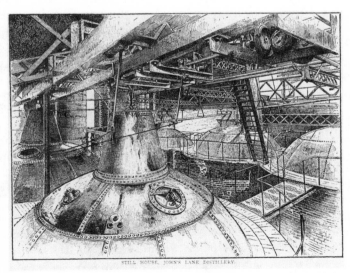

The still house at the John Power and Sons distillery, John's Lane, Dublin, as Alfred Barnard found it in the 1880s. Note the massive, squat pot stills characteristic of Irish whisky making at the time. Behind the ladder at *right center* one may discern the peculiar, off-center still head used to accommodate a mechanical rummager. Wondrich Collection.

That first, incontrovertible, dated mention of grain distilling in Ireland comes from 1556, when an act of the (Anglo-Irish) Parliament of Ireland was passed "to prevent the making of aqua vitae," or distilled spirits, a drink "nothing profitable to be daily drunken and used." See AQUA VITAE. The rationale given was that this drink, made "especially in the borders of the Irishry [i.e., the parts of Ireland outside the pale of English settlement], and for the furniture [i.e., supply] of Irishmen," consumed "much corn, grain, and other things" to the "great hindrance, cost, and damage of the poor inhabitants of this realm" (large property holders and peers, who would be English, were of course excepted, as long as their distilling was for personal use).

This establishes several things: that grain distilling was widespread and that grain spirit was drunk by the common people—the Irish, not the English—but made, and possibly introduced, by the English (or else the distillation would be in the "Irishry," not on its borders). This English trade in grain aqua vitae with the Irish seems to date at least to the 1530s, when in an undated legal note Baron Finglas, one of Henry VIII's magistrates in Ireland, recorded that only one distiller was to be allowed in each town and that the only way wheat malt could be exported to the Irishry was in the form of "bread, ale, and aqua vitae."

In 1603, the English traveler Fynes Moryson, who was secretary to the commander of the English forces in Ireland from 1600 to 1603, gave a description of this "usquebaugh" (the English mangling of *uisce beatha*, the Irish Gaelic translation of "aqua vitae," or "water of life"). "The usquebaugh," Morison wrote, "is preferred before our aqua vitae, because the mingling of raisins, fennel seed, and other things, mitigating the heat, and making the taste pleasant, makes it less inflame." Indeed, he noted that this spirit, consumed by men and women alike, often to excess, was "held the best in the world of that kind."

But this appears to have been the manor-house spirit, so to speak; the version made from good barley malt, flavored with expensive, imported botanicals (saffron was another that was often used), and served to important English guests like Moryson (Irish usquebaugh would go on to be exported widely and, under the name "escubac," become a standard European apothecary's recipe; see USQUE-BAUGH). But if usquebaugh was, as one Dublin historian put it in 1772, the "entertainment . . . of the

great men at their feasts," the "entertainment of the vulgar" was something quite different.

By the 1600s, the Irishry was distilling its own grain spirit from rough black oats, perhaps with a little barley malt mixed in to help fermentation, and it was not flavored. It may predate the English grain spirit, but if so, we have no documentation of that. In any case, it was drunk "by beer glassfuls," as James Howell described Irish drinking habits in 1645, with breakfast, lunch, and dinner. Its nickname, *balcaan*, or, roughly, "bust-head," described its effect. Eventually, the two spirits began to merge: by the early eighteenth century, the bust-head got better and the usquebaugh lost the flavorings. Now, it was all "whisky," as they began calling it in the 1730s.

At that point, there was little to differentiate Irish whisky from the whisky being made in Scotland. The two whiskies only really began to diverge at the end of the century, in the wake of a 1785 law favoring the use of large stills over (harder to regulate) small ones and a duty on malt imposed that same year. Many of the smaller Irish distillers couldn't meet the resulting costs and either went out of business or went underground (*poitín*, or "little pot" was the new nickname attached to their spirit). Meanwhile, the larger distilleries, chiefly in Dublin but also in Cork in the south and Coleraine in the north, bought bigger and bigger stills and switched to making their wash from a portion of the expensive malt, essential to start fermentation, and a mix of raw barley, rye, and oats. All things being equal, raw grain makes for a much more pungent, oily spirit than malt does, and one that needs skillful management to yield a broadly palatable product.

The distillers who made a similar switch in Lowland Scotland at the time were therefore the first to invest in continuous distillation, making a highly rectified, very light whisky that was mostly redistilled into gin (in the Highlands, they mostly went off the grid). See STILL, CONTINUOUS. In Ireland, however, they worked on making the best of the technology they had. The larger the still, the more the reflux, allowing some of the heavier components of the spirit to drop out. See REFLUX. The Irish therefore made their stills extremely large. The big Dublin firms also added a third distillation, as did some of the Lowland Scots. Rather than drying the malt they did use over peat, they used a smokeless hard coal, eliminating smoky, peaty flavors. At some point in the first part of the nineteenth century, Irish distillers took to running the vapor pipe coming off of a spirit still through a tank of cold water and running whatever condensed back into the still. They called this arrangement a "lie pipe" or "lyne arm." (Later it was used occasionally in Scotland, where "lyne arm" survives as the term for a vapor pipe in general.)

Finally, Irish distillers took extra pains to mature their spirit in wood. The result of all this effort was that big Dublin distillers such as John Jameson, John Power, William Jameson, George Roe, and their heirs ended up making a whisky that was clean and elegant but still quite flavorful and not nearly as light as continuous-still whisky. Some distillers even stuck with making malt whisky, cost be damned, but adopted some of the pot-still tweaks used by the mixed-grain distillers (by the 1830s, Bushmills, in Coleraine, had earned a reputation for its "old malt whisky").

As a result, when the Scottish distilling industry adapted to making pot still–continuous still blends, the Irish resisted, and successfully. In 1887, Alfred Barnard found twenty-eight distilleries operating in Ireland, many of them quite large. Of twenty-eight 28, only five had continuous Coffey stills, and four of the five were in the English-associating industrial north. In any case, the five were working for export: Coffey-still whisky was not sold in Ireland. See BARNARD, ALFRED.

Then came the twentieth century. Firstly, the First World War disrupted exports; then the Irish War of Independence severed all but the distilleries in Northern Ireland from the British Commonwealth and its markets; then the United States imposed Prohibition, shutting down that market (mostly, anyway). When that ended, the Great Depression began shortly afterwards, which was only ended by the Second World War, with its ferocious submarine warfare. By 1950, the industry was in real trouble. With a population of under three million people—less than half the population of New York City—Ireland had a domestic market far too small to support multiple large distilleries. Desperate cost cutting led to the introduction of continuous stills and blending in the 1950s, but even the bump in sales caused by the wild popularity of Irish Coffee couldn't help much. See IRISH COFFEE. (Even in Northern Ireland, the two distilleries owned by Bushmills stood alone in the Commonwealth against the juggernaut that was the Scotch whisky industry; they did not fare particularly well.)

In 1966, faced with the loss of the entire industry, John Jameson & Son, John Power & Son, and Cork Distilleries Co, the three surviving distillers, joined forces as Irish Distillers Ltd., consolidating their distilleries in Cork. See IRISH DISTILLERS LTD. In 1972, IDL bought Bushmills. There was then one distilling company in all of Ireland. In 1988, however, it was joined by a second when John Teeling (1946–) opened the Cooley Distillery in a former government potato-spirit plant north of Dublin. Making double-distilled malt whisky in the Scottish style (including even a heavily peated expression, Connemara), Cooley helped to open the door for a new generation of Irish distilling. With an IDL-engineered, Jameson-led boom in export sales beginning in the early 2000s, Irish whisky found its momentum again. Today, there are at least twenty-five operating distilleries in Ireland, with more on the way. Pot-still whisky has enjoyed a remarkable resurgence, to the point that some distillers are even experimenting with restoring rye and oats to their mash bills, eliminated in the 1950s (at present, such a whisky cannot be identified as "pot still," although that may change).

At present, there are seven styles of whisky made in Ireland:

single pot still, triple-distilled in one distillery in pot stills from a mixture of barley malt and unmalted barley
single malt, triple-distilled in one distillery in pot stills from barley malt
single malt, double-distilled in one distillery in pot stills from barley malt
grain whisky, distilled in continuous stills to high proof from a mix of grains
blended whisky: grain whisky blended with
(a) malt whisky
(b) pot-still whisky, or
(c) malt and pot-still whiskies

Irish whiskies are aged almost exclusively in used barrels, most of them American. The triple-distilled ones reach maturity in about five to seven years, the grain whiskies a bit sooner, and the double-distilled malts a bit later. Together, they constitute one of the fastest-growing categories of spirit in the world.

"Baron Finglas' Breviate of Ireland." In *Hibernica*, ed. Walter Harris, 1:100–101. Dublin: 1770.
Harper, William T. *Origins and Rise of the British Distillery*. Lewiston, NY: Edwin Mellen, 1999.

McGuire, E. B. *Irish Whisky*. Dublin: Gill &
MacMillan, 1973.

O'Connor, Fionnán. *A Glass Apart*. Mulgrave,
Australia: Images, 2017.

*The Statutes at Large Passed in the Parliaments Held in
Ireland*, vol. 1. Dublin: 1786.

Townsend, Brian. *The Lost Distilleries of Ireland*.
Glasgow: Neil Wilson, 1997.

David Wondrich

whisky, Japanese. Japan is the youngest of the
"established" whisky-making countries (along with
Scotland, Ireland, United States of America, and
Canada). Whisky first arrived in Japan during the
nineteenth century; when Commander William
Perry opened up trade between the United States
and Japan in 1854, he brought a cask of American
whisky and one of scotch with him as a gift for the
emperor. By the end of the century, various Japanese
firms had begun to specialize in the production of
yo-shu (foreign liquor), whose production involved
adulterating a base alcohol with flavorings to replicate those of the desired spirit. Among these ersatz
spirits was "whisky."

In the twentieth century, some of these firms decided to move into true whisky distillation, among
them Kotobukiya, run by Shinjiro Torii (1879–
1962), and Settsu Shuzo, run by Kihei Abe. In 1919,
the latter sent one of its young chemists, Masataka
Taketsuru (1894–1979), to Scotland to study
chemistry and investigate whisky production. In
1921, he returned (with a Scottish wife), but Settsu
was under financial administration, and its plan for a
distillery had foundered.

Torii meanwhile had bought land at Yamazaki,
close to Kyoto, and established Japan's first purpose-
built whisky distillery. (A license to distill whisky had
previously been issued to White Oak in Akashi but was
never acted upon until the 1960s.) Torii and Taketsuru
were acquaintances, and the latter was hired as distillery manager. In 1924, the first spirit was distilled.

Torii's firm would go on to become Suntory. See
SUNTORY. Taketsuru split with his boss in 1933,
moved to Hokkaido, and founded the firm Nikka.
See NIKKA. The two companies remain the dominant players in Japanese whisky.

Although whisky continued to be made during
the Second World War, Japanese whisky's golden
age started in the 1950s when it became the popular
drink among the new "salaryman" class. More distilleries were built, and consumption rose dramatically, peaking in the early 1980s.

Postwar Japan's tax laws had divided whisky into
three classes. The lower the malt content and alcoholic strength, the lower the tax levied. The bulk
of the whisky consumed in the boom period was
blends from the two lower classes. Sales of domestic
whisky also remained buoyant because of a high import tax levied on imported spirits such as scotch.
When that was scrapped in 1989, the price of scotch
fell, creating a rise in demand, while the domestic
whisky brands suffered. This coincided with a global
trend away from whisky on the part of a new generation. In the West, new drinkers turned to vodka.
In Japan, they began to drink shochu. See SHOCHU.

The slump was to last for twenty-five years.
Many distilleries closed permanently; some went
into short-term working; others were mothballed.
As domestic sales fell, the major distillers began
to look to export and promote their single malts,
rather than the blends that had built the industry. In
2008, Suntory introduced its Yamazaki twelve-year
old and Yamazaki eighteen-year-old single malts to
the American market. Overseas interest grew, albeit slowly. In 2010, however, the domestic market
suddenly revived thanks to an uptake of highball
drinks by a new generation. By 2014, the industry
was selling more whisky but was hampered by lack
of mature stock, as little had been laid down in the
lean years. At the same time, overseas interest began
building up steam. The remaining distilleries have
increased capacity, and a number of new plants have
been built.

The Japanese style, while based on the same
distillation regime as Scotland's, is subtly different.
Ultra-clear wort is used, which eliminates cereal
flavors. Long fermentation is commonplace, as is
the use of a wide range of yeast strains and a wood
policy that often includes Japanese oak (mizunara).
The Japanese climate also has an influence. The
whiskies tend to have a heightened aromatic intensity but are lighter in body than scotch. This allows
them to satisfy the Japanese consumers' demand for
a whisky style that can be mixed and consumed with
Japanese food.

Blends still dominate the market, but as the main
distillers do not exchange stock—as happens in
Scotland—distilleries have been set up to produce
multiple styles. A Japanese single malt can therefore

be a blend of different component malt types from the same plant.

See also EXCISE, TAXES, AND DISTILLATION and WHISKY, SCOTCH.

Broom, Dave. *World Atlas of Whisky: New Edition.* London: Mitchell Beazley, 2014.

Bunting, Chris. *Drinking Japan: A Guide to Japan's Best Drinks and Drinking Establishments.* Clarendon, VT: Tuttle, 2014.

Van Eycken, Stefan. *Nonjatta* (blog). https://nonjatta. blogspot.com/ (accessed April 9, 2021).

Dave Broom

whisky, pot still, is whisky distilled in a pot still, rather than a column still. See STILL, POT; and COLUMN STILL.

whisky, rice. Although not a traditional crop used for whisky production, rice is used as a base grain by distillers internationally. There is debate over whether all of the spirits made from it can be classified as whisky.

Japan's Kirin-Seagram Co., Ltd., launched a rice whisky (saccharified by malted barley) in the 1990s. While some rice-based, oak-aged shochu brands are being marketed in the United States as rice whisky, the use of koji as a saccharification agent means they cannot be legally defined as whisky in Japan, Britain, and the EU. See KOJI.

The term "whisky" is also used to refer to "lao lao," a crude, unaged distillate made in Laos from fermented sticky rice and usually distilled in oil-drum pot stills. See LAO LAO. Similar rice spirits also have a long heritage in Vietnam. Rice is also used in the predominantly molasses-based spirits in Thailand that call themselves "whisky." As molasses is not a grain, these also fall out with the legal definition. Some Asian-style rice spirits are also distilled in the United States.

A more classical whisky style is being made with 100 percent rice in Louisiana, while bourbon distiller Buffalo Trace has also experimented with using rice as part of a mixed mash bill alongside oats and replacing rye/wheat with rice in a bourbon-style mash bill.

See also SHOCHU and WHISKY, JAPANESE.

Barton, Susannah Skiver. "Everything You Need to Know about Rice Whisky." *Whisky Advocate*, Winter 2017.

https://www.whiskyadvocate.com/know-about-rice-whisky/ (accessed April 9, 2021).

Broom, Dave. *The Way of Whisky: A Journey around Japanese Whisky*. London: Mitchell Beazley, 2017.

Dave Broom

whisky, rye. This entry is concerned with the rye whisky made in the United States, as opposed to Canada's "rye whisky," a generic term for Canadian whisky unrelated to its actual rye content. See WHISKY, CANADIAN.

In the summer of 1648 Emanuel and Lucy Downing built a small distillery in Salem, Massachusetts Colony, distilling from both rye and corn, either mixed or separately (the evidence is unclear). By the end of October, according to Emanuel Downing, the "strong water" they were making was preferred by the locals to spirits imported from London. By December, it was all gone. Lucy claimed in a letter that the people of Salem had only two objections to their product: "one, it's too dear; two, not enough of it." Here, in one enterprise, we have the beginning of American rye whisky and, possibly, American corn whisky. This was the first clearly documented grain-distilling in America (it's possible that the distillery William Kieft built in New Amsterdam in 1640 made grain spirits in the Dutch style, but no documentation has survived). Unfortunately, we do not know what happened to the distillery in subsequent years; the Downings went back to England in 1663.

It has long been supposed that American rye whisky is adapted from Scotch-Irish distilling practice. But the Downings' distillery predated the arrival of the Scotch-Irish in America by fifty years. What's more, in a letter to his nephew a few months before he began distilling, Downing asked him for the "German receipt for making strong water with rye meal" that he had. By the mid-1600s, distilling from rye was widespread in Germany and in other countries around the Baltic; in Scotland and Ireland, on the other hand, while some rye was used in the whisky made there, barley was by far the dominant grain. See KORN. There are few mentions of grain distilling between Downing's experiment and the end of the century, and what there are come from the areas of the Middle Atlantic states that had

A coopered wooden three-chamber still, with its (copper) doubler and (wooden) worm tub, 1912. Wondrich Collection.

originally been colonized by the Netherlands and Sweden, where the practice was well known.

In fact, it was not until the middle years of the eighteenth century that grain distilling became widespread in America, and when it did the German influence was also strong. While it is found in North Carolina, Virginia, and Maryland, its stronghold was in southern Pennsylvania (New England by then had switched to making rum from imported molasses). There, the population was largely German, immigrants from the southern Rhineland who had fled war and religious oppression and settled between Philadelphia and the Allegheny Mountains. There they made large amounts of apple and peach brandy, and also a good deal of what they called "Korntram," or "rye dram" (in the English colonies of North America, "dram" was a common generic term for spirits). By the 1740s, this had also acquired the anglicized Gaelic name, "whisky," no doubt through the agency of the Scotch-Irish Protestants who also arrived in Pennsylvania in large numbers beginning in 1728 (the first wave of German immigration had begun in 1683) and brought their own knowledge of distilling.

With the outbreak of the American Revolution, the cheap rum and molasses that had flooded into the Colonies from the British Caribbean were cut off, and the colonists were thrown back on their own resources. As John Adams wrote of Philadelphia in 1777, "Whisky is used here instead of rum, and I don't see but it is just as good." That was perhaps wishful thinking, but good, bad, or indifferent, rye whisky, by far the dominant style, was the spirit of the Revolution. Double-distilled in pot stills from a mix of rye, a little barley malt to start fermentation, and, sometimes, a portion of corn, the spirit was sold unaged. See DOUBLE DISTILLATION and STILL, POT. For the most part, it was an agricultural product, made by farmers from their own grain.

After the war, as Americans moved west beyond the Alleghenies, they brought stills with them. Those who went on to Kentucky soon adapted the loose basic formula to use more corn and less, or even no, rye. In western Pennsylvania and the East, rye still ruled. In 1791, the federal government attempted to tax these producers. This led to the Whisky Rebellion in western Pennsylvania, a semi-organized resistance to the tax and its collectors that George Washington put down in 1794 by personally leading an army into the area (the rebels dispersed before he arrived). Ironically, in 1797 Washington himself went into the rye whisky business, building a model distillery at Mount Vernon. Its purpose-built still house and five pot stills turned out some 120 liters of spirit a day. This made him one of the largest producers in the country. See WASHINGTON, GEORGE.

The beginning of the nineteenth century saw a good deal of technical innovation in the American distilling industry. The small farmhouse distillery was rapidly giving way to larger, professional enterprises like Washington's, although a few small rye distilleries survived until Prohibition. Between 1800 and 1840, a consensus style of rye developed. It was made from a sweet mash (rather than a sour mash, as was becoming common with bourbon) of rye with a small portion of barley malt (in Pennsylvania) or rye malt (in Maryland). See SOUR MASH and WHISKY, BOURBON. It was steam-distilled in wooden or copper three-chamber stills with doublers and put in charred oak barrels (a practice first described in print in a western Pennsylvania how-to book in 1824) at no more than 51 percent ABV. See STILL, THREE-CHAMBER; and DOUBLER, THUMPER, KEG, AND RETORT. The length of aging was still variable, but it increasingly stretched to three or four years. Even as American whisky production became increasingly concentrated and industrialized, the rye distillers of Pennsylvania and Maryland maintained these characteristics even if that meant using huge, coopered 40,000-liter stills for the initial distillation. By the end of the nineteenth century, this style, with the additional characteristic of aging in heated warehouses, became known as "eastern rye." Opposed to it was "western rye," the rye whisky made principally in Kentucky. This was made from a sour mash with a significant portion of corn in it, distilled in pot stills in small distilleries and column stills in large ones and aged in unheated warehouses; in essence, it was bourbon but with more rye than corn.

In 1899, when rye was at its peak of importance, the United States produced 126.2 million liters of whisky, 62 percent of that being bourbon and the rest rye. If, however, one looks at the figures for bonded whisky, the quality side of the market, the picture is rather different. Kentucky, Pennsylvania, and Maryland, the three main whisky-producing states, bottled some 825,000 liters of rye, as opposed to some 850,000 liters of bourbon. All of the bourbon was from Kentucky, but only 15 percent of the rye was, the rest being mostly from Pennsylvania's Twenty-Third District, centered on Pittsburgh. The major brands included Pennsylvania's Old Overholt, Guckenheimer, Large, Moore & Sinott, and Finch, and Maryland's Mount Vernon and Monticello.

The next two decades saw American distillers fighting a futile rearguard action to stave off Prohibition. After 1919, only two rye distilleries had permits to make and sell medicinal whisky, accounting for 25 percent of the country's permitted whisky production (the rest went to bourbon). After Repeal in 1933, the industry tried to rebuild. The conglomerates that took over the dormant business during the dry years kept a few eastern rye distilleries open, but most of their investment went to Kentucky and other states. By the end of World War II, rye was in steep decline, which led to further consolidation. Old Overholt, the leading prestige brand and flagship for the category, was moved from Pennsylvania distillery to Pennsylvania distillery. By the 1960s, it was the last nationwide brand. In 1963, it advertised a new, lighter formula, a likely indication that it abandoned three-chamber distillation for column distillation. It also dropped the proof, abandoning its long-held bonded status. When, in 1987, it was sold to Jim Beam, production was moved to Kentucky. That was the end of eastern rye.

In the twenty-first century, rye came back from the brink of extinction. The handful of bottlings that were (intermittently) available, all Western-style from large producers, were supplemented by a wave of new ryes from micro-distillers, beginning with the Anchor Distilling Co.'s Old Potrero. By the 2010s, rye was growing at 20 percent or more a year (admittedly from a small base), its growth driven by the cocktail revolution: many classic cocktails need rye, and that's what people were drinking. See COCKTAIL RENAISSANCE. In 2015, one of those small distilleries, the Leopold Bros., in Denver, Colorado, installed a three-chamber still for making rye, the first operating in America since at least the 1960s.

Annual Report of the Commissioner of Internal Revenue for the Fiscal Year Ended June 30. 1899, Washington, DC: GPO, 1899.

Downing, Emanuel. "Letters of Emanuel Downing." In *Collections of the Massachusetts Historical Society*, 4th ser., vol. 6. Boston: Massachusetts Historical Society, 1863.

Dunaway, Wayland F. *A History of Pennsylvania*, 2nd ed. New York: Prentice-Hall, 1948.

Neff, Larry M., and Frederick S. Weiser. *Friedrich Heinrich Gelwicks, Shoemaker and Distiller: Accounts, 1760–1783*. Breinigsville, PA: Pennsylvania German Society, 1979.

Parker, M. *The Arcana of Arts and Sciences, or Farmers' and Mechanics' Manual*. Washington, PA: 1824.

"Story of Maryland Rye." *American Spirits Journal*, September 1935, 31.

Wolf, Julius. *Die Branntweinsteuer*. Tübingen, Germany: H. Laupp, 1884.

David Wondrich

whisky, scotch. The current definition of scotch whisky is provided by the Scotch Whisky Regulations passed by the British Government in 2009:

To be labeled "scotch whisky" the spirit must be:

a. Produced at a distillery in Scotland from water and malted barley (to which only the whole grains of other cereals may be added), all of which have been: (i) processed at that distillery into a mash; (ii) converted to a fermentable substrate only by endogenous (i.e., not added) enzyme systems; (iii) fermented only by the addition of yeast

STILL HOUSE, BOWMORE DISTILLERY.

The Bowmore distillery, Islay, as Alfred Barnard found it in the 1880s. Note that each still is different, and the unusual divided outflow arm on the still at *center* (the condensing coils and their worm tubs are kept outside, as was common in Scotland). Wondrich Collection.

b. Distilled at an alcoholic strength by volume of less than 94.8 percent, so that the distillate has an aroma and taste derived from the raw materials used in, and the method of, its production

c. Matured in an excise warehouse in Scotland in oak casks of a capacity not exceeding 700 liters, the period of that maturation being no less than three years

d. In retention of the color, aroma, and taste derived from the raw materials used in, and the method of, its production and maturation

e. Free from the addition of any substance other than water and spirit caramel

f. Bottled at a minimum of 40 percent alcohol by volume

The first written reference in Scotland to distilling from malt comes from an exchequer roll in 1494, although it is likely that aqua vitae (*uisge beatha* in Scots Gaelic, from which the word "whisky" derives) was being made here at least by 1300, for medicinal purposes by monks, physicians, and apothecaries. See WHISKY. There is evidence for the convivial use of aqua vitae from at least the mid-sixteenth century: an act of Parliament in 1579 limited "brewing and stelling [distilling]" to "Gentlemen for their own use" in expectation of a poor harvest, on account of there being "ane greit quantitie of malt consumit in the haill partis of this realm be making of aqua vitae."

In 1609 the statutes of Iona forbade the import of wines and spirits by the Western Isles, on account of the people's "inordinate love of strong wines and aquavite." Private distilling for domestic consumption was allowed, and this remained the case until 1781, by which time the first industrial-scale distilleries were operating, taking advantage of the increased amount of cereals now available owing to improved farming methods.

This new ban on private distilling inevitably led to a massive increase in illicit distilling and smuggling, which reached epic proportions after the conclusion of the Napoleonic War in 1815. Anarchy was averted by the passing of the Excise Act 1823, which encouraged smugglers to take out licenses and laid the foundations of the modern whisky industry. See EXCISE, TAXES, AND DISTILLATION.

By this time two kinds of whisky were being made in Scotland: malt whisky from malted barley and grain whisky from mixed grains. The latter was made in the Lowlands, where there was more grain available, the former in the Highlands, where barley was the traditional "drink crop." The large-scale production of grain whisky was given a boost by the invention of continuous stills by Robert Stein (1828) and Aeneas Coffey (1830). See COFFEY, AENEAS; and STILL, CONTINUOUS. The wide adoption of Coffey's still (the simpler and more effective of the two) for making mixed-grain whisky saw Scotland producing vast amounts of a product that was higher strength, purer (and thus blander), and much cheaper to make than the traditional pot-stilled malt whisky. Spirits merchants soon began to blend it with malt whiskies in order to produce a product with a broad appeal and a consistent flavor, batch by batch. See BLENDING and JOHNNIE WALKER.

Blended scotch whisky became the drink of choice of the English middle classes during the 1880s and 1890s and from this base spread around the British Empire. Very little malt whisky was drunk outside Scotland—almost all of it went for blending.

The boom of the 1890s turned dramatically to bust in 1900: production levels were massively out of balance with sales, Scotch was no longer so fashionable, and the UK economy went into recession. To compound matters further, "the People's Budget" of 1908 increased duty on spirits by one-third: domestic consumption waned, and exports became more important.

Then came World War I, during which the government banned malt whisky distilling in order to preserve barley, reduced the strength at which whisky could be sold to 40 percent ABV, and banned the sale of whisky under three years old. Duty was doubled in 1918, and exports were forbidden for a year.

When Prohibition was introduced in the United States in 1920, the scotch whisky industry's prospects looked grim. In fact, America's taste for scotch was undiminished, and distillers happily shipped ever-growing quantities of whisky to neighboring territories such as the Bahamas, Canada, and Mexico, from which it was bootlegged into the States. By the time Prohibition was repealed in 1933, scotch was the drink of choice, and whisky companies were quick to appoint legal distributors, many of whom had formerly been bootleggers. By the outbreak of World War II in 1939, the United States was scotch whisky's leading export market.

In the home market, grain distilling ceased in 1941 owing to a shortage of cereals, and malt distilling followed in 1943–1944. By 1943 the prewar price of a bottle had been doubled by duty increases; sales in the home market were put on quota—three-quarters of the whisky released had to be sold in export markets, particularly the United States—and barley for distilling continued to be rationed until 1950.

Until the early 1960s mature whisky was in chronically short supply, yet demand for scotch had never been greater. To meet the demand, many distilleries were increased in size, long-closed plants were re-commissioned, and new distilleries were built. During the decade the industry's capacity was doubled, and this continued into the 1970s: stocks of whisky in bond reached unprecedented levels, rising from 2.2 million liters in 1965 to 4.5 *billion* liters in 1975.

Then came a severe slump, prompted by the oil crisis and the effects of the Vietnam War. To make matters worse, scotch was no longer as fashionable as it had been during the past two decades: many consumers were switching to vodka, white rum, or wine. During 1981 the world economy slipped rapidly into recession, and unemployment rose alarmingly throughout the Western world. Blending houses cut their spirit orders, and thirty distilleries closed between 1980 and 1985, ensuring by the end of the decade that the balance of production capacity with demand was restored.

One of the side effects of the economic downturn in the mid-1970s was an increase in the number of malts being bottled by their owners as singles. William Grant & Sons had blazed the trail in this regard, promoting Glenfiddich as a "pure malt" from the early 1960s. By 1970, around thirty single malts were available, mostly from independent bottlers in small quantities. See GLENFIDDICH. By 1980 the number of available expressions had doubled, and this continued during the 1990s and beyond. Currently, over five hundred expressions are released each year, including some off the most highly prized bottlings on the market. See MACALLAN.

The demand for blended scotch also began to increase during the late 1990s and early twenty-first century, with new markets emerging, particularly in Asia and South America, and since 2004 there has been a boom in production capacity not seen since the 1890s, with twenty-four new distilleries being commissioned, a further forty proposed or under construction, and many existing distilleries being expanded. Already production capacity has been increased by about one-third. At the same time, the steady popularity of Scottish single-malt whiskies has inspired a growing boom in malt-whisky distilling around the world, with scotch-style malts from places such as Australia, India, Sweden, France, Austria, and Taiwan stepping up to join the already-established ones from Japan and India as pillars of a growing category. See INDIA AND CENTRAL ASIA and WHISKY, JAPANESE.

See also SINGLE MALT.

Craig, H. Charles. *The Scotch Whisky Industry Record: An Industry History and Reference Book*. Glasgow: Index, 1994.

MacLean, Charles. *Scotch Whisky: A Liquid History*. London: Cassell Illustrated, 2004.

Moss, Michael S., and John R. Hume. *The Making of Scotch Whisky: A History of the Scotch Whiskey Distilling Industry*. Edinburgh: Canongate, 1981.

Scotch Whisky Regulations, 2009. https://www.legislation.gov.uk/uksi/2009/2890/contents/made (accessed April 8, 2020).

Charles MacLean

whisky, single-malt, global. From being a specialty of Scotland and to a lesser extent Ireland, single malt whisky is now being made globally, mostly on the back of the upsurge in interest in single-malt scotch.

While some European distillers have been making the style since the nineteenth century—Germany's Schraml has been distilling whisky since 1818—the explosion in European single malt is a more recent phenomenon starting in the late 1990s. There are in excess of 150 distillers in Germany, Austria, Switzerland, and Liechtenstein making single malt, many of whom have added a malt distillate to an existing range of fruit spirits or grain-based korn. See GERMANY, SWITZERLAND, AND AUSTRIA and KORN.

This approach extends to the distillation equipment used, often copper pot stills with water baths and rectifying columns, and an approach to the raw material in which the distiller treats the malted barley in the same way as fruit and tries to capture the essence of the cereal character. See STILL, HYBRID.

Some others approach whisky making from a brewing heritage, for example, using different roasts of barley, and temperature-controlled fermentation. Some smoke their barley over either peat or wood, while local wine casks are extensively used.

That France has a burgeoning single malt movement is perhaps not surprising; this is the world's largest market for scotch in volume terms. A cluster in Brittany follow a traditional Scottish template, while those in Alsace take a more fruit-spirit-oriented approach, with barley being pushed further forward. The rest are spread geographically and philosophically, with different yeasts being used and deep exploration of terroir (including food culture for smoking techniques) and, in Cognac, a fusion between Cognacais approaches to distillation and maturation. Oak tends to be used as a frame rather than a dynamic element. See COGNAC; ÉLEVAGE; and FRANCE.

Single malt is also made in the Netherlands and Belgium. There is an argument that genever is closer to whisky than to London Dry gin, which would mean the Dutch have been whisky distillers (albeit by another name) since the sixteenth century; indeed, much of the genever they made in the nineteenth century used minimal amounts of botanicals or none at all to flavor the basic malt spirit. There are also two single malt producers in Spain, one of which, Destillerias y Crianzas, has been producing since 1959. The oldest central European whisky distiller is the Czech Republic's Golden Cock.

Single malt is now made in Denmark, Finland, Iceland, Norway, and Sweden. Although whisky production was trialed in Sweden and Denmark in the 1950s, and Finland had the Kosenkorva distillery, which ran from 1981 to 2000, making the Alko and Viski 88 brands, the boom is a recent one, partly driven by rising consumer interest and the easing of monopoly control of spirit sales in Sweden, Norway, and Finland. See SCANDINAVIA.

Distillers have a wide range of approaches, and while a Scottish model is followed, different barley varieties are used, as is local oak, and different smoking techniques using not just peat but juniper and, in Iceland's case, sheep dung. Climate also plays a part (there are two distilleries north of the Arctic Circle), and the extreme fluctuations in temperature in the northern part of region are considered to have an impact on flavor.

Until World War II, Australia was the largest market for scotch whisky. It had also distilled its own from 1791 until the 1980s when the last two large distilleries in the state of Victoria closed. The new Australian single malt industry started in Tasmania—where most of the country's distilleries are now concentrated—in 1992 when distiller Bill Lark succeeded in persuading the Australian government to rewrite existing legislation regarding the minimum size of a still, thereby permitting small-scale distillation to commence. See AUSTRALIA AND NEW ZEALAND.

Although it is too early to say that an identifiable Australian style has emerged, distillers in Tasmania tend to use local brewing malt (and often buy in wash). The local peat contains a different range of microflora, producing a different range of aromatics, while Australian wine and fortified wine casks are used, often of a smaller size than is common in Scotland. New Zealand and Fiji have both started single malt production as well, or restarted in the former's case.

Much of the "whisky" produced in India is molasses-based, thereby placing it outside the recognized definition of whisky as a non-neutral, cereal-based, aged spirit. Some single malt whisky is produced domestically however, with Amrut, Mohan Meakin's Rampur, and Paul John all exported. McDowell's single malt is available on the domestic market. (There is also a single malt distillery, Muree, in Pakistan.) Barley tends to come from Rajasthan, while the ambient temperature results in rapid maturation cycle. While evaporation rates (angel's share) are 2–5 percent in Scotland, in southern India they can reach up to 16 percent per annum. Similar subtropical conditions exist in Taiwan, which has had two malt whisky distilleries—Kavalan and Nantou—built since 2005. The temperature results in whiskies reaching full maturity in four to five years.

Single malt has been a significant part of the experimentation of the new wave of small-scale American and Canadian distillers, and moves are underway to create a definition for this new style. As in the rest of the world, while the approach may take its lead from Scotland, the whiskies also have their own style, with considerable input from the craft brewing industry in terms of levels of malt roasting and yeast. A wide range of raw material has also been used for smoke, from local peat in the Pacific Northwest to mesquite in Sonora and Texas.

There has been whisky made in Brazil since the late 1970s, while Argentina, Peru, and Mexico all now have single malt distilleries (Mexico, at least, has a tradition of grain distilling dating back at least to the seventeenth century). So far, there are only two single malt producers in the African continent, both in South Africa. See ANDEAN SOUTH AMERICA; BRAZIL; and MEXICO.

Single malt is also now being made close to Scotland. Many of the new distilleries in Ireland are making single malt as well as single pot-still whisky (indeed, the Bushmills distillery in Northern Ireland has been making single malt since the late eighteenth century), while Wales has had a malt distillery since 2004. England, too, has a growing number of distilleries producing single malt, often in conjunction with other spirits. See WHISKY, IRISH.

Broom, Dave. The World Atlas of Whisky: The New Edition. London: Mitchell Beazley, 2014.
Ronde, Ingvar, ed. Malt Whisky Yearbook 2017. Shrewsbury, UK: MagDig Media, 2016.
Roskrow, Dominic, Gavin D. Smith, Juergen Diebel, and Davin de Kergommeaux. Whisky Opus: The World's Greatest Distilleries and Their Whiskey. New York: DK, 2012.

Dave Broom

whisky, Tennessee, is a style of corn-based whisky made in the state of Tennessee. In addition to traditionally following the requirements for bourbon (a mash bill of at least 51 percent corn [maize]; distilled at no more than 80 percent abv; aged in charred new oak barrels at an entry proof of no more than 62.5 percent ABV; and bottled at no less than 40 percent ABV), Tennessee whisky is typically passed through or "mingled with" large amounts of maple charcoal before barrel aging. Distillers claim that this additional step, known as the Lincoln County process—for the county on Tennessee's southern (Alabama) border where it is said to have originated—removes impurities and imparts a soft, sweet note.

According to legend, the Lincoln County process was invented by Alfred Eaton, a Middle Tennessee farmer and distiller, about 1825; American distilling manuals had been describing the process, however, since the first decade of the century, and, more than likely, Eaton merely laid claim to a process that had been developed by legal and illegal distillers for generations. See RECTIFIER (DEVICE). In any case, the process, though not uncommon in nineteenth-century American whisky making, was a Tennessee specialty and gave the state's whisky, as a trade journal remarked in 1904, "a special flavor very much prized by the people of that state."

Tennessee whisky as a style grows out of Lincoln County whisky, recognized for quality since the beginning of the 1850s, but also out of the whisky made in Robertson County, on the state's northern (Kentucky) border. In fact, from the 1850s through the 1880s, when American whisky more or less grew into its final form, "Robertson County" on a whisky's label was almost as strong a recommendation as "Bourbon County," and indeed Nelson's Green Brier whisky, made in the county, was one of the pioneers of whisky branding.

Unlike bourbon, Tennessee whisky is not defined by the federal Tax and Trade Bureau—United States federal law recognizes no distinction between it and bourbon. There is not even a federal requirement that Tennessee whisky be made in Tennessee; for example, the Leopold Bros. distillery of Colorado has made a "Tennessee Style" whisky. (However, multiple international trade agreements define it as being made exclusively in Tennessee.)

In 2013, the state of Tennessee passed a law requiring all whisky sold within its borders with the label "Tennessee whisky" to be made in the state, using the Lincoln County process. The law was the subject of a media and legislative battle the following year, led by Diageo (owner of the George Dickel Tennessee whisky brand) and Phil Prichard, who produces an eponymous spirit labeled "Tennessee whisky" but does not use the Lincoln County process (though the law made a specific exception for Prichard's whisky). The law's critics claimed that it was too restrictive; however, after substantial public backlash, they dropped their claim.

Only a handful of companies make Tennessee whisky, though the largest producer, Jack Daniel's, a subsidiary of Brown-Forman, sells about 5 million nine-liter cases annually, making it the largest-volume whisky brand in the United States. George Dickel, in Cascade County, makes about 150,000 nine-liter cases a year; other producers include Tenn South. Jack Daniel's and George Dickel differ significantly in their application of the Lincoln County process: the former uses gravity to pass a small but steady stream of distillate through ten vertical feet of charcoal, while the latter places the distillate in a vat filled with charcoal and allows it to mingle for about a week.

See also LINCOLN COUNTY PROCESS.

Gaston, Kay Baker. "Tennessee Distilleries: Their Rise, Fall, and Re-Emergence." *Border States: Journal of the Kentucky-Tennessee American Studies Association* 12 (1999).

Krass, Peter. *Blood and Whiskey: The Life and Times of Jack Daniel.* Hoboken, NJ: John Wiley & Sons, 2004.
"Tennessee Whisky." *Bonfort's Wine and Spirits Circular,* June 25, 1904, 174.

Clay Risen

whisky books are, for the most part, a relatively new phenomenon. While there are some early examples, such as Alfred Barnard's landmark survey of producers from 1887, *The Whisky Distilleries of the United Kingdom,* and his lesser-known *A Visit to Watson's Dundee Whisky Stores,* as well as a handful of books from the early- and mid-twentieth century, such as *Whisky* by "Aeneas MacDonald" (George Malcolm Thomson), from 1930, and Ross Wilson's *Scotch Made Easy* from 1959, the idea that people would want to read anything about whisky longer than a label simply didn't occur to publishers. See BARNARD, ALFRED; and MacDONALD, AENEAS.

That all changed in the 1980s, an otherwise inauspicious time for whisky. In 1987, Michael Jackson published his first whisky book, *The World Guide to Whisky.* It was an overview of what whisky was and how and where it was made, and for the first time it presented tasting notes to hundreds of whiskies. It was authoritative without being stuffy, engaging without being coy or cute. It changed whisky writing and created a path that would widen into a variety of types of whisky book. See JACKSON, MICHAEL.

Overviews

The overview book attempts to present the full scope of whisky, either the totality or one of the major regions, with an inclusive narrative sweep that takes in history, process, individual producers, and sometimes cocktails and food pairings as well. Recent examples of the totality type would include *The World Atlas of Whisky,* 2nd ed., by Dave Broom (2014); *Tasting Whisky,* by Lew Bryson (2014); and *Whiskey Distilled: A Populist Guide to the Water of Life,* (2015) by Heather Greene. Charles MacLean's *Whiskypedia* (2010) takes a bite-sized approach in a single-volume encyclopedia of scotch whisky. Davin de Kergommeaux's *Canadian Whisky: The Portable Expert* (2012) and *The Book of Bourbon and Other Fine American Whiskies,* by Gary Regan and Mardee Haidin Regan (1998, and still quite relevant), are good examples of the regional type. See REGAN, GARY.

Ratings Collections

Intended as a guide to selecting whiskies of similar quality and caliber or for opening the range of whiskies to the readers' experience, the ratings collection presents a large array of tasting notes on various expressions, with or without a rating scheme. Timeliness in reviewing and publishing such a book is critical. Clay Risen's *American Whisky, Bourbon and Rye* focuses on US whiskies and looks to be doing regular revisions. Although it is controversial both for some of its opinions and for how they are often expressed, no list of this kind would be complete without *Jim Murray's Whisky Bible*, an annual roundup of thousands of tasting notes of whiskies from around the world. See MURRAY, JIM.

Technical Books

There are those who want to learn much more about how whisky is made, right down to the chemical and physical processes. Authors who can make this kind of information accessible yet accurate find this niche. One of the better books is *The Science and Commerce of Whisky*, by Ian Buxton and Paul S. Hughes (2013).

Memoirs and Company Histories

Memoirs of people who have worked in whisky are still relatively rare; an excellent example is that of outspoken master blender Richard Paterson (written with the help of Gavin D. Smith), *Goodness Nose* (2010). Company histories are often done in cooperation with the company, as with F. Paul Pacult's *American Still Life: The Jim Beam Story* (2003) and Dr. Nicholas Morgan's Johnnie Walker history, *A Long Stride* (2020).

Histories

Historical accounts of various aspects of whisky vary from Charles Craig's magisterial *The Scotch Whisky Industry Record* (1994), to Reid Mitenbuler's business portrait *Bourbon Empire* (2015), to Gavin D. Smith's history of illicit scotch, *The Scottish Smuggler* (2004), to Noah Rothbaum's lavishly illustrated *The Art of American Whiskey* (2015). Sometimes a book will completely rewrite the assumed history of a category, as is the case with *A*

Glass Apart: Irish Single Pot Still Whisky, by Fionnán O'Connor (2015).

Cookbooks and Cocktails

Books that focus on whisky-related cooking and cocktails have found eager readers. Amy Zavatto's *Big Book of Bourbon Cocktails* (2019) and Jane Danger and Alla Lapuschik's *Bourbon Bartender* (2017) are fine introductions to mixing with the spirit. Whisky's delicious sweet, smoky character works well with food in books like *The Kentucky Bourbon Cookbook*, by Albert W. A. Schmid and Dean Fearing (2010).

Narratives

Books that read like fiction but tell true whisky-related stories have a special place in this category. The classic may be *Raw Spirit*, by acclaimed Scottish science fiction author Iain Banks (1994), a rambling—literally—self-education in scotch whisky. Another is *Sea Spray and Whisky*, by Norman Freeman (1993), a remembrance of crewing a freighter carrying a cargo of whisky and what happens when the crew realizes the nature of the cargo.

Novelties

Whisky can lead to whimsy, and to introspection, and thus to books that stand alone. The title of *The Essential Scratch and Sniff Guide to Becoming a Whisky Know-It-All*, by Richard Betts (2015), says it all, as does *Whisky and Philosophy: A Small Batch of Spirited Ideas* by Fritz Allhoff and Marcus P. Adams (2009).

See also MIXOGRAPHY and SPIRITS WRITING.

Lew Bryson

Whisky Smash is a member of the julep-like smash family that had its heyday in the nineteenth century, though even then it was less popular than the Brandy Smash. See JULEP; SMASH; and BRANDY SMASH.

The **Whisky Sour** is a cocktail composed of whisky (usually, but not always, American bourbon or rye), lemon juice, and sugar (some recipes also call for egg white). Although it first appears in print as early as 1826, in a list of ways that whisky could be drunk, it does not appear again until 1862, at which point it is immediately inducted into the canon of A-merican drinks. Along with the related drinks made with brandy and gin, the Whisky Sour marked a par-ticularly attractive hybrid of the large-format punch and the single-serving cocktail. Its particular genius, however, lay in the way the lemon juice softened the sharp, woody tang of the American whisky without masking it, turning what some people found objec-tionable into something compelling. See COCKTAIL; PUNCH; and SOUR.

From the 1860s until the 1960s, the Whisky Sour was one of the more popular drinks in the canon, until its place was essentially usurped by the Margarita. See MARGARITA. As the *Atlanta Daily Constitution* put it in 1879, "When American meets American then comes the Whisky Sour." The drink's properties did shift slightly over time. Early recipes (such as in Haney's *Steward and Barkeeper's Manual* from 1869) suggest making the sour with an ample measure of water and a light hand with the lemon, resulting in a sweeter, longer punch-style drink, whereas later recipes eliminate the water and nudge forward the lemon, producing a shorter, sharper drink. Flourishes also followed: a dash of curaçao made its way into the mix in the 1887 edition of Jerry Thomas's bartender's book; a float of red wine atop the sour earned many fans starting in the 1880s (as the Continental Sour, Southern Whisky Sour, Greenwich Sour, or, finally, New York Sour); and, beginning in the 1920s, a touch of egg white to add foam and body, a European addition that by the 1940s had become more or less de rigueur in America, too and is still considered essential in some circles. See NEW YORK SOUR and SOUR MIX. The plain Whisky Sour has not been at the forefront of the twenty-first-century cocktail revival, but its variations and derivatives are ubiquitous.

Recipe: Stir 7 ml sugar in 15 ml lemon juice; add 60 ml bourbon or straight rye whisky (or indeed any other whisky) and (optionally) 15 ml egg white; shake, strain into large cocktail glass and garnish with cherry and orange slice.

Embury, David. *The Fine Art of Mixing Drinks.* New York: Doubleday, 1948.

Steward and Barkeeper's Manual. New York: Haney & Co, 1869.
"When American Meets American." *Atlanta Daily Consti-tution*, February 20, 1879, 2.
Wondrich, David. *Imbibe!*, 2nd ed. New York: Perigee, 2015.

Paul Clarke

white dog is an American term for fresh spirit destined to be whisky as it comes off the still, before has been put into oak. For many years "white dog" was industry jargon, rarely heard outside of profes-sional whisky distilleries. Many ideas regarding the origin of the name exist, none of them verifiable. The most obvious provenance would be simply that fresh spirit is clear and strong, so it is "white," and it bites, like a dog. (The distinctive color of whisky comes not from the spirit itself but from the barrels in which it is aged.) As the popularity of dis-tillery tours grew and more people tasted the new, high-proof spirit, interest in white dog grew. In the early years of the twenty-first century, as small dis-tilleries proliferated, many distilleries decided to release their distillate without aging it and called it white dog. While some distillers were clearly enthu-siastic about bottling an unaged spirit for its own sake, others saw an opportunity to sell a product that was at least related to whisky without having to barrel it and wait for it to age. Bigger distilleries soon followed suit, releasing their own white dogs.

See also BARREL.

Rodewald, James. *American Spirit.* New York: Sterling Epicure, 2014.
Watman, Max. *Chasing the White Dog.* New York: Simon & Schuster, 2010.

Max Watman

White Lady is the name attributed to two quite different art-deco-era cocktails. The first was re-putedly created by Harry McElhone, a Scottish bartender who worked at London's Ciro's Club, and was included in the 1922 edition of his *Harry's ABC of Mixing Cocktails*. See MCELHONE, HENRY "HARRY". His White Lady was brandy, crème de menthe, and Cointreau, shaken and strained into a cocktail glass.

The other White Lady, with equal parts gin, lemon juice, and Cointreau, was closely associated with the bar at London's Savoy Hotel, although—according to a correspondent of the *New York Sun*'s Along the Wine Trail column—it may in fact have been invented at the bar at the popular Quaglino's restaurant in the same city. By early 1929 this version was popular enough to be mentioned in the same breath as the Manhattan and the Sidecar and other favorites. See FOUGNER, G. SELMER.

Harry Craddock provided the first recipe for this drink a year later in his *Savoy Cocktail Book*; it would go on to entirely supplant McElhone's version. In some modern variations of this classic sour, egg white is added to increase the creaminess and froth of the drink (the addition goes back to New York in the late 1930s). However, barmen such as the Savoy's head barman, Peter Dorelli, prefer to shake the drink to the proper consistency than to add more ingredients. See DORELLI, GIAMPIERO "PETER."

Recipe: Shake well with ice 45 ml London dry gin, 22 ml Cointreau, and 22 ml lemon juice (Quaglino's used lime). Add before shaking 15 ml egg white, if desired.

See also EGGS and SOUR.

Cocktails as Served at the Hotel Martinique, New York City. New York: American Hotels Corp, 1938.

Dorelli, Peter. Personal interview, September 12, 2013.

Fougner, G. Selmer. "Along the Wine Trail." *New York Sun*, September 13, 1934, 32.

McElhone, Harry. *Harry's ABC of Mixing Cocktails*. London: Dean & Son, 1922.

Anistatia R. Miller and Jared M. Brown

The **White Russian** is a cocktail in which coffee liqueur (usually Kahlúa) and heavy cream are shaken up with vodka and enough ice to make the whole suitably frosty. Its origins can be traced to the 1930s, when vodka was still something of a novelty to most non-Slavic drinkers. In that era, a number of cocktail curiosities came into being to put the spirit to use. The Russian Cocktail, as found in the 1930 *Savoy Cocktail Book*, combined vodka with gin and crème de cacao in equal parts. The arguably more agreeable (and feminine) sounding Barbara, from the same book, blended two parts of vodka with one part each crème de cacao and cream, to make what is essentially a vodka Alexander. See ALEXANDER and COCKTAIL. By 1936, Parisian master barman Frank Meier had stolen the "Russian" name and attached it to the Barbara. See MEIER, FRANK. Four years later, Crosby Gaige further tweaked that into the "Russian Bear," a name that the determinedly macho, postwar 1950s preferred to the feminine Barbara. See GAIGE, CROSBY. This is the likeliest progenitor of the White Russian.

The drink took its final form, and name, in 1965, when Southern Comfort, the American liqueur brand, used the drink to promote its short-lived Coffee Southern spinoff, replacing the crème de cacao with the new liqueur and renaming it the White Russian, to contrast with the then-popular Black Russian (vodka and Kahlúa, the coffee-flavored Mexican liqueur). The drink is closer to light beige than white, but who wants to order a Beige Russian? In any case, it didn't take long for Kahlúa to replace the Coffee Southern. The result was one of the most successful drinks of its era, and one that still enjoys wide popularity.

To some drinkers it is a guilty pleasure, but its milk-shakey charms are resisted by only the most hard-hearted. It is the sole reason many dive bars grudgingly keep a carton of cream (or, among the less committed, milk), in their lowboy refrigerators. As a motif in the Coen Brothers' cult film *The Big Lebowski*—in which the White Russian is the Dude's main source of sustenance—it has become something of a cult drink, whether consumed ironically or with the Dude's earnestness. See FILM, SPIRITS AND COCKTAILS IN.

Recipe: Shake 45 ml vodka, 22 ½ ml Kahlúa, and 22 ½ ml heavy cream well with cracked ice and strain into an Old-Fashioned glass. This can also be served as a layered drink, with the cream as a float.

See also KAHLÚA.

Gaige, Crosby. *Cocktail Guide and Ladies' Companion*. New York: Fireside, 1941.

"How to Make 46 Great Drinks the Way the Experts Do" (advertising supplement). *Philadelphia Inquirer*, March 7, 1965, 8.

Wondrich, David. "How to Make a White Russian." *Esquire*, March 8, 2015. http://www.esquire.com/food-drink/drinks/recipes/a3872/white-russian-drink-recipe/ (accessed March 15, 2021).

Rosie Schaap

The **Widow's Kiss**, a cocktail best known from George J. Kappeler's well regarded 1895 book, *Modern American Drinks*, is an improbable assemblage of apple brandy, yellow Chartreuse, and Bénédictine—unless it's Bénédictine, green Chartreuse, maraschino, and an egg (Harry Johnson), or yellow Chartreuse, Bénédictine, maraschino, and Parfait Amour, with egg white (William Schmidt), or rye whisky, sugar, and egg yolk, with seltzer (Jack Grohusko), or simply Bénédictine and cream, as the *New Orleans Times-Democrat* held in 1903. See JOHNSON, HARRY; SCHMIDT, WILLIAM; and GROHUSKO, JACOB ABRAHAM "JACK". In point of fact, the name seems to have been applied not specifically but generically, to any strong, sweet mixture, widows' kisses being semi-proverbial at the time as "hot stuff." They were generally intended as after-dinner drinks. The first person recorded using the name for a drink was Schmidt, in 1891. The most popular version, however, was Kappeler's.

Modern mixologists will occasionally deploy Kappeler's Widow's Kiss, since classic cocktails with an apple brandy base are few.

Recipe (Kappeler's): Shake with ice 45 ml apple brandy, 22 ml yellow Chartreuse, and 22 ml Bénédictine; strain into coupe. Note: while drinks without citrus are traditionally stirred, the high strength of everything in here means the drink responds best to shaking.

See also STINGER and KAPPELER, GEORGE J.

"He Could Not Be a Barmaid." *New York Sun*, October 20, 1891, 5.

Pitkin, Helen. "In Feminine Fields." *New Orleans Times-Democrat*, November 8, 1903, 32.

David Wondrich

The **Wild Turkey** distillery is dramatically sited on a cliff overlooking the Kentucky River, outside of Lawrenceburg, Kentucky. Distilling had been going on there in the early 1800s, but James P. Ripy (1844–1922) built his Old Hickory Spring Distillery there in 1891. After a reorganization, it would become the Ripy Brothers Distillery, the name it retained until 1949 (with a nineteen-year break for Prohibition), when it was sold to Robert and Alvin Gould, who would produce their J. T. S. Brown Bourbon there.

The Ripys sold whisky to wholesalers, including a New York company, Austin, Nichols. The story

is that the Wild Turkey brand grew out of a wild turkey hunt in 1940, hosted by Thomas McCarthy, the president of Austin, Nichols, who brought along several bottles of bourbon from company stocks. His friends asked for more of "that wild turkey whiskey," and in 1942, the company branded and bottled a whisky by that name.

Gould sold to Austin, Nichols in 1972, who renamed the facility the Boulevard Distillery. They in turn sold to Pernod-Ricard in 1980. Pernod-Ricard would sell to the Campari Group in 2009. Campari funded a new distillery and visitor center (and new warehouses); the new distillery came on-line in 2011. It is now known as the Wild Turkey Distillery.

Wild Turkey is now somewhat synonymous with master distiller Jimmy Russell (1934–), who began working at the distillery in 1954. Russell and his son Eddie are the current co-master distillers. The distillery's Russell's Reserve brand is a tribute to their work. It should be noted that Wild Turkey was an important brand during the early cocktail renaissance because it had a straight rye whisky at a respectable 50.5 percent ABV that was well aged, widely distributed, and made great Manhattan Cocktails.

The brand includes the Wild Turkey whiskies, the Russell's Reserve line, and American Honey and American Honey Sting flavored whiskies.

See also MANHATTAN COCKTAIL; PERNOD-RICARD; and WHISKY, RYE.

Zoeller, Chester. *Bourbon in Kentucky: A History of Distilleries in Kentucky*. Louisville: Butler, 2009.

Lew Bryson

Wiley, Harvey W. (1844–1930), was an American chemist who was largely responsible for the passage of the 1906 Pure Food and Drug Act and served as the first commissioner of the Food and Drug Administration. A Civil War veteran (he served in the Indiana Volunteers), Wiley earned both medical and chemistry degrees and taught Greek and Latin and then chemistry at various Indiana universities before accepting a position as chief chemist of the United States Department of Agriculture. There, he devoted his energies to studying and combating the adulteration of food and beverages. A convivial, charismatic type, Wiley was a whisky drinker and made sure that it, and other spirits, were included

Dr. H. W. Wiley in 1898. Getty Images.

in his studies. (Charles A. Crampton and Lucius M. Tolman, who conducted the pioneering 1908 Bureau of Internal Revenue study of whisky aging, were Wiley's protégés.) Wiley advocated a strict definition of whisky under the Pure Food and Drug Act, limiting the permissible ingredients to spirits and water, aged in oak, and forcing anything else to be called "imitation whisky." Although he lost that battle and, at least for whisky cut with unaged neutral spirit, "imitation" was replaced by the far softer "blended," modern "straight" whisky still follows his definition.

Crampton, C. A., and L. M. Tolman. "A Study of the Changes Taking Place in Whiskey Stored in Wood." *Journal of the American Chemical Society*, January 1908, 98–136.

Wiley, Harvey W. *Beverages and Their Adulteration*. Philadelphia: P. Blakiston's Son, 1919.

David Wondrich

Willard, Orsamus (1792–1876), universally known as "Willard of the City Hotel," was the most famous bartender in America and the second most famous one in New York City (after Cato Alexander). More importantly, he was a pioneer in mixing individual drinks to order using ice—and thus of the American school of mixology and the modern bar in general. See Alexander, Cato.

Willard was born in north-central Massachusetts and may have worked briefly as a schoolteacher. By the time he turned twenty-one, however, he had secured a position as office boy at the City Hotel in New York. At the time, this was the largest and fanciest hotel in America. Willard had natural gifts, however, that fitted him for higher office: he was ambidextrous and possessed a photographic memory. In 1816, he parlayed those gifts, along with his natural energy and dry New England wit, into a position as desk clerk and bartender (at the time, those were one and the same job: hotel guests checked in at the bar). One day that year, as he later told one of his customers, a "Virginia gentleman," himself a customer at the bar, taught Willard the "art" of making Mint Juleps with ice, a drink then almost exclusively southern. See Mint Julep. Willard, in turn, brought the drink to such a pitch of perfection that soon it was popular in New York, and when the gospel of the iced drink spread from that city throughout America and then the world, the julep spread with it.

At this point it is probably impossible to corroborate that story in detail, but we can say with certainty that by the late 1820s Willard and the bar of the City Hotel had a transatlantic reputation for Mint Juleps— indeed, as the *London Morning Post* observed in 1829, the "bar manager" of the City Hotel, "by his acknowledged skill in mixing mint julep, etc., is said to be a most valuable appendage to the concern." Such was his reputation in New York that one of his nicknames was "Napoleon of the Bar." Among the other drinks in Willard's repertoire we find mention of standards such as Whisky Punch, the Gin Sling, the Cock-Tail, and the Apple Toddy, and also of fancy drinks such as "Willard's Extra-Extra Peach Brandy Punch" (alas, no recipe survives for that). See Punch; Gin Sling; Cock-Tail; and Toddy.

By the mid-1830s, Willard was famous—"The name of this remarkable personage is familiar to every American, and to every foreigner who has visited the States," as one British traveler noted. Stories of his legendary feats of memory were common, such as the time a passing guest sailed to England,

The City Hotel, where Orsamus Willard spent so much of his life, in 1831. The bar was behind the windows at the *bottom right* of the building. Wondrich Collection.

remained there ten years, and returned to New York. When he walked into the bar, Willard welcomed him by name, recalled his old room number, and observed "how quickly ten years roll away." There was also no shortage of stories of his eccentricities—how he almost never left the hotel, how he would do anything possible to accommodate a guest's desires, how he would mix drinks with both hands while answering questions about the whereabouts of his guests and anything else under the sun.

In 1836, after twenty years behind the bar, Willard joined Chester Jennings, the hotel's manager, in retiring. As Jennings's partner, he had made a good deal of money and bought a large farm in Still River, Massachusetts, near his birthplace. (The farmhouse boasted number plates on every room door.) He also bought land in the West—almost 1,600 hectares (4,000 acres) of land in Michigan and Wisconsin—and took to raising prize cattle.

In 1843, however, the City Hotel having failed, he and Jennings were lured out of retirement to restore it to its past fortunes. Willard once again stood behind the bar, where he stayed for a further five years until he and Jennings called it quits again. From 1848 until his death at the age of eighty-four, little is heard from him. Indeed, the sporting fraternity in New York assumed that, like Jennings, who died in 1854, he was no more. Willard left a large estate, and his house in Still River still stands. He is buried nearby on a sunny hillside, surrounded by his wife and descendants. He was America's, and the world's, first celebrity bartender.

See also CITY HOTEL.

Alexander, J. E. *Transatlantic Sketches*. Philadelphia: Key & Biddle, 1833.
"City Hotel, N.Y." *Batavia (NY) Spirit of the Times*, January 24, 1843, 2.
Murray, Charles Augustus. *Travels in North America*. London: Richard Bentley, 1839.
"Notes on America." *London Morning Post*, January 20, 1829, 2.
Nourse, Henry S. *History of the Town of Harvard, Massachusetts, 1792–1893*. Harvard, MA: W. Hapgood, 1894.

David Wondrich

The **Willard Hotel** in Washington, DC, was once among the most celebrated hotels in America. Opened in 1847 by Henry Augustus Willard of Vermont (1822–1909) and completely rebuilt in 1853, the hotel played an important part of diplomacy before the Civil War. The current Willard (erected on the same site in 1901) has a plaque out front commemorating the Peace Congress that was held there in 1861 in an attempt to avert the Civil War. (Another historical legacy of the Willard is that

Julia Ward Howe penned "The Battle Hymn of the Republic" there.)

A large part of the hotel's popularity was due to its bar, which, although "located in a retired part of the building" (as an 1853 article noted), was a locus for some of the most famous figures in early American life. Among those who drank there were Mark Twain, Walt Whitman, and Abraham Lincoln. According to the hotel, it was also there where early American statesmen Henry Clay, of Kentucky, introduced Washington, DC, bartenders to the Mint Julep. While this is not true—in 1836, the Mint Julep was already one of the drinks for which the city's bars set a fixed price (12 ½ cents)—the julep was certainly the Willard bar's signature, and many a person first encountered it there.

Today the hotel, part of the Intercontinental chain, hosts the circular Round Robin Bar, located off the side of the lobby, where hang portraits of historical figures. The bar is still well known for its Mint Juleps and for its legendary barman, Jim Hewes (1953–), who has worked there since 1986. In 2010 Hewes was awarded the DC Craft Bartender Guild's Silver Shaker Award for Lifetime Achievement in Bartending, and he has often been tapped to discuss presidential drinks. The Round Robin Bar also houses an extensive scotch collection and a list of locally invented classic cocktails.

See JULEP.

"Established Prices of the Washington City Refectories." *Washington Globe*, October 2, 1836, 3.

"A Place in History: The Story of the Willard Intercontinental." n.d. http://washington.intercontinental.com/files/pdfs/WillardInterContinental-History%20Sheet-Oct2015.pdf (accessed April 4, 2016).

"Willard InterContinental's Jim Hewes receives DC Craft Bartender's Guild Lifetime Achievement Award." *FB Confidential Blog*, December 13, 2010. http://www.fbconfidential.com/2010/12/13/willard-intercontinental%E2%80%99s-jim-hewes-receives-dc-craft-bartender%E2%80%99s-guild-lifetime-achievement-award (accessed April 4, 2016).

"Willard's Hotel." *Washington Union*. November 23, 1853, 2.

Derek Brown

Wine & Spirit Education Trust (WSET) is

a London-based organization that offers education and training in a variety of wine, sake, and spirits topics for bartenders and sommeliers as well as the general public. WSET administers four levels of credentials, ranging from Level 1 Awards in wine or spirits, given after one-day classes, to the Level 4 Diploma, which requires extensive study in six different subject areas. As of 2015, classes are given in fifteen languages in seventy countries around the world, with more than sixty thousand candidates seeking qualifications annually (a Hong Kong office opened in 2016 and an American one in 2019).

The organization was founded in 1969 as an offshoot of the UK trade group the Wine & Spirit Association, and its board of trustees today includes representatives from that group as well as the Worshipful Company of Vintners, the Worshipful Company of Distillers, and the Institute of Masters of Wine.

Wine & Spirit Education Trust website. https://www.wsetglobal.com/ (accessed March 15, 2021).

Jason Horn

A **wineglass** is an unofficial but widely used British liquid measure of the eighteenth and nineteenth centuries, holding half a gill, or two ounces (roughly 60 ml). It is based on the small, conical glasses British drinkers used to consume the fortified wines that accounted for the bulk of British wine drinking. Their small size facilitated the drinking of multiple toasts, as was customary. As toasting fell out of fashion, wine glasses grew in size, and by the end of the nineteenth century one finds writers adapting older recipes often falling into confusion and treating a wine glass as four ounces (120 ml) or more. The wineglass as a bar measure was replaced by the jigger. See JIGGER.

Ward, Artemas. *The Grocers' Handbook and Directory for 1886*. Philadelphia: Philadelphia Grocer Publishing, 1886.

David Wondrich

wines, fortified, are a class of wines to which distilled spirits, such as a neutral brandy, have been added; they are almost always then aged in oak. In the EU, these are also known as "liqueur wines" (by law, ranging from 15 percent to 24 percent alcohol). Such wines are often sweet or flavored, often through the addition of sugar, grape must, aromatic herbs, and/or spices. Fortified wines, such as vermouth, sherry, port, Madeira, marsala, and mistelle, are often mass-produced and can range from the most prized wines in the world to low-end plonk. The fortification process has historically been used as a method to cover up lesser or even inferior wines, including those that are thin and neutral in character, such as ones made from the Italian trebbiano grape (French: ugni blanc) used in vermouths or the Spanish palomino, used in sherry. See SHERRY and VERMOUTH. Conversely, these grapes can be the ideal foils for such winemaking and wine maturation practices.

Fortification may occur at any one of three points during wine production: before, during, and after fermentation. The first practice is exemplified by Cognac's pineau des Charentes, in which high-proof spirit is added to unfermented ugni blanc must, thus killing any yeasts and stopping fermentation, but still making for a beverage of between 17 percent and 20 percent alcohol, with fruity, sweet flavors. The French refer to this category of fortified wine as mistelle; the EU recognizes this classification for all such beverages, though the primary examples are French, including also floc de Gascogne, pommeau (in Calvados), and ratafia champagne. See MISTELLE.

When fortification happens mid-fermentation, yeast is again inhibited from converting sugar to alcohol, though a portion of the sugar has already been transformed. Port is the most famous of such sweet fortified wines. The timing of the fortification will determine the sweetness of the beverage, and port producers use this sweetness to help differentiate their brands one from another. Most Madeira wines are made in this fashion, as well as most other historically significant fortified wines: moscato de Setubal from Portugal, marsala from Italy, Australian "stickies", muscat beaume de Venise, and the myriad muscat and grenache-based fortified wines of the Rhône valley.

The third method of fortification sees distilled spirit added to the product after the fermentation is complete, bolstering the ABV of the wine. Sherry is the most famous of these: most sherries begin as wines with about 11 percent alcohol and are fortified to between 15 and 20 percent, depending on the style and producer.

Distilled spirits used for fortification are most often neutral in character, run through a column still. See STILL, CONTINUOUS. In most cases, grape-based neutral spirits or brandies are used, but some categories of fortified wine (especially some aromatized wines such as vermouth) may include either grain-, cane-, or beet-based spirits. The spirit used in fortification is highly dependent on the category and region where the wine is made; sherries use a neutral spirit made from the airén grape, produced in bulk in La Mancha.

Fortification offers a means for extending the life of a wine; the most famous fortified wine categories were primarily created for export markets, especially the United Kingdom. Fortification provided greater stability and longevity, sufficient to survive a long ocean voyage. Thus some of the most notable wines between the sixteenth and eighteenth centuries were fortified and were consumed prominently in European colonies, especially colonial America. Madeira was used to toast the completion of the Declaration of Independence and was a favorite of the first US president, George Washington. When punch was first introduced into British drinking circles, in the late seventeenth century, it was consumed in opposition to the old-fashioned fortified wines, but by the mid-eighteenth century it was found on the same table as the punch bowl, and even in it. Fortified wines also became popular in American mixed drinks such as juleps and the Sherry Cobbler in the nineteenth century. See JULEP; PUNCH; SANGAREE; and SHERRY COBBLER.

Fortified wines became a prominent mixer in cocktails in the latter half of the nineteenth century, especially vermouth, which is a major component of cocktails such as the Manhattan and Martini. See MANHATTAN COCKTAIL and MARTINI. (Vermouth is not only an aromatized wine, but it is also fortified, and barrel aged as well.) See VERMOUTH. But other fortified wines such as port, sherry, and Madeira can be found in early cocktail manuals and are increasingly being rediscovered in new cocktails as well.

Dominé, André. *The Ultimate Guide to Spirits and Cocktails*. Königswinter, Germany: H. F. Ullmann, 2008.

OIV Regulations

Sherry Wines website. https://www.sherry.wine (accessed April 9, 2021).

Wondrich, David. *Punch!*. New York: Perigee, 2010.

Derek Brown

wood/barrel finishing • 793

wines, sparkling and still, have a long and varied cocktail history. While not as frequently used as fortified or, especially, aromatized wines, still wines from Bordeaux and burgundies, to Rieslings and Chablis, to Ohio catawbas and California cabernets have been featured in a number of popular drinks. These "light wines"—as they were often called to distinguish them from the heavier, stronger, fortified wines—were used in some eighteenth-century punches but saw their greatest use in the early Victorian era, when wine-based cups such as the Claret Cup and Moselle Cup were the height of fashion in British society and, to a lesser degree, in America. Americans, however, were as likely to incorporate the wine into a Mint Julep or float it on top of a Whisky Sour, as in the famous New York Sour. See JULEP and NEW YORK SOUR.

There is a much richer history of including sparkling wine in cocktails. In fact, many common drinks can be topped with, and arguably improved by, a splash of bubbly. This works particularly well with punches such as Regent's Punch and Chatham Artillery Punch and cocktails from the sour family, including the Margarita and Daiquiri. See CHATHAM ARTILLERY PUNCH; REGENT'S PUNCH; and SOUR. Perhaps the most popular use is in the French 75, which can be made with a base of either gin or cognac, lemon juice, and sparkling wine, although in recent years the prosecco-topped Aperol Spritz may have edged it out. See APEROL SPRITZ and FRENCH 75.

You can also often successfully substitute sparkling wine in drinks that call for sparkling water or beer, like using bubbly in place of the club soda in a Mojito (this yields Audrey Saunders's modern classic the Old Cuban). See MOJITO and SAUNDERS, AUDREY. The historic Italian cocktail the Negroni Sbagliato, or "mistaken Negroni" (invented at Milan's Bar Basso in 1972) is simply a Negroni but made with prosecco replacing the gin and carbonated water. See NEGRONI.

Traditionally, the addition of champagne or sparkling wine to a concoction is noted by the addition of the term "imperial" to its name, just as making it with wine instead of water or beer made it "royal." See ROYAL.

There are also a handful of other modern and historic drinks that call for wine, including the Black Velvet (Guinness stout beer and sparkling wine) and the St-Germain Cocktail (St-Germain Elderflower Liqueur and still or sparkling wine). See BLACK VELVET and COOPER SPIRITS.

Noah Rothbaum

wood/barrel finishing. The technique of "finishing" (otherwise known as "secondary maturation") involves taking a mature spirit, which has spent years maturing in one type of cask, and transferring it into another, different cask type for a short period of time. A typical example would be a scotch single malt whisky, which has been matured in "refill" (used) American oak casks being given a few months "finishing" in ex-sherry casks.

The initial maturation tends to take place in refill casks, which give lower impact of oak-derived flavor compounds. In this environment the normal mechanism of removal of aggressive elements, addition of oak-derived flavors, and prolonged interaction between those elements, oxygen, and the spirit have all taken place. See MATURATION.

The finishing cask, on the other hand, is very active. The short period of time the spirit spends in this new environment means there is no time for slow interaction to take place. Rather, the most significant impact is additive. The spirit absorbs flavor compounds created when the cask's original liquid had interacted with the oak. Finishing is not simply a matter of adding, for example, sherry flavor to a spirit. The brief resting in the new cask adds another layer of flavor born from the interaction between the cask's former spirit, its current one, and the cask itself.

In 1987 Glenmorangie's 1963 Vintage was the first whisky to declare itself to have been "finished." In 1993 Balvenie launched Double Wood, the first finished brand, and in 1996 Glenmorangie released the first wood-finished range comprising sherry, port, and Madeira finishes.

Finishing is now a widespread practice in scotch, Irish, and Canadian whisky. Some rum producers have also started to experiment with the technique. The big United States bourbon and rye distillers have been rather more cautious but have made the occasional experiment, such as Jim Beam's pioneering Distiller's Masterpiece bottling, created in 1999 by master distiller Booker Noe (1929–2004), which finished a sixteen-year-old bourbon in cognac casks.

A wide range of types of finishing casks are used, with sherry (of different types), port, Madeira, and marsala the most commonly seen. Wine casks (mostly red or sweet white wine) are also popular with producers, and some whiskies, such as the Jameson's Caskmates range, are even finished in beer or ale casks. The Scotch Whisky Association has created a list of permitted cask types, all of which are deemed to have historical precedent as being used for maturing scotch. Calvados casks, for example, are banned.

See also WHISKY, IRISH; and WHISKY, SCOTCH.

Bryson, Lew. *Whiskey Master Class*. Beverly, MA: Harvard Common, 2020.

Dave Broom

wood chemistry. There are five considerations when aging spirits in a wooden barrel: color, wood extraction, absorption, oxidation, and diffusion. Each plays an important role in the overall wood chemistry within a cask.

When distilled spirits are produced, whether it is in a column or a pot still, whether they are heavy or light in flavor, the liquid is as clear as water. Subsequent storage in barrels provides color intensity ranging from pale yellow to straw to gold to amber or even mahogany. Factors that affect a barrel's influence on a spirit's color include the number of times the barrel has been used previously and for how long, what the barrel was previously filled with, the size of the barrel, warehouse temperatures, and the duration of time the spirit will spend in the barrel. But wood is an organic product, and aging is complex; it is challenging to maintain a consistent color for spirits, and the same spirit placed in the same warehouse for the same amount of time in two different first-refill bourbon barrels from the same source can come out two different shades. Depending on spirit category, blenders can add caramel coloring to achieve a consistent color. See CARAMEL.

Wood extracts are byproducts of the burning process of the inside of a barrel. The charring or toasting can be controlled either by the intensity or by the length of time the staves are exposed to a flame. By controlling the flame, one can control the degree to which chemical bonds between the cellulose, hemicellulose, and lignin are degraded into smaller units, which will then be extracted into the spirit or wine. See LIGNIN. Depending on the cooper and the requirements of the customer, the inside of the cask is exposed to intense heat for some fifteen to sixty seconds. In general, the extracts provide the vanilla, smoky, caramel, and toffee notes found in the spirit.

The burning of wood's surface provides a layer of activated carbon (char) that is important for absorptive or subtractive reactions, which remove undesirable sulfur components from the spirit. In whisky, for example, sulfur either comes from the malting process, the raw grain, or is a byproduct of yeast metabolism. Any of these can give garlicy, burnt-match, rotten-egg, or vegetable notes to the spirit. Those can also be removed by a copper interaction in the still, but if there is not enough copper contact time (as with some continuous stills), then the alternative is to use barrels with a thick char layer to absorb any remaining sulfur in the spirit. Charring can be a double-edged sword, however: a thicker layer of char will remove more sulfur, but at the same time it reduces the amount of wood extracts. A 2-mm burn produces more vanilla, caramel, and toffee notes than a 4-mm burn.

Casks are porous and expand and contract due to heating and cooling cycles in a warehouse. This allows movement of oxygen into casks, which causes oxidative reactions. For example, coniferyl and sinapyl alcohols are extracted into the spirit from a barrel and are oxidized into their corresponding aldehydes—coniferaldehyde and sinapaldehyde. The tannins from a barrel also react with oxygen, which releases hydrogen peroxide and converts the tannin to a quinone complex (quinones are brownish in color and also contribute to the overall color of aged spirits). See TANNIN. In a further reaction, that hydrogen peroxide oxidizes ethanol to form acetaldehyde, which has a green, unripe, and raw aroma. Acetaldehyde further oxidizes into acetic acid and then ultimately ethyl acetate, which gives a green apple or pear drop flavor to the spirit. See ACETALDEHYDE. Oxidative reactions are temperature dependent. In warmer climates, such compounds form more quickly than they do in cooler climates.

Barrel-finishing spirits—resting an already aged spirit for a brief period in a barrel that has previously held another spirit or a wine or beer—can create interesting brand expressions and is a popular trend. Quite simply, wood acts like a sponge and absorbs spirits into its pores. By nature, flavor molecules move from an area of higher concentration to a lower concentration until equilibrium is achieved—this is called diffusion. So flavors in a barrel from a previous fill will diffuse into the next spirit that is to be aged.

See also BARREL and MATURATION.

Cadahia, E., S. L. Varea, B. Muñoz, M. Fernandez de Simon, and C. Garcia-Vallejo. "Evolution of Ellagitannins in Spanish, French, and American Oak Woods During Natural Seasoning and Toasting." *Journal of Agriculture and Food Chemistry* 49 (2001): 3677–3684.

Ingledew, W. M. "Alcohol Production by *Saccharomyces cerevisiae*: A Yeast Primer." In *The Alcohol Textbook: A Reference for the Beverage, Fuel and Industrial Alcohol Industries*, 3rd ed., ed. K. Jaques, T. P. Lyons, and D. R. Kelsall, 49–88. Nottingham, UK: Nottingham University Press, 1999.

Livermore, D. "Quantification of Oak Wood Extractives Via Gas Chromatography – Mass Spectrometry and Subsequent Calibration of Near Infrared Reflectance to Predict the Canadian Whisky Ageing Process." PhD diss., Heriot Watt University, 2012.

Pastor-Villegas, J., J. M. Meneses Rodriguez, J. F. Pastor-Valle, and M. Garcia Garcia. "Changes in Commercial Wood Charcoals by Thermal Treatments." *Journal of Analytical and Applied Pyrolysis* 80 (2007): 507–514.

Piggott, J. R, K. Y. Lee, and A. Paterson. "Origins of Flavour in Whiskies and a Revised Flavour Wheel: A Review." *Journal of the Institute of Brewing* 107 (2001): 287–313.

Don Livermore

Woo Woo, like the Fuzzy Navel and Sex on the Beach, is one of several peachy drinks that became popular in the mid-1980s following the successful launch of peach schnapps in the American market from companies such as DeKuyper and National Distillers. Its precise origin is unclear, although there is some evidence that points to the singles bars of New York City's Upper East Side. Although the Woo Woo, a combination of vodka, cranberry juice, and peach schnapps, may be served as a shooter, it's more commonly encountered over ice in a highball glass. In some university bars, it is occasionally available by the pitcher.

Recipe: To an ice-filled highball glass, add 60 ml vodka, 15 ml peach schnapps, and 75 ml cranberry juice. Stir.

See also DE KUYPER; HIGHBALL; SEX ON THE BEACH; SCHNAPPS; SHOOTER.

Abou-Ganim, Tony. "The Evolution of Mixology." In *The Modern Mixologist: Contemporary Classic Cocktails*, 21–33. Evanston, IL: Agate, 2010.

Goldberg, Howard G. "Everyone Is Making a Schnapps." *Scranton Times-Tribune*, October 21, 1986, 16.

"Schnapps, the Cordial Spirit." *New York Times*, October 27, 1985.

David Mahoney

Worcestershire sauce is a pungent bottled vinegar-based condiment flavored with anchovies, tamarinds, and spices that has seen occasional use in mixing drinks since the late nineteenth century; today, it is principally found in the Bloody Mary and its derivatives. Worcestershire sauce was invented in the English city of Worcester by John Wheely Lea and William Perrins, a pair of local apothecaries, and introduced to market in 1838. It first found its way behind the bar in the 1880s, as an added touch in the Prairie Oyster, a raw egg seasoned with salt, pepper, and vinegar and drunk from a cocktail glass, and then in the Oyster Cocktail, which was roughly the same but with a real oyster. From there the condiment was rapidly adopted as a hangover cure, drunk straight (or, as the composer Victor Herbert took it, sprinkled in champagne) and then, in the 1920s, found its home in the Tomato Juice Cocktail, which with the addition of gin or vodka became the aforementioned Bloody Mary.

See also BLOODY MARY and BULL SHOT.

Paul, Charlie. *American and Other Drinks*. London: T. F. Shaw, 1884.

Sobol, Louis. "New York Cavalcade: The Immortal Victor Herbert." *San Francisco Examiner*, December 7, 1939, 15.

David Wondrich

worm is a time-honored tool for condensing the alcohol vapor coming off a still. It consists of a coiled copper tube bathed in a tub of cold water.

Its invention is attributed to the Italian physician-alchemist Taddeo Alderotti in the thirteenth century. See also CONDENSER.

Wormwood is the common name for plants in the *Artemisia* genus, comprising between three hundred to four hundred species, many of which contain "wormwood" as part of their English common name. They include familiar species such as the western sagebrush, *Artemisia tridentata*, and many similar scrubby, shrub-like, wasteland-inhabiting plants.

The most commonly used species in beverage alcohol are *Artemisia absinthium* (grand wormwood) and *Artemisia pontica* (petite wormwood), best known as flavoring botanicals in the aperitif spirit absinthe and the aromatic fortified wine vermouth. Also common are *Artemisia genipi* (black genipi) and *Artemisia glacialis* (alpine wormwood), used in the traditional alpine liqueur génépy.

Artemisia absinthium, from which the plant takes its common French name, *grande absinthe*, has been used in medicine and beverages since the time of the ancient Egyptians, generally as an appetite stimulant, gastric tonic, and vermifuge. Its effectiveness in expelling intestinal parasites is the likely origin of the name wormwood. When macerated, it is extremely bitter. When distilled, as in absinthe, the bitter compounds remain behind and the sweeter alpine herbal flavors and aromas dominate.

Culpeper, Nicholas. *Pharmacopœia Londinensis, or The London Dispensary*. London: 1651.

Gwydion Stone

wort is a term typically used in the production of scotch whisky to describe the sugar-rich liquid drawn off the grain after mashing. See also MASHING and WHISKY, SCOTCH.

Wuliangye is a Chinese distillery best known as the inventor of the mixed-grain variety of strong-aroma-style baijiu. The distillery is located in Sichuan Province's Yibin, a strategic port city along the Yangtze River that has been a winemaking center for more than a thousand years. During the Song dynasty (960–1269), the local Yao clan began brewing alcohols from a complex blend of grains, a secret recipe that was passed down through the generations. Strong-aroma baijiu appeared in Yibin during the Ming dynasty (1366–1644), and Wuliangye still operates sixteen fermentation pits dating from the era. In the early twentieth century, Deng Zijun, proprietor of Yibin's Lichuanyong Distillery, used the multigrain recipe to develop Wuliangye's signature baijiu mash, which contains sorghum, long-grain rice, sticky rice, wheat, and maize. The Chinese government established the modern company in 1957 from eight local distilleries as the Yibin Distillery, later renamed Wuliangye ("Five-grain liquid").

Wuliangye is the prototypical Chinese state-run enterprise, and the Chinese Communist Party does nothing on a small scale. Its base of operations in Yibin is a veritable fortress that spans ten square kilometers. Staffed by some forty thousand workers, it has a stated annual output of 400 million liters. In the 1990s, Wuliangye became the world's leading baijiu distillery by sales volume, with successful brands at every price point. It became a privately listed company in 1998 and has since acquired a handful of smaller distilleries such as Jinliufu and Liuyanghe. In 2014 Wuliangye entered an agreement with Brown-Forman, the Louisville-based owner of Jack Daniels, to develop new nontraditional products for the emerging Chinese bar scene.

See also STRONG-AROMA-STYLE BAIJIU.

Wang Guochun 王国春, ed. *Bai nian zhui qiu bai nian fen jin* 百年追求百年奋进. Chengdu: Wuliangye 五粮液, 2009.

Wang Kai 王恺, ed. *San lian sheng huo zhou kan* 三联生活周刊 675, March 26, 2012.

Wang Zhuoqiong. "Brown-Forman, Wuliangye Sign Cooperation Deal." *China Daily USA*, December 16, 2014.

Derek Sandhaus

X

xiao ("small") qu is a rice-based culture of wild yeasts and other microorganisms, formed into cakes and used in traditional Chinese wine and spirit fermentation. See QU.

XO, an abbreviation for "extra old," is a designation used on the labels of cognac and other French brandies to indicate a very mature bottling. It was first used by Hennessy in 1870. The current official requirement for XO cognac, Armagnac, and calvados is that its youngest component must be aged in oak casks for no less than ten years. In practice, many XO brandies incorporate eaux-de-vie aged significantly longer. As with VS and VSOP brandies, XO-marked brandies produced in the United States are not restricted to minimum age requirements. See VSOP and VS.

See also COGNAC and HENNESSY.

Bureau National Interprofessionnel du Cognac. *L'encyclopédie du Cognac.* https://www.pediacognac.com (accessed March 15, 2021).

David Mahoney

yeast, the single-celled fungus that causes fermentation, has been the constant companion of humans since before we even knew that it existed. It's no wonder that early words describing fermentation are often related to the phrase "godlike." In the 1718 guide to spirits production "The Practical Distiller," fermentation was described as follows:

> "The exaltation of parts is most conspicuously discerned in those things destined to human use, in as much as by fermentation they obtain a greater vigor and perfection. . . . Amongst the aliments applicable to human use, bread, beer, wine, cyder etc. deserve the first rank: for whatsoever they have of virtue or power, may be most justly ascribed to fermentation."

All virtue to fermentation—and hence to yeast.

Yeasts are truly exceptional creatures. They are approximately ten times larger than bacteria, but still many times smaller than a single human hair. There are hundreds of different species of yeast and countless strains within each species, each specialized to thrive in a particular microscopic environment. Yeasts are ubiquitous in the natural world. They are present on your skin, your plants, your pets, and even in the air, resting on dust motes or bits of pollen.

Some spirits incorporate wild yeasts in their production processes, especially in the tropics, where in particular *Schizosaccharomyces pombe*, or pombe yeast, often plays a part in fermentation for rums and arracks. See BAIJIU; FERMENTATION; and KWEICHOW MOUTAI. Brewers and distillers, however, most commonly rely on one particular species of cultivated yeast, *Saccharomyces cerevisiae*, which has evolved to thrive in the acidic, oxygen-limited environment of beverage fermentations. In order for this yeast to be readily available to commercial brewers and distillers, the strain must be carefully separated out and precisely reared to maintain a healthy, consistent population free of contamination—no simple task when dealing with a creature characterized by a rapid life cycle, fluid

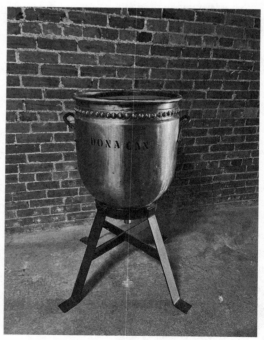

A "dona can" aka "dona tub," in which yeast is propagated before being added to an American whisky mash. Courtesy of Michter's.

genetic exchanges, and high sensitivity to environmental changes and possessing not one but two possible methods of reproduction.

Why go to all of this trouble? Brewers and distillers need yeast for two very important tasks in beverage production. The first is fermentation, the process by which yeast metabolize simple sugars such as glucose, fructose, sucrose, and maltose and in turn excrete carbon dioxide and the hallmark of social beverages—ethanol. Yeast will take, for instance, one fructose molecule $(C_6H_{12}O_6)$ and break it down into two ethanol molecules (C_2H_5OH) and two carbon dioxide molecules (CO_2). Other, more complex sugars go through intermediate stages but end up in the same place.

The other task assigned to these industrious creatures by hopeful brewers and distillers is to improve the flavor of their fermented beverage through the production of a coterie of desirable compounds, such as esters (fruity, floral, spicy), and the destruction of undesirable compounds, such as diacetyl (old buttered popcorn) and acetaldehyde (sour, green apple, solvent). See ESTERS.

The role of fermentation in creating the character and flavor of a spirit is often underappreciated. It is more complex than distinctions in ingredients (e.g., different mash bills) and less romantic than flowing water springs and warehouses full of maturing casks. To appreciate the impact of fermentation, consider the difference between ale and lager beer. Both generally begin with the same raw ingredient—malted barley—but are fermented with different yeasts under different conditions to produce vastly different flavor profiles in the finished beer.

The same principle holds true for distilled spirits, and in many ways the effect is amplified through the selection and concentration of flavors that occur during the distillation process. For unaged spirits, the fermentation phase is the producer's last opportunity to create new flavors. The distillation phase can only select and separate compounds that already exist; it cannot generate new ones. The amount of flavor that can be generated reaches its apex in strong-aroma- and sauce-aroma-style baijius, where repeated fermentations of the same, bland grains produce a uniquely broad palette of strongly asserted aromas and flavors, from the crispest, fruitiest green apple to the most concentrated wild-mushroom broth, all in the same spirit.

The factors that influence the outcomes of fermentation are numerous. The selection of the yeast strain; the quality and availability of nutrients in the mash; environmental conditions such as temperature, pH, oxygen level, and osmotic pressure; the initial health and size of the yeast population; the presence of competitors; alcohol levels—all will impact the yeast's activities and therefore impact the final character of the fermented product. In order to produce a consistent product, the distiller must work diligently to control each of these factors throughout the fermentation process. Natural changes in the raw materials (quality of growing season, storage conditions, etc.) and in the distillery environment (seasonal changes, cleanliness, etc.) introduce further potential for variability in the fermentation.

Examples of Fermentation Products

ethyl acetate, amyl acetate	fruity, solvent, pear
higher alcohols or fusel alcohols (propanol, butanol, amyl alcohol, glycerol, phenylethanol)	musty, oily, floral
sulfur compounds	rotten egg, vegetal
organic acids (acetic, caproic, caprylic, lactic, pyruvic, succinic, butyric)	rancid, sweat, barnyard, cheesy, sour
phenols	spicy, pepper, clove, smoke, medicinal
esters	citrus, floral, fruit, spice

In facing the challenge of controlling fermentation, distillers have both advantages and disadvantages over their brewer cousins. For distillers, the beer is not the final product. Distillers have further production phases (distillation and maturation) that will present opportunities to modify the flavor and character of their final product. Many undesirable compounds that a brewer would be stuck with can be effectively removed or diminished during distillation, while many desirable compounds can be selected, concentrated, and emphasized. This is a distinct advantage for removal of undesirable compounds, but it creates also a new set of questions. Which fermentation products should be removed, and which should be kept?

Fermentation compounds that have undesirable characteristics on their own may change or react during maturation to produce rich and desirable flavor elements. Esterification, the process by which an alcohol and an acid combine to form an ester, can produce a wealth of desirable spirit characteristics such as clove, honey, geranium, rose, pineapple, pear, cherry, orange, cinnamon, and spearmint, but it cannot occur unless the raw ingredients (the alcohol and the acid) are present and the maturation conditions are conducive for that type of reactions. So a distillate that initially smells of musty basements and sour cheese may, over time, begin to smell of tropical fruit and spice cake. Or it may end up smelling like sour cheese that has been sitting for a long time in a musty basement.

The rich, subtle complexity of fermentation is so chaotic and multifarious that it can feel magical to the most seasoned distillers. Even now the nature of yeast eludes artificial reproduction and the achievement of soulless perfection. Of course, that is also what makes these beverages so seductive. This is both the challenge and art of spirits production, which requires a careful, purposeful, and thoughtful producer to produce a truly exceptional elixir.

See also ETHANOL and QU.

Russell, Inge. *Whisky Technology, Production and Marketing*. Amsterdam: Academic Press, 2003.

Walker, Graeme M. *Yeast Physiology and Biotechnology*. Chichester, UK: J. Wiley & Sons, 1998.

White, Chris, and Jamil Zainasheff. *Yeast: The Practical Guide to Beer Fermentation*. Boulder, CO: Brewers Publications, 2010.

Nicole Austin

zest, citrus—the aromatic, oil-rich outer skin of the citrus fruit—is a common flavoring for spirits and mixed drinks. Today, lemon and sweet or Valencia orange zests are the most commonly used in mixed drinks; bitter or Seville orange zests, formerly popular in punch, are now used mostly in distillation, as are citron zests. See CURAÇAO. Lime and grapefruit zest are also occasionally used in both.

The use of citrus zest in distillation dates back at least to the early 1600s, when dried lemon, orange, and citron peels (consisting of the zest plus the bitter white pith that lies beneath) appear in some distiller's manuals. By the end of that century, the fresh peel of lemons and bitter oranges was being used as an ingredient in making punch and other mixed drinks, as in the recipe for "Limonado" (a punch in all but name) found in Hannah Wooley's 1670 *Queene-Like Closet*, which adds to sack wine, brandy, sugar, and water, "the juice of two limons and some of the pill." By the 1730s, the thinly cut, largely pith-free zests were an integral part of punch making. James Ashley's London Punch House, the most famous of its kind, had a ceiling decorated with the dried orange zests rescued from finished bowls of punch.

By the nineteenth century, the state of the art in punch making called for extracting the oil from the zest with sugar, thus forming an "oleo-saccharum," although as punch faded from daily use, so did this technique. See OLEO-SACCHARUM. At the same time, zest began to find a new role as a finishing touch on a cocktail. This practice dates back to at least 1850, when a New Orleans newspaper mentions "an idea of lemon peel" as one of the components of the drink. At first, it seems to have just been floated on top. Only in the 1870s do we find mention of "twisting" the peel to express a fragrant sheen of oil onto the surface of the drink (by 1889, this had led to the swatch of lemon or orange peel used being labeled a "twist"). See COCKTAIL.

Although recent years have seen the return of oleo-saccharum, the twist is still the most common use of zest in mixed drinks; lemon and orange are still the most popular by far, although grapefruit is occasionally used and sometimes even lime zest, despite—or perhaps because of—its bitterness. Primarily deployed with spirit-forward cocktails such as Old-Fashioneds, Martinis, and Negronis, the twist contributes a brightness of aroma and some sweet citrus notes that, while perhaps not obvious in the taste of the drink, nonetheless contribute to the full flavor experience and help to change the drink's whole profile. Some bartenders like to express the oils through the flame of a lit match, which results in an impressive little ball of fire. See FLAME OF LOVE MARTINI and FLAMING A TWIST.

Though the zest's contribution to a drink's flavor isn't debated, both when it should be used and what should happen to it once its oil has been expressed have, beginning in the nineteenth century. In his foundational 1862 bartender's guide, Jerry Thomas falls on both sides of both debates. In some drinks, he suggests squeezing the peel into the drink before stirring and in others using it as a garnish to the final product. Likewise, some recipes call for the used peel to be dropped into the drink, but others call for it to be discarded. The debate continues today, but it's mainly a matter of personal preference, with Thomas's authority cited on both sides.

To make a twist, cut a rectangular swatch of citrus zest with a minimal amount of pith attached

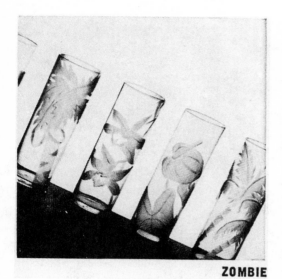

ZOMBIE

All drink fads end in glassware. Fancy Zombie glasses, 1940. Wondrich Collection.

(a vegetable peeler makes this easy). You should be able to see the pores in the cut side of the peel. With the colorful side facing the drink, twist the peel to release the oils. You should be able to see a thin sheen of oil on its surface.

Cademan, Thomas, and Theodore de Mayerne. *The Distiller of London*. London: 1639.

H. L. W. *The American Bar-Tender*. New York: Hurst, 1874.

"Summer Drinks." *Louisville Courier-Journal*, July 21, 1889, 21.

"What to Eat and What to Drink." *New Orleans Weekly Delta*, August 5, 1850, 8.

Wondrich, David. *Imbibe!*, 2nd ed. New York: Perigee, 2015.

Wooley, Hannah, *The Queene-Like Closet*. London: 1670.

Clair McLafferty and David Wondrich

The **Zombie** was created in 1934 by Donn Beach at Don the Beachcomber's in Hollywood, California; this powerful punch was the first famous "tiki drink." Even though the recipe was a trade secret and served only at his bar, it became a coast-to-coast media sensation when radio comedians, newspaper columnists, and editorial cartoonists made its potency the subject of innumerable gags and gossip items. "Beware, in your Hollywood visit," as one columnist wrote, "never to have a Zombie . . . for you will never be the same."

It didn't hurt the buzz that Donn Beach's bar was a hangout for movie stars, or that Beach refused to serve more than two Zombies per customer. Neither did it hurt that his "mender of broken dreams" was addictively rich, complex, and balanced. Inevitably, the Zombie's glowing press coverage prompted rival bars to try reverse-engineering the drink, none more successfully or persistently than New York nightclub impresario Monte Proser (1904–1973), who unapologetically built an empire on it in the early 1940s. Hundreds of these bogus Zombie recipes were published over the past eighty years, but none even comes close to Beach's. The original secret formula, which Beach took to his grave, was discovered by this writer in 2006 in the notebook of former Beachcomber's headwaiter Richard Santiago.

Recipe: Combine 22.5 ml lime juice, 15 ml falernum, 45 ml each gold Puerto Rican rum and gold Jamaican rum, 30 ml 151-proof Lemon Hart demerara rum, 1 tsp grenadine, 6 drops Pernod, a dash of Angostura bitters, and 15 ml "Don's Mix" (two parts grapefruit juice to one part cinnamon syrup) in an electric blender with 3/4 cup crushed ice, then blend at high speed for no more than five seconds. Pour into a tall glass, add ice to fill, and garnish with a mint sprig.

See also BEACH, DONN; PUNCH; and TIKI.

Berry, Jeff. *Beachbum Berry's Sippin' Safari*. San Jose, CA: Club Tiki, 2007.

Sampas, Charles G. "N.Y.—Hollywood." *Lowell (MA) Sun*, August 27, 1938.

Jeff Berry

The **Zoom** is an indulgent cocktail that combines honey and cream with a spirit, usually that most dependable of post-dinner tipples, cognac. The result is a drink that is as sweetly decadent as it is silky smooth. As such, it is fitting that it was either invented or popularized by Frank Meier at the Ritz Hotel in Paris (the original version used Bacardi rum). See MEIER, FRANK. As arguably "the last cocktail in the alphabet," no A-to-Z mixing guide would be complete without a mention of the Zoom. In 1980s London, this post-dinner champion filled that sweet and narrow void between drink and dessert with a river of dairy and alcohol. In any case, it is a welcome addition to the creamy cocktail sector—much more concentrated than a Brandy Alexander, lighter than eggnog, and a hell of a lot more fun than pudding.

Recipe (Brandy Zoom): Shake well with ice 60 ml cognac (or rum, bourbon whisky, or gin), 15 ml heavy cream, and 15 ml honey syrup. Strain into a chilled cocktail glass. Optional: garnish with a light dusting of cocoa powder.

See also BRANDY ALEXANDER; EGGNOG; and COGNAC.

Fougner, G. Selmer. "Along the Wine Trail." *New York Sun*, March 13, 1940, 19.

Meier, Frank. *The Artistry of Mixing Drinks.* Paris: Fryam, 1936.

Tristan Stephenson

Żubrówka is a brand of flavored rye vodka produced since 1928 by Polmos Białystok, the only distiller authorized to make this deeply traditional Polish spirit, which was already well documented by the sixteenth century. See VODKA. The name is derived from *żubr* ("bison") in recognition of the last several hundred European bison that roam Puszcza Białowieska, a primeval forest and protected UNESCO World Heritage site in northeast Poland. Żubrówka is infused with wild-harvested bison grass (*Hierochloe odorata*), said to be favored by the bison, and one of several sweet-scented grasses traditionally used across northern Europe in confectionery, perfumes, incense, folk medicines, and various other beverages. Like tonka beans and sweet woodruff (*Waldmeister*), the comparatively rare Polish bison grass contains coumarin, an aromatic benzopyrone with overtones of vanilla and newly-mown hay, found in other plants and spices such as green tea, carrots, and cassia. Until the United States Food and Drug Administration enacted a controversial ban on coumarin as a food additive in 1954, coumarin was generally recognized as safe. Because of coumarin's supposed toxicity and blood-thinning properties, however, Polmos Białystok developed a coumarin-free version of the original spirit for the American market. Coumarin-containing grasses generally must be dried to release their aroma; each bottle of Żubrówka, whether traditional or American version, is graced with a single blade of dried bison grass. In its native Poland, this flavored vodka is often mixed with approximately two parts apple juice for a drink known as *szarlotka* (literally "Charlotte" but commonly rendered "apple pie").

See also BOTANICAL and FLAVORINGS.

Bączek, K., M. Angielczyk, K. Mosakowska, O. Kosakowska, and Z. Węglarz. "Setting of Southern Sweet-Grass Plantation with Stem Cuttings Obtained by Division of Maternal Plants." *Herba Polonica* 60, no. 4 (2015): 9–21.

Krasińska, M., and Z. A. Krasiński. "Food and Use of the Environment." In *European Bison*, 157–179. Berlin: Springer, 2013.

Michaels, D. "Name Your Poison: How a Banned Polish Vodka Buffaloed Its Way into the U.S." *Wall Street Journal*, January 18, 2011.

Zubrowka: Polish Vodka and Cultural Geographic Indicators. http://mandalaprojects.com/giant-project/polish-vodka.htm (accessed April 9, 2021).

Matthew Rowley

THE WIDE WORLD OF SPIRITS

David Wondrich and Doug Frost

The world of distilled spirits is quite complex, with a great variety of base materials and several styles of distillation and post-distillation treatment. This attempted taxonomy is intended to be neither comprehensive nor exhaustive, but it should at least cover the main bases, suggest the variety of spirits that exist or have existed, and provide a framework for further exploration. Where the spirit has a headword in this book, it is printed in SMALL CAPITALS.

The main organizing division of this taxonomy is by base material. According to this, spirits can be roughly divided by whether they are

A. Based on materials that contain fermentable sugars ("wines")
B. Based on materials that contain starches, which must first be converted to sugars before fermentation ("beers")
C. Based on a mixture of A and B, or
D. Prepared in such a way that the base material is irrelevant

Beyond this, spirits are further subdivided into **rich spirits**, distilled to under 85 percent alcohol (as is typical of spirits made in pot stills), and **clean spirits**, distilled to over 85 percent alcohol (as is typical with continuous-still spirits). Finally, these can be even further divided by their maturation, into **unaged, wood-aged** (stored in wooden barrels or vats), and **oxidated** (aged in clay or other porous, non-extractive materials) spirits.

These subdivisions are marked with letters following the spirit's name as if they were so many postgraduate degrees: **R** or **C** for rich or clean; **U, W,** or **O,** for unaged, wood-aged, or oxidated. Each spirit will have at least two letters: one for distillation,

followed by a dash, and one for maturation. If the spirit is distilled or matured in more than one way, additional letters are added. Where more than one is marked, the most common is first, where that can be determined. Thus a spirit that is only distilled to high proof in continuous stills and bottled unaged will be marked (C-U), while one that is made sometimes in pot stills but occasionally in column stills and is usually bottled after barrel aging, but not always, will be marked (RC-WU). Finally, if the spirit has or can have other flavorings added to it besides the material that directly or indirectly provides its fermentable sugars or the yeast to ferment them, that will be marked with another dash and an **F**, so that if that (C-U) is additionally flavored with whortleberries, it will be marked (C-U-F)

THE SPIRITS

(Note that a spirit may appear in more than one place, if it is made in more than one way.)

R = Rich	C = Clean	
U = Unaged	W = Wood-Aged	O = Oxidated
F = Flavored		

A. Spirits based on materials that contain fermentable sugars

These can be subdivided into:

1. Spirits from fruit
2. Spirits from cane
3. Spirits from sap
4. Spirits from flowers and honey
5. Spirits from milk

6. Spirits from (sweet) roots and tubers
7. Spirits from flowers

A1 (Fruit) includes:
Grape Spirits
  BRANDY
    Brandies, Grape
      AGUARDIENTE (R-U)
      Aguardiente de Catamarca (R-U)
      Armenian BRANDY (R-W)
      ARZENTE (R-W)
      BRANDY DE JEREZ (R-W)
      American Brandies (R-W)
        CALIFORNIA BRANDY (R-W)
      French BRANDY (R-W)
        ARMAGNAC (R-W)
          ARMAGNAC "La Blanche" (R-U)
          Floc de Gascogne (R-W)
        COGNAC (R-W)
          Pineau des Charentes (R-W)
        FINE DE LA MARNE (R-W)
          Ratafia Champenois (C-W)
      Georgian BRANDY (R-W)
      Chilean PISCO (R-UW)
      Peruvian PISCO (R-UO)
      Rakia (Bulgaria) (R-U)
        ARRACK (Lebanese) (R-O)
      Some SAMOGON (R-U)
      SINGANI (R-UW)
      Some CHACHA (R-UW)
      South African BRANDY (R-W)
    POMACE BRANDY
      GRAPPA/Pistapauta (R-UW)
      MARC (R-UW)
      BAGACEIRA (R-UW)
      TSIPOURO/Tsikoudia (R-U)
      Some CHACHA (R-UW)
      Witblitz (R-U)
    Raisin BRANDY (R-UW)
    Fruit-Flavored BRANDY
      APRICOT BRANDY (R-WU-F)
      CHERRY BRANDY (R-WU-F)
      PEACH BRANDY (R-WU-F)
Apple and Pear Spirits
  APPLEJACK (R-W)
  Jersey Lightning (R-U)
  CALVADOS (R-W)
    Pommeau (R-W)
  POIRE WILLIAMS (R-U)
Stone Fruit Spirits
  BARACK PALINKA

EAU-DE-VIE (various) (R-UW)
KIRSCHWASSER (R-U)
MARASCHINO (R-U)
PEACH BRANDY (R-W)
  Mampoer (R-U)
PRUNELLE (R-UW)
QUETSCH (R-U)
RAKIJA (R-U)
SLIVOVITZ (R-UW)
Tresterbrand (R-U)
Berry Spirits
  Himbeergeist (R-U)
Date Spirits
  Date ARRACK (R-U)
Fig Spirits
  BOUKHA (R-U)
  Fig ARRACK (R-U)
  MAHIA (R-U)
Other Fruit Spirits
  Banana BRANDY and GIN (R-U)
  Buckwheat Spirits
    Buckwheat "WHISKY" (R-W)
  Cashew FENI (R-U)
  Mango BRANDY (R-U)
  OBSTLER (R-U)
  Paw Paw BRANDY (R-W)
  Watermelon BRANDY (R-U)

A2 (Cane) includes:
Sugarcane Spirits
  Sugarcane Juice Spirits
    Some AKPETESHIE (R-U)
    CACHAÇA (R-UW)
    CLAIRIN (R-UW)
    GUARO (R-U)
    RHUM AGRICOLE (R-UW)
    Some Rums (RC-UW)
    Some Charandas (RC-UW)
  Molasses Spirits
    Pure
      Some Rums (CR-UW-F)
    Mixed (with cane juice or skimmings)
      Some Rums (R-UW)
      Some Charandas (RC-UW)
  Sugarcane Syrup Spirits
    AGUARDIENTE (RC-UW)
    Caña Paraguaya (RC-UW)
  Sugar Spirits
    MOONSHINE (sometimes mixed with maize) (RC-U-F)

Poitin (sometimes mixed with
barley) (RC-U)
KACHASU (mixed with maize) (R-U)
Other Cane Spirits
Sorghum-Cane RUM/WHISKY (R-UW)
Cornstalk RUM/WHISKY (R-UW)

A3 (Sap) includes:
Palm-Wine Spirits
Coconut Palm
ARRACK (Goa/Sri Lanka) (RC-UW)
Some LAMBANOG (RC-U-F)
Nipa Palm
BATAVIA ARRACK (original) (R-W)
Some LAMBANOG (RC-U-F)
NIPA
Raffia Palm
AKPETESHIE (R-U)
OGOGORO (R-U)
Sodabi (R-U)
Maple Spirits
Maple RUM (R-UW)
Maple VODKA (C-U)
Siberian Hogweed (*Heracleum sphondylium
sibiricum*) Vodka (RC-U)
Aguardiente de Pulque (R-U)

A4 (Honey) includes:
Honey/Mead Nectar (R-U)
VODKA (C-U)

A5 (Milk) Includes:
Arkhi (R-U)
VODKA (C-U)

A6 (Sweet Roots and Tubers [Dicots]) includes:
Beet Spirit (C-U)
Gentian Spirit (R-U)
Jerusalem Artichoke Spirit (RC-U)
Madder Spirit (CU)
SOJU (various) (CR-U-F)
Sweet Potato SHOCHU (R-UW)
VODKA (various) (C-U)
Yam Spirits (RC-U)

A7 (Flowers) includes:
MAHUA (R-U)

**B. SPIRITS BASED ON MATERIALS THAT
CONTAIN STARCHES THAT MUST BE
CONVERTED INTO FERMENTABLE SUGARS**
These can be subdivided into:
1. Spirits from grain
2. Spirits from starchy roots and tubers
3. Spirits from other flowering plants
4. Spirits from pulses

B1 (Grain) includes:
BAIJIU (CR-UO)
KAO LIANG (R-U)
CHANGA'A (R-U)
GENEVER (RC-UW)
Some KORN (RC-UW)
Some American MOONSHINE (CR-UW)
Some Irish Poitin (RC-U)
SAMOGON (RC-U)
Dutch and German SCHNAPPS (CR-U)
Some Shochus (R-UW)
Some Sojus (CR-U)
USQUEBAUGH (R-UW-F)
ESCUBAC (C-U-F)
Some Vodkas
Polugar (R-UW)
STARKA (C-W)
Single-Grain VODKA (C-U)
Mixed-Grain VODKA (C-U)
Whiskies
Malt Whiskies
Barley Malt WHISKY (R-W)
Rye Malt WHISKY (R-W)
Some KORN (R-UW)
Single-Grain Whiskies
Some Canadian Corn Whiskies (R-W)
Some KORN (R-UW)
Some RYE Whiskies (R-W)
Sorghum WHISKY (R-W)
Mixed-Grain Whiskies
American WHISKY
BOURBON (R-WU-F)
CORN (R-UW)
RYE (R-WU)
TENNESSEE WHISKY (R-WU-F)
WHEAT (R-WU)
CANADIAN WHISKY (RC-W-F)
GRAIN WHISKY (C-W-F)

B2 (Starchy Roots and Tubers) Includes:
Carrot SHOCHU (R-U)
Cassava Spirits
    KACHASU (R-U)
    KWETE (R-U)
    SOJU (CR-U-F)
Potato Spirit
    Some Vodkas (C-U)

B3 Other Flowering Plants (monocots, specifically Asparagales) includes:
Agave Spirits
    COCUY (R-UW)
    MEZCAL (R-UW)
        BACANORA (R-U)
        RAICILLA (R-U)
        TEQUILA (R-UW)
    OKOLEHAO (*Cordyline fruticosa*) (R-UW)
    SOTOL (*Dasylirion wheeleri*) (R-UW)

B4 Pulses (dicots) includes:
Some Baijius (peas mixed with grain in mash) (RC-UO)

C. SPIRITS MADE FROM MATERIALS THAT CONTAIN FERMENTABLE SUGARS MIXED WITH ONES THAT CONTAIN STARCHES
Perevara (honey and beer)
BATAVIA ARRACK (molasses, rice, and palm wine) (R-W)
    SWEDISH PUNCH (Batavia Arrack–Based) (R-W-F)

Some Cachaças (cane juice and maize) (R-UW)
Some KACHASU (cane juice and maize) (R-U)
Some American MOONSHINE (sugar and maize) (RC-U)
Some Baijius (various) (RC-UO)

D. FLAVORED SPIRITS MADE WITH NEUTRAL SPIRIT, WHERE THE BASE FERMENTATE DOES NOT MATERIALLY INFLUENCE THE FLAVOR OF THE FINAL SPIRIT

D1 Unsweetened or Lightly Sweetened Spirits
ABSINTHE (C-U-F)
    Colombian AGUARDIENTE (C-U-F)
    Anesone/MISTRÀ/Anice/RAKI/Anis/ OUZO/PASTIS (CR-U-F)
    AQUAVIT/Akvavit (C-UW-F)
    Aromatic and other BITTERS (C-UW-F)
    English-Style GIN (C-UW-F)
Flavored VODKA (C-U-F)

D2 Sweetened Spirits
Amari (C-UW-F)
    Spirituous Aperitives (C-U-F)
    CORDIALS (C-U-F)
    Digestives (C-UW-F)
    LIQUEURS (C-U-F)
    CURAÇAO (with exception of those blended with brandy) (CR-UW-F)
Some American MOONSHINE (C-U-F)
American SCHNAPPS (C-U-F)

A SIMPLE TIMELINE OF DISTILLATION

David Wondrich and Eleanor Brine

This is an anything-but-definitive attempt to sketch out some of the most basic landmarks in the history of distilled spirits (note that some of the dates are speculative or possible). Rather than give exact dates, most of which are merely when something was first observed, entries are grouped by century, or by half century for dates after 1500. Within each section, the arrangement is more or less chronological. The main entries drawn on here are ARRACK; BAIJIU; DISTILLATION, HISTORY; RUM; SPIRITS TRADE, HISTORY OF, and the various regional entries found in the "World of Spirits and Cocktails, by Region" section of the Topical Outline of Entries.

3500–3000 BCE	Simple internal-condensation clay stills may be in use in Mesopotamia.
1500–1000 BCE	Similar stills may be in use in the Balkans.
400–300 BCE	Possible beginning of distillation in India.
200–100 BCE	Possible construction of distillery/pothouses in Gandharan kingdom of northern India, using external condensation stills.
0–100 CE	Pliny describes Falernian wine as being flammable at room temperature.
100–200	Spirits made by freezing wine are common in the northwestern parts of China. Hellenistic alchemists in Egypt experiment with distilling wine.
200–300	Sophisticated internal condensation stills are producing spirits in China.
600–700	Proto-brandy (grapes mixed with qu and steamed) becomes a specialty of the Uighur silk-road oasis of Turpan. Chinese Buddhist monk Yuan Chwang travels to northern India and finds the Vaishya caste drinking "a strong distilled spirit," perhaps made from grapes, cane, or both.
700–800	Distillers in what is now Thailand and Burma are shipping palm spirits to ports around the Andaman Sea and Bay of Bengal. Chinese begin making *chiu* (wine or spirit) from sugarcane molasses.
800–900	The Mongol-style internal condensation still is in use in northern China.
900–1000	Arab philosophers and physicians explore distilling alcohol.
1000–1100	Chinese traders import spirits from Thailand. The Chinese-style side-tube internal condensation still is introduced.
1100–1200	European alchemists begin experimenting with distilled spirits, using air-cooled internal condensation stills.

1200–1300   The Delhi Sultanate in northern India supports a widespread cane-spirit industry.

In Europe, wine distilling spreads widely, chiefly for medicinal use.

Taddeo Alderotti of Florence describes the water-cooled condenser.

Italian distillers are using multiple redistillations to make a high-proof spirit.

1300–1400   Grain distilling takes root in the German lands north of the Alps.

Grape distillation documented in Armagnac.

Arrack distilling spreads throughout the Ottoman lands in southeastern Europe and the Middle East.

Chinese baijiu begins to assume its modern form.

First documented soju production in Korea.

1400–1500   Grain distilling spreads throughout northern Europe, including Ireland and Scotland in the west and Russia in the east.

Cheap grape spirit is being sold in the marketplaces of northern Italy.

Genever distilling begins in the Netherlands.

Mahua flowers are distilled in India.

Kao liang, a strong, unflavored baijiu, is made in Tianjin, China.

1500–1550   Portuguese traders find distillation thriving in many parts of India.

Agave distillation first documented in Mexico.

Likely beginning of rum distillation in Brazil and Spain's American colonies.

Early versions of vodka are in wide use in Poland and Russia.

1550–1600   The Parliament of Ireland passes an act to limit distillation from grain.

Ivan the Terrible of Russia establishes *kabaki*, government-run taverns, to use vodka as a tool for indirect taxation.

Chinese distillers begin making rice-palm arrack in Java.

Fruit eau-de-vie distilling recorded in Alsace.

Filipino sailors bring the Chinese-style internal condensation still to Mexico, where it is used to distill palm wine, and then cane and agave.

Grape distillation begins in the Spanish viceroyalty of Peru.

1600–1650   Punch spread by British sailors throughout the world.

Cognac distillers begin barrel-aging their brandy.

Rum distillation documented in Brazil, Spanish America, and then the French and British Caribbean.

Grain spirits and fruit brandies made in British North America.

Spanish officials in Mexico and Portuguese officials in Brazil attempt to ban the production and sale of cane spirits.

In Europe, copper stills largely replace glass or earthenware ones, and external-condensation stills largely replace internal-condensation ones.

Batavia arrack is shipped from Java to the Netherlands.

1650–1700   Sauce-aroma baijiu is distilled in Kweichow (Guizhou), China.

London distiller John French describes and illustrates the doubler or retort.

English colonists begin making rum in Jamaica.

Molasses is added to the cane-juice skimmings from which Caribbean rum is made.

Distillers in England and New England begin making rum from molasses alone.

Richard Stoughton creates the first bitters in London.

English distillers begin making their version of Dutch genever, known as "geneva" or "gin."

1700–1750   Gin craze in England.

Britain passes excise laws that divide distillers from rectifiers.

Scotch whisky begins to assume its modern form.

The hydrometer is introduced to measure the alcoholic content of spirits.

Rum distillers in the British Caribbean practice an early version of sour mashing, by mixing spent stillage in with their skimmings and molasses.

Admiral Edward Vernon orders the daily rum ration issued to British sailors on foreign station to be mixed with water, creating grog.

Maraschino liqueur takes shape in Zara, on the Croatian coast.

1750–1800

Rye whisky takes shape as a distinctive American style.

Potato spirit is first made in Germany.

Vermouth is first commercialized in Turin.

Scotch and Irish whiskies begin to diverge in response to British excise laws; both begin to be deliberately barrel-aged.

Irish whisky begins to assume its current form.

Curaçao is introduced by Dutch distillers.

The benefits of charring the insides of barrels are described in European scientific journals.

Cognac distillers move to using double distillation exclusively.

1800–1850

Direct steam distillation enters wide use in the United States, and the three-chamber still becomes common.

Indirect steam heating of stills is introduced in Europe.

Bourbon whisky comes together as a style.

Many American distillers adopt the sour mash process.

Some American distillers begin maturing their whisky in charred barrels.

Commercial distilling begins in Canada.

Continuous stills are introduced in France and Great Britain.

Rise of lightly sweetened Old Tom gin.

Grain whisky is introduced in the Scottish Lowlands.

Distilling begins in Madagascar.

Carthusian monks introduce green Chartreuse.

Fernet Branca is introduced.

Dry vermouth is developed in Marseille.

Peruvian pisco flows into Gold Rush San Francisco.

1850–1900

Merchants in Scotland begin blending malt whiskies with grain whiskies.

The first whisky conglomerate, the Distillers Company Ltd., is formed in Scotland.

Distilling spreads through Central Africa and begins in West Africa.

Trademark protection becomes common in Europe and the Americas.

Distilleries begin branding, bottling, and labeling their own spirits.

Vodka distillation achieves its modern form.

Unsweetened London dry gin supplants Old Tom gin.

1900–1950

Bottle making is successfully automated.

Periods of Prohibition are enforced in Canada, the Soviet Union, and the United States.

The Chinese baijiu industry begins to industrialize.

Distillery or rectifier bottling of spirits definitively replaces retailer bottling.

Column-still rums or pot still–column still blends begin to supplant pure pot still rums.

Rhum agricole becomes standardized in the French West Indies.

Whisky begins to be made in Japan.

The Jinro brand of modernized soju is launched in Korea.

Widespread palm spirit distillation begins in West Africa.

1950–2000   American straight rye whisky fades as a popular style.

Irish whisky makers move to making blended whisky from pure pot-still or pure malt.

Jamaican distillers move to making pot still–column still blends from pure pot still.

Spirits companies in Europe, North America, eastern Europe, and China undergo voluntary or government-imposed consolidation.

Ireland consolidates all remaining distilleries into one.

Tequila makes great inroads into the United States market and begins to catch on globally.

The Royal Navy eliminates its daily rum ration.

Single malt scotch whiskies become fashionable worldwide, partially eclipsing premium blends.

Some scotch whisky distillers begin "finishing" their whiskies in casks that have held other wines or spirits.

Vodka becomes the largest-selling spirit in America, replacing whisky.

The cocktail renaissance begins.

2000–2020   Micro- or craft distilleries spring up in the United States and elsewhere.

Malt whisky distilling begins in many countries worldwide.

The cocktail renaissance spurs the revival of many old brands and styles of spirit.

Bourbon and rye whiskies regain their markets in the United States and worldwide.

Mezcal finds an international market as a premium spirit.

Baijiu begins to break out of China and find foreign markets.

HOW TO MIX DRINKS

Although this book offers detailed instructions on how to mix drinks—see, e.g., MIXOLOGY (HOW TO MIX DRINKS)—and well over two hundred rather telegraphic cocktail recipes, we thought it might also be helpful to outline the basic procedures in one place. Below you'll find simple, step-by-step instructions for mixing four drinks: a stirred one, a shaken one, a hot one, and a bowl of punch. Where a word or phrase is written in SMALL CAPITALS, that is also the title of its entry.

First, though, you'll need some things.

The basic bartender's kit:
    a JIGGER (or a set of them) for measuring
    a BAR SPOON for measuring and stirring
    a COCKTAIL SHAKER for shaking drinks (either the three-piece COBBLER SHAKER, with built-in strainer, or the MIXING GLASS and MIXING TIN combination known as a BOSTON SHAKER, which will need a COCKTAIL STRAINER)
    a MUDDLER for mashing things that need mashing
    a JUICER for extracting fresh citrus juice
    a paring knife or citrus knife
    (optional) a vegetable peeler

An ICE MALLET and a LEWIS BAG are also helpful for cracking ice for stirred drinks, such as MARTINIS and MANHATTANS, and for various TIKI drinks, SWIZZLES, and JULEPS.

You'll also need some GLASSWARE—cocktail glasses, if you're serving your drinks straight up (see GLASS, COCKTAIL), Old-Fashioned glasses, if they're going on the rocks (see GLASS, OLD-FASHIONED), and some kind of tall glasses for the LONG DRINKS and mugs for the hot ones.

If you're the type who enjoys a fancy garnish and doesn't mind arts and crafts, you might want to invest in a CHANNEL KNIFE AND ZESTER. If you're gregarious, PUNCH BOWLS AND PUNCH PARAPHERNALIA and a NUTMEG GRATER will come in handy.

A short drink, stirred:
Dry MARTINI, pre-Prohibition style
1. Put a cocktail glass into the freezer, or fill it with ice and stir a few times.
2. Into a mixing glass, measure 60 ml LONDON DRY GIN and 30 ml dry French VERMOUTH and (optional) add 2 dashes ORANGE BITTERS.
3. Fill the glass ¾ of the way with cracked ice (you can either crack it with a mallet and Lewis bag or crack it one cube at a time by cupping each cube in one hand and whacking it swiftly with the bowl of your bar spoon).
4. Using the bar spoon, STIR. A slow fifteen count should be long enough. (Bear in mind that stirring elegantly requires practice.)
5. Retrieve your glass, emptying it of ice if necessary, and, using your julep strainer (place it concave side up in the glass and hold it in place with your index finger), strain the drink into the glass.
6. With a paring knife or vegetable peeler, cut a thin strip of lemon peel, roughly 1 cm wide by 3 cm long. Squeeze the peel over the surface of the drink, shiny-side down, and drop it in or discard it as desired.

A short drink, muddled:
Whisky OLD-FASHIONED, 1880s style
1. Put a level bar spoon of sugar and a bar spoon of water in an Old-Fashioned glass and add 2

or 3 dashes of ANGOSTURA bitters (or other BITTERS).

2. Using a muddler, grind the sugar, water, and bitters into a syrup.

3. Add 2–4 ice cubes; if desired, two of them can be cracked, as above.

4. Add 60 ml straight bourbon (WHISKY, BOURBON) or rye (WHISKY, RYE).

5. Using the bar spoon, stir; a slow fifteen count should be long enough.

6. With a paring knife or vegetable peeler, cut a thin strip of orange peel (if using bourbon) or lemon peel (if using rye), roughly 1 cm wide by 3 cm long. Squeeze the peel over the surface of the drink, shiny-side down, and drop it in or discard it as desired.

A short drink, shaken:
Original Cuban-style DAIQUIRI

1. Put a cocktail glass into the freezer, or fill it with ice and stir a few times.

2. With a juicer, squeeze half a lime; you want 15 ml (½ oz) of juice.

3. Put the juice in the bottom of a cocktail shaker (if using a glass-and-tin Boston shaker, build the drink in the glass part), along with 1 level bar spoon of granulated white sugar. Stir briefly.

4. Add 60 ml of good, flavorful white rum.

5. Fill shaker ¾ of the way with ice cubes.

6. Close the shaker (if using the Boston, fit the tin over the glass) and SHAKE well for a slow ten count.

7. Retrieve your glass, emptying it of ice if necessary, and, using a Hawthorne-style cocktail strainer, strain the drink into it.

A Hot TODDY:

1. Bring 250 ml of water to a boil; while it is heating, with a paring knife or vegetable peeler,

cut a thin strip of lemon peel, roughly 1 cm wide by 3 cm long.

2. Pour approximately 90 ml of the water into an earthenware mug and swirl it around to warm it.

3. Empty the mug and add a level bar spoon of demerara sugar and the lemon peel.

4. Add 1 oz of the hot water and stir briefly to dissolve the sugar.

5. Add 60 ml single-malt scotch whisky (WHISKY, SCOTCH) and stir briefly.

6. Add another 30 ml of the hot water and give it a final brief stir. To make an Irish HOT WHISKY, use Irish whisky (WHISKY, IRISH) and add a wedge of lemon with three cloves stuck through it.

A bowl of Georgian-style Rum PUNCH:

1. At least 8 hours before you need the punch, make an OLEO-SACCHARUM by using a vegetable peeler to remove the peels of 4 lemons in long spirals. Seal the peels in a glass jar with 180 ml white sugar; shake and let sit.

2. Half an hour before you need the punch, open the jar, add 180 ml fresh-squeezed, strained lemon juice, seal it again, and shake until the sugar has dissolved.

3. Pour the contents of the jar—your SHRUB— into a 4-liter (1 gallon) punch bowl half full of ice cubes (alternatively, you can use a 1-liter block of ice, made by freezing a liter container of water overnight).

4. Add a 700- or 750-ml bottle of aged, pot-distilled rum such as RUM, JAMAICA, and 1 liter cold water.

5. Stir well and grate NUTMEG over the top with a NUTMEG GRATER.

6. Ladle forth in 90-ml servings; makes 20–25 glasses.

David Wondrich

DIRECTORY OF CONTRIBUTORS

Alia Akkam

Alia Akkam is a native of New York who now lives in Budapest. She writes about design, travel, food, and drink. She is the author of *Behind the Bar: 50 Cocktail Recipes from the World's Most Iconic Hotels.*

Eric Alperin

Eric Alperin is an NYC native who attended Rutgers University, where he received his BFA in theater. His experience on the boards led him to get behind the stick. He moved to Los Angeles and opened the Varnish in 2009. A decade later, after six more bar openings, he coauthored his first book, *Unvarnished,* in 2020.

Matt Alt

Matt Alt is a Tokyo-based writer and translator. He is the author of the 2021 book *Pure Invention: How Japan Made the Modern World.*

Michael Anstendig

Michael Anstendig is editor in chief at Hanna Lee Communications, an award-winning PR agency based in New York City. He has also written for the *New York Times,* the *New York Observer, Time Out New York,* and *Nation's Restaurant News* and reviewed over two hundred restaurants for *New York Magazine's* website.

Konrad A. Antczak

Konrad A. Antczak is Marie Skłodowska-Curie Postdoctoral Fellow at Universitat Pompeu Fabra, Barcelona, as well as historical archaeologist at the Unidad de Estudios Arqueológicos, Universidad Simón Bolívar, in Caracas, Venezuela. His research focuses on the historical archaeology of commodities, seafaring, and everyday life in the sixteenth-through nineteenth-century southern Caribbean.

Anna Archibald

Anna Archibald writes about cocktails and spirits for the *Daily Beast, Wine Enthusiast,* and other publications.

Dave Arnold

Dave Arnold is a bartender, bar owner, and author and a pioneer in the use of new technology to make cocktails. His James Beard Award–winning 2014 book *Liquid Intelligence* has become an enduring classic for its explanation of the science behind the fine art of mixing drinks.

Nicole Austin

Nicole Austin is the general manager and distiller at Cascade Hollow Distilling Co., the maker of George Dickel Tennessee Whiskey. Previously, she was the master blender for Kings County Distillery in Brooklyn, New York. She was a founding board member of the American Craft Spirits Association and is cochair of its Legislative, Convention and State Guild Committees.

Jeff Berry

Jeff "Beachbum" Berry, one of *Imbibe* magazine's "25 Most Influential Cocktail Personalities of the Past Century," is the author of six critically acclaimed books about vintage tiki drinks and cuisine. He has lectured across Europe and the Americas, and in 2014 opened Beachbum Berry's Latitude 29 in New Orleans.

Julie Besonen

Julie Besonen, a graduate of the University of Arkansas, learned to appreciate quality food and alcohol as a Fulbright Scholar in Brussels, Belgium, and shortly thereafter moved to New York City to pursue writing about such passions, including travel.

Richard Boccato

Richard Boccato cut his teeth as a bartender at Little Branch and Milk & Honey in NYC. He is the owner of Dutch Kills and Hundredweight Ice, both located in Queens. Boccato loves motorcycles.

Marcus Boon

Marcus Boon teaches literature at York University in Toronto. He is the author of *The Road of Excess: A History of Writers on Drugs, In Praise of Copying*, and *The Politics of Vibration* (forthcoming).

Dave Broom

Dave Broom is an internationally acclaimed drinks writer who has been writing on the subject for nearly thirty years as both journalist and author. He is regarded as one of the world's foremost writers on Japanese whisky.

Derek Brown

Derek Brown is a writer, bar owner, and chief spirits advisor to the US National Archives Foundation. In 2019, he wrote *Spirits, Sugar, Water, Bitters: How the Cocktail Conquered the World*. His latest book, *Mindful Mixology: A Comprehensive Guide to No- and Low-Alcohol Cocktails*, will be released January 2022.

Jared M. Brown

Anistatia R. Miller and Jared M. Brown research and write award-winning histories of spirits and drinks, including the two-volume *Spirituous Journey: A History of Drink*. Brown is also cofounder and master distiller of Sipsmith Limited in London. Miller's doctoral thesis at the University of Bristol explores early-modern brewing in England's west country.

Lew Bryson

Lew Bryson was the managing editor of *Whisky Advocate* for twenty years. He is the author of *Tasting Whiskey* and *Whiskey Master Class,* and seven brewery guidebooks. He resides in rural Pennsylvania and is a sworn enemy of the state's liquor control board.

John C. Burton

John C. Burton, owner of Santa Rosa Bartenders School since 1978, teacher, mentor, former beverage manager and consultant of hotels and wineries since 1962, founder of the San Francisco chapter and life member of the USBG.

Maggie Campbell

Maggie Campbell is a spirits distiller, blender, wine expert, flavor and aroma specialist, and writer with both production and executive experience in the global drinks business. She studied distillation technology at Siebel, holds a WSET diploma in both wine and spirits, and studies at the Institute of Masters of Wine.

Fernando Castellon

Fernando Castellon is a bar and spirits historian, consultant, and collector. He is the editor of *MintSling* and the founder of the traveling exhibition *Cocktail Heritage*.

Martin Cate

Martin Cate is a rum and exotic cocktail expert and the owner of the San Francisco bars Smuggler's Cove and Whitechapel. He conducts educational seminars and adjudicates rum and cocktail competitions around the world. His book, *Smuggler's Cove: Exotic Cocktails, Rum, and the Cult of Tiki* was published in 2016.

Joanne Chen

Joanne Chen is an editor and writer in New York City. She has covered the intersection of food and health for many publications including *Vogue, Martha Stewart Living,* and the *Daily Beast.* She is the author of *The Taste of Sweet: Our Complicated Love Affair with our Favorite Treats.*

Lauren Clark

Lauren Clark writes about cocktails, spirits, and beer. She is the author of *Crafty Bastards: Beer in New England from the Mayflower to Modern Day,* and she wrote the blog drinkboston.com. She also helped launch the Boston chapter of Ladies United for the Preservation of Endangered Cocktails.

Paul Clarke

Paul Clarke is the executive editor of *Imbibe* magazine. Since 2005 he's written about spirits, cocktails, and the culture of drink for publications ranging from his *Cocktail Chronicles* blog (dating to the early cocktail renaissance, and revamped as a book in 2015) to the *New York Times.*

Brother Cleve

Brother Cleve (aka Robert Toomey) is a bartender, a musician, and a DJ who has been at the forefront of the contemporary cocktail revival since its inception. He is based in Boston, Massachusetts.

Jennifer Colliau

Jennifer Colliau is an award-winning bartender who manages the innovative, highly successful bar programs at the Interval and the Perennial in San Francisco, while overseeing Small Hand Foods, a popular line of hand-crafted cocktail syrups focusing on pre-Prohibition-era cocktails and their ingredients.

Tony Conigliaro

Tony Conigliaro is known for his innovative cocktails, influenced by the realms of art, perfume, food, and liquid flavor. He owns London's 69 Colebrooke Row and Bar Termini and runs the Drinks Factory Laboratory, a research and development space. He is the author of the James Beard Award–winning *Drinks*.

Wayne Curtis

Wayne Curtis has written frequently about cocktails, spirits, travel, and history for numerous publications for more than two decades, including the *Atlantic, New York Times, Imbibe,* the *Daily Beast, American Scholar, Wall Street Journal,* and *Garden and Gun*. He lives in New Orleans and Maine.

Alexander Paul Day

Alexander Paul Day is the author of *Cocktail Codex: Fundamentals, Formulas, Evolutions, Death and Co: Modern Classic Cocktails,* and *Death and Co Welcome Home*. He is also a managing partner of the hospitality company Gin & Luck, with the notable cocktail bar family Death & Company.

Dale DeGroff

Dale DeGroff was the head bartender at New York's Rainbow Room from 1988 to 1998. There, he reminded the world of the enduring appeal of a well-made cocktail. He is the author of *The Craft of the Cocktail, The Essential Cocktail,* and *The New Craft of the Cocktail*.

Leo DeGroff

Leo DeGroff is a New York City–based bartender and beverage consultant who specializes in the logistics of preparing craft cocktails for large events such as the annual Life Is Beautiful festival in Las Vegas, where the system he created and manages will serve thirty thousand drinks in a weekend.

Davin de Kergommeaux

Davin de Kergommeaux began analyzing, writing, and talking about whisky, as an independent commentator, in 1998. His book, *Canadian Whisky: The Portable Expert,* is the definitive work on Canadian whisky. He writes for *Whisky Advocate* and other magazines and is Canadian contributing editor for *Whisky Magazine*.

Maria del Mar Calpena

Mar Calpena is an internationally published journalist and bartender from Barcelona, Spain. She teaches history of bartending at CETT-UB and consults for Ferran Adrià's elBullifoundation on cocktails and spirits, for which she is writing a book, *Sapiens of Cocktails*.

Michael Dietsch

Michael Dietsch is a freelance writer, editor, and researcher based in Reston, Virginia. He is the author of *Shrubs: An Old-Fashioned Drink for Modern Times*.

Martin Doudoroff

Martin Doudoroff is a content management consultant, early fixture of the cocktail renaissance, publisher of popular drinks-related apps, librarian/archivist for Cocktail Kingdom, and grump.

Philip Duff

Philip Duff is a bar and spirits educator from Ireland who spent almost two decades living and working in Holland, where he studied the history and production of genever. He is also a former bartender and bar owner.

Martin Duffy

Martin Duffy, the North American Brand Representative for the Glencairn Glass, has also been a bartender, a Diageo Master of Whisky, the national brand ambassador for Bénédictine, and a cofounder of the Chicago Independent Spirits Expo. He also cohosts the weekly online whisky talk show, *A Sip of Knowledge*.

Sam Eilertsen

Sam Eilertsen is the host of *Cocktail History*, a podcast on all things history and booze. Based in Providence, Rhode Island, he is a cinematographer and film editor and a partner in Woodhaven Media production studios. He occasionally appears behind the bar serving up history-inspired cocktails at Fortnight Wine Bar.

Camper English

Camper English is a cocktails and spirits writer, speaker, and educator. His specialty is the science and technology behind spirits and cocktail production, and he has a particular interest in clear ice. His website is Alcademics.com.

Jennifer Eremeeva

Jennifer Eremeeva is an American expatriate writer based in Moscow, who writes about Russian history, cuisine, and culture. She is the award-winning author of *Lenin Lives Next Door: Marriage, Martinis, and Mayhem in Moscow* and *Have Personality Disorder, Will Rule Russia: A Concise History of Russia*.

Tomas Estes

Tomas Estes (1945–2021) left a career as an English teacher in his native California in 1976 to open a tequila bar in Amsterdam. Café Pacifico helped to introduce Europe to tequila and Mexican food, and in 2003 Mexico appointed him its official tequila ambassador for the EU. In 2008, he launched the pioneering artisanal brand Tequila Ocho.

Nicholas Faith

Nicholas Faith (1933–2018) was a distinguished veteran journalist, a former senior editor at the *Economist* and the London *Sunday Times*. He founded the International Spirits Challenge, the most prestigious event of its kind in the world, and wrote over twenty books on a wide variety of topics, including the definitive *Cognac*.

Andrew Faulkner

Andrew Faulkner served the American Distilling Institute for fourteen years, rising to vice president and managing editor of *Distiller* magazine. He was the architect of ADI's International Judging of Craft Spirits. Faulkner is the coauthor of *The Art of Distilling: Revised and Expanded* and writes for several magazines.

Alice Feiring

Alice Feiring is the author of the natural wine newsletter, *The Feiring Line*, and several books on wine and culture.

Eric Felten

Eric Felten is a cocktail columnist, who won a 2007 James Beard Award while writing for the *Wall Street Journal*. He continues to write about drinks for the journal and others, including the *Daily Beast* and the *Washington Examiner*. His books include *How's Your Drink?*

Omar Foda

Omar Foda is a historian of the modern Middle East. His book, *Egypt's Beer: Stella, Identity, and the Modern State*, was published in 2019. He received his PhD from the University of Pennsylvania and has taught at Bryn Mawr College, the University of Pennsylvania, and Towson University.

Chloe Frechette

Chloe Frechette is the senior editor of *PUNCH*, a digital platform dedicated to booze, and the author of *Easy Tiki*. She also earned distinction for her master's degree dissertation on the material culture of cocktail consumption from the Royal College of Art.

Alexi Friedman

Alexi Friedman graduated from Boston University with a degree in journalism and has been a reporter and editor in New York and New Jersey for twenty-five years.

St. John Frizell

St. John Frizell is the proprietor of Fort Defiance and founding partner of Gage & Tollner, both restaurants in Brooklyn. He writes about cocktails and spirits and aspires to the lifestyle of Charles H. Baker, Jr.

Doug Frost

Doug Frost is one of only three individuals in the world to hold the Master of Wine and Master Sommelier titles. The *Wine Spectator* has bestowed the accolade of Master of Spirits on Frost, who has authored three wine books and is an Emmy Award–winning TV host/writer.

Stefan Gabányi

Stefan Gabányi worked in Schumann's Bar for twenty-three years, has run his own bar in Munich since 2012, and is the author of *Schumann's Whisk(e)y Lexicon*.

Elizabeth Gabay

Elizabeth Gabay, a Master of Wine, lives in rural southeastern France and writes about the wines of Provence, the Mediterranean, and Hungary, often from a historic and cultural perspective. She is also working on a book on the global history and evolution of punch, her other passion.

Alexandre Gabriel

Alexandre Gabriel is the owner and master blender of Maison Ferrand in Cognac and West Indies Rum Distillery in Barbados and is a specialist in producing and resurrecting award-winning artisanal spirits.

Darra Goldstein

Darra Goldstein is the founding editor of *Gastronomica* and editor-in-chief of *The Oxford Companion to Sugar and Sweets*. She's a member of the advisory "kitchen cabinet" of the Smithsonian National Museum of American History. Her most recent cookbook is *Beyond the North Wind: Russia in Recipes and Lore*.

Heather Greene

Heather Greene is the author of *Whiskey Distilled: A Populist Guide to the Water of Life*. She has written extensively on the topic of whisky, sits on numerous whisky-judging panels, and even makes her own under the brand Milam and Greene.

Philip Greene

Philip Greene is a cofounder of the Museum of the American Cocktail in New Orleans, author of *To Have and Have Another: A Hemingway Cocktail Companion*, *The Manhattan: The Story of the First Modern Cocktail*, and *A Drinkable Feast: A Cocktail Companion to 1920s Paris*, and a *Daily Beast* cocktail columnist.

Jacob Grier

Jacob Grier is a bartender and writer in Portland, Oregon. His credits include tending bar at acclaimed establishments such as Expatriate and the Multnomah Whiskey Library, founding the international Aquavit Week, writing the books *Cocktails on Tap* and *The Rediscovery of Tobacco*, and (rather dubiously) popularizing the drinking ritual known as the "bone luge."

William Grimes

William Grimes is a retired reporter for the *New York Times*, where he covered the arts and for several years and was the paper's restaurant critic. He is also the author of *Straight Up or on the Rocks: The Story of the American Cocktail*.

Jason Grizzanti

Jason Grizzanti is the cofounder and master distiller at Black Dirt Distillery in Warwick, NY. He is a pioneer in the craft alcohol industry, with over twenty years' experience crafting ciders and artisanal spirits.

Edgar Harden

Edgar Harden was educated as an art historian and entered the spirits trade from the world of art and antiques via museums and auction houses. He combined his love of antiques and wine into a new career, founding Old Spirits Company in London in 2009.

Sean Harrison

Sean Harrison is the master distiller of Plymouth Gin. A former lieutenant in the Royal Navy, he was hired by the brand as an assistant manager in 1994, and he has been making gin there ever since.

Robert Hess

Robert Hess is a cocktail expert, cofounder of the Museum of the American Cocktail, and author of *The Essential Bartender's Guide*. He pioneered the craft cocktail revival with Drinkboy.com, a fertile think tank that influenced mixologists globally. His "The Cocktail Spirit" videos continue to inspire both bartenders and home enthusiasts.

Jason Horn

Jason Horn is former senior editor at *Liquor.com* and has been writing about food and drinks for his entire career, for publications including *Cooking Light*, *Playboy*, *Wine Enthusiast*, and *Serious Eats*.

Emma Janzen

Emma Janzen is the author of *Mezcal: The History, Craft and Cocktails of the World's Ultimate Artisanal Spirit*. In addition to working as digital content editor at *Imbibe Magazine*, she has also written for publications including *PUNCH*, *Bon Appetit*, *Serious Eats*, and *Food Republic*.

Misty Kalkofen

Misty Kalkofen is a bartender, writer, and spirits educator and the coauthor of *Drinking Like Ladies*. She lives in Boston and Oaxaca, Mexico.

Allen Katz

Allen Katz is the cofounder of New York Distilling Company in Brooklyn, where he focuses on rye whiskey and gin. He is also the director of spirits education for Southern Glazer's Wine & Spirits of New York.

Kaspar Keller

Kaspar Keller has been working as an editor for the Swiss bar and beverage magazine *BAR NEWS* since 2017. Before and during his studies in business administration, he worked in the hospitality industry in various bars, restaurants, and hotels, and hosted a radio show.

Samuel Lloyd Kinsey

Samuel Lloyd Kinsey writes and evangelizes about spirits and cocktails, often explaining relevant scientific principles for the layperson, and has frequently contributed to cocktail development as an interlocutor and sounding board.

Eben Klemm

Eben Klemm is a bar and restaurant consultant, whose creditability was forged during the New York Cosmo Wars of the early aughts. He is presently coasting off that reputation in Portland, Oregon.

Aaron Knoll

Aaron Knoll writes about botanical spirits (especially gin) for *Gin Magazine*, *Artisan Spirit*, and others. He has authored several books, including *Gin: The Art and Craft of the Artisan Revival*. He was inducted into the Gin Guild in 2019 for his contributions to spirits education.

Alice Lascelles

Alice Lascelles writes about wine, spirits, and cocktail culture for the *Financial Times* and has been covering the drinks industry as a trade and consumer journalist for almost twenty years.

Virginie Lauret

Virginie Lauret teaches Film Studies (PhD from New York University) and works as a screenwriter. She also writes about spirits for the *Daily Beast* and lives between Paris and New York.

Michael A. Lerner

Michael A. Lerner is the author of *Dry Manhattan: Prohibition in New York City*. He has a PhD in history from NYU and has consulted on numerous documentaries, including Ken Burns and Lynn Novick's *Prohibition*. He is the principal at Bard High School Early College, a partnership between Bard College and the NYC Department of Education.

Leonardo Leuci

Leo Leuci is a co-owner of three bars in Rome, including the world-famous Jerry Thomas Speakeasy. After fifteen years of traveling around the world as a bartender, especially in the Caribbean, he returned home to open the first Italian speakeasy. He is an advocate for the traditions of Italian bartending, both at his bars and on Italian television, and a father of the craft vermouth renaissance.

Don Livermore

Don Livermore is the master blender for the Hiram Walker Distillery in Windsor, Ontario. He holds a 2012 PhD in brewing and distilling from Heriot Watt University and was awarded Master Blender of the Year at the Canadian Whisky Awards in 2019 and 2020.

Ariel Lombán

Ariel Lombán has been a bartender since the late 1980s and is passionate about the history of Argentine bartending. A veteran of El Balero Bar on the Argentine coast and several bars in Buenos Aires, he is currently at the classic Los Galgos bar. He also writes the blog *El Barman Clásico Argentino*.

Sean Ludford

Sean Ludford has written innumerable articles on wine and spirits over the decades, read by disconsolate people eager to impress at cocktail parties. He regularly judges in spirits competitions around the globe and assists distilleries in product development.

Jordan Mackay

Jordan Mackay is a veteran writer on beverage and food. Over more than a decade as a drinks columnist in San Francisco, he chronicled the rise of the craft cocktail and spirits movement.

Charles MacLean

Charles MacLean has been writing about scotch whisky since 1981 and has published eighteen books on the subject; in 2005 he won the James Beard Award for Best Book on Wines and Spirits. He is a Master of the Quaich and an inductee of the Whisky Hall of Fame. In 2021 he was appointed MBE for "services to Whisky."

Tom Macy

Tom Macy is part owner of the Brooklyn cocktail bars Leyenda and Clover Club, where he is head bartender. His website and blog, socialhourcocktails.com, is an in-depth look at cocktail recipes, techniques, and tools. He also teaches cocktail classes and has dozens of cocktail videos on YouTube.

David Mahoney

David Mahoney has been writing and editing magazine articles about travel, wine, and spirits for longer than he'd care to admit. He was a senior editor at *Sunset*, editor-in-chief of *Minnesota Monthly*, and founding editor of *Drinks*.

Brett Martin

Brett Martin's first two apartments in New Orleans were just off Bourbon Street, a condition that demands one learn to love Bourbon Street. He is a longtime contributor to *GQ*, among many other publications, and the author of *Difficult Men: Behind the Scenes of a Creative Revolution*.

Chantal Martineau

Chantal Martineau writes about wine, spirits, food, and culture. Her writing has appeared in *Vogue*, *Bon Appetit*, *Food and Wine*, *Saveur*, the *Atlantic*, the *Financial Times*, *AFAR*, and others. She is the author of *How the Gringos Stole Tequila* and coauthor of *Finding Mezcal*. She was raised in Montreal and now lives in the Hudson Valley with her partner and two daughters.

May Matta-Aliah

May Matta-Aliah is an accredited wine and spirits educator. She has represented Armagnac as their ambassador in the United States since 2009 and has traveled extensively in the region.

Lance J. Mayhew

Lance J. Mayhew brings a wealth of experience in the spirits and cocktails world. He is the former contributing whisky writer for About.com and the author of the cocktail books *Whisky Made Me Do It* and *Quarantine Made Me Do It*, as well as a speaker, consultant, and former bartender.

Mike McCaw

Mike McCaw is a cofounder of the Amphora Society and the coauthor of *The Compleat Distiller*, widely recognized as the primary technical publication concerning small-scale distillation. He spent twenty-three years working on microbiological control and process optimization in pulp and paper mills and is the author of several scientific papers.

Clair McLafferty

Clair McLafferty is the author of *Romantic Cocktails* and *The Classic and Craft Cocktail Recipe Book* and has written articles on bartending culture and cocktails for publications including *Mental Floss*, *Eater*, *Adweek*, *The Food Network*, and the *Washington Post*. She also has seven years of bartending under her belt.

Jim Meehan

Jim Meehan is the author of *The PDT Cocktail Book*, *Meehan's Bartender Manual*, and a forthcoming book, *The Bartender's Pantry*. He resides in Portland, Oregon, where he works on behalf of clients of his consulting firm, Mixography Inc.

Chris Middleton

Chris Middleton busies himself scribbling about whisky history and trends, distillation science, and socioeconomic matters affecting liquor. One of the founders and a director of STARWARD, the Whisky Academy, and once global brand director Jack Daniel's, he is blessed with an indomitable liver.

Anistatia R. Miller

Anistatia R. Miller and Jared M. Brown research and write award-winning histories of spirits and drinks, including the two-volume *Spirituous Journey: A History of Drink*. Brown is also cofounder and master distiller of Sipsmith Limited in London. Miller's doctoral thesis at the University of Bristol explores early-modern brewing in England's west country.

Fred Minnick

Fred Minnick is the author of several whiskey books.

Reid Mitenbuler

Reid Mitenbuler is the author of *Bourbon Empire: The Past and Future of America's Whiskey* and *Wild Minds: The Artists and Rivalries That Inspired the Golden Age of Animation*.

Ivy Mix

Ivy Mix is co-owner of the pan-Latin inspired bar Leyenda in Brooklyn and the shop Fiasco! Wine and Spirits. She's the author of *Spirits of Latin America* and cofounder of cocktail competition Speed Rack, which creates a platform for female bartenders while simultaneously raising money for breast cancer–related charities.

François Monti

François Monti is a Belgian cocktail writer based in Madrid. He is the author of *Prohibitions*, *101 Cocktails*, and *El Gran Libro del Vermut* and has written for numerous international medias on the history of the cocktail.

Dave Moo

Dave Moo is a bartender, bar owner, cocktail and bar-operations consultant, voice actor, and theater artist originally from Boston, Massachusetts. Long a promoter of the New York City borough of Brooklyn, he has lived there since 1993 and opened Quarter Bar in 2007.

Nicholas Morgan

Nicholas Morgan's career as a historian was rudely interrupted by a thirty-year, award-winning spell in the scotch whisky business. He has now returned to the relative sanity of the past and recently published *A Long Stride,* the official history of Johnnie Walker.

Jeffrey Morgenthaler

Jeffrey Morgenthaler is the bar manager of Portland, Oregon, bars Clyde Common and Pépé Le Moko. He's the coauthor of *The Bar Book: Elements of Cocktail Technique* and author of *Drinking Distilled.* In 2013, he was named Bartender of the Year at the Nightclub and Bar Show.

Robert F. Moss

Robert F. Moss writes about food, drink, and travel. Based in Charleston, South Carolina, he is the contributing barbecue editor for *Southern Living* and author of *Southern Spirits: Four Hundred Years of Drinking in the American South* and *Barbecue: The History of an American Institution.*

Charles Neal

Charles Neal is an importer of fine wine and spirits based in San Francisco. He has authored books on Armagnac and calvados, and is currently working on a book about cognac.

Kara Newman

Kara Newman is spirits editor for *Wine Enthusiast* magazine. She's the author of seven cocktail books, including *Shake.Stir.Sip.* and *Nightcap.*

Pat Nourse

Pat Nourse is an Australian food, drinks, and travel writer and was an editor of *Gourmet Traveller* magazine for fifteen years.

Garrett Oliver

Garrett Oliver is the brewmaster of Brooklyn Brewery, the author of *The Brewmaster's Table,* the editor-in-chief of *The Oxford Companion to Beer,* and the founder of the Michael James Jackson Foundation for Brewing and Distilling.

Steven Olson

Steven Olson has been helping to shape the beverage industry for over forty years as aka wine geek: writer, consultant, educator, and lecturer. He is a founding partner of Beverage Alcohol Resource and is the global mezcal advocate, aka maguey geek, for Del Maguey Single Village Mezcal.

Darcy O'Neil

Darcy O'Neil is the author of *Fix the Pumps: The History of the American Soda Fountain,* a writer at *Art of Drink,* chemist, and doer of things.

Bill Owens

Bill Owens is a brewer, publisher, photographer, and raconteur. In 1983, he founded one of the first brewpubs in America, before founding the magazines *Beer* and *American Brewer.* In 2003, he founded the seminal American Distilling Institute (ADI), an organization that promotes the art and commerce of craft distilling.

F. Paul Pacult

F. Paul Pacult is a multiple award-winning educator, journalist, and author. He has been honored in Scotland, France, and the United States. His latest books are *The New Kindred Spirits* and *Buffalo, Barrels, and Bourbon,* both published in 2021.

Chad Parkhill

Chad Parkhill is the author of *Around the World in 80 Cocktails* and the owner of Trouble in Dreams, a cocktail and wine bar in Melbourne, Australia.

Antonio Parlapiano

Antonio Parlapiano is the co-owner of the renowned Roman cocktail bar (and bartending academy) the Jerry Thomas Project. He is an IS Master Class sommelier and a holder of the BAR Ready certificate. He is also a coauthor of the Jerry Thomas Project's 2018 book *Twist on Classic.*

Charles Passy

Charles Passy is an award-winning journalist who writes about all things food and drink for the *Wall Street Journal* and the *MarketWatch* website. His Weekend Sip column for *MarketWatch* covers the latest in wine, spirits, and beer.

Garrett Peck

Garrett Peck is a historian and tour guide in Santa Fe and is the author of *The Prohibition Hangover: Alcohol in America from Demon Rum to Cult Cabernet.*

Christopher Pellegrini

Christopher Pellegrini was born and raised in Vermont and took his brewing experience to Japan in 2002. He soon fell in love with the country's indigenous spirits, awamori and shochu, and spends much of his time lecturing and writing about these traditions. In 2018 he was awarded the Brewing Culture Prize by Japan's National Research Institute of Brewing.

Matt Pietrek

Matt Pietrek was a software writer for thirty years, then abandoned that calling to become a spirits writer, educator, historian, and consultant, with a particular predilection for rum and tropical cocktails. Although he lives in New Orleans, he would reside in the British National Archives if given the opportunity.

Dennis J. Pogue

Dennis J. Pogue, PhD, is adjunct associate professor and the interim director of the Historic Preservation Program in the School of Architecture at the University of Maryland. As vice president for Preservation at George Washington's Mount Vernon Estate, he directed the research and oversaw the reconstruction of Washington's whiskey distillery.

Cauré Portugal

Cauré Portugal has a PhD in oenology and food science and has written about yeast, fermentation, and cachaça. He is the founder and CEO of the Smart Yeast company and lives outside of São Paulo, Brazil.

Elva Ramirez

Elva Ramirez is a veteran journalist who spent a decade at the *Wall Street Journal* before becoming a freelance writer and consultant. She is the author of *Zero Proof: 90 Non-Alcoholic Recipes for Mindful Drinking*.

Gary Regan

Gary 'gaz' Regan (1951–2019) was raised in a pub in Lancashire, spent twenty years tending bar in New York, and then turned to writing about drinks. He was one of the founding fathers of the craft cocktail movement, although nobody's sure whether he was its Benjamin Franklin or its Ethan Allen.

Elizabeth Rhoades

Elizabeth Rhoades is a technical distiller with an MS in food and fermentation science and a diploma distiller through IBD; she's helped make spirits on five continents and periodically authors technical articles for various spirits' publications.

Clay Risen

Clay Risen writes about spirits for the *New York Times*. He is the author of two books about whisky, *Single Malt: A Guide to the Whiskies of Scotland* and the bestselling *American Whiskey, Bourbon and Rye: A Guide to the Nation's Favorite Spirit*. He also sits on the judging panel for the Ultimate Spirits Challenge.

Jack Robertiello

Jack Robertiello has worked with or written about food and drink for most of his adult life. He speaks, teaches, and consults about spirits, and judges frequently at international competitions.

Noah Rothbaum

Noah Rothbaum is the editor of the *Daily Beast*'s award-winning Half Full section. He also co-hosts the podcast *Life Behind Bars*, which won the 2018 Tales of the Cocktail Spirited Award for Best Podcast Series. Rothbaum is the author *The Art of American Whiskey*, *The Business of Spirits*, and the forthcoming *The Whiskey Bible*.

Rebecca Rothbaum

Rebecca Rothbaum has written about everything from film to food. Along the way, she's interviewed Salman Rushdie, tramped through a water buffalo dairy, and scoured Central Park for migratory birds. Her work has appeared in publications such as the *New Yorker*, the *New York Times*, and the *Wall Street Journal*.

Matthew Rowley

Matthew Rowley is the author of *Moonshine!* and *Lost Recipes of Prohibition*. The former museum curator holds a master of historic administration and museum studies degree from the University of Kansas and lives in California.

Jeff Ruby

Jeff Ruby served as the chief dining critic of *Chicago* magazine for ten years and has written about bars for *GQ*, *Esquire*, and *Playboy*.

Tony Sachs

Tony Sachs has been writing about spirits and cocktails since 2007 for numerous publications, including *Robb Report*, *Huffington Post*, *Serious Eats*, and the *Daily Beast*, among many others.

Dinah Sanders

Dinah Sanders is the author of *The Art of the Shim: Low-Alcohol Cocktails to Keep You Level* and *Discardia: More Life, Less Stuff*. She is now developing Kabalor, a new spellcasting and storytelling game.

Derek Sandhaus

Derek Sandhaus is the author of *Baijiu: The Essential Guide to Chinese Spirits, Drunk in China*, and other books on Chinese history. In 2018 he cofounded Ming River Sichuan Baijiu with China's oldest continuously operating distillery.

Audrey Saunders

Audrey Saunders is one of the leading pioneers of modern mixology and the visionary behind New York's legendary Pegu Club. Pegu is globally renowned as the bar that catapulted the twenty-first-century craft cocktail movement and also spawned a number of America's finest mixologists.

Rosie Schaap

Rosie Schaap is the author of *Drinking with Men: A Memoir* and *Becoming a Sommelier*. From 2011 to 2017, she wrote the Drink column for the *New York Times Magazine*.

Peter Schaf

Peter Schaf has been an antique bottle hunter since 1969. He moved to Paris in 1999 and became a forefather of the modern renaissance of absinthe. He cofounded Tempus Fugit Spirits and has since devoted his time to the revival of forgotten or neglected historic beverages.

Bernhard Schafer

Bernhard Schafer went from being a top bartender in his native Germany to being a writer, an educator, and a professional spirits taster and judge, specializing in whisky, rum, gin, and champagne. His friends say to him, "I would once like to spend my vacation doing what you are calling work."

Mark L. Schrad

Mark L. Schrad is an assistant professor of political science at Villanova University. He is also the author of several books, including *Vodka Politics: Alcohol, Autocracy, and the Secret History of the Russian State*.

Stephen Shellenberger

Stephen Shellenberger is a beverage technologist who maintains the *Bostonapothecary* blog. His work ranges from collecting and translating a century of works on spirits production to experimentation aimed at unlocking the secrets of heavy rum production.

Robert Simonson

Robert Simonson is the longtime cocktail and spirits writer for the *New York Times*. He is the author of several books, including *The Old-Fashioned, 3-Ingredient Cocktails, The Martini Cocktail*, and *Mezcal and Tequila Cocktails*. In *A Proper Drink*, he told the story of the modern cocktail revival.

Frederick H. Smith

Frederick H. Smith is assistant professor in the Department of Liberal Studies at North Carolina A&T State University. He is author of *Caribbean Rum: A Social and Economic History* and *The Archaeology of Alcohol and Drinking*.

Kevin Smith

Kevin Brent Smith is the technical services manager and microbiologist at the Jack Daniel Distillery in Lynchburg, Tennessee. His broad experience in the fermentation industry includes the management of a fuel ethanol distillery, Commonwealth Agri-Energy, and being a technical manager with Lallemand Ethanol Technology.

David Solmonson

David Solmonson is the cofounder of *12bottlebar.com*, twice nominated for *Saveur* magazine's Best Cocktail Blog, and coauthor of *The 12 Bottle Bar*, a 2015 Best New Cocktail/Bartending Book nominee at Tales of the Cocktail.

Chad Solomon

Chad Solomon began bartending at the renowned New York bar Milk & Honey. He is now the director of trade advocacy and innovation for the Cooper Spirits Company and cofounder of the Midnight Rambler bar in Dallas, Texas.

Shawn Soole

Shawn Soole, a native of Australia, made his reputation at Clive's Classic Lounge in Victoria, British Columbia, where he went on to open several other groundbreaking bars before returning to Clive's. He is also a hospitality and spirits consultant and the author of *Cocktail Culture* and *Great Northern Cocktails*.

Colin Spoelman

Colin Spoelman is cofounder and head distiller at Kings County, New York City's premier craft distillery and wrote *The Guide to Urban Moonshining* and *Dead Distillers* about American whiskey. He grew up in the moonshine (not the bourbon) part of Kentucky and graduated from Yale University.

Doug Stailey

Doug Stailey is a cocktail history enthusiast and obsessive researcher who lives in Washington, DC, with his wife and two cats and blogs as *Libation Legacy*.

Tristan Stephenson

Tristan Stephenson is a UK-based bar operator who has a particular fondness for whisky and rum. He's visited over three hundred distilleries and has written a few books about them under the "Curious Bartender" moniker.

Gwydion Stone

Gwydion Stone is an artisan distiller based in Seattle, Washington. In 2004 he founded the Wormwood Society, a nonprofit association focused on providing accurate scientific and historical information about absinthe.

Theodora Sutcliffe

Theodora Sutcliffe is British-born but Bali-based, and she is often found with a Negroni in hand. She has contributed to the *Guardian*, BBC, CNN, *National Geographic Travel*, and more and cut her cocktail teeth at *CLASS* magazine (now *Difford's Guide*).

Duane Sylvestre

Duane Sylvestre is a bartender-turned-spirits educator. A native of Trinidad, he was the bar manager at Bourbon and Steak in Washington, DC, for many years before becoming a spirits specialist at Campari Group America. He lectures frequently on African American bartenders and their history.

Chuck Taggart

Chuck Taggart has been writing about New Orleans food, drink, and culture at his website *The Gumbo Pages* since 1994, and about cocktails and spirits at his weblog *Looka!* since 1999. He worked in public broadcasting in Los Angeles for twenty years and currently works as an audiovisual tech in the film/television industry.

Sother Teague

Sother Teague is the award-winning bartender and beverage director at New York's Amor y Amargo and a partner at Blue Quarter and Windmill. He is the cohost of *Speakeasy* on Heritage Radio Network and the author of *I'm Just Here for the Drinks*.

Tara Q. Thomas

Tara Q. Thomas specializes in the wines and spirits of the Mediterranean, with a focus on Greece. She has been an editor and wine critic for *Wine and Spirits Magazine* for twenty years and is the assistant editor on the fifth edition of *The Oxford Companion to Wine*.

William Tipper

William Tipper is an associate editor for books at the *Wall Street Journal*. His past occupations have included professor of literature, podcast host, and bookseller.

Guillermo L. Toro-Lira

Guillermo L. Toro-Lira, a native of Lima, Peru, has lived most of his life in Silicon Valley, California. As a historian of American viticulture he is the author of several books, including the groundbreaking *Wings of Cherubs*, a history of pisco and Pisco Punch in San Francisco.

Steve Ury

Steve Ury maintained the popular and influential *Sku's Recent Eats* blog, focused on the world of whisky, and craft whisky in particular, from 2007 to 2017. At present, his energies are directed toward running the Serious Brandy group on Facebook.

Ana G. Valenzuela-Zapata

Ana G. Valenzuela-Zapata is a Mexican scientist in agave spirits; her 2004 book *Tequila: A National and Cultural History* is well known in the United States among tequila aficionados.

Dmitri van den Bersselaar

Dmitri van den Bersselaar teaches African history at Leipzig University, Germany and is the author of *The King of Drinks*, on the long history of genever in West Africa.

Lauren Viera

Lauren Viera wrote about spirits and cocktails for the *Chicago Tribune* and many other publications during the height of the cocktail renaissance; she maintains a well-stocked home bar.

Charlotte Voisey

Charlotte Voisey is the head of ambassadors for William Grant & Sons and host of the video series *The Proper Pour with Charlotte Voisey*. Her cocktail recipes have been published in menus worldwide, and she is the two-time winner of the Golden Spirit Award at Tales of the Cocktail.

Max Watman

Max Watman is, among other things, the author of *Chasing the White Dog: An Amateur Outlaw's Adventures in Moonshine.*

Angus Winchester

Angus Winchester is a peripatetic Brit who has worked in good bars and drunk in better ones in an effort to know all there is about drinks, drinkers and those that serve them.

David Wondrich

David Wondrich is the author of *Imbibe!* and *Punch.* He has a 1997 PhD in comparative literature from New York University; his dissertation was on European scientific poetry from antiquity to the Renaissance.

Frederic Yarm

Frederic Yarm is a home enthusiast and blogger turned book author, professional bartender, and whiskey brand ambassador. His two books, *Drink and Tell: A Boston Cocktail Book* and *Boston Cocktails: Drunk and Told,* capture the recipes, players, and energy of the Boston cocktail renaissance.

Dushan Zaric

Dushan Zaric is a leader in the craft bartending movement and co-owner of the esteemed New York bar Employees Only. He has published numerous cocktail books, including *Speakeasy: Classic Cocktails Reimagined* in 2010.

INDEX OF PEOPLE AND PLACES

People and places that have an entry in the *Companion* are not listed in the index.

The publishers are grateful to all copyright holders for permission to reproduce the photographs and illustrations. Although every effort has been made to contact copyright holders, it has not been possible in every case and we apologize for any that have been omitted. If notified the publisher will be pleased to rectify any errors or omissions at the earliest opportunity.